T0402702

The Palgrave Handbook of Operations Research

Saïd Salhi · John Boylan
Editors

The Palgrave
Handbook
of Operations
Research

palgrave
macmillan

Editors
Saïd Salhi
Kent Business School
University of Kent
Canterbury, UK

John Boylan
Lancaster University
Lancaster, UK

ISBN 978-3-030-96934-9   ISBN 978-3-030-96935-6   (eBook)
https://doi.org/10.1007/978-3-030-96935-6

© The Editor(s) (if applicable) and The Author(s), under exclusive license to Springer Nature
Switzerland AG 2022
This work is subject to copyright. All rights are solely and exclusively licensed by the Publisher, whether
the whole or part of the material is concerned, specifically the rights of translation, reprinting, reuse
of illustrations, recitation, broadcasting, reproduction on microfilms or in any other physical way, and
transmission or information storage and retrieval, electronic adaptation, computer software, or by similar
or dissimilar methodology now known or hereafter developed.
The use of general descriptive names, registered names, trademarks, service marks, etc. in this publication
does not imply, even in the absence of a specific statement, that such names are exempt from the relevant
protective laws and regulations and therefore free for general use.
The publisher, the authors, and the editors are safe to assume that the advice and information in this book
are believed to be true and accurate at the date of publication. Neither the publisher nor the authors or
the editors give a warranty, expressed or implied, with respect to the material contained herein or for any
errors or omissions that may have been made. The publisher remains neutral with regard to jurisdictional
claims in published maps and institutional affiliations.

Cover illustration: Andriy Onufriyenko

This Palgrave Macmillan imprint is published by the registered company Springer Nature Switzerland AG
The registered company address is: Gewerbestrasse 11, 6330 Cham, Switzerland

Said would like to dedicate this book to his beloved wife Pauline for her patience and hard work in keeping our family of five wonderful children, namely, Riadh, Tarek, Louisa, Nassim and Salim, safely under one roof. Said would also like to dedicate this book to all his Ph.D. students through the last thirty years and also to his first beatiful grand-daughter Izabella Molly who was born to our fantastic daughter-in law Francesca and our amazing son Riadh during the preparation of this manuscript.
John would like to dedicate this book to his wife, Jan, in acknowledgement of all her love and support, and to all those OR people he has worked with over the years, both in academia and in industry.

Preface

Operations Research (OR) is a fast-evolving field, which is having a significant impact on its neighbouring disciplines of Business Analytics and Data Science, and on contemporary business and management practices. It can be a difficult field to navigate, because of the multiplicity of academic journals devoted to it, and the need for extensive prior knowledge to comprehend the more technical articles in OR. We have therefore set ourselves the ambitious task of synthesising the state of the art in major aspects of Operations Research, as well as showcasing some of the latest developments, both in theory and in practical application.

Views differ on what should be included within the scope of Operations Research. Most would agree that optimisation (including heuristics) and simulation methods, that can be used for Prescriptive Analytics, would fall under the banner of OR. But what about forecasting methods that can be used for Predictive Analytics? At a more fundamental level, should 'soft OR' be in scope or out of scope? We have taken the view that an inclusive stance is the most helpful, both for theory and practice. Real-world problems often require consideration from both 'softer' and 'harder' perspectives and need consideration of both predictive and prescriptive problems.

In accordance with our inclusive approach to OR, we have divided the book into six parts, more or less evenly balanced, making up 28 chapters. Part I covers Discrete (Combinatorial) Optimisation (DO); Part II deals with Continuous (Global) Optimisation (CO); Part III discusses Heuristic Search Optimisation (HSO); Part IV covers Forecasting, Simulation and Prediction

(FSP); and Part V treats Problem Structuring and Behavioural OR (PSB). The book finishes with Part VI, which presents some 'Recent OR Applications' (RORA), including big data.

The part on Discrete (Combinatorial) Optimisation, which also includes combinatorial optimisation, contains five chapters. The first chapter covers bilevel discrete optimisation with a focus on computational complexity, by Kochetov, Plyasunov and Panin. This is followed by location problems with uncertainty, namely single source, covering and hub hubs, by Azizi, Sergio and Irawan. The next chapter presents a survey on integrated routing problems, including inventory routing and location routing, by Guastaroba, Mor and Speranza. Models and applications for various knapsack problems are discussed by Wilbaut, Hanafi, Coelho and Lucena. The fifth and last chapter in this part of the book is on models and algorithms for rank aggregation by Alcaraz, Landete and Monge.

Combinatorial (Global) Optimisation, which also includes global optimisation, has five chapters starting with the work of Jones and Florentino on multi-objective optimization, with an emphasis on compromise programming and its applications. Chapter 7 is given by T. Drezner, where she covers competitive location problems. Fernandez and Toth discuss the interval tools that are used in branch and bound including potential software. This is followed by Chapter 9, on continuous location problems, by Z. Drezner. Recent developments and challenges in Data Envelopment Analysis (DEA) are presented by Emrouznejad, Yang, Khoveyni and Michali in the last chapter of this part.

Heuristic Search Optimisation five chapters, starting with an overview on heuristics and metaheuristics by Salhi and Thompson, followed by a chapter on formulation space search by Mladenovic, Brimberg and Urosevic. Chapter 13 deals with an evolutionary approach, namely, sine cosine algorithm which is produced by Rawat, Singh and Bansal. A new methodology on heuristic search called less is more is introduced by Mladenovic, Z. Drezner, Brimberg and Urosevic while the last chapter in this part outlines the new era of metaheuristics including hybridisation and learning by Salhi and Thompson.

Forecasting, Simulation and Prediction deals with stochasticity in general and contains six chapters. The first chapter, Chapter 16, is by Goodwin and Fildes on forecasting with judgment, followed by an analysis on simulation with input uncertainty, produced by Barton, Lam and Eunhye. Chapter 18 is given by Xu and Zhang on fuzziness for multi-attribute decision making. An introductory chapter on measures in reliability is delivered by Wu and Coolen, followed by Chapter 20, which deals with queueing theory, with an emphasis on variable speeds by, Yajima and Phun-Duc. The last chapter in this part discusses forecasting and its beneficiaries by Rostami-Tabar and Boylan.

Problem Structuring and Behavioural OR covers the 'softer' aspects of OR. It consists of three chapters, starting with the work of Kunc and Katsikopoulos on recent developments and future perspectives on behavioural OR, followed by a chapter on problem structuring methods (PSM) by Franco and Rouwette. The last chapter of this part, Chapter 24, is presented by Lami and White, and also discusses PSM but with a focus on its impact and relevance in the digital age.

The last part, on Recent OR Applications, contains four chapters. It starts with a discussion on recent advances in big data analytics by Li, Kong, Zheng and Pan, followed by a chapter on OR models for humanitarian logistics by Ghavamifar and Torabi. A chapter on the delivery with drones with an emphasis on the last mile is given by Chen and Demir, followed by the last chapter of the book, Chapter 28, on an application of radiotherapy using DEA by Ehrgott, Raith, Shentall, Simpson and Stubington.

This handbook aims to cover a wide spectrum of OR, though we appreciate there are areas that we would love to have covered but could not due to authors' circumstances, especially some theoretical areas of OR and other applications. We are also pleased and proud to note that our contributing authors are drawn from a diverse pool of people, coming from a large number of countries, gender, religion and seniority.

We hope this edited Handbook on OR will be a useful addition to researchers, students and practitioners alike.

Canterbury, UK   Saïd Salhi
Lancaster, UK   John Boylan
November 2021

Acknowledgments

We would like to thank all the authors who worked very hard during this difficult time of Covid to produce such interesting and well informative chapters. Without their invaluable contributions, we would not be in a position to produce such a diverse and comprehensive OR handbook.

We are grateful to Jessica Harrison, former editor for scholarly business in Palgrave, for the invite and the opportunity to edit such a handbook in this interesting and challenging area of Science, Engineering and Management which we call Operation (or Operational) Research.

We would also like to thank Srishti Gupta and Alec Selwyn from Palgrave, and Punitha Balasubramanian from Springer Nature, who took over Jessica in the last few months for their help and understanding in providing us with a smooth transition.

Contents

Contributors

Javier Alcaraz Center of Operations Research, Miguel Hernández University of Elche, Elche (Alicante), Spain

Nader Azizi Business School, University of Edinburgh, Edinburgh, Scotland, UK

Jagdish Chand Bansal South Asian University, New Delhi, India

Russell R. Barton Penn State University, University Park, PA, USA

John E. Boylan Department of Management Science, Lancaster University, Lancaster, England

Jack Brimberg Royal Military College of Canada, Kingston, ON, Canada

Cheng Chen School of Transportation and Civil Engineering, Fujian Agriculture and Forestry University, Fuzhou, China

Igor Machado Coelho Programa de Pós-Graduação em Ciências Computacionais, Universidade do Estado do Rio de Janeiro, Rio de Janeiro, Brazil; Instituto de Computação, Universidade Federal Fluminense, Niterói, Brazil

Frank Coolen Department of Mathematical Sciences, Durham University, Durham, England

Emrah Demir PARC Institute of Manufacturing, Logistics and Inventory, Cardiff Business School, Cardiff University, Cardiff, Wales, UK

Tammy Drezner College of Business and Economics, California State University, Fullerton, CA, USA

Zvi Drezner College of Business and Economics, California State University, Fullerton, CA, USA

Matthias Ehrgott Department of Management Science, Lancaster University, Lancaster, UK

Ali Emrouznejad Surrey Business School, The University of Surrey, Guildford, Surrey, UK

José Fernández Department Statistics and Operations Research, University of Murcia, Murcia, Spain

Robert Fildes Lancaster Centre for Marketing Analytics and Forecasting, Lancaster University, Lancaster, UK

Helenice O. Florentino Institute of Biosciences, São Paulo State University (Unesp), Botucatu, Brazil

L. Alberto Franco Loughborough University, Loughborough, UK;
Radboud University, Nijmegen, The Netherlands;
Universidad del Pacifico, Lima, Peru

Boglárka G.-Tóth Institute of Informatics, University of Szeged, Szeged, Hungary

Sergio García School of Mathematics, University of Edinburgh, Edinburgh, Scotland, UK

Ali Ghavamifar School of Industrial Engineering, College of Engineering, University of Tehran, Tehran, Iran

Paul Goodwin University of Bath, Bath, UK

Gianfranco Guastaroba Department of Economics and Management, University of Brescia, Brescia, Italy

Saïd Hanafi LAMIH, CNRS, UMR 8201, University Polytechnique Hauts-de-France, Valenciennes, France;
INSA Hauts-de-France, Valenciennes, France

Chandra Ade Irawan Nottingham University Business School, University of Nottingham Ningbo China, Ningbo, China

Dylan F. Jones Centre for Operational Research and Logistics, School of Mathematics and Physics, University of Portsmouth, Portsmouth, UK

Konstantinos V. Katsikopoulos Southampton Business School, University of Southampton, Southampton, England

Mohammad Khoveyni Department of Applied Mathematics, Yadegar-e-Imam Khomeini (RAH) Shahre Rey Branch, Islamic Azad University, Tehran, Iran

Yury Kochetov Sobolev Institute of Mathematics, Novosibirsk, Russia

Yinfei Kong Department of Information Systems and Decision Sciences, California State University, Fullerton, CA, USA

Martin Kunc Southampton Business School, University of Southampton, Southampton, England

Henry Lam Columbia University, New York, NY, USA

Isabella M. Lami Politecnico di Torino, Turin, Italy

Mercedes Landete Center of Operations Research, Miguel Hernández University of Elche, Elche (Alicante), Spain

Daoji Li Department of Information Systems and Decision Sciences, California State University, Fullerton, CA, USA

Abilio Lucena Programa de Engenharia de Sistemas e Computação, Universidade Federal do Rio de Janeiro, Rio de Janeiro, Brazil

Maria Michali Aston Business School, Aston University, Birmingham, UK

Nenad Mladenović Industrial System Engineering, Khalifa University, Abu Dhabi, UAE

Juan F. Monge Center of Operations Research, Miguel Hernández University of Elche, Elche (Alicante), Spain

Andrea Mor Department of Management, Economics and Industrial Engineering, Politecnico di Milano, Milan, Italy

Jianxin Pan School of Mathematics, The University of Manchester, Manchester, UK

Arteam Panin Sobolev Institute of Mathematics, Novosibirsk, Russia

Tuan Phung-Duc Faculty of Engineering, Information and Systems, University of Tsukuba, Ibaraki, Japan

Alexander Plyasunov Sobolev Institute of Mathematics, Novosibirsk, Russia

Andrea Raith Department of Engineering Science, The University of Auckland, Auckland, New Zealand

Anjali Rawat South Asian University, New Delhi, India

Bahman Rostami-Tabar Cardiff Business School, Cardiff University, Cardiff, UK

Etiënne A. J. A. Rouwette Radboud University, Nijmegen, The Netherlands

Saïd Salhi Kent Business School, University of Kent, Canterbury, UK

Glyn Shentall Rosemere Cancer Centre, Royal Preston Hospital, Preston, UK

John Simpson Department of Radiation Oncology, Calvary Mater Newcastle, Waratah, NSW, Australia

Shitu Singh South Asian University, New Delhi, India

Eunhye Song Penn State University, University Park, PA, USA

M. Grazia Speranza Department of Economics and Management, University of Brescia, Brescia, Italy

Emma Stubington STOR-i, Lancaster University, Lancaster, UK

Jonathan Thompson School of Mathematics, Cardiff University, Cardiff, UK

S. Ali Torabi School of Industrial Engineering, College of Engineering, University of Tehran, Tehran, Iran

Dragan Urošević Mathematical Institute of the Serbian Academy of Sciences and Arts, Belgrade, Serbia

Leroy White Management Department, University of Exeter, Exeter, UK

Christophe Wilbaut LAMIH, CNRS, UMR 8201, University Polytechnique Hauts-de-France, Valenciennes, France;
INSA Hauts-de-France, Valenciennes, France

Shaomin Wu Kent Business School, University of Kent, Canterbury, England

Zeshui Xu Business School, Sichuan University, Sichuan, China

Moeko Yajima Department of Mathematical and Computing Sciences, Tokyo Institute of Technology, Tokyo, Japan

Guo-liang Yang Institutes of Science and Development, Chinese Academy of Sciences, Beijing, China

Shen Zhang Business School, Sichuan University, Sichuan, China

Zemin Zheng International Institute of Finance, School of Management, University of Science and Technology of China, Hefei, China

List of Figures

List of Tables

Part I

Discrete (Combinatorial) Optimisation

1

Bilevel Discrete Optimisation: Computational Complexity and Applications

Yury Kochetov⦿, Alexander Plyasunov, and Arteam Panin

1.1 Introduction

The first bilevel optimisation problem was formulated by the German economist Heinrich Freiherr von Stackelberg as the economic two players game in 1934 [1]. Therefore, bilevel optimisation problems are sometimes called Stackelberg games and their solutions are called the Stackelberg equilibria. In 1973, Jerome Bracken and James T. McGill proposed a modern formulation of the bilevel programming problems (BPPs) [2]. These problems contain two levels of decision-making: upper and lower. Each level has its optimisation problem. The upper-level problem is called the leader's problem. The lower-level problem is the follower's problem. Each problem has its objective function, constraints, and decision vector as variables. The lower-level problem is a parametric optimisation problem with an upper-level decision vector as the parameter. The follower's problem is used to form an

Y. Kochetov (✉) · A. Plyasunov · A. Panin
Sobolev Institute of Mathematics, Novosibirsk, Russia
e-mail: jkochet@math.nsc.ru

A. Plyasunov
e-mail: apljas@math.nsc.ru

A. Panin
e-mail: a.panin@g.nsu.ru

© The Author(s), under exclusive license to Springer Nature
Switzerland AG 2022
S. Salhi and J. Boylan (eds.), *The Palgrave Handbook of Operations Research*,
https://doi.org/10.1007/978-3-030-96935-6_1

extreme constraint to the leader's problem. This constraint is usually written as a set-theoretic inclusion [3]. It implies that the lower-level variables are the optimal solution to the lower-level problem parameterised by the upper-level variables.

This extreme constraint is the reason why the bilevel problems turned out to be surprisingly difficult to solve. For example, the linear programming problem is polynomially solvable, but its bilevel analogue is NP-hard in the strong sense. Moreover, to check the feasible domain is empty or not is an NP-hard problem in the strong sense too. This property is preserved for very special cases of the bilevel linear programming problems with the follower's variables in the leader's constraints.

Currently, there are no direct or simple modifications of standard approaches to design exact and approximate algorithms for the bilevel cases. The main reason is that the set of feasible solutions usually turns out to be non-convex and disconnected. For the bilevel mixed-integer linear problems, the optimal value of its linear programming relaxation cannot guarantee a lower bound for the integer global minimum. Moreover, if the optimal solution to the relaxed problem is a feasible solution to the original bilevel problem, then it does not follow that it is the optimal solution to the original problem. If we look at one of the standard approaches for solving optimisation problems, namely local search, then even in this case we will not be successful. This is due to the non-polynomiality of even the simplest neighbourhoods since they require the optimal solution to the follower's problem which, as a rule, is NP-hard.

What makes bilevel models highly relevant is that they are typically characterised by very large unexpected effects on the economy and surrounding environment. Given the far-reaching future impacts of the decisions, it is not surprising that the interest in bilevel optimisation has grown strong especially among researchers dealing with large-scale public sector decision-making problems. To date, a huge number of articles have appeared that study the bilevel models from theoretical and empirical sides. Similarly, there is a rapid increase in the number of papers devoted to bilevel programming applications in various fields of science and industry.

This chapter is organised as follows. Section 1.2 presents bilevel discrete optimisation in general formulation, definitions of feasible and optimal solutions for this ill-posed problem, main concepts, and examples. The relationship of the bilevel problems with Stackelberg games and multi-objective problems is discussed here. A short survey of exact and approximate methods, including metaheuristics as the most strong technique for application, is given in Sect. 1.3. Section 1.4 addresses important questions related to the computational complexity of bilevel discrete optimisation and the approximation complexity. Section 1.5 provides an overview of the literature with practical bilevel problems in economics, industry, transport, engineering, facility location, network design, etc. Finally, Sect. 1.6 concludes the paper and shows some future research directions and perspectives.

1.2 Main Definitions and Properties

Let us consider a sequential game where the first player (leader) chooses her solution (vector $x \in X$) and incorporates the optimal reaction (vector $y \in Y$) of the second player (follower) into her optimisation process. This game can be described mathematically as *bilevel programming problem*:

$$\min_{x \in X, y \in Y} F(x, y)$$

$$\text{s.t. } G(x, y) \leq 0,$$

$$y \in opt(x),$$

where $opt(x)$ is the set of optimal solutions to the follower's problem parameterised by the vector x:

$$\min_{y \in Y} f(x, y)$$

$$\text{s.t. } g(x, y) \leq 0.$$

In this formulation, $F(x, y)$ is the leader's objective function and $f(x, y)$ is the follower's objective function. The leader's and the follower's constraints are defined by the vector functions $G(x, y)$ and $g(x, y)$, respectively. In this program, the leader is free, whenever the set $opt(x)$ does not shrink to a singleton, to select an element of $opt(x)$ that suits her best. This case corresponds to the *optimistic* formulation. Alternatively, in the *pessimistic* formulation, we consider the case when the leader protects herself against the worst possible situation. To this end, we change the objective function of the leader as follows:

$$\min_{x \in X} \max_{y \in opt(x)} F(x, y)$$

and must guarantee that the follower cannot violate the upper-level constraints. In other words, all optimal solutions for the follower's problem must satisfy these joint (or coupling) constraints [4]. As a result, the pessimistic bilevel problems are very difficult to solve. Most theoretical and algorithmic contributions relate to the optimistic formulations. Detail discussion of the pessimistic formulations can be found in [4, 5].

In real-world applications, we often know nothing about follower behaviour. In such a case, the optimistic and pessimistic solutions show the lower and upper bounds for the optimal value of the objective function of the leader. We deal with the ill-posed problem indeed in the case of the multiple optimal solutions for the follower's problem. The difference between the optimistic and pessimistic approaches can also be explained from the follower viewpoint. The optimistic solution results from the friendly or cooperative behaviour of the players, while an aggressive follower produces the pessimistic solution.

Program BPP is often called the *upper (first level, outer, leader)* problem. The mathematical program parameterised by the vector x is the *lower (second level, inner, follower)* problem. The set of follower's optimal solutions $opt(x) = \{y \mid y \in \arg\min\{f(x, y') \mid y' \in sol(x)\}\}$ is also called the set of *rational reactions* where $sol(x) = \{y \mid g(x, y) \leq 0\}$ is the set of follower's feasible solutions.

The set of *feasible optimistic solutions* for the BPP is defined as $Sol = \{(x, y) \mid G(x, y) \leq 0, y \in opt(x)\}$. This set is usually non-convex and might be disconnected. Sometimes, it is called the *inducible region*. The set of *optimal optimistic solutions* for the BPP is the set of the best feasible optimistic solutions for the leader, that is the set $\{(x, y) \mid (x, y) \in \arg\min\{F(x', y') \mid (x', y') \in Sol\}\}$. The *relaxed constraint region* is defined as $S = \{(x, y) \mid G(x, y) \leq 0, g(x, y) \leq 0\}$.

For a better understanding of the bilevel formulations, let us consider an example of the bilevel knapsack problem [6]. Two players hold their own knapsacks and choose items from a common item set. Firstly, the leader packs some items into her knapsack. Later on, the follower packs some of the remaining items into his knapsack. The objective of the follower is to maximise the total profit of the items in his knapsack. The objective of the hostile leader is to minimise this profit. In other words, we face the following bilevel discrete optimisation problem with n items, p_i is the profit of item i, coefficients a_i and b_i are its weights for the leader and the follower, A and B

are the capacities of the leader's and the follower's knapsacks, respectively.

$$\min_{x,y \in \{0,1\}} \sum_{i=1}^{n} p_i y_i$$

$$\sum_{i=1}^{n} a_i x_i \leq A;$$

$$y \in opt(x),$$

where $opt(x)$ is the set of optimal solutions of the lower-level problem:

$$\max_{y \in \{0,1\}} \sum_{i=1}^{n} p_i y_i$$

$$\sum_{i=1}^{n} b_i y_i \leq B;$$

$$y_i \leq 1 - x_i, \quad 1 \leq i \leq n.$$

Note that we have to solve the NP-hard problem for arbitrary feasible solution x to calculate the value of the leader's objective function. Thus, the finding of the best leader's solution is a very hard problem. Below, we will see that it is harder than NP-complete problem, unless P = NP. This example is also interesting because the optimistic and pessimistic solutions coincide here even if the set $opt(x)$ contains multiple solutions. The upper-level constraint contains only the leader's variables. The follower cannot violate them. It is a simple case of BPPs.

For the pessimistic case, we have to modify the definition of feasible solution. The set of feasible pessimistic solutions is the set of pairs $(x, y) \in Sol$ which satisfy two conditions:

- $G(x, \overline{y}) \leq 0, \quad \forall \overline{y} \in opt(x);$
- $F(x, y) \geq F(x, \overline{y})), \quad \forall \overline{y} \in opt(x).$

For given x, all optimal follower's solutions must satisfy the joint constraints and y is the worst answer of the follower according to the leader objective function [7]. Optimal solution in pessimistic case is the best feasible pessimistic solution for the leader.

Consider some properties of the bilevel discrete optimisation problems. Let us find the minimum of the leader's objective function $F(x, y)$ for $(x, y) \in S$ in the relaxed constraint region. In other words, the leader makes a decision instead of the follower. It is so called *high point relaxation*. In that case, the optimal solution (with rare exceptions) will be infeasible for original bilevel problem. This is due to the non-optimality of the follower's response to the leader's decision. But we have got a lower bound for the global optimum.

The next unusual property deals with the integrality constraints. For the classical discrete optimisation, relaxation of this type of constraints lead to a lower bound. Moreover, if the optimal solution to the relaxed problem is integer, we have got the optimal solution to the initial discrete problem. It is not the case for the bilevel discrete optimisation. Let us consider an illustrative example of the pure integer bilevel linear problem proposed by James T. Moore and Jonathan F. Bard [8]:

$$\min_{x, y} F(x, y) = -x - 10y$$

$$\text{s.t. } x \geq 0, \text{ integer }; \quad y \in opt(x);$$

$$\min_{y} f(x, y) = y$$

$$\text{s.t. } -25x + 20y \leq 30; \quad x + 2y \leq 10;$$

$$2x - y \leq 15; \quad 2x + 10y \geq 15; \quad y \geq 0, \text{ integer }.$$

The solution $(x, y) = (8, 1)$ with the value $F(x, y) = -18$ is optimal to the relaxation and it is integer. But the optimal integer solution is $(x^*, y^*) = (2, 2)$ with the value of -22 (see Fig. 1.1).

The lower green lines show the feasible domain to the relaxation. As we can see, it is a non-convex area for this linear bilevel program. Moreover, the feasible domain of linear BPP, even with continuous variables, may be disconnected in general case [9]. Therefore, the idea of the simplex method does not work here. The red domain is the convex hull for the feasible discrete points. It is a small part of the relaxed constraint region S.

Let us slightly modify this example and include a new upper-level constraint $x + y = 5$. Now only three integer points $(2, 3)$, $(3, 2)$, $(4, 1)$ satisfy all constraints. The first one is the most interesting for the leader with value of -32 but $y = 3$ is not optimal for the follower's problem with $x = 2$. For the second point, we have the same property. Hence, the last point is

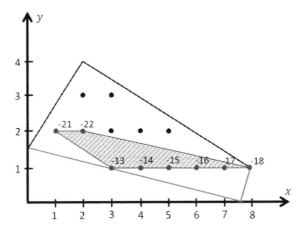

Fig. 1.1 The illustrative example

optimal now with a value of -15. Note that it is not a vertex of the convex hull of the integer feasible discrete points. Moreover, if we move this new constraint to the lower level, we have got another bilevel problem with an optimal value of -32.

Bilevel programming problems can be divided into three categories: (1) all solutions are real-valued vectors; such problems are known as continuous BPPs, (2) all solutions are discrete-valued vectors, discrete BPPs, (3) all solutions are vectors of continuous or discrete components, mixed BPPs. Further in this section, we consider various reformulations and generalisations of bilevel problems and their connections with Stackelberg games and multi-criteria optimisation problems.

The bilevel optimisation problem can be considered as a generalisation of the two-stage Stackelberg game [10]. For the first time, such a game was studied by Von Stackelberg in the context of unbalanced economic markets [1]. Indeed, BPPs are more or less similar to Stackelberg games in game theory [11]. In Stackelberg games, the lower-level problem is an equilibrium problem, while in bilevel optimisation, an optimisation problem arises in the lower level. A Stackelberg game may differ from the BPP when the reaction set of the lower-level decision-maker is not a singleton for some decisions of the leader. As a result, a solution of the static Stackelberg game may not be a solution to the BPP [12].

The optimal solution of the BPP is not necessarily a Pareto optimal solution of the corresponding bi-objective problem composed with the upper-level and the lower-level objectives and vice versa [13, 14]. The relationship between the bilevel problem and bicriteria optimisation is illustrated in [15–18]. In [19–23] the authors propose a methodology in which the

BPP is transformed to an equivalent multi-objective optimisation problem. A specific cone dominance concept is used. An application of these results to solve linear bilevel optimisation problems is given in [24]. The discrete bilevel problems with multiple followers are studied in [25–27]. The bilevel problems with multiple leaders are considered in [28, 29]. Nine different kinds of relationships between followers can be found in [30]. A surprising fact is that the globally optimal solutions to the bilevel optimisation problem need not remain globally optimal if a constraint is added to the lower-level problem which is inactive at the optimal solution [31, 32].

1.3   Computational Methods

The main purpose of this section is to present some state-of-the-art exact methods, metaheuristics, and hybrids of metaheuristics with exact methods to bilevel discrete optimisation. We have to skip the approximation schemes and polynomial-time approximation algorithms with a guaranteed performance. Some negative results in this area for the BPPs establish the inapproximability of various Σ_2^P-hard optimisation problems [33–35], unless P $=$ NP. Nevertheless, the first approximation scheme for a Σ_2^P-hard optimisation problem is designed in [36]. It is excellent result for the bilevel knapsack problem from Sect. 1.2 for the case $b_i = a_i, \forall i$. To the best of our knowledge, it is the first and still unique PTAS for the Σ_2^P-hard BPP.

1.3.1   Exact Methods

This class of methods can be divided into four types. The first one includes reformulation approaches. The BPP is reformulated as a single-level optimisation problem with a large number of variables and (or) constraints. Another approach here is the mathematical decomposition to reduce the original bilevel problem to the single-level problems. The second type includes branch and bound/branch and cut techniques. It is the basis of the mixed-integer bilevel optimisation solvers [37, 38] (see also [39, 40]). The third type includes the parametric programming approaches. The fourth type includes hybrid methods which may have the characteristics of the first three types.

The methods are based on reformulations. An algorithm based on the Benders decomposition method is proposed in [41]. The KKT optimality conditions are used as a reformulation procedure. The only assumption of the proposed algorithm is that although integer variables could appear in both levels, they should be controlled by the upper optimisation problem.

In [42], the linear BPP with binary leader variables and continuous follower variables is considered. The bilevel problem is reduced to a single-level problem using KKT conditions, a suitable linearisation technique, and the Benders decomposition method is applied.

In [43], a decomposition algorithm based on a column-and-constraint generation scheme using a single-level reformulation is proposed to solve the general bilevel mixed-integer linear problem. Another approach for binary lower-level problems is recently proposed in [44].

An algorithm for solving bilevel problems with boolean variables based on optimal value reformulation and the cutting plane technique is proposed in [45]. A similar technique is used in [46]. Some new results in this area are obtained in [47, 48].

The branch and bound/branch and cut methods. The first branch and bound method for discrete bilevel optimisation is developed in [8]. The bilevel problems with the linear programming problem at the lower level and the integer programming problem at the upper level are studied in [49]. A branch and bound method is designed for this special case.

In [50], a class of the BPP is considered where the leader controls continuous and discrete variables and wants to minimise a convex nonlinear objective function. The follower's objective function is a convex quadratic in a continuous decision space. All constraints are linear. A branch and bound algorithm is developed to find the global optima.

A new version of the branch and bound method for the mixed-integer upper- and lower-level problems with joint constraints at the upper level is proposed in [51]. The linking variables are discrete and all discrete variables are bounded. The high point relaxation is used to find the optimal solution in optimistic case.

In [52], two exact algorithms are proposed. The first one is based on the cutting plane technique, and the second one belongs to the class of branch and cut algorithms. In [6, 53], an algorithm based on a branch and cut approach is proposed for the BPP problems without continuous variables and without joint constraints at the upper level. A generalisation of this algorithm that allows a mixed-integer environment at both levels is proposed in [54]. Other efficient cutting plane algorithms can be found in [51, 55–58]. Some valid inequalities and facets for the network pricing problem with connected toll arcs and its variants are designed in [59].

Parametric programming approaches. Two exact algorithms for the integer and mixed-integer bilevel programming problems via multi-parametric programming are proposed in [60]. The first algorithm addresses the integer case of the linear BPP and employs a reformulation linearisation technique to construct a parametric convex hull representation of the inner problem constraint set. The second algorithm addresses the mixed-integer case and employs a similar convexification procedure as the previous algorithm. In contrast to the first algorithm, where a continuous multi-parametric programming approach is used, the second algorithm utilises multi-parametric mixed-integer programming to solve the inner problem.

In [61], exact global optimisation algorithms are presented for two classes of BPP, namely: the mixed-integer linear BPP and the mixed-integer convex quadratic BPP. The proposed algorithms are a result of multi-parametric programming theory. The main idea here is to recast the lower-level problem as a multi-parametric programming problem where the optimisation variables of the upper-level problem (both continuous and integer) are considered as parameters for the lower-level problem. The resulting exact parametric solutions are then substituted into the upper-level problem and it is solved as a set of single-level deterministic mixed-integer programs.

A BPP with only integer decision variables at the lower level and constraints at both levels is studied in [62]. The leader has integer or continuous decision variables. The solution approach is based on the theory of parametric integer programming and runs in polynomial time when the number of decision variables of the follower is fixed.

Non-standard solution methods. In [63], an algorithm based on the concept of k-th best solution, first developed for the linear case, is developed for the integer linear fractional BPP. The correctness of this algorithm is shown in [64]. Upper approximations of the optimal objective function value of the lower-level problem are used for solving mixed-integer BPP in [65].

A multi-way branching method is used for solving the mixed-integer bilevel linear program in the case all leader variables are integer and bounded [66]. An exact algorithm for solving the discrete linear bilevel optimisation problems using multi-way disjunction cuts to remove infeasible solutions for the bilevel problem from the search space is presented in [67]. Additional information about the exact methods for solving (mixed-integer) linear bilevel optimisation can be found in [61].

1.3.2   Metaheuristics

The word heuristic (from the Greek word heuriskein) means the art of discovering new strategies to solve problems. The suffix meta (Greek) means upper-level methodology. The term metaheuristic has been introduced by

Fred Glover [68]. Unlike exact methods, metaheuristics allow finding effective approximate solutions to large-scale problem instances in a reasonable time without guarantee to get global optimal solutions or even solutions with small deviation from the optimal value. Metaheuristics became popular in the last 30 years. They demonstrate efficiency and effectiveness to solve large and sophisticated problems in many applications [69–71].

Due to the intrinsic complexity of bilevel models, BPPs have been recognised as one of the most difficult classses to solve. Hence, metaheuristic algorithms have been applied here. We can divide them into two classes [70]: population-based search and single-solution-based search. Single-solution-based algorithms (e.g. local search, variable neighbourhood search, tabu search, simulated annealing) manipulate and transform a single solution during the search while in population-based algorithms (e.g. particle swarm, evolutionary algorithms) a whole population of solutions is evolved. These two families have complementary characteristics: single-solution-based metaheuristics are exploitation-oriented. They have the power to intensify the search in local regions. Population-based metaheuristics are exploration-oriented. They allow better diversification in the whole search space.

Metaheuristics are approximate algorithms. In bilevel problems, there is a limitation that forces us to solve the lower-level problem exactly. This fact makes it impossible to use metaheuristics directly to the bilevel problems. The following classification distinguishes metaheuristics according to the way they work with the lower-level problem: (1) Single-level transformation approach; (2) Nested sequential approach; (3) Multi-objective approach; (4) Co-evolutionary approach.

In the single-level transformation approach, we try to reformulate the BPP into a single-level optimisation problem. Then, the classical metaheuristics can be used to solve the single-level problem.

In the nested sequential approach, the lower-level optimisation problem is solved in nested and sequential ways to evaluate the solutions generated at the upper level of the BPP.

In the multi-objective approach, the BPP is transformed into a multi-objective optimisation problem. Then, any multi-objective metaheuristic can be used to solve the generated problem.

Finally, the co-evolutionary approach is the most general methodology to solve the BPPs. In this case, metaheuristics for different levels of the problem coevolve in parallel and exchange information during the search.

A detailed description of this classification with links to corresponding algorithms can be found in [70]. For solving bilevel linear problems, heuristic approaches such as evolution algorithms, tabu search, simulated annealing, grid search, and other algorithms can be found in [71, 72]. Computational results for the metaheuristics to the $(r|p)$-centroid problem and other bilevel competitive facility location models can be found in [70, 73]. Implementation of genetic and memetic algorithms, ant colony systems, tabu search, local search, particle swarm optimisation, simulated annealing, and other heuristic approaches are presented in [70, 71, 74, 75].

Let us return to the definition of a feasible solution to the BPP. The set of feasible solutions is defined as $Sol = \{(x, y) \mid G(x, y) \leq 0, y \in opt(x)\}$. Hence, we need an optimal solution to the follower's problem to get a feasible solution for given x. As a result, metaheuristics have to include an exact method for this aim. Thus, they are hybrid methods. Now we will consider the case when the follower's problem has multiple solutions. For the optimistic case, we face an additional problem to pick up the best solution for the leader in the set $opt(x)$. To this end, we must solve the following optimisation problem for given x:

$$\min_{y \in Y} F(x, y)$$

$$\text{s.t. } G(x, y) \leq 0,$$

$$f(x, y) = f^*(x),$$

$$g(x, y) \leq 0,$$

where $f^*(x)$ is the optimal value to the follower's problem. If this auxiliary problem is infeasible then we must change the solution for the leader. Note that we need the optimal solution here. Hence, we need an exact method again.

In the pessimistic case, we have a more sophisticated position. As we have noted in Sect. 1.2, the leader wishes to protect herself against the worst possible answer of the follower and upper-level joint constraints must be satisfied for all possible answers. Hence, we need to solve the following bilevel optimisation problem:

$$\min_{x \in X} \max_{y \in opt(x)} F(x, y),$$

$$\text{s.t. } G(x, y) \leq 0, \forall y \in opt(x), \ x \in X.$$

For given x, we can find the worst follower's answer by solving new auxiliary problem:

$$\max_{y \in Y} F(x, y)$$

$$\text{s.t. } f(x, y) = f^*(x),$$

$$g(x, y) \leq 0.$$

Later on, we must be sure that all optimal solutions to the follower's problem satisfy the joint constraints. If the follower's variables are not presented in the upper-level constraints then this step can be omitted [3]. Otherwise, we need to check all solutions in the set $opt(x)$.

Let $G(x, y) = (G_1(x, y), \ldots, G_m(x, y))$ and we wish to find an optimal solution for the follower which does not satisfy the leader's constraints. Thus, we solve m problems for given x:

$$\alpha_j = \max\{G_j(x, y) | f(x, y) = f^*(x), g(x, y) \leq 0\}, \quad j = 1, \ldots, m.$$

If $\max \alpha_j > 0$ then we have infeasible solution in pessimistic case and the point x must be replaced. The pessimistic case is the most difficult and interesting line for future research.

The following simple example illustrates that the optimistic and pessimistic bilevel problems are similar but their optimal solutions can differ considerably [4].

$$\min_{x \in \{-1, 0, 1\}} x$$

$$x \geq y, \quad y \in opt(x),$$

and $opt(x)$ is the set of optimal solutions to the follower's problem:

$$\max_{y \in \{-1, 0, 1\}} y^2$$

The follower's problem is optimised by $y \in \{-1, 1\}$, independent of the leader's decision. The pessimistic bilevel problem requires x to exceed 1, resulting in an optimal objective value of 1. In contrast, the optimistic bilevel problem requires x to exceed -1, which results in an optimal objective value of -1.

1.4   Computational and Approximation Complexity

According to the principle of bounded rationality [76], economic agents cannot use excessively large resources to find the optimal solution. In operations research, the interaction of economic agents is described by mathematical models. Therefore, computational resources are the most critical type of resource here. From this point of view, the theory of computational complexity is a natural mathematical tool for describing and investigating the behaviour of economic agents based on the principle of bounded rationality [77]. Thus, the knowledge of the relations of the optimisation problem with complexity classes allows us to estimate what computational resources are needed to find a rational solution.

When we discuss the computational complexity of the single-level problems, we usually refer to the complexity classes P and NP for the decision problems and the classes PO, NPO for the optimisation problems. The peculiarity of bilevel (multi-level) problems is that many of them are outside of these classes. Therefore, we are forced to introduce the concepts of a polynomial and approximation hierarchy of complexity classes for the BPP.

1.4.1   Polynomial Hierarchy

We remind the notations used in computational complexity theory to describe the polynomial hierarchy of complexity classes [78, 79]. The first two main classes of the decision problems P and NP are defined with deterministic and non-deterministic Turing machines [78]. The class P contains the decision problems solvable in polynomial time on deterministic Turing machines. The class NP is defined as the class of the decision problems solvable in polynomial time on non-deterministic Turing machines. It means that we can verify the answer *Yes* in time polynomial in the size of the input data of the problem. The third class co-NP consists of decision problems whose complements belong to the class NP. It means that we can verify the answer *No* in time polynomial in the size of the input data of the problem. These classes form the first level of the polynomial hierarchy. They are denoted as Δ_1^P, Σ_1^P, and Π_1^P, respectively. The second level of the polynomial hierarchy is defined with deterministic and nondeterministic oracle Turing machines [78].

A decision problem belongs to the class Δ_2^P if there exists a deterministic Turing machine with an oracle that solves this problem in polynomial time, using as oracle some language (decision problem) from the class NP. A

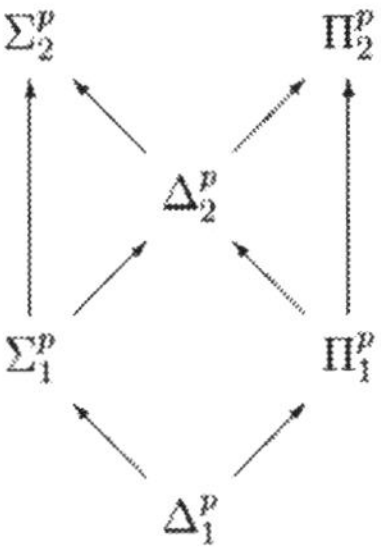

$$\Sigma_2^p = NP^{NP}, \quad \Pi_2^p = co - NP^{NP};$$

$$\Delta_2^p = P^{NP} = P^{co-NP};$$

$$\Sigma_1^p = NP, \quad \Pi_1^p = co - NP;$$

$$\Delta_1^p = \Sigma_0^p = \Pi_0^p = P.$$

Fig. 1.2 The first two levels of hierarchy

decision problem belongs to the class Σ_2^P if there exists a non-deterministic Turing machine with an oracle that solves this problem in polynomial time, using as oracle some language from the class NP. The class Π_2^P consists of decision problems whose complements belong to Σ_2^P. The class Δ_2^P is often denoted as P^{NP} and the class Σ_2^P is denoted as NP^{NP}. Figure 1.2 shows all inclusions between hierarchy classes on the first two levels.

It is clear that this hierarchy can be expanded if we take the class Σ_{k-1}^P as the oracle. It is known that if NP $\neq$ co-NP then these inclusions are strict [78]. The notions of completeness and hardness commonly used for the class NP are translated directly to the classes Σ_k^P. In particular, the k-level optimisation problems with binary variables, linear constraints, and linear objective functions are Σ_k^P-hard [80]. We will focus our attention on the class Σ_2^P as the most appropriate for the BPP and difficult from the point of view of optimisation methods. A compendium of Σ_2^P-complete/hard problems can be found in [81], [82], with more recent updates available online.

1.4.2 Σ_2^P-Hard Bilevel Programming Problems

The structure of the bilevel problems makes their standard decision problem a natural candidate for membership in the Σ_2^P class. This is the case if the lower-level parametric problem lies in the class NPO. If the standard decision problem for the lower-level parametric problem is NP-complete, then as a rule, the corresponding bilevel problems turn out to be Σ_2^P-hard.

Three Σ_2^P-hard bilevel knapsack problems can be found in [36]. One of them we have discussed in Sect. 1.2. Let us formulate two remaining problems. In the first one [83], the leader controls the capacity x of the knapsack while the follower controls all items and decides which of them are packed into it. The objective function of the leader depends on the capacity x and the packed items, whereas the objective function of the follower solely depends on the packed items.

$$\min_{x,y}\left\{ Ax + \sum_{i=1}^{n} a_i y_i \right\} \text{ s.t. } C \leq x \leq C', y \in opt(x),$$

where $opt(x)$ is the set of optimal solutions of the lower-level problem:

$$\max_{y} \sum_{i=1}^{n} b_i y_i \text{ s.t. } \sum_{i=1}^{n} b_i y_i \leq x; y_i \in \{0, 1\}, 1 \leq i \leq n.$$

In the second problem [84], players pack items into the same knapsack with a prespecified capacity of C. The leader controls part of the item set. The follower controls the rest of this set. The leader starts the game by packing some of her items into the knapsack. Later on, the follower adds some further items from his set. The objective function of the leader depends on all items packed by the leader and the follower, whereas the objective function of the follower solely depends on his items.

$$\min_{x,y}\left\{ \sum_{j=1}^{m} a_j x_j + \sum_{i=1}^{n} a_i' y_i \right\} \text{ s.t. } x_j \in \{0, 1\}, 1 \leq j \leq m, y \in opt(x),$$

where $opt(x)$ is the set of optimal solutions of the lower-level problem:

$$\max_{y} \sum_{i=1}^{n} b_i y_i \text{ s.t. } \sum_{i=1}^{n} c_i' y_i \leq C - \sum_{j=1}^{m} c_j x_j, y_i \in \{0, 1\}, 1 \leq i \leq n.$$

To show the Σ_2^P-hardness of these bilevel knapsack variants, the following Σ_2^P-complete decision problem (Subset-Sum-Interval) is used [85].

Instance: A sequence $q_1, q_2, \ldots, q_k$ of positive integers; two positive integers R and r with $r \leq k$.

Question: Does there exist an integer S with $R \leq S < R + 2^r$ such that none of the subsets $I \subseteq \{1, \ldots, k\}$ satisfies $\Sigma_{i \in I} q_i = S$?

Reducibilities guarantee Σ_2^P-hardness of all three bilevel knapsack variants under the optimistic and pessimistic scenarios [36].

In the field of bilevel facility location, we have some variants of $(r|p)$-centroid problem which are Σ_2^P-hard [86, 87]. Let us consider a two-dimensional Euclidean plane in which n clients are located. We assume that each client j has a positive demand w_j. Let X be the set of p points where the leader opens her facilities and let Y be the set of r points where the follower opens his facilities. The distances from client j to the closest facility of the leader and the closest facility of the follower are denoted as $d(j, X)$ and $d(j, Y)$, respectively. The client j prefers Y over X if $d(j, Y) < d(j, X)$ and prefers X over Y otherwise. By

$$U(Y \prec X) := \{j \mid d(j, Y) < d(j, X)\}$$

we denote the set of clients preferring Y over X. The total demand captured by the follower by locating his facilities at Y while the leader locates her facilities at X is given by

$$W(Y \prec X) := \sum (w_j \mid j \in U(Y \prec X)).$$

For X given, the follower tries to maximise his own market share. The maximal value $W^*(X)$ is defined to be

$$W^*(X) := \max_{Y, |Y|=r} W(Y \prec X).$$

This maximisation problem will be called the *follower problem*. The leader tries to minimise the market share of the follower. This minimal value $W^*(X^*)$ is defined to be

$$W^*(X^*) := \min_{X, |X|=p} W^*(X).$$

For the best solution X^* of the leader, her market share is $\sum_{j=1}^{n} w_j - W^*(X^*)$. In the $(r|p)$-centroid problem, the goal is to find X^* and $W^*(X^*)$.

The discrete $(r|p)$-centroid problem and the $(r|p)$-centroid problem on a network are Σ_2^P-hard [86]. The hardness proof uses a reduction from the Σ_2^P-complete decision problem $\exists \forall 3SAT$ [86]. It is shown in [87] that the $(r|p)$-centroid problem in the plane is Σ_2^P-hard. The hardness proof uses a reduction from the Σ_2^P-complete decision problem $\exists \forall 3, 4SAT$ [87]. Based on this reducibility, the following results are also obtained:

- the discrete $(r|p)$-centroid problem is Σ_2^P-hard even the clients and facilities are placed in the two-dimensional Euclidean plane;
- the $(r|p)$-centroid problem on a network is Σ_2^P-hard even for planar graphs with vertices in the two-dimensional Euclidean plane and weights of the edges are Euclidean distances between corresponding points.

Another Σ_2^P-hard problem of competitive facility location is considered in [88]. The hardness proof uses a reduction from the Σ_2^P-complete decision problem $\exists_1 \forall_3 Sat$ [88].

In [89, 90], there is a leader–follower location and pricing problem that is also Σ_2^P-hard. In [89] the hardness proof uses a reduction from the Σ_2^P-complete standard decision problem of the $(r|p)$-centroid problem. In [90] the hardness proof uses a reduction from the Σ_2^P-complete decision problem $\exists \forall 3, 4SAT$ [87].

The bilevel problem of strategic base station placement in cognitive radio networks is studied in [91]. It is shown that the problem is Σ_2^P-hard. The proof uses a reduction from the Σ_2^P-complete decision problem $\exists \forall 3, 4SAT$ [87].

Σ_2^P-hard problems of public–private partnership can be found in [92, 93]. In [92], it is shown that the problem without tax benefits and infrastructure projects still remains Σ_2^P-hard even in the case of a three-year planning horizon and the optimistic and pessimistic setting. The hardness proofs use a reduction from the Σ_2^P-complete decision problem Subset-Sum-Interval [85].

1.4.3 Approximation Hierarchy

Let us consider the computational complexity of finding near optimal solutions for bilevel discrete optimisation problems. In the classical case, we study the computational complexity from the point of view of approximate algorithms with a performance guarantee for the optimisation problems from the class NPO [79]. By definition, this class consists of optimisation problems for which the standard decision problem belongs to class NP. The class PO is the subclass of the NPO problems that admitting an exact polynomial-time algorithm.

Remind some definitions from [79]. Given an optimisation problem Q in NPO, an approximation algorithm A for Q, and a function $r : N \mapsto (1, \infty)$, we say that A is an $r(n)$-approximate algorithm for Q if, for any instance x with a non-empty set of feasible solutions, the performance ratio of the feasible solution $y = A(x)$ with respect to x verifies the following inequality:

$$R(x, A(x)) = \max \left(\frac{f(x, y)}{f^*(x)}, \frac{f^*(x)}{f(x, y)} \right) \leq r(|x|),$$

where $f(x, y)$ is the value of the objective function of the problem on a feasible solution y for x, $f(x^*)$ is the optimal value of the objective function for x.

An algorithm A is said to be a polynomial-time approximation scheme (PTAS) for Q if, for any instance x and for any rational value $r > 1$, A returns an r-approximate solution of x in time polynomial in $|x|$.

An algorithm A is said to be a fully polynomial-time approximation scheme (FPTAS) for Q if, for any instance x and for any rational value $r > 1$, A returns an r-approximate solution of x in time polynomial both in $|x|$ and $1/(r - 1)$.

The class FPTAS is the class of NPO problems that admitting a fully polynomial-time approximation scheme, while the class PTAS is the class of NPO problems that admitting a polynomial-time approximation scheme.

Given a class of functions F, F-APX is the class of all NPO problems Q such that, for some function $r \in F$, there exists a polynomial-time $r(n)$-approximate algorithm for Q.

Denote by APX, Log-APX, $Poly$-APX, Exp-APX classes F-APX with F equal to the set of constant functions, to the set $O(\log n)$ functions, to the set $\cup_{k>0} O(n^k)$ functions, and to the set $\cup_{k>0} O(2^{n^k})$ functions, respectively.

The classes APX, Log-APX, $Poly$-APX, and Exp-APX consist of the problems for which there exist polynomial approximate algorithms with constant, logarithmic, polynomial, and exponential performance guarantee, respectively. In the last three cases, the values of the above-mentioned functions depend on the length of the problem input data.

To determine the approximation complexity of an optimisation problem, it is enough to find its position in the hierarchy of approximation classes:

$$PO \subseteq FPTAS \subseteq PTAS \subseteq APX \subseteq Log\text{-}APX \subseteq Poly\text{-}APX$$
$$\subseteq Exp\text{-}APX \subseteq NPO.$$

Assuming $P \neq NP$, these inclusions are proper [79, 94].

This hierarchy is used to describe the properties of optimisation problems from the class NPO. To compare the approximability properties of arbitrary two problems from the class NPO, reducibility that preserves approximability is used [79, 94]. Similar approximation classes for the BPPs can be found in [89]. The definition of each of these new approximation classes is obtained from the original one by replacing the polynomial-time deterministic algorithm by a polynomial-time deterministic algorithm with an oracle from the class NP.

Bilevel knapsack problems are studied in [36, 95]. In [36], a polynomial-time approximation scheme is developed for the bilevel knapsack problem proposed in [6]. It is the first approximation scheme for a Σ_2^P-hard optimisation problem in the history of approximation algorithms.

The question of the complexity of the approximation of optimisation problems associated with pricing processes is presented in [96–100]. In [96], it is shown that the unit demand envy-free pricing problem is APX-hard. APX-hardness of the Stackelberg network pricing problem is shown in [97]. The Stackelberg minimum spanning tree game is also APX-hard [98]. In [99], it is shown that the bilevel problem with the mill pricing belongs to the class *Log*-APX.

The approximability of the bilevel facility location and pricing problems is discussed in [100]. It is shown that such problems with different pricing strategies are *Poly*-APX-hard if we can open a fixed number of facilities. Without the last constraint, such problems are complete in the class *Poly*-APX. The approximability of the discrete bilevel strategic planning model for public–private partnership is discussed in [101]. It is shown that this problem is NPO-hard, and the investor's problem is NPO-complete. As in the previous case, AP-reducibility is used to give these results. Unless P=NP, there cannot exist polynomial-time approximate algorithms with guaranteed perfomance that correspond to the classes *APX*, *Log-APX*, *Poly-APX*, and *Exp-APX*, and there also cannot exist polynomial-time approximation schemes for the investor's problem at the lower level. Hence, we have the same negative result for the bilevel linear problem.

1.5   Applications

The mixed-integer bilevel programming problems have a wide range of applications in various spheres of life. A comprehensive overview of such applications can be found in [9, 71]. A lot of results are related to the chemical industry, network design, environmental problems, military applications, competitive facility location, pricing, interdiction problems, and many others. Moreover, the review [9] contains some studies on the natural gas cash-out problem, the deregulated electricity market equilibrium problem, biofuel problems, a problem of designing coupled energy carrier networks, and so forth. Most part of them deals with the bilevel models with continuous variables. Below we present some applications of integer or mixed-integer bilevel models.

Network design. The term *network design* means any model that involves the variables to define the structure of a graph or a network. In many cases, we discuss a transportation network. Usually, the objective of network design models is to satisfy data communication requirements and minimise the total expenses. Requirement scope can vary widely from one network design project to another based on geographic particularities and the nature of the data requiring transport.

The network design problem is first modelled as a bilevel program by Gao et al. [102]. The leader determines new road links to minimise the system travelling costs. The follower's problem is design to characterise the user equilibrium. Fontaine and Minner [103] reformulate the network design problem as a mixed-integer linear problem using the same approach as Labbé et al. [104]. An improved Benders decomposition technique is devised. In a recent paper, Fontaine and Minner [105] apply this decomposition method to an extended version of the problem. Different vehicle flow patterns are considered in a time-varying fashion. Bagloee et al. [106] study the interaction of two types of vehicles in the follower's problem, and propose a hybrid algorithm that combines a generalised Benders decomposition with the branch and bound approach. In [107] the joint design and pricing problems are considered. These problems are related to designing freight carrying services and determining their associated prices as observed by the shipper firms. In [108] the bilevel model for the discrete network design problem on trains and its solution method based on the genetic algorithm are proposed.

Interdiction games play an important role in military and drug enforcement applications. In both cases, the goal is to disrupt elements of a transportation network to reduce as much as possible the enemy's movements on the network. In [109] a bilevel problem of network interdiction is proposed and studied. In [110], the discrete network design problem is defined as a bilevel optimisation problem. The leader wants to identify the optimal network structure and minimise the network travel time. The follower problem represents the network user's reaction as a static traffic assignment problem under user equilibrium. The bilevel optimisation model for the hazardous materials (hazmat) transportation problem with lane reservation is studied in [74]. The problem lies in selecting lanes to be reserved in the network and planning paths for hazmat transportation tasks. The trade-off among transportation cost, risk, and impact on normal traffic is considered. In the context of vehicle transportation in congested roads, an optimisation framework to integrate the operator decisions on network pricing, regulation, and expansion while accounting for the shipments of hazardous materials is proposed in [75].

Defence and cybersecurity applications. The literature on the Stackelberg security games and the bilevel defender–attacker models is quite extensive. A large part of publications are devoted to applied problems of ensuring the security of objects (see [111–113] and references in them). For example, in security resource optimisation problems, research has led to decision aids for real-world security agencies which need to deploy patrols and checkpoints to protect targets from terrorists and criminals. Stackelberg security games are a powerful tool to study *a competition* between a defender and an adversary. The defender commits to a mixed strategy—a randomised resource allocation specified by a probability distribution over deterministic schedules—which takes into account the adversary's best response to his observation of the mixed strategy.

In [73, 114–120], another line of research deals with the r-interdiction median problems with fortification are studied. The leader protects q objects, and the follower attacks r unprotected objects. The defensive maximal covering location model as a leader–follower attacker–defender game–theoretic model is studied in [73].

Among modern publications, we can also highlight papers [121–123]. In the *attacker–defender* model [121], a more general situation is considered. The attacker and the defender have various means (methods) for attacking and defending objects, respectively. The losses of the attacking side and the result of the attack depend on the means. In such a situation, the attacking side enters into a game interaction with the defence side and take into account the response of the other side which, choosing its solution, aims to inflict maximum losses for the attacker. To find the optimal solution of the bilevel mixed-integer problem, the feasible region is split into subsets and the bilevel problem is reduced to a sequence of bilevel subproblems. Each bilevel subproblem is reformulated as a mixed-integer programming problem. Previously, the same idea was used to design exact polynomial-time algorithms for the bilevel problems with knapsack problem and continuous variables at the lower level [7, 124–127].

In [122], the leader does not know the attack scenario and the follower's priorities for selecting targets for the attack. But, she can consider several possible scenarios that cover the follower's plans. The leader's problem is to select the set of objects for protection to minimise the total costs of protecting the objects and eliminating the consequences of the attack associated with the reassignment of the facilities for customer service. Reformulation of the bilevel problem as some single-level problems is proposed.

In the bilevel optimisation framework, a leader chooses her solution assuming that a follower answers by an optimal reaction according to the lower-level problem. However, the lower-level problems might be nontrivial. In practice, it might be inexactly solved by metaheuristics. Zare et al. [123] study a broad class of bilevel optimisation problems where the follower might not optimally react to the leader's actions. The authors provide algorithmic implementations of a new framework for a class of nonlinear bilevel knapsack problems and illustrate the impact of incorporating this realistic feature in the context of defender-attacker problems.

Recently proposed attacker-defender models for power system vulnerability assessment perform a worst-case analysis considering both natural-occurring events and malicious attacks. The worst-case analysis is crucial for vulnerability assessment and mitigation of critical infrastructure such as power systems. Defence applications including electric grid defence planning and defence models in interdiction problems can be found in [71].

Information protection and cybersecurity discrete bilevel problems can be found in review [9]. In the bilevel formulation from [128], the goal of the destructive agent is to minimise the number of power system components that must be destroyed in order to cause a loss of load greater than or equal to a specified level. The system operator will implement all feasible corrective actions to minimise the level of system load shed. The resulting nonlinear mixed-integer bilevel programming formulation is transformed into an equivalent single-level mixed-integer linear program and solved by commercially available software.

The bilevel model specifically allows one to define different objective functions for the terrorist and the system. Researchers have begun to look into some new ways of addressing the security assessment problem. For example, in [129], a multiagent system is proposed capable of assessing power system vulnerability, monitoring hidden failures of protection devices, and providing adaptive control actions to prevent catastrophic failures and cascading sequences of events.

Attack tree is another widely used combinatorial model in the cybersecurity analysis [130]. Defence trees have been developed to investigate the effect of defence mechanisms using measures such as attacker's cost and security cost, return on investment and return on the attack. In an attack response tree, an attacker–defender game is used to find an optimal policy from the countermeasures' pool.

Cybersecurity is becoming an area of growing concern in the electric power industry with the development of the smart grid. A false data injection attack has recently attracted the ever wider interest of researchers. A special type of false data injection attack or a Load redistribution (LR) attack is developed in [131]. The damage from LR attacks to power system operations can manifest in an immediate or a delayed fashion. For the immediate attacking goal, the most damaging attack can be identified through a max–min attacker–defender model.

Facility location. Facility location problems arise as real-life applications in both public and private sectors try to determine the optimal location for facilities such as warehouses, plants, distribution centres, shopping malls, hospitals, and post offices. They can have different objectives such as maximisation of the profit obtained from customers and minimisation of the total cost incurred by locating facilities and serving customers. There are many different bilevel settings for the facility location models [71, 73, 132, 133]. For example, mathematical models and computational methods for the classical competitive facility location model so-called $(r|p)$-centroid problem, can be found in [70].

The facility location problems with customer's preferences are studied in [134–141]. In these problems, the upper-level problem describes the facility location process as opposed to the lower-level problem that describes the customer allocation process. In [142], there is the problem of locating differentiated waste collection centres. Another bilevel programming problem of locating waste collection centres can be found in [143]. The model of competitive facility location and pricing is investigated in [90]. The choice of prices is based on the Bertrand model of price competition and the possibility of splitting a client's demand if it is profitable for both players. In [144], a firm wants to open p facilities to enter a market and maximise its market share, where other firms already operate. Customers can patronise any open facility and maximise their utility function. A comprehensive overview of bilevel facility location models can be found in [145].

The mixed-integer bilevel problem of strategic base stations placement in cognitive radio networks is considered in [91]. Two operators want to exploit the unused capacity of the primary network and maximise their profits derived from operating the base stations installed and clients served. The leader is aware of the future arrival of the follower, who is able to capture clients by placing its own base stations. It has also to limit the interference power at some measurement points defined by the primary user. The authors develop a matheuristic where a mixed-integer program derived from the follower's problem is solved by CPLEX software.

An interesting leader–follower facility location model for 5G high-speed networks is presented in [146]. Two mobile operators compete to attract customers with high-speed internet connections. The leader acts first by opening some base stations, anticipating that the follower will react by creating her own base stations and renting some leader's stations. Each customer patronises an operator with the highest speed of connection for him. The leader and the follower maximise their profits at the first and second levels, respectively and the customers move from one operator to another until the Nash equilibrium is reached.

Another line of interesting application is presented by the leader–follower hub location problems. The discrete hub network design model in a competitive environment is investigated in [147] with a flow threshold. Two firms, a leader and a follower, compete with each other to maximise their profits. The level of captured passengers is determined by the logit function and each route contains one hub only.

In [148] the authors consider the bilevel problem which extends the p-hub median problem [149], taking into account intentional hub disruptions. In this formulation, the leader chooses p hubs and additionally the emergency hub to minimise two objectives, one of which corresponds to the total transportation cost in the normal situation while the other corresponds to the total transportation cost in the worst-case after r-interdiction. Two formulations, the multiple allocation hub interdiction problem and hub protection problem are studied in [150]. The first formulation refers to the bilevel programming problem and the second one to the three-level programming problem. For the multiple allocation hub interdiction problem, two reductions to mixed-integer problems are proposed. The first one is based on the dual problem to the linear programming lower-level problem. The second reduction is based on replacing the lower-level problem with an equivalent system of closest assignment constraints. The ideas developed on the multiple allocation hub interdiction problem are used to solve the hub protection problem (see also [151, 152]).

The paper [153] addresses the $(r|p)$-hub centroid problem. The leader locates p hubs, later on, the follower locates r hubs. The customers choose one firm with respect to provided service levels. The goal of each firm is market share maximisation. An exact solution method is proposed.

Three variants of the bilevel hub interdiction problem are presented in [154]: the multiple allocation p-hub median, the p-hub maximal covering, and the p-hub centre problems under intentional disruptions. In these problems, the leader locates p hubs, whereas the follower tries to interdict r such hubs that their loss would diminish the network performance the most. The simulated annealing heuristic is applied as a solution approach.

In [155] the leader–follower hub location problem under fixed markups is introduced deploying an alternating heuristic as a solution approach. In [156] the authors investigate the leader–follower single allocation hub location problem under fixed markups. Two variants of this Stackelberg competition are addressed: deterministic and robust. For the deterministic variant, a mixed-integer linear reformulation of the follower's model is given. For the robust variant, it is shown how to reformulate the follower's program as a mixed-integer conic quadratic one. As a solution approach for the leader, the alternating heuristic is used also.

The $(r|p)$-hub centroid problem under the price war can be found in [157]. It was shown that there is a solution when the objective is profit maximisation, and the customer demand is split according to the logit model. The equilibrium price equations are presented, accompanied by some computational complexity observations. In [158], an extension of this model is presented. The paper provides a theoretical indication of the effect of the price sensitivity parameter on profit. It is shown that the optimal routes under the Bertrand-Nash price equilibrium are among the lowest cost ones. As a solution approach is used the basic variable neighbourhood search algorithm, based on a novel local search stopping rule and objective function estimation.

Supply chain. A bilevel optimisation problem to model the planning of a distribution network is proposed in [159]. In this problem, there are manufacturing plants, depots, and customers. The purpose is to decide which depots should be used and how the product should be distributed from depots to customers and from plants to depots aiming to minimise the total fixed costs and delivery costs. A metaheuristic approach based on evolutionary algorithms is developed.

The paper [160] formulates the joint configuration of a product family and its supply chain. The upper-level problem optimises the selection of modules, module instances, and product variants. The lower-level problem responds to decisions of the upper level in order to determine an optimal supply chain configuration and inventory policies. To solve this nonlinear optimisation model, a bilevel nested genetic algorithm with constraint reasoning is developed and implemented.

The distribution centre problem is represented in [161]. The upper and lower levels are to find the minimum transportation cost of shipping products from plants to distribution centres and from distribution centres to customers, respectively.

Bilevel models associated with timberlands systems are proposed in [162, 163]. The paper [162] investigates the economic impact of a new biorefinery on an established timberlands system. The work [163] studies the supply allocation problem for an established timberlands supply chain with an additional decision of new biorefinery investments. The paper [164] focuses on a multi-product vendor–buyer supply chain considering environmental factors in the product manufacturing process. The model determines the optimal selling prices, advertising expenditures, wholesale prices, vendor's environmental improvements, and ordering policies of the vendor and the buyer.

Scheduling problems. The bilevel flow shop scheduling problem is proposed in [165, 166]. The shop owner (upper level) assigns the jobs to the machines in order to minimise the flow time while the customer is at the lower level and decides on a job schedule in order to minimise the makespan. The authors use the concepts of tolerance membership function at each level to define a fuzzy decision model for generating optimal (satisfactory) solutions for the bilevel flow shop scheduling problem.

The bilevel multi-objective job-shop scheduling problem is considered in [167]. At the upper level, idle time on the system bottleneck is minimised. At the lower level, a decision is made to plan other machines while maintaining the maximum use of the bottleneck and gaining improvements in other performance measures.

The problem of scheduling inbound trucks at the inbound doors of a cross-dock facility under truck arrival time uncertainty is proposed in [168]. A single-level and a bilevel optimisation problem are formulated. A genetic algorithm and its modification are discussed for the single- and bilevel optimisation problems.

Multi-job scheduling problems are considered in [169, 170]. In these problems, the variation of energy consumption with the performance of servers is taken into account for cloud computing. Moreover, task-scheduling strategies depend directly on data placement policies. To solve the bilevel discrete model efficiently, specific-design encoding and decoding methods are designed. Based on these, an effective genetic algorithm is proposed, in which a local search operator is introduced to accelerate the convergent speed and enhance searching ability.

Other application. A new approach to the development of a strategic program for a mineral resource region based on public–private partnership mechanisms is proposed in [92, 93, 101, 171–173]. The government not only carries out general-purpose infrastructural projects but also provides a part of the costs related to compensating for ecological losses caused by the investment projects. As we discussed in Sect. 1.4.2, these bilevel problems are Σ_2^P-hard even in case of a three-year planning horizon.

Evacuation models are proposed in [174, 175]. In [174] to enable an efficient evacuation, a network optimisation model which integrates lane-based reversal design and routing with intersection crossing conflict elimination for evacuation is constructed. The proposed bilevel model minimises the total evacuation time to leave the evacuation zone. A tabu search algorithm is applied to find an optimal lane reversal plan in the upper level. The lower level utilises a simulated annealing algorithm. The paper [175] develops a model to optimise the issuance of evacuation orders with explicit consideration of the highly uncertain evolution of the storm and the complexity of the behavioural reaction to evolving storm conditions. A solution procedure based on progressive hedging is developed. A realistic case study for the eastern portion of the state of North Carolina is presented.

1.6   Conclusion

In this chapter, we have presented discrete bilevel optimisation models, discussed their computational complexity and applications. We have pointed out some lines for future research and wish to discuss below one of them without details. In real-world applications, we often try to choose a solution that is strong (optimal or near optimal) not only for the current input data but also for a wide range of similar instances. Common methods for analysing such situations lead us to solve more computationally difficult problems than the original ones [176]. A new idea in this area had been suggested based on a threshold approach [177, 178]. Let us consider a single-level income maximisation problem with uncertainty in the input data. Now instead of maximising the income, we wish to maximise the norm of possible variations in the input data subject to the income is at least as the given threshold. This elegant approach allows us to significantly improve the quality of the solution obtained in terms of stability with small degradation of the income. In [178], this approach is applied to the facility location problems and analysed as bi-objective optimisation.

Another line of research is related to the uncertainty arising from the rationality of the follower behaviour. As we have mentioned above, economic agents cannot use excessively large resources to find the optimal solution. A new approach which deals with the solution method uncertainty at the lower level is developed in [123]. Earlier we assume that the follower must respond by the optimal solution to the leader's solution. However, the follower has to respond by a feasible solution using some approximate algorithms in case of resource constraints, time or computational resources. Three approaches are presented for this case in [123]. The leader does not know the algorithm that is used by the follower but knows a set of possible follower's solution methods. A similar approach in a simplified form was used in [179, 180]. The optimistic and pessimistic models and the strong-weak approach from

[181–184] of the standard bilevel optimisation also can be viewed as special cases of approach from [123]. We guess that it is a promising area for future research.

Acknowledgements Many thanks to Ivan Davydov and Andrey Melnikov for useful discussions and their efforts in improving the presentation of the paper. The research is supported by the Russian Science Foundation, Project No. 21-41-09017.

References

1. von Stackelberg, H.: Marktform und Gleichgewicht. Springer, Vienna (1934)
2. Bracken, J., McGill, J.: Mathematical programs with optimization problems in the constraints. Oper. Res. **21**, 37–44 (1973)
3. Dempe, S.: Foundations of Bilevel Programming. Nonconvex Optimization and Its Applications (Book seriesL NOIA, volume 61). Springer (2002)
4. Wiesemann, W., Tsoukalas, A., Kleniati, P.-M., Rustem, B.: Pessimistic bilevel optimization. SIAM J. Optim. **23(1)**, 353–380 (2013)
5. Liu, J., Fan, Y., Chen, Z., Zheng, Y.: Pessimistic bilevel optimization: A survey. Int. J. Comput. Intell. Syst. **11(1)**, 725–736 (2018)
6. DeNegre, S.: Interdiction and discrete bilevel linear programming. Ph.D. dissertation, Lehigh University (2011)
7. Kochetov, Y.A., Plyasunov, A.V.: A polynomial solvable class of two-level linear programming problems. Diskret. Anal. Issled. Oper. **4(2)**, 23–33 (1997) (in Russian)
8. Moore, J.T., Bard, J.: The mixed integer linear bilevel programming problem. Oper. Res. **38(5)**, 911–921 (1990)
9. Kalashnikov, V.V., Dempe, S., Pérez-Valdés, G.A., Kalashnykova, N.I., Camacho-Vallejo, J-F.: Bilevel programming and applications. Math. Probl. Eng. **2015**, Article ID 310301 (2015)
10. Ungureanu, V.: Pareto-Nash-Stackelberg Game and Control Theory. Springer (2018)
11. Fudenberg, D., Tirole, J.: Game Theory. MIT Press (1993)
12. Shi, C.: Linear bilevel programming technology—Models and algorithms. PhD thesis, University of Technology, Sydney, Australia (2005)
13. Soismaa, M.: A note on efficient solutions for the linear bilevel programming problem. Eur. J. Oper. Res. **112**, 427–431 (1999)
14. Dempe, S.: Comment to "interactive fuzzy goal programming approach for bilevel programming problem" by S.R. Arora and R. Gupta. Eur. J. Oper. Res. **212(2)**, 429–431 (2011)
15. Candler, W.: A linear bilevel programming algorithm: A comment. Comp. Oper. Res. **15**, 297–298 (1988)

16. Marcotte, P., Savard, G.: A note on the Pareto optimality of solutions to the linear bilevel programming problem. Comp. Oper. Res. **18**, 355–359 (1991)
17. Migdalas, A.: When is Stackelberg equilibrium Pareto optimum? In: Pardalos, P. et al. (eds.) Advances in Multicriteria Analysis. Kluwer Academic Publishers, Dordrecht (1995)
18. Wen, U., Hsu, S.: A note on a linear bilevel programming algorithm based on bicriteria programming. Comp. Oper. Res. **16**, 79–83 (1989)
19. Fliege, J., Vicente, L.N.: Multicriteria approach to bilevel optimization. J. Optim. Theory. Appl. **131**, 209–225 (2006)
20. Fülöp, J.: On the equivalence between a linear bilevel programming problem and linear optimization over the efficient set. Technical Report WP 93-1, Laboratory of Operations Research and Decision Systems, Computer and Automation Institute, Hungarian Academy of Sciences, Budapest, Hungary (1993)
21. Ivanenko, D.S., Plyasunov, A.V.: Reducibility of bilevel programming problems to vector optimization problems. J. Appl. Ind. Math. **2**, 179–195 (2008)
22. Pieume, C.O., Fotso, L.P., Siarry, P.: Solving bilevel programming problems with multicriteria optimization techniques. OPSEARCH. **46**, 169–183 (2009)
23. Ruuska, S., Miettinen, K., Wiecek, M.M.: Connections between single-level and bilevel multiobjective optimization. J. Optim. Theory Appl. **153**, 60–74 (2012)
24. Glackin, J., Ecker, J.G., Kupferschmid, M.: Solving bilevel linear programs using multiple objective linear programming. J. Optim. Theory Appl. **140**, 197–212 (2009)
25. Jing Y., Zhang S.: The solution to a kind of stackelberg game systems with multi-follower: Coordinative and incentive. In: Bensoussan A., Lions J.L. (eds.) Analysis and Optimization of Systems. Lecture Notes in Control and Information Sciences, **111** Springer, Berlin, Heidelberg, pp. 593–602 (1988)
26. Zhang, G., Lu, J.: Fuzzy bilevel programming with multiple objectives and cooperative multiple followers. J. Glob. Optim. **47**, 403–419 (2010)
27. Alekseeva, E., Kochetov, Y., Talbi, E.-G.: A matheuristic for the discrete bilevel problem with multiple objectives at the lower level. I. Trans. Oper. Res. **24(5)**, 959–981 (2017)
28. Sherali, H.: A multiple leader Stackelberg model and analysis. Oper. Res. **32**, 390–404 (1984)
29. DeMiguel, V., Xu, H.: A stochastic multiple-leader Stackelberg model: Analysis, computation, and application. Oper. Res. **57(5)**, 1220–1235 (2009)
30. Lu, J., Shi, C., Zhang, G.: On bilevel multi-follower decision making: General framework and solutions. Inf. Sci. **176(11)**, 1607–1627 (2006)
31. Dempe, S.: Dependence of bilevel programming on irrelevant data. Technical Report 2011-01, TU Bergakademie Freiberg, Department of Mathematics and Computer Science. www.optimization-online.org (2011)

32. Macal, C.M., Hurter, A.P.: Dependence of bilevel mathematical programs on irrelevant constraints, Comput. Oper. Res. **24**, 1129–1140 (1997)

33. Ko, K., Lin, C.L.: On the complexity of min-max optimization problems and their approximation. In Du, D.-Z. and Pardalos, P.M. (eds.) Minimax and Applications. Kluwer Academic Publishers, Dordrecht, 219–239 (1995)

34. Umans, C.: Hardness of approximating Σ_2^P minimization problems. In Proceedings of the 40th Annual Symposium on Foundations of Computer Science (FOCS'1999), Los Alamitos, CA, 465–474 (1999)

35. Umans, C.: Optimization problems in the polynomial-time hierarchy. In Proceedings of the 3rd International Conference on Theory and Applications of Models of Computation (TAMC'2006). Lect. Notes in Comput. Sci. **3959**, 345–355 (2006)

36. Caprara, A., Carvalho, M., Lodi, A., Woeginger, G.J.: A study on the computational complexity of the bilevel knapsack problem. SIAM J. Optim. **24(2)**, 823–838 (2014)

37. Solvebilevel. https://yalmip.github.io/command/solvebilevel/

38. MibS. https://github.com/coin-or/MibS

39. Pyomo. https://pyomo.readthedocs.io/en/stable/modeling_extensions/bilevel.html

40. GAMS. https://www.gams.com/latest/docs/UG_EMP_Bilevel.html

41. Saharidis, G.K., Ierapetritou, M.G.: Resolution method for mixed integer bilevel linear problems based on decomposition technique. J. Global Optim. **44(1)**, 29–51 (2009)

42. Fontaine, P., Minner, S.: Benders decomposition for discrete-continuous linear bilevel problems with application to traffic network design. Transp. Res. Part B: Methodol. **70**, 163–172 (2014)

43. Zeng, B., An, Y.: Solving bilevel mixed integer program by reformulations and decomposition. Optimization online (2014)

44. Shi, X., Prokopyev,O., Ralphs, T.K.: Mixed integer bilevel optimization with k-optimal follower: A hierarchy of bounds. COR@L Technical Report 20T-012. http://www.optimization-online.org/DB_HTML/2020/06/7874.html (2020)

45. Dempe, S., Kue, F.M.: Solving discrete linear bilevel optimization problems using the optimal value reformulation. J. Global Optim. **68(2)**, 255–277 (2017)

46. Lozano, L., Smith, J.: A value-function-based exact approach for the bilevel mixed-integer programming problem. Oper. Res. **65(3)**, 768–786 (2017)

47. Bolusani, S., Coniglio, S. Ralphs, T.K., Tahernejad, S.: A unified framework for multistage mixed integer linear optimization. In: Dempe, S. and Zemkoho, A. (eds.) Bilevel Optimization: Advances and Next Challenges. Springer, Cham, pp. 513–560 (2020)

48. Bolusani, S., Ralphs, T.K.: A framework for generalized Benders' decomposition and its application to multilevel optimization. COR@L Technical

Report 20T-004. http://www.optimization-online.org/DB_HTML/2020/04/7755.html (2020)

49. Wen, U., Yang, Y.: Algorithms for solving the mixed integer two-level linear programming problem. Comput. Oper. Res. **17**, 133–142 (1990)
50. Edmunds, T., Bard, J.F.: An algorithm for the mixed-integer nonlinear bilevel programming problem. Ann. Oper. Res. **34**, 149–162 (1992)
51. Fischetti, M., Ljubic, I., Monaci, M., Sinnl, M.: On the use of intersection cuts for bilevel optimization. Math. Program. **172(1)**, 77–103 (2018)
52. Caramia,M., Mari, R.: Enhanced exact algorithms for discrete bilevel linear problems. Optim. Lett. **9(7)**, 1447–1468 (2015)
53. DeNegre, S.T., Ralphs,T.K.: A branch-and-cut algorithm for integer bilevel linear programs. Oper. Res./Comput. Sci. Interfaces Ser. **47**, 65–78 (2009)
54. Tahernejad, S., Ralphs, T.K., DeNegre, S.T.: A branch-and-cut algorithm for mixed integer bilevel linear optimization problems and its implementation. Math. Program. Comput. **12**, 529–568 (2020)
55. Fischetti, M., Ljubic, I., Monaci, M., Sinnl, M.: A new general-purpose algorithm for mixed-integer bilevel linear programs. Oper. Res. **65(6)**, 1615–1637 (2017)
56. Fischetti, M., Monaci, M.: A branch-and-cut algorithm for mixed-integer bilinear programming. Eur. J. Oper. Res. **282**, 506–514 (2020)
57. Beresnev, V., Melnikov, A.: Approximation of the competitive facility location problem with MIPs. Comput. Oper. Res. **104**, 139–148 (2019)
58. Hemmati, M., Smith, J.C.: A mixed-integer bilevel programming approach for a competitive prioritized set covering problem. Discr. Optimiz. **20**, 105–134 (2016)
59. Heilporn, G., Labbé, M., Marcotte, P., Savard, G.: A polyhedral study of the network pricing problem with connected toll arcs. Networks. **55(3)**, 234–246 (2010)
60. Domínguez, L.F., Pistikopoulos, E.N.: Multiparametric programming based algorithms for pure integer and mixed-integer bilevel programming problems. Comput. Chem. Eng. **34(12)**, 2097–2106 (2010)
61. Avraamidoua, S., Pistikopoulos, E.N.: A multi-parametric optimization approach for bilevel mixed-integer linear and quadratic programming problems. Comput. Chem. Eng. **125**, 98–113 (2019)
62. Köppe, M., Queyranne, M., Ryan, C.T.: Parametric integer programming algorithm for bilevel mixed integer programs. J. Optim. Theory Appl. **146(1)**, 137–150 (2010)
63. Thirwani, D., Arora, S.R.: An algorithm for the integer linear fractional bilevel programming problem. Optim. **39(1)**, 53–67 (1997)
64. Calvete, H.I., Gal, C.: A note on bilevel linear fractional programming problem. Europ. J. Open Res. **152(1)**, 296–299 (2004)
65. Mitsos, A.: Global solution of nonlinear mixed-integer bilevel programs. J. Global Optim. **47(4)**, 557–582 (2010)

66. Xu, P., Wang, L.: An exact algorithm for the bilevel mixed integer linear programming problem under three simplifying assumptions. Comput. Oper. Res. **41**, 309–318 (2014)
67. Wang, L., Xu, P.: The watermelon algorithm for the bilevel integer linear programming problem. SIAM J. Optim. **27**(3), 1403–1430 (2017)
68. Glover, F.: Future paths for integer programming and links to artificial intelligence. Comput. Ops. Res. 13(5), 533–549 (1986)
69. Talbi, E-G. (Ed.): Metaheuristics—From Design to Implementation. Computer Science (2009)
70. Talbi, E-G. (Ed.): Metaheuristics for bi-level optimization. Stud. Comput. Intell. **482** (2013)
71. Dempe, S., Zemkoho, A.: Bilevel Optimization Advances and Next Challenges. Springer Optimization and Its Applications (Book Series: SOIA, **161**) (2020)
72. Bard, J.F.: Practical Bilevel Optimization: Algorithms and Applications. Part of the Nonconvex Optimization and Its Applications. Springer (1998)
73. Mallozzi, L., D'Amato, Eg., Pardalos, P. (Eds.): Spatial Interaction Models Facility Location Using Game Theory. Springer Optimization and Its Applications (2017)
74. Zhang, S., Hui, Q., Bai, X., Sun, R.: Bilevel optimization for the Hazmat transportation problem with lane reservation. J. Adv. Transp. **2020**(34), 1–14 (2020)
75. López-Ramosa, F., Nasinib, S., Guarnaschelli, A.: Road network pricing and design for ordinary and Hazmat vehicles: Integrated model and specialized local search. Comput. Oper. Res. **109**, 170–187 (2019)
76. Simon, H.: Theories of bounded rationality. In: Radner, R., (ed.) Decision and Organization. North-Holland, New York (1972)
77. Deng, X., Papadimitriou, C.H.: On the complexity of cooperative solution concepts. Math. Oper. Res. **19**(2), 257–266 (1994)
78. Attallah, M.: Algorithms and Theory of Computation Handbook. CRC Press, Boca Raton (1999)
79. Ausiello, G., Crescenzi, P., Gambosi, G., et al.: Complexity and Approximation: Combinatorial Optimization Problems and Their Approximability Properties. Springer-Verlag, Berlin (1999)
80. Jeroslow, R.G.: The polynomial hierarchy and a simple model for competitive analysis. Math. Program. **32**(2), 146–164 (1985)
81. Schaefer, M., Umans, C.: Completeness in the polynomial-time hierarchy: A compendium. SIGACT News. **33**(3), 32–49 (2002)
82. Garey, M.R., Johnson, D.S.: Computers and Intractability: A Guide to the Theory of NP-Completeness, San Francisco (1978)
83. Dempe, S., Richter, K.: Bilevel programming with Knapsack constraints. Centr. Eur. J. Oper. Res. **8**, 93–107 (2000)
84. Mansi, R., Alves, C., de Carvalho, J.M.V., Hanafi, S.: An exact algorithm for bilevel 0–1 knapsack problems. Math. Probl. Eng., Article ID 504713 (2012)

85. Eggermont, C., Woeginger, G.J.: Motion planning with pulley, rope, and baskets. In Proceedings of the 29th International Symposium on Theoretical Aspects of Computer Science (STACS–2012), 374–383 (2012)

86. Noltemeier, H., Spoerhase, J., Wirth, H.: Multiple voting location and single voting location on trees. Europ. J. Oper. Res. **181**, 654–667 (2007)

87. Davydov, I., Kochetov, Y., Plyasunov, A.: On the complexity of the $(r|p)$-centroid problem on the plane. TOP. **22(2)**, 614–623 (2014)

88. Melnikov, A.: Computational complexity of the discrete competitive facility location problem. J. Appl. Indust. Math. **8**, 557–567 (2014)

89. Panin, A.A., Pashchenko, M.G., Plyasunov, A.V.: Bilevel competitive facility location and pricing problems. Autom. Remote Control. **75(4)**, 715–727 (2014)

90. Kononov, A.V., Panin, A.A., Plyasunov, A.V.: A bilevel competitive location and pricing model with nonuniform split of demand. J. Appl. Indust. Math. **13(3)**, 500–510 (2019)

91. Iellamo, S., Alekseeva, E., Chen, L., Coupechoux, M., Kochetov, Yu.: Competitive location in cognitive radio networks. 4OR. **13(1)**, 81–110 (2015)

92. Lavlinskii, S., Panin, A., Plyasunov, A.: The Stackelberg model in territorial planning. Automat. Remote Control. **80(2)**, 286–296 (2019)

93. Lavlinskii S., Panin A., Plyasunov A.: Bilevel models for investment policy in resource-rich regions. Commun. Comput. Inf. Sci. **1275**, 36–50 (2020)

94. Bazgan, C., Escoffier, B., Paschos, V.Th.: Completeness in standard and differential approximation classes: Poly-(D)APX- and (D)PTAS-completeness. Theor. Comput. Sci. **339**, 272–292 (2005)

95. Qiu, X., Kern, W.: Improved approximation algorithms for a bi-level knapsack problem. Theor Comput Sci. **595**, 120–129 (2015)

96. Guruswami, V., Hartline, J.D., Karlin, A.R., Kempe, D., Kenyon, C., McSherry, F.: On profit-maximizing envy-free pricing. In Proceedings of the Annual ACM-SIAM Symposium on Discrete Algorithms, 1164–1173 (2005)

97. Joret, G.: Stackelberg network pricing is hard to approximate. Networks. **57(2)**, 117–120 (2011)

98. Cardinal, J., Demaine, E.D., Fiorini, S., Joret, G., Langerman, S., Newman, I., Weimann, O.: The Stackelberg minimum spanning tree game. Algorithmica. **59(2)**, 129–144 (2011)

99. Plyasunov, A.V., Panin, A.A.: The pricing problem. Part 2. The computational complexity. J. Appl. Indust. Math. 7**(3)**, 420–430 (2013)

100. Panin, A., Plyasunov, A.: On complexity of the bilevel location and pricing problems. J. Appl. Indust. Math. **8(4)**, 574–581 (2014)

101. Lavlinskii, S., Panin, A., Plyasunov, A.: A bilevel planning model for public-private partnership. Autom. Remote Control. **76(11)**, 1976–1987 (2015)

102. Gao, Z., Wu, J., Sun, H.: Solution algorithm for the bi-level discrete network design problem. Transp. Res. Part B. **39(6)**, 479–495 (2005)

103. Fontaine, P., Minner, S.: Benders decomposition for discrete–continuous linear bilevel problems with application to traffic network design. Transp. Res. Part B. **70**, 163–172 (2014)
104. Labbé, M., Marcotte P., Savard, G.: A bilevel model of taxation and its application to optimal highway pricing. Manage. Sci. **44**, 1608–1622 (1998)
105. Fontaine, P., Minner, S.: A dynamic discrete network design problem for maintenance planning in traffic networks. Ann. Oper. Res. **253**, 757–772 (2017)
106. Bagloee, S.A., Sarvi, M., Patriksson, M.: A hybrid branch-and-bound and benders decomposition algorithm for the network design problem. Comput.-Aided Civ. Infrastruct. Eng. **32**, 1–25 (2016)
107. Tawfik, C., Limbourg, S.: A bilevel model for network design and pricing based on a level-of-service assessment. Transp. Sci. **53(6)**, 1609–1626 (2019)
108. Tian, Y., Dong, H.-H., Jia, L.-M., Qin, Y., Li, S.-Y.: The bilevel design problem for communication networks on trains: Model, algorithm, and verification. Mathematical Problems in Engineering. N 840619 (2014)
109. Labbé, M., Marcotte, P.: Bilevel Network Design (hal-01937014). https://hal.inria.fr/hal-01937014 (2019)
110. Rey, D.: Computational benchmarking of exact methods for the bilevel discrete network design problem. Transp Res Procedia. **47**, 11–18 (2020)
111. Delle Fave, F.M., Jiang, A.X., Yin, Z., Zhang, C., Tambe, M., Kraus, S., Sullivan, J.P.: Game-theoretic security patrolling with dynamic execution uncertainty and a case study on a real transit system. J. Artif. Intell. Res. **50**, 321–367 (2014).
112. Jain, M., Tsai, J., Pita, J., Kiekintveld, C., Rathi, S., Tambe, M., Ordónez, F.: Software arshal service. Interfaces. **40(4)**, 267–290 (2010)
113. Jiang, A.X., Yin, Z., Zhang, C., Tambe, M., Kraus, S.: Game-theoretic randomization for security patrolling with dynamic execution uncertainty. In Proceedings of the 12th International Conference on Autonomous Agents Multiagent Systems, Saint Paul, MN, USA, May 6–10, 2013 (Int. Found. Autonomous Agents Multiagent Syst., Richland, SC, 2013), 207–214 (2013)
114. Church, R.L., Scaparra, M.P.: Protecting critical assets: The r-interdiction median problem with fortification. Geogr. Anal. **39(2)**, 129–146 (2007)
115. Scaparra, M.P., Church, R.L.: A bilevel mixed integer program for critical infra-structure protection planning. Comput. Oper. Res. **35(6)**, 1905–1923 (2008)
116. Scaparra, M.P., Church, R.L.: An exact solution approach for the interdictionmedian problem with fortification. Europ. J. Open Res. **189(1)**, 76–92 (2008)
117. Scaparra, M.P., Church, R.L.: A bilevel mixed-integer program for critical infrastructure protection planning. Comput. Oper. Res. **35**, 1905–1923 (2008)

118. Aksen, D., Piyade, N., Aras, N.: The budget constrained r-interdiction median problem with capacity expansion. Central Europ. J. Oper. Res. **18(3)**, 269–291 (2010)

119. Zhu, Y., Zheng, Z., Zhang, X., Cai, K.Y.: The r-interdiction median problem with probabilistic protection and its solution algorithm. Comput. Oper. Res. **40**, 451–462 (2013)

120. Aksen, D., Aras, N.: A bilevel fixed charge location model for facilities under imminent attack. Comput. Oper. Res. **39(1)**, 1364–1381 (2012)

121. Beresnev, V., Melnikov, A.: A bilevel attacker-defender model to choosing the composition of attack means. J. Appl. Indust. Math. **13(4)**, 612–622 (2019)

122. Beresnev, V., Davydov, I., Kononova, P., Melnikov, A.: Bilevel defender–attacker model with multiple attack scenarios. J. Appl. Indust. Math. **12(3)**, 417–425 (2018)

123. Zare, M.H., Prokopyev, O.A., Sauré, D.: On bilevel optimization with inexact follower. Decis. Anal. **17(1)**, 1–22 (2020)

124. Kochetov,Y.A., Pljasunov, A.V.: Efficient algorithm for a class of bilevel linear programming problems. In Operations Research Proceedings 1996. Berlin, Springer, 10–13 (1997)

125. Kochetov, Y.A., Plyasunov, A.V.: The problem of selecting a number of products with partial exterior financing. Diskret. Anal. Issled. Oper., Serija 2. **9(2)**, 78–96 (2002) (in Russian)

126. Plyasunov, A.V.: A polynomially solvable class of bilevel nonlinear programming problems. Diskret. Anal. Issled. Oper., Seriya 2. **7**, 89–113 (2000) (in Russian)

127. Plyasunov, A.V.: A bilevel linear programming problem with a multivariant knapsack at the lower level. Diskret. Anal. Issled. Oper. **10(1)**, 44–52 (2003) (in Russian)

128. Arroyo, J.M., Galiana, F.D.: On the solution of the bilevel programming formulation of the terrorist threat problem. IEEE Trans. Power Syst. **20(2)**, 789–797 (2005)

129. Liu, C.-C., Jung, J. Heydt, G.T., Vittal, V., Phadke, A.G.: The strategic power infrastructure defense (SPID) system. A conceptual design. IEEE Control. Syst. Mag. **20(4)**, 40–52 (2000)

130. Roy,A., Kim, D.S., Trivedi, K.S.: Cyber security analysis using attack counter-measure trees. In Proceedings of the 6th Annual Workshop on Cyber Security and Information Intelligence Research (2010)

131. Yuan,Y.-L., Li,Z.-I., Ren, K.-I.: Quantitative analysis of load redistribution attacks in power systems. IEEE Transactions on Parallel and Distributed Systems. **23(9)**, 1731–1738 (2012)

132. Karakitsiou, A.: Modeling Discrete Competitive Facility Location. Springer, Cham, Heidelberg (2015)

133. Kononov, A.V., Kochetov, Yu.A., Plyasunov, A.V.: Competitive facility location models. Comput. Math. Math. Phys. **49(6)**, 994–1009 (2009)

134. Hansen, P., Kochetov, Y., Mladenovic, N.: Lower bounds for the uncapacitated facility location problem with user preferences. Technical Report, Les Cahiers du GERAD, G-2004-24 (2004)
135. Vasilyev, I.L., Klimentova, K.B., Kochetov, Yu.A.: New lower bounds for the facility location problem with clients' preferences. Comput. Math. Math. Phys. **49(6)**, 1010–1020 (2009)
136. Vasilyev, I.V., Klimentova, K.B., Boccia, M.: Polyhedral study of simple plant location problem with order. Oper. Res. Lett. **41(2)**, 153–158 (2013)
137. Cánovas, L., García, S., Labbé, M., Marín, A.: A strengthened formulation for the simple plant location problem with order. Operat. Res. Letts. **35(2)**, 141–150 (2007)
138. Casas-Ramírez, M.-S., Camacho-Vallejo, J.-F., Martínez-Salazar, I.-A.: Approximating solutions to a bilevel capacitated facility location problem with customer's patronization toward a list of preferences. Appl. Math. Comput. **319**, 369–386 (2018)
139. Calvete, H.I., Galé, C., Iranzo, J.A., Camacho-Vallejo, J.-F., Casas-Ramírez, M.-S.: A matheuristic for solving the bilevel approach of the facility location problem with cardinality constraints and preferences. Comput. Oper. Res. **124**, N 105066 (2020)
140. Beresnev, V.L., Melnikov, A.A.: The branch-and-bound algorithm for a competitive facility location problem with the prescribed choice of suppliers. J. Appl. Ind. Math. **8**, 177–189 (2014)
141. Beresnev, V.L., Melnikov, A.A.: Exact method for the capacitated competitive facility location problem. Comp. Oper. Res. **95**, 73–82 (2018)
142. Caramia, M., Giordani, S.: Location of differentiated waste collection centers with user cooperation: A bilevel optimization approach. Optim. Lett. **14**, 85–99 (2020)
143. Caramia, M., Dalla Costa, M.: An application of bilevel optimisation to the waste collection centres location problem. Int. J. Math. Oper. Res. **16(1)**, 118–137 (2020)
144. Casas-Ramírez, M.-S., Camacho-Vallejo, J.-F., Díaz, J.A., Luna, D.E.: A bilevel maximal covering location problem. Oper. Res. **20**, 827–855 (2020)
145. Drezner, T., Drezner, Z.: Leader-follower models in facility location. In: Mallozzi, L., D'Amato, E., and Pardalos, P.M. (eds.) Spatial Interaction Models Facility Location Using Game Theory. Springer, pp. 73–104 (2017)
146. Davydov, I., Kochetov, Y., Dempe, S.: Local search approach for the competitive facility location problem in mobile networks. Int. J. Artif. Intell. **16(1)**, 130–143 (2018)
147. Sasaki, M.: Hub network design model in a competitive environment with flow threshold. J. Oper. Res. Soc. Japan. **48**, 158–171 (2005)
148. Parvaresh, F., Moattar Husseini, S.M., Hashemi Golpayegany, S.A., Karimi, B.: Hub network design problem in the presence of disruptions. J. Intell. Manuf. **25**, 755–774 (2014)

149. Hamacher, H.W., Labbé, M., Nickel, S., Sonneborn, T.: Adapting polyhedral properties from facility to hub location Problems. Discret. Appl. Math. **145(1)**, 104–116 (2004)
150. Ramamoorthy, P., Jayaswal, S., Sinha, A., Vidyarthi, N.: Multiple allocation hub interdiction and protection problems: Model formulations and solution approaches. Eur. J. Oper. Res. **270(1)**, 230–245 (2018)
151. Lei, T.L.: Identifying critical facilities in hub-and-spoke networks: A hub interdiction median problem. Geogr. Anal. **45(2)**, 105–122 (2013)
152. Ghaffarinasab N., Atayi R.: An implicit enumeration algorithm for the hub interdiction median problem with fortification. Eur. J. Oper. Res. **267(1)**, 23–39 (2018)
153. Mahmutogullari, I., Kara, B.: Hub location under competition. Eur. J. Oper. Res. **250(1)**, 214–225 (2016)
154. Ghaffarinasab, N., Motallebzadeh, A.: Hub interdiction problem variants: Models and metaheuristic solution algorithms. Eur. J. Oper. Res. **267(2)**, 496–512 (2018)
155. Ćvokić, D.D., Kochetov,Y.A., Plyasunov, A.V.: A leader-follower hub location and pricing problem under fixed markups. Lect. Notes Comput. Sci. **9869**, 350–363 (2016)
156. Ćvokić, D.D.: A leader-follower single allocation hub location problem under fixed markups. Filomat. **34(8)**, 2463–2484 (2020).
157. Ćvokić, D.D., Kochetov, Y.A., Plyasunov, A.V.: The competitive hub location under the price war. Lect. Notes Comput. Sci. **11548**, 133–146 (2019)
158. Ćvokić, D.D., Kochetov, Y.A., Plyasunov, A.V., Savić, A.: A variable neighborhood search algorithm for the $(r|p)$ hub-centroid problem under the price war. J. Glob. Optim. https://doi.org/10.1007/s10898-021-01036-9 (2021)
159. Calvete, H.I., Galé, C., Iranzo, J.A.: Planning of a decentralized distribution network using bilevel optimization. Omega. **49**, 30–41 (2014)
160. Yang, D., Jiao, J., Ji, Y., Du, G., Helo, P., Valente, A.: Joint optimization for coordinated configuration of product families and supply chains by a leader-follower Stackelberg game. Eur. J. Oper. Res. **246(1)**, 263–280 (2015)
161. Saranwong, S., Likasiri, C.: Bi-level programming model for solving distribution center problem: a case study in Northern Thailand's sugarcane management. Comput. Ind. Eng. **103**, 26–39 (2017)
162. Yeh, K., Realff, M.J., Lee, J.H., Whittaker, C.: Analysis and comparison of single period single level and bilevel programming representations of a pre-existing timberlands supply chain with a new biorefinery facility. Comput. Chem. Eng. **68**, 242–254 (2014)
163. Yeh, K., Whittaker, C., Realff, M.J., Lee, J.H.: Two stage stochastic bilevel programming model of a pre-established timberlands supply chain with biorefinery investment interests. Comput. Chem. Eng. **73**, 141–153 (2015)
164. Wang, M., Zhang, R., Zhu, X.: A bi-level programming approach to the decision problems in a vendor-buyer eco-friendly supply chain. Comput. Ind. Eng. **105**, 299–312 (2017)

165. Karlof, J.K., Wang, W.: Bilevel programming applied to the flow shop scheduling problem. Comput. Oper. Res. **23**, 443–451 (1996)
166. Abass, S.A.: Bilevel programming approach applied to the flow shop scheduling problem under fuzziness. Comput. Manag. Sci. **2(4)**, 279–293 (2005)
167. Kasemset, C., Kachitvichyanukul, V.: A PSO-based procedure for a bi-level multi-objective TOC-based job-shop scheduling problem. Int. J. Oper. Res. **14(1)**, 50–69 (2012)
168. Konur, D., Golias, M.M.: Analysis of different approaches to cross-dock truck scheduling with truck arrival time uncertainty. Comput. Ind. Eng. **65(4)**, 663–672 (2013)
169. Wang, X., Wang, Y., Cui, Y.: A new multi-objective bi-level programming model for energy and locality aware multi-job scheduling in cloud computing. Future Gener. Comput. Syst. **36**, 91–101 (2014)
170. Wang, X., Wang, Y., Cui, Y.: An energy-aware bi-level optimization model for multi-job scheduling problems under cloud computing. Soft Comput. **20(1)**, 303–317 (2016)
171. Lavlinskii, S., Panin, A., Plyasunov, A.: Stackelberg model and public-private partnerships in the natural resources sector of Russia. Lect. Notes Comput. Sci. **11548**, 158–171 (2019)
172. Lavlinskii, S., Panin, A., Plyasunov, A. Public-private partnership models with tax incentives: Numerical analysis of solutions. Commun. Comput. Inf. Sci. **871**, 220–234 (2018)
173. Lavlinskii, S., Panin, A., Plyasunov, A.: Comparison of models of planning public-private partnership. J. Appl. Indust. Math. **10(3)**, 356–369 (2016)
174. Zhao, X., Feng, Z.-Y., Li, Y., Bernard, A.: Evacuation network optimization model with lanebased reversal and routing. Math. Prob. Eng. **13**, N 1273508 (2016)
175. Yi, W., Nozick, L., Davidson, R., Blanton, B., Colle, B.: Optimization of the issuance of evacuation orders under evolving hurricane conditions. Transp. Res. B Methodol. **95**, 285–304 (2017)
176. Beresnev, V.L., Melnikov, A.A.: ε-Constraint method for bi-objective competitive facility location problem with uncertain demand scenario. Eur. J. Comput. Optim. **8**, 33–59 (2020)
177. Carrizosa, E., Nickel, S.: Robust facility location. Math. Meth. Oper. Res. **58**, 331–349 (2003)
178. Carrizosa, E., Ushakov, A., Vasilyev, I.: Threshold robustness in discrete facility location problems: A bi-objective approach. Optim. Lett. **9**, 1297–1314 (2015)
179. Smith, J.C., Lim, C., Sudargho, F.: Survivable network design under optimal and heuristic interdiction scenarios. J. Global Optim. **38(2)**, 181–199 (2007)
180. Shan, X., Zhuang, J.: Hybrid defensive resource allocations in the face of partially strategic attackers in a sequential defender attacker game. Eur. J. Oper. Res. **228(1)**, 262–272 (2013)

181. Aboussoror, A., Loridan, P.: Strong-weak Stackelberg problems in finite dimensional spaces. Serdica Math. J. **21(2)**, 151–170 (1995)
182. Cao, D., Leung, L.: A partial cooperation model for non-unique linear two-level decision problems. Eur. J. Oper. Res. **140(1)**, 134–141 (2002)
183. Zheng, Y., Wan, Z., Jia, S., Wang, G.: A new method for strong-weak linear bilevel programming problem. J. Indust. Management Optim. **11(2)**, 529–547 (2015)
184. Zare M.H., Özaltin O.Y., Prokopyev O.A.: On a class of bilevel linear mixed-integer programs in adversarial settings. J. Global Optim. **71(1)**, 91–113 (2018)

2

Discrete Location Problems with Uncertainty

Nader Azizi⊙, Sergio García, and Chandra Ade Irawan⊙

2.1 Introduction

Location Science has been a very active area of research for more than half a century with an ever-increasing interest among practitioners and the academic community. It is a wealthy field that substantially interacts with both traditional and modern subject fields such as mathematics, economics, computer science, and geography. Partly due to its interaction with other disciplines, the research on location problems has rapidly developed in recent years and many new real-world application areas such as logistics, telecommunications, routing, and transportation have emerged and are widely recognized. This research area encompasses a variety of problems such as covering

N. Azizi
Business School, University of Edinburgh, Edinburgh, Scotland, UK
e-mail: Nader.Azizi@ed.ac.uk

S. García (✉)
School of Mathematics, University of Edinburgh, Edinburgh, Scotland, UK
e-mail: sergio.garcia-quiles@ed.ac.uk

C. A. Irawan
Nottingham University Business School, University of Nottingham Ningbo China, Ningbo, China
e-mail: chandra.irawan@nottingham.edu.cn

© The Author(s), under exclusive license to Springer Nature Switzerland AG 2022
S. Salhi and J. Boylan (eds.), *The Palgrave Handbook of Operations Research*,
https://doi.org/10.1007/978-3-030-96935-6_2

43

problems, *p*-centre location problems, location and routing problems, and hub location problems. Probably, the uncapacitated facility location problem is widely known as its core problem [57].

Location problems are commonly organized in three categories according to the location space: discrete problems, continuous problems, and network problems. Particularly, discrete facility location problems [82] consist in finding the best set of facilities over a finite set of potential sites so that a certain service is provided: goods delivered from a warehouse, emergency vehicles that provide first aid or take sick people to hospitals, shops that are near the potential customers, etc.

Regardless of the type of space, examples of information usually required are volume of demand, supply cost, commodity price, or travel time. Traditionally, deterministic approaches are used to model these problems assuming a priori knowledge of the value of the associated parameters. In a practical context, however, one or more of these parameters are likely to be uncertain with known, partially known, or completely unknown underlying probability distributions. If probabilistic information is available, the uncertain parameters are represented by random variables and stochastic programming is used to model the problem. In other cases, robust optimization approaches are likely to be employed to deal with the problem under uncertainty. Motivated by the importance of accounting for uncertainty, in this chapter we will survey three of the most important families of problems in discrete facility location: the single-source capacitated facility location problem, covering problems, and hub location problems. The main contributions and solution methods in the area are reviewed for these problems, including formulations for some of the models and solution methods. For more general reviews on facility location problems with uncertainty, the interested reader can check [29, 95].

2.2   The Single-Source Capacitated Facility Location Problem with Uncertainty

The single-source capacitated location problem (SSCFLP), the capacitated variant of the original uncapacitated facility location problem introduced in [16], seeks to find the number of facilities to open, their locations, and the customer allocation to these open facilities in order to minimize the total cost without violating the capacity of any of the open facilities. In addition, each customer demand is served from one single facility. This problem has been widely studied in the literature due to its many applications, such as oil wells allocation [34] and humanitarian logistics [55, 56].

Let I be a set of customers indexed by i where the demand of customer i is denoted by d_i. Let J be a set of potential locations to locate the facilities which is indexed by j. The cost of opening a facility at location $j \in J$ is f_j, whereas b_j is the capacity if we build a facility on this location. An allocation cost c_{ij} is incurred if customer $i \in I$ is assigned to facility $j \in J$. Binary decision variable y_j takes value 1 if and only if location j hosts a facility. Binary variable x_{ij} takes value 1 if and only if customer i is assigned to facility j. The SSCFLP can be modelled as follows:

$$\text{Min.} \sum_{j \in J} f_j y_j + \sum_{i \in I} \sum_{j \in J} c_{ij} x_{ij} \tag{2.1}$$

$$\text{s.t.} \sum_{j \in J} x_{ij} = 1, \quad i \in I, \tag{2.2}$$

$$x_{ij} \leq y_j, \quad i \in I, \ j \in J, \tag{2.3}$$

$$\sum_{i \in I} d_i x_{ij} \leq b_j y_j, \quad j \in J, \tag{2.4}$$

$$y_j \in \{0, 1\}, \quad j \in J,$$
$$x_{ij} \in \{0, 1\}, \quad i \in I, \ j \in J.$$

The objective function (2.1) seeks to minimize the total cost (facility location plus customer allocation). Constraint (2.2) ensures that a customer is assigned to exactly one facility. Constraint (2.3) states that a customer can be served only by an open facility. Constraint (2.4) imposes that the demand supplied from any facility does not exceed its capacity.

As many location problems deal with long-term strategic decisions, uncontrolled changes may occur on the underlying conditions, and the SSCFLP is no exception. According to [92], the uncertainty in the facility location problem can be divided into three types: receiver-side uncertainty, provider-side uncertainty, and in-between uncertainty. In the receiver-side uncertainty, the most common uncertain parameter used is the randomness on demands. The provider-side uncertainty may consist of uncertain supply capacity, lead time, and facility status (operational or failed). The in-between uncertainty includes uncertain transportation costs or times and arc status.

In the literature, most researchers study the SSCFLP under the receiver-side uncertainty where customer demands are stochastic and follow certain probability distributions. Laporte et al. [58] investigate the problem with stochastic customer demands which is formulated as a two-stage mixed integer model where the first and second stages deal with binary and continuous variables, respectively. The model is then solved using a branch-and-cut algorithm. Albareda-Sambola et al. [1] investigate the stochastic problem with Bernoulli demands which is also formulated as a two-stage stochastic program. The first stage decides facility locations and customer assignments before knowing the customers who will actually require to be served. In the second-stage service decisions are taken according to the actual requests. The expected value of the recourse function is added into the objective function, which can occur by reassigning customers to another facility. In their model, the recourse function includes the service and outsourcing costs.

Still on the receiver-side uncertainty category, Lin [62] considers uncertain demand while requiring a specific service level. The problem is modelled using chance constraints. By assuming that the demands follow Poisson and normal distributions, the models can be transformed into deterministic models. A hybrid heuristic based on Lagrangean relaxation with a multi-exchange heuristic within a branch-and-bound framework is developed. Albareda-Sambola et al. [2] and Bieniek [24] study methods to tackle the problem proposed in [1]. Bieniek [24] considers the customer demands to be arbitrary discrete, continuous, or mixed distributions. The deterministic equivalent formulations for the stochastic formulations are obtained. Theoretical results for general distributions (exponential and Poisson distributions) are also presented. In [1] the authors propose a heuristic method that comprises a greedy randomized adaptive search technique followed by a path relinking algorithm to solve the problem with general Bernoulli demands. The performance of the proposed method is assessed by comparing its solutions with those obtained by a sample average approximation procedure.

Robust optimization approaches have also been used to solve the SSCFLP with uncertain demands. We can find in [18] a method called "almost robust discrete optimization" (ARDO) that is based on chance constraints. A decomposition methodology is used consisting of a deterministic master problem and a single subproblem that checks the master problem solution under different realizations. This method is used to solve the SSCFLP with uncertain demand. Other works closely related to the SSCFLP with uncertain demands are [55, 56], where the stochastic SSCFLP is extended to solve a shelter site location problem and to investigate a multi-criteria location problem respectively.

Under provider-side uncertainty, Aydin and Murat [10] address the unreliability of facilities in the *capacitated reliable facility location problem*. The authors propose a two-stage stochastic programming model that utilizes a scenario-based strategy to convert the stochastic problem into several deterministic problems with different probabilities. Location decisions are determined on the first stage whereas the allocation problem following the facility failures is solved on the second stage. The problem is solved with a hybrid algorithm that uses particle swarm optimization and a sample average approximation technique.

To the best of our knowledge, there is no work that studies the SSCFLP with in-between uncertainty. Therefore, we propose here a generic stochastic SSCFLP model under this category. In particular, it is assumed that allocation costs c_{ij} are not known in advance and they are considered as uncertain parameters. However, these costs can be captured by a probability distribution. Here, the decision to open facilities has a long-lasting effect. Therefore, this is a strategic decision which is typically determined before having precise information about the customer allocation in the future. On the other hand, the decision about the customer allocation is often considered as an operational decision that can be made when perfect information is available, after uncertainty is revealed.

To include the random nature of the allocation cost in the problem, we consider a two-stage stochastic model. We assume that strategic decision variable y must be determined before the actual realization of the customer allocation at the first stage. The second stage decides the customer allocation which is related to the operational decision variable x. Recourse decisions are considered at this stage because they are determined in such a way that the best response to the occurring scenario is given to the setting defined by the first-stage decisions.

The allocation costs c_{ij} are assumed to be random, and thus the random vector underlying the problem is $\xi = [c_{ij}]_{i \in I, \, j \in J}$, where I and J have the same meaning as earlier. Each realization of this random vector is a scenario and it is assumed that it is possible to compute or estimate accurately the probability associated with each scenario. Here all possible scenarios of future conditions are explored. The goal is to minimize the expected cost of the system.

If the random vector ξ is discrete and of finite size, we can index the scenarios in the set $S = \{1, \ldots, |S|\}$. Let p_s be the probability associated with scenario $s \in S$. The uncertain parameter can also be indexed as c_{ijs} which represents the allocation cost of customer $i \in I$ to facility $j \in J$ under scenario $s \in S$. Accordingly, the allocation decision variable is x_{ijs}. A parameter $\hat{c}$ is introduced to penalize each unit of unmet demand. The introduction of this parameter aims to achieve the feasibility of the obtained solutions over the scenario realizations [70]. Therefore, variables u_{is} are added to determine the amount of unmet demand for customer $i \in I$ for scenario $s \in S$. This stochastic SSCFLP with scenario-based approach can be formulated as follows:

$$\text{Min.} \sum_{j \in J} f_j y_j + \sum_{s \in S} p_s \left(\sum_{i \in I} \sum_{j \in J} c_{ijs} x_{ijs} + \sum_{i \in I} \hat{c} u_{is} \right) \quad (2.5)$$

$$\text{s.t.} \quad \sum_{j \in J} x_{ijs} = 1, \quad i \in I, \ s \in S,$$

$$x_{ijs} \leq y_j, \quad i \in I, \ j \in J, \ s \in S,$$

$$\sum_{i \in I} (d_i - u_{is}) x_{ijs} \leq b_j y_j, \quad j \in J, \ s \in S, \quad (2.6)$$

$$u_{is} \leq d_i, \quad i \in I, \ s \in S,$$

$$y_j \in \{0, 1\}, \quad j \in J,$$

$$x_{ijs} \in \{0, 1\}, \quad i \in I, \ j \in J, \ s \in S,$$

$$u_{is} \in \mathbb{Z}^+, \quad i \in I, \ s \in S. \quad (2.7)$$

In the objective function (2.5), the total penalty cost has been added to the cost of the deterministic model. The interpretation of constraint (2.6) is the same as constraint (2.4). In addition, this constraint also determines the amount of unmet demand for each customer for scenario $s \in S$. Constraint (2.7) ensures that the unmet demand does not exceed the customer demand.

This two-stage stochastic programming model is hard to solve as it is challenging to assess the expected value of the objective function for the stochastic model: an integer programming model for each scenario that corresponds to an uncertain parameter realization needs to be solved. A tool that can be used for solving this problem is the sample average approximation method [88], where a set of sample scenarios are generated using the Monte Carlo sampling method. Nevertheless, solving this model is beyond the scope of this chapter.

2.3   Covering Location Problems with Uncertainty

In a discrete covering location problem there is a finite set of potential sites that can host facilities that provide some kind of service and there is a set of customers that need this service. The particularity of a covering problem is that a customer can receive this service only if they are within a certain distance from a facility. When this happens, it is said that the customer is covered. Otherwise, when that distance is exceeded, the customer is uncovered. A typical example is deciding where to locate ambulances such that any call can be reached in at most a certain number of minutes established beforehand to satisfy some regulation. Covering location problems are among the most widely studied in facility location due to their many applications: location of emergency services such as ambulances and fire trucks, nature reserve selection, crew scheduling, bus stops, etc.

Unless said otherwise, here we are discussing models where the demand is generated only at the nodes of the network and the facilities can be installed only at the nodes. Although the basic models assume that the data are deterministic, this is not true in most of the applications, where there is some kind of uncertainty (for example, on the demand or on the distances). In this section we will focus on reviewing different covering models from the literature that include uncertainty in different ways. Reviews on deterministic covering models can be found in [42, 96]. We can find also reviews such as [61, 81] that deal exclusively with emergency vehicles, one of the main applications of covering problems.

There are two main types of (deterministic) covering problems. In the *set covering problem* introduced in [98] all the customers must be covered at minimum cost. As covering all the customers is usually not possible unless very high costs are incurred, in the *maximal covering problem* introduced by [30] the goal is to maximize the demand covered subject to some constraints (such as a limited budget or number of facilities that can be set up). Therefore, we will structure our review by classifying the models discussed into extensions of these two models where uncertainty is included.

2.3.1   Set Covering Models with Uncertainty

The most basic models seek to achieve robustness simply by covering the nodes more than once without any explicit consideration to uncertainty.

Back-ups are installed for some of the opened facilities, that is, some nodes are covered by more than one facility. Examples of such models can be found in [32, 50], where the idea of their *hierarchical objective set covering problem* and *backup coverage model*, with some minor differences, is to minimize the number of located facilities and to maximize the number of nodes covered more than once.

In a probabilistic extension of the set covering model it is assumed that each facility has a certain probability p of being busy, the same for all of them, and the event that one facility is busy is independent from any other facility being busy. It is required that each node can be covered with a certain minimum probability α, that is, this is the probability of at least one facility not being busy. With this information, a chance constraint is proposed that can be easily written as a constraint that imposes the minimum number of facilities able to cover this node that must be open to meet this threshold:

$$\sum_{j \in N_i} x_j \geq \left\lceil \frac{\log(1 - \alpha)}{\log p} \right\rceil,$$

where x_i takes value 1 if a facility is located at node i, N_i is the set of nodes that can cover node i, and $\lceil a \rceil$ is the smallest integer greater than or equal to a. This is a deterministic constraint that is included in the model. See [33] for details on this model, initially introduced by Chapman and White at the 1974 ORSA/TIMS conference. It must be noted that the constraint is very sensitive numerically, as a change on the right-hand side from 0.99 to 1.01 will double the number of facilities necessary to cover a node. An analysis on this sensitivity can be found in [84]. A similar constraint, but obtained using the estimation of the period of time that the servers are busy, is proposed in [83].

In [7], one of the earliest papers on covering models with uncertainty, we find a similar approach to the set covering model with chance constraints explained above, but here the authors assume that the demand is a random variable uniformly distributed over a certain region. As a consequence, travel times are also random. Formulations with chance constraints and with expected values are proposed.

An extension of the constraint written above can be found in [48] in the context of nature reserve selection. The authors propose a model that maximizes the number of species that can be protected with at least a certain threshold decided beforehand. As the species are counted as protected or not protected, their model can be easily rewritten as a set covering model that minimizes the number of species that are not protected. In addition, they allow for different and independent probabilities for different sites, where the busy probabilities of the classical facility location models now mean the probability of a species being present at a site. Although the constraint that they propose is nonlinear, it can be linearized easily by taking logarithms and they end up solving a mixed integer linear model.

In [20] we find a probabilistic set covering model where the right-hand side of the covering constraints is substituted by a random vector, and it is required that the constraints are satisfied with a certain probability. Independence of the individual right-hand side values for the constraints is not required. The authors study probabilistically efficient points of binary random vectors and suggest a specialized branch-and-bound method to solve the problem. The problem is later analysed in depth in [89], where several properties and model simplifications are studied.

In a different approach from the main body of models that include the uncertainty on the demand, we find in [67] a set covering model with stochastic critical distances. Here the critical distance that determines whether a customer is covered or not is stochastic. As a consequence, customers patronize a facility with a certain probability. In order to find an optimal location of the facilities at minimum cost an algorithm based on two searching paths is proposed.

Lutter et al. [63] use robust optimization to deal with the uncertainty, as the authors argue that the necessary statistical parameters required are not known with enough precision. They develop a mixed integer linear programming model that includes what they call "Γ-robust α-covering constraints", which is a concept based on the Γ-scenario sets introduced in [23]. See these two references for further details.

2.3.2 Maximum Covering Models with Uncertainty

With the same idea and justification than in the backup models presented for the set covering model, Storbeck [97] introduces a maximum covering model that maximizes covering and multiple covering in the objective function.

Moving on to models that consider explicitly the uncertainty, in the *maximum expected covering location problem* (MECLP) introduced in [31] each server has a probability p of not being available, either because it has failed or because it is busy serving other customers. It is assumed that this probability is the same for all the locations and that two facilities failing at the same time are independent events. Distances between customers and facilities are deterministic. The objective is to maximize the expected covered demand.

The problem can be written as a mixed integer linear programming model as follows:

$$\text{Max.} \quad \sum_{k=1}^{n} \sum_{j=1}^{m} w_j h_k y_{jk}$$

$$\text{s.t.} \quad \sum_{j=1}^{m} y_{jk} \leq \sum_{i=1}^{n} a_{ki} x_i, \quad k \in \{1, \ldots, n\},$$

$$\sum_{i=1}^{n} x_i \leq m,$$

$$x_i \in \{0, 1, \ldots, m\}, \quad i \in \{1, \ldots, n\},$$

$$y_{jk} \in \{0, 1\}, \quad j \in \{1, \ldots, m\}, \forall k \in \{1, \ldots, n\},$$

where $y_{jk} = 1$ if node k is covered by at least j facilities (and $y_{jk} = 0$ otherwise), x_i is the number of facilities located at node i, h_k is the demand at node k, and $w_j = (1 - p)p^{j-1}$. The value $w_j h_k$ is the increase in expected coverage at node k when the number of facilities that cover this node is increased from $j - 1$ to j. It must be noted that this model allows for more than one facility to be opened at the same node, what is known as *co-location*. After having formulated the model, the paper discusses some properties of the solutions and a heuristic solution method is proposed. The performance of genetics algorithms to solve the MECLP is analysed in [11] and several additional metaheuristics are developed in [77]: an evolutionary algorithm, tabu search, simulated annealing, and a hybridized hill-climbing algorithm.

The MECLP is revisited in [19] to relax three of the assumptions of the original models: that the servers are independent, that the servers have the same busy probabilities, and that the server probabilities are the same for all the locations. The authors show that there is a disagreement between the MECLP and their model (which is based on a hypercube optimization procedure, see [59]) regarding the coverage predicted, but that there is an important agreement on the locations for the facilities.

An extension of the MECLP, Polasky et al. [75] assume probabilities that are different for each site and independent to maximize the number of expected covering species in an application to nature reserve selection. The model that they propose is nonlinear (a sum of products) and the authors use a greedy heuristic algorithm. The same model is studied in [25] with the slight difference that now the budget constraint is specifically a constraint that imposes the exact number of nature reserves to be located (that is, a p-median constraint). In order to solve the problem, it is proposed a mixed integer linear model that provides an arbitrarily close approximation to the original objective function. The first ever linear formulation for the MECLP is proposed in [71], where the concept of probability chains is used to calculate compound probability terms that allow the authors to develop an efficient linearization technique for some facility location problems with unreliability. Some lower bounds are calculated and several valid inequalities are proposed to strengthen their model, which is solved with a branch-and-cut algorithm.

The *maximum availability location problem*, introduced in [85], is a probabilistic extension of the maximum covering location problem that seeks to locate p facilities so that the population that can be covered by at least one of the servers is maximized with a certain level of reliability decided beforehand. The paper proposes two models, one in which all the servers are equally busy, and another one in which busy fractions are adjusted by zone. Later a unified approach to the maximum availability location problem and to the maximum expected covering location problem is discussed in [43], where the authors discuss similarities and differences between the two models.

In the context of emergency vehicles some approaches that maximize covered demand are analysed in [33], including backup and maximum expected covering models. In [66] we find an extension of the maximum expected covering model that considers two types of servers, with a hypercube queuing model being used to measure the dependencies between the servers. Van den Berg and Aardal [100] consider a model where not only the expected coverage is maximized but also the number of open locations and relocated vehicles is minimized. Their model is time-dependent and the day horizon is split into several time periods. So, the busy probabilities of the emergency vehicles depend on the time of the day. Instead of assuming the classic but strict 0–1 coverage, some models may allow fractional coverage, for example when dealing with stochastic response times. If the maximum expected covering location problem formulation is extended to allow for this, then the formulation is nonlinear. However, in [100] the authors present a linear integer programming formulation that they show to be much more efficient than the nonlinear formulation. In [8] the location and dispatch of the emergency vehicles is decided through district design, and uncertainty on both the travel times and the availability of the ambulances is considered.

The authors of [21] study a maximum covering location problem on a network where there is uncertainty on travel times, which is modelled through different scenarios. Three different models (expected covering, robust covering, and expected p-robust covering) are proposed, being explained how each of them is appropriate for a different type of facilities.

A different approach to deal with uncertainty is the *maximal cover location problem with hedging* introduced in [80]. The authors propose a multi-objective extension of the deterministic maximal cover location problem and introduce a lexicographic ordering of the objectives that are related to the uncertainty on the demands. The model is applied to the design of a network of screening facilities to detect exposure to lead contamination.

2.3.3   Other Covering Location Models

Moving further from the classification on set covering and maximum covering models, in [65] we can find a general model that considers uncertainty and time-dependent aspects. The authors show that several covering models from the literature are particular cases and solve their general model with a heuristic based on Lagrangean relaxation.

In [102] we can find a formulation for a multi-period maximal covering location problem with server uncertainty that is applied to the location of primary health centres where there is a high uncertainty on the availability of doctors (which are the servers in the context of this facility location problem). The authors explain that assigning probabilities to the different scenarios is a challenging experience and they circumvent this problem by using robust optimization to solve a minimax regret approach. In order to solve instances of large size, an algorithm based on Benders decomposition is used.

2.4   Hub Location Problems with Uncertainty

In today's global economy, logistics and supply chain networks play an important role in transporting a massive number of shipments around the globe by facilitating the movement of commodities at a lower cost. Hub-and-spoke is one of the paradigms that is employed by many companies operating in air and freight transport, parcel delivery, and telecommunication and computer networks. A *hub system*, or simply a *hub location problem*, is concerned with the optimal location of *hubs* (special nodes in the network that collect the demand from the origins and redirect it towards the destinations), the hub network design and directing the flow through this network in such a way to minimize the total transportation cost. A hub system has a number of advantages over a network with direct links between all origin-destination pairs including lower transportation and transmission cost. The saving is usually achieved by exploiting economy of scales in hub links and having fewer direct links, which ultimately leads to lower operational costs.

According to the type of node allocation scheme, hub location problems are divided into two distinctive groups: single allocation and multiple allocation problems. In the former, all incoming and outgoing traffic to and from every node is transferred via a single hub, while in the latter each node is allowed to receive and send flow through more than one hub. Hub-and-spoke systems can be also categorized as capacitated and uncapacitated. When constraints exist that limit the amount of flow being transported through the network, the problem is called capacitated [6]. Depending on the problem, capacity constraints may refer to the nodes, to the links, or to both. With regard to hub capacity, either there is a constraint on the total flow transported through a hub (as in [26]), or only the amount of non-processed flow entering a hub is restricted (as in [41]). In hub location problems, hubs often form a complete graph, which means all hubs are directly connected to each other. In other cases a direct hub link between a hub pair is made only if it is necessary [4]. These type of problems are known as hub location with incomplete hub networks. Hub location problems are usually modelled using path-based formulations [26, 94] or flow-based formulations [40]. The path-based formulations of [94] are known to provide tight linear programming relaxation bounds.

Traditional approaches to hub location are widely deterministic assuming very limited or no uncertainty. However, research has shown that deterministic hub location models often lead to sub-optimal networks. From a practical point of view, two types of uncertainty could significantly affect the design of a hub network: (1) variation in demand (dependent or independent demand), cost (fixed or variable), and time, and (2) supply availability (e.g., hubs or arcs failure). The first type of uncertainty is highly related to the level of inaccuracy in input data while the second type is associated with the risk of supply disruption. Regardless of the source, researchers have found that the impact of uncertainty on networks operation is significant ranging from excessive transportation cost and low service level to customer dissatisfaction. Motivated by the importance of uncertainty modelling, in recent years a growing interest has been developing on hub location problems with demand and cost variation, supply disruption, and hub fortification. These studies provide recommendations on how different uncertainty aspects can be taken into account when designing hub networks. To model hub location problems with uncertainty, researchers often recommend stochastic programming, robust optimization, and reliability approaches. In the following we will briefly review some of these studies.

2.4.1 Demand, Cost, and Time Uncertainty

In practice, variation on demand, cost, price, or time are largely unavoidable, and are considered an inherent part of logistics, supply chain, and telecommunication networks. They are often measured as the amount of deviation from the expected values of the interested data. Sim et al. [93] is one of the first studies to consider time variability in hub location models. A stochastic p-hub centre problem is introduced to minimize the longest transportation time assuming a specified service level in delivery times. The formulation uses chance constraints to model the minimum service-level requirement without addressing hub installation and operating costs.

We find in [103] stochastic formulations for hub location problems with uncertain demand and variable discount factor. Here demand is governed by a discrete probability distribution, and direct interaction between non-hub nodes is allowed. A two-stage network design model is proposed where the first stage looks for the number and location of hubs for different demand levels and the second stage attempts to determine the transport paths and flow allocation in response to demand change.

Another pioneer work on modelling uncertainty in hub location is [28], that studies stochastic uncapacitated hub location problems with demand and transportation cost uncertainty. It is shown that problems with stochastic demand or dependent transportation costs are equivalent to their associated deterministic expected value problems but this may not be the case if transportation costs are uncertain and independent. The *uncapacitated hub location problem with stochastic demands* proposed in this paper is as follows:

$$\text{Min.} \sum_{i \in H} f_i z_i + E_\xi \left[\sum_{i,j \in H} \sum_{k \in K} W_k(\xi) F_{ijk} x_{ijk}(\xi) \right]$$

$$\text{s.t.} \quad \sum_{i,j \in H} x_{ijk}(\xi) = 1, \quad k \in K, \ \xi \in \Xi,$$

$$\sum_{j \in H} x_{ijk}(\xi) + \sum_{j \in H} x_{jik}(\xi) \leq z_i, \quad i \in H, \ k \in K, \ \xi \in \Xi,$$

$$x_{ijk}(\xi) \geq 0, \quad i, j \in H, \ k \in K, \ \xi \in \Xi,$$

$$z_i \in \{0, 1\}, \quad i \in H,$$

where E_ξ is the mathematical expectation with respect to a random event ξ whose support is Ξ. H is the set of hubs and K is the set of commodities. Variable z_i takes value 1 if and only if a hub is located at node i, and variable x_{ijk} takes value 1 if and only if commodity k is transits through the

network via hub i first and then via hub j. In addition, f_{ijk} is the unit transportation cost of routing commodity k via hubs i and k, f_i is the fixed set-up
cost for locating a hub at node i, and W_k is the amount of commodity k to be
routed. The first term of the objective function represents the total set-up cost
of the hub facilities and the second term is the total expected transportation
cost. The constraints are the same as those proposed for the uncapacitated
hub location problem with multiple assignments in [49] though now defined
for every possible realization of ξ.

The impact of different sources of uncertainty on the solution of a hub
location problem with uncertainty is studied in [6]. Representing uncertainty
as a finite set of scenarios, the authors study first the two cases in which
sources of uncertainty are set-up cost and demand, and then develop an integrated case where the two sources of uncertainty are simultaneously present.
Several formulations are proposed: a minimax regret formulation to deal with
uncertainty in the set-up costs, a two-stage stochastic program with recourse
to model the problem with uncertain demand, and a two-stage minimax
regret program to address the case with uncertain demand and fixed costs.
It is demonstrated that in hub location problems the structure of the solutions with and without uncertainty are likely to be different, and that optimal
solutions are sensitive to the presence of uncertainty.

The authors of [90] propose robust formulations for the uncapacitated
single and multiple allocation hub location problem with demand uncertainty, where limited features of the demand distribution are assumed to be
known. They model the problem as a mixed integer nonlinear program which
is subsequently transformed into a mixed integer conic quadratic program.
Regarding uncertainty, the approach of [27] is adopted: the uncertain parameters (demand) are assumed to be in an ellipsoidal uncertainty set and can be
expressed by a known mean and a number of independent variables. Numerical experiments are conducted to highlight the difference between robust and
deterministic solutions.

The case where demand distribution is not fully specified is also studied
in [44, 45]. The authors propose formulations for the capacitated single and
multiple allocation hub location problem assuming that transported flows
between any pair of nodes in the network are independent symmetric random
variables. They consider the uncertainty in the capacity constraints, employ
a budget of uncertainty and use the nominal demand value in the objective function. A mixed integer programming model for the deterministic
problem and a robust counterpart of the original model are presented, and
three variants of polyhedral uncertainty are considered: the hose, the hybrid,

and the budget in a multiple allocation p-hub median problem. A tabu search algorithm is used to solve the different instances.

Merakli and Yaman [68] present a robust uncapacitated multiple allocation hub location problem under polyhedral demand uncertainty where hose uncertainty and a hybrid model are used to characterize demand uncertainty. The authors propose linear mixed integer programming formulations with minimax criteria and use two Benders decomposition-based algorithms to solve problem instances with up to 75 nodes. After having discussed the impact of demand uncertainty on the location of hubs, it is argued that demand uncertainty may not significantly affect the decision on where to locate hub facilities. Another paper on robust optimization, Zetina et al. [105] consider uncertainty on transportation costs and its interaction with demand uncertainty. Three models and solution techniques are presented for robust counterparts of the well-known uncapacitated hub location problem with multiple allocation considering uncertainty on demand, transportation cost, and on both parameters simultaneously. Demands between origin-destination pairs in the first model and transportation costs for all links in the second model are assumed to be uncertain values lying in a known interval. In the third model, the uncertainties on both demand and transportation costs are assumed to be independent. The authors then use a budget of uncertainty to control the desired level of conservatism for both demand and transportation costs as suggested in [22]. Finally it is shown that commodities are routed through multiple paths when the transportation costs are uncertain. De Sa et al. [37] propose a robust optimization approach for multiple allocation incomplete hub networks under demand and set-up cost uncertainty. Similar to previous studies, the model is based on the approach proposed in [22]. The worst case with respect to a budget of uncertainty is minimized.

In [76] it is studied a stochastic single allocation hub location problem with deterministic fixed costs and uncertain demand. The problem is formulated as a quadratic program where the location and allocation decisions are taken on the first stage, and the routing is decided on the second. The authors show that the proposed stochastic quadratic program is equivalent to a deterministic quadratic program for the special case of continuous and strictly increasing distribution functions that model the uncertainty.

Rostami et al. [87] highlight the importance of postponing demand allocation due to its uncertain nature. The single allocation hub location problem under demand uncertainty is studied and a two-stage stochastic program is proposed where the optimal location of the hubs is decided on the first stage and the allocation of the spokes on the second stage, once the uncertainty on the demand is observed. To solve larger instances of the nonlinear program, the authors formulate an efficient cutting plane approach that outperforms a commercial solver and the L-shaped decomposition technique.

Demand Uncertainty from the Congestion Perspective

The design of hub location networks with demand uncertainty has been also studied from the hub congestion perspective. Grove and O'Kelly [46] is one of the earliest studies to investigate the effect of congestion in hub-and-spoke networks. A simulation is made for a single allocation hub network with fixed hub locations and it is demonstrated how schedule delays of airline systems are influenced by the amount of flow at hubs.

Studies on congestion at hub systems address the congestion either by restricting the amount of flow passing through the hubs or by explicitly modelling the congestion effects in the objective functions. The latter often use performance measures such as average waiting time or the probability distribution of the queue length to measure congestion. A number of studies have shown that explicitly modelling congestion more accurately captures its effects as it allows to imitate its exponential nature. Alumur et al. [5] propose mixed-integer linear programming formulations for the single and multiple allocation hub location problems with service time limit considering congestion at hubs. Their focus is on capacity decisions and service time limit to reflect the effects of congestion. Ozgun-Kibiroglu et al. [74] address the multiple allocation hub location problem in which a penalty cost in the objective function represents the congestion effects on respective hubs. The proposed model captures the congestion effects using a convex cost function similar to the one used in [38]. The authors proposed a particle swarm optimization algorithm to solve the problem.

Another stream of research attempts to capture congestion effects by modelling hubs as spatially distributed queues. Examples of such studies are [15, 39, 47, 64, 78]. A nonlinear model to design hub-and-spoke networks with capacity and fixed cost is presented in [47]. The authors consider congestion both on links and at hub facilities. Hubs are modelled as M/M/1 queues and congestion is computed using mean waiting time at hubs. Marianov and Serra [64] provide models and solution methods for a hub location problem with congestion. Hub airports are represented as M/D/c queues and a formula is derived for the probability of the number of customers in the system. This formula is used as a capacity constraint in the model for hub location with congestion. Elhedhli and Hu [38] propose the use of a power law function to represent the congestion cost in the objective function. The hubs are modelled as M/M/1 queues and congestion is computed as the ratio of the total flow to the surplus capacity. A Lagrangean heuristic is used to solve the nonlinear mixed integer programming formulation of the problem.

De Camargo et al. [35] address the multiple allocation hub location problem under hub congestion. The authors model congestion as a convex cost function and propose a Benders decomposition algorithm to solve instances of the problem with up to 81 nodes. The single allocation version of the problem with congestion was later studied in [36], where a procedure that concurrently generates outer approximation and Benders cuts is proposed to solve large problem instances.

A hub covering location problem with congestion is studied in [78]. The problem is modelled as an M/M/1/k queuing system with the objective of minimising the probability of flow exceeding a hub capacity. The authors adopt a bi-objective modelling framework to minimize total transportation cost and the maximum travel time between each pair of origin-destination nodes. Azizi et al. [15] analyse a capacitated single allocation hub p-hub location problem with stochastic demand and congestion. The authors model hubs as spatially distributed M/G/1 queues and congestion is captured using the expected queue lengths at hub facilities. The authors use a simple transformation and a piecewise linear approximation technique to linearize the resulting nonlinear model proposed for the problem. Two solution approaches are presented to solve medium and large problem instances: a cutting plane approach and a heuristic.

Alkaabneh et al. [3] consider a hub-and-spoke network design problem with inter-hub economies-of-scale and hub congestion. The authors model the problem as a nonlinear mixed integer program similar to that proposed in [38] but with flow dependent costs. The authors propose a Lagrangian approach to obtain tight upper and lower bounds. Karimi-Mamaghan et al. [52] study a single allocation multi-commodity hub location problem with congestion. Congestion at the hubs is modelled as a general GI/G/c queuing system and a stochastic flow is used to account for congestion in hub-to-hub connection links. A learning-based metaheuristic is proposed.

In summary, the research on hub location with uncertain data has begun approximately a decade ago and it is still in early stages. As shown here, the main focus of the papers that have been published so far has been on demand and cost variations. Few papers have simultaneously considered demand and cost uncertainty, and there is very limited research on time uncertainty alone or in combination with other sources of uncertainty. Most of the works reviewed above attempt to deal with data uncertainty in general without addressing a particular application. Regarding the objective function, the most common objective is the minimization of cost. A large majority of the research so far assumes no capacity restriction and a fixed discount factor in inter-hub links. The popular methodology utilized in modelling data uncertainty is the use of budget of uncertainty. Very few research can be found on link congestion or simultaneous consideration of hub and link congestion. Apart from [3], all of the studies reviewed above assume a flow independent discount factor. Finally, an important practical factor, which is the impact of time dimension of demand in modelling uncertainty in hub location, is yet to be explored.

2.4.2 Network Reliability and Resilience

The second type of uncertainty in hub location is associated with the risk of supply disruption. The cause of hub failure or disruption vary from severe weather condition and natural disasters to labour dispute and sabotage. While some disruptions like earthquakes may occur less frequently, a large number of other causes are likely to strike the network at any time. Traditional approaches to hub-and-spoke network design ignore the possibility of hub disruption. These approaches are mainly concerned with the location of the hubs and the allocation of demand to these facilities to minimize the total network cost. In comparison with other location problems, the number of studies dealing with reliability and facility disruption in the context of hub-and-spoke is limited. Some of these studies are briefly discussed next.

Among the earliest studies in this area are those presented in [51, 73], where the authors propose response strategies such as delaying, cancelling, and rescheduling to deal with facility failure. These measures, though important for coping with disruptions, are reactive in nature and could be expensive to implement. A more robust approach to hub disruption management is to consider the possibility of hub failure and backups at the design stage. Kim and O'Kelly [54] formulate two p-hub location problems in telecommunication networks with reliability. The authors investigate both single and multiple allocation cases but do not consider backup hubs or rerouting of the affected flow. Kim [53] extends the work on hub-and-spoke reliability found in [54] and proposes a series of hub location models to mitigate hub failures, including two variants in which disrupted flows can be rerouted through a single intermediate backup hub.

An et al. [9], Azizi et al. [14], Rostami et al. [86], and Tran et al. [99] have also successfully used backup hubs to design a reliable network. An et al. [9] study the uncapacitated reliable single and multiple allocation hub location problems with backup facilities and propose a mixed integer nonlinear formulation. The paper considers the routes connecting pairs of origin-destination nodes. In a route with two hubs, for example, it is assumed that either the first or the second hub may fail and the affected flow is reassigned to an operating facility in the network. Their reliability model is suitable for networks with symmetric flow. Instances with up to 25 nodes are solved using branch-and-bound and Lagrangian methods. By comparing the solutions from single and multiple disruption scenarios, it is empirically shown that the impact of multiple hub disruptions to the system performance is small.

Several mixed integer linear and nonlinear formulations are introduced in [14] to design uncapacitated hub-and-spoke networks taking into account the probability of hub failure and rerouting costs. The authors study a special case when disrupted flow needs to be reassigned to a single hub. This assumption is relaxed in [12] to allow affected nodes to be re-allocated to any hub in the network. Unlike [9, 14] model implicitly p (the number of hubs) hub failure scenarios and the affected nodes are reassigned to the operating hubs in the network. The proposed model is therefore suitable for both networks with symmetric and asymmetric flow. The objective is to minimize the weighted sum of the transportation cost in normal and in disrupted situations. Instances with up to 81 nodes are solved with a commercial software and with genetic and particle swarm optimization algorithms. The computational results show that by considering hub failure at the design stage significant savings can be achieved without a substantial increase in day-to-day operating costs. A similar uncapacitated problem is studied in [99], where a mixed integer nonlinear model is formulated to find the optimal location of a pre-determined number of hubs taking into account the possibility of hub failure. The model is linearized with a specialized flow network called probability lattice, which is based on the methodology introduced in [71]. The linear formulation is used to solve small instances with up to 20 nodes in extended computational times. Larger instances of the problem are solved using a tabu search algorithm.

Similar to [14, 86] considers the case where a single backup hub is used to completely reroute the flow affected by the failing hubs and proposes a two-stage formulation for the problem. The authors use an interesting approach that keeps the resulting formulation similar to the classical single allocation problem and therefore the model can be easily linearized. A branch-and-cut framework based on Benders decomposition is proposed to solve large problem instances. Their computational results confirm the importance of considering hub breakdowns in the strategic planning phase of a transportation network.

Zhalechian et al. [104] propose a bi-objective two-stage stochastic program that takes into consideration both operational and disruption risks. Mohammadi et al. [69] study a bi-objective reliable p-hub location model that considers hubs and links uncertainties to minimize both the total cost and the maximum transportation time. The authors solve randomly generated large instances using a hybrid algorithm based on genetics algorithms and variable neighbourhood search. We find in [17] a multi-allocation reliable p-hub network problem where more than one hub may be disrupted simultaneously. A nonlinear formulation is proposed and a heuristic is used to solve the problem.

A path-based reliable uncapacitated hub location formulation is proposed in [91] to minimize the sum of the fixed hub installation cost, the expected transportation cost, and the penalty cost under random disruptions. Similar to the work of [17], the authors allow simultaneous (correlated) network disruptions. Numerical studies for an instance with 25 nodes validate the efficiency of the formulation. Larger instances are solved with heuristics.

Azizi and Salhi [13] use the uncapacitated FLOWLOC formulation introduced by [72] to develop reliable models for the single allocation p-hub location problem with multiple capacity levels and flow dependent discount factor. These models aim at simultaneously determining (a) the optimal location of the hubs, (b) the allocation of demand to these hubs, (c) the backup facilities for each demand point, (d) the hub capacity level to handle the normal flow, (e) the additional capacity to handle excessive rerouted flows due to possible hub disruption, (f) the values of discount factor for inter-hub links at normal, and (g) the discount factor to be applied on inter-hub links should volume of flow increase because of hub disruption. The authors demonstrate the need to consider simultaneously hub failure likelihood, inter-hub flow dependent cost and non-exogenous hub capacity in designing a reliable hub system. Instances with up to 170 nodes are solved with a commercial solver and a reduced variable neighbourhood search algorithm.

In summary, as the research on hub location problems with uncertain data, a growing interest has been developing on the design reliable hub systems. A popular approach to this problem is to consider backup hubs and rerouting the affected flow through these facilities. With the exception of [13, 91], all the studies reviewed above assume a fixed discount factor in the inter-hub links. The latter partially addresses flow dependent inter-hub discount model that allows discount factors to be arc dependent while the former explicitly models the network with a flow dependent discount factor. The performance of reliable hub networks with backup hub relies heavily on the availability of adequate capacity in the network. This short review indicates that in a large majority of previous studies it is assumed that hub facilities have unlimited capacities and there is no fixed cost associated with hub installation. Incorporating capacity and flow dependent discount factors may lead to even more challenging and highly nonlinear optimization problems which are worth further investigation.

2.4.3   Hub Interdiction and Fortification

A field closely related to hub-and-spoke reliability is hub interdiction and fortification. Interdiction problems involve two players: a defender, also called the "operator", and an attacker, which is called "interdictor". The operator wishes to optimally utilize some facilities or a network to, for example, transfer flow through least cost paths. The attacker will try to compromise the network in order to deteriorate the operator's optimal solution. Interdiction problems have been widely studied in the areas of network flows (or network interdiction) and facility location-allocation (or facility interdiction) problems. A few studies have recently proposed hub location interdiction and protection (fortification) problems. These problems have been developed based on earlier studies that address facilities and critical infrastructures protection against possible interdictors.

Lei [60] studies a hub interdiction median problem to identify critical hub facilities in a hub network. Two bilevel formulations are proposed to locate hubs in anticipation of a worst-case facility loss and to fortify a subset of existing hubs in a network. Ghaffarinasab and Atayi [44] also study this problem with fortification. The authors model the problem as a leader-follower Stackelberg game and propose a bilevel formulation. To solve the problem, they use an exact solution algorithm based on implicit enumeration. Ramamoorthy et al. [79] study the same problem and offers a more efficient solution technique. Two methods are proposed to reduce the bilevel hub interdiction model to a single level optimization problem: the first approach uses the dual formulation of the lower level problem and the second replace the lower level by a set of closest assignment constraints.

2.5   Conclusions

In this chapter we have presented a survey on three important types of discrete facility location problems with uncertainty. As has been shown, uncertainty can be considered in many different ways, either implicitly (by adding extra facilities that take into account potential failures) or explicitly (by including failure probabilities or probability distributions of the parameters). One way or the other, what is widely recognized in the location community is the need to develop and to solve models that include uncertainty, even at the cost of having models much more difficult to solve, as they usually become much more larger in size than standard deterministic models, sometimes even turning up to be nonlinear models. Therefore, this area of research in facility location will play an important role in the coming years, specially if solution techniques are developed that can be applied to other problems beyond discrete facility location problems.

References

1. Albareda-Sambola, M., Fernández, E., and Saldanha-da-Gama, F. The facility location problem with Bernoulli demands. Omega-Int. J. Manage. S. **39**, 335–345 (2011).
2. Albareda-Sambola, M., Fernández, E., and Saldanha-da-Gama, F. Heuristic solutions to the facility location problem with general Bernoulli demands. INFORMS J. Comput. **29**, 737–753 (2017).
3. Alkaabneh, F., Diabat, A., and Elhedhli, S. A Lagrangian heuristic and GRASP for the hub-and-spoke network system with economies-of-scale and congestion. Transport. Res. C-Emer. **102**, 249-273 (2019).
4. Alumur, S.A., Bahar, Y.K., and Karasan, O.E. The design of single allocation incomplete hub networks. Transport. Res. B-Meth. **43**, 936–951 (2009).
5. Alumur, S.A., Nickel, S., Rohrbeck, B., and Saldanha-da-Gama, F. Modelling congestion and service time in hub location problems. Appl. Math. Model. **55**, 13-32 (2018).
6. Alumur, S.A., Nickel, S., and Saldanha-da-Gama, F. Hub location under uncertainty. Transport. Res. B-Meth. **46**, 529-543 (2012).
7. Aly, A.A., and White, J.A. Probabilistic formulation of the emergency service location problem. J. Oper. Res. Soc. **29(12)**, 1167-1179 (1978).
8. Ansari, S., McLay, L.A., and Mayorga, M.E. A maximum expected covering problem for district design. Transp. Sci. **51(1)**, 376-390 (2017).
9. An,Y., Zhang, Y., and Zeng, B. 2015. The reliable hub-and-spoke design problem: Models and algorithms. Transport. Res. B-Meth. **77**, 103–122 (2015).
10. Aydin, N., and Murat, A. A swarm intelligence based sample average approximation algorithm for the capacitated reliable facility location problem. Int. J. Prod. Econ. **145**, 173–183 (2013).
11. Aytug, H., and Saydam, C. Solving large-scale maximum expected covering location problems by genetic algorithms: A comparative study. Eur. J. Oper. Res. **141**, 480-494 (2002).

12. Azizi, N. Managing facility disruption in hub-and-spoke networks: Formulations and efficient solution methods. Ann. Oper. Res. **272**, 159–185 (2019).

13. Azizi, N., and Salhi, S. Reliable hub-and-spoke systems with multiple capacity levels and flow dependent discount factor. Eur. J. Oper. Res. **298**(3), 834–854 (2022).

14. Azizi, N., Chauhan, S., Salhi, S., and Vidyarthi, N. The impact of hub failure in hub-and-spoke networks: Mathematical formulations and solution techniques. Comput. Oper. Res. **65**, 174–188 (2016).

15. Azizi, N., Chauhan, S., and Vidyarthi, N. Modelling and analysis of hub-and-spoke networks under stochastic demand and congestion. Ann. Oper. Res. **264**, 1–40 (2018).

16. Balinski, M.L., Integer programming: Methods, uses, computations. Manage. Sci. **12**, 253–313 (1965).

17. Barahimi, P., and Vergara, H.A. Reliable p-hub network design under multiple disruptions. Netw. Spat. Econ. **20**, 301–327 (2020).

18. Baron, O., Berman, O., Fazel-Zarandi, M.M., and Roshanaei, V. Almost robust discrete optimization. Eur. J. Oper. Res. **276**, 451–465 (2019).

19. Batta, R., Dolan, J.M., and Krishnamurthy, N.N. The maximal expected covering location problem: revisited. Transp. Sci. **23**(4), 277-287 (1989).

20. Beraldi, P., and Ruszczynsky, A. The probabilistic set-covering problem. Oper. Res. **50**(6), 956-967 (2002).

21. Berman, O., Hajizadeh, I., and Krass, D. The maximum covering problem with travel time uncertainty. IIE Trans. **45**, 81-96 (2013).

22. Bertsimas, D., and Sim, M. Robust discrete optimization and network flows. Math. Program. **98**, 49–71 (2003).

23. Bertsimas, D., and Sim, M. The price of robustness. Oper. Res. **52**(1), 35–53 (2004).

24. Bieniek, M. A note on the facility location problem with stochastic demands. Omega-Int. J. Manage. S. **55**, 53–60 (2015).

25. Camm, J.D., Norman, S.K., Polasky, S., and Solow, A.R. Nature reserve site selection to maximize expected species covered. Oper. Res. **50**(6), 946-955 (2002).

26. Campbell, J.F. Integer programming formulations of discrete hub location problems. Eur. J. Oper. Res. **72**, 387–405 (1994).

27. Chen, X., Sim, M., Sun, P., and Zhang, J.2008. A linear decision-based approximation approach to stochastic programming. Oper. Res. **56**, 344–357 (2008).

28. Contreras, I., Cordeau, J.F., and Laporte, G. Stochastic uncapacitated hub location. Eur. J. Oper. Res. **212**, 518-528 (2011).

29. Correia, I. and Saldanha-da-Gama, F. Facility location under uncertainty. In: Laporte, G., Nickel, S., and Saldanha-da-Gama, F. (eds.) Location science (2nd Edition), pp. 185-213. Springer (2019).

30. Church, R.L., and ReVelle, C. The maximal covering location problem. Pap. Reg. Sci. Assoc. **32(1)**, 101–118 (1974).
31. Daskin, M.S. A maximum expected covering location model: formulation, properties and heuristic solution. Transp. Sci. **17(1)**, 48–70 (1983).
32. Daskin, M.S., and Stern, E.H. A hierarchical objective set covering model for emergency medical service vehicle deployment. Transport. Sci. **15**, 137-152 (1981).
33. Daskin, M.S, Hogan, K., and ReVelle, C. Integration of multiple, excess, backup, and expected covering models. Environ. Plann. B **15**, 15-35 (1988).
34. Devine, M.D., and Lesso, W.G. Models for the minimum cost development of offshore oil fields. Manage. Sci. **18**, 378–387 (1972).
35. De Camargo, R.S., Miranda, G., Ferreira, R.P.M., and Luna, H.P. Multiple allocation hub-and-spoke network design under hub congestion. Comput. Oper. Res. **36**, 3097–3106 (2009).
36. De Camargo, R.S., Miranda, G., and Ferreira, R.P.M. A hybrid outer-approximation/Benders decomposition algorithm for the single allocation hub location problem under congestion. Oper. Res. Lett. **39**, 329–337 (2011).
37. De Sa, E.M., Morabito, R., and de Camargo, R.S. Benders decomposition applied to a robust multiple allocation incomplete hub location problem. Comput. Oper. Res. **89**, 31-50 (2018).
38. Elhedhli, S., and Hu, F.X. Hub-and-spoke network design with congestion. Comput. Oper. Res. **32**, 1615-1632 (2005).
39. Elhedhli, S., and Wu, H. A Lagrangean heuristic for hub-and-spoke system design with capacity selection and congestion. INFORMS J. Comput. **22**, 282–296 (2010).
40. Ernst, A.T., and Krishnamoorthy, M. Efficient algorithms for the uncapacitated single allocation p-hub median problem. Locat. Sci. **4**, 139–154 (1996).
41. Ernst, A.T., and Krishnamoorthy, M. Solution algorithms for the capacitated single allocation hub location problem. Ann. Oper. Res. **86**, 141–159 (1999).
42. García, S., and Marín, A.: Covering location problems. In: Laporte, G., Nickel, S., and Saldanha-da-Gama, F. (eds.) Location Science (2nd Edition), pp. 99-119. Springer (2019).
43. Galvao, R.D., Chiyoshi, F.Y., and Morabito, R. Towards unified formulations and extensions of two classical probabilistic location models. Comput. Oper. Res. **32**, 15-33 (2005).
44. Ghaffarinasab, N., and Atayi, R. An implicit enumeration algorithm for the hub interdiction median problem with fortification. Eur. J. Oper. Res. **267**, 23-39 (2018).
45. Ghaffarinasab, N., Ghazanfari, M., and Teimoury, E. Robust optimization approach to the design of hub-and-spoke networks. Int. J. Adv. Manuf. Tech. **76**, 1091-1110 (2015).
46. Grove, P.G., and O'Kelly, M.E. Hub networks and simulated schedule delay. Pap. Reg. Sci. Assoc. **59**, 103–119 (1986).

47. Guldmann, J.M., and Shen, G. A general mixed integer nonlinear optimization model for hub network design. Working paper, Department of City and Regional Planning, The Ohio State University, Columbus, Ohio (1997).

48. Haight, R.G., Revelle, C., and Snyder, S.A. An integer optimization approach to a probabilistic reserve site selection problem. Oper. Res. **47(5)**, 697-708 (2000).

49. Hamacher, H.W., Labbé, M., Nickel, S., and Sonneborn, T., Adapting polyhedral properties from facility to hub location problems. Discrete Appl. Math. **145**, 104–116 (2004).

50. Hogan, K., and ReVelle, C. Concepts and applications of backup coverage. Manag. Sci. **32(11)**, 434–1444 (1986).

51. Janić, M. Modelling the large scale disruptions of an airline network. J. Transp. Eng. **131**, 249-260 (2005).

52. Karimi-Mamaghan, M., Mohammadi, M., Pirayesh, A., Karimi-Mamaghan, A.M., and Irani, H. Hub-and-spoke network design under congestion: A learning based metaheuristic. Transport. Res. E-Log. **142**, 1-26 (2020).

53. Kim, H. p-Hub protection models for survivable hub network design. J. Geogr. Syst. **14(4)**, 437-461 (2012).

54. Kim, H., and O'Kelly, M.E. Reliable p-hub location problems in telecommunication networks. Geogr. Anal. **41**, 283–306 (2009).

55. Kinay, O.B., Kara, B.Y., Saldanha-da-Gama, F., and Correia, I. Modeling the shelter site location problem using chance constraints: A case study for Istanbul. Eur. J. Oper. Res. **270**, 132–145 (2018).

56. Kinay, O.B., Saldanha-da-Gama, F., and Kara, B.Y. On multi-criteria chance-constrained capacitated single-source discrete facility location problems. Omega-Int. J. Manage. S. **83**, 107–122 (2019).

57. Krarup J., and Pruzan, P.M. The simple plant location problem: survey and synthesis. Eur. J. Oper. Res. **12**, 36–81 (1983).

58. Laporte, G., Louveaux, F.V., and van Hamme, L. Exact solution to a location problem with stochastic demands. Transport. Sci. **28**, 95–103 (1994).

59. Larson, R.C. A hypercube queuing model for facility location and redistricting in urban emergency services. Comput. Oper. Res. **1**, 67-95 (1974).

60. Lei, T.L. Identifying critical facilities in hub-and-spoke networks: A hub interdiction median problem. Geogr. Anal. **45**, 105–122 (2013).

61. Li, X., Zhao, Z., Zhu, X., and Wyatt, T. Covering models and optimization techniques for emergency response facility location and planning: a review. Math. Method. Oper. Res. **74**, 281-310 (2011).

62. Lin, C.K.Y. Stochastic single-source capacitated facility location model with service level requirements. Int. J. Prod. Econ. **117**, 439–451 (2009).

63. Lutter, P., Degel, D., Büsing, C., Koster, A.M.C.A., and Werners, B. Improved handling of uncertainty and robustness in set covering problems. Eur. J. Oper. Res. **263**, 35-49 (2017).

64. Marianov, V., and Serra, D. Location models for airline hubs behaving as M/D/c queues. Comput. Oper. Res. **30**, 983–1003 (2003).

65. Martín, A., Martínez-Merino, L.I., Rodríguez-Chía, A.M., and Saldanha-da-Gama, F. Multi-period stochastic covering location problems: Modeling framework and solution approach. Eur. J. Oper. Res. **268**, 432-449 (2018).

66. McLay L.A. A maximum expected covering location model with two types of servers. IIE Trans. **41(8)**,730-741 (2009).

67. Meng, S., and Shia, B.-C. Set covering location models with stochastic critical distances. J. Oper. Res. Soc. **64**, 945-958 (2013).

68. Merakli, M. and Yaman, H. 2017. A capacitated hub location problem under hose demand uncertainty. Transport. Res. B-Meth. **86**, 66-85 (2017).

69. Mohammadi, M., Jula, P., and Tavakkoli-Moghaddam, R. Reliable single-allocation hub location problem with disruptions. Transport. Res. E-Log. **123**, 90-120 (2019).

70. Mulvey, J.M., Vanderbei, R.J., and Zenios, S.A., 1995. Robust optimization of large-scale systems. Oper. Res. **43**, 264–281 (1995).

71. O'Hanley, J.R., Scaparra, M.P., and García, S. Probability chains: A general linearization technique for modeling reliability in facility location and related problems. Eur. J. Oper. Res. **230**, 63-75 (2013).

72. O'Kelly, M.E., and Bryan, D.L. Hub location with flow economies of scale. Transport. Res. B-Meth. **32(8)**, 605-616 (1998).

73. O'Kelly, M.E., Kim, H., and Kim, C. Internet reliability with realistic peering. Environ. Plann. B **33**, 325-343 (2006).

74. Ozgun-Kibiroglu, C., Serarslan, N., and Topcu, I. Particle swarm optimization for uncapacitated multiple allocation hub location problem under congestion. Expert Syst. Appl. **119**, 1-19 (2019).

75. Polasky, S., Camm, J.D., Solow, A.R., Csuti, B., White, D., and Ding, R. Choosing reserve networks with incomplete species information. Biol. Conserv. **94**, 1-10 (2000).

76. Qin, Z., and Gao, Y. Uncapacitated p-hub location problem with fixed costs and uncertain flows. J. Intell. Manuf. **28**, 705–716 (2017).

77. Rajagopalan, H.K., Vergara, F.E., Saydam, C., and Xiao, J. Developing effective meta-heuristics for a probabilistic location model via experimental design. Eur. J. Oper. Res. **177**, 83-101 (2007).

78. Rahimi, Y., Tavakkoli-Moghaddama, R., Mohammadi, M., and Sadeghi, M. Multi-objective hub network design under uncertainty considering congestion: An M/M/c/K queue system. Appl. Math. Model. **40**, 4179-4198 (2016).

79. Ramamoorthy, P., Jayaswal, S., Sinha, Λ., and Vidyarthi, N. Multiple allocation hub interdiction and protection problems: Model formulations and solution approaches. Eur. J. Oper. Res. **270**, 230-245 (2018).

80. Ratick, S., Osleeb, J., and Kangping, S. The maximal cover location model with hedging: Siting facilities under uncertainty, a lead poisoning screening network for the Dominican Republic. Int. Regional Sci. Rev. **39(1)**, 77-107 (2015).

81. ReVelle, C. Review, extension and prediction in emergency service siting models. Eur. J. Oper. Res. **40**, 58-69 (1989).

82. ReVelle, C., Eiselt, H.A., and Daskin, M.S. A bibliography for some fundamental problem categories in discrete location science. Eur. J. Oper. Res. **184**, 817-848 (2008).

83. ReVelle, C., and Hogan, K. A reliability-constrained siting model with local estimates of busy fractions. Environn. Plann. B **15**, 143-152 (1988).

84. ReVelle, C., and Hogan, K. The maximum reliability location problem and α-reliable p-median problem: Derivatives of the probabilistic location set covering problem. Ann. Oper. Res. **18**, 155-174 (1989).

85. ReVelle, C., and Hogan, K. The maximum availability location problem. Transport. Sci. **23(3)**, 192-200 (1989).

86. Rostami, B., Kämmerling, N., Buchheim, C., and Clausen, U. Reliable single allocation hub location problem under hub breakdowns. Comput. Oper. Res. **96**, 15-29 (2018).

87. Rostami, B., Kämmerling, N., Naoum-Sawayac, J., Buchheim, C., and Clausen, U. Stochastic single-allocation hub location. Eur. J. Oper. Res. **289**, 1087-1106 (2021).

88. Santoso, T., Ahmed, S., Goetschalckx, M., and Shapiro, A. A stochastic programming approach for supply chain network design under uncertainty. Eur. J. Oper. Res. **167**, 96–115 (2005).

89. Saxena, A., Goyal, V., and Lejeune, M.A. MIP reformulations of the probabilistic set covering problem. Math. Program. **121**, 1-31 (2010).

90. Shahabi, M., and Unnikrishnan, A. Robust hub network design problem. Transport. Res. E-Log. **70**, 356-373 (2014).

91. Shen, H., Liang, Y., and Shen, Z.-J.M. Reliable hub location model for air transportation networks under random disruptions. M&SOM-Manuf. Serv. Op. **23**, 388-406 (2021).

92. Shen, Z.J.M., Zhan, R.L., and Zhang, J. The reliable facility location problem: Formulations, heuristics, and approximation algorithms. INFORMS J. Comput. **23**, 470–482 (2011).

93. Sim, T., Lowe, T.J., and Thomas, B.W. The stochastic p-hub centre problem with service-level constraints. Comput. Oper. Res. **36**, 3166–3177 (2009).

94. Skorin-Kapov, D., Skorin-Kapov, J., and O'Kelly, M.E. Tight linear programming relaxations of uncapacitated p-hub median problems. Eur. J. Oper. Res. **94**, 582–593 (1996).

95. Snyder, L.V. Facility location under uncertainty: a review. IIE Trans. **38**, 537–554 (2006).

96. Snyder, L.V. Covering problems. In: Eiselt, H.A., and Marianov, V. (eds). Foundations of location analysis, pp. 109-135. Springer (2011).

97. Storbeck, J.E. Slack, natural slack and location covering. Socio. Econ. Plann. Sci. **16(3)**, 99-105 (1982).

98. Toregas, C., Swain, A., ReVelle, C., and Bergman, L. The location of emergency service facilities. Oper. Res. **19(6)**, 1363–1373 (1971).

99. Tran, T.H., O'Hanley, J.R., and Scaparra, M.P. Reliable hub network eesign: Formulation and solution techniques. Transport. Sci. **51**, 358–375 (2017).

100. Van den Berg, P.L., Kommer, G.J., and Zuzáková, B. Linear formulation for the maximum expected coverage location model with fractional coverage. Oper. Res. Health Care **8**, 33-41 (2016).
101. Van den Berg, P.L., and Aardal, K. Time-dependent MEXCLP with start-up and relocation cost. Eur. J. Oper. Res. **242**, 383-389 (2015).
102. Vatsa, A.K., and Jayaswal, S. A new formulation and Benders decomposition for the multi-period maximal covering facility location problem with server uncertainty. Eur. J. Oper. Res. **251**, 404-418 (2016).
103. Yang, T.H. Stochastic air freight hub location and flight routes planning. Appl. Math. Model. **33**, 4424-4430 (2009).
104. Zhalechian, M., Torabi, A.S., and Mohammadi, M. Hub-and-spoke network design under operational and disruption risks. Transport. Res. E-Log. **109**, 20-43 (2018).
105. Zetina, C.A., Contreras, I., Cordeau, J.F., and Nikbakhsh, E. Robust uncapacitated hub location. Transport. Res. B-Meth. **106**, 393–410 (2017).

3

Integrated Vehicle Routing Problems: A Survey

Gianfranco Guastaroba⊙, Andrea Mor⊙,
and M. Grazia Speranza⊙

3.1 Introduction

The literature on vehicle routing problems is huge, due to the practical interest in this class of problems, the enormous number of interesting variants, and the related computational challenges [65]. In fact, while the Traveling Salesman Problem is considered a well-solved problem, vehicle routing problems are considered among the hardest combinatorial optimization problems. However, exact methods for problems of this class can solve larger and larger instances and many effective heuristics are available, especially for the most studied variants. This progress, combined with the technological advances, has encouraged researchers to study integrated problems, that is problems that jointly optimize two or more previously studied sub-problems.

G. Guastaroba · M. G. Speranza
Department of Economics and Management, University of Brescia, Brescia, Italy
e-mail: gianfranco.guastaroba@unibs.it

M. G. Speranza
e-mail: grazia.speranza@unibs.it

A. Mor (✉)
Department of Management, Economics and Industrial Engineering,
Politecnico di Milano, Milan, Italy
e-mail: andrea.mor@polimi.it

© The Author(s), under exclusive license to Springer Nature
Switzerland AG 2022
S. Salhi and J. Boylan (eds.), *The Palgrave Handbook of Operations Research*,
https://doi.org/10.1007/978-3-030-96935-6_3

The solution of integrated problems, that are computationally harder to solve, offers substantial advantages with respect to the sequential solutions of the sub-problems. Examples of these benefits are presented in [4] for the Inventory Routing Problem and in [16] for the Two-Echelon Capacitated Vehicle Routing Problem. The primary purpose of this chapter is to provide an overview of the foremost classes of *integrated routing problems*, along with a synthesis of the most recent trends in the related literature. Quoting from [7], Integrated Vehicle Routing Problems (IVRP) can be defined as: "[...] problems where the VRP arises in combination with other optimization problems within the broader context of logistics and transportation." Based on the research interest that their study has arisen, as measured by the number of publications and citations, we have identified four main classes of IVRP: inventory routing problems, location routing problems, loading and routing problems, and two-echelon routing problems. In fact, other sub-problems have been considered jointly with routing problems, for instance, order batching and production scheduling. Given the limits in length of a book chapter, these integrated problems are not covered here.

Figure 3.1 provides a tree representation of the classes of IVRP surveyed in this chapter (the leaves), explicitly stating for each class the optimization problem arising in combination with the routing problem (the child of the root node).

The literature covering the above-mentioned classes of IVRP is extremely vast. It is out of the scope of the present survey to provide a thorough review of the research conducted on these classes of problems, also because dedicated surveys are already available. For each class of IVRP we provide

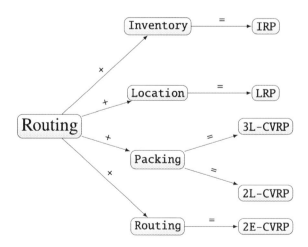

Fig. 3.1 A tree representation of the classes of IVRPs covered in this survey

a general description of the class, detail a prototypical basic problem, and review the most recent trends in the literature. References to previous surveys are provided, where the reader interested in the earlier literature is referred to. For some classes, namely the Inventory Routing Problem and Location Routing Problem, the surveys are very recent. In these cases, we do not provide a literature overview, but only refer the reader to the appropriate review papers.

Regarding the bibliographic search methodology, manuscripts have been searched by querying the Scopus database. The search was limited to articles published in top-tier international Operational Research (OR) journals (see Table 3.1). Papers that appeared in other journals were added, based on their research impact, as measured by the number of citations received. Figure 3.2 displays the distribution among the various OR journals, in percentage, of the papers mentioned in the present survey.

Table 3.1 Journals considered for the initial Scopus research

Journals (in alphabetical order)
4OR
Annals of Operations Research
Asia Pacific Journal of Operational Research
Central European Journal of Operations Research
Computers and Operations Research
Euro Journal on Computational Optimization
Euro Journal on Transportation And Logistics
European Journal of Operational Research
Expert Systems with Applications
Informs Journal on Computing
Interfaces
International Journal of Production Research
International Transactions in Operational Research
Journal of Heuristics
Journal of Scheduling
Journal of the Operational Research Society
Management Science
Networks
Omega United Kingdom
Operations Research
Operations Research Letters
OR Spectrum
TOP
Transportation Research Part B: Methodological
Transportation Science

Table 3.2 A summary of the main abbreviations used in the paper (in alphabetical order)

Problem		Algorithm	
Abbreviation	Description	Abbreviation	Description
2E-CVRP	Two-Echelon CVRP	ALNS	Adaptive LNS
2E-VRP	Two-Echelon VRP	B&C	Branch-and-Cut
2L-CVRP	CVRP with two-dimensional loading constraints	LNS	Large Neighborhood Search
3L-CVRP	CVRP with three-dimensional loading constraints	SA	Simulated Annealing
CVRP	Capacitated VRP	TS	Tabu Search
IRP	Inventory Routing Problem	VNS	Variable Neighborhood Search
IVRP	Integrated VRP		
LRP	Location Routing Problem		
TSP	Traveling Salesman Problem		
VRP	Vehicle Routing Problem		

Table 3.2 summarizes the main abbreviations used in the paper to identify optimization problems and solution algorithms.

The chapter is organized as follows. In Sect. 3.2, the class of Inventory Routing Problems is discussed, whereas Location Routing Problems are presented in Sect. 3.3. Section 3.4 reviews the class of routing problems combined with loading constraints. In particular, the issues related to loading two-dimensional items are discussed in Sect. 3.4.2, whereas the three-dimensional case is presented in Sect. 3.4.3. The combination of routing with routing, i.e., the class of Two-Echelon Routing Problems, is discussed in Sect. 3.5. Finally, conclusions are drawn in Sect. 3.6.

3.2   Inventory Routing Problems

The Inventory Routing Problems (IRP) have been studied for several decades, starting from the eighties, when the combination of routing optimization and inventory management was studied in some real settings. In [8], the first paper where the integrated problem is studied, an example is provided to show that, even when no inventory cost is considered and the transportation cost only is minimized, key decisions in distribution problems are when to

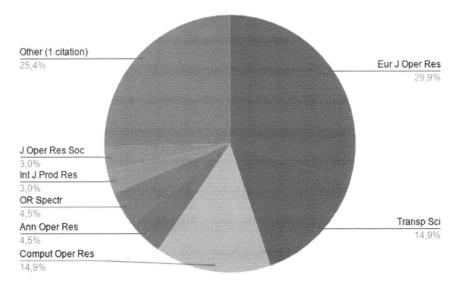

Fig. 3.2 The distribution among the various OR journals, in percentage, of the papers covered in this survey

serve customers and how much to deliver to them and that these decisions determine the routing cost.

In general, in IRPs the decisions to be taken are about when to serve customers, how much to deliver to them, which is the sequence of visits for each of the used vehicles. Formally, the main elements of the basic IRP are as follows. Let $G = (V, A)$ be a complete weighted graph. Set $V = \{0, 1, 2, \ldots, n\}$ is the set of vertices, where 0 represents the depot, and set $V\backslash\{0\}$ is the set of customers. In IRPs, often the depot represents the supplier and customers represent the retailers. Set A is the set of arcs (i, j), each being associated with a non-negative traveling cost c_{ij}. A planning horizon $T = 1, \ldots, |T|$ is defined. The depot and the customers have an initial inventory level, with customers also being characterized by a maximum inventory capacity. At each period $t \in T$, the quantity r_{0t} is made available at the supplier and the quantity r_{it} is consumed at retailer i. A unit inventory holding cost is defined for both the supplier and the retailers. A fleet of K homogeneous vehicles is available at the depot to serve all the customers. Each vehicle has a maximum capacity Q.

The minimization of the total inventory and routing costs is sought, subject to the following constraints. From a routing perspective, any feasible solution must satisfy the following conditions: in each period,

(RC1) each route starts and ends at the depot;

(RC2) each customer served in that period must be visited by exactly one vehicle;

(RC3) no more than K vehicles are used;

(RC4) the quantity assigned to a vehicle does not exceed its maximum capacity Q.

Any feasible inventory management pattern must not violate the following additional constraints: in each period,

(IM1) inventory definition for the depot (customers): the inventory must be consistent with the inventory at the previous period, the quantity made available (received) and the quantity distributed (consumed);

(IM2) stockout definition at the depot (customers): the quantity in inventory must be not lower than the quantity delivered.

A formulation of the basic IRP is defined in [5] for the case with a single vehicle. This class of integrated routing problems has been recently covered in [46], where a survey dedicated to routing problems that have a timing component is provided. A classification of the problems in the class is presented [15] and tutorials on the IRPs can be found in [9] and [10].

3.3   Location Routing Problems

Classical facility location problems (see [51]) aim at finding the best possible locations for facilities, that is, the locations that minimize the sum of the fixed cost for the chosen facilities and the transportation cost for a direct visit from facilities to customers. The cost for direct shipments from the facilities to the customers may be seen as an approximation of the real transportation cost in a tactical/strategic facility planning phase where detailed information about the demands of customers is unknown. However, in general, the assumption of direct shipments may lead to an overestimation of the real transportation cost. This is the reason for studying the Location Routing Problems (LRP), that is, problems where the location decision is taken jointly with the decisions about from which facilities to serve customers and the sequence of visits of the vehicles used for the service.

Formally, the LRP is defined as follows. Let $G = (V, A)$ be a complete weighted graph. Set $V = D \cup C$ is the set of vertices, where D is the set of potential facilities and C is the set of customers to be served. Set A is the set of arcs (i, j), each being associated with a non-negative traveling cost

c_{ij}. Each facility is characterized by an opening cost and a capacity. Each customer is characterized by a demand. A set K of vehicles is available, each with capacity Q.

The minimization of the total facility opening cost and routing cost is sought, subject to the following constraints. From a routing perspective, any feasible solution must satisfy the following conditions:

(RC1) each route starts and ends at an open facility;
(RC2) each customer must be served by exactly one vehicle;
(RC3) no more than K vehicles are used;
(RC4) the quantity assigned to a vehicle does not exceed its maximum capacity Q.

From a facility location perspective, the following constraint must hold:

(FL1) the demand of each customer must be satisfied;
(FL2) customers are supplied only from open facilities;
(FL3) the demand served from an open facility does not exceed its capacity.

We refer the interested reader to the following recent surveys on the LRP. [54] survey the literature on the LRP presented since the survey of [48]. Drexl and Schneider [25] present a survey of variants and extensions of the LRP whereas a survey on the standard LRP is presented in [60]. Finally, the most recent classification of the literature on the LRP is presented in [43].

3.4   Routing in Combination with Packing: Routing with Loading Constraints

The present section is structured as follows. We first provide a general introduction to the class of VRPs integrated with packing problems, often called Routing Problems with Loading Constraints or Routing and Packing Problems. Then, we define the Capacitated Vehicle Routing Problem with Two-dimensional Loading constraints (hereafter referred to as the *2L-CVRP*) and the Capacitated Vehicle Routing Problem with Three-dimensional Loading constraints (henceforth called the *3L-CVRP*), which are two prototypical members of this class of problems. Finally, we review the recent trends in the literature on VRPs combined with packing problems.

3.4.1   Introduction to the Class of Problems

Until recently, the typical approach in Capacitated VRPs, such as the CVRP, has been to assume that the demand of each customer is expressed by a single value, which usually represents the total weight (or volume) of the items requested. Thereby, the capacity of each vehicle measures the maximum weight (or volume) it can carry. Thus, assuming that all the other constraints are satisfied, a solution is feasible if the total weight (or volume) assigned to each vehicle does not exceed its capacity. Nevertheless, in several application contexts, the former assumptions are too restrictive, as it cannot be neglected that the demand of a customer consists of one or multiple items, which are characterized not only by weight (or volume) but also by shape. In these situations, a solution that is feasible to the CVRP may turn out to be infeasible in practice, as it is not possible to determine a feasible loading pattern that allocates all the items within the loading area of each vehicle. Further complications arise when special equipment is required for carrying out loading and unloading operations, or when the items transported are fragile or heavy. In the latter case, unloading must be carried out without reshuffling the loaded items. This is also true whenever the items transported cannot be moved inside the load compartment (or it is preferable not to do so) once they have been loaded. In these situations, the loading plan imposes a strict constraint on the sequence of visits to the customers. As an example, if the items requested by a customer are positioned in the deepest section of the load compartment, that customer has to be visited at the end of the route, as otherwise unloading the items requested is blocked by those demanded by other customers visited later in the route. On the other hand, the sequence of visits of a vehicle constrains the loading plan. All the previous observations highlight that loading and routing are two strictly inter-twinned problems that, if solved sequentially, may lead to sub-optimal solutions.

Based on the shape of the items requested, two major classes of integrated routing and packing problems can be identified. In some transportation applications, the customers request two-dimensional (also called rectangular-shaped) items that, because of their fragility or weight, cannot be stacked on top of each other. Examples of such applications are the transportation of large or heavy items—such as furniture, household appliances, and some mechanical components—or fragile items—such as pieces of catering equipment like food trolleys (e.g., see [53]). In all these cases, the routing problem must incorporate additional constraints to guarantee a feasible packing of the two-dimensional items requested.

In other transportation applications, the customers request three-dimensional items that can be superposed (possibly, with some limitations). Examples of such applications are the transportation of soft drinks and staple goods (e.g., see [59]). In these cases, additional constraints must be added to the routing problem to impose a feasible packing of the three-dimensional items requested by the customers.

The two packing problems mentioned above are multi-dimensional packing problems, which arise as extensions of the classical (one-dimensional) bin packing problem. In their basic forms, they are known as the Two-dimensional Bin Packing Problem (2BPP) and the Three-dimensional Bin Packing Problem (3BPP), respectively (see [32] and the references cited therein). In integrated routing and packing problems, additional restrictions are added to the 2BPP and the 3BPP to capture several loading issues, as detailed below.

In the following, we describe two prototypical problems integrating routing and packing. First, we illustrate the 2L-CVRP and, then, the 3L-CVRP, which can be seen as an extension of the former (e.g., see [32]).

It is worth highlighting that, given the scope of this survey, we focus on the two former problems. Nevertheless, the area of combined routing and packing problems is wider, including the VRPs with multiple compartments, the Traveling Salesman Problems (TSP) with pickups and deliveries and specific unloading restrictions, the double TSPs with multiple stacks. For more general overviews that include also the latter problems, we refer the interested reader to the surveys by [32, 33], and, more recently [53].

3.4.2 The Capacitated Vehicle Routing Problem with Two-Dimensional Loading Constraints

In the 2L-CVRP the customers request rectangular-shaped items (i.e., each item is characterized by width and length). For each vehicle, the loading surface available is also expressed in two dimensions (width and length). The 2L-CVRP models transportation applications where the items are heavy or fragile, such as refrigerators, or pieces of catering equipment, such as food trolleys, or when customer requests are loaded onto pallets which cannot be stacked on top of each other (e.g., see [16]).

Formally, the 2L-CVRP can be defined as follows. Let $G = (V, E)$ be a complete undirected and weighted graph. Set $V = \{0, 1, 2, \ldots, n\}$ is the set of vertices, where 0 represents the depot, and set $V \setminus \{0\}$ is the set of customers. Set E is the set of edges (i, j), each being associated with a non-negative traveling cost c_{ij}.

A fleet of K homogeneous vehicles is available at the depot to serve all the customers. Each vehicle has a maximum capacity Q, and a rectangular loading surface that is accessible from the rear for loading/unloading operations. The loading surface of each vehicle has a given width and length denoted by W and L, respectively.

Each customer $j \in V \setminus \{0\}$ has a known and deterministic demand comprising m_j items, each one having a specific width and length, denoted as w_j^p and l_j^p (with $p = 1, \ldots, m_j$), respectively. Let q_j denote the total weight of the items demanded by customer j.

The 2L-CVRP calls for the determination of a minimum-cost set of routes traveled by the fleet of vehicles available to serve all the customers, subject to the following set of constraints. From a routing perspective, any feasible solution must satisfy the following conditions:

(RC1) each route starts and ends at the depot;
(RC2) each customer must be served by exactly one vehicle;
(RC3) no more than K vehicles are used;
(RC4) for each vehicle, the total weight of the items assigned does not exceed its maximum capacity Q.

Any feasible loading pattern must not violate the following two additional constraints:

(LC1) each item must be loaded with its edges parallel to those of the vehicle (*orthogonality constraints*);
(LC2) there must exist a non-overlapping loading pattern of all the items assigned to a vehicle into its loading surface (*bin packing constraints*).

Additional constraints that define the feasibility of a loading pattern depend on the variant studied. It is worth now recalling the classification proposed in [27] for the 2L-CVRP. This classification is based on the possible loading configurations, and is as follows:

(i) *Sequential Loading* (SL) or rear loading or Last-In First-Out (LIFO) policy, when items must be loaded in reverse order with respect to the customers visits, as they cannot be reshuffled inside the load compartment;
(ii) *Unrestricted Loading* (UL), when items are allowed to be rearranged while visiting a customer;

and,

(I) *Oriented Loading* (OL), when items have a fixed orientation and cannot be rotated;

(II) *Non-oriented Loading* (NL) or rotated loading, when items are allowed to be rotated by 90°.

The possible combinations of the latter four constraints lead to four *basic 2L-CVRP variants*: (a) Two-dimensional Sequential and Oriented Loading (2|*SL*|*OL*); (b) Two-dimensional Sequential and Non-oriented Loading (2|*SL*|*NL*); (c) Two-dimensional Unrestricted and Oriented Loading (2|*UL*|*OL*); (d) Two-dimensional Unrestricted and Non-oriented Loading (2|*UL*|*NL*).

The majority of the problems studied in the literature assume the presence of SL constraints. Such restrictions impose that when customer j is visited, the requested items must be freely available for unloading through a sequence of straight movements (one per item) parallel to the length edge of the loading compartment. In other words, there must not be any item requested by another customer, that will be visited later in the route, blocking the unloading, i.e., between the items requested by customer j and the doors of the vehicle.

Figure 3.3 shows an example of a feasible solution to a 2|*SL*|*OL*.

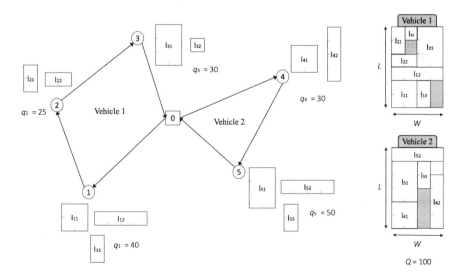

Fig. 3.3 An example of a feasible solution to a 2|*SL*|*OL* variant

Iori et al. [34] show that the 2L-CVRP reduces to the classical CVRP by assigning to each customer a single item having both width and length equal to 1, and setting the dimension of the loading surface of each vehicle equal to the total number of customers.

Côté et al. [16] quantify the potential benefits produced by tackling directly the 2L-CVRP with a unified solution approach, with respect to solving separately the individual routing and packing problems, by means of three non-integrated approaches. As a proof of concept, the authors consider a $2|SL|OL$ variant and show, by using worst-case analysis, that the cost of a solution obtained with one of the considered non-integrated approaches may be as large as twice the cost of the solution produced by an integrated exact approach. Furthermore, the authors provide empirical results to show the cost increase when a non-integrated approach is adopted with respect to an integrated approach.

3.4.2.1 Recent Trends in the Literature on the 2L-CVRP

Since its introduction by [34], the 2L-CVRP has received an ever-increasing academic attention. As mentioned above, surveys on routing problems that incorporate loading constraints, which obviously cover also the 2L-CVRP, are available in [32, 33], and [53]. Hence, in the following, we limit the overview to the recent trends on the 2L-CVRP, and refer the reader to the above-mentioned surveys for the earlier literature.

Basic 2L-CVRP variants are studied in [16, 31, 67], and [68], where the authors propose heuristic or exact solution methods for their solution. The exact solution approaches are proposed for the solution of a $2|SL|OL$ variant, whereas the heuristic algorithms are applied to the solution of the latter and some other basic variants. More particularly, [31] develop for the $2|SL|OL$ variant a Branch-and-Cut (B&C) algorithm, which incorporates several packing routines based on branch-and-bound, constraint programming, and metaheuristic approaches. For the same variant, [16] implement a B&C, derived from the approach proposed [17] for its stochastic counterpart. As mentioned above, to gauge the benefits of addressing the problem by using a unified solution approach, the authors compare the solutions obtained by such approach with those produced by three non-integrated approaches that consider separately the routing and the loading sub-problems. [67] design a heuristic for the solution of the $2|SL|OL$ and $2|UL|OL$ variants. The general idea is to employ a Variable Neighborhood Search (VNS) to address the routing sub-problem, and a skyline heuristic (i.e., a sort of sequence-based Tabu Search - TS) to check the loading feasibility of the routes produced by the VNS. All four basic variants (i.e., 2|*SL*|*OL*, 2|*SL*|*NL*, 2|*UL*|*OL*, 2|*UL*|*NL*) are solved by the Simulated Annealing (SA) algorithm proposed in [68]. This algorithm is based on four neighborhood structures, which are employed probabilistically, and on an open space local search heuristic to check the loading feasibility.

Extensions of the basic variants are studied in the following articles, where the solution approach proposed is, in the majority of the cases, heuristic. [23] and [69] investigate extensions where both collection and distribution of items may occur in the same route. More specifically, [23] analyze 2|*SL*|*OL* and 2|*SL*|*NL* problems with backhaul customers, where a precedence constraint imposes that on each route the backhaul customers, if any, are visited after all linehaul customers (see [65], Chap. 9). For the solution of this problem, the authors develop a hybrid algorithm that combines a Large Neighborhood Search (LNS) heuristic with biased-randomized versions of classical routing and packing heuristics. Based on applications arising in reverse logistics, [69] extend each of the four basic 2L-CVRP variants to problems where customers require simultaneous pickup and delivery services. The heuristic framework developed consists of a local search method for optimizing the routing sub-problem and a packing heuristic to produce feasible loading plans.

The time dimension is considered in the extensions investigated by [2] and [62]. In the former article, the authors study a time-dependent 2|*UL*|*OL*, where the travel time between a given pair of nodes is a function of the departure time from the origin node. The problem is formulated as a bi-objective optimization model, where the two objective functions are the minimization of the total travel time, on one hand, and the balance of the weight distribution among the vehicles achieved by using a minimax approach, on the other hand. A method called elitist non-dominated sorting local search is developed to solve this problem. Inspired by an application encountered in the food services industry, [62] study a multi-product 2L-CVRP with time windows constraints. In addition, the authors consider a modified SL constraint (called Adapted LIFO) where straight movements parallel to both the length edge and the width edge of the loading compartment are allowed. A generalized VNS algorithm is designed for the solution of this problem.

Dominguez et al. [24] extend the two UL basic variants (i.e., 2|*UL*|*OL* and 2|*UL*|*NL*) to consider a heterogeneous fleet of vehicles, where each vehicle type has a different weight capacity, width, length, as well as fixed and variable costs. The objective function considered aims at minimizing the total cost, which includes the driving distances and the fixed and variable costs associated with the vehicles routed. To solve this problem, the authors develop a multi-start algorithm based on biased-randomized versions of routing and packing heuristics previously proposed in the literature. Based on an application arising in the grocery distribution, [50] investigate a multi-compartment 2L-CVRP where the size of the compartments is flexible and has to be determined as part of the optimization. The objective function proposed aims at minimizing the sum of routing, loading, and unloading costs. For its solution, the authors implement both an exact (B&C) and a heuristic (LNS) algorithm. To the best of our knowledge, [17] are the only authors that study a stochastic 2L-CVRP. In particular, they address a $2|SL|OL$ variant where item sizes and weights are not known with certainty when vehicle routes are planned, but are stochastic and, hence, associated with discrete probability distributions. The authors model this problem as a two-stage stochastic program and solve it by means of an exact integer L-shaped method.

3.4.3 The Capacitated Vehicle Routing Problem with Three-Dimensional Loading Constraints

The 3L-CVRP is a natural extension to three dimensions of the 2L-CVRP presented above. In the 3L-CVRP customers request rectangular boxes, that is, besides width and length, the shape of each item is also characterized by height. Similarly, the loading surface available in a vehicle is three-dimensional and defined by width, length, and height. This problem is often encountered in the distribution of soft drinks, staple goods, and certain types of furniture and household appliances (e.g., see [53]) where some items can be superposed on top of each other. Introducing the height dimension implies that some additional loading issues might have to be taken into consideration. Of particular relevance are the issues concerning the fragility of the items, which limits the items that are stackable, and those concerning the stability of the items, when items are superposed on top of others.

Compared to the formal definition provided above for the 2L-CVRP, in the 3L-CVRP the loading surface of each vehicle is further characterized by its height, denoted as H. Similarly, each item demanded by a given customer $j \in V \setminus \{0\}$ has a specific height, denoted as h_j^p (with $p = 1, \ldots, m_j$). Furthermore, each item is also associated with a fragility flag f_j^p that takes value 1 if item p demanded by customer j is fragile, and 0 otherwise.

The 3L-CVRP calls for the determination of a minimum-cost set of routes to be traveled by the given fleet of vehicles to serve all the customers, subject to the above-mentioned routing constraints (RC1)–(RC3), and the loading constraints (LC1)–(LC2) plus the following additional loading constraints:

(LC3) no non-fragile item is stacked on top of a fragile one, whereas a fragile item can be superposed on fragile as well as non-fragile items (*fragility constraints*)

(LC4) when an item is stacked on top of others, its base must be supported by a minimum supporting area to guarantee the vertical stability of the cargo (*stability constraints*).

Regarding the latter constraints, it is worth highlighting that the supporting area of a given item is determined by the area touched by the base of that item. The packing is feasible only if such an area is not smaller than a given percentage of the base of the item itself.

The classification proposed by [27] for the 2L-CVRP (see Sect. 3.4.2) can be extended to the 3L-CVRP with the following specifications:

(I') SL constraints: when a customer j is visited, there must not be any item requested by another customer, that will be visited later in the route, placed over any item requested by j or between these items and the doors of the vehicle;

(II') NL constraints: items are allowed to be rotated by 90° on the horizontal plane, but have a fixed vertical orientation (i.e., they cannot be rotated upside-down).

The basic 3L-CVRP variants can then be identified by using a labeling notation analogous to the one introduced for the 2L-CVRP: 3|*SL*|*OL*, 3|*SL*|*NL*, 3|*UL*|*OL*, and 3|*UL*|*NL*.

Figure 3.4 shows an example of a feasible solution for a 3|*SL*|*OL* where items I_{12}, I_{22}, and I_{32} are assumed to be non-fragile. A feasible loading plan for vehicle 1 is shown in Fig. 3.5.

3.4.3.1 Recent Trends in the Literature on the 3L-CVRP

The introduction of the 3L-CVRP by [28] has inspired a large stream of research. As mentioned above for the 2L-CVRP, in the following we concentrate on the latest advances found in the literature on the 3L-CVRP, and refer the interested reader to the above-mentioned surveys for the earlier literature.

Basic 3L-CVRP variants are studied in [40, 64], and [31]. The first two papers propose heuristics for the basic 3|*SL*|*NL* variant. In more details, [64] design a TS, which iteratively invokes two greedy packing heuristics for the loading sub-problem, whereas [40] propose a column generation-based

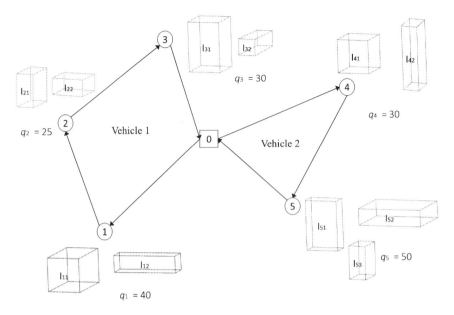

Fig. 3.4 An example of a feasible solution to a 3L-CVRP

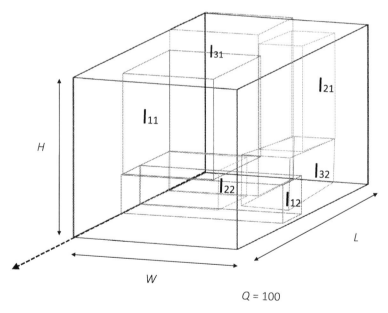

Fig. 3.5 A feasible loading plan for vehicle 1 from Fig. 3.4

heuristic. Hokama et al. [31] extend the exact approach mentioned above for the 2L-CVRP to a basic 3L-CVRP variant.

Extensions of the basic 3L-CVRP variants are studied by the following authors, where the solution approach developed is always heuristic. Significant attention has been devoted to extensions of the $3|SL|NL$ basic variant where both collection and distribution of items may occur in the same route. In more details, [12] study a $3|SL|NL$ variant with backhauls and propose two hybrid heuristics for its solution. Both solution approaches employ a tree search heuristic to solve the loading sub-problem, and they differ in terms of the procedure applied for the routing sub-problem (an Adaptive LNS-ALNS - versus a VNS). Koch et al. [37] study a $3|SL|NL$ variant with mixed backhauls, where the precedence constraint present in classical VRPs with backhauls is relaxed (see [65], Chap. 9) so that linehaul and backhaul customers can be visited in any arbitrary sequence. As in such extension items associated with linehaul and backhaul customers might be simultaneously carried on the same vehicle, the loading sub-problem becomes particularly challenging. For its solution, the authors implement a hybrid heuristic consisting of a reactive TSfor the routing sub-problem and different packing heuristics for the loading sub-problem. Koch et al. [36] address a $3|SL|NL$ variant with simultaneous pickup and delivery, where each customer demands the delivery of a set of items and the pickup of another set of items (see [65], Chap. 6). Additionally, time windows are associated with each customer, as well as the depot. This problem is solved by means of a hybrid algorithm that consists of an ALNS for solving the routing sub-problem, and several construction and local search heuristics for the loading sub-problem. Time windows are also considered in the extensions addressed by [57], along with some elements tackled in the previous three papers. More particularly, [57] study four extensions, namely a 3L-CVRP with backhauls, with mixed backhauls, with simultaneous pickup and delivery, and with divisible deliveries and pickups (i.e., where delivery and pickup at a customer location may be performed in a single visit or in two separate visits, see [65], Chap. 1). The authors develop a solution approach based on invoking, first, a TSto solve the packing sub-problem, and then solving the resulting VRPwith time windows instance by means of an algorithm that combines a multi-start evolutionary strategy with a TS. Männel and Bortfeldt [41] introduce pickup and deliveries into a $3|SL|NL$ variant. The authors show that in this case the standard SL constraint is not sufficient to avoid any reloading, i.e. any temporary or permanent repositioning and rotating of boxes after loading and before unloading, but some additional restrictions are needed. Hence, they present five variants that differ in terms of the reloading efforts involved.

Three of these five variants are solved in [41] by using a heuristic combining an LNS for the routing sub-problem, and a packing heuristic taken from the literature for the loading sub-problem. The remaining two variants are tackled in [42] by using a heuristic that works along the same general lines of the solution procedure developed in [41].

Zhang et al. [70] address a $3|SL|NL$ variant where the objective function aims at minimizing the total fuel consumption, which is assumed to be a function of both the total weight of the vehicle and the distance traveled. This problem is solved by means of an evolutionary local search, which employs an open space heuristic to verify the feasibility of the loading plans. Bortfeldt and Yi [11] introduce the possibility of split deliveries into a $3|SL|NL$ variant, i.e. a customer can be visited in two or more tours (see [65], Chap. 9). The authors consider two splitting policies: (i) a delivery is split only if the demand of a customer cannot be transported by a single vehicle because it exceeds its volume or weight capacity; (ii) a delivery can be split any number of times. For the solution of both cases, the authors develop a hybrid heuristic consisting of a genetic algorithm and several construction heuristics for the packing sub-problem, and a local search algorithm for the routing sub-problem.

3.5   Routing in Combination with Routing: Two-Echelon Routing Problems

This section is organized as follows. We first provide a general description of the class of two-echelon VRPs. Then, we define the Two-Echelon Capacitated Vehicle Routing Problem (henceforth referred to as the *2E-CVRP*), which is a prototypical member of this class of problems. Finally, we provide an overview of the recent trends in the literature on two-echelon VRPs.

3.5.1   Introduction to the Class of Problems

Modern distribution networks are often structured in multiple *echelons*, where an echelon (sometimes called level of the network) represents a pair of stages (e.g., producer-wholesaler, or retailer-customer) between which the transportation of freight occurs. The number of echelons depends on several factors, including the structure of the supply chain and the characteristics of the freight transported.

In the last two decades, a holistic approach to supply chain management has stimulated scholars working in different research areas to study problems characterized by the presence of more than one echelon; that is problems where freight, from its origin, is hauled to some intermediate facilities (e.g., distribution centers or cross-docks) before being delivered to its final destination. Nevertheless, implementing such an approach raises several issues, the most relevant being how to coordinate the flows of freight moving in one echelon with the flow moving in the following one and, more particularly, how to handle the dependency of the second level from the first one. Although in several cases coordinating the flows of freight moving in two adjacent echelons is too complex, in other cases this has proven to be highly beneficial.

We now recall the labeling notation introduced by [38], and later integrated by [19], to classify multi-echelon location routing problems. The notation is as follows: $\lambda/M_1/\ldots/M_{\lambda-1}$, where λ denotes the number of stages, and M_i the type of distribution mode between stages i and $i + 1$. The distribution mode can be $M_i = R$ if between i and $i + 1$ only return trips (i.e., trips to and from a given vertex) are allowed. On the other hand, if trips leaving from i can be routes visiting a sequence of vertices, then $M_i = T$. Finally, if location decisions are considered at stage i, the corresponding distribution mode identifier is marked with an overline (i.e., $\overline{R}$ or $\overline{T}$).

In the present survey, we focus on Two-Echelon VRPs (from now on, *2E-VRPs*), that is, given the above-mentioned labeling notation, on $3/T/T$ problems. In general terms, a 2E-VRP can be described as follows. The distribution network comprises three disjoint sets of vertices, corresponding to the locations of the origins of the freight (hereafter called *depots*), the locations of the intermediate facilities (from now on called *satellites*), and the locations of the destinations of the freight (henceforth called *customers*). Hence, the distribution network consists of two echelons. Direct deliveries from a depot to a customer are usually not allowed, that is, freight must generally transit through a satellite before being delivered to a customer. Freight is transported by two different fleets of vehicles, one fleet per echelon. Vehicles moving through the first echelon are called *primary vehicles*, whereas those moving across the second echelon are named *secondary vehicles*. Routes are possible at both echelons. Note that in the literature several authors call 2E-VRPa problem where routes are possible at only one echelon, and only return trips are allowed at the other echelon. These papers are out of the scope of this survey and therefore are not covered. Despite we concentrate on distribution networks consisting of two echelons, it is worth noticing that our bibliographic search did not return any recent result concerning networks comprising more than two echelons and where routes are possible at each level. Furthermore, the decisions involved in the 2E-VRP sketched above are mainly at a tactical planning level: the routing of freight through each echelon and the allocation of customers to the satellites. Note that strategic planning decisions, e.g., location decisions, are not considered, as we assume that the set of depots and satellites is given. The bibliographic search returned very few papers where location decisions are considered at any stage of the network. The reader interested in the latter area is referred to [56] and [45], and the references cited therein. Finally, truck and trailer routing problems can also be classified as two-echelon routing problems. The latter class is not covered in this survey. The interested reader is referred to the survey by [20], and the more recent articles by [58] and [1].

Real-life applications that can be modeled as two- or multi-echelon distribution systems can be encountered in city logistics, multi-modal transportation, postal and parcel delivery, and grocery distribution (e.g., see [20]). Among those, the most frequently cited application is city logistics. In fact, the paper by [18], who study a two-echelon distribution network in a city logistics context, is usually regarded as the one that inspired the stream of research on 2E-VRPs, despite the latter expression appeared only later in the literature. The following arguments explain the ever-growing interest in 2E-VRPs applied to urban areas. In this context, freight transportation is one of the major causes of congestion, pollution, noise, and chaos. An effective implementation of a two-echelon distribution system may substantially reduce those externalities. In such systems, the freight demanded by a set of customers, located within the city boundaries, is carried by large trucks (called urban vehicles) from the freight origin to the satellites. The latter are located on the outskirt of the city. At the satellites, the freight is unloaded from the large trucks, sorted, consolidated, and finally loaded onto small and eco-friendly vehicles (named city freighters) that are allowed to travel within the city and can deliver the freight to the customers.

In the following, we describe one prototypical problem where routes are possible at two levels of the distribution network, the 2E-CVRP.

3.5.2 The Two-Echelon Capacitated Vehicle Routing Problem

In the 2E-CVRP one uncapacitated depot and a set of capacitated satellites are available at given locations. Each customer demands a given amount of freight. Two limited fleets of capacitated vehicles are available to carry out the deliveries, one fleet per echelon. The primary vehicles are based at the depot, and are allowed to transport freight from the latter to the satellites.

Each satellite can be served by more than one vehicle, i.e., split deliveries on the first echelon are allowed. The secondary vehicles are shared by the satellites. These vehicles are allowed to transport freight from the satellites to the customers. In other words, in the standard 2E-CVRP direct deliveries from the depot to the customers are not allowed. Each satellite is associated with a capacity expressed as the maximum number of secondary vehicles that can start their route from it. Furthermore, each satellite is associated with a handling cost for loading/unloading operations. Finally, each customer must be served by exactly one vehicle.

Formally, the 2E-CVRP can be defined as follows. Let $G = (V, E)$ be an undirected and weighted graph. Set $V = \{0\} \cup S \cup C$ is the set of vertices, where 0 represents the (uncapacitated) depot, $S = \{1, \ldots, |S|\}$ is the set of satellites, and $C = \{|S| + 1, \ldots, |S| + |C|\}$ is the set of customers. Set $E = E^1 \cup E^2$ is the set of edges (i, j), which are partitioned as follows. Set $E^1 = \{(i, j) : i < j; i, j \in \{0\} \cup S\}$ includes those edges connecting the depot with each satellite, as well as those connecting each pair of satellites. Set $E^2 = \{(i, j) : i < j; i, j \in S \cup C; (i, j) \notin S \times S\}$ comprises the edges connecting each satellite with each customer, as well as those connecting each pair of customers. Each edge $(i, j) \in E^1$ (resp. E^2) is associated with a non-negative traveling cost $c_{ij}^1 (c_{ij}^2)$.

A fleet of K^1 homogeneous primary vehicles is available at the depot. Each primary vehicle has a maximum capacity Q^1, starts its route from depot 0, serves one or more satellites in S, and then returns to the depot (i.e., each primary vehicle traverses only edges in set E^1). A fleet of K^2 homogeneous secondary vehicles is shared by the satellites. Each secondary vehicle has a maximum capacity Q^2 (usually, $Q^2 < Q^1$), starts its route from a given satellite $s \in S$, visits one or more customers in C, and then returns to s (i.e., each secondary vehicle traverses only edges in set E^2). From each satellite $s \in S$ at most K_s^2 secondary vehicles can be routed. Furthermore, a handling cost h_s is paid for each unit of freight shipped through satellite $s \in S$. Note that, if cost-effective, some satellites may be left unused. Finally, each customer $j \in C$ demands a known and deterministic amount q_j of freight. The 2E-CVRP calls for the determination of a minimum-cost set of routes at both echelons such that the demand of all customers is satisfied and that the capacity restrictions of the vehicles and satellites are not violated. Notice that in the 2E-CVRP the cost of a solution is given by two components: on one hand, the cost of routing primary and secondary vehicles and, on the other hand, the handling cost at the satellites. Regarding the routes at the first echelon, any feasible solution must satisfy the following conditions:

(F-RC1)   each route starts and ends at the depot, and visits one or more satellites;
(F-RC2)   each satellite is visited by one or more primary vehicles;
(F-RC3)   no more than K^1 primary vehicles are used;
(F-RC4)   for each primary vehicle, the total amount of freight assigned does not exceed its maximum capacity Q^1.

On the other hand, regarding the routes at the second echelon any feasible solution must satisfy:

(S-RC1)   each route starts and ends at a given satellite, and visits one or more customers;
(S-RC2)   each customer must be served by exactly one secondary vehicle;
(S-RC3)   no more than K^2 secondary vehicles are used;
(S-RC4)   for each satellite $s \in S$, no more than K_s^2 secondary vehicles are used;
(S-RC5)   for each secondary vehicle, the total amount of freight assigned does not exceed its maximum capacity Q^2.

Figure 3.6 depicts an example of a feasible solution to a standard 2E-CVRP.

Guastaroba et al. [30] propose to classify freight transportation planning problems with intermediate facilities according to the type of network (pure or hybrid), the number of intermediate facilities (single facility or

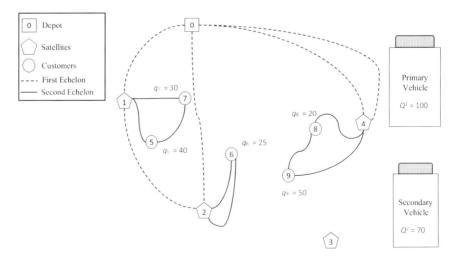

Fig. 3.6   An example of a feasible solution to a standard 2E-CVRP

multi-facility), the origin-destination structure (one-to-one, one-to-many or many-to-many), and the number of commodities (single commodity or multi-commodity). According to such classification, the above 2E-CVRP is a multi-facility problem defined on a pure network, with a one-to-many origin-destination structure, and a single commodity.

3.5.3 Recent Trends in the Literature on 2E-VRPs

The origin of the research on 2E-VRPs is usually associated with the paper by [18], although the first formal definition of the class of 2E-VRPs and of the 2E-CVRP, as described above, can be found in [52]. Surveys on routing problems that cover 2E-VRPs, as well as related problems, are provided in [20] and [30]. Hence, in the following, we concentrate on the recent trends in the literature on 2E-VRPs, and refer the reader to the above-mentioned surveys for the earlier literature.

Most of the recent research efforts are concentrated on the study of variants of the standard 2E-CVRP defined above. The latter basic problem is tackled in [13] by means of a hybrid heuristic that combines local and large neighborhood search with destroy-and-repair principles, and in [44] with a Branch-Cut-and-Price exact algorithm.

We have already highlighted the importance in 2E-VRPs of capturing the dependence of the second level from the first one. The standard 2E-VRP captures a space dependency, that is freight that a secondary vehicle delivers to its customers must be provided to the associated satellite by a primary vehicle. Introducing in such a simple scheme the time dimension makes the problem more realistic but requires capturing the dependency in time between the two levels. Grangier et al. [29] study a 2E-CVRP with time windows constraints associated with customers. As satellites are assumed to have no storage capacity, the arrival of primary and secondary vehicles is explicitly considered by introducing a set of synchronization constraints. Secondary vehicles are allowed to perform multiple trips, which may start at different satellites. The authors present an ALNS to solve this problem. Nolz et al. [49] address a 2E-CVRP with one single satellite, that has a limited capacity, and time windows constraints for the customers. Furthermore, primary vehicles can serve directly a customer, and both primary and secondary vehicles can perform multiple trips. Also in this problem, the synchronization in time between vehicles belonging to the two echelons plays a crucial role. The authors design a three-phase heuristic that combines a genetic algorithm, local search, and integer programming for the solution of this problem. Scheduling synchronized meetings at satellites between vehicles of the two echelons is fundamental also in the 2E-CVRP investigated in [3]. In this problem, customers are grouped into three subsets: a set of customers visited by primary vehicles, a set visited by secondary vehicles, and a set of so-called "grey zone" customers that must be assigned to primary or secondary vehicles. The authors cast this problem as a multi-objective optimization program, by incorporating an economic, an environmental, and a social objective. For its solution, an LNS is integrated into a multi-objective method to find solutions along the Pareto front. Finally, time windows constraints associated with customers are also considered in [21] and [22]. In the former paper, the authors study a 2E-CVRP having a many-to-many origin-destination structure (i.e., there are multiple depots), and where the usage of each vehicle incurs the payment of a fixed cost. The objective function considered aims at minimizing the sum of the total transportation costs and the total fixed cost paid for using vehicles. The authors propose Branch-and-Price algorithms for solving this problem. Dellaert et al. [22] study a 2E-CVRP with time windows, and customer-specific origin-destination, non-substitutable demands. As in [21], the origin-destination structure is many-to-many, and a fixed cost is paid for using a vehicle. The problem is solved by extending the Branch-and-Price approach introduced in [21].

Besides [21] and [22], multi-depot variants are considered also in [61] and [71]. In addition, in the 2E-CVRP addressed by [61] customers can be served by primary vehicles. Based on the method proposed by [6], the authors derive a lower bound, which is then used to obtain an upper bound to the problem at hand. Motivated by applications arising in performing last mile deliveries, [71] tackle a 2E-CVRP where customers can be selected among different delivery options (e.g., direct delivery to home, or pickup at a given location, such as parcel lockers). For the solution of this problem, the authors propose a hybrid multi-population genetic algorithm.

The usage of electric vehicles or, more generally, the consideration of environmental issues is studied in the following papers. Breunig et al. [14] consider a 2E-CVRP where secondary vehicles are electric, so that detours for battery recharging may be necessary because of the limited driving range. The cost of a solution, to be minimized, includes a fixed cost for each vehicle used, and driving costs proportional to the distance traveled. For its solution, the authors extend the approaches developed in [13] and [6] for the standard 2E-CVRP, resulting in a LNS heuristic and an exact algorithm, respectively. In the problem addressed by [35] electric vehicles are present at both levels, which should visit a swapping station to swap their batteries before their battery power runs out. The vehicles are homogeneous within each echelon, in terms of capacity, battery driving ranges, power consumption rate, and battery swapping cost. The objective function aims at minimizing the sum of travel, battery swapping, and handling costs at satellites. For its solution, the authors propose a hybrid algorithm that combines column generation principles with an ALNS algorithm. Environmental considerations connected to the vehicle fuel consumptions and the related emissions characterize the 2E-CVRP tackled by [63]. Furthermore, to account for traffic congestion, in this problem travel times are time-dependent. Soysal et al. [63] cast this problem as a mixed integer linear program, which is solved by means of CPLEX on a small real-world instance inspired by the activities carried out by a supermarket chain operating in the Netherlands. Based on the problem introduced in [63, 66] develop a matheuristic combining VNS and integer programming, where integer programming is employed as a post-optimization technique or to produce minimum-cost routes for primary vehicles.

Liu et al. [39] address a 2E-CVRP where the set of customers is divided upfront in a set of disjoint groups, and a set of additional constraints (called grouping constraints) are added to the problem to ensure that customers from the same group are served by vehicles based at the same satellite. A B&C is developed for the solution of this problem. Similar to [71], in the 2E-CVRP studied by [26] customers can choose among different delivery options (called covering locations) where they can pick up goods themselves. In this variant, there is only one depot available and covering locations can be visited solely by primary vehicles. This problem is solved by means of an ALNS algorithm. Mühlbauer and Fontaine [47] tackle a 2E-CVRP where vans are used as primary vehicles, whereas cargo-bicycles are used as secondary vehicles to perform the final deliveries. As for cargo-bicycles travel distances and times can be significantly asymmetric, the problem is defined on a directed graph. Furthermore, to simplify the cargo transfer at satellites, swap containers are used. These containers are loaded beforehand at the depot according to the second-level routes so that, at a satellite, only the containers are moved from vans to cargo-bicycles. The authors present a parallelized LNS for the solution of this problem. Qiu et al. [55] investigate a 2E-CVRP where production decisions are further integrated into the optimization problem. Because of the production sub-problem, the nature of this variant is multi-period and aims at determining for each day whether and how much to produce; the quantity to deliver from the depot to the satellites, as well as from every satellite to each customer; and the routes of the primary and secondary vehicles at the minimum total cost over the whole planning horizon. For the solution of this problem, the authors present a B&Calgorithm coupled with a matheuristic, where the latter is used to provide feasible initial solutions.

3.6   Conclusions

In this chapter, the most relevant classes of integrated problems with a routing component have been surveyed. Pointers to recent related surveys have been provided and the recent trends in the literature have been discussed.

The research on integrated routing problems is attracting, and we expect it will continue to attract, considerable research efforts, motivated by the clear benefits that integration can bring over more traditional approaches tackling each sub-problem individually. New modeling and algorithmic advancements, together with contributions from other fields such as statistics and computer science, will play an important role in shaping the impact of this topic.

The study of integrated problems contributes to bridge the gap between academic research and real-life applications. Many research directions remain open, from not yet studied integrated routing problems to exact and heuristic methods for the problems that have been already introduced in the literature. Moreover, the majority of papers does not consider dynamic and stochastic aspects that play a relevant role in real-life problems. Considering such characteristics and assessing the benefit of such a consideration is one of the most promising and enticing research directions.

References

1. Accorsi, L. and Vigo, D. A hybrid metaheuristic for single truck and trailer routing problems. *Transportation Science*, 54(5): 1351–1371, 2020.
2. Alinaghian, M., Zamanlou, K., and Sabbagh, M. S. A bi-objective mathematical model for two-dimensional loading time-dependent vehicle routing problem. *Journal of the Operational Research Society*, 68 (11):1422–1441, 2017.
3. Anderluh, A., Nolz, P. C., Hemmelmayr, V. C., and Crainic, T. G. Multi-objective optimization of a two-echelon vehicle routing problem with vehicle synchronization and 'grey zone' customers arising in urban logistics. *European Journal of Operational Research*, 289 (3):940–958, 2021.
4. Archetti, C. and Speranza, M. G. The inventory routing problem: the value of integration. *International Transactions in Operational Research*, 23(3): 393–407, 2016.

5. Archetti, C., Bertazzi, L., Laporte, G., and Speranza, M. G. A branch-and-cut algorithm for a vendor-managed inventory-routing problem. *Transportation Science*, 41 (3): 382–391, 2007.

6. Baldacci, R., Mingozzi, A., Roberti, R., and Wolfler Calvo, R. An exact algorithm for the two-echelon capacitated vehicle routing problem. *Operations Research*, 61 (2): 298–314, 2013.

7. Bektaş, T., Laporte, G., and Vigo, D. Integrated vehicle routing problems. *Computers & Operations Research*, 55: 126, 2015. ISSN 0305-0548.

8. Bell, W. J., Dalberto, L. M., Fisher, M. L., Greenfield, A. J., Jaikumar, R., Kedia, P., Mack, R. G., and Prutzman, P. J. Improving the distribution of industrial gases with an on-line computerized routing and scheduling optimizer. *Interfaces*, 13 (6): 4–23, 1983.

9. Bertazzi, L. and Speranza, M. Inventory routing problems: an introduction. *EURO Journal on Transportation and Logistics*, 1: 307–326, 2012.

10. Bertazzi, L. and Speranza, M. Inventory routing problems with multiple customers. *EURO Journal on Transportation and Logistics*, 2: 255–275, 2013.

11. Bortfeldt, A. and Yi, J. The split delivery vehicle routing problem with three-dimensional loading constraints. *European Journal of Operational Research*, 282 (2): 545–558, 2020.

12. Bortfeldt, A., Hahn, T., Männel, D., and Mönch, L. Hybrid algorithms for the vehicle routing problem with clustered backhauls and 3D loading constraints. *European Journal of Operational Research*, 243 (1): 82–96, 2015.

13. Breunig, U., Schmid, V., Hartl, R. F., and Vidal, T. A large neighbourhood based heuristic for two-echelon routing problems. *Computers & Operations Research*, 76: 208–225, 2016.

14. Breunig, U., Baldacci, R., Hartl, R. F., and Vidal, T. The electric two-echelon vehicle routing problem. *Computers & Operations Research*, 103: 198–210, 2019.

15. Coelho, L., Cordeau, J.-F., and Laporte, G. Thirty years of inventory routing. *Transportation Science*, 48: 1–19, 2013.

16. Côté, J.-F., Guastaroba, G., and Speranza, M. G. The value of integrating loading and routing. *European Journal of Operational Research*, 257 (1): 89–105, 2017.

17. Côté, J.-F., Gendreau, M., and Potvin, J.-Y. The vehicle routing problem with stochastic two-dimensional items. *Transportation Science*, 54 (2): 453–469, 2020.

18. Crainic, T. G., Ricciardi, N., and Storchi, G. Models for evaluating and planning city logistics systems. *Transportation Science*, 43 (4): 432–454, 2009.

19. Crainic, T. G., Sforza, A., and Sterle, C. Location-routing models for two-echelon freight distribution system design. Technical Report CIRRELT-2011-40, CIRRELT, 2011.

20. Cuda, R., Guastaroba, G., and Speranza, M. G. A survey on two-echelon routing problems. *Computers & Operations Research*, 55: 185–199, 2015.

21. Dellaert, N., Saridarq, F. D., Van Woensel, T., and Crainic, T. G. Branch-and-price-based algorithms for the two-echelon vehicle routing problem with time windows. *Transportation Science*, 53 (2): 463–479, 2019.

22. Dellaert, N., Van Woensel, T., Crainic, T. G., and Saridarq, F. D. A multi-commodity two-echelon capacitated vehicle routing problem with time windows: Model formulations and solution approach. *Computers & Operations Research*, 127: 105154, 2021.

23. Dominguez, O., Guimarans, D., Juan, A. A., and de la Nuez, I. A biased-randomised large neighbourhood search for the two-dimensional vehicle routing problem with backhauls. *European Journal of Operational Research*, 255 (2): 442–462, 2016a.

24. Dominguez, O., Juan, A. A., Barrios, B., Faulin, J., and Agustin, A. Using biased randomization for solving the two-dimensional loading vehicle routing problem with heterogeneous fleet. *Annals of Operations Research*, 236 (2): 383–404, 2016b.

25. Drexl, M. and Schneider, M. A survey of variants and extensions of the location-routing problem. *European Journal of Operational Research*, 241 (2): 283–308, 2015.

26. Enthoven, D. L., Jargalsaikhan, B., Roodbergen, K. J., uit het Broek, M. A., and Schrotenboer, A. H. The two-echelon vehicle routing problem with covering options: City logistics with cargo bikes and parcel lockers. *Computers & Operations Research*, 118: 104919, 2020.

27. Fuellerer, G., Doerner, K. F., Hartl, R. F., and Iori, M. Ant colony optimization for the two-dimensional loading vehicle routing problem. *Computers & Operations Research*, 36 (3): 655–673, 2009.

28. Gendreau, M., Iori, M., Laporte, G., and Martello, S. A tabu search algorithm for a routing and container loading problem. *Transportation Science*, 40 (3): 342–350, 2006.

29. Grangier, P., Gendreau, M., Lehuédé, F., and Rousseau, L.-M. An adaptive large neighborhood search for the two-echelon multiple-trip vehicle routing problem with satellite synchronization. *European Journal of Operational Research*, 254 (1): 80–91, 2016.

30. Guastaroba, G., Speranza, M. G., and Vigo, D. Intermediate facilities in freight transportation planning: A survey. *Transportation Science*, 50 (3): 763–789, 2016.

31. Hokama, P., Miyazawa, F. K., and Xavier, E. C. A branch-and-cut approach for the vehicle routing problem with loading constraints. *Expert Systems with Applications*, 47: 1–13, 2016.

32. Iori, M. and Martello, S. Routing problems with loading constraints. *Top*, 18 (1): 4–27, 2010.

33. Iori, M. and Martello, S. An annotated bibliography of combined routing and loading problems. *Yugoslav Journal of Operations Research*, 23 (3): 311–326, 2013.

34. Iori, M., Salazar-González, J.-J., and Vigo, D. An exact approach for the vehicle routing problem with two-dimensional loading constraints. *Transportation Science*, 41 (2): 253–264, 2007.

35. Jie, W., Yang, J., Zhang, M., and Huang, Y. The two-echelon capacitated electric vehicle routing problem with battery swapping stations: Formulation and efficient methodology. *European Journal of Operational Research*, 272 (3): 879–904, 2019.

36. Koch, H., Bortfeldt, A., and Wäscher, G. A hybrid algorithm for the vehicle routing problem with backhauls, time windows and three-dimensional loading constraints. *OR Spectrum*, 40 (4): 1029–1075, 2018.

37. Koch, H., Schlögell, M., and Bortfeldt, A. A hybrid algorithm for the vehicle routing problem with three-dimensional loading constraints and mixed backhauls. *Journal of Scheduling*, 23 (1): 71–93, 2020.

38. Laporte, G. Location-routing problems. In Golden, B. L. and Assad, A. A., editors, *Vehicle Routing: Methods and Studies*. North-Holland, 1988.

39. Liu, T., Luo, Z., Qin, H., and Lim, A. A branch-and-cut algorithm for the two-echelon capacitated vehicle routing problem with grouping constraints. *European Journal of Operational Research*, 266 (2): 487–497, 2018.

40. Mahvash, B., Awasthi, A., and Chauhan, S. A column generation based heuristic for the capacitated vehicle routing problem with three-dimensional loading constraints. *International Journal of Production Research*, 55 (6): 1730–1747, 2017.

41. Männel, D. and Bortfeldt, A. A hybrid algorithm for the vehicle routing problem with pickup and delivery and three-dimensional loading constraints. *European Journal of Operational Research*, 254 (3): 840–858, 2016.

42. Männel, D. and Bortfeldt, A. Solving the pickup and delivery problem with three-dimensional loading constraints and reloading ban. *European Journal of Operational Research*, 264 (1): 119–137, 2018.

43. Mara, S. T. W., Kuo, R., and Asih, A. M. S. Location-routing problem: a classification of recent research. *International Transactions in Operational Research*, 2021.

44. Marques, G., Sadykov, R., Deschamps, J.-C., and Dupas, R. An improved branch-cut-and-price algorithm for the two-echelon capacitated vehicle routing problem. *Computers & Operations Research*, 114: 104833, 2020.

45. Mirhedayatian, S. M., Crainic, T. G., Guajardo, M., and Wallace, S. W. A two-echelon location-routing problem with synchronisation. *Journal of the Operational Research Society*, 72 (1): 145–160, 2021.

46. Mor, A. and Speranza, M. G. Vehicle routing problems over time: A survey. *4OR*, pages 1–21, 2020.

47. Mühlbauer, F. and Fontaine, P. A parallelised large neighbourhood search heuristic for the asymmetric two-echelon vehicle routing problem with swap containers for cargo-bicycles. *European Journal of Operational Research*, 289 (2): 742–757, 2021.

48. Nagy, G. and Salhi, S. Location-routing: Issues, models and methods. *European Journal of Operational Research*, 177 (2): 649–672, 2007.

49. Nolz, P. C., Absi, N., Cattaruzza, D., and Feillet, D. Two-echelon distribution with a single capacitated city hub. *EURO Journal on Transportation and Logistics*, 9 (3): 100015, 2020.

50. Ostermeier, M., Martins, S., Amorim, P., and Hübner, A. Loading constraints for a multi-compartment vehicle routing problem. *OR Spectrum*, 40 (4): 997–1027, 2018.

51. Owen, S. H. and Daskin, M. S. Strategic facility location: A review. *European Journal of Operational research*, 111 (3): 423–447, 1998.

52. Perboli, G., Tadei, R., and Vigo, D. The two-echelon capacitated vehicle routing problem: Models and math-based heuristics. *Transportation Science*, 45 (3): 364–380, 2011.

53. Pollaris, H., Braekers, K., Caris, A., Janssens, G. K., and Limbourg, S. Vehicle routing problems with loading constraints: State-of-the-art and future directions. *OR Spectrum*, 37 (2): 297–330, 2015.

54. Prodhon, C. and Prins, C. A survey of recent research on location-routing problems. *European Journal of Operational Research*, 238 (1): 1–17, 2014.

55. Qiu, Y., Zhou, D., Du, Y., Liu, J., Pardalos, P. M., and Qiao, J. The two-echelon production routing problem with cross-docking satellites. *Transportation Research Part E: Logistics and Transportation Review*, 147: 102210, 2021.

56. Rahmani, Y., Ramdane Cherif-Khettaf, W., and Oulamara, A. The two-echelon multi-products location-routing problem with pickup and delivery: Formulation and heuristic approaches. *International Journal of Production Research*, 54 (4): 999–1019, 2016.

57. Reil, S., Bortfeldt, A., and Mönch, L. Heuristics for vehicle routing problems with backhauls, time windows, and 3d loading constraints. *European Journal of Operational Research*, 266 (3): 877–894, 2018.

58. Rothenbächer, A.-K., Drexl, M., and Irnich, S. Branch-and-price-and-cut for the truck-and-trailer routing problem with time windows. *Transportation Science*, 52 (5): 1174–1190, 2018.

59. Ruan, Q., Zhang, Z., Miao, L., and Shen, H. A hybrid approach for the vehicle routing problem with three-dimensional loading constraints. *Computers & Operations Research*, 40 (6): 1579–1589, 2013.

60. Schneider, M. and Drexl, M. A survey of the standard location-routing problem. *Annals of Operations Research*, 259 (1-2): 389–414, 2017.

61. Song, L., Gu, H., and Huang, H. A lower bound for the adaptive two-echelon capacitated vehicle routing problem. *Journal of Combinatorial Optimization*, 33 (4): 1145–1167, 2017.

62. Song, X., Jones, D., Asgari, N., and Pigden, T. Multi-objective vehicle routing and loading with time window constraints: A real-life application. *Annals of Operations Research*, 291: 99–825, 2020.

63. Soysal, M., Bloemhof-Ruwaard, J. M., and Bektaş, T. The time-dependent two-echelon capacitated vehicle routing problem with environmental considerations. *International Journal of Production Economics*, 164: 366–378, 2015.

64. Tao, Y. and Wang, F. An effective tabu search approach with improved loading algorithms for the 3l-cvrp. *Computers & Operations Research*, 55: 127–140, 2015.

65. Toth, P. and Vigo, D. *Vehicle Routing: Problems, Methods, and Applications, Second Edition, MOS-SIAM Series on Optimization 18*. SIAM, Philadelphia, 2014.

66. Wang, K., Shao, Y., and Zhou, W. Matheuristic for a two-echelon capacitated vehicle routing problem with environmental considerations in city logistics service. *Transportation Research Part D: Transport and Environment*, 57: 262–276, 2017.

67. Wei, L., Zhang, Z., Zhang, D., and Lim, A. A variable neighborhood search for the capacitated vehicle routing problem with two-dimensional loading constraints. *European Journal of Operational Research*, 243 (3): 798–814, 2015.

68. Wei, L., Zhang, Z., Zhang, D., and Leung, S. C. A simulated annealing algorithm for the capacitated vehicle routing problem with two-dimensional loading constraints. *European Journal of Operational Research*, 265 (3): 843–859, 2018.

69. Zachariadis, E. E., Tarantilis, C. D., and Kiranoudis, C. T. The vehicle routing problem with simultaneous pick-ups and deliveries and two-dimensional loading constraints. *European Journal of Operational Research*, 251 (2): 369–386, 2016.

70. Zhang, Z., Wei, L., and Lim, A. An evolutionary local search for the capacitated vehicle routing problem minimizing fuel consumption under three-dimensional loading constraints. *Transportation Research Part B: Methodological*, 82: 20–35, 2015.

71. Zhou, L., Baldacci, R., Vigo, D., and Wang, X. A multi-depot two-echelon vehicle routing problem with delivery options arising in the last mile distribution. *European Journal of Operational Research*, 265 (2): 765–778, 2018.

4

The Knapsack Problem and Its Variants: Formulations and Solution Methods

Christophe Wilbaut⬛, Saïd Hanafi, Igor Machado Coelho, and Abilio Lucena

4.1 Introduction

The knapsack problem asks for the selection of items from a set N with n elements, every item $j \in N$ with a non-negative integer *weight* w_j associated with it. A subset of items $S \subseteq N$ is called *feasible* when $\sum_{j \in S} w_j \leq c$

C. Wilbaut (✉) · S. Hanafi
LAMIH, CNRS, UMR 8201, University Polytechnique Hauts-de-France, Valenciennes, France
e-mail: christophe.wilbaut@uphf.fr

S. Hanafi
e-mail: said.hanafi@uphf.fr

INSA Hauts-de-France, Valenciennes, France

I. M. Coelho
Programa de Pós-Graduação em Ciências Computacionais, Universidade do Estado do Rio de Janeiro, Rio de Janeiro, Brazil
e-mail: igor.machado@ime.uerj.br; imcoelho@ic.uff.br

Instituto de Computação, Universidade Federal Fluminense, Niterói, Brazil

A. Lucena
Programa de Engenharia de Sistemas e Computação, Universidade Federal do Rio de Janeiro, Rio de Janeiro, Brazil
e-mail: abiliolucena@cos.ufrj.br

© The Author(s), under exclusive license to Springer Nature Switzerland AG 2022

S. Salhi and J. Boylan (eds.), *The Palgrave Handbook of Operations Research*,
https://doi.org/10.1007/978-3-030-96935-6_4

applies, where c is the *capacity* of a knapsack for carrying the items. Additionally, a profit is incurred by choosing a feasible subset of items and is measured through a properly defined function of N. The aim is to select a feasible $S \subseteq N$ which maximizes profit. The problem appears in distinct versions, each of them characterized by a different type of objective function. Variants to these versions, in turn, typically impose further restrictions on item selection. The linear and the quadratic objective function versions of the problem are those that attract the most interest, with the latter version lagging well behind the former.

The linear 0-1 Knapsack Problem (KP) maximizes a linear objective function. It associates a non-negative integer profit p_j with the selection of every $j \in N$ and relies on binary variables, $x \in \{0, 1\}^n$, for its standard formulation. Accordingly, $x_j = 1$ holds if j is selected and $x_j = 0$ applies otherwise. The Quadratic Knapsack Problem (QKP) is similarly formulated but its objective function involves cross profits $q_{ij} \in \mathbb{Z}$, $i, j \in N$, $i \leq j$, to account for eventual fringe benefits attained by simultaneously selecting items i and j (for simplicity, we assume that $q_{ii} = p_i$ holds for every $i \in N$). Additional versions of the problem will not be treated here since they only attract very marginal interest. The standard formulation of KP is given by:

$$\max \quad \sum_{j=1}^{n} p_j x_j \tag{4.1}$$

$$\text{subject to:} \quad \sum_{j=1}^{n} w_j x_j \leq c \tag{4.2}$$

$$x_j \in \{0, 1\} \qquad\qquad j \in N = \{1, \ldots, n\} \tag{4.3}$$

Furthermore, to avoid trivial solutions, conditions

$$\max\{w_j : j \in N\} < c < \sum_{j=1}^{n} w_j \tag{4.4}$$

are generally assumed. A formulation for QKP is obtained by noting that $x_i = x_i x_i$ holds for every $i \in N$ and replacing objective function (4.1) by

$$\max \sum_{i=1}^{n-1} \sum_{j=i}^{n} q_{ij} x_i x_j. \tag{4.5}$$

Given that the overwhelming majority of Knapsack Problem references are associated with KP, we will assume here that QKP and all its variants simply correspond to KP variants.

Historically, the first mention of KP dates back to 1896 [145], with references to the subject appearing on early studies in [41] (in folklore, the problem was probably studied under different names hundreds of years before). In the 1950s, the first dynamic programming (DP) approach for solving KP was introduced by Bellman in [13], and in the 1960s the branch-and-bound (B&B) paradigm brought additional solution alternatives to the problem. From that point on, KP has been intensively investigated, starting especially with the works in [73, 129] or [150]. Due to the number of knapsack variants and the associated contributions some books were dedicated to knapsack problems, such as [111, 143].

KP has a wide range of practical applications, such as: cargo loading, cutting stock, capital budgeting or project selection (see, e.g., [129, 150]). The problem can be solved by DP, which means it is not *strongly* $\mathcal{N}\mathcal{P}$-Hard [70], only being limited by the integral magnitude of capacity c (the complexity of such a DP algorithm is $O(n \cdot c)$). A first survey on solution approaches for KP appears in [166].

A few variants of KP directly follow from the standard formulation of the problem. Among these we consider first the fractional or the continuous knapsack problem, FKP, where $(0, 1)$ fractions of the items are also allowed to be selected. A formulation for FKP is obtained by simply replacing (4.3) in the standard formulation of KP by

$$x_j \in [0, 1] \quad \forall j \in N. \tag{4.6}$$

This allows greedy techniques to work, as suggested by Dantzig in [40]. Indeed it is well-known that FKP can be solved in $O(n \log n)$ time, by greedily selecting the items in *descending order* of the ratios $\frac{p_j}{w_j}$, $j \in N$.

It is also possible to allow an integral selection of multiple items, leading to the unbounded knapsack problem. From the standard KP formulation we just need to replace (4.3) by

$$x_j \in \mathbb{Z}_{\geq 0} \quad \forall j \in N, \tag{4.7}$$

in order to formulate the problem.

Finally, the mixed (linear) knapsack problem consists in a collection composed by $n_{\mathcal{D}}$ discrete and $n_{\mathcal{F}}$ fractional items (see, e.g., when $n_{\mathcal{F}} = 1$ [136]). This problem has several practical applications (see, e.g., [200]) and can be modeled in a generalized format, by allowing distinct lower and upper bounds for each item, namely l_j and u_j:

$$\max \quad \sum_{j=1}^{n_{\mathcal{D}}+n_{\mathcal{F}}} p_j x_j \tag{4.8}$$

$$\text{s.t. :} \quad \sum_{j=1}^{n_{\mathcal{D}}+n_{\mathcal{F}}} w_j x_j \le c \tag{4.9}$$

$$l_j \le x_j \le u_j \qquad \forall j \in \{1, \ldots, n_{\mathcal{D}} + n_{\mathcal{F}}\} \tag{4.10}$$

$$x_j \text{ integer} \qquad \forall j \in \{1, \ldots, n_{\mathcal{D}}\} \tag{4.11}$$

$$x_j \in \mathbb{R} \qquad \forall j \in \{n_{\mathcal{D}} + 1, \ldots, n_{\mathcal{D}} + n_{\mathcal{F}}\} \tag{4.12}$$

In practice, instances of the KP variants we have just described involving hundreds of thousands of items are routinely solved by most of mixed-integer programming solvers. Among others, these solvers benefit from preprocessing techniques and the use of facet defining inequalities for the knapsack polytope, i.e., the convex hull of the feasible (integral) solutions to KP (see, e.g., [128] for details).

For the remaining of this chapter we consider several additional KP variants, classical or new. All of them can be formulated by changing the objective function or adding constraints to the standard KP formulation. In practice, these variants are generally much harder to solve than KP and while selecting them we focused on those associated with new interesting applications. First, in Sect. 4.2, we consider variants where a single knapsack constraint must be satisfied. Next, in Sect. 4.3, we discuss additional variants involving two or more knapsack constraints. We conclude the chapter in Sect. 4.4 by considering some future research directions on the topic.

4.2   Variants with a Single Knapsack Constraint

Several extensions of KP where only one knapsack constraint must be enforced can be identified in the literature. In this section we consider some of these variants where additional constraints conduct to some challenging problems.

4.2.1 The Multiple-Choice Knapsack Problem

The Multiple-Choice Knapsack Problem (MCKP) is a well-known variant of the KP in which the set of items is partitioned into classes (or groups). In this case the binary choice of taking an item or not in the knapsack is replaced by the selection of exactly one item out of each class of items. Let us denote by n^g the number of disjoint groups $N_1, \ldots, N_{n^g}$ of items and by n_k the number of items in group N_k. Then, $N = \bigcup_{k=1}^{n^g} N_k$ and the total number of items is $n = \sum_{k=1}^{n^g} n_k$. As for KP, every item $j \in N_k$ is associated with a profit p_{kj} and a weight w_{kj} and MCKP aims at choosing exactly one item from each class such that the profit sum is maximized and the knapsack capacity c is respected. By defining variable $x_{kj} = 1$ if and only item j in class N_k is chosen, MCKP can be mathematically formulated as follows:

$$\max \quad \sum_{k=1}^{n^g} \sum_{j \in N_k} p_{kj} x_{kj} \tag{4.13}$$

$$\text{s.t.:} \quad \sum_{k=1}^{n^g} \sum_{j \in N_k} w_{kj} x_{kj} \leq c \tag{4.14}$$

$$\sum_{j \in N_k} x_{kj} = 1 \qquad\qquad k = 1, \ldots, n^g \tag{4.15}$$

$$x_{kj} \in \{0, 1\}, \qquad\qquad k = 1, \ldots, n^g, j \in N_k \tag{4.16}$$

Like KP it is always assumed that all coefficients p_{kj}, w_{kj} and c are non-negative integers. It is interesting to observe that some additional variants of KP may be derived directly from MCKP. For instance when $p_{kj} = w_{kj}$ for all $k = 1, \ldots, n^g$ and for all $j \in N_k$ MCKP is called the multiple-choice subset-sum problem. In addition, the Multidimensional Multiple-Choice Knapsack Problem (MMCKP) can also be obtained by allowing into MCKP one or more properly defined additional knapsacks. Finally, the discounted 0-1 knapsack problem (see Sect. 4.2.2) can be viewed as a particular case of MCKP.

Several very efficient approaches were proposed to solve MCKP as those described in [51, 155, 173]. In particular, Pisinger developed in [155] an efficient dynamic programming-based algorithm using a list representation and a core problem. Classes are consecutively added to the core and reduction rules are also used to fix some of the variables. Kellerer et al. provided in their book [, Chap. 11] experiments to compare the performance of the approaches described in the last three articles cited above. The results demonstrated the efficiency of all the three approaches for all types of instances, except for strongly correlated ones for which only Pisinger's approach was able to provide results in the fixed time limit of one hour to solve 100 instances. However, these works showed that MCKP can be solved in very reasonable time for large instances.111

The situation is quite different for the multidimensional case. Some of the current best approaches dealing with MMCKP are based on hybrid approaches combining mathematical programming and heuristic strategies like in [32, 33] where authors considered the use of column generation techniques, whereas authors in [38] extended an iterative relaxation-based procedure proposed in [83]. The proposed method was more general and introduced what authors called the semi-continuous relaxation, where variables are constrained to take values close to zero or one. Mansi et al. proposed some variants of an hybrid strategy consisting of new cuts and a reformulation procedure used at each iteration to improve the iterative relaxation-based heuristic framework in [132]. Chen et Hao developed in [31] a "*reduce and solve*" heuristic combining problem reduction techniques (based on group-fixing and variable-fixing rules) with an optimal solution of the resulting integer linear problem. Another interesting work is presented in [183] where authors introduced a reformulation of MMCKP as a set partitioning problem allowing to reduce the decision variable dimension regarding the classical model to one dimension, even if the total number of variables and constraints remain the same. Experiments were conducted to compare this new model with the classical one when using CPLEX and GUROBI solvers. The results showed that the new model improved on average the objective function values and the required computational time to converge to the best solutions. In addition the use of this new formulation was competitive when compared to some state-of-the-art approaches for solving MMCKP. We also noted the work in [69] where authors proposed an iterative pseudo-gap enumeration approach which is a two-step procedure. In the first step, a family of pseudo-cuts is derived from the reduced cost constraints with regarding what authors called a "*pseudo-gap*". In the second step the original problem enriched by these pseudo cuts is solved with CPLEX. The pseudo-gap is used as a hypothesized gap between the upper bound and the lower bound of the original problem and authors proposed a strategy to enumerate it. When the pseudo-gap become valid the proposed iterative approach converges to an optimal solution. This approach obtained very good results compared with other state-of-the art methods for solving MMCKP. Mansini and Zanotti proposed very recently in [135] a new and very effective core-based exact approach. It solves subproblems of increasing size by means of a recursive variable-fixing process and stops when an optimality condition is satisfied. The proposed method obtained 10 new optimal solutions on open benchmark instances in the literature and improved several other best-known solutions.

MCKP and MMCKP have a wide range of classical applications including resources allocation [71, 173], capital budgeting [157], telecommunication networks [93], the management of resources in multimedia systems [113], the VLSI design [146] or the reliability of complex systems [177]. They also appear as a subproblem in several other diverse applications: in nurse scheduling [78], in generalized assignment problems [10] or in the context of warehouse optimization [11]. Fisher showed that MCKP appears when using Lagrangian relaxation of several integer programming problems [62], whereas Kellerer [110] proposed an approximation algorithm for a scheduling problem based on a relaxation formulated as MCKP.

Several additional applications dealing with MCKP or MMCKP can be found in the literature as in [179] where authors introduced what they called the "*selective* MCKP" in the context of QoS-aware service evaluation and selection. The formulation corresponds to the MCKP in which the choice constraints are relaxed as $\sum_{j \in N_k} x_{kj} \leq 1$. Zhong and Young used the MCKP to obtain optimal solutions of transportation programming problems when alternative versions of projects are under consideration in [202]. Authors provided six steps to build a MCKP and solved it with the method from [51]. Bae et al. considered in [9] the MCKP as a subproblem when solving a problem of finding a reconnaissance route of an unmanned combat vehicle in a terrain modeled as a grid. They proposed a two-phases method in which all feasible partial routes are generated in a first step. They showed that the problem of selecting partial routes from the set of candidates corresponds to a MCKP. Caserta and Voß solved the reliability Redundancy Allocation Problem (RAP) via the MCKP in [25]. They introduced the fact that the RAP corresponds to look for an optimal distribution of resources among subsystems. Then, they showed that RAP can be optimally solved in two steps: in the first one a multidimensional knapsack problem (see Sect. 4.3.1) associated to each subsystem is solved, whereas in the second a MCKP is solved to select the specific amount of resources to be assigned to each subsystem. Ykman-Couvreur et al. showed in [199] how the MPSoC runtime management can be modeled as MMCKP, whereas Fischer et al. considered MCKP in a classification problem in [61]. Zhao et al. considered in [201] the optimization of the quality of experience of multiple clients for video streaming over wireless network. They showed that the problem of finding an optimal allocation of bitrate level for multiple wireless clients can be modeled via a MCKP. Tisch et al. dealt with the configuration of learning factories as a MMCKP combined with a two-dimensional bin-packing problem in [178]. Al-Dulaimy et al. showed in [3] that the placement of virtual machines selected for migration in the context of energy efficient cloud data centers management can be modeled as a MCKP, whereas authors in [148] considered an inventory problem under uncertain demand in which a seller stocks an item in anticipation of a single selling season. The corresponding problem is non-convex and they showed that it can be solved via the solution of a polynomial number of particular MCKPs called "*two-sided*" MCKP in which both lower and upper bounds exist on the knapsack capacity. They proposed a DP-based algorithm and a heuristic and showed their methods obtained better results than a global optimizer for non-convex mixed-integer nonlinear problems. Diallo et al. introduced in [48] a model for a selective maintenance problem for serial systems and proposed a two-phase approach in which the problem is transformed into a MMCKP. Finally, Rogeau et al. introduced very recently what they called a "*coupling constraint*" into MMCKP to model a retrofit planning problem at territory scale, with a building-level resolution [161].

4.2.2   The Discounted Knapsack Problem

An interesting variant of the KP is the discounted 0-1 knapsack problem (DKP), where items are selected from 3-sized item groups [89, 163]. Although much harder than KP, fully polynomial approximation schemes and DP-based solution approaches have been developed for it.

Given n^g item groups having three items each, and one knapsack with capacity c, where the items in the i-th ($i = 0, 1, \cdots, n^g - 1$) group are denoted as $3i, 3i + 1$ and $3i + 2$, with value coefficients p_{3i}, p_{3i+1} and $p_{3i+2} = p_{3i} + p_{3i+1}$, and weights w_{3i}, w_{3i+1} and w_{3i+2} (discounted weight), $w_{3i} + w_{3i+1} > w_{3i+2}$, $w_{3i+2} > w_{3i}$, and $w_{3i+2} > w_{3i+1}$, the goal is to maximize the profits by selecting at most one item in a group. We assume profits and weights to be positive integers, so as the capacity c. DKP can be formulated by (4.17)–(4.20):

$$\max \quad \sum_{i=0}^{n^g-1} (p_{3i}x_{3i} + p_{3i+1}x_{3i+1} + p_{3i+2}x_{3i+2}) \qquad (4.17)$$

$$\text{s.t. :} \quad \sum_{i=0}^{n^g-1} (w_{3i}x_{3i} + w_{3i+1}x_{3i+1} + w_{3i+2}x_{3i+2}) \leq c \quad\quad (4.18)$$

$$x_{3i} + x_{3i+1} + x_{3i+2} \leq 1 \quad\quad \forall i \in \{0, \ldots, n^g - 1\} \quad\quad (4.19)$$

$$x_{3i}, x_{3i+1}, x_{3i+2} \in \{0, 1\} \quad\quad \forall i \in \{0, l \ldots, n^g - 1\} \quad\quad (4.20)$$

DKP has been introduced in the Master's Thesis by Guldan [80] and it can be viewed as a particular case of MCKP where the number of items in each group is set to three. Specific relations between items in a group are defined in DKP, which is not the case in MCKP.

DP-based algorithms were proposed to deal with DKP in [80, 89, 163]. Experiments reported in these works show that DP can be used to solve instances with up to $n^g = 1,000$ groups in reasonable time under the condition of having sufficient memory resources. A fully polynomial-time approximation scheme, a 2-approximation algorithm and a particle swarm optimization heuristic were also proposed in [89]. Several other population-based metaheuristics have then been proposed to deal with DKP: genetic algorithm [87], differential evolution algorithms [203], multi-strategy monarch butterfly optimization heuristic [58], moth search [56]. Recently, He et al. proposed a new kind of method to design an evolutionary algorithm by using algebraic theory in [86]. The approach used two evolution operators using the addition, multiplication and inverse operation of the direct product of rings. Wu et al. proposed in [195] a discrete hybrid teaching-learning-based optimization algorithm. Very recently, Wilbaut et al. proposed to combine Variable Neighborhood Search (VNS) with DP and showed that all the instances from the literature can be solved in less than 2 seconds thanks to reduction procedures [192].

4.2.3 The Knapsack Problem with Setup

Another feature which is common to several distinct KP variants is the presence of setup costs [27]. The setup knapsack problem (SKP) originates from (and is named after) a particular machine scheduling problem which involves setup costs [49]. SKP asks for the selection of items from families $\mathcal{F}$, where each item family needs to be set up before usage. Such a condition is modeled through additional variables z_f, which indicate whether or not family f corresponding to item $j \in \mathcal{N}_f$ has been set up [27]. A formulation for SKP is given by:

$$\max \quad \sum_{f \in \mathcal{F}} \left(u_f z_f + \sum_{j \in \mathcal{N}_f} p_j x_j \right) \tag{4.21}$$

$$\text{s.t.} \quad \sum_{f \in \mathcal{F}} \left(s_f z_f + \sum_{j \in \mathcal{N}_f} w_j x_j \right) \leq c \tag{4.22}$$

$$z_f - x_j \geq 0 \qquad \forall f \in \mathcal{F}, j \in \mathcal{N}_f \tag{4.23}$$

$$z_f - \sum_{j \in \mathcal{N}_f} x_j \leq 0 \qquad \forall f \in \mathcal{F} \tag{4.24}$$

$$z_f, x_j \in \{0, 1\} \qquad \forall f \in \mathcal{F}, j \in \mathcal{N}_f \tag{4.25}$$

Note that, in this case, we have $u_f, p_j \in \mathbb{R}$, $s_f, w_j \in \mathbb{Z}^+$ and $N = \bigcup_{f \in \mathcal{F}} \mathcal{N}_f$, with $\mathcal{N}_{f_1} \cap \mathcal{N}_{f_2} = \emptyset$, $\forall f_1, f_2 \in \mathcal{F}$, $f_1 \neq f_2$. Since KP can be reduced to SKP, it is also $\mathcal{NP}$-Hard [70].

A similar SKP variant is called the Multiple-class Integer Knapsack problem with Setups (MIKS), where items are organized in distinct classes with setups and multiplicity constraints [147]. From this perspective, the weight of item at a given class is a multiple of the class weight, while also allowing multiple items to be selected within lower and upper class limits. A more constrained version of MIKS eliminates multiplicity constraints and allows whole integer interval, being called Integer Knapsack Problem with Setups (IKS), that allows the development of more efficient algorithms. In this sense, class weights are restricted to negative factors. A further relaxation of IKS yields the Continuous Knapsack Problem with Setups (CKS), and further adaptations can generate the classic binary knapsack problem. CKS appears as subproblem for capacitated multi-item lot sizing problems, and IKS as subproblem for cutting stock problems. An interesting point is that the relaxation of the binary knapsack with multiple choices is equivalent to CKS [147]. When dealing with numerical experimentation, most success is achieved by hybrid approaches that involve B&B and DP.

Regarding the SKP Khemakhem and Chebil proposed in [114] a tree-search-based combination heuristic which is based on the Filter-and-Fan method. The approach is an iterative local search in which moves are generated according to a tree-search strategy. The main particularity of the method lies in a new technique that makes a bijection between a solution of SKP and an integer index. The algorithm obtains better average results as CPLEX. The same authors proposed in [28] two DP-based algorithms for SKP. The first one considers a stage associated with every item in the problem and computes the optimal values of two auxiliary problems. In the second one authors introduces a space reduction technique to exploit the bijection mentioned above. The DP algorithm considers only the setup variables and a complete solution is obtained by solving a particular KP. This approach is able to solve large correlated instances with up to 10,000 items in reasonable CPU time.

4.2.4 The Knapsack Problem with Neighbor Constraints

For the 1-Neighbor Knapsack Problem (1-NKP), an item can be selected only if at least one of its neighbours is also selected while items with no neighbors can always be selected. Contrary to that, for the all-neighbours knapsack problem (All-NKP), an item can be selected only if all its neighbors are also selected. Approximation algorithms and hardness results for 1-NKP and All-NKP are provided in [16, 17]. These two NKPs can be generalized as described by the following 0-1 linear program NKP_k:

$$\max \quad \sum_{i \in N} p_i x_i \tag{4.26}$$

$$\text{s.t.:} \quad \sum_{i \in N} w_i x_i \leq c \tag{4.27}$$

$$\min(k, n_i) x_i \leq \sum_{j \in N_i} x_j \qquad \forall i \in N, N_i \neq \emptyset \tag{4.28}$$

$$x_i \in \{0, 1\} \qquad \forall i \in N \tag{4.29}$$

where N_i is the set of neighbors of vertex i in the graph G and k is an integer less or equal to the maximum degree of vertices in G, i.e. $k \leq \Delta = \max\{|N_i| : i \in N\}$. Note that NKP_1 is equivalent to 1-NKP and NKP_Δ is equivalent to All-NKP, while NKP_0 corresponds to KP.

The Subset-Union Knapsack Problem (SUKP) is a special case of All-NKP in which the input graph is directed and bipartite and such that the vertex set is partitioned into vertices associated with *items* and vertices associated with *elements* and every arc points from an *item vertex* to an *element vertex*. The precedence-constrained knapsack problem [15] and the partially ordered knapsack problem [118] are also special cases of All-NKP on directed graph. The general, undirected 1-neighbor knapsack problem generalizes several maximum coverage problems including the budgeted variant considered in [116].

4.2.5 The Knapsack Constrained Maximum Spanning Tree Problem

The Knapsack Constrained Maximum Spanning Tree problem (KCMST) is a combination of the knapsack problem and the maximum spanning tree problem, introduced in [197]. The weight-constrained Minimum Spanning Tree (MST) problem is to find a spanning tree of total edge weights at most a given capacity and minimum total edge costs. A spanning tree of a graph G is a subgraph connecting all vertices of G. For a spanning tree T of G, we define its profit $p(T)$ and weight $w(T)$, respectively, as the sum of the profits and weights of its constituent edges. A spanning tree T is feasible for KCMST if it satisfies $w(T) \leq c$. The problem is to fill the knapsack with a feasible spanning tree such that the tree profit is maximized, which can be formulated as follows:

$$\max \quad p(T) \tag{4.30}$$

$$\text{s.t.:} \quad w(T) \leq c \tag{4.31}$$

$$T \text{ is a spanning tree of } G \tag{4.32}$$

Based on the connectivity requirements of a tree, four distinct IP formulations for MST are discussed in [55], namely subtour elimination, cut set, single-commodity flow and Martin's formulation. A subtour elimination formulation is based on the fact that a tree T has no cycles and contains $n-1$ edges [53] and is described as follows:

$$\max \quad \sum_{e \in E} p_e x_e \tag{4.33}$$

$$\text{s.t.:} \quad \sum_{e \in E} w_e x_e \leq c \tag{4.34}$$

$$\sum_{e \in E} x_e = n - 1 \tag{4.35}$$

$$\sum_{e \in E(S)} x_e \leq |S| - 1 \qquad \forall S \subset N \tag{4.36}$$

$$x_e \in \{0, 1\} \qquad\qquad e \in E \qquad\qquad (4.37)$$

Martin's formulation (see [35, 144]) uses binary variables y_{ji}^k if j is the father of i in the tree structure obtained by rooting T at k, 0 otherwise:

$$\max \quad \sum_{e \in E} p_e x_e \qquad\qquad\qquad (4.38)$$

$$\text{s.t.:} \quad \sum_{e \in E} w_e x_e \le c \qquad\qquad\qquad (4.39)$$

$$\sum_{e \in E} x_e = n - 1 \qquad\qquad\qquad (4.40)$$

$$x_{ij} = y_{ij}^k + y_{ji}^k \qquad\qquad \forall (i, j) \in E, k \in N \qquad (4.41)$$

$$\sum_{j \in N} y_{ij}^k = 1 \qquad\qquad \forall i \ne k \in N \qquad (4.42)$$

$$y_{kj}^k = y_{ii}^k = 0 \qquad\qquad \forall (i, j) \in E, k \in N \qquad (4.43)$$

$$x_e \in \{0, 1\} \qquad\qquad e \in E \qquad\qquad (4.44)$$

The KCMST problem can be extended directly to generalized variants of KP where the MST is replaced by Generalized Maximum Spanning Tree. Pop presented in [158] a survey on different integer programming formulations of the generalized MST problem.

4.2.6 The Set Union Knapsack Problem

In the Set-Union knapsack Problem (SUKP), introduced in [77], we are given a set N of n elements and a set M of m items. Each item $i \in M$ is characterized by its profit $p_i > 0$ and by its set of associated elements $N_i \subseteq N$. For any subset $I \subseteq M$, the profit of I is given by $\sum_{i \in I} p_i$, while the weight of I is $\sum_{j \in \cup_{i \in I} N_i} w_j$, where w_j is the weight of element j. The objective of the SUKP is to select a maximum profit subset of M, while respecting the capacity $c > 0$ of the knapsack. A generic set based formulation of SUKP can be expressed as follows:

$$\max \quad p(I) \tag{4.45}$$

$$\text{s.t.:} \quad w(\cup_{i \in I} N_i) \leq c \tag{4.46}$$

$$I \subseteq N \tag{4.47}$$

The graph $G = (M \cup N, E)$, where an edge $(i, j) \in E$ only for $i \in M$ and $j \in N_i$, is a bipartite graph (also known as a bigraph) and sets M and N form a partition of the vertex set. It may be observed that SUKP includes KP as a special case when $N_i \cap N_{i'} = \emptyset \ \forall i, i' \in M$ and $|N_i| = 1 \ \forall i \in M$. Since KP is $\mathcal{NP}$-hard, SUKP is $\mathcal{NP}$-hard as well. SUKP has various domain-specific applications including information security systems, financial decision-making [7, 111], flexible manufacturing machine [77, 116], database partitioning [76], smart city [180] and data stream compression [198]. A mixed-integer programming model can be derived from the previous set-based formulation. It is based on two sets of binary variables. The first one is associated with items whereas the second one is associated with elements. More precisely, we define binary variables x_i and y_j for each item $i \in M$ and for each element $j \in N$, respectively, as:

$$x_i = \begin{cases} 1 & \text{if item } i \text{ is selected} \\ 0 & \text{otherwise} \end{cases}$$

$$y_j = \begin{cases} 1 & \text{if element } j \text{ is selected} \\ 0 & \text{otherwise.} \end{cases}$$

Using these variables SUKP can be formulated as:

$$\max \quad \sum_{i \in M} p_i x_i \tag{4.48}$$

$$\text{s.t.:} \quad \sum_{j \in N} w_j y_j \leq c \tag{4.49}$$

$$x_i \leq y_j \qquad \forall i \in M, \forall j \in N \tag{4.50}$$

$$x_i, y_j \in \{0, 1\} \qquad \forall i \in M, \forall j \in N \tag{4.51}$$

The objective (4.48) maximizes the total profit associated with the selected items whereas constraint (4.49) is the knapsack constraint. Constraints (4.50) imply that the selection of item i forces the selection of all elements in N_i.

Several algorithms have been proposed to solve SUKP. Goldschmidt et al. developed in [77] an exact DP algorithm for SUKP and derived sufficient conditions for having a polynomial run time. Arulsevan showed in [7] that a greedy algorithm for the budgeted maximum coverage problem approximates SUKP within a constant factor. Following the same research direction, Taylor proposed in [175] an approximation algorithm relying on an algorithm for the densest k-subhypergraph problem. Other recent papers dealing with SUKP can be found in the literature. He et al. developed a binary artificial bee colony algorithm and used greedy repairing and optimization to handle infeasibility of a solution in [88], whereas authors in [57] proposed several versions of discrete moth search, while a hybrid approach that combines a genetic algorithm and particle swarm optimization was developed in [151]. Wei and Hao proposed in [184] an iterated two-phase local search (I2PLS) approach for solving SUKP, whereas the same authors proposed in [186] a multistart solution-based tabu search and in [185] a kernel-based tabu search. The last two algorithms conduct to the current best-known solutions for several benchmark instances used in the literature.

4.2.7 The Precedence Constrained Knapsack Problem

The Precedence Constraint Knapsack Problem (PCKP), also called partially ordered knapsack problem, is a generalization of KP which includes a partial order on items described by an acyclic directed graph $G = (N, A)$ with weights and profits associated to its vertices. An arc $(i, j) \in A$ means that "*item i precedes item j*", and implies that if item j is selected then item i must be also selected.

Formally, PCKP can be described by the following 0-1 integer linear program:

$$\max \quad \sum_{i \in N} p_i x_i \tag{4.52}$$

$$\text{s.t.:} \quad \sum_{i \in N} w_i x_i \leq c \tag{4.53}$$

$$x_i \geq x_j \qquad\qquad (i, j) \in A \tag{4.54}$$

$$x_i \in \{0, 1\} \qquad\qquad i \in N \qquad\qquad (4.55)$$

PCKP appears in many applications as network design, investment, management problems, scheduling, production planning, see, e.g., [50, 103, 171, 174].

Johnson and Niemi were the first to propose DP algorithms when G is out-tree, called left-right approach in [106]. Then, Samphaiboon and Yamada presented heuristics and DP algorithms for general acyclic graph G in [167].

Beyond the wide range of applications available for PCKP, precedence constraints are of theoretical and computational interest because by themselves they define a polyhedron with integer vertices. More precisely, the convex hull of feasible integer points is the same as the region obtained by relaxing the integrality restrictions. As a consequence, this property allows to solve the Lagrangian relaxation of PCKP associated with the knapsack constraint in polynomial time. Several researchers investigated the polyhedral structure of PCKP by exploiting this property and the rich and large existing results on the knapsack polytope, see e.g., [19, 152].

4.2.8 The Disjunctively Constrained Knapsack Problem

The knapsack problem with conflicts, also known as the Disjunctively Constrained Knapsack Problem (DCKP), was introduced in [196]. Given a conflict graph $G = (N, E)$ describing incompatibilities between items, DCKP consists in determining a maximum profit set of compatible items to be packed into the knapsack. A compact integer linear programming formulation for DCKP makes use of a set of binary variables x_i associated with every item $i \in N$ and taking value 1 if item i is packed in the knapsack, 0 otherwise, and can be stated as:

$$\max \quad \sum_{i \in N} p_i x_i \qquad\qquad (4.56)$$

$$\text{s.t.:} \quad \sum_{i \in N} w_i x_i \leq c \qquad\qquad (4.57)$$

$$x_i + x_j \leq 1 \qquad\qquad (i, j) \in E \qquad\qquad (4.58)$$

$$x_i \in \{0, 1\} \qquad\qquad i \in N \qquad\qquad (4.59)$$

Additional DCKP formulations are found in [92] where an aggregated formulation is proposed, and in [14] where the authors suggest an equivalent MIP based on the determination of a family of cliques in the conflict graph G. Pferschy and Schauer showed in [153] that DCKP is strongly $\mathcal{NP}$-hard and presented pseudo-polynomial algorithms for graphs of bounded tree width and chordal graphs. DCKP is also known as KP with conflicts and is a combination of the Maximum Weighted Independent Set Problem (MWISP) and the KP. When no conflicts are considered, i.e., $E = \emptyset$, the problem reduces to KP whereas when the knapsack constraint is omitted the problem becomes the MWISP.

Several exact and heuristic approaches are considered in the literature. We note in particular the B&B algorithms proposed in [14, 36, 165, 168, 196]. From a heuristic perspective Yamada et al. proposed a local search algorithm [196], whereas more sophisticated approaches based on Tabu Search (TS) were developed in [91] and [168]. The local branching framework was also considered in [2]. Other metaheuristics were considered as scatter search in [94] or the guided neighborhood search in [95], probabilistic tabu search in [164]. Finally we note the memetic algorithms proposed in [164] and very recently in [187].

4.2.9 The Product Knapsack Problem

The Product Knapsack Problem (PKP) is one of the most recent KP variants. It was introduced in [52] and is defined as we describe next. It aims at determining a subset of items $S \subseteq N$ that maximizes $\prod_{j \in S} p_j$ and such that $\sum_{j \in S} w_j \leq c$ holds. With the usual binary variable x_j equal to 1 iff item j is selected, a mixed-integer nonlinear formulation of PKP is described as follows:

$$\max \prod_{j \in N} \max\{1, p_j x_j\} = \prod_{j \in N} (1 + (p_j - 1)x_j) \tag{4.60}$$

$$\text{s.t.:} \sum_{j \in N} w_j x_j \leq c \tag{4.61}$$

$$x \in \{0, 1\}^n \tag{4.62}$$

Denoting by $N^- = \{j \in N : p_j < 0\}$ the sets of items with negative profits and based on the observation that an optimal solution to PKP must include an even number of items $j \in N^-$, D'Ambrosio et al. proposed the following mixed-integer linear formulation for the problem:

$$\max \quad \sum_{j \in N} \log(|p_j|x_j) \tag{4.63}$$

$$\text{s.t.:} \quad \sum_{j \in N} w_j x_j \leq c \tag{4.64}$$

$$\sum_{j \in N^-} w_j x_j = 2y \tag{4.65}$$

$$(x, y) \in \{0, 1\}^n \times \mathbb{Z}_+ \tag{4.66}$$

As for solution approaches to PKP, D'Ambrosio et al. proposed a DP algorithm and a mixed-integer linear programming one. Pferschy et al. showed in [154] that PKP is weakly $\mathcal{NP}$-Hard and proposed a fully polynomial-time approximation scheme for the problem.

4.3   Variants with Multiple Knapsack Constraints

Some KP variants involve more than one knapsack constraints, a requirement that is straightforward to implement directly over the KP formulation. Additionally, they may eventually combine that feature with, among others, different types of objective functions. In this section we consider a few KP variants that fall in such a group, starting with the simplest (from the formulation point of view) of them, the multidimensional knapsack problem.

4.3.1   The Multidimensional Knapsack Problem

The 0-1 Multidimensional Knapsack Problem (MKP) is the most natural generalization of the KP in which several capacity constraints have to be satisfied. MKP is defined for a set $M = \{1, \ldots, m\}$ of $m > 1$ capacity constraints. Denoting by w_{ij} the weight of item $j \in N$ in constraint $i \in M$ and by c_i the capacity of knapsack $i \in M$, MKP can be formulated as follows:

$$\max \sum_{j=1}^{n} p_j x_j \tag{4.67}$$

$$\text{s.t.} : \sum_{j=1}^{n} w_{ij} x_j \leq c_i \qquad\qquad i \in M \qquad\qquad (4.68)$$

$$x_j \in \{0, 1\} \qquad\qquad j \in N \qquad\qquad (4.69)$$

As for KP it is assumed that all coefficients p_j, w_{ij} and c_i are non-negative integers values. Some weights can be equal to 0, i.e. $w_{ij} = 0$, as long as $\sum_{i=1}^{m} w_{ij} \geq 1$ holds for all items $j \in N$. In addition, it is generally assumed that $w_{ij} \leq c_i, \forall j \in N, \forall i \in M$ to guarantee that every item can be selected. Finally, in the same way as (4.4) for KP it is assumed that $\sum_{j=1}^{n} w_{ij} \geq c_i, \forall i \in M$. It can be observed that MKP is also known under other names such as m-dimensional KP or multi-constraint KP.

As mentioned in previous sections, many applications of KP and its variants can be listed in the selection and packing area. In most of the cases, real-world applications require more than one constraint. Thus MKP can be considered to deal with these practical problems. In addition, MKP is a particular case of the general 0-1 integer programming problem. The first references dedicated to the MKP include [129, 137, 188]. Cutting stock [73] and loading problems [13] are other classical applications. The MKP was also used in [182] to model the daily management of a satellite like SPOT. In the computer science context, MKP enables to model the resource allocation in distributed data processing [71] and the planning of data-processing programs [176]. Other recent applications can be listed. For instance Mansini and Speranza showed in [133] how the problem of optimally selecting the assets for leasing can be modeled as a MKP. Holte pointed out an equivalence between a multi-unit combinatorial auction and a MKP in [97]. Kelly considered in [112] a variety of auction winner determination problems and their corresponding family of KPs. He also highlighted the fact that existing algorithms dedicated for these problems can be applied effectively to solve the corresponding auction winner determination problems. Finally, Chen et al. considered a stochastic variant of MKP as an allocation resource problem in which the demand may change over time in [30].

Theoretical works demonstrated that MKP is $\mathcal{NP}$-hard and that it has no fully polynomial-time approximation scheme unless $\mathcal{P} = \mathcal{NP}$ (see, e.g., [72]). In fact, despite its simple formulation, the problem remains very difficult to solve at optimality, especially when the number of constraints increases. This is undoubtedly what explains the success of MKP, which is often used to calibrate and evaluate new approaches, in particular metaheuristics and hybrid methods. However, one can observe that the number of papers dedicated to exact methods is comparatively small. It is not possible to present a summary of all interesting publications dealing with the MKP in a few pages. We restrict our presentation to some of the recent approaches leading to the current best-known solutions over the instances of the literature. Interested readers can find surveys dedicated specifically to MKP, see, e.g., [64, 119, 159, 190]. We do not consider either in this section the particular case when $m = 2$ for which many references can also be found in the literature.

Efficient recent approaches dealing with the MKP concern mainly metaheuristics and hybrid methods combining mathematical programming with specific components dedicated to the problem. One of the current best approach to solve hard MKP instances is described in [18]. Authors proposed a multi-level search strategy based on the reduced costs of the non-basic variables of the LP-relaxation solution. In their approach the top-level branches of the search tree were enumerated following resolution search [34], the middle-level branches were enumerated using a B&B and the lower-level branches were enumerated with a depth first search enumeration strategy. Mansini and Speranza proposed in [134] another approach using similar concepts: the exact solving of a sequence of sub-problems, each with a different cardinality constraint, and the use of a reduced-cost constraint based on the objective function of the continuous relaxation. Each sub-problem is built in a first phase through a recursive variable-fixing process up to a predefined size, and is optimally solved in a second phase. Promising results, especially in terms of running time were reported. Defining small-sized subproblems and considering different branching strategies to solve 0-1 integer programming and mixed-integer programming models have also been considered in other works, as in [85, 189, 191] where authors proposed several iterative schemes where pseudo-cuts are added to strengthen the problem and direct the search. Angelelli et al. applied the *kernel search* to identify a restricted set of promising items [5]. Starting from an optimal solution of the LP-relaxation, new items are then identified and added in the kernel according to solutions of small to moderate size sub-problems. Della Croce and Grosso proposed in [46] another heuristic closely related to these works and using an LP-based core problem. This heuristic is embedded in a partial enumeration where the branching scheme is based on reduced costs of the corresponding LP-relaxation solution value to fix variables. Very recently, an interesting approach was proposed in [169, 170] in which the aim is to reduce the number of constraints. The method reduces the number of dimensions to be constrained by using new basis vectors to represent the optimal item set with less coordinates. Promising results are reported on the largest instances available in the literature, i.e., when $m = 30$ in the OR-Library instances[1] and the instances generated by Glover and Kochenberger in [74]. In particular, the proposed approach provides the optimal or best-known objective values for most instances. It also improves the currently best-known value of one of the Glover and Kochenberger MKP instances and proves the optimality of one other best-known solution.

Concerning metaheuristics we note in particular the scatter search-based algorithm in [84] and the TS-based approach in [115] where authors proposed an hybrid tree-search algorithm that combined TS with a dynamic and adaptive neighborhood search procedure. A two-phase tabu-evolutionary algorithm was also proposed recently in [124]. Authors introduced two solution-based TS methods into the evolutionary framework. They also used a diversity-based population updating rule to keep an efficient population. Computational experiments demonstrated the robustness of the approach since it converged to many best-known solutions and it provided few new best lower bounds. Metaheuristics field is constantly evolving and new approaches are proposed regularly. A very large share of these new methods are tested on MKP. Fingler et al. considered in [60] a parallel implementation of Ant Colony Optimization (ACO) using CUDA and under the GPGPU. They compared the results of this approach with a hybrid DP method, a kernel search and a nested partition and showed that parallel ACO can be an interesting alternative to deal with MKP. Very recently, Lai et al. introduced in [123] a new quantum Particle Swarm Optimization (PSO) that integrates a distance-based diversity preserving strategy and a variable neighborhood descent-based local search method. The results are encouraging and authors showed that the method performs well for instances with a limited number of constraints. It provides better solutions in average than another quantum PSO approach proposed in [81] in very reasonable running time for larger instances. Several other nature-inspired or bio-inspired methods can be identified such as the binary grey wolf optimizer proposed in [130] with some specific components to deal with MKP: an initial elite population generator, a pseudo-utility based repair operator. The results showed that the approach obtained average better results than a few other nature-inspired and bio-inspired methods. Abdel-Basset et al. introduced a modified multi-verse optimization algorithm to solve binary problems [1]. They evaluated this new approach on KP, MKP and MMKP. The results show an interesting behavior of this metaheuristic to tackle different variants of KPs.

To conclude this section it should be observed that in many works dedicated to population-based approaches some of the large instances in the

---

[1] http://people.brunel.ac.uk/~mastjjb/jeb/info.html.

literature are not considered and that authors do not necessarily compare their results with the state-of-the-art, making it difficult objective comparison.

4.3.2 The Multidimensional Knapsack Problem with Demand Constraints

The 0-1 Multidimensional Knapsack Problem with Demand Constraints (MKPD) is generalization of the MKP in which a set of q *greater than* constraints, $q \geq 1$, complements its multiple knapsack constraints. Accordingly, MKPD extends the MKP formulation as follows:

$$\max \quad \sum_{j=1}^{n} p_j x_j \tag{4.70}$$

$$\text{s.t.}: \quad \sum_{j=1}^{n} w_{ij} x_j \leq c_i \qquad i \in \{1, \ldots, m\} \tag{4.71}$$

$$\sum_{j=1}^{n} w_{ij} x_j \geq c_i \qquad i \in \{m+1, \ldots, m+q\} \tag{4.72}$$

$$x_j \in \{0, 1\} \qquad j \in N = \{1, \ldots, n\} \tag{4.73}$$

In this formulation we distinguish the first m classical knapsack constraints from the subsequent q which are the *demand* constraints. Comparing with MKP and other extensions of KP the MKPD can be viewed as a recent variant if we consider the references to this problem in the literature. Indeed, to the best of our knowledge the MKPD has been formally introduced at the beginning of the twentieth century by Cappanera and Trubian, firstly in [21] and then in the associated paper [22]. Like MKP the MKPD is embedded in the models of many practical applications, in particular in obnoxious and semiobnoxious facility location problems (see, e.g., [20, 162]) and portfolio-selection problems [12]. More recently a possible application in the context of the ideal product mix for a mobile retailer where a resource constraint represents the space of the retailer whereas a demand constraint models the fact the product mix has to meet or exceed a given revenue threshold was considered in [193]. We also noted the work presented in [96] where author considers the constrained problem of multi-robot tasks allocation and compares dedicated algorithms with approaches presented in [6, 102] for solving the more general MKPD. The main conclusion is that a direct application of MKPD dedicated methods does not allow to obtain efficient solutions even for medium-sized instances.

It is interesting to observe that finding a feasible solution of the MKPD is an $\mathcal{NP}$-complete problem [22] due to the presence of conflicting binary constraints. Like for the MKP and other variants a large set of 810 instances is available in the literature to compare the proposed approaches. Most of the proposed approaches dealing with MKPD are based on heuristics and metaheuristics. This can probably be explained by its practical difficulty and the fact that exact methods cannot solve instances with more than 100 items in reasonable running and memory limits. Concerning theoretical works we noted the promising work in [45] in which the author introduced the use of equality rather than inequalities in cutting planes (called equality cuts) in binary programming in general to reduce the linear relaxation space, and the concept of *anticover* inequality. He applied it on the MKPD and showed that using these equality cuts with CPLEX improved the computational effort by about 7% when considering instances with up to 250 items and $m = 10$ and $q = 10$. Wishon and Villalobos introduced in [194] new efficiency measure calculations and some properties and showed that these measures are applicable to all KP variants with a single linear objective function and linear constraints of any quantity. They validated these measures with three solution algorithms (a fixed-core algorithm, a kernel search algorithm and a Genetic Algorithm (GA)) on instances randomly generated with up to 1,000 items and $m + q \leq 25 + 25$.

Among the heuristic and metaheuristic approaches, Cappanera and Trubian proposed in [22] a sophisticated local search algorithm into two phases, which combines a standard attribute-based TS with an oscillation method based on the one proposed for the MKP in [74], but is restricted to the feasible space. The approach was not able to provide a feasible solution to every instance but provided better solutions in general than CPLEX. Arntzen et al. proposed in [6] an adaptive memory search procedure which uses a dynamic TS mechanism and a weighting scheme to manage infeasible solutions. The computational results demonstrated the efficiency of the approach which was able to provide a feasible solution for every instance, except one. Then, Hvattum and Løkketangen conducted in [102] several implementations of Scatter Search (SS) for the MKPD based on some proposals about SS in general [75]. They performed extensive experiments and obtained good results compared with CPLEX and Cappanera and Trubian's algorithm. Gortázar et al. introduced in [79] a black box SS method for general classes of binary optimization problems. According to its general description three of the five methods used in SS are problem-dependent. Authors considered some diversification generators and combination methods and evaluated the approach on four optimization problems among which is the MKPD. The results showed that the approach was dominated by the one in [6] but converged quickly to good solutions compared with commercial solvers. Hvattum et al. proposed in [101] an alternating control tree-search framework related to the relaxation-based heuristics proposed in [189] for the MKP. The approach is based on three components: the first one solves an LP-relaxation of the current problem; the second one partitions the set of variables and build sub-problems that can be solved efficiently; the third one updates the problem by adding inequalities and ensuring the convergence of the approach. The overall method can be also used as a heuristic. The algorithm is evaluated on the MKPD and the MKP. The results revealed that the method was very effective for the MKPD compared to the TS algorithm proposed in [6] and the SS algorithm proposed in [102]. It was also competitive for the MKP when compared with some of the best solution approaches. Recently, Lai et al. introduced in [125] a two-stage TS-based algorithm for solving MKPD. The TS uses one-flip and swap neighborhoods and a hash-based mechanism to determine the tabu status of neighbor solutions. In the approach the fist stage aimed to identify a promising hyperplane within the whole search space. The second stage is dedicated to the search for an improved solution by examining both feasible and infeasible solutions on the identified hyperplane. The computational results reported on a subset of the available instances show that this approach performs well and provides efficient solutions in reasonable running times. Very recently, Al-Shihabi proposed a core-based optimization framework and evaluate it over the MDMKP [4]. The main idea is to define a new core problem iteratively using a kind of local search where the aim is to find the *best* neighbouring core problem. The initial core problem is built from the reduced costs of variables and a probing technique is used to control the number of changes in two consecutive core problems. Author evaluates this framework when using CPLEX and the approach proposed in [125] to solve the core problems. Promising results are presented and the method leads to several new best-known solutions.

4.3.3 The Multiple Knapsack Problem

The Multiple Knapsack Problem (M-KP) is a generalization of KP in which a set M of $m \geq 2$ knapsacks are available for carrying the items. This problem, one should note, is different from the multidimensional knapsack problem (see Sect. 4.3.1) and the multidimensional multiple-choice knapsack problem (see Sect. 4.2.1) since in the M-KP every item has to be assigned to one knapsack (at most). In the formulation of the M-KP a binary variable x_{ij} is associated with knapsack i and item j and is set to 1 if item $j \in N$ is assigned to knapsack i (0 otherwise). The problem aims at maximizing total profit while respecting the capacity of every individual knapsack and can be formulated as follows:

$$\max \quad \sum_{i=1}^{m} \sum_{j=1}^{n} p_j x_{ij} \tag{4.74}$$

$$\text{s.t. :} \quad \sum_{j=1}^{n} w_{ij} x_{ij} \le c_i \qquad\qquad i \in M \tag{4.75}$$

$$\sum_{i=1}^{m} x_{ij} \le 1 \qquad\qquad j \in N \tag{4.76}$$

$$x_{ij} \in \{0, 1\} \qquad\qquad i \in M, j \in N \tag{4.77}$$

Constraints (4.76) guarantee that every item is placed in at most one knapsack. A special case of the M-KP is obtained if all the knapsacks have an identical capacity c. This variant is generally referred to as the multiple knapsack problem with identical capacities. Additionally, one also finds subset-sum variants for both models, with $p_j = w_j, \forall j \in N$, thus applying. The M-KP is also related to the classical bin-packing problem (BPP). Three main differences can be listed: (i) items have both a weight and a profit in the M-KP, whereas items only have a weight in BPP; (ii) bins (knapsacks) in the M-KP have varying sizes, while bin capacities are uniform in BPP; (iii) the aim of the M-KP is to maximize the total profits of the items packed in a set of bins (knapsacks), and some items are not assigned, whereas all items must be packed in the BPP. Finally one can observe that the M-KP is a special case of the generalized assignment problem in which a profit p_{ij} is defined if item j is assigned to knapsack i. The M-KP and its variants are strongly $\mathcal{NP}$-Hard problems and it was proved that even when $m = 2$ the subset-sum variants do not admit a fully polynomial-time approximation scheme unless $\mathcal{P} = \mathcal{NP}$ (see, e.g., [111]). Polynomial-time approximation schemes were developed in [29] for the MKP and in [24] for the subset-sum variant.

Eilon and Christofides [54] were among the first to consider the M-KP as a cargo loading problem. Ferreira et al. used in [59] a generalization of the M-KP to solve real-world problems in the design of processors for mainframe computers, in the layout of electronic circuits, and in sugar cane alcohol production in Brazil. Another application can be found in [107] where authors considered the M-KP for task allocation among autonomous agents, continuous double-call auctions. The M-KP was also used to model multiprocessor scheduling and the assignment of files to storage devices in order to maximize the number of files stored in the fastest storage devices in [122]. More recently Laalaoui and M'Hallah [121] addressed a single machine scheduling problem with machine unavailability as a M-KP, whereas Simon et al. modeled problems of maintaining operational capability without external support through M-KPs in [172]. Additional constraints occur among which are demand constraints and some others related to the application.

Some B&B methods were proposed to solve the M-KP as in [140] where Martello and Toth solved at each node a relaxed version of the M-KP where the assignment constraint is omitted. The branching item is chosen among those which had been assigned to $\bar{m} > 1$ knapsacks and the branching operation generates $\bar{m}$ nodes by assigning the item to one of the $\bar{m} - 1$ knapsacks or excluding it from all of these. Next year, Martello and Toth [141] proposed one of the most well-known B&B for the M-KP known as MTM. In this algorithm a lower bound is derived at each node of the tree by solving m individual KPs in the following way: the first KP is solved optimally. Then, the chosen items are removed and the next KP can be solved and so on until all the m knapsacks are filled. Upper bounds are computed from a surrogate relaxation. The branching scheme is based on the obtained solution by generating two nodes: the first one assigning the next item of a greedy solution to the chosen knapsack, while the other excluding this item from the knapsack. Pisinger [156] proposed a more efficient procedure starting from MTM. In this approach called Mulknap lower bounds are derived by solving a series of subset-sum problems which are also used for tightening the capacity constraints of the knapsacks. He introduced efficient reduction rules to determine which items cannot be packed into any of the knapsacks and he derived upper bounds through surrogate relaxation. He compared the results of MTM and Mulknap and showed that the latter approach was able to solve very efficiently and optimally large-size instances of the M-KP with up to $n = 100,000$ items and $m = 10$ knapsacks. However, Fukunaga showed in [66] that Mulknap performs less effectively when the ratio of items to knapsacks (n/m) falls between 2 and 5 or when the data are strongly correlated. Fukunaga and Korf [67] introduced a B&B algorithm called *bin-completion* and based on a bin-oriented branching structure and a powerful dominance criterion. Authors showed that this new method is particularly competitive for solving MKP instances when the ratio of items to knapsacks is small (i.e., $n/m < 4$). This work was extended in [66] by integrating additional techniques from constraint programming like path-symmetry and path-dominance criteria for pruning nodes in the M-KP B&B search space. Experimental results confirmed the competitiveness of the approach for instances with a small ration n/m and the integration of Mulknap algorithm significantly improved the results for higher ratios. Very recently, Dell'Amico et al. presented in [47] two pseudo-polynomial formulations for the M-KP based on arc-flow and reflect models. Authors proposed a new effective hybrid method combining B&B, Master/Slave decomposition, Benders's cuts and constraint programming. This approach outperforms other exact methods and is able to solve optimally 1,988 instances over the 2,100 instances considered in the paper in reasonable running time.

Papers related to heuristics for the M-KP can also be found in the literature, especially the well-known MTHM polynomial-time heuristic based on greedy algorithm and local search procedure proposed in [142], which was tested on instances with up to $n = 10,000$ and $m = 40$ in [143]. More recently, Lalami et al. proposed a heuristic based on the core concept [126]. The approach recursively solves the core of different KPs through DP. The method is tested on randomly generated instances with up to 100,000 items and $m = 100$ and compared with MTHM. The results showed that the approach provided good solutions in very short time. Laalaoui [120] proposed two simple extensions of the MTHM. It consists in applying a local search starting from the solution of MTHM and considering two swap moves: the replacement of one item currently assigned to a knapsack by one or two others currently not assigned; or the replacement of two items currently assigned by one item currently not assigned. The results demonstrates that this method improves by around 15% the solution value provided by MTHM with a reasonably increased execution time. Final solutions were at less than 1% in average of the solutions obtained by GAs proposed in [68]. Laalaoui and M'Hallah considered in [121] a single machine scheduling problem with machine unavailability periods corresponding to maintenance periods and modeled it as a M-KP. They proposed a VNS that helps to yield better results than MTHM and other heuristics on scheduling instances with up to 4,800 items and 2,400 knapsacks.

To conclude this section we would like to underline another variant of the M-KP in the literature introduced in [109] and named the multiple knapsack assignment problem. In this variant items are partitioned into subsets and additional constraints impose that a knapsack can only contain items of the same class. This interesting problem which has managerial applications in transportation logistics was considered very recently in [139] where authors proposed some upper bounds derived from Lagrangian and surrogate relaxation and a heuristic procedure.

4.3.4   The Compartmentalized Knapsack Problem

The Compartmentalized Knapsack Problem (CKP) is a variant of KP where items are classified under some criteria or affinities and divided into several classes, like for instance in the MCKP. However, in the CKP items of different classes cannot be mixed in the knapsack. To select items some compartments have to be built. The compartments are not predetermined and have to be added inside the knapsack such that each compartment contains items of the same class. Moreover, building a compartment incurs a fixed cost and a fixed loss of the capacity in the original knapsack, and the compartments are lower and upper bounded. The objective is to find the compartments while maximizing the total value of the items loaded in the overall knapsack minus the cost of the compartments. Like in KP each item has a weight and an utility value.

CKP takes its origin from cutting application where it models a particular two-stage cutting process where items are grouped into classes and only items of the same class can be cut from an intermediate roll. It arises for instance in the case of cutting steel coils in two phases in the metallurgical industry [160]. Items are associated to ribbon coils (corresponding to the classes of items) that are grouped by their thickness. The ribbons are obtained by cutting the steel coils available in stock, which correspond to the knapsack to be filled. Another example in the literature is steel roll cutting where items are grouped according to their thickness [127]. In that case the first cut on the original roll generates different intermediate rolls (corresponding to the compartments in the knapsack), which have the same thicknesses as the original roll. In these applications items are modeled by integer variables. Hoto was among the first to introduce and to define the CKP in his Ph.D. thesis [98]. He distinguished the *restricted* (or *constrained*) version where the number of copies for an item is bounded and the *unrestricted* (or *unconstrained*) case where this bound does not exist. He provided an integer nonlinear optimization model for the unrestricted CKP and he proposed a B&B algorithm to solve it. Then, Marques and Arenales proposed in [138] three new heuristics and a model for the restricted case. Hoto et al. considered the cutting stock problem where each cutting pattern is restricted to be compartmentalized [99]. They presented a concise formulation of CKP and proposed heuristic and exact methods for the unrestricted case. They also presented an integer nonlinear programming formulation of the restricted CKP and proposed a two-phase heuristic which obtained better results than the heuristic proposed in [138]. Later, Hoto et al. [100] introduced techniques based on column generation for the restricted CKP, whereas Leão et al. proposed a linear treatment for the restricted CKP and a hybrid heuristic to solve it in [127]. The natural formulation of CKP is nonlinear and some works in the literature were devoted to propose a linear formulation like in [104] where author extended previous works in [39, 100] by proposing new linearity studies of CKP together with a new exact algorithm, called the exhaustive decomposition algorithm, to solve it. More recently, Inarejos et al. [105] proposed an integer linear optimization model for the restricted CKP and proved its linearity. This model was strengthened in [160]. It can be observed from the literature that several variants of the restricted CKP exist. The main difference among these variants is the objective function which is considered. Very recently, Baazaoui et al. proposed in [8] a new variant of CKP with a formulation involving only binary variables. This formulation is related to the one presented in [105] and is introduced below to illustrate CKP. Let c be the capacity of the knapsack and N the set of items which is partitioned into a set M of n^g classes: $N = \cup_{k \in M} N_k$ with $N_k \cap N_{k'} = \emptyset$, $k \neq k' \in M$. Each item j in class k is characterized by a utility and a weight denoted by p_j^k and w_j^k, $j \in N_k, k \in M$, respectively. In addition, for each class $k \in M$ there is a maximum and a minimum capacity to be consumed by a compartment, namely c_{max}^k and c_{min}^k, respectively, whereas building a compartment involves a fixed loss cost f_k. In the formulation a set P_k of all the possible compartments associated with group k is used to define the set of variables (one can observe that the size of P_k can be simply bounded by the number of items in N_k). Binary variable x_j^k is introduced to know if item j in set N_k is selected, whereas binary variable y_{ij}^k is used to know if item $j \in N_k$ is assigned to compartment $i \in P_k$. Finally, binary variable z_i^k is equaled to 1 if compartment $i \in P_k$ is built. Then, a binary variant of CKP can be stated as follows:

$$\max \quad \sum_{k \in M} \left(\sum_{j \in N_k} p_j^k x_j^k - \sum_{i \in P_k} f_k z_i^k \right) \tag{4.78}$$

$$\text{s.t.:} \quad \sum_{k \in M} \sum_{j \in N_k} w_j^k x_j^k \leq c \tag{4.79}$$

$$c_{min}^k \leq \sum_{j \in N_k} w_j^k y_{ij}^k \leq c_{max}^k \qquad \forall k \in M, j \in P_k \tag{4.80}$$

$$\sum_{j \in P_k} y_{ij}^k = x_i^k \qquad\qquad k \in M, i \in N_k \qquad\qquad (4.81)$$

$$x_j^k, y_{ij}^k, z_i^k \in \{0, 1\} \qquad\qquad k \in M, j \in N_k, i \in P_k \qquad\qquad (4.82)$$

Interested readers are invited to consult [105, 160] for other linear formulations with integer variables.

4.3.5 The Multiple Knapsack Problem with Color Constraints

The Multiple Knapsack Problem with Color constraints (MKPC) is another generalization of KP in which: (*i*) a new attribute, called *color*, is associated with every item ; (*ii*) assignment restrictions are introduced regarding the compatibility of items in a given knapsack. MKPC can also be formulated in different ways. The problem was first introduced with this name in [42] motivated by a real application in the steel industry called the surplus inventory matching problem. Here the orders correspond to items and the slabs correspond to knapsacks. The goal of the problem is to maximize the total weight of the surplus used to fulfill orders in the order book. Other objectives can be considered as the minimization of the leftover weight of each used slab. To introduce more formally the problem we have to provide some details about the correspondence between MKPC and the related application [42]. For each item (order) $j \in N$ characterized by a weight w_j, a set M_j of applicable knapsacks (slabs) from the surplus inventory can be identified. These assignment restrictions are based on quality and physical dimension considerations. In addition only knapsacks that are of the same quality or better can be applied for any given item. Then, for each slab (knapsack) $i \in M$ with a weight b_i a set N_i of applicable orders (items) is defined. The thickness and width requirements for each item need to be compatible with those of the applicable knapsacks. Another important notion in MKPC is the color associated with each item. Color constraints restrict the sets of items that can be matched to the same knapsack in the surplus inventory. In fact not all items assignable to a given knapsack can be packed together on that knapsack, due to processing considerations in the finishing line of a steel mill. A route associated with each item that specifies the set of process operations that need to be applied is given. A unique color is associated with each route and the number of colors on a knapsack is restricted (in practice to two). The color can be introduced with parameter k_j to denote the color of order $j \in N$ and with $\mathcal{K}_i$ to denote the set of colors incident on slab $i \in M$.

Forrest et al. proved in [63] that the problem of applying orders against an existing surplus inventory is the surplus inventory matching problem and can be formulated as a multiple knapsack problem with color and assignment constraints considering only one objective. This is achieved by introducing the following binary variables: $x_{ij}, \forall i \in M, j \in N$ which is set to 1 if item j is assigned to knapsack i; $y_{ki}, \forall i \in M, k \in \mathcal{K}_i$ which has value 1 if items of color k obtain material from knapsack i; and $z_i, \forall i \in M$ which is set to 1 if any item is incident to knapsack i. Then, MKPC can be modeled as follows [63]:

$$\max \quad \sum_{j \in N} \sum_{i \in M_j} w_j x_{ij} - \sum_{i \in M}(b_i - \sum_{j \in N_i} w_j x_{ij})z_i \qquad (4.83)$$

$$\text{s.t.} : \quad \sum_{j \in N_i} w_j x_{ij} \leq b_i z_i \qquad\qquad i \in M \qquad (4.84)$$

$$\sum_{i \in M_j} x_{ij} \leq 1 \qquad\qquad j \in N \qquad (4.85)$$

$$\sum_{c \in \mathcal{K}_i} y_{ci} \leq 2 \qquad\qquad i \in M \qquad (4.86)$$

$$x_{ij} \leq y_{c_j,i} \qquad\qquad i \in M, j \in N \qquad (4.87)$$

$$x_{ij} \in \{0, 1\} \qquad\qquad i \in M, j \in N \qquad (4.88)$$

$$y_{ci} \in \{0, 1\} \qquad\qquad c \in \mathcal{K}_i, i \in M \qquad (4.89)$$

$$z_i \in \{0, 1\} \qquad\qquad i \in M \qquad (4.90)$$

As mentioned by [63] nonlinear objective function (4.83) can be rewritten as

$$\sum_{j \in N} \sum_{i \in M_j} 2w_j x_{ij} - \sum_{j \in N} b_i z_i \qquad (4.91)$$

since $z_i = 0$ implies $x_{ij} = 0, \forall i \in N_j$, whereas $z_i = 1$ implies $x_{ij}z_i = x_{ij}$ for all feasible solutions.

Some variants and formulations of MKPC can be found in the literature. Dawande and Kalagnanam [42] proposed two integer linear programming formulations, one by separating the set of variables for modeling the color constraints and another where these color constraints are implicitly modeled without introducing new variables. They presented a polyhedral study of the problem and showed that the color constraints significantly change the classical multiple knapsack integer polytope. In addition they demonstrated that under certain sufficient conditions color constraints define the facets of the integer polytope. Kalagnanam et al. considered a bi-objective version in [108] where the second objective minimizes the unused weight of the slabs that are matched with orders. Authors proposed a mathematical formulation of the problem as well as a network flow-based heuristic. Experiments performed on real instances proved the efficiency of the heuristic approach to provide near-optimal solutions within a reasonable amount of time. Forrest et al. proposed in [63] a branch-and-price algorithm to deal with the previous formulation that helps in solving a real-life instance of MKPC, called mkc. However, the method could not solve a larger real-life instance, called mkc7 (mkc and mkc7 are two well-known instances in the MIPLIB[2]).

MKPC is also related to the variable-sized bin packing problem with color constraints which consists in assigning to each used bin a capacity from a set of available capacities. Each item is also characterized by a weight and a color among a set of colors. The objective is to minimize the residual capacity in the used bins such that: (i) each item is assigned to exactly one type of the bins, (ii) the total weights of items assigned to each bin do not exceed its capacity and (iii) no more than two colors appear in each used bin. This variant was introduced in [42] where authors presented an asymptotic polynomial approximation scheme that serves to classify the complexity of the problem. Later, Dawande et al. [44] proposed several approximation algorithms. They first considered the case where the maximum number of colors is set to two and then the general case. Then, Dawande et al. [43] developed an efficient heuristic algorithm which is used in a real context and the steel plant savings achieved $2.5 million per year. In a recent work, Kochetov and Kondakov [117] applied a VNS-based matheuristic to a special case where each item has zero weight and arbitrary number of colors with the objective of minimizing the number of bin used. VNS is used for the pricing problem as well as for approaching near-optimal solutions for randomly generated instances. Crévits et al. [37] considered another special case where each color is assigned to only one item. They considered several different linear formulations for that special case of the problem, including some standard ones. Out of the computational experiments reported by the authors, the one that

---

[2] http://miplib.zib.de.

appears to be the most promising is called the *matching formulation*. Experiments provided promising results for this formulation when it is compared to other classical ones. This work was extended in [82] where authors showed that for that special case instances with up to 20 bin sizes can be solved in less than 2 seconds.

Finally the constraint programming community also considered MKPC as a bin-packing problem with color constraints. The corresponding problem is problem number 38 in the CSPLIB[3] and consists of 380 benchmark instances. Frisch et al. proposed in [65] a constraint-based model for the problem and added symmetry-breaking techniques as well as efficient implied constraints that help reducing significantly the search space. Heinz et al. solved all the 380 instances of CSPLIB using a column generation-based algorithm in [90]. The approach also solved the mkc instance but was not able to solve the mkc7 one. The problem was also efficiently solved in [181] where authors used constraint programming with an improved symmetry breaking scheme.

4.4   Conclusion and Suggestions

In this chapter we review a few variants of KP which are associated with recently introduced interesting applications. Our choice of variants is obviously personal and is restricted by writing space limitations. Accordingly, numerous existing KP variants are not addressed here. For each KP variant we consider, at least one formulation is provided, together with a list of existing applications for it. Then, we focused on the most recent and the most effective approaches for solving the problem. Quite clearly, we could have considered many other KP variants including quadratic knapsack problems or multi-objective knapsack problems for instance. Likewise, stochastic and robust versions of KPs have also been considered in the literature. For instance Caserta and Voß introduced in [26] a robust version of the MMCKP and studied the relation between the deterministic and the robust problems. They showed that a given nonlinear model arising from the use of robust optimization can be transformed into an equivalent linear model and thus that the complexity of the deterministic version can be preserved. Online or bilevel knapsack problems are other examples of interesting variants (see., e.g., [23, 149]).

---

[3] http://www.csplib.org/Problems/prob038/.

In our opinion the number of publications dealing with KP variants is not about to decrease, for the following reasons: (i) many of KP variants remain extremely challenging problems, even when considering very simple versions of them; (ii) as shown in this chapter and in the literature several recent works identify KP variants as sub-problems within even more difficult problems. Thus, the need of very effective approaches to solve KPs is still relevant; (iii) we can imagine that other new variants will emerge in the next few years, in particular by combining the characteristics of existing KPs. For instance Mansini et al. introduced recently the multiple multidimensional knapsack with family-split penalties which combines the M-KP and the MKP in [131]. In this problem the profit is not associated with each single item but with the family as a whole and to earn this profit it is necessary to select all the items of the family. A splitting penalty incurs when items from the same family are assigned to different knapsacks. The problem arises in distributed computing resource management items that are grouped into families. As noted by the authors efficiently handling large instances can be an interesting challenge. Thus, we encourage interested readers to consider both theoretical and more practicable works to help resolve the more emerging and difficult knapsack problems.

Acknowledgments Saïd Hanafi wishes to thank the support of the Chaire Française at Rio of Janeiro State University, 2019 that initiated this project.

References

1. Abdel-Basset, M., D. El-Shahat, H. Faris, and S. Mirjalili (2019). A binary multi-verse optimizer for 0-1 multidimensional knapsack problems with application in interactive multimedia systems. *Computers & Industrial Engineering 132*, 187–206.
2. Akeb, H., M. Hifi, and M. E. O. A. Mounir (2011). Local branching-based algorithms for the disjunctively constrained knapsack problem. *Computers & Industrial Engineering 60*(4), 811–820.
3. Al-Dulaimy, A., W. Itani, R. Zantout, and A. Zekri (2018). Type-aware virtual machine management for energy efficient cloud data centers. *Sustainable Computing: Informatics and Systems 19*, 185–203.
4. Al-Shihabi, S. (2021). A novel core-based optimization framework for binary integer programs—The multidemand multidimensional knapsack problem as a test problem. *Operations Research Perspectives 8*, 100182.

5. Angelelli, E., R. Mansini, and M. Grazia Speranza (2010). Kernel search: A general heuristic for the multi-dimensional knapsack problem. *Computers & Operations Research 37*(11), 2017–2026.

6. Arntzen, H., L. M. Hvattum, and A. Løkketangen (2006). Adaptive memory search for multidemand multidimensional knapsack problems. *Computers & Operations Research 33*, 2508–2525.

7. Arulselvan, A. (2014). A note on the set union knapsack problem. *Discrete Applied Mathematics 169*, 214–218.

8. Baazaoui, M., S. Hanafi, R. Todosijevic, M. Ratli, and C. Wilbaut (2021). A note on the compartmentalized knapsack problem. Technical Report, Université Polytechnique Hauts-de-France.

9. Bae, K.-Y., Y.-D. Kim, and J.-H. Han (2015). Finding a risk-constrained shortest path for an unmanned combat vehicle. *Computers & Industrial Engineering 80*, 245–353.

10. Barcia, P. and K. Jörnsten (1990). Improved Lagrangean decomposition: An application to the generalized assignment problem. *European Journal of Operational Research 46*, 84–92.

11. Basnet, C. and J. Wilson (2005). Heuristics for determining the number of warehouses for storing non-compatible products. *International Transactions in Operational Research 12*(5), 527–538.

12. Beaujon, G. J., S. P. Marin, and G. C. McDonald (2001). Balancing and optimizing a portfolio of R&D projects. *Naval Research Logistics 48*, 18–40.

13. Bellman, R. (1957). *Dynamic Programming*. Princeton, NJ, USA: Princeton University Press.

14. Bettinelli, A., V. Cacchiani, and E. Malaguti (2014). Bounds and algorithms for the knapsack problem with conflict graph. Technical report, OR-14-16, DEIS—University of Bologna, Bologna, Italy.

15. Boland, N., G. Fricke, C.and Froyland, and R. Sotirov (2005). Clique-based facets for the precedence constrained knapsack problem. Technical Report, Tilburg University Repository, The Netherlands.

16. Borradaile, G., B. Heeringa, and G. Wilfong (2011). The 1-neighbour knapsack problem. In *International Workshop on Combinatorial Algorithms*, pp. 71–84. Berlin and Heidelberg: Springer.

17. Borradaile, G., B. Heeringa, and G. Wilfong (2012). The knapsack problem with neighbour constraints. *Journal of Discrete Algorithms 16*, 224–235.

18. Boussier, S., M. Vasquez, Y. Vimont, S. Hanafi, and P. Michelon (2010). A multi-level search strategy for the 0-1 Multidimensional Knapsack Problem. *Discrete Applied Mathematics 158*(2), 97–109.

19. Boyd, E. A. (1993). Polyhedral results for the precedence-constrained knapsack problem. *Discrete Applied Mathematics 41*(3), 185–201.

20. Cappanera, P., G. Gallo, and F. Maffioli (2003). Discrete facility location and routing of obnoxious activities. *Discrete Applied Mathematics 133*, 3–28.

21. Cappanera, P. and M. Trubian (2001). A local search based heuristic for the demand constrained multidimensional knapsack problem. Technical Report TR-01-10, Dipartimento di Informatica, Università di Pisa.
22. Cappanera, P. and M. Trubian (2005). A local-search-based heuristic for the demand-constrained multidimensional knapsack problem. *INFORMS Journal on Computing 17*(1), 82–98.
23. Caprara, A., M. Carvalho, A. Lodi, and G. J. Woeginger (2016). Bilevel knapsack with interdiction constraints. *INFORMS Journal on Computing 28*(2), 319–333.
24. Caprara, A., H. Kellerer, and U. Pferschy (2000). A PTAS for the multiple subset-sum problem with different knapsack capacities. *Information Processing Letters 73*(3), 111–118.
25. Caserta, M. and S. Voß (2015). An exact algorithm for the reliability redundancy allocation problem. *European Journal of Operational Research 244*, 110–116.
26. Caserta, M. and S. Voß (2019). The robust multiple-choice multidimensional knapsack problem. *Omega 86*, 16–27.
27. Chajakis, E. D. and M. Guignard (1994). Exact algorithms for the setup knapsack problem. *INFOR: Information Systems and Operational Research 32*(3), 124–142.
28. Chebil, K. and M. Khemakhem (2015). A dynamic programming algorithm for the knapsack problem with setup. *Computers & Operations Research 64*, 40–50.
29. Chekuri, C. and S. Khanna (2000). A PTAS for the multiple knapsack problem. In *Proceedings of the 11th Annual ACM-SIAM Symposium on Discrete Algorithms*, pp. 213–222.
30. Chen, F., T. La Porta, and M. B. Srivastava (2012). Resource allocation with stochastic demands. In *2012 IEEE 8th International Conference on Distributed Computing in Sensor Systems*, Hangzhou, Zhejiang, China, pp. 257–264.
31. Chen, Y. and J. K. Hao (2014). A "reduce and solve" approach for the multiple-choice multidimensional knapsack problem. *European Journal of Operational Research 239*, 313–322.
32. Cherfi, N. and M. Hifi (2009). Hybrid algorithms for the multiple-choice multi-dimensional knapsack problem. *International Journal of Operational Research 5*(1), 89–109.
33. Cherfi, N. and M. Hifi (2010). A column generation method for the multiple-choice multi-dimensional knapsack problem. *Computational Optimization and Applications 46*, 51–73.
34. Chvátal, V. (1997). Resolution search. *Discrete Applied Mathematics 73*, 81–99.
35. Conforti, M., G. Cornuéjols, and G. Zambelli (2010). Extended formulations in combinatorial optimization. *4OR 8*(1), 1–48.

36. Coniglio, S., F. Furini, and P. San Segundo (2020). A new combinatorial branch-and-bound algorithm for the knapsack problem with conflicts. *European Journal of Operational Research 289*(2), 435–455.
37. Crévits, I., S. Hanafi, A. R. Mahjoub, R. Taktak, and C. Wilbaut (2019). A special case of variable-sized bin packing problem with color constraints. In *6th International Conference on Control, Decision and Information Technologies (CoDIT'19)*, Paris, France, pp. 1150–1154.
38. Crévits, I., S. Hanafi, R. Mansi, and C. Wilbaut (2012). Iterative semicontinuous relaxation heuristics for the multiple-choice multidimensional knapsack problem. *Computers & Operations Research 39*(1), 32–41.
39. Cruz, E. P. (2010). *A linear heuristic approach to constrained compartmentalized knapsacks*. Master thesis, Londrina State University, Londrina, Brazil.
40. Dantzig, G. B. (1957). Discrete-variable extremum problems. *Operations Research 5*(2), 266–288.
41. Dantzig, T. (1930). *Number the Language of Science*. Free Press.
42. Dawande, M. and J. Kalagnanam (1998). The multiple knapsack problem with color constraints. Technical Report RC21138, IBM Research Division.
43. Dawande, M., J. Kalagnanam, H. S. Lee, C. Reddy, S. Siegel, and M. Trumbo (2004). The slab-design problem in the steel industry. *Interfaces 34*(3), 215–225.
44. Dawande, M., J. Kalagnanam, and J. Sethuraman (2001). Variable sized bin packing with color constraints. *Electronic Notes in Discrete Mathematics 7*, 154–157.
45. Delissa, L. (2014). *The existence and usefulness of equality cuts in the multidemand multidensional knapsack problem*. Master thesis, Kansas State University.
46. Della Croce, F. and A. Grosso (2012). Improved core problem based heuristics for the 0/1 multi-dimensional knapsack problem. *Computers & Operations Research 39*(1), 27–31.
47. Dell'Amico, M., M. Delorme, M. Iori, and S. Martello (2019). Mathematical models and decomposition methods for the multiple knapsack problem. *European Journal of Operational Research 274*, 886–899.
48. Diallo, C., U. Venkatadri, A. Khatab, and Z. Liu (2018). Optimal selective maintenance decisions for large serial k-out-of-n: G systems under imperfect maintenance. *Reliability Engineering and System Safety 175*, 234–245.
49. Dietrich, B. L. (1988). *Scheduling on parallel unrelated machines with set-ups*. IBM TJ Watson Research Center.
50. Dietrich, B. L. and L. F. Escudero (1991). New procedures for preprocessing 0-1 models with knapsack-like constraints and conjunctive and/or disjunctive variable upper bounds. *INFOR: Information Systems and Operational Research 29*(4), 305–317.
51. Dyer, M. E., N. Kayal, and J. Walker (1984). A branch and bound algorithm for solving the multiple choice knapsack problem. *Journal of Computational and Applied Mathematics 11*(2), 231–249.

52. D'Ambrosio, C., F. Furini, M. Monaci, and E. Traversi (2018). On the product knapsack problem. *Optimization Letters 12*(4), 691–712.

53. Edmonds, J. (1971). Matroids and the greedy algorithm. *Mathematical Programming 1*(1), 127–136.

54. Eilon, S. and N. Christofides (1971). The loading problem. *Management Science 17*, 259–268.

55. Fan, N. and M. Golari (2014). Integer programming formulations for minimum spanning forests and connected components in sparse graphs. In *International Conference on Combinatorial Optimization and Applications*, Cham, Springer, pp. 613–622.

56. Feng, Y.-H. and G.-G. Wang (2018). Binary moth search algorithm for discounted 0-1 knapsack problem. *IEEE Access 6*, 10708–10719.

57. Feng, Y., H. An, and X. Gao (2019). The importance of transfer function in solving set-union knapsack problem based on discrete moth search algorithm. *Mathematics 7*(1).

58. Feng, Y., G.-G. Wang, W. Li, and N. Li (2018). Multi-strategy monarch butterfly optimization algorithm for discounted 0-1 knapsack problem. *Neural Computing and Applications 30*(10), 3019–3036.

59. Ferreira, C., A. Martins, and R. Weismantel (1996). Solving multiple knapsack problems by cutting planes. *SIAM Journal on Optimization 6*(3), 858–877.

60. Fingler, H., E. N. Caceres, H. Mongelli, and S. W. Song (2014). A CUDA based solution to the multidimensional knapsack problem using the Ant Colony Optimization. *Procedia Computer Science, ICCS 2014. 14th International Conference on Computational Science 29*, 84–94.

61. Fischer, L., B. Hammer, and H. Wersing (2016). Optimal local rejection for classifiers. *Neurocomputing 214*, 445–457.

62. Fisher, M. L. (1981). The Lagrangian relaxation method for solving integer programming problems. *Management Science 27*, 1–18.

63. Forrest, J. J. H., J. Kalagnanam, and L. Ladanyi (2006). A column generation approach to the multiple knapsack problem with color constraints. *INFORMS Journal on Computing 18*(1), 129–134.

64. Fréville, A. and S. Hanafi (2005). The multidimensional 0-1 knapsack problem—Bounds and computational aspects. *Annals of Operations Research 139*(1), 195–227.

65. Frisch, A. M., I. Miguel, and T. Walsh (2001). Symmetry and implied constraints in the steel mill slab design problem. In *CP'01 Workshop on Modelling and Problem Formulation*, pp. 8–15.

66. Fukunaga, A. S. (2011). A branch-and-bound algorithm for hard multiple knapsack problems. *Annals of Operations Research 184*(1), 97–119.

67. Fukunaga, A. S. and R. Korf (2007). Bin completion algorithms for multi-container packing, knapsack, and covering problems. *Journal of Artificial Intelligence Research 28*, 393–429.

68. Fukunaga, A. S. and S. Tazoe (2009). Combining multiple representations in a genetic algorithm for the multiple knapsack problem. In *2009 IEEE Congress on Evolutionary Computation*, pp. 2423–2430.

69. Gao, C., G. Lu, and J. Li (2017). An iterative pseudo-gap enumeration approach for the multidimensional multiple-choice knapsack problem. *European Journal of Operational Research 260*, 1–11.

70. Garey, M. R. and D. S. Johnson (1979). *Computers and Intractability: A Guide to the Theory of NP-Completeness*. New York: W. H. Freeman and Company.

71. Gavish, B. and H. Pirkul (1982). Allocation of databases and processors in a distributed computing system. In J. Akoka (Ed.), *Management of Distributed Data Processing*, pp. 215–231.

72. Gens, G. V. and E. V. Levner (1979). Computational complexity of approximation algorithms for combinatorial problems. In G. Goos, J. Hartmanis, P. Brinch Hansen, D. Gries, C. Moler, G. Seegmüller, J. Stoer, N. Wirth, and J. Bečvář (Eds.), *Mathematical Foundations of Computer Science 1979*, Volume 74, pp. 292–300. Berlin and Heidelberg: Springer.

73. Gilmore, P. C. and R. E. Gomory (1966). The theory and computation of knapsack functions. *Operations Research 14*(6), 1045–1074.

74. Glover, F. and G. A. Kochenberger (1996). Critical event tabu search for multidimensional knapsack problems. In I. H. Osman and J. P. Kelly (Eds.), *Meta-Heuristics*, pp. 407–427. Boston, MA: Springer.

75. Glover, F., M. Laguna, and R. Martí (2003). Scatter search. In A. Ghosh and S. Tsutsui (Eds.), *Advances in Evolutionary Computation: Theory And Applications*, pp. 519–537. Springer.

76. Goldschmidt, O., D. Nehme, and G. Yu (1993). On a generalization of the knapsack problem with applications to flexible manufacturing systems and database partitioning. Technical report, Department of Management Science and Information Systems, Working Paper No. 92193-3-7, University of Texas at Austin.

77. Goldschmidt, O., D. Nehme, and G. Yu (1994). Note: On the set-union knapsack problem. *Naval Research Logistics 41*(6), 833–842.

78. Goodman, M. D., K. Dowsland, and J. M. Thompson (2009). A GRASP-knapsack hybrid for a nurse-scheduling problem. *Journal of Heuristics 15*, 351–379.

79. Gortázar, F., A. Duarte, M. Laguna, and R. Martí (2010). Black box scatter search for general classes of binary optimization problems. *Computers & Operations Research 37*, 1977–1986.

80. Guldan, B. (2007). *Heuristic and exact algorithms for discounted knapsack problems*. Master thesis, University of Erlangen-Nürnberg, Germany.

81. Haddar, B., M. Khemakhem, S. Hanafi, and C. Wilbaut (2016). A hybrid quantum particle swarm optimization for the multidimensional knapsack problem. *Engineering Applications of Artificial Intelligence 55*, 1–13.

82. Hanafi, S., A. R. Mahjoub, R. Taktak, and C. Wilbaut (2021). Variable-sized bin packing problem with color constraints. In *JPOC 12—Journées Polèdres et Optimisation Combinatoire, 22-25 juin 2021.*

83. Hanafi, S., R. Mansi, and C. Wilbaut (2009). Iterative relaxation-based heuristics for the multiple-choice multidimensional knapsack problem. In M. J. Blesa, C. Blum, L. Di Gaspero, A. Roli, M. Sampels, and A. Schaerf (Eds.), *Hybrid Metaheuristics, HM 2009*, Volume 5818 of Lecture Notes in Computer Science, pp. 73–83. Berlin and Heidelberg: Springer.

84. Hanafi, S. and C. Wilbaut (2008). Scatter search for the 0-1 multidimensional knapsack problem. *Journal of Mathematical Modelling and Algorithms 7*(2), 143–159.

85. Hanafi, S. and C. Wilbaut (2011). Improved convergent heuristics for the 0-1 multidimensional knapsack problem. *Annals of Operations Research 183*(1), 125–142.

86. He, Y., X. Wang, and S. Gao (2019). Ring Theory-Based Evolutionary Algorithm and its application to D{0-1} KP. *Applied Soft Computing 77*, 714–722.

87. He, Y., X. Wang, W. Li, X. Zhang, and Y. Chen (2016). Research on genetic algorithm for discounted 0-1 knapsack problem. *Chinese Journal of Computers 39*(12), 2614–2630.

88. He, Y., H. Xie, T. L. Wong, and X. Wang (2018). A novel binary artificial bee colony algorithm for the set-union knapsack problem. *Future Generation Computer Systems 78*, 77–86.

89. He, Y.-C., X.-Z. Wang, Y.-L. He, S.-L. Zhao, and W.-B. Li (2016). Exact and approximate algorithms for discounted {0–1} knapsack problem. *Information Sciences 369*, 634–647.

90. Heinz, S., T. Schlechte, R. Stephan, and M. Winkler (2012). Solving steel mill slab design problems. *Constraints 17*(1), 39–50.

91. Hifi, M. and M. Michrafy (2006). A reactive local search-based algorithm for the disjunctively constrained knapsack problem. *Journal of the Operational Research Society 57*(6), 718–726.

92. Hifi, M. and M. Michrafy (2007). Reduction strategies and exact algorithms for the disjunctively constrained knapsack problem. *Computers & Operations research 34*(9), 2657–2673.

93. Hifi, M., M. Michrafy, and A. Sbihi (2004). Heuristic algorithms for the multiple-choice multidimensional knapsack problem. *Journal of the Operational Research Society 55*(12), 1323–1332.

94. Hifi, M. and N. Otmani (2012). An algorithm for the disjunctively constrained knapsack problem. *International Journal of Operational Research 13*(1), 22–42.

95. Hifi, M., S. Saleh, and L. Wu (2015). A hybrid guided neighborhood search for the disjunctively constrained knapsack problem. *Cogent Engineering 2*(1), 2–24.

96. Hojda, M. (2017). Task allocation for multi-robot teams in dynamic environments. In W. Mitkowski, J. Kacprzyk, K. Oprzedkiewicz, and P. Skruch (Eds.), *Trends in Advanced Intelligent Control, Optimization and Automation*, Volume 577 of Advances in Intelligent Systems and Computing, pp. 483–492. Cham: Springer.

97. Holte, R. C. (2001). Combinatorial auctions, knapsack problems, and hill-climbing search. In G. Goos, J. Hartmanis, J. van Leeuwen, E. Stroulia, and S. Matwin (Eds.), *Advances in Artificial Intelligence*, Volume 2056, pp. 57–66. Berlin and Heidelberg: Springer.

98. Hoto, R. (2001). *The compartmentalized knapsack problem applied to the steel roll cutting*. Ph.D. thesis, Rio de Janeiro Federal University, Brazil.

99. Hoto, R., M. N. Arenales, and N. Maculan (2007). The one-dimensional compartmentalised knapsack problem: A case study. *European Journal of Operational Research 183*(3), 1183–1195.

100. Hoto, R., N. Maculan, and A. Borssoi (2010). A study of the compartmentalized knapsack problem with additional restrictions. *IEE Latin America Transactions 8*(3), 269–274.

101. Hvattum, L. M., H. Arntzen, A. Løkketangen, and F. Glover (2010). Alternating control tree search for knapsack/covering problems. *Journal of Heuristics 16*, 239–258.

102. Hvattum, L. M. and A. Løkketangen (2007). Experiments using scatter search for the multidemand multidimensional knapsack problem. In K. F. Doerner, M. Gendreau, P. Greistorfer, W. Gutjahr, R. F. Hartl, and M. Reimann (Eds.), *Metaheuristics*, Volume 39 of *Operations Research/Computer Science Interfaces Series*, pp. 3–24. Boston, MA: Springer US.

103. Hwan, S. S. and A. W. Shogan (1989). Modelling and solving an FMS part selection problem. *International Journal of Production Research 27*(8), 1349–1366.

104. Inarejos, O. (2015). *On the non-linearity of the compartmentalized backpack problem*. Master thesis, Londrina State University, Londrina, Brazil.

105. Inarejos, O., R. Hoto, and N. Maculan (2019). An integer linear optimization model to the compartmentalized knapsack problem. *International Transactions in Operational Research 26*(5), 1698–1717.

106. Johnson, D. S. and K. Niemi (1983). On knapsacks, partitions, and a new dynamic programming technique for trees. *Mathematics of Operations Research 8*(1), 1–14.

107. Kalagnanam, J., A. Davenport, and H. Lee (2001). Computational aspects of clearing continuous call double auctions with assignment constraints and indivisible demand. *Electronic Commerce Research 1*, 221–238.

108. Kalagnanam, J., M. Dawande, M. Trumbo, and H. S. Lee (2000). The surplus inventory matching problem in the process industry. *Operations Research 48*(4), 505–516.

109. Kataoka, S. and T. Yamada (2014). Upper and lower bounding procedures for the multiple knapsack assignment problem. *European Journal of Operational Research 237*, 440–447.
110. Kellerer, H. (2008). An approximation algorithm for identical parallel machine scheduling with resource dependent processing times. *Operations Research Letters 36*, 157–159.
111. Kellerer, H., U. Pferschy, and D. Pisinger (2004). *Knapsack Problems*. Berlin and Heidelberg: Springer.
112. Kelly, T. (2006). Generalized knapsack solvers for multi-unit combinatorial auctions: Analysis and application to computational resource allocation. In P. Faratin and J. A. Rodríguez-Aguilar (Eds.), *Agent-Mediated Electronic Commerce VI. Theories for and Engineering of Distributed Mechanisms and Systems*, Volume 3435 of Lecture Notes in Computer Science pp. 73–86. Berlin and Heidelberg: Springer.
113. Khan, S., K. F. Li, and E. G. Manning (1997). The utility model for adaptive multimedia system. In *International Workshop on Multimedia Modeling*, pp. 111–126.
114. Khemakhem, M. and K. Chebil (2016). A tree search based combination heuristic for the knapsack problem with setup. *Computers & Industrial Engineering 99*, 280–286.
115. Khemakhem, M., B. Haddar, K. Chebil, and S. Hanafi (2012). A filter-and-fan metaheuristic for the 0-1 multidimensional knapsack problem. *International Journal of Applied Metaheuristic Computing 3*(4), 43–63.
116. Khuller, S., A. Moss, and J. Naro (1999). The budgeted maximum coverage problem. *Information Processing Letters 70*(1), 39–45.
117. Kochetov, Y. and A. Kondakov (2017). VNS matheuristic for a bin packing problem with a color constraint. *Electronic Notes in Discrete Mathematics 58*, 39–46.
118. Kolliopoulos, S. G. and G. Steiner (2007). Partially ordered knapsack and applications to scheduling. *Discrete Applied Mathematics 155*(8), 889–897.
119. Laabadi, S., M. Naimi, H. Amri, and B. Achchab (2018). The 0/1 multidimensional knapsack problem and its variants: A survey of practical models and heuristic approaches. *American Journal of Operations Research 8*(5), 395–439.
120. Laalaoui, Y. (2013). Improved swap heuristic for the multiple knapsack problem. In I. Rojas, G. Joya, and J. Gabestany (Eds.), *Advances in Computational Intelligence: 12th International Work-Conference on Artificial Neural Networks—IWANN 2013*, pp. 547–555. Heidelberg: Springer and Berlin.
121. Laalaoui, Y. and R. M'Hallah (2016). A binary multiple knapsack model for single machine scheduling with machine unavailability. *Computers & Operations Research 72*, 71–82.
122. Labbé, L., G. Laporte, and S. Martello (2003). Upper bounds and algorithms for the maximum cardinality bin packing problem. *European Journal of Operational Research 149*, 490–498.

123. Lai, X., J.-K. Hao, Z.-H. Fu, and D. Yue (2020). Diversity-preserving quantum particle swarm optimization for the multidimensional knapsack problem. *Expert Systems with Applications 149*, 113310.
124. Lai, X., J.-K. Hao, F. Glover, and Z. Lü (2018). A two-phase tabu-evolutionary algorithm for the 0-1 multidimensional knapsack problem. *Information Sciences 436–437*, 282–301.
125. Lai, X., J.-K. Hao, and D. Yue (2019). Two-stage solution-based tabu search for the multidemand multidimensional knapsack problem. *European Journal of Operational Research 274*, 35–48.
126. Lalami, M., M. Elkihel, D. El Baz, and V. Boyer (2012). A procedure-based heuristic for 0-1 multiple knapsack problems. *International Journal of Mathematics in Operational Research 4*(3), 214–224.
127. Leão, A. A. S., M. O. Santos, R. Hoto, and M. N. Arenales (2011). The constrained compartmentalized knapsack problem: Mathematical models and solution methods. *European Journal of Operational Research 212*, 455–463.
128. Letchford, A. N. and G. Souli (2020). Lifting the knapsack cover inequalities for the knapsack polytope. *Operations Research Letters 48*(5), 607–611.
129. Lorie, J. H. and L. J. Savage (1955). Three problems in rationing capital. *The Journal of Business 28*(4), 229–239.
130. Luo, K. and Q. Zhao (2019). A binary grey wolf optimizer for the multidimensional knapsack problem. *Applied Soft Computing 83*, 105645.
131. Mancini, S., M. Ciavotta, and C. Meloni (2021). The multiple multidimensional knapsack with family-split penalties. *European Journal of Operational Research 289*(3), 987–998.
132. Mansi, R., C. Alves, J. M. V. de Carvalho, and S. Hanafi (2013). A hybrid heuristic for the multiple choice multidimensional knapsack problem. *Engineering Optimization 45*(8), 983–1004.
133. Mansini, R. and M. G. Speranza (2002). A multidimensional knapsack model for asset-backed securitization. *Journal of the Operational Research Society 53*(8), 822–832.
134. Mansini, R. and M. G. Speranza (2012). CORAL: An exact algorithm for the multidimensional knapsack problem. *INFORMS Journal on Computing 24*(3), 399–415.
135. Mansini, R. and R. Zanotti (2020). A core-based exact algorithm for the multidimensional multiple choice knapsack problem. *INFORMS Journal on Computing 32*(4), 1061–1079.
136. Marchand, H. and L. A. Wolsey (1999). The 0-1 knapsack problem with a single continuous variable. *Mathematical Programming 85*(1), 15–33.
137. Markowitz, H. M. and A. S. Manne (1957). On the solution of discrete programming problems. *Econometrica 25*(1), 84–110.
138. Marques, F. P. and M. N. Arenales (2002). The compartmentalized knapsack problem and applications. *Pesquisa Operacional 22*(3), 285–304.
139. Martello, S. and M. Monaci (2020). Algorithmic approaches to the multiple knapsack assignment problem. *Omega 90*, 102004.

140. Martello, S. and P. Toth (1980). Solution of the zero-one multiple knapsack problem. *European Journal of Operational Research 4*, 276–283.

141. Martello, S. and P. Toth (1981a). A bound and bound algorithm for the zero-one multiple knapsack problem. *Discrete Applied Mathematics 3*, 275–288.

142. Martello, S. and P. Toth (1981b). Heuristic algorithms for the multiple knapsack problem. *Computing 27*(2), 93–112.

143. Martello, S. and P. Toth (1990). *Knapsack Problems: Algorithms and Computer Implementations*. Wiley-Interscience Series in Discrete Mathematics and Optimization. Chichester and New York: Wiley.

144. Martin, R. K. (1991). Using separation algorithms to generate mixed integer model reformulations. *Operations Research Letters 10*(3), 119–128.

145. Mathews, G. B. (1896, 11). On the partition of numbers. *Proceedings of the London Mathematical Society s1-28*(1), 486–490.

146. Mejia-Alvarez, P., E. V. Levner, and D. Mosse (2002). An integrated heuristic approach to power-aware real-time scheduling. In *International Workshop on Power Aware Computer Systems (PACS'02)*, Volume 2325 of Lecture Notes in Computer Science. Springer.

147. Michel, S., N. Perrot, and F. Vanderbeck (2009). Knapsack problems with setups. *European Journal of Operational Research 196*(3), 909–918.

148. Mohammadivojdan, R. and J. Geunes (2018). The newsvendor problem with capacitated suppliers and quantity discounts. *European Journal of Operational Research 271*, 109–119.

149. Navarra, A. and C. M. Pinotti (2017). Online knapsack of unknown capacity: How to optimize energy consumption in smartphones. *Theoretical Computer Science 697*, 98–109.

150. Nemhauser, G. L. and Z. Ullmann (1969). Discrete dynamic programming and capital allocation. *Management Science 15*(9), 494–505.

151. Ozsoydan, F. B. and A. Baykasoglu (2019). A swarm intelligence-based algorithm for the set-union knapsack problem. *Future Generation Computer Systems 93*, 560–569.

152. Park, K. and S. Park (1997). Lifting cover inequalities for the precedence-constrained knapsack problem. *Discrete Applied Mathematics 72*(3), 219–241.

153. Pferschy, U. and J. Schauer (2009). The knapsack problem with conflict graphs. *Journal of Graph Algorithms and Applications 13*(2), 233–249.

154. Pferschy, U., J. Schauer, and C. Thielen (2020). The product knapsack problem: Approximation and complexity.

155. Pisinger, D. (1995). A minimal algorithm for the multiple-choice knapsack problem. *European Journal of Operational Research 83*, 394–410.

156. Pisinger, D. (1999). An exact algorithm for large multiple knapsack problems. *European Journal of Operational Research 114*, 528–541.

157. Pisinger, D. (2001). Budgeting with bounded multiple-choice constraints. *European Journal of Operational Research 129*, 471–480.

158. Pop, P. C. (2009). A survey of different integer programming formulations of the generalized minimum spanning tree problem. *Carpathian Journal of Mathematics 25*(1), 104–118.

159. Puchinger, J., G. R. Raidl, and U. Pferschy (2010). The multidimensional knapsack problem: Structure and algorithms. *INFORMS Journal on Computing 22*(2), 250–265.

160. Quiroga-Orozco, J. J., J. M. V. de Carvalho, and R. S. V. Hoto (2019). A strong integer linear optimization model to the compartmentalized knapsack problem. *International Transactions in Operational Research 26*(5), 1633–1654.

161. Rogeau, A., R. Girard, Y. Abdelouadoud, M. Thorel, and G. Kariniotakis (2020). Joint optimization of building-envelope and heating-system retrofits at territory scale to enhance decision-aiding. *Applied Energy 264*, 114639.

162. Romero-Morales, D., E. Carrizosa, and E. Conde (1997). Semi-obnoxious location models: A global optimization approach. *European Journal of Operational Research 102*(2), 295–301.

163. Rong, A., J. R. Figueira, and K. Klamroth (2012). Dynamic programming based algorithms for the discounted 0-1 knapsack problem. *Applied Mathematics and Computation 218*(12), 6921–6933.

164. Salem, M. B., S. Hanafi, R. Taktak, and H. Ben-Abdallah (2017). Probabilistic tabu search with multiple neighborhoods for the disjunctively constrained knapsack problem. *RAIRO-Operations Research 51*(3), 627–637.

165. Salem, M. B., R. Taktak, A. R. Mahjoub, and H. Ben-Abdallah (2018). Optimization algorithms for the disjunctively constrained knapsack problem. *Soft Computing 22*(6), 2025–2043.

166. Salkin, H. M. and C. A. D. Kluyver (1975). The knapsack problem: A survey. *Naval Research Logistics Quarterly 22*(1), 127–144.

167. Samphaiboon, N. and Y. Yamada (2000). Heuristic and exact algorithms for the precedence-constrained knapsack problem. *Journal of optimization theory and applications 105*(3), 659–676.

168. Senisuka, A., B. You, and T. Yamada (2005). Reduction and exact algorithms for the disjunctively constrained knapsack problem. In *International Symposium on OR and Its Applications*, pp. 241–254.

169. Setzer, T. and S. M. Blanc (2020a). Corrigendum to "empirical orthogonal constraint generation for multidimensional 0/1 knapsack problems". *European Journal of Operational Research 286*(2), 791–795.

170. Setzer, T. and S. M. Blanc (2020b). Empirical orthogonal constraint generation for multidimensional 0/1 knapsack problems. *European Journal of Operational Research 282*(1), 58–70.

171. Shaw, D. X., G. Cho, and H. Chang (1997). A depth-first dynamic programming procedure for the extended tree knapsack problem in local access network design. *Telecommunication Systems 7*(1), 29–43.

172. Simon, J., A. Apte, and E. Regnier (2017). An application of the multiple knapsack problem: The self-sufficient marine. *European Journal of Operational Research 256*(3), 868–876.

173. Sinha, A. and A. Zoltners (1979). The multiple-choice knapsack problem. *Operations Research 27*, 503–515.

174. Stecke, K. E. and I. Kim (1988). A study of FMS part type selection approaches for short-term production planning. *International Journal of Flexible Manufacturing Systems 1*(1), 7–29.

175. Taylor, R. (2016). Approximations of the densest k-subhypergraph and set union knapsack problems.

176. Thesen, A. (1972). *Scheduling of computer programs in a multiprogramming environment*. Ph.D. thesis, University of Illinois at Urbana-Champaign.

177. Tillman, I. A., C. L. Hwang, and W. Kuo (1980). *Optimization of System Reliability*. New York: Marcel Dekker.

178. Tisch, M., H. Laudemann, A. Kreß, and J. Metternich (2017). Utility-based configuration of learning factories using a multidimensional, multiple-choice knapsack problem. In *Procedia Manufacturing*, Volume 9, pp. 25–32.

179. Tsesmetzis, D., I. Roussaki, and E. Sykas (2008). QoS-aware service evaluation and selection. *European Journal of Operational Research 191*, 1101–1112.

180. Tu, M. and L. Xiao (2016). System resilience enhancement through modularization for large scale cyber systems. In *2016 IEEE/CIC International Conference on Communications in China (ICCC Workshops)*, pp. 1–6.

181. Van Hentenryck, P. and L. Michel (2008). The steel mill slab design problem revisited. In *International Conference on Integration of Artificial Intelligence (AI) and Operations Research (OR) Techniques in Constraint Programming*, pp. 377–381.

182. Vasquez, M. and J.-K. Hao (2001). A "logic-constrained" knapsack formulation and a tabu algorithm for the daily photograph scheduling of an earth observation satellite. *Computational Optimization and Applications 20*(2), 137–157.

183. Voß, S. and E. Lalla-Ruiz (2016). A set partitioning reformulation for the multiple-choice multidimensional knapsack problem. *Engineering Optimization 48*(5), 832–850.

184. Wei, Z. and J. K. Hao (2019). Iterated two-phase local search for the set-union knapsack problem. *Future Generation Computer Systems 101*, 1005–1017.

185. Wei, Z. and J. K. Hao (2021a). Kernel based tabu search for the set-union knapsack problem. *Expert Systems with Applications 165*, 113802.

186. Wei, Z. and J. K. Hao (2021b). Multistart solution-based tabu search for the set-union knapsack problem. *Applied Soft Computing Journal 105*, 107260.

187. Wei, Z. and J. K. Hao (2021c). A threshold search based memetic algorithm for the disjunctively constrained knapsack problem.

188. Weingartner, H. M. (1966). Capital budgeting of interrelated projects: Survey and synthesis. *Management Science 12*(7), 485–516.

189. Wilbaut, C. and S. Hanafi (2009). New convergent heuristics for 0-1 mixed integer programming. *European Journal of Operational Research 195*(1), 62–74.

190. Wilbaut, C., S. Hanafi, and S. Salhi (2007). A survey of effective heuristics and their application to a variety of knapsack problems. *IMA Journal of Management Mathematics 19*(3), 227–244.

191. Wilbaut, C., S. Salhi, and S. Hanafi (2009). An iterative variable-based fixation heuristic for the 0-1 multidimensional knapsack problem. *European Journal of Operational Research 199*(2), 339–348.

192. Wilbaut, C., R. Todosijevic, S. Hanafi, and A. Fréville (2021). Heuristic and exact fixation-based approaches for the discounted 0-1 knapsack problem.

193. Wishon, C. and J. R. Villalobos (2016a). Alleviating food disparities with mobile retailers: Dissecting the problem from an OR perspective. *Computers & Industrial Engineering 91*, 154–164.

194. Wishon, C. and J. R. Villalobos (2016b). Robust efficiency measures for linear knapsack problem variants. *European Journal of Operational Research 254*, 398–409.

195. Wu, C., J. Zhao, Y. Feng, and M. Lee (2020). Solving discounted 0-1 knapsack problems by a discrete hybrid teaching-learning-based optimization algorithm. *Applied Intelligence 50*, 1872–1888.

196. Yamada, T., S. Kataoka, and K. Watanabe (2002). Heuristic and exact algorithms for the disjunctively constrained knapsack problem. *Information Processing Society of Japan Journal 43*(9), 2864–2870.

197. Yamada, T., K. Watanabe, and S. Kataoka (2005). Algorithms to solve the knapsack constrained maximum spanning tree problem. *International Journal of Computer Mathematics 82*(1), 23–34.

198. Yang, X., A. Vernitski, and L. Carrea (2016). An approximate dynamic programming approach for improving accuracy of lossy data compression by bloom filters. *European Journal of Operational Research 252*(3), 985–994.

199. Ykman-Couvreur, C., V. Nollet, F. Catthoor, and H. Corporaal (2016). Fast multi-dimension multi-choice knapsack heuristic for MP-SoC run-time management. *ACM Transactions on Embedded Computing Systems (TECS) 10*, 1–4.

200. Zhang, B. and Z. Hua (2012). Simple solution methods for separable mixed linear and quadratic knapsack problem. *Applied Mathematical Modelling 36*(7), 3245–3256.

201. Zhao, M., X. Gong, J. Liang, W. Wang, X. Que, Y. Guo, and S. Cheng (2017). QoE-driven optimization for cloud-assisted DASH-based scalable interactive multiview video streaming over wireless network. *Signal Processing: Image Communication 57*, 157–172.

202. Zhong, T. and R. Young (2010). Multiple choice knapsack problem: Example of planning choice in transportation. *Evaluation and Program Planning 33*, 128–137.

203. Zhu, H., Y. He, X. Wang, and E. C. C. Tsang (2017). Discrete differential evolutions for the discounted 0-1 knapsack problem. *International Journal of Bio-Inspired Computation 10*(4), 219–238.

5

Rank Aggregation: Models and Algorithms

Javier Alcaraz⬤, Mercedes Landete⬤, and Juan F. Monge⬤

5.1   Introduction

Nowadays, we live in an interconnected society where we constantly need to order elements to form a ranking in very different contexts: a ranking of the best universities, a ranking of the political parties that will participate in the next elections, a ranking of the companies with the highest turnovers last year or the ranking of university teachers who achieved the best student scores, to give just a few examples. In all the rankings, elements are ordered based on a given criterion or a set of them. Sometimes, we need to draw up a ranking that reflects, in the best possible way, the preferences of different users, preferences which are also expressed in particular rankings, which is known as rank aggregation. For example, to elaborate a ranking of the best companies in which to invest on the stock market, we have the rankings prepared

J. Alcaraz · M. Landete (✉) · J. F. Monge
Center of Operations Research, Miguel Hernández University of Elche, Elche (Alicante), Spain
e-mail: landete@umh.es

J. Alcaraz
e-mail: jalcaraz@umh.es

J. F. Monge
e-mail: monge@umh.es

© The Author(s), under exclusive license to Springer Nature
Switzerland AG 2022
S. Salhi and J. Boylan (eds.), *The Palgrave Handbook of Operations Research*,
https://doi.org/10.1007/978-3-030-96935-6_5

by different experts. Rankings are part of the ubiquitous information society aggregation and they are very common issues in current reports.

There are complete and partial rankings depending on the output information. In a complete ranking any pair of elements can be compared while in a partial ranking some pairs cannot. For example, in a partial ranking we can group and order the different companies by commercial sector and the companies belonging to the same group are considered tied or not comparable. In these types of problems, a group of elements is referred in the literature as a bucket or a cluster. The difference between a bucket and a cluster is the origin of the group. If these groups are previously formed and are known as an input of the problem, the group is referred to as a cluster. Otherwise, if the grouping of the elements is induced by the data and is an output of the problem, it is considered a bucket. Most times, the order of the elements is given by an order of the groups they belong to.

Sometimes, if the input data are cycle judgments, such as cyclic sequences, the output is called cycle ranking. Otherwise, the term "non-cycle rankings" can also be used.

The aggregation of the rankings has a crucial role in the decision-making process. Mathematically, the problem of the ranking aggregation is a combinatorial problem which looks for the best permutation of a set of elements assuming a certain criterion.

The common input for all the ranking aggregation problems is a preference matrix. A preference matrix is a squared matrix that measures value judgments. These value judgments are generally individual although sometimes they may differ between categories. Rank aggregation problems seek to unite the different judgments. Sometimes the preference matrix is not explicitly provided by the system and it must be carefully computed beforehand. Rankings are often represented as a permutation of the elements to be ordered. In this sense, the terms *ranking*, *rank ordering* and *permutation* are considered to be equivalent in the rank aggregation literature.

Most of the ranking problems can be classified into two different groups:

Ranking of elements: The input data is a preference matrix for a set of elements. Alternatively it can be a non-squared matrix of data from which the preference matrix can be computed. The goal is to provide the best ranking of the elements in the sense that it is the rank ordering that best fits with the matrix. If the matrix rows are seen as different rank orderings, the ranking of elements is a rank aggregation of the matrix row information.

Ranking of sets from a ranking of elements: The input can be a single ranking of elements or several ranking of elements or sometimes the preference matrix for the elements. Then, it might happen that the elements belong to different known clusters and the rank of the clusters is aimed. It might also happen that the elements can be grouped into different indistinguishable buckets and the goal is again the rank of these unknown buckets.

Other ranking problems could tackle the ranking of elements from several rankings of some of their subsets.

This chapter is organized as follows. In Sect. 5.2, four different ways of obtaining ranking of elements are revised, in particular the Linear Ordering Problem, the Rank Aggregation Problem in Cyclic sequences, the Target Visitation Problem and the Center Ranking Problem are studied. In Sect. 5.3, different problems of the second class defined above are presented, problems in which the aim is to get an order of sets in which different rankings of the elements are taken as inputs. In the Optimal Bucket Order Problem, the elements are grouped in different buckets as an output of the problem. In the Linear Ordering Problem with Clusters, elements have been previously grouped in clusters and the output of the problem is a ranking of these clusters. The Linear Ordering Problem of Sets looks for a ranking of subsets of a set from the ranking of the elements in that set. Finally, the Center Ranking Problem of Sets is a variant of the Linear Ordering Problem of Sets. In the last section, a small example is presented so that the different problems presented in this chapter can be easily compared.

5.2 Ranking of Elements

Let us suppose that $V = \{1, \ldots, n\}$ is the set of elements to rank. Given paired comparisons over elements in V, these comparisons can be saved in a square $n \times n$ matrix D, namely the preference matrix. The row i of D has the information for comparing i with the rest of elements in V. The value d_{ij} is a measure of the goodness of the statement "element i goes before element j". Given the preference matrix D, the goal of the rankings in this section is to obtain a complete ranking of all elements in V that best represent the data. If the preference matrix D represents non-cyclic judgments, the most popular way of obtaining a ranking is the well-known Linear Ordering Problem. Contrarily, if matrix D represents cyclic judgments, the ranking is the solution of the Rank Aggregation Problem in Cyclic sequences. Another approach when the judgments are cyclic is the Target Visitation Problem that combines the ranking aggregation and travelling salesman problem goals. If apart from the preference matrix D, the list of judgments which led to it is available, the center ranking problem can be considered.

Rankings are permutations of elements. Given σ_1 and σ_2 two permutations of the elements in V, the distance between both permutations can be measured as the number or pairwise disagreements between them, known as the Kendall-tau distance.

Definition 5.1 The Kendall-tau distance between two permutations σ_1 and σ_2 is given by:

$$K(\sigma_1, \sigma_2) = |\{(i, j) : i < j, ((\sigma_1(i) < \sigma_1(j) \wedge \sigma_2(i) > \sigma_2(j))$$
$$\vee (\sigma_1(i) > \sigma_1(j) \wedge \sigma_2(i) < \sigma_2(j)))\}|$$

where, $\sigma_1(i)$ and $\sigma_2(i)$ are the positions of the element i in σ_1 and σ_2, respectively.

The larger the Kendall-tau distance is, the more different the permutations are. For instance, if we had three elements, the distance to the permutation (1,2,3) from (1,3,2), (2,3,1) and (3,2,1) will be 1, 2 and 3, respectively. Frequently, the ranking problems make use of the Kendall-tau distance for the definition of the optimal ranking.

5.2.1 Linear Ordering Problem

The Linear Ordering Problem (LOP) states that the optimal ranking is the one which maximizes the distance of the path induced by the rank ordering. The input is the square matrix D and each element d_{ij} of this matrix can be seen as the *distance* from i to j. A rank of the elements in V entails a path of a certain distance and by D definition, the larger is the distance d_{ij}, the stronger is the consensus that "i must precede j". Thus, the goal is to find the path with the maximum distance. Since V has n elements, there are $n!$ ranks/paths with potential different distances.

The LOP was firstly proposed in [1] where a pioneer heuristic method was introduced. It was proved to be NP-hard in [2]. It has multiple and diverse applications in archaeology, economy, graph theory, automatic translation, mathematical psychology, scheduling with preferences or machine programming among others. The book [3] is an essential comprehensive textbook on the LOP since it surveys both exact methods and approximation algorithms. LOP continues to deserve authors' attention. We can see in [4] and [5] how two new efficient algorithms are developed.

The LOP can be solved as a triangulation problem. Given the matrix $D = (d_{ij})$, the goal is to determine the simultaneous permutation of the rows and columns for which the addition of all the elements above the diagonal is maximal. This triangulation problem is common for entrance/exit matrices in economic theory.

In order to illustrate the LOP and some other problems described later, we consider the following example.

Example 5.1 Five voters rank the elements in $V = \{a, b, c, d, e, f\}$. The rank for the first voter is (a, b, c, d, e, f), for the second (a, c, b, d, f, e), for the third (a, c, d, b, f, e), for the fourth (d, f, c, a, b, e) and for the fifth (c, f, e, d, b, a) (it corresponds with an instance in [6]). These preferences are represented in Table 5.1. The preference matrix D follows from these judgments, d_{ij} is the fraction of rankings in which i goes before j, for instance $d_{ab} = 4/5$ because 4 of the 5 voters say that a goes before b. Table 5.2 shows the input matrix D. The LOP solution is (a, c, d, b, f, e) and the optimal value is 11.2. If there were a consensus ranking to which everyone agrees, the optimal value would be 15: the sum of super-diagonal positions. Somehow, $74.6\% = (11.2/15) \times 100$ is the percentage at which the LOP solution maintains the voters' judgments.

There are different models for the LOP: binary linear, quadratically constrained quadratic program or integer quadratic program. In his paper, the one binary linear described in [3] is presented. For all $i, j \in V$, let z_{ij} be

Table 5.1 Candidate rankings: list of five total orders

Voter 1:	a	b	c	d	e	f
Voter 2:	a	c	b	d	f	e
Voter 3:	a	c	d	b	f	e
Voter 4:	d	f	c	a	b	e
Voter 5:	c	f	e	d	b	a

Table 5.2 D matrix for Example 5.1

	a	b	c	d	e	f
a		0.8	0.6	0.6	0.8	0.6
b	0.2		0.2	0.4	0.8	0.6
c	0.4	0.8		0.8	1.0	0.8
d	0.4	0.6	0.2		0.8	0.8
e	0.2	0.2	0.0	0.2		0.2
f	0.4	0.4	0.2	0.2	0.8	

the following binary variable

$$z_{ij} = \begin{cases} 1 & \text{if } i \text{ is ranked before } j \\ 0 & \text{otherwise} \end{cases}$$

The LOP can be modelled as the following linear problem:

$$\max \sum_{i \in V} \sum_{j \in V : j \neq i} d_{ij} z_{ij} \tag{5.1}$$

$$\text{s.t. } z_{ij} + z_{ji} = 1 \quad \forall i, j \in V : i < j \tag{5.2}$$

$$z_{ij} + z_{jk} + z_{ki} \leq 2 \quad \forall i, j, k \in V : i \neq j, j \neq k, i \neq k \tag{5.3}$$

$$z_{ij} \in \{0, 1\} \quad \forall i, j \in V : i \neq j \tag{5.4}$$

Effectively, the objective function (5.1) is the total distance of the path. The first family of constraints (5.2) states that either element i goes before element j or element j goes before element i. The second condition (5.3) rules out the existence of forbidden precedences; if i goes before j and j goes before k, then k cannot go before i. If $V = \{1, 2, 3, 4\}$, the ranks (4,3,2,1) and (2,4,3,1) will be associated to the solutions

$$z_{ij} = \begin{pmatrix} - & 0 & 0 & 0 \\ 1 & - & 0 & 0 \\ 1 & 1 & - & 0 \\ 1 & 1 & 1 & - \end{pmatrix} \text{ and } z_{ij} = \begin{pmatrix} - & 0 & 0 & 0 \\ 1 & - & 1 & 1 \\ 1 & 0 & - & 0 \\ 1 & 0 & 1 & - \end{pmatrix}.$$

respectively.

Despite the computational complexity of the LOP, it has been proved that any random permutation and its inverse provides a solution to the problem that is at least 50% of the optimal solution. In the particular case when the preference matrix has been randomly generated by a uniform distribution, all the permutations/solutions look similar; these results are presented in [7].

A particular problem arises when the preferences are 0 or 1. This problem is known in the literature as the minimum feedback arc set problem, i.e., the minimum number of arcs that must be removed to obtain an acyclic graph. In [8], a bound for the integrality gap of the minimum feedback arc set problem is given, this being 3/4. This result implies that the integrality gap of LOP converges to 4/3 if the preference matrix is in a certain normal form.

When the optimal permutation is the closest to a given set of permutations and the distances among permutations are measured with the Kendall-tau distance, the problem is called the Rank Aggregation Problem (RAP), also known as the Kemeny problem . If T is a set of rankings of elements, the RAP can be expressed as

$$(\text{RAP}) \quad \arg \min_{\rho} \sum_{t \in T} K(\rho, t).$$

The RAP is a classic problem in combinatorial optimization: some papers in the literature concentrate on giving good algorithms for solving it [9–14], some concentrate on giving properties of the solution [15, 16] while others compare different strategies for ranking [17, 18]. LOP and RAP are closely related and it can be shown that the RAP reduces to the LOP under a suitable transformation [19].

Example 5.2 (cont. Example 5.1) The LOP solution (a, c, d, b, f, e) can be alternatively obtained as the RAP solution, i.e., as the closest permutation to all the five permutations given in Table 5.1. The Kendall-tau distances of the LOP solution from each preference in Table 5.1 are 3, 1, 0, 6 and 9, therefore the optimal solution of the RAP is 19. Note that the optimal value of the LOP can be obtained as $v(LOP) = n(n-1)/2 - V(RAP)/|T| = 6 \cdot 5/2 - 19/5 = 11.2$.

5.2.2 Rank Aggregation Problem in Cyclic Sequences

The Rank Aggregation Problem in Cyclic sequences (RAPC) consists in finding the sequence that best represents a set of cyclic sequences. Cyclic rankings are required when the last element in ranking is once more that which precedes the first. The elements in the input matrix D keep representing the distance between elements, while a ranking of the elements in V represents a tour instead of a path. There are a lot of permutations of elements (rankings) representing the same tour. Again, the larger is the distance d_{ij}, the stronger is the consensus that "i must precede j" and the goal is to find the tour with the maximum distance.

The RAPC was first proposed in [19] where a binary linear model and some solution properties were introduced. It is an NP-hard problem and it has multiple applications. In the same way that scheduling with preferences is an application of the LOP, cyclic scheduling with preferences is an application of RAPC. The cyclic scheduling problem is the problem that appears when the set of tasks is to be repeated infinitely many times. A second application of this problem is the position of the slices in a pie chart when there is a matrix of preferences, even if any permutation represents the same fractions, only some of them respect the aggregation of preferences. The third application is to aggregate preferences in routing problems.

Cyclic orderings split the set of linear orderings into a set of equivalence classes. Each equivalence class is represented by a representative cyclic ranking. Let R be the set of representative cyclic rankings. The RAPC is the problem of finding the cyclic sequence closest to all cyclic sequences in R.

$$(RAPC) \quad \arg\min_{\rho} \sum_{r \in R} K(\rho, r).$$

Making use of the same binary variables z_{ij} in the LOP model, the RAPC can be modelled as follows:

$$\max \sum_{i \in V - \{1\}} \sum_{j \in V - \{1\}: j \neq i} (d_{ij} + d_{1i} + d_{j1}) z_{ij} \tag{5.5}$$

$$\text{s.t. } z_{ij} + z_{ji} = 1 \quad \forall i, j \in V : i < j \tag{5.6}$$

$$z_{ij} + z_{jk} + z_{ki} \leq 2 \quad \forall i, j, k \in V : i \neq j, j \neq k, i \neq k \tag{5.7}$$

$$z_{1i} = 1 \quad \forall i \in V - \{1\} \tag{5.8}$$

$$z_{ij} \in \{0, 1\} \quad \forall i, j \in V : i \neq j \tag{5.9}$$

The set of constraints is the same as the set of constraints in LOP but for the equalities $z_{1i} = 1$ for all $i \in V$, (5.8). So, in this model, and with loss of generality all the feasible cycle rankings start with 1. Any solution of the system (5.6), (5.7), (5.9) is a permutation of the elements in V: all the nodes are relatively sorted and transitivity holds. (5.8) forces node 1 to be the first node of any cyclic sequence. The feasible region of RAPC is a subset of the feasible region of LOP. It is given by the subset of rankings starting with 1. The objective function (5.5) is isomorphic to the distance of the tour while it is not the distance. The interested reader can read the mathematical calculations that transform the distance of the tour indicated by variables z_{ij} into the expression (5.5). Alternatively, the distance can be computed afterward from the optimal solution.

LOP and RAPC are equivalents in the sense that each instance of the LOP can be transformed to an instance of the RAPC adding an additional null row and null column to the matrix of distances, and each instance of the RAPC is by definition an instance of the LOP when the arc weight has been properly transformed.

5.2.3   Target Visitation Problem

The Target Visitation Problem (TVP) is a combination of the Travelling Salesman Problem and the LOP. As in the RAPC, the elements in the input matrix D represent the distance between elements and the permutations of elements (rankings) represent tours. Apart from matrix D, the TVP has another input $(n + 1) \times (n + 1)$ matrix that is the cost of travelling from i to j for all $i, j \in V$ plus the cost to a depot, namely the arc weight matrix C. D and C are both positive matrices. The TVP consists of finding a tour, i.e., a path that visits each vertex of V exactly once, starting and finishing at the same node, which best fits with matrix D. Nodes are called targets because the TVP was introduced for humanitarian purposes and the nodes were the target group. The profit of a tour depends on two weights, it is the sum of pairwise preferences between the targets corresponding to their visiting sequence minus the sum of costs travelled. It is the difference of the objective function of LOP and the objective function of the Travelling Salesman Problem. So, the TVP consists of finding a tour which maximizes the difference of the sum of the met preferences and the total travel cost.

The TVP was first proposed in [20] and [21] both theoretically wise. The paper [22] is the first exact approach. Recent works focusing on the TVP are [23, 24] and [25]. The last one proves some polyhedral properties and gives a branch and cut algorithm that manages to solve the problem efficiently.

The TVP has applications in environment assessment, combat search, rescue and disaster relief [20] and applications to the delivery of emergency supplies [27]. There is a twofold objective in all the applications: firstly, to minimize the total travelled cost and secondly, to respect a sequence. On the other hand, all the application fields for the TVP can be seen as application fields for RAPC.

Let $\bar{z}_{ij}$ be the opposite to z_{ij}, i.e., the binary variable which takes the value of one if i is ranked after j. Defining a new family of binary variables for recording the length of the tour,

$$x_{ij} = \begin{cases} 1 & \text{if the arc } (i, j) \text{ is used} \\ 0 & \text{otherwise} \end{cases} \quad \forall i, j \in V,$$

a mixed-integer linear formulation of the Target Visitation Problem is the following:

$$\max \sum_{i \in V} \sum_{j \in V: j \neq i} [(d_{ij} - d_{ji})\bar{z}_{ij} + d_{ij}] - \sum_{i \in V} \sum_{j \in V: j \neq i} c_{ij} x_{ij} \qquad (5.10)$$

$$\text{s.t.} \sum_{i \in V} \sum_{j \in V: j \neq i} c_{ij} x_{ij} = n - 1 \qquad (5.11)$$

$$\sum_{j \in V: j \neq i} x_{ij} \leq 1 \quad \forall i \in V \qquad (5.12)$$

$$\sum_{i \in V: i \neq j} x_{ij} \leq 1 \quad \forall j \in V \qquad (5.13)$$

$$x_{ij} - \bar{z}_{ij} \leq 0 \quad \forall i, j \in V : i \neq j \qquad (5.14)$$

$$0 \leq \bar{z}_{ij} + \bar{z}_{jk} - \bar{z}_{ik} \leq 1 \; \forall i, j, k \in V : i \neq j, j \neq k, i \neq k \qquad (5.15)$$

$$\bar{z}_{ij} \in \{0, 1\} \quad \forall i, j \in V : i \neq j \qquad (5.16)$$

$$x_{ij} \in \{0, 1\} \quad \forall i, j \in V : i \neq j \qquad (5.17)$$

The objective function (5.10) is equivalent to

$$\sum_{i \in V} \sum_{j \in V: j \neq i} d_{ij} z_{ij} - \sum_{i \in V} \sum_{j \in V: j \neq i} c_{ij} x_{ij}$$

when $\bar{z}_{ij}$ is substituted by $1 - z_{ji}$. Details can be consulted in [25]. Constraints (5.11), (5.12) and (5.13) model the tour. The subtour elimination constraints have been removed since that have been proven to be unnecessary in [25]. Inequalities (5.14) make sure that the two families of variables match up: if i is visited directly before j, the variable z_{ij} must be equal to 1. Constraints (5.15) are equivalent to constraints (5.3) and equalities (5.2) have been ruled out because of redundancy. The correctness of the model is shown in [25].

Recently, the Target Visitation Arc Routing problem has been introduced in [26]. This problem combines the undirected rural postman problem and the LOP, where pairwise preferences between the required edges are considered.

5.2.4 The Center Ranking Problem

The Center Ranking Problem (CRP) was introduced in [28]. The author shows that the CRP is NP-complete and illustrates the application of this new problem in the field of bioinformatics. The input for the CRP is not the preference matrix but the non-squared matrix of data from which the preference matrix is computed. The CRP consists on identifying the ranking of elements such that the maximum Kendall-tau distance to the rankings expressed by the rows of the non-squared matrix is the smallest.

Let T be the rows of this non-squared matrix, i.e., a set of rankings of elements, then the CRP can be expressed as

$$\arg\min_{\rho}\{\max_{\pi \in T} K(\rho, \pi)\} \tag{5.18}$$

The following example illustrates the solution the CRP is looking for.

Example 5.3 (cont. Example 5.1). There are six voters and the candidate rankings are proposed in Table 5.1. The solution of the LOP is (a, c, d, b, f, e) and the optimal value is 11.2. This ranking of candidates satisfies 74.6% of the preferences expressed by the voters and can be interpreted as a consensus among voters. However, the value of 74.6% is very unevenly distributed among the voters: the ranking (a, c, d, b, f, e) satisfies 80%, 93.3%, 100%, 60% and 40% of the preferences expressed for each voter. Conversely, ranking (c, a, d, f, e, b) satisfies 68% of the preferences expressed by the voters and 60%, 73.3%, 80%, 66.6% and 60% of the preferences expressed for each voter. Thus, the second ranking is a more robust solution. The CRP aims to find the most robust ranking.

Let T be the set of preferences expressed for a set of voters/agents. Let d_{ij}^{π} be a constant equal to one if element i is preferred to j for the agent/voter who has expressed the preference $\pi \in T$, and zero otherwise. The CRP can be modeled as the following linear problem:

$$\max \quad k$$

$$\text{s.t.} \quad k \leq \sum_{i \in V} \sum_{j \in V: j \neq i} d_{ij}^{\pi} z_{ij} \quad \forall \pi \in T$$

$$z_{ij} + z_{ji} = 1 \quad \forall i, j \in V : i < j$$

$$z_{ij} + z_{jt} + z_{ti} \leq 2 \quad \forall i, j, t \in V : i \neq j, j \neq t, i \neq t$$

$$z_{ij} \in \{0, 1\} \quad \forall i, j \in V : i \neq j.$$

Note that the minimization of the maximum in expression (5.18) is equivalent to the maximization of d in the above model. Analogously, the LOP was minimizing the Kendall-tau distance and maximizing the super-diagonal values of the preference matrix.

5.3   Ranking of Sets from a Ranking of Elements

The problems described in Sect. 5.2 obtain total orders, i.e., they do not leave any elements unordered. If only a partial ranking of the elements is desired, the solution would be a bucket or cluster order. In a bucket order, elements are grouped in different buckets, so that all the elements of the same bucket are assumed to be tied or incomparable and the order between two elements of different buckets is given by the relative ordering of the buckets they belong to. In a bucket order, the grouping of the elements is an output of the problem, i.e., they are induced by the data. On the other hand, in a cluster order, the clusters of elements are inherent to the data, that is, it is known a priori to the cluster each element belongs to. Now, the order of the elements is given by a permutation of the clusters, where an element representing each cluster need to be chosen and the belonging of an element to a cluster is not part of the solution but of the data.

In [29], the author introduces the concept of bucket in order to approximate the Rank Aggregation Problem with ties. Several works studied the Optimal Bucket Order Problem (OBOP) later [6, 12, 29, 30] and it has been used to discover serialization of information in very different contexts such as Ecology [31], Archeology [32] or Paleontology [33, 34] to cite just a few. When the elements are grouped in clusters and the aim is to choose a representative of each element and order these elements, giving a permutation of them we have the Linear Ordering Problem with Clusters (LOPC), introduced in [35], where the authors propose a linear formulation and a metaheuristic to solve it. This problem is also given in many different contexts, for example when scheduling tasks which are grouped in different types, so that only one task of each group needs to be scheduled.

In the following, the symbol "|" would represent a tie in the ranking. For instance, $(a, b|c, d, e|f|g)$ would represent the ranking in which a goes first, the second position is shared by b and c, b and c are tied, the third position is for d and the last in the ranking are e, f or g, the three being equivalent in terms of the ranking.

5.3.1 The Optimal Bucket Order Problem

In the Optimal Bucket Order Problem (OBOP), which was first introduced in [29] the solution is formed by a ranking of the elements in V, but in that ranking ties are permitted. The elements which are tied form a bucket. Therefore, the solution of the problem represents an ordered list of the buckets.

Example 5.4 Let us suppose that there are four voters and the candidate rankings proposed in Table 5.3. It is obvious that all the voters think that candidates 1 and 2 are better than candidates 3 and 4. However, there is no preference between 1 and 2, or between 3 and 4. In this case, ties between 1 and 2 and between 3 and 4 arise from the collective opinion and the most reasonable solution would be (1|2, 3|4). Two buckets are formed, which are inherent from the data. In other cases, the ties come from the individual opinion of the agents or voters. If none of the four previous voters would have expressed any preference between candidates 1 and 2, i.e., candidates 1 and 2 tie in all the individual preferences, why should this tie be broken in a solution ranking? In this case, candidates 1 and 2 form a bucket, which arises from the ties in the individual preferences.

Following [36] a bucket order is an ordered partition of V into k disjoint subsets (buckets): $V = B_1 \cup B_2 \cdots B_k$, where $1 \le k \le n$ and $B_r \cap B_s = \emptyset$ for all $r, s \in \{1, \ldots, k\}$ $r \ne s$. $\beta(i)$ represents the bucket to which element $i \in V$ belongs to. A bucket order has an associated square matrix $B = (b_{ij})$, such that $b_{ij} = 1$ if $\beta(i)$ is ordered before $\beta(j)$, $b_{ij} = 0$ if $\beta(j)$ is ordered before $\beta(i)$ and $b_{ij} = 0.5$ if i and j tie and therefore belong to the same

Table 5.3 Candidate rankings: list of four total orders

Voter 1:	a	b	c	d
Voter 2:	b	a	c	d
Voter 3:	a	b	d	c
Voter 4:	a	b	d	c

Table 5.4 D' matrix for Example 5.4

	a	b	c	d
a	0.5	0.75	1	1
b	0.25	0.5	1	1
c	0	0	0.5	0.5
d	0	0	0.5	0.5

bucket. Then, given a paired comparison matrix $D' = (d'_{ij})$, which is defined as $D = (d_{ij})$ as defined above, but setting the elements in the diagonal equal to 0.5, $d'_{ii} = 0.5$ for all $i \in \{1, \ldots, n\}$, as it is shown in Table 5.4, the bucket order problem consists in finding a bucket order for which the associated square matrix $B = (b_{ij})$ optimizes the function:

$$\min \sum_{i \in V} \sum_{j \in V} |b_{ij} - d'_{ij}| \qquad (5.19)$$

It is compulsory that the paired comparison matrix D' has all the values in $[0, 1]$, i.e., $d'_{ij} \in [0, 1]$. If $d_{ij} \notin [0, 1]$ for some i, j, matrix D has to be normalized before computing matrix D'.

Given that the problem is NP-complete [30], several approaches have been proposed in order to solve it or, at least, approximate quality solutions. In [6], the authors propose a method to discover bucket orders but only in the case when a set of full rankings is available. This limitation is avoided by the Bucket Pivot Algorithm (BPA) [30, 37] which is, nowadays, the most used method for solving the bucket order problem because it obtains quite good results [30, 37, 38]. However, in [36] the authors point out some drawbacks of BPA, mainly related to the random way in which this algorithm chooses the unique pivot, which decides the positions of the rest of the items in the bucket order. To overcome these weaknesses, the authors propose a new approach based on two points: to use more than one item as a pivot and not to choose these pivots randomly. This work presents a statistical analysis comparing the proposed method with BPA, which demonstrates that the proposal achieves an important increase in the accuracy of the solutions and a significant decrease of the output variance. Later, in [39] an evolutionary metaheuristic to solve the OBOP is designed and compared with current state-of-the-art algorithms, improving the accuracy of the solutions by more than 10%.

5.3.2 The Linear Ordering Problem with Clusters

In this problem, the set V is partitioned into h disjoint subsets (clusters): $V = V_1 \cup V_2 \cdots V_h$ and $V_r \cap V_s = \emptyset$ for all $r, s \in \{1, \ldots, h\}$ $r \neq s$. H is the set of subsets, $H = \{1, \ldots, h\}$. The objective is to choose only one representative of each cluster in order to find the best linear order of them.

In order to formulate a model for the Linear Ordering Problem with Clusters (LOPC), the following families of binary variables are defined: for all $i \in V$, variable y_i takes the value of one, if and only if index i is the element chosen from its cluster as representative; for all $i, j \in V$ belonging to different clusters, z_{ij} takes the value of one if and only if indexes i and j are representative of their clusters and the cluster to which i belongs goes before the cluster to which j belongs.

The linear integer formulation of LOPC is presented in [35] as follows:

$$\max \quad \sum_{r,s \in H : r \neq s} \sum_{\substack{i \in V_r \\ j \in V_s}} c_{ij} z_{ij} \tag{5.20}$$

$$\text{s.t.} \quad \sum_{\substack{k \in V_t \\ j \in V_s}} z_{kj} - \sum_{\substack{i \in V_r \\ j \in V_s}} z_{ij}$$

$$- \sum_{\substack{k \in V_t \\ i \in V_r}} z_{ki} \leq 0 \quad r, s, t \in H : \text{ pairwise disjoint} \tag{5.21}$$

$$\sum_{j \in V_r} (z_{ij} + z_{ji}) - y_i = 0 \qquad r \in H, i \notin V_r \tag{5.22}$$

$$\sum_{i \in V_r} y_i = 1 \qquad r \in H \tag{5.23}$$

$$z_{ij} \in \{0, 1\} \qquad i \in V_r, j \in V_s, r \neq s \tag{5.24}$$

$$y_i \in \{0, 1\} \qquad i \in V \tag{5.25}$$

In the previous model, the objective function is to maximize the weighted sum of the z-variables. (5.21) ensure transitivity in the order of clusters. Constraints (5.22) state that given i is the representative of a cluster, for any different cluster V_r, we can find a representative which will be ordered before or after element i. Constraints (5.23) determine that each cluster has only one representative. Any solution satisfying all the constraints induces a permutation of m elements in V, which are representative of the clusters and thus a permutation of the same.

Example 5.5 (cont. Example 5.1). Following with the example given before, let us now suppose that voters are grouped in three different clusters. Let $V_1 = \{a, b\}$, $V_2 = \{c, d\}$ and $V_3 = \{e, f\}$. The optimal solution for the

Table 5.5 Voter preferences on selected candidates

Voter 1:	b	c	e
Voter 2:	c	b	e
Voter 3:	c	b	e
Voter 4:	c	b	e
Voter 5:	c	e	b

LOPC is $(c, b, e) \equiv (\mathbf{c}|d, a|\mathbf{b}, \mathbf{e}|f)$ and the optimal value is 2.6. If the preferences of non-selected candidates are removed, the list of preferences would be the list in Table 5.5 and a consensus permutation with zero disagreement would give an objective value of 3. Then, the optimal solution (c, b, e) guarantees $86.6\%((2.6/3) \times 100)$ of voter preferences.

Besides, the LOP solution does not lead to the LOPC solution. The LOP solution is (a, c, d, b, f, e), then the first three elements of different clusters are $(a, c, f) \equiv (\mathbf{a}|b, \mathbf{c}|d, e|\mathbf{f})$, which is not the LOPC solution. In fact, the objective value for the solution (a, c, f) in the LOPC is 2, which only guarantees the $66.6\%((2/3) \times 100)$ of voter preferences.

The LOP can be seen as a particular case of LOPC when all the clusters have only one element. Therefore, the LOPC is also NP-hard. In this sense, in [35] authors state that LOPC is more difficult than LOP because the relaxation of the transitivity constraint in the LOPC does not provide a integer solution unlike the LOP.

The computational study provided in [35] shows some insights of how the complexity of the problem increases in line with the number of clusters. When the same number of elements are split into more clusters, the computation time needed to solve the problem increases. This makes it difficult to solve medium or large-sized instances through the binary linear model presented above in reasonable computation times. Therefore, the authors also propose a metaheuristic which is compared to the exact approach. This algorithm outperforms the model in terms of computational time. The metaheuristic proposed is a hybrid scatter search which employs genetic operators designed to exploit the problem-specific knowledge in an efficient way. As far as we know, this is the only metaheuristic proposed to solve the problem.

5.3.3   The Linear Ordering Problem of Sets

The problem of determining a ranking of subsets from a ranking of the elements of the set, namely Linear Ordering Problem of Sets (LOPS) or Kendall-τ partition ranking, was introduced in [8]. In the same paper, the authors apply the LOPS for ranking the OECD countries from the ranking of schools obtained from the Programme for International Student Assessment (PISA). Let π be a ranking of the elements of V and let $V_1, V_2,..., V_h$ be a partition of $V = \cup_{r=1}^{h} V_r$ with $V_r = \{1, \ldots, n_r\}$ for all $r \in \{1, \ldots, h\}$. The ranking of the subsets in the partition ρ is defined as the ranking of elements π_ρ such that elements in V_r for all r are consecutively listed and the Kendall-tau distance $K(\pi, \pi_\rho)$ is minimized, i.e., the number of pairwise disagreements from π is minimized. If m_{rs}^π is the number of times that an element of subset V_r is ranked before an element of subset V_s in π, then the solution of LOPS is the solution of the LOP for matrix $M^\pi = m_{rs}^\pi$.

Example 5.6 (cont. Example 5.1). Following with the example given before, let us now suppose that the candidates are listed in ranking $\pi = (a, c, d, b, f, e)$. Candidates are grouped into three different political parties, let $V_1 = \{a, b\}$, $V_2 = \{c, d\}$ and $V_3 = \{e, f\}$. The LOPS provides a linear order of the political parties $\rho = (V_1, V_2, V3)$, where ρ is the solution of the LOP for matrix:

$$M^\pi = \begin{pmatrix} - & 2 & 4 \\ 2 & - & 4 \\ 0 & 0 & - \end{pmatrix}$$

Note that $\rho = (V_2, V_1, V3)$ is also an optimal solution for this problem.

The authors in [8] present the properties of the LOPS and compare it with classical mean and median-based rank approaches. These properties are extracted from social choice theory and are adapted to a partition ranking, see [40, 41]. Two of these properties are only true for the LOPS: the Condorcet and Deletion Independence properties. The Condorcet property establishes that the most preferred subset must be listed before any other in any ranking; and the Deletion Independence property establishes that if any subset is removed, then the induced order of subsets does not change.

The problem in obtaining a ranking of sets from a ranking of elements is an easier problem than the LOP because the preference matrix already comes from a linear order of elements. The authors in [8] establish that the integrality gap of the LOPS converges to 8/7, when the preference matrix is done in normal form, i.e., $m_{rs}^\pi + m_{sr}^\pi = 1$ for all $r \neq s$.

The distance $K(\pi, \pi_\rho)$ between the ranking of sets from the ranking of elements can be normalized by the maximum number of disagreements that may occur between them, i.e., the maximum disorder for a permutation of elements. This distance, which is the number of pairwise disagreements needed in a permutation of elements to reach a permutation that establishes a total order between treatments, is denominated by the disorder of a permutation by the authors of the work [8], and allows to define the relative disorder of a permutation of elements as:

$$relative\ disorder\ of\ \pi = \frac{K(\pi, \pi_\rho)}{\sum_{r<s} n_r n_s - (GB_o + \sum_{r<s} \frac{n_r n_s}{2})}$$

where GB_o is the pentagonal number and o the number of sets with odd cardinality.

In [42], the authors use the relative disorder of a permutation to define the *Concordance Coefficient* which is that used to measure the ordinal association between quantity and quality measures when two or more samples are considered. The authors propose this new measure as an alternative to the non-parametric mean rank-based methods for comparing two or more samples, and compare it with the classical Kruskal-Wallis method. An R-package to solve this problem is presented in [43]. Additionally, the R-package provides routines for solving the LOP problem; it calculates the Kendal-tau distance between two permutations and the relative disorder of a permutation of elements.

5.3.4   The Center Ranking Problem of Sets

An extension to the LOPS, when different linear orders of elements are available, is the problem of determining the best ranking of sets close to the linear orders of elements. The next example illustrates two ways to aggregate these linear orders of elements; the LOP and the center ranking problem of sets (CRPS).

Example 5.7 Let $\pi^1 = (a, b, c, b)$, $\pi^2 = (b, b, c, a)$ and $\pi^3 = (b, c, a, b)$ be three ranking of elements in $V = A \cup B \cup C : A = \{a\}$, $B = \{b, b\}$ y $C = \{c\}$. Each ranking establishes a preference matrix of the subsets A, B and C.

$$M^{\pi_1} = \begin{pmatrix} - & 2 & 1 \\ 0 & - & 1 \\ 0 & 1 & - \end{pmatrix} \quad M^{\pi_2} = \begin{pmatrix} - & 0 & 0 \\ 2 & - & 2 \\ 1 & 0 & - \end{pmatrix} \quad M^{\pi_2} = \begin{pmatrix} - & 1 & 0 \\ 1 & - & 1 \\ 1 & 1 & - \end{pmatrix}$$

The optimal solution of LOP for $M = M^{\pi_1} + M^{\pi_2} + M^{\pi_3}$ is the ranking ρ such that the elements of A, B and C are listed consecutively and the number of pairwise disagreements from π^1, π^2 and π^3 is minimized. $M^{(\pi_1,\pi_2,\pi_3)} =$

$$M^{\pi_1} + M^{\pi_2} + M^{\pi_3} = \begin{pmatrix} - & 3 & 1 \\ 3 & - & 4 \\ 2 & 2 & - \end{pmatrix}$$

The optimal solution of the Linear Ordering Problem (LOP) for $M^{(\pi_1,\pi_2,\pi_3)}$ is the permutation $\rho = (B, C, A)$ with a objective value of 9. Therefore, permutation ρ needs 6 disagreements from π^1, π^2, y π^3, i.e., 15-9=6. Distances of ρ from π_1, π_2 and π_3 are $K(\pi^1, \rho) = 4$, $K(\pi^2, \rho) = 0$, and $K(\pi^1, \rho) = 2$,, respectively.

Notice that ρ, which is the optimal solution of the LOP, provides an unbalanced optimal solution, i.e., ρ presents 4 disagreements from π_1 while it is the optimal solution for π_1 but in reverse order.

Conversely, ranking $\rho^* = (A, B, C)$ needs 1,3 and 3 disagreements from π^1, π^2, y π^3, therefore ranking ρ is a more robust solution of our problem than the classical mean solution.

Ranking $\rho^* = (A, B, C)$ is the optimal solution for center ranking problem of sets (CRPS).

Let T be a set of ranking of elements. The CRPS can be modeled as the following linear problem:

$$\max \quad k$$

$$\text{s.t.} \quad k \le \sum_{r \in M^\pi} \sum_{s \in M^\pi : j \ne i} m_{rs}^\pi z_{rs} \quad \forall \pi \in T \tag{5.27}$$

$$\text{s.t.} \ z_{rs} + z_{sr} = 1 \quad \forall r, s \in H : r < s \tag{5.28}$$

$$z_{rs} + z_{st} + z_{tr} \le 2 \quad \forall r, s, t \in H : r \ne s, s \ne t, t \ne r \tag{5.29}$$

$$z_{rs} \in \{0, 1\} \quad \forall r, s \in H : r \ne s \tag{5.30}$$

5.4 Feasible Regions Similarities and Differences Through a Small Example

In this section, the feasible region of the seven different presented models is illustrated with a small example. It helps to go deep into the scope and the applications of the models.

Let D be the following 3×3 preference matrix:

$$D = \begin{pmatrix} - & 0 & 2 \\ 4 & - & 1 \\ 1 & 3 & - \end{pmatrix}$$

If D represents the number of times that player i has beaten player j, the LOP looks for the ranking of the players. Three players participate in a tournament. Player 1 has played 7 games, he has beaten player 3 twice and he has lost four times against player 2 and once against player 3. Moreover, player 2 has played 4 games with player 3 and he has won only one of these. The LOP looks for the ranking of the players that best fits with this situation.

If D represents the number of orders in which task i must be executed before task j every day, the RAPC looks for the sequential ranking of tasks. Each week a certain number of orders is received, in none of them task 1 precedes task 2, in two of them task 1 precedes task 3 and so on. The RAPC looks for the best ranking of tasks from this data and on the premise that when the last task is finished the first one will start again.

If D represents the benefit of serving target i before target j and a 4×4 cost matrix C is known, the TVP looks for the route/ranking that best balances preferences and distances. The first row and column of the cost matrix corresponds with the depot, let us say 0. W.l.o.g. Let us suppose $c_{0i} = c_{i0} = c_{ii} = 0$ for all $i \in \{1, 2, 3\}$, $c_{32} = c_{21} = 2$ and $c_{ij} = 0.5$ otherwise.

Table 5.6 shows the feasible solutions, with its values, for the LOP, RAPC and TVP (all of them for obtaining a ranking of elements). Columns LOP, RAPC and TVP give the set of all the feasible solutions and v(LOP), v(RAPC) and v(TVP) the associated objective values. All the feasible solutions for the LOP are all the permutations of the three players. The first value in column v(LOP) indicates that 1 goes before 2, 1 also goes before 3 and 2 goes before 3, $d_{12} + d_{13} + d_{23} = 0 + 2 + 1 = 3$, the rest of values are computed

Table 5.6 Solutions and values for three ranking of elements: LOP, RAPC and TVP

LOP	v(LOP)	RAPC	v(RAPC)	TVP	v(TVP)
(1, 2, 3)	3	(1, 2, 3)	10	(0, 1, 2, 3, 0)	1.5
(1, 3, 2)	5	(1, 3, 2)	20	(0, 1, 3, 2, 0)	2
(2, 1, 3)	7			(0, 2, 1, 3, 0)	4
(2, 3, 1)	3			(0, 2, 3, 1, 0)	1.5
(3, 1, 2)	4			(0, 3, 1, 2, 0)	2.5
(3, 2, 1)	8			(0, 3, 2, 1, 0)	3.5

analogously. All the feasible solutions for RAPC are the two representatives of the two equivalence classes. The first value in column v(RAPC) is the addition of the values in column v(LOP) for the elements of the equivalence class with representative (1,2,3), i.e., 3+3+4=10. All the feasible solutions for the TVP are all the possible routes starting from and arriving to the depot and visiting all the three players. The first value in column v(TVP) is $d_{12} + d_{13} + d_{23} - c_{01} - c_{12} - c_{23} - c_{30} = 1.5$, that is the value that represents that 1 goes before 2, 1 also goes before 3 and 2 goes before 3 and the route goes from 0 to 1, from 1 to 2, from 2 to 3 and from 3 to 0. The optimal solution for each problem is in bold. In this small example, the optimal value for RAPC is the representative for the class to which the optimal value of LOP belongs, however it does not hold in general.

Let us suppose again that D represents the number of times that player i has beaten player j but that the goal is to split the players into two teams (buckets) and rank the buckets, then the OBOP looks for the best solution.

If it is known that players 1 and 2 belong to the same team A and that player 3 belongs to a second team B, LOPC looks for a good representative of each team and a good ranking of the selected representatives.

Table 5.7 shows the feasible solutions, with its values, for the OBOP and LOPC (both for obtaining ranking of sets). All the feasible solutions for the OBOP are all the permutations of two non-overlapped sets, one with one player and another with two players. For the values in column v(OBOP), the B matrices are the following:

$$B^1 = \begin{pmatrix} 0.5 & 1 & 1 \\ 0 & 0.5 & 0.5 \\ 0 & 0.5 & 0.5 \end{pmatrix}, B^2 = \begin{pmatrix} 0.5 & 0 & 0.5 \\ 1 & 0.5 & 1 \\ 0.5 & 0 & 0.5 \end{pmatrix}, B^3 = \begin{pmatrix} 0.5 & 0.5 & 0 \\ 0.5 & 0.5 & 0 \\ 1 & 1 & 0.5 \end{pmatrix},$$

$$B^4 = \begin{pmatrix} 0.5 & 0 & 0 \\ 1 & 0.5 & 0.5 \\ 1 & 0.5 & 0.5 \end{pmatrix}, B^5 = \begin{pmatrix} 0.5 & 1 & 0.5 \\ 0 & 0.5 & 0 \\ 0.5 & 1 & 0.5 \end{pmatrix}, B^6 = \begin{pmatrix} 0.5 & 0.5 & 1 \\ 0.5 & 0.5 & 1 \\ 0 & 0 & 0.5 \end{pmatrix}.$$

Moreover, matrix D' can be obtained from D filling the diagonal with the value 0.5 and projecting the values in [0, 1] by performing $d'_{ij} = d_{ij}/(d_{ij} + d_{ji})$, i,e,

$$D' = \begin{pmatrix} 0.5 & 0 & 0.67 \\ 1 & 0.5 & 0.25 \\ 0.33 & 0.75 & 0.5 \end{pmatrix}.$$

The first value in the column v(OBOP) is $\sum_{i=1}^{3} \sum_{j=1}^{3} |b^1_{ij} - d'_{ij}| = 3.16$.

All the feasible solutions for the LOPC are all the permutations for one representative of each team. The first value in column v(LOPC) is $d_{13} = 2$. The optimal solution for each problem is in bold. In this small instance there are two optimal solutions for the OBOP, data support that player 2 goes before player 1 but player 3 can belong to player 2's team or to player 1's team. It is not common that data cannot discriminate between different solutions but, as this example illustrates, it might happen.

CRP, LOPS and CLOPS cannot be illustrated by using matrix D since all of them require different inputs and do not make use of D.

CRP requires a preference list. Let's consider that three players hold the positions in Table 5.8 in six different and equally prestigious tournaments.

All the feasible solutions for the CRP are all the permutations of the three players, see Table 5.9. The value in column v(CRP) is the minimum between the distance of the solution/ranking and each of the rankings in each tournament; these distances are reported in the last column of the table.

LOPS requires a ranking of elements and the affiliation of the elements to the clusters. Let's consider that it is known that there are still three players, the best is player 3, the second is player 2 and the third is player 1 and that players 1 and 2 belong to the same team A and that player 3 belongs to a second team B. Thus, the input is $\pi = (3, 2, 1) \equiv (B, A, A)$. All the feasible solutions for the LOPS are all the permutations of two consecutive A and one consecutive B, see Table 5.10. Values in column v(LOPS) are the LOP values

Table 5.7 Solutions and values for two ranking of sets: OBOP and LOPC

OBOP	v(OBOP)	LOPC	v(LOPC)
(1, 2|3)	3.16	(1, 3)	2
(**2**, **1**|3)	1.84	(2, 3)	1
(3, 1|2)	2.84	(3, 1)	1
(**2**|**3**, **1**)	1.84	(**3**, **2**)	3
(1|3, 2)	2.84		
(1|2, 3)	3.16		

Table 5.8 Player rankings in the four tournaments

	Winner	Second	Third
Tournament 1:	1	2	3
Tournament 2:	1	3	2
Tournament 3:	1	3	2
Tournament 4:	2	1	3
Tournament 5:	2	3	1
Tournament 6:	3	1	2

Table 5.9 Solutions and values for CRP

CRP	v(CRP)	distance from the 6 tournaments
(1, 2, 3)	2	=max{0, 1, 1, 1, 2, 2}
(1, 3, 2)	3	=max{1, 0, 0, 2, 3, 2}
(2, 1, 3)	3	=max{1, 2, 2, 0, 1, 3}
(2, 3, 1)	3	=max{2, 3, 3, 1, 0, 2}
(3, 1, 2)	3	=max{2, 1, 1, 3, 2, 0}
(3, 2, 1)	3	=max{3, 2, 2, 2, 1, 1}

for matrix

$$M^{\pi} = \begin{pmatrix} - & 0 \\ 2 & - \end{pmatrix}$$

($m_{AB}^{\pi} = 0$ is the number of times that an element of subset $V_A = \{1, 2\}$ is ranked before an element of subset $V_B = \{3\}$ in π). Alternatively, the optimal solution for LOPS is the one with the smallest Kendall-tau distance to the input.

CRPS requires several rankings of elements and the affiliation of the elements to the clusters. Let's consider the rankings in Table 5.8 and that player 3 is still in a cluster and players 1 and 2 in another. All the feasible solutions for the LOPS are all the permutations of two consecutive A and one consecutive B, see Table 5.10. Values in column v(CRPS) are the maximum of the distances to the rankings in Table 5.8. It is not common that data cannot discriminate between different solutions but, as this example illustrates, it might happen.

Acknowledgements The authors thank the grant PID2019-105952GB-I00 funded by Ministerio de Ciencia e Innovación/Agencia Estatal de Investigación /10.13039/501100011033. This work was partially also supported by the Generalitat Valenciana under grant PROMETEO/2021/063.

Table 5.10 Solutions and values for two ranking of sets: LOPS and CLOPS

LOPS	v(LOPS)	CLOPS	v(CLOPS)
(A, A, B)	0	(A, A, B)	2 =max{0, 1, 1, 0, 1, 2}
(B, A, A)	2	(B, A, A)	2 =max{2, 1, 1, 2, 1, 0}

References

1. Chenery, H.B. and Watanabe,T.: International comparisons of the structure of production. Econometrica **26**, 487–521 (1958)
2. Garey, M.R. and Johnson, D.S.: Computers and intractability: A guide to the theory of NP-completeness. W. H. FREEMAN AND COMPANY, New York (1979)
3. Martí, R. and Reinelt, G.: The lineal ordering problem. Exact and heuristic methods in combinational optimization. Springer. (2011)
4. Ceberio, J., Mendiburu, A. and Lozano, J.A.: The linear ordering problem revisited. European Journal of Operational Research **241**, 686–696 (2015)
5. Qian, Y., Lin, J., Li, D. and Hu, H.: Block-insertion-based algorithms for the linear ordering problem. Computers & Operations Research **115**, 1048–61 (2020)
6. Feng, J., Fang, Q. and Ng, W.: Discovering Bucket Orders from full Rankings. Proceedings of the 2008 ACM SIGMOD international conference on Management of data, 55–66 (2008).
7. Boussaïd, I., Lepagnot, J. and Siarry, P.: A survey on optimization metaheuristics. Information Sciences **237**, 82-117 (2013)
8. Aparicio, J., Landete, M. and Monge, J.F.: A linear ordering problem of sets. Annals of Operations Research. **288**, 45–64 (2020)
9. Aledo, J.A., Gàmez, J.A. and Molina, D.: Tackling the rank aggregation problem with evolutionay algorithms. Applied Mathematics and Computation. **222**, 632–644. (2013).
10. Andoni, A., Fagin, R., Kumar, R., Patrascu, M. and Sivakumar, D.: Efficient similarity search and classification via rank aggregation. In Proceedings of the ACM SIG-MOD International Conference on Management of Data, 1375–1376 (2008)
11. Dwork, C., Kumar, R., Naor, M. and Sivakumar, D.: Rank aggregation methods for the web. In Proceedings of the Tenth International World Wide Web Conference(WWW'01), 613–622 (2001)
12. Fagin, R., Kumar, R. and Sivakumar, D.: Eficient similarity search and classification via rank aggregation. In Proceedings of the ACM SIGMOD International Conference on Management of Data, 301–312 (2003)
13. Schalekamp, F. and Zuylen, A.V.: Rank aggregation: Together we're strong. ALENEX 38–51 (2009)
14. Yasutake, S., Hatano, K., Takimoto, E. and Takeda, M: Online Rank Aggregation. JMLR: Workshop and Conference proceedings, Asian Conference on Machine Learning **25**, 539–553 (2012)
15. Betzler, N., Brederec, R. and Niedermeier, R.: Theoretical and empirical evaluation of data reduction for exact kemeny rank aggregation. Autonomous Agents and Multi-Agent Systems **28**, 721–748 (2014)

16. Conitzer, V., A. Davenport, A. and Kalagnanam, J.: Improved bounds for computing kemeny rankings. In: proceedings of the 21st national conference on Artificial intelligence, 620–626 (2006)
17. Ali, A. and Meilă, M.: Experiments with Kemeny ranking: What works when?. Mathematical Social Sciences **64**, 28–40 (2012)
18. Gattaca, L.: An Analysis of Rank Aggregation Algorithms. *Data Structures and Algorithms* (2014) arXiv:1402.5259v5.
19. García-Nové, E.M., Alcaraz, J., Landete, M., Puerto, J. and Monge, J.F. Rank aggregation in cyclic sequences. Optimization Letters **11**, 667–678 (2017)
20. Grundel, D.A. and Jeffcoat, D.E.: Formulation and solution of the target visitation problem. Proceedings of the AIAA 1st Intelligent systems technical conferences (2004)
21. Arulselvan, A., Commander, C.W. and Pardalos, P.M.: A hybrid genetic algorithm for the target visitation problem. Naval Research Logistics 1-20 (2007)
22. Lörwald, S.: Exact solving methods for the target visitation problem, *Diploma thesis* (2014)
23. Hildenbrandt, A.: The Target Visitation Problem. PhD (2015) http://www.ub.uni-heidelberg.de/archiv/17993
24. Hildenbrandt, A. and Reinelt, G.: Inter Programming Models for the Target Visitation Problem. Informatica **39** 257–260 (2015)
25. Hildenbrandt, A.: A branch-and-cut algorithm for the target visitation problem. EURO J Comput Optim **7**, 209–242 (2019)
26. Rodríguez-Pereira, J., Laporte, G. The target visitation arc routing problem. TOP (2021). https://doi.org/10.1007/s11750-021-00601-5
27. Claiborne Price, C.: Applications of Operations Research models to problems in Health Care. University of Maryland (2009)
28. Popov, V.Y.: Multiple genome rearrangement by swaps and by element duplications. Theoretical Computer Science, **385**, 115–126 (2007)
29. Fagin, R., Kumar, R., Mahdian, M., Sivakumar, D. and Vee, E: Comparing and aggregating rankings with ties. In Proceedings of the ACM Symposium on Principles of Database Systems(PODS), 47–58, (2004)
30. Gionis, A. Mannila, H., Puolamaki, K. and Ukkonen, A.: Algorithms for Discovering Bucket Orders from Data. Proceedings of the 12th ACM SIGKDD International Conference on Knowledge Discovery and Data Mining, 561–566 (2006)
31. Miklos, I., Somodi, I. and Podani, J.: Rearrangement of ecological matrices via markov chain monte carlo simulation. Ecology, **86**, 3398–3410 (2005)
32. Halekoh, U. and Vach, W.: A bayesian approach to seriation problems in archeology. Computational Statistics and Data Analysis **45**, 651–673 (2004)
33. Fortelius, M., Gionis, A., Jernvall, J. and Mannila, H.: Spectral ordering and biochronology of european fossil mammals. Paleobiology, 206-214 (2006)

34. Puolamaki, M., Fortelius, M. and Mannila, H.: Seriation in paleontological data matrices via markov chain monte carlo methods. PLoS Computational Biology, **2** (2006).

35. Alcaraz, J., Garcìa-Novè, E.M., Landete, M. and Monge, J.F.: The linear ordering problem with clusters: a new partial ranking. TOP **28**, 646-671 (2020).

36. Aledo, J.A., Gàmez, J.A. and Rosete, A.: Utopia in the solution of the Bucket Order Problem. Decision Support Systems **97**, 69–80 (2017)

37. Ukkonen, A., Puolamäki, K., Gionis, A. and Mannila, H.: A randomized approximation algorithm for computing bucket orders. Information Processing Letters, **109**, 356–359 (2009)

38. Kenkre, S., Khan, A. and Pandit, V.: On Discovering Bucket Orders from Preference Data. Proceedings of the 2011 SIAM International Conference on Data Mining: 872–883 (2011)

39. Aledo, J.A., Gàmez, J.A. and Rosete, A.: Approaching rank aggregation problems by using evolution strategies: The case of the optimal bucket order problem. European Journal of Operational Research **270**, 982-998 (2018).

40. Arrow, K.J.: Social Choice and Individual Values. Wiley, New York (1951)

41. Kemeny, J.: Mathematics Without Numbers. Daedalus, 88, 577–591 (1959)

42. Monge, J.F.: The Concordance coefficient: An alternative to the Kruskal-Wallis test (2019), arXiv:1912.12880v2

43. Alcaraz, J.; Anton-Sanchez, L.; Monge, J: ConcordanceTest: An Alternative to the Kruskal-Wallis Test Based on the Kendall Tau Ideas. R Package. 2020. https://CRAN.R-project.org/package= ConcordanceTest (accessed on 15 January 2021).

Part II

Continuous (Global) Optimisation

6

Multi-Objective Optimization: Methods and Applications

Dylan F. Jones and Helenice O. Florentino

Multi-objective optimization is concerned with finding solutions to a decision problem with multiple, normally conflicting objectives. This chapter focusses on multi-objective optimization problems that can be characterized within the paradigm of mathematical programming. Three modelling techniques that are well established in the literature are presented: Pareto set generation, goal programming and compromise programming. Each method is described, along with its strengths, weaknesses and areas of application. The underlying assumptions and philosophies of each method, nature of interaction of decision makers and nature of solutions produced are discussed and compared between the three methods. A small but representative example is given for each method and the results are discussed and conclusions are drawn.

D. F. Jones (✉)
Centre for Operational Research and Logistics, School of Mathematics and
Physics, University of Portsmouth, Portsmouth, UK
e-mail: dylan.jones@port.ac.uk

H. O. Florentino
Institute of Biosciences, São Paulo State University (Unesp), Botucatu, Brazil
e-mail: helenice.silva@unesp.br

© The Author(s), under exclusive license to Springer Nature
Switzerland AG 2022
S. Salhi and J. Boylan (eds.), *The Palgrave Handbook of Operations Research*,
https://doi.org/10.1007/978-3-030-96935-6_6

6.1   Introduction to Multi-Objective Optimization

Multi-objective optimization involves the formulation and solution of decision problems with two or more normally conflicting objectives by which the value of a solution can be measured. The field of multi-objective optimization falls within the wider field of multiple criteria decision-making or analysis (MCDM/A), which is concerned in supporting decision makers who are encountered with problems with multiple, normally conflicting criteria. In this chapter, the overview of multiple objective optimization concentrates on problems that can be specified within a mathematical programming framework. That is, the decision maker(s) problem can be mathematically specified as:

$$\text{Min} \qquad \bar{z} = \left(f_1(\bar{x}), f_2(\bar{x}), \ldots, f_Q(\bar{x}) \right) \qquad (6.1)$$

$$\text{Subject to,}$$
$$\bar{x} \in F, \qquad (6.2)$$

where $f_q(\bar{x})$ represents the objective function of the $q'th$ objective, where $q=1,\ldots, Q$. That is there exist Q underlying criteria of importance to the decision maker. In the case that an objective is naturally of maximization type, its negative $(-f_q(\bar{x}))$ can be used without loss of generality. $\bar{x}$ represents a vector with the decision variables over which the decision maker(s) have control, which is bounded by the set F of constraints and sign restrictions. The nature of $\bar{x}$, F and $f_q(\bar{x})$, $q=1,\ldots,Q$ will determine the type of multiple objective optimization model (e.g. linear, non-linear, integer, binary, stochastic), following the same nomenclature and rules as in the wider mathematical programming field.

As formulation (6.1)–(6.2) normally does not have a unique, single optimal value for all objectives, the concept of a Pareto-optimal solution is key to generating solutions that will aid the decision maker in understanding the range of solutions available and hence making a choice of preferred solution. A solution in decision space $\bar{x}$ to (6.1)–(6.2) is termed Pareto optimal (sometimes termed Pareto efficient) if no objective can be improved without worsening another objective. If at least one objective can be improved without worsening any other objective then solution $\bar{x}$ is termed Pareto sub-optimal (sometimes termed Pareto inefficient) and the corresponding vectors $\bar{z}$ in objective space are termed nondominated and dominated, respectively. A widely accepted theory is that no decision maker will willingly choose a Pareto sub-optimal solution if they know of the existence of a Pareto optimal solution that dominates it. The field of multi-objective optimization therefore concentrates on the search for Pareto-optimal solution(s), with different models and solution methods arising depending on the characteristics of the decision problem, the number of objectives involved, the assumed underlying philosophies of the decision maker and their ability or willingness to express preferential information at different stages of the modelling and solution process and the number and characteristics of Pareto optimal solutions required. The different multi-objective optimization modelling and solution techniques have been well described in seminal books over their period of development such as [4, 14, 18, 43, 54, 62]. This chapter concentrates on three of the most prolific techniques within the field of multi-objective optimization: Pareto set generation, goal programming and compromise programming. These are developed in Sects. 6.2–6.4, respectively. Section 6.5 presents some recent applications and recommendations for usage and Sect. 6.6 draws overall conclusions.

6.2 Solving a Multi-objective Problem

Ehrgott and Gandibleux [19] present two classes of multi-objective methods: **Generating methods**, which aim at the generation of optimal Pareto points without advance contribution from the decision maker and **methods based on preferences**, in which the solutions are generated with information from the decision maker.

6.2.1 Basic Concepts

For a better understanding of optimality used in multi-objective optimization, some basic concepts are necessary.

Definition 6.1 Pareto Dominance A solution $\bar{x}^1 \in F$ to (6.1)–(6.2) dominates another solution $\bar{x}^2 \in F$ (or $\bar{x}^2$ is dominated by $\bar{x}^1$) if $f_q(\bar{x}^1) \leq f_q(\bar{x}^2)$ for $q = 1, \ldots, Q$ and $f_i(\bar{x}^1) < f_i(\bar{x}^2)$ for at least one objective function $i \in \{1, \ldots, Q\}$.

If $\bar{x}^1$ dominates $\bar{x}^2$ and $f_i(\bar{x}^1) = f_i(\bar{x}^2)$ for at least one objective function, $i \in \{1, \ldots, Q\}$, it is said that the vector objective $\bar{z}^1$ weakly dominates the vector objective $\bar{z}^2$ where $\bar{z}^1 = (f_1(\bar{x}^1), f_2(\bar{x}^1), \ldots, f_Q(\bar{x}^1))$ and $\bar{z}^2 = (f_1(\bar{x}^2), f_2(\bar{x}^2), \ldots, f_Q(\bar{x}^2))$.

If $\overline{x}^1$ dominates $\overline{x}^2$ and $f_q(\overline{x}^1) < f_q(\overline{x}^2)$, for all $q = 1, \dots, Q$, it is said that the vector objective $\overline{z}^1$ (or point $\overline{z}^1$) strictly dominates the vector objective $\overline{z}^2$. In both cases it is said that $\overline{z}^2$ is dominated by $\overline{z}^1$.

Definition 6.2 Pareto-optimal (or Pareto efficient or Nondominated) solution A solution $\overline{x}^* \in F$ is termed Pareto optimal (or Pareto efficient, or Nondominated) if there does not exist a point $\overline{z}$ that dominates $\overline{z}^*$, where $\overline{z} = (f_1(\overline{x}), f_2(\overline{x}), \dots, f_Q(\overline{x}))$ for all $\overline{x} \in F$, $\overline{x} \neq \overline{x}^*$ and $\overline{z}^* = (f_1(\overline{x}^*), f_2(\overline{x}^*), \dots, f_Q(\overline{x}^*))$. However, if weak dominance exists, $\overline{x}^*$ is termed Pareto sub-optimal (or Pareto inefficient).

Definition 6.3 Pareto-optimal Set The Pareto-optimal Set (or nondominated solution set) is a set of all Pareto-optimal solutions.

Definition 6.4 Pareto-optimal front The Pareto-optimal front is the boundary defined by the set of all points mapped from the Pareto-optimal set.

Definition 6.5 Ideal Point (Ideal Vector) $(I_1, I_2, \dots, I_Q)$ is an Ideal Point if $I_q = \min(f_q(\overline{x}), \overline{x} \in F)$, $q \in \{1, \dots, Q\}$.

Definition 6.6 Lexicographic Points $L_q = (f_1(\overline{x}_{Lq}), \dots, f_{q-1}(\overline{x}_{Lq}), I_q, f_{q+1}(\overline{x}_{Lq}), \dots, f_Q(\overline{x}_{Lq}))$ is an Lexicographic Point if $I_q = \min(f_q(\overline{x}), \overline{x} \in F)$ and $\overline{x}_{Lq} = \arg\min(f_q(\overline{x}), \overline{x} \in F)$, $q \in \{1, \dots, Q\}$.

We present an example in order to illustrate the elements defined.

Example 6.1 Consider the bi-objective optimization model

$$\text{Min} \qquad \overline{z} = \left(x_1^2 + x_2, -x_1^2 - x_1 x_2 - x_2^2 + 10\right) \qquad (6.3)$$

Subject to,

$$1.5x_1^2 + x_2^2 \leq 6, \qquad (6.4)$$

$$-0.75x_1^2 + 2.75x_1 + x_2 \geq 2.5, \qquad (6.5)$$

$$x_1 \geq 0 \quad \text{and} \quad x_2 \geq 0. \qquad (6.6)$$

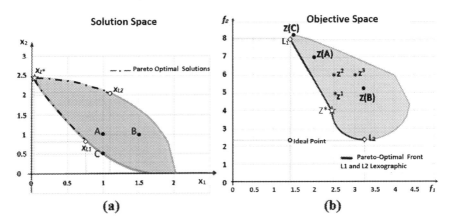

Fig. 6.1 **a** Solution (decision) space for the problem in Example 6.1. **b** Objective space for the problem in Example 6.1

In this example $Q = 2$, $\overline{x} = (x_1, x_2)$, $f_1(\overline{x}) = x_1^2 + x_2$, $f_2(\overline{x}) = -x_1^2 - x_1 x_2 - x_2^2 + 10$ and $F = \{(x_1, x_2) : 1.5x_1^2 + x_2^2 \leq 6, -0.75x_1^2 + 2.75x_1 + x_2 \geq 2.5, x_1 \geq 0 \text{ and } x_2 \geq 0\}$.

The set F of constraints is shown in Fig. 6.1a. This figure also shows the Pareto-optimal set (all points shown along the dotted line), the points x_{L1} and x_{L2} whose images are the lexicographic points, and some other feasible points in the solution space (A, B, C, x_{z*}), aimed at giving a better understanding of these spaces. Looking at Fig. 6.1b, which shows the objective space, the images of the points represented in the solution space can be seen. Note also that point z^1 weakly dominates the point z^2 and strictly dominates z^3. The point z^*, image of x_z^*, is not dominated by any other feasible point, therefore it belongs to the Pareto-optimal front. All points of the Pareto-optimal front are shown in a darker colour in Fig. 6.1b. In this figure the Ideal and Lexicographic Points can also be observed.

6.2.2 Pareto Set Generation

The multi-objective optimization process is basically composed of two stages: (i) the search for solutions and (ii) decision-making. This process allows for the determination of the elements of the Pareto-optimal Set and the quantification of trade-offs. According to [13], to assist the decision maker it is necessary to find Pareto-optimal solutions using procedures that obtain preferential information and generate solutions based on these preferences. In this way, the Pareto set generation methods consist of a process divided into two phases: In the first phase the Pareto-optimal solutions are generated. After

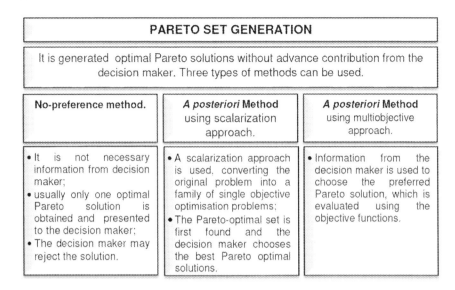

Fig. 6.2   Characteristics of the Pareto set generation methods

that, the decision maker selects from among all the possible alternatives, the most preferred solution, as summarized in Fig. 6.2.

The advantage of the Pareto set generation methods is that they convey a lot of information to the decision maker since these methods generate the Pareto front, which may assist in more informed, and hence safer decision-making. However, generating the optimal Pareto complete set is a very difficult and often even impossible task, and hence the most used strategy is the generation of some points of this front. Thus, some authors characterize the quality of the results of a multi-objective study based on a set of factors, such as: obtaining the greatest possible number of elements from the optimal Pareto set; the points on the Pareto-Optimal front must be evenly distributed in order for the decision maker to obtain an accurate picture of the trade-offs; the determined points on the Pareto front must capture the entire spectrum of the Pareto front (the Pareto front must have a large range); if approximate processes are used to determine the Pareto front, the points found must be as close as possible to the real Pareto front and not contain dominated points [17, 63].

According to [40] the most widely used among the generation methods are the Weighted Sum Method and the ϵ-Constraint Method. These methods can determine a representative subset of the Pareto set. This author points out some advantages of ϵ-Constraint Method over Weighted Sum Method, which are: contrary to the Weighted Sum Method, the ϵ-Constraint is able to produce non-extreme efficient solutions for linear problems, produce unsupported efficient solutions in multi-objective integer and mixed-integer programming problems and it is not necessary to put the objective functions onto a common scale. In this context, the focus in this section is the ϵ-Constraint Method.

6.2.2.1 ϵ-Constraint Method

Considering the multobjective problem (6.1)–(6.2), the ϵ-Constraint Method proposed by [29] consists in keeping f_i ($i \in \{1, \ldots, Q\}$) as the only objective function and limiting the other objective functions to ϵ_q ($q = 1, \ldots, Q$ and $q \neq i$), hence using them as constraints, as shown in the mono-objective optimization problem (6.7)–(6.9).

$$\text{Min} \qquad\qquad f_i(\overline{x}) \qquad\qquad (6.7)$$

Subject to,

$$f_q(\overline{x}) \leq \epsilon_q \text{ for all } q \in \{1, \ldots, Q\} \text{ and } q \neq i, \qquad (6.8)$$

$$\overline{x} \in F. \qquad (6.9)$$

According to [14], different Pareto-optimal solutions can be found by varying the values of the parameters ϵ_q, for convex or non-convex image set in objective space. This is the great advantage of this method when compared with other Pareto set generation methods, as Weighted Sum Method. Example 6.2 illustrates this method for different values of the ϵ_q.

Considering the bi-objective optimization model in Example 6.1, the ϵ-Constraint Method is used to generate 30 and 60 points of the Pareto-Optimal Set. For this, the objective function 2 is minimized and the objective function 1 is placed as a constraint, as shown in the following model.

Example 6.2 Consider the bi-objective optimization model

$$\text{Min} \qquad \overline{f}_2(\overline{x}) = (-x_1^2 - x_1 x_2 - x_2^2 + 10) \qquad (6.10)$$

Subject to,

$$x_1^2 + x_2 \leq \epsilon_1, \qquad (6.11)$$

$$1.5x_1^2 + x_2^2 \leq 6, \qquad (6.12)$$

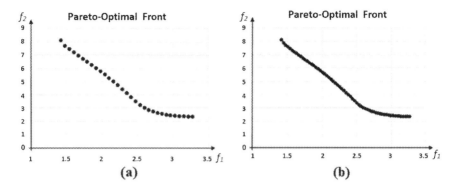

Fig. 6.3 **a** 30 points generated by the ϵ-constraint method for the Pareto-Optimal Set of the problem in Example 6.1. **b** 60 points generated by the ϵ-constraint method for the Pareto-Optimal Set of the problem in Example 6.1

$$-0.75x_1^2 + 2.75x_1 + x_2 \geq 2.5, \qquad (6.13)$$

$$x_1 \geq 0 \text{ and } x_2 \geq 0. \qquad (6.14)$$

To generate k points of the Pareto-Optimal Set it is necessary to solve k sub-problems using k different values of ϵ_1. For this example, the ideal point is (1.42, 2.35) and the lexicographic point L_2 is (3.28, 2.35), in this way, we take k values from ϵ_1 equally spaced in the range [1.42, 3.28]. Figure 6.3 shows the results of the ϵ-constraint method for the $k=30$ and $k=60$ different values of ϵ_1.

A disadvantage of this method is the need to choose an appropriate range to take the values of the parameter ϵ_1.

6.2.2.2   Multi-Objective Evolutionary Algorithms

The aim of a Multi-objective Evolutionary Algorithm (MOEA) is to find an approximation of the Pareto-optimal set that capture the trade-offs among objective functions. This technique was inspired by Darwin's theory of evolution by natural selection, such as mutation, selection and crossover that occur in a population, where each individual represents a solution to the problem investigated [26]. The selection operator has a great influence on the performance of the MOEAs and the improvement of these algorithms in the last decades was based, in a way, on the adequacy of the form of selection, as discussed in [12].

Schaffer [52] proposed the Vector Evaluated Genetic Algorithm (VEGA) where, for model (6.1)–(6.2), it creates Q subpopulations, in which the fitness of individuals in each subpopulation q is based on the f_q objective and the crossover is carried out among the best individuals of all subpopulations, using some random selection process. According to [12] this method is very simple and naive, therefore it does not perform well. This and other works developed in the 70s and 80s had many practical limitations, but they were very important historically [30, 52].

Goldberg in 1989 [26] proposed some ideas for MOEAs using selection based on Pareto optimality, creating a ranking for the selection scheme, giving to all nondominated solutions the best rank possible and also discussed the idea of elitism to increase the population diversity of solutions, what guarantee the convergence to optimal in Pareto sense [50]. These ideas favoured the emergence of several MOEAs from the 90s, as an example: Multi-Objective Genetic Algorithm (MOGA) [24], Nondominated Sorting Genetic Algorithm (NSGA) [53], Strength Pareto Evolutionary Algorithm (SPEA) [65], Nondominated Sorting Genetic Algorithm-II (NSGA-II) [16], among others.

In the last 20 years, decision-making in all areas has become more complex due to the dimensions of the problems, often encompassing the fulfillment of social, economic, political, environmental demands, increasing the number of objectives to be addressed. In this way, the Pareto-based MOEAs have been presented with many challenges [12, 67]. In an attempt to obtain different type of algorithmic designs that works with many-objective problems (more than three) and with a more efficient selection scheme, indicator-based selection [64] and decomposition-based selection [66] were proposed.

Indicator-Based Evolutionary Algorithm (IBEA) [64], S Metric Selection Evolutionary Multi-objective Algorithm (SMS-EMOA) [5, 20] and Hypervolume Estimation Algorithm for Multi-Objective Optimization (HyPE) [3] are examples of the indicator-based MOEAs, which are algorithms that incorporate any performance indicator into the selection mechanism [12]. Among the performance indicators, the most used and which has strong theoretical properties is the hypervolume indicator. However, a practical difficulty of the hypervolume measure is the high computation cost, especially for many-objectives problems. An alternative is to use an approximation of the exact hypervolume values [3], although this does not present competitive results [12].

Decomposition-based MOEAs are being actively researched. Multi-Objective Evolutionary Algorithm based on Decomposition (MOEA/D) [66] and Nondominated SortingGenetic Algorithm-III (NSGA-III) [15] are examples of this type of the MOEA. The decomposition-based MOEAs consist in the use of scalarization methods (see Fig. 6.2) to generate nondominated solutions. According to [12], these kinds of algorithms have the advantage of generating non-convex portions of the Pareto front, work with disconnected Pareto fronts, and can deal with many-objective problems.

All of the metaheuristics discussed above have limitations associated with the number of objectives addressed, so MOEAs are still the subject of much ongoing research [12]. A promising approach that has been investigated in recent years is the hyper-heuristic. A hyper-heuristic is a learning mechanism or investigation method for selecting or generating heuristics to solve computational problems [7]. It generates or chooses, among a given number of the heuristics, one that solves the problem. Therefore, the hyper-heuristic works on a heuristic search space, solving the problem indirectly by recommending which heuristic can be applied at which stage of the solution process, where the source of feedback information during the execution process can be without a learning mechanism and the selection made by a heuristic process (no-learning), or with knowledge in the form of rules (offline learning), or the learning occurs while the algorithm is solving an instance of a problem (online learning).

In the field of multi-objective optimization, many hyper-heuristics have been developed and applied, for example: Markov Chain hyper-heuristic (MCHH) [41], multi-objective Optimization, controlling and combining (NSGA-II, SPEA2, and MOGA) [39], MOEA/D Hyper-Heuristic (MOEA/D-HH) [28], multi-objective sequence-based hyper-heuristic (MOSSHH) [56], hyper-heuristic combining the strengths and compensates for the weaknesses of different scalarizing functions [27].

As discussed in this section, MOEAs have supported multi-objective (including many-objective) problem solution, but research in this area is still intense and necessary.

6.2.2.3 Quality of the Pareto-Optimal Set

As previously discussed, there is a range of exact and heuristic techniques for Pareto-optimal set generation. However, methods to evaluate and compare the quality of the solution sets generated by these techniques are also necessary. According to [14], when the preferences are unknown *a priori*, this quality is associated with the number of solutions (cardinality) close to the true Pareto-optimal front (convergence) and the ability to span the entire Pareto-optimal region uniformly (coverage (spread) and uniformly), as shown in Fig. 6.4. In Fig. 6.4, nondominated solutions generated by 4 hypothetical

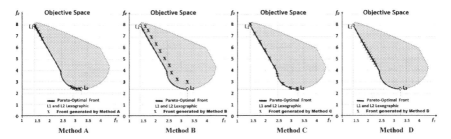

Fig. 6.4 Visual analysis of the quality of hypothetical methods A, B, C and D: Method A: good in convergence and cardinality, poor in coverage and uniformly. Method B: good in cardinality and uniformly, poor in convergence. Method C: good in convergence, cardinality, coverage and uniformly. Method D: good in convergence, poor in coverage and uniformly

methods are visually compared. Method C is the one with the best quality when compared with the others, because the method A is good in convergence to the Pareto-optimal front, but does not present diversity (coverage and uniformly) of the solutions, method B is poor in convergence and its points are dominated by solutions of the all other methods, and method D is good in convergence but poor in Pareto-optimal front coverage.

The greater the quantity of objectives of the problem, the greater the difficulty of analysing the quality of the solution set. In this way, many methods and algorithms use mechanisms (such as weight vectors, niching, clustering, cellular structures, etc.) to obtain a solution set with better quality [14, 37]. There are also indicators that were proposed to measure quantitatively the quality of the set of points found using methods or heuristics (cardinality of the found solution set, convergence to the Pareto-optimal front, coverage over the Pareto front and uniformly among solutions), these metrics help in the comparison of results achieved by different multi-objective problem-solving techniques. Deb [14] presents a very broad discussion on metrics for analysing the quality of a set of solutions generated for multi-objective problems and other solution quality approaches. Li and Yao [37] discuss current approaches of multi-objective solution sets quality evaluation, categorising 100 quality indicators for convergence, spread, uniformity, cardinality, for both spread and uniformity, and for combined quality of the four quality aspects. The authors present examples detailing indicators and their desirable properties. An important conclusion of these is that the choice of the quality indicator to be used depends on the characteristics of the problem and the solution set obtained.

6.3   Goal Programming

Goal programming was introduced by [11] in the context of an extension of linear programming in order to satisfy multiple goals related to executive remuneration. The technique was formalized by [8], who introduced the term goal programming and gave formulations that allowed for pre-emptive prioritization of goals by the decision maker (now commonly termed lexicographic GP) or without the pre-emptive prioritization of goals, instead of aggregating them according to their relative preferences to the decision maker (now commonly termed weighted GP). The goal programming technique has an underlying satisficing philosophy [51], that is the decision maker wishes to achieve a set of multiple, conflicting goals as closely as possible, penalizing any unwanted deviations from the goals. This results in the transformation of the set of objectives into the following generic goal programming model [35]:

$$\text{Min} \qquad \overline{z} = g(n_1, \ldots, n_Q, p_1, \ldots, p_Q) \qquad (6.15)$$

Subject to,

$$f_q(\overline{x}) + n_q - p_q = b_q, q = 1, \ldots, Q, \qquad (6.16)$$

$$\overline{x} \in F, \qquad (6.17)$$

$$n_q \geq 0 \text{ and } p_q \geq 0, q = 1, \ldots, Q. \qquad (6.18)$$

Figure 6.5 demonstrates the progression of goal programming since the formative work of [8]. Significant variants in terms of preferential modelling include Chebshev GP [23], also termed Minmax GP, which introduces the concept of balance between goals. The Extended GP [47] and Meta GP [55] variants allow for a combination of the weighted (optimization) and Chebyshev (balance) by means of parametric analysis and formation of meta-goals, respectively. Multi-Choice GP [9] allows decision makers to set multiple target levels. The extended network variant [34] allows for the consideration of balance, optimization and the effect of centralization over a multi-objective network of stakeholders. Additionally to the above, there are many GP variants based around the nature of the goals, target values, constraints and decision variables. Many of these are given in detail in [32] and summarized in [35]. These variants include fuzzy GP, stochastic GP, non-linear GP, integer GP and binary GP.

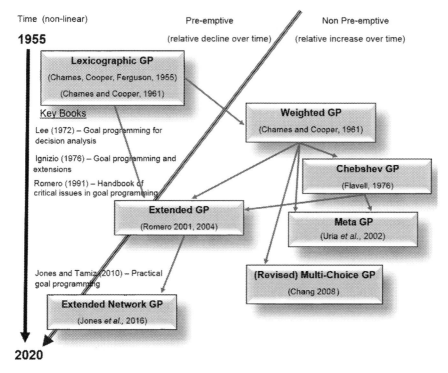

Fig. 6.5 Evolution of goal programming paradigm 1955–2020

The usage of one of the most used recent goal programming variants, extended GP [47] in its non-pre-emptive form, is demonstrated via Example 6.3.

Example 6.3 Consider the model

$$\text{Min} \quad a = \alpha\lambda + (1-\alpha)(\frac{v_1 p_1}{20} + \frac{u_2 n_2}{30} + \frac{u_3 n_3}{35} + \frac{u_4 n_4 + v_4 p_4}{30}) \tag{6.19}$$

Subject to,

$$x_1 + x_2 + x_3 + n_1 - \underline{p_1} = 20, \tag{6.20}$$

$$2x_1 + x_2 - x_3 + \underline{n_2} - p_2 = 30, \tag{6.21}$$

$$x_1 - x_2 + 2x_3 + \underline{n_3} - p_3 = 35, \tag{6.22}$$

$$-x_1 + 2x_2 + x_3 + \underline{n_4} - \underline{p_4} = 30, \tag{6.23}$$

$$\frac{v_1 p_1}{20} \leq \lambda, \tag{6.24}$$

$$\frac{u_2 n_2}{30} \leq \lambda, \tag{6.25}$$

$$\frac{u_3 n_3}{35} \leq \lambda, \tag{6.26}$$

$$\frac{u_4 n_4 + v_4 p_4}{30} \leq \lambda, \tag{6.27}$$

$$x_i \geq 0, \ n_j \geq 0, \ p_j \geq 0, \ i = 1, \ldots, 3, \ j = 1, \ldots, 4. \tag{6.28}$$

Table 6.1 gives the results of a parametric analysis with respect to the parameter α, which is set by the analyst in order to give the decision maker an indication of the range of available solutions between optimization ($\alpha = 0$) and balance ($\alpha = 1$). The variable λ represents the maximal unwanted, weighted, normalized deviation from among the set of goal target values. The example includes all three principal goal types, that is goals (6.21) and (6.22) require penalisation of just negative deviations from the goal (e.g. a profit target). Goal (6.20) requires just penalization of positive deviations from the target (e.g. a cost target). Finally, goal (6.23) requires penalization of both types of deviation (e.g. a number of required workers target). The preferential weights v_1, u_2, u_3, u_4 and v_4 represent the relative importance of their deviational variable in the achievement function (6.19) to the decision maker(s). Many schemes have been used for the elicitation of these weights, with Analytical Hierarchy Process Based methodologies [25] among the most popular. Although goal programming is traditionally used as an *a priori* technique (see Fig. 6.2), weight sensitivity algorithms such as [33] allow for its usage as *a posteriori* technique. For the sake of simplicity of demonstration, an equal weight solution: $v_1 = u_2 = u_3 = u_4 = v_4 = 1$ is used to solve goal programming model (6.19)–(6.28).

Table 6.1 demonstrates the extended goal programming model solutions in parameter, decision and unwanted deviational variable space. The first column gives the ranges of parameter α, at 0.01 fidelity, where each of the

Table 6.1 Solutions to goal programming model (6.19)–(6.28)

α range	x_1	x_2	x_3	p_1	n_2	n_3	n_4	p_4	λ
0.00-0.12	16.07	14.64	16.79	27.50	0	0	0	0	1.38
0.13-0.33	10.57	16.48	7.62	14.67	0	25.67	0	0	0.73
0.34-1.00	9.52	8.68	9.95	8.15	12.22	14.26	12.22	0	0.41

three distinct solutions is found. Columns 2–4 represent the solutions in decision ($\bar{x}$) space. Columns 5–9 give the solutions in terms of the values of the
unwanted deviational variables. All other deviational variables (n_1, p_2, p_3)
took the value zero in all three solutions, although this is co-incidental to
this example. The final, tenth column gives the value of λ, the maximal,
unwanted, weighted deviation. Table 6.1 demonstrates the change from an
unbalanced yet efficient solution to a more balanced solution as α increases.
For instance the first row solution ($\alpha \in [0, 0.12]$) has a total normalized
deviational sum of $\frac{27.50}{20} = 1.38$ to 2sf and also an λ value of 1.38 (as a single
deviation, p_1, comprises both measures). However, the third row solution has
a total normalized deviational sum of $\frac{8.15}{20} + \frac{12.22}{30} + \frac{14.26}{35} + \frac{12.22}{30} = 1.63$
to 2dp and a λ value of 0.41, indicating a poorer level of efficiency but a
higher level of balance. It should also be noted that three of the four goals
are satisfied in the first row solution but none of the goals are in the third
row solution, thus showing the compromise necessary to provide a balance
between the achievement of goals for this example. Furthermore, the fact that
the α solution ranges (0.12, 0.2, 0.66) are unequal shows that care should be
taken when conducting parameter sensitivity analysis or with respect to α or
choosing an appropriate number of α values to generate solutions that accurately demonstrate the transition from efficiency to balance. Finally, it should
also be noted that setting $\alpha = 0$ (the first row solution) gives a weighted goal
programme and setting $\alpha = 1$ (the third row solution) gives a Chebyshev
goal programme [47].

6.4 Compromise Programming

The technique of compromise programming is first introduced by [60] and
further detailed by [62]. The main principle is to find a subset of Pareto efficient solutions which have the specific solution of minimizing an L_p distance
between the feasible set and the ideal point, for some value of $1 \le p \le \infty$.
The set of Pareto efficient solutions fulfilling his property is known as the
compromise set. Utilizing the notation of Sect. 6.2, the minimization to find
a point in the compromise set corresponding to a specific distance metric p
is given by:

$$\text{Min} \qquad Z = \left[\sum_{i=1}^{Q} \left(\frac{I_q - f_q(\bar{x})}{I_q - N_q} \right)^p \right]^{\frac{1}{p}} \qquad (6.29)$$

Subject to,

$$\overline{x} \in F. \tag{6.30}$$

Similar to the extended goal programming model presented in Sect. 6.3, the compromise set allows the decision maker to investigate a set of solutions that range from efficiency (represented by the L_1 distance metric) to balance (represented by the L_∞ distance metric). The mathematical connections between goal and compromise programming are detailed by [49]. However, there are some important differences in underlying philosophy to be noted. The principal difference is that the goal programming models minimize the distance between a set of decision maker specified goals and the set of achieved values whereas the compromise programming model minimizes the difference between the ideal values and the set of achieved values. Furthermore, the goal programming model often tends, by convention, to utilize percentage normalization (scaling by division by the target value), whereas the compromise programming model utilizes zero-one scaling. That is, the normalizing factor in (6.29) is the difference between the ideal value (Iq) and a measure of the worst value (Nq). The latter is either the nadir value (the worst value from among the Pareto efficient set of solutions) or the anti-ideal value (the worst value within the feasible set F). It should also be noted that in this chapter, formulation (6.29)–(6.30) includes the simplifying assumption that all objectives are of equal importance to the decision maker, as the main emphasis of compromise programming is the investigation of the trade-off between balance and efficiency. In the case of unequally weighted objectives, weights can be added to objective function (6.29).

Example 6.4 A regional government is considering investing in some of a set of regional development projects. Each project has a cost (in £100,000s),

Table 6.2 Cost, environmental payoff and economic payoff for the projects

Project	Cost (£1,000s)	Environmental Payoff (1–10)	Economic Payoff (1–10)
1	1.2	1.3	1.5
2	6.8	10.0	3.8
3	6.0	6.3	4.2
4	5.5	5.7	5.2
5	5.8	1.1	10.0
6	6.3	3.7	6.2
7	7.0	7.1	7.4
8	6.6	9.3	3.4
9	4.5	8.2	1.0
10	8.3	9.1	9.0

an environmental payoff (as it replaces older, less environmentally friendly infrastructure) and an economic payoff. All economic and environmental payoffs are standardized onto a 1–10 scale where 10 is the highest payoff and 1 is the worst payoff. The regional government has a budget of 25 million pounds which cannot be exceeded. The cost, environmental payoff and economic payoff for each potential project are given in Table 6.2.

Indexing the projects as $i = 1, \ldots, 10$ allows the assignment of a cost c_i, an environmental payoff r_i and an economic payoff e_i. The binary decision variables are defined as:

$$x_i = \begin{cases} 1 & \text{if project i is selected.} \\ 0 & \text{otherwise} \end{cases} \quad i = 1, \ldots, 10. \tag{6.31}$$

The first phase of solution is to find the ideal (maximum) total environmental payoff, termed $R_{\max}$ and the ideal (maximum) total economic payoff, termed $E_{\max}$. These are found by the single objective optimizations of

$$\text{Max} \qquad z = \sum_{i=1}^{10} r_i x_i \tag{6.32}$$

and

$$\text{Max} \qquad z = \sum_{i=1}^{10} e_i x_i \tag{6.33}$$

Subject to

$$\sum_{i=1}^{10} c_i x_i \leq 60, \tag{6.34}$$

$$x_i = 0 \; or \; 1, \; i = 1, \ldots, 10. \tag{6.35}$$

The solution to (6.32), (6.34) and (6.35) yields the ideal environmental value $R_{\max}$. Furthermore, as the problem is bi-objective, the term $\sum_{i=1}^{10} e_i x_i$ will yield the nadir economic value, which can be denoted as $E_{\min}$. Similarly, the solution to (6.33), (6.34) and (6.35) yields the ideal economic value $E_{\max}$, and the term $\sum_{i=1}^{10} r_i x_i$ will yield the nadir environmental value, which can be denoted as $R_{\min}$. Note that this logic does not always hold in three or more objective problems, in which case the anti-ideal value or an approximation of the nadir should be used instead. In the case of the example, the optimizations yield the ideal and nadir values of $R_{max} = 35.1$, $E_{max} = 31.2$, $R_{min} = 17.7$ and $E_{min} = 21.7$. Thus, the compromise programming model is:

$$\text{Min} \quad z = \left[\left(\frac{R_{max} - \sum_{i=1}^{10} r_i x_i}{R_{max} - R_{min}} \right)^p + \left(\frac{E_{max} - \sum_{i=1}^{10} e_i x_i}{E_{max} - E_{min}} \right)^p \right]^{\frac{1}{p}}, \quad 1 \le p \le \infty. \tag{6.36}$$

Subject to the budget constraint (6.34) and sign restrictions (6.35), the two ends of the compromise set are found at the distance metrics $p = 1$ and $p = \infty$. These can be found by the two respective minimizations:

$$\text{Min} \quad z_1 = \left(\frac{R_{max} - \sum_{i=1}^{10} r_i x_i}{R_{max} - R_{min}} \right) + \left(\frac{E_{max} - \sum_{i=1}^{10} e_i x_i}{E_{max} - E_{min}} \right) \tag{6.37}$$

Subject to

$$\text{(6.34) and (6.35)}. \tag{6.38}$$

and

$$\text{Min} \quad\quad\quad z_\infty = \lambda \tag{6.39}$$

Subject to

$$\text{(6.34), (6.35) and} \tag{6.40}$$

$$\left(\frac{R_{max} - \sum_{i=1}^{10} r_i x_i}{R_{max} - R_{min}} \right) \le \lambda, \tag{6.41}$$

$$\left(\frac{E_{max} - \sum_{i=1}^{10} e_i x_i}{E_{max} - E_{min}} \right) \le \lambda, \tag{6.42}$$

where λ is the maximum of the two unwanted deviations. Romero et al. [49] details the similarities between formulations (6.37)–(6.38) and weighted goal programming and formulations (6.396.40)–(6.42) and Chebyshev goal programming. Furthermore, [60] demonstrates that in the case of a linear, bi-objective model such as (6.32)–(6.35) the compromise set is a straight line in objective space with the co-ordinates of z_1 and z_∞ solutions as end points. In this case, the compromise set can be defined in objective space by the parametric equation:

$$z_c = \alpha z_\infty + (1 - \alpha)z_1, \ 0 \le \alpha \le 1.$$

which is based on the same underlying philosophy as the extended goal programming model (6.19)–(6.28), that is a parametric mix between efficiency and balance. The compromise set in three or more objectives exhibits more erratic behaviour, with some observations regarding its nature given by [6].

Therefore the compromise set for a bi-criteria linear model can be found by solving four linear programmes: the maximizations of (6.32), (6.34)–(6.35) and (6.33)–(6.35) to find the ideal and nadir points and the minimizations of (6.37)–(6.38) and (6.396.40)–(6.42) to find the two endpoints of the compromise set. Returning to our example, we note that the model is binary in nature, so not every point in the compromise set may be available to the decision maker or lying exactly on the line given by z_c due to the integer restrictions. In fact, conducting a parametric analysis with respect to p or α with fidelity 0.1 for p or 0.01 for α yields the results given in Fig. 6.6 and Table 6.3.

Table 6.3 gives the properties of the three solutions in terms of the parametric, decision and objective spaces of the problem, respectively. Columns 2 and 3 give the α and p ranges that generate the solution, respectively. Column 4 gives the value of $\overline{x}$ in decision space in the form of the chosen projects, i.e.

Table 6.3 Compromise Set Solutions to Example 6.4

Solution	α range	p range	Projects	Environment	Economic
A	[0, 0.41]	[1, 1.5]	1, 2, 4, 7, 9	32.3	18.9
B	[0.42, 0.66]	[1.6, 10.5]	1, 2, 7, 10	27.5	21.7
C	[0.67, 1]	[10.6, ∞]	2, 5, 7, 9	26.4	22.2

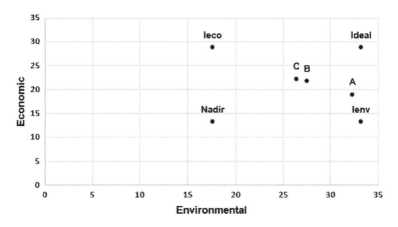

Fig. 6.6 Compromise set of Example 6.4

those where $x_i = 1$. Columns 5 and 6 give the solution in objective space, containing the total environmental score, $\sum_{i=1}^{10} r_i x_i$ and the total economic score $\sum_{i=1}^{10} e_i x_i$. Figure 6.6 portrays the solutions graphically, where solution A is the most efficient in terms of the scaled Manhattan ($p = 1$) distance from the ideal and solution C is the most balanced ($p = \infty$) with respect to the environmental and economic objectives. As solution B is slightly displaced from the line $(\overrightarrow{AC})$ due to the aforementioned integer restrictions, the compromise set is piecewise linear and defined by the lines $(\overrightarrow{AB})$ and $(\overrightarrow{BC})$. It is finally due to the decision maker(s) preferences regarding balance and efficiency as to which of the three available compromise solutions they prefer.

6.5   Applications and Usage

6.5.1   Application of Techniques

The fields of application of the multi-objective techniques described in Sects. 6.2–6.4 are many and diverse. The list of applications is continually expanding as new fields of discovery give rise to novel situations with multiple, conflicting criteria. Jones and Tamiz [35] highlight the combined usage of multi-objective techniques with techniques from the wider fields of MCDM/A and Operational Research to gain more insight into arising, complex decision problems. Recently this has been supplemented by combination with techniques from the wider fields of artificial intelligence, machine learning and analytics. Due to the volume of literature involved, it is not possible to give an exhaustive list of all multi-objective applications, but the remainder of this sub-section highlights some recent examples from emerging fields.

Firstly, considering the field of renewable energy, sustainability and the environment, decisions in this field can be inherently multi-objective, for example consideration of economic, environmental, social and technical sustainability criteria. Akbari et al. [1] give an example of interval coefficient goal programming and cluster analysis applied to selection of marine renewable energy projects with sustainability criteria. Wang et al. [57] use the ϵ-Constraint Method to solve a non-linear, integer model pertaining to optimal design and operation of a hybrid renewable energy system. Miao et al. [42] use compromise programming to investigate trade-offs between economic and environmental criteria for combined solar and wind energy systems.

The wide field of healthcare, including humanitarian, disaster and public health management gives rise to a varied range of conflicting criteria on many levels of planning, management, organization and assisted treatment. For instance, [2] use revised multi-choice goal programming to model a blood supply network considering environmental, social and cost criteria. Farughi et al. [21] use the MOEA2 multiple objective genetic algorithm to generate solutions to a healthcare district partitioning problem. Ferrer et al. [22] use compromise programming for last-mile logistical planning of disaster relief aid. They consider time, cost, equity, priority, security and reliability aspects of the problem.

The field of logistics, supply chain management and transportation has also given rise to multiple objective problems across the strategic, tactical and operational decision-making levels. These frequently require heuristic solution techniques because of the complexity of the underlying problems. Zajac and Huber [61] provide a recent review of multi-objective routing advances and applications. Homayouni et al. [31] utilize multi-choice goal programming to design green supply chains under uncertainty. Wang et al. [58] use a revised version of the evolutionary multi-objective algorithm NSGA-II, along with Tabu search and clustering techniques to devise collaborative logistics distribution networks for fresh and perishable products. Onat et al. [44] use compromise programming to calculate the optimal distribution of alternative (sustainable) vehicles following life cycle-assessments, and demonstrate their methodology on a Qatari case study.

Finally, considering the field of risk, safety and security management, the arising multiple objective challenges include designing systems that have sufficient levels of safety and security, but also maximize efficiency, effectiveness and usability. Lin et al. [38] consider data security in an internet of things (IoT) environment, and design an ant colony optimization heuristic to generate a Pareto front considering maximization of data security and minimization of unwanted side effects. Yu et al. [59] utilize weighted goal programming in an iterative fashion to solve a hazardous waste transportation problem considering risk and cost objectives. They illustrate the methodology on a Chinese case study. Pla-Santamaria et al. [45] utilize compromise programming to provide a balance between debt quality and risk concentration in a credit risk management problem. They demonstrate their methodology with a case study arising from the Spanish stock market.

6.5.2   Use of Techniques

To attempt to produce a global ranking of multi-criteria or multi-objective techniques is, in the authors' opinion, a nugatory exercise. As detailed in Sects. 6.2–6.4, different techniques have their own set of characteristics. Thus, the discussion in the multi-objective field has correctly evolved to answering the question of which techniques are better for which classes of problems. With this in mind, we note that compromise programming is the most clearly delineated of the three techniques considered, in that it has attractive properties for linear, bi-objective problems where the complete compromise set can be characterized by a relatively small (four) number of optimizations. It does, however, produce a smaller portion of the efficient set, restricted to solutions which are optimal for an L_p distance metric, $1 \leq p \leq \infty$. So if the decision maker is looking for a restricted set of potential solutions to a bi-objective problem that explore the range from optimization to balance, then compromise programming appears a good choice.

For a wider exploration of the set of available Pareto efficient solutions, with a still relatively low number of global objectives (typically in the range of two to four, but possibly up to seven), then Pareto efficient set generation has some advantages. With a good methodology for selecting and presenting a representative set of solutions to the decision maker(s) for discussion, it can be an effective technique. However, the computational burden can be large, particularly for higher criteria problems. Efficient set generation is thus perhaps at its best where a strategic multi-objective decision of high importance but few criteria must be considered and decision maker(s) wish to invest effort in considering the full range of options available.

The goal programming technique is designed to allow the decision maker to achieve a set of multiple, conflicting goals as closely as possible. It is hence at its strongest when the underlying problem structure has this format. It can hence deal effectively with problems with many criteria, including those with networks of sub-criteria. Its additional computational solution load for considering the multi-objectives is low compared to some other multi-objective techniques, making it suitable for computationally challenging multi-objective problems, at either the strategic or operational level, especially with high numbers of objectives. Conversely, it may not be the natural choice for bi-objective models as other techniques, such as compromise programming or Pareto set generation may provide a better representation and visualization of the trade-offs involved in two dimensions.

6.6 Conclusions

This chapter has reviewed the development, principles and usage of three of the most prolific multi-objective programming techniques. Sections 6.2–6.4 showed their ability in providing decision maker(s) with solutions that demonstrate the nature of the available solutions and the trade-offs between them. The discussion of applications in Section 6.5.1 showed their continued relevance in emerging and expanding fields such as renewable energy and sustainability; healthcare and humanitarian aid management; modern logistics, supply chain and transportation systems management and risk, security and safety management. Section 6.5.2 outlined the fact that all of the discussed techniques have specific strengths and situations in which they are recommended. Furthermore, the discussions on recent advances and applications throughout this chapter demonstrate that the field of multi-objective optimization is continuing to evolve and hence future techniques, variants, combinations with techniques from other fields and applications should be anticipated and looked forward to.

Acknowledgements The authors would like to thank the following Brazilian grant-making organizations: CNPq (grant 312551/2019-3), FAPESP (grant 2013/07375-0), CAPES (Finance Code 001), UNESP-PROPE and UNESP-FUNDUNESP.

References

1. Akbari, N., Jones, D., Arabikhan, F.: Goal programming models with interval coefficients for the sustainable selection of marine renewable energy projects in the UK. European Journal of Operational Researsh. **293**, 748–760 (2020)
2. Arani, M., Chan, Y., Liu, X., Momenitabar, M.: A lateral resupply blood supply chain network design under uncertainties. Applied Mathematical Modelling. **93**, 165–187 (2021)
3. Bader J., Zitzler, E.: HypE: an algorithm for fast hypervolume-based many-objective optimization. Evol Comput. **19**, 45–76 (2011)
4. Belton, V., Stewart, T.: Multiple criteria decision analysis: an integrated approach. Springer Science & Business Media (2002)
5. Beume N., Naujoks, B., Emmerich, M.: SMS-EMOA: multiobjective selection based on dominated hypervolume. Eur J Oper Res. **181**, 1653–1669 (2007)
6. Blasco, F., Cuchillo-Ibanez, E., Moron, M. Romero, C.: On the monotonicity of the compromise set in multicriteria problems. Journal of Optimization Theory and Applications. **102**, 69–82 (1999)

7. Burke, E.K., Gendreau, M., Hyde, M., Kendall, G., Ochoa, G., özcan, E., Qu, R.: Hyper-heuristics: a survey of the state of the art. J Oper Res Soc. **64**, 1695–1724 (2013)

8. Chambers, D., Charnes, A.: Inter-temporal analysis and optimization of bank portfolios. Management Science. **7**, 393–410 (1961)

9. Chang, C.T.: Revised multi-choice goal programming. Applied Mathematical Modelling. **32**, 2587–2595 (2008)

10. Charnes, A., Cooper, W.: Management models and industrial applications of linear programming. John Wiley and Sons, New York (1961)

11. Charnes, A., Cooper, W., Ferguson, R.O.: Optimal estimation of executive compensation by linear programming. Management Science. **1**, 138–151 (1955)

12. Coello, C.A.C., Brambila, S.G., Gamboa, J.F., Tapia, M.G.C., Gomez, R.H.G.: Evolutionarymultiobjective optimization: open research areas and some challenges lying ahead. Complex & Intelligent Systems. **6**, 221–236 (2020)

13. Cohon, J.L., Marks, D.H.: A review and evaluation of multiobjective programing techniques. Water Resources Research. **11**, 208–220 (1975)

14. Deb, K.: Multi-Objective Optimization Using Evolutionary Algorithms. John Wiley & Sons Inc, New York, NY, USA (2001)

15. Deb, K, Jain, H.: An evolutionary many-objective optimization algorithm using reference-point-based nondominated sorting approach, Part I: solving problems with Box constraints. IEEE Trans Evol Comput. **18**, 577–601 (2014)

16. Deb, K., Pratap, A., Agarwal, S., Meyarivan, T.: A fast and elitist multiobjective genetic algorithm: NSGA-II. IEEE Trans Evol Comput. **6**, 182–197 (2002)

17. Demir, E., Bekta, T., Laporte, G.: The bi-objective pollution-routing problem. European Journal of Operational Research. **232**, 464–478 (2014)

18. Ehrgott, M.: Multicriteria optimization. Springer Science & Business Media (2005)

19. Ehrgott, M., Gandibleux, X.: Multiple criteria optimization. Lecture Notes in Economics and Mathematical Systems. **491** (2002)

20. Emmerich, M., Beume, N., Naujoks, B.: An EMO algorithm using the hypervolume measure as selection criterion. In: Coello CAC, Aguirre AH, Zitzler E Evolutionary multi-criterion optimization. Lecture notes in computer science, vol 3410. Third international conference, EMO2005. Springer, Guanajuato, México. 62–76 (2005)

21. Farughi, H., Tavana, M., Mostafayi, S., Arteaga, F.J.: A novel optimization model for designing compact, balanced, and contiguous healthcare districts. Journal of the Operational Research Society, **71**, 1740–1759 (2020)

22. Ferrer, J.M., Javier Martin-Campo, F., Teresa Ortuno, M., Pedraza-Martinez, A.J., Tirado, G., Vitoriano, B.: Multi-criteria optimization for last mile distribution of disaster relief aid: Test cases and applications. European Journal of Operational Research. **269**, 501–515 (2018)

23. Flavell, R.B. and others.: A new goal programming formulation. Omega. **4**, 731–732 (1976)

24. Fonseca, C.M., Fleming, P.J.: Genetic algorithms for multiobjective optimization: formulation, discussion and generalization. In: Forrest S Proceedings of the fifth international conference on genetic algorithms. Morgan Kauffman Publishers, San Mateo, California, USA. 416–423 (1993)
25. Gass, S.I.: A process for determining priorities and weights for large-scale linear goal programmes. Journal of the Operational Research Society. **37**, 779–785 (1986)
26. Goldberg, D.E.: Genetic algorithms in search, optimization and machine learning. Addison-Wesley Publishing Company, Reading (1989)
27. Gómez, R.H., Coello, C.A.C.: A hyper-heuristic of scalarizing functions. In: 2017 genetic and evolutionary computation conference (GECCO'2017), ACM Press, Berlin, Germany. 577–584 (2017)
28. Gonçalves, R.A., Kuk, J.N., Almeida, C.P., Venske, S.M. MOEA/D-HH: a hyper-heuristic for multi-objective problems. In: Evolutionary multi-criterion optimization, 8th international conference, EMO 2015. Lecture notes in computer science, vol 9018, Springer, Guimarães, Portugal. 94–108 (2015)
29. Haimes, Y.: On a bicriterion formulation of the problems of integrated system identification and system optimization. IEEE Transactions on Systems, Man, and Cybernetics. **1**, 296–297 (1971)
30. Holland, J.: Adaptation in natural and artificial systems. The University of Mihcigan Press (1975)
31. Homayouni, Z. Pishvaee, M. S., Jahani, H., Ivanov, D.: A robust-heuristic optimization approach to a green supply chain design with consideration of assorted vehicle types and carbon policies under uncertainty. Annals of Operations Research (2021). https://doi.org/10.1007/s10479-021-03985-6
32. Ignizio, J.P.: Goal programming and extensions. Lexington Books (1976)
33. Jones, D.: A practical weight sensitivity algorithm for goal and multiple objective programming. European Journal of Operational Research. **213**, 238–245 (2011)
34. Jones, D., Florentino, H., Cantane, D., Oliveira, R.: An extended goal programming methodology for analysis of a network encompassing multiple objectives and stakeholders. European Journal of Operational Research. **255**, 845–855 (2016)
35. Jones, D., Tamiz, M.: Practical goal programming. Springer (2010)
36. Lee, S.M.: Goal programming for decision analysis. Philadelphia: Auerbach Publishers. 252–260 (1972)
37. Li, M., Yao, X.: Quality evaluation of solution sets in multiobjective optimisation: a survey. ACM Comput Surv. **52**, 1–38 (2019)
38. Lin, J.C.W., Srivastava, G., Zhang, Y., Djenouri, Y., Aloqaily, M.: Privacy-Preserving Multiobjective Sanitization Model in 6G IoT Environments. IEEE Internet of Things Journal. **8**, 5340–5349 (2021)
39. Maashi, M.: An investigation of multi-objective hyperheuristics for multi-objective optimisation. PhD thesis, The University of Nottingham, UK (2014)

40. Mavrotas, G.: Effective implementation of the ε-constraint method in multi-objective mathematical programming problems. Applied Mathematics and Computation. **213**, 455–465 (2009)

41. McClymont, K., Keedwell, E.C.: Markov chain hyperheuristic (MCHH): an online selective hyper-heuristic for multiobjective continuous problems. In: 2011 genetic and evolutionary computation conference (GECCO'2011), ACM Press, Dublin, Ireland. 2003–2010 (2011)

42. Miao, P., Yue, Z., Niu,T., Alizadeh, A. Jermsittiparsert, K.: Optimal emission management of photovoltaic and wind generation based energy hub system using compromise programming. Journal of Cleaner Production. **281** (2021). https://doi.org/10.1016/j.jclepro.2020.124333.

43. Miettinen K.: Non-linear Multi-objective Optimization. Springer (1998)

44. Onat, N.C., Aboushaqrah, N.N.M., Kucukvar, M., Tarlochan, F., Hamouda, A.M.: From sustainability assessment to sustainability management for policy development: The case for electric vehicles. **216** (2020). https://doi.org/10.1016/j.enconman.2020.112937

45. Pla-Santamaria, D., Bravo, M., Reig-Mullor, J., Molina, F.S.: A multicriteria approach to manage credit risk under strict uncertainty. TOP (2020). https://doi.org/10.1007/s11750-020-00571-0

46. Romero, C.: A general structure of achievement function for a goal programming model. European Journal of Operational Research. **153**, 675–686 (2004)

47. Romero, C.: Extended lexicographic goal programming: a unifying approach. Omega. **29**, 63–71 (2001)

48. Romero, C.: Handbook of critical issues in goal programming. Elsevier. (1991)

49. Romero, C., Tamiz, M., Jones, D.F.: Goal programming, compromise programming and reference point method formulations: linkages and utility interpretations. Journal of the Operational Research Society. **49**, 986–991 (1998)

50. Rudolph G., Agapie A.: Convergence properties of some multi-objective evolutionary algorithms. In: Proceedings of the 2000 conference on evolutionary computation, vol 2, IEEE Press, Piscataway, New Jersey. 1010–1016 (2000)

51. Simon, H.: A behavioral model of rational choice. The Quarterly Journal of Economics. **69**, 99–118 (1955)

52. Schaffer, J.D.: Multiple objective optimization with vector evaluated genetic algorithms. In: Genetic algorithms and their applications. Proceedings of the first international conference on genetic algorithms, Lawrence Erlbaum, 93–100 (1985)

53. Srinivas, N., Deb, K.: Multiobjective optimization using nondominated sorting in genetic algorithms. Evol Comput. **2**, 221–248 (1994)

54. Steuer, R.E.: Multiple criteria optimization: Theory, computation and application. John Wliey & Sons, New York, NY, USA (1986)

55. Uria, M.V.R., Caballero, R., Ruiz, F., Romero, C.: Meta-goal programming. European Journal of Operational Research. **136**, 422–429 (2002)

56. Walker, D.J., Keedwell, E.: Multi-objective optimisation with a sequence-based selection hyper-heuristic. In: Proceedings of the 2016 on genetic and evolutionary computation conference companion, ACM Press, New York, USA. 81–82 (2016)
57. Wang, F., Xu, J., Liu, L., Yin, G., Wang, J., Yan, J.: Optimal design and operation of hybrid renewable energy system for drinking water treatment. Energy. **219**, (2021), https://doi.org/10.1016/j.energy.2020.119673
58. Wang, Y., Zhang, J., Guan, X., Xu, M., Wang, Z., Wang, H.: Collaborative multiple centers fresh logistics distribution network optimization with resource sharing and temperature control constraints. Expert Systems With Pplications. **165** (2021). https://doi.org/10.1016/j.eswa.2020.113838
59. Yu, H., Sun, X., Solvang, W.D., Laporte, G., Lee, C.K.M.: A stochastic network design problem for hazardous waste management. Journal of Cleaner Production (2020). https://doi.org/10.1016/j.jclepro.2020.123566
60. Yu, P.L.: A class of solutions for group decision problems. Management Science. **19**, 936–946 (1973)
61. Zajac, S., Huber, S.: Objectives and methods in multi-objective routing problems: a survey and classification scheme. European Journal of Operational Research. **290**, 1–25 (2021). https://doi.org/10.1016/j.ejor.2020.07.005
62. Zeleny, M.: Multiple Criteria Decision Making. McGraw-Hill, Company, London (1982)
63. Zitzler, E., Deb, K., Thiele, L.: Comparison of multiobjective evolutionary algorithms: Empirical results. Evolutionary Computation **8**, 173–195 (2000)
64. Zitzler, E., Künzli, S.: Indicator-based selection in multiobjective search. In: Yao X Parallel problem solving from nature-PPSN VIII. Lecture Notes in Computer Science, vol 3242. Springer, Birmingham, UK. 832–842 (2004)
65. Zitzler, E.,Thiele, L.: Multiobjective evolutionary algorithms: a comparative case study and the strength pareto approach. IEEE Trans Evol Comput. **3**, 257–271 (1999)
66. Zhang, Q., Li, H.: MOEA/D: a multiobjective evolutionary algorithm based on decomposition. IEEE Trans Evol Comput. **11**, 712–731 (2007)
67. Zou, X., Chen, Y., Liu, M., and Kang, L.: A new evolutionary algorithm for solving many-objective optimization problems. IEEE Trans. on Systems, Man, and Cybernetics: Part B - Cybernetics. **38**, 1402–1412 (2008)

7

Competitive Facilities Location

Tammy Drezner

7.1 Introduction

The competitive facilities location problem is the location of one or more facilities among existing competing facilities. The facilities attract demand generated by customers in the area. The objective is to maximize the market share captured by the new facilities. Over the years many ways to estimating the market share captured by each facility were proposed. It is assumed that customers divide their buying power among facilities according to the facilities' attractiveness and their distance relative to other facilities. Once the market share attracted by one or more facilities can be estimated, a procedure for finding the best locations for the new facilities can be constructed. The objective function is not convex. Therefore, only heuristic procedures, that do not guarantee optimality, were proposed for solving most models.

The basic competitive model is to find the location of one or more facilities that maximize the market share captured by the new facilities. Some extensions/variations to the basic model were investigated. These extensions are listed below and are detailed in Sect. 7.4.

T. Drezner (✉)
College of Business and Economics, California State University, Fullerton, CA, USA
e-mail: tdrezner@fullerton.edu

© The Author(s), under exclusive license to Springer Nature Switzerland AG 2022
S. Salhi and J. Boylan (eds.), *The Palgrave Handbook of Operations Research*, https://doi.org/10.1007/978-3-030-96935-6_7

Minimax Regret: Incorporating future market conditions, such as future changes in demand, into the model. Future market conditions are defined by a set of possible scenarios. For each scenario there is an optimal location for a facility yielding the maximum possible market share for that scenario. We find a location for a facility to accommodate the individual scenarios. For each scenario, some market share is lost at a location, compared to the optimal value at the best location for that scenario. The objective is to minimize the maximum loss in market share across all scenarios.

The Threshold Criterion: Rather than the objective of maximizing the total buying power attracted by the chain, there is a minimum buying power threshold to be met. If the chain fails to attract the threshold buying power, the company fails. The proposed objective is minimizing the probability that the company fails to meet the threshold.

The Leader-Follower: (Von Stackelberg equilibrium [121]). We find the best location in anticipation of future competition. The leader locates his facility and the follower (competitor) locates his facility *knowing* the leader's location. The follower has all the necessary information for his location decision. Therefore, the follower's problem is the standard competitive location problem. The leader's problem is more complicated. The objective is to maximize his market share *following* the follower's decision.

Location and Design: A limited budget is available. The improvement in the attractiveness of a facility depends on the budget allocated to it. We find the location of a new facility, its attractiveness, and possibly improving existing facilities subject to the limited budget.

Lost Demand: Customers may choose a substitute product if the product they are looking for is located too far. For example, if potential customers are interested in a Chinese restaurant but the closest one is too far, they may choose a non-Chinese restaurant which is close by, or eat at home.

Cannibalization: Minimize the cannibalization of one's chain facilities when constructing new ones. Cannibalization at the retail chain facilities is important, especially in the case of franchises. Franchisees may lose sales, which may be more than is allowed by the contract they signed with the company.

Recent reviews of competitive facilities location models are Berman et al. [6], Drezner [23, 24], Drezner and Eiselt [48], Eiselt [59], Eiselt et al. [60], Kress and Pesch [87], Lederer [90], Marianov et al. [96], Pelegrín et al. [109].

7.2   Approaches to Estimating Market Share

7.2.1   Deterministic Rules

According to the deterministic rules all customers residing at the same demand point patronize the same facility.

Proximity Rule: Hotelling [79] proposed that competitors compete by charging different mill prices and customers select the facility that provides the lowest mill price plus the cost of travel. This approach led to many papers, for example [50, 64, 69–72, 116, 119], that apply the proximity rule, i.e., customers patronize the closest facility. The proximity rule implies that all facilities charge the same price and thus are equally attractive.

Utility Function: The utility model is an extension of the proximity rule [16, 18]. A list of M quality measures, Q_i, $i = 1, \ldots, M$, each with a weight w_i, is determined. The utility function is $\sum_{i=1}^{M} w_i Q_i - d$, where d is the distance to the facility. A customer selects the facility with the maximum utility.

7.2.2   Probabilistic Rules

By the probabilistic rules, customers residing at the same demand point divide their patronage among several competing facilities. It can be interpreted as "each facility is patronized with a certain probability".

Random Utility: The random utility rule [25, 91] is an extension of the utility rule. The utility function parameters, except for the distance, are randomly distributed. Each customer patronizes the facility with the largest utility according to his assessment of the parameters. Therefore, not all customers residing at the same demand point patronize the same facility.

Gravity Model: The gravity model, sometimes referred to as the "Huff" model, was proposed by Reilly [115] and refined by Huff [80, 81]. According to the gravity model, the probability that a customer patronizes a facility is proportional to its attractiveness and declines according to a distance decay function. The basic gravity model is based on p competing facilities and n demand points that exist in an area [17]. A distance decay function $f(d, \lambda)$ with a parameter λ depending on the retail category is defined. For example, the distance decay function for grocery stores is different from the one for shopping malls. Let:

B_i	be the buying power at demand point i for $i = 1, \ldots, n$,
A_j	be the attractiveness level of facility j for $j = 1, \ldots, p$,
d_{ij}	be the distance between demand point i and facility j,
$f(d, \lambda)$	be the distance decay function,
λ	be the parameter of the distance decay function which depends on the retail category.
M_j	be the expected market share captured by facility j.

The estimated market share captured by facility j according to the gravity model is:

$$M_j = \sum_{i=1}^{n} B_i \frac{A_j f(d_{ij}, \lambda)}{\sum_{k=1}^{p} A_k f(d_{ik}, \lambda)} . \tag{7.1}$$

where the distance decay function $f(d, \lambda)$ is the same for all competing facilities in the same retail category. Note that some models assume a decay function $f(d)$ without a parameter λ.

In the original gravity model [115] it is assumed that the distance decay parallels gravity decay and thus $f(d) = \frac{1}{d^2}$. Huff [80, 81] suggested a decay function $f(d, \lambda) = \frac{1}{d^\lambda}$. Other distance decay functions include: exponential decay $f(d, \lambda) = e^{-\lambda d}$ [77, 132], $f(d) = e^{-1.705 d^{0.409}}$ [5], and a logit function [56]. Based on a real data set, Drezner [20] showed that exponential decay $f(d, \lambda) = e^{-\lambda d}$ fits the data better than a power decay $f(d, \lambda) = \frac{1}{d^\lambda}$. It is well recognized that the decay function varies across retail categories. For example, for the decay function $f(d, \lambda) = \frac{1}{d^\lambda}$ it was found that $\lambda = 3$ for grocery stores [81], $\lambda = 3.191$ for clothing stores [80], $\lambda = 2.723$ for furniture stores [80], and $\lambda = 1.27$ for shopping malls [20].

Flow Interception: Berman and Krass [8] introduced a competitive location model where demand is attracted from customers traveling en route to some destination while passing by a facility ("impulsive" shoppers) and demand originated at nodes of the network (planned purchase trips). Customers may change their mind on the way to the selected facility and stop at a less attractive facility just because they noticed it on the way. The latter issue is discussed in [37] concluding with a recommendation to locate a small retail facility "on the way" to a large shopping mall.

Cover Based Model: Launhardt [89] and Fetter [62] coined the term "Economic law of market areas". This concept was formalized by defining a "radius of influence", which is at the core of central place theory [11, 94]. According to central place theory there is a maximum "range of the good", depending on retail category, that customers are willing to travel to obtain the good. Drezner et al. [38, 39] proposed that each competing facility has a "sphere of influence" determined by its attractiveness level. More attractive facilities have a larger sphere of influence. The buying power spent by a customer in the sphere of influence of several facilities is divided among the competing facilities. The buying power of a customer located outside all the spheres of influence is lost. Drezner et al. [42] refined the model by assuming that patronage does not drop abruptly at the radius of influence, but declines gradually near that radius.

7.2.3 Estimating Attractiveness

The models for estimating the captured market share (except for the proximity rule) rely on a good estimate of the facilities' attractiveness levels. Therefore, estimating the attractiveness of a facility is an important component required for a successful implementation of the models.

Nakanishi and Cooper [101] suggested to determine a list of properties and calculated the attractiveness of a facility as a product of these properties' values, each raised by a power. Many researchers conducted public opinion surveys to determine the attributes affecting the attractiveness of the competing facilities and then establish their attractiveness. Properties that were found by opinion surveys to affect attractiveness include:

Supermarkets: Square footage [81]; price [113]; price, freshness, availability, convenience, quality service, parking [118]; choice range for daily/non-daily goods, price for daily/non-daily goods, parking [127]; store image, layout, appearance, accessibility, service, employee composition [83]; cleanliness, brands I like, better produce, low prices [16]; cost of products [5].
Furniture: Square footage [80].
Clothing: Square footage [80]; parking availability, choice range [126].
Central Business District: price, visual appearance, reputation, range of goods, shopping hours, atmosphere, design, service [15].
Shopping Malls: variety of stores, mall appearance, favorite brand names [49]. They tested 6 more attributes that were not found significant: Mall prices, distance to mall, adequate parking, mall safety, food court/restaurants, movies/entertainment.

There are other approaches to estimating and analyzing attractiveness levels:

* Drezner and Drezner [29] observed that the annual sales of a retail facility are a clear indication of its attractiveness. Higher attractiveness level is

reflected in higher sales figures. However, sales figures alone cannot be directly used as the attractiveness measures because sales are also dependent on the affluence (or buying income) of potential customers in a retail facility's trade area. The proposed procedure adjusts the sales figures by the demographic characteristics of the area, thus deriving the attractiveness measures of the retail facilities mainly from these two pieces of data.

- Drezner [20] estimated the attractiveness of facilities by asking shoppers about the zip code they came from and determined the attractiveness level by a least squares approach. She found the best fit to the observed distances by defining the attractiveness levels as variables.

- Drezner et al. [46] refined the gravity model by assigning different decay functions to different facilities. Customers patronize a more attractive facility at greater distances. A more attractive facility has a flatter decay function. The multiplicative attractiveness values are replaced by different decay functions. This approach is easier to implement because there is no need for public opinion surveys. It yielded more accurate results on a real data set. They modified the Drezner [20] approach by replacing the multiplicative attractiveness coefficients A_j as variables, with different decay parameter λ_j as variables. There is no multiplicative attractiveness level, i.e., $A_j = 1 \forall j$. Drezner et al. [47] incorporated the attractiveness level A_j in addition to variable decay parameters λ_j into the model.

- Drezner et al. [45] observed that not all customers perceive the same attractiveness level for the same facility. They proposed that the attractiveness level A_j is normally distributed with some mean and variance. Existing models use the mean attractiveness as A_j. Drezner et al. [45] defined an "effective" attractiveness level which is found to be lower than the average attractiveness assumed in gravity models. Greater variances yield lower effective attractiveness because the loss in market share by a given decline in attractiveness is greater than the gain in market share by increasing the attractiveness by the same amount.

7.3   Distance Correction

In most location models it is assumed that demand is generated at demand "points". In reality demand is generated in neighborhoods and not all residents in a neighborhood reside at the same distance from a facility. Demand generated in an area (for non-competitive location models) is investigated in, for example, [55, 122, 131].

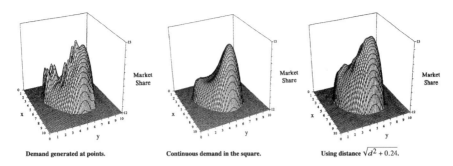

Fig. 7.1 Discrete and continuous market share surfaces

Drezner and Drezner [26] proposed a distance correction to the gravity model. Data may be available by zip codes or census tracts. Listing all individual customers is impractical. The distance correction incorporates these considerations. Drezner and Drezner [26] suggested that if the area of a demand "point" is A, the distance to a facility from the center of the area (the demand point) is d, then the corrected distance to be used in the gravity model is about $\sqrt{d^2 + 0.24A}$.

Drezner and Drezner [26] used an example problem of 100 demand points in a square of size 10 by 10 with seven existing facilities. This example problem was used in many papers, for example [18, 106]. Each demand point has an area of 1. The market share captured by the new facility is plotted in Drezner and Drezner [26], and depicted in Fig. 7.1. On the left, the surface plot of the "standard" gravity model using $f(d) = \frac{1}{d^2}$ as the decay function is depicted. In the middle, the market share captured when demand is continuous in the 10 by 10 square is shown. On the right, the market share surface using a decay function of $f(d) = \frac{1}{d^2 + 0.24}$ (distance correction) is depicted. When demand is generated at demand "points" there are many local maxima at various locations. The surface on the right is "smooth" and very close to the continuous surface with two local maxima.

7.4 Extensions

7.4.1 Minimax Regret Criterion

Drezner [21] incorporated future market conditions into the gravity model for the retail facility location. Future market conditions were analyzed as a set of possible scenarios. The best location for a new retail facility is at a location where the market share captured at that location is as close to the maximum as possible regardless of which future scenario takes place. Each scenario may also span different time horizons. The objective is the minimax regret which is used in other models of location analysis, for example [4, 13, 114].

Suppose there are K possible scenarios, $k = 1, \ldots, K$. For each scenario we can calculate the market share $M_k(X)$ at location X. The maximum buying power that can be captured according to each scenario, $M_k^* = \max\limits_{X}\{M_k(X)\}$, is calculated. The minimax regret objective $R(X)$, to be minimized, is then

$$ R(X) = \max_{k=1,\ldots,K} \left\{ M_k^* - M_k(X) \right\} $$

Drezner [21] applied the multi-start heuristic approach to find M_k^* and minimize $R(X)$ for the location of one facility in the plane.

7.4.2   The Threshold Objective

Drezner et al. [44] suggested a different objective for competitive location models. Rather than the objective of maximizing the total buying power attracted by a chain, there is a minimum buying power threshold T to be met. If the chain fails to attract the buying power T, the company fails. The proposed objective is minimizing the probability that the company fails to meet the threshold. The threshold concept has been employed in financial circles as a form of insurance on a portfolio, either to protect the portfolio or to protect a firm's minimum profit, for example [82, 84, 107].

In competitive facility location, let the buying power at demand point $1 \leq i \leq n$ be distributed according to some distribution with a mean of μ_i and a standard deviation σ_i. The buying powers of two demand points i and j are correlated with a correlation coefficient r_{ij}. The total buying power attracted by the chain has a mean of μ and a standard deviation σ (see [44] for detailed calculations). The objective function is to minimize $p(X) = P\left(Z \leq \frac{T-\mu}{\sigma}\right)$. By the Central Limit Theorem $M(X)$ can be assumed Normal but this is unnecessary because any cumulative distribution is monotonically increasing, thus minimizing $p(X)$ is equivalent to minimizing $\frac{T-\mu}{\sigma}$.

This problem was solved heuristically in [44]. It is possible to solve it optimally using BTST [53], but to the best of our knowledge no such attempt was made.

7.4.3 Leader-Follower Models

Drezner and Drezner [36] provide a review of the leader-follower model. Other papers on the topic are Küçükaydın et al. [112], Plastria and Vanhaverbeke [88].

There are two well researched two players' games: Nash equilibrium [102] and the leader-follower game also termed the von-Stackelberg equilibrium [121] and in voting theory is known as Simpson's problem [120]. In the Nash equilibrium game no player can improve his objective when the other player does not change his strategy. In many cases no equilibrium exists. In the leader-follower game the leader adopts a strategy and the follower adopts his best strategy knowing the leader's strategy. The follower's goal is to maximize his objective function while the leader's goal is to maximize his objective function *following* the follower's action.

Early contributions to Nash equilibrium location problems include Eaton and Lipsey [58], Hotelling [79], Lerner and Singer [92], Wendell and McKelvey [130]. The leader-follower location problem was introduced to competitive location models by Hakimi [69], and published in Hakimi [70–72], for location on network nodes using the Hotelling [79] premise that each customer patronizes the closest facility, see also Hansen and Labbè [73].

Drezner [50] analyzed two competitive location models in the plane. One is the location of a new facility that will attract the most buying power from an existing facility (the follower's problem). The other is the location of a facility that will secure the most buying power against the best location of a competing facility to be set up in the future (the leader's problem). The proximity rule using Euclidean distances is assumed.

Let n demand points be located in the plane. A buying power $b_i > 0$ is associated with demand point i for $i = 1, \ldots, n$. The leader locates his facility at X and the follower locates his facility at Y. Customers will patronize the follower's facility Y if the Euclidean distance between the customer and Y is less than the distance between the customer and X. Two problems are considered:

The follower's problem: Given the location of an existing facility X serving the demand points, find a location for a new facility Y that will attract the most buying power from demand points.

The leader's problem: Find a location for X such that it will retain the most buying power against the best possible location for the follower's facility Y.

For given locations X and Y, the distribution of the buying power can be found by constructing the perpendicular bisector to the segment connecting X and Y. This perpendicular bisector divides the plane into two half planes. All points in the closed half plane which includes X (including points on the perpendicular bisector itself) will patronize X and all the points in the other open half plane which includes Y, will patronize Y. This is a generalization of Hotelling's analysis on a line [79].

It is shown in [50] that one of the optimal locations for Y when X is given is infinitesimally close to X but not on X. It follows that the best location for the follower, Y^*, is "adjacent" (close) to X. The variable yet to be determined is the direction in which Y is "touching" X. In conclusion, finding an optimal location for Y is equivalent to finding the best line through X such that the open half plane defined by this line contains the most buying power for Y. Finding the best line by simple enumeration is detailed in [50].

The algorithm that solves the leader's problem is based on the algorithm used for solving the follower's problem. It can be found whether attracting a certain market share P_0 or higher by Y is possible by finding whether there is a feasible solution to a linear program. The algorithm is based on a bisection on the value of P_0. Complete details are given in [50].

The two problems can be modified by an extra restriction that the follower cannot locate his facility closer than a given distance R from the leader's facility. To solve the modified follower's problem for a given X it can be shown that the best solution for Y is determined by open half planes defined by tangent lines to the circle centered at X with a radius of $\frac{1}{2}R$ rather than lines through X. The details of the algorithms for solving the modified problems are available in [50].

Drezner and Zemel [57] considered the following problem: a large number of customers are spread uniformly over a given region $A \subseteq \mathbb{R}^2$. What configuration of facilities that cover the area will best protect against a future competing facility? The proximity rule is assumed, i.e., each customer patronizes the closest facility. There are three evenly spread configurations that cover the whole $\mathbb{R}^2$ plane with equilateral polygons depicted in Fig. 7.2: a triangular grid; a square grid; and an hexagonal grid (beehive). No other cover of the plane by identical equilateral polygons exists. Drezner and Zemel [57] found that the solution to the problem of covering the whole $\mathbb{R}^2$ plane is the hexagonal pattern. Then they analyzed the finite area problem and found bounds on the difference between the configurations as the number of facilities increases.

Since customers are attracted to the closest facility, the market share captured by each facility is proportional to the area attracted to the closest

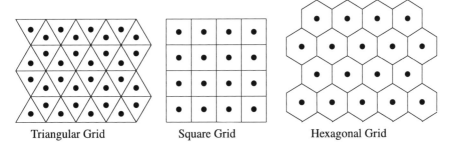

Triangular Grid   Square Grid   Hexagonal Grid

Fig. 7.2 Various configurations

facility. This is similar to the Voronoi diagram concept [3, 104, 124, 129]. In the configurations depicted in Fig. 7.2, the market share attracted by each facility is the area of the polygon. Let A be the area attracted by each facility (the area of the triangle, square, or hexagon). It is shown in [57] that:

* For the triangular grid the competitor's facility can attract a maximum of $\frac{2}{3}A$.
* For a square grid the competitor's facility can attract a maximum of $\frac{9}{16}A = 0.5625A$.
* For an hexagonal grid the competitor's facility can attract a maximum of $0.5127A$.

The hexagonal pattern provides the best protection from a future competitor. It is interesting that for hexagonal and square grids the competitor captures at least half of A at any point in the plane.

Hexagonal pattern is optimal for many location problems with numerous facilities covering a large area. For example:

* packing the largest number of circles in an area [12, 76, 125],
* p-median [105], p-center [122] and p-cover [54],
* p-dispersion [52, 93, 95, 103],
* equalizing the load covered by facilities [123].

It is also the preferred arrangement for a beehive in nature which has developed over the years in the evolutionary process.

Drezner and Drezner [27] proposed three heuristic approaches for finding a good solution to the leader-following model where market share is estimated by the gravity model: brute force, pseudo mathematical programming, and gradient search.

The Brute Force Approach: A grid of potential locations for the leader that cover the area is generated. For each grid location, the market share attracted by the follower is found and the market share attracted by the leader (after the follower locates at his best location) is calculated. If the grid is dense enough, the vicinity of the global maximum can be identified. If a more precise location is sought, a finer grid can be evaluated in that vicinity.

The Pseudo Mathematical Programming Approach: If the market share captured by the leader and the follower were concave, the following mathematical programming formulation (termed the "pseudo" problem) would have solved the problem: Maximize the market share captured by the leader subject to the derivative of the market share captured by the follower equal to zero (indicating a local maximum for the follower).

The Gradient Search Approach: A gradient search that directly finds a local maximum for the leader-follower problem is suggested. It guarantees termination at a local maximum once the optimal market share attracted by the follower can be found. It is recommended that this procedure is repeated many times in order to have a reasonable chance of getting the global optimum.

Drezner et al. [40] investigated a leader-follower competitive location model incorporating facilities' attractiveness (design) subject to limited budgets for both the leader and follower. The competitive model is based on the concept of cover [38, 39]. The leader and the follower, each has a budget to be spent on the expansion of their chains either by improving their existing facilities or by constructing new ones. The objective of the leader is to maximize his market share following the follower's reaction. The follower's problem is identical to the three problems analyzed in [39] because market conditions are fully known to the follower. A branch and bound algorithm as well as a tabu search [65–67] were proposed in [39] for the solution of each of these three strategies. For complete details the reader is referred to [85].

7.4.4   Location and Design

Combining the location decision with the design (treating the attractiveness level of the facility as a variable) was investigated, for example, in [1, 19, 61, 111, 128].

Drezner [19] assumed that the facilities' attractiveness are variables. A budget is available for locating new facilities and for establishing the new facilities' attractiveness levels. The problem is determining the facilities' attractiveness levels within the available budget. It is solved by a gradient search when the budget constraint is kept as equality. Plastria and Vanhaverbeke [112] combined the limited budget model with the leader-follower model.

The analysis in [19] for various assumptions about the attractiveness as a function of the investment in the facility leads to some interesting insights:

1. For firms with a decreasing marginal return on investment curve, the fixed budget allocation solution with equally divided budget among the new facilities is very close to optimality.
2. For firms with a fixed (constant) marginal return on investment the fixed budget allocation solution with equally divided budget works well, and can be used if the computational effort required to obtain the flexible budget allocation solution is prohibitive.
3. For a rapidly increasing marginal return, one should consider opening only one new facility investing all the budget in it.
4. Mildly increasing marginal return leads to a middle ground solution and none of the extreme budget allocation strategies is appropriate. In this case it is recommended to find the best budget allocation by applying the algorithm in [19].

Aboolian et al. [1] studied the problem of simultaneously finding the number of facilities, their location, and their design. For the problem with discrete design scenarios the TLA (tangent line approximation) procedure (see Sect. 7.5.3) can be applied. Aboolian et al. [1] assume that A_j, the attractiveness of facility j, is a function of K attraction attributes. These attributes can be continuous (e.g. facility size, product price) or discrete (e.g. number of parking spots, product variety). Moreover, it is assumed that for any potential facility j there is a basic design γ_j and K levels of improvement y_{jk} $j \in \bar{E}$, $k \in \{1, \ldots, K\}$ over the basic design. The attractiveness of facility j can now be expressed as:

$$A_j = I_j \gamma_j \prod_{k=1}^{K} (1 + y_{jk})^{Q_k}$$

where Q_k is the sensitivity parameter of the utility function with respect to attribute k, $0 \leq Q_k \leq 1$, and $I_j = 1$ if facility j is open and 0 otherwise. When y_{jk} is continuous, it is assumed to belong to an interval $[0, y_{jk}^{\max}]$, and when it is discrete it is assumed to belong to a certain discrete set (note that $y_{jk}^1 > y_{jk}$ if y_{jk}^1 is preferred to y_{jk}). The utility u_{ij} is now defined as: $u_{ij} = A_j (d_{ij} + 1)^{-\beta}$.

Two heuristics are introduced: an adapted weighted greedy and a steepest descent. The adapted greedy heuristic starts with an empty set of facilities and at each iteration the location design pair that results in the largest improvement per unit cost is added as long as it is within the available budget. The ascent approach starts with a given location set Q_0 and at each iteration either a new facility in the neighborhood of Q_0 is added to Q_0, or a facility is removed from Q_0 or an exchange of a new facility with one of the facilities from Q_0 takes place.

Drezner et al. [41] suggested the model assuming that the market can be partitioned into mutually exclusive sub-markets. For example, expanding a franchise around the world in New York, Paris, Tokyo, Beijing, etc., that customers residing in one sub-market patronize facilities only in that sub-market. Suppose that a procedure for finding the market share at each sub-market for a given budget allocated to the sub-market is available. The problem is then to determine the allocation of the budget among the sub-markets. A constraint that the sum of these individual budgets is equal to the available budget is added.

Three objectives were investigated: (i) maximizing the firm's profit, (ii) maximizing the firm's return on investment, and (iii) maximizing profit subject to a minimum threshold return on investment. Once the market share for a given budget at each individual market can be determined, the allocation of the budget among the markets is found by dynamic programming. For complete details see [41].

7.4.5   Lost Demand

Standard competitive location models assume that the total expenditures of each customer are a constant and are not affected by the location or number of service facilities. Therefore, locating new facilities only changes the allocation of the market share between the existing and new facilities. However, if there are no facilities nearby, customers may choose a substitute facility and the potential demand is lost.

As an example consider Chinese restaurants. There exists a certain buying power in the area which people who "love" Chinese food are willing to spend in Chinese restaurants. If there is at least one Chinese restaurant close to a customer, the available buying power will likely be completely spent at Chinese restaurants. If the closest Chinese restaurant is quite far from the customer, this customer may patronize a closer non-Chinese restaurant or eat at home rather than travel a long distance, and thus the buying power will be lost by the chain of Chinese restaurants.

Drezner and Drezner [33] suggested the following approach to estimating lost demand. The buying power at a demand point will be completely spent at a facility which is at distance "0" from the community. Furthermore, let k retail facilities be located at distances $d_1, \ldots, d_k$ from a community with buying power B. We assume that the probability that a customer located at the community will *not* spend his/her buying power at facility j is $1 - e^{-\lambda_j d_j}$ for some constant λ_j. The probability that a customer will not spend his buying power at any of the facilities is $\prod_{j=1}^{k} [1 - e^{-\lambda_j d_j}]$. The total buying power spent at all competing facilities is therefore:

$$B \left\{ 1 - \prod_{j=1}^{k} \left[1 - e^{-\lambda_j d_{ij}} \right] \right\} \tag{7.2}$$

and the buying power lost is

$$B \prod_{j=1}^{k} \left[1 - e^{-\lambda_j d_{ij}} \right] \tag{7.3}$$

Drezner and Drezner [33] suggested to adjust the buying power at each community by Eq. (7.2).

Another approach to modeling lost demand is proposed in [35]. They assume that there is a maximum distance D that customers are willing to drive to a facility. A "dummy" competitor is created at an imaginary location which is at a distance D from all demand points. This dummy competitor attracts the lost demand. By the proximity rule, if the distance to the closest facility is greater than D, demand is lost. By the gravity model, the dummy competitor attracts the lost demand and the total market share is that attracted by "real" facilities. By Eq. (7.1) $\sum_{j=1}^{p} M_j = \sum_{i=1}^{n} B_i$. However, not including the dummy facility in the sum, $\sum_{j=1}^{p} M_j < \sum_{i=1}^{n} B_i$ and the difference is the lost market share.

7.4.6 Cannibalization

Marketers commonly use a definition of cannibalization that focuses on a company eating into its own market by introducing a new product to an existing product line or an established brand (product line extension and multi-brand strategies) at the expense of the old brand. For example, if Coca

Cola introduces Coke2, and customers buy Coke2 instead of the original Coke, sales may be up for the new product, but these sales may be eating into Coke's sales of the original Coke. In such cases, overall company sales may not be increasing. This form of cannibalization is well recognized and well researched in the marketing literature. See for example [10, 22, 97, 98, 100].

Another form of cannibalization occurs at the retail level of chain facilities, especially in the case of franchises. In this form of cannibalization, opening a new retail outlet in close proximity to an existing outlet, the new outlet cannibalizes the sales of the existing one. Though not a franchise, this applies to Starbucks coffee and other chain retailers. Unlike cannibalization in new product development and introduction that is well researched, cannibalization at the retail level has been overlooked for the most part. With the growth of franchise operations, this emerges as an important and timely issue. For as long as companies wish to grow and expand, managers will be faced with the strategic decision of optimally locating new, additional facilities so that cannibalization of existing chain members is minimized.

Schneider et al. [117] report cases of lawsuits regarding cannibalization in fast food franchise systems such as Arby's, Burger King, KFC, McDonald's, Subway, and Taco Bell. This phenomenon is referred to as encroachment. A similar problem is observed and documented in the hospitality/lodging industry for such franchise systems as Holiday Inn, Days Inn, Howard Johnson, Ramada, Comfort Inn, and Quality Inn [108]. Many franchisees believe they have lost business as a result of cannibalization from new units in the same chain, a phenomenon referred to in the lodging industry as "impact".

When a retail chain plans an expansion in a market by building additional outlets, two not necessarily compatible objectives should be considered: (1) Maximize the market share captured by the expanding chain (if the expansion cost is fixed, profit is an increasing function of the market share captured and therefore maximizing market share is equivalent to maximizing profit). (2) Minimize cannibalization of existing chain outlets so as not to gain market share at the expense of member outlets. Cannibalizing chain members may render them nonprofitable and may result in channel conflict (both horizontal and vertical conflict). This consideration is especially critical when the outlets are franchised and gain in market share at the expense of member franchisees may be damaging to the profitability of the whole chain.

Drezner [22] formulated and solved the problem of maximizing the market share captured by the chain facilities subject to a given limit of cannibalization. The market share captured, and consequently the cannibalized portion of it, was calculated using the gravity model [80, 81].

Plastria [110] applied the utility function model [17] in which the optimal solution to maximizing market share usually is not unique but there is an area in the plane such that a facility located at any point in that area attracts the same (maximal) market share. Plastria [110] suggested to locate the facility at the point in that region that minimizes cannibalization, thus maintaining the maximum market share. When the gravity model is used, there is only one optimal solution point that maximizes chain's market share and the planner must accept the cannibalization at that point if he or she does not wish to consider sub-optimal location solutions regarding the market share captured.

Zeller et al. [133] considered the market share captured by an expanding chain. The franchisor attempts to maximize the total market share of the chain (thus implicitly considers the cannibalization of existing outlets) while the new franchisee considers the market share captured by his new outlet. They conclude that the franchisee of a new store may choose a different location for his store than the franchisor. In reality, the franchisee has no input into the location decision and thus his objective is ignored.

Ghosh and Craig [63] developed the FRANSYS model for franchise system growth. Firms seeking to expand franchise distribution systems have to balance two incompatible goals, maximizing system revenues and minimizing the cannibalization of sales of existing outlets. The model uses two constraint types: (1) constraints that disallow new unit locations that do not provide a minimum revenue threshold for the new unit, (2) disallow new units that fail to either protect current revenue for existing units as a group, or, protect current revenue for each existing unit. The first, weaker constraint is not very satisfying to existing franchisees because individual units may lose revenue. The "best" location in terms of maximizing system revenues while protecting current revenue for all existing units, results in a mediocre new location that barely meets its minimum revenue threshold [117]. Application of the FRANSYS model to the hospitality industry would require modification of data input to conform to the market and product characteristics of the hospitality industry [108].

Fernández et al. [61] proposed a related model. Their model is a bi-objective model of maximizing profit while minimizing cannibalization. They consider the location of the new facility along with its attractiveness as a decision variable. The construction cost of the new facility is included in the profit function. In addition, they added constraints forbidding the location of a facility in the vicinity of demand points. All of these components lead to a complicated model that requires extensive data collection and relies on many modeling assumptions.

7.5   Solution Methods

7.5.1   Single Facility

Drezner and Drezner [30] optimally solved the single facility gravity-based competitive location problem by applying the Big Triangle Small Triangle (BTST) global optimization algorithm [53]. The procedure BTST requires effective upper and lower bounds on the market share captured when the facility is located anywhere in a triangle. The procedure is very efficient and finds the optimal solution for 10,000 demand points in less than six minutes of computer time. The generalized Weiszfeld algorithm [51] repeated from 1,000 different starting solutions required about the same time for all 1,000 runs but does not guarantee optimality. However, it found the optimal solution at least 17 times out of 1,000 on a set of test problems.

7.5.2   Multiple Facilities

Drezner et al. [43] proposed five heuristic procedures for the maximization of the market share by locating p new facilities with given attractiveness levels using the gravity rule. The most successful heuristic was found to be:

1. Applying a simulated annealing approach [86] for locations restricted to grid points.
2. Finding a good location for each facility, one at a time, by the generalized Weiszfeld algorithm [51].
3. The two steps are repeated 100 times from randomly generated starting solutions and the best one is selected.

7.5.3   The TLA Method

The TLA (tangent line approximation) method [2] can find an optimal solution to the gravity model within a given accuracy. For its implementation, the objective function should be a concave function, twice differentiable and non-decreasing of a linear function. These conditions hold for the gravity model. The idea is to replace the objective function by a piece-wise linear function. The feasible range is divided into segments and a tangent line is constructed in each segment touching the objective function at the segment's center. The objective function is formulated by adding a binary variable for each segment and maintaining the original constraints. Optimal solutions of the modified problem are then found by non-linear solvers. The number of segments is determined by the pre-specified accuracy. For details see [2].

7.6 Applying the Gravity Rule to Other Objectives

The gravity rule can be applied to other commonly used non-competitive location objectives. Rather than assuming that a user gets services from the closest facility, he chooses a facility according to the gravity rule. The probability of patronizing a facility is proportional to the facility's attractiveness and to some decay function of the distance.

7.6.1 Gravity p-Median

In the standard p-median model [14] it is assumed that each user travels to the closest facility. This implicitly implies that facility choice is centrally controlled or that all facilities charge the same price for the service. Drezner and Drezner [31, 32] proposed the gravity p-median model. It is assumed that users choose from among the facilities providing services according to the gravity rule rather than from the closest facility. Users consider facilities' attractiveness in their choice. Similar to the standard p-median problem, the objective is to minimize the sum of the expected weighted distances.

Brimberg et al. [9] suggested a similar p-median model based on this idea that customers do not necessarily patronize the closest facility. A list of probabilities $P_1 \geq P_2, \ldots, \geq P_p$ that add up to 1 is constructed. The probability that a customer patronizes the closest facility is P_1. The probability he patronizes the second closest facility is P_2, and so on.

7.6.2 Gravity Hub Location

Drezner and Drezner [28] applied the gravity rule to the hub location problem. A traveler needs to fly from one airport to another. Several potential hubs are available. If the origin or the destination is a hub airport, the traveler chooses a non-stop flight. Otherwise, the probability that a certain hub is selected is proportional to the hub's attractiveness (price, walking distance from the arrival gate to the connecting one, chance of inclement weather, etc.) and to a distance decay function such as the total travel distance (or time) raised to a given inverse power. Such a model can be generalized to selecting a sequence of two or more hubs.

7.6.3   Gravity Multiple Server

Drezner and Drezner [34] considered the gravity rule version of the multiple server location problem [7]. Total service time consists of travel time to the facility, waiting time in line, and service time. There is a given number of servers to be distributed among the facilities. Each facility acts as an M/M/k queuing system. In [34] customers select a server with a probability proportional to its attractiveness and to a decay function of the distance, not necessarily the closest one. Two models are proposed: a stationary one and an interactive one. In the stationary model it is assumed that customers do not consider the expected waiting time in line and service time at the facility in their facility selection decision simply because they do not know these values. In the interactive model it is assumed that customers know the expected waiting time in line and service time at the facility and do consider them in their facility selection decision.

7.7   Summary and Suggestions for Future Research

In this chapter we reviewed competitive location models which are part of the field of facility location. Facility location models investigate the location of one or more facilities to achieve a certain objective. In competitive location models the objective is to attract as much buying power as possible from competitors' facilities by constructing new facilities and/or improving existing ones. A main component of such models is the estimation of how customers select the facility to patronize. Demand attracted by a facility depends on its attractiveness, on the buying power customers are planning to spend, and on the distance customers need to travel to get to the facility. What distinguishes different models is the assessment of the relationship between these factors and the market share captured. It is clear that higher attractiveness and buying power lead to higher market share, and a greater distance lowers the expected market share captured.

The gravity model [80, 81, 115] estimates the probability of patronizing a facility by these three components. Other approaches include the proximity rule (customer patronize the closest facility), utility and random utility models, cover-based models, and the flow interception model (all discussed in Sects. 7.2.1 and 7.2.2). One important implementation issue is the assessment of these components, especially the attractiveness level of a facility.

Many extensions to the basic models were investigated. For example, anticipating future changes in the market, considering lost demand due to long distances, cannibalization of one's chain facilities. Optimal location of one facility can be found by branch and bound algorithms such as Big Square Small Square [75], or Big Triangle Small Triangle [53]. Location of multiple facilities is usually solved heuristically by various approaches tailored to the specific model, or metaheuristic methods such as tabu search [65–67], simulated annealing [86], genetic algorithms [68, 78], variable neighborhood search [74, 99] and others.

There are many opportunities for future research. Improving and fitting the models better to real circumstances; obtaining better estimates for attractiveness of facilities. There are many solution methods for multiple facilities location models and constrained models that can be improved by designing more efficient heuristic algorithms that will enable practitioners to solve larger problems.

References

1. Aboolian, R., Berman, O., and Krass, D. (2007a). Competitive facility location and design problem. *European Journal of Operations Research*, 182:40–62.
2. Aboolian, R., Berman, O., and Krass, D. (2007b). Competitive facility location model with concave demand. *European Journal of Operations Research*, 181:598–619.
3. Aurenhammer, F., Klein, R., and Lee, D.-T. (2013). *Voronoi Diagrams and Delaunay Triangulations*. World Scientific, New Jersey.
4. Averbakh, I. and Berman, O. (2000). Minmax regret median location on a network under uncertainty. *INFORMS Journal on Computing*, 12:104–110.
5. Bell, D., Ho, T., and Tang, C. (1998). Determining where to shop: Fixed and variable costs of shopping. *Journal of Marketing Research*, 35(3):352–369.
6. Berman, O., Drezner, T., Drezner, Z., and Krass, D. (2009). Modeling competitive facility location problems: New approaches and results. In Oskoorouchi, M., editor, *TutORials in Operations Research*, pages 156–181. INFORMS, San Diego.
7. Berman, O. and Drezner, Z. (2007). The multiple server location problem. *Journal of the Operational Research Society*, 58:91–99.
8. Berman, O. and Krass, D. (1998). Flow intercepting spatial interaction model: A new approach to optimal location of competitive facilities. *Location Science*, 6:41–65.

9. Brimberg, J., Maier, A., and Schöbel, A. (2021). When closest is not always the best: The distributed p-median problem. *Journal of the Operational Research Society*, 72:200–216.

10. Chandy, R. K. and Tellis, G. J. (1998). Organizing for radical product innovation: The overlooked role of willingness to cannibalize. *Journal of Marketing Research*, 35:474–487.

11. Christaller, W. (1966). *Central Places in Southern Germany*. Prentice-Hall, Englewood Cliffs, NJ.

12. Coxeter, H. S. M. (1973). *Regular Polytopes*. Dover Publications.

13. Daskin, M., Hesse, S., and Revelle, C. (1997). α-reliable p-minimax regret: A new model for strategic facility location modeling. *Location Science*, 5:227–246.

14. Daskin, M. S. (1995). *Network and Discrete Location: Models, Algorithms, and Applications*. John Wiley & Sons, New York.

15. Downs, R. M. (1970). The cognitive structure of an urban shopping center. *Environment and Behavior*, 2:13–39.

16. Drezner, T. (1994a). Locating a single new facility among existing unequally attractive facilities. *Journal of Regional Science*, 34:237–252.

17. Drezner, T. (1994b). Optimal continuous location of a retail facility, facility attractiveness, and market share: An interactive model. *Journal of Retailing*, 70:49–64.

18. Drezner, T. (1995). Competitive facility location in the plane. In Drezner, Z., editor, *Facility Location: A Survey of Applications and Methods*, pages 285–300. Springer, New York, NY.

19. Drezner, T. (1998). Location of multiple retail facilities with limited budget constraints—In continuous space. *Journal of Retailing and Consumer Sevices*, 5:173–184.

20. Drezner, T. (2006). Derived attractiveness of shopping malls. *IMA Journal of Management Mathematics*, 17:349–358.

21. Drezner, T. (2009a). Location of retail facilities under conditions of uncertainty. *Annals of Operations Research*, 167:107–120.

22. Drezner, T. (2011). Cannibalization in a competitive environment. *International Regional Science Review*, 34:306–322.

23. Drezner, T. (2014). A review of competitive facility location in the plane. *Logistics Research*, 7:1–12.

24. Drezner, T. (2019). Gravity models in competitive facility location. In Eiselt, H. A. and Marianov, V., editors, *Contributions to Location Analysis—In Honor of Zvi Drezner's 75th Birthday*, pages 253–275. Springer, Cham.

25. Drezner, T. and Drezner, Z. (1996). Competitive facilities: Market share and location with random utility. *Journal of Regional Science*, 36:1–15.

26. Drezner, T. and Drezner, Z. (1997). Replacing discrete demand with continuous demand in a competitive facility location problem. *Naval Research Logistics*, 44:81–95.

27. Drezner, T. and Drezner, Z. (1998). Facility location in anticipation of future competition. *Location Science*, 6:155–173.
28. Drezner, T. and Drezner, Z. (2001). A note on applying the gravity rule to the airline hub problem. *Journal of Regional Science*, 41:67–73.
29. Drezner, T. and Drezner, Z. (2002). Validating the gravity-based competitive location model using inferred attractiveness. *Annals of Operations Research*, 111:227–237.
30. Drezner, T. and Drezner, Z. (2004). Finding the optimal solution to the Huff competitive location model. *Computational Management Science*, 1:193–208.
31. Drezner, T. and Drezner, Z. (2006). Multiple facilities location in the plane using the gravity model. *Geographical Analysis*, 38:391–406.
32. Drezner, T. and Drezner, Z. (2007). The gravity p-median model. *European Journal of Operational Research*, 179:1239–1251.
33. Drezner, T. and Drezner, Z. (2008). Lost demand in a competitive environment. *Journal of the Operational Research Society*, 59:362–371.
34. Drezner, T. and Drezner, Z. (2011). The gravity multiple server location problem. *Computers & Operations Research*, 38:694–701.
35. Drezner, T. and Drezner, Z. (2012). Modelling lost demand in competitive facility location. *Journal of the Operational Research Society*, 63:201–206.
36. Drezner, T. and Drezner, Z. (2017). Leader-follower models in facility location. In *Spatial Interaction Models*, pages 73–104. Springer.
37. Drezner, T., Drezner, Z., and Eiselt, H. A. (1996). Consistent and inconsistent rules in competitive facility choice. *Journal of the Operational Research Society*, 47:1494–1503.
38. Drezner, T., Drezner, Z., and Kalczynski, P. (2011). A cover-based competitive location model. *Journal of the Operational Research Society*, 62:100–113.
39. Drezner, T., Drezner, Z., and Kalczynski, P. (2012). Strategic competitive location: Improving existing and establishing new facilities. *Journal of the Operational Research Society*, 63:1720–1730.
40. Drezner, T., Drezner, Z., and Kalczynski, P. (2015). A leader-follower model for discrete competitive facility location. *Computers & Operations Research*, 64:51–59.
41. Drezner, T., Drezner, Z., and Kalczynski, P. (2016). The multiple markets competitive location problem. *Kybernetes*, 45:854–865.
42. Drezner, T., Drezner, Z., and Kalczynski, P. (2020a). A gradual cover competitive facility location model. *OR Spectrum*, 42:333–354.
43. Drezner, T., Drezner, Z., and Salhi, S. (2002a). Solving the multiple competitive facilities location problem. *European Journal of Operational Research*, 142:138–151.
44. Drezner, T., Drezner, Z., and Shiode, S. (2002b). A threshold satisfying competitive location model. *Journal of Regional Science*, 42:287–299.
45. Drezner, T., Drezner, Z., and Zerom, D. (2018). Competitive facility location with random attractiveness. *Operations Research Letters*, 46:312–317.

46. Drezner, T., Drezner, Z., and Zerom, D. (2020b). Facility dependent distance decay in competitive location. *Networks and Spatial Economics*, 20:915–934.

47. Drezner, T., Drezner, Z., and Zerom, D. (2022). An extension of the gravity model. *Journal of the Operational Research Society*. https://doi.org/10.1080/016 05682.2021.2015256

48. Drezner, T. and Eiselt, H. A. (2002). Consumers in competitive location models. In Drezner, Z. and Hamacher, H. W., editors, *Facility Location: Applications and Theory*, pages 151–178. Springer-Verlag, Berlin.

49. Drezner, T., Marcouldies, G., and Drezner, Z. (1998a). Methods for comparing the attractiveness of shopping centers. In *Proceedings of the DSI meeting, Las Vegas*, vol. 2, pages 1090–1092. November, 1998.

50. Drezner, Z. (1982). Competitive location strategies for two facilities. *Regional Science and Urban Economics*, 12:485–493.

51. Drezner, Z. (2009b). On the convergence of the generalized Weiszfeld algorithm. *Annals of Operations Research*, 167:327–336.

52. Drezner, Z. and Erkut, E. (1995). Solving the continuous p-dispersion problem using non-linear programming. *Journal of the Operational Research Society*, 46:516–520.

53. Drezner, Z. and Suzuki, A. (2004). The big triangle small triangle method for the solution of non-convex facility location problems. *Operations Research*, 52:128–135.

54. Drezner, Z. and Suzuki, A. (2010). Covering continuous demand in the plane. *Journal of the Operational Research Society*, 61:878–881.

55. Drezner, Z. and Wesolowsky, G. O. (1980). Optimal location of a facility relative to area demands. *Naval Research Logistics Quarterly*, 27:199–206.

56. Drezner, Z., Wesolowsky, G. O., and Drezner, T. (1998b). On the logit approach to competitive facility location. *Journal of Regional Science*, 38:313–327.

57. Drezner, Z. and Zemel, E. (1992). Competitive location in the plane. *Annals of Operations Research*, 40:173–193.

58. Eaton, B. C. and Lipsey, R. G. (1975). The principle of minimum differentiation reconsidered: Some new developments in the theory of spatial competition. *The Review of Economic Studies*, 42:27–49.

59. Eiselt, H. A. (2011). Equilibria in competitive location models. In Eiselt, H. A. and Marianov, V., editors, *Foundations of Location Analysis*, pages 139–162.

60. Eiselt, H. A., Marianov, V., and Drezner, T. (2015). Competitive location models. In Laporte, G., Nickel, S., and da Gama, F. S., editors, *Location Science*, pages 365–398. Springer, Cham.

61. Fernández, J., Pelegrín, B., Plastria, F., and Tóth, B. (2007). Planar location and design of a new facility with inner and outer competition: An interval lexicographical-like solution procedure. *Networks and Spatial Economics*, 7:19–44.

62. Fetter, F. A. (1924). The economic law of market areas. *The Quarterly Journal of Economics*, 38:520–529.

63. Ghosh, A. and Craig, C. S. (1991). FRANSYS: A franchise location model. *Journal of Retailing*, 67:212–234.
64. Ghosh, A. and Rushton, G. (1987). *Spatial Analysis and Location-Allocation Models*. Van Nostrand Reinhold Company, New York, NY.
65. Glover, F. (1977). Heuristics for integer programming using surrogate constraints. *Decision Sciences*, 8:156–166.
66. Glover, F. (1986). Future paths for integer programming and links to artificial intelligence. *Computers & Operations Research*, 13:533–549.
67. Glover, F. and Laguna, M. (1997). *Tabu Search*. Kluwer Academic Publishers, Boston.
68. Goldberg, D. E. (2006). *Genetic Algorithms*. Pearson Education, Delhi, India.
69. Hakimi, S. L. (1981). On locating new facilities in a competitive environment. In *Presented at the ISOLDE II Conference*, Skodsborg, Denmark.
70. Hakimi, S. L. (1983). On locating new facilities in a competitive environment. *European Journal of Operational Research*, 12:29–35.
71. Hakimi, S. L. (1986). *p*-Median theorems for competitive location. *Annals of Operations Research*, 6:77–98.
72. Hakimi, S. L. (1990). Locations with spatial interactions: Competitive locations and games. In Mirchandani, P. B. and Francis, R. L., editors, *Discrete Location Theory*, pages 439–478. Wiley-Interscience, New York, NY.
73. Hansen, P. and Labbè, M. (1988). Algorithms for voting and competitive location on a network. *Transportation Science*, 22:278–288.
74. Hansen, P. and Mladenović, N. (1997). Variable neighborhood search for the *p*-median. *Location Science*, 5:207–226.
75. Hansen, P., Peeters, D., and Thisse, J.-F. (1981). On the location of an obnoxious facility. *Sistemi Urbani*, 3:299–317.
76. Hilbert, D. and Cohn-Vossen, S. (1932). *Anschauliche Geometrie*. Springer, Berlin. English translation published by Chelsea Publishing Company, New York (1956): Geometry and the Imagination.
77. Hodgson, M. J. (1981). A location-allocation model maximizing consumers' welfare. *Regional Studies*, 15:493–506.
78. Holland, J. H. (1975). *Adaptation in Natural and Artificial Systems*. University of Michigan Press, Ann Arbor, MI.
79. Hotelling, H. (1929). Stability in competition. *Economic Journal*, 39:41–57.
80. Huff, D. L. (1964). Defining and estimating a trade area. *Journal of Marketing*, 28:34–38.
81. Huff, D. L. (1966). A programmed solution for approximating an optimum retail location. *Land Economics*, 42:293–303.
82. Jacobs, B. I. and Levy, K. N. (1996). Residual risk: How much is too much? *Journal of Portfolio Management*, 22:10–16.
83. Jain, A. K. and Mahajan, V. (1979). Evaluating the competitive environment in retailing using multiplicative competitive interactive models. In Sheth, J. N., editor, *Research in Marketing*, vol. 2, pages 217–235. JAI Press, Greenwich, CT.

84. Johansson, F., Seiler, M. J., and Tjarnberg, M. (1999). Measuring downside portfolio risk. *The Journal of Portfolio Management*, 26:96–107.

85. Kalczynski, P. (2019). Cover-based competitive location models. In Eiselt, H. A. and Marianov, V., editors, *Contributions to Location Analysis—In Honor of Zvi Drezner's 75th Birthday*, pages 277–320. Springer, Cham.

86. Kirkpatrick, S., Gelat, C. D., and Vecchi, M. P. (1983). Optimization by simulated annealing. *Science*, 220:671–680.

87. Kress, D. and Pesch, E. (2012). Sequential competitive location on networks. *European Journal of Operational Research*, 217:483–499.

88. Küçükaydın, H., Aras, N., and Kuban Altınel, İ. (2012). A leader–follower game in competitive facility location. *Computers & Operations Research*, 39:437–448.

89. Launhardt, W. (1885). *Mathematische Begründung der Volkswirthschaftslehre*. W. Engelmann.

90. Lederer, P. J. (2019). Location-price competition with delivered pricing and elastic demand. *Networks and Spatial Economics*. In press.

91. Leonardi, G. and Tadei, R. (1984). Random utility demand models and service location. *Regional Science and Urban Economics*, 14:399–431.

92. Lerner, A. P. and Singer, H. W. (1937). Some notes on duopoly and spatial competition. *The Journal of Political Economy*, 45:145–186.

93. Locatelli, M. and Raber, U. (2002). Packing equal circles in a square: A deterministic global optimization approach. *Discrete Applied Mathematics*, 122:139–166.

94. Lösch, A. (1954). *The Economics of Location*. Yale University Press, New Haven, CT.

95. Maranas, C. D., Floudas, C. A., and Pardalos, P. M. (1995). New results in the packing of equal circles in a square. *Discrete Mathematics*, 142:287–293.

96. Marianov, V., Eiselt, H., and Lüer-Villagra, A. (2020). The follower competitive location problem with comparison-shopping. *Networks and Spatial Economics*, 20, 367–393.

97. Mason, C. H. and Milne, G. R. (1994). An approach for identifying cannibalization within product line extensions and multi-brand strategies. *Journal of Business Research*, 31:163–170.

98. Mazumdar, T., Sivakumar, K., and Wilemon, D. (1996). Launching new products with cannibalization potential: an optimal timing framework. *Journal of marketing theory and practice*, 4:83–93.

99. Mladenović, N. and Hansen, P. (1997). Variable neighborhood search. *Computers & Operations Research*, 24:1097–1100.

100. Moorthy, K. S. and Png, I. P. (1992). Market segmentation, cannibalization, and the timing of product introductions. *Management Science*, 38:345–359.

101. Nakanishi, M. and Cooper, L. G. (1974). Parameter estimate for multiplicative interactive choice model: Least squares approach. *Journal of Marketing Research*, 11:303–311.

102. Nash, J. (1951). Non-cooperative games. *Annals of Mathematics*, 54:286–295.

103. Nurmela, K. J. and Oestergard, P. (1999). More optimal packings of equal circles in a square. *Discrete & Computational Geometry*, 22:439–457.

104. Okabe, A., Boots, B., Sugihara, K., and Chiu, S. N. (2000). *Spatial Tessellations: Concepts and Applications of Voronoi Diagrams*. Wiley Series in Probability and Statistics. John Wiley, Hoboken, NJ.

105. Okabe, A. and Suzuki, A. (1997). Locational optimization problems solved through Voronoi diagrams. *European Journal of Operational Research*, 98:445–456.

106. O'Kelly, M. E. (1995). Inferred ideal weights for multiple facilities. In Drezner, Z., editor, *Facility Location: A Survey of Applications and Methods*, pages 69–88. Springer New York.

107. Olsen, R. A. (1997). Investment risk: The experts' perspective. *Financial Analysts Journal*, 53:62–66.

108. Patel, D. and Corgel, J. B. (1995). An analysis of hotel-impact studies. *The Cornell Hotel and Restaurant Administration Quarterly*, 36:27–37.

109. Pelegrín, B., Fernández, P., and García, M. D. (2018). Computation of multi-facility location nash equilibria on a network under quantity competition. *Networks and Spatial Economics*, 18:999–1017.

110. Plastria, F. (2005). Avoiding cannibalisation and/or competitor reaction in planar single facility location. *Journal of the Operational Research Society of Japan*, 48:148–157.

111. Plastria, F. and Carrizosa, E. (2004). Optimal location and design of a competitive facility. *Mathematical Programming*, 100:247–265.

112. Plastria, F. and Vanhaverbeke, L. (2008). Discrete models for competitive location with foresight. *Computers & Operations Research*, 35:683–700.

113. Prosperi, D. C. and Schuler, H. J. (1976). An alternate method to identify rules of spatial choice. *Geographical Perspectives*, 38.

114. Puerto, J., Rodríguez-Chía, A. M., and Tamir, A. (2009). Minimax regret single-facility ordered median location problems on networks. *INFORMS Journal on Computing*, 21:77–87.

115. Reilly, W. J. (1931). *The Law of Retail Gravitation*. Knickerbocker Press, New York, NY.

116. ReVelle, C. (1986). The maximum capture or sphere of influence problem: Hotelling revisited on a network. *Journal of Regional Science*, 26:343–357.

117. Schneider, K. C., Johnson, J. C., Sleeper, B. J., and Rodgers, W. C. (1998). A note on applying retail location models in franchise systems: A view from the trenches. *Journal of Consumer Marketing*, 15:290–296.

118. Schuler, H. J. (1981). Grocery shopping choices: Individual preferences based on store attractiveness and distance. *Environment and Behavior*, 13:331–347.

119. Serra, D. and ReVelle, C. (1995). Competitive location in discrete space. In Drezner, Z., editor, *Facility Location: A Survey of Applications and Methods*, pages 367–386. Springer, New York, NY.

120. Simpson, P. B. (1969). On defining areas of voter choice: Professor tullock on stable voting. *The Quarterly Journal of Economics*, 83:478–490.

121. Stackelberg, H. V. (1934). *Marktform und Gleichgewicht*. Julius Springer, Vienne.
122. Suzuki, A. and Drezner, Z. (1996). The *p*-center location problem in an area. *Location Science*, 4:69–82.
123. Suzuki, A. and Drezner, Z. (2009). The minimum equitable radius location problem with continuous demand. *European Journal of Operational Research*, 195:17–30.
124. Suzuki, A. and Okabe, A. (1995). Using Voronoi diagrams. In Drezner, Z., editor, *Facility Location: A Survey of Applications and Methods*, pages 103–118. Springer, New York.
125. Szabo, P. G., Markot, M., Csendes, T., and Specht, E. (2007). *New Approaches to Circle Packing in a Square: With Program Codes*. Springer, New York.
126. Timmermans, H. (1982). Consumer choice of shopping centre: An information integration approach. *Regional Studies*, 16:171–182.
127. Timmermans, H. (1988). Multipurpose trips and individual choice behaviour: An analysis using experimental design data. *Behavioural Modelling in Geography and Planning*, pages 356–67.
128. Toth, B., Fernandez, J., Pelegrin, B., and Plastria, F. (2009). Sequential versus simultaneous approach in the location and design of two new facilities using planar Huff-like models. *Computers & Operations Research*, 36:1393–1405.
129. Voronoï, G. (1908). Nouvelles applications des paramètres continus à la théorie des formes quadratiques. deuxième mémoire. recherches sur les parallélloèdres primitifs. *Journal für die reine und angewandte Mathematik*, 134:198–287.
130. Wendell, R. and McKelvey, R. (1981). New perspectives in competitive location theory. *European Journal of Operational Research*, 6:174–182.
131. Wesolowsky, G. O. and Love, R. F. (1971). Location of facilities with rectangular distances among point and area destinations. *Naval Research Logistics Quarterly*, 18:83–90.
132. Wilson, A. G. (1976). Retailers' profits and consumers' welfare in a spatial interaction shopping mode. In Masser, I., editor, *Theory and Practice in Regional Science*, pages 42–59. Pion, London.
133. Zeller, R. E., Achabal, D. D., and Brown, L. A. (1980). Market penetration and locational conflict in franchise systems. *Decision Sciences*, 11:58–80.

8

Interval Tools in Branch-and-Bound Methods for Global Optimization

José Fernández⊙ and Boglárka G.-Tóth⊙

8.1 Introduction

Given the set $A \subseteq \mathbb{R}^n$, and the functions $f : A \longrightarrow \mathbb{R}$, $g : A \longrightarrow \mathbb{R}^m$ and $h : A \longrightarrow \mathbb{R}^k$, we deal with the nonlinear programming (NLP) problem

$$
\begin{aligned}
\min \ & f(x) \\
\text{s.t. } & g(x) \le 0 \\
& h(x) = 0 \\
& x \in \pmb{x}^0
\end{aligned}
\tag{8.1}
$$

where $\pmb{x}^0 \subseteq A$ is an n-dimensional interval of $\mathbb{R}^n$. It is assumed that f and/or g and/or h are nonlinear functions and the variables can take any value within $\pmb{x}^0$, i.e., we have a *continuous* NLP problem. If at least one

J. Fernández
Department Statistics and Operations Research, University of Murcia, Murcia, Spain
e-mail: josefdez@um.es

B. G.-Tóth (✉)
Institute of Informatics, University of Szeged, Szeged, Hungary
e-mail: boglarka@inf.u-szeged.hu

© The Author(s), under exclusive license to Springer Nature Switzerland AG 2022
S. Salhi and J. Boylan (eds.), *The Palgrave Handbook of Operations Research*,
https://doi.org/10.1007/978-3-030-96935-6_8

of the variables is constrained to take integer values, then we have a Mixed-Integer Nonlinear Programming (MINLP) problem. Problem (8.1) is said to be a global optimization problem when it has local minimum points different from the global minimum points. If x^* is a global minimum point, we will denote by $f^* = f(x^*)$ the corresponding global minimum value. Checking that $h(x)$ is exactly equal to 0 is usually impossible in practice. That is why in most applications the equality constraints are changed to $\varepsilon^1 \le h(x) \le \varepsilon^2$, where $[\varepsilon^1, \varepsilon^2] \ni 0$ and the problem is assumed to have only inequality constraints.

In general, problem (8.1) is NP-hard. Depending on the mathematical properties of the functions involved, different methods can be devised to cope with it [44]. Branch-and-bound (B&B) algorithms are among the most successful ones. They manage a working list of subregions of the feasible set still to be investigated, initially composed by x^0. At each iteration, a subregion from the list is chosen and investigated. The subregion is discarded if it is found to be infeasible, if the minimum objective value that can be attained by any of its feasible points is greater than the current best value $\tilde{f}$ found so far by the algorithm, or if the optimal solution of the problem within the subregion can be found. Also, the subregion is no further investigated and sent to the solution list if the difference between a lower bound and an upper bound of the objective function over the subregion is less than a given tolerance ε_f. Otherwise, the subregion is subdivided, and the new subregions are inserted in the working list. Every time that $\tilde{f}$ is updated (when evaluating the objective function at some feasible point) the subregions whose lower bound is greater than $\tilde{f}$ are also discarded. The process finishes when the working list is empty. The subregions in the solution list contain then any global optimal solution, and any point in those subregions differs from f^* less than ε_f.

8.1.1   Interval Analysis

The difficulty in designing a B&B method lies in obtaining the lower and upper bounds of the objective function in a given subregion. And it is here where *interval analysis* comes into play. Interval analysis started in the early sixties with the seminal work by R. E. Moore [63, 64] about automatic error analysis in digital computing, although its application in B&B methods for solving global optimization problems dates back to the seventies [39, 46, 86]. In a nutshell, interval analysis is similar to real analysis, but it uses closed and bounded intervals instead of real numbers.

We follow the notation suggested in [50]. According to it, intervals are denoted by boldface letters, the corresponding endpoints with lower- and over-lines, $x = [\underline{x}, \overline{x}]$, the midpoint by $\operatorname{mid} x = (\underline{x} + \overline{x})/2$ and the width by $\operatorname{wid} x = \overline{x} - \underline{x}$. An n-dimensional interval, also called as a *box*, is denoted in the same way, and its components are then distinguished with the use of subscripts, $x = (x_1, \ldots, x_n)$. The midpoint of a box should be understood component-wise, and the width as $\operatorname{wid} x = \max\{\operatorname{wid} x_i : i = 1, \ldots, n\}$. The set of intervals will be denoted by $\mathbb{IR}$ and the set of n-dimensional boxes by $\mathbb{IR}^n$.

The arithmetic operations should be understood logically, in the sense that for $\otimes \in \{+, -, \times, \div\}$ we define

$$x \otimes y = \{x \otimes y : x \in x, y \in y\}.$$

There are simple formulae which allow us to compute the result intervals:

$$
\begin{aligned}
x + y &= [\underline{x} + \underline{y}, \overline{x} + \overline{y}] \\
x - y &= [\underline{x} - \overline{y}, \overline{x} - \underline{y}] \\
x \times y &= [\min\{\underline{x}\underline{y}, \underline{x}\overline{y}, \overline{x}\underline{y}, \overline{x}\overline{y}\}, \max\{\underline{x}\underline{y}, \underline{x}\overline{y}, \overline{x}\underline{y}, \overline{x}\overline{y}\}] \\
x \div y &= x \times [\tfrac{1}{\overline{y}}, \tfrac{1}{\underline{y}}] (\text{only defined when } 0 \notin y)
\end{aligned}
$$

When implemented in a computer, *directed rounding* is required, as the endpoints may not be exactly represented in the binary system employed by the computer.

Unfortunately, the use of those formulae may not give the exact expected result, due to the so-called *interval dependence*. For instance, the result of $x - x$ for $x = [0, 1]$ is $[0, 1] - [0, 1] = [-1, 1]$. This is because what is computed is $x - y$, with $x = [0, 1]$ and $y = [0, 1]$ but assuming that $x \in x$ and $y \in y$ vary *independently*. In general, this may lead to an over-estimation of the result. For example, $(x + 1)(x - 1)$ when $x = [-2, 2]$ gives $[-9, 3]$ when the true range is $[-1, 3]$. Notice, however, that the result always contains the true range, so the bounds are valid. This follows from the so-called *inclusion isotony*:

$$a \subseteq b, c \subseteq d \Rightarrow a \otimes c \subseteq b \otimes d, \forall a, b, c, d \in \mathbb{IR}.$$

This property helps to construct inclusion functions, which is the main tool employed in B&B methods. Given a real function $f : A \subseteq \mathbb{R}^n \to \mathbb{R}$, a function $f : \mathbb{I}(A) \to \mathbb{I}$ is said to be an *inclusion function* for f provided that $\operatorname{range} f(x) \subseteq f(x)$ for all $x \subseteq \mathbb{I}(A)$. Here, $\mathbb{I}(A)$ denotes the set of all boxes included in A and $\operatorname{range} f(x) = \{f(x) : x \in x\}$ is the range of f over x. Observe that if f is an inclusion function for f then we can directly

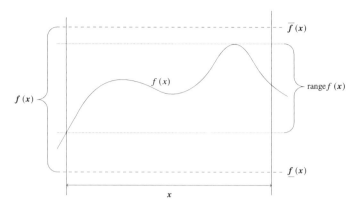

Fig. 8.1 $f(x)$ is an inclusion function of $f(x)$

obtain lower and upper bounds of f over any box x just by taking $\underline{f}(x)$ and $\overline{f}(x)$, respectively (see Fig. 8.1). Inclusion functions for vector-valued functions should be understood component-wise.

For a function f *predeclared* in some programming language (like sin or exp) it is not difficult to obtain a corresponding inclusion function since the monotonicity of predeclared functions is well-known, and then we can take $f(x) = \text{range} f(x)$. For a general function $f : A \subseteq \mathbb{R}^n \to \mathbb{R}$ there are several methods which allow to obtain an inclusion function [75]. The easiest one (and the quickest one from the computational point of view) is to replace each occurrence of a variable by its corresponding interval, each predeclared function by its corresponding predeclared inclusion function and the real arithmetic operations by their interval counterparts. The inclusion function so obtained is called *natural inclusion function*.

If the function f is differentiable, another inclusion function that could be used is the *centered form*, given by $f(x) = f(c) + (x - c)^T \nabla f(x)$ where c is any point of x (usually its midpoint) and $\nabla f(x)$ an inclusion function of the gradient ∇f of f at x (usually obtained as the natural interval extension of ∇f). Whereas the centered form usually gives over small boxes tighter bounds as compared to the natural interval extension, the opposite usually holds over big boxes. For instance, the natural interval extension of $f(x) = x^2 - x + 1$ at $x = [-1, 1]$ gives $[-1, 1]^2 - [-1, 1] + 1 = [0, 3]$ and the centered form (using $c = \text{mid}[-1, 1] = 0$, and $\nabla f(x) = [-3, 1]$) gives $1 + ([-1, 1] - 0)[-3, 1] = [-2, 4]$, whereas $\text{range} f([-1, 1]) = [3/4, 3]$. In general, given a function and a box, it is not known which of the possible inclusion functions will provide the tightest inclusion for the range [90].

Regardless of the inclusion function employed, it will provide valid lower and upper bounds automatically, which allows us to build a B&B method easily.

Surprisingly, although we can find in the literature B&B methods designed to cope with MINLP problems (see for instance [1, 8, 9, 87]), and even some of them use interval analysis tools in some steps, the general machinery of interval B&B methods commonly used for continuous problems has seldom been applied to MINLP problems.

8.1.2   Aim of the Chapter

The aim of this chapter is twofold. First, we want to do a review of the most relevant publications about interval B&B methods for single-objective optimization problems from 2011 to March 2021. The following search was done in Scopus within article title, abstract or keywords: (interval W/0 "branch-and-bound") OR (interval W/0 branch W/1 bound) OR (interval W/0 analysis AND (optimiz* OR optimis* OR minim* OR maxim* OR contract* OR filter* OR extension)) OR (interval W/0 method* AND (optimiz* OR optimis* OR minim* OR maxim* OR contract* OR filter* OR extension)) OR (interval W/0 tool* AND (optimiz* OR optimis* OR minim* OR maxim* OR contract* OR filter* OR extension)) OR (interval W/0 arithmetic* AND (optimiz* OR optimis* OR minim* OR maxim* OR contract* OR filter* OR extension)) OR (interval AND constraint W/0 pro*) OR (interval W/2 optimiz*) OR (interval W/2 optimis*) OR (interval W/2 contract*). In all, 4148 references were found. To select the most relevant ones, they were exported to a .ris file, and the ASReview software (https://asr eview.nl/) was used with the default strategies. ASReview uses artificial intelligence techniques to improve the screening process. The revision of abstracts was stopped when 20% of the papers had been checked. At that moment, 195 non-relevant papers in a row were discarded. As a result, 81 papers were selected and investigated in depth, although only some of them are finally included in this revision.

To put the new research in context, first, in Sect. 8.2 we briefly comment some of the most important strategies used in interval B&B methods up to 2010. The books [37, 40, 47, 49, 76, 89] provide a broader coverage of the research done in interval B&B methods until that date. It is in Sects. 8.3–8.6 where the review is done. We do not include in the review papers devoted exclusively to constraint programming techniques for constraint satisfaction problems nor hybrid techniques which combine interval B&B with heuristic procedures, so as not to make the chapter excessively long. For the same reason, research work devoted to applications of interval B&B methods to the solution of real optimization problems is also left out. However, we do include a section concerning the software available as of May 2021 to implement interval B&B methods (see Sect. 8.7).

The second aim of the paper is to highlight which of the interval tools designed for continuous NLP problems could also be employed, maybe with some modifications, to cope with MINLP problems, as well as tools specifically designed for MINLP problems (see Sect. 8.8).

8.2   Prototype Interval B&B Method

The prototype interval B&B algorithm is as pseudo-coded in Algorithm 1.

Algorithm 1: A general interval B&B algorithm.

Funct IBB(x^0, f, g, h)
1: Set the working list $\mathcal{L}_W := \{x^0\}$ and the final list $\mathcal{L}_S := \emptyset$
2: **while** ($\mathcal{L}_W \neq \emptyset$) **do**
3:     Select a box x from $\mathcal{L}_W$ *Selection rule*
4:     Compute $f(x)$ *Bounding rule*
5:     **if** x cannot be eliminated   *Elimination rule*
6:         Divide x into x^j, $j = 1, \ldots, p$, subboxes   *Division rule*
7:         **for** $j = 1, \ldots, p$ **do**
8:             **if** x^j satisfies the termination criterion   *Termination rule*
9:                 Store x^j in $\mathcal{L}_S$
10:            **else**
11:                Store x^j in $\mathcal{L}_W$
12:            **endif**
13:        **endfor**
14:    **endif**
15: **endwhile**
16: **return** $\mathcal{L}_S$

Depending on how the steps are carried out, different algorithms can be obtained. And how a specific step is designed depends on the mathematical properties of the problem. Usually it is assumed that the functions defining the problem are continuous, although it is possible to construct inclusion functions for non-continuous functions, too [30, 31, 49, 72]. In many cases, it is assumed that f is differentiable, and that an inclusion function $\nabla f = (\nabla_1 f, \ldots, \nabla_n f)^T$ of the gradient $\nabla f = (\frac{\partial f}{\partial x_1}, \ldots, \frac{\partial f}{\partial x_n})^T$ is available. In some cases, f is required to be twice differentiable; in that case, the inclusion of the Hessian matrix $H(f) = (\frac{\partial^2 f}{\partial x_i \partial x_j})_{i,j=1}^n$ will be denoted by $\boldsymbol{Hf} =$

$(H_{ij}f)_{i,j=1}^{n}$. Usually, the inclusions for the gradient and the Hessian matrix are obtained via *automatic differentiation* [36, 74].

Next, we briefly discuss some of the most commonly used rules in the literature up to 2010.

8.2.1 Bounding Rule

In interval B&B methods, the usual way to obtain bounds for the range of a function f over a box x is to evaluate an inclusion function. Apart from the natural inclusion function [64] and the center form mentioned above [38, 56], other inclusion functions have been proposed in the literature, such as the Baumann's optimal centered form [7] (which uses a particular point $c \in x$ in the centered form to minimize the range overestimation), the slope form [77] (where instead of inclusion of derivatives, inclusion of *slopes* are used), or the affine form [22] (which uses *affine arithmetic* instead of the classical interval arithmetic).

Notice that if $f^1, \ldots, f^r$ are inclusion functions for f, then a tighter interval containing range $f(x)$ can be obtained as $\cap_{i=1}^{r} f_i(x)$.

8.2.2 Elimination/Filtering Rules

Usually, several tests are applied successively to the same box to try to discard it or to reduce its size. Most of the tests in the literature are designed for the unconstrained version of problem (8.1).

Cut-off test: A box x is rejected whenever $\underline{f}(x) > \tilde{f}$, where $\tilde{f}$ is the best known upper bound of the global minimum f^*. $\tilde{f}$ is usually updated evaluating the objective function at the midpoint of the boxes, that is why this test is also known as *midpoint test*.

Monotonicity test: It can only be used when the objective function is differentiable. If $0 \notin \nabla f(x)$ for a given box x, then the objective function is monotonous over it. Hence, if x is not on the boundary of the search region, it can be rejected; otherwise it can be narrowed to the intersection of x and the boundary of the search region.

Non-convexity test: The objective function must be twice differentiable. If for some $i \in \{1, \ldots, n\}$ the condition $H_{ii}f(x) < 0$ holds, then f cannot be convex at x. Hence, if x is not on the boundary of the search region, it can be rejected; otherwise it can be narrowed to the intersection of x and the boundary of the search region.

Newton step: The objective function must be twice differentiable. It consists of applying an interval version of Newton's method to the system $\nabla f(x) = 0$, by iterating

$$N\left(\pmb{x}^{(k+1)}\right) = \text{mid}\left(\pmb{x}^{(k)}\right) - \left[\pmb{H}f\left(\pmb{x}^{(k)}\right)\right]^{-1} \nabla f\left(\text{mid}\left(\pmb{x}^{(k)}\right)\right)$$

$$\pmb{x}^{(k+1)} = N\left(\pmb{x}^{(k+1)}\right) \cap \pmb{x}^{(k)}$$

until $\pmb{x}^{(k+1)} = \emptyset$ or $\pmb{x}^{(k+1)} = \pmb{x}^{(k)}$ for some k. In the first case it is proved that there is no global optimizer in the box $\pmb{x}$, while in the later case all local optimizers of $\pmb{x}$ are included in $\pmb{x}^{(k+1)}$, if any. Moreover, if $N(\pmb{x}^{(k+1)}) \subset \pmb{x}^{(k)}$ for some k, then it is proved that there exists a unique local optimizer in the interval $\pmb{x}^{(k+1)}$. This procedure is rather costly, due to the computation of the Hessian matrix and its inverse matrix. On the other hand, even if it converges to a local optimum, maybe the box could be deleted a few steps later by the cut-off test. That is why it is recommended to perform only one step of the Newton method [40, 49, 66].

Except for the cut-off test, the rest of the discarding test mentioned above can only be applied to unconstrained (or bound constrained) problems. If there are inequality constraints, it is first needed to know whether the box is feasible or not. This can be done using the

Feasibility test: We say that a box $\pmb{x}$ *satisfies* the constraint $g_j(x) \leq 0$ if $\overline{\pmb{g}}_j(\pmb{x}) \leq 0$ and that $\pmb{x}$ *does not satisfy* it if $\underline{\pmb{g}}_j(\pmb{x}) > 0$. A box $\pmb{x}$ is said to be *feasible* if it satisfies all the constraints, *infeasible* if it does not satisfy at least one of the constraints, and *undetermined* otherwise. A box $\pmb{x}$ is said to be *strictly feasible* if $\overline{\pmb{g}}_j(\pmb{x}) < 0$, $j = 1, \ldots, m$. The Feasibility test [76] discards boxes that are infeasible. It also provides information about the feasibility of a box. Notice that to apply this test, we just need an inclusion function $\pmb{g}_j$ for each of the functions g_j defining the inequality constraints.

The monotonicity and non-convexity tests can be applied to a box $\pmb{x}$ whenever it is feasible. However, in [29] some conditions are described under which the monotonicity test can be applied to undetermined boxes as well. Something similar is done in [91] for the non-convexity test.

The Newton step can be applied as described above if the box is feasible, and it could be applied to the Karush-Kuhn-Tucker of Fritz John optimality conditions if the box is undetermined. Also, in [29] a *projected one-dimensional interval Newton method* is proposed which can be applied to feasible boxes, and also, under some conditions, to undetermined boxes.

Other discarding tests suitable for being applied to feasible boxes try to make an efficient use of the gradient information, by constructing a linear lower bounding function of the objective function (similarly to what is done in Lipschitz optimization [41]). See for instance [17, 88, 94].

Discarding tests specially designed for inequality constrained problems can be found in [28], such as the *best corner test* and, for the case of undetermined boxes for which only one linear constraint is not satisfied, the *monotonicity-border test* and the *reduction test*.

8.2.3 Selection Rule

Since (8.1) is a minimization problem, usually the box x such that $\underline{f}(x) = \min\{\underline{f}(x^j) : x^j \in \mathcal{L}_W\}$ is selected, as it is thought to be the most likely box to contain a global optimum solution.

In some papers, instead of using $\underline{f}(x)$ as a proxy for the likelihood of the optimality of the box x, other indexes have been suggested. For instance, in [18, 20] the *RejectIndex*

$$p(f^*, x) = \frac{f^* - \underline{f}(x)}{\text{wid } f(x)}$$

is suggested for unconstrained problems, and the box with the highest index is selected. The index was modified in [59] to handle inequality constrained problems, in order to take the feasibility degree of the box into account, and substituted by

$$pup(f^*, x) = pu(x) \cdot p(f^*, x),$$

where

$$pu(x) = \prod_{j=1}^{m} \min\left\{ \frac{-\underline{g}_j(x)}{\text{wid } g_j(x)}, 1 \right\}.$$

In the implementations, the unknown optimal value f^* is approximated by the objective value of the best feasible point found so far by the algorithm, $\tilde{f}$. The computational studies in those papers showed that in some cases the CPU time required by the interval B&B algorithm could be reduced considerably with the new rules.

8.2.4 Division Rules

Two things have to be decided when subdividing a box $\boldsymbol{x}$: (1) along which coordinate direction (or directions) should the box be cut and (2) how many cuts should be performed perpendicularly to the chosen direction(s). The division procedure employed in most of the literature is the bisection along the direction of maximum width.

Selecting the direction of maximum width allows a uniform subdivision of the searching region $\boldsymbol{x}^0$. However, for unconstrained problems, other rules which try to select the coordinate direction along which the objective function varies the most, have proved to be successful. For instance, among other rules, in [21, 78] it is suggested to select the direction r where the maximum $\max\{\text{wid}\,(\nabla_i f(\boldsymbol{x})(\boldsymbol{x}_i - \text{mid}\,\boldsymbol{x}_i)) : i = 1, \ldots, n\}$ is attained (see also [52] for a related rule). Note, however, that this rule is more time-consuming.

Bisection avoids that the B&B tree grows too fast, specially when it is anticipated that some of the subboxes generated will be discarded by the discarding tests. However, around the global optimal solutions many boxes are usually evaluated (the so-called *cluster effect*) because it is difficult to discard them, and in those cases a multisection may be more advantageous [12]. In fact, in [19] an adaptive multisection technique is suggested, where the box is subdivided into a larger number of subboxes when if it is located in the neighborhood of a minimizer point, it is bisected when it is far, and tetrasected otherwise. The index $p(f^*, \boldsymbol{x})$ is used as a surrogate to measure the proximity of a box to a minimizer point. See also [59].

8.2.5 Termination Rule

A box $\boldsymbol{x}$ is sent to the final list $\mathcal{L}_S$ whenever $\tilde{f} - \underline{f}(\boldsymbol{x}) < \varepsilon_f$. Sometimes, the more demanding condition wid $\boldsymbol{f}(\boldsymbol{x}) < \varepsilon_f$ is employed instead. Both rules work with absolute units, which may be inconvenient in some cases. That is why the rule

$$\frac{\tilde{f} - \underline{f}(\boldsymbol{x})}{\max\{\tilde{f}, 1\}} < \varepsilon_f$$

is also commonly employed. Furthermore, this last rule has the advantage of reducing both the cluster problem and the excess processing that occurs when an infinity of equivalent non-isolated solutions exists, as pointed out in [71].

Sometimes, due to the overestimation, the criteria above alone are not enough, and in order to avoid that the computer runs out of memory, a box is also sent to $\mathcal{L}_S$ if wid $x < \varepsilon_s$ for some $\varepsilon_s > 0$.

8.2.6 Interval B&B Methods for MINLP Problems

Interval B&B methods have rarely been applied to MINLP problems. In [40] (see also [97]) it is suggested to add, for any integer variable x_i, the constraint $\sin(\pi x_i) = 0$ and to apply the interval B&B method for continuous problems. Although this can, at least theoretically, solve the problem, in practice has not proved to be a good strategy.

In [40] it is also suggested to use the prototype algorithm to problem (8.1) when some of the variables can only take integer values. To take advantage of the integrity of a variable $x_i \in \mathbb{Z}$, when subdividing the box x perpendicularly to coordinate direction i through the point c, instead of generating the subboxes $x^1 = (x_1, \ldots, x_{i-1}, [\underline{x}_i, c], x_{i+1}, \ldots, x_n)$ and $x^2 = (x_1, \ldots, x_{i-1}, [c, \overline{x}_i], x_{i+1}, \ldots, x_n)$, in x^1 the point c can be changed to $\lfloor c \rfloor$ and in x^2 to $\lceil c \rceil$ (note that no integer solution is lost). In this way, the endpoints of the intervals of integer variables are always integer numbers. The monotonicity test can also be adapted to integer variables: if x is a feasible box and $0 \notin \nabla_i f(x)$ for an integer variable x_i, then the box can be reduced to the facet containing the minimum values in the box. For instance, if $\nabla_i f(x) < 0$, x can be reduced to $(x_1, \ldots, \overline{x}_i, \ldots, x_n)$ (see Fig. 8.2).

This strategy was put in practice in [62] (see also [32]) to solve a constrained MINLP problem (although only the feasibility and cut-off tests were used) and in [93], where other discarding tests were also proposed.

In [9], Belotti et al. introduced the software package COUENNE for MINLP problems. It follows a B&B scheme, and uses interval analysis in some steps. Some ideas introduced in [9] could also be of help in a general interval B&B algorithm for MINLP problems.

To our knowledge, no more relevant work has been presented in the literature up to 2010.

8.3 Bounding Techniques

Having tight lower bounds of the objective function over boxes is important, because they may allow to discard the boxes thanks to the cut-off test. In [11] the case of single variable functions that can be decomposed into

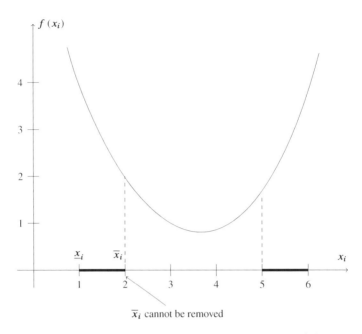

$\overline{x}_i$ cannot be removed

Fig. 8.2 The facet corresponding to the upper bound $\overline{x}_i \in \mathbb{Z}$ of the interval x_i of the integer variable x_i cannot be discarded, since the monotonicity of the objective function may change in the box $(x_1, \ldots, [\overline{x}_i, \overline{x}_i + 1], \ldots, x_n)$

sub-functions is investigated. The basic idea is to compute bounds for the sub-functions, and then put together at work all those bounds to compute a bound for the original function. In particular, in [11] the case of additively separable functions is analyzed, i.e., functions $f : A \subseteq \mathbb{R} \rightarrow \mathbb{R}$ which can be written as $f(x) = \sum_{j=1}^{p} f_j(x)$. Notice that

$$\min_{x \in A} f(x) \geq \sum_{j=1}^{p} \min_{x \in A} f_j(x).$$

In particular, if $\underline{F}_j$ is a lower bound of f_j over A then $\sum_{j=1}^{p} \underline{F}_j$ is a lower bound for f over A, and sometimes it may be tighter than the bound obtained with the natural inclusion function or the centered form. In their paper, the authors work with the Baumann's optimal centered form and the so-called Lower Boundary Value Form (LBVF), a centered form that uses the evaluation at the endpoints of the interval. The latter seems to provide better bounds, although when applied to solving a test bed of problems it does not speed-up the interval B&B algorithms.

Posypkin and Khamisov [73] also work with single variable functions, and again, they decompose them into sub-functions. However, their approach is rather different. They try to exploit the monotonicity and the convexity/concavity of the sub-functions in order to obtain better bounds of the original function. They can even handle nondifferentiable composite functions. Their approach restricts the objective function's range even if the latter is not convex neither concave, and it was experimentally proved that the technique can significantly reduce the bounds on the function's range and enhance the interval B&B algorithm for global optimization. For this, a set of rules for deducing monotonicity, concavity, and convexity of a univariate function are proposed, which are then implemented via operator overloading.

Araya et al. [4] also try to exploit the monotonicity of the sub-functions in which the original function is decomposed. They present their procedure for functions of several variables. Assume that f is monotonous on the variables $x_1, \ldots, x_q$ (we assume they are the first q out of the n variables of f without loss of generality). And consider the values x_i^- and x_i^+ such that: if f is increasing (resp. decreasing) along x_i, then $x_i^- = \underline{x}_i$ and $x_i^+ = \overline{x}_i$ (resp. $x_i^- = \overline{x}_i$ and $x_i^+ = \underline{x}_i$). Let us denote $w = (x_{q+1}, \ldots, x_n)$ the non-monotonic variables and consider the functions

$$f_{\min}(w) = f(x_1^-, \ldots, x_q^-, w)$$
$$f_{\max}(w) = f(x_1^+, \ldots, x_q^+, w)$$

Then, an interval containing the image of f over a box x can be obtained as $[\underline{f}_{\min}(w), \overline{f}_{\max}(w)]$, which is sharper (smaller) than the one produced by the natural interval inclusion function of f. If f is monotonous with respect to all its variables, then the exact range is obtained. When f is not monotonic with respect to a variable x_i, but is monotonic w.r.t. a subgroup of occurrences of x_i, the paper groups the occurrences of x_i into three sets, increasing, decreasing and non-monotonic auxiliary variables, and exploits the monotonicity of the first two sets. One could think about grouping all increasing variables in the first group, all decreasing variables in the second one, and the non-monotonic variables in a third one. However, the evaluation by monotonicity of the new function will provide the same result as the natural interval extension. The key point is to include in the first group (resp. second group) some decreasing (resp. increasing) or non-monotonic variables so that, when considered together, the corresponding sub-function is still increasing (resp. decreasing). For instance, $f(x) = -x^3 + 2x^2 + 14x$ is not monotonous in the interval $[-2, 1]$. Its exact range is $[-13.18, 15]$ while the natural inclusion functions gives $[-29, 30]$. If we group $f^{og}(x_a, x_b) =$

$-x_b^3 + 2x_a^2 + 14x_a$, notice that the interval derivative of the group corresponding to x_a is $4[-2, 1] + 14 = [6, 18]$, which is positive, so the function is increasing. And the group corresponding to x_b is decreasing. Hence, evaluating both parts using their monotonicity, we obtain the inclusion $[2(-2)^2 + 14(-2), 2 \cdot 1^2 + 14 \cdot 1] + [-1^3, -(-2)^3] = [-21, 24]$. Notice, however, that the interval extension by occurrence grouping is not unique for a function f since it depends on the occurrence grouping used. For instance, in the previous example, we could also have used the grouping $f^{og}(x_a, x_c) = -x_a^3 + 2x_c^2 + 14x_a$ (where x_c groups the non-monotonic variables) and then the inclusion $[-20, 21]$ would be obtained. That is why the authors also present in [4], first, a 0-1 linear program to automatically select the grouping, and second, a continuous linear program to do the grouping using a linear convex combination of the variables. The computational studies show that the methodology is useful when applied to solving systems of equations.

Makino and Berz [58] propose to use Taylor models (which combine Taylor polynomials and remainder error enclosures) to obtain sharper inclusion functions, alleviating the overestimation provoked by the dependency problem. Although it is more time-consuming to work with Taylor models than with classical interval inclusion functions, it can be done in an automatic way (as interval arithmetic) and provides much better bounds. In particular, it is suggested that the use of first and second order Taylor models provides improved bounds quickly.

Moscato et al. [65] present a formalization of the affine arithmetic [22] which only supports polynomial expressions. Computational experiments show that when dealing with problems with a high level of coupling between sub-expressions (and hence, where the dependency problem is high), the affine method performs significantly better than the classic interval arithmetic.

Ninin et al. [71] propose to use a *simplified* affine arithmetic form to compute bounds for the objective function and the functions defining the constraints. Furthermore, they use those affine forms to generate a linear programming problem which is a linear relaxation of the global optimization problem. The linear problem has the same number of variables than the original global optimization problem, and its number of constraints is at most twice. New tighter bounds can be obtained in this way for the objective function since in the computation of those bounds the constraints are also taken into account. This new technique is specially useful at discarding small boxes. The authors included those techniques in a branch-and-bound algorithm, where constraint programming techniques were also included. The constraint programming techniques were specially useful at discarding/reducing bigger boxes. The combination of both affine techniques and constraint programming techniques leads to a fast and reliable algorithm.

The use of auxiliary linear programming problems to compute better bounds is also proposed in Araya et al. [5], although in a different context. In this paper the authors propose an interval Newton-like operator called *X-Newton*, which constructs a convexification of the problem over a given box by using a mean value form (for each of the functions defining the constraints) but based on two opposite extreme points of the box (instead of using as base point the midpoint of the box). Then, the box hull containing the polytope produced by the linear convexification is found by calling the simplex algorithm twice per variable. This procedure is included in a recursive procedure where constraint programming tools are used to reduce the search space. X-Newton does not require the system to be preconditioned, and it can handle both well-constrained as well as under-constrained systems. And the computational studies show its usefulness when applied to solve constrained global optimization problems and constraint satisfaction problems.

Araya et al. [92] and Trombettoni et al. [6] also use auxiliary linear programming problems to compute bounds. This time, the authors exploit "inner regions" in the upper bounding phase. Although equality constraints lead to empty inner regions, the procedure can also be applied to equality constraints provided that equations can be defined with a tiny admissible precision error. The strategy proposed to obtain an inner region constructs a linear upper bounding function for each constraint using again a mean value form based on a corner of the box. And doing something similar for the objective function, a linear optimization problem is obtained. If it is infeasible, nothing can be said, since the linear problem is more constrained than the original problem. If it has an optimal solution, it can be used to update the best upper bound of the original global optimization problem. Another procedure base on constraint programming techniques is also proposed in [6]. Similarly, an "outer" linearization of the constraints can be built, leading to another linear programming problem, where this time infeasibility means that the box contains no feasible points and can be discarded, and in case the problem has an optimal solution, it can be used to update the best lower bound of the original problem on the box.

In all the previous cases, the use of the simplex method with floating-point arithmetic may lead to unsafe results. That is why it is suggested to employ the methodology introduced in [68] to have those errors always under control.

Kearfott [53] investigates how to obtain rigorous upper bounds when the problem has equality constraints or the optimal solution is active at some inequality constraints. As in [6, 92], equality constraints are transformed into inequality constraints with a tiny admissible precision error. A procedure to compute a feasible point from an approximate infeasible (but almost feasible) solution is proposed. The computational results show the procedure is usually successful at finding feasible points, and when included in an interval B& B algorithm can speed-up its convergence, as it allows to update the best upper bound of the objective function.

8.4   Discarding Tests

Araya [2] shows through a computational study that interval B&B methods can be speed-up if an upper bound close to the optimal value is available. A good upper bound makes the cut-off test more efficient. In interval B&B methods, the best upper bound is usually updated by evaluating the objective function at feasible points. The proposal in [2] is instead to estimate upper bounds UB_{est} during the execution of the algorithm based on the actual values of the global lower bound LB and upper bound $\tilde{f}$ of the problem and in the estimation of the upper bound previously generated, UB_{est}^{prev}. In particular, the following estimation is suggested:

$$UB_{est} = \tilde{f} - h(\Delta, \alpha)(\tilde{f} - LB)$$

where $\Delta = (UB_{est}^{prev} - \tilde{f})/(UB_{est}^{prev} - LB)$ and

$$h(\Delta, \alpha) = \begin{cases} \frac{\alpha \Delta}{1-\alpha} & \text{if } \Delta \leq 1 - \alpha \\ \frac{\Delta(1-\alpha)-1}{\alpha} + 2 & \text{if } \Delta > 1 - \alpha \end{cases}$$

Here α is a parameter which controls how much risky we want the estimation of the upper to be. When $\alpha = 0$ we are pessimistic, and we set $UB_{est} = UB$. When $\alpha = 1$ we are extraordinarily optimistic and we set $UB_{est} = LB$. Note that when $UB_{est} < f(x^*)$ extra work is required to complete the search, as the boxes wrongly discarded should be reprocessed. In practice, α is suggested to have a value in the interval $[0.1, 0.5]$. In fact, in [2] an adaptive approach is suggested which increases or decreases the value of α depending on whether the previous estimate was correct (an increase is then performed) or wrong (a decrease is performed). The computational studies reported in the paper show that the so-called *abrupt_decline* adaptive strategy can reduce the CPU time by more than 20%.

As already mentioned above, the use of a simplified affine arithmetic is proposed in Ninin et al. [71] to generate a linear relaxation of the global optimization problem. In particular, if for a given box the corresponding linear relaxation is infeasible, the box can be discarded. The computational studies in [71] show that this test is specially useful at discarding small boxes.

Domes and Neumaier [25] also propose a test specially suitable for discarding small boxes, but their aim is to discard boxes around the global optimum, where usually many small boxes have to be processed due to the difficulty at discarding them (the so-called *cluster effect*). Their idea is to apply a local optimizer to hopefully find a global optimal solution of the problem. If the point obtained is (nearly) feasible, then the Lagrange multipliers are used to add to the problem a redundant constraint. On the contrary, if the point is far from being feasible, then a different redundant constraint is added which makes use of the infeasibility information of the point. With this constraint aggregation technique the information in the redundant constraint is used to obtain bounds on the feasible set. In some cases, it may discard the whole box, whereas in other cases the size of the box is reduced. The usefulness of the constraint aggregation technique within a interval B&B algorithm is still to be investigated.

Schichl et al. [83] also try to avoid the cluster effect, but using a very different approach. The idea is, given a approximate local optimum, to generate an exclusion region R_e and an inclusion region R_i such that any solution of the problem inside R_e must lie within R_i. Thus, the region $R_e \setminus R_i$ can be removed from further consideration. Under some conditions, it can be proven that the local minimum inside R_i is unique, which may also allow to discard R_i if a better feasible solution is known. To construct the exclusion and inclusion regions third-order information is required. The Krawczyk operator applied to the first order necessary Frit John optimality conditions plays a key role in the process. Despite the fact that this may be time-consuming, its application may avoid or alleviate the cluster effect in some problems, making them from unsolvable to solvable.

On the other hand, Granvilliers [35] proposes a new filtering method for bound-constrained global optimization problems specially designed to cope with the facets of the boxes when the facets lie on the boundary of the box defining the bounds of the variables. The method exploits the necessary first-order Karush-Kuhn-Tucker optimality conditions and in the computational studies proved to be useful specially for problems with many variables.

An extension of the classical interval arithmetic, called *interval union arithmetic* is proposed in Schichl et al. [82]. It allows to work with sets of disjoint intervals, and in particular provides a natural way to represent the division of two intervals when the one in the denominator contains to 0. In the paper it is proved that the new interval union arithmetic allows to speed-up the interval Newton method for functions of a single variable, as well as the solution of interval linear systems of equations. See also [24]. The usefulness of the new interval arithmetic within an interval B&B strategy for solving global optimization problems is still to be investigated.

8.5   Selection of the Next Box to Be Processed

In [69], Neveu et al. study different selection rules. In all of them the best first rule plays a role, since it is computationally proven that the only promising selection rules select the box with the lowest lower bound at certain nodes of the search tree. One of the most promising ones, called *LBvUB*, randomly selects either the node in the working list $\mathcal{L}_W$ with the lowest lower bound or the one with the lowest upper bound. Both the lower and upper bound of a box x are made more accurate with the use of some constraint programming techniques. The selection of the box with the highest *RejectIndex* instead of the one with the lowest upper bound also offers competitive results when used randomly with the best first strategy. But the best strategy seems to be the one in which the node with the lowest lower bound is chosen, but then, a greedy dive in search of feasible points is performed. The *FeasibleDiving* procedure performs a depth-first search that keeps the more promising node at each iteration (the one with the lowest lower bound). No backtracking is performed.

For optimization problems with interval coefficients in the objective function, Karmakar and Bhunia [48] propose to use an order relation for intervals which takes into account the *pessimistic* view of the decision-maker, according to which a decision-maker prefers the best alternative with less uncertainty. They propose to use a branch-and-bound method at which, in each iteration, a multisection of the selected box is performed (the selected box is bisected perpendicularly to all the coordinate directions) and the box selected is the best one according to the pessimistic order.

8.6   Subdivision Rule

Concerning the subdivision rule, it seems that, apart from the papers [12, 19, 59], bisection perpendicular to a selected coordinate direction is the strategy followed in all research works.

More research has been devoted to the selection of the coordinate direction chosen to perform the bisection. In the seminar work of Kearfott and Novoa [51], the *smear* value was first introduced. Given a function g_j and a box x, the smear value of the variable x_i on g_j at the box x is given by:

$$smear(x_i, g_j) = |\nabla_i g_j(x)| \cdot \operatorname{wid} x_i,$$

where $\nabla_i g_j(x)$ is an inclusion of $\frac{\partial g_j}{\partial x_i}$ over x, and $|y| = \max\{|\underline{y}|, |\overline{y}|\}$ denotes the *magnitude* of the interval $y \in \mathbb{IR}$. The rationale behind the smear value is that it estimates the reduction of the image size of g_j after a reduction of the domain of x_i. Selection methods based on the smear values select as coordinate to be split the one which maximizes an aggregation of the smear values associated to each of the constraints g_j and to the objective function. There are different ways to carry out that aggregation. The *smearmax* strategy selects the variable x_i which maximizes

$$\max\{smear(x_i, f), \max\{smear(x_i, g_j) : j = 1, \dots, m\}\}.$$

The *smearsum* selects the variable with maximizes

$$smear(x_i, f) + \sum_{j=1}^{m} smear(x_i, g_j).$$

The variant proposed in [92] uses a *relative* smear value,

$$smear_{rel}(x_i, g_j) = \frac{smear(x_i, g_j)}{\sum_{k=1}^{n} smear(x_k, g_j)},$$

and the strategy *smearsumrel* selects the variable x_i which maximizes

$$smear_{rel}(x_i, f) + \sum_{j=1}^{m} smear_{rel}(x_i, g_j).$$

Recently, in Araya and Nevey [3] a new variant, *lsmear* has been proposed, which first weights the constraints by using the optimal Lagrangian multipliers of a linearization of the original optimization problem. Specifically, each constraint $g_j(x)$ function (and also the objective function) is approximated by the first-order term of its Taylor expansion around the midpoint of the box,

$$gl_j(x) = g_j(\text{mid } x) + \sum_{i=1}^{n} \text{mid } \nabla_i g_j(x) \cdot (x_i - \text{mid } x_i).$$

The dual of the corresponding linear problem is solved using the simplex method for linear programming, and the dual variables λ_j^* are used to construct the Lagrange-like function

$$L(x) = f(x) + \sum_{j=1}^{m} \lambda_j^* g_j(x).$$

lsmear selects the variable which maximizes the smear value on L. The computational results reported in [3] show that the new *lsmear* strategy is superior to all the previous smear strategies, and also the classical rule which selects the variable of maximum width.

On the other hand, Huang et al. [45] compare three bisection strategies, namely, bisection perpendicular to the direction maximum width, a smear-like strategy, and a so-called *lookahead* strategy, which takes into account the effect of pruning along a given variable in previous steps. They carry out a sound computational study on more than 11000 instances on constraint satisfaction problem (no optimization problems) and, interestingly, none of the strategies dominates the other.

8.7 Software

When talking about software for interval B&B methods, there are two different groups to mention. The first one includes available interval arithmetic libraries which can be used to build an interval B&B method. The second group consists of software packages which are different implementations of interval B&B methods and alike. Some of those packages use some of the libraries of the first group, but others use interval arithmetic implementations which are just developed inside the code.

8.7.1 Libraries

First, let us discuss the most used interval arithmetic libraries. Most of them are written in C++, and contain not only the basic interval arithmetic, but automatic differentiation and other useful techniques as well. The most relevant libraries are C-XSC[1] [43, 54], PROFIL/BIAS[2] [55], BOOST[3] [15] and filib++[4] [57]. C-XSC and PROFIL/BIAS were built in the 90s but work robustly, although they needed some updates due to the newer compiler versions. The BOOST interval package is part of a huge library, thus it is the best option if you would need the other features of BOOST anyway. The newer KV[5] library is based on BOOST and contains in addition implementations of affine arithmetic and Taylor forms. KV and filib++ are the newest libraries in the C++ category.

There is also an implementation of the basics of IEEE Standard for Interval Arithmetic in the *Moore: Interval Arithmetic in C++20*.[6] In [61] the efficiency of that library was compared to filib++ and Boost IA, and the results showed that in many cases it was the best, whereas in a few cases it had a similar performance. Its drawback is that it uses the novel feature of the C++ language called *concepts*.

There are also implementations where the type of precision for the floating-point numbers can be arbitrary: *Multiple Precision Floating-point Interval Library* MPFI[7] [79] and *Arbitrary precision arithmetics in C-XSC*[8] implements it using C-XSC and MPFR, see [13].

On top of these libraries, there are additional bounding techniques that are implemented in some packages. In [26] the authors describe ACETAF[9] made for the validated computation of bounds for Taylor coefficients and for Taylor remainder series of analytic functions. Similarly, libraries exist for slope arithmetic[10] [14] and Modal Interval Arithmetic (ivalDb[11]) [42]. Slope arithmetic works similarly as automatic differentiation, but enclosing the tangent of all

---

[1] C-XSC: http://www2.math.uni-wuppertal.de/wrswt/xsc/cxsc.html.

[2] PROFIL/BIAS: https://www.tuhh.de/ti3/software/profil.shtml.

[3] BOOST: https://www.boost.org/doc/libs/1_77_0/libs/numeric/interval/doc/interval.htm.

[4] filib++: https://www2.math.uni-wuppertal.de/org/WRST/software/filib.html.

[5] KV: http://verifiedby.me/kv/index-e.html.

[6] Moore IA: for the code directly email `walter.mascarenhas@gmail.com`.

[7] MPFI: https://gitlab.inria.fr/mpfi/mpfi.

[8] Arbitrary precision arithmetics in C-XSC: http://www2.math.uni-wuppertal.de/wrswt/xsc/cxsc_software.html#mpfr-mpfi.

[9] ACETAF: http://www2.math.uni-wuppertal.de/wrswt/xsc/cxsc_software.html#acetaf.

[10] Slope arithmetic: http://www2.math.uni-wuppertal.de/wrswt/xsc/cxsc_software.html#slope.

[11] ivalDB: http://www.ti3.tuhh.de/, https://sites.google.com/site/pauherrero/IVALDB.zip.

possible slopes from a given base point. The main contribution of MIA is its inherent capability to deal with a more complex class of problems involving logical quantifiers (like ∃, ∀) respecting an ordering of the quantifiers.

There are also a few libraries in other languages. The most used one is Intlab[12] for Matlab [80] which is not a standalone library, but a package for Matlab containing also methods for many algorithms using interval arithmetic, automatic differentiation, slope arithmetic, affine arithmetic and so on. The newest and most promising way to implement software with interval arithmetic is to use Julia[13] [95], a new language for high performance scientific computations (https://julialang.org/). Apart from the basic IA package, there is a multiple-precision interval arithmetic library based on MPFR[14], Taylor models[15] [10] and an implementation of interval arithmetic with variable precision ("ubounds") called Unums[16]. There is also a Python implementation for interval arithmetic, called PyInterval[17] although containing less complex techniques than Intlab or Julia.

8.7.2   Packages with Interval B&B Implementations

For the second group, we list only the software available and ready to use in 2021. We can start the list with the already mentioned Intlab, since based on the several interval arithmetics implemented there is a branch-and-bound method to solve global optimization problems. Similarly, based on the C-XSC library, there is a *Numerical toolbox for C-XSC*[18] [37] which contains a general interval branch-and-bound method.

Ibex[19] [70] implements an interval branch-and-bound based method, which uses *constraint propagation* techniques, thus it works well on constrained global optimization problems. The software pyIbex[20] is a python binding of Ibex. In Julia, there is an implementation of an *Easy Advanced Global Optimization* (EAGO[21]) method [96], that use McCormick arithmetic and many bound tightening techniques.

---

[12] Intlab: https://www.tuhh.de/ti3/rump/intlab/.

[13] Julia IA: https://github.com/JuliaIntervals/IntervalArithmetic.jl.

[14] MPFR IA in Julia: https://github.com/andrioni/Intervals.jl.

[15] Taylor models in Julia: https://github.com/JuliaIntervals/TaylorModels.jl.

[16] Unums in Julia: https://github.com/JuliaComputing/Unums.jl.

[17] PyInterval: https://pypi.org/project/pyinterval/.

[18] Toolbox for C-XSC: http://www2.math.uni-wuppertal.de/wrswt/xsc/cxsc_software.html#cxsc-toolbox.

[19] Ibex: http://www.ibex-lib.org/.

[20] pyIbex: https://github.com/codac-team/pyIbex.

[21] EAGO: https://github.com/PSORLab/EAGO.jl.

Last but not least, we mention the Coconut Environment[22], a modular environment for developing solvers for nonlinear continuous global optimization problems. It provides rigorous computational tools using interval arithmetic to promote the development of reliable computational methods. See [60, 67, 83, 84] for the advanced techniques available. Among them, Coconut includes: STOP (a heuristic starting point generator), Karush-John-condition generator using symbolic differentiation, Point Verifier (for verifying solution points), Exclusion Box generator (which computes an exclusion region around local optima), interval constraint propagation techniques, Linear Relaxation generator using slopes, wrappers for state of the art linear programming solvers, a wrapper for DONLP3 (a general purpose nonlinear local optimizer for continuous variables), Basic Splitter (computing difficult variables and split variants), BCS (a box covering solver), Convexity detection (for simple convexity analysis), and more.

All the above packages are open-source to facilitate the research on the development of methods and/or its adjustment for solving special problems.

A somewhat outlier software is GloptLab[23] [23] which implements a configurable framework for the rigorous global solution of quadratic constraint satisfaction problems, because it uses interval branch-and-bound techniques only partially. It is made to build a solution strategy in the graphical user interface by inserting, editing or removing tasks like scaling, constraint propagation, linear relaxations, strictly convex enclosures, conic methods, and also branch-and-bound methods.

Finally, there is an interesting software which is not directly related to interval branch-and-bound methods, but implements an Optimization Test Environment[24] [27] which enables users to choose and compare diverse solver routines, organize and solve large test problem sets, select interactively subsets of test problem sets, and perform a statistical analysis of the results.

8.8   Interval B&B Methods for MINLP Problems

Although interval tools are used in some of the few software packages available for MINLP problems, such as COUENNE [9] or BARON [81], to our knowledge there is no *publicly available* package for MINLP problems mainly based in interval B&B methods.

---

[22] Coconut: https://www.mat.univie.ac.at/~coconut/coconut-environment/.

[23] GloptLab: https://www.mat.univie.ac.at/~dferi/gloptlab.html.

[24] TestEnv: http://www.mat.univie.ac.at/~dferi/testenv.html.

The code of the IBBA algorithm developed by F. Messine and J. Ninin and used to solve some MINLP problems (see for instance [16, 32]) includes constraint propagation techniques and linear relaxations based on interval and affine arithmetic [71]. But it is not publicly available.

The way in which Schöbel and Scholz [85] cope with MINLP problems differs slightly from the classical interval B&B method. They assume that for any subbox of the continuous variables it is possible to obtain a lower bound of the objective function over the corresponding box obtained by adding the domains of the integer variables. In that case, it is suggested to carry out a B&B procedure on the continuous variables only. Some bounding procedures are proposed for concave as well as D.C. functions. And a new discarding test is proposed assuming that for each integer assignment of the integer variables it is possible to solve exactly the corresponding continuous optimization problem. Their method is suitable for problems with a small number of continuous variables, but again is not publicly available.

However, notice that it is not difficult to adapt available implementations of interval B&B algorithm for global optimization (see Sect. 8.7) to deal with MINLP problems following the ideas highlighted in the second paragraph of Subsection 8.2.6. In fact, this is what is done in [33] (see also [34]). The basic idea is to assume that the integer variables are continuous, and then, when the moment of discarding/filtering subregions arrives, to take the integrity of the variables back into account so as not to remove any optimal solution (see for instance the modification of the monotonicity test described in Subsection 8.2.6 when the objective function is found to be monotonous along an integer variable).

Special care is also required when updating the best upper bound $\tilde{f}$ for the problem, since the point $\tilde{x}$ such that $f(\tilde{x} >) = \tilde{f}$ must be feasible, in particular the components of $\tilde{x}$ corresponding to the integer variables must be integer values. The feasibility test can be of help here. When a box $\boldsymbol{x}$ is declared as feasible by the feasibility test (considering that the integer variables are continuous), then, from any integer assignment within the box of the integer variables we can obtain an integer feasible point, which can be used to update $\tilde{f}$.

Other discarding tests/filtering techniques can be adapted following the same ideas. Consider for instance the non-convexity test. Let $\boldsymbol{x}$ be a strictly feasible box and denote by $\nabla^2 \boldsymbol{f}(\boldsymbol{x})$ an inclusion of the Hessian matrix of f at $\boldsymbol{x}$. If $\nabla^2_{ii} \boldsymbol{f}(\boldsymbol{x}) < 0$ for some i, the objective function cannot be convex at $\boldsymbol{x}$. Thus, we know that the solution cannot lie inside the box. However, it may be on one of the facets corresponding to an integer variable x_i. Hence, we can remove the interior of the box and reduce it to the facets corresponding to integer variables. Since $x \in \mathbb{IR}^n$, it has $2n$ facets, given by $(x_1, \ldots, \underline{x}_i, \ldots, x_n)$ and $(x_1, \ldots, \overline{x}_i, \ldots, x_n)$, for $i = 1, \ldots, n$. This is somehow related to the *peeling* procedure described in Section 5.2.3 in [49]. As in the monotonicity test, we cannot remove the whole box now, since the non-convexity certification may no longer hold between an integer value $\underline{x}_i$ (or $\overline{x}_i$) and the following one $\underline{x}_i - 1$ (or $\overline{x}_i + 1$).

Something similar can be done with the interval Newton method (applying it only to the continuous variables while fixing the integer variables at their current values), the projected one-dimensional Newton method [29], the best corner test, [28] or the monotonicity-border test [28].

Some of the techniques reviewed in sections 8.3 and 8.4 are also suitable for being adapted to MINLP problems, such as the bounding techniques in [4, 11, 73]. Also the linearization techniques described in [5, 6, 92] which make use the mean value form based on corners of the box seem that could be easily adapted. The use of estimated upper bounds described in [2] can also be used directly, as well as the selection rule *LBvUB* in [69]. And the *FeasibleDiving* strategy could be adapted to find integer feasible solutions. The subdivision rules based on the smear value described in Sect. 8.6 can also be applied without modifications.

In general, the interval techniques designed for continuous NLP problems should be revised to investigate whether they can be adapted to handle MINLP problems too. Hopefully, when cleverly combined in an interval B&B algorithm, they will allow to solve difficult MINLP problems which still cannot be solved by the existing solvers. Some of those techniques could also be incorporated in other software packages for MINLP problems so that they can solve broader classes of problems.

Acknowledgements This research has been supported by grants from Fundación Séneca (The Agency of Science and Technology of the Region of Murcia, 20817/PI/18) and Junta de Andalucía (P-18-RT-1193), in part financed by the European Regional Development Fund (ERDF).

References

1. C. Adjiman, L. Androulakis, and C. Floudas. Global optimization of mixed-integer nonlinear problems. *American Institute of Chemical Engineers Journal*, 46:176–248, 2000.
2. I. Araya. Estimating upper bounds for improving the filtering in interval branch and bound optimizers. In *Proceedings—International Conference on Tools*

with Artificial Intelligence, ICTAI, volume 2014-Decem, pages 24–30. IEEE Computer Society, 2014.

3. I. Araya and B. Neveu. lsmear: a variable selection strategy for interval branch and bound solvers. *Journal of Global Optimization*, 71(3):483–500, 2018.

4. I. Araya, B. Neveu, and G. Trombettoni. An interval extension based on occurrence grouping. *Computing*, 94(2-4):173–188, 2012.

5. I. Araya, G. Trombettoni, and B. Neveu. A contractor based on convex interval Taylor. In *Proceedings of the 9th International Conference on Integration of Artificial Intelligence and Operations Research Techniques in Constraint Programming, CPAIOR 2012*, volume 7298 LNCS, pages 1–16, 2012.

6. I. Araya, G. Trombettoni, B. Neveu, and G. Chabert. Upper bounding in inner regions for global optimization under inequality constraints. *Journal of Global Optimization*, 60:145–164, 2014.

7. E. Baumann. Optimal centered forms. *BIT*, 28:80–87, 1988.

8. P. Belotti, C. Kirches, S. Leyffer, J. Linderoth, J. Luedtke, and A. Mahajan. Mixed-integer nonlinear optimization. *Acta Numerica*, 22:1–131, 2013.

9. P. Belotti, J. Lee, L. Liberti, F. Margot, and A. Wachter. Branching and bounds tightening techniques for non-convex MINLP. *Optimization Methods & Software*, 24(4-5):597–634, 2009.

10. L. Benet and D. P. Sanders. Taylorseries.jl: Taylor expansions in one and several variables in julia. *Journal of Open Source Software*, 4(36):1043, 2019.

11. J. L. Berenguel, L. G. Casado, I. García, E. M. T. Hendrix, and F. Messine. On lower bounds using additively separable terms in interval B&B. In *12th International Conference on Computational Science and Its Applications, ICCSA 2012*, volume 7335 LNCS, pages 119–132, 2012.

12. S. Berner. New results on verified global optimization. *Computing*, 57:323–343, 1996.

13. F. Blomquist, W. Hofschuster, and W. Krämer. C-XSC-Langzahlarithmetiken füer reelle und komplexe intervalle basierend auf den bibliotheken MPFR und MPFI. Preprint, Universität Wuppertal, 2011 (in German).

14. M. Bräuer, W. Hofschuster, and W. Krämer. Steigungsarithmetiken in C-XSC. Preprint, Universität Wuppertal, 2001.

15. H. Brönnimann, G. Melquiond, and S. Pion. The design of the boost interval arithmetic library. *Theoretical Computer Science*, 351(1):111–118, 2006. Real Numbers and Computers.

16. S. Cafieri, F. Messine, and A. Touhami. On solving aircraft conflict avoidance using deterministic global optimization (sBB) codes. In *Proceedings of the XIII Global Optimization Workshop*, pages 149–152, Braga, Portual, 2016.

17. L. Casado, I. García, J. Martínez, and Y. Sergeyev. New interval analysis support functions using gradient information in a global minimization algorithm. *Journal of Global Optimization*, 25:345–362, 2003.

18. L. Casado, J. Martínez, and I. García. Experiments with a new selection criterion in a fast interval optimization algorithm. *Journal of Global Optimization*, 19(3):247–264, 2001.

19. L. G. Casado, I. García, and T. Csendes. A new multisection technique in interval methods for global optimization. *Computing*, 65:263–269, 2000.

20. T. Csendes. New subinterval selection criteria for interval global optimization. *Journal of Global Optimization*, 19:307–327, 2001.

21. T. Csendes and D. Ratz. Subdivision direction selection in interval methods for global optimization. *SIAM Journal on Numerical Analysis*, 34:922–938, 1997.

22. L. de Figueiredo and J. Stolfi. *Self-validated numerical methods and applications.* Brazilian Mathematics Colloquium monographs. IMPA/CNPq, Rio de Janeiro, Brazil, 1997.

23. F. Domes. Gloptlab—A configurable framework for the rigorous global solution of quadratic constraint satisfaction problems. *Optimization Methods and Software*, 24:727–747, 2009.

24. F. Domes, T. Montanher, H. Schichl, and A. Neumaier. Rigorous global filtering methods with interval unions. In *Studies in Computational Intelligence*, volume 835, pages 249–267. Springer, 2020.

25. F. Domes and A. Neumaier. Constraint aggregation for rigorous global optimization. *Mathematical Programming*, 155(1-2):375–401, 2016.

26. I. Eble and M. Neher. ACETAF: A software package for computing validated bounds for taylor coefficients of analytic functions. *ACM Transactions on Mathematical Software*, 29(3):263-286, 2003.

27. H. S. F. Domes, M. Fuchs and A. Neumaier. The optimization test environment. *Optimization and Engineering*, 15:443-468, 2014.

28. J. Fernández and B. Pelegrín. Using interval analysis for solving planar single-facility location problems: new discarding tests. *Journal of Global Optimization*, 19(1):61–81, 2001.

29. J. Fernández, B. Pelegrín, F. Plastria, and B. Tóth. Solving a Huff-like competitive location and design model for profit maximization in the plane. *European Journal of Operational Research*, 179(3):1274–1287, 2007.

30. J. Fernández, S. Salhi, and B. G. Tóth. Location equilibria for a continuous competitive facility location problem under delivered pricing. *Computers & Operations Research*, 41(1):185–195, 2014.

31. J. Fernández, B. G. Tóth, J. Redondo, and P. Ortigosa. The probabilistic customer's choice rule with a threshold attraction value: effect on the location of competitive facilities. *Computers & Operations Research*, 101:234–249, 2019.

32. E. Fitan, F. Messine, and B. Nogarède. The electromagnetic actuator design problem: a general and rational approach. *IEEE Transactions on Magnetics*, 40(3):1579–1590, 2004.

33. B. G.-Tóth, L. Anton-Sanchez, J. Fernández, J. Redondo, and P. Ortigosa. A continuous competitive facility location and design problem for firm expansion. In H. Le Thi, H. Le, and T. Pham, editors, *Optimization of complex systems: theory, models, algorithms and applications*, Advances in Intelligent Systems and Computing 991, pages 1013–1022. Springer, 2020.

34. B. G.-Tóth, L. Anton-Sanchez, and J. Fernández A MINLP competitive facility location model with quality adjustment and/or closing of existing facilities. submitted, 2021.

35. L. Granvilliers. Filtering domains of factorable functions using interval contractors. In L. T. H.A., L. H.M., and P. D. T., editors, *Optimization of complex systems: theory, models, algorithms and applications*, Advances in Intelligent Systems and Computing 991, pages 99–108. Springer Verlag, 2020.

36. A. Griewank and G. Corliss, editors. *Automatic differentiation of algorithms: theory, implementation and application*. SIAM, Philadelphia, 1991.

37. R. Hammer, M. Hocks, U. Kulisch, and D. Ratz. *C++ Toolbox for verified computing I: basic numerical problems: theory, algorithms and programs*. Springer-Verlag, Berlin, 1995.

38. E. Hansen. The centered form. In E. Hansen, editor, *Topics in interval analysis*, pages 102–106. Oxford University Press, 1969.

39. E. Hansen. Global optimization using interval analysis—The one-dimensional case. *Journal of Optimization Theory and Applications*, 29:331–344, 1979.

40. E. Hansen and G. W. Walster. *Global optimization using interval analysis— Second edition, revised and expanded*. Marcel Dekker, New York, 2004.

41. P. Hansen and B. Jaumard. *Handbook of global optimization*, chapter Lipschitz optimization, pages 407–494. Kluwer, Dordrecht, 1995.

42. P. Herrero Vinas. *Quantified real constraint solving using modal intervals with applications to control*. Theses, Université d'Angers, Dec. 2006.

43. W. Hofschuster and W. Krämer. C-XSC 2.0: A C++ Library for eXtended Scientific Computing. In R. Alt, A. Frommer, B. Kearfott, and W. Luther, editors, *Numerical software with result verification*, volume 2991 of Springer Lecture Notes in Computer Science, pages 15–35. Springer-Verlag, Heidelberg, 2004.

44. R. Horst and H. Tuy. *Global Optimization: Deterministic Approaches*. Springer, 3rd edition, 1996.

45. C. Huang, S. Kong, S. Gao, and D. Zufferey. Evaluating branching heuristics in interval constraint propagation for satisfiability. In Z. M. and Z. D., editors, *12th International Workshop on Numerical Software Verification, NSV 2019*, volume 11652 LNCS, pages 85–100. Springer Verlag, 2019.

46. K. Ichida and Y. Fujii. An interval arithmetic method for global optimization. *Computing*, 23:85–97, 1979.

47. L. Jaulin, M. Kieffer, O. Didrit, and E. Walter. *Applied interval analysis, with examples in parameter and state estimation, robust control and robotics*. Springer-Verlag, London, 2001.

48. S. Karmakar and A. Bhunia. A new multi-section based technique for constrained optimization problems with interval-valued objective function. *Applied Mathematics and Computation*, 225:487–502, 2013.

49. R. Kearfott. *Rigorous global search: continuous problems*. Kluwer, Dordrecht, 1996.

50. R. Kearfott, M. Nakao, A. Neumaier, S. M. Rump, S. P. Shary, and P. van Hentenryck. Standardized notation in interval analysis. *TOM*, 15(1):7–13, 2010.

51. R. Kearfott and M. Novoa III. ALGORITHM 681. INTBIS, a portable interval Newton/bisection package. *ACM Transactions on Mathematical Software*, 16:152–157, 1990.

52. R. B. Kearfott. Interval Newton/generalized bisection when there are singularities near roots. *Annals of Operations Research*, 25(1):181–196, 1990.

53. R. B. Kearfott. On rigorous upper bounds to a global optimum. *Journal of Global Optimization*, 59(2-3):459–476, 2014.

54. R. Klatte, U. Kulisch, A. Wiethoff, C. Lawo, and R. M. *C-XSC: A C++ class library for eXtended Scientific Computing*. Springer-Verlag, Berlin, 1993.

55. O. Knüppel. PROFIL/BIAS—A Fast Interval Library. *Computing*, 53(1):277–287, 1993.

56. R. Krawczyk and K. Nickel. The centered form in interval arithmetics: Quadratic convergence and inclusion isotonicity. *Computing*, 28:117–137, 1982.

57. M. Lerch, G. Tischler, J. W. Von Gudenberg, W. Hofschuster, and W. Krämer. FILIB++, A fast interval library supporting containment computations. *ACM Transactions on Mathematical Software*, 32(2):299–324, 2006.

58. K. Makino and M. Berz. Verified computations using Taylor models and their applications. In A. A. and B. S., editors, *12th International Workshop on Numerical Software Verification, NSV 2019*, volume 10381 LNCS, pages 3–13. Springer Verlag, 2017.

59. M. Markót, J. Fernández, L. Casado, and T. Csendes. New interval methods for constrained global optimization. *Mathematical Programming Series A*, 106:287–318, 2006.

60. M. C. Markót and H. Schichl. Bound constrained interval global optimization in the COCONUT environment. *Journal of Global Optimization*, 60:751–776, 2014.

61. W. F. Mascarenhas. Moore: Interval Arithmetic in C++20. In G. A. Barreto and R. Coelho, editors, *Fuzzy Information Processing*, pages 519–529. Springer International Publishing, Cham, 2018.

62. F. Messine, B. Nogarède, and J. Lagouanelle. Optimal design of electromechanical actuators: a new method based on global optimization. *IEEE Transactions on Magnetics*, 34:299–308, 1998.

63. R. Moore. *Interval arithmetic and automatic error analysis in digital computing*. Ph.D. Thesis, Department of Mathematics, Stanford University, Stanford, California, November 1962. Published as Applied Mathematics and Statistics Laboratories Technical Report No. 25.

64. R. Moore. *Interval analysis*. Prentice-Hall, New Jersey, 1966.

65. M. M. Moscato, C. A. Muñoz, and A. P. Smith. Affine arithmetic and applications to real-number proving. In Z. X. and U. C., editors, *Proceedings of the*

6th International Conference on Interactive Theorem Proving, ITP 2015, volume 9236, pages 294–309. Springer Verlag, 2015.

66. A. Neumaier. *Interval methods for systems of equations*. Cambridge University Press, Cambridge, 1990.

67. A. Neumaier. Complete search in continuous global optimization and constraint satisfaction. In A. Iserles, editor, *Acta Numerica*, volume 13, pages 271–369. Cambridge University Press, Cambridge, 2004.

68. A. Neumaier and O. Shcherbina. Safe bounds in linear and mixed-integer linear programming. *Mathematical Programming*, 99(2):283–296, 2004.

69. B. Neveu, G. Trombettoni, and I. Araya. Node selection strategies in interval Branch and Bound algorithms. *Journal of Global Optimization*, 64(2):289–304, 2016.

70. J. Ninin. Global optimization based on contractor programming: An overview of the IBEX library. In I. S. Kotsireas, S. M. Rump, and C. K. Yap, editors, *Mathematical aspects of computer and information sciences*, pages 555–559, Cham, 2016. Springer International Publishing.

71. J. Ninin, F. Messine, and P. Hansen. A reliable affine relaxation method for global optimization. *4OR*, 13(3):247–277, 2015.

72. B. Pelegrín, J. Fernández, and B. Tóth. The 1-center problem in the plane with independent random weights. *Computers & Operations Research*, 35(3):737–749, 2008.

73. M. Posypkin and O. Khamisov. Automatic convexity deduction for efficient function's range bounding. *Mathematics*, 9(2):1–15, 2021.

74. L. Rall. *Automatic differentiation, techniques and applications*. Lecture Notes in Computer Science. Springer, Berlin, 1981.

75. H. Ratschek and J. Rokne. *Computer methods for the range of functions*. Ellis Horwood, Chichester, 1984.

76. H. Ratschek and J. Rokne. *New computer methods for global optimization*. Ellis Horwood, Chichester, 1988.

77. D. Ratz. *Automatic slope computation and its application in nonsmooth global optimization*. Shaker Verlag, Aachen, Germany, 1998.

78. D. Ratz and T. Csendes. On the selection of subdivision directions in interval branch-and-bound methods for global optimization. *Journal of Global Optimization*, 7:183–207, 1995.

79. N. Revol and F. Rouillier. Motivations for an arbitrary precision interval arithmetic and the MPFI library. *Reliable Computing*, 11(4):275–290, 2005.

80. S. Rump. INTLAB—INTerval LABoratory. In T. Csendes, editor, *Developments in reliable computing*, pages 77–104. Kluwer Academic Publishers, Dordrecht, 1999.

81. N. V. Sahinidis. *BARON 21.1.13: Global Optimization of Mixed-Integer Nonlinear Programs, User's Manual*, 2017.

82. H. Schichl, F. Domes, T. Montanher, and K. Kofler. Interval unions. *BIT*, 57:531–556, 2016.

83. H. Schichl, M. Markót, and A. Neumaier. Exclusion regions for optimization problems. *Journal of Global Optimization*, 59:569–595, 2014.
84. H. Schichl and M. C. Markót. Algorithmic differentiation techniques for global optimization in the COCONUT environment. *Optimization Methods and Software*, 27(2):359–372, 2012.
85. A. Schöbel and D. Scholz. A solution algorithm for non-convex mixed integer optimization problems with only few continuous variables. *European Journal of Operational Research*, 232(2):266–275, 2014.
86. S. Skelboe. Computation of rational interval functions. *BIT*, 14:87–95, 1974.
87. M. Tawarmalani and N. Sahinidis. Global optimization of mixed-integer nonlinear programs: A theoretical and computational study. *Mathematical Programming*, 99(3):563–591, 2004.
88. B. Tóth and L. Casado. Multi-dimensional pruning from the Baumann point in an interval global optimization algorithm. *Journal of Global Optimization*, 38:215–236, 2007.
89. B. Tóth and J. Fernández. *Interval methods for single and bi-objective optimization problems—Applied to competitive facility location problems.* Lambert Academic Publishing, Saarbrücken, 2010.
90. B. Tóth, J. Fernández, and T. Csendes. Empirical convergence speed of inclusion functions for facility location problems. *Journal of Computational and Applied Mathematics*, 199:384–389, 2007.
91. B. Tóth, J. Fernández, B. Pelegrín, and F. Plastria. Sequential versus simultaneous approach in the location and design of two new facilities using planar Huff-like models. *Computers & Operations Research*, 36(5):1393–1405, 2009.
92. G. Trombettoni, I. Araya, B. Neveu, and G. Chabert. Inner regions and interval linearizations for global optimization. In *Proceedings of the Twenty-Fifth AAAI Conference on Artificial Intelligence*, pages 99–104, 2011.
93. R. Vaidyanathan and M. El-Halwagi. Global optimization of nonconvex MINLP'S by Interval Analysis. In *Global Optimization in Engineering Design*, chapter 6, pages 175–193. Kluwer Academic Publishers, 1996.
94. T. Vinkó, J. Lagouanelle, and T. Csendes. A new inclusion function for optimization: Kite—The one dimensional case. *Journal of Global Optimization*, 30:435–456, 2004.
95. E. Vorontsova. Interval Computations in Julia programming language. In *Summer Workshop on Interval Methods (SWIM) 2019, ENSTA*, Paris, France, July 2019.
96. M. E. Wilhelm and M. D. Stuber. EAGO.jl: easy advanced global optimization in Julia. *Optimization Methods and Software*, 0(0):1–26, 2020.
97. L. Zhang, F. Gao, and W. Zhu. Nonlinear integer programming and global optimization. *Journal of Computational Mathematics*, 17(2):179–190, 1999.

9

Continuous Facility Location Problems

Zvi Drezner

9.1 Introduction

Facility location models investigate the location of one or more facilities, among a set of demand points, to achieve a certain objective. Discrete location models assume that there is a set of potential locations for the facilities, and a partial subset of locations is selected for locating them. Continuous location problems assume that facilities can be located anywhere (usually in the plane) or in a given area, and thus the set of candidate locations is "infinite". In this chapter we review continuous location models.

One of the earliest objectives investigated in the literature is minimizing the weighted sum of distances between the demand points and their closest facility. For example, locating warehouses to serve a given set of outlets. The cost of service is proportional to the distance and if there are two or more facilities, service to a demand point is provided by the closest facility.

Another objective is minimizing the maximum distance to the closest facility so that the customer who gets the worst service is getting the service as quickly as possible. For example, location of emergency facilities, such as ambulances or fire trucks, so that the farthest customer is as close as possible

Z. Drezner (✉)
College of Business and Economics, California State University, Fullerton, CA, USA
e-mail: zdrezner@fullerton.edu

© The Author(s), under exclusive license to Springer Nature Switzerland AG 2022
S. Salhi and J. Boylan (eds.), *The Palgrave Handbook of Operations Research*,
https://doi.org/10.1007/978-3-030-96935-6_9

to a facility. Some types of facilities such as polluting or noisy factories, land-fills, airports, have a negative impact on neighborhoods and thus should be located as far as possible from communities. Such facilities are termed "obnoxious" facilities. Another objective is to locate facilities to provide equi-table service to all demand points. Covering models attempt to cover as many demand points as possible within a given distance from the closest facility. Competitive location models, discussed in Chapter [52] in this book, involve the location of facilities, such as retail outlets, to attract as much demand as possible from competing facilities.

Commonly used distance measures between points (x, y) and (u, v) include:

* Euclidean distance (also termed ℓ_2): $\sqrt{(x-u)^2 + (y-v)^2}$. This is a straight line distance.
* Rectilinear (also termed Manhattan, or ℓ_1) distance: $|x-u| + |y-v|$. This is a distance on a grid where roads are either in a North-South or East-West directions and there are no diagonal roads.
* General ℓ_p distance: $\{|x-u|^p + |y-v|^p\}^{\frac{1}{p}}$. $p = 2$ is the Euclidean distance, and $p = 1$ is the rectilinear distance.

There are extensions to the basic location models. For example, some models are formulated on the surface of a sphere. Distances on the globe are not "straight" lines but great circle distances used by airplanes flying between origin and destination. Spherical models are discussed in Sect. 9.2.5.

9.2 Single Facility Location Problems

In this section we review single facility location models. The location of multiple facilities is discussed in Sect. 9.3.

9.2.1 The Weber (One-Median) Location Problem

The first and most basic location problem is the Weber problem [202]. A set of demand points with associated weights exist in the area. The problem is to find a location for a facility that minimizes the weighted sum of distances to the set of demand points. The formulation and solution methods are detailed in Sect. 9.4.2.4. The simple form of the problem dates back to the French mathematician Pierre de Fermat who lived in 1601–1665. For historical reviews the reader is referred to [207, 39, 97]. As detailed in [39, 147], Pierre

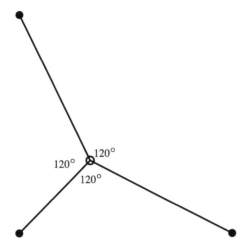

Fig. 9.1 Solution to the minimum sum of distances in a triangle

de Fermat asked the question of finding the point in a triangle that mini-mizes the sum of the distances to the vertices of the triangle. The problem was solved by Torricelli (1608–1647). Torricelli showed (see Fig. 9.1), that the optimal location (Fermat point) is at a point forming three angles of 120° each with the sides of the triangle (and on a vertex if an angle at a vertex is 120° or greater).

   This is the solution to connecting three cities by the shortest possible rail-road. Suppose that we need to connect four cities on the vertices of a square with a side of 1. Connecting three sides, or forming an H shape, has a total length of 3. The two diagonals have a total length of $2\sqrt{2} = 2.828$. The optimal solution to this problem is depicted in Fig. 9.2. The two points in the interior of the square are Fermat's points in the triangles formed by two vertices and the square's center C. Therefore, all the angles are 120°. The total distance is $1 + \sqrt{3} = 2.732$. The general problem of connecting n points by the shortest tree is called the Steiner tree problem [180].

9.2.1.1   Extensions to the Basic Weber Problem

Drezner et al. [90] investigated a model where travel time is not necessarily proportional to the distance. Every trip starts at a speed of zero, then the vehicle accelerates to a cruising speed, stays at the cruising speed for a portion of the trip, and then decelerates back to a speed of zero. A time equiva-lent distance which is equal to the travel time multiplied by the cruising speed is defined. It is proved that every demand point is a local minimum

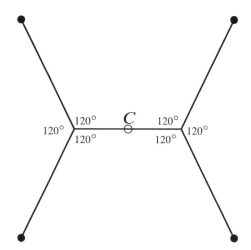

Fig. 9.2 Solution to the minimum sum of distances in a square

for the Weber problem defined by travel time rather than distance. Accurate estimate of travel time is especially important when evaluating hub location [187, 176, 30, 46, 1]. When a flight has one or more stopovers, the underestimation of flight time is increased, in addition to the waiting time at the stopover, because there are more acceleration and deceleration periods. Therefore, when using distances rather than flight times, hub location models may underestimate the decline in quality of service due to stopovers at hubs.

Drezner and Wesolowsky [110] and Drezner and Drezner [61] considered the Weber problem when the distance from point A to point B is not the same as the distance from B to A. This is common in rush hour traffic or for flights that in one direction have tail winds and in the opposite direction have head winds.

Drezner et al. [101] considered the Weber problem on a network where demand points can be on nodes of the network or anywhere in the plane off the network. Distances to demand points located on the network can be either network distances or Euclidean distances, while distances to points off-the network are Euclidean. Travel time on the network is slower by a given factor but is cheaper than using Euclidean distances. Applications include building a hospital providing emergency services either by an ambulance using network roads, or by a helicopter flying directly to the patient, especially when the patient is off the network. The facility can be located anywhere on the network and the optimal solution is not necessarily on a node. The problem is optimally solved by the "Big Segment Small Segment" global optimization algorithm (see also Sect. 9.4.2.3 and Berman et al. [9]). Locating a transfer point where service is switched from one vehicle to another on the way to a demand point or on the way back is investigated in [13, 14, 15].

Drezner [74] considered the Weber problem when there is uncertainty in the location of demand points. Each demand point can be located anywhere in a circle. The set of all possible optimal locations is found.

Farahani et al. [120] investigated the Weber problem with multiple relocation opportunities. The weight associated with each demand point is a known function of time. Relocations can take place at pre-determined times. The objective function is the minimization of the total location and relocation costs.

Drezner and Scott [100] considered the location of a facility that sells goods to a set of demand points. The cost for producing an item and the transportation cost per unit distance are given. The total cost is the sum of the price charged at the source (mill price) and the transportation cost paid by the customers. Demand by customers is elastic and assumed to decline linearly in the total cost to customers.

Drezner [79] found the sensitivity of the optimal location of the Weber problem to changes in the locations and weights of the demand points. An approximate formula for the set of all optimal sites is found when demand points are restricted to given areas and weights are within given ranges.

Drezner and Goldman [94] found the smallest set of points that may include at least one optimal solution to the Weber problem for a given set of demand points and any unknown set of weights.

Drezner and Simchi-Levi [103] proved that when n points with random weights are randomly generated in a unit circle, the probability that the Weber solution point with Euclidean distances is on a demand point is approximately $\frac{1}{n}$. One would expect that when the number of demand points increases to infinity, the probability that a solution is on a demand point converges to 1 because there is no "empty space" left in the circle. This counter-intuitive result was verified by simulation.

The possibility that some of the weights in the Weber problem are negative is proposed in [111, 160, 33, 178]. This problem is also termed "the Weber problem with attraction and repulsion". Schöbel and Scholz [184] generalized it to multiple facilities.

Drezner et al. [72] proposed the Weber obnoxious facility location problem. The facility location is required to be at least a given distance from demand points because it is "obnoxious" to them. For example, locating an airport that generates noise and pollution and thus should not be too close to communities. However, it serves travelers and thus their total travel distance to the airport should be minimized. Kalczynski and Drezner [140] extended this model to multiple facilities.

9.2.2   The Minimax (One-Center) Location Problem

The minimax facility location problem (also termed the one-center problem) is to locate a facility so that the maximum distance to a set of demand points is minimized. For planar Euclidean distances, this problem is equivalent to finding the center of the smallest circle enclosing all points hence the term "center" is used for this problem. When other metrics are used, the one-center problem is equivalent to covering all points with a shape similar to the unit ball of the metric. For example, when rectilinear distances are used, the problem is to cover all points with the smallest possible rhombus (a square rotated by 45°). This objective can be viewed as locating a facility that will provide the best possible service to the farthest community.

The smallest circle problem was first suggested and solved by the renowned English mathematician James Joseph Sylvester [195, 196]. An almost identical algorithm is provided by Chrystal [38]. Chrystal [38] starts with a "large" circle that encloses all the points and reduces the radius of the circle iteratively until the smallest circle is obtained. Drezner [86] reviewed planar center problems and their history. Solution methods are discussed in Sect. 9.4.2.5.

A variation on the weighted one-center problem is proposed in [75]. The objective is to maximize the total weight of n demand points within a given distance from the facility. An optimal procedure of complexity $O(n^2 \log n)$ is proposed. This problem is a single facility covering problem. For its multiple facility version see Sect. 9.3.4.

9.2.3   The Obnoxious Facility Location Problem

In most location problems, the closer is a facility to demand points the better. However, there are facilities that have a negative impact on communities (being "obnoxious") and being farther from communities is better. For example, noisy or polluting factories, garbage dumps, airports, should not be located close to communities. The maximin location problem is to find the point that maximizes the minimum (weighted) distance to all demand points. If no restrictions on the location of the facility are imposed, the best location is at infinity. Therefore, the location is restricted to a finite region, such as the convex hull of the demand points.

Melachrinoudis and Xanthopulos [167] proposed a model of locating a new facility that serves certain demand points. Two objectives are considered: (1) minimize the undesirable effects introduced by the new facility by maximizing its minimum Euclidean distance with respect to all demand points, and (2) minimize the total transportation cost from the new facility to the demand points.

Drezner and Wesolowsky [112] and Drezner et al. [73] found the best location of a facility inside a planar network. Drezner and Wesolowsky [112] found a point that maximizes the minimum weighted distance to the links and nodes of the network. Drezner et al. [73] investigated two equivalent problems. In one problem it is assumed that the links of the network generate a negative impact and the objective is to locate a facility, such as a school or a hospital, where the total impact is minimized. An equivalent problem is locating an obnoxious facility where the total negative impact generated by the facility and inflicted on the links of the network is minimized.

Berman et al. [12] considered the location of an obnoxious facility by a developer that has a given expropriation budget. Each demand point can be bought by the developer at a given price. Demand points closest to the facility are expropriated (bought and eliminated) with the given budget. The objective is to maximize the distance to the closest point not expropriated. This model is similar to minimizing the population that is exposed to the negative impact [40].

Melachrinoudis and Cullinane [165] considered the location of an obnoxious facility when some obnoxious facilities already exist in the area. The facility must be located outside circles centered at the existing facilities.

A review of obnoxious facilities models is [41]. A review of single obnoxious facility location models is [164]. Solution approaches are discussed in Sect. 9.4.2.4

9.2.4 Equity Models

The purpose of equity models is to provide equitable service to demand points. Eiselt and Laporte [115] list nineteen equity objectives. Below are some single facility location models with equity objectives. Models involving location of multiple facilities are discussed in Sect. 9.3.6.

1. Minimizing the range of the distances to all demand points [55, 105].
2. Minimizing the variance of the distances to the facility [55, 159, 31, 5, 54].

3. Minimizing the quintile share ratio [119]. The quintile share ratio is the ratio of total weight of the 20% of the demand points with the largest distance (top quintile) to the weight of the 20% of the demand points with the lowest distance (lowest quintile) [64].

9.2.5 Location on a Sphere

In this section we review several location models on the surface of a sphere. For solution approaches see Sect. 9.4.2.7.

9.2.5.1 Calculating Spherical Distances

The distance between any two points on the sphere can be calculated by the "great circle" formula, which is the shortest distance between two points on the surface of a sphere, utilized by airplanes [106]. The distance $\hat{d}$ along the great circle between two points whose latitudes are φ_1, φ_2 and longitudes θ_1, θ_2 is:

$$\hat{d} = R \arccos\{\cos\varphi_1 \cos\varphi_2 \cos(\theta_1 - \theta_2) + \sin\varphi_1 \sin\varphi_2\} \tag{9.1}$$

where R is the sphere's radius (3959 miles, or 6371 kilometers, for the earth).

This formula can be re-written to avoid large round-off errors for small distances when $\cos\frac{\hat{d}}{R} \approx 1$ [93]. The identity $\cos\alpha = 1 - 2\sin^2\frac{\alpha}{2}$ is used:

$$\cos\varphi_1 \cos\varphi_2 \cos(\theta_1 - \theta_2) + \sin\varphi_1 \sin\varphi_2 = \cos\varphi_1 \cos\varphi_2 + \sin\varphi_1 \sin\varphi_2$$
$$- (1 - \cos(\theta_1 - \theta_2)) \cos\varphi_1 \cos\varphi_2 = \cos(\varphi_1 - \varphi_2)$$
$$- 2\sin^2\frac{\theta_1 - \theta_2}{2} \cos\varphi_1 \cos\varphi_2$$

yielding

$$\cos\frac{\hat{d}}{R} = 1 - 2\sin^2\frac{\hat{d}}{2R} = \cos(\varphi_1 - \varphi_2) - 2\sin^2\frac{\theta_1 - \theta_2}{2}\cos\varphi_1 \cos\varphi_2$$

$$\rightarrow 2\sin^2\frac{\hat{d}}{2R} = 2\sin^2\frac{\varphi_1 - \varphi_2}{2} + 2\sin^2\frac{\theta_1 - \theta_2}{2}\cos\varphi_1 \cos\varphi_2$$

$$\rightarrow \hat{d} = 2R \arcsin\sqrt{\sin^2\frac{\varphi_1 - \varphi_2}{2} + \sin^2\frac{\theta_1 - \theta_2}{2}\cos\varphi_1 \cos\varphi_2}$$

$$\tag{9.2}$$

Another way to calculate the great circle distance [146] is to convert the points on the surface of the sphere to three-dimensional coordinates (x, y, z) so that $x^2 + y^2 + z^2 = R^2$. A point (φ, θ) is transformed to: $x = R \cos \varphi \sin \theta$; $y = R \cos \varphi \cos \theta$; $z = R \sin \varphi$. The distance d between the points (x_1, y_1, z_1), (x_2, y_2, z_2) in a three-dimensional space is

$$d = \sqrt{(x_1 - x_2)^2 + (y_1 - y_2)^2 + (z_1 - z_2)^2}. \tag{9.3}$$

The angle of the segment connecting the two points seen from the sphere's center is $\alpha = 2 \arcsin \frac{d}{2R}$. Therefore, the great circle distance $\hat{d}$ is:

$$\hat{d} = R\alpha = 2R \arcsin \frac{d}{2R} \tag{9.4}$$

because the great circle is on the plane connecting the two points and the center of the sphere. $\hat{d} > d$ for $d > 0$ because $\arcsin \alpha > \alpha$ for $\alpha > 0$. For very small values of $\frac{d}{R}$, $\arcsin \alpha \approx \alpha$ and thus $\hat{d} \approx d$.

Drezner and Wesolowsky [106] showed that the spherical distance is convex up to a distance of $\frac{\pi R}{2}$ and not convex for greater distances. Therefore, if all demand points are within a circle of radius $\frac{\pi R}{4}$ (about 5000 kilometers or 3100 miles on earth), the Weber problem on the sphere is convex and has one local minimum which is the global one. They also constructed an example of a problem with all demand points in a circle of radius $\frac{\pi R}{4} + \varepsilon$ for any $\varepsilon > 0$ that has two local optima with different values of the objective function. Drezner et al. [93] analyzed small multiple facility location problems on the surface of a sphere.

9.2.5.2 Various Location Models on the Sphere

The antipode of a point on a sphere is a point on the line connecting the point with the center of the sphere "on the other side". For example, the antipode of Hong Kong is near Rio de Janeiro. The antipode of a point (φ, θ) is $(-\varphi, \theta \pm \pi)$. Every circle, centered at the sphere's center, passing through these two points is a "great circle", and the distance between the point and its antipode is πR which is the largest possible distance between any two points on the sphere. This distance is obtained by the three formulas above.

By Eq. (9.1), $\hat{d} = R \arccos\{-\cos^2 \varphi - \sin^2 \varphi\} = R \arccos\{-1\} = \pi R$.
By Eq. (9.2), $\hat{d} = 2R \arcsin\{\sin^2 \varphi + \cos^2 \varphi\} = 2R \arcsin\{1\} = \pi R$.

By Eq. (9.3), $d = 2R$. Then, by Eq. (9.4), $\hat{d} = 2R \arcsin\{1\} = \pi R$.

The concept of the antipode can be useful for analyzing spherical problems. The distance between any point X and point Y plus the distance between X and the antipode of Y is equal to πR. Therefore, if there are negative weights in a location problem, a point with a negative weight can be replaced by its antipode with a positive weight. The maximin problem based on a set of points, is equivalent to the minimax problem based on the antipodes of these points. This property was utilized in [109] for solving the maximin and minimax problems on the sphere, and in [76] for solving constrained maximin and minimax problems on the sphere.

Drezner [81] investigated the Weber objective on a surface of a sphere when the demand points and weights are randomly generated. It is proven that when the number of demand points increases to infinity: (i) the ratio between the maximum value of the objective function and the minimum value converges to one, and (ii) the expected number of points that are a local minimum converges to one.

9.3   Multiple Facilities Location Problems

Most multiple facilities location models assume that customers are getting their services from, or are affected by, the closest facility. If only one facility is located, all customers are served by that facility. However, if several facilities are located, the set of demand points is partitioned into subsets so that all demand points in each subset are closest to the facility located in that subset. When Euclidean distances are used, the plane is partitioned into polygons based on the perpendicular bisectors between all pairs of facilities which is a Voronoi diagram (see Sect. 9.4.2.2). Such problems are not convex and may have several (may be many) local optima. Most of the solution methods proposed for such problems are heuristics. For solution methods see Sect. 9.4.3. Models that do not assume that services are provided by the closest facility are discussed in Sect. 9.3.7.

9.3.1   Conditional Models

Conditional location models investigate locating one or more facilities when some facilities already exist in the area. Customers select the closest existing or new facility. Many of the models listed in the rest of this section can also be formulated as conditional problems. The first to suggest such models was Minieka [168]. Some papers investigating conditional models are [174, 135, 7, 83, 80, 36, 35, 18].

9.3.2 The *p*-Median Location Problem

The continuous *p*-median problem [89, 99], also known as the multi-source Weber problem [22, 150, 132], or continuous location-allocation problem [158, 23] is an extension of the single facility Weber problem [202] discussed in Sect. 9.2.1. The problem is to find *p* sites for facilities that minimize a weighted sum of distances from a set of demand points to their closest facility.

Let $X_i = (x_i, y_i)$ denote the location of facility $i \in \{1, \ldots, p\}$, and $A_j = (a_j, b_j)$; $w_j > 0$ the known location of demand point j and its associated weight for $j \in N = \{1, \ldots, n\}$. For distances measured by the Euclidean norm: $d(X_i, A_j) = \sqrt{(x_i - a_j)^2 + (y_i - b_j)^2}$.

The planar *p*-median problem is: $\min_{\mathbf{X} \subset \mathbb{R}^2} \left\{ f(\mathbf{X}) = \sum_{j=1}^{n} w_j \min_{1 \leq i \leq p} \{d(X_i, A_j)\} \right\}$,

where $\mathbf{X} = \{X_1, \ldots, X_p\}$.

This model was originally proposed by Cooper [47, 48], who also observed that the objective function $f(\mathbf{X})$ is not convex, and may contain several local optima. The problem was later shown to be NP-hard [163]. For a recent review of the planar *p*-median problem see Brimberg and Hodgson [24]. In the discrete version of this problem (reviewed in Daskin and Maass[51, 50]), there is a list of potential locations for the facilities, rather than locating facilities anywhere in the plane.

It can be easily shown that in the optimal solution for Euclidean distances, the facilities must be located in the convex hull of the demand points. The proof is based on the theorem in Wendell and Hurter [206]: if a point is located outside the convex hull of the demand points, then there exists a point in the convex hull that is closer to all demand points. Therefore, if a facility is located outside the convex hull, there is a better location for it in the convex hull.

An extension to the *p*-median problem was proposed in Brimberg and Drezner [20] based on the procedure proposed in Drezner et al. [67]. Suppose that the set of demand points can be separated into *k* disconnected subsets, such as a subset in New-York, a subset in Tokyo, etc., so that demand points get their services from a facility assigned to a subset and not a facility assigned to another subset. $p > k$ facilities are to be built in these subsets. The problem is finding how many facilities to assign to each subset so that the sum of the individual p-median objectives, which is the p-median objective for the whole set, is minimized.

9.3.3 The p-Center Location Problem

The p-center location problem is an extension of the 1-center problem discussed in Sect. 9.2.2. The objective is to minimize the maximum (weighted) distance of demand points to their closest facility. The problem was proposed in a network environment [145]. Solution approaches are discussed in Sect. 9.4.3.2.

9.3.4 Cover Models

Facilities need to be located in an area to provide as much cover as possible. A demand point is covered by a facility within a certain distance [44, 183]. Such models are used for cover provided by emergency facilities such as ambulances, police cars, or fire trucks. They are also used to model cover by transmission towers such as cell-phone towers, TV or radio transmission towers, and radar coverage. For a review see [179, 124, 188, 43]. Drezner et al. [65, 66] applied the cover concept to competing facilities. Each competing facility has a "sphere of influence" [151, 121, 157, 37, 182], and customers patronize a facility up to a certain distance.

9.3.4.1 Gradual Cover Models

In the gradual cover models, up to a certain distance R_1 the demand point is fully covered and beyond a greater distance R_2 it is not covered at all. Between these two extreme distances the demand point is partially covered. Suppose that the cover distance in traditional cover models is 3 miles. At a distance of 2.99 miles the demand point is fully covered, while at a distance of 3.01 miles it is not covered at all. This assumption may be convenient for analyzing and solving covering problems. However, in reality cover does not drop abruptly but the decline in cover is gradual.

Church and Roberts [45] were the first to propose the gradual cover model (also referred to as partial cover). The facilities must be located within a finite set of potential locations. The network version with a step-wise cover function is discussed in [16]. The network and discrete models with a general non-increasing cover function were analyzed in [17]. The single facility planar model with a linearly decreasing cover function between R_1 and R_2 was optimally solved in [114], and its stochastic version (randomly distributed R_1 and R_2) analyzed and optimally solved in [62]. Additional references include [143, 116, 60, 10].

Drezner et al. [68] proposed the directional gradual cover. Communities are usually areas and not points. Not all residents are at the same distance from a facility and in many instances only some of the residents, that are closer to the facility, are covered. Suppose that customers residing at a demand "point" reside in a disc (centered at the demand point) of radius r, and the facility is located at a point. The facility covers customers within a given distance D. All the points in the disc centered at the facility with a radius D are covered. The intersection area between this disc and the disc centered at the demand point of radius r is covered. Therefore, the partial cover by one facility is the ratio between this intersection area and the area of the demand disc. A facility within a distance $D - r$ from the demand point covers the whole disc, and at a distance exceeding $D + r$ it covers none. Follow-up papers extending the concept of the directional cover are [69, 71].

A different gradual covering model where facilities "cooperate" in providing cover was proposed in [8]. Each facility emits a signal (such as light posts in a parking lot) whose strength declines according to a distance decay function. A point is covered if the combined signal from all facilities exceeds a certain threshold. Recent papers on the cooperative cover are [170, 144, 201, 3].

It is not obvious how to estimate the total partial cover of a demand point when it is partially covered by several facilities. This issue is discussed in [10]. Let c_j be the partial cover of a demand point by facility j for $j = 1, \ldots, p$. Eiselt and Marianov [116] proposed a total partial cover of $\min \left\{ \sum_{j=1}^{p} c_j, 1 \right\}$. Partial cover can be interpreted as the probability of cover. Assuming that the partial covers are not correlated, the total partial cover is: $1 - \prod_{j=1}^{p} \left(1 - c_j \right)$ [12, 113, 57]. In the directional gradual cover [68], if a demand point is partially covered by two or more facilities, the total cover (area) depends on the distances between the facilities and the demand point, and on the *directions* of the facilities from the demand point. For example, if two facilities are located North of the demand point, the cover areas overlap and the total cover is equal to the larger cover area. If one facility is to the North and one to the South, total cover is greater than the larger cover area unless the demand point is fully covered by one of the facilities. Total cover is at least the largest cover by one of the facilities and cannot exceed the sum of the covers by individual facilities. When $r = 0$, the demand point is either fully covered or not covered at all. The cover is identical to the cover applied in the standard non-gradual cover models.

9.3.5   The Multiple Obnoxious Facilities Location Problem

In all models of locating obnoxious facilities, all facilities must be located in a finite feasible area. Otherwise, facilities will be located "at infinity". For a review of obnoxious facilities models see [41].

One of the models for the multiple obnoxious facilities location problem is to locate p facilities, that are at least a distance D from one another, with the objective of maximizing the shortest distance between facilities and demand points [205, 96]. The problem is "extremely" non-convex. The surface of the shortest distance to the communities is depicted in Fig. 9.3. The hilltops are Voronoi points discussed in Sect. 9.4.2.2. There are 202 hilltops in the figure. Drezner et al. [96] proposed to find locations on hilltops for p facilities that are at least a given distance D from one another with the objective of maximizing the shortest distance between demand points and facilities. Kalczynski

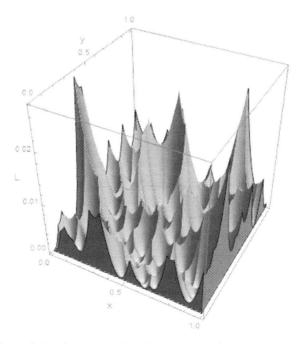

Fig. 9.3 Surface of the distance to the closest demand point in a square

and Drezner [139] improved this procedure. Kalczynski et al. [141] generalized this problem to include weights associated with demand points. Rather than maximizing the minimum distance, the objective is maximizing the minimum weighted distance. Solution methods are described in Sect. 9.4.3.3

Eiselt and Marianov [117] modeled the locations of landfills and transfer stations. The model is formulated as a bi-objective problem. One objective is cost-minimization, while the other is minimizing pollution. Melachrinoudis et al. [166] proposed a multi-objective model for the location of landfills. Teran-Somohano and Smith [199] present a model for the obnoxious, multiple capacitated facility location problem on a Euclidean plane. The problem is solved using a bi-objective evolutionary strategy algorithm that seeks to minimize social and non-social costs. The effects of under and over capacitating the facility are included in the cost functions.

Kalczynski and Drezner [138] proposed solving two variants of obnoxious multi-facilities problems with the objective of maximizing the sum of the shortest distances rather than the minimum, which can be termed p-maxian following the terminology of [42]. Since there is no advantage to locating facilities close to one another, there is no need to require a minimum distance between facilities. One problem's objective is maximizing the sum of weighted distances between each demand point and its closest obnoxious facility. The second objective is maximizing the sum of weighted distances between each facility and its closest obnoxious demand point. They first solved the problems using three general purpose nonlinear software packages from many randomly generated starting solutions: Matlab's [129] interior point, SNOPT [125], and MSLP (Multi-start Sequential Linear Programming [95] which performed the best of the three). However, as in [96], the best quality solutions and shortest run times were obtained by selecting p starting locations among the Voronoi points.

Drezner et al. [70] defined a different objective function. The negative impact emitted by the facilities declines by the square of the distance and is additive. The facilities "cooperate" in inflicting the disturbance. The objective is to minimize the disturbance inflicted on the most affected community. Since locating two facilities at the same location doubles the disturbance generated at that location, there is no need to require a minimum distance between facilities. The model is a generalization of the single facility location model proposed by Hansen et al. [133].

The p-dispersion problem, originally described by Shier [186] on a tree network, deals with facility to facility interactions as no demand points are included in the model. The objective is maximizing the minimum distance between facilities. Kuby [149] designed an integer programming formulation for the discrete case. It was approached in the continuous space by [92, 161]. For the continuous case, there is a bounded area with no demand points. An equivalent problem is circle packing in a convex area (finding p non-intersecting circles inside a convex area with the greatest possible radius [154, 161, 173, 197]). Common convex areas investigated in the literature include a square, a rectangle, a disk, and an equilateral triangle [197, 155].

9.3.6 Equity Models

Equity models aim to provide similar service to the demand points rather than minimizing or maximizing some objective. Single facility models are discussed in Sect. 9.2.4. Examples of multiple facilities models include:

1. Minimizing the Gini coefficient of the Lorenz curve [156, 126] calculated by service distances to the closest facility [63].
2. Equalizing the load serviced by the facilities [193, 4, 11].
3. The set of demand points is partitioned into groups. These groups are not necessarily divided by their locations but by characteristics such as neighborhoods' wealth. The objective is to provide equitable service to the groups by locating one or more facilities. For example, poor neighborhoods should get comparable service level to rich neighborhoods [59].

9.3.7 Not Necessarily Patronizing the Closest Facility

Most multiple facility location problems assume that customers get their services from the closest facility. There are a few papers that do not assume that. Brimberg et al. [26] assumed that there is a sequence of probabilities $p_1, p_2, \ldots$. A customer is served by the closest facility with probability p_1, by the second closest with probability p_2, and so on. In competitive location, discussed in Chapter [52] in this book, one approach termed the gravity or Huff model [181, 136, 137] assumes that customers split their patronage among several competing facilities rather than patronize the closest one. The probability of patronizing a facility declines by a distance decay function.

Some models propose that customers obtain their services according to the gravity rule. Drezner and Drezner [56, 54] proposed the gravity p-median model. It is assumed that users choose from among the facilities providing services according to the gravity rule rather than getting them from the closest facility.

Drezner and Drezner [53] applied the gravity rule to the hub location problem. A traveler needs to fly from one airport to another. Several potential hub airports are available. If the origin or the destination is a hub airport, the traveler chooses a non-stop flight. Otherwise, the probability that a certain hub is selected is governed by the gravity rule.

Drezner and Drezner [58] considered the gravity rule version of the multiple server location problem [6]. Total service time consists of travel time to the facility, waiting time in line, and service time. There is a given number of servers to be distributed among the facilities. Each facility acts as an M/M/k queuing system [162]. Customers select a server with a probability proportional to its attractiveness and to a decay function of the distance, not necessarily selecting the closest one.

9.4   Solution Methods

9.4.1   Generating Replicable Test Problems

In order to compare computational results of test problems in future research, access to the parameters of the test problems is required. Drezner et al. [96] suggested a simple method, that was used in many follow-up papers, to generate a pseudo-random sequence of numbers distributed uniformly in the open range between 0 and 1 based on the idea of Law and Kelton [152]. Such test problems can be easily replicated without a need for an access to a data base.

A starting seed r_1 and a multiplier λ, which are odd numbers not divisible by 5, are selected. Note that r_1 can be an even number not ending with a zero. Drezner et al. [96] used $\lambda = 12, 219$. The sequence is generated by the following rule for $k \geq 1$:

$$r_{k+1} = \lambda r_k - \lfloor \frac{\lambda r_k}{100, 000} \rfloor \times 100, 000$$

The number r_k is an integer between 1 and 99,999, so $\frac{r_k}{100,000}$ is a number in the open range between 0 and 1. If a random number between a and b is sought, we can use $a + (b - a)\frac{r_k}{100,000}$. It turns out that $r_{5001} = r_1$ and if a sequence of more than 5,000 points is needed, the 100,000 can be replaced by 1,000,000 and sequences of up to 50,000 numbers can be generated [142]. Drezner et al. [96] used $r_1 = 97$ to generate the x coordinates, and $r_1 = 367$ to generate the y coordinates of their test problem. The surface plot for $n = 100$ for the obnoxious facility problem depicted in Fig. 9.3 is based on the points generated this way.

9.4.2 Solving Single Facility Problems

9.4.2.1 Solving with the Solver in Excel

Convex single facility location problems can be solved with the Solver in Excel, mainly for instruction purposes. Expression (9.5) is easy to program. There are only two variables (x, y). For the one-center problem, it is better to formulate it as minimize $\{L\}$ subject to the constraints that each distance $\leq L$. The distances (9.1) for problems on the sphere are somewhat more complicated to program, but spherical problems can serve as a good example for a global FedEx idea of planes flying to a central airport, exchange packages and fly back. If the company serves 20 cities all over the world, flying directly between all pairs of cities will require 380 airplanes to fly daily, while this scheme requires only 20 airplanes.

If a problem is not convex, it can be heuristically solved by Solver using VBA (Visual Basic for Applications) in a multi-start approach (for example repeating the process 100 times). Each starting solution is randomly generated, and the problem is solved by calling Solver in the VBA code, and the best solution is selected.

9.4.2.2 Voronoi Diagram and Delaunay Triangulation

A Voronoi diagram [200] is constructed by a set of generator points. The plane is partitioned into polygons so that all the points inside a polygon are closest to one generator point. The sides of the polygons are equidistant from two generator points (and closest to them), and the vertices of the polygons (termed Voronoi points) are equidistant from three generator points. So, for example, if the generator points are facilities, the plane is partitioned into polygons so that the points inside a polygon are closest to the same facility. If a demand point gets its services from the closest facility, each facility provides service to the set of demand points in its polygon.

The Delaunay triangulation [153] is based on the Voronoi diagram. A polygon whose interior is the feasible set, has demand points in its interior (and boundary). The polygon is partitioned into non-overlapping triangles so that the vertices of the triangles are demand points, and the union of the triangles covers the whole feasible polygon. Figure 9.4 depicts an example

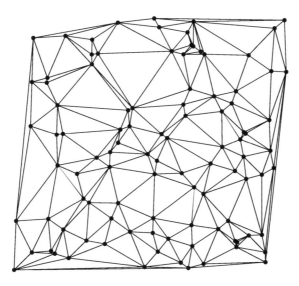

Fig. 9.4 Delaunay triangulation of the convex hull

of a Delaunay triangulation of the convex hull of a set of points. The Delaunay triangulation can be generated by Mathematica [208]. For a review of Voronoi Diagrams and Delaunay triangulation see [2, 194, 175].

9.4.2.3 General Global Optimization Algorithms

The first global optimization procedure suitable for the location of a single facility is the "Big-Square-Small-Square" (BSSS) proposed by Hansen et al. [133]. It is a branch and bound algorithm. A relative accuracy $\varepsilon > 0$ is given. A square that covers the feasible region is defined, and a formula (or procedure) for finding lower and upper bounds in a square is needed. The following steps are executed for a minimization problem. A procedure for maximization is very similar.

1. Find the lower bound LB_1 and the upper bound UB_1 in the square. The upper bound is at a feasible point. The list of squares has one member. The best upper bound (best solution found so far) in the list is $UB = UB_1$.
2. Select the square i in the list with the minimum LB_i. If $LB_i > UB(1 - \varepsilon)$, stop with UB as the solution.
3. Remove square i (the "big" square) from the list and create four "small" squares by perpendicular lines, parallel to its sides, through the big square's center.
4. For each of the four small squares:

    a. Calculate the lower bound $\overline{LB}$ and the feasible upper bound $\overline{UB}$ in the square.

    b. Update UB if $\overline{UB} < UB$.

    c. If $\overline{LB} \leq UB(1 - \varepsilon)$, add the small square to the list.

5. If UB was updated in Step 4b, check all the squares in the list and remove squares for which $LB_i > UB(1 - \varepsilon)$.

6. If the list of squares is empty, stop with UB as the solution within a relative accuracy ε. Otherwise, go to Step 2.

The BSSS branch and bound algorithm was modified in several ways. Drezner and Suzuki [104] constructed the "Big-Triangle-Small-Triangle" (BTST) procedure. The feasible set, such as the convex hull of the demand points, is triangulated by the Delaunay triangulation [153] described in Sect. 9.4.2.2. The initial list consists of the Delaunay triangles. In the first phase bounds are calculated for each triangle, and some triangles are removed from the list. The second phase is similar to BSSS. Four "small triangles" are created by connecting the centers of the sides of the selected "big triangle". The BTST algorithm is more efficient, especially when the feasible area is not the whole square. In order to evaluate the bounds for BSSS, the feasibility of points in a square needs to be considered. In BTST all Delaunay triangles and consequently all small triangles are feasible by design and no feasibility check is required.

Drezner [85] constructed a general algorithm for solving by BTST any location problem whose objective is a sum of individual terms, one for each demand point. Specific bounds are constructed when each term can be expressed as a difference between two convex functions *of the distance* which are not necessarily convex in the coordinates x and y. For example, $-\ln(d)$ is convex for $d > 0$ but it is not convex (or concave) in the coordinates. Drezner and Nickel [98] constructed general bounds for problems that can be formulated as an ordered median problem [172].

Drezner et al. [72] constructed the "Big-Arc-Small-Arc" (BASA) algorithm for solving location problems on peripheries of circles. Berman et al. [9] designed the "Big-Segment-Small-Segment" algorithm for solving problems on networks. Schöbel and Scholz [184] proposed the "Big-Cube-Small-Cube" (BCSC) algorithm for solving problems in k-dimensional space for $k \geq 3$.

9.4.2.4 Solving the Weber Problem

The first algorithm for solving the Weber [202] problem with Euclidean distances was designed by [203] (translated to English in [204]). It is an iterative procedure converging to the optimal solution because the problem is convex [177].

Let (x_i, y_i) for $i = 1, \ldots n$ with weights $w_i > 0$ be a set of demand points in the plane. The objective function is:

$$\min_{x,y} \left\{ \sum_{i=1}^{n} w_i \sqrt{(x - x_i)^2 + (y - y_i)^2} \right\} \tag{9.5}$$

A starting solution $(\hat{x}, \hat{y})$ is selected. The next iterate is obtained by equating the derivatives of Eq. (9.5) by x and y at $(\hat{x}, \hat{y})$ to zero, and solving for (x, y). Define $\widehat{w}_i = \dfrac{w_i}{\sqrt{(\hat{x}-x_i)^2+(\hat{y}-y_i)^2}}$, then

$$\sum_{i=1}^{n} \widehat{w}_i (x - x_i) = 0; \quad \sum_{i=1}^{n} \widehat{w}_i (y - y_i) = 0 \ \rightarrow \ x = \frac{\sum\limits_{i=1}^{n} \widehat{w}_i x_i}{\sum\limits_{i=1}^{n} \widehat{w}_i}; \quad y = \frac{\sum\limits_{i=1}^{n} \widehat{w}_i y_i}{\sum\limits_{i=1}^{n} \widehat{w}_i}.$$
$$\tag{9.6}$$

When the Euclidean distance is replaced by the squared Euclidean distance, the solution is at the center of gravity ($\widehat{w}_i = w_i$). When Manhattan (ℓ_1) distances are used, the problem is separable into two unrelated one dimensional problems. The solution in one dimension (on a line) is at the median point, hence the name "the one-median problem". For ℓ_p distances, a procedure similar to Weiszfeld [203] is designed by Brimberg and Love [25]. For details see [158, 122].

Several improvements of the Weiszfeld algorithm [203] were proposed. Drezner [82] proposed to multiply the change between two consecutive iterations by a factor of 1.8. An "ideal" multiplier that needs to be computed every iteration was also proposed. Drezner [84] proposed to accelerate the procedure by estimating the limit of a geometric series by the ratio of the changes of two consecutive iterations. Drezner [87] proposed the fortified algorithm based on the values of the objective function at 9 points (the present iteration and eight points around it on the vertices and sides' centers of a square depicted in Fig. 9.5), and fitting a paraboloid to these nine values by a least

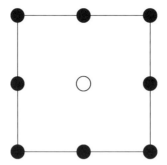

Fig. 9.5 The square configuration for the fortified algorithm

squares quadratic regression. The next iterate is the minimum point of the paraboloid. For details see Drezner [87].

9.4.2.5   Solving the One-Center Problem

Elzinga and Hearn [118] proved that the smallest circle enclosing all points passes through two points (in which case the solution is in the middle between the points), or through three points. They proposed the following algorithm for solving optimally the unweighted 1-center problem:

1. Pick any two points. Construct a circle based on the segment connecting the two points as a diameter.
2. If the circle covers all points, a solution has been found, stop.
3. Otherwise, add a point outside the circle to the pair of points to form a set of three points.
4. If the triangle with the three points at its vertices has an angle of at least 90°, drop the point on the obtuse angle and go to Step 3.
5. If the circle passing through the three points covers all points, a solution has been found, stop.
6. If there is a point outside the circle, choose such a point, and add it as a fourth point. One of the original three points needs to be discarded. Go to Step 4.

Once the solution based on three points is available [108], the following modification is faster and can be used for the weighted case as well.

1. Select a point such as the center of gravity of the demand points.
2. Select the three farthest points (weighted for the general case).
3. Find the solution point based on these three points.
4. This point is the next iterate. Note that the solution point may be based on only two of the points.
5. Find the largest weighted point from the next iterate. If it is within the (weighted) distance obtained in Step 4 stop.
6. Otherwise, replace each of the three points by the farthest point (actually solving the four point problem) and select the center of the best solution as the next iterate. Go to Step 4

Drezner and Shelah [102] constructed a special configuration that shows that the Elzinga and Hearn [118] algorithm can have a complexity of at least $o(n^2)$ even though in practice the complexity is linear for most tested problems.

9.4.2.6 Solving the Obnoxious Facility Problem

In Fig. 9.3 the surface of the shortest distance to a set of 100 randomly generated demand points is depicted. The solution is on the top of the tallest hill. There are 202 hilltops in the figure. It turns out that these hilltops are Voronoi points (see Sect. 9.4.2.2). The Voronoi points can be easily generated by Mathematica [208], or special FORTRAN programs such as Sugihara and Iri [190, 191]. Shamos and Hoey [185] observed this property. Their idea was to generate all the Voronoi points and select the one with the largest shortest distance. Dasarathy and White [49] solved the unweighted maximin problem directly without resorting to Voronoi diagrams. Drezner and Wesolowsky [107] solved the weighted version of the problem.

Hansen et al. [133] observed that the negative impact inflicted by an obnoxious facility usually declines by the square of the distance. Let a facility be located at location X, and the distance between community i for $i = 1, \ldots, n$ and location X is $d_i(X)$. There are w_i residents in community i. The objective is to minimize the cumulative effect on the residents in the area by locating the facility in a pre-determined region S, with the objective:

$$\min_{X \in S} \sum_{i=1}^{n} \frac{w_i}{d_i^2(X)} \tag{9.7}$$

They optimally solved this problem by the Big-Square-Small-Square (BSSS) global optimization method (described in Sect. 9.4.2.3) designed in that paper.

9.4.2.7 Solving Spherical Problems

Hansen et al. [130] and Suzuki [192] constructed global optimization algorithms for location on a sphere's surface based on the algorithms described in Sect. 9.4.2.3. For spherical surfaces, Hansen et al. [130] generalized the BSSS algorithm [133], and Suzuki [192] generalized the BTST algorithm [104]. The spherical Delaunay triangles are found by the method in Sugihara [189].

9.4.3 Multiple Facilities Solution Methods

Most solution methods of continuous multiple facilities locations are heuristic. Only small instances can be optimally solved in reasonable computer time.

9.4.3.1 *p*-Median

The planar *p*-median problem is known to be NP-hard [163], and therefore many heuristics have been developed for its solution. Classical heuristics include the famous alternating procedure [47, 48], the projection method [19], and gradient-based methods [34, 171]. An algorithm that can optimally solve medium size problems is designed by Krau [148]. For recent reviews of solution approaches to the planar *p*-median problem the reader is referred to [88, 89, 27].

Cooper [47, 48] proposed the alternating (sometimes called location-allocation) method. Starting locations for *p* facilities are selected (randomly or otherwise). The set of demand points is partitioned into subsets, each served by one facility. The best location of the facility serving each subset (the Weber problem which is convex) is found, and possibly a different partition is found. The process is continued until the partition into subsets stabilizes

Genetic algorithms [134, 128] in combination of additional heuristics such as variable neighborhood search [169, 131], tabu search [127], were proposed in [198, 21, 123, 88, 99]. The best results were obtained in [91].

9.4.3.2   p-Center

Drezner [78] optimally solved the two-center and the two-median problems on the plane. It is proved that in the optimal solution there is a line separating the set of demand points into two subsets such that the single facility solution point for each subset yields the optimal solution to the two facilities problem. There are at most $\frac{1}{2}n(n-1)$ such lines. Once all separating lines are evaluated, the optimal solution is identified. A lower bound for each subset improves the efficiency of the algorithm.

Drezner [77] suggested two heuristics and one optimal algorithm for the solution of the weighted p-center problem. The two heuristic procedures are similar to the location-allocation algorithm [47, 48]. The optimal algorithm is based on the property that the solution to the one-center problem is based on two or three demand points [118]. There are $\frac{1}{6}n(n^2 + 5)$ possible maximal sets. Based on a proof in [75], the number of relevant maximal sets is bounded by $n(n-1)$. The proposed optimal algorithm is polynomial in n for a fixed p. The extension of the modified center problem [75] is also solved in polynomial time.

Callaghan et al. [28, 29] constructed the best optimal algorithm to solve the p-center problem. They optimally solved problems with up to 1,323 demand points. Earlier solution algorithms were proposed by [32, 34, 36, 35].

9.4.3.3   Multiple Obnoxious Facilities Solution Methods

The Voronoi points (hilltops in Fig. 9.3) are found. The heuristic algorithm proposed in Drezner et al. [96] is to select p hilltops so that the distance between any two hilltops is at least D, and the lowest hilltop is as high as possible. This is done by solving the following Binary Linear Program (BLP).

Let K be the number of hilltops, and d_i be the shortest distance between hilltop i and all demand points (the height of the hilltop). The hilltops are sorted so that $d_1 \geq d_2 \geq \ldots d_K$. The distance between hilltops i and j is D_{ij}, and we select only hilltops that are at least a given distance D from one another. The proposed binary linear program is (For complete details see Drezner et al. [96]):

$$\text{Maximize } \{L\}$$

subject to:

$$\sum_{i=1}^{K} x_i = p$$

$$x_i + x_j \leq 1 \text{ when } D_{ij} < D$$

$$L + x_i(d_1 - d_i) \leq d_1 \text{ for } i = 1, \ldots, K$$

$$x_i \in \{0, 1\} \tag{9.8}$$

9.5 Summary and Suggestions for Future Research

Location models involve locating one or more facilities among a given set of demand points to achieve a certain objective. For example: locating a warehouse that serves a set of stores; locating a landfill to serve communities but should not be close to them; locating cell-phone towers with a certain range to cover the population in an area. In discrete location models, a finite set of potential locations for facilities is given. In continuous location models, facilities can be located anywhere in the plane, or in a finite region with an infinite number of possible locations.

Such problems are modeled as optimization problems, such as nonlinear programming. Some models are convex and can be easily solved to optimality. Single facility location problems can be optimally solved by the algorithms detailed in Sect. 9.4.2.3. However, most multiple facility problems are non-convex and optimal algorithms are difficult to construct. Therefore, specially designed heuristic algorithms, meta-heuristic approaches such as genetic algorithms [134, 128], variable neighborhood search [169, 131], tabu search [127] and others, are applied for their solution.

There are many models that were proposed in discrete space but yet to be investigated in continuous space. In discrete space such problems are combinatorial in nature: selecting p locations for facilities out of the list of potential locations. Well-designed branch and bound algorithms may be able to solve them to optimality. In continuous space, optimal algorithms are difficult to construct, and heuristic algorithms are usually constructed for solving them.

References

1. Alumur, S. A. (2019). Hub location and related models. In *Contributions to Location Analysis—In Honor of Zvi Drezner's 75th Birthday*, pages 237–252. Springer Nature, Switzerland.
2. Aurenhammer, F., Klein, R., and Lee, D.-T. (2013). *Voronoi Diagrams and Delaunay Triangulations*. World Scientific, New Jersey.
3. Bagherinejad, J., Bashiri, M., and Nikzad, H. (2018). General form of a cooperative gradual maximal covering location problem. *Journal of Industrial Engineering International*, 14:241–253.
4. Baron, O., Berman, O., Krass, D., and Wang, Q. (2007). The equitable location problem on the plane. *European Journal of Operational Research*, 183:578–590.
5. Berman, O. (1990). Mean-variance location problems. *Transportation Science*, 24:287–293.
6. Berman, O. and Drezner, Z. (2007). The multiple server location problem. *Journal of the Operational Research Society*, 58:91–99.
7. Berman, O. and Drezner, Z. (2008). A new formulation for the conditional p-median and p-center problems. *Operations Research Letters*, 36:481–483.
8. Berman, O., Drezner, Z., and Krass, D. (2010). Cooperative cover location problems: The planar case. *IIE Transactions*, 42:232–246.
9. Berman, O., Drezner, Z., and Krass, D. (2011). Big segment small segment global optimization algorithm on networks. *Networks*, 58:1–11.
10. Berman, O., Drezner, Z., and Krass, D. (2019). The multiple gradual cover location problem. *Jornal of the Operational Research Society*, 70:931–940.
11. Berman, O., Drezner, Z., Tamir, A., and Wesolowsky, G. O. (2009). Optimal location with equitable loads. *Annals of Operations Research*, 167:307–325.
12. Berman, O., Drezner, Z., and Wesolowsky, G. O. (2003a). The expropriation location problem. *Journal of the Operational Research Society*, 54:769–776.
13. Berman, O., Drezner, Z., and Wesolowsky, G. O. (2005). The facility and transfer points location problem. *International Transactions in Operational Research*, 12:387–402.
14. Berman, O., Drezner, Z., and Wesolowsky, G. O. (2007). The transfer point location problem. *European Journal of Operational Research*, 179:978–989.
15. Berman, O., Drezner, Z., and Wesolowsky, G. O. (2008). The multiple location of transfer points. *Journal of the Operational Research Society*, 59:805–811.
16. Berman, O. and Krass, D. (2002). The generalized maximal covering location problem. *Computers & Operations Research*, 29:563–591.
17. Berman, O., Krass, D., and Drezner, Z. (2003b). The gradual covering decay location problem on a network. *European Journal of Operational Research*, 151:474–480.
18. Berman, O. and Simchi-Levi, D. (1990). The conditional location problem on networks. *Transportation Science*, 24:77–78.

19. Bongartz, I., Calamai, P. H., and Conn, A. R. (1994). A projection method for ℓ_p norm location-allocation problems. *Mathematical Programming*, 66:238–312.

20. Brimberg, J. and Drezner, Z. (2019). Solving multiple facilities location problems with separated clusters. *Operations Research Letters*, 47:386–390.

21. Brimberg, J., Hansen, P., and Mladenović, N. (2006). Decomposition strategies for large-scale continuous location–allocation problems. *IMA Journal of Management Mathematics*, 17:307–316.

22. Brimberg, J., Hansen, P., Mladenović, N., and Taillard, E. (2000). Improvements and comparison of heuristics for solving the uncapacitated multisource Weber problem. *Operations Research*, 48:444–460.

23. Brimberg, J., Hansen, P., Mladonovic, N., and Salhi, S. (2008). A survey of solution methods for the continuous location allocation problem. *International Journal of Operations Research*, 5:1–12.

24. Brimberg, J. and Hodgson, M. J. (2011). Heuristics for location models. In Eiselt, H. A. and Marianov, V., editors, *Foundations of Location Analysis: International Series in Operations Research & Management Science*, Vol. 155, pages 335–355. Springer, New York, NY.

25. Brimberg, J. and Love, R. F. (1993). Global convergence of a generalized iterative procedure for the minisum location problem with l_p distances. *Operations Research*, 41:1153–1163.

26. Brimberg, J., Maier, A., and Schöbel, A. (2021). When closest is not always the best: The distributed p-median problem. *Journal of the Operational Research Society*, 72:200–216.

27. Brimberg, J. and Salhi, S. (2019). A general framework for local search applied to the continuous p-median problem. In *Contributions to Location Analysis— In Honor of Zvi Drezner's 75th Birthday*, pages 89–108. Springer Nature, Switzerland.

28. Callaghan, B., Salhi, S., and Brimberg, J. (2019). Optimal solutions for the continuous p-centre problem and related-neighbour and conditional problems: A relaxation-based algorithm. *Journal of the Operational Research Society*, 70:192–211.

29. Callaghan, B., Salhi, S., and Nagy, G. (2017). Speeding up the optimal method of Drezner for the p-centre problem in the plane. *European Journal of Operational Research*, 257:722–734.

30. Campbell, J. F. (1994). Integer programming formulations of discrete hub location problems. *European Journal of Operational Research*, 72:387–405.

31. Carrizosa, E. (1998). Minimizing the variance of Euclidean distances. *Studies in Locational Analysis*, 12:101–118.

32. Chen, D. and Chen, R. (2009). New relaxation-based algorithms for the optimal solution of the continuous and discrete p-center problems. *Computers & Operations Research*, 36:1646–1655.

33. Chen, P., Hansen, P., Jaumard, B., and Tuy, H. (1992). Weber's problem with attraction and repulsion. *Journal of Regional Science*, 32:467–486.

34. Chen, R. (1983). Solution of minisum and minimax location-allocation problems with Euclidean distances. *Naval Research Logistics Quarterly*, 30:449–459.
35. Chen, R. (1988). Conditional minisum and minimax location-allocation problems in Euclidean space. *Transportation Science*, 22:157–160.
36. Chen, R. and Handler, G. Y. (1993). The conditional p-center in the plane. *Naval Research Logistics*, 40:117–127.
37. Christaller, W. (1966). *Central Places in Southern Germany*. Prentice-Hall, Englewood Cliffs, NJ.
38. Chrystal, G. (1885). On the problem to construct the minimum circle enclosing n given points in the plane. *Proceedings of the Edinburgh Mathematical Society*, 3:30–33.
39. Church, R. L. (2019). Understanding the Weber location paradigm. In Eiselt, H. A. and Marianov, V., editors, *Contributions to Location Analysis—In Honor of Zvi Drezner's 75th Birthday*, pages 69–88. Springer Nature, Switzerland.
40. Church, R. L. and Cohon, J. L. (1976). Multiobjective location analysis of regional energy facility siting problems. Technical report, Brookhaven National Lab., Upton, NY (USA).
41. Church, R. L. and Drezner, Z. (2022). Review of obnoxious facilities location problems. *Computers and Operations Research*, 138, 105468.
42. Church, R. L. and Garfinkel, R. S. (1978). Locating an obnoxious facility on a network. *Transportation Science*, 12:107–118.
43. Church, R. L. and Murray, A. (2018). Location covering models: History, applications, and advancements. *Advances in Spatial Science*.
44. Church, R. L. and ReVelle, C. S. (1974). The maximal covering location problem. *Papers of the Regional Science Association*, 32:101–118.
45. Church, R. L. and Roberts, K. L. (1984). Generalized coverage models and public facility location. *Papers of the Regional Science Association*, 53:117–135.
46. Contreras, I. (2015). Hub location problems. In Laporte, G., Nickel, S., and da Gama, F. S., editors, *Location Science*, pages 311–344. Springer, Heidelberg.
47. Cooper, L. (1963). Location-allocation problems. *Operations Research*, 11:331–343.
48. Cooper, L. (1964). Heuristic methods for location-allocation problems. *SIAM Review*, 6:37–53.
49. Dasarathy, B. and White, L. (1980). A maximin location problem. *Operations Research*, 28(6):1385–1401.
50. Daskin, M. S. (1995). *Network and Discrete Location: Models, Algorithms, and Applications*. John Wiley & Sons, New York.
51. Daskin, M. S. and Maass, K. L. (2015). The p-median problem. In Laporte, G., Nickel, S., and da Gama, F. S., editors, *Location Science*, pages 21–45. Springer, Heidelberg.
52. Drezner, T. (2021). Competitive location problems. In Salhi S. and Boylan J.E., editors, *The Palgrave Handbook of Operations Research*. Palgrave, London.
53. Drezner, T. and Drezner, Z. (2001). A note on applying the gravity rule to the airline hub problem. *Journal of Regional Science*, 41:67–73.

54. Drezner, T. and Drezner, Z. (2006). Multiple facilities location in the plane using the gravity model. *Geographical Analysis*, 38:391–406.
55. Drezner, T. and Drezner, Z. (2007a). Equity models in planar location. *Computational Management Science*, 4:1–16.
56. Drezner, T. and Drezner, Z. (2007b). The gravity p-median model. *European Journal of Operational Research*, 179:1239–1251.
57. Drezner, T. and Drezner, Z. (2008). Lost demand in a competitive environment. *Journal of the Operational Research Society*, 59:362–371.
58. Drezner, T. and Drezner, Z. (2011a). The gravity multiple server location problem. *Computers & Operations Research*, 38:694–701.
59. Drezner, T. and Drezner, Z. (2011b). A note on equity across groups in facility location. *Naval Research Logistics*, 58:705–711.
60. Drezner, T. and Drezner, Z. (2014). The maximin gradual cover location problem. *OR Spectrum*, 36:903–921.
61. Drezner, T. and Drezner, Z. (2021). Asymmetric distance location model. *INFOR: Information Systems and Operational Research*, 59:102–110.
62. Drezner, T., Drezner, Z., and Goldstein, Z. (2010). A stochastic gradual cover location problem. *Naval Research Logistics*, 57:367–372.
63. Drezner, T., Drezner, Z., and Guyse, J. (2009a). Equitable service by a facility: Minimizing the Gini coefficient. *Computers & Operations Research*, 36:3240–3246.
64. Drezner, T., Drezner, Z., and Hulliger, B. (2014). The quintile share ratio in location analysis. *European Journal of Operational Research*, 236:166–174.
65. Drezner, T., Drezner, Z., and Kalczynski, P. (2011). A cover-based competitive location model. *Journal of the Operational Research Society*, 62:100–113.
66. Drezner, T., Drezner, Z., and Kalczynski, P. (2012). Strategic competitive location: Improving existing and establishing new facilities. *Journal of the Operational Research Society*, 63:1720–1730.
67. Drezner, T., Drezner, Z., and Kalczynski, P. (2016a). The multiple markets competitive location problem. *Kybernetes*, 45:854–865.
68. Drezner, T., Drezner, Z., and Kalczynski, P. (2019a). A directional approach to gradual cover. *TOP*, 27:70–93.
69. Drezner, T., Drezner, Z., and Kalczynski, P. (2020a). Directional approach to gradual cover: A maximin objective. *Computational Management Science*, 17:121–139.
70. Drezner, T., Drezner, Z., and Kalczynski, P. (2020b). Multiple obnoxious facilities location: A cooperative model. *IISE Transactions*, 52:1403–1412.
71. Drezner, T., Drezner, Z., and Kalczynski, P. (2021). Directional approach to gradual cover: The continuous case. *Computational Management Science*, 18:25–47.
72. Drezner, T., Drezner, Z., and Schöbel, A. (2018). The Weber obnoxious facility location model: A Big Arc Small Arc approach. *Computers and Operations Research*, 98:240–250.

73. Drezner, T., Drezner, Z., and Scott, C. H. (2009b). Location of a facility minimizing nuisance to or from a planar network. *Computers & Operations Research*, 36:135–148.
74. Drezner, Z. (1979). Bounds on the optimal location to the Weber problem under conditions of uncertainty. *Journal of the Operational Research Society*, 30:923–931.
75. Drezner, Z. (1981). On a modified one-center model. *Management Science*, 27:848–851.
76. Drezner, Z. (1983). Constrained location problems in the plane and on a sphere. *IIE Transactions*, 15:300–304.
77. Drezner, Z. (1984a). The p-center problem—Heuristic and optimal algorithms. *Journal of the Operational Research Society*, 35:741–748.
78. Drezner, Z. (1984b). The planar two-center and two-median problems. *Transportation Science*, 18:351–361.
79. Drezner, Z. (1985). Sensitivity analysis of the optimal location of a facility. *Naval Research Logistics Quarterly*, 32:209–224.
80. Drezner, Z. (1989a). On the conditional p-center problem. *Transportation Science*, 23:51–53.
81. Drezner, Z. (1989b). Stochastic analysis of the Weber problem on the sphere. *Journal of the Operational Research Society*, 40:1137–1144.
82. Drezner, Z. (1992). A note on the Weber location problem. *Annals of Operations Research*, 40:153–161.
83. Drezner, Z. (1995). On the conditional p-median problem. *Computers & Operations Research*, 22:525–530.
84. Drezner, Z. (1996). A note on accelerating the Weiszfeld procedure. *Location Science*, 3:275–279.
85. Drezner, Z. (2007). A general global optimization approach for solving location problems in the plane. *Journal of Global Optimization*, 37:305–319.
86. Drezner, Z. (2011). Continuous center problems. In Eiselt, H. A. and Marianov, V., editors, *Foundations of Location Analysis*, pages 63–78. Springer, New York.
87. Drezner, Z. (2015). The fortified Weiszfeld algorithm for solving the Weber problem. *IMA Journal of Management Mathematics*, 26:1–9.
88. Drezner, Z., Brimberg, J., Salhi, S., and Mladenović, N. (2015). New heuristic algorithms for solving the planar p-median problem. *Computers & Operations Research*, 62:296–304.
89. Drezner, Z., Brimberg, J., Salhi, S., and Mladenović, N. (2016b). New local searches for solving the multi-source Weber problem. *Annals of Operations Research*, 246:181–203.
90. Drezner, Z., Drezner, T., and Wesolowsky, G. O. (2009c). Location with acceleration-deceleration distance. *European Journal of Operational Research*, 198:157–164.
91. Drezner, Z. and Drezner, T. D. (2020). Biologically inspired parent selection in genetic algorithms. *Annals of Operations Research*, 287:161–183.

92. Drezner, Z. and Erkut, E. (1995). Solving the continuous *p*-dispersion problem using non-linear programming. *Journal of the Operational Research Society*, 46:516–520.

93. Drezner, Z., Gelfand, R. J., and Drezner, T. D. (2019b). Sensitivity of large scale facility location solutions. *Journal of Supply Chain and Operations Management*, 17:157–168.

94. Drezner, Z. and Goldman, A. (1991). On the set of optimal points to the Weber problem. *Transportation Science*, 25:3–8.

95. Drezner, Z. and Kalczynski, P. (2020). Solving non-convex non-linear programs with reverse convex constraints by sequential linear programming. *International Transactions in Operational Research*, 27:1320–1342.

96. Drezner, Z., Kalczynski, P., and Salhi, S. (2019c). The multiple obnoxious facilities location problem on the plane: A Voronoi based heuristic. *OMEGA: The International Journal of Management Science*, 87:105–116.

97. Drezner, Z., Klamroth, K., Schöbel, A., and Wesolowsky, G. O. (2002). The Weber problem. In Drezner, Z. and Hamacher, H. W., editors, *Facility Location: Applications and Theory*, pages 1–36. Springer, Berlin.

98. Drezner, Z. and Nickel, S. (2009). Constructing a DC decomposition for ordered median problems. *Journal of Global Optimization*, 45:187–201.

99. Drezner, Z. and Salhi, S. (2017). Incorporating neighborhood reduction for the solution of the planar *p*-median problem. *Annals of Operations Research*, 258:639–654.

100. Drezner, Z. and Scott, C. H. (2010). Optimizing the location of a production firm. *Networks and Spatial Economics*, 10:411–425.

101. Drezner, Z., Scott, C. H., and Turner, J. (2016c). Mixed planar and network single-facility location problems. *Networks*, 68:271–282.

102. Drezner, Z. and Shelah, S. (1987). On the complexity of the Elzinga-Hearn algorithm for the one-center problem. *Mathematics of Operations Research*, 12:255–261.

103. Drezner, Z. and Simchi-Levi, D. (1992). Asymptotic behavior of the Weber location problem on the plane. *Annals of Operations Research*, 40:163–172.

104. Drezner, Z. and Suzuki, A. (2004). The big triangle small triangle method for the solution of non-convex facility location problems. *Operations Research*, 52:128–135.

105. Drezner, Z., Thisse, J.-F., and Wesolowsky, G. O. (1986). The minimax-min location problem. *Journal of Regional Science*, 26:87–101.

106. Drezner, Z. and Wesolowsky, G. O. (1978). Facility location on a sphere. *Journal of the Operational Research Society*, 29:997–1004.

107. Drezner, Z. and Wesolowsky, G. O. (1980a). A maximin location problem with maximum distance constraints. *AIIE Transactions*, 12(3):249–252.

108. Drezner, Z. and Wesolowsky, G. O. (1980b). Single facility lp distance minimax location. *SIAM Journal of Algebraic and Discrete Methods*, 1:315–321.

109. Drezner, Z. and Wesolowsky, G. O. (1983). Minimax and maximin facility location problems on a sphere. *Naval Research Logistics Quarterly*, 30:305–312.

110. Drezner, Z. and Wesolowsky, G. O. (1989). The asymmetric distance location problem. *Transportation Science*, 23:201–207.
111. Drezner, Z. and Wesolowsky, G. O. (1991). The Weber problem on the plane with some negative weights. *Information Systems and Operational Research*, 29:87–99.
112. Drezner, Z. and Wesolowsky, G. O. (1996). Obnoxious facility location in the interior of a planar network. *Journal of Regional Science*, 35:675–688.
113. Drezner, Z. and Wesolowsky, G. O. (1997). On the best location of signal detectors. *IIE Transactions*, 29:1007–1015.
114. Drezner, Z., Wesolowsky, G. O., and Drezner, T. (2004). The gradual covering problem. *Naval Research Logistics*, 51:841–855.
115. Eiselt, H. A. and Laporte, G. (1995). Objectives in location problems. In Drezner, Z., editor, *Facility Location: A Survey of Applications and Methods*, pages 151–180. Springer, New York, NY.
116. Eiselt, H. A. and Marianov, V. (2009). Gradual location set covering with service quality. *Socio-Economic Planning Sciences*, 43:121–130.
117. Eiselt, H. A. and Marianov, V. (2014). A bi-objective model for the location of landfills for municipal solid waste. *European Journal of Operational Research*, 235:187–194.
118. Elzinga, J. and Hearn, D. (1972). Geometrical solutions for some minimax location problems. *Transportation Science*, 6:379–394.
119. Eurostat (2012). Income quintile share ratio (s80/s20) (source: Silc). Eurostat Structural Indicators.
120. Farahani, R., Drezner, Z., and Asgari, N. (2009). Single facility location and relocation problem with time dependent weights and discrete planning horizon. *Annals of Operations Research*, 167:353–368.
121. Fetter, F. A. (1924). The economic law of market areas. *The Quarterly Journal of Economics*, 38:520–529.
122. Francis, R. L., McGinnis Jr., L. F., and White, J. A. (1992). *Facility Layout and Location: An Analytical Approach*. Prentice Hall, Englewood Cliffs, NJ, Second edition.
123. García, S., Labbé, M., and Marín, A. (2011). Solving large p-median problems with a radius formulation. *INFORMS Journal on Computing*, 23:546–556.
124. García, S. and Marín, A. (2015). Covering location problems. In Laporte, G., Nickel, S., and da Gama, F. S., editors, *Location Science*, pages 93–114. Springer, Heidelberg.
125. Gill, P. E., Murray, W., and Saunders, M. A. (2005). SNOPT: An SQP algorithm for large-scale constrained optimization. *SIAM review*, 47:99–131.
126. Gini, C. (1921). Measurement of inequality and incomes. *The Economic Journal*, 31:124–126.
127. Glover, F. and Laguna, M. (1997). *Tabu Search*. Kluwer Academic Publishers, Boston.
128. Goldberg, D. E. (2006). *Genetic Algorithms*. Pearson Education, Delhi, India.

129. Hanselman, D. and Littlefield, B. C. (1997). *Mastering MATLAB 5: A Comprehensive Tutorial and Reference*. Prentice Hall PTR.

130. Hansen, P., Jaumard, B., and Krau, S. (1995). An algorithm for Weber's problem on the sphere. *Location Science*, 3:217–237.

131. Hansen, P. and Mladenović, N. (1997). Variable neighborhood search for the *p*-median. *Location Science*, 5:207–226.

132. Hansen, P., Mladenović, N., and Taillard, É. (1998). Heuristic solution of the multisource Weber problem as a *p*-median problem. *Operations Research Letters*, 22:55–62.

133. Hansen, P., Peeters, D., and Thisse, J.-F. (1981). On the location of an obnoxious facility. *Sistemi Urbani*, 3:299–317.

134. Holland, J. H. (1975). *Adaptation in Natural and Artificial Systems*. University of Michigan Press, Ann Arbor, MI.

135. Horne, J. and Smith, J. (2005). A dynamic programming algorithm for the conditional covering problem on tree graphs. *Networks*, 46:186–197.

136. Huff, D. L. (1964). Defining and estimating a trade area. *Journal of Marketing*, 28:34–38.

137. Huff, D. L. (1966). A programmed solution for approximating an optimum retail location. *Land Economics*, 42:293–303.

138. Kalczynski, P. and Drezner, Z. (2019). Locating multiple facilities using the max-sum objective. *Computers and Industrial Engineering*, 129:136–143.

139. Kalczynski, P. and Drezner, Z. (2021a). Extremely non-convex optimization problems: The case of the multiple obnoxious facilities location. *Optimization Letters*. https://doi.org/10.1007/s11590-021-01731-2.

140. Kalczynski, P. and Drezner, Z. (2021b). The obnoxious facilities planar *p*-median problem. *OR Spectrum*, 43:577–593.

141. Kalczynski, P., Suzuki, A., and Drezner, Z. (2021). Multiple obnoxious facilities with weighted demand points. *Journal of the Operational Research Society*. https://doi.org/10.1080/01605682.2020.1851149.

142. Kalczynski, P., Suzuki, A., and Drezner, Z. (2021). Obnoxious facility location in multiple dimensional space. In review.

143. Karasakal, O. and Karasakal, E. (2004). A maximal covering location model in the presence of partial coverage. *Computers & Operations Research*, 31:15–26.

144. Karatas, M. (2017). A multi-objective facility location problem in the presence of variable gradual coverage performance and cooperative cover. *European Journal of Operational Research*, 262:1040–1051.

145. Kariv, O. and Hakimi, S. L. (1979). An algorithmic approach to network location problems. I: The *p*-centers. *SIAM Journal on Applied Mathematics*, 37:513–538.

146. Katz, I. N. and Cooper, L. (1980). Optimal location on a sphere. *Computers & Mathematics with Applications*, 6:175–196.

147. Krarup, J. and Vajda, S. (1997). On Torricelli's geometrical solution to a problem of fermat. *IMA Journal of Management Mathematics*, 8:215–224.

148. Krau, S. (1997). *Extensions du problème de Weber*. PhD thesis, École Polytechnique de Montréal.

149. Kuby, M. (1987). Programming models for facility dispersion: The *p*-dispersion and maxisum dispersion problems. *Geographical Analysis*, 19(4):315–329.

150. Kuenne, R. E. and Soland, R. M. (1972). Exact and approximate solutions to the multisource Weber problem. *Mathematical Programming*, 3:193–209.

151. Launhardt, W. (1885). *Mathematische Begründung der Volkswirtschaftslehre*. W. Engelmann.

152. Law, A. M. and Kelton, W. D. (1991). *Simulation Modeling and Analysis*. McGraw-Hill, New York, Second edition.

153. Lee, D. T. and Schachter, B. J. (1980). Two algorithms for constructing a Delaunay triangulation. *International Journal of Parallel Programming*, 9:219–242.

154. Locatelli, M. and Raber, U. (2002). Packing equal circles in a square: A deterministic global optimization approach. *Discrete Applied Mathematics*, 122:139–166.

155. Lopez, C. and Beasley, J. E. (2011). A heuristic for the circle packing problem with a variety of containers. *European Journal of Operational Research*, 214:512–525.

156. Lorenz, M. O. (1905). Methods of measuring the concentration of wealth. *Publications of the American Statistical Association*, 9:209–219.

157. Lösch, A. (1954). *The Economics of Location*. Yale University Press, New Haven, CT.

158. Love, R. F., Morris, J. G., and Wesolowsky, G. O. (1988). *Facilities Location: Models & Methods*. North Holland, New York, NY.

159. Maimon, O. (1986). The variance equity measure in locational decision theory. *Annals of Operations Research*, 6:147–160.

160. Maranas, C. D. and Floudas, C. A. (1993). A global optimization method for Weber's problem with attraction and repulsion. In Hager, W. W., Hearn, D. W., and Pardalos, P. M., editors, *Large Scale Optimization: State of the Art*, pages 259–293. Kluwer, Dordrecht.

161. Maranas, C. D., Floudas, C. A., and Pardalos, P. M. (1995). New results in the packing of equal circles in a square. *Discrete Mathematics*, 142:287–293.

162. Medhi, J. (2002). *Stochastic Models in Queueing Theory*. Elsevier, San Diego, CA.

163. Megiddo, N. and Supowit, K. J. (1984). On the complexity of some common geometric location problems. *SIAM Journal on Computing*, 13:182–196.

164. Melachrinoudis, E. (2011). The location of undesirable facilities. In *Foundations of Location Analysis*, pages 207–239. Springer, New York.

165. Melachrinoudis, E. and Cullinane, P. (1985). Locating an undesirable facility within a geographical region using the maximin criterion. *Journal of Regional Science*, 25:115–127.

166. Melachrinoudis, E., Min, H., and Cullinane, P. (1996). A multiobjective model for the dynamic location of landfills. *Location Science*, 3:143–166.

167. Melachrinoudis, E. and Xanthopulos, Z. (2003). Semi-obnoxious single facility location in euclidean space. *Computers & Operations Research*, 30:2191–2209.

168. Minieka, E. (1980). Conditional centers and medians on a graph. *Networks*, 10:265–272.

169. Mladenović, N. and Hansen, P. (1997). Variable neighborhood search. *Computers & Operations Research*, 24:1097–1100.

170. Morohosi, H. and Furuta, T. (2017). Two approaches to cooperative covering location problem and their application to ambulance deployment. In *Operations Research Proceedings 2015*, pages 361–366. Springer, Cham, Switzerland.

171. Murtagh, B. A. and Niwattisyawong, S. R. (1982). An efficient method for the multi-depot location-allocation problem. *Journal of the Operational Research Society*, 33:629–634.

172. Nickel, S. and Puerto, J. (2005). *Facility Location—A Unified Approach*. Springer Verlag, Berlin.

173. Nurmela, K. J. and Oestergard, P. (1999). More optimal packings of equal circles in a square. *Discrete & Computational Geometry*, 22:439–457.

174. Ogryczak, W. and Zawadzki, M. (2002). Conditional median: A parametric solution concept for location problems. *Annals of Operations Research*, 110:167–181.

175. Okabe, A., Boots, B., Sugihara, K., and Chiu, S. N. (2000). *Spatial Tessellations: Concepts and Applications of Voronoi Diagrams*. Wiley Series in Probability and Statistics. John Wiley, Hoboken, NJ.

176. O'kelly, M. E. (1987). A quadratic integer program for the location of interacting hub facilities. *European Journal of Operational Research*, 32:393–404.

177. Ostresh Jr., L. M. (1978). On the convergence of a class of iterative methods for solving the Weber location problem. *Operations Research*, 26:597–609.

178. Plastria, F. (1991). The effects of majority in Fermat-Weber problems with attraction and repulsion. *Yugoslav Journal of Operations Research*, 1:141–146.

179. Plastria, F. (2002). Continuous covering location problems. In Drezner, Z. and Hamacher, H. W., editors, *Facility Location: Applications and Theory*, pages 39–83. Springer, Berlin.

180. Prömel, H. J. and Steger, A. (2012). *The Steiner Tree Problem: A Tour Through Graphs, Algorithms, and Complexity*. Springer Science & Business Media.

181. Reilly, W. J. (1931). *The Law of Retail Gravitation*. Knickerbocker Press, New York, NY.

182. ReVelle, C. (1986). The maximum capture or sphere of influence problem: Hotelling revisited on a network. *Journal of Regional Science*, 26:343–357.

183. ReVelle, C., Toregas, C., and Falkson, L. (1976). Applications of the location set covering problem. *Geographical Analysis*, 8:65–76.

184. Schöbel, A. and Scholz, D. (2010). The big cube small cube solution method for multidimensional facility location problems. *Computers & Operations Research*, 37:115–122.
185. Shamos, M. and Hoey, D. (1975). Closest-point problems. *Proceedings 16th Annual Symposium on the Foundations of Computer Science*, pages 151–162, Berkeley, CA.
186. Shier, D. R. (1977). A min-max theorem for p-center problems on a tree. *Transportation Science*, 11:243–252.
187. Skorin-Kapov, D., Skorin-Kapov, J., and O'Kelly, M. (1996). Tight linear programming relaxations of uncapacitated *p*-hub median problems. *European Journal of Operational Research*, 94:582–593.
188. Snyder, L. V. (2011). Covering problems. In Eiselt, H. A. and Marianov, V., editors, *Foundations of Location Analysis*, pages 109–135. Springer, New York.
189. Sugihara, K. (2002). Laguerre voronoi diagram on the sphere. *Journal for Geometry and Graphics*, 6:69–81.
190. Sugihara, K. and Iri, M. (1992). Construction of the voronoi diagram for "one million" generators in single-precision arithmetic. *Proceedings of the IEEE*, 80:1471–1484.
191. Sugihara, K. and Iri, M. (1994). A robust topology-oriented incremental algorithm for Voronoi diagram. *International Journal of Computational Geometry and Applications*, 4:179–228.
192. Suzuki, A. (2019). Big triangle small triangle method for the Weber problem on the sphere. In Eiselt, H. A. and Marianov, V., editors, *Contributions to Location Analysis—In Honor of Zvi Drezner's 75th Birthday*, pages 109–123. Springer Nature, Switzerland.
193. Suzuki, A. and Drezner, Z. (2009). The minimum equitable radius location problem with continuous demand. *European Journal of Operational Research*, 195:17–30.
194. Suzuki, A. and Okabe, A. (1995). Using Voronoi diagrams. In Drezner, Z., editor, *Facility Location: A Survey of Applications and Methods*, pages 103–118. Springer, New York.
195. Sylvester, J. (1857). A question in the geometry of situation. *Quarterly Journal of Mathematics*, 1:79.
196. Sylvester, J. (1860). On Poncelet's approximate linear valuation of Surd forms. *Philosophical Magazine*, 20 (Fourth series):203–222.
197. Szabo, P. G., Markot, M., Csendes, T., and Specht, E. (2007). *New Approaches to Circle Packing in a Square: With Program Codes*. Springer, New York.
198. Taillard, É. (2003). Heuristic methods for large centroid clustering problems. *Journal of Heuristics*, 9:51–73.
199. Teran-Somohano, A. and Smith, A. E. (2019). Locating multiple capacitated semi-obnoxious facilities using evolutionary strategies. *Computers & Industrial Engineering*, 133:303–316.
200. Voronoï, G. (1908). Nouvelles applications des paramètres continus à la théorie des formes quadratiques. deuxième mémoire. recherches sur les

parallélloèdres primitifs. *Journal für die reine und angewandte Mathematik*, 134:198–287.

201. Wang, S.-C. and Chen, T.-C. (2017). Multi-objective competitive location problem with distance-based attractiveness and its best non-dominated solution. *Applied Mathematical Modelling*, 47:785–795.

202. Weber, A. (1909). *Über den Standort der Industrien, 1. Teil: Reine Theorie des Standortes. English Translation: On the Location of Industries*. University of Chicago Press, Chicago, IL. Translation published in 1929.

203. Weiszfeld, E. (1937). Sur le point pour lequel la somme des distances de n points donnés est minimum. *Tohoku Mathematical Journal, First Series*, 43:355–386.

204. Weiszfeld, E. and Plastria, F. (2009). On the point for which the sum of the distances to n given points is minimum. *Annals of Operations Research*, 167:7–41 (English Translation of Weiszfeld [203]).

205. Welch, S. B., Salhi, S., and Drezner, Z. (2006). The multifacility maximin planar location problem with facility interaction. *IMA Journal of Management Mathematics*, 17:397–412.

206. Wendell, R. E. and Hurter, A. P. (1973). Location theory, dominance and convexity. *Operations Research*, 21:314–320.

207. Wesolowsky, G. O. (1993). The Weber problem: History and perspectives. *Location Science*, 1:5–23.

208. Wolfram, S. (2020). *Mathematica, Version 12.2*. Champaign, IL. https://www.wolfram.com/mathematica.

10

Data Envelopment Analysis: Recent Developments and Challenges

Ali Emrouznejad, Guo-liang Yang, Mohammad Khoveyni,
and Maria Michali

10.1 Introduction

Hitherto many developments have been made by researchers in the field
of Data Envelopment Analysis. These studies are in the context of performance evaluation, finding suitable benchmarks for efficient and inefficient
decision-making units (DMUs), detecting the congestion status of DMUs,

A. Emrouznejad (✉)
Surrey Business School, The University of Surrey, Guildford, Surrey, UK
e-mail: a.emrouznejad@surrey.ac.uk

G. Yang
Institutes of Science and Development, Chinese Academy of Sciences, Beijing,
China
e-mail: glyang@casipm.ac.cn

M. Khoveyni
Department of Applied Mathematics, Yadegar-e-Imam Khomeini (RAH) Shahre
Rey Branch, Islamic Azad University, Tehran, Iran
e-mail: m_khoveyni@azad.ac.ir

M. Michali
Aston Business School, Aston University, Birmingham, UK
e-mail: 180207981@aston.ac.uk

© The Author(s), under exclusive license to Springer Nature
Switzerland AG 2022
S. Salhi and J. Boylan (eds.), *The Palgrave Handbook of Operations Research*,
https://doi.org/10.1007/978-3-030-96935-6_10

estimating the returns to scale (RTS), deciding about the optimal budget allocation, measuring the efficiency of multi-stage DMUs with series and parallel network structures, etc.

One of the most important problems in operations management is to measure the productive efficiency of firms from both the theoretical and economic viewpoints. From the economic point of view, it is significant to know how much a firm can increase its outputs so that its efficiency score increases without reducing any inputs. Besides, from a theoretical viewpoint, a production function concept illustrates the basis of the relationship between the inputs and the outputs of a firm. In principle, the maximum amount of outputs that can be produced without any reduction of the inputs, and the minimum amount of inputs that can be consumed without deterioration of outputs can be explained by the production function.

In the literature, there exist two main methods to estimate efficient frontiers from an economics viewpoint. These methods are denoted as parametric and non-parametric, with the non-parametric method being more common. The focus of this chapter is on the non-parametric method which extends the concept of measuring efficiency scores of DMUs from a single-input and single-output case to a multi-input and multi-output case. This method was proposed by Charnes, Cooper, and Rhodes [5] and was named Data Envelopment Analysis (DEA). DEA has rapidly grown with over 20,000 papers published in the last four decades and applications of DEA appeared in many fields including operational research, economics, accounting, information management, and engineering to measure efficiency scores DMUs, e.g., firms, hospital, banks, airports, etc.

In complex organizations, the production process involves several stages. The standard DEA is a black box model which is not capable to measure the efficiency of the multi-stage production process. Hence, has been introduced to the literature by considering the intermediate products of multi-stage DMUs. It is necessary to mention that the structures of these multi-stage DMUs consist of series and/or parallel network structures.

This chapter reviews some of the recent developments and challenges of DEA and the rest of this chapter is structured as follows. Section 10.2 explains the background of DEA including some related models under the assumptions of constant and variable returns to scale (RTS). Section 10.3 describes a short literature survey of publications. In Sect. 10.4, some recent theoretical developments are provided. This is followed by a review of some applications of DEA. Section 10.5 provides direction for future developments and the conclusion is given in Sect. 10.6.

10.2 Background

In this section, we intend to explain the standard DEA-based models under the constant returns to scale (CRS) and variable returns to scale (VRS) specifications to measure the efficiency scores of DMUs with multiple inputs and multiple outputs.

Here, consider a set of n homogeneous DMUs, where each DMU_j, ($j = 1, 2, .., n$) uses an input vector $X_j = (x_{1j}, ..., x_{rj}, ..., x_{mj}) \geq 0$ to produce an output vector $Y_j = (y_{1j}, ..., y_{rj}, ..., y_{sj}) \geq 0$, such that $X_j \neq 0$ and $Y_j \neq 0$. Further, we define the production possibility set (PPS) as $PPS = \{(X, Y) | Y \geq 0 \text{ can be produced by } X \geq 0\}$.

Definition 10.1 $\text{DMU}_p = \begin{pmatrix} X_p \\ Y_p \end{pmatrix}$ is dominated by $\text{DMU}_q = \begin{pmatrix} X_q \\ Y_q \end{pmatrix}$ if and only if $\begin{pmatrix} -X_p \\ Y_p \end{pmatrix} \leq \begin{pmatrix} -X_q \\ Y_q \end{pmatrix}$, and $\begin{pmatrix} -X_p \\ Y_p \end{pmatrix} \neq \begin{pmatrix} -X_q \\ Y_q \end{pmatrix}$.

10.2.1 The CCR Model in the Envelopment and Multiplier Forms

The production possibility set (PPS), denoted by T_C, under the CRS assumption is as follows:

$$T_C = \{(X, Y) | \sum_{j=1}^{n} \lambda_j X_j \leq X, \sum_{j=1}^{n} \lambda_j Y_j \geq Y, \lambda_j \geq 0; j = 1, 2, ..., n\}$$

$$(10.1)$$

Hereafter, in this study, "*" is used to indicate the optimal solution values.

The input efficiency scores of a target DMU (DMU_p; $p \in \{1, 2..., n\}$) can be assessed by the following input-oriented envelopment model ([5]):

$$
\text{Min } \theta - \varepsilon \left(\sum_{i=1}^{m} s_i^- + \sum_{r=1}^{s} s_r^+ \right)
$$

$$
\text{s.t.} \sum_{j=1}^{n} \lambda_j x_{ij} + s_i^- = \theta x_{ip}, \quad i = 1, ..., m,
$$

$$
\sum_{j=1}^{n} \lambda_j y_{rj} - s_r^+ = y_{rp}, \quad r = 1, ..., s, \tag{10.2}
$$

$$
\lambda_j \geq 0, \quad j = 1, ..., n,
$$

$$
s_i^- \geq 0, \quad i = 1, ..., m, \quad s_r^+ \geq 0, \quad r = 1, ..., s,
$$

where x_{ip} and y_{rp} represent the amount of the ith input and the rth output for DMU_p, respectively. Here, ε is a non-Archimedean small positive number. Moreover, the input and output slacks are denoted by s_i^- ($i = 1, 2, ..., m$) and s_r^+ ($r = 1, 2, ..., s$), respectively.

Definition 10.2 DMU_p is called CCR-efficient in T_C if and only if there is no DMU_j ($j = 1, 2, ..., n$) which can dominate DMU_p, in other words, an optimal solution ($\theta^*, \lambda^*, s^{-*}, s^{+*}$) obtained from model (10.2) satisfies $\theta^* = 1$ and has no slack ($s^{-*} = 0, s^{+*} = 0$). Otherwise, DMU_p is CCR-inefficient.

The dual version of model (10.2), the multiplier model, is as follows:

$$
\text{Max } U^t Y_p
$$

$$
\text{s.t. } U^t Y_j - V^t X_j \leq 0, \quad j = 1, ..., n, \tag{10.3}
$$

$$
V^t X_p = 1, \quad U \geq 0, \quad V \geq 0,
$$

where the vectors V and U denote the decision variables corresponding to the inputs and outputs, respectively.

Definition 10.3 (CCR-efficient) DMU_p is called CCR-efficient in T_C if and only if an obtained optimal solution (U^*, V^*) from model (10.3) satisfies $U^{t*} Y_p = 1$, $U^* > 0$, and $V^* > 0$. Otherwise, DMU_p is CCR-inefficient.

10.2.2 The BCC Model in Envelopment and Multiplier Forms

Now, we consider the PPS under the VRS assumption, denoted by T_V, that is as below:

$$T_V = \left\{ (X, Y) \middle| \sum_{j=1}^{n} \lambda_j X_j \leq X, \sum_{j=1}^{n} \lambda_j Y_j \geq Y, \right.$$

$$\left. \sum_{j=1}^{n} \lambda_j = 1, \lambda_j \geq 0; j = 1, 2, ..., n \right\}. \tag{10.4}$$

The input efficiency scores of the DMU_p under evaluation can be calculated by the following input-oriented envelopment model [3]:

$$\text{Min } \theta - \varepsilon \left(\sum_{i=1}^{m} s_i^- + \sum_{r=1}^{s} s_r^+ \right)$$

$$\text{s.t. } \sum_{j=1}^{n} \lambda_j x_{ij} + s_i^- = \theta x_{ip}, \quad i = 1, ..., m,$$

$$\sum_{j=1}^{n} \lambda_j y_{rj} - s_r^+ = y_{rp}, \quad r = 1, ..., s, \tag{10.5}$$

$$\sum_{j=1}^{n} \lambda_j = 1, \quad \lambda_j \geq 0, \ j = 1, ..., n,$$

$$s_i^- \geq 0, \ i = 1, ..., m, \quad s_r^+ \geq 0, \ r = 1, ..., s,$$

where $x_{ip}, y_{rp}, \varepsilon, s_i^-$ $(i = 1, 2, ..., m)$, and s_r^+ $(r = 1, 2, ..., s)$ are defined as before.

Definition 10.4 (BCC-efficient)
  DMU_p is called BCC-efficient in T_V if and only if there is no DMU_j $(j = 1, 2, ..., n)$ which can dominate DMU_p, in other words, an optimal solution $(\theta^*, \lambda^*, s^{-*}, s^{+*})$ obtained from model (10.5) satisfies $\theta^* = 1$ and has no slack $(s^{-*} = 0, s^{+*} = 0)$. Otherwise, DMU_p is BCC-inefficient.

The dual version of model (10.5), i.e., the multiplier model, is as below:

$$\text{Max } U^t Y_p + u_p$$
$$\text{s.t. } U^t Y_j - V^t X_j + u_p \leq 0, \quad j = 1, ..., n, \tag{10.6}$$
$$V^t X_p = 1, \quad U \geq 0, \quad V \geq 0, \quad u_p \text{ free in sign,}$$

where the vectors V and U are defined as before.

Definition 10.5 (BCC-efficient) DMU_p is called BCC-efficient in T_V if and only if an obtained optimal solution (U^*, V^*, u_p^*) from model (10.6) satisfies $U^{t*} Y_p + u_p^* = 1$, $U^* > 0$, and $V^* > 0$. Otherwise, DMU_p is BCC-inefficient.

10.2.3   The Additive Model

The additive model is a non-radial DEA model given as follows:

$$\text{Max } \sum_{i=1}^{m} s_i^- + \sum_{r=1}^{s} s_r^+$$

$$\text{s.t. } \sum_{j=1}^{n} \lambda_j x_{ij} + s_i^- = x_{ip}, \quad i = 1, ..., m,$$

$$\sum_{j=1}^{n} \lambda_j y_{rj} - s_r^+ = y_{rp}, \quad r = 1, ..., s, \tag{10.7}$$

$$\sum_{j=1}^{n} \lambda_j = 1, \quad \lambda_j \geq 0, \quad j = 1, ..., n,$$

$$s_i^- \geq 0, \quad i = 1, ..., m, \quad s_r^+ \geq 0, \quad r = 1, ..., s,$$

where $x_{ip}, y_{rp}, \varepsilon, s_i^-$ $(i = 1, 2, ..., m)$, and s_r^+ $(r = 1, 2, ..., s)$ are defined as before.

Definition 10.6 DMU_p is called efficient in T_V if and only if an optimal solution $(\lambda^*, s^{-*}, s^{+*})$ obtained from model (10.7) satisfies $s^{-*} = 0$ and $s^{+*} = 0$. Otherwise, DMU_p is inefficient.

Number of papers

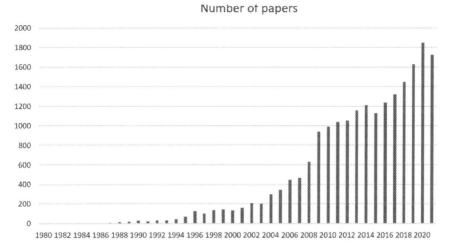

Fig. 10.1 Annual statistics of the number of DEA articles published (1978–2021)

10.3 A Short Literature Survey and Trend of Publications on DEA

10.3.1 Statistics Based on Publication Years

The histogram of the DEA-related articles given in Fig. 10.1 reveals a continuous and rapid growth in the number of DEA-related articles published annually since the first publication of Charnes et al. [5]. Four obvious conclusions can be extracted from Fig. 10.1. Firstly, during the early years of the DEA methodology, i.e., before 1994, less than 100 articles related to DEA were published per year, which reveals that the DEA theory had a relatively narrow scope of innovation. Secondly, articles in the DEA field entered a steadily growing stage during the period from 1994 to 2004, even though the number of DEA-related articles published remained below 200 per year. Thirdly, from 2004 to 2011 is the stage of rapid growth and development of the DEA theory and its applications. The annual average publications are increased substantially. Fourthly, the most obvious growth of the number of articles occurred in the last years, with over 1000 publications per year since 2011.

10.3.2 Statistics Based on Journals

Table 10.1 displays the top 25 journals that have published the largest number of articles concerning DEA and its application from 1978. 3576

Table 10.1 The 25 journals that have published the largest number of DEA-related articles

No.	Journals	Numbers
1	European Journal of Operational Research	731
2	Journal of the Operational Research Society	313
3	Journal of Productivity Analysis	272
4	Annals of Operations Research	213
5	Expert Systems with Applications	196
6	Applied Economics	143
7	Omega	130
8	Journal of Cleaner Production	127
9	Socio-Economic Planning Sciences	125
10	Omega (United Kingdom)	124
11	Computers and Industrial Engineering	112
12	Energy Policy	106
13	Sustainability (Switzerland)	100
14	Applied Mathematics and Computation	95
15	International Journal of Production Economics	92
16	Benchmarking	86
17	Energy Economics	79
18	Computers and Operations Research	78
19	International Journal of Production Research	72
20	Energy	68
21	Health Care Management Science	66
22	Applied Economics Letters	64
23	Journal of Air Transport Management	62
24	Applied Mathematical Sciences	61
25	Applied Mathematical Modeling	61
	Sum	3576

DEA-related articles were published in these 25 journals, which accounts for 30.89% of the total 11554 journal articles. Since DEA theory and most of the applications belong to the field of management science and operations research (MS/OR), the most commonly used periodicals were related to MS/OR, such as *European Journal of Operational Research, Journal of the Operational Research Society, Journal of Productivity Analysis, Annals of Operations Research*, and so on.

10.3.3   Statistics Based on Authors

According to the statistical data, over 20,000 distinct authors are identified in the DEA-related publications. The largest number of DEA-related articles were written by two authors, accounting for about 33% of the total. Almost

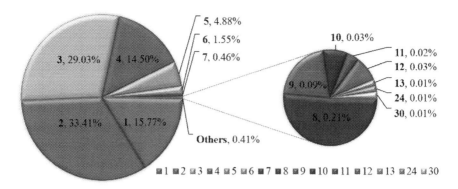

Fig. 10.2 Distribution by number of authors of DEA-related articles

16% of the total investigated articles were written by a single author. Besides, an article was written by 30 distinct authors[1], which is the article with the largest number of authors. More details of the distribution of DEA-related articles by a number of authors are presented in the following Fig. 10.2.

10.3.4 Statistics Based on Keywords

We analyzed the keywords in DEA-related articles, and the top-50 most frequently used keywords are listed in Table 10.2. Undoubtedly, DEA-related terms, e.g., Data Envelopment Analysis, DEA, and DEA models, were the most widely used. In addition, some words referring to efficiency measurement, and decision-making analysis, i.e., efficiency, decision-making, technical efficiency, and so on, were also commonly used keywords.

10.3.5 Statistics Based on Page Numbers (Size)

During the recent 40 years, DEA-related articles have been published in various journals and cover over 140,000 pages, with an average of 13.4 pages per article. Statistics show that three-quarters of the DEA-related articles have 6 to 18 pages, and the DEA-related articles with 10 pages in length are the most frequent, accounting for about 8%. A DEA-related article, with 74 pages, ranked first as the longest one among all the surveyed articles. More

---

[1] Di Giorgio et al. (2016). The potential to expand antiretroviral therapy by improving health facility efficiency: evidence from Kenya, Uganda, and Zambia, BMC Medicine 14, 108. DOI 10.1186/s12916-016-0653-z.

Table 10.2 The 50 most commonly used keywords in DEA-related articles

No.	Keywords
1	Data Envelopment Analysis, Data Envelopment Analysis (DEA), DEA, or DEA models
2	Efficiency
3	Decision-making
4	Technical efficiency
5	Productivity
6	Linear programming
7	Mathematical models
8	Decision-making unit, Decision-making units, Decision-Making units
9	Benchmarking
10	Data reduction
11	Human, Humans
12	Article
13	Efficiency measurement
14	Malmquist index, Malmquist productivity index
15	Optimization
16	China
17	Operations research
18	Performance
19	Data handling
20	Energy efficiency
21	Bootstrap, bootstrapping
22	Performance assessment
23	Regression analysis
24	Efficiency, Organizational
25	Economics
26	Returns to scale
27	data analysis
28	United States
29	Performance evaluation
30	Eurasia
31	Ranking
32	Relative efficiency
33	Banking
34	Industry
35	Resource allocation
36	Efficiency analysis
37	Performance measurement
38	Data envelopment

(continued)

Table 10.2   (continued)

No.	Keywords
39	Problem solving
40	Costs
41	Total factor productivity
42	Europe
43	Sustainable development
44	Decision theory
45	Competition
46	Mathematical programming
47	methodology
48	Organization and management
49	Profitability
50	Efficiency evaluation

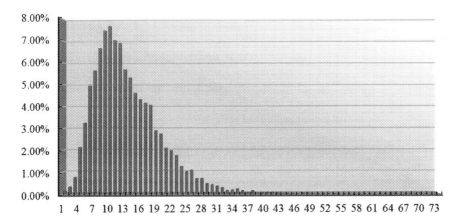

Fig. 10.3   Distribution by page number of DEA articles

details of the number of pages of the DEA-related articles are illustrated in Fig. 10.3.

10.4   Recent Theoretical Developments in DEA

10.4.1   Network DEA

In this section, we intend to clarify the recent contributions presented by researchers in the field. Färe and Grosskopf [9] were those who initially proposed this term to describe multi-stage processes and set the base for its future study.

Consider a set of n DMUs, denoted by DMU_j ($j = 1, 2, .., n$), operating on a two-stage production process with a series network structure (see Fig. 10.4). Note that each DMU_j has at least one positive input, one positive intermediate product, and one positive output.

Guo et al. [11] proposed the following multiplier model (model (10.8)) to estimate the efficiency of a two-stage DMU_0, and then converted this model into the parametric linear model (10.9) given below:

$$
e_0 = \max \left(a \frac{\displaystyle\sum_{d=1}^{D} \eta_d z_{d0}}{\displaystyle\sum_{i=1}^{m} v_i x_{i0}} + (1-a) \frac{\displaystyle\sum_{r=1}^{s} u_r y_{r0}}{\displaystyle\sum_{d=1}^{D} \eta_d z_{d0} + \sum_{h=1}^{H} Q_h x_{h0}^2} \right)
$$

$$
\text{s.t.} \quad \frac{\displaystyle\sum_{d=1}^{D} \eta_d z_{dj}}{\displaystyle\sum_{i=1}^{m} v_i x_{ij}} \leq 1 \quad (\forall j),
$$

$$
\frac{\displaystyle\sum_{r=1}^{s} u_r y_{rj}}{\displaystyle\sum_{d=1}^{D} \eta_d z_{dj} + \sum_{h=1}^{H} Q_h x_{h0}^2} \leq 1 \quad (\forall j),
$$

$$
v_i, u_r, \eta_d, Q_h \geq 0 \quad (\forall d, i, r, h),
$$

$$
0 \leq a \leq 1,
$$

(10.8)

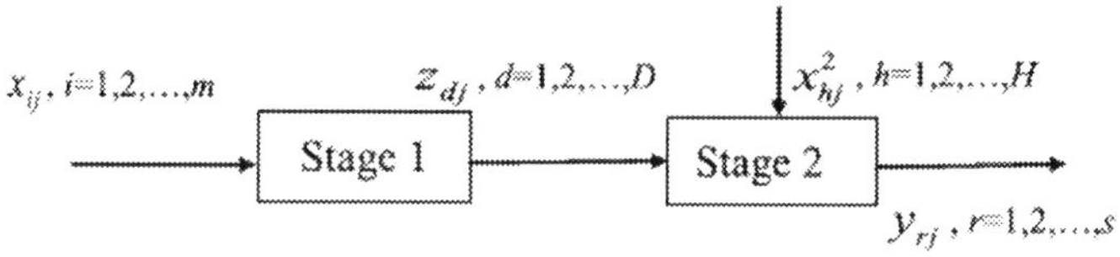

Fig. 10.4 Two-stage series network structure

and

$$e_0 = \max \left(a \sum_{d=1}^{D} \eta_d z_{d0} + (1-a) \sum_{r=1}^{s} u_r y_{r0} \right)$$

$$\text{s.t. } \sum_{d=1}^{D} \eta_d z_{dj} - \sum_{i=1}^{m} v_i x_{ij} \leq 0 \quad (\forall j),$$

$$\sum_{r=1}^{s} u_r y_{rj} - \rho \sum_{d=1}^{D} \eta_d z_{dj} - \sum_{h=1}^{H} Q_h x_{hj}^2 \leq 0 \quad (\forall j),$$

$$\sum_{i=1}^{m} v_i x_{i0} = 1,$$

$$\rho \sum_{d=1}^{D} \eta_d z_{d0} + \sum_{h=1}^{H} Q_h x_{h0}^2 = 1,$$

$$v_i, u_r, \eta_d, Q_h \geq 0 \quad (\forall d, i, r, h),$$

$$0 \leq a \leq 1, \quad \rho > 0.$$

(10.9)

Also, Wang et al. [36] introduced a DEA-based model (model (10.10)) to measure the overall efficiency score of the two-stage DMU_0 under evaluation, in the presence of shared inputs, as shown in Fig. 10.5. They also converted this model into a linear model, (model (10.11)).

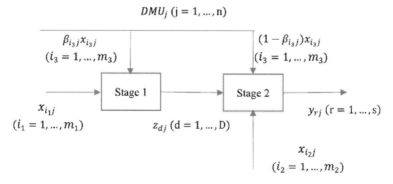

Fig. 10.5 Two-stage series network structure

$$e_0 = \max \left(a \frac{\sum\limits_{d=1}^{D} \eta_d z_{d0}}{\sum\limits_{i_3=1}^{m_3} v_{i_3} \beta_{i_3 0} x_{i_3 0} + \sum\limits_{i_1=1}^{m_1} v_{i_1} x_{i_1 0}} \right.$$

$$+ (1-a) \frac{\sum\limits_{r=1}^{s} u_r y_{r0}}{\sum\limits_{i_3=1}^{m_3} v_{i_3}(1 - \beta_{i_3 0}) x_{i_3 0} + \sum\limits_{i_2=1}^{m_2} v_{i_2} x_{i_2 0} + \sum\limits_{d=1}^{D} \eta_d z_{d0}} \right)$$

$$\text{s.t.} \quad \frac{\sum\limits_{d=1}^{D} \eta_d z_{dj}}{\sum\limits_{i_3=1}^{m_3} v_{i_3} \beta_{i_3 j} x_{i_3 j} + \sum\limits_{i=1}^{m} v_i x_{ij}} \leq 1 \quad (\forall j), \tag{10.10}$$

$$\frac{\sum\limits_{r=1}^{s} u_r y_{rj}}{\sum\limits_{i_3=1}^{m_3} v_{i_3}(1 - \beta_{i_3 j}) x_{i_3 j} + \sum\limits_{i_2=1}^{m_2} v_{i_2} x_{i_2 j} + \sum\limits_{d=1}^{D} \eta_d z_{dj}} \leq 1 \quad (\forall j),$$

$$v_{i_1}, v_{i_2}, v_{i_3}, u_r, \eta_d \geq 0 \quad (\forall i_1, i_2, i_3, r, d),$$

$$0 \leq a \leq 1, \quad 0 \leq \beta_{i_3 j} \leq 1 \quad (\forall i_3, j),$$

and

$$e_0 = \max \left(a \sum_{d=1}^{D} \eta_d z_{d0} + (1-a) \sum_{r=1}^{s} \mu_r y_{r0} \right)$$

$$\text{s.t.} \sum_{d=1}^{D} \pi_d z_{dj} - \left(\sum_{i_3=1}^{m_3} w_{i_3} x_{i_3 j} - \sum_{i_3=1}^{m_3} \sigma_{i_3 j} x_{i_3 j} + \sum_{i_1=1}^{m_1} w_{i_1} x_{i_1 j} \right) \le 0 \quad (\forall j),$$

$$\sum_{r=1}^{s} \mu_r y_{rj} - e \left(\sum_{d=1}^{D} \pi_d z_{dj} + \sum_{i_3=1}^{m_3} \sigma_{i_3 j} x_{i_3 j} + \sum_{i_2=1}^{m_2} w_{i_2} x_{i_2 j} \right) \le 0 \quad (\forall j),$$

$$\sum_{i_3=1}^{m_3} w_{i_3} x_{i_3 0} - \sum_{i_3=1}^{m_3} \sigma_{i_3 0} x_{i_3 0} + \sum_{i_1=1}^{m_1} w_{i_1} x_{i_1 0} = 1,$$

$$e \left(\sum_{d=1}^{D} \pi_d z_{d0} + \sum_{i_3=1}^{m_3} \sigma_{i_3 0} x_{i_3 0} + \sum_{i_2=1}^{m_2} w_{i_2} x_{i_2 0} \right) = 1,$$

$$0 \le \sigma_{i_3 j} \le w_{i_3} \quad (\forall i_3, j),$$

$$0 \le a \le 1, \quad \pi_d, \mu_r, w_{i_1}, w_{i_2}, w_{i_3} \ge 0 \quad (\forall i_1, i_2, i_3, r, d).$$

$$(10.11)$$

where $e < 1/\left(\sum_{i_3=1}^{m_3} \pi_d z_{do} + \sum_{i_3=1}^{m_3} \sigma_{i_3 o} x_{i_3 o} + \sum_{i_2=1}^{m_2} w_{i_2} x_{i_2 o} \right)$ is the efficiency
score of the first stage. Its upper bound can be obtained through the following
two steps: first, the efficiency score of the second stage is maximized. Then,
the efficiency score of the first stage is maximized while maintaining the
optimal efficiency level of the second stage. Further, Guo et al. [12] provided
the following DEA model (model (10.12)) to compute the efficiency of the

system depicted in Fig. 10.4:

$$\min \left(a\theta_0^1 + (1-a)\theta_0^2 \right)$$

$$\text{s.t.} \quad \left. \begin{array}{l} \displaystyle\sum_{j=1}^{n} \lambda_j x_{ij} \leq \theta_0^1 x_{i0} \quad (i=1,...,m), \\[3mm] \displaystyle\sum_{j=1}^{n} \lambda_j z_{dj}^1 \geq z_{d0}^1 + \rho' \tilde{z}_{d0} \quad (d=1,...,D), \end{array} \right\} \text{(Stage 1)}$$

$$\left. \begin{array}{l} \displaystyle\sum_{j=1}^{n} \mu_j z_{dj}^2 \leq \theta_0^2 z_{d0}^2 + \tilde{z}_{d0} \quad (d=1,...,D) \\[3mm] \displaystyle\sum_{j=1}^{n} \mu_j x_{hj}^2 \leq \theta_0^2 x_{h0}^2 \quad (h=1,...,H), \\[3mm] \displaystyle\sum_{j=1}^{n} \mu_j y_{rj} \geq y_{r0} \quad (r=1,...,s), \end{array} \right\} \text{(Stage 2)} \qquad (10.12)$$

$$\lambda_j, \mu_j \geq 0 \quad (\forall j), \quad \theta_0^1, \theta_0^2 \text{ free in sign.}$$

Besides, Li et al. [16] presented the following model (10.13) to compute the efficiency of the series network system shown in Fig. 10.6 and then,

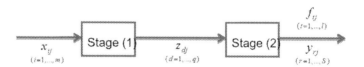

Fig. 10.6 Two-stage series process

converted this model into the linear model (10.14):

$$\min \theta_0 = \theta_0^{1*} \times \theta_0^{2*} = \theta_0^{1*} \times \frac{\sum\limits_{d=1}^{q} w_d z_{d0} + \mu_0^2}{\sum\limits_{r=1}^{s} u_r y_{r0} + \sum\limits_{t=1}^{l} a_t f_{t0}}$$

$$\text{s.t.} \quad \frac{\sum\limits_{i=1}^{m} v_i x_{ij} + \mu_0^1}{\sum\limits_{d=1}^{q} w_d z_{dj}} \geq 1 \quad (\forall j),$$

$$\frac{\sum\limits_{d=1}^{q} w_d z_{dj} + \mu_0^2}{\sum\limits_{r=1}^{s} u_r y_{rj} + \sum\limits_{t=1}^{l} a_t (f_{tj} + \delta_{tj})} \geq 1 \quad (\forall j), \tag{10.13}$$

$$\frac{\sum\limits_{i=1}^{m} v_i x_{ij} + \mu_0^1}{\sum\limits_{d=1}^{q} w_d z_{dj}} = \theta_0^{1*},$$

$$\theta_0^{1*} \in [0, \theta^{1CCR*}],$$

$$v_i, u_r, w_d, a_i \geq 0, \quad \delta_{tj}, \mu_0^1, \mu_0^2 \text{ are free,}$$

and

$$\min \theta_0 = \theta_0^{1*} \times \theta_0^{2*} = \theta_0^{1*} \times \left(\sum_{d=1}^{q} w_d z_{d0} + \mu_0^2 \right)$$

$$\text{s.t.} \quad \sum_{i=1}^{m} v_i x_{ij} - \sum_{d=1}^{q} w_d z_{dj} + \mu_0^1 \geq 0 \quad (\forall j),$$

$$\sum_{d=1}^{q} w_d z_{dj} - \sum_{r=1}^{s} u_r y_{rj} - \sum_{t=1}^{l} a_t (f_{tj} + \delta_{tj}) + \mu_0^2 \geq 0 \quad (\forall j),$$

$$\sum_{i=1}^{m} v_i x_{i0} - \theta_0^{1*} \sum_{d=1}^{q} w_d z_{dj} + \mu_0^1 = 0,$$

$$\sum_{r=1}^{s} u_r y_{r0} + \sum_{t=1}^{l} a_t f_{t0} = 1,$$

$$\theta_0^{1*} \in [0, \theta^{1CCR*}],$$

$$v_i, u_r, w_d, a_i \geq 0, \quad \delta_{tj}, \mu_0^1, \mu_0^2 \text{ are free.}$$

(10.14)

10.4.2   Stochastic DEA

This section explains the recent contributions provided by researchers in stochastic DEA.

As initially defined, DEA is based on deterministic inputs and outputs. While, in the real world, input and output variables may be stochastic. Hence, in the stochastic DEA field, the following DEA model was presented to measure the efficiency of the evaluating DMU (see Olesen and Petersen [19]):

$\min \theta$

s.t. $Pr\left(\sum\limits_{j=1}^{n} \lambda_j \tilde{x}_{ij} \leq \theta \tilde{x}_{kj} \right) \geq 1 - a, \quad (i = 1, ..., m; \forall i \in I_s),$

$\sum\limits_{j=1}^{n} \lambda_j x_{ij} \leq \theta x_{ik}, \quad (i = 1, ..., m; \forall i \in I_D),$

$Pr\left(\sum\limits_{j=1}^{n} \lambda_j \tilde{y}_{rj} \geq \tilde{y}_{rk} \right) \geq 1 - a, \quad (r = 1, ..., s; \forall r \in R_s),$ $\qquad (10.15)$

$\sum\limits_{j=1}^{n} \lambda_j y_{rj} \geq y_{rk}, \quad (r = 1, ..., s; \forall r \in R_s),$

$\sum\limits_{j=1}^{n} \lambda_j = 1, \quad \lambda_j \geq 0 \quad (\forall j), \quad \theta{:}\text{free},$

where I_S set of stochastic inputs, I_D set of deterministic inputs, R_S set of stochastic outputs, and R_D set of deterministic outputs. It is assumed that all the stochastic inputs and outputs follow a (see Tavassoli et al. [35] for more details).

Then, the stochastic model (10.15) can be rewritten as follows:

$$\min \theta$$

$$\text{s.t. } \sum_{j=1}^{n} \lambda_j x_{ij} \le \theta x_{ik}, \quad (\forall i \in I_D),$$

$$\sum_{j=1}^{n} \lambda_j \mu_{ij} - \theta \mu_{ik} \le e \sqrt{\sum_{\substack{j=1 \\ j \ne k}}^{n} \lambda_j^2 \sigma_{ij}^2 + (\lambda_j - \theta)^2 \sigma_{ik}^2 + 2 \operatorname{cov}(\tilde{x}_{ij}, \tilde{x}_{ik})},$$

$$(\forall i \in I_s),$$

$$\sum_{j=1}^{n} \lambda_j y_{rj} \ge y_{rk}, \quad (\forall r \in R_D),$$

$$\sum_{j=1}^{n} \lambda_j \mu_{rj} - \mu_{rk} \ge e \sqrt{\sum_{\substack{j=1 \\ j \ne k}}^{n} \lambda_j^2 \sigma_{rj}^2 + (\lambda_j - \theta)^2 \sigma_{rk}^2 + 2 \operatorname{cov}(\tilde{y}_{rj}, \tilde{y}_{rk})},$$

$$(\forall r \in R_s),$$

$$\sum_{j=1}^{n} \lambda_j = 1, \quad \lambda_j \ge 0 \quad (\forall j), \quad \theta\text{:free.}$$

$$(10.16)$$

Now, suppose that there are n two-stage DMUs as shown in Fig. 10.7. For DMU$_j$ ($j = 1, ..., n$), $\tilde{X}_j = (\tilde{x}_{1j}, ..., \tilde{x}_{mj})$ depicts the random input vector to the first stage and $\tilde{Z}_j = (\tilde{z}_1, ..., \tilde{z}_{tj})$ shows the random output vector from the first stage and also the input to the second stage, hence it is called intermediate product. The random output vector $\tilde{Y}_j = (\tilde{y}_{1j}, ..., \tilde{y}_{sj})$ indicates the output from the second stage.

Zhou et al. [42] introduced the following fractional stochastic leader–follower DEA model (10.17) to evaluate the efficiency of the second stage when it is treated as a follower. To do this, the leader's efficiency is calculated first, and then, the follower's efficiency is maximized, while the leader's efficiency level is maintained at its optimum level. The follower's efficiency

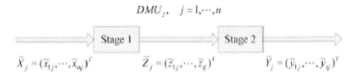

Fig. 10.7 Two-stage series process with stochastic data

can be obtained as given below, where $E_{SL1}^{(a)}$ is the efficiency of the first stage-leader:

$$E_{SF2}^{(a)} = \max \frac{\sum\limits_{r=1}^{s} U_r^1(y_{r0} - F_\zeta^{-1}(a)b_{r0}) + \sum\limits_{r=1}^{s} U_r^2(y_{r0} + F_\zeta^{-1}(a)b_{r0})}{Q\left(\sum\limits_{k=1}^{t} w_k^1(z_{k0} - F_\eta^{-1}(a)c_{k0}) + \sum\limits_{k=1}^{t} w_k^2(z_{k0} + F_\eta^{-1}(a)c_{k0})\right)}$$

$$\text{s.t.} \sum_{k=1}^{t} w_k^1(z_{k0} - F_\eta^{-1}(a)c_{k0}) + \sum_{k=1}^{t} w_k^2(z_{k0} + F_\eta^{-1}(a)c_{k0}) = 1,$$

$$\sum_{k=1}^{t} w_k^1(z_{k0} - F_\eta^{-1}(a)c_{k0}) + \sum_{k=1}^{t} w_k^2(z_{k0} + F_\eta^{-1}(a)c_{k0})$$

$$= E_{SL1}^{(a)}\left(\sum_{i=1}^{m} v_i^1(x_{i0} - F_\zeta^{-1}(a)a_{i0}) + \sum_{i=1}^{m} v_i^2(x_{i0} + F_\zeta^{-1}(a)a_{i0})\right)$$

$$\sum_{k=1}^{t} w_k^1(z_{kj} - F_\eta^{-1}(a)c_{kj}) + \sum_{k=1}^{t} w_k^2(z_{kj} + F_\eta^{-1}(a)c_{kj})$$

$$\leq \sum_{i=1}^{m} v_i^1(x_{ij} - F_\zeta^{-1}(a)a_{ij}) + \sum_{i=1}^{m} v_i^2(x_{ij} + F_\zeta^{-1}(a)a_{ij}), \ (j = 1, ..., n)$$

$$\frac{\sum\limits_{r=1}^{s} U_r^1(y_{rj} - F_\zeta^{-1}(a)b_{rj}) + \sum\limits_{r=1}^{s} U_r^2(y_{rj} + F_\zeta^{-1}(a)b_{rj})}{Q\left(\sum\limits_{k=1}^{t} w_k^1(z_{kj} - F_\eta^{-1}(a)c_{kj}) + \sum\limits_{k=1}^{t} w_k^2(z_{kj} + F_\eta^{-1}(a)c_{kj})\right)} \leq 1,$$

$$(j = 1, ..., n)$$

$$Q \geq 0, \quad v_i^1, v_i^2 \geq 0, \ (i = 1, ..., m), \quad U_r^1, U_r^2 \geq 0, \ (r = 1, ..., s)$$

$$w_k^1, w_k^2 \geq 0, \ (k = 1, ..., t).$$

$$(10.17)$$

Now, when the second stage is treated as a leader and first stage as a follower, the efficiency of first stage-follower can be calculated using the following linearized stochastic leader–follower DEA model (10.18):

$$E_{SF1}^{(a)} = \max \sum_{k=1}^{t} w_k^1(z_{k0} - F_\eta^{-1}(a)c_{k0}) + \sum_{k=1}^{t} w_k^2(z_{k0} + F_\eta^{-1}(a)c_{k0})$$

$$\text{s.t.} \sum_{i=1}^{m} v_i^1\left(x_{i0} - F_\zeta^{-1}(a)a_{i0}\right) + \sum_{i=1}^{m} v_i^2(x_{i0} + F_\zeta^{-1}(a)a_{i0}) = 1,$$

$$\sum_{r=1}^{s} u_r^1(y_{r0} - F_\zeta^{-1}(a)b_{r0}) + \sum_{r=1}^{s} u_r^2(y_{r0} + F_\zeta^{-1}(a)b_{r0})$$

$$= E_{SL2}^{(a)}\left(\sum_{k=1}^{t} w_k^1(z_{k0} - F_\eta^{-1}(a)c_{k0}) + \sum_{k=1}^{t} w_k^2(z_{k0} + F_\eta^{-1}(a)c_{k0})\right),$$

$$\sum_{k=1}^{t} w_k^1(z_{kj} - F_\eta^{-1}(a)c_{kj}) + \sum_{k=1}^{t} w_k^2(z_{kj} + F_\eta^{-1}(a)c_{kj})$$

$$\leq \sum_{i=1}^{m} v_i^1\left(x_{ij} - F_\zeta^{-1}(a)a_{ij}\right) + \sum_{i=1}^{m} v_i^2(x_{ij} + F_\zeta^{-1}(a)a_{ij}), \ (j = 1, ..., n)$$

$$\sum_{r=1}^{s} u_r^1(y_{rj} - F_\zeta^{-1}(a)b_{rj}) + \sum_{r=1}^{s} u_r^2(y_{rj} + F_\zeta^{-1}(a)b_{rj})$$

$$\leq \left(\sum_{k=1}^{t} w_k^1(z_{kj} - F_\eta^{-1}(a)c_{kj}) + \sum_{k=1}^{t} w_k^2(z_{kj} + F_\eta^{-1}(a)c_{kj})\right),$$

$$(j = 1, ..., n)$$

$$v_i^1, v_i^2 \geq 0, \ (i = 1, ..., m), \quad u_r^1, u_r^2 \geq 0, \ (r = 1, ..., s)$$

$$w_k^1, w_k^2 \geq 0, \ (k = 1, ..., t).$$

$$(10.18)$$

10.4.3 Fuzzy DEA

In this section, we describe the recent contributions given by researchers in (See Emrouznejad and Tavana [7]).

Consider a set of n homogenous DMUs so that each one uses m intuitionistic fuzzy inputs and s intuitionistic fuzzy outputs. Let DMU$_k$ denote the DMU under evaluation. Singh [32] presented the following intuitionistic fuzzy DEA/AR (Assurance Region) model (model (10.19)) to measure the efficiency of DMU$_k$:

$$\max \tilde{E}_K^l = \sum_{r=1}^{s} \tilde{v}_r^l \otimes \tilde{y}_{rk}^l + v_0$$

$$\text{s.t.} \sum_{i=1}^{m} \tilde{u}_i^l \otimes \tilde{x}_{ij}^l = \tilde{1},$$

$$\sum_{r=1}^{s} \tilde{v}_r^l \otimes \tilde{y}_{rk}^l \ominus \sum_{i=1}^{m} \tilde{u}_i^l \otimes \tilde{x}_{ij}^l + v_0 \leq \tilde{0}, \, j = 1, 2, ..., n, \qquad (10.19)$$

$$g_{pg}^l \tilde{v}_q^l \ominus \tilde{v}_p^l \leq \tilde{0}, \quad \tilde{v}_p^l \ominus g_{pg}^u \tilde{v}_q^l \leq \tilde{0}, \, \forall p < q = 2, 3, ..., s,$$

$$h_{pg}^l \tilde{u}_q^l \ominus \tilde{u}_p^l \leq \tilde{0}, \quad \tilde{u}_p^l \ominus h_{pg}^u \tilde{u}_q^l \leq 0, \, \forall p < q = 2, 3, ..., m,$$

$$\tilde{u}_i^l \geq \varepsilon > 0, \, i = 1, 2, ..., m$$

$$\tilde{v}_r^l \geq \varepsilon > 0, \, r = 1, 2, ..., s,$$

v_0 is unrestricted in sign.

where $\tilde{x}_{ij}^l = (x_{ij}^1, x_{ij}^2, x_{ij}^3; x_{ij}^{1'}, x_{ij}^2, x_{ij}^{3'})$ and $\tilde{y}_{rj}^l = (y_{rj}^1, y_{rj}^2, y_{rj}^3; y_{rj}^{1'}, y_{rj}^1, y_{rj}^{3'})$ represent the $i^{th} (i = 1, ..., m)$ and $r^{th} (r = 1, ..., s)$ intuitionistic fuzzy input and output of DMU$_j$ $(j = 1, ..., n)$, respectively. Also, $\tilde{u}_{ij}^l = (u_{ij}^1, u_{ij}^2, u_{ij}^3; u_{ij}^{1'}, u_{ij}^2, u_{ij}^{3'})$ and $\tilde{v}_{ij}^l = (v_{ij}^1, v_{ij}^2, v_{ij}^3; v_{ij}^{1'}, v_{ij}^2, v_{ij}^{3'})$ denote the intuitionistic fuzzy weights of the ith intuitionistic fuzzy input and the rth intuitionistic fuzzy output, respectively.

In this area, Peykani et al. [22] proposed a general two-stage series network structure as shown in Fig. 10.8 and provided the novel models (models (10.20) and (10.22)) to measure the overall efficiency of the DMU$_p$ under evaluation, under fuzzy data, for $a \leq \beta$ and $a > \beta$, respectively:

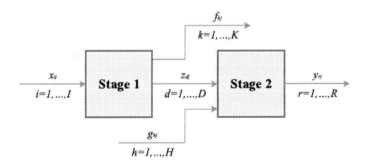

Fig. 10.8 General two-stage series network structure

$$\Psi_{p(a>\beta)}^{Overall} = \max \Omega$$

$$\text{s.t.} \sum_{k=1}^{K} \left(\left(\frac{a}{\beta} \right) f_{k0}^3 + \left(\frac{\beta - a}{\beta} \right) f_{k0}^4 \right) \omega_k + \sum_{d=1}^{D} \left(\left(\frac{a}{\beta} \right) z_{d0}^3 + \left(\frac{\beta - a}{\beta} \right) z_{d0}^4 \right) \gamma_d$$

$$+ \sum_{r=1}^{R} \left(\left(\frac{a}{\beta} \right) y_{r0}^3 + \left(\frac{\beta - a}{\beta} \right) y_{r0}^4 \right) \mu_r \geq \Omega,$$

$$\sum_{i=1}^{I} \left(\left(\frac{\beta - a}{\beta} \right) x_{i0}^1 + \left(\frac{a}{\beta} \right) x_{i0}^2 \right) \tau_i + \sum_{d=1}^{D} \left(\left(\frac{\beta - a}{\beta} \right) z_{d0}^1 + \left(\frac{a}{\beta} \right) z_{d0}^2 \right) \gamma_d$$

$$+ \sum_{h=1}^{H} \left(\left(\frac{\beta - a}{\beta} \right) g_{h0}^1 + \left(\frac{a}{\beta} \right) g_{h0}^2 \right) \pi_h \leq 1,$$

(10.20)

$$\sum_{k=1}^{K} \left(\left(\frac{\beta - a}{\beta} \right) f_{kj}^1 + \left(\frac{a}{\beta} \right) f_{kj}^2 \right) \omega_k + \sum_{d=1}^{D} \left(\left(\frac{\beta - a}{\beta} \right) z_{dj}^1 + \left(\frac{a}{\beta} \right) z_{dj}^2 \right) \gamma_d$$

$$- \sum_{i=1}^{I} \left(\left(\frac{a}{\beta} \right) x_{ij}^3 + \left(\frac{\beta - a}{\beta} \right) x_{ij}^4 \right) \tau_i \leq 0, \ (\forall j),$$

$$\sum_{r=1}^{R} \left(\left(\frac{\beta - a}{\beta} \right) y_{rj}^1 + \left(\frac{a}{\beta} \right) y_{rj}^2 \right) \mu_r - \sum_{d=1}^{D} \left(\left(\frac{a}{\beta} \right) z_{dj}^3 + \left(\frac{\beta - a}{\beta} \right) z_{dj}^4 \right) \gamma_d$$

$$- \sum_{h=1}^{H} \left(\left(\frac{a}{\beta} \right) g_{hj}^3 + \left(\frac{\beta - a}{\beta} \right) g_{hj}^4 \right) \pi_h \leq 0, \ (\forall j)$$

$$\tau_i, \omega_k, \mu_r, \pi_h, \gamma_d \geq 0 (\forall i, k, r, h, d).$$

(10.21)

and

$$\Psi_{p(a \leq \beta)}^{Overall} = \max \Omega$$

$$\text{s.t.}$$

(10.22)

$$\sum_{k=1}^{K} \left(\left(\frac{a-\beta}{1-\beta} \right) f_{k0}^3 + \left(\frac{1-a}{1-\beta} \right) f_{k0}^4 \right) \omega_k + \sum_{d=1}^{D} \left(\left(\frac{a-\beta}{1-\beta} \right) z_{d0}^1 + \left(\frac{1-a}{1-\beta} \right) z_{d0}^2 \right) \gamma_d$$

$$+ \sum_{r=1}^{R} \left(\left(\frac{a-\beta}{1-\beta} \right) y_{r0}^1 + \left(\frac{1-a}{1-\beta} \right) y_{r0}^2 \right) \mu_r \geq \Omega,$$

$$\sum_{i=1}^{I} \left(\left(\frac{1-a}{1-\beta} \right) x_{i0}^3 + \left(\frac{a-\beta}{1-\beta} \right) x_{i0}^4 \right) \tau_i + \sum_{d=1}^{D} \left(\left(\frac{1-a}{1-\beta} \right) z_{d0}^3 + \left(\frac{a-\beta}{1-\beta} \right) z_{d0}^4 \right) \gamma_d$$

$$+ \sum_{h=1}^{H} \left(\left(\frac{1-a}{1-\beta} \right) g_{h0}^3 + \left(\frac{a-\beta}{1-\beta} \right) g_{h0}^4 \right) \pi_h \leq 1,$$

$$\sum_{k=1}^{K} \left(\left(\frac{1-a}{1-\beta} \right) f_{kj}^3 + \left(\frac{a-\beta}{1-\beta} \right) f_{kj}^4 \right) \omega_k + \sum_{d=1}^{D} \left(\left(\frac{1-a}{1-\beta} \right) z_{dj}^3 + \left(\frac{a-\beta}{1-\beta} \right) z_{dj}^4 \right) \gamma_d$$

$$- \sum_{i=1}^{I} \left(\left(\frac{a-\beta}{1-\beta} \right) x_{ij}^1 + \left(\frac{1-a}{1-\beta} \right) x_{ij}^2 \right) \tau_i \leq 0, \ (\forall j),$$

$$\sum_{r=1}^{R} \left(\left(\frac{1-a}{1-\beta} \right) y_{rj}^3 + \left(\frac{a-\beta}{1-\beta} \right) y_{rj}^4 \right) \mu_r - \sum_{d=1}^{D} \left(\left(\frac{a-\beta}{1-\beta} \right) z_{dj}^1 + \left(\frac{1-a}{1-\beta} \right) z_{dj}^2 \right) \gamma_d$$

$$- \sum_{h=1}^{H} \left(\left(\frac{a-\beta}{1-\beta} \right) g_{hj}^1 + \left(\frac{1-a}{1-\beta} \right) g_{hj}^2 \right) \pi_h \leq 0, \ (\forall j)$$

$$\tau_i, \omega_k, \mu_r, \pi_h, \gamma_d \geq 0 (\forall i, k, r, h, d).$$

$$(10.23)$$

where in models (10.20) and (10.22), all inputs and outputs are depicted by fuzzy numbers $\tilde{x}_{ij}, \tilde{f}_{kj}, \tilde{z}_{dj}, \tilde{g}_{hj}$ and $\tilde{y}_{rj}$ with trapezoidal membership functions $\tilde{x}_{ij}(x_{ij}^1, x_{ij}^2, x_{ij}^3, x_{ij}^4)$, $\tilde{f}_{kj}(f_{kj}^1, f_{kj}^2, f_{kj}^3, f_{kj}^4)$, $\tilde{z}_{dj}(z_{dj}^1, z_{dj}^2, z_{dj}^3, z_{dj}^4)$, $\tilde{g}_{hj}(g_{hj}^1, g_{hj}^2, g_{hj}^3, g_{hj}^4)$ and $\tilde{y}_{rj}(y_{rj}^1, y_{rj}^2, y_{rj}^3, y_{rj}^4)$ (see Peykani et al. [23]).

10.4.4 Bootstrapping

This section explains the recent contributions given by researchers on bootstrapping in the DEA context.

In DEA, the efficiency score that a DMU is assigned depends on the difference between its operation compared to the operation of the best-performing DMUs included in the observed set. Any changes in the composition of the observed set, such as adding or removing DMUs, may impact the efficiency scores. Therefore, the standard DEA approach suffers from the lack of sampling noise consideration. This may result in overestimated efficiency scores and lead to the erroneous efficient characterization of some DMUs. As developed by Simar and Wilson [29, 30], the bootstrap DEA deals with this deficiency of DEA by providing a statistical framework for the efficiency scores and allowing for estimations of the true efficiency of a DMU. In what follows, we explain the differences between DEA and bootstrap DEA methods.

In reality, the observed set of DMUs is only a sample drawn from a population through an unknown data generating process. The DEA method, firstly introduced by Simar and Wilson [29], simulates this unknown data generating process by repeatedly drawing random samples from the available set of DMUs and treating them as they were drawn from the population itself. In this way, the bootstrap DEA method allows for estimations of the efficiency scores for each DMU, based on numerous samples. Thus, the bootstrap DEA efficiency scores are more accurate than the DEA ones and have statistical properties which the DEA efficiency scores lack (see Simar and Wilson [30] and Moradi-Motlagh and Emrouznejad [18] for further details).

Some years later, the bootstrapping approach was also used in the literature to make statistical inference in cases where undesirable outputs exist in the production model. Consider a set of N DMUs such that each one uses k positive inputs $\underset{\sim}{x} = (x_1, ..., x_k)^t \in \mathbb{R}^k_+$, to produce m positive desirable (good) outputs, $\underset{\sim}{y} = (y_1, ..., y_m)^t \in \mathbb{R}^m_+$ and r positive undesirable (bad) outputs $\underset{\sim}{u} = (u_1, ..., u_r)^t \in \mathbb{R}^r_+$. Then, the production possibility set (PPS) is defined as the following closed set:

$$\Omega = \left\{ (\underset{\sim}{x}, \underset{\sim}{u}, \underset{\sim}{y}) \middle| \underset{\sim}{x} \text{ can produce } \underset{\sim}{u} \text{ and } \underset{\sim}{y} \right\} \subset \mathbb{R}^{k+r+m}_+ \qquad (10.24)$$

The PPS under the CRS (constant returns to scale) and the VRS (variable returns to scale) specifications, respectively, is obtained as follows:

$$\Omega^{CRS} = \left\{ (\underset{\sim}{x}, \underset{\sim}{u}, \underset{\sim}{y}) \middle| X\underset{\sim}{\lambda} \leq \underset{\sim}{x}, U\underset{\sim}{\lambda} = \underset{\sim}{u}, Y\underset{\sim}{\lambda} \geq \underset{\sim}{y}, \underset{\sim}{\lambda} \geq \underset{\sim}{0} \right\}, \qquad (10.25)$$

$$\Omega^{VRS} = \left\{ (\underset{\sim}{x}, \underset{\sim}{u}, \underset{\sim}{y}) \middle| X\underset{\sim}{\lambda} \leq \underset{\sim}{x}, U\underset{\sim}{\lambda} = \underset{\sim}{u}, Y\underset{\sim}{\lambda} \geq \underset{\sim}{y}, 1'\underset{\sim}{\lambda} = 1, \underset{\sim}{\lambda} \geq \underset{\sim}{0} \right\}, \qquad (10.26)$$

where $X = [\underset{\sim}{x}_1, ..., \underset{\sim}{x}_N]$, $Y = [\underset{\sim}{y}_1, ..., \underset{\sim}{y}_N]$, $U = [\underset{\sim}{u}_1, ..., \underset{\sim}{u}_N]$, $\underset{\sim}{\lambda} = [\underset{\sim}{\lambda}_1, ..., \underset{\sim}{\lambda}_N] \in \mathbb{R}^N_+$ and $\underset{\sim}{0} = [0, ..., 0]$.

The input-oriented technical efficiency of the CCR and BCC models denoted by θ^{CRS} and θ^{VRS}, respectively, are measured as

$$\theta^{CRS} = \inf_{\theta,\underset{\sim}{\lambda}} \left\{ \theta \big| (\theta \underset{\sim}{x}, \underset{\sim}{u}, \underset{\sim}{y}) \in \Omega^{CRS} \right\}, \tag{10.27}$$

$$\theta^{VRS} = \inf_{\theta,\underset{\sim}{\lambda}} \left\{ \theta \big| (\theta \underset{\sim}{x}, \underset{\sim}{u}, \underset{\sim}{y}) \in \Omega^{VRS} \right\}. \tag{10.28}$$

Li [15] extended the bootstrap algorithm presented by Simar and Wilson [29] to account for the presence of undesirable outputs, and calculated the bootstrap efficiencies using the following steps:

Step 1. Measure the input efficiency of all DMUs using (10.27) or (10.28) to calculate $\delta_n = 1/\theta$.

Step 2. Provide $\{(2-\delta_1), ..., (2-\delta_N), \delta_1, ..., \delta_N\}$ that is a random sample of size N to get $\{\tilde{\delta}_1^*, ..., \tilde{\delta}_N^*\}$.

Step 3. Compute $\tilde{\tilde{\delta}}_n = \tilde{\delta}_n^* + \tau \varepsilon_n$ (for $n = 1, ..., N$), in which $\tau = 1.06 \min\{\widehat{S}, \widehat{R}/1.34\} N^{-1/5}$, $\widehat{R}$, and $\widehat{S}$ denote the interquartile range of $\{\delta_1, ..., \delta_N\}$ and the empirical standard deviation, respectively. Also, ε_n represents a random draw from a standard normal distribution.

Step 4. Compute $\tilde{\delta}_n^{**} = \bar{\tilde{\delta}}^* + (\tilde{\delta}_n^* - \bar{\tilde{\delta}}^*)/\sqrt{1 + (\tau^2/\tilde{S}^{*2})}$ for $(n = 1, .., N)$, in which $\bar{\tilde{\delta}}^*$ and $\tilde{S}^{*2}$ are the empirical mean and variance of $\{\tilde{\delta}_1^*, ..., \tilde{\delta}_N^*\}$.

Step 5. Define $\tilde{\tilde{\delta}}_n^{**} = \begin{cases} 2 - \tilde{\delta}_n^{**}, & \text{if } \tilde{\delta}_n^{**} < 1 \\ \tilde{\delta}_n^{**}, & \text{if } \tilde{\delta}_n^{**} \geq 1 \end{cases}$ (for $n = 1, ..., N$).

Step 6. Consider $\underset{\sim}{x}_n^* = \tilde{\delta}_n^{**} \underset{\sim}{x}_n/\delta_n$, $\underset{\sim}{u}_n^* = \underset{\sim}{u}_n$, and $\underset{\sim}{y}_n^* = \underset{\sim}{y}_n$ (for $n = 1, ..., N$).

Step 7. Compute the bootstrap estimate, denoted by θ_n^* (for $n = 1, ..., N$), using a suitable DEA model with the technology characterized by $(\underset{\sim}{X}^*, \underset{\sim}{U}^*, \underset{\sim}{Y}^*)$, in which $\underset{\sim}{X}^* = [\underset{\sim}{x}_1^*, ..., \underset{\sim}{x}_N^*]$, $\underset{\sim}{Y}^* = [\underset{\sim}{y}_1^*, ..., \underset{\sim}{y}_N^*]$, $\underset{\sim}{U}^* = [\underset{\sim}{u}_1^*, ..., \underset{\sim}{u}_N^*]$.

Step 8. Repeat Steps 2 to 7 for B times to obtain bootstrap estimates $\{\theta_{nb}^*\}_{n=1}^N$ for $b = 1, ..., B$.

Also, in this context, the bias-corrected efficiency score is expressed as follows:

$$\tilde{\theta}_k = \hat{\theta}_k - bias(\hat{\theta}_k) = 2\hat{\theta}_k - B^{-1} \sum_{k=1}^{K} \hat{\theta}_{*k}, \tag{10.29}$$

where $bias(\hat{\theta}_k) = E(\hat{\theta}_k) - \hat{\theta}_k = B^{-1} \sum_{k=1}^{K} \hat{\theta}_{*k} - \hat{\theta}_k$ and $\hat{\theta}_k$ for $(k = 1, ..., K)$ is a scalar and indicates the input-oriented efficiency score of each DMU$_k$ (for $k = 1, ..., K$).

Another bootstrap approach commonly encountered in the DEA literature, is that of the second-stage double bootstrap, which is used to investigate the impact of contextual variables on the efficiency of DMUs. For example, Al-Mezeini wt al. [1] applied a second-stage double bootstrap in the investigation of greenhouse's (GH) production performance. So, they considered a set of K GH farms, such that the GH$_k$ $(k = 1, ..., K)$ uses N inputs, $x_{ik}(i = 1, ..., N)$, to produce M outputs, $y_{jk}(j = 1, ..., M)$. To measure the technical efficiency (TE) θ_g of GH$_g$, the following input-oriented CCR model can be used:

$$\begin{aligned}
&\min \theta_g \\
&\text{s.t.} \sum_{k=1}^{K} \lambda_k x_{ik} \leq \theta_g x_{ig}, i = 1, 2, ..., N, \\
&\qquad \sum_{k=1}^{K} \lambda_k y_{jk} \geq y_{jg}, j = 1, 2, ..., M, \\
&\qquad \lambda_k \geq 0, k = 1, 2, ..., K,
\end{aligned} \tag{10.30}$$

where under the VRS specification, the pure technical efficiency (PTE) of GH$_g$ is estimated by adding the constraint $\sum_{k=1}^{K} \lambda_k = 1$ to model (10.30) ([4]). Using this model, a GH$_g$ is CCR-efficient (BCC-efficient) if $TE = 1$ $(PTE = 1)$, otherwise it is inefficient.

Here, let $t_g = (t_{1g}, t_{2g}, ..., t_{pg})$ represent a vector of p contextual variables corresponding to GH$_g$. Since $\theta_g \leq 1$, using a regression model $\theta_g = \boldsymbol{\beta t_g} + \varepsilon$, it is implied that $\boldsymbol{\beta t_g} + \varepsilon \leq 1$ and so $\varepsilon \leq 1 - \boldsymbol{\beta t_g}$, in which $\boldsymbol{\beta} = (\beta_1, \beta_2, ..., \beta_p)$ indicates the model's coefficients and also ε is the error term with $\varepsilon \sim N(0, \sigma_\varepsilon)$. To identify the contextual variables, with the specification level set at $a\%$, the following algorithm of the procedure is used, with

B_1 and B_2 being the number of the first and second bootstrap replications, respectively ([20, 31]).

Step 1. Solve the BCC model for each GH_g to obtain θ_g by considering the original data.

Step 2. Calculate the estimates $\hat{\beta}$ and $\hat{\sigma}_\varepsilon$ for β and σ_ε, respectively, using truncated maximum likelihood estimation.

Step 3. Repeat the next sub-steps for each GH_g B_1 times to produce a set of B_1 bootstrap estimates $\hat{\theta}_{gb}$ for $b = 1, ..., B_1$.

   Sub-step 3.1. Generate the residual error ε_g from the normal distribution $N(0, \hat{\sigma}_\varepsilon)$ with right-truncation at $1 - \hat{\beta}t_g$.

   Sub-step 3.2. Calculate $\theta_g^* = \hat{\beta}t_g + \varepsilon_g$.

   Sub-step 3.3. Construct a pseudo data set (x_g^*, y_g^*), in which $x_g^* = x_g\theta_g/\theta_g^*$ and $y_g^* = y_g$.

   Sub-step 3.4. Use the BCC model with the pseudo data set (x_g^*, y_g^*) to obtain an estimate $\hat{\theta}_g^*$ of the real efficiency score.

Step 4. Compute the bias-corrected estimator $\hat{\hat{\theta}}_g$ for each GH_g using the bootstrap estimator of the bias $\hat{b}_g$, in which $\hat{\hat{\theta}}_g = \theta_g - \hat{b}_g$ and $\hat{b}_g = \frac{1}{B}\sum_{b=1}^{B_1} \hat{\theta}_{gb}^* - \theta_g$.

Step 5. Use the truncated maximum likelihood estimation and provide an estimate $\hat{\beta}^*$ for β and an estimate $\hat{\sigma}^*$ for σ_ε.

Step 6. Repeat the following sub-steps B_2 times to obtain a set of B_2 pairs of bootstrap estimates $(\hat{\beta}_b^{**}, \hat{\sigma}_b^{**})$ for $b = 1, ..., B_2$.

   Sub-step 6.1. Generate ε_g from the normal distribution $N(0, \hat{\sigma}^*)$ with right-truncation at $1 - \hat{\beta}^* t_g$ for each GH_g $(g = 1, ..., K)$.

   Sub-step 6.2. Compute $\hat{\theta}_g^{**}$ for each GH_g $(g = 1, ..., K)$ such that $\hat{\theta}_g^{**} = \hat{\beta}^* t_g + \varepsilon_g$.

   Sub-step 6.3. Use the truncated maximum likelihood estimation and provide an estimate $\hat{\beta}^{**}$ for β and an estimate $\hat{\sigma}^{**}$ for σ_ε.

Step 7. Construct the estimated $(1 - a)\%$ confidence interval of the jth element β_j of the vector β as $\left[Lower_{a_j}, Upper_{a_j}\right] = \left[\hat{\beta}_j^* + \hat{a}_a, \hat{\beta}_j^* + (-\hat{b}_a)\right]$, where $\left(-\hat{b}_a \leq \hat{\beta}_j^{**} - \hat{\beta}_j^* \leq -\hat{a}_a\right) \approx 1 - a$.

10.4.5   Directional Measure and Negative Data

In this section, we describe the recent contributions presented by researchers in the context of the directional measure/directional distance function.

Directional measure has been initially proposed by Färe and Grosskopf [8]. Since negative values might exist in the input and output data of DMUs, Lin and Chen [17] proposed the following VRS radial super-efficiency model (model (10.31)) using a data-independent direction vector:

$$\max \beta_0$$

$$\text{s.t.} \sum_{\substack{j=1 \\ j \neq 0}}^{n} \lambda_j x_{ij} \leq (1 - \beta_0) x_{i0} - a_i \beta_0, \quad (i = 1, ..., m),$$

$$\sum_{\substack{j=1 \\ j \neq 0}}^{n} \lambda_j y_{rj} \geq (1 + \beta_0) y_{r0} - b_r \beta_0, \quad (r = 1, ..., s), \qquad (10.31)$$

$$\sum_{\substack{j=1 \\ j \neq 0}}^{n} \lambda_j = 1, \quad \lambda_j \geq 0 \ (j = 1, ..., n; \ j \neq 0),$$

where $a_i = k \max_{j=1,...,n} \{|x_{ij}|\}$ (for $i = 1, ..., m$) and $b_r = \min_{j=1,...,n} \{y_{rj}\}$ (for $r = 1, ..., s$), in which k is a constant satisfying $k \geq 3$.

Zhou et al. [41] also presented the following non-radial DDF model (model (10.32)) based on second-order cone programming:

$$\min \psi_0$$

$$\text{s.t.} \sum_{j=1}^{n} \lambda_j x_{ij} - \delta_0 x_{i0} + d_{ix} = 0, \ (i = 1, ..., m),$$

$$\sum_{j=1}^{n} \lambda_j y_{tj}^{b} - y_{t0}^{b} + d_{tb} = 0, \ (t = 1, ..., w),$$

$$\psi_0 + d_0^{\psi} = 1,$$

$$\delta_0 - d_0^{\delta} = 1, \tag{10.32}$$

$$\sum_{j=1}^{n} \lambda_j - \delta_0 = 0,$$

$$\left| \frac{\sum_{j=1}^{n} \lambda_j y_{rj} - \psi_0}{2} \right|_2 \leq \frac{\sum_{j=1}^{n} \lambda_j y_{rj} - \psi_0}{2} \sqrt{y_{r0}},$$

$$\lambda_j, d_{tb}, d_{ix}, d_0^{\psi}, d_0^{\delta} \geq 0,$$

where y_{tj}^{b} (for $t = 1, ..., w$) denote the undesirable (bad) outputs of DMU_j and ψ_0^{*} represents the environmental efficiency of DMU_0. DMU_0 is VRS-efficient if and only if $\psi_0^{*} = 1$. Also, under the CRS specification, the constraint $\sum_{j=1}^{n} \lambda_j - \delta_0 = 0$ is removed from model (10.32). In this case, DMU_0 is CRS-efficient if and only if $\psi_0^{*} = 1$.

Also, Portela et al. [27] introduced the following (DDF) model (model (10.33)) to improve performance of the DMU under evaluation (DMU_o), in the presence of both positive and negative input and output data:

$$
\max \beta
$$

$$
\text{s.t.} \sum_{j=1}^{n} \lambda_j x_{ij} \leq x_{io} - \beta R_{io}^-, \ (i = 1, \ldots, m),
$$

$$
\sum_{j=1}^{n} \lambda_j y_{rj} \geq y_{ro} + \beta R_{ro}^+, \ (r = 1, \ldots, s), \tag{10.33}
$$

$$
\sum_{j=1}^{n} \lambda_j = 1, \quad \beta, \lambda_j \geq 0 \ (j = 1, \ldots, n).
$$

Model (10.33) has the following two drawbacks: (1) this model cannot guarantee that the obtained projections are on the Pareto efficient frontier ([2]) and (2) this model is not capable of distinguishing between strongly and weakly efficient DMUs ([6]).

Tavana et al. [34] provided the following non-radial DDF model (model (10.34)) to tackle these two drawbacks stated above:

$$
\min 1 - \frac{1}{m+s} \left(\sum_{i=1}^{m} \frac{\theta_i}{\theta_{io}} + \sum_{r=1}^{s} \frac{\varphi_r}{\varphi_{ro}} \right)
$$

$$
\text{s.t.} \sum_{j=1}^{n} \lambda_j x_{ij} = x_{io} - \theta_i g_{io}^-, \ (\forall i),
$$

$$
\sum_{j=1}^{n} \lambda_j y_{rj} = y_{ro} + \varphi_r g_{ro}^+, \ (\forall r), \tag{10.34}
$$

$$
\sum_{j=1}^{n} \lambda_j = 1, \quad \theta_i, \varphi_r, \lambda_j \geq 0 \ (\forall i, \forall r, \forall j),
$$

where $\bar{\theta}_{io} = \frac{x_{io} - \min\{x_{ij} : \forall j\}}{g_{io}^-}$ and $\bar{\varphi}_{ro} = \frac{\max\{y_{rj} : \forall j\} - y_{ro}}{g_{ro}^+}$.

Moreover, in the presence of negative inputs and outputs, Tavana et al. [34] modified model (10.34) and presented the following non-radial model

(10.35) using the ideal point concept:

$$
\min 1 - \frac{1}{m+s} \left(\sum_{\substack{i=1 \\ R_{io}^- > 0}}^{m} \theta_i + \sum_{\substack{r=1 \\ R_{ro}^+ > 0}}^{s} \varphi_r \right)
$$

$$
\text{s.t.} \sum_{j=1}^{n} \lambda_j x_{ij} = x_{io} - \theta_i R_{io}^-, \quad (\forall i),
$$

(10.35)

$$
\sum_{j=1}^{n} \lambda_j y_{rj} = y_{ro} + \varphi_r R_{ro}^+, \quad (\forall r),
$$

$$
\sum_{j=1}^{n} \lambda_j = 1, \quad \theta_i, \varphi_r, \lambda_j \geq 0 \ (\forall i, \forall r, \forall j),
$$

where $g_{io}^- = R_{io}^- = x_{io} - \min_j\{x_{ij}\}$, $(\forall i)$ and $g_{ro}^+ = R_{ro}^+ = y_{ro} - \max_j\{y_{rj}\}$, $(\forall r)$ denote the lower-sided range for inputs and the upper-sided range for output, respectively.

Tavana et al. [34] explained that model (10.35) is capable of correctly recognizing all kinds of inefficiencies, and also it helps managers to find a suitable benchmark for inefficient DMUs.

They also introduced a pair of pessimistic and optimistic mixed binary non-linear programming (MBNLP) models (models (10.36) and (10.37)) for extending the DDF-based model (10.35) to accommodate the L flexible measures represented by $z_j = (z_{1j}, ..., z_{ij})$. These models not only handle but also consider the flexible measures.

The pessimistic MBNLP model:

$$\underline{\xi_o}^* = \min\ 1 - \frac{1}{m+s+l}\left(\sum_{\substack{i=1\\ R_{io}^->0}}^{m}\theta_i + \sum_{\substack{r=1\\ R_{ro}^+>0}}^{s}\varphi_r + \sum_{\substack{l=1\\ R_{lo}^-.R_{lo}^+>0}}^{L}(\Theta_l+\Phi_l)\right)$$

$$\text{s.t.}\ \sum_{j=1}^{n}\lambda_j x_{ij} \le x_{io} - \theta_i R_{io}^-,\ (\forall i),$$

$$\sum_{j=1}^{n}\lambda_j y_{rj} \ge y_{ro} + \varphi_r R_{ro}^+,\ (\forall r),$$

$$\sum_{j=1}^{n}\lambda_j z_{lj} \le z_{lo} - \bar{\theta}_l \bar{R}_{lo}^- + M d_l,\ (\forall l),$$

$$\sum_{j=1}^{n}\lambda_j z_{lj} \ge z_{lo} + \bar{\varphi}_l \bar{R}_{lo}^+ - M(1-d_l),\ (\forall l),$$ \hfill (10.36)

$$0 \le \Theta_l \le M(1-d_l),\ (\forall l),$$

$$\bar{\theta}_l - M d_l \le \Theta_l \le \bar{\theta}_l,\ (\forall l),$$

$$0 \le \Phi_l \le M d_l,\ (\forall l),$$

$$\bar{\varphi}_l - M(1-d_l) \le \Phi_l \le \bar{\varphi}_l,\ (\forall l),$$

$$\sum_{j=1}^{n}\lambda_j = 1,\quad \lambda_j \ge 0\ (\forall j),$$

$$d_l \in \{0,1\}\ (\forall l),$$

where $\bar{R}_{lo}^- = z_{lo} - \min_j\{z_{lj}\}$, $(\forall l)$ and $\bar{R}_{lo}^+ = \max_j\{z_{lj}\} - z_{lo}$, $(\forall l)$.

The optimistic MBNLP model:

$$\bar{\xi}_o^* = \max \; 1 + \sum_{r=1}^{s} u_r y_{ro} + \sum_{l=1}^{L} \varphi_l^{out} z_{lo} - \sum_{i=1}^{m} v_i x_{io} - \sum_{l=1}^{L} \varphi_l^{in} z_{lo} + u_0$$

$$- M \left(\sum_{r=1}^{s} h_r R_{ro}^+ + \sum_{l=1}^{L} \chi_l^{out} \bar{R}_{lo}^+ + \sum_{i=1}^{m} w_i R_{io}^- + \sum_{l=1}^{L} \chi_l^{in} \bar{R}_{io}^- \right)$$

$$\text{s.t.} \quad \sum_{r=1}^{s} u_r y_{rj} + \sum_{l=1}^{L} \varphi_l^{out} z_{lj} - \sum_{i=1}^{m} v_i x_{ij} - \sum_{l=1}^{L} \varphi_l^{in} z_{lj} + u_0 \le 0, \;\; (\forall j),$$

$$u_r R_{ro}^+ + h_r \ge \frac{1}{m+s+L}, \;\; (\forall r),$$

$$w_l^{out} \bar{R}_{lo}^+ + q_l^{out} \ge \frac{d_l}{m+s+L}, \;\; (\forall l),$$

$$v_i R_{io}^- + w_i \ge \frac{1}{m+s+L}, \;\; (\forall i),$$

$$w_l^{in} \bar{R}_{lo}^- + q_l^{in} \ge \frac{1-d_l}{m+s+L}, \;\; (\forall l),$$

$$0 \le \varphi_l^{out} \le M d_l, \;\; (\forall l),$$

$$\varphi_l^{out} \le w_l^{out} \le \varphi_l^{out} + M(1-d_l), \;\; (\forall l),$$

$$0 \le \varphi_l^{in} \le M(1-d_l), \;\; (\forall l),$$

$$\varphi_l^{in} \le w_l^{out} \le \varphi_l^{in} + M d_l, \;\; (\forall l),$$

$$0 \le \chi_l^{out} \le M d_l, \;\; (\forall l),$$

$$\chi_l^{out} \le q_l^{out} \le \chi_l^{out} + M(1-d_l), \;\; (\forall l),$$

$$0 \le \chi_l^{in} \le M(1-d_l), \;\; (\forall l),$$

$$\chi_l^{in} \le q_l^{in} \le \chi_l^{in} + M d_l, \;\; (\forall l),$$

$$d_l \in \{0,1\}, \;\; (\forall l),$$

$$u_r, v_i, h_r, w_i, \; , \;\; (\forall r, \forall i),$$

$$w_l^{out}, w_l^{in}, q_l^{out}, q_l^{in}, \;\; (\forall l).$$

$$(10.37)$$

10.4.6   Undesirable Factors

This section explains the recent contributions provided by researchers in handling the presence of undesirable factors.

Undesirable factors were introduced in the DEA models over 30 years ago, but many extensions and applications appeared in the last few years. For example, Izadikhah and Saen [13] considered the two-stage series network structure with undesirable factors shown in Fig. 10.9, and introduced the following linear cooperative model (model (10.38)) to measure the overall efficiency score of a DMU_o under evaluation:

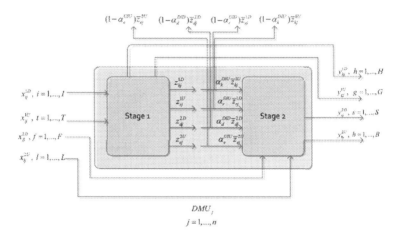

Fig. 10.9   A visual description of the two-stage series network structure

$$\theta^* = \max \left(\sum_{s=1}^{S} \tilde{q}_s^{2D} y_{so}^{2D} + \sum_{k=1}^{K} \tilde{\varphi}_k^{1D} z_{ko}^{1D} + \sum_{e=1}^{E} \tilde{\varphi}_e^{2U} z_{e0}^{2U} + \sum_{l=1}^{L} \tilde{v}_l^{2U} x_{lo}^{2U} \right)$$

$$\text{s.t. } \sum_{g=1}^{G} \tilde{q}_g^{1U} y_{go}^{1U} + \sum_{r=1}^{R} \tilde{w}_r^{1U} z_{ro}^{1U} + \sum_{e=1}^{E} \tilde{w}_e^{2U} z_{eo}^{2U} + \sum_{i=1}^{I} \tilde{v}_i^{1D} x_{io}^{D} = \lambda,$$

$$\sum_{b=1}^{B} \tilde{q}_b^{2U} y_{bo}^{2U} + \sum_{r=1}^{R} \tilde{\varphi}_{ro}^{1U} z_{ro}^{1U} + \sum_{d=1}^{D} \tilde{\varphi}_d^{2D} z_{do}^{2D} + \sum_{f=1}^{F} \tilde{v}_f^{2D} x_{fo}^{2D} = \lambda,$$

$$\sum_{h=1}^{H} \tilde{q}_h^{1D} y_{hj}^{1D} + \sum_{k=1}^{K} \tilde{w}_k^{1D} z_{kj}^{1D} + \sum_{d=1}^{D} \tilde{w}_d^{2D} z_{dj}^{2D} + \sum_{t=1}^{T} \tilde{v}_t^{1U} x_{tj}^{1U} - \sum_{g=1}^{G} \tilde{q}_g^{1U} y_{gj}^{1U}$$

$$- \sum_{r=1}^{R} \tilde{w}_r^{1U} z_{rj}^{1U} - \sum_{e=1}^{E} \tilde{w}_e^{2U} z_{ej}^{2U} - \sum_{i=1}^{I} \tilde{v}_i^{1D} x_{ij}^{1D} \leq 0, \ (\forall j)$$

$$\sum_{s=1}^{S} \tilde{q}_s^{2D} y_{sj}^{2D} + \sum_{k=1}^{K} \tilde{\varphi}_k^{1D} z_{kj}^{1D} + \sum_{e=1}^{E} \tilde{\varphi}_e^{2U} z_{ej}^{2U} + \sum_{l=1}^{L} \tilde{v}_l^{2U} x_{ij}^{2U} - \sum_{b=1}^{B} \tilde{q}_b^{2U} y_{bj}^{2U}$$

$$- \sum_{r=1}^{R} \tilde{\varphi}_r^{1U} z_{rj}^{1U} - \sum_{d=1}^{D} \tilde{\varphi}_d^{2D} z_{dj}^{2D} - \sum_{f=1}^{F} \tilde{v}_f^{2D} x_{fj}^{2D} \leq 0, \ (\forall j),$$

$$\tilde{\varphi}_k^{1D} \leq \tilde{w}_k^{1D}, \ (\forall k),$$

$$\tilde{\varphi}_d^{2D} \leq \tilde{w}_d^{2D}, \ (\forall d),$$

$$\tilde{\varphi}_r^{1U} \leq \tilde{w}_r^{1U}, \ (\forall r),$$

$$\tilde{\varphi}_e^{2U} \leq \tilde{w}_e^{2U}, \ (\forall e),$$

$$\theta_1^L \leq \lambda \leq \theta_1^U,$$

$$\tilde{q}_h^{1D}, \tilde{q}_s^{2D}, \tilde{w}_k^{1D}, \tilde{w}_d^{2D}, \tilde{w}_r^{1U}, \tilde{w}_e^{2U}, \tilde{v}_l^{2U}, \tilde{q}_g^{1U}, \tilde{q}_b^{2U}, \tilde{v}_f^{2D}, \tilde{v}_i^{1D}, \tilde{v}_t^{1U},$$

$$\tilde{\varphi}_k^{1D}, \tilde{\varphi}_d^{2D}, \tilde{\varphi}_r^{1U}, \tilde{\varphi}_e^{2U} \geq 0, \ (\forall h, s, k, d, r, e, l, g, b, f, i, t).$$

$$(10.38)$$

Khodadadipour et al. [14] extended the above concept to stochastic data and provided the following input-output stochastic model (model (10.39)) to estimate the efficiency score of a DMU$_o$, as:

$$E^*_\infty = \max \sum_{r=1}^{s} \mu_{ro} \bar{y}_{ro} + \sum_{p=1}^{k} \varphi_{po} \bar{z}'_{po} + u_0$$

$$\text{s.t. } \sum_{i=1}^{l} \omega_{io} \bar{x}_{io} = 1,$$

$$\sum_{i=1}^{l} \omega_{io} \bar{x}_{ij} - \sum_{r=1}^{s} \mu_{ro} \bar{y}_{rj} - \sum_{p=1}^{k} \varphi_{po} \bar{z}'_{pj} - u_0 + A_j \varphi^{-1}(a) \geq 0, \ j = 1, ..., n,$$

$$A_j^2 = \sum_{i=1}^{m} \sum_{k=1}^{m} \omega_{io} \omega_{ko} \ \text{cov}(\tilde{x}_{ij} \tilde{x}_{kj}) + \sum_{r=1}^{s} \sum_{k=1}^{s} \mu_{ro} \mu_{ko} \ \text{cov}(\tilde{y}_{rj}, \tilde{y}_{kj})$$

$$+ \sum_{p=1}^{k} \sum_{q=1}^{k} \omega_{po} \omega_{qo} \ \text{cov}(\tilde{z}'_{pj}, \tilde{z}'_{qj}) - 2 \sum_{i=1}^{m} \sum_{k=1}^{m} \omega_{io} \mu_{ro} \ \text{cov}(\tilde{x}_{ij}, \tilde{y}_{rj})$$

$$- 2 \sum_{i=1}^{m} \sum_{p=1}^{k} \omega_{io} \varphi_{po} \ \text{cov}(\tilde{x}_{ij}, \tilde{z}'_{pj}) + 2 \sum_{r=1}^{s} \sum_{p=1}^{k} \mu_{ro} \varphi_{po} \ \text{cov}(\tilde{y}_{rj}, \tilde{z}'_{pj}),$$

$$j = 1, ..., n,$$

$$\sum_{r=1}^{s} \mu_{ro} \bar{y}_{rj} + \sum_{p=1}^{k} \varphi_{po} \bar{z}'_{pj} + u_o + B_j \varphi^{-1}(a) \geq 0, \ j = 1, ..., n,$$

$$B_j^2 = \sum_{r=1}^{s} \sum_{k=1}^{s} \mu_{ro} \mu_{ko} \ \text{cov}(\tilde{y}_{rj}, \tilde{y}_{kj}) + \sum_{p=1}^{k} \sum_{q=1}^{k} \varphi_{po} \varphi_{qo} \ \text{cov}(\tilde{z}'_{pj}, \tilde{z}'_{qj})$$

$$+ 2 \sum_{r=1}^{s} \sum_{p=1}^{k} \mu_{ro} \varphi_{po} \ \text{cov}(\tilde{y}_{rj}, \tilde{z}'_{pj}), \ j = 1, ..., n,$$

$$\omega_{io} \geq 0, \ i = 1, ..., m$$

$$\mu_{ro} \geq 0, \ r = 1, .., s$$

$$\varphi_{po} \geq 0, \ p = 1, ..., k,$$

$$u_d \text{ free,}$$

$$A_j, B_j \geq 0, \ j = 1, ..., n,$$

$$(10.39)$$

where $\varphi(a)$ represents the standard normal distribution function and $\varphi^{-1}(a)$ denotes the inverse standard normal distribution function for a value.

10.4.7   Directional Returns to Scale in DEA

Panzar and Willig [21] proposed a method to determine the (RTS) of decision-making units (DMUs) based on the production function. The estimation of the RTS of DMUs using the (DEA) method was investigated first by Banker [3] and Banker et al. [4]. Banker [3] introduced the definition of the RTS from classical economics into the framework of the DEA method, and he used the CCR-DEA model with a radial measure to estimate the RTS of the evaluated DMUs. Soon after that, Banker et al. [4] proposed the BCC-DEA model under the assumption of variable RTS and investigated how to apply the BCC-DEA model to estimate the RTS of DMUs. Thus far, in addition to the cost-based measurement of the RTS of DMUs (e.g., [8, 10, 28, 33]), DEA-based studies of DMUs' RTS can be roughly divided into four categories: (1) RTS measurement using CCR-DEA models, (2) RTS measurement using BCC-DEA models, (3) RTS measurement using the FGL-DEA model and quantitative measurement of the scale elasticity (SE) and (4) RTS measurement using non-radial DEA models.

The existing studies on the RTS measurement in DEA models are all based on the definition of RTS proposed in Banker [3]. The RTS is a classic economic concept describing the relationship between changes in the scale of production and output. The traditional definition of RTS in economics is based on the idea of measuring radial changes in outputs caused by all inputs. Following this concept, Banker [3] defined RTS in the DEA framework using the radial changes in outputs caused by all inputs.

In real production practices (e.g., research organizations), it can be seen that the inputs normally do not change proportionally. Podinovski [24, 25] and Podinovski et al. [26] noted the possible non-proportional changes of inputs or outputs in research organizations. It should be noted that the changes over time and RTS are different concepts. However, the observations above do indicate possible change patterns of the inputs; we observed that they may be non-proportional. This motivates us to consider (directional RTS) with non-proportional changes in inputs (or outputs). Of course, the introduction of directional RTS does not mean that the standard RTS is not meaningful, but enables us to consider more increment patterns for inputs and outputs as illustrated in our case studies. Thus, the directional RTS is a generalization of traditional RTS by considering the non-proportional changes of inputs and outputs. Yang [38, 39] and Yang et al. [37] extended the classic definition of RTS in economics to directional RTS and introduced the definition into the DEA framework. They extended the classic definitions of SE or RTS in the DEA, initially proposed by Banker [3], and redefined the left- and right-hand direction SE and the directional RTS based on the

PPS. It should be noted that the directional RTS is still based on the Pareto preference. Yang et al. [40] also investigated directional congestion.

10.5 Recent Applications and Future Developments

To explore the hotspots of the latest DEA research and grasp the development trend of the DEA theory and its applications, we further analyzed the keywords of DEA-related articles published in the recent two years. In Table 10.3, the six types of the most used keywords within DEA-related articles in the recent two years are listed.

Table 10.4 shows the 10 most actively implemented fields of DEA methods in the past two years, i.e., energy, banking, education, environment, hospital, public policy, supply chain, transportation, agriculture, and

Table 10.3 The six most commonly used types of keywords

No.	Keywords
1	Sustainability, Eco-efficiency, Undesirable outputs, Directional distance function (DDF), Environmental efficiency, Sustainable development, Environmental protection, Energy efficiency, CO_2 emissions
2	Efficiency evaluation, Efficiency analysis, Cost efficiency, Technical efficiency, Performance evaluation, Performance assessment, Ranking, Benchmarking
3	Malmquist, Malmquist index, Malmquist productivity Index, DEA-Malmquist index, Total factor productivity
4	Network DEA, Two-stage, Efficiency decomposition
5	Bootstrap, Bootstrapping
6	Returns to scale, Scale efficiency, Congestion

Table 10.4 Top 10 most implemented fields of the DEA method

No.	Keywords
1	Energy
2	Banking
3	Education
4	Environment
5	Hospital
6	Public policy
7	Supply chain
8	Transportation
9	Agriculture
10	Sociology

sociology. Compared with the previous DEA reviews (see references in Sect. 10.2), it is obvious that the application of DEA in the field of energy, education, and environment has increased significantly.

10.6 Conclusions

This chapter reviewed some recent developments and challenges in the context of DEA and its applications. Since the seminal work of Charnes, Cooper and Rhodes [5] in DEA, there has been an "exponential" growth in the number of journal articles in the recent four decades. Until the end of 2021, the total number of journal articles reaches over 20,000. We found that the *European Journal of Operational Research*, *Journal of the Operational Research Society*, *Journal of Productivity Analysis*, *Omega*, and *Annals of Operations Research* are the most utilized journals in this field, while the journal of *Socio-Economic Planning Sciences* has been recognized as the first choice journal for DEA papers with applications in the public sector. In respect to modeling and applications, environmental efficiency and DDF (including eco-efficiency, undesirable outputs, directional distance function (DDF), carbon dioxide emissions, pollution, sustainable development, sustainability, environmental protection), network DEA (including two-stage DEA, efficiency decomposition), bootstrap or bootstrapping and fuzzy DEA, as well as returns to scale (including scale efficiency) are the main fields of current studies. Moreover, we detect eco-efficiency, agriculture, banking, supply chain, transportation, as well as public policy within the application fields of DEA with the greatest numbers of journal articles.

Acknowledgements We would like to acknowledge the support from the National Natural Science Foundation of China (NSFC, No. 72071196).

References

1. Al-Mezeini, N.K., Oukil, A., Al-Ismaili, A.M. (2020). Investigating the efficiency of greenhouse production in Oman: A two-stage approach based on data envelopment analysis and double bootstrapping. Journal of Cleaner Production, 247, 119160.
2. Asmild, M., Pastor, J.T. (2010). Slack free MEA and RDM with comprehensive efficiency measures. Omega, 38(6), 475–483.
3. Banker, R.D. (1984). Estimating most productive scale size using data envelopment analysis. Journal of Operational Research, 17, 35–44.

4. Banker, R.D., Charnes, A., Cooper, W.W. (1984). Some models for estimating technical and scale inefficiencies in data envelopment analysis. Management Science, 30, 1078–1092.

5. Charnes, A., Cooper, W.W., Rhodes, E. (1978). Measuring the efficiency of decision making units. European Journal of Operational Research, 2(6), 429–444.

6. Emrouznejad, A., Anouze, A.L., Thanassoulis, E. (2010). A semi-oriented radial measure for measuring the efficiency of decision making units with negative data, using DEA. European Journal of Operational Research, 200(1), 297–304.

7. Emrouznejad, A. and Tavana, M. (2014). Performance measurement with Fuzzy Data envelopment analysis. In the series of "Studies in Fuzziness and Soft Computing", Springer-Verlag, ISBN 978-3-642-41371-1.

8. Färe, R., Grosskopf. S. (1985). A nonparametric cost approach to scale efficiency. Scandinavian Journal of Economics, 87, 594–604.

9. Färe, R., Grosskopf. S. (2000). Network DEA, Socio-Economic Planning Sciences, 3, 249–267.

10. Färe, R., Grosskopf. S., Lovell, C.A.K. (1994). Production frontiers. Cambridge, UK: Cambridge University Press.

11. Guo, C., Wei, F., Ding, T., Zhang, L., Liang, L. (2017). Multistage network DEA: Decomposition and aggregation weights of component performance. Computers & Industrial Engineering, 113, 64–74.

12. Guo, C., Zhang, J., Zhang, L. (2020). Two-stage additive network DEA: Duality, frontier projection and divisional efficiency. Expert Systems with Applications, 157, 113478.

13. Izadikhah, M., Saen, F.R. (2018). Assessing sustainability of supply chain by chance-constrained two-stage DEA model in the presence of undesirable factors. Computers and Operations Research, 100, 343–367.

14. Khodadadipour, M., Hadi-Vencheh, A., Behzadi, M.H., Rostamy-Malekhalifeh, M. (2021). Undesirable factors in stochastic DEA cross efficiency evaluation: An application to thermal power plant energy efficiency. Economic Analysis and Policy, 69, 613–628.

15. Li, Y. (2020). Analyzing efficiencies of city commercial banks in China: An application of the bootstrapped DEA approach. Pacific-Basin Finance Journal, 62, 101372.

16. Li, Y., Liu, J., Ang, S., Yang, f. (2021). Performance evaluation of two-stage network structures with fixed-sum outputs: An application to the 2018 winter Olympic Games. Omega, 102, 102342.

17. Lin, R., Chen, Z. (2017). A directional distance based super-efficiency DEA model handling negative data. Journal of the operational Research Society, 68, 1312–1322.

18. Moradi-Motlagh, A., Emrouznejad, A. (2022). The origins and development of statistical approaches in non-parametric frontier models: A survey of the first two decades of scholarly literature (1998–2020). Annals of Operations Research, https://doi.org/10.1007/s10479-022-04659-7.

19. Olesen, O.B., Petersen, N.C. (2016). Stochastic Data Envelopment Analysis-A review. European Journal of Operational Research, 251(1), 2–21.
20. Oukil, A., Channouf, N., Al-Zaidi, A. (2016). Performance evaluation of the hotel industry in an emerging tourism destination: The case of Oman. Journal of Hospitality and Tourism Management, 29, 60–68.
21. Panzar, J.C., Willig, R.D. (1977). Economies of scale in multi-output production. Quarterly Journal of Economics, 91(3), 481–493.
22. Peykani, P., Mohammadi, E., Emrouznejad, A. (2021). An adjustable fuzzy chance constrained network DEA approach with application to ranking investment firms. Expert Systems with Applications, 166, 113938.
23. Peykani, P., Mohammadi, E., Emrouznejad, A., Pishvaee, M.S., Rostami-Malkhalifeh, M. (2019). Fuzzy data envelopment analysis: An adjustable approach. Expert Systems with Applications, 136, 439–452.
24. Podinovski, V. V. (2004). Bridging the gap between the constant and variable returns-to-scale models: Selective proportionality in data envelopment analysis. Journal of the Operational Research Society, 55, 265–276.
25. Podinovski, V. V. (2009). Production technologies based on combined proportionality assumptions. Journal of Productivity Analysis, 32, 21–26.
26. Podinovski, V. V., Ismail, I., Bouzdine-Chameeva, T., Wenjuan Zhang, W.J. (2014). Combining the assumptions of variable and constant returns to scale in the efficiency evaluation of secondary schools. European Journal of Operational Research, 239, 504–513.
27. Portela, M.C.A.S., Thanassoulis, E., Simpson, G. (2004). Negative data in DEA: A directional distance approach applied to bank branches. Journal of the Operational Research Society, 55(10), 1111–1121.
28. Seitz, W.D. (1970). The measurement of efficiency relative to a frontier production function. American Journal of Agricultural Economics, 52, 505–511.
29. Simar, L., Wilson, P.W. (1998). Sensitivity analysis of efficiency scores: How to bootstrap in nonparametric frontier models. Management Science, 44(1), 49–61.
30. Simar, L., Wilson, P.W. (2000). Statistical inference in nonparametric frontier models: The state of the art. Journal of Productivity Analysis, 13, 49–78.
31. Simar, L., Wilson, P.W. (2007). Estimation and inference in two-stage, semi-para-metric models of production processes. Journal of Economics, 136(1), 31–64.
32. Singh, S. (2018). Intuitionistic fuzzy DEA/AR and its application to flexible manufacturing systems. RAIRO—Operations Research, 52(1), 241–257.
33. Sueyoshi, T. (1999). DEA duality on returns to scale (RTS) in production and cost analyses: An occurrence of multiple solutions and differences between production-based and cost-based RTS estimates. Management Science, 45, 1593–1608.
34. Tavana, M., Izadikhah, M., Toloo, M., Roostaee, R. (2021). A new non-radial directional distance model for data envelopment analysis problems with negative and flexible measures. Omega, 102, 102355.

35. Tavassoli, M., Farzipoor Saen, R., Mohamadi Zanjirani, D. (2020). Assessing sustainability of suppliers: A novel stochastic-fuzzy DEA model. Sustainable Production and Consumption, 21, 78–91.
36. Wang, Q., Wu, Z., Chen, X. (2019). Decomposition weights and overall efficiency in a two-stage DEA model with shared resources. Computers & Industrial Engineering, 136, 135–148.
37. Yang, G.L., Rousseau, R., Yang, L.Y., Liu, W.B. (2014). A Study on directional returns to scale. Journal of Informetrics, 8, 628–641.
38. Yang, G.L. (2012). On relative efficiencies and directional returns to scale for research institutions. Ph.D thesis. University of Chinese Academy of Sciences, Beijing (in Chinese).
39. Yang, G.L., Liu, W.B. (2017). Estimating directional returns to scale in DEA. INFOR: Information Systems and Operational Research, 55(3), 243–273.
40. Yang, G.L., Ren, Khoveyni, M., Eslami, R. (2020). Directional congestion in the framework of data envelopment analysis. Journal of Management Science and Engineering, 5(1), 57–75.
41. Zhou, Y., Liu, W., Lv, X., Chen, X., Shen, M. (2019). Investigating interior driving factors and cross-industrial linkages of carbon emission efficiency in China's construction industry: Based on Super-SBM DEA and GVAR model. Journal of Cleaner Production, 241, 118322.
42. Zhou, Z., Sun, W., Xiao, H., Jin, Q., Liu, W. (2021). Stochastic leader-follower DEA models for two-stage systems. Journal of Management Science and Engineering, in press. https://doi.org/10.1016/j.jmse.2021.02.004.

Part III

Heuristic Search Optimisation

11

An Overview of Heuristics and Metaheuristics

Saïd Salhi and Jonathan Thompson

11.1 Introduction

We live in a world of limited resources, including food, water and energy. As society becomes more advanced, the need to make efficient use of these limited resources becomes more pressing. The study of optimisation enables many real-life problems to be solved and leads to many positive outcomes. For example scheduling the shift patterns of nurses can lead to optimal use of resources and shift patterns that are conducive to good staff wellbeing. The optimal routing of delivery trucks can lead to reduced carbon dioxide emissions. Optimal scheduling of jobs leads to efficient use of resources and increased profits for manufacturers.

There are many real-life applications that can be solved optimally by one of the exact optimisation techniques known to the Operational Research community such as linear programming, integer programming, non-linear programming and dynamic programming among others. However, there are

S. Salhi (✉)
Kent Business School, University of Kent, Canterbury, UK
e-mail: s.salhi@kent.ac.uk

J. Thompson
School of Mathematics, Cardiff University, Cardiff, UK
e-mail: thompsonjm1@cardiff.ac.uk

© The Author(s), under exclusive license to Springer Nature Switzerland AG 2022
S. Salhi and J. Boylan (eds.), *The Palgrave Handbook of Operations Research*,
https://doi.org/10.1007/978-3-030-96935-6_11

many applications where the combinatorial effect of the problem makes the determination of the optimal solution intractable, and hence, these standard techniques become unsuitable. This is because the computer time needed to find the optimal solution becomes too large to be practical for real-life situations, or specialist software is required that is not easily usable by many companies and organisations. To overcome this drawback, heuristic methods were introduced with the aim of providing the user with reasonably good solutions in a reasonable time. Heuristics can be likened to algorithms which are step-by-step procedures for producing solutions to a class of problems. In many practical situations they seem to be the only way to produce concrete results in a reasonable time. To date, heuristic search methods have been widely used in a large number of different areas including business, economics, sports, statistics, medicine and engineering.

The word 'heuristic' originates from the Greek word 'heuriskein' that means discover and explore. Heuristics are also sometimes referred to as rules of thumb. They have been used throughout history as humans are natural problem solvers and can naturally construct heuristic methods. An example given by Sorenson [101] is that when deciding the trajectory of a spear to throw at a wild animal, it is more important that the trajectory is selected quickly rather than optimally. The time spent to calculate the optimal trajectory will almost certainly mean the creature has disappeared long before the spear is thrown. Therefore a quick but not precise trajectory is superior. However the scientific study of heuristics began more recently and still continues to this day, with numerous academic papers each year proposing new heuristic methods for a wide variety of problems. Figure 11.1 shows the number of publications listed in Scopus with 'heuristic' as a keyword over the last 10 years and shows an increasing trend throughout the decade showing that advancements in computer software and hardware have not removed the need for heuristic solution methods.

The main goal in heuristic search is to construct a model that can be easily understood and that provides good solutions in a reasonable amount of computing time. A good insight into the problem that needs to be addressed is essential. Slight changes to the problem description can lead to major changes to the model being applied, for example a slight change to a problem that was easy to solve exactly may change the complexity of the problem and necessitate the use of a heuristic.

In this chapter we will provide a short introduction to optimisation and state the need for heuristics. Heuristics can be classified into various categories and we will consider improvement-only heuristics in Sect. 11.2, heuristics that accept worsening moves in Sect. 11.3, and population-based heuristics

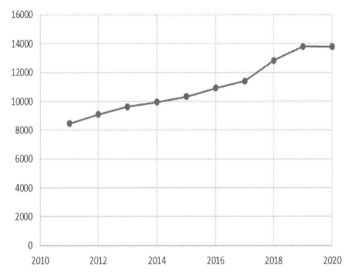

Fig. 11.1 The number of mentions of 'heuristics' on SCOPUS over the last 10 years

in Sect. 11.4. Some examples of applications will be provided in Sect. 11.5 and the chapter concludes with some suggestions for future research.

11.1.1 Optimisation Problems

An optimisation problem for the case of minimisation can be defined in the following form:

$P = $ Minimise $F(X)$

s.t.

$X \in S$

Here, $F(X)$ defines the cost or value of each solution X. When the set S is discrete, (P) falls into the category of discrete optimisation problems (also known as combinatorial optimisation), whereas if it is a continuous set, (P) is referred to as a continuous optimisation problem (also known as global optimisation).

11.1.1.1 Local vs Global Optimality

Consider $X \in S$ and let $N(X) \subset S$ be a given neighbourhood of X. $N(X)$ could be defined as being a set of solutions that are similar to X in some way. The decision of which neighbourhood to use in different applications is a vital one when applying an improvement heuristic.

$\widehat{X}$ is a **local minimum** (maximum) with respect to neighbourhood $N(X)$ if $F(\widehat{X}) \le (\ge)F(X)\forall X \in N(X)$. X^* is a **global minimum** (maximum) if $F(X^*) \le (\ge)F(X)\forall X \in S$. For instance, if Ω represents all the possible neighbourhoods and Λ the set of all local minima (maxima), X^* can also be defined as $X^* =$Arg Min$\{F(X); X \in \Omega(X)\}$ or $X^* =$Arg Min $\{F(\widehat{X}); \widehat{X} \in \Lambda\}$.

In brief, the global minimum (maximum) X^* is the local minimum (maximum) that yields the best solution value of the objective function F with respect to all neighbourhoods.

Local search is the mechanism (i.e. operator or transformation) by which $\widehat{X}$ is obtained from X in a given neighbourhood $N(X)$. In other words, $\widehat{X} =$Arg Min$\{F(X); X \in N(X)\}$ denotes choosing the best member of the neighbourhood.

11.1.1.2 Modelling Approach

When approaching complex real-life problems, a possible modelling approach is to follow the following four steps. Note that this ordered list is not exhaustive as other possibilities do exist.

The aim is to apply:

1. an exact method to the exact (true) problem, if not possible go to (2)
2. a heuristic method to the exact problem, if not possible go to (3)
3. an exact method to a modified (approximated) problem, if not possible go to (4)
4. a heuristic method to the approximated problem.

Though these rules are presented in the above ranking, the complexity in the design of the heuristic in step (2) which aims to retain the true characteristics of the problem, and the degree of modification of the problem in step (3) are both crucial points when dealing with practical problems. It may be argued that steps (2) and (3) could swap places. The idea is to keep the characteristics of the problem as close as possible to the true problem and then try to implement (1) or (2). Another related approach would be to start with a simplified or a relaxed version of (P), find a solution and check whether the solution satisfies the constraints to the original problem. If it is the case, there is no need to worry about the original problem as the solution is optimal. If some constraints are violated, which is likely to happen especially at the beginning of the search, additional characteristics are then introduced gradually. The process is repeated until the problem becomes impractical to solve and hence, the feasible solution found at the previous stage can then be used as the final solution of the problem. The choice of whether to use a heuristic method or to modify the problem into one that can be solved exactly is crucial. It appears that applying a heuristic is a straightforward approach and this concept is highlighted by the following observation that it is better to have a good and acceptable solution to a true problem rather than an optimal solution to a problem that has very little resemblance to the original problem.

11.1.2 The Need for Heuristics

Heuristics are usually used only when exact methods, which guarantee optimal solutions, are impractical because the computational effort required is excessive. They are often used to produce solutions to problems in the class NP-complete, a set of problems for which there are no known efficient ways to find optimal solutions to large problems. However solutions to problems in this category can be verified efficiently. The most well-known example is the Travelling Salesman Problem (TSP) which consists of finding the shortest route to visit a set of cities and return to the starting point. The TSP is a computationally difficult problem and an optimal solution to even a relatively small problem can be difficult to find, leading to the widespread use of heuristics. The decision of whether to use exact or heuristic solution methods also depends on the context of the problem and how much time is available to find a solution. Heuristics may also be used where the problem is ill-defined, or a solution of reasonable quality is all that is required. Salhi [87], [92], [93] provides further reasons for accepting and using heuristics.

11.1.3 Some Characteristics of Heuristics

The following characteristics are worth considering in the design of a given heuristic. Some are by-products of the attributes that make heuristic necessary as mentioned in the previous section, whereas others are added for generalisation purposes. For simplicity these characteristics are only summarised below while more details can be found in [63], [87], [92], [93], [48] among others.

Heuristics should be:

i. Simple and coherent—the method should follow well defined steps which are not ambiguous in any way.

ii. Effective and robust—the method should be reliable enough to provide good or near optimal solutions irrespective of the instances solved.
iii. Efficient—the run time needs to be acceptable. The solution time will depend to some extent on how the method is implemented.
iv. Flexible—so they can be easily adjusted to solve variants of the problem with minimum changes while retaining the strengths of the heuristic. This may include the flexibility to allow interaction with the user so they can take some control over the algorithm.

11.1.4   Performance of Heuristics

One difficulty with heuristics is measuring the quality of their performance, given they are typically used on problems for which the exact solution is unknown. The main criteria for evaluating the performance of a heuristic are the quality of the solutions provided and the computational effort, measured in terms of CPU time, the number of iterations or the number of function evaluations. Other criteria such as simplicity, flexibility, ease of control, interaction and friendliness can also be of interest, but are more difficult to measure precisely.

Solution Quality There are various ways in which the solution quality of a heuristic may be measured. These include:

* Comparison with lower or upper bounds, which is most useful when bounds are tight
* Benchmarking against optimal results for smaller problems where the optimal solutions are known
* A theoretical understanding of worst-case behaviour
* Comparison with other heuristic techniques

Many papers merely use the latter method for evaluating solution quality and this is fraught with danger, particularly where the authors of a particular heuristic have also implemented the other heuristic methods for the comparison. One positive step is that an increasing number of authors are making their code and results available for evaluation by others.

11.1.4.1   Computational Effort

Heuristics are also evaluated in terms of their computational effort. Computational effort is usually measured by how long a heuristic takes, and how much memory it uses. The former describes the computing time the method requires for a given instance whereas the latter measures the storage capacity needed when solving a given instance. Unfortunately, the latter is seldom discussed in the literature. It should be noted that the concept of large or small computer time should be relative to both the nature of the problem (whether it is strategic, tactical or operational) and the availability and quality of the computing resources. The time for interfaces is usually ignored in research though it can constitute an important part of the total computing time in practice. The importance of computing effort is directly related to the importance of the problem. So if the problem relates to short-term planning and needs to be solved several times a day, it is essential that the algorithm is quick, whereas if the problem is solved at a medium or at a strategic level (so once every month or year), the cpu time is less important, and more consideration can be given to the quality of the solution. So for example a supermarket routing delivery vehicles need a quicker solution than a university scheduling its examinations twice per year. It should be noted that for some strategic problems, users may require the need to investigate different options and scenarios in which case the heuristic would need to be run several times and therefore should not be too slow.

11.1.5 Heuristic Classification and Categorisation

There are several ways to classify heuristics. Heuristics can be greedy where solutions are constructed from scratch or improvement where an existing solution is improved over time. Other classifications take into account whether the heuristic is deterministic or stochastic, uses memory or is memory-less, and whether it considers one solution at a time or a population of solutions. Salhi [93] categorises heuristics into four groups, namely, (a) improving solutions only, (b) not necessarily improving solutions, (c) population-based and (d) hybridisation. The first two groups are completely disjoint, whereas the last two could interrelate with each other as well as with the first two. We discuss the first three of these in the next three sections. Hybridisation is discussed in the following chapter.

11.2 Improvement-Only Heuristics

In this section, we briefly discuss approaches that only allow improving moves. The simplest such method is a descent or hill-climbing method but more sophisticated improvement-only methods commonly used include

GRASP (Greedy Randomised Adaptive Search Procedure), multi-level, variable neighbourhood search, perturbation schemes, adaptive large neighbourhood search, iterated local search and guided local search. Some of these will be described below

11.2.1   Hill-Climbing Methods

The basic hill-climbing or descent method has two main components, the generation of an initial solution and the means of improving this solution. The initial solution is typically generated either randomly or using a simple constructive type heuristic that builds the solution piece by piece until the final solution is constructed. For example for the Travelling Salesperson Problem (TSP), the starting solution may be constructed by selecting the nearest unvisited city at each step. Different heuristics may be used instead, which may be more computationally expensive but could result in better quality starting solutions. For example for the TSP, the heuristic could insert an unvisited city into the partial tour in the position which causes the minimum increase in the tour distance. Typically these rules are myopic (short-sighted) so can lead to large increases in cost towards the end of the construction.

The initial solution is then subject to improvement. The process of improvement requires a cost function $F(s)$ which attributes a cost or value to each solution s, and a neighbourhood $N(s)$ that defines a set of solutions that can be reached from the current solution via a small change. For the TSP, the cost is the total length of the tour and the neighbourhood could be defined as the set of solutions constructed by deleting 2 edges from the current solution and then forming a new tour, or swapping the positions of two cities in the tour, etc. A selection mechanism also needs to be defined that determines which neighbouring solutions are sampled. The neighbourhood structures and the selection mechanism adopted are crucial elements that contribute considerably to the success of improving heuristics. The most commonly used selection strategies are (i) the best improving move where we evaluate all or a part of the neighbourhood and select the feasible move that yields the best cost, or (ii) the first improving move where we select the first feasible solution that is better than the current solution. Note that (i) may take longer as all moves have to be evaluated at each stage but do mean the heuristic ends in a locally optimal solution and the search can terminate as soon as none of the neighbouring solutions provides an improvement. In (ii) neighbouring solutions are sampled at random so the selection is much quicker and at first, it is often straightforward to find improving moves. However as the number of iterations increases, fewer moves result in improvements and the search can only estimate that a locally optimal solution has been reached. Such heuristics normally terminate when there have been a certain number of iterations N_{end} without improvement, and the value of this parameter N_{end} depends on the size of the problem/neighbourhood and is problem and instance dependent. In this case, the search may need to be repeated several times as different solutions may be produced depending on the random number stream used.

Algorithm 1 summarises the main features of (a) the best improving move and (b) the first improving move.

Algorithm 1: The Basic Descent method

(a) Best Improvement	(b) First Improvement
Select initial solution $s \in S$	Select initial solution $s \in S$
Repeat the following steps:	Set max_n = max number of consecutive
Find the best member $s' \in N(s)$	moves without improvement
If $f(s') < f(s)$ then	Set $n = 0$
Let $s = s'$	Repeat the following steps while $n < max_n$
Else	Choose s', a random member of $N(s)$
Terminate run	If $f(s') < f(s)$ then
	Let $s = s'$
	$n = 0$
	Else
	$n = n + 1$

It is also possible to employ a compromise strategy that sits between the best improvement and first improvement methods. This could be achieved in several ways, for example by selecting the best improving move found after a certain time has elapsed since the previous improvement.

These methods typically search a very small part of the solution space, and solution quality depends on the starting solution. Therefore they are of limited use but can provide quick improvements to solutions produced heuristically that may not be local optima.

11.2.2 Classical Multi-Start

The local search procedure is efficient when the objective function is unimodular (i.e. has one local minimum only). However, when there are several minima, it is impossible to get out of the neighbourhood of a local minimum

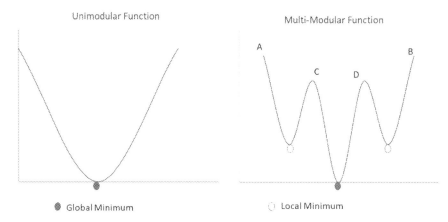

Fig. 11.2 Local optimality

using the same neighbourhood as shown in Fig. 11.2. In the second diagram representing a multi-modular function, if the search begins at position A or B, it converges to a poor quality local optimum whereas if it starts from position C or D, it converges to the global optimum. In practice for many combinatorial optimisation problems there are numerous local optima and the likelihood of finding a high-quality solution using a descent only strategy is quite small.

One way of improving the likelihood of finding a high-quality local optimum is to use a multi-start method where the search is repeated from different starting solutions to ensure a broader section of the solution space is searched. An example is Braysy et al. [8] who apply a multi-start local search method to the vehicle routing problem with time windows. They use a randomised constructive heuristic to generate a set of starting solutions and then apply local search to each. The best solution found is then subject to a further improvement process. In practice they construct 420 starting solutions but only apply the descent phase to solutions consisting of the minimum number of routes.

The basic multi-start method is summarised in Algorithm 2.

Algorithm 2: The multi-start method.

Step 1. Set $best_s = \infty$
Step 2. Repeat the following m times
    (2a) Create an initial solution s
    (2b) Perform a descent move to find a locally optimal solution s''
    (2c) If $f(s'') < best_s$ then set $best_s = f(s'')$

If starting solutions are created randomly, then multi-start methods are well suited to parallelisation which can improve solution quality. However the search can be considered to be blind as it may re-visit local optima that have already been considered. Therefore methods that deliberately create starting solutions that differ to previously visited solutions are more popular. For example for the TSP, a list of the frequency of edges being included in solutions can be maintained, and future starting solutions can be weighted towards selecting edges that have not been frequently selected previously.

11.2.3 Greedy Randomised Adaptive Search Procedure (GRASP)

GRASP is an extension of multi-start methods and was introduced by Feo and Resende [39]. A more formal description is given in Feo and Resende [40]. It is a multi-start heuristic which consists of two phases, the construction phase that constructs an initial solution and a local search phase that improves the initial solution. This is repeated several times. GRASP can be considered as a memory-less multi-start heuristic. GRASP differs from multi-start in the way the initial solution is generated as it combines randomness with greediness. The idea is that at each step of the construction phase a selection rule is used that is less rigid and allows flexibility in choosing not necessarily the best option but to choose any options that are close in some way to the best. Typically a restricted candidate list (RCL) is used made up of either the top k best options or those options that are within a certain deviation from the best. For instance, for the case of minimisation: RCL= {set of attributes e such that $g_{min} \leq g(e) \leq g_{min} + \alpha(g_{max} - g_{min})$} where $0 \leq \alpha \leq 1$ and g_e is the cost of incorporating element e into the solution. The element to be added to the partial solution e^* is then randomly chosen from the RCL. Note that if $\alpha = 0$ this reduces to a greedy method whereas if $\alpha = 1$ the search becomes the classical random multi-start approach. The basic GRASP is described in Algorithm 3.

Algorithm 3: The GRASP method.

Step 1. Set $best_s = \infty$
Step 2. Repeat the following m times
    (2a) Create an initial solution s using a greedy-randomised procedure and an RCL
    (2b) Perform a descent move to find a locally optimal solution s''
    (2c) If $f(s'') < best_s$ then set $best_s = f(s'')$

There are several possible variations to GRASP. For instance the choice of α does not need to be fixed beforehand but can be adjusted from one cycle to another depending on the solution quality found in previous solutions (this is known as reactive grasp). The definition of α can also be defined as a function of the gain/loss at a given iteration, or as a convex or a concave function dependent on the number of iterations. Path-relinking can be introduced which involves exploring the path between different locally optimal solutions to search for better solutions. Learning can also be introduced, either to guide the search towards new unexplored areas of the solution space or to maintain in future solutions attributes that appear to commonly occur in high-quality solutions. For examples see [46], [70] and [94].

11.2.4   Variable Neighbourhood Search (VNS)

Variable Neighbourhood Search (VNS) requires the definition of several neighbourhoods for the given problem. VNS attempts to escape local optima by moving to a new, usually larger, neighbourhood whenever there is no possible improvement through a local search in a given neighbourhood, and then reverts back to the first one, usually the smallest, if a better solution is found. VNS was originally developed by Mladenović and Hansen [75] for solving combinatorial and global optimisation problems. VNS contains mainly three phases, namely, a shaking phase (given a set of neighbourhood structures, a neighbouring solution is generated), an improvement phase (a local search or a local search engine is deployed to improve the currently perturbed solution) and finally a neighbourhood change phase (move or not move). VNS takes advantage of the fact that a local minimum with respect to a given neighbourhood may not be a local minimum for other neighbourhoods, but local optima for several different neighbourhoods are often close to each other. However, a global minimum is a local minimum for all neighbourhoods.

VNS starts from some starting solution x and local search is applied using an initial neighbourhood $N_1(x)$. The locally optimal solution found under the initial neighbourhood is then used as the starting solution for a local search under neighbourhood $N_2(x)$. If an improving move is identified, the search reverts to the first neighbourhood; otherwise the search moves onto neighbourhood $N_3(x)$ and so on. See Algorithm 4 for a description.

Algorithm 4: Variable Neighbourhhod Search (basic VNS).

Step 1.
    (1a) Set $best_s = \infty$
    (1b) Generate an initial solution s and define the neighbourhood structures
        $N_1, N_2, ..., N_{kmax}$
    (1c) Set $k = 1$
Step 2. Repeat until stopping criteria are satisfied
    (2a) Choose a solution s' in the neighbourhood $N_k(s)$ (shaking procedure)
    (2b) Perform a descent move (a local search or a series of local searches) to find a
locally optimal solution s''
    (2c) If $f(s'') < best_s$ then set $best_s = f(s'')$
    (2d) If $f(s'') < f(s)$ then   Move or not
        Set $s = s''$ and $k = 1$
    Else
        Set $k = k + 1$; If $k > kmax$, set $k = 1$

Compared to other powerful heuristics, VNS has the advantage of being simple and easy to implement as it requires only the definition of the neighbourhoods and the local search and there are no parameters to consider. A number of variants have been applied to different combinatorial problems with success. These include:

• Reduced VNS is useful for large problems where local search is too time-consuming and hence omitted from the search. In other words, this is mainly a VNS without the local search (i.e. the use of the shaking procedure and the move or not step) but allows to be used either in a systematic manner (reverting to the first neighbourhood, or to the next one, or a combination).
• VND, short for variable neighbourhood descent, is focused on the local search phase and the move or not move phase. Here the way the local search phase is implemented is critical. Usually there are a number of local searches used either in series or in a VNS type format like the multi-level heuristic described earlier.
• General VNS is a VNS where the local search phase is a VND.
• Skewed VNS explores areas of the solution space which can be far from the current solution by accepting non-improving solutions based on a certain threshold. In other words the move or not move phase is made slightly relaxed.

Note that in the improvement phase within the local search either a first improvement or a best improvement is adopted which can lead to several other variants. The move or not move step can also have several options such as sequential, cyclical or in a pruning way as defined in [49]. For more description on these and other variants, see [48], [49] and [93].

11.2.5   Iterated Local Search (ILS)

This consists of two main phases known as the construction/diversification phase and the local search phase. At each iteration the current solution is diversified, and then is subject to local search. These are performed repeatedly while an acceptance step is embedded to retain the best solution found so far. The aim is to ideally keep using the same local search as a black box while providing interesting solutions to it through diversification. This approach is simple and efficient and has shown to be powerful in obtaining interesting results in several combinatorial problems. One possible implementation of a strong ILS could be the combination of LNS (diversification/construction) with a VND or randomised VND (local search). For more details and possible applications of this heuristic, see [67].

11.2.6   A Multi-Level Composite Heuristic

Multi-level composite heuristics are similar to variable neighbourhood descent and involve improving the solution using a small number of local searches, known as refinement procedures in sequence, with the method stopping when there is no further improvement possible. The resulting solution should be a high-quality solution as it is a local minimum with respect to the selected procedures. The heuristic starts by finding a locally optimal solution using the first refinement procedure, and then this solution becomes a starting solution for a second refinement procedure, etc. In addition, once a new better solution is found, it can be used as an initial solution for any of the other refinements, not necessarily the next one in the list. For simplicity, we can restart the process using the first one which is the simplest refinement in our list of available refinements. This is the backbone of multi-level heuristics initially proposed in Salhi and Sari [90] for the multi-depot routing problem with a heterogeneous vehicle fleet. This approach has now been successfully applied to many other combinatorial and global optimisation problems. The choice of the refinement procedures, the sequence in which these are used and the choice of the refinement to go back to, once a new better solution is found, can be critical. Note that once a solution is found at a given level, it is appropriate to go to any of the other refinements of the earlier levels. A standard approach is to revert back to the first level where computations are relatively fast. More details on this approach can be found in [90], [96].

The way the levels are organised can have a significant effect on the solution quality and this requires careful consideration. The choice of successive refinements may be critical as one may wish to consider the next local search to be drastically different in structure to the previous one so as to provide diversity. The search does not necessarily have to return to the initial refinement once a solution is determined and the choice of the refinement to return to does not need to remain constant throughout the run. It may be that the obtained solution would be better suited to another refinement chosen randomly or based on certain rules that consider the structure of the current solution. It can be a challenging task to match the structure of a given solution with the characteristics of the set of refinements used. The integration of learning within the search could render this approach more adaptive and hence more powerful as demonstrated in [103], [104].

11.2.7 Problem Perturbation Heuristics

The idea of problem perturbation heuristics is to perturb the original problem to obtain a series of gradually perturbed problems. Local search is applied to the initial problem and a locally optimal solution is then obtained. The problem is then perturbed in some way and local search is applied again to this new problem leading to a different solution. It can be considered whether this new solution is a better solution to the original problem than the previously found local optimum.

The perturbed problem may be found by adding a violation that means the current local optimum is infeasible. As there is a well-defined perturbation built up between successive perturbed problems, the successive solutions may have the tendency of retaining some of the important attributes in their respective configurations. After a set of perturbed problems are found, the search may proceed by gradually relaxing the problem by removing the violations again, one by one. This continues until the problem returns to the initial problem again. At this stage a local search to improve the solution can be used again and then either the process starts adding violations again or making the original problem even less restricted by removing some of the constraints. This process can be repeated several times.

For instance, consider the p-median problem where the objective is to identify the optimal location of a fixed number of facilities (say p) with the aim of minimising the total transportation cost. A local search can be performed and a local optimum identified. Then, the solution is allowed purposely to become infeasible in terms of the number of facilities by accepting solutions with more than or less than p (say $p \pm q$ where $q \in [p/4, p/3]$). By solving the modified problems, infeasible solutions can be generated that when transformed into feasible ones may yield a cost improvement. Initially a feasible solution with p facilities is found, then one facility is added at a time and after each, a simple local search is activated. Once we reach $p + q$ facilities, we then start removing one facility at a time till we get to a feasible solution with p facilities where a more powerful local search is applied for intensification purposes to try to obtain a better local minimum. At this stage we also allow the solution to be infeasible by removing one facility at a time until we reach say $p - q$, from where we start adding facilities again until we reach a new feasible solution. This up and down trajectory makes up one full cycle. The process is then repeated until there is either no improvement after a certain number of cycles or the overall computing time is met. When this process is repeated several times going through several cycles, it acts as a filtering process where the most attractive depots will have the tendency to remain in the best configuration, which is a form of survival of the fittest. Such an approach was developed by Salhi [90] and it performed well when tested on a class of large facility location problems with known and unknown values of p. Zainuddin and Salhi [120] adapted this approach to solve the capacitated multisource Weber problem and Elshaikh et al. [38] modified it for the continuous p-centre problem.

A similar strategy is Strategic Oscillation where the search moves between the feasible and infeasible regions. Consider Fig. 11.3 which illustrates a solution space with a disconnected solution space. A search is performed in a

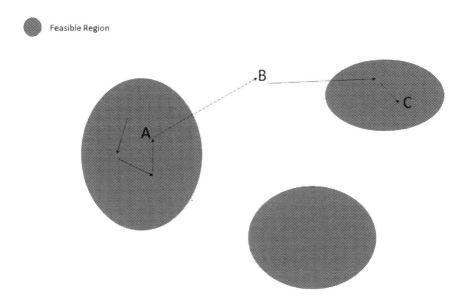

Fig. 11.3 Strategic oscillation to search a disconnected solution space

feasible region, ending in say point A but the constraints are then relaxed, enabling the search to move into the infeasible region (say point B). At this stage, the constraints are re-imposed and the local search is used to guide the search back towards a feasible region, point C in this case. In this way the search investigates a broader area of the solution space and is able to navigate between different parts of a disconnected solution space.

The amount of infeasibility allowed is dealt with by attaching penalties to broken constraints. These penalties are dynamically updated. This concept is useful particularly when the solution space is disconnected or non-convex as it is impossible to cross the infeasible region using only feasible solutions. The only difference with problem perturbation heuristics is that the latter is designed purposely to explore these infeasible solutions in a guided manner without any penalty attached so that some useful and promising attributes could then be identified.

11.2.8   Some Other Improving Only Methods

Large Neighbourhood Search (LNS): The idea is to use not necessarily small neighbourhoods but larger ones as well. The need for these large neighbourhoods is sometimes crucial to get out of local optimality as pointed out by Ahuja et al. [1]. This was proposed by Shaw [100] and can be seen to be similar to the 'ruin and recreate' procedure of Schrimpf et al. [98]. The idea is to perturb the solution configuration in an intelligent way by deleting some of the attributes of the solution using some removal strategies and then reintroducing them using some insertion strategies. This has similarities with perturbation methods described earlier except here the removal of many attributes is performed at the same time. Some of the considerations when implementing this method include the number of attributes to remove, the removal strategies adopted and the insertion or repair strategies used. The way these strategies are implemented and developed is critical to the success of the search. As the method is repeated several times some form of learning is worth exploring to efficiently guide the search. For instance [103], [104] introduced interesting new operators and successfully integrated LNS with VNS in an adaptive way. LNS is now becoming a useful tool to solve many complex combinatorial problems.

Random Noise: A related method that perturbs the problem space by introducing random noises to the data is the noising method developed by Charon and Hudry [13]. The idea is to solve the problem with the perturbed objective function values via a local search where at each iteration, or after a fixed number of iterations, the level of perturbation is reduced until it reaches zero and the problem reverts to the original one. The way the noise is introduced and how randomness is gradually reduced as the search progresses are two key factors that are critical to the success of the method. Relatively recent work by Charon and Hudry [14] explored the self-tuning of the parameters of such a method.

Guided Local Search: This is an adaptive local search which attempts to avoid local optimality and guide the search by using a modified objective function. This objective function contains the original objective and a penalty term which relates to the less attractive features of the configuration of a given local optimum. The local search used can be a simple improvement procedure or a powerful heuristic. In other words, at every locally optimal solution the feature which has a large utility value receives an increase in its unit penalty. For instance, in the case of the TSP, the edges can represent features of the tour and the largest edge of the obtained tour will have its penalty increased. Note that this type of penalty is related to the so-called 'bad' features and not to the amount of infeasibility as usually carried out in constrained optimisation. The way the features are selected and penalised plays an important part in the success of this approach. Voudouris and Tsang [112] provide an interesting review with an emphasis on how to implement this approach when addressing several combinatorial problems.

11.3   Not Necessarily Improving Heuristics

In this section, we discuss those popular heuristics that improve the solution by not necessarily restricting the next move to be an improving move. This enables the search to escape from local optima. However note that allowing such inferior solutions to be chosen needs to be controlled as the search may diverge to even worse solutions. Some of the well-established techniques that are based on this concept are covered here, and include simulated annealing, threshold accepting and tabu search. These methods have been around for many years and are still extremely popular, being used to solve both real-life and academic problems.

11.3.1   Simulated Annealing

The concept of simulated annealing (SA) is derived from statistical mechanics which investigates the behaviour of very large systems of interacting components such as atoms in a fluid in thermal equilibrium, at a finite temperature.

Metropolis et al. [74] studied the simulation of the annealing of solids. This work was built on by Kirkpatrick et al. [59] and later by Cerny [12] who considered how to apply a method based on simulated annealing to large combinatorial optimisation problems. In the context of an optimisation problem, the process of a body cooling is an analogy for a search algorithm seeking a good solution with the aim of approaching the global optimum. The energy function in our case will represent the objective function of the problem. The configuration of the system's particles becomes the solution configuration of the problem. The temperature acts as the control parameter. Cooling too fast resulting in defective crystal is analogous to a neighbour-hood search that yields a poor local optimum. Kirkpatrick et al. adopted these analogies for the context of combinatorial optimisation, to explicitly formu-late the algorithm that is now widely known as Simulated Annealing (SA). The way in which the temperature decreases is called the cooling schedule and the probability function used is that of Boltzmann's Law (see [74]) which is a negative exponential function. The reasoning behind this choice is that it has the tendency to choose more non-improving solutions initially but as the search progresses this random-based technique will have a smaller probability of selecting inferior solutions meaning the search converges to a high-quality local optimum. For more details see [37], [78], [34] and [33]. A simple implementation of SA is shown in Algorithm 5.

Algorithm 5: Basic Simulated Annealing Algorithm

Step 1. Choose an initial temperature T which is sufficiently high that many worsening
      moves are likely to be accepted.

Step 2. Create an initial solution s and evaluate its cost value $f(s)$. Set $best = s$

Step 3. Repeat the following n times.

    (3a) Choose a neighbouring solution s' and evaluate its cost function.
        If $f(s') \leq f(s)$, then set $s = s'$ as it is an improving or equivalent move.
        If $f(s') < f(best)$ set $best = s'$

    (3b) If $f(s') > f(s)$ then calculate $d = exp(-(f(s') - f(s))/T)$ and if a random
        number $r(0, 1) < d$, then accept the move and set $s = s'$. Otherwise reject.

Step 4. Reduce the temperature according to some cooling schedule.

Step 5. If the stopping criteria are not met, return to step 3,
      Otherwise, stop the search and return $best$.

A disadvantage of simulated annealing is that it is heavily dependent on parameters. These relate to the start and end value of the temperature, the means for reducing the temperature and the number of iterations at each temperature.

There are various methods for reducing the temperature (cooling). The most common is $T_{k+1} = \beta T_k, 0 < \beta < 1$ where the closer β is to 1, the better the solution quality will normally be but the run time will increase also. Other possible cooling methods include:

$T_{k+1} = T_k - t$ (t = constant) or $T_{k+1} = T_k - t_k$ where t_k is randomly chosen at each iteration k or $T_{k+1} = 1/t(1 + \beta t)$ [69], etc. Typical stopping criteria are a maximum number of iterations is reached, a time limit is attained or the temperature becomes sufficiently small that the likelihood of accepting any worsening moves is likely to be extremely small, so at this stage it is likely that a local optimum has been reached.

The value of the initial temperature (T_0) should be large enough to accept a large number of moves. Therefore an initial phase may be used where random moves are sampled and an appropriate value of the temperature parameter can be calculated to ensure that a given percentage of these moves would be accepted. However, if the value of T_0 is too large, most solutions will be initially accepted which can be a waste of time as the search is in effect performing a random walk. On the other hand, if the value is too small, too many non-improving solutions will be rejected and the method becomes a simple local search method. See [62] for details of some possible implementations, and see [93] for more details. The temperature T_k theoretically needs to be a non-increasing function of iteration k (e.g. $T_{k+1} = g(T_k) \leq T_k$). However it is possible to allow the temperature to remain constant or to increase marginally at a given iteration. One idea is to reset the temperature at higher values after getting stuck in a flat region, say if no improvement is found after a certain number of iterations (i.e. consecutive uphill rejections). The current solution is locally optimal and since the temperature is low, the SA algorithm becomes self-destructive as it restricts the acceptance of less attractive solutions. These non-improving moves are rejected with a probability of almost one. The following resets are commonly used based on the temperature when the best solution was found, say T_{best} and the last temperature reset T_R: $T_{k+1} = T_{\text{best}}$, or $\alpha T_{\text{best}} + (1 - \alpha)T_k$ or $\beta T_{\text{best}} + (1 - \beta)T_R$ (initially $T_R = T_{best}$), with α, $\beta \in [0, 1]$ representing the corresponding weight factors. Some of these resetting schemes are initially given by Connolly [16], [17] and successfully applied by Osman and Christofide [76] to solve the VRP.

One may argue that the update function using such a reset scheme violates the property of $g(T_k)$ as it should be theoretically a non-increasing function of k. This is true if $g(T_k)$ was optimally defined but not heuristically as derived here. Such a statement needs therefore to be relaxed and allowing such flexibility is appropriate. Another way of relaxing such an update would be to incorporate flexibility by allowing the temperature to increase relatively according to the change in the cost function, see [30] and [31]. If a number of worsening moves are accepted the temperature should be reduced whereas if few worsening moves are being accepted and it appears the search has become trapped in a specific part of the solution space, the temperature should be increased. For more information on SA, see [33].

11.3.2 Threshold-Accepting Heuristics

This heuristic is a simplified version of simulated annealing. It generally involves accepting all moves that fall below some threshold value which varies as the search progresses. This avoids the probabilistic effect of simulated annealing when selecting a non-improving move, as the acceptance decision is entirely deterministic. When implementing threshold acceptance, one again needs to define a starting solution, cost function and neighbourhood. Additionally, the value of the threshold needs to be selected as well as the method for updating it. If the threshold is too high, almost all moves will be accepted and the search will just perform a random walk. If the threshold is too low, no moves will be accepted. Dueck and Scheurer [35] were the first to propose the Threshold Acceptance heuristic formally and they presented empirical studies comparing the results against simulated annealing when solving the TSP. The results were encouraging and Threshold Acceptance has the advantage of requiring fewer parameters and being a simpler method. The method is shown in Algorithm 6.

Algorithm 6: Basic Threshold Accepting Algorithm.

Step 1. Choose an initial threshold value T
Step 2. Create an initial solution s and evaluate its cost value $f(s)$. Set $best = s$
Step 3. Repeat the following n times.
    (3a) Choose a neighbouring solution s' and evaluate its cost function.
    (3b) If $f(s') \leq f(s)$ or $f(s') \leq T$, then set $s = s'$
    (3c) If $f(s') < f(best)$ set $best = s'$
Step 4. Reduce the threshold value according to $T = T * \alpha$ where $\alpha < 1$.
Step 5. If the stopping criteria are not met, return to Step 3,
    Otherwise stop the search and return $best$.

An alternative is to record a list of the top non-improving solutions which can then be used to guide the threshold target (the size of such a list can be made constant or dynamically changing). This is similar to SA except that there is flexibility in accepting a non-improving solution deterministically through thresholding instead.

Threshold Acceptance has proved to be computationally efficient when tackling hard combinatorial problems especially routing-based problems (see [107] and [66]). For further references on TA and its implementation, see [52] and [64].

The following two simple but successful variants of TA have proved to be promising and hence are worth mentioning.

Record to record heuristic: This is developed by Dueck [36] where the threshold is based on the relative deviation from the best solution instead of the absolute deviation from the current solution. Therefore moves are accepted if they improve the current move or if the difference between the two costs is below some threshold value. This takes into account the fact that different problems may have very different magnitudes of costs which can be misleading if the classical TA is blindly implemented. Li et al. [66] adopted this approach for solving the heterogeneous vehicle routing problem.

List-based threshold accepting: This approach is developed by Tarantilis et al. [107] where instead of having a threshold value based on the objective function only, a list containing a number of the top solutions is used with its cardinality being the only parameter (M) that needs to be controlled which makes the search easier to implement. During the search, the list is reduced gradually by decreasing the value of M. The authors produced competitive results when testing this scheme on a class of routing problem with a heterogeneous vehicle fleet.

11.3.3 Tabu Search

This approach was proposed by Glover [43] and independently discussed by Hansen [47] as a meta-heuristic optimisation method. Tabu Search (TS) concepts are derived from artificial intelligence where the intelligent use of memory helps to exploit useful historical information. Tabu Search is a best acceptance method that escapes from local optima by accepting non-improving moves. However merely accepting worsening moves will lead to the search cycling between a small number of solutions. To avoid this, a tabu status is allocated to those attributes involved in recent moves. The search is not permitted to return to solutions with these attributes for a certain number of moves. Tabu Search (TS) shares with SA and TA the ability to accept non-improving moves and to escape from local optima.

An attribute of a solution is recorded rather than the entire solution as it is more efficient, but it can lead to solutions being classed as tabu even if they have not been visited before. Therefore an aspiration criterion is normally used which means that a tabu solution can still be accepted if its cost is better than the best solution found so far.

Tabu search can be considered as an aggressive method as it selects the next best move in a deterministic manner. It will converge quickly to a local optimum before starting to accept worsening moves unlike simulated annealing and threshold methods that may only find locally optimal solutions towards the end of the run. TS also takes into account past information of already found solutions to construct short and/or long-term memories. These memories are useful in guiding the search via diversification to explore other regions of the solution space, and intensification to intensify the search within the same vicinity of the current solution. TS, as other metaheuristics, has also the power of searching over non-feasible regions which, in some situations, can provide an efficient way for crossing the boundaries of feasibility. The general method is shown in Algorithm 7.

Algorithm 7: Basic Tabu Search Algorithm.

Step 1. Create an initial solution s and evaluate its cost value $f(s)$. Set $best = s$
Step 2. Repeat the following n times.
    (3a) If there exists a tabu solution s' in $N(s)$ for which $f(s') < f(best)$ then
        Set $s = s'$ and update Tabu list.
    (3b) Else
        Choose the best non-tabu solution s' in $N(s)$
        Set $s = s'$ and update Tabu list
    (3c) If $f(s) < f(best)$ then $best = s$.

A key question is how to define the right restriction or tabu status. For instance in routing, if the best move was to exchange customer i from route R_k with customer j from route R_s, a very restrictive approach would be to say that both customers cannot be allowed to go back to their original routes, respectively, for a certain number of iterations, a tight restriction would be that either customer i or j is not allowed to go back to its original route but one could return, and a less tight restriction would be that both customers are able to go back to their original routes but cannot be allowed to be inserted between their original predecessors and successors.

The time that a solution remains tabu must also be selected. Small values may increase the risk of cycling whereas large values, on the other hand, may overconstrain the search. Additionally a larger tabu list (size $|Ts|$) can be more computationally demanding. The ideal value may be difficult to decide, and will vary from problem to problem and even instance to instance. It can be defined dynamically so that it updates according to observations made as the search progresses. It can periodically change between a set of values generated randomly within a fixed range at each iteration. This is known as robust tabu as it provides a more flexible approach. Another scheme is to have a rule that the size of the tabu list switches between the two extreme values. This implementation was found to be successful when adopted by Drezner and Salhi [34] for the one-way network design problem. Finally $|T_s|$ can be dependent on the change in the cost function for that selected move. For instance for the p-median problem, a functional setting was successfully adopted by Salhi [88].

The construction of such functions is seldom attempted in the literature as it is challenging but it is an interesting idea as it incorporates both learning and problem characteristics in an integrated way.

The size of the tabu list can also be updated dynamically by increasing or decreasing its value as the search progresses. For example, $|T_s|$ could be increased according to ($|T_s| = (1 + \beta|T_s|)$) with $\beta = 0.1$ or decreased by setting $\beta = -0.1$ depending on the number of repetitions, their risk of collision, etc. Collision is usually identified through hashing functions or other forms of identification. This is originally proposed by Battiti and Tecchiolli [4] who named this variant as reactive TS (RTS). This approach is adopted by several researchers including Wassan [115] who successfully addressed a class of routing problems, namely, the vehicle routing with backhauls problem.

The level for which the aspiration level overrides the tabu status is crucial in the search as it defines the degree of flexibility of the method. The most common method as mentioned above is to relax the tabu restriction if a solution produces a better result than the currently best-known solution. This is obviously correct as the search would be missing out on the opportunity to identify a new best solution. Another consideration that arises in some circumstances is what will happen if all of the solutions are either tabu or non-improving solutions. Is it appropriate to look for the first non-tabu solution down the list or to choose one from those tabu top solutions? The elements which will constitute the decision need to include the tabu status of the attribute for that solution, the objective function value (or the change in the objective function) and other factors such as frequency of occurrence during a certain number of iterations and so on. One possible attempt is to use the scheme developed by Salhi [88] who introduced a softer aspiration level which is based on the concept of criticality in the tabu status.

Most tabu search implementations include a Diversification step with the aim of guiding the search to new, different parts of the solution space. Diversification moves use some form of perturbation (jumps) to explore new regions. It uses long-term memory to guide the search out of regions which appears to be either less promising according to the results provided from the short-term memory, or have not been explored previously. The use of diversification is nowadays embedded into most metaheuristics either as a post optimisation step or as a perturbation step as in large neighbourhood search.

Alternatively intensification can be used which stimulates moves to go to a nearby state (neighbourhood) that looks myopically good. This uses short-term memory as it observes the attributes of all performed moves. This is usually achieved by a local search or a series of local searches where the focus of the search is on promising regions of the solution space. In brief, intensification is aimed at detecting good solutions and performing a deeper exploration.

An important question is how to decide when it is better to carry out an intensification and when it is time to perturb the solution and activate diversification. What is the right balance between intensification and diversification? None of these questions are straightforward as these are related to the problem characteristics, the power of the local search used and the type of perturbation the overall search is adopting.

11.4 Population-Based Heuristics

In this section, we present those methods that generate a set of solutions from one iteration to the next instead of only one solution at a time. We give an overview of the most commonly used approaches in this class which include genetic algorithms, ant systems, bees algorithm and particle swarms. For completeness, we also briefly mention other ones such as path relinking, scatter search, harmony search, heuristic cross-entropy, artificial immune systems and the psycho-clonal algorithm.

11.4.1 Genetic Algorithms

Genetic algorithms (GAs) were initiated to mimic some of the processes observed in natural and biological evolution. This approach was initially developed by John Holland and his associates at the University of Michigan in the 1970s. The method was formally introduced for the context of solving general optimisation problems by Holland [50] and Goldberg [45].

In brief, GA is an adaptive heuristic search method based on population genetics. A GA consists of a population of chromosomes (set of solutions) that evolve over a number of generations (iterations) and are subject to genetic operators (transformations) at each generation. The initial population is typically generated at random and a fitness function is defined to measure the quality of each solution. Parent solutions are chosen from the population, typically with a bias towards selecting high-quality solutions. A crossover operator is defined to combine attributes of the parent solutions to create offspring, and then mutations are used to add random variation to the child solutions. The population is updated according to some rules which usually ensures that better solutions have more chance of surviving into the next generation. The process continues for many generations.

A key decision is the chromosome representation of a solution which may involve a binary, permutation, integer or continuous encoding depending on the nature of the problem. For example for the p-median problem where there are n possible sites for p facilities, a binary representation of length n can be used where position $i = 1$ means the site is used and $i = 0$ means it is not. A permutation representation is more suitable for the TSP where the chromosome can consist of a string of integers listing the cities in the order in which they should be visited. An integer representation may be suited to scheduling problems where the value in position i represents the time job i should start. Thought needs to be given to select the right representation as this can either facilitate or hinder the chromosomes' transformation that will be generated via the crossover and mutation operators.

Crossover operators should ensure that children inherit characteristics of the parent solutions. For binary and integer representations possible crossover operators include 1-point, 2-point and uniform which are illustrated in Fig. 11.4. For 1-point crossover, a random cut point is chosen and the child solutions are made up of the elements before the cut point from one parent, and the elements after the cut point from the other parent. For 2-point crossover, 2 random cut points are selected. The child solutions are made up of the elements before the first cut point and after the second cut point from one parent and the elements between the two cut points from the other parent. Uniform crossover selects each element of the child solutions randomly from either parent. For permutation representations, 1-point crossover is not appropriate as it causes infeasible children due to repeated and missing values. Alternatives for permutation representations include partially mapped crossover and order crossover, which are illustrated in Fig. 11.5. For partially mapped crossover, two random cut points are chosen and mapping systems relate the elements between the cut points. In the example shown the

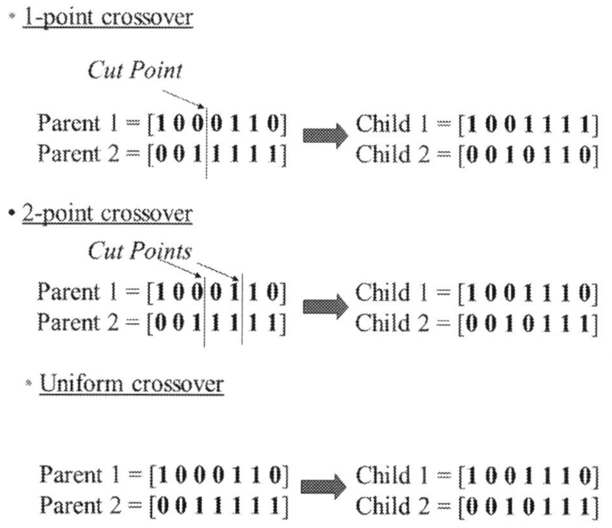

* 1-point crossover

Cut Point

Parent 1 = [1 0 0|0 1 1 0] ⟹ Child 1 = [1 0 0 1 1 1 1]
Parent 2 = [0 0 1|1 1 1 1]   Child 2 = [0 0 1 0 1 1 0]

• 2-point crossover

Cut Points

Parent 1 = [1 0 0|0 1|1 0] ⟹ Child 1 = [1 0 0 1 1 1 0]
Parent 2 = [0 0 1|1 1|1 1]   Child 2 = [0 0 1 0 1 1 1]

* Uniform crossover

Parent 1 = [1 0 0 0 1 1 0] ⟹ Child 1 = [1 0 0 1 1 1 0]
Parent 2 = [0 0 1 1 1 1 1]   Child 2 = [0 0 1 0 1 1 1]

Fig. 11.4 Crossover for binary and integer representations

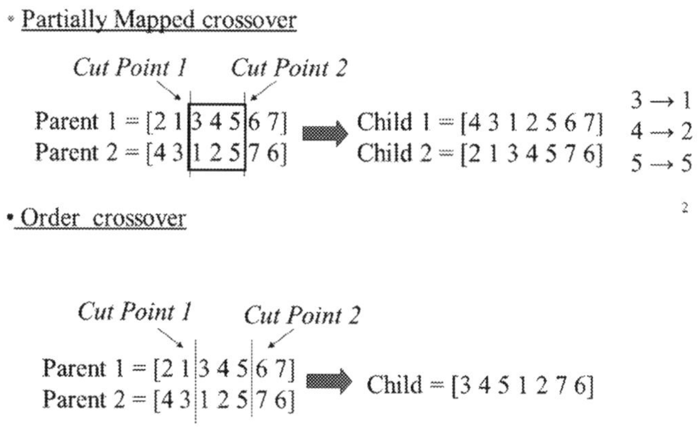

* Partially Mapped crossover

Cut Point 1   Cut Point 2

Parent 1 = [2 1|3 4 5|6 7] ⟹ Child 1 = [4 3 1 2 5 6 7]   3 → 1
Parent 2 = [4 3|1 2 5|7 6]   Child 2 = [2 1 3 4 5 7 6]   4 → 2
                                                              5 → 5

• Order crossover

Cut Point 1   Cut Point 2

Parent 1 = [2 1|3 4 5|6 7] ⟹ Child = [3 4 5 1 2 7 6]
Parent 2 = [4 3|1 2 5|7 6]

Fig. 11.5 Crossover for permutation representations

mapping systems are [3, 1], [4, 2], [5, 5]. These values are swapped and the remaining values are added if they do not cause any conflict. So for Child 1 for example, 6 and 7 can be added in their positions in Parent 1 but 2 and 1 cannot as they are already present in the child solution. Therefore 2 and 1 are replaced according to the mapping systems by 4 and 3, respectively. For the order crossover, two random cut points are chosen. The child solution is made up of the values between the two cut points in the first parent, and the remaining values are added in the order they appear in the second parent.

Mutation operators may flip a binary value $(0- > 1$ or $1- > 0)$, replace the value in an integer representation or swap values in a permutation representation. A mutation rate λ is typically defined, normally in the range $[0.01, 0.1]$ and then a value is subject to mutation if a random value between 0 and 1 is less than λ.

Other decisions that must be made when using a genetic algorithm include which solutions should be chosen as parents. A commonly used selection scheme is the tournament selection where a subset of the population is chosen randomly and the best of these are selected as parents based on their fitness values (i.e, $f(.)$). There are several other ways to select a chromosome k from population P. Roulette wheel selection is commonly used, where the probability of selecting chromosome k is $\text{Prob}(k) = f(k)/\sum_{r \in P} f(r)$. This simple rule seems to suffer where the population contains some outstanding individuals as these tend to be chosen with a high probability and can lead to premature convergence. However if the population contains solutions that are equally fit, then there is insufficient selection pressure. Other selection rules are based on linear ranking, power and exponential ranking, among others. One interesting approach would be to sort the chromosomes according to their fitness, then construct in addition to the top chromosome, three groups consisting of good, not so good and mediocre or bad chromosomes with respective sizes n_1, n_2 and n_3, respectively. The weights of the three respective groups at generation t say $\alpha_1(t) > \alpha_2(t) > \alpha_3(t) > 0$ with $\sum_{j=1}^{3} \alpha_j(t) = 1$ can be defined. We can also assume that the first weight $\alpha_1(t)$ is a non-decreasing function of t with $\lim_{t \to \infty} \alpha(t) \to 1$ while the other weights converge towards zero. Using the roulette wheel, the group will be selected based on these weights and then a chromosome within that group is chosen randomly for crossover or mutation, etc.

It is also important to provide diversity and hence an opportunity for improvement is possible through some form of migration. In a GA, a small number of completely new chromosomes which are generated either randomly or constructed can be injected into the population to provide diversity from time to time. The number of injected chromosomes and when the injection takes place are issues that deserve careful investigation. Usually the injection starts being active once the GA shows some form of stagnation and then from that point onward injection is activated periodically or adaptively depending on the behaviour of the overall results.

Figure 11.6 illustrates the new combined generation scheme which includes both the flexible reproduction and the effect of immigration which

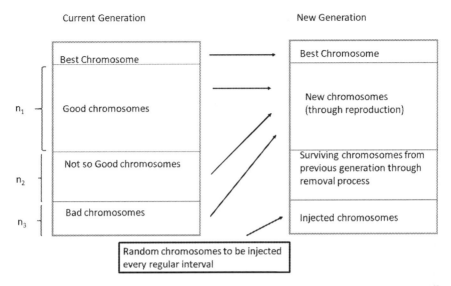

Fig. 11.6 Injection of chromosomes and new generation composition (adapted from [93])

was successfully explored by Salhi and Gama [91], and Salhi and Petch [86] for a class of location and routing problems, respectively. More details can also be found in the recent book on heuristic search in [93].

GAs are powerful at exploring the wider space by identifying promising regions, but lack the fine mechanisms to pinpoint the exact local minima (maxima) that may be required. Therefore many Genetic Algorithms in literature are actually Memetic Algorithms, which are hybrids of GAs and local search. The initial population is produced but is then subject to local search so the population consists of a set of local optima. The algorithm continues as normal but each child that is produced is also subject to descent. In this way, better solutions may be produced but at a cost of additional computational time.

11.4.2 Ant Colony Optimisation

Ant Colony Optimisation (ACO) is a meta-heuristic inspired by the observation of the behaviour of real-life ant colonies, in particular the way in which real ants find the shortest path between food sources and their nest. Ants create paths from the nest to their food and leave pheromone trails which influence the decisions of other ants as to which path to take. The effect of this is the pheromone trail will build up at a faster rate on the shorter paths.

This will influence more ants to follow the shorter paths due to the fact that the ants prefer to follow a path with a higher pheromone concentration. As a greater number of ants choose the shorter path, this in turn causes a greater level of pheromone and hence encourages more ants to follow the shorter path. In time, all ants will have the tendency to choose the shorter path. In other words, the greater the concentration of the pheromone on the ground, the higher the probability that an ant will choose that path. Good quality solutions are developed as a result of this collective behaviour of the ants. For more information see [21].

This real-life behaviour of ants has been adapted to solve combinatorial optimisation problems, as initially proposed by Dorigo et al. [29]. Ant system algorithms employ a set of agents, known as ants, who search in parallel for good solutions using a form of indirect communication. The artificial ants co-operate via the artificial pheromone level deposited on arcs which is calculated as a function of the quality of the solution found. The amount of pheromone an ant deposits is proportional to the quality of the solution generated by that ant helping direct the search towards good solutions. The artificial ants construct solutions iteratively by adding a new node to a partial solution exploiting information gained from past performance using both pheromone levels and a greedy heuristic. A local search could also be introduced to improve the solutions. Once that is completed, a global updating of the pheromone trail levels is activated to reinforce the best solutions by adding an extra amount of pheromone to those arcs of the best solutions. This amount can be based on the length of the best tour as well as the number of ants that produced that best tour.

A variant of ACO named Ant System (AS) was initially proposed by Colorni et al. [15] to solve the travelling salesman problem. The algorithm is illustrated in Algorithm 8. Assume the TSP contains n cities and distance matrix $d(i, j)$ defines the distance between each pair of cities (i, j).

Algorithm 8: Basic Ant System Algorithm.

Step 1. Initialise the placement of M ants and their respective pheromone trail matrix $\tau(i,j)$ to a constant value c where $c > 0$.

Step 2. While none of the stopping criteria witin the inner loop is met, for each ant $(k = 1,\ldots,M)$ perform the following steps:

(2a) Form the complete solution configuration by keep selecting the next customer to visit probabilitistically using the formula:

$\tau(i,j)^{\alpha} * \eta(i,j)^{\beta} / \sum_k \tau(i,k)^{\alpha} * \eta(i,k)^{\beta}$ where η_{ij} is known as the visibility and is the greedy cost of going to unvisited city j from current city i to the tour and equals $1/d(i,j)$. α and β are the respective weights on the trail and the visibility.

(2b) Apply a local search if needed (this can be optional, applied once in a while or adaptively using a learning scheme)

(2c) Record the objective function value for each ant $(L_k, k = 1,\ldots,M)$.

(2d) Use the local update of the trail matrix according to the formula

$\tau(i,k) = (1-\rho)\tau(i,k) + \sum_{k=1}^{n} \Delta\tau^k(i,k)$ where the amount of trail added by ant k, $\Delta\tau^k(i,j) = Q/L_k$ for each path (i,j) included in solution k with Q and ρ being the correction and the evaporation factors respectively.

Step 3. If the stopping criteria for the outer loop is met then stop, otherwise

(3a) Apply the global updating of the pheromone trail by adding a constant $\gamma > 0$ to those arcs that belong to the best solution configurations. For example, $\gamma = N_{best} \ltimes L_{best}$ where N_{best} represents the number of ants that produced the best

objective function value L_{best}.

(3b) Return to Step 2.

Colorni et al. also evaluated a trail update rule which add a constant value to the trail which is independent of the total distance of the tour. This made little difference to solution quality. They also showed that it was better to update the trail matrix after the entire tour had been produced rather than after each construction step.

In addition, an elitism strategy that provides a strong reinforcement to the tour corresponding to the global best solution may be used. Arcs belonging to the global best tour have their pheromone increased by a quantity that favour the number of ants that produce the best tour and the length of the global best tour. The consequence of the global updating rule is that arcs belonging to short tours and arcs which have been used frequently are favoured by receiving a greater amount of pheromone. Dorigo and Gambardella [27] proposed updating the pheromone based only on the global best-found solution. Stutzle and Hoos [102] introduced other variants such as the Max-Min ant system, known as MMAS. Their method is similar to AS using the same state transition rule in the selection process with some modifications, the main one is to restrict the pheromone trail values to be in a certain interval $[\tau_{\min}, \tau_{\max}]$. The aim is to reduce the risk of stagnation and make sure that certain choices do not become either dominant with high trail values, or have such small trail values that the probability of them being selected is approximately zero. It should be noted that although the idea of introducing restrictions on the trail values is interesting as it avoids stagnation and provides a chance for less visited solutions to exist, the choice of these additional parameters τ_{min} and τ_{max} need to be made appropriately. ACO already has many parameters including the parameters α and β that balance the emphasis on trail and visibility, the number of ants, the number of cycles and the evaporation rate.

Bullnheimer et al. [9] introduced another modification to AS by ranking the ants according to their tour length, and using the ranking to weight the amount of pheromone each ant contributes. Wade and Salhi [113] investigated the use of ACO in a class of VRP by incorporating a visibility factor based on the remaining load in the selection rule, the frequency of occurrence of a given arc in the local updating rule and both elitism and ranking are combined to yield a compromise global updating rule. For more information, references and applications on ant systems in general, the review paper [28] and the book [93] can be useful references.

11.4.3   The Bee Algorithm

This optimisation algorithm is inspired by the behaviour of swarms of honey bees when searching for their food. It shares some similarities with the way the ants behave. The best example of individual insects to resolve complex tasks is by the collection and processing of nectar. Each bee finds sources of the nectar by following another bee which has already discovered a patch of flowers. Once the bee returns to the hive with some food, the bee can either abandon the food source and then becomes again an uncommitted follower, continue to forage at the food source without recruiting new bees, or recruit more bees and return to the food source.

The basic bee algorithm, originally developed for continuous optimisation problems, can be found in [81]. In brief, the bees are first assigned to some chosen sites with the idea that those sites that attract more bees are considered more promising. This is repeated several times till a certain stopping criterion is met. The way a site is considered attractive is the most important point. This is measured by the fitness function of each bee at that site where the top sites will receive more bees either in an equal number or proportionally to their fitness.

Another popular and related bee algorithm is the Artificial Bee Colony (ABC) algorithm proposed by Karaboga [56]. The ABC algorithm is inspired by the intelligent foraging behaviour of a swarm of honeybees. The foraging bees are classified into three categories: employed, onlookers and scouts. All bees that are currently exploiting a food source are classified as employed and they provide information to the waiting bees (onlooker bees) in the hive about the quality of the food source sites which they are exploiting. Onlooker bees wait in the hive and decide on a food source to further exploit based on the information shared by the employed bees. Scouts search the neighbouring areas to find a new food source. Scout bees can be visualised as performing the job of exploration or diversification, whereas employed and onlooker bees can be considered as performing the job of exploitation or intensification.

The ABC algorithm is an iterative algorithm that starts by assigning all employed bees to randomly generated food sources (solutions). At each iteration, every employed bee determines a food source in the neighbourhood of its currently associated food source and evaluates its nectar amount (fitness). If the new fitness value is better than the previous one then that employed bee moves to this new food source, otherwise it retains its old food source. When all employed bees have finished this process, the bees share the nectar information of the food sources with the onlookers, each of whom selects a food source according to the food quality. This scheme means that good food sources will attract more onlookers than those of poorer quality. After all onlookers have selected their food sources, each of them determines a food source in its neighbourhood and computes its fitness. If an onlooker finds a better fitness value, it changed the employed food source with this new information. However, if a solution represented by a particular food source does not improve for a predetermined number of iterations then that food source is abandoned by its associated employed bee which becomes a scout (i.e. it will search for a new food source randomly). The whole process is repeated until the termination condition is met. The method is shown in Algorithm 9.

Algorithm 9: Basic Bee Colony Algorithm.

Step 1. Perform the following

    (1a) Initialise the number of bees B and construct B solutions at random. These are the initial food sources (X_i, $i = 1, \ldots, B$). Evaluate the fitness of each, say $F(X_i)$.

    (1b) Initialise T_{max} as the maximum number of iterations and L_{max} as the maximum number of successive iterations without improvement.

    (1c) Set the number of successive iterations without improvement = 0 for all bees i.e. $L_i = 0 \forall i = 1, ..B$ and set the neighbours of X_i, say $S_i = N(X_i) = \emptyset$.

Step 2. Repeat the following until the stopping conditions are met

    (2a) For each food source, X_i, find $X_i' \in N(X_i)$.

    If $F(X_i') < F(X_i)$ set $X_i = X_i'$ and $L_i = 0$. Otherwise let $L_i = L_i + 1$

    (2b) For each onlooker, choose a food source X_i randomly; find $X_i' \in N(X_i)$ and set $S_i = S_i \cup X_i'$

    (2c) For each food source X_i and $S_i \neq \emptyset$, find the member of S_i with the lowest cost = X_i'.

    If $F(X_i') < F(X_i)$ then set $X_i = X_i'$ and $L_i = 0$, else set $L_i = L_i + 1$

    (2d) For each food source i, if $L_i = L_{max}$, then select a random move i.e., select $X_i' \in N(X_i)$ and set $X_i = X_i'$. Set $L_i = 0$.

The main steps of the ABC algorithm can be found in Szeto et al. [105] where efficient implementations are presented for solving the vehicle routing problem.

11.4.4 Particle Swarm Optimisation (PSO)

This is a further meta-heuristic method based on the social behaviour of animals, in this case birds or fish. This evolutionary stochastic heuristic is introduced by Kennedy and Eberhat [58] where a population of individuals which searches a region of solutions that is recognised as promising is called a swarm and individual solutions are referred to as particles. It is interesting to stress the similarities which exist in the classical non-linear numerical optimisation techniques where the next point is based on the previous point and the displacement. In other words, the new point at iteration $(k + 1)$ lies along the direction S_k from the previous point X^k with an optimal step size λ_k (i.e. $X^{k+1} = X^k + \lambda_k S_k$). In these numerical optimisation methods the aim is to design a suitable direction and then to derive optimally or numerically the value of the step size. See for instance the classical textbook in numerical optimisation by Fletcher [41] for further information. Here, a particle i (at position p_i) is flown with a velocity V_i through the search space, but retains in memory its best position $(\overrightarrow{p_i})$. In the global PSO each particle, through communication, is aware of the best position of the particles of the swarm $(\overrightarrow{p_g})$. At a given iteration k, the position of the ith particle ($i = 1, ..., n$) is updated as follows $X_{ik} = X_i(k - 1) + V_i^k$. The velocity (or displacement) is defined as a linear combination of three velocities, namely, (i) the velocity at the previous iteration, (ii) the velocity with respect to the best position of this particle up to this iteration and (iii) the velocity with respect to the global best position of all particles up to this iteration.

PSO has been found to be suitable for solving combinatorial optimisation and especially unconstrained global optimisation problems. As the swarm may become stagnated (early convergence) after a certain number of iterations, a form of diversification or perturbation is often recommended. One way would be to introduce a simple chaotic perturbation that adds diversity to the system and avoids the search from getting stuck.

11.4.5   A Brief Summary of Other Population-Based Approaches

In this subsection, other population-based metaheuristics are briefly described in turn.

Cross-Entropy Based Algorithms (CE): This is an iterative population-based method made up of two steps that are applied in sequence until a stopping criterion is met. These steps are (i) the generation of feasible solutions pseudo-randomly based on a probability distribution representing the frequency of the occurrence of the attributes of a given solution, and (ii) the distribution is then updated. The idea is that this adaptive technique will have the tendency to estimate and learn better probabilities and hence generate better solutions. CE was initially presented by Rubinstein [84] for estimating rare events (financial risk, false alarms, etc) and then Rubinstein and Kroese [85] gave a formal description of this approach and presented its uses in solving combinatorial optimisation problems.

Scatter Search (SS): This is proposed by Glover et al. [44] with the aim of constructing new solutions by combining parts of existing solutions. This method can be considered as one of the earliest steps towards deep learning which is discussed in the next chapter. The idea is to generate a large number of diverse trial solutions which are then improved. The set of these solutions needs to be of high quality while being diverse. A subset of these solutions are classed as the reference solutions; these are typically the best ones but some additional solutions may be included to increase the diversity of the reference set. It could for example consist of 10% of the entire solution set. New solutions are constructed from the solutions in the reference set and these are then improved. Any new solutions that outperform solutions in the reference set are added to it. The process continues until the reference set no longer improves. The main steps of the SS can be found in Marti et al. [72].

Harmony Search (HS): This was originally proposed by Geem et al. [42] to imitate the success of music players in their improvisation when searching for a music harmony that is pleasing to the ear. Such a harmony is made up of a combination of sounds at certain pitches played by different instruments. The aim of the musician is to identify the best pitch for each sound so that when combined they make an excellent harmonious noise. The analogy with optimisation can be seen as follows: A given harmony relates to a given solution configuration, the sounds of the instruments represent the decision variables, their respective pitches are the values of the decision variables, and the quality of the harmony is the objective function value. Each practice by the musician(s) represents the iteration or the generation number. At each practice the musician tries to identify new pitches based on the ones he/she remembers to be of good quality, known as the HS memory, while introducing some extra changes to create a new harmony. This process is repeated until the best harmony already discovered can no longer be improved. HS is a population-based approach where the memory contains the pool of harmonies, similar to the population of chromosomes in GA. However the way the attributes of a new harmony (new solution) are constructed does not depend on two parents only as in GA but on all previously found harmonies. The obtained solution (harmony) is then adjusted for possible improvement with a certain probability. HS relies on its parameter values that are set at the outset. The first attempt to enhance HS was made by Mahdavi et al. [71] followed by a further enhancement by Pan et al. [80].

Artificial Immune Systems (AIS): The immune system's aim is to defend us against diseases and infections. It recognises antigens using immune cells which are known as B-cells whose jobs are to circulate through the blood continuously watching and waiting to encounter antigens (foreign molecules of the pathogens). Each antigen has a particular shape that can be recognised by the receptor of the B cell. AIS is a fast emerging method in some applied areas of computer science such as data analysis and data mining, pattern recognition and has now been adapted to the area of optimisation. In other words, when a pathogen invades the organism it was observed that a number of immune cells which recognise the pathogen will reproduce in large numbers, known as clones. This process is known as reinforcement learning. The clones are then diversified using two methods: (i) a high mutation rate (known as hyper-mutation) which is performed by introducing random changes, and (ii) receptor editing which aims to remove the less attractive antibodies (poor solutions) and replaced them with new ones. In this way, those cells that bind with their antigens are multiplied whereas the others are eliminated following the survival of the fittest. In addition, some of the successful ones are also kept in memory to face future similar invaders. This concept is similar to the intensification of the search in promising regions whereas the hyper-mutation acts as a diversification strategy. In brief, AIS shares some similarities with GA with the exception that there is no crossover but just a hyper-mutation.

Psycho-Clonal Algorithm: This meta-heuristic was initially developed by Tiwari et al. [110] and it is based on the artificial immune system (AIS) as discussed earlier (mainly based on the clonal selection) and the theory of the hierarchy of social needs as proposed by Maslow [73]. This hierarchy is composed of five levels where the lowest level A refers to the physiological needs (each antibody represents a solution), level B refers to safety needs (the evaluation of the objective function), level C refers to the social needs (the best solutions are selected and cloned proportionally to their objective function value), level D refers to the growth needs (diversification used to generate new solutions via hyper-mutation) and finally the highest level E refers to the self-actualisation needs (the best solutions are chosen to be part of the new population including the injection of new ones). This approach can be considered as a mixture of AIS and guided GA where the management of the population is maintained in a guided way based on the quality of cloning whereas diversity is controlled through the hyper-mutation.

There are numerous examples of heuristics being hybridised with other heuristics. Researchers are only limited by their imaginations as to what is possible. These are discussed in detail in the following chapter. Some hybrids have become extremely common. For example memetic algorithms combine a genetic algorithm with a hill climber meaning all members of the population are local optima according to the neighbourhood definition used. This helps the genetic algorithm identify high-quality solutions but adds considerably to the run time. Similarly a hill climber is often added to Ant Colony Optimisation.

11.5 Some Applications

In this section we present some real-life applications that are addressed by meta-heuristic approaches. There are numerous applications of heuristic and metaheuristic so we can only provide a small overview of a few problems. However we hope this gives an idea of the wide range and variety of problems that are solved in practice.

11.5.1   Radio-Therapy

One of the techniques adopted in treating cancerous tumours is the intensity modulated radiotherapy treatment (short for IMRT). This consists of sending a dose of radiation to the cancerous region with the aim to sterilise the tumour while avoiding damage to the surrounding healthy organs and tissues. This is performed by defining the number of angles, their respective angles and the intensity chosen for the radiation beams at each of these angles. For instance, Bertsimas et al. [5] present a hybridisation of a gradient descent and an adaptive Simulated Annealing method. The initial solution is generated by solving an LP based on using equi-spaced angle beams. Their approach is tested on real-life pancreatic cases (kidneys, liver, stomach, skin and pancreas) at the Massachusetts general hospital of Boston, USA. A case study dealing with patients with head-and-neck tumours at the Portuguese Institute of Oncology in Coimbra is conducted by Dias et al. [24] who adopted a hybrid Genetic Algorithm with a Neural Network. Here, each chromosome is binary and represented by 360 genes, one for each possible angle, with the angles selected represented by 1. Also, Dias et al. [25] proposed Simulated Annealing, with a dynamically adjusted neighbourhood (in terms of angles), and successfully tested it on the same case study in Coimbra. Their results suggest that a reduced number of angles (and hence less technical adjustment) is required and an improvement in organ sparing and coverage of the tumours is observed.

11.5.2   Sport Management

A variety of metaheuristics have been used to schedule fixtures across many different sporting activities. Wright [117] uses Tabu Search to schedule the English county cricket fixtures, Willis and Terrill [116] opt for Simulated Annealing to schedule Australian state cricket, Costa [19] adopts an evolutionary Tabu Search to schedule National Hockey League matches in North America while Thompson [109] also uses Tabu Search to schedule the 1999 Rugby World Cup. Wright [119] produces schedules for New Zealand cricket matches using Simulated Annealing whereas Kendall [57] uses a form of local search to schedule English football fixtures over the Christmas period.

11.5.3   Educational Timetabling

Constructing timetables including examination timetables at schools, colleges and universities can be a hugely time-consuming and difficult task if performed manually. Computer systems that incorporate some form of heuristics are nowadays used frequently and reduce the time required to produce solutions considerably. For instance, Wright [118] constructs a tool that incorporates Tabu Search for a large comprehensive school of over 1400 pupils and 80 teachers in Lancashire, England. Dowsland and Thompson [31] construct an examination timetable for the University of Swansea using Simulated Annealing. The examination timetabling problem is also solved by Di Gaspero and Schaerf [26] using Tabu Search and by Pillay et al. [82] using a Genetic Algorithm. The problem of optimising lecture timetables is considered by, amongst others Borchani et al. [6] using Variable Neighbourhood Descent, Corne et al. [18] using evolutionary algorithms and Basir et al. [3] using Simulated Annealing. For more information and references therein on educational timetabling, see [65].

11.5.4   Nurse Rostering

This problem plays an important part in efficiently managing the personnel at a hospital. The aim is to balance the workforce workload while providing flexibility and satisfying preferences whenever possible leading to a reduction in stress, an increase in staff satisfaction and a happier working environment. Dowsland and Thompson [32] integrate ideas from knapsack problems, network flow models and Tabu Search to construct an efficient computer software tool to solve the nurse rostering problem in a large UK hospital in Wales. Aickelin and Dowsland [2] use an indirect Genetic Algorithm to produce nurse rosters. Burke et al. [11] used Variable Neighbourhood Search to solve the same problem. For more information on this area see the review papers by [10] and [111].

11.5.5   Distribution Management (Routing)

Planning routes by efficiently scheduling the sequence of the customers as they are served and in some cases determining strategically the right vehicle fleet constitutes a huge component of logistic costs (in the range of 30%) and therefore any improvement gained will provide the company with a competitive edge over its competitors. For instance, Semet and Taillard [99] used

Tabu Search to solve a real-life distribution problem in Switzerland leading to a 15% reduction in cost. Rochat and Semet [83] developed a Tabu Search approach for a pet food company having 100 farms and stores leading to about 16% a cost saving. Brandao and Mercier [7] also used Tabu Search for the multi-trip problem at a British biscuit company in the UK. Threshold Acceptance was adopted by Tarantilis and Kiranoudis [107] to schedule the fresh meat distribution with heterogeneous fleet in a densely populated area of Athens. Tarantilis and Kiranoudis [108] used a two-phase approach based on Large Neighbourhood Search for both a dairy and a construction company in Greece. The delivery of blood products to Austrian hospitals for the blood bank of the Austrian Red Cross for Eastern Austria was conducted by Hemmelmayr et al. [51] using a combination of integer programming and Variable Neighbourhood Search.

11.5.6   Location Problems

There is always a challenge in deciding where to locate something which may require a massive investment such as plants and warehouses, consolidation points and in some cases less expensive equipment that are required in large numbers. For instance, when it comes to locating emergency facilities such as police stations, fire stations etc, the aim is to locate the facilities in such a way that the longest time to reach the customer is minimised. This type of problem is known as the p-centre problem where the parameter can be changed for scenario analysis purposes. Pacheto and Casado [79] adopted Scatter Search to locate a number of geriatric and diabetic health care clinics in the rural area of Burgos in Spain. Lu [68] implemented Simulated Annealing to locate urgent relief centres in Taiwan to respond to a major earthquake. Cunha and Silva [20] presented an efficient configuration of such a hub and spoke network for one of the top ten trucking companies in Brazil using a Genetic Algorithm. Also, electricity providers seek to locate their large number of protection devices (costing approximately £10K each) on their tree network to protect the users from having an electricity cut in the case of big storms, etc. James and Salhi [53], [54] explored this unusual network location problem for the UK Midland Electricity Board using a constructive heuristic and Tabu Search.

11.5.7 Chemical Engineering

In several industries such as pharmaceutical, wastewater treatment, biotechnology, the control and the regulation of the pH value, which needs to be around 7, is critical. The modelling of pH control is an important issue which turns out to be an operational decision problem that fits into the class of global optimisation. There is a good amount of research into advanced non-linear control techniques but in practice linear control techniques are usually adopted due to their simplicity and robustness. Research on how to monitor some of the parameters that control the pH is carried out for instance by Mwenbeshi et al. [77] who adopted a powerful GA implementation to intelligently control and model pH in reactors using a lab-scale pH reactor. In this study, a strong base, namely sodium hydroxide is used to neutralise the process made up of four acids whose levels need to be determined in real time as the change in the pH in the reservoir keeps changing all the time. Interesting studies along this area can also be found in their references therein.

11.5.8 Civil Engineering Applications

The design of water distribution networks is very important and costly in the area of civil engineering. This can be seen as a hydraulic infrastructure composed of several pipes of different diameters, hydraulic devices with various powers and different reservoirs. The aim of the problem is to determine the minimal diameter for each pipe in such a way that the total cost is minimised and appropriate water pressure is reached at each of the nodes of the network. HS was tested on this complex non-linear problem based on the water distribution network of Hanoi in Vietnam by Geem et al. [42]. A real coding GA that incorporates neighbourhood reduction with several crossover and mutation operators was proposed by Kadu et al. [55] for the same case study. Reservoir management is also one of the key aspects in water resource planning. Each reservoir has several conflicting objectives as well as different operating rules and operating policies due to the land or the cities around it. The aim is to determine the right policy among a large set of possible ones at a given period. For instance two basic conflicting objectives are the minimisation of the lack of irrigation against the maximisation of the generation of electricity (e.g. hydropower generation). The problem is transformed into a weighted multi-objective approach and solved efficiently using an adaptation of Particle Swarm Optimisation by Kumar and Reddy [61]. The same authors a year earlier in 2006 [60] put forward an approach based on Ant Colony Optimisation to solve the multi-purpose reservoir problem.

There are many applications in other areas of engineering such as electrical, chemical, mechanical, environmental and civil engineering where evolutionary methods including GA are commonly used. See for instance the edited book by Dasgupta [22] which can be a useful and informative addition to the reader.

11.6   Conclusion and Research Issues

In this final section we summarise our findings and provide some research avenues that could be worth pursuing.

11.6.1   Conclusion

In this chapter several heuristic-based techniques that are used in solving difficult combinatorial and global optimisation are described and their pros and cons are highlighted. The methods range from those that only accept improving solutions such as hill-climbing, Variable Neighbourhood Search and GRASP, to those that accept non-improving ones while incorporating some form of guidance to avoid the risk of diverging and cycling like Simulated Annealing, Threshold Acceptance and Tabu Search. Those techniques that use simultaneously more than one solution at a time, also known as population or evolutionary methods, are also discussed include Genetic Algorithms, Ant Colony Optimisation and Bee Colony Optimisation. As strengths and weaknesses can be found in any heuristic, many modern implementations hybridise a number of these methods, leading to better results overall. Of particular interest is metaheuristics, where exact and heuristic methods are combined.

The efficiency of heuristics depends on several aspects and one key element is the quality of the implementation. Each meta-heuristic can be applied in different ways and reviewing the academic literature to understand which sorts of methods have worked well on particular problems is crucial. Also key is parameter optimisation and here methods that require fewer parameters e.g. tabu search, threshold acceptance may be considered superior to methods that require many parameters such as simulated annealing and ant colony optimisation. Methods that automatically set parameters or dynamically adjust them as the search proceeds may remove this advantage. The coding is crucial also—much time can be saved by using efficient data structures, reducing neighbourhoods, etc.

Heuristic search has made huge advances in the last 25 years and this is likely to continue as problem complexity and size also increase. Advances in computer technology and commercial optimisation software are enabling larger problems to be solved exactly than previous, however there is still a huge need for high-quality heuristic solution methods.

Heuristics have arisen from a variety of applications, from different people's expertise and sometimes just as a by-product of curiosity of some researchers whose original aim was to disprove their usefulness. We believe this less structured area, known by some as a grey research area, will remain for many years to come and will become even greyer and open to more challenges. Heuristics remain the most appropriate and attractive optimisation approaches for tackling many complex combinatorial and global optimisation problems.

11.6.2   Potential Research Issues

An exciting future topic is hybridisation, be it between purely heuristic methods or heuristic and exact methods. This suggestion will be discussed in another chapter in this book [97].

The understanding of how a given method works and then the design of a data structure that incorporates interesting information found during the search so as to avoid re-computing unnecessary calculations is vital. This process though may increase some level of memory and may require an initial fixed cost in terms of development and computation time, but it does often lead to a massive time saving without affecting the solution quality at all. This aspect can also be enhanced further by the construction of effective neighbourhood reduction schemes that helps the search to avoid checking combinations and operations that are unlikely to result in improving the solution. A note of caution here is that the latter schemes will have a considerable saving in computational time and are usually simple to construct, but could affect the solution quality if they happen to be too restrictive. The compromise in the design between a neighbourhood reduction method which is powerful enough (removing as many as possible irrelevant checks) while not excluding promising moves is exciting and hence worth exploring.

Evolutionary heuristics are relatively easy to be parallelised and hence can be used for larger instances and in a practical setting if the computing facilities are available.

The design of adaptive search that dynamically learns and makes use of the obtained information is crucial. This learning mechanism which ought to be continuously or at least periodically updated is then used to pseudo-randomly select at regular intervals the decision rules to be used. These can include a subset of neighbourhoods to choose from, a number of local searches to be used for intensification purposes, or even the powerful heuristics or exact methods to select from. This kind of search is self-adaptive and also efficient as it uses only what it needs with the expectation that a good solution may be found. This research issue though challenging and practically useful will probably be one of the most popular research areas in the near future as it has the additional benefits of being applicable in several areas ranging from engineering to medicine.

In a related but different aspect, it is well known that most exciting powerful heuristics seem to suffer from parameter tuning. It is therefore worthwhile concentrating on schemes that incorporate ways of reducing the number of parameters or adjusting the parameters' values dynamically and adaptively. This is very welcome and in our view is also one of the ways forward. Results from such studies will provide us with tools that avoid requiring excessive time for fine tuning of the parameters, besides making the heuristic less sensitive to parameter values and hence reliable to use.

References

1. Ahuja RK, Ergun O, Orlin JB and Punnen AP (2002). A survey of very large scale neighbourhood search techniques. Discrete Appl Math 123: 75–102.
2. Aickelin U and Dowsland K (2000). Exploiting problem structure in a genetic algorithm approach to a nurse rostering problem. J Sched 3: 139–153.
3. Basir N, Ismail W and Norwawi, N (2013). A simulated annealing for Tahmidi course timetabling. Procedia Technology 11: 437–445.
4. Battiti R and Tecchiolli G (1994). The reactive tabu search. ORSA J Comput 6: 126–140.
5. Bertsimas D, Cacchiani V, Craft D and Nohadani O (2013). A hybrid approach to beam angle optimization in intensity-modulated radiation therapy. Comput Oper Res 40: 2187–2197.
6. Borchani E, Elloumi A and Masmoudi M (2017). Variable neighbourhood descent search algorithms for course timetabling problem: Application to a Tunisian University. Electronic Notes in Discrete Math. 58: 119–126.
7. Brandao J and Mercer A (1997). A tabu search heuristic for the multiple-trip vehicle routing and scheduling problem. Eur J Oper Res 100: 180–191.
8. Braysy O, Hasle G and Dullaert W (2004). A multi-start local search algorithm for the vehicle routing problem with time windows. Eur J Oper Res 159 (3): 586–605.
9. Bullnheimer B, Harlt R and Strauss C (1998). Applying ant systems to the vehicle routing problem. In Voss S, Martello S, Osman IH and Roucairal

C (eds), Metaheuristics: Advances and Trends in Local Search Paradigms for Optimization. Kluwer Academic Publishers, Boston.

10. Burke EK, De Causmaecker P, Berghe GV and Van Landeghem H (2004). The state of the art of nurse rostering. J Sched 7: 441–499.

11. Burke EK, Curtois T, Post G, Qu R and Veltman B (2008). A hybrid heuristic ordering and variable neighbourhood search for the nurse rostering problem. Eur J Oper Res 188 (2): 330–341.

12. Cerny V (1982). A thermodynamical approach to the travelling salesman problem: an efficient simulation algorithm. J Optim Theory Appl 45: 41–51.

13. Charon I and Hudry O (1993). The noising method—a new method for combinatorial optimization. Oper Res Let 14: 133–137.

14. Charon I and Hudry O (2009). Self-tuning of the noising method. Optimization 58: 1–21.

15. Colorni A, Dorigo M and Maniezzo V (1991). Distributed optimization by ant colonies. In Varela F and Bourgine P (eds) Proceedings of the European Conference on Artificial Life. Elsevier Publishing, Amsterdam, 457–474.

16. Conolly DT (1990). An improved simulated annealing technique for the QAP. Eur J Oper Res 46: 93–100.

17. Conolly D (1992). General purpose simulated annealing. J Opl Res Soc 43: 495–505.

18. Corne D, Ross P and Fang H-L (2005). Fast practical evolutionary timetabling. In: Fogarty T C (ed) Evolutionary Computing. Lecture Notes in Computer Science 865, Srpinger, Berlin, Heidelberg.

19. Costa D (1995). An evolutionary tabu search algorithm and the NHL scheduling problem. INFOR 33: 161–178.

20. Cunha CB and Silva ME (2007). A genetic algorithm for the problem of configuring a hub-and-spoke network for a LTL trucking company in Brazil. Eur J Oper Res 179: 747–758.

21. Daneubourg JL, Aron A, Goss S and Pasteels JM (1990). The self organising exploratory pattern of the argentine ant. J Insec Behav 3: 159–168.

22. Dasgupta D and Michalewicz Z (Eds) (2013). Evolutionary Algorithms in Engineering Applications. Springer, New York.

23. Dasgupta D (Ed) (1999). Artificial Immune System and Their Applications. Springer- Verlag.

24. Dias J, Rocha H, Ferreira B, de Carmo Lopes C (2014). A genetic algorithm with neural network fitness function evaluation for IMRT beam angle optimization. Cent Eur J Oper Res 22: 431–455.

25. Dias J, Rocha H, Ferreira B, de Carmo Lopes C (2014). Simulated annealing applied to IMRT beam angle optimization: a computational study. Physica Medica 31: 747–756.

26. Di Gaspero L and Schaerf A (2001). Tabu search techniques for examination timetabling. In: EK Burke and W Erben (eds) Selected Papers from the Third International Conference on the Practice and Theory of Automated Timetabling. Lecture Notes in Computer Science 2079, 104–117.

27. Dorigo M and Gambardella LM (1997). Ant colony system: a cooperative learning approach to the travelling salesman problem. IEEE Trans Evol Comput 1: 53–66.

28. Dorigi M and Stutzle T (2010). Ant colony optimization: overview and recent advances. In Gendreau M and Potvin JY (eds) Handbook of Metaheuristics (2nd edition). Springer, London, pp 227–264.

29. Dorigo M, Caro G and Gambardella L (1999). Ant algorithms for discrete optimization. Art Life 5: 137–172.

30. Dowsland KA (1993). Some experiments with simulated annealing techniques for packing problems. Eur J Oper Res 68: 389–399.

31. Dowsland KA and Thompson JM (1998). A robust simulated annealing based examination timetabling system. Comp Oper Res 25: 637–648.

32. Dowsland KA and Thompson JM (2000). Solving a nurse scheduling problem with knapsacks, network and tabu search. J Oper Res Soc 51: 825–833.

33. Dowsland KA and Thompson JM (2012). Simulated annealing. In Rozenberg G, Back T and Kok JN (eds) Handbook of Natural Computing. Springer-Verlag, Berlin, pp 1624–1655.

34. Drezner Z and Salhi S (2002). Using hybrid metaheuristics for the one-way and two-way network design problem. Nav Res Logistics 49: 449–463.

35. Dueck G and Scheuer T (1990). Threshold accepting: a general purpose optimization algorithm superior to simulated annealing. J Comput Phy 90: 161–175.

36. Dueck G (1993). New optimization heuristics: the great deluge algorithm and the record-to-record travel. J Comp Phys 104: 86–92.

37. Eglese R (1990). Simulated annealing: a tool for operational research. Eur J Oper Res 46: 271–281.

38. Elshaikh A, Salhi S, Brimberg J, Mladenović N, Callaghan B and Nagy G (2016). An adaptive perturbation-based heuristic: an application to the continuous p-centre problem. Comput Oper Res 75: 1–11.

39. Feo TA and Resende MGC (1989). A probablistic heuristic for a computationally difficult set covering problem. Opns Res Lett 8: 67–71.

40. Feo TA and Resende MGC (1995). Greedy randomized adaptive search procedures. J Glob Opt 6: 109–133.

41. Fletcher R (1989). Practical Methods of Optimisation. John Wiley and Sons, New York.

42. Geem ZW, Kim JH and Loganathan GV (2001). A new heuristic optimization algorithm: harmony search. Simulation 76 (2): 60–68.

43. Glover F (1986). Future paths for integer programming and links to artificial intelligence. Comput Opns Res 13: 533–549.

44. Glover F, Laguna M and Marti R (2003) Scatter search and path relinking: advances and applications. In Glover F and Kochenberger GA (eds) Handbook of Metaheuristics. Kluwer Academic Publisher, London, pp 1–35.

45. Goldberg DE (1989). Genetic Algorithm in Search, Optimization and Machine Learning. Addison-Wesley, New York.

46. Goodman M, Dowsland KA and Thompson JM (2009) A grasp-knapsack hybrid for a nurse-scheduling problem. J Heuristics 15: 351–379.
47. Hansen P (1986). The steepest ascent, mildest descent heuristic for combinatorial programming. Paper presented at the congress on Numerical Methods in Combinatorial Optimization, Capri, Italy.
48. Hansen P, Mladenović N, Brimberg J and Moreno Perez JA (2019). Variable neighbourhood search. In Gendreau M and Potvin JY (eds) Handbook of metaheuristics (latest edition). Springer, Cham, pp 57–97.
49. Hansen P, Mladenović N, Todosijević and Hanafi S (2017). Variable neighborhood search: basics and variants. EURO J Comput Optim 5: 423–454.
50. Holland JH (1975). Adaptation in Natural and Artificial Systems. University of Michigan Press, Ann Harbor.
51. Hemmelmayr V, Doerner KF, Hartl RF and Savelsbergh MWP (2009). Delivery strategies for blood products supplies. OR Spec 31: 707–725.
52. Hu TC, Kahng AB and Tsao CWA (1995). Old bachelor acceptance: a new class of non-monotone threshold accepting methods. ORSA J Comput 7: 417–425.
53. James C and Salhi S (2000). The location of protection devices on electrical tree networks: a heuristic approach. J Oper Res Soc 51: 959–970.
54. James C and Salhi S (2000). A tabu search heuristic for the location of multi type protection devices on electrical tree networks. J Com Opt 6: 81–98.
55. Kadu MS, Gupta R and Bhave P (2008). Optimal design of water networks using a modified genetic algorithm with reduction in search space. J Water Res Plan Manage 134: 147–160.
56. Karaboga D and Basturk B (2007). Artificial bee colony optimization algorithm for solving constrained optimization problems. In Melin P, Castillo O, Aguilar L, Kacprzyk J and Pedrycz, W (eds) Foundations of Fuzzy Logic and Soft Computing. Lecture Notes in Computer Science 4529, Berlin, Heidelberg.
57. Kendall G (2008). Scheduling English football fixtures over holiday periods. J Oper Res Soc 59: 743–755.
58. Kennedy J and Eberhault RC (1995). Particle Swarm Optimization. IEEE Int Conf Neural Networks, Perth, Australia, pp 1942–1948.
59. Kirkpatrick S, Gelat CD and Vecchi MP (1983). Optimization by simulated annealing. Science 220: 671–680.
60. Kumar DN and Reddy MJ (2006). Ant colony optimization for multi-purpose reservoir operation. Water Res Manage 20: 879–898.
61. Kumar DN and Reddy MJ (2007). Multi-purpose reservoir operation using particle swarm optimization. J Water Resour Plann Manag 133 (3): 192–201.
62. Laarhoven PJM and Aarts EHL (1987). Simulated Annealing: Theory and Applications. Reidel, Rotterdam.
63. Laporte G, Gendreau M, Potvin J-Y and Semet F (2000). Classical and modern heuristics for the vehicle routing problem. International Transaction in Operational Research 7: 285–300.

64. Lee DS, Vassiliadis VS and Park JM (2004). A novel threshold accepting meta-heuristic for the job-shop scheduling problem. Comp Oper Res 31 (13): 2199–2213.

65. Lewis R (2008). A survey of meta-heuristic based techniques for university timetabling problems. OR Spektrum 30: 167–190.

66. Li F, Golden B and Wasil E (2007). A record-to-record travel algorithm for solving the heterogeneous fleet vehicle routing problem. Comput Opns Res 34: 2734–2742.

67. Lourenco HR, Martin OC and Stutzle T (2010). Iterated local search: framework and applications. In Gendreau M and Potvin JY (eds) Handbook of Metaheuristics. Springer, London, pp 363–397.

68. Lu C (2013). Robust weighted vertex p-center model considering uncertain data: an application to emergency management. Eur J Oper Res 230: 113–121.

69. Lundy M and Mees A (1986). Convergence of an annealing algorithm. Math Prog 34: 111–124.

70. Luis M, Salhi S and Nagy G (2011). A guided reactive GRASP for the capacitated multi-source Weber problem. Comp Oper Res 38 (7): 1014–1024.

71. Mahdavi M, Fesanghary M and Damangir E (2007). An improved harmony search algorithm for solving optimization problems. Applied Mathematics and Computation 188: 1567–1579.

72. Marti R, Laguna M and Glover F (2006). Principles of scatter search. Eur J Oper Res 169: 359–372.

73. Maslow AH (1954). Motivation and Personality. Harper & Sons, New York.

74. Metropolis N, Rosenbluth A, Rosenbluth M, Teller A and Teller E (1953). Equations of state calculations by fast computing machines. J Chem Phy 21: 1087–1092.

75. Mladenović N and Hansen P (1997). Variable neighbourhood search. Comput Oper Res 24: 1097–1100.

76. Osman IH and Christofides N (1994). Capacitated clustering problems by hybrid simulated annealing and tabu search. Int Trans Oper Res 1: 317–336.

77. Mwenbeshi MM, Kent CA and Salhi S (2004). A genetic algorithm based approach to intelligent modelling and control of pH in reactors. Comp Chem Eng 28 (9): 1743–1757.

78. Osman IH and Laporte G (1996). Metaheuristics: a bibliography. Ann Oper Res 63: 513–623.

79. Pacheto JA and Casado S (2004). Solving two location models with few facilities by using a hybrid heuristic: a real health resources case. Comput Oper Res 32: 3075–3091.

80. Pan QK, Suganthan PN, Tasgetiren MF and Liang JJ (2010). A self-adaptive global best harmony search algorithm for continuous optimization problems. Appl Math Comput 216: 830–848.

81. Pham DT, Ghanbarzadeh A, Koc E, Otri S, Rahim S and Zaidi M (2006). The bees algorithm, a novel tool for complex optimisation problems. In Proc

2nd Virtual International Conference on Intelligent Production Machines and Systems, Elsevier, Oxford, pp 454–459.

82. Pillay N and Banzhaf W (2010). An informed genetic algorithm for the examination problem. Appl Soft Comput 10 (2): 457–467.

83. Rochat Y and Semet F (1994). A tabu search approach for delivering pet food and flour in Switzerland. J Oper Res Soc 45: 1233–1246.

84. Rubinstein RY (1997). Optimization of computer simulation models with rare events. Eur J Oper Res 99: 89–112.

85. Rubinstein RY and Kroese DP (2004). The cross-entropy method: a unified approach to combinatorial optimization, Monte Carlo simulation and machine learning. Springer-Verlag, New York.

86. Salhi S (1997). A perturbation heuristic for a class of location problem. J Oper Res Soc 48: 1233–1240.

87. Salhi S (1998). Heuristic search methods. In Marcoulides GA (ed) Modern methods for business research. Lawrence Erlbaum Associates, New Jersey, pp 147–175.

88. Salhi S (2002). Defining tabu list size and aspiration criterion within tabu search methods. Comput Opns Res 29: 67–86.

89. Salhi S and Rand GK (1987). Improvements to vehicle routing heuristics. J Oper Res Soc 38: 293–295.

90. Salhi S and Sari M (1997). A Multi-level composite heuristic for the multi-depot vehicle fleet mix problem. Eur J Oper Res 103: 78–95.

91. Salhi S and Gamal MDH (2003). A genetic algorithm based approach for the uncapacitated continuous location–allocation problem. Ann Oper Res 123: 203–222.

92. Salhi S (2006). Heuristic search in action: the science of tomorrow. In Salhi S (Ed) OR48 Keynote papers. ORS Bath, pp 39–58.

93. Salhi S (2017). Heuristic Search: The Emerging Science of Problem Solving. Palgrave MacMillan.

94. Salhi S, Gutierrez, Wassan N, Wu S and Kaya R (2020). An effective real time GRASP-based metaheuristic: application to order consolidation and dynamic selection of transshipment points for time-critical freight logistics. Expert Syst Appl 158: 113574.

95. Salhi S and Petch R (2007). A GA based heuristic for the vehicle routing problem with multiple trips. J Math Model Algor 6: 591–613.

96. Salhi S, Imran A and Wassan NA (2014). The multi-depot vehicle routing problem with heterogeneous vehicle fleet: formulation and a variable neighbourhood search implementation. Comput Oprs Res 52: 315–325.

97. Salhi S and Thompson J (2021). The new era of hybridisation and learning in heuristic search design. In Salhi S and Boylan J (eds) The Palgrave Handbook of Operations Research. Palgrave, London.

98. Schrimpf G, Schneider J, Stamm-Wilbrabdt H and Dueck H (2000). Record breaking optimization results-using the ruin and recreate principle. J Comput Phys 159: 139–171.

99. Semet F and Taillard E (1993). Solving real-life vehicle routing problems efficiently using tabu search. Ann Oper Res 41: 469–488.

100. Shaw P (1998). Using constrain programming and local search methods to solve vehicle routing problem. In Proceeding CP-98 (Fourth International Conference on Principles and Practice of Constraint Programming).

101. Sorenson K, Sevaux M and Glover F (2018). A history of metaheuristics. In Marti R, Pardalos P and Resende M (eds) Handbook of Heuristics. Springer, 791–808.

102. Stützle T and Hoos HH (2000). MAX–MIN ant system. Futur Gener Comput Syst 16: 889–914.

103. Sze J, Salhi S and Wassan N (2016). A hybridisation of adaptive variable neighbourhood search and large neighbourhood search: application to the vehicle routing problem. Expert Syst Appl 65: 383–397.

104. Sze J, Salhi S and Wassan N (2017). The cumulative capacitated vehicle routing problem with min-sum and min-max objectives: an effective hybridisation of adaptive variable neighbourhood search and large neighbourhood search. Transp Res Part B 101: 162–184.

105. Szeto WY, Wu Y and Ho SC (2011). An artificial bee colony algorithm for the capacitated vehicle routing problem. Eur J Oper Res 215: 126–135.

106. Tarantilis CD and Kiranoudis CT (2002). BoneRoute: an adaptive memory-based method for effective fleet management. Ann Opns Res 115: 227–241.

107. Tarantilis CD, Kiranoudis C and Vassiliadis V (2003). A list based threshold accepting metahauristic for the heterogeneous fixed vehicle routing problem. J Oper Res Soc 54: 65–71.

108. Tarantilis CD and Kiranoudis CT (2007). A flexible adaptive memory-based algorithm for real-life transportation operations: two case studies from Diary and construction sector. Eur J Oper Res 179: 806–822.

109. Thompson J (1999). Kicking timetabling problems into touch. OR Insight 12: 7–15.

110. Tiwari MK, Prakash A, Kumar A, Mileham AR (2005). Determination of an optimal sequence using the psychoclonal algorithm. J Eng Manuf 219: 137–149.

111. Valouxis G, Gogos C, Goulas G and Alefragis P (2012). A systematic two phase approach for the nurse rostering problem. Eur J Oper Res 219: 425–433.

112. Voudouris C and Tsang EPK (2010). Guided local search. In Gendreau M, and Potvin JY (eds) Handbook of Metaheuristcs. Springer, London, pp 321–361.

113. Wade AC and Salhi S (2003). An ant system algorithm for the mixed vehicle routing problem with backhauls. In Resende MG and de Sousa JP (eds) Metaheuristics: Computer Decision-Making. Kluwer, NY, pp 699–719.

114. Wang H, Yao Y and Salhi S (2021). Tension in big data using machine learning: analysis and applications. Tech For Soc Change 158: 120175.

115. Wassan NA (2006). A reactive tabu search for vehicle routing. J Oper Res Soc 57: 111–116.
116. Willis R and Terrill B (1994). Scheduling the Australian state cricket season using simulated annealing. J Oper Res Soc 45: 276–280.
117. Wright M (1994). Timetabling county cricket fixtures using a form of tabu search. J Oper Res Soc 45: 758–770.
118. Wright M (1996). School timetabling using heuristic search. J Oper Res Soc 47: 347–357.
119. Wright M (2005). Scheduling fixtures for New Zealand cricket. IMA J Manag Math 16: 99–112.
120. Zainuddin ZM and Salhi S (2007). A perturbation-based heuristic for the capacitated multisource Weber problem. Eur J Oper Res 179: 1194–1207.

12

Formulation Space Search Metaheuristic

Nenad Mladenović, Jack Brimberg, and Dragan Urošević

12.1 Introduction

Many methods for solving discrete and continuous global optimization problems are based on changing one formulation to another, which is either equivalent or very close to it, so that by solving the reformulated problem we can easily get the solution of the original one. These types of methods include

 i. dual methods,
 ii. primal-dual methods,
 iii. Lagrange methods,

N. Mladenović
Industrial System Engineering, Khalifa University, Abu Dhabi, UAE
e-mail: nenad.mladenovic@ku.ac.ae

J. Brimberg
Royal Military College of Canada, Kingston, ON, Canada
e-mail: jack.brimberg@rmc.ca

D. Urošević (✉)
Mathematical Institute of the Serbian Academy of Sciences and Arts, Belgrade, Serbia
e-mail: draganu@mi.sanu.ac.rs

© The Author(s), under exclusive license to Springer Nature
Switzerland AG 2022
S. Salhi and J. Boylan (eds.), *The Palgrave Handbook of Operations Research*,
https://doi.org/10.1007/978-3-030-96935-6_12

iv. linearization methods,

v. convexification methods,

vi. (nonlinear) coordinate system change methods (e.g., polar, Cartesian, projective transformations, etc.),

vii. discrete/continuous reformulation methods,

viii. augmented methods,

to mention a few. However, in all those classes, the set of formulations of one problem are not considered as a set having some structure provided with some order relation among formulations. The usual conclusion in papers oriented to a new formulation is that a given formulation is better than another or the best among several. The criteria for making such conclusions are typically the duality or integrality gap provided (difference between upper and lower bounds), precision, efficiency (the CPU times spent by the various methods applied to different formulations of the same instances), and so on.

Formulation space search (FSS) is a metaheuristic first proposed in 2005 by Mladenović et al. [37]. Since then, many algorithms for solving various optimization problems have been proposed that apply this framework. The main idea is to provide the set of formulations used for solving a given class or type of problem with some metric or quasi-metric. In that way, the distance between formulations can be induced from those (quasi) metric functions, and thus, the search space is extended to the set of formulations as well. Therefore, the search space becomes a pair $(\mathcal{F}, \mathcal{S})$, consisting of *formulation space* $\mathcal{F}$ and *solution space* $\mathcal{S}$. Most importantly, in all of the above mentioned method classes (i)–(viii), the discrete metric function between any two formulations can easily be defined. For example, in Lagrange methods, the distance between any two formulations can be defined as the difference between their relaxed constraints (the number of multipliers used); in coordinate change methods the distance between formulations could be the difference between the number of entities (points) presented in the same coordinate system, etc.

The work of Mladenović et al. [37] is also motivated by the following important observation: when solving continuous nonlinear programs (NLPs) with the aid of a solver that uses first-order information, the solution obtained may be a stationary point that is not a local optimum. Stationary points may be induced by the objective function (F) or the constraints. In the first case, they are found at points in the solution space where the first-order partial derivatives of F are all equal to zero. In the second case, they may occur at points on the boundary of one or more constraints where the derivatives of F are not all zero, but no feasible and improving direction of search can be found because of the imposed constraints. Unfortunately, these stationary points are often neither local minima nor local maxima. Checking the second-order conditions may help to identify these artificial local optima and escape them, but may also be computationally expensive, since the number of stationary points can be huge. Alternatively, different formulations of the same problem may have different characteristics that can be exploited in order to move in an efficient manner from these stationary points to better solutions. That is, while the improving search is stuck at a stationary point in one formulation, this solution may not be a stationary point in another formulation.

To illustrate the fact that a local solution in one formulation may behave differently in another, consider the following simple problem in the plane ($\mathbb{R}^2$):

$$\min F(x, y) = x + y, \tag{12.1}$$

subject to

$$x^2 + y^2 \geq 1,$$
$$x \geq 0, y \geq 0.$$

The objective function is linear, and therefore convex, but the feasible region is not a convex set, resulting in a nonconvex program. This problem may be reformulated from Cartesian coordinates in (12.1) to Polar coordinates to obtain an equivalent model:

$$\min G(r, \theta) = r(\cos \theta + \sin \theta), \tag{12.2}$$

subject to

$$r \geq 1, 0 \leq \theta \leq \pi/2.$$

Interestingly, in (12.2), the objective function is nonconvex, while the constraints are linear, and therefore define a convex feasible set. Referring to Fig. 12.1(a) for model (12.1) with (x, y) coordinates, we see that a local solution occurs at the point $(1/\sqrt{2}, 1/\sqrt{2})$. This is because no feasible move direction exists at this point that will improve the solution (i.e., there is an immediate increase in the objective function or no improvement at all). Hence, any (local) improving search would be stuck at this point, even though the iso-contours of F show that this solution is not a local minimum. Referring to Fig. 12.1(b) for model (12.2), we find that the situation is not the same at the corresponding point in (r, θ) space, $(r, \theta) = (1, \pi/4)$.

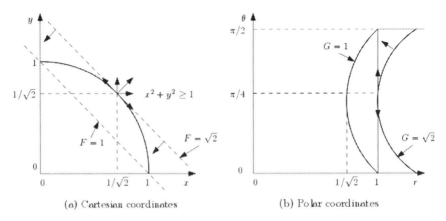

(a) Cartesian coordinates   (b) Polar coordinates

Fig. 12.1 Illustrative example

Moving down (or up) along the vertical line $r = 1$ is a feasible direction that immediately improves the solution. Continuing down (or up) along this vertical line eventually leads to an optimal solution at $(r, \theta) = (1, 0)$ (or $(r, \theta) = (1, \pi/2)$). This is equivalent to moving clockwise (or counter clockwise) along the circumference of the circle in Fig. 12.1(a) from the local solution at $(x, y) = (1/\sqrt{2}, 1/\sqrt{2})$ to the optimal solution at $(x, y) = (1, 0)$ (or $(0, 1)$). Thus, this small example illustrates that a local solution in one coordinate system may not be one in another coordinate system.

The FSS approach was first applied to the circle packing problem (Mladenović et al. [37]), which is a highly nonconvex NLP due to the imposed constraints, and as a result, contains a large number of stationary points. Here the authors used the nonlinear transformation demonstrated in the example above, where the mathematical formulation of the problem switches back and forth between Cartesian and Polar coordinate systems when convergence to a stationary point is detected, and proceeds in this manner until no further improvement is possible in either coordinate system. This simple application of FSS produced excellent results, and several successful applications of FSS have appeared since. The rest of this chapter is organized as follows. In the next section, we do a brief literature review of several papers that examine a range of optimization problems, continuous and discrete, and that have applied FSS in different ways. This is followed in Sect. 12.3 by a discussion of the general procedure or methodology at the base of FSS. Section 12.4 examines in detail how the steps of FSS have been incorporated in solution methods used to solve the circle packing problem, and the graph coloring problem (Hertz et al. [23]). We also examine in this section the reformulation local search methodology proposed in Brimberg et al. [6], which is closely related to FSS and was developed to solve continuous location problems. Section 12.5 provides some conclusions.

12.2 Literature Review

A sample of papers using FSS and related ideas is presented here, and briefly discussed.

Circle Packing - Reformulation Descent (Mladenović et al. [37]). Several years ago, classical Euclidean geometry problems of densest packing of circles in the plane were formulated as nonconvex optimization problems, allowing to find heuristic solutions by using any available NLP solver. The faster NLP solvers use first-order information only, and so may stop at stationary points which are not local optima. A simple switch from Cartesian coordinates to polar, or vice versa, can destroy this stationarity, and thus allow the solver to move further to better solutions. Such formulation switches may of course be iterated. For densest packing of equal circles into a unit circle, this simple feature turns out to yield results close to the best known, while beating second-order methods by a time-factor well over 100. This technique is formalized as a general reformulation descent (RD) procedure, which iterates among several formulations of the same problem until the applied local searches obtain no further improvement.

Circle Packing (Mladenović et al. [38]). This paper extends the RD idea by using several formulations instead of only two. This is formalized as a general search in formulation space. The distance between two formulations is defined as the number of centers whose coordinates are expressed in different systems in each formulation. Therefore, the search is performed through the formulation space as well. Results with up to 100 circles compare favorably with the RD method.

Packing Unequal Circles Using Formulation Space Search (López and Beasley [30]). This paper presents a heuristic algorithm for the problem of packing unequal circles in a fixed size container such as the unit circle, the unit square or a rectangle. The problem is viewed as scaling the radii of the unequal circles so that they can all be packed into the container. The presented algorithm has an optimization phase and an improvement phase. The optimization phase is based on the formulation space search method, while the improvement phase creates a perturbation of the current solution by swapping two circles. The instances considered are categorized into two groups: instances with large variations in radii, and instances with small variations. Six different containers: circle, square, rectangle, right-angled isosceles triangle, semicircle, and circular quadrant are investigated. Computational results show improvements over previous work in the literature.

Packing Unequal Circles in a Fixed Size Circular Container (López and Beasley [32]). This paper considers the problem of packing unequal circles in a fixed size circular container, where the objective is to maximize the value of the circles packed. Two different objectives are examined: maximize the number of circles packed; maximize the area of the circles packed. For the particular case where the objective is to maximize the number of circles packed, the authors prove that the optimal solution has a particular form. A heuristic is developed for the general problem based upon formulation space search. Computational results are given for a number of publicly available test problems involving the packing of up to 40 circles. Computational results are also provided for test problems taken from the literature, relating to packing both equal and unequal circles.

Mixed Integer Nonlinear Programming Problem (López and Beasley [31]). An approach based on FSS to solve mixed-integer nonlinear (zero-one) programming problems is presented. Zero-one variables are presented by a well-known single nonlinear constraint, and an iterative method which adds a single nonlinear inequality constraint of increasing tightness to the original problem, is proposed. Computational results are presented on 51 standard benchmark problems taken from MINLPLib and compared against the Minotaur and minlp_bb nonlinear solvers, as well as against the RECIPE algorithms [28].

Timetabling Problem (Kochetov et al. [26]). This paper examines a well-known NP-hard teacher/class timetabling problem. Variable neighborhood search and tabu search heuristics are developed based on the idea of formulation space search. Two types of solution representation are used in the heuristics. Each representation considers two families of neighborhoods. The first uses swapping of time periods for the teacher (class) timetable. The second is based on the idea of large Kernighan-Lin neighborhoods. Computational results for difficult random test instances show that the proposed approach is highly efficient.

Multi-item Capacitated Lot-Sizing Problem (Erromdhani et al. [16]). This paper proposes a new variant of Variable neighborhood search (VNS) designed for solving Mixed integer programming problems. The procedure is called Variable neighborhood formulation search (VNFS), since the neighborhoods and formulations are both changed during the search. The VNS part is responsible for the integer variables, while an available (commercial) solver is responsible for the continuous variables and the objective function value. The procedure is applied to the multi-item capacitated lot-sizing problem with production time windows and setup times, under the non-customer specific case. This problem is known to be NP-hard and can be formulated as a mixed 0-1 program. Neighborhoods are induced from the Hamming distance in 0-1 variables, while the objective function values in the corresponding neighborhoods are evaluated using different mathematical programming formulations of the problem. The computational experiments show that the new approach is superior to existing methods from the literature.

Graph Coloring (Hertz et al. [23]). This paper studies the k-coloring problem. Given a graph $G = (V, E)$ with vertex set V, and edge set E, the aim is to assign a color (a number chosen in $\{1, \ldots, k\}$) to each vertex of G so that no edge has both endpoints with the same color. A new local search methodology, called Variable Space Search is proposed and then applied to this problem. The main idea is to consider several search spaces, with various neighborhoods and objective functions, and to move from one to another when the search is blocked at a local optimum in a given search space. The k-coloring problem is thus solved by combining different formulations of the problem which are not equivalent, in the sense that some constraints are possibly relaxed in one search space and always satisfied in another. The authors show that the proposed heuristic is superior to each local search used independently (i.e., with a unique search space). It was also found to be competitive with state-of-the-art coloring methods, which consisted of complex hybrid evolutionary algorithms at the time.

Cutwidth Minimization Problem (Pardo et al. [41]). This paper proposes different parallel designs for the VNS schema. The performance of these general strategies is examined by parallelizing a new VNS variant called variable formulation search (VFS). Six different variants are proposed, which differ in the VNS stages to be parallelized as well as in the communication mechanisms among processes. These variants are grouped into three different templates. The first one parallelizes the whole VNS method; the second parallelizes the shake and the local search procedures; the third parallelizes the set of predefined neighborhoods. The resulting designs are tested on the cutwidth minimization problem (CMP). Experimental results show that the parallel implementation of the VFS outperforms previous state-of-the-art methods for the CMP.

Maximum Min-Sum Dispersion Problem (Amirgaliyeva et al. [1]). The maximum min-sum dispersion problem aims to maximize the minimum accumulative dispersion among the chosen elements. It is known to be a strongly NP-hard problem. In Amirgaliyeva et al. [1], the objective functions of two different problems are shifted. Though this heuristic can be seen as an extension of the variable formulation search approach (Pardo et al. [41]) that takes into account alternative formulations of one problem, the important difference is that it allows using alternative formulations of more than one optimization problem. Here it uses one alternative formulation that is of a max-sum type of the originally max-min type, maximum diversity problem. Computational experiments on benchmark instances from the literature show that the suggested approach improves the best-known results for most instances in a shorter computing time.

Continuous Location Problems (Brimberg et al. [6]). This paper presents a new approach called Reformulation local search (RLS), which can be used for solving continuous location problems. The main idea is to exploit the relation between the continuous model and its discrete counterpart. The RLS switches between a local search in the continuous model and a separate improving search in a discrete relaxation in order to widen the search. In each iteration new points obtained in the continuous phase are added to the discrete formulation making the two formulations equivalent in a limiting sense. Computational results on the multi-source Weber problem (a.k.a. the continuous or planar p-median problem) show that the RLS procedure significantly outperforms the continuous local search by itself, and is even equivalent to state-of-the-art metaheuristic-based methods.

12.3 Methodology

The general methodology of FSS and related ideas are presented here. We first analyze two usual types of search methodologies, stochastic and deterministic. Then we present FSS methods that combine both stochastic and deterministic elements.

12.3.1 Stochastic FSS

Let us denote with (φ, x) an incumbent formulation-solution pair, and with $f_{\mathrm{opt}} = f(\varphi, x)$ the current objective function value. One can alternate between formulation space $\mathcal{F}$ and solution space $\mathcal{S}$ in the following ways:

  i. *Monte-Carlo FSS.* This is the simplest search heuristic through $\mathcal{F}$:

a. take formulation - solution pair $(\varphi', x') \in (\mathcal{F}, \mathcal{S})$ at random and calculate the corresponding objective function value f';

b. keep the best solution and value;

c. repeat previous two steps p (a parameter) times.

ii. *Random walk FSS.* For a random walk procedure we need to introduce neighborhoods of both, the formulation and the solution: $(N(\varphi), \mathcal{N}(x))$, $\varphi \in \mathcal{F}$ and $x \in \mathcal{S}$. Then we simply walk through the formulation-solution space by taking a random solution from such a defined neighborhood in each iteration.

iii. *Reduced FSS.* This technique for searching through $\mathcal{F}$ has already been successfully applied in [37]. It represents a combination of Monte-Carlo and random walk stochastic search strategies. Here we take a formulation-solution pair from a given neighborhood as in the random walk. However, we do not move to that solution if it is not better than the current one. We rather return, and take a two-step walk move (in other words, we jump to a random point in the formulation-solution neighborhood of the current solution, and then jump to a random point in the formulation-solution neighborhood of that point (two jumps)). If a better solution is found, we move there and restart the process; otherwise we return and perform a three-step walk, etc. Once we unsuccessfully perform $k_{\max}$ (a parameter) steps, we return to the one-step move again.

In all three FSS routines above, we choose (φ', x') at random and then simply calculate the objective function value. However, (φ', x') could be used as an initial point for any usual descent (ascent) optimization method through $(\mathcal{F}, \mathcal{S})$. Moreover, as an improvement method, one can use a Reformulation descent procedure described below. The final results should be of better quality in that case, but require much more computing time. Thus, some problem specific strategy in balancing the number of calls to an optimization routine is worth considering.

12.3.2 Deterministic FSS

i. *Local FSS.* One can perform local search through $\mathcal{F}$ as well. That is, find local solution x' for any $\varphi' \in N(\varphi)$ (starting from x as an initial solution) and keep the best; repeat this step until there is a formulation in the neighborhood that gives an improvement. Local FSS is probably not as efficient and effective as LS in the solution space, since it is not very likely that many solutions will be different in the neighboring formulations. Moreover, local

FSS is a very time-consuming procedure since for each neighboring formulation, some optimization method is applied. Therefore, we do not give detailed pseudo code for local FSS here.

ii. *Reformulation Descent* (RD). Up to now, we choose the next formulation in the search at random. A procedure that changes the formulation in a deterministic way is called Reformulation descent. The following procedure describes in more detail how we propose to exploit the availability of several formulations of a problem. We assume that at least two ($\ell_{max} \geq 2$) not linearly related formulations of the problem are constructed ($\varphi_\ell, \ell = 1, \ldots, \ell_{max}$), and that initial solution x and formulation ($\ell = 1$) are found. Our RD performs the following steps:

> a. Using Formulation φ_ℓ and an optimization code, find a stationary or local optimum point x' starting from x;
> b. If x' is better than x, move there ($x \leftarrow x'$) and start again from the first formulation ($\ell \leftarrow 1$); otherwise change the formulation ($\ell \leftarrow \ell + 1$);
> c. Repeat the steps above until $\ell > \ell_{max}$.

This algorithm was used for solving the circle packing problem in Mladenović et al. [37]. Results obtained were comparable with the best-known values. Moreover, the RD was 150 times faster than a Newton type method.

iii. *Steepest Descent FSS.* If objective functions f_i of all formulations φ_i, $i = 1, \ldots, \ell_{max}$ are smooth, then, after finding an initial solution x, the Steepest descent FSS may be constructed as follows:

> a. Find descent search directions $-\nabla f_i(x)$.
> b. Perform a line search along all directions (i.e., find $\lambda_i^* > 0$) to get a set of new solutions

$$x^{(i)} \leftarrow x^{(i)} - \lambda_i^* \nabla f_i(x).$$

> c. Let $f_i \leftarrow f_i(x^{(i)})$, and let i^* be the index where f_i is a minimum. Set $x \leftarrow x^{(i^*)}$ and $f_{opt} \leftarrow f_{i^*}$.
> d. Repeat the previous three steps until $f_{opt} \geq f_{i^*}$.

For constrained optimization, replace $\nabla f_i(x)$ by feasible move direction $\Delta_i(x)$ in the formula in step (b), such that the inner product $\nabla f_i(x) \cdot \Delta_i(x) \geq 0$.

12.3.3 Variable Neighborhood FSS and Variants

i. *Variable Neighborhood Formulation Space Search* (VNFSS). As in Variable neighborhood search (VNS), we can combine stochastic and deterministic searches, to get VNFSS. Traditional ways to tackle an optimization problem consider a given formulation, and search in some way through its feasible set X. The fact that the same problem may often be formulated in different ways allows to extend search paradigms to include jumps from one formulation to another. Each formulation should lend itself to some traditional search method, its "local search" that works totally within this formulation, and yields a final solution when started from some initial solution. Any solution found in one formulation should be easily transformed to its equivalent solution in any other formulation. We may then move from one formulation to another using the solution resulting from the former's local search as the initial solution for the latter's local search. Such a strategy will of course only be useful when local searches in different formulations behave differently. This idea was first investigated in [37] while examining the circle packing problem. Only two formulations of the circle packing problem (one with Cartesian coordinates, and the other with polar coordinates) were used. The nonlinear solver used by the authors alternates between these two formulations, each time starting from the solution reached in the previous iteration (but transformed into the corresponding solution (point) in the other formulation) until there is no further improvement. This approach was named Reformulation Descent. The same paper also introduced the idea of *Formulation space search* (FSS) where more than two formulations could be used. In [38], the collection of formulations is enlarged by presenting a subset of circles in Cartesian coordinates, while the rest are presented in polar coordinates. Also, the distance between any two formulations is introduced, and neighborhoods are defined as collections of formulations based on this distance. So, neighborhood $\mathcal{N}_k(\varphi)$ of formulation φ contains all formulations φ' that are at distance k from formulation φ. The basic idea behind FSS is to continue the search in one of the given formulations φ until it gets trapped at a stationary point, then choose a new formulation φ' belonging to the current neighborhood of φ, then transform the stationary point in φ to the corresponding solution in φ', and continue the search in φ' from that point. An improved version of FSS for solving the circle packing problem is proposed in [29]. One methodology that uses the variable neighborhood idea in searching through the formulation space is given in Algorithms 1 and 2. Here φ (φ') denotes a formulation from given formulation space

$\mathcal{F}$, x (x') denotes a solution in the feasible set defined with that formulation, and $\ell \leq \ell_{\max}$ is the formulation neighborhood index. Note that Algorithm 2 uses a reduced VNS strategy [19] in $\mathcal{F}$.

We can extend to the full VNFSS with the following changes:

a. the shake step involves only the random selection of formulation $\varphi' \in \mathcal{N}_\ell(\varphi)$; then set $x' \in \varphi'$ to the same solution as $x \in \varphi$;
b. in between the shake and formulation change steps, add a local search to map x' onto a stationary point under formulation φ': $x' \leftarrow LS_{\varphi'}(x')$.

Algorithm 1: Formulation change function.

```
1  Function FormulationChange(x, x′, φ, φ′, ℓ);
3  if f(φ′, x′) < f(φ, x) then
5  |    φ ← φ′; x ← x′; ℓ ← ℓ_min
6  else
8  |    ℓ ← ℓ + ℓ_step;
9  end
```

Algorithm 2: Reduced variable neighborhood FSS.

```
1  Function VNFSS(x, φ, ℓ_max);
3  repeat
5  |    ℓ ← 1                              // Initialize formulation in F ;
7  |    while ℓ ≤ ℓ_max do
9  |    |    ShakeFormulation(x,x′,φ,φ′,ℓ)  // (φ′,x′)∈(N_ℓ(φ), N(x)) at random;
11 |    |    FormulationChange(x,x′,φ,φ′,ℓ) // Change formulation ;
12 |    end
13 until some stopping condition is met;
```

---

ii. *Variable Objective Search* (VOS). Butenko et al. [10] propose a variant they call Variable Objective Search (VOS). Their idea uses the fact that many combinatorial optimization problems have different formulations (e.g. the maximum clique problem with more than twenty formulations, traveling salesman with more than 40 formulations, quadratic assignment problem, max-cut problem, etc). They assume that all formulations share the same feasible region, but have different objective functions. Also, all formulations have the same neighborhood structures. However,

* a stationary point for one formulation may not correspond to a stationary point with respect to another formulation;

- a global optimum of the considered combinatorial optimization problem should correspond to a global optimum for any formulation of this problem.

Based on the previous assumptions, Butenko et al. [10] propose the following method (named Basic Variable Objective Search):

- Arrange formulations in prespecified order: φ_1, φ_2, ..., φ_n. Denote with f_i the objective function for formulation φ_i.
- Choose an initial feasible solution, and perform a local search in a proposed neighborhood $\mathcal{N}$, yielding local optimum $x^{(1)}$ with respect to formulation φ_1.
- Perform a local search starting from the previous local optimum $x^{(1)}$ in neighborhood $\mathcal{N}$, but with respect to formulation φ_2. In other words the neighbors of current local optimum $x^{(1)}$ are mapped into corresponding points in formulation φ_2, and checked to see if a better solution can be obtained according to formulation φ_2 (and according to objective function f_2). This local search produces a local optimum with respect to formulation φ_2, and this local optimum will be presented (remembered) as a point in the solution space of formulation φ_1.
- After performing local search with respect to formulation φ_i $(i < n)$, local search starting from the last obtained local optimum with respect to formulation φ_{i+1} is performed.
- After performing local search with respect to formulation φ_n, the complete procedure repeats until there is no improvement with respect to all formulations.

A Variable Objective Search is demonstrated on the Maximal Independent Set Problem. A so-called Uniform Variable Objective Search is also proposed in [10]. Instead of local search with respect to a single formulation, this method performs simultaneous local search by exploring the complete neighborhood $\mathcal{N}$ of the current solution, thereby determining a collection of local optima with respect to all formulations. The move is then made to the best of all obtained local optima.

iii. *Variable Formulation Search* (VFS). Many optimization problems in the literature, for example, min–max types, present a flat landscape. This means that, given a formulation of the problem, there are many neighboring solutions with the same value of the objective function. When this happens, it is difficult to determine which neighborhood solution is a more promising one to continue the search. To address this drawback, the use of alternative formulations of the problem within VNS is proposed in [36, 39, 41]. In [41] this approach is named Variable Formulation Search (VFS). It combines the change of neighborhood within the VNS framework, with the use of alternative formulations. In particular, the alternative formulations will be used to compare different solutions with the same value of the objective function, when considering the original formulation.

Let us assume that, beside the original formulation and the corresponding objective function $f_0(x)$, there are p other formulations denoted as $f_1(x), \ldots, f_p(x), x \in X$. Note that two formulations are equivalent if the optimal solution of one is the optimal solution of the other, and vice versa. Without loss of clarity, we will denote different formulations as different objectives $f_i(x), i = 1, \ldots, p$. The idea of VFS is to add the procedure $\texttt{Accept}(x, x', p)$, given in Algorithm 3 in all three steps of Basic VNS (BVNS): $\texttt{Shaking}$, $\texttt{LocalSearch}$ and $\texttt{NeighborhoodChange}$. Clearly, if a better solution is not obtained by any formulation among the p pre-selected, the move is rejected. The next iteration in the loop of Algorithm 3 will take place only if the objective function values according to all previous formulations are equal.

Algorithm 3: Accept procedure with p secondary formulations.

1 **logical function** Accept (x, x', p) ;
2 **for** $i \leftarrow 0$ **to** p **do**
3   condition1 $\leftarrow f_i(x') < f_i(x)$;
4   condition2 $\leftarrow f_i(x') > f_i(x)$;
5   **if** condition1 **then**
6   Accept $\leftarrow$ True; **return**;
7   **else**
8   **if** condition2 **then**
9   Accept $\leftarrow$ False; **return**;
10   **end**
11   **end**
12 **end**
13 Accept $\leftarrow$ False; **return**;

If Accept (x, x', p) is included in the $\texttt{LocalSearch}$ subroutine of BVNS, then it will not stop the first time a non-improved solution is found. In order to stop $\texttt{LocalSearch}$, and thus claim that x' is a local minimum, x' should not be improved by any among the p different formulations. Thus, for any particular problem, one needs to design different formulations of the problem considered and decide the order they will be used in the Accept

subroutine. Answers to those two questions are problem specific and sometimes not easy. The `Accept` (x, x', p) subroutine can obviously be added
to the `NeighborhoodChange` and `Shaking` steps of BVNS as well.

In Mladenović et   al. [39], three evaluation functions, or acceptance
criteria, within the `Neighborhood Change` step are used in solving the
bandwidth minimization problem. This min-max problem consists in finding
permutations of rows and columns of a given square matrix such that the
maximal distance of a nonzero element from the main diagonal in the corresponding row, is a minimum. Solution x may be presented as a labeling of a
graph and the move from x to x' as $x \leftarrow x'$. The three criteria used are:

1. the simplest one which is based on the objective function value $f_0(x)$
   (bandwidth length);
2. the total number of critical vertices $f_1(x)$ (if $f_0(x') = f_0(x)$ and
   $f_1(x') < f_1(x)$);
3. $f_3(x, x') = \rho(x, x') - \alpha$ (if ($f_0(x') = f_0(x)$ and $f_1(x') = f_1(x)$),
   but x and x' are relatively far from each other; that is, the distance between
   solutions x and x', $\rho(x, x') > \alpha$, where α is an additional parameter).

The idea for a move to a mildly worse solution if it is very far, is used
within Skewed VNS [19]. However, a move to a solution with the same value
is performed in [39] only if its Hamming distance from the incumbent is
greater than α.

In [36], a different mathematical programming formulation of the original problem is used as a secondary objective within the `Neighborhood`
`Change` function of VNS. Two combinatorial optimization problems on
graphs are considered here: the *Metric dimension problem* and the *Minimal
doubly resolving set problem.*

iv. *Variable Space Search* (VSS). Hertz et al. [23] developed this variant of
FSS to solve the graph coloring problem (GCP). Their solution method
exploits the relation between the k-coloring problem and the GCP. Three
solution spaces are defined as follows: S_1 containing all k-colorings of a
given graph G, S_2 containing all partially legal k-colorings of G, and S_3
containing all cycle-free orientations of the edges of G. The VSS procedure
cycles through these spaces in an empirically determined sequence. We will
examine their VSS procedure in more detail in a later section.

(v) *Reformulation Local Search* (RLS) was originally proposed for solving
continuous location problems (Brimberg et al. [6]). This approach differs
from FSS in that the different formulations used are not equivalent to

each other. There is a base model, which is a single formulation of a given continuous location problem, and a series of discrete formulations, which are improving approximations of the continuous model.

The RLS switches between the continuous model (the original problem) and a discrete approximation in order to expand the search. In each iteration, new facility locations obtained by the improving search in the continuous phase are added to the discrete formulation. Thus, the two formulations become equivalent in a limiting sense. As in FSS, the solution found using the current formulation becomes the starting point for the next formulation.

There are many ways to construct an RLS-based algorithm (e.g. choice of: rules for inserting promising points or removing non-promising points in the discrete phase, improving searches for both phases, the initial discrete model, and so on). RLS can be applied not only to continuous location problems, but also other types of problems having continuous and discrete formulations. More details are given in the next section.

12.4   Some Applications

12.4.1   Circle Packing Problem

The circle packing problem can be stated in the following way. Given a number n of circular disks of equal radius r, determine how to place them within a unit circle without any overlap in order to maximize the radius r.

  i. *Circle Packing Problem Formulation in Cartesian Coordinates.* The circular container is the unit radius circle with center $(0, 0)$. The circles to be packed within it are given by their centers (x_i, y_i) $(i = 1, \ldots, n)$, and their common radius r, which is to be maximized. This may be formulated as:

$$\max r \tag{12.3}$$

subject to

$$(x_i - x_j)^2 + (y_i - y_j)^2 - 4r^2 \geq 0, \quad \forall\, i, j\ (1 \leq i < j \leq n)$$
$$x_i^2 + y_i^2 \leq (1 - r)^2, \qquad\qquad\qquad \forall\, i\ (1 \leq i \leq n)$$
$$r \geq 0, \quad x_i, y_i \in R, \qquad\qquad\qquad \forall\, i\ (1 \leq i \leq n).$$

The first set of inequalities expresses that any two disks should be disjoint: the squared Euclidean distance between their centers must be at least $(2r)^2$. The second set states that the disks must fully lie within the unit circle. This smoother quadratic form is preferred to the more standard constraint

$$\sqrt{x_i^2 + y_i^2} + r \leq 1.$$

ii. *Circle Packing Problem Formulation in Polar Coordinates.* The circular container is centered at the pole and has unit radius. The disks to be packed within it are given by their centers at polar coordinates (ρ_i, θ_i) $(i = 1, 2, \ldots, n)$, and their common radius r, which is to be maximized. The equivalent problem may be formulated as:

$$\max r \qquad\qquad (12.4)$$

subject to

$$
\begin{aligned}
&\rho_i^2 + \rho_j^2 - 2\rho_i\rho_j \cos(\theta_i - \theta_j) - 4r^2 \geq 0, \forall\, i, j\ (1 \leq i < j \leq n)\\
&\rho_i + r \leq 1, &\forall\, i\ (1 \leq i \leq n)\\
&r \geq 0,\\
&\rho_i \geq 0, \quad \theta_i \in [0, 2\pi], &\forall\, i\ (1 \leq i \leq n).
\end{aligned}
$$

Note that, unlike the Cartesian formulation, the second constraint set, expressing inclusion of the disks inside the container, is now linear.

12.4.1.1 Reformulation Descent

These two formulations are used to solve the circle packing problem in [37], using MINOS (an off-the-self nonlinear program solver). The starting solution is a set of randomly chosen points within the container acting as centers of the circles. The radius of the circles is a maximal number r such that the corresponding circles do not overlap and each circle is completely inside the unit circle. The centers of the circles are first expressed in Cartesian coordinates. As already noted, MINOS is applied to the current solution, in this case, the selected initial solution. After MINOS finishes at some stationary point, the coordinates of the obtained centers are converted to polar coordinates, and MINOS is applied on the optimization problem written in polar coordinates with the set of current centers and current value of r as the initial solution. If MINOS is unable to increase the radius of the circles, the method finishes, and the final solution is the corresponding solution. Otherwise, if

MINOS is able to increase r, the centers of the obtained circles are converted in Cartesian coordinates and a new iteration begins using the current solution as the initial solution.

This procedure, referred to as Reformulation Descent (RD), is illustrated in Fig. 12.2 for $n = 35$ equal circles. As can be seen, seven executions are applied until the final (which is also optimal) solution is obtained.

Reformulation Descent (RD) is implemented in [37] on packing n ($n = 10, 15, 20, \ldots, 100$) circles in the unit circle. For each value of n, RD is

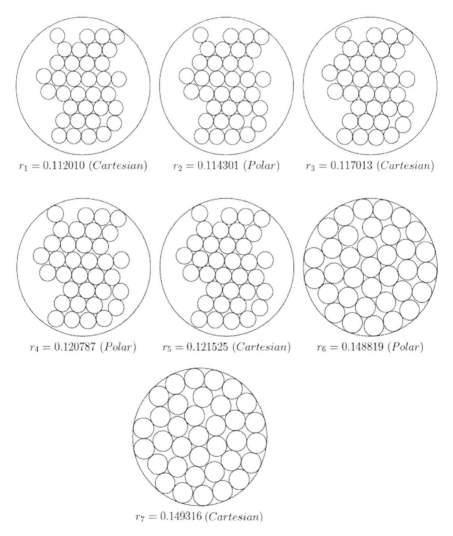

$r_1 = 0.112010 \ (Cartesian)$ $r_2 = 0.114301 \ (Polar)$ $r_3 = 0.117013 \ (Cartesian)$

$r_4 = 0.120787 \ (Polar)$ $r_5 = 0.121525 \ (Cartesian)$ $r_6 = 0.148819 \ (Polar)$

$r_7 = 0.149316 \ (Cartesian)$

Fig. 12.2 Illustration of reformulation descent applied on packing 35 circles in the unit circle ([37])

executed 50 times. The same problem is also executed 50 times using Cartesian coordinates only from the same set of initial solutions, and again in Polar coordinates only from the same set of initial solutions. Initial solutions are generated by choosing at random Polar coordinates ρ and θ and converting them into Cartesian coordinates (if it is necessary). The value of radius ρ is set to $(1 - 1/\sqrt{n}) \cdot \sqrt{rnd}$ where rnd is uniformly distributed on $[0, 1]$. The value of angle θ is uniformly distributed on $[0, 2\pi]$.

Summary results are given in Table 12.1. The first column contains the value of n (number of circles). Column 2 contains the best-known result (radius of the circle) for the corresponding value of n. Columns 3–5 contain the percentage deviation of best results obtained respectively by MINOS with RD, MINOS with Cartesian coordinates only, and MINOS with Polar coordinates only, from the best-known results (radius). Columns 6–8 contain the percentage deviation of average results obtained by RD, Cartesian coordinates, and Polar coordinates, respectively, from the best-known results (radius). Columns 9–11 contain the average running time respectively for RD, Cartesian coordinates, and Polar coordinates.

Table 12.1 Summary results of 50 executions of RD, Cartesian coordinates only, and Polar coordinates only [37]

		% dev. of best			% dev. of avg.			Running time		
n	Best	M_{RD}	M_C	M_P	M_{RD}	M_C	M_P	M_{RD}	M_C	N_P
10	0.262258899	0.00	0.00	0.00	1.03	2.01	0.88	0.00	0.02	0.01
15	0.221172537	0.00	0.13	0.13	0.49	0.65	0.77	0.01	0.03	0.02
20	0.195224535	0.00	0.00	0.00	1.15	2.80	2.49	0.04	0.11	0.08
25	0.173827671	0.00	0.00	0.00	0.62	5.07	3.21	0.08	0.37	0.19
30	0.161349111	0.00	0.00	0.00	0.97	2.49	1.40	0.16	0.52	0.29
35	0.149316779	0.00	0.01	0.02	0.73	12.27	2.17	0.90	1.84	1.73
40	0.140373593	0.00	0.00	0.00	0.97	9.36	4.21	1.11	2.92	1.91
45	0.132049600	0.10	0.11	0.04	0.69	3.75	2.31	1.47	3.08	2.19
50	0.125825494	0.06	0.03	0.00	0.79	6.90	4.26	3.19	5.16	4.41
55	0.121786333	0.00	1.13	1.57	2.09	4.80	2.40	3.37	6.73	5.15
60	0.115657478	0.03	0.10	0.57	1.40	1.58	1.78	4.71	7.54	6.00
65	0.110896748	0.00	0.47	0.44	1.33	5.86	2.79	16.24	12.94	10.43
70	0.106990091	0.10	0.55	0.32	0.99	7.83	2.15	19.56	17.61	14.54
75	0.103323461	0.10	0.22	0.44	0.77	4.56	1.69	26.46	22.67	17.16
80	0.100294988	0.10	0.41	0.29	0.93	3.38	1.69	39.15	30.99	23.62
85	0.098395059	0.72	1.43	1.10	1.75	3.31	1.90	38.79	29.85	24.04
90	0.094822061	0.02	0.02	0.45	1.27	10.59	4.32	96.82	47.19	47.70
95	0.092249178	0.18	0.26	0.48	0.93	11.55	6.87	147.35	59.51	41.84
100	0.090232120	0.30	0.52	0.38	1.01	8.39	3.39	180.32	64.96	45.02

iii. *Mixed formulation of Circle Packing Problem.* There are many possible formulations obtained by expressing the locations of some centers in Cartesian coordinates, and the remaining centers in Polar coordinates. Suppose that centers of circles are numbered $1, 2, 3, \ldots, n$. Then the pair of disjoint sets C_φ and P_φ, whose union is the set $\{1, 2, 3, \ldots, n\}$, determines one formulation (φ) as follows:

$$\max r \tag{12.5}$$

subject to

$$
\begin{aligned}
&(x_i - x_j)^2 + (y_i - y_j)^2 - 4r^2 \geq 0, && \forall \, i, j \in C_\varphi (i < j) \\
&\rho_i^2 + \rho_j^2 - 2\rho_i \rho_j \cos(\theta_i - \theta_j) - 4r^2 \geq 0, && \forall \, i, j \in P_\varphi (i < j) \\
&(x_i - \rho_j \cos(\theta_j))^2 + (y_i - \rho_j \sin(\theta_j))^2 - 4r^2 \geq 0, && \forall \, i \in C_\varphi, \forall \, j \in P_\varphi \\
&x_i^2 + y_i^2 \leq (1 - r)^2, && \forall \, i \in C_\varphi \\
&\rho_i + r \leq 1, && \forall \, i \in P_\varphi \\
&r \geq 0, && \\
&x_i, y_i \in \mathbb{R}, && \forall i \in C_\varphi \\
&\rho_i \geq 0, \quad \theta_i \in [0, 2\pi], && \forall \, i \in P_\varphi.
\end{aligned}
$$

A general reformulation descent procedure could be constructed by replacing the two pure formulations (Cartesian and polar) used above by a specified sequence of mixed and pure formulations.

12.4.1.2   Formulation Space Search

We will call the set of all possible formulations *Formulation Space $\mathcal{F}$*. Each of these formulations can be used by MINOS (or any other NLP solver) for solving the circle packing problem. In Mladenović et al. [38], a distance function in the formulation space is introduced as the cardinality of the symmetric difference of sets representing the subsets of circles which are in Cartesian coordinates:

$$d(\varphi_1, \varphi_2) = |C_{\varphi_1} \Delta C_{\varphi_2}| = |P_{\varphi_1} \Delta P_{\varphi_2}|.$$

The defined distance allows the definition of neighborhoods in the Formulation space:

$$\mathcal{N}_k(\varphi) = \{\varphi' | d(\varphi, \varphi') = k\},$$

and introduces *Formulation Space Search* for the circle packing problem. A pseudo code for FSS is given in Algorithm 4 ([38]).

Algorithm 4: VNFSS heuristic for solving CPP.

```
 1  Function FSSCPP(n, k_min, k_max, k_step, t_max);
 2  (x, y, ρ, θ, r) ← Initial_solution(n);
 3  C ← {1, 2, ..., n};
 4  P ← ∅;
 5  k_curr ← k_min;
 6  (x, y, ρ, θ, r) ← MinosMix(x, y, ρ, θ, P, C);
 7  repeat
 8  │   let Q be a random subset of {1, 2, ..., n} with k_curr elements;
 9  │   P' ← PΔQ;
10  │   C' ← CΔQ;
11  │   (x', y', ρ', θ', r') ← MinosMix(x, y, ρ, θ, P', C');
12  │   if r' > r then
13  │   │    (x, y, ρ, θ, r) ← (x', y', ρ', θ', r');
14  │   │    P ← P';
15  │   │    C ← C';
16  │   │    k_curr ← k_min;
17  │   else
18  │   │    k_curr ← k_curr + k_step;
19  │   │    if k_curr > k_max then
20  │   │    │   k_curr ← k_min
21  │   │    end
22  │   end
23  │   t ← CpuTime();
24  until t > t_max;
25  return r;
```

Execution of FSS for $n = 50$ circles is shown in Fig. 12.3. The starting solution is not randomly selected, but is instead a solution obtained after applying Reformulation Descent. Each picture shows an improved solution obtained by execution of function MinosMix. Below each picture we see the value of circle radius (r) as well as the neighborhood in the Formulation Space in which the improved solution is obtained.

In Mladenović et al. [38], k_{min} and k_{step} are both set to 3, and k_{max} is set to $n = 50$. Note that the first improvement was obtained for $k_{curr} = 12$. This implies that no improvement was found with $k_{curr} = 3, 6$ and 9. Since the initial formulation is all Cartesian, this also means that a mixed formulation with 12 polar and 38 Cartesian coordinates was used ($|C_F| = 38$, $|P_F| = 12$). In the next round, a formulation with 3 randomly chosen circle centers ($k_{curr} = 3$), was unsuccessful, but a better solution was found with 6, and so on. After 10 improvements, the algorithm ends up with a solution with radius $r_{max} = 0.125798$.

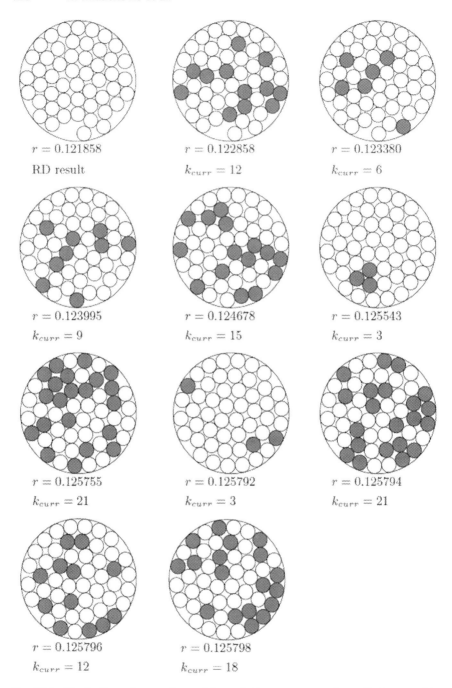

$r = 0.121858$

RD result

$r = 0.122858$

$k_{curr} = 12$

$r = 0.123380$

$k_{curr} = 6$

$r = 0.123995$

$k_{curr} = 9$

$r = 0.124678$

$k_{curr} = 15$

$r = 0.125543$

$k_{curr} = 3$

$r = 0.125755$

$k_{curr} = 21$

$r = 0.125792$

$k_{curr} = 3$

$r = 0.125794$

$k_{curr} = 21$

$r = 0.125796$

$k_{curr} = 12$

$r = 0.125798$

$k_{curr} = 18$

Fig. 12.3 Illustration of execution of formulation space search applied on packing 50 circles in the unit circle. Starting solution is a solution obtained by Reformulation Descent ([38])

Table 12.2 Comparison of reformulation descent and formulation space search on circle packing problem [38]

		RD			FSS		
n	Best known	Best	Avg.	Time	Best	Avg.	Time
50	0.125825494	0.06	0.79	3.19	0.00	0.24	80.54
55	0.121786333	0.00	2.09	3.37	0.00	0.60	72.81
60	0.115657478	0.03	1.40	4.71	0.00	0.95	84.39
65	0.110896748	0.00	1.33	16.24	0.00	0.21	108.25
70	0.106990091	0.10	0.99	19.56	0.01	0.27	151.64
75	0.103323461	0.10	0.77	26.46	0.02	0.20	164.51
80	0.100294988	0.10	0.93	39.15	0.04	0.23	229.49
85	0.098395059	0.72	1.75	38.79	0.18	0.72	256.17
90	0.094822061	0.02	1.27	96.82	0.02	0.56	294.77
95	0.092249178	0.18	0.93	147.35	0.07	0.39	308.34
100	0.09023212	0.30	1.01	180.32	0.12	0.68	326.67

A comparison of results obtained by 50 executions of Reformulation Descent and Formulation Space Search for the circle packing problem is given in Table 12.2. The first column in Table 12.2 contains the number of circles n. The second column contains the value of the best-known solution for the corresponding value of n. Columns 3–5 contain results for Reformulation Descent: percentage deviation of best solution from best-known solution, percentage deviation of the average of solutions and average running time. Columns 6–8 contain the corresponding values for solutions obtained by Formulation Space Search.

The table shows that the average error of the FSS heuristic is smaller, i.e., solutions obtained by FSS are more stable than those obtained with RD.

12.4.2 Graph Coloring Problem

A graph $G = (V, E)$ with vertex set V and edge set E, and an integer k are given. A k-coloring of G is a mapping $c : V \rightarrow \{1, \ldots, k\}$. The value $c(x)$, where x is a vertex is called the color of x. The vertices which have color i ($1 \leq i \leq k$) represent a *color class*, denoted V_i. If two adjacent vertices x and y have the same color i, vertices x and y, the edge (x, y) and color i are said to be conflicting. A k-coloring without conflicting edges is a *legal coloring* and its color classes are called *stable sets*.

The Graph Coloring Problem (GCP for short) requires that the smallest integer k be determined, such that a legal k-coloring of G exists. Number k is also called the chromatic number of G, and is denoted as $\chi(G)$. Given a fixed integer k, the optimization problem k-GCP is to determine a k-coloring of

G which has the minimal number of conflicting edges. If the optimal value of the k-GCP is zero then graph G has a legal k-coloring. A local search algorithm for the GCP can be used to solve the k-GCP by simply stopping the search as soon as a legal k-coloring is found. Also, an algorithm that solves the k-GCP can be used to solve the GCP, by starting with an upper bound k on $\chi(G)$, and then decreasing k as long as a legal k-coloring can be found.

Hertz et al. [23] define three solution spaces for solving the GCP and k-GCP problems. Note that a solution of the k-GCP should satisfy two conditions if possible: there are no edges where both endpoints have the same color, and all vertices must be colored. The first two solution spaces relax one of these two conditions; the third search space satisfies both conditions.

The first proposed solution space S_1 consists of all (not necessarily legal) k-colorings of graph G. In solution space S_1, objective function $f_1(s)$ (for $s \in S_1$) is defined as the number of conflicting edges in coloring s. In solution space S_1, neighborhood $N_1(s)$ consists of all k-coloring s' obtained by changing the color of exactly one vertex. Based on the proposed neighborhood, Hertz and de Werra [22] developed a Tabu search algorithm, also called TabuCol, for solving the k-coloring problem.

The second solution space S_2 consists of all partially legal k-colorings. More precisely each solution is a partition of the set of vertices into $k + 1$ disjoint sets $V_1, V_2, \ldots, V_k, V_{k+1}$, where sets $V_1, V_2, \ldots, V_k$ are stable sets, while V_{k+1} is a set of non-colored vertices. In solution space S_2, the objective function f_2 is defined, such that $f_2(s)$ is the cardinality of subset V_{k+1}. Morgenstern [40] proposed the objective function $f_2'(s) = \sum_{v \in V_{k+1}} d(v)$, where $d(v)$ denotes the number of edges incident to vertex v. Neighborhood $N_2(s)$ consists of all solutions obtained by moving a vertex $v \in V_{k+1}$ in the set (color class) V_i, and moving to V_{k+1} all vertices $u \in V_i$ adjacent to vertex v. Bloechliger and Zufferey [2] obtained very good results by using reactive tabu search and the number of non-colored vertices as the objective function. Solution space S_3 consists of the *cycle-free orientations* of the edges of graph G. Gallai [18], Roy [43], and Vitaver [46] independently proved in the sixties that the length of a longest path in an orientation of graph G is at least equal to the chromatic number of G. As a corollary, the problem of orienting the edges of a graph so that the resulting digraph $\overrightarrow{G}$ is cycle-free, and the length $\lambda(\overrightarrow{G})$ of a longest path in $\overrightarrow{G}$ is minimum, is equivalent to the problem of finding the chromatic number of G.

Indeed, given a $\chi(G)$-coloring c of a graph G, one can easily construct a cycle-free orientation $\overrightarrow{G}$ with $\lambda(\overrightarrow{G}) \leq \chi(G)$ by simply orienting each edge $[u, v]$ from u to v if and only if $c(u) < c(v)$. Conversely, given a cycle-free orientation $\overrightarrow{G}$ of G, one can build a $\lambda(\overrightarrow{G})$-coloring of G by assigning to each vertex v a color $c(v)$ equal to the length of a longest path ending at v in $\overrightarrow{G}$.

So, objective function f_3 can be defined, such that $f_3(s)$ is the length of the longest oriented path. Many local searches can be defined in S_3. One of them is removing all arcs (oriented edges) not contained in the longest path, choosing vertex u and changing the orientation of all arcs ending at vertex u or beginning at vertex u. It can be proved that the length of a longest path in the so obtained graph is bigger by at most one than the length of the longest path in the starting graph.

Translators can be constructed that translate the solution belonging to one of the three solution spaces into the corresponding solution belonging to another solution space. After some preliminary experiments, Hertz et al. [23] found that the sequence $S_1 \rightarrow S_3 \rightarrow S_2 \rightarrow S_1$ of search spaces, called a cycle, appears to be a good choice, each translation from an S_i to its successor being easy to perform.

A variable space search (VSS) algorithm (Hertz et al. [23]) is executed on 16 graphs from the DIMACS Challenge. After a preliminary set of experiments, the following graphs were selected as representative of the most challenging ones.

- Six DSJCn.d graphs: the DSJCs are random graphs with n vertices and a density of $\frac{d}{10}$. It means that each pair of vertices has a probability of $\frac{d}{10}$ to be adjacent. Hertz et al. [23] use the DSJC graphs with $n \in \{500, 1000\}$ and $d \in \{1, 5, 9\}$
- Two DSJRn.r graphs: the DSJRs are geometric random graphs. They are constructed by choosing n random points in the unit square and two vertices are connected if the distance between them is less than $\frac{r}{10}$. Graphs with an added end letter "c" are the complementary graphs. The authors use two graphs with $n = 500$ and, respectively, $r = 1$ and $r = 5$.
- Four flatn_χ_0 graphs: the flat graphs are constructed graphs with n vertices and a chromatic number χ. The end number "0" means that all vertices are incident to the same number of vertices.
- Four len_χx graphs: the Leighton graphs are graphs with n vertices and a chromatic number χ equal to the size of the largest clique (i.e., the largest number of pairwise adjacent vertices). The end letter "x" stands for different graphs with similar settings.

Detailed results of the VSS coloring algorithm are presented in Table 12.3. The first column contains the name of the graph. The second column

Table 12.3 Detailed results of VSS coloring with a time limit of 1 hour ([23])

Instance	χ	UB	k	Succ./run	10^3 iter.	Time
DSJC1000.1	*	20	20	03/10	285,624	2396
			21	10/10	757	11
DSJC1000.5	*	83	88	08/10	55,971	2028
			89	10/10	22,852	820
DSJC1000.9	*	224	224	01/10	48,348	3326
			225	05/10	21,667	1484
			226	10/10	27,429	1751
DSJC500.1	*	12	12	10/10	19,799	97
DSJC500.5	*	48	48	03/10	78,667	1331
			49	10/10	10,524	162
DSJC500.9	*	126	126	08/10	76,927	1686
			127	10/10	7754	169
DSJR500.1c	*	85	85	09/10	48,530	736
			86	10/10	20,020	291
DSJR500.5	*	122	126	09/10	61,849	1409
			127	10/10	9066	183
flat1000_50_0	50	50	50	10/10	625	318
flat1000_60_0	60	60	60	10/10	1242	694
flat1000_76_0	76	82	87	04/06	48,609	1689
			88	10/10	36,924	1155
flat300_28_0	28	28	29	01/10	45,611	867
			30	02/10	217,647	2666
			31	10/10	4173	39
le450_15c	15	15	15	10/10	497	6
le450_15d	15	15	15	10/10	4761	44
le450_25c	25	25	26	10/10	183	1
le450_25d	25	25	26	10/10	117	1

* Chromatic number was not known

contains the chromatic number ("*" when it is not known), and the third column contains the best-known upper bound. The VSS algorithm was run 10 times on each graph with different values of k. The fourth column reports various values of k ranging from the smallest number for which they had at least one successful run, to the smallest number for which they had 10 successful runs. The next columns respectively contain the number of successful runs and the number of tries, the average number of iterations in thousands (i.e., the total number of moves performed using the 3 neighborhoods, divided by 1000) on successful runs, and the average CPU time used (in seconds).

The VSS algorithm is compared with TabuCol [22], PartialCol [2] as well as with three graph coloring algorithms which are among the most effective

Table 12.4 Comparisons between VSS-Col and five other algorithms ([23])

Instance	χ	UB	VSS-Col	TabuCol	PartialCol	GH	MMT	MOR
DSJC1000.1	*	20	20	20	20	20	20	21
DSJC1000.5	*	83	88	89	89	83	83	88
DSJC1000.9	*	224	224	227	228	224	226	226
DSJC500.1	*	12	12	12	12	12	12	12
DSJC500.5	*	48	48	49	49	48	48	49
DSJC500.9	*	126	126	127	127	126	127	128
DSJR500.1c	*	85	85	85	85	–	85	85
DSJR500.5	*	122	126	126	126	–	122	123
flat1000_50_0	50	50	50	50	50	50	50	50
flat1000_60_0	60	60	60	60	60	60	60	60
flat1000_76_0	76	82	87	88	88	83	82	89
flat300_28_0	28	28	29	31	28	31	31	31
le450_15c	15	15	15	16	15	15	15	15
le450_15d	15	15	15	15	15	15	15	15
le450_25c	25	25	26	26	27	26	25	25
le450_25d	25	25	26	26	27	26	25	25

* Chromatic number was not known

ones: the GH algorithm in [17], the MOR algorithm in [40], and the MMT algorithm in [34]. A detailed comparison is given in Table 12.4.

12.4.3 Continuous Location Problems

12.4.3.1 Preliminaries

Location models in the literature typically determine where to place a given number of new facilities in order to serve a given set of demand points (also called existing facilities, fixed points, or customers) in the best way. Continuous models, also known as site-generating models (Love et al. [33]), allow the new facilities to be located anywhere in N-dimensional Euclidean space (E^N) or a sub-region thereof. A specified distance function is required in practical applications in order to measure the distances between new facilities and the customers they will serve. Most applications in the literature occur in the plane ($N = 2$), and use the Euclidean norm as the distance function.

Consider the unconstrained planar p-median problem with Euclidean distances (also known as the multi-source Weber problem (MWP)), which may be written as:

$$\text{(min)}\ \ f(X_1, X_2, \ldots, X_p) = \sum_{j \in [n]} w_j \min\{d(X_i, A_j) : i \in [p]\},$$

$$(12.6)$$

where n denotes the number of demand points; p denotes the number of new facilities to be opened; $[t] = \{1, 2, \ldots, t\}$ for any positive integer t; w_j is a positive weight equivalent to the demand at given point $A_j = (a_j, b_j)$, $j \in [n]$; $X_i = (x_i, y_i)$ denotes the unknown location of new facility $i \in [p]$; and $d(X_i, A_j)$ is the Euclidean distance between X_i and A_j, for all pairs (X_i, A_j).

The objective function f in (12.6) is a weighted sum of distances between the demand points and their closest facilities. Since the minimum of a set of convex functions is nonconvex, the function f is itself nonconvex and may contain several stationary points. This was recognized by Cooper [11, 12], who was also the first to propose this continuous location–allocation problem. Among the methods proposed by Cooper to solve (12.6), one became quite famous, and is referred in the literature as Cooper's algorithm. It is based on the following simple observation. When the facility locations are fixed, the problem reduces to allocating each demand point to its closest facility. Then when the resulting partition of the set of demand points is fixed, the problem reduces to p independent and convex single facility location problems, which are easily solved by gradient descent methods such as the well-known Weiszfeld procedure (Weiszfeld [47]). Cooper's algorithm iterates between location and allocation steps until a local minimum is reached.

Solving the planar p-median problem is equivalent to enumerating the Voronoi partitions of the set of demand points, which is NP-hard (Megiddo and Supowit [35]). The complexity of the problem has been demonstrated in the literature. For example, Brimberg et al. [5] test the well-studied 50-customer problem in Eilon et al. [14] by running Cooper's algorithm from 10,000 randomly generated starting solutions for each $p \in \{5, 10, 15\}$. They obtain 272, 3008, and 3363 different local minima, respectively. The worst deviation from the best solution found (later shown to be optimal by Krau [27]) was, respectively, $47\%, 66\%$ and 70%. The best-found solution was obtained 690 times for $p = 5$, 34 times for $p = 10$, and only once for $p = 15$. Considering that $n = 50$ is a small instance by today's standard, these results demonstrate quite dramatically the complex topology of the objective function. For further reading, see e.g., Brimberg and Salhi [9].

12.4.3.2 Reformulation Local Search for Continuous Location

Any continuous location model can be formulated as a discrete problem by restricting the potential sites of the new facilities to a finite set of given points in the continuous space. The distance between any pair of points is measured by the same distance function used in the continuous model. For example, the continuous p-median problem in (12.6) becomes the classical discrete p-median problem when the facility locations are restricted to the n given demand points. Exploiting the relation between these two formulations was suggested in the original work of Cooper [11, 12]. Hansen et al. [20] proposed an effective heuristic that first solves the discrete p-median exactly using a primal-dual algorithm by Erlenkotter [15], and then completes one iteration of "continuous-space adjustment" by solving the p continuous single facility minisum problems identified by the partition of the set of demand points found in the discrete phase. The excessive computation time needed to solve larger instances of the discrete model limits the size of instances that can be considered (Brimberg et al. [4]). A similar approach is proposed in Salhi and Gamal [44], but this time a heuristic is used to solve the discrete p-median approximately. Kalczynski et al. [25] describe a greedy, random approach to construct good discrete starting solutions. They go on to show the rather counter-intuitive result that using good discrete starting solutions can be more effective and efficient than the optimal discrete solution.

A general procedure known as reformulation local search (RLS) that iterates between the continuous location problem under consideration and discrete approximations of this problem was proposed in [6]. The RLS procedure may be viewed as a special case of formulation space search (FSS), i.e., its extended Reformulation descent variant. In the latter case, two or more equivalent formulations of a given problem are combined in the search process. Meanwhile, in RLS we have the original continuous location model coupled with a series of discrete approximations. Each succeeding discrete formulation presents a better approximation of the original (continuous) problem until the algorithm terminates at a local optimum in both spaces. We will also see later that the series of approximations can be made to converge in an asymptotic sense to an equivalent formulation of the original problem. The general steps of RLS are examined next (see [6] for further details).

Consider a continuous location problem of the following general form:

$$\min \ (\text{or max}) \ f(X_1, X_2, \ldots, X_p), \tag{12.7}$$

requiring p new facility sites $X_i \in \mathbb{R}^N$, $i \in [p]$, to be found. The multi-source Weber problem (MWP) given in (12.6) is an example. Another important, but less-studied class of location problems is given by the continuous p-centre problem,

$$\min g(X_1, X_2, \ldots, X_p) = \max\{\min\{d(X_i, A_j) : i \in [p]\} : j \in [n]\},$$
$$(12.8)$$

where the objective is to minimize the furthest distance from a demand point to its closest facility, and which is used when quality of service (e.g., emergency response) is the main goal. (Note that the unweighted version of MWP, where $w_j = 1$, for all j, minimizes the average distance from a demand point to its closest facility.) The continuous p-dispersion problem is used to locate obnoxious facilities. Here we have a max min min objective:

$$\max h(X_1, X_2, \ldots, X_p) = \min\{\min\{d(X_i, A_j) : i \in [p]\} : j \in [n]\}.$$
$$(12.9)$$

In this case, constraints are required to limit the locations of the new facilities to a closed sub-region of $\mathbb{R}^N$. Constraints specifying a minimum separation distance between the new facilities may also be included. Other types of constraints, such as limits on the capacities of the facilities, may be added to the general model in (12.7) without affecting the discussion below. We will refer to (12.7) (+ any required constraints) as (GLP) for the general location problem in continuous space.

Using the notation in Brimberg et al. [6], let $(GLP)'$ denote the current discrete approximation of (GLP), and S the finite set of potential sites specified in $(GLP)'$. The discrete approximation of the unconstrained (GLP) in (12.7) may be written as:

$$\min \text{ (or max)}_{X \subset S, |X|=p} f(X).$$
$$(12.10)$$

For the case of p homogeneous facilities, and where no constraints are included in (GLP), there are $\binom{M}{p}$ possible solutions to $(GLP)'$. When constraints are included in (GLP), they must also be respected in $(GLP)'$, and so to be effective, the constructed set S should contain several feasible solutions. To complete the preliminaries, let L_C and L_D denote the selected improving searches for (GLP) and $(GLP)'$, respectively. These searches stop at a current solution, if and only if, a better solution cannot be found in the respective neighborhood of the search. The framework for reformulation local search (RLS) is now presented assuming that (GLP) is a minimization problem (see [6]).

Algorithm 5: Basic Reformulation Local Search (RLS).

1   Step 1: Select an initial solution $X^0 = \{X_1^0, \ldots, X_P^0\}$, and initial set S for $(GLP)'$.
2   Step 2 (solving the continuous problem): $L_C(X^0) \to X^C$ (where $X^C \neq X^0$, only if $f(X^C) < f(X^0)$).
3   Step 3 (augmenting S): $S \leftarrow S \cup X^C$.
4   Step 4 (solving the discrete problem): $L_D(X^C) \to X^D$ (where $X^D \neq X^C$, only if $f(X^D) < f(X^C)$).
5   Step 5: If $X^D = X^C$, stop (final solution = X^D); else $X^0 \leftarrow X^D$ and return to step 2.

Referring to Algorithm 5, we can note the following useful features of RLS:

- The initial set S is not restricted to the set of demand points as in other methods that combine a discrete approximation of the original continuous problem. For example, S can include some "attractive" demand points combined with a sufficient number of "attractive" sites obtained by local search from several random initial solutions. The choice of initial solution X^0 is also left up to the analyst. It can be, for example, a randomly generated solution or one obtained by a constructive method (e.g. [8]).
- The analyst also selects the algorithms, L_C and L_D for improving the solution in the continuous and discrete spaces, respectively. These can be the simplest of local searches, metaheuristic based methods, and in the case of L_D, even an exact method. Thus, the RLS framework is very flexible.
- Step 3 (augmenting S) is an important feature. It allows new, attractive facility sites to be added to the discrete model. For example, referring to the continuous p-median problem (12.6), new median points found by L_C in the continuous space allow new partitions of the set of demand points to be investigated in the discrete phase by L_D, which in turn may give improved solutions of the original problem (12.6). We demonstrate this in the following example. (Also see [6] for a different example.)

An Illustration

Consider the small example in Fig. 12.4 with five demand points arranged to form two equilateral triangles, a small one with sides of length $= 1$, and a large one with sides of length $= 3$. The two triangles share a common vertex A_3 located at the origin $(0, 0)$, and the large one is symmetrically inverted above the small one with the vertical axis bisecting the two triangles. The

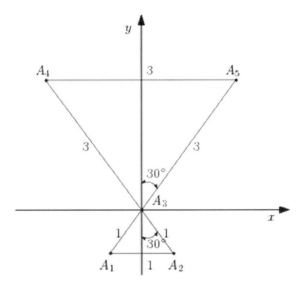

Fig. 12.4 Illustration of RLS

weights at the demand points are all equal to 1; $w_j = 1$, $j = 1, \ldots, 5$, and three facilities are to be located ($p = 3$). The initial set S (step 1) comprises the complete set of demand points. Suppose also that the initial solution consists of p randomly selected demand points (a commonly used procedure), and this time $X^0 = \{A_1, A_2, A_4\}$. Assigning demand points to their nearest facilities, with ties broken arbitrarily, results in the following partition:

$$\{A_1, A_3\}, \{A_2\}, \{A_4, A_5\}$$

The objective value for this solution is $f = d(A_1, A_3) + d(A_4, A_5) = 1 + 3 = 4$. Since the facilities are optimally located with respect to their assigned demand points, the current solution is a local minimum, and L_C (Cooper's algorithm is chosen) cannot improve it in step 2. As a result, no new points are added to S in step 3. Using the common single vertex swap move for L_D in step 4 (where only one facility can move from its current vertex to any unoccupied vertex) leads to an improved solution where X_2 moves from A_2 to A_5, and a better partition of the demand points is achieved:

$$\{A_1, A_2, A_3\}, \{A_5\}, \{A_4\}$$

The objective value is reduced to $f = d(A_1, A_3) + d(A_1, A_2) = 1 + 1 = 2$. In the next iteration of the continuous phase, X_1 moves from A_1 to the median point of its assigned cluster $\{A_1, A_2, A_3\}$, $X_m = (0, -1/\sqrt{3})$, with new $f = d(X_m, A_1) + d(X_m, A_2) + d(X_m, A_3) = 3 \times \frac{1}{\sqrt{3}} = \sqrt{3}$. The new point X_m is added to S. The next iteration of the discrete phase cannot improve this solution; so the algorithm terminates with final solution, $X_1 = X_m$, $X_2 = A_5$, and $X_3 = A_4$, which is also the optimal solution. The summary of RLS moves is as follows:

$$X^0 = \{A_1, A_2, A_4\} \xrightarrow{L_C} X^1 = X^0 \xrightarrow{L_D} X^2 = \{A_1, A_5, A_4\} \xrightarrow{L_C}$$

$$X^3 = \{X_m, A_5, A_4\} \xrightarrow{L_D} X^4 = X^3.$$

A Small Instance (n = 50) from the Literature

Brimberg et al. [6] carry out a detailed computational experiment on the well-studied 50-customer problem from [14]. The aim of the experiment is to compare RLS to Cooper's classical algorithm, which is referred to as MALT to signify multi-start alternating (locate–allocate), and which is used as a basis of comparison to this day for heuristics developed to solve the multi-source Weber problem (12.6). Note that MALT was originally developed for MWP, but can also be adapted to many other classes of location problems, continuous or discrete, such as the p-centre problem, by simply changing the objective function. Five different values of p are tested ($p = 5, 10, 15, 20, 25$). Each of these five instances is run 100 times from random starting solutions generated within the smallest rectangle containing the set of demand points, for both MALT and RLS. The most basic form of RLS is used, where the improving search in the continuous phase (L_C) is the same Cooper algorithm used in MALT, and the improving search in the discrete phase (L_D) is the standard single vertex exchange (Teitz and Bart [45]) discussed above in the illustrative example. The number of distinct local minima (LM), the number of occurrences of the 1st, 2nd, and 3rd best solutions, and the number of solutions within given fractional deviations of the optimal solution (from Krau [27]) are tabulated. Sample results are provided here in Table 12.5.

Some interesting observations are noted.

* The number of distinct local minima is much smaller for RLS than MALT. For $p = 5$, this number = 50 for MALT and only 4 for RLS. For $p = 15$, all 100 runs in MALT produce different local minima, while RLS only produces two different local minima. We may attribute the small number

Table 12.5 Sample results comparing MALT and RLS on 50-customer problem (Brimberg et al. [6])

p	Local minima infos	MALT	RLS
5	# Distinct local minima (LM)	50	4
	# 1st best	7	19
	# 2nd best	3	32
	# 3rd best	4	20
	# LM with dev $\leq$ 0.0005	10	19
	# LM with dev $\leq$ 0.005	19	51
	# LM with dev $\leq$ 0.05	57	96
15	# Distinct local minima (LM)	100	2
	# 1st best	1	70
	# 2nd best	1	30
	# 3rd best	1	0
	# LM with dev $\leq$ 0.0005	0	70
	# LM with dev $\leq$ 0.005	1	70
	# LM with dev $\leq$ 0.05	4	100

of local minima found by RLS to the much larger search neighborhood compared to MALT obtained by adding the discrete phase.

* The first best solution obtained by RLS turns out to be the optimal solution in all five instances tested. However, MALT finds the optimal solution only for the smallest instance, $p = 5$.
* The quality of the few local minima obtained by RLS is very good. Considering the poor quality of the random starting solutions, this would indicate that RLS is able to descend deep down along the surface (or landscape) of the objective function, and certainly avoid many of the local optima traps that MALT gets stuck in. As a result, the quality of the solutions found by RLS is vastly superior to MALT. The improvement for the smallest instance with $p = 5$ is not as dramatic as the larger instances. For example, for $p = 15$ (see Table 12.5), 70 out of 100 runs of RLS produce the optimal solution compared to 0 for MALT. The remaining 30 runs of RLS produce its second best solution, which is within 0.05 (5%) of the optimal, while MALT produces only 4 solutions out of 100 within 0.05 of optimal.

Further analysis (see [6] for details) also reveals that the augmentation step in RLS (step 3), where new median points from the continuous phase are added to the set S containing the nodes of the discrete model, is a useful feature. This step enhances the algorithm by increasing the number of iterations between continuous and discrete phases; i.e., more descent moves and better solutions are obtained.

Table 12.6 Summary of results on larger instances, MALT and RLS (see [6] for details)

Data set (n)	Average deviation (%)		Average CPU time (sec)	
	MALT	RLS	MALT	RLS
287	78.79	0.04	9.86	4.79
654	22.82	0.21	54.82	43.32
1060	4.17	0.21	133.79	119.95

Computational Results on Large Instances

Three other data sets commonly used for the MWP (e.g., see [4]) are also examined in [6]. These are the 287 - customer problem from Bongartz et al. [3], and the 654- and 1060 - customer problems from the TSP library (Reinelt [42]). Values of p were taken from $\{2, 3, 4, \ldots, 15, 20, 25, \ldots, 100\}$ for $n = 287$, and $\{5, 10, 15, \ldots, 150\}$ for $n = 654$ and 1060, giving a total of 91 instances tested. CPU time for each instance and each algorithm was set at 20, 120, and 300 sec, respectively, for $n = 287, 654$, and 1060. The average percentage deviation from the best-known result over all instances run for the specified data set is given in Table 12.6 for MALT and RLS (see [6] for detailed results for each instance). Note that these best-known solutions were shown to be optimal for the $n = 287$ instances (Krau [27]). As we might expect, Table 12.6 shows that RLS significantly outperforms MALT. It is also noteworthy that despite the simple RLS procedure used in Brimberg et al. [6], this algorithm was able to improve on two best-known solutions for $n = 654$, obtained by a much more sophisticated metaheuristic-based method. These results are quite encouraging. They also demonstrate that simple algorithm designs can be as effective (or nearly so) as more complicated ones, in support of the "less is more" (LIMA) philosophy discussed in a separate chapter of this book.

Injection Points

Brimberg et al. [7] suggest that injection points be added to set S once the basic RLS procedure terminates. The idea here is to add "attractive" points to the discrete model in order to improve the discrete approximation of the original model. In that way, the improving search L_D may find a better solution, and hence, jump out of the current local optimum trap. The steps of the new procedure, called augmented reformulation local search (ARLS), are shown in Algorithm 6 below for convenience. Note the new parameter K in step 1 denoting the total number of injection points that will be added.

Otherwise, the procedure is the same as basic RLS (Algorithm 5) until step 5 where the algorithm starts to add the injection points (Y_j) once the basic RLS cannot improve the solution any further. The injection points are added one at a time, and each time one is added, the search in the discrete phase (step 4) is resumed. If a better solution is found than the current best (X^0), the algorithm returns to the continuous phase (step 2) with this new solution, and resumes the basic RLS. The algorithm ends when all K injection points are added, and the solution cannot be improved further.

Algorithm 6: Augmented Reformulation Local Search (ARLS).

1 Step 1: Select an initial solution $X^0 = \{X_1^0, \ldots, X_p^0\}$, an initial set S for $(GLP)'$, and a value for parameter K; set $j = 0$.
2 Step 2: (solving the continuous problem): $L_C(X^0) \rightarrow X^C$ (where $X^C \neq X^0$, only if $f(X^C) < f(X^0)$).
3 Step 3: (augmenting S): $S \leftarrow S \cup X^C$.
4 Step 4: (solving the discrete problem): $L_D(X^C) \rightarrow X^D$ (where $X^D \neq X^C$, only if $f(X^D) < f(X^C)$).
5 Step 5: If $X^D \neq X^C$, $X^0 \leftarrow X^D$ and return to step 2; elseif $j < K$, obtain the next injection point Y_j, set $S \leftarrow S \cup \{Y_j\}$, $j \leftarrow j + 1$, and return to step 4; else stop.

The injection points can be determined in different ways. In Brimberg et al. [7], two strategies are specified. The first requires the injection points to be convex combinations of two or more demand points (or facilities, or combinations of the two). The second strategy involves the use of a local search in the continuous problem that can be different from L_C, and that can generate local optima with new and attractive points to add to the set S. However, in the computational experiments, they only use the first strategy with pairs of randomly selected demand points, e.g.,

$$Y_j = A_{j_1}/2 + A_{j_2}/2,$$

where Y_j is placed at the midpoint of the line segment joining A_{j_1} and A_{j_2}. The computational results are comparable to basic RLS, suggesting this is only a preliminary study, and more work is needed to develop effective strategies for inserting injection points.

Some interesting features of ARLS are noted:

* A small example in [6] demonstrates that a multi-start version of basic RLS is not guaranteed to be globally convergent. In this case, the starting solution is a randomly selected combination of p demand points, and Cooper's algorithm is used to improve the solution in the continuous phase. They show that the optimal solution of the MWP is unattainable under these

conditions. On the other hand, injecting median points into the discrete approximation easily fixes this issue.

* Adding injection points, for example, median points for the MWP, makes the discrete model a better approximation of the original (continuous) model. By generating all possible local solutions, and adding the obtained facility sites to the set S, the discrete model becomes an equivalent formulation of the continuous one. That is, solving one model automatically solves the other. Thus, we may view the RLS approach as falling within the FSS framework in an asymptotic sense.

12.5 Conclusions

Many methods for solving global optimization problems are based on changing one formulation to another. These types of methods include dual, primal-dual, Lagrangian, linearization, surrogation, convexification methods, coordinate system change, discrete/continuous reformulations, to mention a few. The main idea of Formulation Space Search (FSS) is to provide the set of formulations for a given problem with some metric or quasi-metric functions. In that way, the (quasi) distance between formulations is introduced, and the search space is extended to the set of formulations as well. Most importantly, in all solution method classes mentioned, the discrete metric function between any two formulations can easily be defined. Those simple facts open an avenue to a new approach where heuristics are developed within the FSS framework. Instead of a single formulation with corresponding solution space, as in the traditional approach, there are now multiple formulations and solution spaces to explore in a structured way. This opens up immense possibilities in designing new and powerful heuristics. For example, it may be that new types of distances in the formulation space will make some hard problems easier to solve.

Computational results demonstrate that the FSS framework can produce simple and effective heuristics that support the less is more (LIMA) philosophy discussed in a separate chapter of this book. The authors hope they have convinced the reader that FSS is an exciting direction for future research.

A Tribute to Professor Nenad Mladenovic
We sadly announce that Professor Nenad Mladenović passed away in May 2022, before the publication of this book was completed. His sudden death from a heart attack shocked his many friends and colleagues at universities and research institutes around the globe. It was a privilege for me to work with Nenad on this chapter,

and on numerous other projects over the 30 years I have known him. Borrowing on ideas from Variable Neighborhood Search, a popular metaheuristic framework that he pioneered, Nenad later introduced the notion of Formulation Space Search, which is the topic of this chapter. The novel idea in FSS is to structure a formulation space containing different formulations of a problem by using a distance metric in the same way a solution space is structured with defined neighborhoods in VNS.

I consider myself very lucky to have known Nenad. He has had a tremendous impact on my work, as I am sure he has for many others. His ideas will inspire researchers for many years to come. Rest in peace, my good friend.

Jack Brimberg.

Acknowledgements The first author is partially supported by the Khalifa University of Science and Technology under Award No. RC2 DSO, and by the Committee of Science of the Ministry of Education and Science of the Republic of Kazakhstan under the grant number AP08856034. The second author is partially supported by a Natural Sciences and Engineering Research Council of Canada Discovery Grant (NSERC # RGPIN-2020-04846). The work of the third author is partially supported by the Serbian Ministry of Education, Science and Technological Development through Mathematical Institute of the Serbian Academy of Sciences and Arts.

References

1. Amirgaliyeva, Z., Mladenović, N., Todosijević, R., Urošević, D. (2017) Solving the maximum min-sum dispersion by alternating formulations of two different problems. *European Journal of Operational Research*, 260(2): 444–459.
2. Bloechliger, I., Zufferey, N. (2008) A graph coloring heuristic using partial solutions and a reactive tabu scheme. *Computers and Operations Research*, 35: 960–975.
3. Bongartz, I., Calamai, P.H., Conn, A.R. (1994) A projection method for l_p norm location-allocation problems. *Mathematical Programming*, 66: 283–312.
4. Brimberg, J., Hansen, P., Mladenović, N., Taillard, E.D. (2000) Improvement and comparison of heuristics for solving the uncapacitated multisource Weber problem. *Operations Research*, 48(3): 444–460.
5. Brimberg, J., Hansen, P., Mladenović, N. (2010) Attraction probabilities in variable neighborhood search. *4OR-Quarterly Journal of Operations Research*, 8: 181–194.
6. Brimberg, J., Drezner, Z., Mladenović, N., Salhi, S. (2014) A new local search for continuous location problems. *European Journal of Operational Research*, 232(2): 256–265.

7. Brimberg, J., Drezner, Z., Mladenović, N., Salhi, S. (2017) Using injection points in reformulation local search for solving continuous location problems. *Yugoslav Journal of Operations Research*, 27(3): 291–300.

8. Brimberg, J., Drezner, Z. (2021) Improved starting solutions for the planar *p*-median problem. *Yugoslav Journal of Operations Research*, 31(1): 45–64.

9. Brimberg, J., Salhi, S. (2019) A general framework for local search applied to the continuous *p*-median problem. In Eiselt, H.A., Marianov, V. (eds.), *Contributions to Location Analysis*. In Honor of Zvi Drezner's 75th Birthday, Springer, pp. 89–108.

10. Butenko, S., Yezerska, O., Balasundaram, B. (2013) Variable objective search. *Journal of Heuristics*, 19(4): 697–709.

11. Cooper. L. (1963) Location-allocation problem. *Operations Research*, 11: 331–343.

12. Cooper. L. (1964) Heuristics methods for location–allocation problems. SIAM Review, 6: 37–53.

13. Duarte, A., Pantrigo, J. J., Pardo, E. G., Sánchez-Oro, J. (2016) Parallel variable neighbourhood search strategies for the cutwidth minimization problem. *IMA J. Management Mathematics*, 27(1): 55–73.

14. Eilon, S., Watson-Gandy, C.D.T., Christofides, N. (1971) Distribution Management. Hafner, New York.

15. Erlenkotter, D. (1978) A dual-based procedure for uncapacitated facility location. *Operations Research*, 26: 992–1009.

16. Erromdhani, R., Jarboui, B., Eddaly, M., Rebai, A., Mladenović, N. (2017) Variable neighborhood formulation search approach for the multi-item capacitated lot-sizing problem with time windows and setup times. *Yugoslav Journal of Operations Research*, 27(3): 301–322.

17. Galinier, P., Hao J.K. (1999) Hybrid evolutionary algorithms for graph coloring. *Journal of Combinatorial Optimization*, 3(4): 379–397.

18. Gallai, T., (1968) On directed paths and circuits. In Erdös, P., Katobna, G. (eds.), *Theory of Graphs*. Academic Press, New York, pp. 115–118.

19. Hansen, P., Mladenović, N., Moreno Pérez, J. A. (2010) Variable neighbourhood search: methods and applications. *Annals of Operations Research*, 175: 367–407.

20. Hansen, P., Mladenović, N., Taillard, E., (1998) Heuristic solution of the multisource Weber problem as a *p*-median problem. *Operations Research Letters*, 22: 55–62.

21. Hansen, P., Mladenović, N., Todosijević, R., Hanafi, S. (2017) Variable neighborhood search: basics and variants. *EURO Journal on Computational Optimization*, 5: 423–454.

22. Hertz, A., de Werra D. (1987) Using Tabu search techniques for graph coloring. *Computing*, 39: 345–351.

23. Hertz, A., Plumettaz, M., Zufferey, N. (2008) Variable space search for graph coloring. *Discrete Applied Mathematics*, 156(13): 2551–2560.

24. Hertz, A., Plumettaz, M., Zufferey, N. (2009) Corrigendum to "variable space search for graph coloring". *Discrete Applied Mathematics*, 157(7): 1335–1336.
25. Kalczynski, P., Brimberg, J., Drezner, Z. (2021) Less is more: discrete starting solutions in the planar p-median problem. *TOP*. https://doi.org//10.1007/s11 750-021-00599-w.
26. Kochetov, Y., Kononova, P., Paschenko, M. (2008) Formulation space search approach for the teacher/class timetabling problem. *Yugoslav Journal of Operations Research*, 18(1): 1–11.
27. Krau, S. (1999) Extensions du probleme de Weber. PhD thesis.
28. Liberti, L., Nannicini, G., Mladenovié, N. (2011) A recipe for finding good solutions to MINLPs. *Mathematical Programming and Computing* 3(4): 349–390.
29. López, C. O., Beasley, J. E. (2011) A heuristic for the circle packing problem with a variety of containers. *European Journal of Operational Research*, 214(3): 512–525.
30. López, C. O., Beasley, J. E. (2013) Packing unequal circles using formulation space search. *Computers and Operations Research*, 40(5): 1276–1288.
31. López, C. O., Beasley, J. E. (2014) A note on solving MINLP's using formulation space search. *Optimization Letters*, 8(3): 1167–1182.
32. López, C. O., Beasley, J. E. (2016) A formulation space search heuristic for packing unequal circles in a fixed size circular container. *European Journal of Operational Research*, 251(1): 65–73.
33. Love, R. F., Morris, J. G., Wesolowsky, G. O. (1988) Facilities Location: Models and Methods. North-Holland, New York.
34. Malaguti, E., Monaci, M., Toth, P. (2005) A metaheuristic approach for the vertex coloring problem. *Technical Report OR/05/3*, University of Bologna, Italy.
35. Megiddo, M., Supowit, K.J. (1984) On the complexity of some common geometric location problems. *SIAM Journal on Computing*, 13: 182–196.
36. Mladenović, N., Kratica, J., Kovačević-Vujčić, V., Čangalović, M. (2012) Variable neighborhood search for metric dimension and minimal doubly resolving set problems. *European Journal of Operational Research*, 220: 328–337.
37. Mladenović, N., Plastria, F., Urošević, D. (2005) Reformulation descent applied to circle packing problems. *Computers and Operations Research*, 32(9): 2419–2434.
38. Mladenović, N., Plastria, F., Urošević, D. (2007) Formulation space search for circle packing problems. In "Engineering stochastic local search algorithms. Designing, implementing and analyzing effective heuristics". Proceedings of the International Workshop, SLS 2007, Brussels, Belgium (2007), pp. 212–216.
39. Mladenović, N., Urošević, D., Pérez-Brito, D., García-González, C. (2010) Variable neighbourhood search for bandwidth reduction. *European Journal of Operational Research*, 200: 14–27.
40. Morgenstern, C. (1996) Distributed coloration neighborhood search. *DIMACS Series in Discrete Mathematics and Theoretical Computer Science*, 26: 335–357.

41. Pardo, E. G., Mladenović, N., Pantrigo, J. J., Duarte, A. (2013) Variable formulation search for the cutwidth minimization problem. *Applied Soft Computing*, 13(5): 2242–2252.
42. Reinelt, G. (1991) TSLIB—a travelling salesman library. *ORSA J Computing*, 3: 376–384.
43. Roy, B. (1967) Nombre chromatique et plus longs chemins d'un graphe. *Revue AFIRO*, 1: 127–132.
44. Salhi, S., Gamal, M.D.H. (2003) A genetic algorithm based approach for the uncapacitated continuous location–allocation problem. *Annals of Operations Research*, 123: 203–222.
45. Teitz, M., Bart, P., Heuristic methods for estimating the generalized vertex median of a weighted graph. *Operations Research*, 16(5). https://doi.org/10.1287/opre.16.5.955.
46. Vitaver, L.M. (1962) Determination of minimal coloring of vertices of a graph by means of boolean powers of the incidence matrix. *Doklady Akademii Nauk SSSR*, 147: 758–759 (in Russian).
47. Weiszfeld, E. (1937) Sur le point pour lequel la somme des distances de *n* points donnés est minimum. *Tohoku Mathematical Journal*, 43: 355–386.

13

Sine Cosine Algorithm: Introduction and Advances

Anjali Rawat, Shitu Singh, and Jagdish Chand Bansal ⓘ

13.1 Introduction

A Metaheuristic is a problem-independent algorithmic framework that provides a near-global optimal solution to an optimization problem. Meta-heuristic algorithms can be categorized into two categories—single solution-based algorithms and population-based algorithms. A population-based algorithm begins with a set of randomly generated solutions that are updated iteratively until the end condition (or termination criteria) is satisfied. On the other hand, in the single solution-based algorithm, a single solution is generated and updated iteratively until the end condition is satisfied. Although both the categories have their own advantages and disadvantages, the researchers use population-based algorithms more due to their higher exploratory behavior than single solution-based algorithms. Examples of some of the population-based meta-heuristic algorithms are Particle Swarm Optimization (PSO) [1], Artificial Bee Colony (ABC) [2], Differential Evolution (DE) [3], Ant Colony Optimization (ACO) [4] Genetic Algorithm (GA) [5], Gravitational Search Algorithm (GSA) [6], Teaching-Learning Based Optimization (TLBO) [7], Grey wolf Optimization algorithm (GWO) [8],

A. Rawat · S. Singh · J. C. Bansal (✉)
South Asian University, New Delhi, India
e-mail: jcbansal@sau.ac.in

© The Author(s), under exclusive license to Springer Nature Switzerland AG 2022
S. Salhi and J. Boylan (eds.), *The Palgrave Handbook of Operations Research*,
https://doi.org/10.1007/978-3-030-96935-6_13

Spider Monkey Optimization (SMO) [9], Sine Cosine Algorithm (SCA) [10], etc.

Sine Cosine Algorithm is one of the recently developed promising population-based metaheuristic algorithms introduced by Mirjalili [10] in 2016. The main idea behind SCA is to use the cyclic pattern of the sine and cosine functions to locate the next position of its search agents in the search space. Since 2016, to deal with the various challenging research problems, a lot of research has been carried out to make it more efficient and robust. This chapter covers its mathematical model, its important parameters, and some of its variants developed to overcome the weaknesses of the SCA.

The proceeding sections of this chapter are arranged in the following manner: Section 13.2 provides the mathematical model of the SCA and its pseudo code, Section 13.3 discusses its important parameters, Section 13.4 presents its advances, and Section 13.5 concludes the whole chapter, respectively.

13.2   Sine Cosine Algorithm (SCA)

Sine Cosine Algorithm, being a population-based optimization technique, begins with a set of randomly generated solutions (called population) of size 'N' where each solution is a 'D' dimensional vector. The random solutions are then evaluated repeatedly with the help of the objective function and are relocated in the search space using the following two main mathematical equations:

$$X_{ij}^{t+1} = X_{ij}^t + r_1 \times \sin(r_2) \times |r_3 \times P_{gj}^t - X_{ij}^t| \tag{13.1}$$

$$X_{ij}^{t+1} = X_{ij}^t + r_1 \times \cos(r_2) \times |r_3 \times P_{gj}^t - X_{ij}^t| \tag{13.2}$$

where, $i = 1, 2, 3, \ldots, N$, $j = 1, 2, 3, \ldots, D$ and t is the iteration counter. $X_i^t = (X_{i1}^t, X_{i2}^t, \ldots, X_{iD}^t)$ is the position of an ith individual solution at the tth iteration, $P_{gj}^t = (P_{g1}^t, P_{g2}^t, \ldots, P_{gD}^t)$ is the global best solution (called destination point) in the tth iteration. r_2 and r_3 are two uniform random values in the range $[0, 2\pi]$ and $[0,2]$, respectively. r_1 is a function of t, calculated using Eq. (13.3).

The most crucial aspect of any population-based algorithm is to ensure an adequate balance between exploration of the search region at initial iterations to explore the maximum possible area and exploitation at later iterations to speed up the convergence. To maintain a proper balance between the global exploration and local exploitation ability of the algorithm, the parameter r_1 is designed as the linear decreasing function of 't' given by the following expression:

$$r_1 = a - a \times \left(\frac{t}{T} \right) \tag{13.3}$$

where a is a constant and T is the maximum number of iteration.

To decide whether the solution is updated using Eq. (13.1) or Eq. (13.2), a switch probability $p(p = 0.5)$ is used, and the solutions update its position based on a random number $r_4 \in [0, 1]$ using the following update mechanism:

$$X_{ij}^{t+1} = \begin{cases} X_{ij}^t + r_1 \times \sin(r_2) \times |r_3 \times P_{gj}^t - X_{ij}^t| & \text{if } r_4 < p \\ \\ X_{ij}^t + r_1 \times \cos(r_2) \times |r_3 \times P_{gj}^t - X_{ij}^t| & \text{if } r_4 \geq p \end{cases} \tag{13.4}$$

For each search agent, the Eq. (13.4) gives 50% chance to both Eq. (13.1) and Eq. (13.2) in each iteration and each dimension.

The procedure of the SCA can be summarized in Algorithm 1.

Algorithm 1: Sine Cosine Algorithm (SCA)

Initialize the population $\{X_1, X_2, ..., X_N\}$ randomly
Initialize the parameter 'a'
For each candidate solution, calculate the objective function value
Identify the best solution obtained X_D so far as P_g
initialize $t = 0$
while Termination criteria is meet **do**
   Calculate r_1, using Eq. (13.3) and generate the parameters r_2, r_3, r_4 randomly
   for each candidate solution **do**
      update the position using Eq. (13.4)
   endfor
   $t = t + 1$
endwhile
Return the best solution X_D

13.3 Parameters Involved in the SCA

The main parameters of the SCA are r_1, r_2, r_3, and r_4. The performance of the SCA is sensitive to the choices of these parameters. These parameters help the algorithm avoid the local optima and maintain a perfect balance between the exploratory and exploitative behavior of the algorithm.

In the SCA, r_1 is a random parameter responsible for controlling both the global and the local search process. It dictates the direction of the movement of the search agents by deciding whether the solution should move toward the destination point ($r_1 > 1$) or away from it ($r_1 < 1$). It plays a significant role in ensuring that the exploration behavior decreases with the number of iterations and the exploitation behavior increases. Its value decreases linearly from the predefined parameter 'a' to 0.

The parameter r_2 is another important parameter that decides to what extent the search agents should move toward or away from the destination point. It is a uniformly distributed random number in the range $[0, 2\pi]$.

In the SCA, the parameter r_3 is the random weight given to the destination point. It indicates the magnitude of the contribution of the best solution in updating the next position of the search agents in each iteration. It is responsible in emphasizing ($r_3 > 1$) or de-emphasizing ($r_3 < 1$) the effect of the best solution in defining the extent of movement. Its value lies in the range $[0,2]$.

The parameter r_4 is utilized to choose between the sine and cosine components randomly. It helps the algorithm in skipping the local optima. Its value lies in the range $[0,1]$.

One more parameter plays a key role in SCA, which is the constant 'a'. This parameter makes sure that the algorithm transits smoothly from the exploration phase to the exploitation phase. The value of the parameter 'a' is generally chosen to be 2.

13.4 Advances in the Sine Cosine Algorithm

The original version of the Sine Cosine Algorithm (SCA) was meant to solve single-objective unconstrained problems with continuous (real-valued) variables. But apart from real-valued representation, there are other types of representation, including binary, discrete and mixed. Furthermore, based on the existence of the constraints and the number of the objective functions involved, there are other types of optimization problems like constrained, multi-objective, etc. These types of problems can not be easily dealt with by the traditional SCA. Although SCA has been able to avoid local optima, explore different regions of a search space, exploit promising regions of a search space, and converge toward the global optimum effectively, still it has certain limitations like slow convergence in some of the complex optimization problems, premature convergence to local optima due to the adoption of a fixed switch probability, lack of internal memory. To deal with these limitations, some of the modified and hybridized versions of SCA were also proposed.

Since its first introduction in 2016, SCA has continued to attract the interest of investigators from diverse disciplines across the globe. Till now, several papers have been widely published on the SCA. Based on the papers available online, the work done on SCA so far can be broadly categorized into four categories—extension, modifications, hybridizations, and performance review. Figure 13.1 shows the classification of the various works done on the SCA. Since significant work has been done on the extension of the SCA, it is discussed further in detail in the following subsection:

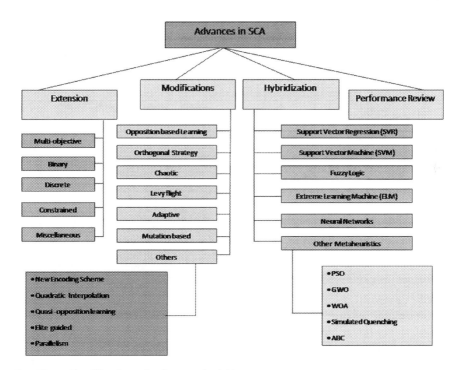

Fig. 13.1 Classification of advances in SCA

13.4.1 Extension of SCA

The success of the SCA in solving single-objective optimization problems within continuous search spaces has motivated the researchers to extend it to solve other optimization problems like multi-objective, discrete, binary, constrained, etc. These variants of the SCA are explained in detail in the following subsections:

13.4.1.1 Multi-Objective

In most real-life optimization problems, there can be more than two objectives that often conflict. These problems are called multi-objective optimization problems, where rather than a single objective multiple conflicting objectives are optimized concurrently. In multi-objective problems, a unique optimal solution does not exist that optimizes all the objective functions simultaneously. Instead, there is a set of non-dominated solutions, known as Pareto-optimal solutions, in which no solution that exists is superior to the other solution. Conceptually, a multi-objective version should follow the same mechanism of the parent optimization algorithm to update the position of solutions. However, several modifications were made to SCA due to the existence of so-called Pareto-optimal solutions in multi-objective problems. There have been four attempts in the literature to deal with the multi-objective problems with the SCA algorithm. The main mechanisms used in these works are elitist non-dominated sorting, Crowding Distance (CD) and archives.

Tawhid et al. [11], in 2019, presented an extended version of SCA to solve engineering design problems using elitism-based non-dominated sorting and crowding distance (CD) method of NSGA-II [12]. In this algorithm, the whole population of size N is first arranged into different non-domination levels. Then it is assigned a Non-Domination Rank (NDR) using the concept of Pareto dominance. Then for each objective function f_l ($l = 1, 2, \ldots, m$), all the solutions in the population of a particular non-dominated set are sorted in ascending order. In order to maintain the diversity of the solutions, the individuals with the lowest and the highest objective function values are assigned an infinite crowding distance so that they are always selected, while other solutions are assigned the crowding distance (cd_j^i) as follows:

$$cd_l^i = \frac{f_l^{i+1} - f_l^{i-1}}{f_l^{max} - f_l^{min}} \quad \forall\, l = 1, 2, \ldots, m \tag{13.5}$$

The final crowding distance value (CD_i) for each solution ($X_i, i = 1, \ldots, N$) is computed by adding the solution's crowding distance values (cd_l) in each objective function. After this, the SCA is operated to generate the new population P_k. The new and the parent population (P_o) are then merged to form a merged population P_{new} of size greater than N. In order to maintain a constant population size N, the NDR and the crowding distance (CD) are then used to select N solutions from the P_{new} number of solutions using a simple rule, where the solution with the lower NDR is selected and in case of a tie, one with the higher CD is selected. The proposed method was tested and approved on various engineering design problems and multi-objective benchmark functions. Compared with the other well-known multi-objective optimization algorithms, the results indicated that the proposed method was better in some instances and at par in others.

In radial distribution networks, Selim et al. [13] introduced another Pareto-based multi-objective optimization technique to install multiple Distribution STATic COMpensators (DSTATCOMs) optimally. In this technique, the Multi-Objective Sine Cosine Algorithm (MOSCA), similar to the Multi-objective Grey Wolf Optimization (MGWO) [14], was formulated and was integrated with fuzzy logic decision making to get better results. In MOSCA, three operators—an archive, a grid mechanism and a leader selection mechanism, are integrated into the SCA to maintain, improve and replace the non-dominated solutions in the archive. Once a set of Pareto-optimal solutions are produced using the MOSCA, the fuzzy logic decision controller is then used to choose the best compromise solutions. To verify its proficiency, the MOSCA was tested on the IEEE-33 and 69-bus distribution systems and was compared with the well-known MOPSO [15]. The experimental results demonstrated the higher efficiency of the MOSCA over MOPSO in overall voltage profile and total power losses.

To optimally place Distributed Generators (DGs) in radial distribution systems, Raut et al. [16] proposed an enhanced version of the multi-objective Sine Cosine Algorithm [11]. This algorithm used the fuzzy logic decision controllers to select the best solution and the two multi-objective operators—elitist non-dominated ranking and crowding distance—to sort the population. However, to get better results, the authors replaced the linearly decreasing parameter (r_1) with an exponentially decreasing parameter (given by Eq. (13.6)) in the traditional SCA. They then applied a self-adapting levy mutation strategy on the solutions obtained from it.

$$r_1 = a \times e^{\frac{t}{T}} \qquad (13.6)$$

In order to validate its efficiency, it was applied on 33 and 69-bus distribution systems under four different voltage-dependent load models and was compared with other multi-objective algorithms like NSGA-II and MOPSO. The results showed that the approach outperformed other algorithms in different performance metrics.

In 2021, Wan et al. [17] introduced another multi-objective variant of the SCA for image spatial-spectral clustering. In the proposed algorithm, the individual solutions are first updated using the original update equation of SCA. The results are then merged with the parent population of size N to form a new population with $2N$ solutions. The newly generated population is then sorted and ranked based on the non-dominated ranking. Out of these $2N$ solutions, N individuals with the higher crowding distance are selected (known as density estimation sorting). This density estimation sorting helps an algorithm preserve the diversity of the optimal solution set and maintain the original size of the population. In addition to this, a knee-point-based automatic selection approach [18] is used to automatically obtain the best solution (destination point) from the Pareto-optimal solution set. The proficiency of the presented approach was tested using the ten UCI data sets and clustering experiments involving four real remote sensing images. The evaluation of the results showed that the proposed approach performed somewhat better than several popular clustering methods.

13.4.1.2 Binary

Some optimization problems involve variables taking only two possible values, namely, 0 and 1. As the SCA was initially designed for continuous optimization problems, it was hard to apply the main position updating equation of SCA to problems with a binary-valued domain. Hence, some essential changes in the SCA mechanism need to be adopted to put the continuous metaheuristic SCA to work in binary-valued domains. Different binarization methods like normalization, rounding, transfer functions, angle modulation, quantum approach, binary operators, etc., are available in the literature to develop a binary algorithm.

In 2016, Hafez et al. [19] developed a binary version of SCA that uses the standard binarization rule of rounding off to address feature selection problems. In the proposed approach, the range of all the variables is limited to {0, 1} using the rounding method, where first the values of each decision variable were rounded to the nearest integer using the Eq. (13.7) and then the features corresponding to the variable value one are selected. At the same time, the features with variable value 0 are rejected.

$$f_{ij} = \begin{cases} 1 \text{ if } X_{ij} > 0.5 \\ 0 \text{ otherwise} \end{cases} \tag{13.7}$$

where f_{ij} is the ith individual's fitness value, X_{ij} is the value for i^{th} search agent at the jth dimension.

In 2018, Reddy et al. [20] proposed four variants of SCA to solve the binary-natured Unit Commitment Problem (UCP). The proposed four variants of Binary SCA used four different transfer function to convert the local version of SCA to a binary version. Those transfer functions are—(a) The tangent hyperbolic transfer function, (b) Sigmoidal transfer function, (c) A modified sigmoidal transfer function and (d) Arctan transfer function. The performance of different transfer functions to solve a binary-natured Profit-Based Unit Commitment (PBUC) problem was investigated. The adequacy of the proposed approach, in terms of convergence and quality of solutions, was explored in test systems with the two market mechanisms that were (a) energy-only market participation and (b) energy and reserve market participation. In the second market, two different reserve payment scenarios were considered separately. The convergence characteristics of the transfer function in solving UCP were found in the following order:

arctan transfer function> the tangent hyperbolic transfer function> modified sigmoidal transfer>sigmoidal transfer function.

In terms of the solution quality, the arctan transfer function showed superior results out of all the four variants, and the simple sigmoidal transfer function showed inferior results. The simulation findings were compared with other existing approaches. It demonstrated the effectiveness and superiority of the proposed approaches in solving the PBUC problem in the perfectly competitive electricity market.

In the same year, another binary variant of SCA called Binary Percentile Sine Cosine Algorithm (BPSCA) was introduced by Fernandez et al. [21], in which percentile concept was utilized to conduct the binary adaptation of the Sine Cosine Algorithm (SCA). The main issue with the Binary percentile operator is that it generates infeasible solutions. To deal with the infeasible solutions, the authors used the percentile binary operator along with a heuristic operator. To assess the contribution of the percentile operator in obtaining the solutions, BPSCA was applied to resolve one of the classic combinatorial problems called the Set Covering Problem (SCP). The experimental results demonstrated that the operator plays an important role in providing accurate and good-quality solutions. In addition, comparison with the two best Metaheuristic algorithm that has solved SCPs, namely, Jumping PSO (JPSO) [22] and Multi Dynamic Binary Black Hole (MDBBH) [23] algorithms showed that results obtained using BPSCA were quite close to the one obtained using the JPSO. It generated superior results than the MDBBH. The authors emphasized that, unlike JPSO, the percentile technique used in BPSCA allows binarizing any continuous swarm intelligence algorithm.

In 2019, they proposed another percentile-based binary SCA [24], which used a repair operator instead of the heuristic operator to address the infeasible solutions. To evaluate the usefulness of the percentile concept in the binarization process, the authors applied it to resolve the multidimensional knapsack problem (MKP). The results showed that the operator improved the precision and the quality of the solutions. The proposed method was contrasted with the Binary Artificial Algae (BAAA) [18] and K-means Transition Ranking (KMTR) [26] algorithms. The results clearly showed that the proposed method outperformed the other algorithms in the best value indicator in 9 out of 30 instances. However, it was found ineffective in the average indicator.

Following this work, Taghian et al. [27] proposed two other binary versions of SCA using the two-step binarization technique. The first version is called S-shaped Binary Sine Cosine Algorithm (SBSCA). In SBSCA, the S-shaped transfer function, defined in Eq. (13.8), is used to define a bounded probability of changing a position of the search agents.

$$S(X_{ij}^{t+1}) = \frac{1}{1 + e^{-X_{ij}^t}} \tag{13.8}$$

Then the standard binarization rule, given in Eq. (13.9), is used to transform the solutions into a binary space.

$$(X_{ij}^{t+1}) = \begin{cases} 1 \text{ if rand} < S(X_{ij}^{t+1}) \\ 0 \text{ otherwise} \end{cases} \tag{13.9}$$

The second version is called the V-shaped binary Sine Cosine Algorithm (VBSCA). In VBSCA, the V-shaped transfer function is used to calculate the position changing probabilities given as:

$$V(X_{ij}^{t+1}) = |\frac{2}{\pi} \arctan(\frac{\pi}{2})(X_{ij}^t)| \tag{13.10}$$

Then the complement binarization rule, given by Eq. (13.11), is utilized to transform the solution into a binary domain.

$$(X_{ij}^{t+1}) = \begin{cases} \text{complement of } X_{ij}^{t+1} & \text{if rand} < V(X_{ij}^{t+1}) \\ (X_{ij}^{t}) & \text{otherwise} \end{cases} \qquad (13.11)$$

The performance of both the proposed algorithms was assessed and compared with four popular binary optimization algorithms, including binary GSA [28] and Binary GWO [29], over five UCI medical datasets: Pima, Lymphography, Heart, Breast Cancer and Breast-WDBC. The experimental results demonstrated that both the binary SCA variants have effectively enhanced the classification accuracy and yielded competitive or even better results compared to the others.

13.4.1.3 Discrete

There exist several optimization problems in the real world whose search space is restricted to take discrete values. Such problems are called discrete optimization problems. To tackle these problems, a Discrete Sine Cosine Algorithm (DSCA) was devised by Tawhid et al. [30] to resolve the Traveling Salesman Problem (TSP). To make the original SCA suitable for discrete combinatorial problems such as TSP, the authors operated two local search techniques—the heuristic crossover [31] and the 2-opt [32] on the best solution based on two randomly generated numbers between 0 and 1 (say R_1 and R_2), in the following manner:

If $R_1 < R_2$, Heuristic crossover is operated

Otherwise, 2-opt local search is operated

The DSCA was tested on 41 different benchmark instances of symmeterical TSP. The results indicated that the technique provided optimal solutions for 27 benchmark problems and near-optimal solutions for the remaining ones. When the results were compared with other state-of-the-art techniques, the DSCA demonstrated promising and competitive performance over the others.

In the same year, another discrete version of the Sine Cosine Algorithm [33] was put forward to tackle the discrete truss structures optimization problem. In this algorithm, the solutions obtained from the traditional SCA are rounded to their nearest integer to speed up the process significantly. However, the solutions generated by the unintelligent round-offs might lie in an infeasible region, and their fitness values might differ drastically from that of the optimal solutions. The two main strategies—regeneration and mutation operator—are incorporated with it to address these issues. These two strategies were found to help the algorithm explore and exploit the design space better. In the regeneration strategy, individual solutions of the population of size N are first arranged based on their objective function values in ascending order as follows:

$$\text{sort}(X^t) = [X_1^t, X_2^t, \ldots, X_{k-1}^t, X_k^t, X_{k+2}^t, \ldots, X_{N-1}^t, X_N^t] \quad (13.12)$$

where $\text{sort}(X^t)$ is the sorted current population, and X_k^t to X_N^t are the worst solutions at the current iteration (t) that needed to be regenerated. Then, $\lambda \times N$ number of worst particles (X_k^t to X_N^t) are removed from the population, and then the best solution found so far, $X* = [X_1^*, X_2^*, \ldots, X_j^*, \ldots, X_D^*]$ are added $\lambda \times N$ times in the population, that is,

$$\text{For} \quad l = k, k+1, \ldots, N, \text{ Replace } X_l^t \text{ by } X_l^t = [X_1^*, X_2^*, \ldots, X_D^*]$$
$$(13.13)$$

Then a randomly selected design variable $j \in [1, 2, \ldots, D]$ from each of these solutions X_k^t to X_{N-1}^t is regenerated on a random basis as follows:

$$X_j^* = \text{round}(X_j^L + r \times X_j^U + X_j^L) \quad (13.14)$$

where X_j^L and X_j^U are lower and upper limits of the jth design variable, and r is a random number in [0,1].

The regenerated variables of the individuals X_k^t to X_{N-1}^t are then substituted in the last particle (X_N^t), thus increasing the chances of finding promising regions of the search space. In the second strategy, a mutation operator is added to it to escape the local optima trap. In this, for each particle ($X_i, i = 1, 2, \ldots, N$), a random number in [0,1] is generated and if for the ith particle, the selected random number is less than a predefined parameter mutation rate (mr), X_i will be regenerated using the following equation:

$$X_i^{t+1} = \text{round}\left(X_i^t + \left(\frac{t}{T}\right) \times R^t \otimes (X_{\text{best}}^t - X_r^t)\right) \quad (13.15)$$

where R^t is a D dimensional vector of random numbers in the range [0, 1] in the tth iteration; X_{best}^t is the best solution of the current population, and

X_r^t is a randomly selected solution from the current population in the tth iteration. In this paper, the values of λ and mr were assumed to be 0.2 and 0.05, respectively. The proposed algorithm was applied on five well-known benchmark truss optimization problems, and the outcomes were compared with the original SCA and many optimization algorithms. The experimental findings represented the superiority of the proposed technique over the original SCA. In fact, in most of the cases, the proposed MSCA outperformed the other algorithms as well.

In 2019, another discrete version of the Sine Cosine Algorithm (DSCA) [34] was developed to solve community detection problems. In this algorithm, a population of N individuals is generated via Label Propagation [35] and the individuals are updated based on the following updating rules:

$$
X_i^{t+1} = \begin{cases} X_i^t \ \Phi \ [S(r_1 \times \sin(r_2) \times |r_3 \times P_{gj}^t \oplus X_{ij}^t| & \text{if } r_4 < p \\ X_i^t \ \Phi \ [S(r_1 \times \sin(r_2) \times |r_3 \times P_{gj}^t \oplus X_{ij}^t| & \text{if } r_4 \geq p \end{cases} \tag{13.16}
$$

where $\oplus$ represents XOR operation. The Φ operator is defined as follows:

Let $Y = [y_1, y_2, \ldots, y_D]$ and $X = [x_1, x_2, \ldots, x_D]$ be any two D dimensional vectors, then $W = X \Phi Y$ is defined as:

$$
W_i = \begin{cases} x_j & \text{if } y_j = 0 \\ Nbest_j, & \text{otherwise} \end{cases} \tag{13.17}
$$

where $Nbest_j$ is the label identifier that most neighborhood individuals in the jth dimension.

The S function is defined as follows:
Y= S(X) such that

$$
y_i = \begin{cases} 1 \text{ if rand}() < \text{sigmoid}(x_k) & \forall \, k = 1, 2 \ldots N \\ 0 \text{ otherwise} \end{cases} \tag{13.18}
$$

where the sigmoid function is given by Eq. (13.18)

$$
\text{sigmoid}(x) = \frac{1}{1 + e^x} \tag{13.19}
$$

In addition to this, the locus-based adjacency mutation is applied to maintain the diversity of individual solutions. After the new individuals are generated, the greedy selection technique is applied to retain the better individuals.

13.4.1.4   Constrained

An optimization problem refers to finding the optimum value of the given objective function. Based on the existence of constraints, an optimization problem can be classified as constrained or unconstrained. If there are no constraints involved on the variables, the problem is called unconstrained Optimization problems, else is called constrained optimization problem. The unconstrained optimization problems are easier than the constrained ones. Most of the real-life problems are constrained (i.e., it involves various constraints such as resource constraint, time constraint, cost constraint, design constraint, etc., depending on the nature of the problem to be optimized). These constraints have a significant effect on the performance of the algorithms applied to them. All the stochastic optimization algorithms are inherently suited to solve unconstrained optimization problems. Applying these algorithms directly to the constrained optimization problems could be problematic; thus, they need to adapt themselves. The most common and the oldest approach of incorporating constraints into an unconstrained optimization algorithm is penalty functions. The basic idea behind this method is to convert a constrained problem into an unconstrained problem by simply subtracting or adding a particular function from or to the objective functions based on the violation degree of constraints in a solution.

In 2020, Chen et al. [36] proposed a multi-strategy enhanced SCA (MSCA) and then incorporated the death penalty function with it to solve three constrained engineering problems—welded beam design problem, tension/compression spring design problem, and pressure vessel design problem. The MSCA, as the name suggests, uses multiple strategies that include Cauchy Mutation (CM) operator, Chaotic Local Search (CLS) mechanism, Opposition-Based Learning (OBL) strategy and, Mutation and Crossover Strategy (MCS) of Differential Evolution (DE). The death penalty function is a simple and easiest way to handle constraints. It penalizes the primary objective function of the problem with a factor that measures the point of infeasibility and ensures that infeasible solutions are automatically rejected in each iteration. The experimental results demonstrated that the approach is very efficient and effective in solving various engineering problems and provides competitive and potential results than its competitors. The authors concluded that the proposed algorithm could effectively solve real-world optimization problems with complex search space.

13.4.1.5 Miscellaneous

In 2017, Rizk et al. [37] proposed a new approach named novel Sine Cosine Algorithm (NSCA) for solving the non-smooth environmental/economic load dispatch (EELD) problem in both single and multi-objective frameworks. In the proposed algorithm, an opposition-based learning strategy is employed in the initialization stage and after each iteration to improve the diversity and the quality of solutions. Opposition-based learning (OBL), originally introduced by Tizhoosh in [38] is a machine learning technique that takes into consideration the opposite position of solutions in the search space. Given population $X = \cup X_i$, the opposite position $\overline{X_i}$ of each individual (X_i) is calculated as follows:

$$\overline{X_i} = [\overline{X_{i1}}, \overline{X_{i2}}, ...\overline{X_{iD}}] \tag{13.20}$$

where $\overline{X_{ij}} = u_j + l_j + X_{ij}$, $i = 1, 2, \ldots, N$; $j = 1, 2, \ldots, D$ and $X_i = [X_{i1}, X_{i2}, \ldots, X_{iD}]$ is a randomly generated individual of dimension D in a population of size N. This leads to the generation of a new population $\overline{X} = \cup \overline{X_i}$. The basic idea behind this is to consider the current estimate (guess) and its corresponding opposite simultaneously to obtain the optimal solution. After calculating the opposite population, the fitness of each individual (X_i) and its opposites $\overline{X_i}$ are calculated, and then the population is brought back to the original size (N) by selecting the N best solutions from the population $(\overline{X} \cup X)$.

The algorithm begins with initializing random solutions, their opposite positions, and their evaluation for the single or multi-objective cases accordingly. After that, the solutions update themselves to obtain an approximated optimal solution in the single-objective case or Pareto-optimal solutions in the multi-objective case, where the weighted sum method is used to transform the multiple objective functions into a single one with the help of different weights. The authors used the traditional SCA for single-objective cases and introduced some modifications in the update mechanism to deal with the multiple objective cases. The authors used two separate external archives M and K, for the multiple objective cases to store the dominated solutions and the non-dominated solutions, respectively, according to the Pareto front concepts. Further, the new solutions are generated based on mutation probability (p_i) using the following modified updating mechanism of the SCA:

$$X_{ij}^{t+1} = \begin{cases} \begin{cases} X_{ij}^t + r_1 \times \sin(r_2) \times |r_3 \times P_{gj}^t - X_{ij}^t| & \text{if } r_4 < p \\ X_{ij}^t + r_1 \times \cos(r_2) \times |r_3 * P_{gj}^t - X_{ij}^t| & \text{if } r_4 \geq p \end{cases} & \text{if } r_5 > p_i \\ \\ \begin{cases} X_{ij}^t + r_1 \times \sin(r_2) \times |r_3 \times P_a^t - X_{ij}^t| & \text{if } r_4 < p \\ X_{ij}^t + r_1 \times \cos(r_2) \times |r_3 \times P_a^t - X_{ij}^t| & \text{if } r_4 \geq p \end{cases} & \text{if } r_5 \leq p_i \end{cases}$$

$$(13.21)$$

and

$$p_i = 0.4 - 0.4 \times \frac{t}{T}, \ i = 1, 2, \ldots, K \qquad (13.22)$$

where r_5 is a switch parameter lying in [0, 1], and P_a^t is a solution chosen randomly from the archive K. To boost its exploration and exploitation capabilities, the authors tuned the parameter r_1 using the following non-linear strategy:

$$r_1 = \alpha \times \left(a^{\max} - \left(\frac{t \times (a^{\max} - a^{\min})}{T} \right) \right), \ \alpha = 0.98^t \qquad (13.23)$$

where $a^{\min}$ and $a^{\max}$ are the minimum and the maximum limits set by the user, respectively. In order to evaluate the performance of the proposed approach, the authors used two benchmarking systems- 6-unit and 10-unit, with fuel cost and emission issues. It concluded that MSCO could be a promising and competent alternative for solving EELD problems in both single and multi-objective cases, as compared to other techniques present in the literature.

They again, in 2018 [39], proposed a new update mechanism for the same economic emission load dispatch (EELD) problem with the same update equations but with a slight twist. Instead of using an opposition-based strategy in both the initialization and solution update mechanism, the authors only used it in the solution update mechanism. Apart from this, only one external archive $A(t)$ is used instead of two archives, which stores only the non-dominated solutions and discards the dominated solutions. The performance of the proposed approach was investigated on the IEEE 30 bus test system with 6, 10 and 40 generating units. The results clearly demonstrated the proposed mechanism's effectiveness and robustness in tackling the EELD problem in both single and multi-objective frameworks.

In 2019, a multi-objective discrete version of SCA (MOSCA) [40] was proposed for optimal band selection of Hyperspectral remote Sensing Images (HSI). In MOSCA, a novel discrete SCA is proposed where the incremental part (v_{ij}) given by Eq. (13.25) taken from the original SCA become a version of the probability in updating the position of the individual solutions, in the following way:

$$X_{ij}^{t+1} = \begin{cases} 0 & \text{if rand}() \leq \text{sig}(v_{ij}) \text{ and } v_{ij} \leq 0 \\ 1 & \text{if rand}() \leq \text{sig}(v_{ij}) \text{ and } v_{ij} > 0 \\ X_{ij}^{t} & \text{if rand}() > \text{sig}(v_{ij}) \end{cases} \tag{13.24}$$

$$v_{ij} = \begin{cases} r_1 \times \sin(r_2) \times |r_3 \times P_{ij}^{t} - X_{ij}^{t}| & \text{if } r_4 < p \\ r_1 \times \cos(r_2) \times |r_3 \times P_{ij}^{t} - X_{ij}^{t}| & \text{if } r_4 \geq p \end{cases} \tag{13.25}$$

$$\text{sig}(v_{ij}) = \begin{cases} 1 - \frac{2}{1+e^{v_{ij}}} & \text{if } v_{ij} \leq 0 \\ \frac{2}{1+e^{v_{ij}}} - 1 & \text{otherwise} \end{cases} \tag{13.26}$$

After updating the individual solutions by the discrete SCA, Pareto domination ranking and density ranking strategies are used, and the best solution (destination point) is updated using the knee point-based method [41]. The proposed band selection method was investigated on two real HSI scenes provided by the Remote Sensing group (RSIDEA group). The results proved that MOSCA produces better results than other optimization methods in terms of accuracy and stability.

13.5 Conclusion

SCA is a simple and relatively new population-based stochastic approach, originally developed to tackle single-objective unconstrained optimization problems over continuous spaces. Its success in solving single-objective optimization problems within continuous spaces motivated the researchers to extend it to other types of optimization problems like multi-objective optimization, binary optimization, constrained optimization, discrete optimization, etc. Since there is no single best algorithm, SCA, too, failed to provide near-optimal solutions in many cases. Hence, the SCA was modified by using specialized operators, local search, etc., and by hybridizing it with other algorithms, to improve its capability and efficiency.

This chapter attempted to highlight the SCA and its extended versions that were developed to solve various other types of optimization problems like multi-objective, discrete, binary, etc., only. The hybridized version of SCA and its modification using various specialized operators are not covered in this chapter. Based on the papers considered, it is observed that the SCA is capable of tackling almost all types of optimization problems, including multi-objective, discrete and binary optimization problems.

SCA, as a stochastic algorithm, has fewer control parameters, is easy to execute, and could be modified and hybridized with other techniques. Over five years have passed since its introduction, and in these five years, SCA proved itself to be a powerful and robust algorithm. Even though the SCA has been modified in many ways, there are still various dimensions where this algorithm can be enhanced. Its potential advantage of being simple and easy to implement makes it viable for being continuously utilized in various areas (with or without modifications) in the coming years.

References

1. Kennedy, J., Eberhart, R.: Particle swarm optimization. In: Proceedings of ICNN'95 - International Conference on Neural Networks. **4**, pp. 1942–1948. (1995)
2. Karaboga, D.: An idea based on honey bee swarm for numerical optimization. Technical report-tr06, Erciyes university, engineering faculty, computer engineering department. **200**, pp. 1–10. (2005)
3. Storn, R., Price, K.: Differential evolution—a simple and efficient heuristic for global optimization over continuous spaces. Journal of Global Optimization. **11**, 341–359 (1997)
4. Gambardella, M.D.L.M., Martinoli, M.B.A., Stützle, R.P.T.: Ant colony optimization and swarm intelligence. In: 5th international Workshop. Springer (2006)
5. Mitchell, M. An introduction to genetic algorithms. MIT Press (1998)
6. Rashedi, E., Nezamabadi-Pour, H., Saryazdi, S.: GSA: a gravitational search algorithm. Information Sciences. **179**, 2232–2248 (2009)
7. Rao, R.V., Savsani, V.J., Vakharia, D.P.: Teaching-learning-based optimization: an optimization method for continuous non-linear large scale problems. Information Sciences. **183**, 1–15 (2012)
8. Mirjalili, S., Mirjalili, S.M., Lewis, A.: Grey wolf optimizer. Advances in Engineering Software. **69**, 46–61 (2014)
9. Bansal, J.C., Sharma, H., Jadon, S.S., Clerc, M.: Spider monkey optimization algorithm for numerical optimization. Memetic Computing. **6**, 31–47 (2014)

10. Mirjalili, S.: SCA: a sine cosine algorithm for solving optimization problems. Knowledge-Based Systems. **96**, 120–133 (2016)
11. Tawhid, M.A., Savsani, V.: Multi-objective sine-cosine algorithm (MO-SCA) for multi-objective engineering design problems. Neural Computing and Applications. **31**, 915–929 (2019)
12. Deb, K., Pratap, A., Agarwal, S., Meyarivan, T.A.M.T.: A fast and elitist multiobjective genetic algorithm: NSGA-II. IEEE Transactions on Evolutionary Computation. **6**, 182–197 (2002)
13. Selim, A., Kamel, S., Jurado, F.: Voltage profile enhancement using multi-objective sine cosine algorithm for optimal installation of dstacoms into distribution systems. In: 2019 10th International Renewable Energy Congress (IREC), pp. 1–6. IEEE (2019)
14. Mirjalili, S., Saremi, S., Mirjalili, S.M., Coelho, L.D.S.: Multi-objective grey wolf optimizer: a novel algorithm for multi-criterion optimization. Expert Systems with Applications. **47**, 106–119 (2016)
15. Coello, C.A.C., Pulido, G.T., Lechuga, M.S.: Handling multiple objectives with particle swarm optimization. IEEE Transactions on Evolutionary Computation. **8**, 256–279 (2004)
16. Raut, U., Mishra, S.: A new Pareto multi-objective sine cosine algorithm for performance enhancement of radial distribution network by optimal allocation of distributed generators. Evolutionary Intelligence. 1–22 (2020)
17. Wan, Y., Ma, A., Zhang, L., Zhong, Y.: Multiobjective sine cosine algorithm for remote sensing image spatial-spectral clustering. IEEE Transactions on Cybernetics. (2021)
18. Zhang, X., Tian, Y., Jin, Y.: A knee point-driven evolutionary algorithm for many-objective optimization. IEEE Transactions on Evolutionary Computation. **19**, 761–776 (2014)
19. Hafez, A.I., Zawbaa, H.M., Emary, E., Hassanien, A.E.: Sine cosine optimization algorithm for feature selection. In: 2016 International Symposium on Innovations in Intelligent Systems and Applications (INISTA), pp. 1–5. (2016)
20. Reddy, K.S., Panwar, L.K., Panigrahi, B.K., Kumar, R. A new binary variant of sine-cosine algorithm: development and application to solve profit-based unit commitment problem. Arabian Journal for Science and Engineering. **43**, 4041–4056 (2018)
21. Fernández, A., Peña, A., Valenzuela, M., Pinto, H.: A binary percentile sin-cosine optimisation algorithm applied to the set covering problem. In: Proceedings of the Computational Methods in Systems and Software, pp. 285–295. Springer, Cham (2018)
22. Balaji, S., Revathi, N.: A new approach for solving set covering problem using jumping particle swarm optimization method. Natural Computing. **15**, 503–517 (2016)
23. García, J., Crawford, B., Soto, R., García, P.: A multi dynamic binary black hole algorithm applied to set covering problem. In: International Conference on Harmony Search Algorithm, pp. 42–51. Springer, Singapore (2017)

24. Pinto, H., Peña, A., Valenzuela, M., Fernández, A.: A binary sine-cosine algorithm applied to the knapsack problem. In: Computer Science On-line Conference, pp. 128–138. Springer, Cham (2019)

25. Zhang, X., Wu, C., Li, J., Wang, X., Yang, Z., Lee, J.M., Jung, K.H.: Binary artificial algae algorithm for multidimensional knapsack problems. Applied Soft Computing. **43**, 583–595 (2016)

26. García, J., Crawford, B., Soto, R., Castro, C., Paredes, F.: A k-means binarization framework applied to multidimensional knapsack problem. Applied Intelligence. **48**, 357–380 (2018)

27. Taghian, S., Nadimi-Shahraki, M.H.: Binary sine cosine algorithms for feature selection from medical data. Advanced Computing: An International Journal (ACIJ). **10** (2019)

28. Rashedi, E., Nezamabadi-Pour, H., Saryazdi, S.: BGSA: binary gravitational search algorithm. Natural Computing. **9**, 727–745 (2010)

29. Emary, E., Zawbaa, H.M., Hassanien, A.E.: Binary grey wolf optimization approaches for feature selection. Neurocomputing. **172**, 371–381 (2016)

30. Tawhid, M.A., Savsani, P.: Discrete sine-cosine algorithm (DSCA) with local search for solving traveling salesman problem. Arabian Journal for Science and Engineering. **44**, 3669–3679 (2019)

31. Liu, W.P., Zheng, J.H., Wu, M.L., Zou, J.: Hybrid crossover operator based on pattern. In: Seventh International Conference on Natural Computation, **2**, pp. 1097–1100. IEEE (2011)

32. Croes, G.A.: A method for solving traveling-salesman problems. Operations Research. **6**, 791–812 (1958)

33. Gholizadeh, S., Sojoudizadeh, R.: Modified sine-cosine algorithm for sizing optimization of truss structures with discrete design variables. International Journal of Optimization in Civil Engineering. **9(2)**, 195–212. (2019)

34. Zhao, Y., Zou, F., Chen, D.: A discrete sine cosine algorithm for community detection. In: International Conference on Intelligent Computing, pp. 35–44. Springer, Cham (2019)

35. Gong, M., Cai, Q., Li, Y., Ma, J.: An improved memetic algorithm for community detection in complex networks. In: 2012 IEEE Congress on Evolutionary Computation, pp. 1–8. (2012)

36. Chen, H., Wang, M., Zhao, X: A multi-strategy enhanced sine cosine algorithm for global optimization and constrained practical engineering problems. Applied Mathematics and Computation. **369**, 124872 (2020)

37. Rizk-Allah, R.M., Abdel Mageed, H.M., El-Sehiemy, R.A., Abdel Aleem, S.H.E., El Shahat, A.: A new sine cosine optimization algorithm for solving combined non-convex economic and emission power dispatch problems. International Journal of Energy Conversion. **5**, 180–192 (2017)

38. Tizhoosh, H.R.: Opposition-based learning: a new scheme for machine intelligence. In: International Conference on Computational Intelligence for Modelling, Control and Automation and International Conference on

Intelligent Agents, Web Technologies and Internet Commerce (CIMCA-IAWTIC'06), **1**, pp. 695–701. IEEE (2005)

39. Rizk-Allah, R.M., El-Sehiemy, R.A.: A novel sine cosine approach for single and multiobjective emission/economic load dispatch problem. In: 2018 International Conference on Innovative Trends in Computer Engineering (ITCE), pp. 271–277. IEEE (2018)

40. Wan, Y., Zhong, Y., Ma, A., Zhang, L.: Hyperspectral remote sensing image band selection via multi-objective sine cosine algorithm. In: IGARSS 2019—2019 IEEE International Geoscience and Remote Sensing Symposium, pp. 3796–3799. IEEE (2019)

41. Branke, J., Deb, K., Dierolf, H., Osswald, M.: Finding knees in multi-objective optimization. In: International Conference on Parallel Problem Solving from Nature, pp. 722–731. Springer, Heidelberg (2004)

14

Less Is More Approach in Heuristic Optimization

Nenad Mladenović⬭, Zvi Drezner⬭, Jack Brimberg,
and Dragan Urošević⬭

14.1 Introduction

Whichever creative work people undertake, if the inclination to improve it by adding more and more new elements prevails, there comes a moment when the obtained result is perceived to be far from the desired and expected outcome. A response to this "more and more" attitude is an approach usually

N. Mladenović
Industrial System Engineering, Khalifa University, Abu Dhabi, UAE
e-mail: nenad.mladenovic@ku.ac.ae

Z. Drezner
College of Business and Economics, California State University-Fullerton,
Fullerton, CA 92834, USA
e-mail: zdrezner@fullerton.edu

J. Brimberg
Royal Military College of Canada, Kingston, ON, Canada
e-mail: jack.brimberg@rmc.ca

D. Urošević (✉)
Mathematical Institute of the Serbian Academy of Sciences and Arts, Belgrade,
Serbia
e-mail: draganu@mi.sanu.ac.rs

© The Author(s), under exclusive license to Springer Nature
Switzerland AG 2022
S. Salhi and J. Boylan (eds.), *The Palgrave Handbook of Operations Research*,
https://doi.org/10.1007/978-3-030-96935-6_14

called "less is more". It is the case in almost all the scientific and art disciplines: in Architecture (Van der Rohe, 1886–1969), Genetic Networks [7], Medicine Treatment [52], Cancer Immunotherapy [87], Neuro-sciences [19], Signaling [5], Education [67], Functional Materials [6], and so on. In the venerable *Science* journal there are more than 20 articles with the title "Less is more". Even the last article written by Lenin in 1923 that considered the five-year macro-economic plan, had a title "Less is more". He wrote: "We must follow the rule: better fewer, but better". In Search Engine Optimization (SEO) and Marketing, the *less is more* principle is used to find a keyword. Indeed, industry best practices recommend focusing each page on a single keyword, rather than trying to optimize for several at once. This helps with SEO and makes it easy for consumers to find targeted information. If too many terms are added on a page, the keyword density required for search engines will not be achieved.

Optimization problems (OP) may be defined in general as

$$(\min)\{f(x)|x \in X, X \subseteq S\}, \tag{14.1}$$

where x, f, X, S are solution, objective function, feasible set, and solution space, respectively. OPs occur in the private and public sectors, and small or huge enterprises. The main difficulty in solving them is the existence of multiple local optima, often in the millions, among which there are only one or a few global optima. Such problems are classified as NP-hard, and vastly outnumber those problems solvable in polynomial time. Many methods, both exact and heuristic, have been proposed to avoid the so-called *local optimum trap*, or to describe how to continue the search once a local minimum is reached. To do that, various methods use different ingredients and ideas. Meta-heuristics, or frameworks for building heuristics, are methods to overcome local optimum traps. Most popular among them are Simulated Annealing [62], Tabu Search (TS) [44], Variable neighborhood search (VNS) [49], and the Genetic algorithm [97]. Researchers have frequently adopted the *more is more approach* by combining different meta-ideas to get complex hybrid algorithms. In that way, over a hundred different combined strategies may be proposed, resulting in procedures that are often hard to understand.

The less is more approach (LIMA) has been recently proposed for solving global optimization problems. Its main idea is to find the minimum number of combinatorial or search elements (ingredients, or control variables) when solving an optimization problem that would make some optimization method more efficient and effective than the currently best. LIMA has appeared as a reaction to more and more complex hybrid heuristic methods that combine many different ideas and metaphors, yet giving no proper explanations for such combinations. Combining several heuristics to get a new hybrid method comes at a price of losing efficiency and user friendliness, two very important and desired properties of any heuristic. Indeed, despite the simplicity of LIMA, significantly better results have been reported compared to more complex, "state-of-the-art" heuristics used to solve several classical optimization problems. A few such examples will be presented later. Thus, including many ideas in the search does not necessarily lead to better computational results. On the contrary, sometimes less can yield more.

In this chapter we follow the opposite research direction from *more is more*; i.e., we advocate the *less is more approach* (LIMA) in optimization. In the next section, we give a quick overview of LIMA successes from the literature on optimization. To make the LIMA concept more general and more precise, we define a dominance relation between two algorithms in Sect. 14.3 that measures and compares their relative simplicity/complexity. Section 14.3 also outlines a general approach for constructing algorithms that follow the LIMA principle. Section 14.4 discusses various applications that reinforce the LIMA principle, and also expand the scope of LIMA. Section 14.5 concludes the chapter.

14.2 Literature Review of LIMA Implementations

We give here a brief survey of some successful implementations of LIMA that adhere to the interpretation of the LIMA approach presented in Sect. 14.3. Most of these LIMA applications are based on the Variable neighborhood search (VNS) meta-heuristic, since the developed heuristics are usually less complex than heuristics based on other principles.

Minimum Differential Dispersion Problem Mladenović et al. [74] were the first to solve an optimization problem by LIMA. It was proposed in 2016. The basic VNS (BVNS) suggested here uses a random initial solution and only one neighborhood structure, while providing much better results than the hybrid heuristic which was state-of-the-art at that time. We will give more details of this LIMA application later in Sect. 14.4.

Balanced Minimum Sum-of-Squares Clustering Costa et al. [25]. Given a set of entities or points, the clustering addresses the problem of finding homogeneous and well-separated subsets of those entities. In balanced clustering, the constraints impose that the entities be equally spread among the different subsets. Again, a basic VNS (BVNS) is implemented. Computational experiments and statistical tests showed that the proposed algorithm outperformed the more complex state-of-the-art algorithm at that time.

Max-Mean Diversity Problem Brimberg et al. [15]. Given a set of elements, this problem requires finding a subset that maximizes the quotient of the sum of all edges belonging to that subset and the cardinality of the subset. The authors developed a new application of general VNS for solving this problem. Extensive computational results showed that the new heuristic, while simpler in design, significantly outperformed the current state-of-the-art heuristic. The best-known solutions were improved on 58 out of 60 large test instances from the literature.

Discrete Obnoxious p -Median Problem Mladenović et al. [72]. Given a set J of possible facility locations and a set of customers I, as well as the distance between each customer $i \in I$ and facility location $j \in J$, the Obnoxious p-median problem consists in choosing p facility locations from the set J so that the sum of the distances between each customer and its nearest facility is maximized. LIMA is successfully applied to solve this problem in [72]. A basic variable neighborhood search is developed, where a single search ingredient, an interchange neighborhood structure, is used. According to the results obtained on benchmark instances, the LIMA heuristic turns out to be highly competitive with the existing ones, while establishing new state-of-the-art results. For example, four new best-known solutions and 133 ties are claimed in testing a set of 144 instances.

An Integrated Production and Assembly Scheduling Problem in Smart Manufacturing Lu et al. [66]. The authors also use a LIMA-VNS algorithm. The problem is divided into two stages: the production stage and the assembly stage. Then it is proved that the investigated problem is NP-hard. The computational experiments indicate that the designed LIMA-VNS has an advantage over other heuristics in terms of convergence speed, solution quality, and robustness, especially for large-scale problems.

The Traveling Repairman Problem with Profits Pei et al. [80]. This problem generalizes the Traveling Repairman Problem, by taking into account the variability of the repairman's profit over different time steps in order to maximize the total profit. Detailed experiments on benchmark instances show that the new LIMA-GVNS-based method outperforms all previous heuristics. Out of 60 instances tested, it was able to replicate the best-known solutions in 20 of them and find new best solutions in the remaining 40.

The Capacitated Modular Hub Location Problem Mikić et al. [70]. This problem belongs to the class of single assignment hub location problems, where a terminal can be assigned to only one hub. In addition, the problem imposes capacity constraints on both the hubs and the edges that connect them. It is directly related to air traffic control where the number of flights between pairs of cities directly determines the conditions of the capacity. In order to tackle the problem the authors propose a general variable neighborhood search (GVNS) based heuristic. They show through exhaustive testing that the GVNS method gives superior results in comparison to earlier methods. This is especially reflected in the number of best solutions that were obtained in a much shorter time. Statistical tests are applied showing conclusively that GVNS is superior to the earlier methods.

Unconstrained Continuous Optimization Gonçalves Silva et al. [46]. The Nelder-Mead method (NM) [77] for solving continuous nonlinear optimization problems is probably the most cited and most used method in the optimization literature and in practical applications, too. It belongs to the class of direct search methods. The popularity of NM is based on its simplicity. In [46] an even simpler algorithm for larger instances, following the NM idea, is proposed. It is called Simplified NM (SNM): instead of generating all $n + 1$ simplex points in R^n, the search uses many fewer simplex points, say $q + 1$. Though the results cannot be better than the original NM with $n + 1$ points, a substantial speed-up allows the authors to run SNM many times from different starting solutions, usually getting better results than those obtained by the full NM within the same cpu time. A computational analysis is performed on 10 classical convex and non-convex instances, where the number of variables n can be arbitrarily large. The obtained results with n as large as 10,000, show that SNM is more effective than the original NM, confirming that LIMA can yield good results when solving a continuous optimization problem. Furthermore, such a dimensional simplification may be used in many other numerical methods.

Solving a System of Nonlinear Equations Pei et al. [79]. A continuous VNS for finding all the solutions to a nonlinear system of equations (NSEs) is proposed. The NSE problem is transformed into an equivalent optimization problem, such that a new objective function allows them to find all the zeros. Instead of the usual sum-of-squares, our objective function is presented as the sum of absolute values. Despite its simpler form, a theoretical investigation confirms that the new objective function provides more accurate solutions regardless of the optimization method used. Secondly, a basic VNS is developed to solve the transformed problem. Computational analysis of standard test instances shows that the proposed method is more precise, much faster, and simpler than two recently developed methods. Similar conclusions are reached when comparing the proposed method with many other methods in the literature.

Binary Bipartite Quadratic Programming Problem Urošević et al. [93]. Given a complete bipartite graph G with given weights assigned to vertices and edges, the *Boolean/Binary Bipartite Quadratic Programming problem* (BBQP) (in the literature also called *maximum weighted induced sub-graph*, *maximum weight bi-clique* or *maximum cut on bipartite graphs*) consists of selecting a sub-graph which maximizes the sum of the weights assigned to the chosen vertices, and the edges that connect them. Applications of the BBQP are present in mining discrete patterns from binary data, approximating matrices by rank-one binary matrices, computing the cut-norm of a matrix, and so on. Since the problem is NP-hard, many heuristic methods have been proposed in the literature to solve it. In [93] a simple LIMA heuristic based on Tabu search is proposed. It uses two neighborhood structures and a relatively simple rule for implementation of a short-term memory operation. In addition, a simple rule for automatic calculation of the tabu list length is proposed, without increasing the method's complexity. Despite its simplicity, this heuristic showed better performance than the current state-of-the-art, with six new best-known solutions of well-studied test instances.

14.3   LIMA Algorithm

When designing a LIMA-type algorithm, one must consider what method to choose to compare with, let us say method A vs. our method B. It is easier to design a LIMA-based method B if we have some method A to compare with. Naturally, a method A should be the most successful in the literature for the problem considered. If problem P in (14.1) is new, then method A could be an exact solution procedure.

14.3.1   What Is More and What Is Less in Algorithm Design

Here we will answer a fundamental question of how to define more precisely *what is more and what is less* in solving an optimization problem? If we accept the natural assumption that *less* means fewer ingredients used in the search for a better solution, then the question is how to define the set of search ingredients U? There are two possible ways of defining the control set U.

i. The simple way is just to analyze the state-of-the-art algorithm A, and collect the ingredients it uses; then set $U = U_A$. A LIMA type algorithm will first specify an order of ingredients $u_\ell \in U$, and after solving this part, add and drop those ingredients in a given order. The aim is to get $U_B \subseteq U_A$ for a proposed LIMA algorithm B. Of course, an order of ingredients could be an interesting question by itself. Up to now, most of the successful implementations of LIMA from the literature follow the general procedure above.

ii. Another, more general and harder way is to design some set of ingredients U, that we call the control or universal set. Elements u_i of the universal set U define the heuristic method that is currently used. By changing the arrangement of these elements, by swapping, adding, removing, and so on, we automatically change the method within our LIMA algorithm. Possible elements of U could signal if a heuristic uses an initial solution obtained by some constructive heuristic or not, if it uses local search or not, if it uses memory or not, etc.

The usual way to compare methods in solving OPs is by their precision and speed. However, there is no measure of an algorithm's simplicity in the literature. The *worst-case analysis* cannot usually give answers in a practical comparison of computer results. Consequently, hybrid methods with several heuristic ideas have been claimed as the best, without checking if a smaller subset of algorithmic ingredients would provide results with better quality. Here we introduce a different dominance relation for algorithms solving minimization problem (14.1) that measures also the simplicity of the compared algorithms.

Definition 1 The cardinality of the set of ingredients U_A used to solve minimization problem (14.1) on data set D by algorithm A is called the *LIMA number* of A.

Definition 2 We say that algorithm B is *LIMA-dominant* over algorithm A in solving problem (14.1) on data set D, if and only if

(a) the objective function value $f_B \leq f_A$;
(b) the running time $t_B \leq t_A$;
(c) the cardinality of the ingredient set of B (LIMA number of B) $|U_B| \leq |U_A|$;

and at least one of these inequalities is strictly satisfied.

The LIMA dominance relation could be too strong if applied to each run and each test instance. Therefore, we can easily define weak or *average LIMA- dominance*, i.e., after many runs on the same problem, by requiring that average values $f_B \leq f_A$, $t_B \leq t_A$, and $|U_B| \leq |U_A|$, on all runs.

14.3.2 Steps of the LIMA Algorithm

We next present in Algorithm 1 the general steps of LIMA that will satisfy those three relations (a), (b), and (c), and minimize the LIMA number. To include efficacy (precision) and efficiency (speed) in the algorithm quality, let us introduce the following:

* f_*, t_* the objective function value and the running time of algorithm A (state-of-the-art), respectively;
* f^*, t^* the objective function value and the running time of algorithm B (LIMA), respectively (Fig. 14.1).

In step 1 the set of ingredients U is defined. As discussed before, the simple way is just to analyze the state-of-the-art algorithm A, collect ingredients it uses, and then set $U \subseteq U_A$. The initial solution of the problem is found in step 2, while the main loop starts from step 3. It consists of an enumeration of elements from U, selected in step 1, until CPU time exceeds an imposed limit ($t_{\max}$). In step 4 the optimization problem with objective cut constraint obtained by the best-known value, is solved, where the cut represents the original best value. If the solution is feasible (satisfying the objective cut constraint as well) and if obtained in a time less than t_* (step 6), then the LIMA-based algorithm is successful, and it can stop in step 7. Alternatively, the search for even better solutions can continue (go to step 12). If a better solution is not found within t_* (step 9), then we can either stop and admit that we did not get a better solution than algorithm A in t_* time, or continue the search for a better solution using more time (step 10).

14.4 Applications of LIMA

In this section we demonstrate the LIMA approach with the following four optimization problems: minimum differential dispersion problem; planar p-median problem; continuous obnoxious facility location problem and gray patterns problem.

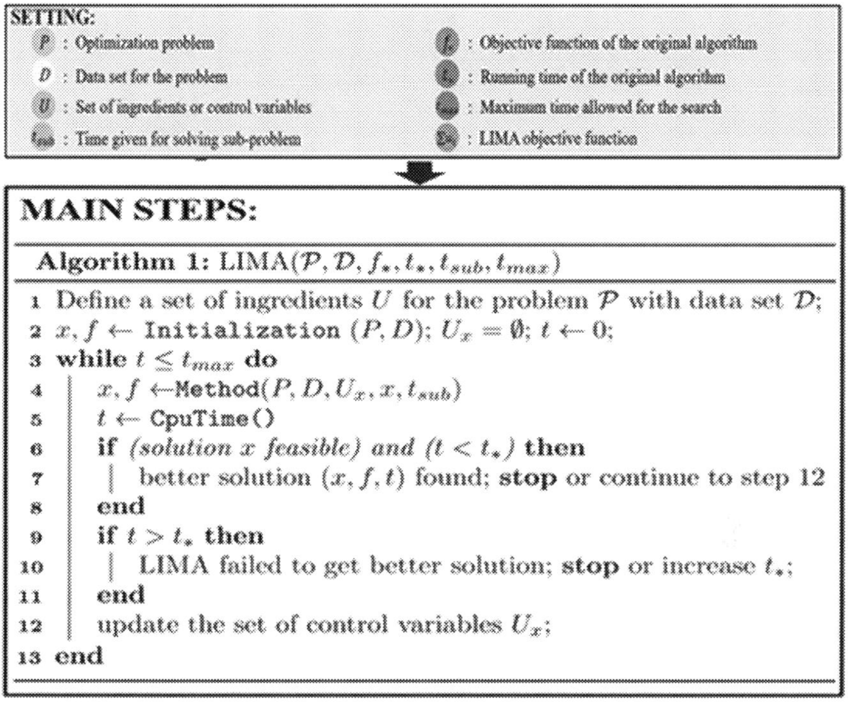

SETTING:

$\mathcal{P}$: Optimization problem	: Objective function of the original algorithm
$\mathcal{D}$: Data set for the problem	: Running time of the original algorithm
$\mathcal{U}$: Set of ingredients or control variables	: Maximum time allowed for the search
: Time given for solving sub-problem	: LIMA objective function

MAIN STEPS:

Algorithm 1: $\mathrm{LIMA}(\mathcal{P}, \mathcal{D}, f_*, t_*, t_{sub}, t_{max})$

1 Define a set of ingredients U for the problem $\mathcal{P}$ with data set $\mathcal{D}$;
2 $x, f \leftarrow$ Initialization (P, D); $U_x = \emptyset$; $t \leftarrow 0$;
3 **while** $t \le t_{max}$ **do**
4 $\quad$ $x, f \leftarrow$ Method (P, D, U_x, x, t_{sub})
5 $\quad$ $t \leftarrow$ CpuTime()
6 $\quad$ **if** *(solution x feasible)* and *(t < t*)* **then**
7 $\quad\quad$ better solution (x, f, t) found; **stop** or continue to step 12
8 $\quad$ **end**
9 $\quad$ **if** $t > t_*$ **then**
10 $\quad\quad$ LIMA failed to get better solution; **stop** or increase t_*;
11 $\quad$ **end**
12 $\quad$ update the set of control variables U_x;
13 **end**

Fig. 14.1 A general algorithm for implementing the less is more approach (LIMA)

14.4.1 Minimum Differential Dispersion Problem

We are given a set N of n elements and the distances d_{ij} between all pairs of elements (i, j). Let S be a subset of N whose cardinality is equal to m. The differential dispersion of the subset S is calculated as follows

$$\delta(S) = \max_{i \in S} \Delta(i) - \min_{j \in S} \Delta(j)$$

where $\Delta(i)$ represents the sum of distances of element i from all remaining elements in S. The minimum differential dispersion problem consists in finding subset S (of cardinality m) with the minimum differential dispersion. The mathematical programming formulation is as follows [82]:

$$\min_{t,r,s,x} \{ t \}$$

subject to:

$$r \ge \sum_{j, j \ne i} d_{ij} x_j - U_i(1 - x_i) + M^-(1 - x_i), \quad i \in N$$

$$s \leq \sum_{j,j\neq i} d_{ij}x_j - L_i(1-x_i) + M^+(1-x_i), \quad i \in N$$

$$t \geq r - s$$

$$\sum_{i\in N} x_i = m$$

$$x \in \{0,1\}^n$$

where

$$L_i = \sum_{j\in N, j\neq i} \min\{0, d_{ij}\}, \quad U_i = \sum_{j\in N, j\neq i} \max\{0, d_{ij}\},$$

and M^- and M^+ denote the lower bound of U_i and the upper bound of L_i values, respectively.

The following ingredients are adopted in the state-of-the-art algorithm to solve the minimum differential dispersion problem: GRASP for the initialization, and then hybridizing TS, Path Re-linking (PR), and VNS-based heuristics for the improvement [41]. The binary variables u_1, u_2, u_3, and u_4 are defined to be 1 or 0 if GRASP, TS, PR, and VNS are included or not in the algorithm, respectively. The LIMA type objective function (LIMA number) for algorithm A in this case is equal to 4 ($f = u_1 + \cdots + u_4$). Using Algorithm 2, we are looking for a method with LIMA number less than or, equal to 4. Following the steps of LIMA, a random initial solution is constructed, and the VNS-based heuristic is adopted as the only selected ingredient of the improvement phase in the heuristic developed in [74] (see Algorithm 2).

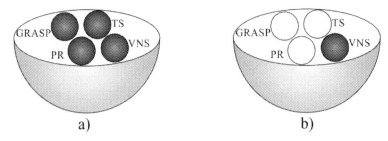

Fig. 14.2 Ingredients for GRASP_EPR (left) and VNS_LIMA (right)

Algorithm 2: VNS heuristic for solving Min-DiffDP.

1 **Function** VNS_MinDiff(S, k_{max}, t_{max});
2 $S \leftarrow$ Initial_solution();
3 **repeat**
4    $k \leftarrow 1$;
5   **while** $k \leq k_{max}$ **do**
6        $S' \leftarrow$ Shake(S, k);
7        $S'' \leftarrow$ LS(S');
8        $k \leftarrow k + 1$;
9   **if** S'' *is better than* S **then**
10           $S \leftarrow S''$; $k \leftarrow 1$;
11   **end**
12   **end**
13   $t \leftarrow$ CpuTime();
14 **until** $t > t_{max}$;
15 **return** S;

Its LIMA objective (LIMA number) is obviously equal to 1 ($f = u_4 = 1$). Surprisingly, there are 170 new best-known solutions found, and another 20 solutions remain the same as before, but are obtained in less time (Fig. 14.2). The average improvement on solution quality is over 10% (Table 14.1).

14.4.2 Planar *p*-Median Problem

The continuous *p*-median problem [32, 39], also known as the multi-source Weber problem [11, 50, 60], or continuous location-allocation problem [12, 65], requires finding *p* sites for facilities in Euclidean space in order to minimize a weighted sum of distances from a set of demand points to their closest facility. Let X_i denote the location of facility $i \in \{1, \ldots, p\}$, and A_j the known location of demand point $j \in N = \{1, \ldots, n\}$. The points $X_i = (x_i, y_i)$ and $A_j = (a_j, b_j)$ are all located in the plane. Distances are

Table 14.1 Average results on each data set group SOM, GKD, and MDG. Each instance was run 10 times, getting 1900 runs in total

Data set (# ins.)	GRASP_EPR		VNS_LIMA				(%)imp.		
	Best	Time	Best	Avg.	Worst	Time	Best	Avg.	Worst
SOM (20)	23.35	173.41	18.40	20.09	21.75	121.47	21.82	15.20	9.32
GKD (70)	52.57	56.99	45.08	46.85	49.13	129.44	24.78	19.46	13.70
MDG (100)	3567.63	1472.35	3052.07	3290.12	3521.92	1040.30	14.60	8.43	2.89
Average (190)	1214.52	567.58	1038.52	1119.02	1197.60	430.40	20.40	14.37	8.64

assumed to be measured by the Euclidean norm:

$$d(X_i, A_j) = \sqrt{(x_i - a_j)^2 + (y_i - b_j)^2}. \qquad (14.2)$$

The weights (or demands) at the A_j's are given by $w_j > 0$, $j \in \{1, \ldots, n\}$. The formulation of the planar p-median problem is:

$$\min_{X \subset \mathbb{R}^2} \left\{ f(X) = \sum_{j=1}^{n} w_j \min_{1 \le i \le p} \{d(X_i, A_j)\} \right\}, \qquad (14.3)$$

where $X = \{X_1, \ldots, X_p\}$ denotes the set of location variables.

This model was originally proposed by Cooper [23, 24], who also observed that the objective function $f(X)$ is non-convex, and may contain several local optima. The problem was later shown to be NP-hard [68]. For recent reviews of the discrete p-median problem see [28], and for the planar p-median problem see [13].

The single facility (1-median) problem termed the Weber problem [95] has a long history dating back to the French mathematician Pierre De Fermat of the 1600s. Recent reviews of the Weber problem are [20, 37, 96].

Kalczynski et al. [53] proposed to use solutions to the discrete p-median problem, where facility locations are restricted to demand points, as starting solutions for algorithms that heuristically solve the planar p-median problem. They applied the RATIO algorithm [9], which is a small modification of the IALT algorithm [8], on the set of starting solutions. Cooper [23, 24] suggested the original ALT (alternating) algorithm. Since each demand point gets its services from the closest facility, each facility attracts a subset of demand points. The ALT algorithm alternates between determining the subsets attracted by each facility, and re-locating the facilities to the optimal location for each subset, until stabilization. Once Cooper's algorithm terminates, the IALT algorithm finds for each demand point the difference between the distances to the closest facility and the second closest, and considers re-assigning the demand points with the L smallest differences (they used $L = 20$) individually from the closest facility to the second closest. The RATIO algorithm selects the L smallest *ratios* between the distances rather than differences. It was found in [9] that this small modification significantly improves the performance of the IALT algorithm.

The connection between the discrete p-median problem, where potential facility locations are restricted to a given set of nodes (or demand points), and its continuous counterpart, where the facility sites are modeled as unknown points in the plane, has been a topic of study since the introduction of the continuous problem by [23, 24]. Hansen et al. [50] propose a heuristic that first finds an optimal solution of the discrete problem, and then performs one step of continuous adjustment starting from this solution to obtain the final one. Very good computational results are reported, but as observed in Brimberg et al. [11], the CPU time to find an optimal solution to the discrete p-median becomes prohibitively high for larger problem instances. Kalczynski et al. [53] showed, through extensive computational tests, a rather counterintuitive result that "good" discrete starting solutions can actually be better than optimal (or best-known) ones. The implication is that heuristics that interface between discrete and continuous versions of the p-median (e.g., [11, 50]), should not focus efforts on obtaining exact solutions in the discrete phase, but rather introduce some randomness by using multiple good discrete solutions as starting points for the continuous phase. This will save considerable execution time, and may, depending on the improving search, produce as good or better continuous solutions.

The following formulation for finding the best set (or optimal discrete solution) is similar to the one in [27, 28, 56, 85]. Let $x_j \in \{0, 1\}$ be a binary variable. $x_j = 1$ if demand point j is selected for locating a facility, and zero otherwise. $y_{ij} = 1$ if selected demand point j is the closest facility to demand point i. The BLP (binary linear programming) optimization problem is:

$$\min \left\{ \sum_{i=1}^{n} \sum_{j=1}^{n} [w_i d_{ij}] y_{ij} \right\}$$

subject to:

$$\sum_{j=1}^{n} x_j = p$$

$$y_{ij} \leq x_j \qquad\qquad \text{for } i, j = 1, \ldots, n$$

$$\sum_{j=1}^{n} y_{ij} = 1 \qquad\qquad \text{for } i = 1, \ldots, n$$

$$x_j \in \{0, 1\} \qquad\qquad \text{for } j = 1, \ldots, n$$

$$y_{ij} \in \{0, 1\} \qquad\qquad \text{for } i, j = 1, \ldots, n \qquad (14.4)$$

In formulation (14.4) there are $n^2 + n$ variables, and $n^2 + n + 1$ constraints not including the last two.

To get the kth best optimal solution the following procedure is followed. Let $P^{(1)}$ be the optimal set. In order to get the second best solution add the constraint

$$\sum_{j \in P^{(1)}} x_j \leq p - 1$$

getting the second best set $P^{(2)}$. Once the best $k \geq 1$ sets are found, the $(k + 1)^{th}$ best solution is obtained by adding to the original problem (14.4), k constraints:

$$\sum_{j \in P^{(m)}} x_j \leq p - 1 \text{ for } m = 1, \ldots, k \qquad\qquad (14.5)$$

Kalczynski et al. [53] also designed and tested a genetic algorithm. We report only the computational experiments with the 10 best solutions. One would expect that the optimal discrete solution will result in the best continuous solution. However, confirming the less is more approach, it is not the case for the continuous p-median problem. They first tested the approaches on the 50 randomly generated instances of problems used in [9]. The number of demand points is $n = 100, 200, \ldots, 1000$, and the number of facilities is $p = 5, 10, 15, 20, 25$, for a total of 50 instances. They also tested problems that were extensively investigated in the literature, and reported results on two of them with $n = 654$ and 1060 demand points [84].

The best discrete solution for the 50 random instances was obtained by solving (14.4) using CPLEX [26]. Some of the largest problem sets required several days of computing time. Applying RATIO on the best discrete solution required a negligible fraction of one second by a FORTRAN program.

The results are disappointing. The best-known (BK) continuous solution was found for only 12 of the 50 instances. The average percentage above the best-known solution was 0.048%.

When the top 10 discrete solutions were used as starting solutions, the improvement in the results was again disappointing. The best-known continuous solution was obtained at least once in 21 of the 50 instances, an increase of only 9 instances. The average best result was 0.035% above the best-known solution, down from 0.048%. There are also some unusual results. In eleven instances the same continuous solution was found for all ten discrete starting solutions, but it was not the best-known solution.

In conclusion, for this set of test problems, the best discrete solutions are not recommended as starting solutions confirming the less is more principle. On the other hand, good discrete solutions were generated quickly using a greedy heuristic with a random component to achieve some diversity. Using these solutions as starting solutions for RATIO resulted, to the surprise of the authors, in the same or better results in a small fraction of the run time. In other words. "good may be better than best" as starting solutions for problems of this type.

In the next subsections we report on two papers that have a "less is more" component, and verify the "less is more" philosophy. In [55] it was found that infeasible starting solutions resulted in a better final solution, and in [35] it was found that of the two formulations proposed by the authors, the one with many more variables and constraints performed much faster than the streamlined model to their surprise.

14.4.3 Multiple Obnoxious Facility Location Problem

In most location problems, the closer a facility is to communities the better. However, there are facilities that have a negative impact on communities (being "obnoxious"), and being farther from communities is preferred. For example, noisy or polluting factories, garbage dumps, airports, should not be located close to communities. The obnoxious facility location problem was initiated in the 1970s, for example [3, 4, 22, 76], and intensively analyzed in the literature (for reviews see [21, 51, 69, 81]).

Suppose that n communities are located in an area. One needs to locate $p \geq 1$ obnoxious facilities in that area. Most of the papers on the subject are modeled in discrete space, i.e., there is a limited number of potential locations for the facilities (for example in a network environment). However, in most of these applications, the negative impact propagates "by air". Therefore, the use of planar Euclidean distances is appropriate. Also, locations of facilities are usually in open spaces far from the communities, and thus not limited to a list of locations. So location anywhere in the area is appropriate as well.

Drezner et al. [36] investigated the model of locating obnoxious facilities in the plane with the objective of maximizing the shortest distance between facilities and communities subject to a minimum distance D between facilities. Let $A_i = (a_i, b_i)$ for $i = 1, \ldots n$ be the given locations of the communities, and $X_j = (x_j, y_j)$ for $j = 1, \ldots, p$ be the unknown locations of the p facilities. The nonlinear programming formulation is:

$$\max\{L\}$$

subject to:

$$(x_j - a_i)^2 + (y_j - b_i)^2 \geq L \text{ for } i = 1, \ldots, n; \ j = 1, \ldots p$$
$$(x_i - x_j)^2 + (y_i - y_j)^2 \geq D^2 \text{ for } 1 \leq i < j \leq p . \quad (14.6)$$

In addition, constraints that restrict the facilities' locations to a convex polygon or any finite region are needed. Otherwise, the solution is to locate the facilities "at infinity".

This problem is extremely non-convex. The surface plot for one facility among $n = 100$ communities (tested in [36]) is plotted in Fig. 14.3. There

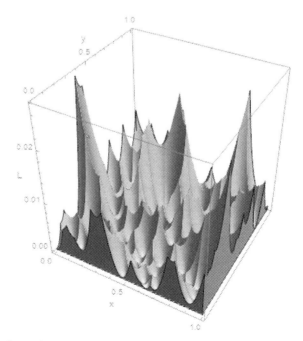

Fig. 14.3 Surface of squared distances to the closest community for 100 communities

are 202 "hilltops" (for $n = 1000$ there are 2002 hilltops), and the solution for the $p = 1$ instance is on the top of the highest hill. The hilltops are located at Voronoi points [2, 78, 89, 94] that can be found by Mathematica [98] or FORTRAN codes (for example [88]). Okabe et al. [78] showed that for n generating points there are about $2n$ Voronoi points. Shamos and Hoey [86] recognized this property and optimally solved the $p = 1$ case by finding all Voronoi points generated by the set of demand points, and selecting the one with the maximum objective.

Drezner et al. [36] generated a data set of 76 instances in a 10 miles by 10 miles square, that can be easily replicated. There are two values of $n = 100, 1000$, 19 values of $2 \leq p \leq 20$, and two values of $D = \frac{10}{\sqrt{p}}; \frac{10}{\sqrt{2p}}$. They first solved the problem 100 times by the nonlinear solver SNOPT [43]. For example, the best results for the $n = 1000$, $p = 20$, and $D = \frac{10}{\sqrt{2p}}$ instance had a minimum distance of 1.63 miles between the facilities and the communities. It required about 5 hours of computer time. They then suggested to select the highest p hilltops (Voronoi points) that have at least a distance D between them. Note that any feasible selection of p hilltops is a local maximum. The objective function is determined by the facility with the minimum distance to all communities. An infinitesimal move of this facility can only decrease its minimum distance, and thus decrease the value of the objective function, and infinitesimal moves of other facilities have a zero impact on the value of the objective function.

The selection of the best p locations from the list of v Voronoi points, that satisfies the requirement of a minimum distance D between facilities can be found by a binary linear program (BLP) (see [36]). Let the distance between potential locations i and j be D_{ij}, and d_i is the minimum distance between Voronoi point i and all communities. Also, $\hat{d} = \max_{1 \leq i \leq v} \{d_i\}$.

$$\text{Maximize } \{L\}$$

subject to:

$$\sum_{i=1}^{v} x_i = p$$

$$x_i + x_j \leq 1 \text{ when } D_{ij} < D$$

$$L + x_i(\hat{d} - d_i) \leq \hat{d} \text{ for } i = 1, \ldots, v$$

$$x_i \in \{0, 1\} . \tag{14.7}$$

The objective function L in an optimal solution is the maximum possible minimum distance between any p feasible Voronoi points and all communities.

They found that the obtained solution by the BLP (14.7) is much better than applying a multi-start approach using general purpose nonlinear solvers. It could not be improved by SNOPT because it is a local maximum. For example, the results for the $n = 1000$, $p = 20$, and $D = \frac{10}{\sqrt{2p}}$ instance had a minimum distance of 4.02 miles between the facilities and the communities, and required only 24 seconds of computer time. It is almost 150% better than the best solution found by SNOPT from 100 random starting solutions, and was found in a tiny fraction of the run time.

Kalczynski and Drezner [55] found that the results of Drezner et al. [36] can be further improved if an inferior selection of the p Voronoi points is used. Three approaches to selecting starting solutions were proposed.

The p selected Voronoi points $i_1, \ldots, i_p$ found by BLP (14.7), are sorted so that $d_{i_1} \geq d_{i_2} \geq \ldots \geq d_{i_p}$. The value of the objective function is d_{i_p}.

In each iteration of the first Algorithm, the facility i_p is replaced by a facility located at a feasible optimal location while keeping the other $p - 1$ facilities at their current locations. The algorithm is stopped when no improvement is found.

In the second algorithm, the selected location i_p is removed from the list of selected locations and the set of all Voronoi points for which $d_i > d_{i_p}$: $I = \{1, 2, \ldots, i_p - 1\}$, plus locations not selected by BLP (14.7), is considered. There is no feasible selection of locations in the set I. Otherwise, such a selection would have been found by the BLP. The maximum $D_0 \leq D$ for which a selection of p points in I that satisfy $D_{ij} \geq D_0$, is found by bisection for a given accuracy $\varepsilon > 0$. This non-feasible solution is used as a starting solution for a Sequential Linear Programming algorithm (SLP, [34]). If a better feasible solution is found, this is the result of the algorithm.

The third algorithm is a small modification of the second algorithm. Facilities on taller hilltops can be moved more than facilities on lower hilltops before their height falls below the lowest hilltop. Therefore, smaller D_{ij} distances can be accommodated for distances between high hilltops. d_{i_p} is the height of the lowest selected hilltop. $d_i - d_{i_p}$ is the extra height between hilltop i and the lowest hilltop. $d_i + d_j - 2d_{i_p}$ is the total extra height of hilltops i and j above the lowest hilltop. Therefore, the bisection to find D_0 in the second algorithm, is replaced by a bisection to find the minimum θ that satisfies $D_{ij} + \theta(d_i + d_j - 2d_{i_p}) \geq D$.

Algorithms 2 and 3 confirm the less is more approach. Rather than selecting the optimal set of Voronoi points, non-feasible sets are selected and in 33 out of 76 instances these selections improved the solution found in Drezner et al. [36]. The average improvement of these 33 instances is 2.7% with a maximum improvement of 14.6%. That is, starting with inferior initial solutions (in this case infeasible) leads to better final solutions.

There are other obnoxious facility models where solution methods based on selecting the best potential locations from the set of Voronoi points were suggested [29, 54, 56, 57]. It is possible to be able to improve the final solutions for these and similar models by starting with inferior selections of Voronoi points.

14.4.4 Gray Patterns

The Gray Pattern Problem proposed by Taillard [90] is based on a rectangle of dimensions n_1 by n_2. A gray pattern of p black points is selected from the $n = n_1 \times n_2$ points in the rectangle while the rest of the points remain white. This forms a "gray pattern" of density $\frac{p}{n}$ with rectangles covering the whole plane. The objective is to have a gray pattern where the black points are distributed as uniformly as possible in the rectangle considering identical patterns in adjacent rectangles.

To achieve maximum uniformity, Taillard [90] created a distance matrix $[d_{ij}]$ between locations i and j by the principle of minimum entropy in Physics. For details see also [35]. A non-convex quadratic integer program can be formulated as follows. Let $x_i = 1$ if point i is black, and zero otherwise. The formulation is:

$$\min\left\{ \sum_{i=1}^{n} \sum_{j=1}^{n} d_{ij} x_i x_j \right\}$$

subject to:

$$\sum_{i=1}^{n} x_i = p$$

$$x_i \in \{0, 1\} \tag{14.8}$$

The initial formulation of the Gray Pattern Problem (GPP) was made in the context of the generation of gray (black-white) patterns [92], but the problem can also be well applicable to color halftones [58, 63]. Finding a cluster of p out of n points which minimizes the total distance between all pairs of points in the cluster [30], and the maximum diversity problem [61] can also be formulated as a GPP.

The GPP can be formulated as a Quadratic Assignment Problem (QAP, [31]). Solving the QAP optimally is an extremely difficult problem [33, 48, 64]. The QAPLIB website [18] provides up-to-date information about the QAP.

Drezner et al. [38] exploited the structure of this specific QAP, and were able to establish optimal solutions for relatively large problems. Misevicius et al. [71] improved some best-known solutions.

Drezner et al. [35] proposed two new formulations for the gray pattern problem. They converted the quadratic binary program (14.8) to a linear Mixed Integer Program (MIP) in two ways. For simplicity we assume that $d_{ij} = d_{ji}$ and $d_{ii} = 0$ as in the gray pattern problem.

In the first formulation they defined (continuous) variables z_{ij} so that $z_{ij} = x_i x_j$, and linearized in a standard way to get:

$$\min \left\{ 2 \sum_{i=1}^{n-1} \sum_{j=i+1}^{n} d_{ij} z_{ij} \right\}$$

subject to:

$$\sum_{i=1}^{n} x_i = p$$

$$z_{ij} \geq x_i + x_j - 1 \text{ for } 1 \leq i < j \leq n$$

$$x_j \in \{0, 1\}; \quad z_{ij} \geq 0 \quad \quad (14.9)$$

In this formulation there are n binary variables, $\frac{1}{2}n(n-1)$ continuous variables, and $\frac{1}{2}n(n-1) + 1$ constraints.

A second formulation is based on (14.8). The objective function can be written as $\sum_{i=1}^{n} x_i \left[\sum_{j=1}^{n} d_{ij} x_j \right]$. Define $\underline{b_i}$ for $i = 1, \ldots, n$ as the sum of the p smallest d_{ij}'s and $\overline{b_i}$ as the sum of the p largest ones. Clearly,

$$\underline{b_i} \leq \sum_{j=1}^{n} d_{ij} x_j \leq \overline{b_i} . \quad \quad (14.10)$$

They added to the formulation n continuous variables z_i for $i = 1, \ldots, n$ which will satisfy, after the optimum is found, $z_i = x_i \left[\sum_{j=1}^{n} d_{ij} x_j \right]$. To achieve that, they formulated the following MIP:

$$\min \left\{ \sum_{i=1}^{n} z_i \right\}$$

subject to:

$$\sum_{i=1}^{n} x_i = p$$

$$z_i \geq x_i \underline{b}_i \text{ for } 1 \leq i \leq n$$

$$z_i + (1 - x_i) \overline{b}_i \geq \sum_{j=1}^{n} d_{ij} x_j \text{ for } 1 \leq i \leq n$$

$$x_i \in \{0, 1\} \tag{14.11}$$

Formulation (14.11) has n binary variables, n continuous variables, and $2n + 1$ constraints.

Which of the two formulations is "better"? The second formulation is much smaller. For example, for $n = 64$ both have 64 binary variables but formulation (14.9) has 2,016 continuous variable and 2,017 constraints while formulation (14.11) has only 64 continuous variables and 129 constraints. One would expect that Gurobi [47], for example, will solve the second formulation much more efficiently. However, confirming the "less is more" principle, the first large formulation was solved much more efficiently. Run times usually increase as p increases. Drezner et al. [38] proved optimality of all instances up to $p = 25$ with the largest one requiring about 12 days of computer time. By the first formulation (14.9), all $2 \leq p \leq 32$ were optimally solved, each requiring less than 80,000 seconds of computer time. The instances $p > 32$ were not tested because they are equivalent to $p < 32$ instances when the black and white points are switched. When applying the second formulation (14.11), they proved optimality only up to $p = 13$, which took almost a day of computer time. $p \geq 14$ instances required more than a day. The increase in run time was very significant. For example, $p = 12$ required only about 10% of the run time of $p = 13$. The $p = 13$ instance required only about 5,000 seconds by the first formulation.

Researchers normally try to derive compact formulations, assuming that available solvers will be more efficient as a result. In this example, a smaller formulation does not give better results. Similar findings occur in other scenarios, for example, weak and strong formulations of hub location problems. In other words, more sophisticated derivations do not necessarily perform better, confirming the less is more approach (that can be stated as less is better).

14.4.5 Discussion

Four optimization problems are presented in this section to demonstrate the "*less is more*" approach (LIMA). We summarize here some common characteristics of each.

1. The general LIMA methodology of Sect. 14.3 is applied on the *minimum differential dispersion problem* in a straightforward way. The state-of-the-art method (Algorithm A) contains four ingredients, given by $U_A = \{GRASP, TS, PR, VNS\}$, and hence, has LIMA number $|U_A| = 4$, which is used to measure the complexity of this method. (A higher LIMA number indicates a higher complexity when comparing two methods.) The goal is to find a new Algorithm B that is LIMA dominant with respect to A. The authors propose to use a single ingredient from U_A, the VNS component (with standard random initial solution); thus, $U_B = \{VNS\}$, and $|U_B| = 1$. The computational study reveals the surprising and counter-intuitive result that Algorithm B performs significantly better than A. We can say that B *strongly* dominates A in the LIMA sense, since all three conditions in Definition 2 are strictly satisfied.

2. The second example, the *planar p-median problem*, is very different, in that the general LIMA approach is not followed. The aim of the authors here is to study the effect that the quality of starting solutions has on the local optima obtained by a powerful local search from the literature (which we will refer here as LS). There is no attempt to find an Algorithm B that dominates the state-of-the-art algorithm in a LIMA way. Yet there are some interesting LIMA results. In one part of their study, two algorithms are proposed and compared. The first one uses the optimal solution of the corresponding discrete p-median problem as the starting solution, which is found by solving a binary linear program using a general MIP solver (call this ingredient OPT). The second one constructs a starting solution in a greedy, random way similar to GRASP, and in a miniscule fraction of the time. We can summarize as follows: $U_A = \{OPT, LS\}$, $U_B = \{GRASP, LS\}$, and both methods have LIMA number $= 2$. The authors find a surprising and counter-intuitive result that Algorithm A is

LIMA-dominated by B. This refutes earlier best knowledge that recommends using the optimal discrete solution. Researchers can also use this information to construct new state-of-the-art algorithms, for example, by developing an Algorithm C with $U_C = \{GRASP, VNS\}$.

3. The third example considers the *multiple obnoxious facility location problem*. As in example 2, the authors study the effect of different starting solutions on the final solution. The base algorithm (call it A) uses a general nonlinear solver to find local optima from random initial solutions. This method has a single ingredient, $U_A = \{LS\}$. The second algorithm (call it B) finds an optimal solution of a discrete approximation of the OP, where facility locations are restricted to the set of Voronoi points. The LIMA number of B is also equal to 1. Since better results are obtained in a fraction of the time by Algorithm B, LIMA dominates A. In a later study, it was found that the results from state-of-the-art Algorithm B could be further improved by constructing infeasible solutions in two prescribed ways as starting solutions for a sequential linear programming algorithm (SLP). The added ingredient (SLP) means that the new algorithms cannot LIMA dominate B, since these newer methods have LIMA number $= 2$. Nonetheless, the newer algorithms advance the state-of-the-art by obtaining better solutions to test instances, implying that "*more is more*" can also be useful at times, particularly when LIMA numbers are low.

4. The last example studies the *gray pattern problem* (GPP). In this case, three different mathematical formulations of the problem are considered. Another interesting feature is that optimal solutions are sought, therefore requiring an exact solution method. So we are not comparing heuristics here. The first formulation is the original quadratic binary integer program of the GPP from the literature. The authors then propose two linear models of GPP, which are both mixed binary integer (MILP). These two new models were solved using a general MIP solver. The unexpected result was that the first model, which is substantially larger in terms of number of variables and number of constraints than the second, performed much better. Solving the first model (Algorithm B) produced optimal solutions in a miniscule fraction of the time, and allowed larger instances to be solved exactly, compared to the second (Algorithm A). Thus, Algorithm B dominates A in the LIMA sense. We may conclude that the formulation of *more* compact mathematical programs can be counter-productive, again a counter-intuitive result as in most cases where the *less is more* phenomenon is observed.

14.5 Conclusions

In this chapter, we study a recently proposed philosophy for heuristic design known as the "*less is more*" approach (LIMA). To date, more than a dozen papers in the optimization literature have applied this philosophy with surprising success. They show that the popular trend to implement more and more complex algorithms can be counter-productive, and actually produce inferior results. LIMA algorithms with fewer ingredients may not only find better solutions, but tend also to be more user friendly and easier to understand.

A brief review of LIMA implementations on various optimization problems is given at the beginning of the chapter. This is followed by a description of the general steps that are needed to build LIMA-dominant algorithms. The concept of LIMA dominance involves a new parameter, the LIMA number, which measures the number of ingredients (or identifiable components or subroutines) used by an algorithm, and may be used to compare different algorithms in a simple and quantitative manner. We then review in detail four applications of LIMA that further illustrate the practical benefit of finding better solutions in less time, but also perhaps more importantly, the intangible benefit of better understanding the nature of the considered optimization problems.

The "*less is more*" approach is just getting started, and we hope that this chapter will inspire readers to advance this methodology in new and exciting ways.

A Tribute to Professor Nenad Mladenovic

We sadly announce that Professor Nenad Mladenović passed away in May 2022, before the publication of this book was completed. His sudden death from a heart attack shocked his many friends and colleagues at universities and research institutes around the globe. Nenad introduced several important ideas in Operations Research. He is known principally for his pioneering work in Variable Neighborhood Search, which was later extended to Formulation Space Search (the topic of another chapter in this book). The VNS methodology has been applied with great success on many combinatorial and global optimization problems. It is interesting that while heuristic methods have tended to become more and more complex in order to obtain a competitive edge over other heuristics, Nenad has argued for the principle of simple designs. This is the *less-is-more* principal, which is the topic of this chapter. Simple heuristic designs are not only competitive; they also lead to a better understanding of the underlying nature of the problem.

The passing of Nenad is a great loss to the Operations Research community. His work has stopped, but it will continue to inspire us for many years to come. Rest in peace, my good friend.

Jack Brimberg.

Acknowledgements The first author is partially supported by the Khalifa University of Science and Technology under Award No. RC2 DSO, and by the Committee of Science of the Ministry of Education and Science of the Republic of Kazakhstan under the grant number AP08856034. The work of the fourth author is partially supported by the Serbian Ministry of Education, Science and Technological Development through the Mathematical Institute of the Serbian Academy of Sciences and Arts.

References

1. Amirgaliyeva, Z., Mladenović, N., Todosijević, R., and Urošević, D. (2017) Solving the maximum min-sum dispersion by alternating formulations of two different problems. *European Journal of Operational Research*, 260(2):444–459.
2. Aurenhammer, F., Klein, R., and Lee, D.-T. (2013). *Voronoi Diagrams and Delaunay Triangulations*. World Scientific, New Jersey.
3. Austin, C. M. (1974). The evaluation of urban public facility location: An alternative to benefit-cost analysis. *Geographical Analysis*, 6:135–145.
4. Austin, C. M., Smith, T. E., and Wolpert, J. (1970). The implementation of controversial facility-complex programs. *Geographical Analysis*, 2:315–329.
5. Bannard, O. M. and Cyster, J. G. (2012). When less signaling is more. *Science*, 336:1120–1121.
6. Bassiri-Gharb, N. (2020). Less can be more in functional materials. *Science*, 369:252–253.
7. Bornholdt, S. (2005). Less is more in modeling large genetic networks. *Science*, 310:449–451.
8. Brimberg, J. and Drezner, Z. (2013). A new heuristic for solving the p-median problem in the plane. *Computers & Operations Research*, 40:427–437.
9. Brimberg, J. and Drezner, Z. (2021). Improved starting solutions for the planar p-median problem. *Yugoslav Journal of Operations Research*, 31:45–64.
10. Brimberg, J., Drezner, Z., Mladenović, N., and Salhi, S. (2014). A new local search for continuous location problems. *European Journal of Operational Research*, 232:256–265.
11. Brimberg, J., Hansen, P., Mladenović, N., and Taillard, E. (2000). Improvements and comparison of heuristics for solving the uncapacitated multisource Weber problem. *Operations Research*, 48:444–460.

12. Brimberg, J., Hansen, P., Mladonovic, N., and Salhi, S. (2008). A survey of solution methods for the continuous location allocation problem. *International Journal of Operations Research*, 5:1–12.

13. Brimberg, J. and Hodgson, M. J. (2011). Heuristics for location models. In Eiselt, H. A. and Marianov, V., editors, *Foundations of Location Analysis: International Series in Operations Research & Management Science, Vol. 155*, pages 335–355. Springer, New York, NY.

14. Brimberg, J., Janićijević, S., Mladenović, N., and Urošević, D. (2017). Solving the clique partitioning problem as a maximally diverse grouping problem. *Optimization Letters*, 11(6):1123–1135

15. Brimberg, J., Mladenović, N., Todosijević, R., and Urošević, D. (2017). Less is more: solving the max-mean diversity problem with variable neighborhood search. *Information Sciences*, 382:179–200.

16. Brimberg, J., Mladenović, N., and Urošević, D. (2016). Solving the maximally diverse grouping problem by skewed general variable neighborhood search. *Information Sciences*, 295:650–675.

17. Brimberg, J., Mladenović, N., Todosijević, R., and Urošević, D. (2019). Solving the capacitated clustering problem with variable neighborhood search. *Annals of Operations Research*, 272 (1-2):289–321.

18. Burkard, R. E., Karisch, S. E., and Rendl, F. (1997). Qaplib–a quadratic assignment problem library. *Journal of Global optimization*, 10:391–403. https://www.opt.math.tugraz.at/qaplib/.

19. Chong, L.D. (2011). Exosomes Deliver. *Science*, 332:515.

20. Church, R. L. (2019). Understanding the Weber location paradigm. In Eiselt, H. A. and Marianov, V., editors, *Contributions to Location Analysis - In Honor of Zvi Drezner's 75th Birthday*, pages 69–88. Springer Nature, Switzerland.

21. Church, R. L., and Drezner, Z. (2022). Extensions to the weber problem. *Computers and Operations Research*, 138:105468.

22. Church, R. L. and Garfinkel, R. S. (1978). Locating an obnoxious facility on a network. *Transportation Science*, 12:107–118.

23. Cooper, L. (1963). Location-allocation problems. *Operations Research*, 11:331–343.

24. Cooper, L. (1964). Heuristic methods for location-allocation problems. *SIAM Review*, 6:37–53.

25. Costa, L. R., Aloise, D., and Mladenović, N. (2017). Less is more: basic variable neighborhood search heuristic for balanced minimum sum-of-squares clustering. *Information Sciences*, 415:247–253.

26. CPLEX, IBM ILOG (2019). 12.10: User's Manual for CPLEX. *International Business Machines Corporation, Incline Village, NV*.

27. Daskin, M. S. (1995). *Network and Discrete Location: Models, Algorithms, and Applications*. John Wiley & Sons, New York.

28. Daskin, M. S. and Maass, K. L. (2015). The p-median problem. In Laporte, G., Nickel, S., and da Gama, F. S., editors, *Location science*, pages 21–45. Springer.

29. Drezner, T., Drezner, Z., and Kalczynski, P. (2020). Multiple obnoxious facilities location: A cooperative model. *IISE Transactions*, 52:1403–1412.
30. Drezner, Z. (2006). Finding a cluster of points and the grey pattern quadratic assignment problem. *OR Spectrum*, 28:417–436.
31. Drezner, Z. (2015). The quadratic assignment problem. In Laporte, G., Nickel, S., and da Gama, F. S., editors, *Location Science*, pages 345–363. Springer, Chum, Heidelberg.
32. Drezner, Z., Brimberg, J., Salhi, S., and Mladenović, N. (2016). New local searches for solving the multi-source Weber problem. *Annals of Operations Research*, 246:181–203.
33. Drezner, Z., Hahn, P. M., and Taillard, É. D. (2005). Recent advances for the quadratic assignment problem with special emphasis on instances that are difficult for meta-heuristic methods. *Annals of Operations Research*, 139:65–94.
34. Drezner, Z. and Kalczynski, P. (2020). Solving non-convex non-linear programs with reverse convex constraints by sequential linear programming. *International Transactions in Operational Research*, 27:1320–1342.
35. Drezner, Z., Kalczynski, P., Misevicius, A., and G. Palubeckis. (2022). Finding optimal solutions to Several gray pattern instances. *Optimization Letters*, 16:713–722.
36. Drezner, Z., Kalczynski, P., and Salhi, S. (2019). The multiple obnoxious facilities location problem on the plane: A Voronoi based heuristic. *OMEGA: The International Journal of Management Science*, 87:105–116.
37. Drezner, Z., Klamroth, K., Schöbel, A., and Wesolowsky, G. O. (2002). The Weber problem. In Drezner, Z. and Hamacher, H. W., editors, *Facility Location: Applications and Theory*, pages 1–36. Springer, Berlin.
38. Drezner, Z., Misevičius, A., and Palubeckis, G. (2015). Exact algorithms for the solution of the grey pattern quadratic assignment problem. *Mathematical Methods of Operations Research*, 82:85–105.
39. Drezner, Z. and Salhi, S. (2017). Incorporating neighborhood reduction for the solution of the planar *p*-median problem. *Annals of Operations Research*, 258:639–654.
40. Duarte, A., Laguna, M., Martí, R., and Sánchez-Oro, J. (2014). Optimization procedures for the bipartite unconstrained 0-1 quadratic programming problem. *Computers & operations research*, 51:123–129.
41. Duarte, A., Sánchez-Oro, J., Resende, M. G., Glover, F., and Martí, R. (2015). Greedy randomized adaptive search procedure with exterior path relinking for differential dispersion minimization. *Information Sciences*, 296:46–60.
42. Galinier, P., Boujbel, Z., and Fernandes, M. C. (2011). An efficient memetic algorithm for the graph partitioning problem. *Annals of Operations Research*, 191:1–22.
43. Gill, P. E., Murray, W., and Saunders, M. A. (2005). SNOPT: An SQP algorithm for large-scale constrained optimization. *SIAM Review*, 47:99–131.
44. Glover, F., and Laguna, M. (1998). *Tabu Search*. Kluwer Academic Publishers, Boston/Dordrecht/London.

45. Glover, F., Ye, T., Punnen, A. P., and Kochenberger, G. (2015). Integrating tabu search and vlsn search to develop enhanced algorithms: A case study using bipartite boolean quadratic programs. *European Journal of Operational Research*, 241:697–707.

46. Gonçalves Silva, K., Aloise, D., Xavier-De-Souza, S., Mladenović, N. (2018). Less is more: simplified Nelder-Mead method for large unconstrained optimization. *Yugoslav Journal of Operations Research*, 28:153–169.

47. Gurobi Optimization Incorporated (2018). Gurobi optimizer reference manual. URL http://www. gurobi. com.

48. Hahn, P. M., Zhu, Y.-R., Guignard, M., Hightower, W. L., and Saltzman, M. J. (2012). A level-3 reformulation-linearization technique-based bound for the quadratic assignment problem. *INFORMS Journal on Computing*, 24:202–209.

49. Hansen, P. and Mladenović, N. (1997). Variable neighborhood search. *Computers and operations research*, 24(11):1097–1101.

50. Hansen, P., Mladenović, N., and Taillard, É. (1998). Heuristic solution of the multisource Weber problem as a p-median problem. *Operations Research Letters*, 22:55–62.

51. Hosseini, S. and Esfahani, A. M. (2009). Obnoxious facility location. In *Facility Location*, pages 315–345. Springer.

52. Kaiser, J. (2017). When less is more. *Science*, 355:1144–1146.

53. Kalczynski, P., Brimberg, J., and Z, Drezner. (2022). Less is more: Discrete starting solutions in the planar p-median problem. *TOP*, 30:34–59.

54. Kalczynski, P. and Drezner, Z. (2019). Locating multiple facilities using the max-sum objective. *Computers and Industrial Engineering*, 129:136–143.

55. Kalczynski, P., and Z, Drezner. (2022). Extremely non-convex optimization problems: The case of the multiple obnoxious facilities location. *Optimization Letters*, 16:1153–1166.

56. Kalczynski, P. and Drezner, Z. (2021b). The obnoxious facilities planar p-median problem. *OR Spectrum*, 43:577–593.

57. Kalczynski P., Suzuki, A., and Z. Drezner. (2022). Multiple obnoxious facilities with weighted demand points. *Journal of the Operational Research Society*, 73:598–607.

58. Kang, H. R. (1999). *Digital color halftoning*. SPIE press.

59. Karapetyan, D., Punnen, A. P., and Parkes, A. J. (2017). Markov chain methods for the bipartite boolean quadratic programming problem. *European Journal of Operational Research*, 260:494–506.

60. Kuenne, R. E. and Soland, R. M. (1972). Exact and approximate solutions to the multisource Weber problem. *Mathematical Programming*, 3:193–209.

61. Kuo, C.-C., Glover, F., and Dhir, K. S. (1993). Analyzing and modeling the maximum diversity problem by zero-one programming. *Decision Sciences*, 24:1171–1185.

62. van Laarhoven, P. J. M., Aarts, E. H. L. (1987). Simulated annealing. In: *Simulated Annealing: Theory and Applications. Mathematics and Its Applications*, vol 37, pages 7–15, Springer, Dordrecht.

63. Lau, D. L. and Arce, G. R. (2018). *Modern digital halftoning*. CRC Press.
64. Loiola, E. M., de Abreu, N. M. M., Boaventura-Netto, P. O., Hahn, P., and Querido, T. (2007). A survey for the quadratic assignment problem. *European Journal of Operational Research*, 176:657–690.
65. Love, R. F., Morris, J. G., and Wesolowsky, G. O. (1988). *Facilities Location: Models & Methods*. North Holland, New York, NY.
66. Lu, S., Pei, J., Liu, X., Qian, X., Mladenovic, N., and Pardalos, P. M. (2020). Less is more: variable neighborhood search for integrated production and assembly in smart manufacturing. *Journal of Scheduling*, 23:649–664.
67. McCartney, M. (2011). Calendar effects. *Science*, 334:1324–1324.
68. Megiddo, N. and Supowit, K. (1984). On the complexity of some common geometric location problems. *SIAM Journal on Computing*, 18:182–196.
69. Melachrinoudis, E. (2011). The location of undesirable facilities. In *Foundations of location analysis*, pages 207–239. Springer, New York.
70. Mikić, M., Todosijević, R., Urošević, D. (2019). Less is more: General variable neighborhood search for the capacitated modular hub location problem. *Computers and Operations Research*, 110:101–115.
71. Misevicius, A., Palubeckis, G., and Drezner, Z. (2021). Hierarchicity-based (self-similar) hybrid genetic algorithm for the grey pattern quadratic assignment problem. *Memetic Computing*, 13:69–90. https://doi.org/10.1007/s12293-020-00321-6.
72. Mladenovi?, N., Alkandari, A., Pei, J., Todosijevi?, R., and Pardalos, P. M. (2020). Less is more approach: basic variable neighborhood search for the obnoxious p-median problem. *International Transactions in Operational Research*, 27:480–493.
73. Mladenović, N., Todosijević, R., and Urošević, D. (2013). An efficient general variable neighborhood search for large travelling salesman problem with time windows. *Yugoslav Journal of Operations Research*, 23(1):19–30.
74. Mladenović, N., Todosijević, R., and Urošević, D. (2016). Less is more: basic variable neighborhood search for minimum differential dispersion problem. *Information Sciences*, 326:160–171.
75. Mladenović, N., Urošević, D., aand Pérez-Brito, D. (2016). Variable neighborhood search for minimum arrangement problem. *Yugoslav Journal of Operations Research*, 26(1):3–16.
76. Mumphrey, A. J. and Wolpert, J. (1973). Equity considerations and concessions in the siting of public facilities. *Economic Geography*, 49:109–121.
77. Nelder, J. A. and Mead, R. (1965). A simplex method for function minimization. *Computer Journal*, 7:308–313.
78. Okabe, A., Boots, B., Sugihara, K., and Chiu, S. N. (2000). *Spatial Tessellations: Concepts and Applications of Voronoi Diagrams*. Wiley Series in Probability and Statistics. John Wiley, Hoboken, NJ.
79. Pei, J., Dražić, Z., Dražić, M., Mladenović, N., and Pardalos, P. M. (2019). Continuous variable neighborhood search (c-vns) for solving systems of nonlinear equations. *INFORMS Journal on Computing*, 31:235–250.

80. Pei, J., Mladenović, N., Urošević, D., Brimberg, J., and Liu, X. (2020). Solving the traveling repairman problem with profits: A novel variable neighborhood search approach. *Information Sciences*, 507:108–123.

81. Plastria, F. and Carrizosa, E. (1999). Undesirable facility location in the Euclidean plane with minimal covering objectives. *European Journal of Operational Research*, 119:158–180.

82. Prokopyev, O., Kong, N., and Martinez-Torres, D. (2009). The equitable dispersion problem. *European Journal of Operational Research*, 197:59–67.

83. Ratli, M., Urošević, D., El Cadi, A.A., Brimberg, J., Mladenović, N., and Todosijević, R. (2020). An efficient heuristic for a hub location routing problem. *Optimization Letters*, DOI: https://doi.org/10.1007/s11590-020-016 75-z,

84. Reinelt, G. (1991). TSLIB a traveling salesman library. *ORSA Journal on Computing*, 3:376–384.

85. ReVelle, C. S. and Swain, R. W. (1970). Central facilities location. *Geographical analysis*, 2:30–42.

86. Shamos, M. and Hoey, D. (1975). Closest-point problems. *Proceedings 16th Annual Symposium on the Foundations of Computer Science, Berkeley, CA*, pages 151–162.

87. Shi, L. Z. (2020). Less is more for adoptive immunotherapy? *Science Translational Medicine*, 12.

88. Sugihara, K. and Iri, M. (1992). Construction of the Voronoi diagram for "one million" generators in single-precision arithmetic. *Proceedings of the IEEE*, 80:1471–1484.

89. Suzuki, A. and Okabe, A. (1995). Using Voronoi diagrams. In Drezner, Z., editor, *Facility Location: A Survey of Applications and Methods*, pages 103–118. Springer, New York.

90. Taillard, É. D. (1995). Comparison of iterative searches for the quadratic assignment problem. *Location Science*, 3:87–105.

91. Todosijević, R., Urošević, D., Mladenović, N., Hanafi, S. (2017). A general variable neighborhood search for solving the uncapacitated r-allocation p-hub median problem. *Optimization Letters*, 11(6):1109-1121.

92. Ulichney, R. (1987). *Digital halftoning*. MIT press.

93. Urošević, D., Alghoul, Y. I. Y., Amirgaliyeva, Z., and Mladenović, N. (2019). Less is more: Tabu search for bipartite quadratic programming problem. In *International Conference on Mathematical Optimization Theory and Operations Research*, pages 390–401.

94. Voronoï, G. (1908). Nouvelles applications des paramètres continus à la théorie des formes quadratiques. deuxième mémoire. recherches sur les parallélloèdres primitifs. *Journal für die reine und angewandte Mathematik*, 134:198–287.

95. Weber, A. (1909). *Über den Standort der Industrien, 1. Teil: Reine Theorie des Standortes. English Translation: on the Location of Industries*. University of Chicago Press, Chicago, IL. Translation published in 1929.

96. Wesolowsky, G. O. (1993). The Weber problem: History and perspectives. *Location Science*, 1:5–23.
97. Whitley, D. (1994). A genetic algorithm tutorial. *Statistics and Computing*, 4:65–85.
98. Wolfram, S. (2020). *Mathematica, Version 12.2*. Champaign, IL. https://www.wolfram.com/mathematica.

15

The New Era of Hybridisation and Learning in Heuristic Search Design

Saïd Salhi and Jonathan Thompson

15.1 Hybridisation Search

The metaheuristics presented in the earlier chapter [51] though are useful and some proved to be superior to others when tested on certain classes of instances, these could be made even more powerful if they are somehow complementing each other. This can be done between the methods or within the method themselves. In this section we explore these various aspects of hybridisation. The simplest way of hybridisation is obviously to put one heuristic after another which is usually known as post-optimisation. A more exciting approach is to extend such integration to cater to intermediate stages of the search by hybridising rules whenever needed within the search. In this section three main approaches are described, namely, the hybridisation of heuristics with heuristics, the hybridisation of heuristics within exact methods, and finally the hybridisation of exact methods within heuristics.

S. Salhi (✉)
Kent Business School, University of Kent, Canterbury, UK
e-mail: s.salhi@kent.ac.uk

J. Thompson
School of Mathematics, Cardiff University, Cardiff, UK
e-mail: thompsonjm1@cardiff.ac.uk

© The Author(s), under exclusive license to Springer Nature Switzerland AG 2022
S. Salhi and J. Boylan (eds.), *The Palgrave Handbook of Operations Research*,
https://doi.org/10.1007/978-3-030-96935-6_15

15.1.1 Hybridisation of Heuristics with Heuristics

The most common integration of heuristics is usually a two-phase method where one heuristic calls the other at the end making the latter behave as a simple post-optimiser. This approach is now extended to incorporate the integration within each of the heuristic or metaheuristic. This view seems to attract more attention in recent years. The most used ones include hyper-heuristics and memetic algorithms.

15.1.1.1 Hyper-Heuristics

These are originally designed to construct a good quality feasible solution using several instead of one constructive/greedy heuristic only. The reasoning behind this is that each heuristic has strengths and weaknesses, and it is thought to be appropriate if those aspects are taken into account during the search. Though this notion has been hinted at in the literature from time to time since the 1960s [43], these methods, known as hyper-heuristics, were revisited and intensively studied by [10]. There are two ways of implementing this kind of approach which we refer to as constructive and improvement hyper-heuristics.

Constructive Hyper-Heuristics

The idea is to use, at each iteration during the construction of the solution, a chosen heuristic from a list of low level heuristics either randomly or intelligently. The design of such a high level heuristic that controls the evolution of the incomplete solution and hence decides which low level heuristic is more appropriate at each iteration is known as a hyper-heuristic. This can be achieved by (i) *a brute force approach* where all the low level heuristics at each step of the construction of the solution are first used, and the one that produces the best solution is chosen by selecting the next attribute from that best configuration to add to the incomplete solution configuration. The process is repeated until all attributes are included to make up a complete feasible solution. This mechanism guarantees that the obtained solution is either better or the same as the solution found by the best individual low level heuristic. In (ii), the idea is to apply *a random scheme* where the selection is to choose at each step of the construction of the solution configuration, one of these low level heuristics randomly and with equal probability. This is obviously much quicker than (i) but may produce a solution which is inferior to the one that could be generated by the best low level heuristic. Finally in (iii), *a learning-based approach* made up of two stages can be adopted. In stage one (i.e., the training stage), each low level heuristic is applied over the set of instances (or just over a training subset) where useful information are recorded. In stage two, this information is then used to choose the low level heuristic at each step of the construction of the new solution as used in the above two schemes. The only weakness is that the approach needs to be run more than once or at least on a smaller subset of instances which leads to biases towards the selected subset. Another slightly more finely tuned version is based on the brute force approach to record the information in stage one which can be performed based on the first steps that are used to construct the incomplete solutions only. This information is then passed to stage two where in subsequent steps the selection of the low level heuristics is performed pseudo-randomly. This approach is quicker than the brute force method but could produce relatively less competitive results as it may miss some good opportunities when selecting the next attribute. Note that both the first and the third methods could be made more focussed if a smaller subset of promising low level heuristics that produce good but diverse solutions are chosen a priori so as to avoid unnecessary computations used by those heuristics that are proved to behave poorly in most cases.

Improvement Hyper-Heuristics

Here, an initial solution is already found and the use of hyper-heuristic is adopted to act as a post-optimiser or a local search. However, instead of using one particular metaheuristic, say TS or SA, to improve the solution, the hyper-heuristic philosophy is adopted. Note that it is common and simpler to use local searches as low level heuristics in these type of hyper-heuristics though the use of metaheuristics is also attempted by a few authors. The question is how to spread the total computing time between each run of a given metaheuristic and how long the short periods in the training and the launching stages should be. For instance, Garcia-Villoria et al. [19] obtained superior results with this strategy when solving a class of scheduling problems. This approach is displayed in Fig. 15.1.

Note that hyper-heuristics could also be considered as a form of an expert system that guides iteratively the selection of the heuristics within the search in order to solve a given optimisation problem, irrespective of whether these heuristics are low or high level. The strategy for selecting the low level heuristic at a given iteration and the choice of the pool of these low level heuristics to be used can be challenging. Burke et al. [10] give an interesting

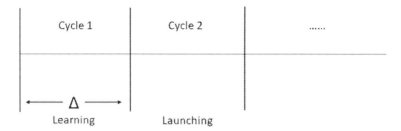

Fig. 15.1 A representation of the improvement hyper-heuristics (adapted from [46])

classification of hyper-heuristics and provide further references on this issue, with a focus on timetabling problems.

15.1.1.2 Memetic Algorithm and Its Variants

These are based on a population of solutions like a GA except that each solution (chromosome) within the same generation is improved via intensification by a refinement/improvement procedure like a local search. Memetic algorithms (MA) can therefore be considered more aggressive than their classical GAs. Obviously this combination can be seen as a hybridisation of a GA and local search. Such a heuristic was originally put forward by [31] and an overview of this approach can be found in [31] and [32] though other authors have also implemented a similar strategy indirectly, see for instance [56] for the case of multi-depot routing. Here, the multi-level heuristic of [48] was integrated with a GA to improve the obtained chromosomes at each generation. The questions may include how long the improvement procedure is allowed to run? Is the local search necessary at each generation or just for specific chromosomes? And how to avoid the risk of early stagnation due to such intensifications? To control diversity and to answer the last question, one attempt was performed by [53] who introduced schemes to manage the population (PM) which they refer to as MA/PM. An efficient implementation of MA/PM for solving an integrated distribution/production system is also proposed by [6]. The above authors put emphasis on how to better manage the population so as to maintain diversity and to guide the search more efficiently. The idea is to use a smaller population size than in a typical GA (say 20 or 30), and also to control diversity, not through mutation as in a GA, but via a measure of diversity which is embedded into the generation of the chromosomes, such as dissimilarity or distance between solutions. In simple terms, MA/PM can be considered as a guided MA, though it has more parameters than a GA and the classical MA. One may argue that this avenue may suffer from its additional parameters and computational burden, but, in our view, this has scope for improvement as this can be overcome and hence could lead to a much more promising outcome.

15.1.1.3   A Brief Summary of Other Metaheuristic Hybridisations

The above population-based hybridisation is also valid for any other population-based heuristics described in the earlier chapter as these are successful at finding promising regions of the search space but not powerful enough to localise the exact local optima. In this case, some form of local search or those one point solution (or trajectory) methods as discussed in the earlier chapter are usually better suited for the job. For instance, a local search or small runs of those metaheuristics described in the earlier chapter could be combined with ACO after global updating is performed, with the bee algorithm ABC once some sites are dropped or reinforced, with PSO when global velocity update is activated, with HS once the new set of harmonies are selected, etc. For more information on these population-based metaheuristics, see [46] and the earlier chapter in this volume by [51]. The interested reader could consider any of the above by thoroughly investigating the time to activate the local search, how intensive this is implemented and which solutions are better suited for such improvement. The choice of the subset of solutions can be based on the top quality solutions as well as those with high level of diversity. Other integrations of metaheuristics have also been attempted. For instance, for the vehicle routing problem, interesting results were obtained by [63] who integrate VNS with SA, Akpinar [3] who consider the hybridisation of LNS with ACO, and [54] who hybridise VNS with LNS. For more information on hybridisation of metaheuristics the reader will find the review in [39] and the relevant chapters in [46] and the references therein informative and useful.

15.1.2   Integrating Heuristics within Exact Methods

Exact methods can be slow and inappropriate for some applications but could be made useful if combined with heuristic search. In this section we shall present some schemes that are shown to be promising and worth considering.

Injection of Upper Bounds The simplest way is to introduce the value of a feasible solution from a heuristic as an upper bound say within Branch and Bound (B& B). Note that this extra information will fathom any unnecessary branches from being explored but may incur an extra computational effort due to this additional constraint.

Tightening of Lower and Upper Bounds There are some approaches that aim to tighten both the upper and the lower bounds simultaneously. These include

Lagrangean Relaxation Heuristics (LRH) This approach takes into account the advantages of both exact and heuristic methods for generating proven lower bounds and corresponding upper bounds, respectively. LRH was first proposed by [23] and [24] and proved to be successful at solving many classes of optimization problems. The main concept of LRH is to identify the set of constraints of a general integer program that results in an increase of the computational complexity of the problem making it intractable. These constraints are then introduced into the objective function in a Lagrangean fashion by attaching to them unit penalties, that will be reduced as the search progresses with the aim of reducing the amount of feasibility violation. This transformation should be constructed to render the new relaxed problem easier to solve optimally (usually by inspection or a basic polynomial optimal type algorithm) and hence produce lower bounds for the original problem. Note that the relaxed problem could, after mathematical manipulations, turn into a subset of separable subproblems, instead of a single one only. These subproblems are solved individually and their respective optimal objective function values and their corresponding decision variables values are then used to make up the overall solution for the relaxed problem. A feasible solution of the original problem (an upper bound in the case of a minimization problem) is then derived using a usually quick heuristic method. The penalties are adjusted based on the violation and the process is repeated until one of the stopping criteria is met. This could include, for instance, the gap between the best lower and upper bound is small enough, a negligible change in the solution configuration is detected, the step size is nearly zero, and the maximum computing time is reached, among others. Theoretically after several iterations this approach should lead to a near or optimal solution. It is worth noting that it is effective to add a simple local search as a mini step that aims to improve the upper bound before the updating is performed. This yields a tighter upper bound which in turn will speed up the process when adjusting the penalties, etc. A schematic graph of LRH is given in Fig. 15.2. This mechanism was successfully applied for a class of discrete location problems by [2] and [33].

Note that not all problems fit nicely into this category as both the lower bound problem (LB) and its corresponding feasible problem may not be always easy to solve. It is also worth mentioning that there is no guarantee

Feasible Solution
(Upper Bounds)

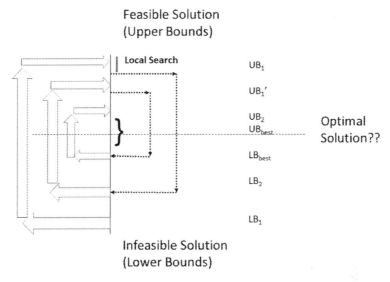

Infeasible Solution
(Lower Bounds)

Fig. 15.2 Principle of Lagrangean relaxation heuristics (adapted from [46])

that the new corresponding upper bound found at a given iteration of LRH is always an improving feasible solution. This is due to the heuristic procedure used to transform the lower bound into a feasible solution. In this case, extra care is required to guide the search by referring to the best upper bound so far when updating the lagrangean multipliers, etc. LRH can also be integrated within heuristics or metaheuristics to act at optimally solving subproblems within a larger problem that are implemented in a recursive way. For instance, in vehicle routing problems, Bouzid et al. [7] used LRH to obtain an optimal split of the giant tour into optimal routes and the VNS is applied as a diversification tool to build a new giant tour. This hybridisation showed to be more efficient than using the classical ILP to split the giant tour.

Reduction/relaxation-based schemes The idea is based on a dynamic variable fixation mechanism obtained by solving a series of relaxed problems with an efficient way of recording useful information using memory and frequency. For instance, a variable that is never used is more likely to not belong to the optimal solution and a variable which has been used most often could be fixed permanently. This is an iterative process that continues until no change in the solution is found. One approach, which seems to have gained more pace recently, is to solve a series of reduced problems exactly by fixing some of the variables to their integer values as found by the LP relaxation. The problem is then augmented by an additional constraint (or a small number of constraints) every time leading to a new lower bound and hence to a new fixation of the variables for the new reduced problem. This process is then repeated until the gap between lower and upper bound is either zero or negligible. This concept is adopted by [21] and [61] for solving the multi-dimensional knapsack problem. An interesting review by [60] discusses some of these aspects with a focus on knapsack problems.

A similar view that is based on solving a succession of subproblems optimally while adding at each iteration a few attributes (say r) is successively presented by [12] and recently enhanced by [11] for solving a class of continuous p-centre problems. This approach though sensitive to the values of r has the advantage that the optimal solution if it exists can be identified whenever the optimal solution of the last reduced problem happens to be feasible for the original one. One approach that also incorporates solutions and useful information from heuristics to tighten both the upper and lower bounds in the corresponding ILP formulation is presented by [49] for the vertex p-centre problem.

Kernel Search This is an iterative approach introduced by [4] for solving MILP problems. The idea is to define a succession of smaller related MILP problems where promising values, usually those with positive values, are used to make up a reduced and smaller problem with the idea that at each iteration, additional variables are added to the subproblem whereas some may be removed. At the initial phase, the LP is usually solved and all positive variables are used to make up the subset of promising variables which is referred to as the kernel from which Kernel Search (KS) was named. The rest of the variables are put into groups known as buckets. At each iteration one bucket is added to make up a larger problem. This approach is adapted to allow for the removal of some variables from the kernel and the sequence in which the buckets are added. For instance, the variables to be removed from the kernel can be those which happen not to be part of the optimal solutions in the last few iterations. This removal strategy can be extended to identify a performance measure for the variables based on frequency of occurrence, their shadow prices if not selected, etc. This process continues until the last bucket is utilised. Guastaroba and Speranza [20] explore these issues for the case of a large capacitated facility location problem with competitive results. Besides, in this iterative approach, at each iteration the new objective function value, if it is found to be an improved and feasible solution, is considered as the new upper bound which is then added to tighten the formulation. The choice of the bucket to add and the selection of the variables to remove from the kernel constitute a challenging part of this approach that could be critical to the success of KS.

Regular seeking of new upper bounds Another option which is more challenging is to integrate heuristics and exact methods more intensively by

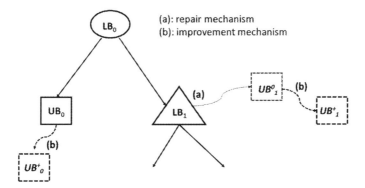

Fig. 15.3   Integrating heuristics within B&B (adapted from [46])

calling a heuristic which transforms (a) an infeasible solution (lower bound) into a feasible one at certain nodes of the B&B tree and (b) improve the best upper bound or even other promising but less attractive already found upper bounds. The question is to determine which nodes are worthwhile exploring and also which type of heuristics are better suited for (a) or (b). A basic representation of (a) and (b) is shown in Fig. 15.3.

In other words, instead of applying the optimal method (B&B, Branch & Cut) till the end, we can at intermediate points of the search that need to be identified, inject extra information. For instance, in B&B, one way would be to take a solution at a given node and see whether that solution (upper or lower bound) can be either improved or transformed from lower to upper bound. For example, if the node is a feasible node as mentioned in (b) with a value UB_0 (see Fig. 15.3), a metaheuristic or just a simple heuristic that uses that feasible solution as a starting point may improve it (say UB_0^+) and hence provide a tighter upper bound for quick fathoming. This mechanism can be either applied each time a new upper bound within B&B is obtained even if it is not better than the best, or if the new upper bound happens to be slightly worse than the best incumbent upper bound but passes a certain threshold, as commonly used in TA, see earlier chapter. The new improved upper bound, if it exists, may be proved to be even optimal if it happens to match the best lower bound so far or satisfies certain optimality rules. Similarly in (a), if an infeasible solution is at a node (lower bound, LB_1), before branching a repair mechanism that transforms such an infeasible solution (i.e., lower bound) into a feasible one (say UB_1^0) could be used. If this solution happens to be better than the best upper bound so far, this will become the incumbent upper bound leading to further fathoming in the B&B tree. This temporary node with UB_1^0 can then be improved via (b) again to obtain an even tighter bound, say UB_1^+. One obvious way would be to choose those attributes with higher values close to 1 (in case of binary optimisation) while checking feasibility.

Local branching There are however interesting studies that aim to find feasible solutions, the first of which is the idea of local branching (LoBr) developed by [16]. For simplicity consider a binary optimisation problem where a lower bound is found at a given node (including the source node) with $\bar{X}_i = \lceil X_i^* \rceil$ for all $i \in E_1$ where the set $E_1 \subset E$ is the required subset of binary variables and $\bar{X}_i = \lceil X_i^* \rceil$ for all $i \in E - E_1$ (those not required to be binary or integer say). The idea is to solve the original problem with the addition of the following linear constraint given a suitable value of k which aims to restrict the distance between X and $\bar{X}$ to be within k only using $\Delta(X, \bar{X}) = \sum_{i \in E_1 : X_i = 0} X_i + \sum_{i \in E_1 : X_i = 1} X_i \leq k$. This is updated and the process is repeated until a feasible solution is found. In other words, if the solution is not improved after a certain time limit at a node, k is halved, however if no solution was found in that time limit or the solver proved infeasibility the new linear constraint is relaxed by setting $k = k + k/2$. An enhanced method, which avoids some of these parameters, is known as feasibility pump (FP). This is presented by Fischetti et al. [17] whose idea is to solve the auxiliary subproblem by substituting the original objective function with $Min \Delta(X, \bar{X}) = \sum_{i \in E_1 : X_i = 0} X_i + \sum_{i \in E_1 : X_i = 1} X_i$ instead. This is repeated until a feasible solution is obtained. Extra refinements to reduce the computing time and to get a good quality solution are also examined. As both (LoBr) and (FP) run under a certain time limit, the obtained solution if it exists is obviously a feasible MIP solution. Very competitive results are produced for a variety of difficult combinatorial problems, see [17] for more details. An interesting adaptation of (LoBr) by [22] is to use a general VNS structure within (LoBr). Here, the initial step at the root node is found as in (LoBr) as this is the initial solution found by a commercial solver such as CPLEX. In the shaking step of the VNS, the values of the parameter follow the VNS structure instead where the neighbourhood is defined by: $N_k(\bar{X}) = \{X | \Delta(X, \bar{X}) \leq k\}; k = K_{min}, \ldots, K_{max}$.

In the local search, a VND is applied where a solver is also used to find the local minimum based on $N_l(\bar{X}); l = 1, \ldots, l_{max}$ defined as the new linear constraint. Very competitive results are discovered when compared against the classical (LoBr) results. Other examples that use such a similar hybridisation include the work by [34] who combined B&B with SA to solve the binary and the mixed ILPs. A depth first of B&B is incorporated to generate an initial feasible solution and SA is used to determine feasible ones whenever infeasibility is encountered. This is a hybrid approach that is based on sharing information between concurrent runs of B&B and SA. Wilbaut et al. [61]

combined heuristic solutions and ILP formulations to design an adaptive search for solving the 0–1 knapsack problem. Lazic et al. [28] also embedded VNS with ILP formulation to tackle 0–1 mixed integer programs with very good results.

15.1.3   Integration of ILP within Heuristics/Metaheuristics

In some cases the original problem reduces to manageable and relatively easier subproblems to be solved optimally when the promising attributes are identified only or when the problem is split into separable subproblems that are also easy to solve optimally. We present one approach for the former (heuristic concentration) and a brief on the latter (problem decomposition).

15.1.3.1   Heuristic Concentration (HC)

This is a two-stage process where in stage 1, a large number of solutions are generated randomly using multi-start, for instance, or through a heuristic such as GRASP. The selected attributes of those solutions are then put together to make up the concentration set which is obviously a relatively much smaller subset. The aim of the selected subset is to represent the original problem with those promising attributes only without considering the large number of irrelevant ones. The reasoning behind this idea is that the optimal or the final best solution is likely to consist of those attributes. Note that HC shares some similarities with the metaheuristic Cross Entropy (CE) described in earlier chapter in [51] in terms of identifying the subset of promising attributes. In the second stage, an exact method or an intensive-based metaheuristic or even a powerful local search is then applied on this small subset. This idea is originally developed by [41] with some variants being later proposed by [42] for solving the p-median problem. For instance, in stage 1 only those attributes (potential sites) that belong to all the solutions are considered as fixed to make up the potential sites and hence will be part of the optimal solution and in stage 2 a reduced problem, made up of these potential selected sites, is then solved either optimally or heuristically with a powerful metaheuristic. Another stricter way is to choose the concentration set from those attributes that happen to exist in $k(k > 1)$ times in the solutions configurations. The reasoning behind this is that some attributes with very low frequency of occurrence (i.e., $k = 1$) could have been chosen by luck and hence may distort the basic principle of this method. The value of k can affect the final solution and hence linking k to the number of solutions generated could be one way forward.

15.1.3.2   Problem Decomposition

The idea here is to decompose the original problem into separable problems which are solved optimally. As the splitting is not optimal a recursive approach is usually adopted. As an example solving the capacitated or the single source location problem, once the facilities are sited the problem reduces to either a transportation problem (TP) or a generalised assignment problem (GAP). In the former a customer may not need to be served from one facility only whereas in the former a customer is entirely served by one facility only. Both the TP and the GAP can be solved using standard commercial optimisation solvers such as CPLEX, LINDO, Xpress-MP, and GuRobi just to cite a few. A metaheuristic is then used to relocate some of the facilities. As the number of calls to the TP (or the GAP) can be too excessive, an approximation technique or heuristic could be used instead and only once in a while the allocation is performed optimally. The balance between the use of approximation and optimality depends on the complexity of the ILP problem and the problem size. As an example the TP is relatively much easier to solve than the GAP so the number of calls to optimally solve the TP could be used more often than its counterpart the GAP if found necessary. It could also be emphasised that the use of a two-phase method, such as the 'locate-allocate' approach commonly used in multi-source Weber problem (or its discrete counter part the p-median problem) is also another example. Here, in phase one p clusters are obtained and in phase two the optimal p-median problem is optimally solved within each cluster. The new locations are then used to construct the new p clusters for phase one and the process continues until there is no change in the location of any of the p facilities. This approach is originally proposed by [13] and applied by several authors including [18] and [30].

A similar example, commonly encountered in routing strategies, is the cluster-first routing-second strategy. Here, the clusters are first constructed and then in each cluster a small TSP is optimally solved. The search is to guide the search by identifying other sets of clusters usually through performing a certain level of perturbations on existing clusters.

Another approach that also deals with the same routing problem is to remove from a feasible tour some sequences, as in ILS, and then insert them back optimally to the split points of the tours through solving optimally the corresponding set partitioning problem where this ruin/repair mechanism is repeated several times. This approach is successfully adopted by [14].

15.1.3.3   Data Mining

Here the idea is similar to the above two schemes. This can be organised into two phases where in phase one (learning phase) many solutions are obtained and the elite solutions, say the top $k\%$, are identified with their attributes being considered as potential. For instance, in the p-median problem like in HC, those attributes (facilities sites) that belong to the elite solutions and having a high frequency of occurrence are assumed to belong to the best final solution. In phase two, the local search will be relatively much faster as it starts with a solution which already has good quality. This can be implemented in two ways where those attributes are kept unaffected reducing the search space even further or free them for potential improvement. Note that the former may be limited in terms of improvement whereas the latter though slighter slower will explore a larger search space. This concept can also be used in routing where in phase one, common subsequences that belong to the elite solutions with a high frequency, usually known as bones in the routing literature, are identified. These routes can then be augmented through suitable insertion mechanisms. This type of implementation can also be used in a GA where parts of the chromosome, that are considered to be promising, can be treated differently by retaining them from one generation to the next during the execution of the operators such as crossover or mutation. In phase two, these subsequences can either be retained or made free throughout the rest of the local search. As discussed earlier, in the former the problem is reduced into a more constrained and smaller problem. An interesting approach that relies on identifying good subsequences of nodes in routing is developed by [55]. This can be used in stage two to fix these subsequences either in the local search or if an exact approach is adopted making the problem much reduced and hence easier to solve. This concept of identifying bits of the solution configuration can be adopted to solve several combinatorial optimisation problems including knapsack, bin packing, location, routing, and graph colouring, among others. For example, the use of data mining for the p-median problem is explored by [36] and for combinatorial optimisation in general an interesting and informative paper can be found in [37].

In summary, the power of an individual approach can be very strong, taking advantage of the strengths of more than one approach when searching for a good quality solution. This mechanism of intelligently integrating various methods leads to the design of efficient hybridisations which can be

challenging is worth the effort especially the matheuristic-based ones as these have the added advantage in guaranteeing optimality or at least providing interesting bounds even though at the expense of extra computational burden.

15.2   Big Data and Machine Learning

When there is a large volume of data and the aim is to extract some interesting information either known a priori or completely unknown (patterns, clusters, relationships, classification), schemes that are inspired from heuristics and sometimes supported by statistical modelling and exact methods are worth the investigation. For example, in loan insurance or mortgages, customers get a yes or a no score to assess whether the customer is eligible for the loan or not. This solution is based on the customers attributes and historic past information (such as age, gender, salary, home ownership, etc.). This can be seen as a classification issue where the instance here is to decide if the customer is put into a specific category (yes or no). A neural network or decision tree-based approaches such as random forest are usually used to provide the user with such an important decision which is useful for the company and vital for the customer.

In many cases, the problem is so large that there will be interesting features and patterns in the data that cannot be easily discovered but are still worth identifying. Note that if the size of the problem is that big, modelling through standard optimisation or statistical modelling becomes inappropriate. The idea is to approach such combinatorial problems with massive data using Artificial Intelligence (AI) based methods, known as machine learning (ML), with recent ones exploiting deep learning within their search. We will briefly discuss some of these issues but the reader will find the review on deep learning by [29] with a focus on neural network to identify images or texts, interesting and informative.

Due to the internet and the advances in computer technology and novelty in algorithm design a lot of information is now stored providing a rich source of discovery while requiring some ways of digging deep to find the right information as highlighted in [58].

Big data can be defined using the following five attributes which are usually referred to as the 5Vs:

- Volume- relates to the massive scale of the data.

- Variety- describes the data structure such as structured, semi-structured, or unstructured.
- Velocity- defines how the data presents itself such as streams, real time, batches.
- Veracity- highlights the reliability of the data.
- Value- provides the amount of knowledge and possible insight that can be gained from it.

The same data can lead to various outcomes depending on the aim of the exercise. Exploiting this massive content is not easy and can be even confusing and in some cases misleading. There are heuristic type methods known as artificial intelligence or machine learning algorithms that attempt to provide answers. These techniques are well suited to discover implicit relationships within big data with high dimensions which were impossible to analyse in the recent past.

These techniques are now also easy to implement on personal computers due to the advances in computer technology, the popular programming languages such as R or Python, and the simple connection to popular statistical and optimisation tools. Although the understanding of these algorithms can be mathematically demanding in some cases, these algorithms are now made accessible to a wider audience. We will present briefly three supervised ML algorithms that are commonly used in the OR community. These include random forest, support vector machines, and neural network, all three have shown to be promising at classification tasks. Other techniques include k-nearest neighbour, decision trees, and logistic regression, among others. Note that methods for prediction are usually based on regression such as linear/nonlinear types and those for clustering include k mean, for instance, though the above techniques can be adapted to tackle this kind of problems too. These techniques are also commonly used in the OR literature especially linear/nonlinear regression in prediction, and k mean and k-nearest neighbours in combinatorial optimisation mainly in clustering such as location analysis. Other applications that require other types of MLs are not discussed. Unsupervised learning techniques can be considered as exploratory techniques given there is no a priori target to compare against and aim at discovering new patterns or hidden answers. This will be discussed as part of the section in deep learning.

15.2.1   Decision Trees and Random Forest (RM)

This is one of the most popular machine learning (ML) techniques adopted especially in classification and in regression such as in bioinformatics, banking, insurance, etc. This is a supervised learning which is an ensemble algorithm of random trees (RTs). For simplicity let us first introduce briefly a decision tree as a machine learning technique as this forms the basis for several known techniques such as branch and bound, genetic programming, and particularly RF.

Decision Trees A decision tree is the simplest supervised ML technique for several problems including classification and regression problems. The idea is to choose the best feature (i.e., age) and feature values (say 30, 50, and 65) to split the data into two distinct cohorts for a given value. How to split and in which order the features and their values are chosen is a critical issue that may not have an optimal solution. This is similar to the key issues found in branch and bound implementation (which decision variable to branch from, depth or width first, among others). For the case of decision trees, one way is to use the splitting based on the Information Gain by [38], or the GINI impurity by [8]. See [40] for more information on this aspect. Though decision trees are simple to implement and can handle various types of features (i.e., from real to categorical), they are however sensitive to bias and variance as a minimal change in the data set may result in a big change in the configuration of the chosen decision tree and therefore may cause the risk of overfitting.

Random Forest (RF) aim to overcome some of the drawbacks that arise in decision trees by constructing a number (say n) of random trees, RTs, instead. Given the randomness of these RTs, a subset of good features (say $m <<$ total number of features) and the thresholds for these best features that will be used to split a node $(Th_k; k = 1, \ldots, m_k)$ with m_k being the number of thresholds used for the kth feature are also chosen. For instance, a salary feature could have 3 thresholds leading to four ranges, namely low, medium, high, and very high defined by the three thresholds such as £20K, £50K, and £90K. In other words, each RT can have a depth of at least $\sum_{k=1}^{m} m_k$.

As in most MLs, RF also uses mainly two subsets, the training set and the testing set, approximately accounting for 2/3 and 1/3 of the entire set, respectively. Note that this split is commonly used but it was also found recently that a smaller size for the training set, say approximately 20–25%, could be promising when tested on a variety of applications and also in many MLs including RF, see [59]. Using the training set, each RT will result in a score and the average score (or other appropriate performance measures) of all these n RTs is then used to assess the prediction of the RF when used in the data set. RF has a high predictive accuracy and also a good identification of important variables or attributes for classification. A comprehensive and critical review can be found in [9]. The number of the best features to split (m) and the chosen best features are critical parameters impacting the depth of the tree. The order to choose the best features with their corresponding thresholds at a given level can be performed randomly for diversification purposes or based on a guided split using one of the performance measures that will be briefly given later. RF has the advantage of being simplistic to implement while incorporating randomness due to the choice of the m best attributes and also the way the split is followed at intermediary nodes.

These n RTs can be constructed independently or iteratively taking account of information already identified in earlier RTs and then introducing weights to bias towards those features accordingly. Note that the former is easier to parallelise whereas the latter is not. The latter can however, be more powerful as in Adaboost split but can be less robust especially in terms of output noise when compared to bagging or random split that use the former. An interesting point was also shown by [9] that having a larger number of trees will not provide overfitting due to the strong law of large numbers but will not add extra valuable information. In other words, after a certain number of RTs the added value is minimal and hence getting a critical value is important as the added computational burden may not be worthwhile. RFs have usually a lower risk of overfitting though this advantage can be affected if too much pruning is adopted (i.e., if a large number of best features is used, rendering the process similar to decision trees). In addition, RFs have shown to be robust to outliers, can respond well to nonlinear data and above all can yield better accuracy than most other ML techniques. However, RFs can be biased towards categorical data, are found to be relatively slow and may not be suitable for sparse features. One way to enhance the robustness of the iterative approach is to construct a small number of trees instead of one at a time and then based on the information found this is then introduced to guide the construction of the next lot. In other words this can be not only efficient at learning but also can take advantage of parallelisation within each lot. The number of random trees within each lot does not have to be fixed a priori either as a dynamic approach could be even more efficient.

15.2.2 Support Vector Machines (SVM)

This supervised ML technique also uses training and testing data sets. These are for classification and regression but showed to be more effective at the former especially in text recognition and image detection. The idea is to construct a hyperplane that will split the data set into two subsets. For instance, in 2D that will be a line whereas in 3D this becomes a plane, etc. The hyperplane is defined by the two nearest points to the hyperplane resulting in a distance margin. The larger is this margin the better at classifying the data is the hyperplane, and hence a data that is far away from the hyperplane can be considered classified with a high probability. In other words, if one of these nearest points is removed, the dividing hyperplane is affected and hence this helps in defining the hyperplane. However, when using the training set it is unlikely that there would be one hyperplane that completely classifies all these data sets and therefore a compromise between having a large margin and a small number of classification is adopted. One commonly adopted approach is to start with a lower dimension, evaluate the margin and then increase the dimension until segregation or near segregation is discovered. This procedure can be time consuming and hence SVM are accurate and effective for small data sets with low dimension mainly due to the computational burden. Also, this technique may not be as promising in producing a high level of misclassification on data sets with overlapping classes.

Mathematically this is a challenging non-convex problem given the issue of weight determination that is associated with these two conflicting objective functions. An interesting approach is to solve the problem by solving a sequence of quadratic programming problems as given in [35]. In addition, how to measure the overall margin is also challenging question as this can be based on a maximin or maxisum minimisation problem. A recent study that considers this issue and incorporates various norms is given by [27].

In the OR sphere, this concept is indirectly used, though not referred to as SVM or hyperplane, when solving location and also multi-depot routing problems. In the case of latter, customers are assigned to their nearest depots and hyperplanes can be formed based on the borderline customers resulting in forming a Voronoi diagram where each customer is classified within the region of a given depot, see [48]. Those not borderline customers are classified or considered to belong to their respective depot with confidence when routing is adopted whereas the borderline customers, those that are close to the hyperplane can be assigned to either of their nearest depots and hence could be misclassified. A similar reasoning is also applied in location analysis where the clusters are defined by their hyperplanes.

15.2.3 Neural Networks (NN)

This approach was not well received in the early eighties as it was considered to be a black box with little mathematical rigour, therefore suffering the same problem as heuristic search. Neural networks due to their rich applicability have now become well studied resulting in several interesting developments. The standard architecture for the supervised learning NN is the well known multilayer feed forward neural network proposed by [44]. The network consists of input, hidden, and output layers with weights representing the importance of the connections between two nodes. Based on a set of given input patterns and their corresponding target outputs, the training is applied to minimise the sum of the errors between the unknown output patterns and the known target patterns. This problem turns out to be an optimisation problem with the weights as the decision variables and the objective as the minimisation of the sum of square of the errors. Initially, the problem is solved by back propagation with a descent method as its optimiser. Given the problem is non-convex there is a risk of hitting a poor local minimiser. This is where metaheuristics flourish and become important part to incorporate within the search. For example, a more powerful optimiser that includes adaptive tabu search within the optimisation is developed by [52] to identify cancer recurrence. Another approach developed by [29] is to adopt a stochastic gradient descent where a subset of samples is used to estimate the gradient of the objective function when small changes in the weights are performed. The weights are then increased or decreased in the opposite sign of the average gradient values. NN can be applied in two ways either as a black box where a new entry detail (e.g., the input of a customer requesting a loan) is entered into the network which is already well defined and hence the decision comes as either accept or reject the applicant, or the black box could also have the facility to incorporate new entries and fine tune the network dynamically or once in a while to produce even more reliable solutions.

15.2.4 MLs Evaluation Measures

When training these supervised MLs, depending on the task there are suitable evaluation metrics. For instance, in regression the commonly used metric includes the mean square error though others such as mean absolute error or max absolute error could be useful in area where worst cases are of more relative importance. For classification, the measures used are based on ratios (or probabilities) reflecting the correctly classified and vice versa. These include

Accuracy is the ratio of correctly classified either as true positive (TP) or true negative (TN) over all possibilities including false negative (FN) and false positive (FP);

$$\text{Accuracy} = \frac{(TP+TN)}{(TF+TN+FP+FN)}$$

Sensitivity or Recall can be even more useful as it refers to the ratio of correctly classified in the target class, i.e., $\text{Sensitivity} = \frac{TP}{(TP+FN)}$; for example the percentage of those who may get cancer.

A similar measure is specificity which represents the ratio of correctly classified in the target class, i.e., $\text{Specificity} = \frac{TN}{(TN+FP)}$; for example percentage of those who may not get cancer. Finally, precision refers to the ratio of those correctly classified in the target class that are really in the target class; i.e., $\text{Precision} = \frac{TP}{(TP+FP)}$

Other measures that attempt to combine the above measures include the F1score which is defined as $\text{F1score} = \frac{2(Recall \times Precision)}{(Recall+Precision)}$ and the area under the receiver operator curve (ROC) which measures the true positive rate vs the false positive rate for varying thresholds setting.

>**Observation** It is worth noting that one of the main concerns is that though most users found these ML techniques very useful and practical, we believe it is important to stress that the results provided are by no means guaranteeing optimality though some may be. This is because the problems addressed are usually non-convex and the ML techniques are just heuristic in nature and hence do not guarantee optimality. This anomaly needs to be made aware of as it is important for the user to know. For example, this has been demonstrated by [59] who showed using applications from different areas and a number of MLs including RF, SVM, and NN, that using a fraction of the data set for the training (say about 20%) can be much more effective and robust than using a larger sample, for instance, the 70–30 split as usually suggested. This is just one of the issues among others where the decision maker ought to be aware of this potential hidden aspects that appear to be either ignored, not emphasised enough or just not taken that seriously.

15.3 Deep Learning Heuristics

MLs with no supervision (unsupervised learning) could exploit the large volume of data and through correction and self-improvement, like a child learns through experience, identify important features, useful patterns that could not have been found otherwise, and even discover exciting new models that one would not have thought about. This is because in some cases, it is hard to identify before hand the output a user is looking for. This can also be seen as an extension of reinforcement learning which focusses on the search path based on earlier outcome and then reward positive outcome as the search progresses and then by taking into account such information it biases the search accordingly. A more advanced learning is transfer learning which considers any good information (this refers to useful characteristics as well as non-promising ones) found during the search to be incorporated in future exploration. This continuous learning mechanism tends to identify promising search areas and discard others. The above two concepts of learning can obviously be considered in supervised learning too though their impact is more intensified in unsupervised learning as the search space is even more open and unstructured.

One possible approach which we think to be worth exploring and could enhance the quality of the above ML techniques mentioned above can be outlined as follows:

This is based on a multi-phase approach consisting of say K phases. At the beginning of the search (i.e., phase 1) and as no information is available, we can start by taking a few samples randomly and perform some simple analysis using very quick selection rules. This leads to some attributes that could be worth recording. At this stage the technique used is either optimisation-based or statistical and can be rather crude and fast. This is repeated for a certain number of rounds until T_1 say, where those individual results could be analysed using a simple heuristic leading to useful information to be selected. In the next round of sampling, given some of the useful information are already embedded in, a similar analysis is carried out again. The choice of the samples and their sizes can be identified by heuristic rules as well. At this point, the technique that will be used becomes slightly more powerful and the sampling strategies relatively more sophisticated. This process of gathering information and increasing the level of solution quality by adopting a slightly more powerful heuristic as the search progresses is repeated several times. The switching to a higher calibre heuristic can be either dynamically identified or set at fixed points, say. Note that at this stage enough information is collected and the problem sizes become more manageable until T_k is reached where we can then adopt till the end a more powerful metaheuristic, or even an exact method based on mathematical programming, dynamic programming or just pure statistical modelling if necessary. The number of phases, K, the time spent in each phase (i.e., the T_j; $j = 1, \ldots, K$), the number of samples within each strip and their sizes all contribute to the final solution leading to challenging and exciting questions that need answers. This is one of the methodologies that can be explored further to efficiently discover some of the important hidden attributes of big data arising from classification, clustering, regression, and so forth.

For example, a similar but slightly simpler methodology using sampling, VNS, and ILP formulation was presented with interesting results by [25] and [26] for large p-median and the p-centre problems, respectively. Some of the ideas can also be inspired from data mining where interesting patterns are first found as discussed in the previous section. A schematic representation that shows the level of focus and the depth and power of the methods (solution quality) with the reduction of the problem size as the search progresses is shown in Fig. 15.4.

In summary, hybridisation is carried out using higher and higher level heuristics as the search progresses. In other words, crude heuristics or even simple rules are first used to perform the sampling as well as to analyse them, then followed by more advanced approaches such as composite heuristics or metaheuristics but applied within a small computing time or based on a reduced number of neighbourhoods, then finally a well defined and structured problem could be defined which is then addressed in a standard

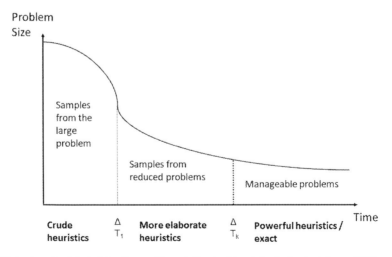

Fig. 15.4 Level of hybridisation of heuristics in big data (adapted from [46])

optimisation or statistical manner where powerful metaheuristics or exact methods are adopted if possible. This type of hybridisation which is heavily recursive and time dependent on the progress of the search may not be that simple to explore but, in our view, this is worth the challenge.

15.4 Implementation Issues in Heuristic Search Design

Since metaheuristics are computer intensive, any intelligent way of reducing the computer time without (or significantly) affecting the solution quality is a welcome way forward. Such a saving in computer time can be reallocated if necessary to perform additional iterations which may lead to even better quality solutions. There are many ways of enhancing the implementation of a given heuristic to improve its efficiency. The following key aspects which include data structure, duplication identification, cost approximation , neighbourhood reduction schemes, efficient way of parameter estimation, and the use of parallelisation could be of some help and guidance when designing a powerful metaheuristic including an ML technique.

15.4.1 Data Structure

Some ideas that may help in emphasising this concept of data structure (DS) while designing a computer program are outlined below. Note that DS does not affect the quality of solutions.

Avoidance of the Recomputation of Already Computed Information This can be achieved by storing the necessary intermediate information. These data will usually be not kept and hence not taken advantage of if DS is not used. Though there is obviously an initial fixed cost to bear and a small computational burden linked to recording and updating the information, this effort is relatively negligible considering the large number of iterations that needs to be performed in metaheuristics-based methods. For example, Sze et al. [54] developed an efficient scheme on how to record information for the case of the vehicle routing problem which yields a massive saving in computational time.

Elimination of Common Tasks which are Used in Several Parts of the Method For instance, in routing problems where a move is based on customer removal or exchange, the cost (total demand or time) of a vehicle route without a given customer remains unchanged from its insertion in all potential routes. This information though small helps enormously in cutting redundant calculations as shown by [47] when solving the vehicle routing with heterogeneous vehicle fleet. This obviously requires an additional storage requirement but this is usually not a severe restriction. This clue is worth incorporating in other applications where intermediate information could be identified.

Avoidance of Extra Unnecessary Computation This can be performed by detecting as early as possible the possible conditions or restrictions that may not permit a given move to be worth evaluating. For instance, in any constrained type problem, say the vehicle routing problem, if a given customer is introduced into a vehicle route which violates capacity or time constraints, it would be economical if such an information was made available as early as possible in the search so as to cut down on any earlier worthless computation. We assume we base our search on feasible moves only, otherwise extra care is needed as the amount of violation can be used as a target to whether or not it is worth exploring such moves. Another example is the vertex p-centre problem where the aim is to locate p facilities among the existing customer sites such that the furthest customer from its nearest chosen facility is minimised. This problem relates to emergency services such as the case of locating hospitals, fire service, or police stations. One of the approaches is based on reducing the gap between lower and upper bounds (thresholds or response times) by applying a bisection method in the range to define the new threshold for which a set covering problem is applied. This is repeated until there is nothing left in the range. One interesting view is to sort the distances between nodes and therefore identify quickly those distance elements that lie in a range (between the current lower and upper bound) at any iteration without considering the others which will be many. The bisection point, which will be used as the next threshold, is then computed but chosen as the nearest existing distance element in that range and not as its original value which may not be necessarily one of the elements in the range. Besides, if there are only 1 or 2 elements left in the range even if the range is still wide, a complete enumeration of these elements used as thresholds can be conducted instead which can be much faster. The search then terminates much quicker without searching for a bisection point all the way until there is a range of size one. Irawan et al. [25] incorporated this scheme within their hybrid exact/VNS framework to produce optimal solutions for large instances for both the p-median and the vertex p-centre problems for the first time.

Quadtree-based DS One well known data compression technique is the quadtree-based DS commonly used in computer science. This was successfully adopted by [50] to solve very large p-median problems. Here the data is first classified under quadtrees which are well defined by their corners. The idea is to construct a tree starting from the first node representing the overall region, which is then split into 4 branches (the initial space is split into four equal spaces usually rectangles), this splitting continues until the number of lowest level is reached. This mechanism requires a high fixed cost at the beginning of the search which is then compensated by the massive saving in later stages of the search. The idea is that once the four corners of each quadrant are assigned to their nearest facility, all those nodes (customers) inside that quadtree are systematically assigned to that facility as one block instead of individual nodes resulting in a massive saving in computational time. This DS is practically useful if the size of the problem is very large and many runs are required as the construction of the DS can be time consuming though performed once only.

15.4.2 Duplication Identification

In addition to the basic data structures some of which can be problem specific, there are several ways on how to identify duplicate solution configurations during the search. These mechanisms are introduced to avoid the risk of cycling as well as the unnecessary recording of similar already found information that do not need to be examined again. Some of these schemes are presented here.

Hashing Function and Its Related Versions A hashing function is one way to efficiently record and detect previously found solutions, see [62]. These functions which are defined from the solution configuration set, need to be assigned integer numbers while being bijective. In other words, each value of the hashing function will relate to one single solution configuration only (i.e., a one to one relationship). The construction of such functions is not easy as these functions need to be theoretically proven to guarantee the unique interdependency between the hashing function value and the corresponding configuration. In practice, a nearly bijective function is usually adopted as a proxy with a small degree of inaccuracy. For instance, in vehicle routing possible functions may include the objective function value namely the total cost, some index function based on route configuration such as the number of routes, for each route with the same number of customers, and cost of the sequence of customers in those routes, among others. However, when these are put together will reduce the risk of missing the 'one to one relationship' property. For instance, in the case of routing problems, we can use the following checks in sequence. We can conclude that if the total cost is different, then the new solution is different, otherwise, we check if the number of routes is different, then if the number of customers in each route is different, if the load in each route, etc.

Subset-Based Configuration It is worth noting that the issue of duplication can be relatively easier to deal with in those applications where the solution configuration is defined by a selected subset of integer numbers instead of a sequence. For instance, in the p-median problem where the configuration is made up of p integer numbers denoting the site number of the facilities, we can sort each configuration in ascending (or descending) order of its sites numbers as the order in this situation has no practical meaning. If the total cost (or the objective function value of the problem studied) happens to be the same as some of the previous configurations, the following two rules can be applied. We can either turn each solution configuration into a string and then compare the strings only, or perform the checks column by column starting from the first one. For example, if the two elements (i.e., the location in this case) at a given position of the two solution configurations are different, the new configuration must be different and therefore there is no need to check the remaining positions. This overall check of the new configuration, if, for instance, m other already found configurations have the same cost, will take $0(pm)$ in the worst case. This is performed successfully in [18] where a cellular approach is used for the Weber problem making the problem easier to identify its small pieces, referring to the cells in this example.

15.4.3   Cost Function Approximation

The computation of the objective function, once the move is selected, can require an excessive computational effort. As there will be a lot of moves to evaluate, if such an evaluation is too heavy computationally, it could be important to apply a good but quick approximation of the cost evaluation instead. To add flexibility and reduce the risk of missing good solutions, the top K moves will be rechecked properly using the full cost evaluation. Note that if K represents all the possible moves, this will reduce to the original implementation but if $K = 1$, the chosen move will be based on the best one using the approximation only. The former could be too time consuming whereas the latter is quick but could be too myopic and hence could miss good quality moves. Having K as a fraction of the problem size or just based on the number of possible moves could be a good way forward. Such implementation is proved to be successful in solving capacitated location problem where the full transportation problem is solved optimally using the selected moves only and the approximation is based on assigning customers to the open facilities using the nearest proximity criterion or the regret cost (difference between the second nearest and the nearest facility to a customer) instead. The main idea is that the approximation needs to be easy to compute while being as close as possible to the real objective function and robust in the sense that all moves are similarly approximated irrespective of whether they are all over or under estimated.

15.4.4 Reduction Tests/Neighbourhood Reduction

The reduction in computing time can be obtained by introducing some neighbourhood reductions which eliminate from the testing certain cases that are unlikely to influence the global best solution. There will be a trade-off between speed by which the best solution is obtained and the quality of the solution. This important aspect is crucial when designing a heuristic. When implementing a heuristic it is important to understand the problem which will help in defining the right size of the restricted neighbourhood for each attribute that only will be considered. This mechanism, also known as a reduction test, can be built to be either dynamic or deterministic that is set from the outset. For instance, Salhi and Sari [48] introduced some reduction tests when studying the multi-depot vehicle routing and saved over 85% of the cpu time with a negligible loss in solution quality. A good neighbourhood reduction scheme has also the added benefits in matheuristics in some circumstances, as it transforms the original problem into a new reduced problem that could be manageable to be optimally solvable. A similar approach that considers the power of neighbourhood reduction is the interesting paper on granular tabu search by [57] where restricted neighbourhoods are defined making the overall search relatively much faster. It is worth mentioning that the use of neighbourhood reduction may slightly affect the solution quality though the challenge is to construct such schemes which only exclude with high probability those unnecessary moves. This risk presents an exciting challenge with the aim to thrive towards finding the right balance between a strong reduction test (remove as much as possible) while not affecting seriously the solution quality.

For illustration purposes, we shall present some of those neighbourhood reductions that are originally proposed for the vehicle routing by [48] and revisited by [54]. We show two rules, namely, rule 1 which is proximity based and rule 2 which is depot based.

Proximity-based scheme (Rule 1) For each node i, let us define the subset of nodes that should not be excluded for subsequent moves where node i is involved. This can be distance-based (those nodes that are within a certain threshold from i) or cardinality-based (a certain number of neighbouring nodes from i), or a combination of the two measures. For each node i, we define the following logical flag as $flag(i, j)$ to false if node j is not excluded due to the above conditions. Initially all flags are set to true. Note that when no reduction scheme is adopted, this is equivalent to setting all flags to true.

Depot-based (Rule 2) Some customers may be far away from each other but could be close to the trajectory of leaving the depot or returning to the depot. This observation can be taken into account by considering node j to be a neighbour of i if its insertion cost between the depot, say 0, and node i is less than a defined insertion-based threshold. The above two rules that define the two neighbourhood reductions are represented in Fig. 15.5 for a VRP example of three routes.

Another test that considers those pairs of nodes (i, j) which happen to be within a certain angle with respect to the depot, $\theta(i, 0, j)$, or not too far apart but within proximity to the depot is also worth incorporating as part of the overall pruning mechanism. For more details on all the neighbourhood reductions , see [46].

It is important to make the link between neighbourhood reduction and valid inequalities. Both are defined as some form of cuts to eliminate

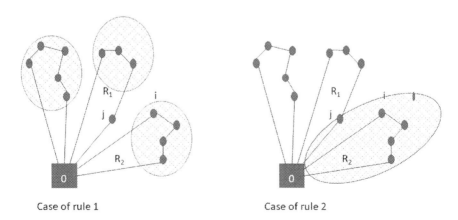

Case of rule 1   Case of rule 2

Fig. 15.5 Two neighbourhood reductions for a 3 routes VRP (adapted from [46])

some regions from being searched. However these two schemes differ in the following. The former eliminates feasible regions that are unlikely to, though still could, contain the optimal solution whereas the latter retains the optimality property of not missing the optimal solution. In addition, the former tends to eliminate a relatively much larger portion of feasible regions contrarily to the latter by making the search even much faster. An interesting potential research view related to these schemes is also discussed in the suggestion section.

15.4.5 Parameters and Hyper Parameters Optimisation

One of the weakest and most criticised aspect within heuristics and machine learning is the reliance on good estimate and fine tuning of the parameters used. For example, in a GA we can consider the crossover rates, type of crossover, mutation rate, number of chromosomes in a population, whereas for the RF we need to identify the number of RTs, the number of best attributes, their threshold, depth of the RTs, etc. Some of these parameters can be continuous, discrete, categorical within their domain spaces which can be also large making this global/combinatorial problem even more complex to study.

This task is usually performed on a training set. Two commonly adopted approaches are grid search and manual search with the latter incorporating random search. The former is used by evaluating the entire space (all combinations in the grid space) for all the dimensions which could be impractical and time consuming. This is because this approach may suffer from the curse of dimensionality and hence not always appropriate and even not promising due to the defined grid adopted. Note that this grid could be adaptively redesigned to focus on the promising areas. For instance, one can start with a uniform grid and as the search progresses, many areas could be discarded and the rest made more granulated. This process of continuously granulating the grid search approach is a useful and promising area to pursue within the sphere of deep learning. Random search on the other hand is very simple but can be blind so one common strategy is to adopt a combination of the two, see [5]. However, random search can also take advantage of the same enhancement mentioned above to make the search pseudo random while giving more weight to certain regions instead. In practice, there are usually four ways to select the parameters:

(a) *Experimental work.* This is one of the most used techniques which aid to find the most appropriate values after performing preliminary testing usually conducted on a subset of instances, known as training sets, using grid search, random search, or a combination of the two.

(b) *Matching methods*. The idea is to assign the parameters already found in other studies to similar classes of problems.

(c) *Analytical forms*. This aims to determine analytically these values which can be derived statistically via linear/nonlinear regression for example.

(d) *Adaptive learning*. This is based on dynamically adjusting the parameter values depending on the solution quality as the search progresses.

The first two approaches are the commonly applied ones with (a) mainly in the computer science/artificial intelligence areas where machine learning is core whereas (b) is more used in the OR areas. In (c) it can be difficult to define an analytical function that works all the time. For instance, Salhi [45] put forward an analytic formulae for defining tabu length and aspiration level within tabu search, Dorigo and Gambardella [15] gave a formula for the number of ants based on the other parameters within ant systems, and [1] conducted a statistical investigation for a metaheuristic which is applicable for other ones. Also, there are several studies related to simulated annealing for setting the initial temperature say. The fourth category (d) is the most challenging and also one that starts to gain more attention. This is because it shows to be robust besides yielding more competitive results when compared to the above static measures. Here, some form of control is embedded into the search so corrective measures are added to either avoid the risk of early convergence or to control the problem of divergence. The use of information to control the search is successfully applied in several applications. As examples, consider the reactive TS where the tabu size goes up or down depending on the solution quality and the risk of collision. In SA, the temperature is reset to previously found values, in VNS for larger and complex problems, the use of a smaller number of promising neighbourhoods is restricted in pseudo-random way to a smaller but promising subset among the original set of neighbourhood structures. The same idea is applied to the use of a subset of local searches instead of the full set which may require an excessive computational effort. The choice of such subsets is performed dynamically that is based on those good solutions found earlier in the search. In GA the rate of selection between the elite solutions and the less well-off ones can also be controlled dynamically as the search progresses. Note that learning is now also integrated in both (a) and (b) to strengthen the search and hence provide better estimates of the parameters. One way forward is to adopt a two-phase approach where in phase 1 we start with random search for a while then identify interesting and promising regions where in phase two a grid search could then be employed in those well defined spaces only. Here the grid coverage in a given dimension could take advantage of the learning to assess whether the objective function is relatively more sensitive to certain dimensions than others. The first phase is similar in principle to manual search where regions are first identified but there it is not easy to reproduce the results. In other words, this first phase is systematic and problem independent. In addition, the search could be made even more efficient if parallelisation is applied as both random search and grid search, for instance, can easily be parallelised.

At a higher level, the hyper parameter optimisation could be dealt with in two layers that are nested. For instance, in layer one an evolutionary approach such as GA, PSO, or Ant colony is used with parameters provided to the lower layer say VNS, TS, SA, or RF to solve the problem that yields the fitness function values. The parameters of the first layer are usually fixed. This iterative process could be time consuming as the lower level itself will require some time to complete and hence a good learning on how to cut on the calls to the higher level or how to approximate the result at the lower level relatively quickly is paramount. Note that the two levels could obviously be interchanged where in level one the parameters are updated given the parameters of lower lev are made fixed. In machine learning, for instance, a higher level could be GA that optimise the parameters of a neural network (number of layers, number of inputs, etc.) or RF (number of RTs, type of branching, number of attributes, etc.).

15.4.6   Impact of Parallelisation

There exist various models on how to parallelise a given algorithm including master slave, fine grained, island, and obviously a hybridisation of the above. The first one is to use several computers (or processors) and carry out a scheduling task between them, whereas the others especially the island model focusses on exploiting the power of course grain parallel computers. Even a computer with one processor only which happens to have dual or multi-core (internal parallel processing) can be taken advantage of its architecture. In addition, parallel random access model, or known as PRAM, could also make use of memory better and hence activate the processing accordingly. Recently, GPU short for Graphics Processing Units, which is originally used in the video game industry, can be explored. Note that GPU handles thousands of cores whereas CPU has only multiple cores only. However, it is worth noting that each GPU core runs significantly much slower than its counterpart CPU core. The strength of GPU is for those applications that are or can be massively parallelised so each little job can be performed separately even if it is slower. The idea is to offload parts of a given job to the GPU and leave the hard part to run on the normal CPU.

There are some techniques though that may not be so powerful but their performance can easily be enhanced as their structure fits naturally with parallelism. These include random forests where each random tree can be exploited separately, population-based metaheuristics such as GA and PSO can be parallelised easily as each chromosome in GA or a particle in PSO can be exploited separately and then their overall result is then combined before the process starts again. This is also the case for ant colony and bees optimisation.

15.5   Conclusion and Research Issues

In this final section we summarise the main aspects we discussed and provide some research avenues that could be worth pursuing.

In this chapter, we extend on chapter [51] where strengths and weaknesses can be found in any heuristic. Hybridisation which is one way forward to overcome this limitation, is covered with an emphasis on exact methods with heuristics, heuristics with exact methods and heuristics with heuristics. A possible hybridisation for big data that adopts a series of heuristics with increasing complexity as the search progresses is also proposed. As the search progresses, the effect of learning is briefly discussed. Due to the advance in computer technology and algorithm design, three commonly used machine learnings, namely, random forest, support vector machines, and neural network are briefly described with their strong links to heuristic optimisation highlighted. The efficiency of heuristics depends on several aspects including the hidden key elements when it comes to their implementation. This delicate issue has a massive practical importance is put across where the benefits of constructing effective data structure, neighbourhood reductions, duplication identification schemes, parameters estimation, and parallel processing, among others are highlighted.

The following research aspects could be worth exploiting.

1. The first issue is the hybridisation of heuristic and exact methods. This is a nested approach (heuristics within exact methods, or exact methods within heuristics), which in our view, will remain a hot topic for many years to come. The issue here is to dynamically identify those nodes of the B&B tree which are worth examining further. Some of these could have (a) infeasible solutions (i.e., lower bound values) or (b) feasible ones

(upper bounds) not only the incumbent one. Embedding some form of repair mechanism followed by an improvement scheme, such as a local search or even a small version of a powerful heuristic, can be used for (a) whereas the improvement scheme is better suited for (b). In (a) the aim is to first transform the infeasible solution into a feasible one whereas in (b) the idea is to improve the feasible solution if possible. Note that the improvement scheme is used not only on the best upper bound as applied in integer programming for fathoming purposes but also on the other upper bounds for which their feasible solutions display some form of diversity or promising attributes. This mechanism could lead to improving upon the best incumbent upper bound while strengthening the improvement scheme adopted for diversification purposes as is commonly used in TS or via the injection operators as in GA.

2. The view of identifying promising attributes or patterns as the search progresses is an exciting avenue that is likely to yield excellent results in the future. The idea is to obtain, through a simpler heuristic which could be called several times such as a smaller version of GRASP, guided LP relaxations, or even a GA, to generate several solution configurations. These solution configurations when merged together in either subsequent reduced problems or an augmented problem will control the search in a guided manner towards optimal or near optimal solutions due to their promising attributes. This aspect has shown to be worth pursuing in various powerful heuristics such as concentration set approach, harmony search, relaxation methods, and bucket search, among others.

3. The understanding of how a given method works and then to design a data structure that incorporates as much as possible those interesting intermediate found information so to avoid re-computing unnecessary calculations is vital. This process though may increase some level of memory and may require an initial fixed cost in terms of development and computation time, it does often lead to a massive time saving without affecting the solution quality at all.

4. Another aspect that enhances the implementation is the construction of effective neighbourhood reduction schemes. These help the search to avoid even checking combinations and operations that are unlikely to result in improving the solution. A note of caution here is that the latter schemes though will have a considerable saving in computational time and are usually simple to construct, could affect the solution quality. This is contrarily to valid inequalities which retain optimality. It would be interesting to create a new flexible scheme that sits between the two by

developing a powerful neighbourhood reduction while guaranteeing optimality within $1 - \alpha$ with α being the risk (or probability) of missing optimality. In other words, this is a compromise between controlling the restricted neighbourhood which is powerful enough (remove as many as possible irrelevant checks) while not excluding promising moves which may lead to optimal solutions is exciting and hence worth exploring.

5. As the decision problems tackled by machine learning are combinatorial or global optimisation type problems that are often not convex, with the added complexity of very big data, it is important to stress that the solutions usually provided are feasible solutions only which by no mean guarantee optimality. It is therefore important that as the engine of the machine learning is mainly linked to optimisation, which is usually not made aware of as it should be, more research and involvement of the OR community in general and heuristic optimisation in particular is crucial. This not only opens a massive opportunity for applications but also a massive boost to research in combinatorial and global optimisation general.

6. Evolutionary heuristics are relatively easier to be parallelised and hence can be used for larger instances and in practical setting if the computing facilities are available. The integration of GPU and CPU, as briefly highlighted earlier, can be a useful addition to the mix which may entice researchers, mainly in the computer science community, to be more excited about. Though this is a technical issue, it may require some interesting developments that could be worth exploring.

7. The design of adaptive search that dynamically learns and makes use of the obtained information is crucial. This learning mechanism which ought to be continuously or at least periodically updated is then used to pseudo-randomly select at each iteration or just after a certain number of iterations the decision rules to be used. These can include a subset of neighbourhoods to choose from, a number of local searches to be used for intensification purposes, or even the powerful heuristics or exact methods to opt from. This kind of search is self-adaptive and also efficient as it uses what it needs only rather than having everything with the expectation that a good solution may be found! This research issue though challenging and practically useful would probably be one of the most popular research areas in the near future as it has the additional benefits of being applicable in several areas ranging from engineering to medicine.

8. In a related but different aspect, it is well known that most exciting powerful heuristics seem to suffer from parameter tuning. It is therefore worthwhile concentrating on schemes that incorporate ways of reducing

the number of parameters or adjusting the parameters values dynamically and adaptively. This is very welcome and in our view is also one of the ways forward. Results from such studies will provide us with tools on how to avoid the excessive time for fine tuning of the parameters, besides making the heuristic less sensitive to parameter values and hence more reliable to use.

References

1. Adenso-Diaz B and Laguna B (2006). Fine tuning of the algorithms using fractional experimental designs and local search. Oper Res **54**: 99–114.
2. Agar M and Salhi S (1998). Lagrangean heuristics applied to a variety of large capacitated plant location problems. J Oper Res Soc **49**: 1072–1084.
3. Akpinar S (2014). Hybrid large neighbourhood search algorithm for capacitated vehicle routing problem. Exp Syst Appl **61**: 28–38.
4. Angelelli E, Mansini R and Speranza MG (2010). Kernel Search: A general heuristic for the multi-dimensional knapsack problem. Comput Oper Res **37**: 2017–2026.
5. Bergstra J and Bengio Y (2012). Random search for hyper-parameter optimisation. J Mach Learn Res **13**: 281–305.
6. Boudia M and Prins C (2009). A memetic algorithm with dynamic population management for an integrated production-distribution problem. Eur J Oper Res **195**: 703–715.
7. Bouzid MC, Haddadene HA and Salhi S (2017). A new integration of Lagrangean split and VNS: The case of the capacitated vehicle routing problem. Comput Oper Res **78**: 513–525.
8. Breiman L, Friedman J, Stone CJ and Olshen RA (1984). Classification and regression trees. CRC Press.
9. Breiman L (2001). Random forests. Mach Learn **45**: 5–32.
10. Burke EK, Hyde M, Kendall G, Ochoa G, Ozcan E and Woodward J (2010). A classification of hyper-heuristics approaches. In Gendreau M and Potvin JY (eds). Handbook of Metaheuristics (2nd edition). Springer, London, pp 449–468.
11. Callaghan B, Salhi S and Brimberg J (2019). The continuous p-centre problem and related α-neighbour and the conditional problems: Optimal relaxation algorithms and managerial insights. JORS **70**: 192–211.
12. Chen D and Chen R (2009). New relaxation-based algorithms for the optimal solution of the continuous and discrete p-centre problems. Comput Oper Res **36**: 1646–1655.
13. Cooper L (1964). Heuristic methods for location–allocation problem. SIAM Rev **6**: 37–53.

14. De Franceschi R, Fischetti M and Toth P (2006). A new ILP-based refinement heuristic for vehicle routing problems. Math Progam B **105**: 471–499.
15. Dorigo M and Gambardella LM (1997). Ant colony system: A cooperative learning approach to the travelling salesman problem. IEEE Trans Evol Comput **1**: 53–66.
16. Fischetti M and Lodi A (2003). Local branching. Math Program **98**: 23–47.
17. Fischetti M, Glover F and Loti A (2005). The feasibility pump. Math Program B **104**: 91–104.
18. Gamal MDH and Salhi S (2008). A cellular heuristic for the multisource Weber problem. Comput Oper Res **30**: 1609–1624.
19. Garcia-Villoria A, Salhi S, Corominas A and Pastor R (2011). Hyper-heuristic approaches for the response time variability problem. Eur J Oper Res **211**: 160–169.
20. Guastaroba G and Speranza MG (2012). Kernel search for the capacitated facility problem. J Heuristics **18**: 877–917.
21. Hanafi S and Wilbaut C (2006). Mixed integer programming relaxation based Heuristics to solve the 0–1 multidimensional knapsack problem. Paper given at COR/Optimization Days May 2006, Montreal, Canada.
22. Hansen P, Mladenović N and Urosević D (2006). Variable neighbourhood search and local branching. Comput Oper Res **33**: 3034–3045.
23. Held M and Karp RM (1970). The traveling salesman problem and minimum spanning trees. Oper Res **18**: 1138–1162.
24. Held M and Karp RM (1971). The traveling salesman problem and minimum spanning trees: Part II. Math Program **1**: 6–25.
25. Irawan CA, Salhi S and Scaparra P (2016). An adaptive multiphase approach for large unconditional and conditional p-median problems. Eur J Oper Res **237**: 590–605.
26. Irawan CA, Salhi S and Drezner Z (2014). Hybrid metaheuristics with VNS and exact methods: Application to large unconditional and conditional vertex p-centre problems. J Heuristics **22**: 507–537.
27. Ke T, Zhang L, Ge X, Lv H and Li M (2021). Construct a robust least squares support vector machine based on Lp-norm and $L\infty$-norm. Eng Appl Artif Intell **99**: 104134 https://doi.org/10.1016/j.engappai.2020.104134.
28. Lazic J, Hanafi S, Mladenović N and Urosevic D (2010). Variable neighbourhood decomposition search for 0-1 mixed integer programs. Comput Oper Res **37**: 1055–1067.
29. LeCun Y, Bengio Y and Hinton G (2015). Deep learning. Nature **521**: 436–444.
30. Luis M, Salhi S and Gabor N (2011). A guided reactive GRASP for the capacitated Multi-source Weber problem. Comput Oper Res **38**: 1014–1024.
31. Moscato P and Norman MG (1992). A memetic approach for the travelling salesman problem-implementation of a computational ecology for combinatorial optimization on message passing systems. In Valero M. et al. (eds). Parallel Computing and Transputer Applications. IOS Press, Amsterdam, pp 177–186.

32. Moscato P and Cotta C (2003). A gentle introduction of memetic algorithms. In Glover F and Kochenberger GA (eds). Handbook of Metaheuristics. Kluwer, London, pp 105–144.

33. Nezhad AM, Mazour H and Salhi S (2013). Lagrangean relaxation heuristucs for the uncapacitated single-source multi-product facility location problem. Int J of Prod Econ **145**: 713–723.

34. Nwana V, Darby-Dowman K and Mitra G (2005). A co-operative parallel heuristic for mixed zero-one linear programming: Combining simulated annealing with branch and bound. Eur J Oper Res **164**: 12–23.

35. Osuna E, Freund R and Girosi F (1997). An improved training algorithm for support vector machines. In Neural Network for Signal Processing VII, Proceeding of the 1997 IEEE Signal Processing Society Workshop, Florida, USA, 276–285.

36. Plastino A, Fuchshuber R, Martins S, Freitas AA and Salhi S (2011). A hybrid data mining meta-heuristic for the p-median problem. Stat Anal Data Min J **4**: 313–335.

37. de Holland Maia MR, Plastino A and Vaz Penna PH (2020). MineReduce: An approach based on data mining for problem size reduction. Comput Oper Res **122**: 104995.

38. Quinlan JR (1983). Learning efficient classification procedures and their application to chess end games. In Michalski RS, Carbonell JG, and Mitchell TM (eds). Machine Learning: An Artificial Intelligence Approach, pp. 463–482.

39. Raidl GR (2006). A unified view on hybrid metaheuristics. In Hybrid Meta-heuristics. Springer Berlin Heidelberg, pp. 1–12.

40. Raileanu LE and Stoffel K (2004). Theoretical comparison between the gini index and information gain criteria. Ann Math Artif Intell **41**: 77–93.

41. Rosing KE and ReVelle CS (1997). Heuristic concentration: Two stage solution construction. Eur J Oper Res **97**: 75–86.

42. Rosing KE, ReVelle CS and Schilling DA (1999). A Gamma heuristic for the p-median problem. Eur J Oper Res **117**: 522–532.

43. Ross P (2005). Hyper-heuristics. In Burke EK and Kendall G (eds). Search Methodologies: Introductory Tutorials in Optimization and Decision Support Techniques. Springer, London, pp 529–556.

44. Rumelhart D and McClelland J (1986). Parallel distributed processing. MIT Press, Cambridge, MA.

45. Salhi S (2002). Defining tabu list size and aspiration criterion within tabu search methods. Comput Oper Res **29**: 67–86.

46. Salhi S (2017). Heuristic Search: The Emerging Science of Problem Solving. Springer, Chan.

47. Salhi S and Rand GK (1987). Improvements to vehicle routing heuristics. J Oper Res Soc **38**: 293–295.

48. Salhi S and Sari M (1997). A Multi-level composite heuristic for the multi-depot vehicle fleet mix problem. Eur J Oper Res **103**: 78–95.

49. Salhi S and Al-Khedhairi A (2010). Integrating heuristic information into exact methods: The case of the vertex p-centre problem. J Oper Res Soc **61**: 1619–1631.

50. Salhi S and Irawan CA (2015). A quadtree-based allocation method for a class of large discrete Euclidean location problems. Comput Oper Res **55**: 23–35.

51. Salhi S and Thompson J (2021). An overview of heuristic and metaheuristics. In Salhi S and Boylan J (eds). The Palgrave Handbook of Operations Research. Palgrave, London.

52. Smithies R, Salhi S and Queen N (2004). Adaptive hybrid learning for neural networks. Neural Comput **16**: 139–157.

53. Sorensen K and Sevaux M (2006). MA/PM: Memetic algorithms with population management. Comput Oper Res **33**: 1214–1225.

54. Sze JF, Salhi S and Wassan NA (2016). A hybridisation of adaptive variable neighbourhood search and large neighbourhood search: Application to the vehicle routing problem. Exp Syst Appls **65**: 383–397.

55. Tarantilis CD and Kiranoudis CT (2002). Boneroute: An adaptive memory-based method for effective fleet management. Ann Oper Res **115**: 227–241.

56. Thangiah SR and Salhi S (2001). Genetic clustering: An adaptive heuristic for the multi depot vehicle routing problem. Appl Art Int **15**: 361–383.

57. Toth P and Vigo D (2003). The granular tabu search and its applications to the vehicle routing problem. Informs J Comput **15**: 333–346.

58. Wang Y, Kung L and Byrd TA (2018). Big data analytics: Understanding its capabilities and potential benefits for healthcare organizations. Technol Forecast Soc Chang **126**: 3–13.

59. Wang H, Yao Y and Salhi S (2021). Tension in big data using machine learning: Analysis and applications. Technol Forecast Soc Change **158**: 120175.

60. Wilbaut C, Hanafi S and Salhi S (2008). A survey of effective heuristics and their application to a variety of knapsack problems. IMA J Manage Math **19**: 227–244.

61. Wilbaut C, Salhi S and Hanafi S (2009). An iterative variable-based fixation heuristic for the 0-1 multidimensional knapsack problem. Eur J Oper Res **199**: 339–348.

62. Woodruff DL and Zemel E (1993). Hashing vectors for tabu search. Ann Oper Res **41**: 123–137.

63. Xiao Y, Zhao Q, Kaku I and Mladenovic N (2014). Variable neighbourhood simulated annealing algorithm for capacitated vehicle routing problems. Eng Opt **46**: 562–579.

Part IV

Forecasting, Simulation and Prediction

16

Forecasting with Judgment

Paul Goodwin and Robert Fildes

16.1 Introduction

Despite the rise of Big Data and predictive analytics, most forecasts in organisations still rely heavily on people's judgments (Fildes and Petropoulos [41]; Fildes et al. [39]). For example, forecasts of the demand for a new product may be based wholly on managers' guestimates. Similarly, in the case of exceptional events such as sales promotions, forecasters may make judgmental adjustments to statistical or algorithm-based forecasts. The forecasts may be made by an individual, or, alternatively, aggregated from a group of individual judgments. They can be based on nothing more than a holistic view of the problem or prompted by information cues , both quantitative or qualitative (such as a competitive price rise, a statistical forecast or a rise of pneumonia in China).

P. Goodwin
University of Bath, Bath, UK
e-mail: p.goodwin@bath.ac.uk

R. Fildes (✉)
Lancaster Centre for Marketing Analytics and Forecasting, Lancaster University, Lancaster, UK
e-mail: r.fildes@lancaster.ac.uk

© The Author(s), under exclusive license to Springer Nature
Switzerland AG 2022

S. Salhi and J. Boylan (eds.), *The Palgrave Handbook of Operations Research*,
https://doi.org/10.1007/978-3-030-96935-6_16

Alternatively, judgment can have an indirect influence on forecasts. For example, it can be used to decide which statistical forecasting method to employ, the length of historical data that should be used to estimate the parameters of a statistical forecasting model or the variables which should be included in the model. The key element of judgment is that it is subjective and cannot be exactly reproduced by an algorithm or a set of explicit rules.

In some circumstances, forecasts reflect the judgments of potential customers on their likelihood of purchasing a particular product or service or the views of the electorate on their voting intentions. These judgments are elicited in intentions surveys and typically translated into forecasts of demand, market share or election outcomes (Morwitz et al. [101]). However, for brevity, this aspect of forecasting will not be considered here.

The tasks faced by judgmental forecasters making direct judgments can take several forms. They can involve forecasting a numeric quantity, such as next month's demand for a product or the rate of a country's inflation over the next quarter. Alternatively, they can entail forecasting whether an event will occur, for example will the next US President be a Democrat or will a human land on Mars by 2040? In both cases the forecast can be expressed with or without probabilities. A manager might simply forecast that next month's demand for a product will be 320 units (a so-called point forecast) or they may provide a complete probability distribution for possible levels of demand (a density forecast). An intermediate position would be to forecast specific quantiles of the distribution. A special case of this involves the estimation of a prediction interval. For example, a manager may estimate that there is a 95% probability that the interval from 280 to 360 units will contain next month's level of demand. In the case of events, the forecaster may simply report what they consider to be the most probable event, for example that the UK will not rejoin the EU within the next decade or they may attach a probability to this event (e.g., "I estimate there is an 85% chance that the UK will not rejoin the EU within the next decade").

Given that judgment is frequently used in such a wide variety of forecasting tasks, all fundamental in OR, this chapter first explores why judgment has such a prevalent role in forecasting. We then review what the latest research tells us about the benefits and drawbacks of using judgment to perform these different forecast tasks. In the third section we examine and evaluate strategies that are designed to support and improve the role of judgment in forecasting, highlighting the many under-researched questions, followed by our conclusions on the role of judgment.

16.2   Why Is the Use of Judgment so Widespread in Forecasting?

There are several reasons why forecasts often rely heavily on judgment. Quantitative forecasting methods such as exponential smoothing, regression or artificial neural networks (ANNs) require past data, often in significant quantities, before they can be used. Many forecasting situations are unique or have only a few close analogies, so large amounts of data may not be available. For example, a product due to be launched next week may be unlike anything previously seen on the market, or an established product may be the subject of a sales promotion strategy that has not been tried before. Even when data is available, it may no longer be relevant, as when a once-in-a-century pandemic has a profound disruptive and long-lasting impact on demand. Alternatively, the cost of acquiring relevant data may not be justified by the relatively limited benefits of accurate forecasts. In these circumstances, forecasters may have no option but to rely on judgment.

However, there is plenty of evidence that, even when inexpensive and useful data can be accessed, people still resort to judgment. There are several reasons for this (Fildes and Goodwin [36]).

i. Many forecasters may lack the training or facilities (such as software) that are required to apply quantitative methods (Watson [141], Hoover et al. [72]);

ii. They may be unaware of the potential benefits of such models;

iii. They may suffer from egocentric discounting of advice, or from algorithm aversion—the human tendency to abandon algorithms quickly after they see them err (Dietvorst et al. [27]; Önkal et al. [108]); but also see Logg et al. [92] who reported 'algorithm appreciation';

iv. They may have a fear of being deskilled if their role as forecasters is replaced by algorithms (De Baets and Harvey [22]);

v. They may require a sense of ownership of the forecasts (Önkal and Gönül [106]);

vi. They may see forecasts, based on their judgments, as a means of demonstrating their expertise (Fildes and Goodwin [36]);

vii. They may be subject to a range of cognitive or motivational biases, which cause them to reject reliable statistical forecasts;

viii. Misunderstanding the forecasting task, they may confuse targets, plans or decisions with forecasts (Goodwin [48]; Fildes et al. [38]); or

ix. They may believe that they have valid extra information that complements or contradicts the information already incorporated into the
quantitative model.

In addition, when models or algorithms are available, people often prefer
to use judgment because they suffer from 'deluded self-confidence' (Kleinmuntz [85]), overconfident that they will 'beat the odds' because they have
real expertise in a domain. Their false perception of expertise can be exacerbated by hindsight bias (Goodwin [51]), which can encourage people to
think that they are better forecasters than they really are, and an illusion that
they have control over the variable they are forecasting (Durand [30]).

16.2.1   The Benefits of Judgment in Forecasting

Although early researchers advised against the widespread use of judgment
in forecasting (Meehl [97]; Carbone and Gorr [17]), there is evidence that,
under the right conditions, judgmental forecasters can provide reliable forecasts and even outperform quantitative methods when a comparison between
the two approaches is possible. These conditions relate to the nature of
the forecasters, the forecasting environment and the characteristics of the
forecasting task.

Moritz et al. [100] have suggested that judgmental forecasters could be
selected based on a cognitive reflection test, which assesses their ability to
balance intuitive judgment with cognitive deliberation. Those performing
well on the test produced more accurate forecasts in an experiment—though
a study by De Baets and Vanderheyden [24] did not find any effect of cognitive reflection on the susceptibility to forecasting biases. Qualities associated
with judgmental forecasting ability have also been extensively explored by
Tetlock [131]. In a study of the performance of experts in estimating the
probabilities of future economic and political events, he found that those he
referred to as 'hedgehogs' were less accurate than guesswork in their predictions. Hedgehogs were characterised by a 'dogged perseverance in believing
in their limited vision of the world', a tendency to 'know one big thing and
toil devotedly within one tradition' and 'a belief that history occurs as a result
of deep underlying laws'. These forecasters were less successful than those
labelled as 'foxes'—experts who are sceptical of dogmatic theories and are
open to re-adjustment in light of recent findings. In later work, Tetlock and
Gardner [132] were able to identify relatively rare people who they termed
superforecasters. Working in groups, these people were able to outperform
intelligence specialists in their prediction of world events. Unlike hedgehogs,

the superforecasters were open-minded, able to blend conflicting arguments, emotionally detached from what they were forecasting, open to challenge, analytical and numerate, and accepting that the world is complex, contradictory and untidy. Subsequent work by Katsagounos et al. [80] suggests that superforecasters can be identified and employed within organisations, even where there is a small pool of potential forecasters to select from. However, it is important to note that these studies relate to probabilistic event forecasting over shorter horizons and it is unclear whether the notion of superforecasters could be successfully applied to situations such as month-to-month product demand forecasting in companies (Goodwin [52], p. 112) or to longer term forecasting problems (Scoblic and Tetlock [122] and associated commentaries).

Even where superforecasters are not available, some environments have characteristics that can favour judgmental forecasters. Psychologists have found that humans have evolved mental shortcuts, known as heuristics, that reduce the information processing demands of judgment and decision-making (Tversky and Kahneman [136]). Heuristics consist of simple rules that people can apply quickly and effortlessly. For example, the recognition heuristic states that when faced with a choice between two products, only one of which is recognised, a purchaser should choose the one that is recognised (Gigerenzer et al. [46]). This rule will work well in an environment where better known products tend to be superior, or more generally where a propensity to recognise an option correlates with its performance. This can apply in some forecasting contexts. For example, Gigerenzer et al. ([46], p. 69) found that laypeople outperformed experts when asked to select stocks that they thought would offer the best future returns. While the experts selected less well-known stocks, the laypeople tended to select stocks that they recognised-dominant companies with large market shares tend to be more profitable and more recognisable. Similar results have been found in sports forecasting. More recognisable football teams and tennis players tend to have a greater probability of winning games (Ayton et al. [5]; Scheibehenne and Broder [121]; Serwe and Frings [123]). The recognition heuristic is an example of where 'less can be more'. The less a person knows about the situation they are forecasting the less likely they are to be distracted by non-diagnostic information that is not useful in the forecasting task.

Other experiments by Gigerenzer and his colleagues (Gigerenzer et al. [46]) have revealed that so-called fast and frugal heuristics can outperform multiple regression when the environment has particular structural characteristics. For example, when a single cue dominates others in its association with the variable to be predicted, judgmental forecasts based on this cue alone can be more accurate than regression models based on multiple cues. This is because, when many cues are available, there is a likelihood that the regression model will reflect accidental correlations in the training dataset between cues and criterion—correlations which fail to be sustained outside this dataset. When data is relatively scarce this is more likely to be an issue because the ratio of the number of cues to the number of available observations may be high.

Several other aspects of the forecasting environment can be advantageous to judgmental rather than algorithmic forecasts. Human forecasters may be able to draw on non-linear relationships between cues and outcomes (Seifert et al. [124]) and configural cues. For example, combinations of cues may have emergent non-linear properties which provide indications that cannot easily be captured by formal models (Einhorn [32])—though developments in artificial intelligence research may mean that this advantage is becoming less marked (e.g., Veksler et al. [140]).

In addition, judgment may perform relatively well in environments where accurate forecasts depend on the ability to adapt speedily to change or disruption (Blattberg and Hoch [12]). The extent to which this advantage applies depends upon the forecaster's ability to identify changed or abnormal circumstances and distinguish these from variation arising from noise (O'Connor et al. [102]). We discuss later the factors that may restrict this ability. However, when changed or abnormal circumstances can be anticipated (e.g., as in the case of forthcoming sales promotions or price increases) research in organisations suggests that judgmental adjustments to statistical forecasts can improve accuracy under some conditions. These include a high level of expertise by those making the adjustments (Alvarado-Valencia et al. [2]) and statistical forecasts that are relatively inaccurate and lacking in credibility (Alvarado-Valencia et al. [2]; Franses and Legerstee [44]). However, empirical studies with a number of supply chain company data sets by Fildes and colleagues ([37, 38]), found that only negative adjustments (i.e., those that reduced the size of the statistical forecast) consistently proved beneficial, possibly because positive adjustments were subject to optimism bias (see later). When sales histories were presented graphically in a laboratory study, Goodwin and Fildes [53] found that judgmental adjustments tended to improve statistical forecasts when the sales promotion effect was strong and the series in normal periods was stationary or subject to low noise. This meant that spikes on a sales graph representing past promotion effects were salient. Recent work (Sroginis et al. [126]) found that it is the most recent promotional peak that has the most influence.

Effectively, when making an adjustment, the forecaster is weighting the statistical forecast and the corresponding conditional judgment. A re-analysis of the Franses and Legerstee and Fildes et al. data (Fildes et al. [37]) has confirmed the weightings are typically inefficient. Nevertheless, in some circumstances such as positive adjustments reweighting leads to improved accuracy. The Covid-19 pandemic of 2020–2021 has provided a particularly pertinent example as in the initial stages of the pandemic, the statistical forecasts for many products were irrelevant and as the pandemic progressed, the relative weights to judgment and the statistical forecast needed updating.

The performance of human judges in selecting appropriate statistical forecasting methods is an area that has only recently been researched. However, two studies suggest that people are proficient in identifying the most accurate method when asked to make a choice between candidates (Petropoulos et al. [116]; De Baets and Harvey [23]). Both studies involved the selection of statistical time series methods, such as variants of exponential smoothing, where past observations were presented on graphs. In [116], judgmental selection rivalled that based on algorithmic selection using the Akaike information criterion (AIC) and it tended to avoid the selection of the worst method more often than algorithmic selection. In [23], participants' ability to identify the best method improved as the difference in the true accuracy of two candidate methods widened. Also, when invited to adjust forecasts judgmentally, people were more influenced by the better performing method. Further research could usefully examine the quality of judgmental selection when contextual information is available in addition to time series data: model specification through the use of dummy event variables is featured in SAP's popular F&R software.

16.2.2 The Drawbacks of Using Judgment in Forecasting

16.2.2.1 Motivational Biases

In some circumstances, judgmental forecasters may be motivated to produce forecasts that do not conform to their true assessment of future outcomes. When their forecast's accuracy is subject to scrutiny, forecasters may be tempted to play safe and set their prediction close to those of other people - a process known as herding (e.g., Hong et al. [71]; Christoffersen and Stæhr [19]). In contrast, other forecasters may have a tendency towards contrarianism (or anti-herding) because they want to stand out from the crowd (e.g., Pierdzioch et al. [117]). The odd extreme forecast that fortuitously turns out to be accurate may be enough to establish your reputation, particularly if it eclipses a record of inaccuracy in people's minds (Henry [69]; Denrell and Fang [25]). Preserving one's reputation may also be a reason for forecasters' reluctance to change forecasts when relevant new information becomes available because such changes may be regarded as a sign of incompetence (Kirchgässner and Müller [83]). When it comes to probability-based forecasts, users may discount overly wide prediction intervals or probabilities that are not close to certainties, even when such forecasts are well calibrated (e.g., Keren [81]; Yaniv and Foster [144]) so forecasters may feel pressurised to exaggerate the level of confidence they have in their predictions (Løhre and Teigen [93]).

Politics can be a major cause of bias in judgmental forecasting (Deschamps [26]). For example, pressure groups may produce distorted forecasts to try to influence government policy or public opinion (Goodwin [52], p. 157). Even respected international institutions are not immune. There is evidence that the International Monetary Fund (IMF) produces 'better' forecasts of growth and inflation when a country is politically aligned to the United States—the IMF's major funder (Dreher et al. [29]). At the company level, forecasts may be exaggerated to attract funding to the forecaster's project (Tyebjee [137]) or to meet the requirements of senior managers. Alternatively, they may be set at unreasonably low levels when people will gain kudos by exceeding the forecast. In financial services, brokerage houses may produce overly optimistic forecasts for investors to attract more trade (Mehran and Stulz [98]). Mello [99] has provided a comprehensive account of the game playing that can be associated with forecasting in supply chain companies. Supply chain planning sees functional biases and political conflict coming into play and these can be seriously damaging. Oliva and Watson[104] showed how these could be overcome through a coordination system that made underlying assumptions explicit and shared information across functions.

Even where forecasts are produced by apparently objective quantitative methods, there is a danger that motivated judgments will distort forecasts. It is known that predictive algorithms can reflect the biases of their authors (Kirkpatrick [84]; O'Neil [105]). Some forecasting software products enable users to manipulate the selection of methods and their parameters and data histories until they obtain forecasts that they are happy with -effectively leading to judgmental forecasts 'by the back door' (Fildes and Goodwin [36]; Ioannidis et al. [74]).

16.2.2.2 Cognitive Factors

Although the human brain is remarkable in its ability to carry out complex tasks of pattern recognition, such as instant facial recognition and language construction, there are limits on its information processing capacity and working memory and this can be detrimental to the performance of judgmental forecasters. Han et al. [62] used brain imaging to show that when more difficult forecasting tasks, such as discerning systematic patterns in noisy time series, placed a higher cognitive load on forecasters, their performance deteriorated. While the heuristics we have evolved to reduce cognitive effort can often provide efficient ways of solving problems as we showed earlier, they can also be unsuited to some tasks and environments and can lead to oversimplifications and cognitive biases (Harvey [65]).

The Effect of Heuristics

In addition to pattern recognition, heuristics that people may rely on in judgmental forecasting include representativeness, availability and anchoring and adjustment (Tversky and Kahneman [136]). Biases can result from each of these heuristics and there is evidence that they can interact and that their effects are prevalent in many organisational forecasts (Karelse [79]). The representativeness heuristic is used to judge the probability that a phenomenon belongs to a particular category, or has originated from a particular process, based on how representative it appears to be of that category or process. For example, in judgmental time series extrapolation, it may be used to assess the likelihood that a time series has been generated by a random process based on the forecaster's assessment of how representative the observed time series is of what they perceive to be a random process. In general, people have a poor conception of randomness and may perceive systematic patterns in the noise appearing in time series (Eggleton [31]). These illusory patterns are then extrapolated when future values of the series need to be forecast because people aim to make these representative of what they have observed in the past series (Harvey [65]). If statistical forecasts are available, these can be subject to damaging adjustments because forecasters may regard forecast errors arising from noise as evidence that the statistical method has failed to recognise predictable patterns (Goodwin and Fildes [53]).

The availability heuristic is used to assess the probability of a given event occurring based on how easily the forecaster can recall or imagine similar events occurring. For example, a recent crash in the stock prices may cause the forecaster to estimate a high probability of the event reoccurring within a specified period. Biases arise when ease of recall or imagination are not associated with an event's probability. Recent vivid or dramatic events and those highlighted in the news media can be unduly influential causing people to estimate high probabilities of reoccurrence, even when they are rare. The availability heuristic can also lead to illusory correlation. This occurs where forecasters have an unsubstantiated prior belief that an independent variable is correlated with the forecast variable, for example that machines manufactured in a given country have higher probability of failure. They may tend to recall instances that confirm their belief, while disconfirming evidence is forgotten. As a result, their conviction that the two variables are related persists.

The anchoring and adjustment heuristic involves a forecaster making an estimate by starting with an initial value (the anchor) and adjusting from it to reach their final estimate. For example, a forecast of next month's sales may start with the current month's sales or perhaps the most recent forecast; this is then adjusted to take in any new information about next month's market conditions. However, people tend to under adjust from the anchor. This can lead to the under estimation of trends because people stay too close to the most recent value when making forecasts (Bolger and Harvey [13]). It is also one reason why prediction intervals tend to be too narrow, given their stated coverage probability, because people anchor on the most likely value and under adjust from it when estimating the interval's bounds (Doyle et al. [28]). This tendency, known as overconfidence, can also occur when forecasters are estimating the range of density forecasts. When estimating subjective probabilities for multiple future events there is evidence that people start by assigning an equal probability to all the events and then adjust from these to reflect their beliefs on the relative likelihood of the events. However, anchoring on their initial equal probabilities causes the resulting probabilities to be too close to a uniform distribution (Fox and Clemen [42]).

Other Cognitive Factors

Several other cognitive factors may have an impact on the quality of judgmental forecasts. Forecasters are more likely to pay attention to items of information that are relatively salient, irrespective of their true value to the forecasting process (Fildes et al. [39]). Recent data, such as the latest observation or forecast error, is likely to be particularly salient (Petropoulos et al. [114]) as will recent contextual information. Recent events may be highly influential when the forecast lead time is short, and this may account for the finding in a study by van den Broeke et al. [138] that company fore-casters made increasing adjustments to statistical forecasts as the sales period got closer, even though these damaged accuracy. Narratives are also likely to attract more attention and be more memorable than statistical informa-tion, even when they are unreliable (Taleb [129]). Statistical forecasts may be adjusted based on persuasive narratives that have no diagnosticity, being based merely on rumours, speculation or samples of one observation (Fildes et al. [39]).

Forecasters may also suffer from the false consensus effect where, for example, they expect that their own preferences for products will be shared by most potential consumers (Belvedere and Goodwin [9]). They may also egocentrically discount advice from experts (or computerised advice) because they have a better understanding of their own rationale for producing a given set of forecasts than those provided by the adviser (Bonaccio and Dalal, 2006). Confidence in an advisor can also be lost when their advice leads to a rare large forecasting error, despite their general track record of accuracy.

The perception of a substantive signal in noise can be exacerbated by people's ability to invent elaborate narratives to explain random movements in series (Fildes and Goodwin [35]). For example, a recent random rise in sales can activate attention to factors that are consistent with higher sales and a neglect of negative factors that are present (Krizan and Windschitl [87]).

The system neglect hypothesis proposed by Massey and Wu [96] provides an additional explanation of why people have a propensity to adjust statis-tical forecasts in the light of recent errors. Variation within a time series and statistical forecast errors are salient while the underlying signal is latent. As a result, there is a tendency to overreact to forecast errors when the environ-ment is relatively stable but underreact in relatively unstable environments when the errors are signalling genuine disruptions or change (O'Connor et al. [102]; Kremer et al. [86]; Petropoulos et al. [114]). This can undermine the potential value of judgment in times of change or disruption.

When a particular future outcome is desired, information favouring the outcome may be accepted at a lower quality threshold, while disconfirming information may be more carefully scrutinised so that its weaknesses are more likely to be uncovered (Krizan and Windschitl [87]). Alternatively, forecasters may deliberately search for information that is consistent with what they hope will happen, thereby manifesting confirmation bias. All of this can result in optimism bias (Fildes et al. [38]).

If statistical point forecasts are accompanied by best- and worst-case narra-tive scenarios intended to highlight the uncertainty associated with the forecast, this may also damage accuracy (Goodwin et al. [55]). The scenario that is congruent with the latest movement in the series (e.g., a best-case sales scenario and an upward movement) can exacerbate the tendency to focus on this recent movement, while the opposite scenario is discounted. The presentation of opposite scenarios has also been found to have a contrast effect (e.g., Herr et al. [70]). For example, when participants in a study by Goodwin et al. [56] were asked to make a forecast, under the assumption a pessimistic scenario would prevail, they tended to make even more pessimistic forecasts when an optimistic scenario was also presented. Normatively, the opposing scenarios belong to different independent possible future worlds and hence the presentation of (say) a best-case scenario should have no effect on forecasts based on the opposite scenario. There is also a danger of forecasts being distorted by scenario bias. The more detailed a scenario is, the more probable it may appear to be, while its true probability of occurring diminishes as more details are added (Kahneman [78], p. 159). Nevertheless, some of the evidence on the benefits or disbenefits of providing scenarios to forecasters is contradictory and the area would benefit from more research (Önkal et al. [110]).

When estimating the probability of future events, such as the probability that a new business will survive for the next twelve months, forecasters may be tempted to discount relevant statistical information when it is available in the form of a base rate. Their focus on the specific case they are forecasting can cause them to neglect the wider picture and what this may reveal. For example, statistics may reveal that only 20 per cent of similar business survive for a year (this is the base rate) but a person planning a new business may be tempted to regard their own plans as unique and estimate there is a 90 per cent chance of survival. In one study this tendency was intensified because the focus of prospective entrepreneurs was on formulating their own detailed financial plans. (Cassar [18]). This fostered what Kahneman [78] has called an 'inside view', which is to be contrasted with an outside view that involves considering the percentage of similar cases that have succeeded. People's preference for narratives, at the expense of statistical information, can also lead to base rate neglect, the two factors reinforcing each other.

Finally, in organisations, forecasts are often finalised by groups of people in meetings (Fildes and Goodwin [36]). As a result, they can reflect the views of the most loquacious, domineering, or high-status group members, irrespective of their ability to forecast. Where the group is highly cohesive, insulated, under stress and has a dictatorial leader who spurns methodological procedures, there can be insufficient debate about possible future outcomes and a pressure to conform. This phenomenon, known as groupthink (Janis [75]), can be associated with an unwillingness to search for new information and selective bias when processing information that is available. The result can be unmerited optimism and a failure to acknowledge the risk associated with forecasts. Groupthink can also adversely affect the judgment of analysts applying quantitative models when they select methods or relevant variables (Ioannidis et al. [74]).

16.3 Strategies for Improving the Role of Judgment in Forecasting

16.3.1 Providing Feedback

Feedback on the performance of judgmental forecasts can be provided with the aim of helping forecasters to learn how to make improvements. However, to be effective, feedback needs to be timely, unambiguous, easily comprehended and indicative of how improvements can be achieved. It should also avoid oversensitivity to recent forecast errors, which may merely reflect noise, while simultaneously being responsive to underlying changes in a forecaster's performance.

In the case of point forecasts, simply feeding back the latest observation or forecast error, known as outcome feedback, fails to meet these criteria. It provides no indication of how future forecasts might be improved and exacerbates the tendency to focus on the most recent observation. Forecasters will be unable to discern whether their latest error is due to noise or a deficiency in their forecast and they may overreact unnecessarily. Feeding back accuracy, averaged over several periods, can mitigate this problem to some extent, but an accuracy metric alone will still provide no guidance on the cause of any deficiencies. In contrast, feeding back a measure of bias, such as the mean error, will indicate whether forecasts tend to be too high or too low by a certain amount and thereby specify potential improvements (Petropoulos et al. [115]). The value of feedback may also be greater when it is provided in a variety of forms and combined with formal training (Legerstee and Franses [90]).

For probability forecasts several forms of feedback are available, including simple outcome feedback, which reveals whether the event in question occurred, and calibration feedback, which reveals the extent to which estimated probabilities conformed to the percentage of times an event occurred on those occasions when given probabilities were put forward. Outcome feedback was ineffective in a study where participants were asked to estimate the probability of college football teams winning sporting contests in a study by

Benson and Önkal [10]. However, calibration feedback improved probability forecasts because it indicated whether these probabilities tended to be too high or low. It was also the most effective form in a study of stock market probability forecasting by Önkal and Muradoglu [109].

There is, however, some evidence that outcome feedback is more effective in helping judgmental forecasters to produce better calibrated prediction intervals. This is because people estimating overly narrow intervals will frequently experience outcomes that fall outside their intervals (Goodwin et al. [57]). Nevertheless, where the time period between the production of a forecast and the outcome feedback is long people may fail to recall how their previous estimates fared. In this case, the provision of calibration reports, such as: 'Your 95% prediction intervals only captured the true outcome on 30% of occasions', is likely to be more effective (Bolger and Önkal-Atay [14]).

In short, based on a number of studies, feedback is of limited value in improving accuracy. Research on the benefits with regard to bias and calibration has been limited, but perhaps because both measures suggest an easily implemented action, there is greater potential for improvement (and further influential research).

16.3.2 Providing Advice

Advice on forecasting can come from a human or be produced from software. In the latter case, an algorithm-based forecast can be regarded as a form of advice. To be useful, advice has not only to be accurate, but it must also overcome the barriers of egocentric discounting and scepticism (Bonaccio and Dalal [15]). There is evidence that advice from a machine is more likely to attract scepticism than that for a human (Önkal et al. [108]). However, if advice is from a human, their presumed credibility, based on their status, can interact in complex ways with their credibility as experienced from their track record, when determining the extent to which their advice is used (Önkal et al. [107]). When multiple advisors are available, people are better at assessing the relative quality of their advice than using this advice to produce a forecast, suggesting that it is best to combine the advice mechanically based on the judges' estimates of quality (Harvey et al. [66]). When there are some advisors with dissenting opinions, people tend to discount their views. However, feedback on the advisors' accuracy can enable them to learn to rely on outlying opinions when these are accurate (Harries et al. [68]).

Advice can have a stronger effect if people are asked to suspend making their judgment until after they have received it (Yaniv and Choshen-Hillel

[143]). However, when forecasters are less knowledgeable than their advisors, they should consider avoiding making their own forecasts altogether (Harvey and Harries [67]). Other research has indicated that, although advice suggesting a particular forecast is likely to improve the final adjusted forecast's accuracy, such advice is likely to be less successful in promoting learning than informative guidance (i.e., the provision of unbiased, relevant information without a specific suggestion) (Parikh, Fazlollahi, and Verma [112]). Explanations behind the proffered advice can increase trust, (Gönül et al. [47]), but the most appropriate format for these explanations requires further research (Alvarado-Valencia and Barrero [1]). This issue is of developing importance when the advice is derived from an opaque machine learning algorithm. Baker [7] has made interesting suggestions as to how 'fuzzy' advice can nudge forecasters towards a desired adjustment. In his study machine learning classification techniques were used to predict whether a judgmental adjustment would improve or reduce a forecast's accuracy. A requirement to document reasons for contravening this 'advice', for example, would be likely to nudge forecasters away from frivolous adjustments (Goodwin [49]).

16.3.3   Restrictiveness

An alternative to providing advice to people is to restrict their judgments to circumstances where they are likely to improve accuracy. Research in organisations indicates that forecasters often make small adjustments to statistical forecasts which tend to slightly reduce accuracy and transparently waste time (Fildes et al. [38]). This suggests that restricting adjustments to those above a certain size may be beneficial (see for example, Petropoulos et al. [114]). However, a study by Goodwin et al. [54] found that this simply encouraged forecasters to make larger adjustments to get around the constraint, even though these were unnecessary, and this further damaged accuracy. Nevertheless, there have only been a limited number of studies on the effectiveness of restrictiveness and it is an area which merits further research.

16.3.4   Decomposition

Decomposition aims to make the judgmental task easier, and hence more accurate, by breaking down the hard-to-forecast whole into easier components before reconstituting the resulting judgments to make the overall forecast. This also has the advantage that it can yield a documented and defensible rationale to underpin the forecast.

MacGregor [94] summarised the evidence in favour of decomposition in the early 2000s, suggesting that its use should be confined to situations where uncertainty about the target quantity is high. In other situations, a component might have greater uncertainty than the target quantity and lead to a less accurate forecast than a holistic estimate. Webby et al. [142] found that point forecasts of the combined effect of multiple special events that were due to impact on future demand were more accurate when the effect of each event was assessed individually. Similarly, Lee and Siemsen [89] found that breaking down newsvendor order quantity decisions into point forecasts, uncertainty judgments, and service level decisions led to improved performance, especially when it was accompanied by decision support in the form of advice. The process also enabled specific issues associated with each type of judgment to be addressed individually. Decomposition also allows the forecasting task to be divided into components best performed by algorithmic models and those where judgment is advantageous (Seifert et al. [124]). For example, compartmentalising the use of judgment and hard data can be exploited when event trees are used to obtain forecasts of the probability of rare events (Goodwin and Wright [58]).

Some research has suggested that the tendency of judgmental forecasters to estimate overly narrow prediction intervals can be reduced through decomposition. People are generally better at estimating a probability for a given interval (e.g. the probability that the interval £300 to £500 units will capture the unit cost of materials) than they are at estimating a prediction interval that will have a fixed probability (e.g. a 95% prediction interval for unit costs) (Teigen and Jørgensen [130]). A simple decomposition method called SPIES (Subjective Probability Interval Estimates) allows this advantage to be exploited (Haran and Moore [63]). For example, in a cost forecasting task, forecasters would first estimate the lowest and highest possible costs. This range is then divided into subranges and points assigned to each to reflect their relative probability of including the actual unit cost. Probabilities for the subranges are obtained by normalising the points so they sum to 100. SPIES appears to improve the calibration of prediction intervals (Haran et al. [64]), but can also be used to elicit complete density forecasts. The technique also forces decision makers to consider the possibility of extreme outcomes and hence decreases overconfidence (Ren and Croson [118]).

Decomposition can also be applied to obtain density forecasts when possible outcomes depend on several factors by using Monte-Carlo simulation (Sugiyama [127]). For example, to forecast the demand for a product, a probability distribution is estimated for each factor for which the outcome is uncertain, such as weather conditions, advertising effectiveness and competitors' actions. Some of these distributions may be obtained empirically while others will be based on judgment. Outcomes from each distribution are then sampled and combined to determine the resulting demand. A probability distribution for the forecast variable is obtained by repeating this process thousands of times and recording the relative frequency of occurrence of different levels of demand.

Despite what we judge to be the popularity of decomposition in practice, for example in new product forecasting, there has been little documentation and evaluation of its effectiveness since MacGregor's summary [94]. It offers a means for overcoming the complexities in any forecasting study and deserves more attention by researchers.

16.3.5 Correcting Forecasts

Biases caused by motivational or cognitive factors can significantly reduce the accuracy of forecasts based on judgment. Mean bias occurs in point forecasts when they exhibit a systematic tendency to forecast too high or low. Regression bias is evident where the systematic discrepancy between the forecasts and outcomes is associated with the size of the forecast. It occurs where a unit increase in the judgmental point forecast tends to be systematically greater or less than a unit increase in the outcome so that, for example, relatively low forecasts may be too high while relatively high forecasts tend to be too low (Davydenko and Goodwin [21]). Theil [133] showed that both biases can be removed from a set of past forecasts by fitting the regression line: $A_t = a + b \times F_t$, where A_t = the actual outcome for period t and F_t is the forecast for that period, and replacing A_t in the equation with a corrected forecast, C_t where $C_t = a + b \times F_t$. This equation can be used to correct future forecasts on the assumption that biases observed in the past will continue (e.g., see Blanc and Setzer [11]). This process is likely to be unsuccessful if forecasters react by putting less effort into their forecasts or by trying to pre-empt the correction.

Where the forecaster is using multiple cues, any inconsistency in their use can be removed by regressing their past forecasts on to these cues in a process known as judgmental bootstrapping (O'Connor et al. [103]). The resulting equation is then used to replace the forecaster in the future. The success of this strategy depends on knowing which cues the forecaster has been using, which is particularly problematical in time series extrapolation. It also depends on the assumption that the forecaster has not been exploiting non-linear relationships between the forecast variable and the cues. Fildes [34] showed that forecasts, where there are biases in the weights attached to cues, can be corrected by regressing past forecast errors on to the values of the cues and adjusting future forecasts by the predicted errors. This has been applied to judgmental adjustments with positive results (Fildes et al. [38]).

Where biases of different departments in an organisation are intentional, they may act in opposite directions because some groups favour over-forecasting while others aim to under forecast. Pennings et al. [113] simulated this situation in a laboratory experiment and found that estimating and removing 'constant' biases could lead to substantial increases in forecast accuracy. One key under-researched issue is (again) organisational implementation of forecast correction.

16.3.6 Other Improvement Strategies

Researchers have tested several other strategies for improving judgmental forecasts. Theocharis and Harvey [135] found that judgmental time series extrapolations were more accurate when the time series presented to them were either very short (even involving just one observation) or relatively long (20 to 40 observations). Presenting an intermediate number of observations (such as five) apparently tempted people to see false patterns in the series. In contrast, one observation forced them to make a naive forecast (i.e., a forecast that equals the most recent observation)—such forecasts can be relatively accurate in many situations—while over 20 observations allowed them to discern real patterns within the data. The same researchers found that when the judgmental extrapolation is required for several periods into the future, the common bias of underestimating the trend can be overcome by eliciting the forecast for the most distant horizon first. Judgmental interpolation can then be used to obtain forecasts for the intermediate periods (Theocharis and Harvey [134]).

Moritz et al. [100] found that point forecasts of time series could be improved by constraining the amount of time allowed for making forecasts between a lower and upper bound. This avoided errors arising from tendencies to either underthink the forecast by making it too quickly or overthinking it by having too much time available. In another time series forecasting experiment, Kim et al. [82] found that competition between forecasters improved accuracy for those who were told, truthfully or otherwise, that their accuracy was inferior to those of other forecasters.

When it comes to estimating probabilities for future events people tend to produce better calibrated estimates when the elicitation questions are framed in terms of relative frequencies. This is because such judgments accord with the natural way in which people think (Gigerenzer and Hoffrage [45]). For example, it would be preferable to ask: 'Out of 100 new restaurants of this type, how many do you think will still be in business after one year?' as opposed to: 'What is the probability that this new restaurant will still be in business after one year?'

16.3.7 Improving Forecasts from Groups

Many judgmental forecasts are made by groups of people, particularly those of strategic importance. Groups have the power to draw on a wider range of information sources and perspectives than individuals and when people submit forecasts independently, their average forecast can be relatively accurate because of the so-called wisdom of crowds (Surowiecki [128]). Diversity among group members is likely to be particularly advantageous even where some members tend to produce relatively inaccurate forecasts (Brown and Reade [16]). Competition and feedback to group members can also improve their individual forecast accuracy and hence improve the group estimate (Atanasov et al. [4]). However, the advantage of the wisdom of crowds can be diminished if people are aware of each other's forecasts and devices designed to restrict them to their own private information have been found to be effective (Da and Huang [20]). Where people have access to shared information, an alternative is to use an approach called pivoting where people are asked to estimate the average forecast of the group in addition to making their own forecast (Palley and Soll [111]). This allows an estimate to be made of the extent to which an individual's forecast results from shared information, leading to an adjusted group forecast.

While there are advantages to restricting access to other group members' information and forecasts, these methods also exclude the potential benefits of interaction that can be found in meetings, such as learning from others and exchanging information. Nevertheless, when people meet to agree forecasts, pressures to conform and the dominance of some group members can restrict debate and reduce accuracy. The Delphi method tackles these problems by ensuring the anonymity of group members while, allowing an, albeit restricted, interchange of information and discussion (Rowe and Wright [119, 120]). The method involves carefully selected panellists providing forecasts anonymously to a convenor. The convenor then feeds back statistical summaries (e.g. medians and ranges) of the group's estimates to the panel members and asks them to reconsider their original forecasts in the light of this feedback. The process usually proceeds for two to three rounds and there is evidence that its use can improve forecast accuracy (e.g., Lin et al. [91]).

Belton et al. [8] provide guidelines for the effective application of Delphi. One of the most important is that panellist's forecasts should be accompanied by an anonymous written rationale, allowing the convenor to circulate these alongside the feedback. Without this, panellists may have little reason to adjust their original forecasts.

Where probabilistic forecasts are required, an alternative is to use prediction markets where assets are bought and sold that have a final value depending on whether a specified event occurs or not (Vaughan Williams et al. [139]). The current price of the asset is assumed to reflect the market's view of the probability that the event will occur. Unlike the Delphi method , these markets aim to benefit accuracy by providing incentives for people to produce accurate forecasts and by allowing the group's forecasts to instantly react to new information. However, they have several limitations, including the fact that the only shared information is the current price of the asset. This can lead to cascades where small initial price changes lead to large unwarranted larger changes because people believe others have new information that they are not privy to. They react by buying or selling assets and so amplify the original price change. Green et al. [61] and Graefe and Armstrong [59] have provided a detailed comparison of the relative benefits of the Delphi method and prediction markets.

Atanasov et al. [4] discuss a form of group forecasting for probabilities, called team polling, that is more open than Delphi. This involves teams, typically 15 forecasters, working online to share information and views. Team members encourage each other to update their forecasts when appropriate. A team is not required to reach a consensus, instead they make individual predictions and the average of these becomes the group's forecast. The team members receive feedback on accuracy in the form of Brier scores. and a leader board fosters a competitive attitude. This approach was found to lead to more accurate forecasts than prediction markets, when individuals' forecasts were weighted based on past performance, and how recently the forecast was made, and then recalibrated.

16.3.8 Integrating Judgment with Algorithm-based Forecasts

Integrating judgmental and algorithmic forecasts can lead to greater accuracy when it draws on the complementary strengths of the different methods (e.g., Song et al. [125]). It is one of the most common approaches in supply chain forecasting [126]. As with group forecasting, integrating the approaches also allows forecasts to draw on a wider range of information sources. Arvan et al. [3] have provided an extensive review of integration methods.

Integration can be carried out in several ways. Algorithm-based forecasts can be judgmentally adjusted; independent judgmental and statistical forecasts can be combined, for example through averaging; judgmental forecasts can be treated as an independent variable in a regression model alongside other cues; and Bayesian methods can treat judgmental forecasts as priors that can be updated as statistical data becomes available. In the latter case there has been relatively little progress where time series forecasts are concerned since initial developments in the 1980s and evidence for the relative efficacy of Bayesian methods is sparse (Arvan et al. [3]).

When algorithmic forecasts of time series require judgmental adjustment because of forthcoming special events, Marmier and Cheikhrouhou [95] recommended a three-stage structured approach. This involved first removing nonperiodic events from time series and using statistical methods to forecast the 'cleansed' series. Next, factors that influence the likely future disruption to the regular time series are identified along with judgmental assessments of the nature of their effect (e.g., transient or trend change). The forecaster's judgments of the size of each effect are then quantified using a formal scale. These effects are summed in the third stage and added to the statistical forecast. As we saw earlier, Baker [7] has also made proposals for implementing a process that advises on the circumstances when adjustments should be made, with conditional recommendations on the direction and size of adjustment.

The accuracy of adjustments is likely to improve with better quality information. Eksoz et al. [33] conducted a survey of European and North American food manufacturers and reported that collaboration and information sharing both within and between organisations improved accuracy. In some cases, useful information about forthcoming special events is likely to be retrievable from the past. In an experiment relating to product promotions, Lee et al. [88] found that a support system that identified the most similar past promotions, displayed their details and estimated their effect on demand, enabled people to produce more accurate adjustments for future promotions.

There is a danger that adjustments to statistical forecasts will suffer from a tendency of people to anchor on the statistical forecasts and under adjust from them (de Baets and Harvey [22]; Fildes et al. [39]). Combining independent statistical and judgmental forecasts, through averaging for example, can overcome this problem, and this approach has worked well in areas such as sales and election forecasting (Blattberg and Hoch [12]; Graefe et al. [60]).

Combining can be effective where there is tendency for judgmental adjustments to be in the right direction but too large -though it has proved to be sub-optimal compared to 'correction' (Fildes et al. [38]; Goodwin [50]). However, as judgment should usually be reserved for periods where there are special circumstances, the indiscriminate application of combining to all periods does not seem sensible.

Other researchers have investigated the effectiveness of incorporating judgmental forecasts as another predictor variable in the statistical forecasting model. Franses and Legerstee [44] found that this approach worked best where the model forecasts were poor in an application to the demand forecasts of a pharmaceutical company. Baecke et al. [6] found that it improved demand forecasts for an international publishing company in all circumstances they examined. The approach even appears to improve accuracy where judgmental point forecasts are less accurate than algorithmic forecasts because the algorithm filters out the inconsistency of the human forecaster (Ibrahim et al. [73]).

Implementing more effective methods of integration presents problems in practice in that every procedure posits an authoritative forecaster with the power to over-ride and modify the initial judgmental input, thereby down-weighting the individual expert. Yet again, we point out there is no research as to the feasibility of the various suggestions beyond straightforward judgmental adjustment.

16.4   Conclusions

Judgment has proved its value in domains as diverse as macroeconomic forecasting (Franses et al. [43]), demand planning for the supply chain (Fildes et al. [38]) and software engineering (Jørrgensen [76], Jørrgensen et al. [77]). Some researchers have recently argued that, in an era of enhanced artificial intelligence and machine learning, human judgment will soon have no role to play in forecasting. However, even if forecasts from these advanced technologies prove to be generally more accurate than judgment, it seems unlikely that judgmental forecasters will become redundant any time soon. In fact, Jørgensen [76] argues that it is the particular circumstances that will define the relative performance characteristics. Accuracy too is not the only criterion for the choice of forecasting methods. The need to have a sense of ownership of forecasts and to display one's expertise, unwarranted belief in judgment, scepticism about machine-based forecasts, particularly those that lack transparency, and a lack of access to advanced software and the specialist knowledge needed to apply it-these are all factors that are likely to sustain a pivotal role for humans in many situations. Moreover, in a turbulent world where historical data has limited predictive potential, it is not clear that machine-based methods will always have the upper hand when it comes to accuracy: the Covid-19 pandemic provides a graphic example. Continuing research to improve the role of judgment in forecasting is therefore warranted. In particular, the provision of enhanced forecasting software, designed to support judgment, is likely to be as desirable in the future as the development of more sophisticated forecasting algorithms.

References

1. Alvarado-Valencia, J. A., and Barrero, L. H. (2014). Reliance, trust and heuristics in judgmental forecasting. Computers in Human Behavior, 36, 102–113.
2. Alvarado-Valencia, J., Barrero, L. H., Önkal, D., and Dennerlein, J. T. (2017). Expertise, credibility of system forecasts and integration methods in judgmental demand forecasting. International Journal of Forecasting, 33(1), 298–313.
3. Arvan, M., Fahimnia, B., Reisi, M., and Siemsen, E. (2019). Integrating human judgement into quantitative forecasting methods: A review. Omega, 86, 237–252.
4. Atanasov, P., Rescober, P., Stone, E., Swift, S.A., Servan-Schreiber, E., Tetlock, P., Ungar, L., and Mellers, B. (2017). Distilling the wisdom of crowds: Prediction markets vs. prediction polls. Management Science, 63(3), 691–706.
5. Ayton, P., Önkal, D., and McReynolds, L. (2011). Effects of ignorance and information on judgments and decisions. Judgment and Decision Making, 6(5), 381–391.
6. Baecke, P., De Baets, S., and Vanderheyden, K. (2017). Investigating the added value of integrating human judgement into statistical demand forecasting systems. International Journal of Production Economics, 191, 85–96.
7. Baker, J. (2021). Maximizing forecast value added through machine learning and "nudges". Foresight: The International Journal of Applied Forecasting, 60, 8–15.
8. Belton, I., MacDonald, A., Wright, G., and Hamlin, I. (2019). Improving the practical application of the Delphi method in group-based judgment: A six-step prescription for a well-founded and defensible process. Technological Forecasting and Social Change, 147, 72–82.
9. Belvedere, V., and Goodwin, P. (2017). The influence of product involvement and emotion on short-term product demand forecasting. International Journal of Forecasting, 33(3), 652–661.

10. Benson, P. G., and Önkal, D. (1992). The effects of feedback and training on the performance of probability forecasters. International Journal of Forecasting, 8(4), 559–573.

11. Blanc, S. M., and Setzer, T. (2015). Analytical debiasing of corporate cash flow forecasts. European Journal of Operational Research, 243(3), 1004–1015.

12. Blattberg, R. C., and Hoch, S. J. (2010). Database models and managerial intuition: 50% model+ 50% manager. Management Science, 36, 887–899.

13. Bolger, F., and Harvey, N. (1993). Context-sensitive heuristics in statistical reasoning. The Quarterly Journal of Experimental Psychology Section A, 46(4), 779–811.

14. Bolger, F., and Önkal-Atay, D. (2004). The effects of feedback on judgmental interval predictions. International Journal of Forecasting, 20(1), 29–39.

15. Bonaccio, S., and Dalal, R. S. (2006). Advice taking and decision-making: An integrative literature review, and implications for the organizational sciences. Organizational Behavior and Human Decision Processes, 101(2), 127–151.

16. Brown, A., and Reade, J. J. (2019). The wisdom of amateur crowds: Evidence from an online community of sports tipsters. European Journal of Operational Research, 272, 1073–1081.

17. Carbone, R., and Gorr, W. L. (1985). Accuracy of judgmental forecasting of time series. Decision Sciences, 16(2), 153–160.

18. Cassar, G. (2010). Are individuals entering self-employment overly optimistic? An empirical test of plans and projections on nascent entrepreneur expectations. Strategic Management Journal, 31, 822–840.

19. Christoffersen, J., and Stæhr, S. (2019). Individual risk tolerance and herding behaviors in financial forecasts. European Financial Management, 25(5), 1348–1377.

20. Da, Z., and Huang, X. (2020). Harnessing the wisdom of crowds. Management Science, 66, 1847–1867.

21. Davydenko, A., and Goodwin, P. (2021). Assessing point forecast bias across multiple time series: Measures and visual tools. International Journal of Statistics and Probability, 10, 46-69.

22. De Baets, S., and Harvey, N. (2018). Forecasting from time series subject to sporadic perturbations: Effectiveness of different types of forecasting support. International Journal of Forecasting, 34(2), 163–180.

23. De Baets, S., and Harvey, N. (2020). Using judgment to select and adjust forecasts from statistical models. European Journal of Operational Research, 284(3), 882–895.

24. De Baets, S., and Vanderheyden, K. (2021). Individual differences in the susceptibility to forecasting biases. Applied Cognitive Psychology, 35(4), 1106-1114.

25. Denrell, J., and Fang, C. (2010). Predicting the next big thing: Success as a signal of poor judgment. Management Science, 56(10), 1653–1667.

26. Deschamps, E. (2004). The impact of institutional change on forecast accuracy: A case study of budget forecasting in Washington State. International Journal of Forecasting, 20(4), 647–657.

27. Dietvorst, B. J., Simmons, J. P., and Massey, C. (2018). Overcoming algorithm aversion: People will use imperfect algorithms if they can (even slightly) modify them. Management Science, 64(3), 1155–1170.

28. Doyle, J., Ojiako, U., Marshall, A., Dawson, I., and Brito, M. (2021). The anchoring heuristic and overconfidence bias among frontline employees in supply chain organizations. Production Planning and Control, 32, 549–566.

29. Dreher, A., Marchesi, S., and Vreeland, J. R. (2008). The political economy of IMF forecasts. Public Choice, 137(1–2), 145–171.

30. Durand, R. (2003). Predicting a firm's forecasting ability: The roles of organizational illusion of control and organizational attention. Strategic Management Journal, 24(9), 821–838.

31. Eggleton, I. R. (1982). Intuitive time-series extrapolation. Journal of Accounting Research, 20, 68–102.

32. Einhorn, H. J. (1974). Cue definition and residual judgment. Organizational Behavior and Human Performance, 12(1), 30–49.

33. Eksoz, C., Mansouri, S. A., Bourlakis, M., and Önkal, D. (2019). Judgmental adjustments through supply integration for strategic partnerships in food chains. Omega, 87, 20–33.

34. Fildes, R. (1991). Efficient use of information in the formation of subjective industry forecasts. Journal of Forecasting, 10(6), 597–617.

35. Fildes, R., and Goodwin, P. (2007). Good and bad judgement in forecasting: Lessons from four companies. Foresight, 8, 5–10.

36. Fildes, R., and Goodwin, P. (2021). Stability in the inefficient use of forecasting systems: A case study in a supply chain company. International Journal of Forecasting, 37(2), 1031-1046.

37. Fildes, R., Goodwin, P., De Baets, S., and Sroginis, A. (2021). Stylised facts of forecast value added, a meta-analysis—Where do judgmental adjustments improve accuracy? International Symposium on Forecasting: ISF2021.

38. Fildes, R., Goodwin, P., Lawrence, M., and Nikolopoulos, K. (2009). Effective forecasting and judgmental adjustments: An empirical evaluation and strategies for improvement in supply-chain planning. International Journal of Forecasting, 25(1), 3–23.

39. Fildes, R., Goodwin, P., and Önkal, D. (2019). Use and misuse of information in supply chain forecasting of promotion effects. International Journal of Forecasting, 35(1), 144–156.

40. Fildes, R., Ma, S., and Kolassa, S. (in press). Retail forecasting: Research and practice. International Journal of Forecasting.

41. Fildes, R., and Petropoulos, F. (2015). Improving forecast quality in practice. Foresight: The International Journal of Applied Forecasting, 36, 5–12.

42. Fox, C. R., and Clemen, R. T. (2005). Subjective probability assessment in decision analysis: Partition dependence and bias toward the ignorance prior. Management Science, 51(9), 1417–1432.

43. Franses, P. H., Kranendonk, H. C., and Lanser, D. (2011). One model and various experts: Evaluating Dutch macroeconomic forecasts. International Journal of Forecasting, 27, 482–495.

44. Franses, P. H., and Legerstee, R. (2013). Do statistical forecasting models for SKU-level data benefit from including past expert knowledge? International Journal of Forecasting, 29, 80–87.

45. Gigerenzer, G., and Hoffrage, U. (1995). How to improve Bayesian reasoning without instruction: Frequency formats. Psychological Review, 102(4), 684–704.

46. Gigerenzer, G., Todd, P. M., and the ABC Team. (2000). Simple heuristics that make us smart. Oxford: Oxford University Press.

47. Gönül, S., Önkal, D., and Goodwin, P. (2009). Expectations, use and judgmental adjustment of external financial and economic forecasts: An empirical investigation. Journal of Forecasting, 28(1), 19–37.

48. Goodwin, P. (1996). Statistical correction of judgmental point forecasts and decisions. Omega, 24(5), 551–559.

49. Goodwin, P. (2000a). Improving the voluntary integration of statistical forecasts and judgment. International Journal of Forecasting, 16(1), 85–99.

50. Goodwin, P. (2000b). Correct or combine? Mechanically integrating judgmental forecasts with statistical methods. International Journal of Forecasting, 16(2), 261–275.

51. Goodwin, P. (2010). Why hindsight can damage foresight. The International Journal of Applied Forecasting, 17, 5–7.

52. Goodwin, P. (2017). Forewarned: A Sceptic's guide to prediction. London: Biteback Publishing.

53. Goodwin, P., and Fildes, R. (1999). Judgmental forecasts of time series affected by special events: Does providing a statistical forecast improve accuracy? Journal of Behavioral Decision Making, 12(1), 37–53.

54. Goodwin, P., Fildes, R., Lawrence, M., and Stephens, G. (2011). Restrictiveness and guidance in support systems. Omega, 39(3), 242–253.

55. Goodwin, P., Gönül, M. S., and Önkal, D. (2019a). When providing optimistic and pessimistic scenarios can be detrimental to judgmental demand forecasts and production decisions. European Journal of Operational Research, 273(3), 992–1004.

56. Goodwin, P., Gönül, S., Önkal, D., Kocabıyıkoğlu, A., and Göğüş, C. I. (2019b). Contrast effects in judgmental forecasting when assessing the implications of worst and best case scenarios. Journal of Behavioral Decision Making, 32(5), 536–549.

57. Goodwin, P., Önkal-Atay, D., Thomson, M. E., Pollock, A. C., and Macaulay, A. (2004). Feedback-labelling synergies in judgmental stock price forecasting. Decision Support Systems, 37(1), 175–186.

58. Goodwin, P., and Wright, G. (2010). The limits of forecasting methods in anticipating rare events. Technological Forecasting and Social Change, 77(3), 355–368.
59. Graefe, A., and Armstrong, J. S. (2011). Comparing face-to-face meetings, nominal groups, Delphi and prediction markets on an estimation task. International Journal of Forecasting, 27(1), 183–195.
60. Graefe, A., Armstrong, J. S., Jones Jr, R. J., and Cuzán, A. G. (2014). Combining forecasts: An application to elections. International Journal of Forecasting, 30(1), 43–54.
61. Green, K., Armstrong, J. S., and Graefe, A. (2007). Methods to elicit forecasts from groups. Delphi and prediction markets compared. Foresight: The International Journal of Applied Forecasting, 8, 17–20.
62. Han, W., Wang, X., Petropoulos, F., and Wang, J. (2019). Brain imaging and forecasting: Insights from judgmental model selection. Omega, 87, 1–9.
63. Haran, U., and Moore, D. A. (2014). A simple tool for making better forecasts. http://blogs.hbr.org/2014/05/a-simple-tool-for-making-better-forecasts/
64. Haran, U., Moore, D. A., and Morewedge, C. K. (2010). A simple remedy for overprecision in judgment. Judgment and Decision Making, 5(7), 467–476.
65. Harvey, N. (2007). Use of heuristics: Insights from forecasting research. Thinking and Reasoning, 13(1), 5–24.
66. Harvey, N., Harries, C., and Fischer, I. (2000). Using advice and assessing its quality. Organizational Behavior and Human Decision Processes, 81(2), 252–273.
67. Harvey, N., and Harries, C. (2004). Effects of judges' forecasting on their later combination of forecasts for the same outcomes. International Journal of Forecasting, 20(3), 391–409.
68. Harries, C., Yaniv, I., and Harvey, N. (2004). Combining advice: The weight of a dissenting opinion in the consensus. Journal of Behavioral Decision Making, 17(5), 333–348.
69. Henry, G. B. (1989). Wall Street economists: Are they worth their salt? Business Economics, 10, 44–48.
70. Herr, P. M., Sherman, S. J., and Fazio, R. H. (1983). On the consequences of priming: Assimilation and contrast effects. Journal of Experimental Social Psychology, 19(4), 323–340.
71. Hong, H., Kubik, J. D., and Solomon, A. (2000). Security analysts' career concerns and herding of earnings forecasts. The Rand Journal of Economics, 121–144.
72. Hoover, J. and the UFO Project Team. (2021). The UFO project: Initial survey results. Foresight: The International Journal of Applied Forecasting, 60, 45–48.
73. Ibrahim, R., Kim, S. H., and Tong, J. (2021). Eliciting human judgment for prediction algorithms. Management Science, 67(4), 2314-2325.

74. Ioannidis, J. P., Cripps, S., and Tanner, M. A. (2021). Forecasting for COVID-19 has failed. International Journal of Forecasting. Forthcoming

75. Janis, I. (1991). Groupthink. In E. Griffin (Ed.) A First Look at Communication Theory, pp. 235–246. New York: McGrawHill.

76. Jorgensen, M. (2007). How should we compare forecasting models with expert judgement? International Journal of Forecasting, 23, 473–474.

77. Jørgensen, M., Boehm, B., and Rifkin, S. (2009). Software development effort estimation: Formal models or expert judgment?. IEEE Software, 26(2), 14–19.

78. Kahneman, D. (2011). Thinking, Fast and Slow. London: Allen Lane.

79. Karelse, J. (2021). Mitigating unconscious bias in forecasting. Foresight: The International Journal of Applied Forecasting, (61), 5–14.

80. Katsagounos, I., Thomakos, D. D., Litsiou, K., and Nikolopoulos, K. (2020). Superforecasting reality check: Evidence from a small pool of experts and expedited identification. European Journal of Operational Research, 289(1), 107–117.

81. Keren, G. (1997). On the calibration of probability judgments: Some critical comments and alternative perspectives. Journal of Behavioral Decision Making, 10, 269–278.

82. Kim, H. Y., Lee, Y. S., and Jun, D. B. (2018). The effect of relative performance feedback on judgmental forecasting accuracy. Management Decision, 57, 1695–1711.

83. Kirchgässner, G., and Müller, U. K. (2006). Are forecasters reluctant to revise their predictions? Some German evidence. Journal of Forecasting, 25(6), 401–413.

84. Kirkpatrick, K. (2016). Battling algorithmic bias: How do we ensure algorithms treat us fairly?. Communications of the ACM, 59(10), 16–17.

85. Kleinmuntz, B. (1990). Why we still use our heads instead of formulas: Toward an integrative approach. Psychological Bulletin, 107(3), 296.

86. Kremer, M., Moritz, B., and Siemsen, E. (2011). Demand forecasting behavior: System neglect and change detection. Management Science, 57(10), 1827–1843.

87. Krizan, Z., and Windschitl, P. D. (2007). The influence of outcome desirability on optimism. Psychological Bulletin, 133(1), 95.

88. Lee, W. Y., Goodwin, P., Fildes, R., Nikolopoulos, K., and Lawrence, M. (2007). Providing support for the use of analogies in demand forecasting tasks. International Journal of Forecasting, 23(3), 377–390.

89. Lee, Y. S., and Siemsen, E. (2017). Task decomposition and newsvendor decision making. Management Science, 63(10), 3226–3245.

90. Legerstee, R., and Franses, P. H. (2014). Do experts' SKU forecasts improve after feedback?. Journal of Forecasting, 33(1), 69–79.

91. Lin, V. S., Goodwin, P., and Song, H. (2014). Accuracy and bias of experts' adjusted forecasts. Annals of Tourism Research, 48, 156–174.

92. Logg, J. M., Minson, J. A., and Moore, D. A. (2019). Algorithm appreciation: People prefer algorithmic to human judgment. Organizational Behavior and Human Decision Processes, 151, 90–103.

93. Løhre, E., and Teigen, K. H. (2017). Probabilities associated with precise and vague forecasts. Journal of Behavioral Decision Making, 30(5), 1014–1026.

94. MacGregor, D. (2001). Decomposition for judgemental forecasting and estimation. In J. S. Armstrong (Ed.), Principles of forecasting (pp. 107–123). Norwell, MA: Kluwer.

95. Marmier, F., and Cheikhrouhou, N. (2010). Structuring and integrating human knowledge in demand forecasting: A judgemental adjustment approach. Production Planning and Control, 21(4), 399–412.

96. Massey, C., and Wu, G. (2005). Detecting regime shifts: The causes of under- and overreaction. Management Science, 51(6), 932–947.

97. Meehl, P. E. (1954). Clinical versus statistical prediction: A theoretical analysis and review of the evidence. Minneapolis, MN: University of Minnesota Press.

98. Mehran, H., and Stulz, R. M. (2007). The economics of conflicts of interest in financial institutions. Journal of Financial Economics, 85(2), 267–296.

99. Mello, J. (2009). The impact of sales forecast game playing on supply chains. Foresight: The International Journal of Applied Forecasting 13, 13–22.

100. Moritz, B., Siemsen, E., and Kremer, M. (2014). Judgmental forecasting: Cognitive reflection and decision speed. Production and Operations Management, 23(7), 1146–1160.

101. Morwitz, V. G., Steckel, J. H., and Gupta, A. (2007). When do purchase intentions predict sales?. International Journal of Forecasting, 23(3), 347–364.

102. O'Connor, M., Remus, W., and Griggs, K. (1993). Judgemental forecasting in times of change. International Journal of Forecasting, 9(2), 163–172.

103. O'Connor, M., Remus, W., and Lim, K. (2005). Improving judgmental forecasts with judgmental bootstrapping and task feedback support. Journal of Behavioral Decision Making, 18(4), 247–260.

104. Oliva, R., and Watson, N. (2009). Managing functional biases in organizational forecasts: A case study of consensus forecasting in supply chain planning. Production and Operations Management, 18, 138–151.

105. O'Neil, C. (2016). Weapons of Math destruction: How Big Data Increases Inequality and Threatens Democracy. New York: Penguin Random House.

106. Önkal, D., and Gönül, S. (2005). Judgmental adjustment: A challenge for providers and users of forecasts. Foresight: The International Journal of Applied Forecasting, 1(1), 13–17.

107. Önkal, D., Gönül, M. S., Goodwin, P., Thomson, M., and Öz, E. (2017). Evaluating expert advice in forecasting: Users' reactions to presumed vs. experienced credibility. International Journal of Forecasting, 33(1), 280–297.

108. Önkal, D., Goodwin, P., Thomson, M., Gönül, S., and Pollock, A. (2009). The relative influence of advice from human experts and statistical methods on forecast adjustments. Journal of Behavioral Decision Making, 22(4), 390–409.

109. Önkal, D., and Muradoglu, G. (1995). Effects of feedback on probabilistic forecasts of stock prices. International Journal of Forecasting, 11(2), 307–319.

110. Önkal, D., Sayım, K. Z., and Gönül, M. S. (2013). Scenarios as channels of forecast advice. Technological Forecasting and Social Change, 80(4), 772–788.

111. Palley, A. B., and Soll, J. B. (2019). Extracting the wisdom of crowds when information is shared. Management Science, 65, 2291–2309.

112. Parikh, M., Fazlollahi, B., and Verma, S. (2001). The effectiveness of decisional guidance: An empirical evaluation. Decision Sciences, 32(2), 303–332.

113. Pennings, C. L., van Dalen, J., and Rook, L. (2019). Coordinating judgmental forecasting: Coping with intentional biases. Omega, 87, 46–56.

114. Petropoulos, F., Fildes, R., and Goodwin, P. (2016). Do 'big losses' in judgmental adjustments to statistical forecasts affect experts' behaviour? European Journal of Operational Research, 249(3), 842–852.

115. Petropoulos, F., Goodwin, P., and Fildes, R. (2017). Using a rolling training approach to improve judgmental extrapolations elicited from forecasters with technical knowledge. International Journal of Forecasting, 33(1), 314–324.

116. Petropoulos, F., Kourentzes, N., Nikolopoulos, K., and Siemsen, E. (2018). Judgmental selection of forecasting models. Journal of Operations Management, 60, 34–46.

117. Pierdzioch, C., Rülke, J. C., and Stadtmann, G. (2012). A note on forecasting emerging market exchange rates: Evidence of anti-herding. Review of International Economics, 20(5), 974–984.

118. Ren, Y., and Croson, R. (2013). Overconfidence in newsvendor orders: An experimental study. Management Science, 59(11), 2502–2517.

119. Rowe, G., and Wright, G. (1999). The Delphi technique as a forecasting tool: Issues and analysis. International Journal of Forecasting, 15, 353–375.

120. Rowe, G., and Wright, G. (2011). The Delphi technique: Past, present, and future prospects—Introduction to the special issue. Technological Forecasting and Social Change, 78(9), 1487–1490.

121. Scheibehenne, B., and Bröder, A. (2007). Predicting Wimbledon 2005 tennis results by mere player name recognition. International Journal of Forecasting, 23(3), 415–426.

122. Scoblic, J. P., and Tetlock, P. (2021). A better crystal ball. Foresight: The International Journal of Applied Forecasting. 61 Quarter 3.

123. Serwe, S., and Frings, C. (2006). Who will win Wimbledon? The recognition heuristic in predicting sports events. Journal of Behavioral Decision Making, 19(4), 321–332.

124. Seifert, M., Siemsen, E., Hadida, A. L., and Eisingerich, A. B. (2015). Effective judgmental forecasting in the context of fashion products. Journal of Operations Management, 36, 33–45.

125. Song, H., Gao, B. Z., and Lin, V. S. (2013). Combining statistical and judgmental forecasts via a web-based tourism demand forecasting system. International Journal of Forecasting, 29(2), 295–310.

126. Sroginis, A., Fildes, R., and Kourentzes, N. (2019). Use of contextual and model-based information in behavioural operations. In Lancaster University Department of Management. Science, Working Paper 5. Lancaster.

127. Sugiyama, S. (2007). Forecasting uncertainty and Monte Carlo simulation. Foresight: The International Journal of Applied Forecasting, 6, 29–37.

128. Surowiecki, J. (2005). The Wisdom of Crowds. Anchor.

129. Taleb, N. (2005). The Black Swan: Why Don't We Learn That We Don't Learn. New York: Random House.

130. Teigen, K. H., and Jørgensen, M. (2005). When 90% confidence intervals are 50% certain: On the credibility of credible intervals. Applied Cognitive Psychology, 19, 455–475.

131. Tetlock, P. E. (2005). Expert Political Judgment: How Good Is It? How Can We Know? New edition. Princeton: Princeton University Press.

132. Tetlock, P. E., and Gardner, D. (2016). Superforecasting: The Art and Science of Prediction. London: Random House.

133. Theil, H. (1966). Applied Economic Forecasting. Amsterdam: North Holland Publishing Company.

134. Theocharis, Z., and Harvey, N. (2016). Order effects in judgmental forecasting. International Journal of Forecasting, 32(1), 44–60.

135. Theocharis, Z., and Harvey, N. (2019). When does more mean worse? Accuracy of judgmental forecasting is nonlinearly related to length of data series. Omega, 87, 10–19.

136. Tversky, A., and Kahneman, D. (1974). Judgment under uncertainty: Heuristics and biases. Science, 185(4157), 1124–1131.

137. Tyebjee, T. T. (1987). Behavioral biases in new product forecasting. International Journal of Forecasting, 3, 393–404.

138. Van den Broeke, M., De Baets, S., Vereecke, A., Baecke, P., and Vanderheyden, K. (2019). Judgmental forecast adjustments over different time horizons. Omega, 87, 34–45.

139. Vaughan Williams, L., Sung, M., and Johnson, J. E. V. (2019). Prediction markets: Theory, evidence and applications. International Journal of Forecasting, 35(1), 266–270.

140. Veksler, V. D., Buchler, N., LaFleur, C. G., Yu, M. S., Lebiere, C., and Gonzalez, C. (2020). Cognitive models in cybersecurity: Learning from expert analysts and predicting attacker behavior. Frontiers in Psychology, 11, 1049.

141. Watson, M. C. (1996). Forecasting in the Scottish electronics industry. International Journal of Forecasting, 12(3), 361–371.

142. Webby, R., O'Connor, M., and Edmundson, B. (2005). Forecasting support systems for the incorporation of event information: An empirical investigation. International Journal of Forecasting, 21(3), 411–423.

143. Yaniv, I., and Choshen-Hillel, S. (2012). Exploiting the wisdom of others to make better decisions: Suspending judgment reduces egocentrism and increases accuracy. Journal of Behavioral Decision Making, 25(5), 427–434.

144. Yaniv, I., and Foster, D. P. (1995). Graininess of judgment under uncertainty: An accuracy-informativeness trade-off. Journal of Experimental Psychology: General, 124(4), 424.

17

Input Uncertainty in Stochastic Simulation

Russell R. Barton, Henry Lam, and Eunhye Song

17.1 Introduction

A stochastic simulator refers to a computer model that takes random inputs in and generates outputs by following a set of deterministic system rules. The simulation outputs are collected and used to estimate a performance measure of interest. For instance, a simple queueing simulator may prescribe the system rules on how jobs are processed by servers, where the goal is to estimate the expected waiting time of jobs in the queue. The inputs to the simulator consist of interarrival times of jobs and service times of the servers. These inputs are typically generated from probability distributions referred to as *input models*. According to the system rules, the simulator calculates each job's waiting time in the queue from the inputs and returns it as an output. Simulating many such jobs, the expected waiting time can be estimated

R. R. Barton (✉) · E. Song
Penn State University, University Park, PA, USA
e-mail: rrb2@psu.edu

E. Song
e-mail: eus358@psu.edu

H. Lam
Columbia University, New York, NY, USA
e-mail: khl2114@columbia.edu

© The Author(s), under exclusive license to Springer Nature
Switzerland AG 2022
S. Salhi and J. Boylan (eds.), *The Palgrave Handbook of Operations Research*,
https://doi.org/10.1007/978-3-030-96935-6_17

by averaging the outputs. Typically, the estimated performance measure is subject to stochastic error since one can only generate finitely many simulation outputs. As the simulation sample size increases, the hope is that the estimated performance measure converges to the true performance measure in some probabilistic sense.

When the simulator is built to mimic a real-world system, the input models may be estimated from *input data* (e.g., interarrival and service times) collected from the system. Then, there is statistical error in estimating the input models from the finite input data. As a result, any simulation outputs computed from the inputs generated from these models are subject to the estimation error. In turn, the performance measure estimate now has additional uncertainty caused by the input-model estimation error. The latter is referred to as *input uncertainty* and is the main focus of this chapter.

To summarize, the two sources of stochastic variability in the performance measure estimate are: (i) the finiteness of the simulation output sample, and (ii) the finiteness of the input data used to fit the input models. These two sources of variability in the simulation literature have been given a number of different names. Perhaps most intuitive are *simulation variability* and *parameter variability* by Cheng and Holland [26], with the former characterizing uncertainty or error in a (deterministic) function of the simulation output random variable due to the stochastic nature of the output, and the latter characterizing uncertainty in estimated input model's parameters. Other names for simulation variability include *simulation error*, *Monte Carlo error*, *variance error*, *stochastic uncertainty*, *sampling error*, and *intrinsic output uncertainty*. Other terms used for parameter variability (and beyond to cover other errors stemming from input fitting) include *input uncertainty*, *input-model uncertainty*, *bias error*, and *extrinsic error*. In the Bayesian setting, *structural uncertainty* captures both model uncertainty (probability model forms and system logic) and probability model parameter uncertainty. See [6, 7, 28, 29, 63, 75, 92, 120] and Chapter 7 of [92] for additional information. For this chapter we will use *Monte Carlo error* and *input uncertainty* to name the two sources of variability in simulation output.

We distinguish analyzing input uncertainty from *uncertainty quantification* (UQ) of a computer model. For UQ, the computer models typically are differential equation-based and have deterministic outputs; the uncertainty is in the values of model parameters. For instance, [121] perform UQ of a fire-spread model, which calculates the spread speed of forest fire based on a set of differential equations. Here, the source of uncertainty is the unknown values of wind speed, moisture level in the air, size of the fuel in the forest, etc. Closely related to UQ is the topic of *sensitivity analysis*, again typically associated with differential equation models. See [107] for an overview. Examples of this work include [94, 97] and, more recently, [95]. A main distinction of input uncertainty from computer model UQ is the stochasticity of the considered model, which adds variability on top of real data noise that complicates estimation. Another distinction is the type of data used. Input uncertainty often considers the availability of observations that directly inform the input distributions while UQ can involve output-level data [11, 33, 70, 124]. The latter, which is sometimes known as calibration [64, 125, 134] or simulation-based inference [32], has nonetheless been also considered in the stochastic simulation literature in the context of model validation [4, 73, 108, 112] and more recently [58, 59, 101], though still relatively open.

Concepts closely related to Monte Carlo error and input uncertainty from the UQ setting are named *aleatory uncertainty* and *epistemic uncertainty* [114]. *Aleatory* refers to inherent randomness in the output, and this variability cannot be reduced by better modeling or using more data. On the other hand, *epistemic* refers to lack of knowledge of model parameter value and model bias, and can be reduced by modeling or more data. While these terms have erudite philosophical roots, they are not as widely known in stochastic simulation and it would benefit to have more systematic connections.

Another related topic is *robust analysis*. We review some of robust analysis methods applied to stochastic simulation. See for example, [42, 53, 66, 75, 99].

17.2 Characterizing Input Uncertainty

Consider the estimation of a performance measure ψ that depends on the input distributions $\mathbf{P} = (P_1, \ldots, P_m)$, where $P_1, \ldots, P_m$ denote the individual distributions for independent random sources. For instance, in queueing models, P_1 and P_2 can denote the interarrival time and service time distributions, respectively. Sets of dependent random sources can be considered to be captured by multivariate distribution P_j of $\mathbf{P}$. The performance measure ψ, given $\mathbf{P}$, can be evaluated with error via simulation runs, i.e., we can generate $\widehat{\psi}_r, r = 1, \ldots, R$ where R is the simulation budget, and output the average $\widehat{\psi} = (1/R) \sum_{r=1}^{R} \widehat{\psi}_r$ as a natural point estimate of ψ. We call $\widehat{\psi} - \psi$ Monte Carlo error.

Input uncertainty arises when the ground-truth $\mathbf{P}$ is not known but only observed via data. Thus, $\mathbf{P}$ needs to be estimated, and this statistical error can propagate to the output and affect the accuracy of the point estimate of ψ.

Typically, the data set to inform each P_i is assumed independent of others and comprises i.i.d. observations (though can be generalized to serial dependence with sufficient mixing). In the parametric regime, we assume P_i is from a parametric family, say P_θ with unknown true parameter vector θ. In this case, an estimate of P_i reduces to estimating θ. In the nonparametric regime, no parametric assumption is placed on P_i, and a natural estimate of P_i is the empirical distribution (or its smoothed variants).

While simulation output analysis in general may consider any characterization of the probability distribution of simulation output, $\widehat{\psi}$, there are two main, and closely related, approaches to quantify input uncertainty. First is the construction of confidence interval (CI) on ψ that accounts for both the input uncertainty and Monte Carlo error. Second is the estimation of the variance of the point estimate $\widehat{\psi}$, which involves decomposition of the variance into the input uncertainty variance and Monte Carlo error variance components. The input uncertainty variance component is typically more difficult to estimate than the Monte Carlo variance, as the latter can be quite readily estimated by using the sample variance of replicate simulation runs. The former, however, not only involves a variance of a nonlinear functional, but also can only be evaluated with added Monte Carlo error. The CI approach and the variance estimation approach are closely connected as the variance estimate provides the standard error for a variance-based (as opposed to quantile-based) CI. Note, however, that when ψ is a steady-state measure such as average queue length or average time in system, $\widehat{\psi}$ may have infinite expectation and its variance is undefined [111]. In this case CIs may still be obtained, but they cannot be variance-based.

17.3 Confidence Interval Construction and Variance Estimation

A $(1 - \alpha)$-level CI for ψ is an interval $[L, U]$ that satisfies

$$\mathbb{P}(\psi \in [L, U]) \geq 1 - \alpha$$

where $\mathbb{P}$ refers to the probability with respect to both input data and Monte Carlo runs. We say that a CI is asymptotically valid if

$$\liminf_{n\to\infty} \mathbb{P}(\psi \in [L, U]) \geq 1 - \alpha$$

for some scaling parameter n. We call CI asymptotically exact if

$$\lim_{n\to\infty} \mathbb{P}(\psi \in [L, U]) = 1 - \alpha.$$

Besides coverage, the efficiency of the CI measured by the length of the interval (in expectation) is also important. Obviously, the infinite interval $L = -\infty, U = \infty$ is asymptotically valid but not useful.

As will be described in further detail in the following sections, we typically have

$$\text{Var}(\widehat{\psi}_{point}) = V_{IU} + V_{MC} \qquad (17.1)$$

where $\widehat{\psi}_{point}$ is a natural point estimate of ψ, by "plugging in" the point estimate of the input parameter and conducting simulation runs based on the resulting input model, and Var refers to the variance from both input uncertainty and Monte Carlo error. (17.1) implies that the variance of the natural point estimate of ψ can be decomposed into an input uncertainty variance component, V_{IU}, and a simulation Monte Carlo error variance component V_{MC}. The variance estimation approach in input uncertainty often refers to the estimation of this decomposed variance, in particular V_{IU} which is the more challenging piece as mentioned before.

CIs and variance estimation are closely connected. Under suitable regularity conditions, not only (17.1) holds, but also we have a central limit theorem (CLT) for $\widehat{\psi}_{point}$ such that it is approximately $N(\psi, \text{Var}(\widehat{\psi}_{point}))$. Thus, to construct a CI for ψ, it suffices to estimate the variance of $\widehat{\psi}_{point}$ and then use

$$[L, U] = \left[\widehat{\psi}_{point} - z_{1-\alpha/2}\sqrt{\text{Var}(\widehat{\psi}_{point})}, \widehat{\psi}_{point} + z_{1-\alpha/2}\sqrt{\text{Var}(\widehat{\psi}_{point})} \right]$$

where $\text{Var}(\widehat{\psi}_{point})$ is plugged in with the variance estimate, and $z_{1-\alpha/2}$ denotes the $(1 - \alpha/2)$-level normal critical value, given by the $(1 - \alpha/2)$-quantile of standard normal.

In the following, we divide our review into methods that primarily apply to parametric regimes (i.e., when the input model is specified up to a parametric family with unknown parameters), and methods that can handle nonparametric settings (which typically are also applicable to parametric cases). Moreover, we will focus on the problem of CI construction as, in view of our discussion above, variance estimation often serves as an intermediate step in obtaining the CI.

17.3.1   Parametric Methods

When the input probability distributions are assumed to have a parametric form, the uncertainty characterization is simplified. For each P_j, rather than dealing with an unknown functional form (restricted to the class of probability distribution functions), the uncertainty is over a finite set of parameters that define a particular member of the assumed parametric family. While easier to handle, parametric assumption should be viewed with caution: In real-world systems, random phenomena rarely follow any parametric distributions (or mixtures) exactly [20], and sometimes this error ignored by the existing frequentist and Bayesian input uncertainty quantification methods described below could be substantial.

17.3.1.1   Central Limit Theorem and Delta Method

To highlight the dependence on θ, we denote $\psi = \psi(\theta)$ where $\psi(\cdot)$ is a map from the input parameter to the performance measure value. From input data, we give an estimate of the ground-truth parameter vector θ given by $\hat{\theta}$. Then, given $\hat{\theta}$, we estimate $\psi(\hat{\theta})$ by running and averaging R simulation runs, each denoted by $\widehat{\psi}_r(\theta)$, to get $\widehat{\psi}(\hat{\theta})$. This point estimate $\widehat{\psi}(\hat{\theta})$ is contaminated by both the input and Monte Carlo noises, with the two "hats" indicating the two sources of noises.

From the decomposition

$$\widehat{\psi}(\hat{\theta}) - \psi(\theta) = [\widehat{\psi}(\hat{\theta}) - \psi(\hat{\theta})] + [\psi(\hat{\theta}) - \psi(\theta)]$$

it can be inferred that

$$\widehat{\psi}(\hat{\theta}) - \psi(\theta) \approx N\left(0, \mathrm{Var}(\psi(\hat{\theta})) + \frac{\mathrm{Var}(\widehat{\psi}_r(\theta))}{R}\right), \qquad (17.2)$$

where $\mathrm{Var}(\psi(\hat{\theta}))$ is the input variance, with Var on the randomness of input data, and $\mathrm{Var}(\widehat{\psi}_r(\theta))/R$ is the variance of the Monte Carlo error, with Var on the simulation noise in $\widehat{\psi}_r$ (see, e.g., [24, 57]).

Moreover, by the delta method, asymptotically as the input data size increases,

$$\text{Var}(\psi(\hat{\theta})) \approx \nabla_\theta \psi(\theta)' \frac{\Sigma}{n} \nabla_\theta \psi(\theta) \qquad (17.3)$$

where $\frac{\Sigma}{n}$ is the estimation variance of $\hat{\theta}$, typically scaling in a data size parameter n (e.g., a parameter linear in all the individual data sizes for different input models) and $\nabla_\theta \psi$ is the gradient of ψ with respect to θ, known as the sensitivity coefficient. If we use maximum likelihood for instance, then Σ would comprise the inverse Fisher information matrices.

Thus, when both the input data size and simulation replication size are large, we have

$$\widehat{\psi}(\hat{\theta}) - \psi(\theta) \approx N\left(0, \frac{\nabla_\theta \psi(\theta)' \Sigma(\theta) \nabla_\theta \psi(\theta)}{n} + \frac{\text{Var}(\widehat{\psi}_r(\theta))}{R}\right)$$

which then can be used to generate $[L, U]$ in Section 17.3. Note that $\nabla_\theta \psi(\theta)$ needs to be estimated by simulation (as ψ itself also needs to be estimated by such), via one of the following ways:

Unbiased gradient estimator: $\nabla_\theta \psi(\theta)$ estimated via unbiased methods such as the likelihood ratio or score function method [55, 103, 106]. This, however, may have high variance especially for long-horizon problems.

Finite-difference or zeroth-order gradient estimator: $\nabla_\theta \psi(\theta)$ estimated by using finite difference that requires only unbiased function evaluations [47, 140]. The rate of convergence, however, is subcanonically slow, and a precise complexity analysis for the use in (17.3) is not available in the literature.

Two-point methods: $\nabla_\theta \psi(\theta)$ estimated by using finite difference, but only using a couple of "perturbation directions" for the θ vector, judicially chosen (the "two points"). [25, 26] show some advantages in this approach.

Though the delta method is based on the normality approximation common in statistics, in the context of input uncertainty its implementation requires the estimation of a gradient or sensitivity coefficient that may not always be easy. Moreover, in finite-sample situations this method may undercover [8]. This partially motivates the alternatives that are discussed later in this section.

17.3.1.2   Bayesian Methods

The delta method and the resulting CI discussed above take the classical frequentist perspective. In the input uncertainty literature, Bayesian methods provide an alternate approach. Assume we have data D for a single input model parametrized by the unknown parameter vector θ, which is distributed according to $p(\xi|\theta)$. In the Bayesian framework, we impose a prior distribution $p_{prior}(\theta)$ on θ, and compute the posterior distribution

$$p_{post}(\theta|D) \propto p_{prior}(\theta)p(D|\theta) \qquad (17.4)$$

where $p(D|\theta)$ is the likelihood of the data D, which is often a product of terms $p(\xi|\theta)$ (note that we could have multiple input models each with its own set of parameters, in which case we multiply these likelihoods together if the data are all independent). Computing the posterior $p_{post}(\theta|D)$ is a subject of long-standing interest, where in some cases (e.g., conjugate prior) it is readily computable, while in other cases more elaborate techniques such as Markov chain Monte Carlo (MCMC) are required [27]. Compared to the frequentist interpretation, a commonly viewed advantage of a Bayesian approach is the flexibility in specifying prior belief about uncertain parameters, which can be used to incorporate expert knowledge [63]. Moreover, Bayesian approaches are especially convenient in handling dynamic problems where data are sequentially assimilated, since the posterior distribution can be naturally used as an updating mechanism to reflect all the historical information.

In translating the above into inference on $\psi = \psi(\theta)$, note that, much like the frequentist case, we encounter two sources of uncertainty, one from the statistical error in estimating θ, and one from the simulation error. There are two views in handling this combination of uncertainties:

Direct Combination: This approach uses a distribution to capture the overall uncertainty that "lumps" the two sources together. More precisely, the sampling scheme repeatedly draws a sample from the posterior of θ, and given this sample that is used to calibrate the input model, a simulation run is conducted. The distribution of all these simulation outputs comprises a quantification of the combined input-simulation error. This approach is conceptually straightforward, and is used in, e.g., [27].

Variance Decomposition: The second approach resembles more closely the frequentist approach described in the last subsection. It consists of a two-layer sampling, where at each outer layer, a posterior sample of θ is drawn, and given this value that calibrates the input model, several (i.e., R) simulation runs are conducted which forms the inner sampling layer. Then the input variance and the simulation variance can be estimated via methods much like the analysis-of-variance to be presented in the variance-based bootstrap in Section 17.3.2.1. This approach is used by [143, 144].

17.3.1.3 Metamodel-Based Methods

The direct bootstrap, whether used to construct variance-based or quantile-based CIs (to be discussed in Section 17.3.2.1), is corrupted by Monte Carlo error. When the Monte Carlo error is large relative to the input uncertainty, the result can be significant overcoverage of CIs, providing the experimenter with lower precision than what they should be.

For the parametric setting, constructing a metamodel for $\psi(\theta)$ can greatly reduce the impact of Monte Carlo error on the bootstrap distribution of $\widehat{\psi}(\theta_b)$, where the bootstrap resamples are indexed by b. This phenomenon is easiest to see by considering the case where ψ can be modeled with linear regression (to full fidelity), and then considering prediction in the CLT case. To further simplify the motivation for metamodeling, assume that ψ includes a transformation of the simulation output so that $\widehat{\psi}_r(\theta)$ has homogeneous variance with respect to θ.

That is, we have the full-fidelity metamodel:

$$\psi(\theta) = g(\theta)'\beta + \varepsilon, \varepsilon \sim N(0, \mathrm{Var}(\widehat{\psi}_r/R)) \qquad (17.5)$$

where g is the vector-valued regression function. Denoting the fitted regression metamodel prediction by $\widehat{\psi}_{mm}$, the approximate variance decomposition of $\widehat{\psi}_{mm}(\widehat{\theta}) - \psi(\theta)$ can be compared with (17.2), where $\mathrm{Var}(\psi_r/R)$ in (17.2) is multiplied by

$$(g(\theta)'(G'G)^{-1}g(\theta)), \qquad (17.6)$$

and G is the design matrix of g values used to fit the metamodel. This assumes that the design matrix has one row per different design condition, which would result in R replications of each row in G. The multiplier will be smaller than one for θ values inside the design space. For simple linear regression with $\theta \in \mathbb{R}^d$, design region scaled to $(+/-1)^d$ and a 2^d factorial design, the largest value for $\theta'(G'G)^{-1}\theta$ occurs at the corners of the hypercube, with value $(d+1)/2^d$. This provides one motivation for metamodeling: using metamodel-predicted bootstrap estimates for $\widehat{\psi}$ can have greatly reduced Monte Carlo error. The second motivation is that the bootstrap resamples of θ each requires an inexpensive evaluation of the metamodel, rather than several replications of the expensive simulation model. If the metamodel fitting design has fewer runs than the bootstrap, the computational effort will be less.

Linear regression metamodels are essentially identical to the delta method reviewed in Chapter 17.3.1.1. Here we focus on the use of nonlinear metamodels with the bootstrap to characterize the distribution of $\psi(\hat{\theta})$.

When the input data is limited, the potential for highly nonlinear response of the simulation as a function of θ makes low-order polynomial regression less attractive, since Taylor's Theorem is less likely to apply. Further, the assumption of homoscedastic variance (independence of $\text{Var}(\hat{\psi}_r/R)$ from θ) is harder to support.

In a series of papers [9, 137, 138], Xie, Nelson, and Barton employed stochastic kriging [1] to provide metamodel-based bootstrap CIs for input uncertainty. The work covers frequentist, Bayesian, and dependent input variable cases.

Key to the method was the experiment design strategy. Unlike linear regression, prediction error for stochastic kriging models increases when the prediction point is far from any experiment design point. In this setting, space-filling designs are preferred to traditional factorial experiment designs. Since the metamodel is used to evaluate bootstrap-resampled θ_b values, the design should focus on the bootstrap-resample space. The design proposed by the authors had two phases. In the first phase, a large number of bootstrap sample θ_b values were generated (without simulating the resulting performance), then a hyperellipse enclosing a high fraction (e.g., 99%) of the θ_b values was fitted. In the second phase, a space-filling design for a hypercube (e.g., Latin hypercube design) was transformed to cover the fitted ellipsoid.

The experiment design was executed (with replications) for specified θ values to fit a stochastic kriging metamodel. Then bootstrap-resampled θ_b values were used with the metamodel to generate approximate bootstrap $\psi(\theta_b)$ values to assess input uncertainty.

Metamodel-assisted bootstrapping has two advantages over direct bootstrapping. It makes efficient use of simulation budget by assigning simulation effort through a designed experiment that evenly covers the uncertain θ input space. The direct bootstrap over-emphasizes simulation effort in the design region of the most commonly occurring realizations of θ_b, which are unlikely to contribute much to confidence interval or quantile estimation. Second, the metamodeling approach produces the reduction in Monte Carlo uncertainty described above. This makes bootstrapping not only efficient but also robust to Monte Carlo error.

But metamodel-assisted bootstrapping may have disadvantages over the direct bootstrap when θ is high-dimensional. The number of simulation experiment runs required to fit a high-fidelity metamodel can increase rapidly with the dimension of θ. Thus, for a simulation model with many input parameters, the number of runs for the metamodel fitting experiment may exceed the number of direct bootstrap simulation model runs required for adequate input uncertainty characterization.

17.3.1.4   Green Simulation

Green simulation is an application of the likelihood ratio method, where simulation replications made to estimate $\psi(\theta)$ are reused to construct an estimator of $\psi(\theta')$ for $\theta' \neq \theta$ [44, 45].

Green simulation has been applied to reduce the computational cost of input uncertainty quantification. We focus on the Bayesian setting in this section, although the same approach can be applied in the frequentist setting as well. Suppose $\theta_1, \theta_2, \ldots, \theta_B$ are sampled from the posterior, $p_{post}(\theta|D)$. At each $\theta_b, 1 \leq b \leq B$, R simulation replications, $\widehat{\psi}_1(\theta_b), \widehat{\psi}_2(\theta_b), \ldots, \widehat{\psi}_R(\theta_b)$, are made and let $\widehat{\psi}(\theta_b)$ denote their sample mean. Moreover, let ζ_r^b be the vector of input random variables generated within the r-th replication given θ_b and $f(\cdot|\theta_b)$ denote the probability density function of ζ_r^b. Thus, $\widehat{\psi}_r(\theta_b)$ is a deterministic function of ζ_r^b. The following change of measure allows us to reuse the inputs and outputs generated from the R replications made at θ_b to estimate $\psi(\theta_{b'})$ for $\theta_{b'} \neq \theta_b$:

$$\psi(\theta_{b'}) = \mathrm{E}\left[\widehat{\psi}_r(\theta_b)\frac{f(\zeta_r^b|\theta_{b'})}{f(\zeta_r^b|\theta_b)}\right] = \int_\zeta \widehat{\psi}_r(\theta_b)\frac{f(\zeta|\theta_{b'})}{f(\zeta|\theta_b)}f(\zeta|\theta_b)d\zeta.$$

Here, an implicit assumption is that the support of the input vector does not depend on θ. Therefore, $\tilde{\psi}^b(\theta_{b'})$ below is an unbiased estimator of $\psi(\theta_{b'})$:

$$\tilde{\psi}^b(\theta_{b'}) = \frac{1}{R}\sum_{r=1}^R \widehat{\psi}_r(\theta_b)\frac{f(\zeta_r^b|\theta_{b'})}{f(\zeta_r^b|\theta_b)}.$$

Using this trick, [43] propose pooling all BR replications to estimate each $\psi(\theta_b)$ to improve computational efficiency. However, this approach should be taken with caution; although $\tilde{\psi}^b(\theta_{b'})$ is unbiased, its variance may be unbounded. The exact derivation of $\mathrm{Var}(\tilde{\psi}^b(\theta_{b'}))$ cannot be obtained in general, but it can be estimated. Thus, one can choose not to pool replications made at some θ_b to estimate $\theta_{b'}$, if the estimated variance is large.

Expanding on the idea, [46] study an experiment design scheme to minimize the total number of replications so that the resulting pooled estimators have (approximately) the same variances as the original two-layer design that requires BR replications. The experiment design can be optimized prior to running any replications as long as $f(\cdot|\theta_b)$ is known. For a special case, they show that the minimized simulation budget is $O(B^{1+\varepsilon})$ for any $\varepsilon > 0$, which is a significant reduction from BR.

17.3.2 Nonparametric Methods

We now turn to methods that apply to nonparametric regimes in which the input distribution is not assumed to follow any parametric family. Following Section 17.2, we write $\psi = \psi(\mathbf{P})$, where $\mathbf{P} = (P_1, \ldots, P_m)$ is a collection of m input distributions. Suppose we have a collection of data sets $\mathbf{D} = (D_1, \ldots, D_m)$, where each $D_i = (\xi_{i1}, \ldots, \xi_{in_i})$ is the data set of size n_i distributed under P_i. Suppose the data are all independent. Then, naturally we construct empirical distributions $\widehat{\mathbf{P}} = (\widehat{P}_1, \ldots, \widehat{P}_m)$ from these data sets, where

$$\widehat{P}_i(\cdot) = \frac{1}{n_i} \sum_{j=1}^{n_i} \delta_{\xi_{ij}}(\cdot)$$

for Dirac measure $\delta_{\xi_{ij}}(\cdot)$. With these input distributions, we generate R simulation runs to obtain

$$\widehat{\psi}(\widehat{\mathbf{P}}) = \frac{1}{R} \sum_{r=1}^{R} \widehat{\psi}_r(\widehat{\mathbf{P}})$$

where $\widehat{\psi}_r, r = 1, \ldots, R$ are independent simulation runs.

Under regularity conditions, we have a CLT

$$\widehat{\psi}(\widehat{\mathbf{P}}) - \psi(\mathbf{P}) \approx N\left(0, \text{Var}(\psi(\widehat{\mathbf{P}})) + \frac{\text{Var}(\widehat{\psi}_r(\mathbf{P}))}{R}\right) \qquad (17.7)$$

much like the parametric case in Section 17.3.1.1 [57].

Though conceptually similar, a main difference between the nonparametric and parametric setups is the representation of the input variance

$\text{Var}(\psi(\hat{\mathbf{P}}))$. In particular, to specify this quantity, we would need to employ the nonparametric delta method, which involves the notion of functional derivatives. More specifically, the so-called influence function [61] $IF(\xi; \mathbf{P}) = (IF_1(\xi_1; \mathbf{P}), \ldots, IF_m(\xi_m; \mathbf{P}))$, which maps from the image of random variable $\xi = (\xi_1, \ldots, \xi_m)$ to $\mathbb{R}^m$, is a function satisfying the property

$$\psi(\mathbf{Q}) \approx \psi(\mathbf{P}) + \int IF(\xi; \mathbf{P})d(\mathbf{Q} - \mathbf{P}) + \text{remainder} \qquad (17.8)$$

where $\mathbf{Q} = (Q_1, \ldots, Q_m)$ is a sequence of independent distributions Q_i each defined on the same space as P_i, $\int IF(\xi; \mathbf{P})d(\mathbf{Q} - \mathbf{P})$ is defined as

$$\int IF(\xi; \mathbf{P})d\mathbf{Q} = \sum_{i=1}^{m} \int IF_i(\xi_i; \mathbf{P})d(Q_i - P_i),$$

and the remainder in (17.8) goes to zero at a higher order than $\mathbf{Q} - \mathbf{P}$ (which can be rigorized). Note that we can replace $\int IF(\xi; \mathbf{P})d(\mathbf{Q} - \mathbf{P})$ by $\int IF(\xi; \mathbf{P})d\mathbf{Q}$, by redefining $IF(\xi; \mathbf{P})$ as $IF(\xi; \mathbf{P}) - E_{\mathbf{P}}[(\xi; \mathbf{P})]$. Thus, without loss of generality, we can use a canonical version of IF that satisfies (17.8) and also the mean-zero property (under $\mathbf{P}$). From (17.8), we see that the influence function dictates the linearization of $\psi(\mathbf{P})$ as $\mathbf{P}$ perturbs to $\mathbf{Q}$, and plays a distributional analog of the derivative in Euclidean space, which leads to the notion of Gateaux, Frechet or most relevantly Hadamard derivatives [128].

With the influence function IF, it turns out that the input variance $\text{Var}(\psi(\hat{\mathbf{P}}))$ is given by

$$\text{Var}(\psi(\hat{\mathbf{P}})) = \sum_{i=1}^{m} \frac{\text{Var}(IF(\xi_i; \mathbf{P}))}{n_i} \qquad (17.9)$$

where the variance in the RHS is on the random variable ξ_i generated from P_i. This formula is a nonparametric analog to (17.3).

A major challenge in the nonparametric case that distinguishes from parametric is that the influence function generally requires more effort to estimate than the sensitivity coefficient for parametric input models. Efficient estimation of the variance of influence function is potentially doable [84], but quite open in the literature, and the input uncertainty literature has focused on resampling, cancellation methods or nonparametric Bayesian approaches, as we describe below. We also note that many of these approaches, by design, also apply naturally for parametric settings.

17.3.2.1 Bootstrap: Elementary Schemes

The bootstrap method in input uncertainty can be roughly categorized into two frameworks, quantile-based and variance-based.

Quantile-based bootstrap: The bootstrap approach is principled on the observation that the variability of a statistic, under the data distribution, can be approximated by the counterpart of a resampled statistic, conditioned on the realized data [34, 40]. To be more precise, suppose we have a point estimate of $\psi(\mathbf{P})$ given by $\psi(\widehat{\mathbf{P}})$, and we want to construct a $(1 - \alpha)$-level CI. This problem can be recast as the search of $[\underline{q}, \overline{q}]$ such that $P(\underline{q} \leq \psi(\widehat{\mathbf{P}}) - \psi(\mathbf{P}) \leq \overline{q}) = 1 - \alpha$ which then gives $[\psi(\widehat{\mathbf{P}}) - \overline{q}, \psi(\widehat{\mathbf{P}}) - \underline{q}]$ as the CI. The bootstrap stipulates that

$$P_*(\underline{q} \leq \psi(\mathbf{P}^*) - \psi(\widehat{\mathbf{P}}) \leq \overline{q}) \approx P(\underline{q} \leq \psi(\widehat{\mathbf{P}}) - \psi(\mathbf{P}) \leq \overline{q}) \qquad (17.10)$$

where $\mathbf{P}^*$ is a resampled distribution, namely the empirical distribution formed by sampling with replacement from the data with the same size (or, in the case of m independent input distributions, the resampling is done independently from each input data set), and P_* denotes the probability conditional on the data. Thanks to (17.10), we can use Monte Carlo to approximate $\underline{q}$ and $\overline{q}$, say $\underline{q}^*$ and $\overline{q}^*$, which then gives $[\psi(\widehat{\mathbf{P}}) - \overline{q}^*, \psi(\widehat{\mathbf{P}}) - \underline{q}^*]$ as our CI.

The above principle has been used in constructing CIs for $\psi(\theta)$ under input uncertainty. A main distinction in this setting compared to conventional usage of the bootstrap is that the performance function ψ itself needs to be estimated from running many simulation runs. Thus, applying the bootstrap in the input uncertainty setting typically requires a *nested simulation*, where in the first layer, we resample the input distributions B times, and then given each resampled input distribution, we draw in the second layer a number, say R, of simulation runs driven by the resampled input distribution. The overall simulation complexity is BR.

The *basic bootstrap* method gives precisely the interval $[\widehat{\psi}(\widehat{\mathbf{P}}) - \overline{q}^*, \widehat{\psi}(\widehat{\mathbf{P}}) - \underline{q}^*]$, where $\widehat{\psi}(\widehat{\mathbf{P}})$ is a point estimate that uses the empirical distribution and enough simulation runs, and $\underline{q}^*$ and $\overline{q}^*$ are obtained as described above, using R large enough to approximate ψ sufficiently accurately in each resampled performance measure $\widehat{\psi}(\mathbf{P}^*)$.

On the other hand, (Efron's) *percentile bootstrap* uses the interval $[\underline{q}^*, \overline{q}^*]$ directly, where $\underline{q}^*$ and $\overline{q}^*$ are defined as in the basic bootstrap above. This approach does not require computing the point estimate, and is justified with the additional assumption that the limiting distribution of the statistic (centered at the true quantity of interest) is symmetric, which is typically true because this limiting distribution in many cases is a mean-zero normal distribution. Barton [10, 5] studies this approach.

Variance-based bootstrap: Instead of using quantiles $\underline{q}$ and $\overline{q}$ to construct CI, we can also estimate $\mathrm{Var}(\psi(\widehat{\mathbf{P}}))$ directly and then use the CLT (17.7) to deduce the interval

$$\left[\widehat{\psi}(\widehat{\mathbf{P}}) \pm z_{1-\alpha/2} \sqrt{ \mathrm{Var}(\psi(\widehat{\mathbf{P}})) + \frac{\mathrm{Var}(\widehat{\psi}_r(\mathbf{P}))}{R} } \right] \qquad (17.11)$$

where $z_{1-\alpha/2}$ is the $1 - \alpha/2$-level normal critical value. Note that in (17.11) the simulation variance $\mathrm{Var}(\widehat{\psi}_r(\mathbf{P}))$ is typically easy to estimate by simply taking the sample variance of all simulation runs in the experiment, and the difficulty, as noted in the introduction, is the input variance.

To estimate $\mathrm{Var}(\psi(\widehat{\mathbf{P}}))$ using the bootstrap, we once again invoke the approximation principle of resampling distribution for the original distribution of a statistic, that

$$\mathrm{Var}_*(\psi(\mathbf{P}^*)) \approx \mathrm{Var}(\psi(\widehat{\mathbf{P}})) \qquad (17.12)$$

where Var_* is the variance of the resampling randomness conditional on the data. Note that in the simulation setting, ψ has to be estimated from an enough number, say R, of simulation runs for each resampled input distribution $\mathbf{P}^*$. Thus, once again, this approach typically requires a nested simulation like in the quantile-based method.

Note that the accuracy of estimating $\mathrm{Var}_*(\psi(\mathbf{P}^*))$ can be improved by using analysis-of-variance (ANOVA) to debias the effect coming from finite simulation runs. To explain, note that a naive approach to estimate $\mathrm{Var}_*(\psi(\mathbf{P}^*))$, with B first-layer resampling and R second-layer simulation is

$$\frac{1}{B-1} \sum_{b=1}^{B} (\widehat{\psi}(\mathbf{P}^{*b}) - \overline{\psi(\mathbf{P}^*)})^2 \qquad (17.13)$$

where $\mathbf{P}^{*b}$ denotes the b-th resample distribution, $\widehat{\psi}$ denotes the sample mean from R runs, and $\overline{\psi(\mathbf{P}^*)}$ denotes the sample mean of B resample performance measures. Viewing the resample simulation experiment as a random-effect model, where each resample corresponds to a group and the simulation per resample corresponds to the sample within a group, we can readily see that the mean of (17.13) is actually

$$\mathrm{Var}_*(\psi(\mathbf{P}^*)) + \frac{\mathrm{E}_*[\mathrm{Var}(\widehat{\psi}_r(\mathbf{P}^*)|\mathbf{P}^*)]}{R} \tag{17.14}$$

where $\widehat{\psi}_r$ refers to the r-th inner simulation run, and E_* refers to the expectation on the resampling randomness of $\mathbf{P}^*$ conditional on the data. Thus, since we are interested in estimating the between-group variance in (17.14), we can use

$$\frac{1}{B-1}\sum_{b=1}^{B}(\widehat{\psi}(\mathbf{P}^{*b}) - \overline{\psi(\mathbf{P}^*)})^2 - \frac{1}{BR(R-1)}\sum_{b=1}^{B}\sum_{r=1}^{R}(\widehat{\psi}_r(\mathbf{P}^{*b})$$
$$- \widehat{\psi}(\mathbf{P}^{*b}))^2 \tag{17.15}$$

to remove the within-group variance. The formula (17.15) is used in, e.g., [117].

Note that both quantile-based and variance-based frameworks can be applied to the case when the parametric bootstrap is adopted. In parametric bootstrapping, an input model and its parameter vector $\widehat{\theta}$ are first fitted from the data, then bootstrap samples are generated by sampling from the input model.

17.3.2.2   Bootstrap: Computational Enhancements

The bootstrap methods discussed above, though natural and straightforward to understand, unfortunately require high-computational load in general. This computational load arises from the need of running nested simulation (resampling at the outer layer, and simulation runs per resampled input model at the inner layer), which requires a multiplicative amount of simulation runs where, in order to control the overall error that is convoluted by both the input and simulation noises, the sampling effort in each layer has to be sufficiently large. To explain more concretely, consider the variance-based bootstrap where we use B outer samples and R inner samples. Under suitable assumptions and using [123], we obtain that the variance (conditional on the data as we are using the bootstrap) of (17.15) is

$$O\left(\frac{1}{Bn^2} + \frac{1}{BR^2}\right) \tag{17.16}$$

where n is a scaling for the data size (i.e., the input data n_i for each input-model i is assumed to scale proportionally with n for some proportional constant). Now, note that the target quantity that (17.15) estimates is the input variance given by (17.9), which is of order $1/n$. Since this input variance shrinks to 0 as n increases, if we want to get a good input variance estimator, a basic requirement is relative consistency, which means the ratio of (17.16) and $1/n^2$ needs to go to 0. This in turn means, from the first term in (17.16), that B needs to go to ∞ and, from the second term, that R needs to be at least order n, which then gives a total required effort of strictly larger order than the data size n. [82] calls this a *simulation complexity barrier* for using naive variance-based bootstrap.

Some methods that improve the computational complexity motivated from the barrier above include subsampling, which has been used in the variance-based bootstrap framework, and shrinkage, which has been used in the quantile-based framework.

Subsampling: On a high level, the difficulty in using nested simulation to accurately estimate $\mathrm{Var}_*(\psi(\mathbf{P}^*))$, or subsequently $\mathrm{Var}(\psi(\widehat{\mathbf{P}}))$, is due to the small magnitude of these quantities that are in the order of $1/n$. This small magnitude requires one to wash away the noise coming from the inner sampling and necessitates the use of a large inner sample size. This issue manifests explicitly when we analyze the variance of the variance estimator in (17.16).

[82, 83] proposes to use subsampling to reduce sampling effort. Their main insight is the following. Suppose we had a smaller data size, say with a scale s, to begin with. Then, from our discussion above, this becomes an *easier* problem and in particular we would only need a larger order than s (instead of n) total simulation effort to ensure relative consistency. Of course, s is not the original scale of the sample size. However, we can utilize the reciprocal form of the input variance in terms of data size shown in (17.9) to rescale our estimate in the s-scale back to the n-scale.

To make the argument above more precise, denote the bootstrap input variance as

$$\mathrm{Var}_*(\psi(\mathbf{P}_n^*))$$

where we introduce a subscript n in $\mathbf{P}_n^*$ to explicitly denote the data size in the resample. From (17.9) and (17.12), we know

$$\text{Var}(\psi(\widehat{\mathbf{P}})) \approx \text{Var}_*(\psi(\mathbf{P}_n^*)) \approx \sum_{i=1}^{m} \frac{\text{Var}(IF(\xi_i; \mathbf{P}))}{n_i} \tag{17.17}$$

Now, if we use a resample size of scale s, or more precisely we use $s_i = \rho n_i$ for some factor $0 < \rho < 1$, then the bootstrap input variance becomes

$$\text{Var}_*(\psi(\mathbf{P}_s^*)) \approx \sum_{i=1}^{m} \frac{\text{Var}(IF(\xi_i; \mathbf{P}))}{s_i} \tag{17.18}$$

which now requires order larger than s effort instead of n effort due to (17.16). Now, comparing (17.17) and (17.18), we see that we have

$$\rho \text{Var}_*(\psi(\mathbf{P}_s^*)) \approx \sum_{i=1}^{m} \frac{\rho \text{Var}(IF(\xi_i; \mathbf{P}))}{s_i}$$

$$= \sum_{i=1}^{m} \frac{\text{Var}(IF(\xi_i; \mathbf{P}))}{n_i} \approx \text{Var}_*(\psi(\mathbf{P}_n^*)) \tag{17.19}$$

So, by subsampling input distributions using a size scale s, running the nested simulation to estimate the bootstrap input variance, and then multiplying back by a factor of ρ gives rise to a valid estimate of the input variance, now with a total computational effort controlled by s instead of n. We could choose s to be substantially smaller than n, in principle independent of the data size.

Shrinkage: The principle of quantile-based bootstrap relies on the closeness between the distribution of a resampled estimate $\psi(\mathbf{P}^*)$ (conditional on data) and the original estimate $\psi(\widehat{\mathbf{P}})$, when suitably scaled and centered. In other words,

$$\psi(\mathbf{P}^*) - \psi(\widehat{\mathbf{P}}) \approx \psi(\widehat{\mathbf{P}}) - \psi(\mathbf{P})$$

where $\approx$ denotes approximation in distribution, conditional on data for the LHS, which then gives rise to (17.10) as a way to generate CI for $\psi(\mathbf{P})$. When $\psi(\cdot)$ needs to be computed via simulation, then the point estimate becomes $\widehat{\psi}(\widehat{\mathbf{P}})$, and we would use

$$\widehat{\psi}(\mathbf{P}^*) - \psi(\widehat{\mathbf{P}}) \approx \widehat{\psi}(\widehat{\mathbf{P}}) - \psi(\mathbf{P})$$

where each $\widehat{\psi}(\cdot)$ is estimated from a number of simulation runs. To use the basic bootstrap, we would use the quantiles of the LHS above to approximate the quantiles of the RHS. Unfortunately, this means we also need to estimate the "center" quantity $\psi(\widehat{\mathbf{P}})$ in the LHS via simulation. Moreover, we need to use enough simulation to wash away this noise so that

$$\widehat{\psi}(\mathbf{P}^*) - \widehat{\psi}(\widehat{\mathbf{P}}) \approx \widehat{\psi}(\widehat{\mathbf{P}}) - \psi(\mathbf{P}) \tag{17.20}$$

In other words, we need a large simulation size, say R_0, to get a point estimate $\widehat{\psi}(\widehat{\mathbf{P}})$ that has negligible simulation error. And if we do so, then the bootstrap-resample estimate $\widehat{\psi}(\mathbf{P}^*)$ in (17.20) would each require a matching simulation size R_0, and at the end the computation load is $R_0 B$ where B is the bootstrap size, which could be very demanding.

The shrinkage method proposed by [8] is an approach to reduce the simulation size in each bootstrap-resample estimate, while retaining the approximation (17.20). The approach is inspired from a similar concept to adjust for variances in statistical linear models [34]. Suppose each bootstrap-resample estimate $\widehat{\psi}(\mathbf{P}^*)$ uses $R < R_0$ runs (while the point estimate $\widehat{\psi}(\widehat{\mathbf{P}})$ uses R_0 runs), then the quantity

$$\widehat{\psi}(\mathbf{P}^*) - \widehat{\psi}(\widehat{\mathbf{P}}) \tag{17.21}$$

has a larger variance than

$$\widehat{\psi}(\widehat{\mathbf{P}}) - \psi(\mathbf{P}).$$

To compensate for this, we scale down the variability of the outcomes of (17.21) by a *shrinkage factor*

$$S = \sqrt{\frac{\mathrm{Var}(\psi(\widehat{\mathbf{P}}))}{\mathrm{Var}(\psi(\widehat{\mathbf{P}})) + \frac{\mathrm{Var}(\widehat{\psi}_r(\mathbf{P}))}{R}}}$$

which comes from the ratio between the standard deviation of (17.21) when $\widehat{\psi}(\mathbf{P}^*)$ is estimated using R_0 simulation runs (which is assumed so large that the simulation noise becomes negligible) and R simulation runs. To execute this shrinkage, we can either scale the resample estimate, i.e., multiply each $\widehat{\psi}(\mathbf{P}^*)$ by S before applying the basic bootstrap, or scale the quantile obtained from the basic bootstrap directly. The shrinkage factor itself is estimated using ANOVA described in Section 17.3.2.1. Moreover, a similar shrinkage approach can be applied to the percentile bootstrap.

17.3.2.3   Batching, Sectioning, and Sectioned Jackknife

Recall the CLT in (17.7) that, when combined with (17.9), gives

$$
\widehat{\psi}(\mathbf{P}) - \psi(\mathbf{P}) \approx N\left(0, \sum_{i=1}^{m} \frac{\mathrm{Var}(IF(\xi_i; \mathbf{P}))}{n_i} + \frac{\mathrm{Var}(\widehat{\psi}_r(\mathbf{P}))}{R}\right) \qquad (17.22)
$$

The batching method studied by [57] utilizes a pivotal t-statistic constructed from asymptotic normal variables in (17.22) to efficiently generate a CI. Divide the input data for each input-model i into say K batches, each of size m_i (so that $Km_i = n_i$, ignoring integrality). For each batch (which includes the data corresponding to all input models), we construct the empirical distribution $\mathbf{F}^k$ and run R simulation runs to obtain the k-th batched estimate $\widehat{\psi}(\mathbf{F}^k)$. When K is a fixed, small number (e.g., $K = 5$), then as $n_i \to \infty$ we have the CLT

$$
\left(\widehat{\psi}(\widehat{\mathbf{P}}^k) - \psi(\mathbf{P})\right)_{k=1,\ldots,K}
$$
$$
\approx \left(N\left(0, \sum_{i=1}^{m} \frac{\mathrm{Var}(IF(\xi_i; \mathbf{P}))}{m_i} + \frac{\mathrm{Var}(\widehat{\psi}_r(\mathbf{P}))}{R}\right)\right)_{k=1,\ldots,K} \qquad (17.23)
$$

where the normal variables are all independent. Thus, we can form a t-statistic

$$
\frac{\bar{\psi} - \psi(\mathbf{P})}{S/\sqrt{K}}
$$

where

$$
\bar{\psi} := \frac{1}{K}\sum_{k=1}^{K}\widehat{\psi}(\widehat{\mathbf{P}}^k), \quad S^2 = \frac{1}{K-1}\sum_{k=1}^{K}(\widehat{\psi}(\widehat{\mathbf{P}}^k) - \bar{\psi})^2
$$

which is distributed as t_{K-1}, the t-distribution with degree of freedom $K-1$. This gives a CI

$$
\left[\bar{\psi} - t_{K-1,1-\alpha/2}\frac{S}{\sqrt{K}}, \bar{\psi} + t_{K-1,1-\alpha/2}\frac{S}{\sqrt{K}}\right]
$$

where $t_{K-1,1-\alpha/2}$ is the $(1-\alpha/2)$-quantile of t_{K-1}. This idea resembles the batch means method commonly used in steady-state analysis [56, 109, 110], but here as a means to generate a CI capturing input uncertainty. The main strength of this approach is its light computation effort. To use batching with K number of batches, we need a simulation effort KR, and K in principle can be as small as 2. The caution here is that a small K would give a long interval (note the critical value $t_{K-1,1-\alpha/2}$ is large when K is small). Nonetheless, as K increases from 2, the decrease in interval width is steep and then stabilizes quickly [109]. In general, K equal to 5 would already reasonably approach the limiting critical value, i.e., the normal critical value $z_{1-\alpha/2}$.

If we have a point estimate $\widehat{\psi}(\widehat{\mathbf{P}})$ constructed from using all the input data, then we can also use the interval

$$\left[\widehat{\psi}(\widehat{\mathbf{P}}) - t_{K-1,1-\alpha/2}\frac{S}{\sqrt{K}}, \widehat{\psi}(\widehat{\mathbf{P}}) + t_{K-1,1-\alpha/2}\frac{S}{\sqrt{K}}\right].$$

where now the simulation effort for each sectioned estimate needs to be $1/K$ of the effort used for the point estimate $\widehat{\psi}(\widehat{\mathbf{P}})$ to elicit a proper self-normalization. This corresponds to the sectioning method.

The above can also be generalized to the jackknife, resulting in a sectioned jackknife method [2] for constructing CI under input uncertainty. The roadmap for deriving such a CI is similar in that a pivotal statistic is proposed, the difference being that due to the leave-one-section-out estimates in jackknife the cancellation needed in the pivotal statistic becomes more delicate to analyze. The benefit of sectioned jackknife, however, is that its resulting point estimate has a lower-order bias [2, 88], and that it is less sensitive, or more robust, against the adverse effect of a small batch size, because it uses all data *except* the batch.

17.3.2.4 Mixture-Based and Nonparametric Bayesian

When the sample size of the input data is relatively small, selecting a single parametric input model may be difficult. Instead of taking a purely nonparametric approach, Zouaoui and Wilson [144] propose to apply the Bayesian model averaging (BMA) scheme to construct a mixture of candidate input distributions and account for parametric as well as model uncertainties in their input uncertainty quantification framework.

Recall the Bayesian framework for modeling uncertainty about θ discussed in Section 17.3.1.2. The posterior update in (17.4) implicitly assumes that the distribution family is known. In BMA, in addition to imposing a prior distribution for each candidate distribution's parameter vector, a prior is assumed for the weights that determine the mixture. Given the real-world data, both priors are updated to their posteriors. Using both posteriors, Zouaoui and Wilson [144] propose variance decomposition method that accounts for Monte Carlo error and estimation error in θ as well as uncertainty about the parametric distribution family, which they refer to as model uncertainty.

Although BMA provides flexibility in choosing the parametric family, one must come up with a set of candidate distributions. Bayesian bootstrap [105], on the other hand, is a Bayesian analog to the frequentist's bootstrap method. For the (nonparametric) bootstrap scheme discussed in Section 17.3.2.1, recall that $\mathbf{P}^*$ is an empirical distribution of resampled observations from the original data set, say, $\mathbf{D} = \{\xi_1, \xi_2, \ldots, \xi_n\}$, with replacement. Therefore, $\mathbf{P}^*$ can be written as a n-dimensional probability simplex assigning a probability mass to each ξ_j in $\mathbf{D}$. For $\mathbf{P}^*$, each ξ_j is assigned with a multiple of $1/n$, e.g., $0, 1/n, 2/n, \cdots$. In Bayesian bootstrap, the probability simplex is modeled as a realization of a Dirichlet distribution whose density function is proportional to

$$\prod_{j=1}^{n} p_j^{\delta_j - 1} \mathbf{1}\left\{\sum_{j} p_j = 1\right\},$$

where p_j is the probability mass assigned to ξ_j and $\{\delta_1, \delta_2, \ldots, \delta_n > 0\}$ are the concentration parameters. Therefore, the Bayesian bootstrap allows more flexibility in modeling $\mathbf{P}^*$ than the frequentist's bootstrap. The Dirichlet distribution is a conjugate prior for the multinomial distribution with probabilities $\{p_j\}$; the resulting posterior distribution of $\{p_j\}$ is still Dirichlet.

In the input uncertainty context, [10] show their uniform resampling method to be a kind of Bayesian bootstrap, [116] and [130] include nonparametric input models in their stochastic kriging metamodels by sampling the probability simplex from the Dirichlet posterior given data, and [136] study the use of Dirichlet process mixture to construct credible intervals for simulation outputs.

17.3.2.5   Robust Simulation

In recent years, an approach based on (distributionally) robust optimization has been studied to quantify input uncertainty. Robust optimization [15, 16] is a framework that originated from optimization under uncertainty, in which the decision-maker uses a worst-case perspective, i.e., makes a decision that optimizes the worst-case performance over the unknown or uncertain parameter in the optimization problem. This uncertain parameter is postulated to lie in a so-called *uncertainty set* or *ambiguity set* that reflects the belief of the modeler which, roughly speaking, is a set where the truth is likely to lie in. The approach thus typically results in a minimax optimization problem, where the outer optimization is over the decision and the inner optimization computes the worst-case scenario constrained within the uncertainty set.

Distributionally robust optimization (DRO) [35, 60, 133] can be viewed as a branch of robust optimization when the uncertain parameter is the underlying probability distribution in a stochastic optimization. The uncertainty set can take a variety of forms, but mainly falls into two categories. The first consists of neighborhood balls surrounding a baseline distribution, where the ball size is measured by statistical distance such as φ-divergence [12, 14, 68], which includes for instance Kullback-Leibler (KL) and χ^2-distance, and Wasserstein distance [19, 23, 41, 48]. The second class consists of distributional summary constraints including moments and support [50, 62], marginal information [22, 36, 37], and distribution shape such as unimodality [79, 89, 102, 127].

The DRO approach, when applied to input uncertainty, can be viewed as a nonparametric approach, since the uncertainty sets can be created nonparametrically. The goal of this approach, much like the methods described above, is to construct intervals that cover the truth. This can be attained by imposing a worst-case optimization problem over the uncertainty set. Here, we use the term DRO broadly to refer to worst-case optimization, not necessarily having a decision to determine but only standard output analysis. More concretely,

$$\max / \min \psi(\mathbf{Q}) \quad \text{subject to} \quad \mathbf{Q} \in \mathcal{U} \qquad (17.24)$$

where max / min refers to a pair of maximization and minimization, and $\mathcal{U}$ is the uncertainty set in the probability space, and the decision variable is the unknown input distribution $\mathbf{Q}$. When the uncertainty set $\mathcal{U}$ is a confidence region on the unknown input distribution, then the worst-case optimization pair above would output an interval covering the true target quantity with at least the same confidence level. This implication can be readily seen and forms the basis of data-driven DRO [14, 17].

Regarding the construction of CIs, a main benefit of DRO is the flexibility to capture certain types of uncertainties beyond traditional statistical methods. For instance, in some problems, the modeler might be concerned about the misspecification of, say, i.i.d. assumptions, but is confident about the marginal distribution specification of the input process. In this case, the modeler can constrain the marginal information in the uncertainty set, but leave the dependence structure open to some extent. Then the resulting values of the optimization pair (17.24) would give the worst-case interval subject to this level of uncertainty or information. As another example, in other problems with little knowledge or very few data on the input distribution, one cannot fit a distribution and needs to rely on expert knowledge or crude a priori information. In this situation, the modeler can impose an uncertainty set on the first-order moments only.

In general, the DRO problems (17.24) need to be solved via simulation optimization, since the objective function is the target performance measure that can be only be approximated via the simulation model. (17.24) is thus a constrained stochastic optimization where the constraints are built from the uncertainty set, and moreover the decision variable is probability distribution, i.e., constrained by probability simplex constraints. When $\psi(\cdot)$ is a linear function in $\mathbf{Q}$, i.e., an expectation, the problem can be solved by sample average approximation [53, 54, 66, 67]. In more general cases such as discrete-event systems where $\psi(\cdot)$ is nonlinear in the input distributions, [51, 52, 85] devise approaches using stochastic approximation to iteratively solve these problems, which involve stochastic Frank-Wolfe or mirror descent that specializes to a variety of uncertainty sets.

Another perspective that has been taken to utilize (17.24) is to conduct local sensitivity analysis. In this context, the modeler imposes an uncertainty set whose size signifies the deviation of some model parameters away from a baseline value, with auxiliary constraints in the uncertainty set that capture the model structure or quantity that is kept unchanged. When the size shrinks, the values of the worst-case optimization (17.24) are expressible as a Taylor-type expansion around the baseline value in terms of the ball size, with the coefficients representing the worst-case sensitivity of the performance measure due to these input model changes subject to the auxiliary constraints. [76] develops these expansions when the balls are measured in KL, and [77] further develops expansions under auxiliary constraints on p-lag serial dependency and when the ball size is measured by Pearson's φ^2-coefficient.

17.3.3 Empirical Likelihood

Relating to the last subsection, when $\mathcal{U}$ is set as the neighborhood ball measured by a statistical distance surrounding the empirical distribution, the optimization (17.24) has a close connection to the empirical likelihood (EL) method [96]. The latter is a nonparametric analog to the celebrated maximum likelihood estimator (MLE) in parametric inference, and operates with the nonparametric MLE that turns out to equate to the (empirical, reverse) KL distance. EL uses a so-called profile likelihood that is the optimal value of an optimization problem with objective being this reverse KL distance and constraint being the quantity to be estimated, and conducts inference based on an analog to the classical Wilks' theorem.

It can be readily seen that when $\mathcal{U}$ uses the reverse KL distance, then (17.24) becomes the dual of the EL in the sense that the roles of objective and constraint in the profile likelihood are now reversed. This implies that the optimal value of (17.24) gives rise to CI that matches those generated from EL, when we choose the ball size of $\mathcal{U}$ to be a suitable χ^2-quantile [39, 87]. In other words, (17.24) provides an alternate approach to construct asymptotically exact CIs that is different from the delta method and the bootstrap. Notably, this interpretation goes beyond the rationale of data-driven DRO presented in Section 17.3.2.5 [78]. Lastly, it is notable that the statistical distance in $\mathcal{U}$ does not have to be reverse KL, but can also be any of a wide class of φ-divergence, and more recently Wasserstein distance [18].

Lam and Qian [80, 81] use the EL, in the form of the DRO (17.24), to construct CI under input uncertainty. More precisely, [81] use a tractable approximation of (17.24), via linearization, to obtain solution of the worst-case distributions encoded in terms of probability weights on the data points. They then run simulation using input distributions that are weighted by these worst-case probability weights to obtain upper and lower bounds. Compared to the delta method, this approach demonstrates better finite-sample performance because its bound construction does not rely on linearization directly, which can give poor coverage especially for performance measures that are close to some "natural boundaries" (e.g., small probability estimation). Compared to the bootstrap, it does not involve nested simulation whose configuration can be difficult to optimize, but instead replace the resampling with solving a pair of optimization problems derived from (17.24).

17.4 Other Aspects

In addition to the construction of CIs and variance estimation, there are a few other aspects regarding the handling of input uncertainty.

17.4.1   Bias Estimation

Input uncertainty affects not only the variance of $\widehat{\psi}$, but also its bias relative to ψ as well. With small input data samples and highly nonlinear simulation response, this bias can be substantial. Morgan [91] employs a quadratic linear regression metamodel to compute a bias estimate:

$$\hat{b} = \frac{1}{2}\mathrm{tr}(\widehat{\Omega}\widehat{\mathrm{H}}(\hat{\theta})), \qquad (17.25)$$

where $\widehat{\Omega}$ is the estimated covariance matrix of the MLE $\hat{\theta}$ and $\widehat{\mathrm{H}}$ approximates the Hessian of $\psi(\theta)$, computed via a quadratic regression metamodel. In addition to providing a bias estimate, the authors construct a hypothesis test to identify statistically significant bias.

17.4.2   Online Data

Zhou and Liu [141] first study an online input uncertainty quantification problem, where additional real-world observations are sequentially made available and the posterior distribution on θ, $p_{post}(\theta|D)$, is updated at each stage. They apply green simulation techniques (see Section 17.3.1.4) to reuse replications made at the parameters sampled from a previous stage in the current stage.

17.4.3   Data Collection vs Simulation Expense

In some applications, additional data collection is feasible at a cost. A natural question in this setting is how to allocate the finite resource for data collection among a number of data sources so that input uncertainty can be minimized. Ng and Chick [93] study this problem for a parametric Bayesian setting where all input distributions are independent. They also consider a joint resource allocation problem among simulation and data collection when the cost of a simulation replication is relatively expensive. Xu et al. [139] expand this framework to the case with correlated inputs.

Relatedly, Song and Nelson [117] focus on decomposing the total input uncertainty into each input distribution's contribution when there are m independent input distributions; note a nonparametric version of such decomposition is shown in (17.9). They also propose a sample-size sensitivity measure that indicates how much input uncertainty can be reduced by collecting an extra observation from each data source.

17.4.4   Model Calibration and Inverse Problems

While the input uncertainty literature has focused on situations where the input models are observable from direct data, in some applications the *output*-level instead of input-level data are observed. In these cases, calibrating the input model becomes an inverse problem where the unknown parameters or input distributions can only be observed through the input-output relation described by the simulation model, which is usually analytically intractable but evaluatable only via noisy simulation runs. This problem resembles the UQ literature in computer experiments [64, 70, 125, 134], but now with additional stochastic noise in the simulator (recall our introduction). In discrete-event simulation, the problem of informing input parameter values through output data falls traditionally under the umbrella of model validation and calibration [4, 73, 108, 112], in which a modeler would compare the simulation model output with real output data using statistical tests or Turing tests, re-calibrate or enhance the model if the test concludes a mismatch, and iterate the process.

Recently, some approaches have been suggested to directly calibrate the input unknowns by setting up (simulation) optimization problems. In particular, [59] use entropy maximization, and [3, 58] use DRO with an uncertainty set constructed from a statistical distance between simulated and real output data. Furthermore, [86, 101] study the correction of output discrepancies between the simulated and real data at the distribution level.

17.5   Simulation Optimization under Input Uncertainty

Thus far, the focus was on quantifying input uncertainty of a simulation model. In this section, we discuss how one can formulate and solve a simulation optimization problem in the presence of input uncertainty. We first define the generic simulation optimization problem with the following form:

$$x^* = \arg\max_{x \in \mathcal{X}} \psi(x, \mathbf{P}), \tag{17.26}$$

where $\mathcal{X}$ is a feasible solution set, and $\mathbf{P}$ and ψ are as before. The parametric form is:

$$x^* = \arg\max_{x \in \mathcal{X}} \psi(x, \theta). \tag{17.27}$$

The performance measure is parameterized by both solution x and input parameter vector θ. What makes (17.26) and (17.27) "simulation" optimization problems is that $\psi(x, \theta)$ must be estimated by running simulations. When $\psi(x, \theta)$ is replaced with its estimate, $\widehat{\psi}(x, \theta)$, Monte Carlo error is introduced. Therefore, as long as the simulation budget is finite, we cannot find x^* with certainty in general. Instead, a simulation optimization algorithm aims to provide an estimate $\hat{x}^*$ of x^* with some statistical guarantee on closeness of $\hat{x}^*$ to x^*. One such guarantee may be

$$\mathbb{P}\{|\psi(\hat{x}^*, \theta) - \psi(x^*, \theta)| \le \varepsilon\} \ge 1 - \alpha$$

for some $\varepsilon > 0$ and $0 < \alpha < 1$, where the probability is taken with respect to the Monte Carlo error in simulation. This implies that the probability that the optimality gap between $\hat{x}^*$ and x^* is within a tolerable level ($< \varepsilon$) is at least $1 - \alpha$.

In the traditional simulation optimization setting, $\mathbf{P}$ or θ is assumed to be given. Thus, the only source of stochasticity is Monte Carlo error in estimating $\widehat{\psi}(x, \theta)$, which can be reduced by running more simulation replications. The problem becomes more complex once input uncertainty is considered in conjunction with Monte Carlo error.

One may be tempted to solve the "plug-in" version by replacing the input distributions with their "best estimates" given the data. For instance, in the parametric case, θ may be replaced with its point estimate $\hat{\theta}$ in (17.27) to find

$$x^*(\hat{\theta}) = \arg\max_{x \in \mathcal{X}} \psi(x, \hat{\theta}),$$

which is the conditional optimum given $\hat{\theta}$. In general, $x^*(\hat{\theta}) \neq x^*$ as $x^*(\hat{\theta})$ depends on the random vector, $\hat{\theta}$. However, when a generic simulation optimization algorithm is applied to the plug-in problem, it provides a statistical guarantee for finding $x^*(\hat{\theta})$, not x^*. Therefore, to properly account for the effect of input uncertainty in simulation optimization, one must explicitly consider dependence of $\psi(x, \theta)$ on θ when designing the simulation optimization algorithm to provide a statistical guarantee for finding x^*.

Once again, consider the delta method:

$$\psi(x, \hat{\theta}) \approx \psi(x, \theta) + \nabla_\theta \psi(x, \theta)'(\hat{\theta} - \theta).$$

If this linear model is exact for all x and the gradient, $\nabla_\theta \psi(x, \theta)$, does not depend on x, then $x^*(\hat{\theta}) = x^*$. However, this is an unrealistic assumption for many practical problems as $\psi(x, \hat{\theta})$ tends to have an interaction effect between x and $\hat{\theta}$.

Suppose we compare performance measures at x and given $x^*\hat{\theta}$. We have from the delta method,

$$\psi(x^*, \hat{\theta}) - \psi(x, \hat{\theta}) - \{\psi(x^*, \theta) - \psi(x, \theta)\}$$
$$\approx [\nabla_\theta \psi(x^*, \theta) - \nabla_\theta \psi(x, \theta)]'(\hat{\theta} - \theta). \quad (17.28)$$

The distribution of (17.28) lets us infer the value of $\psi(x^*, \theta) - \psi(x, \theta)$ from that of $\psi(x^*, \hat{\theta}) - \psi(x, \hat{\theta})$. Here, $\nabla_\theta \psi(x^*, \theta) - \nabla_\theta \psi(x, \theta)$ quantifies how differently the performance measures at x^* and x are affected by a small change in the parameter vector. [118] refer to the right-hand side of (17.28) as the common-input-data (CID) effect since it captures the impact of input uncertainty caused by the same set of real-world data in comparing x^* and x. Notice that the CID effect is random due to the uncertainty in $\hat{\theta}$. If $\hat{\theta}$ is a maximum likelihood estimator, then from the asymptotic distribution of $\hat{\theta}$, (17.28) is approximately distributed as

$$N\left(0, [\nabla_\theta \psi(x^*, \theta) - \nabla_\theta \psi(x, \theta)]'\frac{\Sigma(\theta)}{n}[\nabla_\theta \psi(x^*, \theta) - \nabla_\theta \psi(x, \theta)]\right).$$
$$(17.29)$$

Observe that uncertainty about $\hat{\theta}$ measured by $\Sigma(\theta)/n$ is amplified or reduced by the gradient difference. For instance, if the gradient difference is near 0 along a dimension of $\hat{\theta}$, then even if its marginal variance is large, it may have very little impact on the variance of the CID effect. On the other hand, if the gradient difference is large, then the variance of (17.29) becomes large, which makes it difficult to infer that $\psi(x^*, \theta) - \psi(x, \theta) > 0$.

In fact, we do not observe $\psi(x^*, \hat{\theta}) - \psi(x, \hat{\theta})$, either. Suppose $\psi(x, \hat{\theta})$ is estimated by a sample average of noisy simulation outputs, i.e., $\hat{\psi}(x, \hat{\theta}) = \frac{1}{R(x)} \sum_{r=1}^{R(x)} \psi_r(x, \hat{\theta})$, where $R(x)$ is the number of replications run at x. Assuming that all simulations are run independently, the variance of $\hat{\psi}(x^*, \hat{\theta}) - \hat{\psi}(x, \hat{\theta}) - \{\psi(x^*, \theta) - \psi(x, \theta)\}$ is approximately

$$[\nabla_\theta \psi(x^*, \theta) - \nabla_\theta \psi(x, \theta)]'\frac{\Sigma(\theta)}{n}[\nabla_\theta \psi(x^*, \theta) - \nabla_\theta \psi(x, \theta)]$$
$$+ \frac{\text{Var}(\psi_r(x^*, \hat{\theta}))}{R(x^*)} + \frac{\text{Var}(\psi_r(x, \hat{\theta}))}{R(x)}.$$
$$(17.30)$$

Clearly, the latter two terms can be reduced by increasing $R(x^*)$ and $R(x)$, whereas the first term may be reduced only by collecting more real-world data.

In the following subsections, we first discuss the case when the data size, n, is fixed (17.5.1 and 17.5.2) and when streaming data are available (17.5.3).

17.5.1   Selection of the Best under Input Uncertainty

In this section, we consider the case when the set of feasible solutions, $\mathcal{X}$, contains a finite number of solutions. In particular, when $|\mathcal{X}|$ is relatively small, say k, we are able to simulate them all and compare their estimated performance measures to select the best (ranking and selection) or return a set of solutions that contains the best (subset selection). We refer the readers to Kim and Nelson [72] for foundations of ranking and selection, subset selection, and related work. Our main focus in this section is integration of input uncertainty into these methodologies.

17.5.1.1   Ranking and Selection

A classical problem formulation for ranking and selection (R&S) is

$$k^* = \arg\max_{1 \le k \le K} \psi(k, \theta) \tag{17.31}$$

where θ is assumed known. Notice that we replaced x with its index k given that the total number of alternatives in comparison is K. Typically, $\psi(k, \theta)$ is assumed to be the expectation of a stochastic simulation output, $\psi_r(k, \theta)$. A R&S procedure controls the numbers of replications assigned to each alternative in comparison given the total budget, N, so that it achieves the statistical guarantee that it is designed to provide upon termination. Depending on how the allocation is made, R&S procedures can be categorized into single-stage [13], two-stage [104], or sequential [71] procedures. Upon termination, an estimate of k^*, $\hat{k}^*$, is returned. Typically, $\hat{k}^*$ is the alternative that has the best sample mean given the simulation replications made throughout the procedure, namely,

$$\hat{k}^* = \arg\max_{1 \le k \le K} \widehat{\psi}(k, \theta),$$

where $\widehat{\psi}(k, \theta) = \frac{1}{R(k)} \sum_{r=1}^{R(k)} \psi_r(k, \theta)$ and $R(k)$ is the number of replications allocated to the k-th alternative.

To provide a statistical guarantee for selecting k^*, R&S procedures typically control the probability of correct selection (PCS)

$$\text{PCS} = \mathbb{P}\{\hat{k}^* = k^*\}$$

to be at least $1/K < 1-\alpha < 1$. Equivalently, one may control the probability of false selection (PFS)

$$\text{PFS} = \mathbb{P}\{\hat{k}^* \neq k^*\}$$

to be lower than $0 < \alpha < 1 - 1/K$. There are two main approaches to provide the PCS guarantee: one is to control the exact PCS given finite simulation budget N and the other is to control the asymptotic convergence rate of PFS assuming N is sufficiently large.

For the former, most procedures assume the simulation outputs are normally distributed to get a handle on the distribution of $\hat{\psi}(k, \theta)$ and its variance estimator is given finite $R(k)$. Moreover, the procedures adopt the indifference zone (IZ) assumption, which states that all suboptimal alternatives have performance measures that are at least δ less than the best for some known $\delta > 0$. Mathematically, this can be written as

$$\psi(k^*, \theta) - \psi(k, \theta) \geq \delta, \forall k \neq k^*. \tag{17.32}$$

First introduced by Bechhofer [13], the IZ assumption turns out to be crucial for providing the finite-sample PFS guarantee; without the assumption, any suboptimal alternative's performance measure can be arbitrarily close to the best solution so that they may not be distinguished given finite N. The PCS under the IZ assumption is denoted as

$$\text{PCS}_\delta = \mathbb{P}\{\hat{k}^* = k^* | \psi(k^*, \theta) - \psi(k, \theta) \geq \delta, \forall k \neq k^*\}$$

to differentiate it from the PFS. Under the normality assumption, several procedures have been designed to guarantee $\text{PCS}_\delta \geq 1 - \alpha$ after spending a finite amount of simulation budget, N, for any chosen $\delta > 0$.

When input uncertainty is considered, Problem (17.31) must be reformulated as θ is unknown. As discussed for the generic simulation optimization problem, one can construct the "plug-in" version of (17.31) by replacing θ with its point estimate $\hat{\theta}$. The corresponding optimum of the plug-in problem, $k^*(\hat{\theta})$, is then conditional on $\hat{\theta}$. Song et al. [119] propose to consider the following average PCS

$$\overline{\text{PCS}}_\delta = \text{E}_{\widehat{\theta}}[\mathbb{P}\{\widehat{k}^*(\widehat{\theta}) = k^*|\widehat{\theta}\}|\psi(k^*, \theta) - \psi(k, \theta) \geq \delta, \forall k \neq k^*],$$

where the outer expectation is with respect to the distribution of $\widehat{\theta}$. In words, $\overline{\text{PCS}}_\delta$ evaluates the probability that $\widehat{k}^*(\widehat{\theta})$ is indeed k^*. Of course, we have a single realization of $\widehat{\theta}$ computed from the set of real-world observations. Nevertheless, if $\overline{\text{PCS}}_\delta \geq 1 - \alpha$ can be guaranteed, then in expectation (over both Monte Carlo error and input uncertainty), the PCS guarantee is achieved.

From the definition of $\widehat{k}^*$, $\overline{\text{PCS}}_\delta$ can be rewritten as

$$\overline{\text{PCS}}_\delta = \text{E}_{\widehat{\theta}}[\mathbb{P}\{\widehat{\psi}(k^*, \widehat{\theta}) > \widehat{\psi}(k, \widehat{\theta}), \forall k \neq k^*|\widehat{\theta}\}|\psi(k^*, \theta) - \psi(k, \theta)$$
$$\geq \delta, \forall k \neq k^*].$$

Thus, computing $\overline{\text{PCS}}_\delta$ requires characterizing the joint distribution of

$$\left\{\widehat{\psi}(k^*, \widehat{\theta}) - \widehat{\psi}(k, \widehat{\theta}) - [\psi(k^*, \theta) - \psi(k, \theta)]\right\}_{\forall k \neq k^*}. \tag{17.33}$$

Applying the delta method as in the beginning of Chapter 17.5, the joint distribution of (17.33) can be approximated with a multivariate normal distribution whose mean is the $(K - 1)$-dimensional zero vector and the elements of its variance-covariance matrix can be computed similarly as in (17.30). Under some additional assumptions on the variance-covariance matrix, Song et al. [119] derive the expression for $\overline{\text{PCS}}_\delta$ for a single-stage R&S procedure.

However, unlike any $\delta > 0$ is allowed for the generic R&S problem, the values of α and δ may not be chosen as desired when there is input uncertainty. To see this, consider the minimum indifference zone parameter, $\delta^\alpha_{\min}$, given α defined as

$$\delta^\alpha_{\min} = \inf\{\delta : \lim_{N \to \infty} \overline{\text{PCS}}_\delta \geq 1 - \alpha\}.$$

Loosely speaking, $\delta^\alpha_{\min}$ is the smallest performance measure difference one can detect with desired precision $(1 - \alpha)$ in the presence of input uncertainty captured by estimation error of $\widehat{\theta}$. Note that $\delta^\alpha_{\min}$ is an increasing function of α and may be strictly positive when the input data sample size, n, and α are small. For any δ smaller than $\delta^\alpha_{\min}$, we cannot guarantee $\text{PCS}_\delta \geq 1 - \alpha$ even with an infinite simulation budget. Such a positive lower bound on the

IZ parameter is a result of input uncertainty. Derivation of $\delta^{\alpha}_{\min}$ depends on the specific R&S procedure; Song et al. [119] derive the expression for a single-stage R&S procedure.

This challenge motivates one to consider formulations other than the plug-in version of (17.31). One popular variant studied by Fan et al. [42] is the distributionally robust R&S problem:

$$\underline{k} = \arg\max_{1 \leq k \leq K} \min_{\theta \in \mathcal{U}} \psi(k, \theta), \qquad (17.34)$$

where $\mathcal{U}$ is the uncertainty set that contains the possible values of θ. Specifically, they consider when $\mathcal{U}$ has a finite number of candidate θ values; namely, $\mathcal{U} = \{\theta_1, \theta_2, \ldots, \theta_B\}$. The inner problem of (17.34) finds the worst-case input parameter θ_b in $\mathcal{U}$ for each alternative k, whereas the outer problem selects the alternative with the best worst-case performance. Similar to the generic R&S problem, $\underline{k}$ is estimated by

$$\hat{\underline{k}} = \arg\max_{1 \leq k \leq K} \min_{\theta_b \in \mathcal{U}} \hat{\psi}(k, \theta_b),$$

where the number of replications allocated to each (k, θ_b) is determined by the procedure. Under this formulation, the probability of correct selection is modified to

$$\text{PCS} = \mathbb{P}\{\hat{\underline{k}} = \underline{k}\}. \qquad (17.35)$$

A benefit of Formulation (17.34) is that the input uncertainty is completely characterized by solving the inner minimization problem. By limiting θ to be among a finite number of candidates in $\mathcal{U}$ and simulating all alternative-parameter pairs, it eliminates the need to model the effect of $\hat{\theta}$ to $\psi(k, \hat{\theta})$ for each k. Thus, one only needs to control the Monte Carlo error in $\hat{\psi}(k, \theta_b)$ for each (k, θ_b) to achieve correct selection.

To provide a finite-sample probability guarantee for solving (17.34), Fan et al. [42] extend the IZ formulation in classical R&S procedures. First, they relabeled the performance measures at solution-parameter pairs $\{\psi(k, \theta_b)\}_{1 \leq k \leq K, 1 \leq b \leq B}$ such that $\psi_{k,1} \leq \psi_{k,2} \leq \cdots \leq \psi_{k,B}$ for all $1 \leq k \leq K$ and $\psi_{1,1} > \psi_{2,1} \geq \cdots \geq \psi_{K,1}$. Therefore, $\underline{k} = 1$. The IZ formulation is modified to

$$\psi_{\underline{k},1} - \psi_{2,1} > \delta \qquad (17.36)$$

for given $\delta > 0$. That is, the worst-case performance measure of $\underline{k}$ is at least δ better than those of other $k - 1$ alternatives. Instead of providing the PCS guarantee under the IZ assumption, they guarantee the following probability of good selection (PGS):

$$\mathbb{P}\{\psi_{\underline{k},1} - \psi_{\widehat{\underline{k}},1} \leq \delta\} \geq 1 - \alpha. \tag{17.37}$$

In words, (17.37) grants that the selected solution's worst-case performance is within δ from that of $\underline{k}$. If (17.36) holds, then (17.37) is equivalent to (17.35) $\geq 1 - \alpha$. Therefore, δ here can be interpreted as the allowable error tolerance.

Fan et al. [42] further split δ to $\delta_I = \delta_O = \delta/2$, where δ_I is the allowable error in solving the inner-level minimization problem of (17.34). Specifically, they aim to achieve

$$\psi_{k,b^k} - \psi_{k,1} \leq \delta_I, \quad \forall 1 \leq k \leq K,$$

where $b^k = \min_{\theta_b \in \mathcal{U}} \widehat{\psi}(k, \theta_b)$. Assuming the IZ assumption holds, this implies that to make a correct selection at the outer level, ψ_{k,b^k} and ψ_{1,b^1} must be at least $\delta - \delta_I = \delta_O$ apart for all $1 \leq k \leq K$. Similarly, they also split the error level α for inner-level and outer-level comparisons so that the overall probability error is no larger than α. Based on these parameters, Fan et al. [42] propose two-stage and sequential R&S procedures that provide PGS guarantee (17.37) after spending a finite number of replications.

We close this subsection by mentioning that Gao et al. [49] also study (17.34). Instead of creating a R&S procedure with a finite-sample guarantee, they develop an optimal computing budget allocation scheme for (17.34) aiming to maximize the convergence rate of $1 - PCS$ as the simulation budget increases. Shi et al. [115] further extend Gao et al. [49] to solve stochastically constrained version of (17.34).

17.5.1.2   Subset Selection and Multiple Comparisons with the Best

The objective of a subset selection procedure is to return a set of alternatives $\mathcal{I}$ that contains k^* defined in (17.31) with probability $1 - \alpha$:

$$\mathbb{P}\{k^* \in \mathcal{I}\} \geq 1 - \alpha. \tag{17.38}$$

A subset selection procedure does not necessarily guarantee $|\mathcal{I}| = 1$, but when $|\mathcal{I}| = 1$, then the element of $\mathcal{I}$ is indeed k^* with probability of at least $1 - \alpha$.

Corlu and Biller [30] first consider accounting for input uncertainty in a subset selection procedure aiming to guarantee (17.38) under the IZ assumption (17.32). Similar to Song et al. [119], they also find that there is a positive lower bound to δ to guarantee (17.38) when there is input uncertainty. Corlu and Biller [31] take an approach to average out both input uncertainty and Monte Carlo error when they define the optimum. That is, their subset $\mathcal{I}$ contains

$$\bar{k} = \arg\max_{1 \leq k \leq K} E_\theta[\psi(k, \theta)] \qquad (17.39)$$

with probability no less than $1 - \alpha$, where the expectation is taken with respect to the posterior distribution of θ conditional on the input data. A benefit of this approach is that one is guaranteed to have $|\mathcal{I}| = 1$ for sufficiently large simulation budget. However, this formulation may be misleading when the size of the input data is small as no warning is given regarding the risk caused by uncertainty about θ.

The multiple comparisons with the best (MCB) procedure provides simultaneous confidence intervals $[L_k, U_k]$ for all $1 \leq k \leq K$ such that

$$\mathbb{P}\{\psi(k, \theta) - \psi(k^*, \theta) \in [L_k, U_k], 1 \leq k \leq K\} \geq 1 - \alpha, \qquad (17.40)$$

where $\{L_k, U_k\}_{1 \leq k \leq K}$ can be constructed from the confidence intervals of the pairwise difference between performance measures [65]:

$$\mathbb{P}\{\psi(k, \theta) - \psi(\ell, \theta) \in [\widehat{\psi}(k, \theta) - \widehat{\psi}(\ell, \theta) \pm w_{k\ell}], \forall k \neq \ell\} \geq 1 - \alpha. \qquad (17.41)$$

In words, the intervals in (17.40) cover the difference between each alternative's performance and the optimum's. By design, either L_k or U_k is equal to 0 for each k and if we define $\mathcal{S} = \{k : U_k > 0\}$, then we have $\mathbb{P}\{k^* \in \mathcal{S}\} \geq 1 - \alpha$.

With input uncertainty, θ is unknown. Thus, $\widehat{\psi}(k, \theta)$ in (17.41) is replaced with $\widehat{\psi}(k, \widehat{\theta})$ for each k. As a result, $w_{k\ell}, \forall k \neq \ell$ that satisfy (17.41) comes down to estimating (17.30) under a normality assumption on the simulation outputs for each alternative and regularity conditions on $\widehat{\theta}$. Focusing on the case that all K alternatives' simulators share the same input models, Song and Nelson [118] propose to split $w_{k\ell}$ into two parts, where one covers the difference in the CID effects for solutions k and ℓ, $\{\nabla_\theta \psi(k, \theta) - \nabla_\theta \psi(\ell, \theta)\}'(\widehat{\theta} - \theta)$, and the other covers the stochastic error difference in $\widehat{\psi}(k, \widehat{\theta}) - \widehat{\psi}(\ell, \widehat{\theta})$ conditional on $\widehat{\theta}$. Upon choosing the coverage error appropriately for each interval, they show that the resulting

$\{w_{k\ell}\}_{1\le k\neq \ell\le K}$ provide MCB intervals with asymptotically correct coverage probability.

17.5.2 Global Optimization under Input Uncertainty

Continuous optimization in the stochastic simulation setting is also affected by uncertainty in input distributions used to drive the simulation model. Both searching for the optimal solution and characterizing its error should take input uncertainty into account.

Consider the continuous optimization problem (17.26) where $\mathcal{X}$ is a nonempty subset of $\mathbb{R}^n$. Zhou and Xie [142] provided one of the first approaches for this setting by defining a risk measure, ρ (e.g., expected value, mean-variance, Value-At-Risk). For the parametric case, this can be written $\rho_{\mathbf{P}_\theta|\xi}$ where $\mathbf{P}_\theta|\xi$ is the posterior distribution for $\mathbf{P}$ (i.e., for θ) given the observed input data ξ. Their approach replaces the optimization in (17.27) with $H^\rho(x) = \rho_{\mathbf{P}_\theta|\xi}(\psi(x|\mathbf{P}))$. Although the development was for the parametric case, the authors suggested that the approach could be applied in a nonparametric setting using a Dirichlet process prior. Under general conditions, as the input data sample size goes to infinity, they show that the risk-based objective using posterior $\psi_{\mathbf{P}_\theta|\xi}$ converges in probability to the risk-based objective using $\mathbf{P}$. A stochastic approximation method for this approach and associated stochastic gradient estimators are presented in [21].

When the performance measure ψ can be modeled as a Gaussian process (GP) over x, θ space, Bayesian methods can be employed to include input uncertainty in the GP model optimization process given a prior distribution $\mathbf{G}$ for the unknown θ. Then the optimization is of $\mathbf{E}_{\mathbf{G}(\theta)}(\psi(x, \theta))$. In [98] efficient global optimization (EGO—see [69]) and knowledge gradient (KG—see [113]) sequential optimization methods were modified to include input uncertainty. Also in the GP setting, [74] proposed a robust optimization method based on Kullback-Leibler distance with a modified EGO criterion.

Wang et al. [131] modified the method of Pearce and Branke [98] to determine the next x, θ pair sequentially (x then θ) rather than simultaneously. The θ value is selected by minimizing IMSE or IMSE weighted by the posterior distribution for θ. They showed somewhat better results for KG search with small data samples and similar results in EGO and other KG settings while reducing computational time. In addition to EGO and KG, they also incorporated the two-stage search with Informational Approach for Global Optimization (IAGO—[129]) and Expected Excursion

Volume (EEV—[100]) metrics for selecting search points in the GP-based optimization.

Bayesian optimization has also been employed for handling the nonparametric optimization case posed in (17.26). In two recent papers, Wang et al. [130, 132] approached the simulation optimization problem similarly to [98] but employed Bayesian updating of the unknown input distribution, beginning with a (presumably diffuse) Dirichlet process prior.

When there is the option to collect more input-model data or continue an optimization, Ungredda et al. [126] suggest an extension to the approach in Pearce et al. [98] that they call Bayesian Information Collection and Optimisation (BICO). The decision is based on a Value of Information (VoI) measure for an additional simulation evaluation (at cost c_f) vs. the VoI for an additional input data sample (at cost c_s).

17.5.3   Online Optimization with Streaming Input Data

Thus far, our discussion in Section 17.5 has focused on the case when a batch of finite input data is available, but no additional data can be collected. In many practical problems, however, a stream of input data may be collected continuously. Assuming that the input data-generating process is stationary, Wu and Zhou [135] propose a R&S framework to solve Problem (17.39) by continuously updating the posterior distribution of θ from the sequence of incoming data. They also consider the case when there is a trade-off between real-world data collection versus simulation replication and study a computational budget allocation scheme.

Song and Shanbhag [122] study a simulation optimization problem with continuous variables when a sequence of streaming data is made available at each period. Their propose to update $\hat{\theta}$ at each period using the cumulative data and solve the plug-in version of (17.27) given $\hat{\theta}$ using stochastic approximation (SA). Under a strong convexity assumption, they derive an upper bound on the expected optimality gap of the solution returned from SA for the original problem (17.27) as a function of number of SA steps taken as well as the sample size of accumulated data in the period. From the upper bound, they propose a stopping criterion for SA at each period, i.e., they take SA steps until the error rate of SA matches that from the finite-sample size.

Both work mentioned here assume that the streaming data are independent and identically distributed. A framework that can account for a nonstationary data-generating process will broaden the applicability of the online simulation optimization schemes.

17.6   Future Research Directions

As computation resources increase in power with decreasing cost, simulation analysis has evolved from accepting the point estimate of the input distribution as *the truth* to incorporating the estimation error in uncertainty quantification and in simulation optimization. However, many open questions remain to be addressed.

First, the majority of work introduced in this chapter assumes the collected data are i.i.d. observations from real-world distributions that do not change over time. In many applications, such assumptions fail to hold due to dependence among the sequence of observations or nonstationarity of the data-generating process. Also, even if the real-world distribution can be characterized as generating i.i.d. input vectors, only marginal observations may be available so that the dependence structure cannot be estimated in a straightforward way. Among the tools that have been investigated in the input uncertainty literature, robust optimization and robust simulation come closest to handling such issues, but there remains much work to be done including: (i) making the methodology computationally efficient, (ii) quantifying the reliability when facing nonstationarity in a rigorous statistical sense, and (iii) exploring alternative methods to tackle these challenges.

In some cases, the input data themselves are unobservable and we can only access the "output data" from the real-world system. For instance, in a queueing system, we may observe the departure times of the jobs, but not their arrival times nor service times. In this case, finding the "right" input model for the simulator can be viewed as a calibration problem. However, unlike a typical calibration problem in the computer experiment literature that calibrates the model parameter so that the model output matches a given benchmark, here, we need to choose the input model so that the sequence of outputs generated from the simulator matches the real-world output data. This can be a high-dimensional inference problem that faces difficult statistical challenges, including the unavailability of the likelihood function, non-identifiability issues for over-parametrized models (i.e., more than one set of parameter values give the simulation-real output match), and model bias (i.e., the best fitting model in the class has parameter values bearing a discrepancy with reality). Both traditional model validation tools and more recent approaches on this problem require further developments. Moreover, there are several other open questions, including what metric should be adopted to measure the discrepancy between real and simulation outputs, and how to incorporate uncertainty from both input and output data.

Lastly, creating more application-specific methods and addressing challenges in these areas will enrich the literature. Although input uncertainty appears ubiquitous in simulation applications, there has been little work in applying input uncertainty methods to support decision-making. For instance, a company may run a market simulation study where the key input being the utility parameters that customers use to decide which product to buy (if any) among the competing offers. One way to estimate the utility parameters is to survey (often a very small fraction of) the customer basis. Thus, the estimation error of the utility parameters may cause significant uncertainty in the sales prediction obtained from the simulation study. Without quantifying input uncertainty, the company may face a significant risk. How to quantify and mitigate the uncertainty, both statistically and in a computationally efficient way, is an important question to resolve.

References

1. Ankenman, B., Nelson, B. L., and Staum, J. (2010). Stochastic kriging for simulation metamodeling. *Operations Research,* 58(2):371–382.
2. Asmussen, S. and Glynn, P. W. (2007). *Stochastic Simulation: Algorithms and Analysis,* volume 57. Springer Science & Business Media.
3. Bai, Y., Balch, T., Chen, H., Dervovic, D., Lam, H., and Vyetrenko, S. (2021). Calibrating over-parametrized simulation models: A framework via eligibility set. *arXiv preprint* arXiv:2105.12893.
4. Balci, O. and Sargent, R. G. (1982). Some examples of simulation model validation using hypothesis testing. In *Proceedings of the 14th Winter Simulation Conference,* volume 2, pages 621–629.
5. Barton, R. R. and Schruben, L. W. (2001). Resampling methods for input modeling. In *Proceedings of the 2001 Winter Simulation Conference,* pages 372–378. IEEE.
6. Barton, R. R. (2012). Tutorial: Input uncertainty in outout analysis. In *Proceedings of the 2012 Winter Simulation Conference,* pages 67–78. IEEE.
7. Barton, R. R., Chick, S. E., Cheng, R. C., Henderson, S. G., Law, A. M., Schmeiser, B. W., Leemis, L. M., Schruben, L. W., and Wilson, J. R. (2002). Panel discussion on current issues in input modeling. In *Proceedings of the 2002 Winter Simulation Conference,* pages 353–369. IEEE.
8. Barton, R. R., Lam, H., and Song, E. (2018). Revisiting direct bootstrap resampling for input model uncertainty. In *Proceedings of the 2018 Winter Simulation Conference,* pages 1635–1645. IEEE.
9. Barton, R. R., Nelson, B. L., and Xie, W. (2014). Quantifying input uncertainty via simulation confidence intervals. *INFORMS Journal on Computing,* 26(1):74–87.

10. Barton, R. R. and Schruben, L. W. (1993). Uniform and bootstrap resampling of empirical distributions. In *Proceedings of the 1993 Winter Simulation Conference*, pages 503–508. IEEE.

11. Bayarri, M. J., Berger, J. O., Paulo, R., Sacks, J., Cafeo, J. A., Cavendish, J., Lin, C.-H., and Tu, J. (2007). A framework for validation of computer models. *Technometrics*, 49(2):138–154.

12. Bayraksan, G. and Love, D. K. (2015). Data-driven stochastic programming using phi-divergences. In *Tutorials in Operations Research*, pages 1–19. INFORMS.

13. Bechhofer, R. E. (1954). A single-sample multiple decision procedure for ranking means of normal populations with known variances. *The Annals of Mathematical Statistics*, 25(1):16 – 39.

14. Ben-Tal, A., Den Hertog, D., De Waegenaere, A., Melenberg, B., and Rennen, G. (2013). Robust solutions of optimization problems affected by uncertain probabilities. *Management Science*, 59(2):341–357.

15. Ben-Tal, A., El Ghaoui, L., and Nemirovski, A. (2009). *Robust Optimization*. Princeton University Press.

16. Bertsimas, D., Brown, D. B., and Caramanis, C. (2011). Theory and applications of robust optimization. *SIAM Review*, 53(3):464–501.

17. Bertsimas, D., Gupta, V., and Kallus, N. (2018). Robust sample average approximation. *Mathematical Programming*, 171(1-2):217–282.

18. Blanchet, J., Kang, Y., and Murthy, K. (2019). Robust Wasserstein profile inference and applications to machine learning. *Journal of Applied Probability*, 56(3):830-857.

19. Blanchet, J. and Murthy, K. (2019). Quantifying distributional model risk via optimal transport. *Mathematics of Operations Research*, 44(2):565–600.

20. Box, G. E. P. (1976). Science and statistics. *Journal of the American Statistical Association*, 71(356):791–799.

21. Cakmak, S., Wu, D., and Zhou, E. (2020). Solving Bayesian risk optimization via nested stochastic gradient estimation. *arXiv:2007.05860*.

22. Chen, L., Ma, W., Natarajan, K., Simchi-Levi, D., and Yan, Z. (2018). Distributionally robust linear and discrete optimization with marginals. *Available at SSRN 3159473*.

23. Chen, R. and Paschalidis, I. C. (2018). A robust learning approach for regression models based on distributionally robust optimization. *Journal of Machine Learning Research*, 19(13):1–48.

24. Cheng, R. C. and Holland, W. (1997). Sensitivity of computer simulation experiments to errors in input data. *Journal of Statistical Computation and Simulation*, 57(1–4):219–241.

25. Cheng, R. C. and Holland, W. (1998). Two-point methods for assessing variability in simulation output. *Journal of Statistical Computation and Simulation*, 60(3):183–205.

26. Cheng, R. C. H. and Holland, W. (2004). Calculation of confidence intervals for simulation output. *ACM Transactions on Modeling and Computer Simulation*, 14(4).

27. Chick, S. E. (2001). Input distribution selection for simulation experiments: Accounting for input uncertainty. *Operations Research*, 49(5):744–758.

28. Chick, S. E. (2006). Bayesian ideas and discrete event simulation: Why, what and how. In Perrone, L. F., Wieland, F. P., Liu, J., Lawson, B. G., Nicol, D. M., and Fujimoto, R. M., editors, *Proceedings of the 2006 Winter Simulation Conference*, pages 96–106. IEEE.

29. Corlu, C. G., Akcay, A., and Xie, W. (2020). Stochastic simulation under input uncertainty: A Review. *Operations Research Perspectives*, 7:100162.

30. Corlu, C. and Biller, B. (2013). A subset selection procedure under input parameter uncertainty. In *Proceedings of the 2013 Winter Simulation Conference*, pages 463–473. IEEE.

31. Corlu, C. G. and Biller, B. (2015). Subset selection for simulations accounting for input uncertainty. In *Proceedings of the 2015 Winter Simulation Conference*, pages 437–446. IEEE.

32. Cranmer, K., Brehmer, J., and Louppe, G. (2020). The frontier of simulation-based inference. *Proceedings of the National Academy of Sciences*, 117(48):30055–30062.

33. Currin, C., Mitchell, T., Morris, M., and Ylvisaker, D. (1991). Bayesian prediction of deterministic functions, with applications to the design and analysis of computer experiments. *Journal of the American Statistical Association*, 86(416):953–963.

34. Davison, A. C. and Hinkley, D. V. (1997). *Bootstrap Methods and their Application*. Number 1. Cambridge University Press.

35. Delage, E. and Ye, Y. (2010). Distributionally robust optimization under moment uncertainty with application to data-driven problems. *Operations Research*, 58(3):595–612.

36. Dhara, A., Das, B., and Natarajan, K. (2021). Worst-case expected shortfall with univariate and bivariate marginals. *INFORMS Journal on Computing*, 33(1):370–389.

37. Doan, X. V., Li, X., and Natarajan, K. (2015). Robustness to dependency in portfolio optimization using overlapping marginals. *Operations Research*, 63(6):1468–1488.

38. Duchi, J., Glynn, P., and Namkoong, H. (2016). Statistics of robust optimization: A generalized empirical likelihood approach. *arXiv preprint* arXiv:1610.03425.

39. Duchi, J. C., Glynn, P. W., and Namkoong, H. (2021). Statistics of robust optimization: A generalized empirical likelihood approach. *Mathematics of Operations Research*, 46(3):946–969.

40. Efron, B. and Tibshirani, R. J. (1994). *An Introduction to the Bootstrap*. CRC press.

41. Esfahani, P. M. and Kuhn, D. (2018). Data-driven distributionally robust optimization using the Wasserstein metric: Performance guarantees and tractable reformulations. *Mathematical Programming*, 171(1-2):115–166.

42. Fan, W., Hong, L. J., and Zhang, X. (2020). Distributionally robust selection of the best. *Management Science*, 66(1):190–208.

43. Feng, M. and Song, E. (2019). Efficient input uncertainty quantification via green simulation using sample path likelihood ratios. In *Proceedings of the 2019 Winter Simulation Conference*, pages 3693–3704. IEEE.

44. Feng, M. and Staum, J. (2015). Green simulation designs for repeated experiments. In *Proceedings of the 2015 Winter Simulation Conference*, pages 403–413. IEEE.

45. Feng, M. and Staum, J. (2017). Green simulation: Reusing the output of repeated experiments. *ACM Transactions on Modeling and Computer Simulation*, 27(4):1–28.

46. Feng, M. B. and Song, E. (2021). Optimal nested simulation experiment design via likelihood ratio method. *arXiv preprint* arXiv:2008.13087v2.

47. Fox, B. L. and Glynn, P. W. (1989). Replication schemes for limiting expectations. *Probability in the Engineering and Informational Sciences*, 3(3):299–318.

48. Gao, R. and Kleywegt, A. J. (2016). Distributionally robust stochastic optimization with Wasserstein distance. *arXiv preprint* arXiv:1604.02199.

49. Gao, S., Xiao, H., Zhou, E., and Chen, W. (2017). Robust ranking and selection with optimal computing budget allocation. *Automatica*, 81:30–36.

50. Ghaoui, L. E., Oks, M., and Oustry, F. (2003). Worst-case value-at-risk and robust portfolio optimization: A conic programming approach. *Operations Research*, 51(4):543–556.

51. Ghosh, S. and Lam, H. (2015). Mirror descent stochastic approximation for computing worst-case stochastic input models. In *Proceedings of the 2015 Winter Simulation Conference*, pages 425–436. IEEE.

52. Ghosh, S. and Lam, H. (2019). Robust analysis in stochastic simulation: Computation and performance guarantees. *Operations Research*, 67(1):232–249.

53. Glasserman, P. and Xu, X. (2014). Robust risk measurement and model risk. *Quantitative Finance*, 14(1):29–58.

54. Glasserman, P. and Yang, L. (2018). Bounding wrong-way risk in CVA calculation. *Mathematical Finance*, 28(1):268–305.

55. Glynn, P. W. (1990). Likelihood ratio gradient estimation for stochastic systems. *Communications of the ACM*, 33(10):75–84.

56. Glynn, P. W. and Iglehart, D. L. (1990). Simulation output analysis using standardized time series. *Mathematics of Operations Research*, 15(1):1–16.

57. Glynn, P. W. and Lam, H. (2018). Constructing simulation output intervals under input uncertainty via data sectioning. In *Proceedings of the 2018 Winter Simulation Conference*, pages 1551–1562. IEEE.

58. Goeva, A., Lam, H., Qian, H., and Zhang, B. (2019). Optimization-based calibration of simulation input models. *Operations Research*, 67(5):1362–1382.

59. Goeva, A., Lam, H., and Zhang, B. (2014). Reconstructing input models via simulation optimization. In *Proceedings of the 2014 Winter Simulation Conference*, pages 698–709. IEEE.

60. Goh, J. and Sim, M. (2010). Distributionally robust optimization and its tractable approximations. *Operations Research*, 58(4):902–917.

61. Hampel, F. R. (1974). The influence curve and its role in robust estimation. *Journal of the American Statistical Association*, 69(346):383–393.

62. Hanasusanto, G. A., Roitch, V., Kuhn, D., and Wiesemann, W. (2015). A distributionally robust perspective on uncertainty quantification and chance constrained programming. *Mathematical Programming*, 151(1):35–62.

63. Henderson, S. G. (2003). Input modeling: Input model uncertainty: Why do we care and what should we do about it? In Chick, S., Sánchez, P. J., Ferrin, D., and Morrice, D. J., editors, *Proceedings of the 2003 Winter Simulation Conference*, pages 90–100. IEEE.

64. Higdon, D., Gattiker, J., Williams, B., and Rightley, M. (2008). Computer model calibration using high-dimensional output. *Journal of the American Statistical Association*, 103(482):570–583.

65. Hsu, J. C. (1984). Constrained simultaneous confidence intervals for multiple comparisons with the best. *Annals of Statistics*, 12(3):1136–1144.

66. Hu, Z., Cao, J., and Hong, L. J. (2012). Robust simulation of global warming policies using the DICE model. *Management Science*, 58(12):2190–2206.

67. Hu, Z. and Hong, L. J. (2015). Robust simulation of stochastic systems with input uncertainties modeled by statistical divergences. In *2015 Winter Simulation Conference*, pages 643–654. IEEE.

68. Jiang, R. and Guan, Y. (2016). Data-driven chance constrained stochastic program. *Mathematical Programming*, 158(1):291–327.

69. Jones, D. R., Schonlau, M., and Welch, W. J. (1998). Efficient global optimization of expensive black-box functions. *Journal of Global Optimization*, 13(4):455–492.

70. Kennedy, M. C. and O'Hagan, A. (2001). Bayesian calibration of computer models. *Journal of the Royal Statistical Society. Series B, Statistical Methodology*, 63(3):425–464.

71. Kim, S.-H. and Nelson, B. L. (2001). A fully sequential procedure for indifference-zone selection in simulation. *ACM Transactions on Modeling and Computer Simulation*, 11(3):251–273.

72. Kim, S.-H. and Nelson, B. L. (2006). Chapter 17 selecting the best system. In Henderson, S. G. and Nelson, B. L., editors, *Simulation*, volume 13 of *Handbooks in Operations Research and Management Science*, pages 501–534. Elsevier.

73. Kleijnen, J. P. (1995). Verification and validation of simulation models. *European Journal of Operational Research*, 82(1):145–162.

74. Lakshmanan, S. and Venkateswaran, J. (2017). Robust simulation based optimization with input uncertainty. In *Proceedings of the 2017 Winter Simulation Conference*, pages 2257–2267. IEEE.

75. Lam, H. (2016a). Advanced tutorial: Input uncertainty and robust analysis in stochastic simulation. In *Proceedings of the 2016 Winter Simulation Conference*, pages 178–192. IEEE.

76. Lam, H. (2016b). Robust sensitivity analysis for stochastic systems. *Mathematics of Operations Research*, 41(4):1248–1275.

77. Lam, H. (2018). Sensitivity to serial dependency of input processes: A robust approach. *Management Science*, 64(3):1311–1327.

78. Lam, H. (2019). Recovering best statistical guarantees via the empirical divergence-based distributionally robust optimization. *Operations Research*, 67(4):1090–1105.

79. Lam, H. and Mottet, C. (2017). Tail analysis without parametric models: A worst-case perspective. *Operations Research*, 65(6):1696–1711.

80. Lam, H. and Qian, H. (2016). The empirical likelihood approach to simulation input uncertainty. In *Proceedings of the 2016 Winter Simulation Conference*, pages 791-802. IEEE.

81. Lam, H. and Qian, H. (2017). Optimization-based quantification of simulation input uncertainty via empirical likelihood. *arXiv preprint* arXiv:1707. 05917.

82. Lam, H. and Qian, H. (2018a). Subsampling to enhance efficiency in input uncertainty quantification. *Operations Research*, published online in *Articles in Advance*, 03 Dec 2021.

83. Lam, H. and Qian, H. (2018b). Subsampling variance for input uncertainty quantification. In *2018 Winter Simulation Conference*, pages 1611–1622. IEEE.

84. Lam, H. and Qian, H. (2019). Random perturbation and bagging to quantify input uncertainty. In *2019 Winter Simulation Conference*, pages 320–331. IEEE.

85. Lam, H. and Zhang, J. (2020). Distributionally constrained stochastic gradient estimation using noisy function evaluations. In *Proceedings of the 2020 Winter Simulation Conference*, pages 445–456. IEEE.

86. Lam, H., Zhang, X., and Plumlee, M. (2017). Improving prediction from stochastic simulation via model discrepancy learning. In *Proceedings of the 2017 Winter Simulation Conference*, pages 1808–1819. IEEE.

87. Lam, H. and Zhou, E. (2017). The empirical likelihood approach to quantifying uncertainty in sample average approximation. *Operations Research Letters*, 45(4):301–307.

88. Lewis, P. A. and Orav, E. J. (2017). *Simulation Methodology for Statisticians, Operations Analysts, and Engineers*. Chapman and Hall/CRC.

89. Li, B., Jiang, R., and Mathieu, J. L. (2017). Ambiguous risk constraints with moment and unimodality information. *Mathematical Programming*, 173:151–192.

90. Miller, B. L. and Wagner, H. M. (1965). Chance constrained programming with joint constraints. *Operations Research*, 13(6):930–945.

91. Morgan, L. E., Nelson, B. L., Titman, A. C., and Worthington, D. J. (2019). Detecting bias due to input modelling in computer simulation. *European Journal of Operational Research*, 279(3):869–881.
92. Nelson, B. (2013). *Foundations and Methods of Stochastic Simulation: A First Course*. Springer Science & Business Media.
93. Ng, S. H. and Chick, S. E. (2006). Reducing parameter uncertainty for stochastic systems. *ACM Transactions on Modeling and Computer Simulation*, 16(1):26–51.
94. Oakley, J. E. and O'Hagan, A. (2004). Probabilistic sensitivity analysis of complex models: a Bayesian approach. *Journal of the Royal Statistical Society: Series B (Statistical Methodology)*, 66(3):751–769.
95. Oakley, J. E. and Youngman, B. D. (2017). Calibration of stochastic computer simulators using likelihood emulation. *Technometrics*, 59(1):80–92.
96. Owen, A. B. (2001). *Empirical Likelihood*. CRC press.
97. O'Hagan, A., Kennedy, M. C., and Oakley, J. E. (1999). Uncertainty analysis and other inference tools for complex computer codes. In Bernardo, J., Berger, J., Dawid, A., and Smith, A., editors, *Bayesian Statistics 6: Proceedings of the Sixth Valencia International Meeting*, pages 503–524. Oxford Science Publications.
98. Pearce, M. and Branke, J. (2017). Bayesian simulation optimization with input uncertainty. In *Proceedings of the 2017 Winter Simulation Conference*, pages 2268–2278. IEEE.
99. Phuong Le, H. and Branke, J. (2020). Bayesian optimization searching for robust solutions. In *Proceedings of the 2020 Winter Simulation Conference*, pages 2844–2855. IEEE.
100. Picheny, V. (2015). Multiobjective optimization using Gaussian process emulators via stepwise uncertainty reduction. *Statistics and Computing*, 25(6):1265–1280.
101. Plumlee, M. and Lam, H. (2016). Learning stochastic model discrepancy. In *Proceedings of the 2016 Winter Simulation Conference*, pages 413–424. IEEE.
102. Popescu, I. (2005). A semidefinite programming approach to optimal-moment bounds for convex classes of distributions. *Mathematics of Operations Research*, 30(3):632–657.
103. Reiman, M. I. and Weiss, A. (1989). Sensitivity analysis for simulations via likelihood ratios. *Operations Research*, 37(5):830–844.
104. Rinott, Y. (1978). On two-stage selection procedures and related probability-inequalities. *Communications in Statistics - Theory and Methods*, 7(8):799–811.
105. Rubin, D. B. (1981). The Bayesian bootstrap. *The Annals of Statistics*, 9(1):130–134.
106. Rubinstein, R. Y. (1986). The score function approach for sensitivity analysis of computer simulation models. *Mathematics and Computers in Simulation*, 28(5):351–379.
107. Saltelli, A., Tarantola, S., Campolongo, F., and Ratto, M. (2004). *Sensitivity Analysis in Practice: A Guide to Assessing Scientific Models*. John Wiley & Sons.

108. Sargent, R. G. (2005). Verification and validation of simulation models. In *Proceedings of the 2005 Winter Simulation Conference*, pages 130–143. IEEE.

109. Schmeiser, B. (1982). Batch size effects in the analysis of simulation output. *Operations Research*, 30(3):556–568.

110. Schruben, L. (1983). Confidence interval estimation using standardized time series. *Operations Research*, 31(6):1090–1108.

111. Schruben, L. and Kulkarni, R. (1982). Some consequences of estimating parameters for the M/M/1 queue. *Operations Research Letters*, 1(2):75–78.

112. Schruben, L. W. (1980). Establishing the credibility of simulations. *Simulation*, 34(3):101–105.

113. Scott, W., Frazier, P., and Powell, W. (2011). The correlated knowledge gradient for simulation optimization of continuous parameters using Gaussian process regression. *SIAM Journal on Optimization*, 21(3):996–1026.

114. Shafer, G. (1976). Statistical evidence. In *A Mathematical Theory of Evidence*, pages 237–273. Princeton University Press.

115. Shi, Z., Gao, S., Xiao, H., and Chen, W. (2019). A worst-case formulation for constrained ranking and selection with input uncertainty. *Naval Research Logistics*, 66(8):648–662.

116. Song, E. (2021). Sequential bayesian risk set inference for robust discrete optimization via simulation. *arXiv preprint* arXiv:2101.07466.

117. Song, E. and Nelson, B. L. (2015). Quickly assessing contributions to input uncertainty. *IIE Transactions*, 47(9):893–909.

118. Song, E. and Nelson, B. L. (2019). Input–output uncertainty comparisons for discrete optimization via simulation. *Operations Research*, 67(2):562–576.

119. Song, E., Nelson, B. L., and Hong, L. J. (2015). Input uncertainty and indifference-zone ranking & selection. In *Proceedings of the 2015 Winter Simulation Conference*, pages 414–424. IEEE.

120. Song, E., Nelson, B. L., and Pegden, C. D. (2014). Advanced tutorial: Input uncertainty quantification. In *Proceedings of the 2014 Winter Simulation Conference*, pages 162–176. IEEE.

121. Song, E., Nelson, B. L., and Staum, J. (2016). Shapley effects for global sensitivity analysis: Theory and computation. *SIAM/ASA Journal on Uncertainty Quantification*, 4(1):1060–1083.

122. Song, E. and Shanbhag, U. V. (2019). Stochastic approximation for simulation optimization under input uncertainty with streaming data. In *Proceedings of the 2019 Winter Simulation Conference*, pages 3597–3608. IEEE.

123. Sun, Y., Apley, D. W., and Staum, J. (2011). Efficient nested simulation for estimating the variance of a conditional expectation. *Operations Research*, 59(4):998–1007.

124. Tarantola, A. (2005). *Inverse Problem Theory and Methods for Model Parameter Estimation.* SIAM.

125. Tuo, R., Wu, C. J., et al. (2015). Efficient calibration for imperfect computer models. *The Annals of Statistics*, 43(6):2331–2352.

126. Ungredda, J., Pearce, M., and Branke, J. (2020). Bayesian optimisation vs. input uncertainty reduction. *arXiv:2006.00643.*

127. Van Parys, B. P., Goulart, P. J., and Kuhn, D. (2016). Generalized Gauss inequalities via semidefinite programming. *Mathematical Programming*, 156(1-2):271–302.

128. Van der Vaart, A. W. (2000). *Asymptotic Statistics*, volume 3. Cambridge University Press.

129. Villemonteix, J., Vazquez, E., and Walter, E. (2008). An informational approach to the global optimization of expensive-to-evaluate functions. *Journal of Global Optimization*, 44(4):509.

130. Wang, H., Ng, S. H., and Zhang, X. (2020a). A Gaussian process based algorithm for stochastic simulation optimization with input distribution uncertainty. In *Proceedings of the 2020 Winter Simulation Conference*, pages 2899–2910. IEEE.

131. Wang, H., Yuan, J., and Ng, S. H. (2020b). Gaussian process based optimization algorithms with input uncertainty. *IISE Transactions*, 52(4):377–393.

132. Wang, H., Zhang, X., and Ng, S. H. (2021). A nonparametric Bayesian approach for simulation optimization with input uncertainty. *arXiv:2008.02154.*

133. Wiesemann, W., Kuhn, D., and Sim, M. (2014). Distributionally robust convex optimization. *Operations Research*, 62(6):1358–1376.

134. Wong, R. K. W., Storlie, C. B., and Lee, T. C. M. (2017). A frequentist approach to computer model calibration. *Journal of the Royal Statistical Society: Series B (Statistical Methodology)*, 79(2):635–648.

135. Wu, D. and Zhou, E. (2017). Ranking and selection under input uncertainty: fixed confidence and fixed budget. *arXiv preprint*arXiv:1708.08526.

136. Xie, W., Li, C., Wu, Y., and Zhang, P. (2021). A Bayesian nonparametric framework for uncertainty quantification in simulation. *SIAM Journal on Uncertainty Quantification*, 9(4):1527–1552.

137. Xie, W., Nelson, B. L., and Barton, R. R. (2014). A Bayesian framework for quantifying uncertainty in stochastic simulation. *Operations Research*, 62(6):1439–1452.

138. Xie, W., Nelson, B. L., and Barton, R. R. (2016). Multivariate input uncertainty in output analysis for stochastic simulation. *ACM Transactions on Modeling and Computer Simulation*, 27(1):5:1–5:22.

139. Xu, J., Zheng, Z., and Glynn, P. W. (2020). Joint resource allocation for input data collection and simulation. In *Proceedings of the 2020 Winter Simulation Conference*, pages 2126–2137. IEEE.

140. Zazanis, M. A. and Suri, R. (1993). Convergence rates of finite-difference sensitivity estimates for stochastic systems. *Operations Research*, 41(4):694–703.

141. Zhou, E. and Liu, T. (2018). Online quantification of input uncertainty for parametric models. In *Proceedings of the 2018 Winter Simulation Conference*, pages 1587–1598. IEEE.

142. Zhou, E. and Xie, W. (2015). Simulation optimization when facing input uncertainty. In *Proceedings of the 2015 Winter Simulation Conference*, pages 3714–3724. IEEE.

143. Zouaoui, F. and Wilson, J. R. (2003). Accounting for parameter uncertainty in simulation input modeling. *IIE Transactions*, 35(9):781–792.

144. Zouaoui, F. and Wilson, J. R. (2004). Accounting for input-model and input-parameter uncertainties in simulation. *IIE Transactions*, 36(11):1135–1151.

18

Fuzzy multi-attribute decision-making: Theory, methods and Applications

Zeshui Xu and Shen Zhang

18.1 Introduction

When it comes to fuzzy multi-attribute decision-making (MADM), we firstly need to briefly introduce the fuzzy sets. The concept "fuzzy" was proposed by L.A. Zadeh [1] in 1965. It means that the denotation of a concept is uncertain, or its denotation is not clear. Instead, it is fuzzy. For example, the connotation of the concept "youth" is clear to us. But for its denotation, that is, at what age a person is young, it is difficult to make it clear. Because there is no definite boundary between "young" and "not young", it is a fuzzy concept. There are a few other things to note about fuzzy: (1) When people try to understand fuzziness, they are allowed to have subjectivity. That is to say, everyone is not exactly the same on the boundary of fuzzy things. To recognize a certain subjectivity is a characteristic of fuzzy understanding. For example, if we ask 100 people to name the age range of "young", we may get 100 different answers. Even so, when we use the method of fuzzy statistics

Z. Xu (✉) · S. Zhang
Business School, Sichuan University, Chengdu, Sichuan 610064, China
e-mail: xuzeshui@263.net

S. Zhang
e-mail: zhsh_227@163.com

© The Author(s), under exclusive license to Springer Nature
Switzerland AG 2022
S. Salhi and J. Boylan (eds.), *The Palgrave Handbook of Operations Research*,
https://doi.org/10.1007/978-3-030-96935-6_18

to analyze, the distribution of the age limit of "young" has a certain regularity; (2) Fuzzy is the opposite of accuracy, but it should not be understood as a negative representation of backward productivity. On the contrary, we often resort to fuzzy when dealing with objective things. It is not difficult, for example, to find a "tall old man" in a room full of people. The words "old" and "tall" here are fuzzy concepts, but we can quickly find a person in a crowd by analyzing these fuzzy concepts in our minds. If we ask a computer to do such a search, we have to put the exact data of the ages and heights of all the people into the computer, and then we can find such people from the crowd; (3) Fuzziness is often confused with randomness, but there is a fundamental difference between them. Randomness itself has a clear meaning, but due to the occurrence of insufficient conditions, there can be no definite causal relationship between the conditions and the event, so that the occurrence of the event shows an uncertainty. The fuzziness of things means that the concept of things we want to deal with is itself fuzzy, that is, it is difficult to determine whether an object conforms to this concept. It is the uncertainty caused by the fuzzy concept denotation.

Since the birth of fuzzy sets, scholars have done a lot of research on the basis of it, and put forward a lot of extension forms. Among them, intuitionistic fuzzy sets (IFS) [2, 3], hesitant fuzzy sets (HFS) [4, 5] and probabilistic hesitant fuzzy sets (P-HFS) [6, 7] are widely used in the field of decision-making. It is worth mentioning that the concept of fuzzy has also been applied to linguistic decision-making, forming tools such as the hesitant fuzzy linguistic set (HFLS) [8] and the probabilistic linguistic term set (PLTS) [9]. Following the previous introduction to fuzzy, we will continue to briefly introduce the fuzzy set and its several extended forms and their applications in decision-making.

The core idea of fuzzy set theory is the concept of membership degree. It uses the membership function to express the degree to which something belongs to a set. That's a good solution to the problem of young people that we talked about earlier. In fact, using the concept of membership, we can use a real number between 0 and 1 to express the extent to which a person belongs to the youth. However, generally speaking, this kind of evaluation has strong subjectivity. Moreover, many evaluators are not entirely sure of their estimates. At this point, they can use an interval instead of a precise value as the membership, or they can set a hesitant degree for their assessment. The former can obtain interval-valued fuzzy sets, while the latter can obtain IFS. IFS adds a hesitant degree to the fuzzy set, which means that the evaluator is not entirely sure about his or her own evaluation. The greater the degree of hesitation, the greater the degree of the uncertainty. IFS can better express the real thoughts of decision-makers, and is more in line with the process of people's judgment. With the increasing complexity of practical decision-making problems, we gradually need to integrate multiple evaluation values into a single information unit. At this point, the former information expression tools are difficult to sustain. HFS can meet this need very well. HFS is essentially the consolidation of multiple membership degrees into a single set. It can include more information in the decision-making process. But it also has the problem of missing information. It pays more attention to the difference between membership degrees but ignores the weight information behind different membership degrees. P-HFS preserves the weight information behind different membership degrees by adding the corresponding probability after each membership degree in the elements, which effectively improves the HFS. It is the latest research result of fuzzy decision-making development and it is an important supplement of fuzzy decision-making.

The emergence of the fuzzy set and its extension forms provides very important tools for decision-making science and greatly promotes the development of decision-making theory. You could even say that, strictly speaking, most of today's decision-making problems require fuzzy decision-making methods. In fuzzy decision-making, fuzzy MADM is undoubtedly the one with the fastest development and widest application.

MADM refers to the decision-making problems of choosing the best alternative or ranking the schemes under the condition of considering multiple attributes. Its theories and methods have been widely applied in many fields. The main problems of MADM are evaluation and selection. It can be seen that MADM is to comprehensively consider the performance of a finite number of alternative schemes under multiple attributes, and select the best or give a ranking among them. Then, how do you evaluate the quality of each alternative in terms of each attribute? Is each one good or bad? How good are the good ones, and how bad are the bad ones? At this time, the application of fuzzy information to answer these questions is very appropriate. The application of the fuzzy set and its extended forms in MADM is usually based on the following forms: (1) information integration; (2) distance measures; (3) preference relations. (They will be discussed in more detail later). In the past few decades, many scholars have done in-depth research on the related fuzzy theory. With the development of fuzzy theory, fuzzy MADM has been evolving. Every new achievement of fuzzy set theory can bring many new methods to solve the problem of MADM. Of course, this is not to say that as new methods come into being, the old ones become completely ineffective. In fact, the old methods, while less applicable, can still solve a lot of practical problems in the areas where they are applicable. Moreover, they are also the basis of new methods and can provide important inspirations for the research of new methods. At the same time, even if the new method has higher accuracy and wider application range, it may also have problems of complex calculations and unstable mathematical properties, etc. In many practical decision-making problems, the effect is not as good as the old methods. Therefore, we need to understand that the actual decision-making problems are very complex and there is no perfect decision-making method. What we have to do is to choose the appropriate decision-making method under every different decision-making condition.

The purpose of this paper is to introduce the research process, the research content, the differences between different methods and the scope of application of fuzzy MADM in detail. We hope our work can provide an effective reference for scholars in related fields, and can also help people with decision-making needs.

18.2 Literature Review of Fuzzy MADM

In this chapter, we will give a brief description of the literature under the topic "fuzzy MADM", so that we can see the research status more intuitively. We use the data on the "Web of Science" as a reference. By inputting the topic "fuzzy multi-attribute decision-making", we can get the following search results. Figures 18.1 and 18.2 describe the number of articles published and cited on the topic "fuzzy MADM".

Figures 18.3 and 18.4 describe the number of document types of the search results and source titles on the topic "fuzzy MADM":

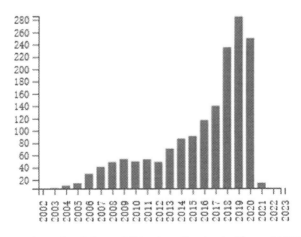

Fig. 18.1 The number of articles published on the topic "fuzzy MADM" every year since 2002

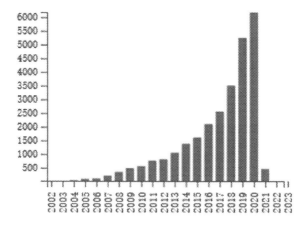

Fig. 18.2 The number of articles cited on the topic "fuzzy MADM" every year since 2002

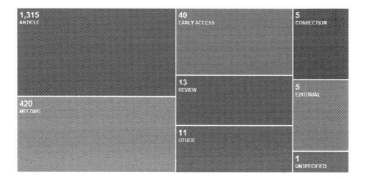

Fig. 18.3 Document types of the search results on the topic "fuzzy MADM"

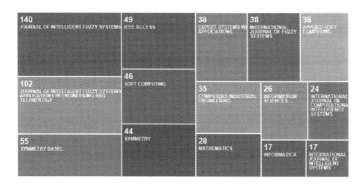

Fig. 18.4 Source titles of the search results on the topic "fuzzy MADM"

Table 18.1 Retrieval and citation of fuzzy MADM-related literatures

Results found	1685
Sum of the Times Cited	27716
Average Citations per Item	16.45
h-index	78

The following table 18.1 describes the retrieval and citation of fuzzy MADM-related literatures:

As you can see from the figures and table above, among the 1685 articles retrieved, most of them are regular articles or conference articles. The total number of citations of these articles is 27716, with an average of 16.45 citations per article, and the h-index is as high as 78. The number of citations in 2020 is more than 6000. Moreover, the number of articles published in this field continues to rise every year. Especially in the last five years, the growth has been extremely rapid except for a slight decrease in 2020, which may be due to the influence of COVID-19 epidemic. In addition, quite a number of articles have been published in such authoritative journals as *Journal of Intelligent & Fuzzy Systems, Expert Systems with Applications* and *Information Sciences* in the field of fuzzy decision-making and computer science. The above data show that the research results in this direction are very rich and of high quality. Moreover, the research of fuzzy MADM has a bright future.

We can continue refining the search results by inputting "aggregation":

Through similar operations, we can get the following two tables by inputting "preference" and "measure":

It can be seen from Table 18.2, Table 18.3 and Table 18.4 that there are 589 articles on aggregation with 10952 citations; 489 articles on preference with 9914 citations; and 400 articles on measure with 6407 citations. A total of 1478 articles in three directions were cited 27273 times. There is, of course,

Table 18.2 Retrieval and citation of the topic "fuzzy MADM + aggregation"

Results found	589
Sum of the Times Cited	10952
Average Citations per Item	18.59
h-index	52

Table 18.3 Retrieval and citation of the topic "fuzzy MADM + preference"

Results found	489
Sum of the Times Cited	9914
Average Citations per Item	20.27
h-index	49

Table 18.4 Retrieval and citation of the topic "fuzzy MADM + measure"

Results found	400
Sum of the Times Cited	6407
Average Citations per Item	16.02
h-index	40

a small amount of repetition. However, these data are enough to illustrate the three directions "aggregation", "preference" and "measure" account for the vast majority of the related researches of fuzzy MADM. This is also in line with the general law of decision-making science. Therefore, we will elaborate the research of fuzzy MADM from these three perspectives in the rest of this paper.

18.3 Fuzzy MADM Based on the Information Integration

18.3.1 Information Integration and Fuzzy MADM

Information integration is a concept of organically integrating and optimizing the use of related multiple information. In today's society, the era of big data is gradually coming, and we need to generate and acquire massive amounts of information every day. In this case, information integration appears more and more frequently and gradually occupies an important position in our life. At the same time, research on its application in decision-making processes is increasing. So why do we need information integration in decision-making? It stems from the fragmentation of information. This means that it is not enough to judge a person or an event from only one or a few aspects of information, we need to integrate information from multiple perspectives, and then make an evaluation of the whole. This kind of integration is not a simple accumulation of information, but a dynamic process of organically integrating and optimizing multi-dimensional information resources according to the needs of a specific user in a specific field. Based on the above description, it can be seen that information integration is an indispensable tool for solving MADM problems. For every alternative solution, we need to integrate their evaluation values under all attributes. The method of information integration can effectively consider all attributes and enable the MADM problems to get more reasonable decision-making results.

Fuzzy set theory is an important foundation of information integration. The fuzzy set uses a real number on the interval [0, 1] to represent the membership degree, which allows uncertainty in the integration process of many aspects of information to be directly expressed in the calculation process. If some systematic methods are used to model the uncertainty in the process of information integration, consistent fuzzy inference can be obtained. The actual value of fuzzy set theory for information integration lies in its extension to fuzzy logic, which is a kind of multi-valued logic. And membership degree can be regarded as an inaccurate representation of the truth value of data. In the process of information integration, the uncertainty can be directly represented by fuzzy numbers, and then the data from different angles can be combined according to various calculation methods of fuzzy set theory, and then the information integration can be realized. Compared with traditional probability and statistics methods, the expression and processing of information by fuzzy reasoning are closer to the way of thinking of human beings. Therefore, information integration based on fuzzy information is very suitable for application in the social sciences such as MADM. There is much research on the application of fuzzy information integration in MADM, the most common being the study of aggregation operators.

As an important information integration tool, aggregation operators can fuse different information together. It is mostly used for sorting. Aggregation operators actually evolved from common practices in real life. For example, five judges grade a contestant. When calculating a player's final score, we often remove the highest score, remove the lowest score and then average the rest. From this method, Prof. Yager [10–12] extracted the OWA operator. Actually, aggregation operators are widely and deeply used in decision-making. Compared with the aggregation operators of real numbers, fuzzy aggregation operators can integrate fuzzy information. This can better express the real thinking of decision-makers. There are many kinds of fuzzy integration operators, each of which has its own characteristics and specific scope of application. Next, we will make a detailed introduction to fuzzy aggregation operators.

18.3.2 Fuzzy Aggregation Operators

Based on the properties of fuzzy information and the advantages of aggregation operators, fuzzy aggregation operators are widely used in MADM. Among them, different operators have different characteristics. In terms of the types of fuzzy information, fuzzy aggregation operators can be divided into fuzzy integration operators, intuitionistic fuzzy integration operators, hesitant fuzzy integration operators, probabilistic hesitant fuzzy integration operators and so on. These operators are produced with the development of fuzzy theory and more and more complex decision-making requirements. Fuzzy aggregation operators use the concept of membership degree to better express the decision-makers' initial ideas. Intuitionistic fuzzy integration operators give decision-makers a space of hesitation. Hesitant fuzzy integration operators allow multiple membership degrees to appear in the same element at the same time. The probabilistic hesitant fuzzy integration operator adds a corresponding probability value for each membership degree, which can completely express the importance of each membership degree. However, the structure of aggregation operators based on each kind of fuzzy information is similar. Therefore, this paper introduces fuzzy aggregation operators from another perspective, that is, the types of operators themselves.

Firstly, we look at the fuzzy weighted average (FWA) operators [5, 13].

$$FWA_\omega(\alpha_1, \alpha_2, \cdots, \alpha_n) = \omega_1\alpha_1 \oplus \omega_2\alpha_2 \oplus \cdots \oplus \omega_n\alpha_n \,, \qquad (18.1)$$

where α_i, $i = 1, 2, \cdots, n$ can be fuzzy numbers, they can also be intuitionistic fuzzy numbers, hesitant fuzzy elements, etc. The core of this operator is to assign a weight to each part of information in a specific way, and then integrate the corresponding information. The calculation process of this operator fully considers the importance of each part of the information. Therefore, in MADM, it is more applicable to the problem that the importance degree of each attribute is relatively balanced. If one or more properties are particularly important, the fuzzy geometric average (FGA) [5, 14–17] operator is needed.

$$FWG_\omega(\alpha_1, \alpha_2, \cdots, \alpha_n) = \alpha_1^{\omega_1} \otimes \alpha_2^{\omega_2} \otimes \cdots \otimes \alpha_n^{\omega_n} \,, \qquad (18.2)$$

Compared with FWA, the biggest feature of FGA operator is that it can highlight the status of one or several attributes, such as the very familiar one-vote system. The FWA and FGA are like brothers, so to speak. FWA applies to the situation where the importance of all attributes is balanced, while FGA applies to the situation where a few attributes have significant importance. Another typical kind of aggregation operator is the fuzzy ordered average/geometric [5, 13, 14, 18–22] operator.

$$FOWA_\omega(\alpha_1, \alpha_2, \cdots, \alpha_n) = \omega_1\alpha_{\sigma(1)} \oplus \omega_2\alpha_{\sigma(2)} \oplus \cdots \oplus \omega_n\alpha_{\sigma(n)} \,, \qquad (18.3)$$

$$FOWG_\omega(\alpha_1, \alpha_2, \cdots, \alpha_n) = \alpha_{\sigma(1)}^{\omega_1} \otimes \alpha_{\sigma(2)}^{\omega_2} \otimes \cdots \otimes \alpha_{\sigma(n)}^{\omega_n} \,, \qquad (18.4)$$

Where $(\sigma(1), \sigma(2), \cdots, \sigma(n))$ is substitution of $(1, 2, \cdots, n)$. For any j, there holds $\alpha_{\sigma(j-1)} > \alpha_{\sigma(j)}$. This operator first sorts the elements participating in the integration by size, and then integrates. The essence of this kind of operator is the integration of locations, not each element. The scoring method just mentioned, which removes the highest and lowest scores, is a typical application of it. The above are four basic fuzzy aggregation operators. It can be said that most of the subsequent operators are derived from the generalization of these four operators.

As you can see, FWA and FGA focus only on the importance of each piece of data, while FOWA and FOGA focus only on the importance of different locations. In fact, in many cases, we need to focus on the weight of both. In this case, we need some fuzzy hybrid (FHWA/FHGA) operators [5, 13, 14, 23–27].

$$
FHA_{\omega,w}(\alpha_1, \alpha_2, \cdots, \alpha_n) = w_1\dot{\alpha}_{\sigma(1)} \oplus w_2\dot{\alpha}_{\sigma(2)} \oplus \cdots \oplus w_n\dot{\alpha}_{\sigma(n)} ,
\tag{18.5}
$$

$$
FHG_{\omega,w}(\alpha_1, \alpha_2, \cdots, \alpha_n) = \dot{\alpha}_{\sigma(1)}^{w_1} \otimes \dot{\alpha}_{\sigma(2)}^{w_2} \otimes \cdots \otimes \dot{\alpha}_{\sigma(n)}^{w_n} ,
\tag{18.6}
$$

where $w = (w_1, w_2, \ldots, w_n)$ is the weight vector of the corresponding operator. $\dot{\alpha}_j = n\omega_j\alpha_j$, $\dot{\alpha}_{\sigma(j)} \geq \dot{\alpha}_{\sigma(j+1)}$. $\omega = (\omega_1, \omega_2, \ldots, \omega_n)$ is the weight vector of α_j. In essence, the fuzzy hybrid operator can be seen as a two-step integration, in which different elements and different positions are integrated respectively. This type of operator takes into account the importance of both data and location and is more comprehensive than the previous operators. We can use these operators flexibly in practical decision-making problems.

With the development of society, the decision-making environment is becoming more and more complex, and scholars have been deepening their research on decision-making theory and methods. In addition to the most basic aggregation operators mentioned above, some newer and more complex operators have been proposed to deal with more complex decision-making scenarios. The fuzzy Bonferroni average (FBM) operator [28–34] can be used for the integration between the Max operator and the Min operator, as well as the logical "or" and "and" operator. Its biggest advantage is that it can describe different relationships between different elements by adjusting the value of parameters. None of the above operators restrict the weight conditions. In the application of these operators, we usually give the corresponding weights directly. In fact, in many cases, there is often correlation between various attributes, that is to say, the weights of some attributes are also related. Therefore, after considering this situation, many scholars have given some fuzzy aggregation operators based on the idea of derivation [35, 36]. The typical ones are fuzzy Choquet integral operator [37–39], fuzzy Dempster-Shafer operator [40, 41], etc. When we encounter decision-making problems with obvious correlation between attributes, we can consider applying these operators to solve them. It is worth noting that almost all fuzzy aggregation operators currently are based on algebraic T-norm and T-conorm, which are determined by their operation methods. Therefore, given a fuzzy weighted average operator based on Archimedean T-norm and T-conorm (ATS-FWA) [42] and a fuzzy geometric average operator based on Archimedean T-norm and T-conorm (ATS-FGA)[42], almost all fuzzy aggregation operators can be regarded as special cases of them. Of course, there are exceptions. One such operator is the fuzzy-precedence "or" operator [43–45], which we will look at below. In MADM problems, if all attributes have the same priority level, that is to say, we allow mutual compensation among attributes. Then the operators mentioned above can solve the problem. However, in many cases, we do not allow compromises between attributes. That is, there are priority differences between attributes. For example, if someone buys a piece of clothing, no matter how beautiful it is, he will not consider buying it if there is no suitable size for him. Thus, the fuzzy-precedence "or" operators are needed for this kind of MADM problem.

18.3.3   Supplementary Instruction

In this chapter, we introduce fuzzy information integration and its application in MADM. Fuzzy information integration is a very big research field, and there are thousands of related literatures. It is impossible for us to introduce it in great detail due to the lack of space. Therefore, in this paper, we do not distinguish fuzzy sets and their extended forms in detail, such as FS, Type-2 FS, IFS, HFS, P-HFS, etc. On the contrary, we only introduce the characteristics and application environment of different fuzzy aggregation operators. Readers can refer to the corresponding references for specific formulas in each kind of fuzzy environment.

In addition to being the basis of many fuzzy MADM methods, fuzzy aggregation operators can also be directly used to solve practical decision-making problems. The application of aggregation operators in MADM is very simple and clear. We only need to determine the decision-making matrix and select the appropriate aggregation operator to integrate the evaluation information of each attribute. Finally, we should calculate the score value of the final result of each scheme after integration and rank them. We describe this process in detail with the following flow chart (Fig. 18.5):

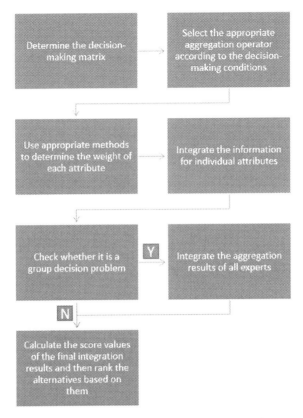

Fig. 18.5   Flow chart of the fuzzy-aggregation-operator-based MADM method

18.4   Fuzzy Measures and MADM

18.4.1   Fuzzy Measures

As a mathematical concept, fuzzy measures can express the relationship between different fuzzy sets. Based on this feature, it is widely used in MADM. It is also an important basis for many MADM methods. At present, the research on fuzzy measures mainly includes distance and similarity measures, correlation measures and entropy measures.

Distance measure and similarity measure are a pair of concepts, which express the distance between two fuzzy sets or fuzzy elements. In general, the greater the distance, the lower the similarity. This pair of concepts is often applied in MADM, such as the famous TOPSIS method. The research on fuzzy distance measure is mainly based on some classical distance formulas, such as Euclidean distance, Manhattan distance and so on.

The first is fuzzy Euclidean distance [46–52]. The most straightforward way to understand Euclidean distance is to find the straight-line distance between two points (in two or three dimensions). Because of its similar form, it is often used to calculate the distance between two fuzzy sets (or elements). Here is the formula for the Euclidean distance between two hesitant fuzzy elements:

$$d(A_1, A_2) = \left[\frac{1}{n} \sum_{i=1}^{n} \left(\frac{1}{l_{x_i}} \sum_{j=1}^{l_{x_i}} \left| h_{A_1}^{\sigma(j)}(x_i) - h_{A_2}^{\sigma(j)}(x_i) \right|^2 \right) \right]^{\frac{1}{2}}, \qquad (18.7)$$

And it's important to note that the Euclidean distance here is the normalized Euclidean distance. In the original Euclidean distance, each coordinate contributes equally to the Euclidean distance. Taking the hesitant fuzzy element (HFE) as an example, in the process of MADM, if we use each membership degree in HFE to represent different attributes, then in the traditional Euclidean distance, it means that each attribute has the same contribution to the decision result, which is obviously not in line with the reality. The standardized Euclidean distance is weighted to coordinates. When each component is a quantity of different nature, the magnitude of the "distance" is related to the unit of the index. It improves the original formula by treating the differences between different attributes of samples (i.e. each index or variable) differently to some extent.

Now let's look at the fuzzy Manhattan distance [46–52]. We still use Manhattan distance formula of HFEs as an example:

$$d(A_1, A_2) = \frac{1}{n} \sum_{i=1}^{n} \left(\frac{1}{l_{x_i}} \sum_{j=1}^{l_{x_i}} \left| h_{A_1}^{\sigma(j)}(x_i) - h_{A_2}^{\sigma(j)}(x_i) \right| \right), \qquad (18.8)$$

As you can see, the fuzzy Manhattan distance is different from the fuzzy Euclidean distance. Imagine you're driving from one intersection to another in Manhattan. Is that the distance as the crow flies between the two points? Obviously not, unless you can get through the building. The actual driving distance is this "Manhattan distance". This is where the name Manhattan distance comes from (also called City Block distance). Note that the formula for the Manhattan distance given above is also standardized. Compared with Euclidean distance, the calculation of Manhattan distance is simpler but more likely to cause confusion, especially in a fuzzy environment because it's always more intuitive to calculate the straight-line distance between two points.

In general, the research direction of fuzzy distance measure is to generalize some commonly used distance measure in measure theory to different types of fuzzy sets, so as to deal with fuzzy information better and solve fuzzy decision problems. In these research results, the above two kinds are the most commonly used. Of course, there are other types of fuzzy distance measures. We don't need to go into details here. Readers can refer to the related work for more specific studies.

Another tool used to describe the relationship between fuzzy elements is the fuzzy correlation coefficient [53–59]. Unlike the distance measure, which focuses on the distance between two elements, the correlation coefficient calculates the "included angle" between two elements. It measures the degree of correlation between two fuzzy elements. The greater the correlation coefficient, the greater the correlation between the two elements, and vice versa. The common fuzzy correlation coefficient is mainly based on the Pearson correlation coefficient in the fuzzy environment, such as the hesitant fuzzy correlation coefficient below:

$$c(h_1, h_2) = \frac{\sum_{i=1}^{l}\left(h_1^{\sigma(i)}h_2^{\sigma(i)}\right)}{\left(\sum_{i=1}^{l}\left(h_1^{\sigma(i)}\right)^2 \sum_{i=1}^{l}\left(h_2^{\sigma(i)}\right)^2\right)^{\frac{1}{2}}}, \tag{18.9}$$

In MADM, the fuzzy correlation coefficient can be used to test the correlation between different attributes, making it a very practical tool. The fuzzy entropy and cross entropy measures [60–64] are also very commonly used in fuzzy decision-making. Entropy is originally a thermodynamic concept that describes how messy things are. In the field of decision-making, entropy measure and cross entropy measure can also be used to compare the correlation degree between fuzzy elements. It can be said that entropy measure is a bridge between thermodynamics and decision-making science. At present, there are also many scholars in the relevant research.

In general, fuzzy measures are mainly used to measure the distance or correlation between fuzzy elements. We look at their use in MADM in more detail in the next section.

18.4.2 Application of Fuzzy Measures in MADM

The application of fuzzy distance measures and similarity measures in MADM is mainly in some decision-making methods. The most important and most widely used method is TOPSIS. TOPSIS (Technique for Order Preference by Similarity to an Ideal Solution) was first proposed by C.L. Hwang and K. Yoon in 1981 [65]. TOPSIS is a method to rank limited evaluation objects according to their proximity to the idealized target, and it is used to evaluate the relative merits of existing objects. There are two ideal solutions, one is the positive ideal solution (PIS), the other is the negative ideal solution (NIS). The best object should be the closest to the PIS, while the farthest from the NIS. The calculation of distance can use the commonly used Euclidean distance or Manhattan distance, etc.

TOPSIS method is a sequential optimization technique of ideal target similarity, and it is a very effective method in multi-attribute decision analysis. It finds out the optimal target and the worst target (represented by PIS and NIS, respectively) in multiple targets through the normalized data normalization matrix. And then, the distance between each evaluation target and PIS and NIS is calculated, respectively, and the closeness degree of each target and the ideal solution is obtained. The closeness degree of each target and ideal solution is sorted according to the closeness degree of ideal solution, which is used as the basis for evaluating the merits and demerits of the target. The closeness degree is between 0 and 1, and the closer this value is to 1, the closer the corresponding evaluation target is to the optimal level. On the contrary, the closer the value is to 0, the closer the evaluation target is to the worst level. TOPSIS has been successfully applied in many fields such as land use planning, material selection and evaluation, project investment, medical and health care, and has significantly improved the, accuracy and operability of MADM.

In order to make readers better understand the fuzzy TOPSIS method, we take the hesitant fuzzy TOPSIS as an example to elaborate in more detail. For TOPSIS methods in other fuzzy environment, readers can refer to relevant literature [66–69]. Hesitant fuzzy TOPSIS is proposed by Xu and Zhang [70]. Its main idea is to use the distance between each alternative and the hesitant fuzzy positive and negative ideal solutions (HF-PIS and HF-NIS) to rank the alternatives. The HF-PIS and HF-NIS can be defined as follows:

$$A^+ = \left\{ x_j, max_i \langle \gamma_{ij}^{\sigma(\lambda)} \rangle | j = 1, 2, \cdots, n \right\} \qquad (18.10)$$

$$
= \left\{ \begin{array}{l} \langle x_1, ((\gamma_1^1)^+, (\gamma_1^2)^+, \cdots, (\gamma_1^l)^+) \rangle, \langle x_2, ((\gamma_2^1)^+, (\gamma_2^2)^+, \cdots, (\gamma_2^l)^+) \rangle \\ \cdots, \langle x_n, ((\gamma_n^1)^+, (\gamma_n^2)^+, \cdots, (\gamma_n^l)^+) \rangle \end{array} \right\} \tag{18.11}
$$

$$
A^- = \left\{ x_j, \, min_i \langle \gamma_{ij}^{\sigma(\lambda)} \rangle \mid j = 1, 2, \cdots, n \right\} \tag{18.12}
$$

$$
= \left\{ \begin{array}{l} \langle x_1, ((\gamma_1^1)^-, (\gamma_1^2)^-, \cdots, (\gamma_1^l)^-) \rangle, \langle x_2, ((\gamma_2^1)^-, (\gamma_2^2)^-, \cdots, (\gamma_2^l)^-) \rangle \\ \cdots, \langle x_n, ((\gamma_n^1)^-, (\gamma_n^2)^-, \cdots, (\gamma_n^l)^-) \rangle \end{array} \right\} \tag{18.13}
$$

After that, the distances between the alternatives and the HF-PIS and HF-NIS can be calculated through the using of the hesitant fuzzy Euclidean distance [70]. And then we can get:

$$
d_i^+ = \sum_{j=1}^n d\left(h_{ij}, h_j^+\right) w_j = \sqrt{\frac{1}{l} \sum_{\lambda=1}^l \left| h_{ij}^{\sigma(\lambda)} - \left(h_{ij}^{\sigma(\lambda)}\right)^+ \right|^2},
$$
$$
i = 1, 2, \cdots, n , \tag{18.14}
$$

$$
d_i^- = \sum_{j=1}^n d\left(h_{ij}, h_j^-\right) w_j = \sqrt{\frac{1}{l} \sum_{\lambda=1}^l \left| h_{ij}^{\sigma(\lambda)} - \left(h_{ij}^{\sigma(\lambda)}\right)^- \right|^2},
$$
$$
i = 1, 2, \cdots, n , \tag{18.15}
$$

Next, the relative closeness coefficient of an alternative and the HF-PIS is defined as follows:

$$
C_i = \frac{d_i^-}{d_i^+ + d_i^-} , \tag{18.16}
$$

Finally, alternatives can be sorted with the relative closeness coefficients. According to the previous introduction, the higher the relative closeness coefficient C_i , the closer the distance is to the HF-PIS.

A similar method is the fuzzy VIKOR method [36, 71–73]. It is a method to solve the MADM problem with conflicting attributes, which is based on the special measure of the paste progress from alternative to ideal solution. The basic measure for compromise ranking in this method is derived from the integration function L_p- metric used in compromise programming. In this method, we first need to find the ideal solutions. For the profit type attribute, the ideal solution is the maximum value of each column of the fuzzy decision matrix. On the contrary, for cost attributes, the ideal solution is the minimum value of each column of the fuzzy decision matrix. The operation of this step is very simple. However, ideal solutions are usually infeasible solutions because conflicting properties cannot be satisfied at the same time. Fuzzy VIKOR integrates the maximum "group utility" and the minimum "individual regret" in the process of mutual concession, so as to find the optimal compromise solution.

Fuzzy correlation measures and entropy measures are usually used in fuzzy clustering algorithms. The method of fuzzy cluster analysis originates from introducing fuzzy mathematics method into cluster analysis. Fuzzy clustering analysis methods can be roughly divided into two kinds: one is fuzzy clustering method based on fuzzy relation. It is also called systematic clustering analysis. The other method is called non-systematic clustering method, which first divides the samples roughly, and then classifies them according to their optimal principle. After several iterations, the classification is relatively reasonable. This method is also called step-by-step clustering method. Fuzzy clustering analysis usually requires the following four steps :

1. Determining the complete set of clustering units;
2. Determine clustering criteria and clustering factors;
3. Survey and collate data according to clustering criteria and factors;
4. Meta-dimensional processing of statistical data, also known as normalization.

Fuzzy clustering analysis is widely used in MADM, especially in large-scale MADM. In large-scale MADM, the amount of data is very large. There are some problems in the decision-making process, such as dimensionality confusion and information complexity. This makes information very difficult to use. At this time, the fuzzy clustering method can classify the alternative schemes or attributes, which makes the initial decision-making information more concise and easier to use, thus greatly simplifying the decision-making problem. It can be said that cluster analysis is a necessary step for most large-scale decision problems. At present, there is much research on fuzzy clustering. In terms of clustering methods, it can be classified into algorithms based on condensed hierarchical clustering [74, 75], algorithms based on K-means clustering [76], clustering algorithms based on graph theory [77] and so on [78–81]. When we are faced with large-scale MADM problems, we can choose the appropriate fuzzy clustering method to deal with the decision-making information, and lay a solid foundation for the decision-making processes.

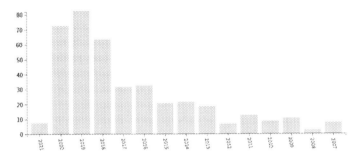

Fig. 18.6 Research trend of Fuzzy measures

In general, the application of fuzzy measure theory in fuzzy MADM is a relatively new kind of research. The application of thermodynamics principle and cluster analysis to decision analysis is also a decision model that has gradually emerged in recent years. Since 2018, there has been an explosion of the related research about fuzzy measures. We can see the research trend in Fig. 18.6 below:

We believe that in the next few years, the study of fuzzy measure theory and its application in MADM will definitely become a hot direction.

18.5   Fuzzy Preference Relations and MADM

18.5.1   Fuzzy Preference Relations

In many cases, it is difficult for decision-makers to give a specific evaluation of an alternative. But it is easy to compare the two schemes. Of course, using fuzzy information to express this preference is more in line with the subjective thinking of decision-makers. This is the fuzzy preference relation. There are two kinds of fuzzy preference relations: fuzzy additive preference relation (complementary judgment matrix) and fuzzy multiplicative preference relation (reciprocal judgment matrix). The main difference between the two is scale. The additive preference relation uses $0 - 1$ scale, while the multiplicative preference relation uses $1/9 - 9$ scale. Fuzzy preference relation is an important part of fuzzy decision-making. At present, there are many related researches. The research on it can be divided into the following four parts:

1. direct derivation of alternative ranking or weight vector from judgment matrix [82–85];
2. consistency of judgment matrix [86–89];
3. consensus process [90–93];

4. analytic hierarchy process (AHP) [94–97].

Among them, consensus process is to study how to make multiple decision-makers reach consensus, which is mainly applied to group decision-making (GDM). Therefore, the application of preference relation in MADM is mainly the other three.

In MADM, if we want to get the ranking of alternatives directly from a set of judgment matrices, we need to integrate the scores of each alternative in all attributes with the help of fuzzy aggregation operators. Finally, we get the ranking result according to the comprehensive score of each scheme. This idea is very simple and direct, and it is the most basic application of fuzzy preference relation in MADM.

The research on the consistency of fuzzy preference relations generally follows the following steps. Firstly, for a new kind of fuzzy information, such as IFS and HFS, we need to give a definition of its consistency, which must be well defined. Secondly, the definitions are generally complex and obscure. We need to give some sufficient and necessary conditions to obtain ways to judge whether a certain preference relation is consistent. Then, for those inconsistent preference relations, we need to give some adjustment algorithms to make them consistent. For some complex preference relations which satisfy the consistency, we need to use their good properties to degenerate them into simple preference relations by some methods. In a word, the research on the consistency of fuzzy preference relations is essentially to lay a good foundation for the subsequent derivation of weight or ranking results based on these preference relations, and do a good job of "quality inspector". The judgment matrix without testing cannot be used.

18.5.2 Fuzzy Analytic Hierarchy Process

The analytic hierarchy process (AHP) first takes a complex multi-objective decision-making problem as a system, decomposes the objective into multiple objectives or criteria, and then decomposes it into several levels of multiple indicators (or criteria, constraints). Then, the single rank (or weight) and the total rank are calculated by the fuzzy quantitative method of qualitative index. It decomposes the decision-making problem into different hierarchies according to the order of general objective, sub-objectives of each level, evaluation criteria and specific alternatives. Then, by solving the eigenvector of judgment matrix, the priority weight of each element of each level to a certain element of the upper level is obtained. Finally, the method of weighted sum is used to merge the final weight of each alternative to the general objective hierarchically. The best scheme is the one with the largest final weight.

From the perspective of decision-makers, fuzzy information can better express their ideas. As a classical decision-making method, AHP has been extended to fuzzy environments by many scholars, which forms fuzzy AHP. It is a typical example of comprehensive application of fuzzy preference relation, which uses approaches such as the construction of preference relation, consistency test and weight derivation. Fuzzy AHP is mainly used to derive weights and ranking results, and it is widely used in GDM, MADM and other decision-making problems. Next, we briefly introduce the decision-making process of fuzzy AHP (Fig. 18.7).

Step 1 Determine the objectives, attributes, sub-attributes and alternatives of the decision-making problem, and construct the hierarchical structure of the decision-making problem.

Step 2 Determine the type of fuzzy set to be used through the analysis of decision-making information, and then construct the corresponding fuzzy preference relations through the pairwise comparison of attributes or sub attributes. At the same time, compare each alternative under each attribute, and construct the corresponding fuzzy preference relation. The relative importance of these attributes or schemes is represented by corresponding fuzzy elements.

Step 3 Check the consistency of each fuzzy preference relation is by the corresponding criterion. If all fuzzy preference relations have acceptable consistency, go to step 5, otherwise go to step 4.

Step 4 Use the corresponding algorithm to modify the inconsistent fuzzy preference relations. Or return them to the relevant decision-makers for re-evaluation until they have acceptable consistency.

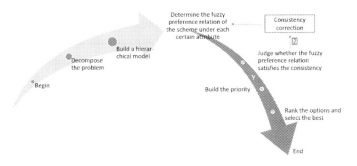

Fig. 18.7 Flow chart of fuzzy AHP

Step 5   Select the corresponding method to calculate the priority of each
         fuzzy preference relationship.

Step 6   Use the operation method of corresponding fuzzy elements to fuse
         all the weight information from the bottom to the top, and then
         compare the comprehensive weight and select the optimal scheme
         in the end.

18.6 Some Other Classical Synthetic Fuzzy MADM Methods

In the previous chapters, we introduced some basic knowledge and methods
of fuzzy MADM. In addition, there are some MADM methods, which integrate the knowledge of fuzzy decision-making, and provide more and more
suitable choices for MADM problems in different situations. In this chapter,
we mainly introduce these methods.

18.6.1 Fuzzy PROMETHEE

The main idea of PROMETHEE method is to derive the partial order or
complete order of alternative schemes according to outgoing flow, entering
flow and net flow of schemes. In recent years, this method has been
extended to various decision-making environments to solve MADM problems in different information forms. The first generation of PROMETHEE
method was characterized by partial order and the second generation of
PROMETHEE method was characterized by complete order, first proposed
by Brans and Mareschal [98]. Subsequently, various versions were produced
one after another, and they were also applied to many fields, such as environmental management [99], business and financial management [100],
information technology [101], project management [102] and so on. For
details, please refer to reference [103]. The PROMETHEE method is mainly
used to deal with the problems with difficulties on pairwise comparison. It
considers two kinds of additional information, that is, information within
and between attributes. It considers the deviation degree of the evaluation
value of every two pairs of alternatives on a specific attribute. The smaller
the deviation, the decision-maker will assign a smaller preference to the
alternative.

Many scholars applied different kinds of fuzzy information to PROMETHEE and established fuzzy PROMETHEE methods. They allow decision-makers to apply fuzzy elements when giving evaluation values for each alternative with respect to different attributes. Then, the preference degrees between every two alternatives with fuzzy elements can be obtained and FPR can be established. They can avoid the deviation of decision-making results caused by the DMs forcibly giving accurate evaluation values under uncertain conditions.

Fuzzy PROMETHEE can be roughly summarized as the following steps:

1. For a certain given decision-making problem, generate the set of alternatives $X = \{X_1, X_2, \cdots, X_m\}$ and determine the set of attributes $A = \{A_1, A_2, \cdots, A_n\}$;
2. The decision-makers give evaluation values of all alternatives in $X = \{X_1, X_2, \cdots, X_m\}$ with respect to the attributes in $C = \{A_1, A_2, \cdots, A_n\}$, respectively, with corresponding information form. At the same time, determine the relative weight vector of all attributes, $\boldsymbol{\omega} = (\omega_1, \omega_2, \cdots, \omega_n)^T$, where $\sum_{j=1}^{n} \omega_j = 1$;
3. Calculate the deviation degrees of each pair of alternatives with respect to different attributes $A = \{A_1, A_2, \cdots, A_n\}$. And then, determine the decision-makers' preference functions, that is, determine the no-difference-threshold q and the strict-preference-threshold p. And then, compute the preference degree μ_{ij}^k between alternatives X_i and X_j with respect to the attribute A_k through the linear preference function (V-shape) [98], and get the preference matrix $U^k (k = 1, 2, \cdots, n)$;
4. Establish the FPR $\boldsymbol{F}^k = (\mu_{ij}^k)_{m \times m}$ with respect to the attributes $A_k (k = 1, 2, \cdots, n)$;
5. Establish the overall FPR $\boldsymbol{F} = (r_{ij})_{m \times m}$;
6. Calculate the outgoing flows and entering flows of all alternatives $X_i (i = 1, 2, \cdots, m)$, denoted as $\varphi^+(X_i)$ and $\varphi^-(X_i)$;
7. Compare the sizes of all $\varphi^+(X_i)(i = 1, 2, \cdots, m)$ and $\varphi^-(X_i)(i = 1, 2, \cdots, m)$ to get the final preference orders of all alternatives.

The above is just a rough explanation of fuzzy PROMETHEE. In fact, the details of the method are slightly different in different fuzzy environments. Please see the detailed algorithm and formulas in Ref. [104–107].

18.6.2 Fuzzy ELECTRE

The ELECTRE method plays an important role in scheme ranking. It was first proposed by Benayoun et al [108]. Subsequently, Roy proposed the ELECTRE I method and improved it continuously [109]. Then, many scholars continue to improve and expand this method, and apply it to many different fields, such as project selection [110], transportation [111], energy management [112] and so on. The ELECTRE method mainly constructs the consistent set and inconsistent set of attributes to get the corresponding dominant matrix and the final ranking results. Compared with traditional ELECTRE method, fuzzy elements applied in fuzzy ELECTRE method can contain more decision information than real information. We can use score value and deviation degree to further divide consistent set and inconsistent set. Thus, we can avoid forcing the decision-makers to take the average preference. Therefore, the fuzzy ELECTRE method is more suitable for the actual decision-making processes. Next, we take hesitant fuzzy ELECTRE as an example to briefly introduce the steps of fuzzy ELECTRE:.

1. Establish the hesitant fuzzy decision-making matrix. And then, determine the weight vector of all attributes $\boldsymbol{\omega} = (\omega_1, \omega_2, \cdots, \omega_n)^T$ and the attitude weight vector of different kinds of hesitant fuzzy concordance (discordance) set $\boldsymbol{w} = (w_c, w_{c'}, w_{\overline{D}}, w_{\overline{D}'})^T$;
2. Calculate the score values and the deviation degrees of all alternatives under every attribute;
3. Construct the hesitant fuzzy concordance (discordance) set and the weakened hesitant fuzzy concordance (discordance) set;
4. Calculate the hesitant fuzzy concordance (discordance) index and the weakened hesitant fuzzy concordance (discordance) index. And then, establish the hesitant fuzzy concordance (discordance) matrix and the weakened hesitant fuzzy concordance (discordance) matrix;
5. Determine the consistent dominant matrix and the inconsistent dominant matrix;
6. Establish the dominant aggregation matrix;
7. Draw the decision-making map and choose the best alternative.

The above is a brief process of hesitant fuzzy ELECTRE I. The purpose of our introduction is to help readers better understand this method. In fact, the specific steps of ELECTRE . are different in different fuzzy environments. And there are some other kinds of ELECTRE, such as ELECTRE II, ELECTRE III, ELECTRE TRI, etc. If you want to know more about other content, you can refer to the corresponding literature [113–117].

18.6.3 Hesitant Fuzzy TODIM

In most decision-making processes, decision-makers usually do not have complete rationality [118]. This means that the psychological behavior of decision-makers will fundamentally have a significant impact on the decision-making processes and results. Unfortunately, most MADM methods, including the famous TOPSIS and ELECTRE, assume that the decision-makers are completely rational. In this way, in many practical decision-making problems, the reliability of these methods is questionable. TODIM considers the bounded rationality of decision-makers. Next, we will take the hesitant fuzzy TODIM method [119] as an example to introduce the specific content of this method in detail:

Let's start with a new measure of HFEs. Let $h = \{\gamma_1, \gamma_2, \cdots, \gamma_n\}$ be an HFE, $Z_\delta(h)$ of h can be defined as follows:

$$Z_\delta(h) = Z_\delta(\gamma_1, \gamma_2, \cdots, \gamma_n) = \left(\frac{(\gamma_1)^\delta + (\gamma_2)^\delta + \cdots + (\gamma_n)^\delta}{n}\right)^{\frac{1}{\delta}},$$
(18.17)

where δ is a parameter given by decision-makers. It can be changed with different problems, and is in the range $0 < \delta \leq 1$. In particular, if $\delta = 1$, then $Z_\delta(h)$ reduces to the score function [5] of HFEs.

After that, we can get a new way to compare two HFEs.

1. If $Z_\delta(h_1) > Z_\delta(h_2)$, then h_1 is superior to h_2, denoted as $h_1 > h_2$;
2. If $Z_\delta(h_1) < Z_\delta(h_2)$, then h_1 is inferior to h_2, denoted as $h_1 < h_2$;
3. If $Z_\delta(h_1) = Z_\delta(h_2)$, then h_1 is equivalent to h_2, denoted as $h_1 \sim h_2$.

Based on the above measure function and the HFE-ranking method, in the following, the hesitant fuzzy TODIM will be introduced as follows:

At first, the attribute with the highest weight A_{i_0} is considered as the reference attribute. Then, we can calculate the relative weight of each attribute A_i which is relative to the reference attribute A_{i_0} with:

$$w_{ii_0} = \frac{w_i}{w_{i_0}}, i = 1, 2, \cdots, n ,$$
(18.18)

Benefitting from the above information, the gain and loss values of the alternative X_i relative to X_j with respect to different attributes can be calculated. Let $A = \{A_1, A_2, \cdots, A_n\}$ be the attribute set, and $X =$

$\{X_1, X_2, \cdots, X_m\}$ be the alternative set. h_{ik} is used to denote the evaluation value of the alternative X_i with respect to the attribute A_k, the weight vector of A is $\boldsymbol{w} = (w_1, w_2, \cdots, w_n)^T$, and largest one among $w_k (k = 1, 2, \cdots, n)$ is w_{k_0}. Then, the perceptual function value of X_i relative to X_j on A_k is:

$$\varphi_k(X_i, X_j)$$
$$= \begin{cases} \sqrt{w_{kk_0} d\left(h_{ik}, h_{jk}\right) / \sum_{k=1}^{n} w_{kk_0}}, & if \, Z_\delta(h_{ik}) - Z_\delta(h_{jk}) > 0 \\ 0, & if \, Z_\delta(h_{ik}) - Z_\delta(h_{jk}) = 0 \\ -\frac{1}{\theta} \sqrt{\left(\sum_{k=1}^{n} w_{kk_0}\right) d\left(h_{ik}, h_{jk}\right) / w_{kk_0}}, & if \, Z_\delta(h_{ik}) - Z_\delta(h_{jk}) < 0 \end{cases}$$

(18.19)

where θ denotes the attenuation factor of the losses, $d(h_{ik}, h_{jk})$ is the Euclidean distance measure of h_{ik} and h_{jk}. If $Z_\delta(h_{ik}) - Z_\delta(h_{jk}) > 0$, the $\varphi_k(X_i, X_j)$ represents "gain"; If $Z_\delta(h_{ik}) - Z_\delta(h_{jk}) = 0$, the $\varphi_k(X_i, X_j)$ represents a "nil"; If $Z_\delta(h_{ik}) - Z_\delta(h_{jk}) > 0$, the $\varphi_k(X_i, X_j)$ represents "losses".

Next, the perceptual function of X_i relative to X_j under all attributes in $A = \{A_1, A_2, \cdots, A_n\}$ can be calculated as follows:

$$\vartheta(X_i, X_j) = \sum_{k=1}^{n} \varphi_k(X_i, X_j), i, j = 1, 2, \cdots, m, \quad (18.20)$$

Finally, the overall perceptual function values of $X_i (i = 1, 2, \cdots, m)$ can be calculated by:

$$\Phi(X_i) = \frac{\sum_{j=1}^{m} \vartheta(X_i, X_j) - min_i \left\{\sum_{j=1}^{m} \vartheta(X_i, X_j)\right\}}{max_i \left\{\sum_{j=1}^{m} \vartheta(X_i, X_j)\right\} - min_i \left\{\sum_{j=1}^{m} \vartheta(X_i, X_j)\right\}},$$
$$i = 1, 2, \cdots, m, \quad (18.21)$$

It can be seen that $0 \leq \Phi(X_i) \leq 1$. Thus, we can rank the alternatives $X_i (i = 1, 2, \cdots, m)$ by their overall perceptual function values.

In different fuzzy environments, the decision-making methods are different. Readers can refer to the relevant literature [120–123] to further understand TODIM methods in other fuzzy environment and their application scenarios.

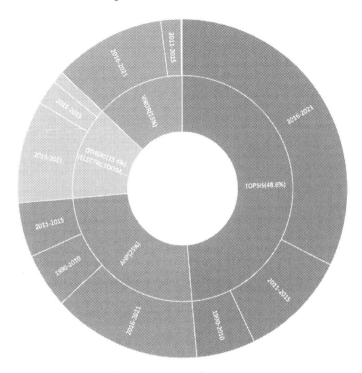

Fig. 18.8 The proportion of the research of fuzzy TOPSIS, AHP, VIKOR and other methods

We introduce three fuzzy MADM methods above. In fact, there are many fuzzy MADM methods, in addition to the above three, there are also fuzzy LINMAP [124–126], fuzzy QUALIFLEX [127–130], fuzzy COPRAS [131] and other classic methods. The following Figs. 18.8 and 18.9 describe the research status of those fuzzy MADM methods in recent decades:

It can be seen from the above two figures that TOPSIS, AHP and VIKOR are the three most commonly used methods in fuzzy multi-attribute decision-making. And since 2016, the number of related studies has increased dramatically. The number of articles published each year is several times higher than before.

18.7   Prospects for Future Research Directions

From the earliest FS to IFS, HFS, until the recent P-HFS, fuzzy theory has been developing. At the same time, fuzzy MADM has been making progress. We believe that in the future, the development direction of fuzzy MADM is mainly the combination of fuzzy and probability. At present, it is P-HFS.

Fig. 18.9 The proportion of the research of some other fuzzy MADM methods

Of course, there may be more perfect fuzzy information expressions in the future.

At present, the research on probabilistic hesitant fuzzy MADM has begun to take shape. The research of P-HFS in information fusion [7, 132, 133], distance measures [134–136] and preference relations [137–142] has formed a basic system, and some scholars have also proposed some related MADM methods [143–149]. However, it is far from IFS and HFS. In fact, since Zhu [6] put forward the concept of P-HFS in 2014, the follow-up research has been carried out. However, for a long time, the related research work has been stagnant for a long time. The reason is that the structure of P-HFS is complex, which makes it very difficult to deal with. In this regard, we think that the future research on probabilistic hesitant fuzzy MADM should focus on the following points:

1. Operation and integration: the operation and integration of P-HFEs is the basis of all subsequent research. Firstly, compared with other fuzzy elements, the difficulty of P-HFEs' operation lies in the processing of probability information. Therefore, we should find some reasonable and

concise ways to deal with the probability information, so as to simplify the operation of P-HFEs as much as possible. In this aspect of research, we think that continuity is a good idea. In fact, probability information brings us not only trouble, but also some good properties. For example, if we make rational use of probability distribution, we can make P-HFEs continuous. After that, we can use computer-based methods and the knowledge of statistics to carry out subsequent operations. If the method is appropriate, it can greatly improve our computational efficiency. We believe that this is a good research direction.

2. Distance measures: from the previous description, we can know that distance measure is the basis of many MADM methods. Therefore, it is very important to study the distance measure of probabilistic hesitant fuzzy information. However, it is difficult to define the distance measure of probabilistic hesitant fuzzy information for the same reason that it is difficult to deal with the probability information. At present, there is no perfect distance measure. Therefore, this is also a key research direction in the future.

3. The MADM methods: the former two directions are both basic research, and they also limit the development of probabilistic hesitant fuzzy MADM method. After solving the above two problems, we should improve the original MADM method based on the advantages of probabilistic hesitant fuzzy information, and construct some new methods. And then we can establish a more perfect MADM method system, so as to better solve the actual MADM problems.

References

1. L.A. Zadeh, Fuzzy sets, Information and Control, 1965, 8: 338–356.
2. K. Atanassov, Intuitionistic fuzzy sets, In: Sgurev V ed. VII ITKR's Session, Sofia, June, 1983.
3. K. Atanassov, Intuitionistic fuzzy sets, Fuzzy Sets and Systems, 1986, 20: 87–96.
4. V. Torra, Hesitant fuzzy sets, International Journal of Intelligent Systems, 2010, 25: 529–539.
5. M.M. Xia, Z.S. Xu, Hesitant fuzzy information aggregation in decision making, International Journal of Approximate Reasoning, 2011, 52: 395–407.
6. B. Zhu, Decision method for research and application based on preference relation, Nanjing: Southeast University, 2014.

7. S. Zhang, Z.S. Xu, Operations and integrations of probabilistic hesitant fuzzy information in decision making, Information Fusion, 2017, 38: 1–11.

8. R.M. Rodriguez, L. Martinez, F. Herrera, Hesitant fuzzy linguistic term sets for decision making, IEEE Transactions on fuzzy systems, 2012, 20(1): 109–119.

9. Q. Pang, H. Wang, Z.S. Xu, Probabilistic linguistic term sets in multi-attribute group decision making, Information Sciences, 2016, 369: 128–143.

10. R.R. Yager, On ordered weighted averaging aggregation operators in multicriteria decision making, IEEE Transactions on Systems, Man, and Cybernetics, 1988, 18: 183–190.

11. R.R. Yager, Generalized OWA aggregation operators, Fuzzy Optimization and Decision Making, 2004, 3: 93–107.

12. R.R. Yager, OWA aggregation over a continuous interval argument with applications to decision making, IEEE Transaction Systems, Man, and Cybernetics, 2004, 34: 1952–1963.

13. Z.S. Xu, Intuitionistic fuzzy aggregation operations, IEEE Transactions on Fuzzy Systems, 2007, 15: 1179–1187.

14. Z.S. Xu, R.R. Yager, Some geometric aggregation operators based on intuitionistic fuzzy sets, International Journal of General System, 2006, 35: 417–433.

15. G.W. Wei, M. Lu, Pythagorean fuzzy power aggregation operators in multiple attribute decision making, International Journal of Intelligent Systems, 2018, 33(1): 169–186.

16. D.J. Yu, Some generalized dual hesitant fuzzy geometric aggregation operators and applications, International Journal of Uncertainty Fuzziness and Knowledge-Based Systems, 2014, 22(3): 367–384.

17. W.Z. Wang, X.W. Liu, Intuitionistic fuzzy geometric aggregation operators based on Einstein operations, International Journal of Intelligent Systems, 2011, 26(11): 1049–1075.

18. S.Z. Zeng, W.H. Su, A.B. Le, Fuzzy generalized ordered weighted averaging distance operator and its application to decision making, International Journal of Fuzzy Systems, 2012, 14(3): 402–412.

19. W. Yang, Z.P. Chen, The quasi-arithmetic intuitionistic fuzzy OWA operators, Knowledge-Based Systems, 2012, 27: 219–233.

20. S.Z. Zeng, J.M. Merigo, D. Palacios-Marques, H.H. Jin, F.J. Gu, Intuitionistic fuzzy induced ordered weighted averaging distance operator and its application to decision making, Journal of Intelligent & Fuzzy Systems, 2017, 32(1): 11–22.

21. J.M. Merigo, M. Casanovas, P.D. Liu, Decision making with fuzzy induced heavy ordered weighted averaging operators, International Journal of Fuzzy Systems, 2014, 16(3): 277–289.

22. X. Liang, C.P. Wei, Z.M. Chen, An intuitionistic fuzzy weighted OWA operator and its application, International Journal of Machine Learning and Cybernetics, 2013, 4(6): 713–719.

23. X.F. Zhao, G.W. Wei, Some intuitionistic fuzzy Einstein hybrid aggregation operators and their application to multiple attribute decision making, Knowledge-Based Systems, 2013, 37: 472–479.

24. H.C. Liao, Z.S. Xu, Some new hybrid weighted aggregation operators under hesitant fuzzy multi-criteria decision making environment, Journal of Intelligent & Fuzzy Systems, 2014, 26(4): 1601–1617.

25. Z.M. Zhang, Several new interval-valued intuitionistic fuzzy Hamacher hybrid operators and their application to multi-criteria group decision making, International Journal of Fuzzy Systems, 2016, 18(5): 829–848.

26. A. Fahmi, S. Abdullah, F. Amin, M.S.A. Khan, Trapezoidal cubic fuzzy number Einstein hybrid weighted averaging operators and its application to decision making, Soft Computing, 2019, 23(14): 5753–5783.

27. M. Riaz, H.M.A. Farid, F. Karaaslan, M.R. Hashmi, Some q-rung orthopair fuzzy hybrid aggregation operators and TOPSIS method for multi-attribute decision-making, Journal of Intelligent & Fuzzy Systems, 2020, 39(1): 1227–1241.

28. W. Yang, Y.F. Pang, New q-Rung orthopair fuzzy Bonferroni mean Dombi operators and their application in multiple attribute decision making, IEEE Access, 2020, 8: 50587–50610.

29. B. Zhu, Z.S. Xu, M.M. Xia, Hesitant fuzzy geometric Bonferroni means, Information Sciences, 2012, 205: 72–85.

30. F. Ates, D. Akay, Some picture fuzzy Bonferroni mean operators with their application to multicriteria decision making, International Journal of Intelligent Systems, 2020, 35(4): 625–649.

31. M.M Xia, Z.S. Xu, B. Zhu, Geometric Bonferroni means with their application in multi-criteria decision making, Knowledge-Based Systems, 2013, 40: 288–100.

32. Y.D. He, Z. He, G.D. Wang, H.Y. Chen, Hesitant fuzzy power Bonferroni means and their application to multiple attribute decision making, IEEE Transactions on Fuzzy Systems, 2015, 23(5): 1655–1668.

33. D.C. Liang, A.P. Darko, Z.S. Xu, M.W. Wang, Aggregation of dual hesitant fuzzy heterogenous related information with extended Bonferroni mean and its application to MULTIMOORA, Computers & Industrial Engineering, 2019, 135: 156–176.

34. Y.D. He, Z. He, H.Y. Chen, Intuitionistic fuzzy interaction Bonferroni means and its application to multiple attribute decision making, IEEE Transactions on Cybernetics, 2015, 45(1): 116–128.

35. M.M Xia, Z.S. Xu, M, Chen, Some hesitant fuzzy aggregation operators with their applications in group decision making, Group Decision and Negotiation, 2013, 22: 259–279.

36. H.C. Liao, Z.S. Xu, A VIKOR-based method for hesitant fuzzy multi-criteria decision making, Fuzzy Optimization and Decision Making, 2013, 12: 373–392.

37. M.S.A. Khan, S. Abdullah, A. Ali, F. Amin, F. Hussain, Pythagorean hesitant fuzzy Choquet integral aggregation operators and their application to multi-attribute decision-making, Soft Computing, 2019, 23(1): 251–267.
38. S. Zhang, D.J. Yu, Some geometric Choquet aggregation operators using Einstein operations under intuitionistic fuzzy environment, Journal of Intelligent & Fuzzy Systems, 2014, 26(1): 491–500.
39. D.C. Liang, Y.R.J. Zhang, W. Cao, q-Rung orthopair fuzzy Choquet integral aggregation and its application in heterogeneous multicriteria two-sided matching decision making, International Journal of Intelligent Systems, 2019, 34(12): 3275–3301.
40. R.R. Yager, An intuitionistic view of the Dempster-Shafer belief structure, Soft Computing, 2014, 18(11): 2091–2099.
41. R.R. Yager, D.P. Filev, Including probabilistic uncertainty in fuzzy-logic controller modeling using Dempster-Shafer theory, IEEE Transactions on Systems Man and Cybernetics, 1995, 25(8): 1221–1230.
42. Z.S. Xu, H. Zhao, Hesitant Fuzzy Sets Theory and Applications, Beijing: Science Press, 2018.
43. R.R. Yager, Prioritized aggregation operators, International Journal of Approximate Reasoning, 2008, 48: 363–274.
44. R. Torres, R. Salas, H. Astudillo, Time-based hesitant fuzzy information aggregation approach for decision-making problems, International Journal of Intelligent Systems, 2014, 29: 579–595.
45. N. Zhao, Z.S. Xu, Z.L. Ren, On typical hesitant fuzzy prioritized "or" operator in multi-attribute decision making, International Journal of Intelligent Systems, 2015, 31: 73–100.
46. P. Diamond, P. Kloeden, Metric Spaces of Fuzzy Sets Theory and Applications, Sinapore: World Scientific Publishing, 1994.
47. J. Kacprzyk, Multistage Fuzzy Control, Chichester: Wiley.
48. B.B. Chaudhuri, A. Rosenfield, A modified Hausdorff distance between fuzzy sets, Information Sciences, 1999, 118: 159–171.
49. P. Grzegorzewski, Distances between intuitionistic fuzzy sets and/or interval-valued fuzzy sets based on the Hausdorff metric, Fuzzy Sets and Systems, 2004, 148: 319–328.
50. E. Szmidt, J. Kacprzyk, Distances between intuitionistic fuzzy sets, Fuzzy Sets and Systems, 2000, 114: 505–518.
51. Z.S. Xu, A survey of preference relations, International Journal of General System, 2007, 36: 179–203.
52. Z.S. Xu, J. Chen, An overview of distance and similarity measures of intuitionistic fuzzy sets, International Journal of Uncertainty Fuzziness and Knowledge-Based Systems, 2008, 16: 529–555.
53. D.H. Hong, Fuzzy measures for a correlation coefficient of fuzzy numbers under T_ω (the weakest t-norm)-based fuzzy arithmetic operations, Information Sciences, 2006, 176: 150–160.

54. T. Gerstenkorn, J. Mako, Correlation of intuitionistic fuzzy sets, Fuzzy Sets and Systems, 1991, 44: 39–43.
55. H. Bustince, P. Burillo, Correlation of interval-valued intuitionistic fuzzy sets, Fuzzy Sets and Systems, 1995, 74: 237–244.
56. W.L. Hung, J.W. Wu, Correlation of intuitionistic fuzzy sets by centroid method, Information Sciences, 2002, 144: 219–225.
57. Z.S. Xu, J. Chen, J.J. Wu, Clustering algorithm for intuitionistic fuzzy sets, Information Sciences, 2008, 178: 3775–3790.
58. E. Szmidt, J. Kacprzyk, Correlation of intuitionistic fuzzy sets, Lecture Notes in Computer Sciences, 2010, 6178: 169–177.
59. Z.S. Xu, M.M. Xia, Distance and similarity measures for hesitant fuzzy sets, Information Sciences, 2011, 181: 2128–2138.
60. A. De Luca, S. Termini, A definition of nonprobabilistic entropy in the setting of fuzzy sets theory, Information and Control, 1972, 20: 301–312.
61. P. Burillo, H. Bustince, Entropy on intuitionistic fuzzy sets and on interval-valued fuzzy sets, Fuzzy Sets and Systems, 1996, 78: 305–316.
62. H.Y.Zhang, W.X. Zhang, C.L. Mei, Entropy of interval-valued fuzzy sets based on distance and its relationship with similarity measure, Knowledge-Based Systems, 2009, 22: 449–454.
63. E. Szmidt, J. Kacprzyk, Entropy for intuitionistic fuzzy sets, Fuzzy Sets and Systems, 2001, 118: 467–477.
64. M.M. Xia, Z.S. Xu, Entropy/cross entropy-based group decision making under intuitionistic fuzzy environment, Information Fusion, 2012, 13: 31–47.
65. C.L. Hwang, K. Yoon, Multiple attribute decision making methods and applications, 1981, Berlin: Springer.
66. C.T. Chen, Extensions of the TOPSIS for group decision-making under fuzzy environment, Fuzzy Sets and Systems, 2000, 114(1): 1–9.
67. F.E. Boran, S. Genc, M. Kurt, D. Akay, A multi-criteria intuitionistic fuzzy group decision making for supplier selection with TOPSIS method, Expert Systems with Applications, 2009, 36(8): 11363–11368.
68. D.F. Li, TOPSIS-based nonlinear-programming methodology for multi-attribute decision making with interval-valued intuitionistic fuzzy sets, IEEE Transactions on fuzzy systems, 2010, 18(2): 299–311.
69. G. Bakioglu, A.O. Atahan, AHP integrated TOPSIS and VIKOR methods with Pythagorean fuzzy sets to prioritize risks in self-driving vehicles, Applied Soft Computing, 2021, 99: 106948.
70. Z.S. Xu, X.L. Zhang, Hesitant fuzzy multi-attribute decision making based on TOPSIS with incomplete weight information, Knowledge-Based Systems, 2013, 52: 53–64.
71. Z.S. Xu, M.M. Xia, On distance and correlation measures of hesitant fuzzy information, International Journal of Intelligent Systems, 2011, 26: 410–425.
72. A. Shemshadi, H. Shirazi, M. Toreihi, M.J. Tarokh, A fuzzy VIKOR method for supplier selection based on entropy measure for objective weighting, Expert Systems with Applications, 2011, 38(10): 12160–12167.

73. A. Sanayei, S. F. Mousavi, A. Yazdankhah, Group decision making process for supplier selection with VIKOR under fuzzy environment, Expert Systems with Applications, 2010, 37(1): 24–30.

74. N. Zhang, G.W. Wei, Extension of VIKOR method for decision making problem based on hesitant fuzzy set, Applied Mathematical Modelling, 2013, 37(7): 4938–4947.

75. X.L. Zhang, Z.S. Xu, Hesitant fuzzy agglomerative hierarchical clustering algorithms, International Journal of Systems Science, 2015, 46(3): 562–576.

76. S. Miyamoto, Information clustering based on fuzzy multisets, Information Processing and Management, 2003, 39: 195–213.

77. N. Chen, Z.S. Xu, M.M. Xia, Hierarchical hesitant fuzzy K-means clustering algorithm, Applied Mathematics-A Journal Chinese Universities Ser. B, 2014, 29: 1–17.

78. X.L. Zhang, Z.S. Xu, A MST clustering analysis method under hesitant fuzzy environment, Control and Cybernetics, 2012, 41: 645–666.

79. J.C. Bezdek, R. Ehrlich, W. Full, FCM-The fuzzy C-means clustering-algorithm, Computers & Geosciences, 1984, 10: 191–203.

80. L. Sirisup; S. Vera, An incremental density-based clustering framework using fuzzy local clustering, Information Sciences, 2021, 547: 404–426.

81. F. Salehi, M. Keyvanpour, A. Sharifi, SMKFC-ER: Semi-supervised multiple kernel fuzzy clustering based on entropy and relative entropy, Information Sciences, 2021, 547: 667–688.

82. M.M. Xia, Z.S. Xu, Managing hesitant information in GDM problems under fuzzy and multiplicative preference relations, International Journal of Uncertainty Fuzziness and Knowledge-Based Systems, 2013, 21: 865–897.

83. N. Chen, Z.S. Xu, M.M. Xia, Interval-valued hesitant preference relations and their applications to group decision making, Knowledge-Based Systems, 2013, 37: 528–540.

84. B. Zhu, Z.S. Xu, J.P. Xu, Deriving a ranking from hesitant fuzzy preference relations under group decision making, IEEE Transactions on Cybernetics, 2017, 44(8): 1328–1337.

85. Z.S. Xu, J. Chen, Some models for deriving the priority weights from interval fuzzy preference relations, European Journal of Operational Research, 2008, 184(1): 266–280.

86. E. Herrera-Viedma, F. Herrera, F. Chiclana, M. Luque, Some issues on consistency of fuzzy preference relations, European Journal of Operational Research, 2004, 154(1): 98–109.

87. W. Yang, S.T. Jhang, S.G. Shi, Z.S. Xu, Z.M. Ma, A novel additive consistency for intuitionistic fuzzy preference relations in group decision making, Applied Intelligence, 2020, 50(12): 4342–4356.

88. H.C. Liao, Z.S. Xu, Consistency of the fused intuitionistic fuzzy preference relation in group intuitionistic fuzzy analytic hierarchy process, Applied Soft Computing, 2015, 35: 812–826.

89. F.F. Jin, Z.W. Ni, H.Y. Chen, Y.P. Li, Approaches to group decision making with intuitionistic fuzzy preference relations based on multiplicative consistency, Knowledge-Based Systems, 2016, 97: 48–59.

90. Z.M. Zhang, S.M. Chen, Group decision making with incomplete q-rung orthopair fuzzy preference relations, Information Sciences, 2021, 553: 376–396.

91. J. Tang, Y.N. Zhang, H. Fujita, X.D. Zhang, F.Y. Meng, Analysis of acceptable additive consistency and consensus of group decision making with interval-valued hesitant fuzzy preference relations, Neural Computing & Applications, 2021, https://doi.org/10.1007/s00521-020-05516-z.

92. E. Herrera-Viedma, S. Alonso, F. Chiclana, F. Herrera, A consensus model for group decision making with incomplete fuzzy preference relations, IEEE Transactions on fuzzy systems, 2007, 15(5): 863–877.

93. Z.M. Zhang, W. Pedrycz, A consistency and consensus-based goal programming method for group decision-making with interval-valued intuitionistic multiplicative preference relations, IEEE Transactions on Cybernetics, 2019, 49(10): 3640–3654.

94. D.Y. Chang, Applications of the extent analysis method on fuzzy AHP, European Journal of Operational Research, 1996, 95(3): 649–655.

95. Y.M. Wang, Y. Luo, Z.S. Hua, On the extent analysis method for fuzzy AHP and its applications, European Journal of Operational Research, 2008, 186(2): 735–747.

96. Z.S. Xu, H.C. Liao, Intuitionistic fuzzy analytic hierarchy process, IEEE Transactions on fuzzy systems, 2014, 22(4): 749–761.

97. B. Zhu, Z.S. Xu, Analytic hierarchy process-hesitant group decision making, European Journal of Operational Research, 2014, 239(3): 794–801.

98. J.P. Brans, B. Mareschal, PROMETHEE methods//J. Figueira, S. Greco, M. Ehrgott, Multiple Criteria Decision Analysis: State of the Art Surveys. Berlin: Springer, 2005.

99. K.J. Zhang, C. Kluck, G. Achari, A comparative approach for ranking contaminated sites based on the risk assessment paradigm using fuzzy PROMETHEE, Environmental Management, 2009, 44: 952–967.

100. A. Albadvi, S.K. Chaharsooghi, A. Esfahanipour, Decision making in stock trading: an application of PROMETHEE, European Journal of Operational Research, 2007, 177: 673–683.

101. A. Albadvi, Formulating national information technology strategies: a preference ranking model using PROMETHEE method, European Journal of Operational Research, 2004, 153: 290–296.

102. N. Halouani, H. Chabchoub, J.M. Martel, PROMETHEE-MD-2T method for project selection, European Journal of Operational Research, 2009, 195: 841–849.

103. M. Behzadian, R.B. Kazemzadeh, A. Albadvi, PROMETHEE: a comprehensive literature review on methodologies and applications, European Journal of Operational Research, 2010, 200: 198–215.

104. M. Goumas, V. Lygerou, An extension of the PROMETHEE method for decision making in fuzzy environment: Ranking of alternative energy exploitation projects, European Journal of Operational Research, 2000, 123(3): 606–613.
105. H.C. Liao, Z.S. Xu, Multi-criteria decision making with intuitionistic fuzzy PROMETHEE, Journal of Intelligent & Fuzzy Systems, 2014, 27(4): 1703–1717.
106. A.S. Fernandez-Castro, M. Jimenez, PROMETHEE: an extension through fuzzy mathematical programming, Journal of the Operational Research Society, 2005, 56(1): 119–122.
107. F. Feng, Z.S. Xu, H. Fujita, M.Q. Liang, Enhancing PROMETHEE method with intuitionistic fuzzy soft sets, International Journal of Intelligent Systems, 2020, 35(7): 1071–1104.
108. R. Benayoun, B. Roy, B. Sussman, ELECTRE: Une methode pour guider le choi xen presence de points de vue multiples, Note de travail 49, SEMA-METRA International, Direction Scientifique, 1966.
109. B. Roy, Classment et choi xen presence de points de vue multiples (la methode ELECTRE), RIRO, 1968, 8: 57–75.
110. J. Buchanan, D. Vanderpooten, Ranking projects for an electricity utility using ELECTRE III, International Transactions in Operational Research, 2007, 14: 309–323.
111. B. Roy, J.C. Hugonnard, Ranking of suburban line extension projects on the Paris metro system by a multicriteria method, Transportation Research, 1982, 16(A): 301–312.
112. E. Georgopoulou, Y. Sarafidis, S. Mirasgedis, S. Zaimi, D. Lalas, A multiple criteria decision-aid approach in defining national priorities for greenhouse gases emissions reduction in the energy sector, European Journal of Operational Research, 2003, 146: 199–215.
113. M. Sevkli, An application of the fuzzy ELECTRE method for supplier selection, International Journal of Production Research, 2010, 48(12): 3393–3405.
114. N. Chen, Z.S. Xu, M.M. Xia, Hesitant fuzzy ELECTRE II approach: A new way to handle multi-criteria decision making problems, Information Sciences, 2015, 292: 175–197.
115. A. Hatami-Marbini, M. Tavana, An extension of the Electre I method for group decision-making under a fuzzy environment, OMEGA-International Journal of Management Science, 2011, 39(4): 373–386.
116. T.Y. Chen, An ELECTRE-based outranking method for multiple criteria group decision making using interval type-2 fuzzy sets, Information Sciences, 2014, 263: 1–21.
117. J.J. Peng, J.Q. Wang, J. Wang, L.J. Yang, X.H. Chen, An extension of ELECTRE to multi-criteria decision-making problems with multi-hesitant fuzzy sets, Information Sciences, 2015, 307: 113–126.
118. C. Camerer, Bounded rationality in individual decision making, Experimental Economics, 1998, 1(2): 163–183.

119. X.L. Zhang, Z.S. Xu, The TODIM analysis approach based on novel measured functions under hesitant fuzzy environment, Knowledge-Based Systems, 2014, 61: 48–58.
120. P.J. Ren, Z.S. Xu, X.J. Gou, Pythagorean fuzzy TODIM approach to multi-criteria decision making, Applied Soft Computing, 2016, 42: 246–259.
121. J.D. Qin, X.W. Liu, W. Pedrycz, An extended TODIM multi-criteria group decision making method for green supplier selection in interval type-2 fuzzy environment, European Journal of Operational Research, 2017, 258(2): 626–638.
122. Q.D. Qin, F.Q. Liang, L. Li, Y.W. Chen, G.F. Yu, A TODIM-based multi-criteria group decision making with triangular intuitionistic fuzzy numbers, Applied Soft Computing, 2017, 55: 93–107.
123. R.A. Krohling, A.G.C. Pacheco, A.L.T. Siviero, IF-TODIM: An intuitionistic fuzzy TODIM to multi-criteria decision making, Knowledge-Based Systems, 2013, 53: 142–146.
124. S.P. Wan, D.F. Li, Fuzzy LINMAP approach to heterogeneous MADM considering comparisons of alternatives with hesitation degrees, OMEGA-International Journal of Management Science, 2013, 41(6): 925–940.
125. D.F. Li, Extension of the LINMAP for multiattribute decision making under Atanassov's intuitionistic fuzzy environment, Fuzzy Optimization and Decision Making, 2008, 7(1): 17–34.
126. X.L. Zhang, Z.S. Xu, Interval programming method for hesitant fuzzy multi-attribute group decision making with incomplete preference over alternatives, Computers & Industrial Engineering, 2014, 75: 217–229.
127. X.L. Zhang, Multicriteria Pythagorean fuzzy decision analysis: A hierarchical QUALIFLEX approach with the closeness index-based ranking methods, Information Sciences, 2016, SI, 330: 104–124.
128. T.Y. Chen, C.H. Chang, J.F.R. Lu, The extended QUALIFLEX method for multiple criteria decision analysis based on interval type-2 fuzzy sets and applications to medical decision making, European Journal of Operational Research, 2013, 226(3): 615–625.
129. T.Y. Chen, Interval-valued intuitionistic fuzzy QUALIFLEX method with a likelihood-based comparison approach for multiple criteria decision analysis, Information Sciences, 2014, 261: 149–169.
130. X.L. Zhang, Z.S. Xu, Hesitant fuzzy QUALIFLEX approach with a signed distance-based comparison method for multiple criteria decision analysis, Expert Systems with Applications, 2015, 42(2): 873–884.
131. M.G. Keshavarz, M. Amiri, J.S. Sadaghiani, G.H. Goodarzi, Multiple criteria group decision-making for supplier selection based on COPRAS method with interval type-2 fuzzy sets, International Journal of Advanced Manufacturing Technology, 2014, 75: 1115–1130.
132. Z.M. Zhang, C. Wu, Weighted hesitant fuzzy sets and their application to multi-criteria decision making, British Journal of Mathematics and Computer Science, 2014, 4: 1091–1123.

133. S. Zhang, Z.S. Xu, X.J. Zeng, X. Yan, Integrations of continuous hesitant fuzzy information in group decision making with a case study of water resources emergency management, IEEE Access, 2020, 8: 146134–146144.

134. J. Yang, Z.S. Xu, A measure of probabilistic hesitant I-fuzzy sets and decision makings for strategy choice, International Journal of Intelligent Systems, 2020, https://doi.org/10.1002/int.22340.

135. B. Farhadinia, Utility of correlation measures for weighted hesitant fuzzy sets in medical diagnosis problems, Mathematical Modelling and Applications, 2016, 1(2): 36–45.

136. B. Farhadinia, U. Aickelin, H.A. Khorshidi, Uncertainty measures for probabilistic hesitant fuzzy sets in multiple criteria decision making, International Journal of Intelligent Systems, 2020, 35(11): 1646–1679.

137. B. Zhu, Z.S. Xu, Probability-hesitant fuzzy sets and the representation of preference relations, Technological & Economic Development of Economy 2018, 24(3): 1029–1040.

138. Z.S. Xu, W. Zhou, Consensus building with a group of decision makers under the hesitant probabilistic fuzzy environment, Fuzzy Optimization and Decision Making, 2017, 16: 481–503.

139. W. Zhou, Z.S. Xu, Probability calculation and element optimization of probabilistic hesitant fuzzy preference relations based on expected consistency, IEEE Transactions on Fuzzy Systems 2018, 26(3): 1367–1378.

140. Z.B. Wu, B.M. Jin, J.P. Xu, Local feedback strategy for consensus building with probability-hesitant fuzzy preference relations, Applied Soft Computing 2018, 67: 691–705.

141. W. Zhou, Z.S. Xu, Group consistency and group decision making under uncertain probabilistic hesitant fuzzy preference environment, Information Sciences, 2017, 414: 276–288.

142. X.L. Tian, Z.S. Xu, H. Fujita, Sequential funding the venture project or not? A prospect consensus process with probabilistic hesitant fuzzy preference information, Knowledge-Based Systems, 2018, 161: 172–184.

143. J. Ding, Z.S. Xu, N. Zhao, An interactive approach to probabilistic hesitant fuzzy multi-attribute group decision-making with incomplete weight information, Journal of Intelligent & Fuzzy Systems, 2017, 32(3): 2523–2536.

144. H.M. Jiang, C.K. Kwong, W.Y. Park. Probabilistic fuzzy regression approach for preference modeling, Engineering Applications of Artificial Intelligence, 2017, 64: 286–294.

145. W. Zhou, Z.S. Xu, Expected hesitant VaR for tail decision making under probabilistic hesitant fuzzy environment, Applied Soft Computing, 2017, 60: 297–311.

146. J. Li, Q.X. Chen, L.L. Niu, Z.X. Wang, An ORESTE approach for multi-criteria decision-making with probabilistic hesitant fuzzy information, International Journal of Machine Learning and Cybernetics, 2020, 11(7): 1591–1609.

147. Y. He, Z.S. Xu, Multi-attribute decision making methods based on reference ideal theory with probabilistic hesitant information, Expert Systems with Applications, 2019, 118: 459–469.
148. J. Li, J.Q. Wang, J.H. Hu, Multi-criteria decision-making method based on dominance degree and BWM with probabilistic hesitant fuzzy information, International Journal of Machine Learning and Cybernetics, 2019, 10(7): 1671–1685.
149. W.K. Zhang, J. Du, X.L. Tian, Finding a promising venture capital project with TODIM under probabilistic hesitant fuzzy circumstance, Technological and Economic Development of Economy, 2018, 24(5): 2026–2044.

19

Importance Measures in Reliability Engineering: An Introductory Overview

Shaomin Wu and Frank Coolen

19.1 Introduction

Modern technical systems are complex and composed of multiple components. The failures of such systems may cause various types of consequences, such as loss of healthy life and well being, economic losses or environmental damage. This requires engineers to design their products with high reliability and maintain them in a good condition to ensure good availability.

In the reliability literature, many approaches have been presented to support system engineers in their tasks to fulfil these requirements. These include, at the product design stage, the optimisation of reliability allocation under constraints on e.g. budget and weight, and at the operation stage, optimal scheduling of preventive and corrective maintenance activities. These approaches can be guided by a widely studied general concept: importance measures.

S. Wu (✉)
Kent Business School, University of Kent, Canterbury, England
e-mail: s.m.wu@kent.ac.uk

F. Coolen
Department of Mathematical Sciences, Durham University, Durham, England
e-mail: frank.coolen@durkam.ac.uk

© The Author(s), under exclusive license to Springer Nature
Switzerland AG 2022
S. Salhi and J. Boylan (eds.), *The Palgrave Handbook of Operations Research*,
https://doi.org/10.1007/978-3-030-96935-6_19

Importance measures in the reliability literature aim to provide a list of priority rankings for a given task. For example, if the system has failed, a list of probabilities of which components may have caused the system to fail can be helpful for the engineers to diagnose the system and ascertain the cause of the failure; if preventive maintenance is carried out on the system, then a ranking which indicates the improvement of the system reliability resulting from maintenance activity on each particular component will be useful. There are many other examples where various types of component importance measures can be applied. That is, importance measures are proposed from different perspectives and can be used for different purposes. The reader is referred to [1] for a monograph and to [2–4] for review papers relating to importance measures. This chapter aims to provide practitioners with an introduction to importance measures in reliability engineering.

19.2   Basic Concepts of Reliability

In many applications, time to the occurrence of an event is a main concern. For example, the event can be the failure of a product or system, or death or recovery of a patient who has been given newly developed medication. While such events seem to be very different, the mathematical methods for quantification of the uncertainty involved are very similar. Hence, while this chapter discusses importance measures from an engineering perspective, the concept is relevant and applicable in many other fields.

19.2.1   Reliability Function

British Standard gives the following definition of reliability [5]:

Definition 19.1 *(Reliability)* [5] Reliability is the ability of an entity to perform a required function under given conditions for a given time interval.

It should be highlighted that, in this definition, *required function*, *given condition*, and *given time interval* are very important. Accordingly, failure is the termination of the ability to perform the required function.

Let T be the time to failure, then the reliability function $R(t) = P(T > t)$, with $t \geq 0$, is of central interest in reliability theory. $R(t)$ is also referred to as the survival function, mainly so in medical applications. So reliability is the probability that an item, which can be a component, a subsystem or a system, works without failure during a time interval $(0, t)$ under given usage intensity and operating environment.

For engineering scenarios, we normally assume the following properties of $R(t)$:

- $R(t_1) \geq R(t_2)$ if $t_1 < t_2$. That is, $R(t)$ is a non-increasing function of t. With time progressing, the reliability of an item becomes smaller;
- $R(0) = 1$. That is, at time $t = 0$, the reliability of the item under study is 1; and
- $R(\infty) = 0$. That is, when time approaches infinite, the item will definitely fail.

19.2.2 System Reliability Analysis

Assume that a system consists of multiple components and the reliability of each component is known. Then we will be able to obtain the reliability of the system, given the assumption that the failure times of the components are statistically independent, and assuming that the system structure function, which describes the system state as function of the component states, is fully known. The assumption of independence will be applied in this chapter for simplicity. It should be remarked that there are important scenarios where component lifetimes are naturally dependent, and this will also affect the important measures. Examples of such scenarios include common failure modes and cascading failures, but also in cases of load-sharing between components, the failure of one component can increase the load on other components, and hence their failure times will not be dependent. The simplest system structures are series systems, parallel systems and k-out-of-n systems, which are briefly introduced.

Definition 19.2 *(Series system)* Suppose a system consists of multiple components. If the failure of any of the components causes the system to fail, then the system is called a series system.

For example, a car has four tyres. If one of the tyres deflates, then the tyre system stops working and the deflated tyre needs to be fixed or replaced with one that functions. As such, the tyre system can be regarded as a series system.

Assume a series system is composed of n components with statistically independent failure times. Denote the cumulative distribution function of the failure time distribution of component i by $F_i(t)$, for $i = 1, 2, \ldots, n$, and the corresponding reliability functions by $R_i(t) = 1 - F_i(t)$. The reliability function of the series system is given by $R_s(t) = \prod_{i=1}^{n} R_i(t) = \prod_{i=1}^{n}(1 - F_i(t))$.

Definition 19.3 (*Parallel system*) Suppose a system consists of multiple components and that the system fails only if all of the components in the system fail. Then the system is called a parallel system.

For example, a human body has two kidneys. Only if both kidneys fail, the kidney system will fail. As such, the kidney system can be regarded as a parallel system composed of two components.

Assume a parallel system is composed of n components, with statistically independent failure times. Then the failure time distribution of the system is given by $F_s(t) = \prod_{i=1}^{n} F_i(t)$, and the reliability function of the system is $R_s(t) = 1 - F_s(t) = 1 - \prod_{i=1}^{n}(1 - R_i(t))$.

Definition 19.4 (*k-out-of-n system*) Suppose a system consists of n components. Assume that the system functions only if at least k components function. Then the system is called a k-out-of-n system.

Clearly, if $k = n$ then such a system is a series system, and if $k = 1$ then it is a parallel system. A real-world example is a V8 engine, which works if and only if four or more of its eight cylinders work, so this is a 4-out-of-8 system.

For the special case that all n components have the same reliability function $R(t)$, the reliability function of a k-out-of-n system is $R_s(t) = \sum_{i=k}^{n} \binom{n}{i} (R(t))^i (1 - R(t))^{n-i}$.

Many real-world systems are more complex as they are composed of subsystems, each of which may have different structures. For example, Fig 19.1 illustrates a system composed of five components: component 1, component 2 and the subsystem composed of components 3, 4, and 5 are structured in series; components 3, 4 and 5 in the subsystem are structured in parallel.

If we denote the reliability functions of the five components in Fig 19.1 by $R_i(t)$, for $i = 1, 2, 3, 4, 5$, respectively, then the reliability function of the system is given by $R_s(t) = R_1(t)R_2(t)[1 - (1 - R_3(t))(1 - R_4(t))(1 - R_5(t))]$.

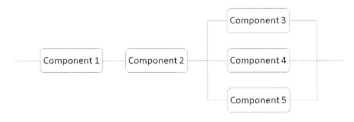

Fig. 19.1 A typical example of a complex system

19.3   Importance Measures

The concept of importance measures was first introduced by Birnbaum [6]. Importance measures are metrics that can be used to rank the components in a technical system from a given perspective. For example, one may need to identify and rank the most important components within a system, and, specifically, to identify where investments should be made to increase the overall system availability, subject to a budget constraint [7]. In such cases, component importance measures are useful decision support tools.

A recurrent theme of interest in reliability theory is to define reliability importance. Importance measures have deep ramifications for researchers in reliability theory. Suppose that a system contains n components, whose reliability functions are $R_1(t)$, $R_2(t)$, $\ldots$, $R_n(t)$, and assume that components failures are independent. The reliability of the system at a given time point t may be expressed as a function of the component reliabilities at that time, say by

$$R_s(t) = f(R_1(t), R_2(t), \ldots, R_n(t)).$$

Importance measures can be categorised into technology-based or utility-based measures. We briefly describe these.

19.3.1   Technology-Based Measures

The *technology-based criterion* reflects the impact of a reliability-related index of a component on its system. In this category, importance measures may be categorised into three classes: structure importance, reliability importance and lifetime importance [6].

19.3.1.1   Structure Importance

Structure importance measures evaluate the importance of the position of a component in the system. As such, the structure importance is evaluated with the knowledge of the position of each component, but reliability-related information of each component is not needed.

A component is critical in a state vector if its failure will cause system failure. The structure importance of component i in binary-state systems is obtained from the following index

$$I_i^S = \frac{The\ total\ number\ of\ different\ state\ \cdot\ vectors\ in\ which\ component\ i\ is\ critical}{2^{n-1}} \qquad (19.1)$$

It is easily seen that all components in a series (or parallel or k-out-of-n) system have the same structure importance. However, components in a series-parallel system may have different structure importance. For example, components 1 and 2 in Fig 19.1 are structured in series, and therefore they have the same structure importance. Similarly, components 3, 4 and 5 have the same structure importance, but components 1 and 3 (or components 4 and 5) have different structure importance.

As can be seen from the definition 19.1, there is no need to use any information about the reliability of each component in the system to calculate the structure importance.

19.3.1.2 Reliability Importance

Reliability importance measures evaluate the importance of a component in the system when the knowledge of the position of each component is known and the reliability function of each component is also known or assumed. This enables the importance of a component for the system functioning to be measured at any specific time. A well-known importance measure which takes time into account is Birnbaum's importance measure, as discussed below.

The Birnbaum measure of the importance of component i is the rate of change of system reliability with respect to component reliability [6]:

$$I_i^B(t) = \frac{\partial R_s(t)}{\partial R_i(t)}. \qquad (19.2)$$

Assuming there is a given amount ΔR of the reliability improvement which can be conducted on any given component, then it can easily be proved that the largest Birnbaum importance for a series system is assigned to the component with the smallest reliability, and for a parallel system it is the component with the largest reliability that has the largest Birnbaum importance. That is, if one is able to improve a component with a given amount of reliability ΔR, then one should choose to improve the weakest component in a series system in order to maximise the improvement of the system reliability, while in a parallel system it is optimal to improve the reliability of the strongest component.

The improvement of the system reliability due to replacing component i with reliability $R_i(t)$ by a component with reliability $\tilde{R}_i(t) > R_i(t)$, is given by

$$I^I_{R_i \to \tilde{R}_i}(t) = f(R_1(t), R_2(t), \ldots, \tilde{R}_i(t), \ldots, R_n(t))$$
$$- f(R_1(t), R_2(t), \ldots, R_i(t), \ldots, R_n(t)). \quad (19.3)$$

$I^I_{R_i \to \tilde{R}_i}(t)$ is called the *improvement potential* of component i at time t. In some publications, when defining the improvement potential, the $\tilde{R}_i(t)$ in (19.3) can be set to 1. Nevertheless, we should note that in practice the reliability of component i is unlikely to be perfect (i.e, $\tilde{R}_i(t) = 1$). As such, the definition shown in Eq. (19.3) fits better with practice. Apparently, one can easily derive the relationship between the Birnbaum importance measure and the improvement potential [8].

19.3.1.3 Lifetime Importance

Lifetime importance measures evaluate the importance of a component in the system, considered over the full lifetime of the system, when the knowledge of the position of each component is known and the reliability of each component is a function of time. The examples of reliability importance measures aforementioned can be extended to their counterparts that fall in this category, for example, the Birnbaum time-dependent lifetime importance measure and the criticality time-dependent lifetime importance measure.

The Barlow-Proschan (BP) importance is defined under the condition that the system is a coherent system and the component lifetimes are independent. It measures the probability that the failure of a given component causes the system to fail [9]. The BP importance measure is defined by

$$I^{BP}_i = \int_0^{+\infty} I^B_i(t) f_i(t) dt, \quad (19.4)$$

where $f_i(t)$ is the probability density function (pdf) of the failure time of component i.

19.3.2   Utility-Based Importance Measures

The *utility-based criteria* are set to compare, in monetary terms, the relevant economic impact of an event caused by a component on its system. Such an event can be the failure of a component, the repair upon a failure, or a preventive maintenance action. For example, the cost-based importance, introduced by Wu & Coolen [10], is a utility-based importance measure which considers the costs incurred due to maintaining a system and its components within a finite time horizon.

Wu & Coolen[10] assume that the total cost of maintaining a system within time period $(0, t)$ includes costs $C_S(t)$ incurred due to system failure and costs $C_i(t)$ for maintaining component i during this period. Hence, the total cost within time interval $(0, t)$ is given by

$$C(t) = C_s(t) + \sum_{i=1}^{n} C_i(t) \tag{19.5}$$

The cost-based importance of component k is defined as

$$I_i^C(t) = -\frac{\partial C(t)}{\partial R_i(t)}. \tag{19.6}$$

where the negative sign in the definition is in order to align $I_i^C(t)$ with conventional importance measures, so that larger importance measures imply more cost savings.

It should also be noted that a system can be coherent or non-coherent. A system is coherent if its reliability function is nondecreasing in terms of the values of its components reliabilities, otherwise it is non-coherent. The above importance measures were proposed for coherent systems but they can be extended to the non-coherent systems. For example, Birnbaum's importance is extended to non-coherent systems by Andrews & Beeson [11] and Beeson & Andrews [12].

19.3.3   Importance Measures Based on the Survival Signature

Importance measures are typically defined per component in a system. However, for large systems, the information required to compute such importance measures may not be available, mainly because a full system structure function may not be available. If a system has many components, but these are only of a few types, then the system reliability computations, and hence importance measures computations, can be simplified through the use of the survival signature, which was introduced by Coolen & Coolen-Maturi [13]. The survival signature is a summary of a system structure function which, together with the probability model for the components' failure times, is sufficient for computing the reliability function of the system failure time.

The survival signature can be used to assess the importance of components of a specific type instead of the importance of each specific component, as presented by Feng et al. [14]. For several practical decision problems, the importance of a component type may be the most relevant information, for example if one needs to decide on immediate availability of spare components in case the system fails, then it may not be crucial to know which specific component is likely to fail next and to lead to system failure, but the type of component to fail next could be sufficient information in order to prepare for a possible maintenance action. Eryilmaz et al.[15] considered marginal and joint component importance for dependent components, based on the survival signature.

In order to make a system more resilient, one may have the opportunity to swap components of the same type within the system. Quantifying the effect of such swaps on the system reliability proved relatively straightforward with the use of the survival signature. Najem & Coolen [16] showed that such possible swaps can also greatly affect the importance of components of specific types. Huang et al.[17] presented a survival signature for phased mission systems, with the possibility that not all components need to function in each phase. Component importance measures in this setting were presented by Huang et al. [18].

19.3.4 Importance Measures and Some Important Concepts

Risk and resilience are crucial concepts in reliability mathematics and engineering. The relationships of these concepts with importance measures are briefly considered next.

19.3.4.1 Importance Measures and Risk

Vesely et al. [19] gives two risk related importance measures: *risk achievement worth* and *risk reduction worth* , which are defined as follows. If $R_s(t)$ is the reliability of a system, then $1 - R_s(t)$, or the unreliability of the system, can be seen as the risk level at given time t. Denote $R_i^-(t)$ as the reliability of the system in which component i is assumed to have failed by time t, then, $1 - R_i^-(t)$ is the increased risk level with component i not functioning. *Risk achievement worth* (RAW), which relates to risk increase potential, is defined as

$$I_i^{\text{RAW}}(t) = \frac{1 - R_i^-(t)}{1 - R_s(t)};\qquad(19.7)$$

$I_i^{\text{RAW}}(t)$ measures the importance of maintaining the current level of reliability for component i at time t.

Denote $R_i^+(t)$ as the reliability of the system in which component i is assumed to be functioning at time t. The risk reduction worth (RRW), which relates to risk decrease potential, is defined as

$$I_i^{\text{RRW}}(t) = \frac{1 - R_s(t)}{1 - R_i^+(t)}.\qquad(19.8)$$

$I_i^{\text{RRW}}(t)$ measures the decrease in risk if the system is assumed to be functioning. The reader is referred to [20] for more detailed discussion on risk importance measures in the design and operation of nuclear power plants, and to [21] for the use of importance measures for risk-informed decision support.

19.3.4.2 Importance Measures and Resilience

Research on reliability theory and engineering traditionally concentrates on single individual systems such as an engine or a car, or a fleet of identical systems. In the last two decades, research on resilience management has received increasing attention. Tierney & Bruneau [22] define resilience as both the inherent strength and ability to be flexible and adaptable after environmental shocks and disruptive events. Resilience is normally studied for large-scale systems such as critical infrastructure systems, including electric power systems, water supply systems, transportation systems, and telecommunication systems, which are the building blocks of the modern society and economy. A large-scale system (or a network) is normally composed of many subsystems, which are connected by components, normally called links.

Barker et al. [23] proposed two importance measures to assess the potential adverse impact on system resilience from a disruption affecting a link, and the potential positive impact on system resilience when a link cannot be disrupted. Baroud et al. [24] proposed two stochastic resilience-based component importance measures to highlight the critical waterway links that contribute to waterway network resilience. Uday & Marais [25] proposed importance measures that rank the constituent systems based on their impact on the performance of systems-of-systems, which are large-scale integrated networks of systems.

19.4 Information Needed for Importance Measures

Since the level of information needed to evaluate the different importance measures becomes more demanding, we can use Fig 19.2 to summarise the information required for different measures. That is, from left to right, the required information is increasing. Importance measures can be categorised into time-independent and time-dependent importance measures [6]. Lifetime importance measures and cost-based importance measures are functions of time and can therefore be categorised into time-dependent importance measures, while structure importance and reliability importance are functions of component reliabilities that are normally regarded as constants, and can therefore be seen as time-independent important measures [26].

If an item (component or system) has only two states, functioning or failed, then it is called a binary item. If an item has more than two states, then it is called a multi-state item. A power plant which has states 0, 1, 2, 3, 4 that correspond to generating electricity at 0%, 25%, 50%, 75%, 100% of its

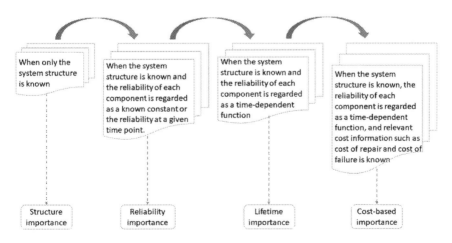

Fig. 19.2 Information needed for different types of importance measures

full capacity, is an example of a multi-state system that has ordered multiple states [27]. Unlike a binary item that has only one functioning state, which implies that its level of performance does not need to be measured when it is functioning, a multi-state item has different performance levels. This can be used to define more general importance measures than for binary systems with binary components. For example, the utility importance of a component can be defined as the proportion of the contribution a multi-state component makes to the system's performance [28].

19.5 Applications of Importance Measures

In reliability engineering, three approaches are commonly used for reliability improvement:

* Assuring reliability through material selection. The approach of component selection aims to select components with certain levels of reliability to assure the reliability of the entire system. Normally, component selection is subject to some constraints such as the cost, weight or volume of the components.
* Achieving the reliability target through adding component redundancy and reliability optimisation.
* Reliability and availability improvement through preventive or corrective maintenance.

The first two approaches are typically implemented at the design stage, while preventive and corrective maintenance are performed at the operation stage, although they are also frequently considered at the design stage, and aspects of possible maintenance may influence the design. In each of these approaches, component importance measures play an important role.

We refer to a component, a set of components, or a subsystem, as an object. In the literature, importance measures of an object are introduced based mainly on three factors:

* The location of the object in the system.
* The technical index of the object in question, where the technical index may be reliability, availability, and repair rates, etc.
* The consequence of an event on the object, where the consequence can, for example, be cost, and the event may be failure, repair, etc.

Below we discuss importance measures for different stages in the lifetime cycle, although in practice these measures may be used at various stages.

Importance measures for the design stage. At the design stage, engineers aim to design their products to achieve the reliability goals, which may be defined by their customers. Reliability allocation and optimisation are commonly used techniques.

Adding a new component onto an active redundant system (such as a parallel system) can increase the reliability of the system. One may use importance measures to find the increment in system reliability by adding a spare component [29]. For example, the structure importance may be used to find the importance index of a given position; the Birnbaum importance measure may be useful for component selection in order to meet a pre-specified reliability target. That is, when only a given amount of reliability of each component in a system can be improved, the engineer may use the Birnbaum importance to prioritise the components in order to maximise the reliability improvement of the system.

Importance measures for the operation stage. At the operation stage, the main focus is to ensure that the system operates at a specific level of availability. At this stage, maintenance plays an important role. As such, importance measures that can be used to help in fault diagnosis and the magnitude of reliability improvement after maintenance are helpful.

For example, Fussell-Vesely's importance measure for a component is the probability that at least one minimal cut set that contains this component has failed by time t, given that the system has failed by time t; the criticality importance measure is the probability that a component has caused the system to fail, when we know that the system fails at time t; and the credible improvement potential measure evaluates the difference between the system reliabilities with a component before and after repair.

Another importance measure that is worth mentioning is the component maintenance priority (CMP), introduced by Wu et al. [30]. Assuming that a component in a system has failed and is being repaired, one may use the repair time to preventively maintain other components in the system. The CMP can be used to prioritise components for preventive maintenance. For example, for the system shown in Fig 19.1, if component 3 fails and if preventive maintenance on a component needs the system to stop operating, then either component 4 or component 5, but not both, can be selected for preventive maintenance. However, if component 1 or component 2 fails, preventive maintenance can be conducted on any of the other components. The CMP can be extended to multi-state systems, as discussed in [31].

19.6   Concluding Remarks

Reliability engineering and mathematics is an important research field involving many methods from operational research and applied statistics. High levels of system reliability and availability are required in many industries such as the railway industry, the aviation industry, and many modern production processes. To assure that a system operates at a specific level of availability requires collaborative work of many people, in particular the design engineers and maintenance engineers, and importance measures can be useful tools to support them in their tasks. This chapter provided a brief introductory overview on the main ideas of reliability importance measures.

We should include some warnings with regard to importance measures. There is a risk that they may lead to over-simplification of complex issues. It is very easy to interpret such measures wrongly, in particular for managers who may lack detailed understanding of (conditional) probability and engineering insight. It may be tempting to think that one importance measure is sufficient to understand the risks in often complex engineering situations, but it is rarely the case that such simple one-dimensional quantities provide an adequate summary to support complex decisions. One may consider several importance measures as input to decision problems, but that also requires deeper understanding as these will not be independent measures. In many scenarios, risks due to single components failing may be well understood, but the results of several components failing simultaneously may be harder to assess, and the likelihood of simultaneous failure of multinomial components may be particularly hard to assess. With new technology, it is also often difficult to foresee all possible failure modes and their likelihood of occurring, making it even harder to provide the required input to derive importance measures. In particular for well designed critical systems, failures frequently occur with unforeseen causes, which would typically not be reflected in any importance measures beyond basic measures based only on the structure of the system. Hence, importance measures should always come with a warning to not use them without detailed insight into their meaning and how they can be used, and how they should not be used.

Reliability engineering is a huge topic area with challenges for both researchers and practitioners. New scenarios of system reliability keep emerging due to ever more advanced techniques, for example increased use of sensors provides more information (which may not be without errors). This opens up opportunities to develop new importance measures, where the actual aim for their use should always be the starting point.

References

1. W. Kuo, X. Zhu, Importance measures in reliability, risk, and optimization: principles and applications, John Wiley & Sons, 2012.
2. W. Kuo, X. Zhu, Some recent advances on importance measures in reliability, IEEE Transactions on Reliability 61 (2) (2012) 344–360.
3. Y. Dutuit, A. Rauzy, Importance factors of coherent systems: A review, Journal of Risk and Reliability 228 (2014) 313–323.
4. S. Si, J. Zhao, Z. Cai, H. Dui, Recent advances in system reliability optimization driven by importance measures, Frontiers of Engineering Management 7 (2020) 335–358.
5. British Standard, 13306: 2017: Maintenance-maintenance terminology, BSI Standards Publication (2017).
6. Z. W. Birnbaum, On the importance of different components in a multicomponent system, in: P. Krishnaiah (Ed.), Multivariate Analysis (vol. 2), Academic Press, New York, USA, 1969, pp. 581–592.
7. J. F. Espiritu, D. W. Coit, U. Prakash, Component criticality importance measures for the power industry, Electric Power Systems Research 77 (5–6) (2007) 407–420.
8. A. Høyland, M. Rausand, System Reliability Theory: Models and Statistical Methods, Vol. 420, John Wiley & Sons, New Jersey, 2009.
9. R. E. Barlow, F. Proschan, Importance of system components and fault tree events, Stochastic Processes and their applications 3 (2) (1975) 153–173.
10. S. Wu, F. Coolen, A cost-based importance measure for system components: An extension of the birnbaum importance, European Journal of Operational Research 225 (1) (2013) 189–195.
11. J. D. Andrews, S. Beeson, Birnbaum's measure of component importance for noncoherent systems, IEEE Transactions on Reliability 52 (2) (2003) 213–219.
12. S. Beeson, J. D. Andrews, Importance measures for noncoherent-system analysis, IEEE Transactions on Reliability 52 (3) (2003) 301–310.
13. F. Coolen, T. Coolen-Maturi, On generalizing the signature to systems with multiple types of components., in: Complex Systems and Dependability, Springer, 2012, pp. 115–130.
14. G. Feng, E. Patelli, M. Beer, F. Coolen, Imprecise system reliability and component importance based on survival signature, Reliability Engineering and System Safety 150 (2016) 116–125.

15. S. Eryilmaz, F. Coolen, T. Coolen-Maturi, Marginal and joint reliability importance based on survival signature, Reliability Engineering and System Safety 172 (2018) 118–128.

16. A. Najem, F. Coolen, System reliability and component importance when components can be swapped upon failure., Applied Stochastic Models in Business and Industry 35 (2019) 399–413.

17. X. Huang, L. Aslett, F. Coolen, Reliability analysis of general phased mission systems with a new survival signature., Reliability Engineering and System Safety 189 (2019) 416–422.

18. X. Huang, F. Coolen, T. Coolen-Maturi, Y. Zhang, A new study on reliability importance analysis of phased mission systems., IEEE Transactions on Reliability 69 (2020) 522–532.

19. W. Vesely, T. Davis, R. Denning, N. Saltos, Measures of risk importance and their applications, Tech. rep., Battelle Columbus Labs. (1983).

20. I. Vrbanic, P. Samanta, I. Basic, Risk importance measures in the designand operation of nuclear power plants, Tech. rep., Brookhaven National Lab.(BNL), Upton, NY (United States) (2017).

21. M. Azarkhail, M. Modarres, A study of implications of using importance measures in risk-informed decisions, in: Probabilistic Safety Assessment and Management, Springer, 2004, pp. 456–461.

22. K. Tierney, M. Bruneau, Conceptualizing and measuring resilience: A key to disaster loss reduction, TR news (250) (2007).

23. K. Barker, J. E. Ramirez-Marquez, C. M. Rocco, Resilience-based network component importance measures, Reliability Engineering & System Safety 117 (2013) 89–97.

24. H. Baroud, K. Barker, J. E. Ramirez-Marquez, et al., Importance measures for inland waterway network resilience, Transportation research part E: logistics and transportation review 62 (2014) 55–67.

25. P. Uday, K. B. Marais, Resilience-based system importance measures for system-of-systems, Procedia Computer Science 28 (2014) 257–264.

26. E. Borgonovo, H. Aliee, M. Glaß, J. Teich, A new time-independent reliability importance measure, European Journal of Operational Research 254 (2) (2016) 427–442.

27. A. P. Wood, Multistate block diagrams and fault trees, IEEE Transactions on Reliability 34 (3) (1985) 236–240.

28. S. Wu, L.-Y. Chan, Performance utility-analysis of multi-state systems, IEEE Transactions on Reliability 52 (1) (2003) 14–21.

29. M. Xie, K. Shen, On ranking of system components with respect to different improvement actions, Microelectronics Reliability 29 (2) (1989) 159–164.

30. S. Wu, Y. Chen, Q. Wu, Z. Wang, Linking component importance to optimisation of preventive maintenance policy, Reliability Engineering & System Safety 146 (2016) 26–32.

31. H. Dui, S. Wu, J. Zhao, Some extensions of the component maintenance priority, Reliability Engineering & System Safety (2021) 107729.

20

Queues with Variable Service Speeds: Exact Results and Scaling Limits

Moeko Yajima and Tuan Phung-Duc

20.1 Introduction

In classical queueing models, the arrival process, the service time distributions and the number of servers are fixed. However, in many real-world situations, models with variable service capacity are more flexible and are used to balance the performance and the operating cost. In this chapter, we attempt to make a thoughtful survey on recent advances of queues with variable service speeds. In Section 20.2, we investigate literature on queues with vacation or setup time which are used to optimize the operating cost of servers, i.e., power consumption, etc. Vacation models are characterized by the feature that a server takes a vacation once it completes a service. In the single vacation policy, the server returns to the normal mode after the vacation regardless whether or not there are waiting customers, while in multiple vacation policy,

M. Yajima (✉)
Department of Mathematical and Computing Sciences, Tokyo Institute of Technology, Meguro-ku, Tokyo, Japan
e-mail: yajima.m.ad@m.titech.ac.jp

T. Phung-Duc
Faculty of Engineering, Information and Systems, University of Tsukuba, Tsukuba, Ibaraki, Japan
e-mail: tuan@sk.tsukuba.ac.jp

© The Author(s), under exclusive license to Springer Nature Switzerland AG 2022
S. Salhi and J. Boylan (eds.), *The Palgrave Handbook of Operations Research*,
https://doi.org/10.1007/978-3-030-96935-6_20

675

the server returns to the normal mode only if there are waiting customers otherwise it takes another vacation.

Setup time is a similar concept to vacation, where the server is turned off upon the completion of a service. When customers arrive, an off server is activated to serve waiting customers but it takes some setup time for a server to change to the active state so as to serve waiting customers.

Section 20.3 is devoted to models with infinitely many servers. In this model, customers are served immediately upon arrivals. The quantity of interest is the number of busy servers which is also the number of customers in the system. In simple cases, the service speed of the system is proportional to the number of jobs in the system which allow various analytical results. These models are challenging when customers arrive in batches for which the stability condition becomes nontrivial. These models also become difficult when the arrivals and services are modulated by a background process such as a Markov chain. In these cases, analytic results are rarely obtained and the main focuses are the fluid/diffusion limits .

20.2   Queues with Vacation/setup time

Queues with variable service speeds naturally arise from various applications. In an energy-saving computer, the CPU adjusts its speeds according to the workload to save energy. In data centers, servers are turned on and off according to the number of jobs in the system. Idle servers are turned off to save energy. However, when there are a certain number of waiting jobs, off servers are turned on to process these jobs. A server needs some setup time to become active. We will review some major results on vacation models in Section 20.2.1 and models with workload-dependent service speeds in Section 20.2.2. Models with setup time are presented in Section 20.2.3 and some open problems are discussed in Section 20.2.4.

20.2.1   Vacation Models

First of all, we start with the M/G/1 vacation queue. In this model, the server goes for a vacation once it becomes empty. After the vacation time if there are waiting customers, the server is active and serve these customers. Upon returning from vacation, if the system is empty, the server takes another vacation (multiple vacations) or becomes active (single vacation). In single server queues with vacation, one of the most important result is the stochastic decomposition in which, the queue length is decomposed into the sum of two independent random variables. The first one is the queue length in the corresponding model without vacation and the second one is the number of arrivals during the residual life of the vacation [15]. A similar theorem for sojourn time is also obtained via the distributional Little's law [25]. For more results on the decomposition in single server queues can be found in [12].

Vacation models are then extended to working vacations ones, where during vacation the server instead of completely stopping its service provides the service at a different speed. After the vacation period, the server returns to the normal mode. Servi and Finn [51] are the first to propose the working vacation M/M/1 queue as a model for optical networks. The model was then extended to M/G/1 with multiple vacations using generating function and Laplace transform in Wu and Takagi [56] and to models with exponential working vacations by matrix analytic methods in Li et al. [29]. Furthermore, the extension to the GI/M/1 working vacation model is presented by Baba [3].

In working vacation models, the queue length is also decomposed into the sum of two independent random variables. The first one is the queue length of the standard model without vacation and the second one is a random variable related to not only the vacation time but also other system parameters for even the M/M/1 settings (See e.g., Servi and Finn [51]).

Multiserver vacation queues are studied by many authors since the pioneer paper by Levy and Yechiali [28]. Generating function and matrix analytic method are the main tools for analyzing these models. Some recent comprehensive surveys and results are presented in a survey by Ke, Wu and Zhang [24] and a book by Tian and Zhang [53]. The main results are that these models are formulated by a quasi-birth-and-death process (QBD) whose phase has a special transition structure allowing explicit solution of the rate matrix. As a result, these models are analytically tractable. Working vacation versions of multiserver queues are also studied and their analysis is the same as the models with vacation.

Similar to the models with working vacation, an important result of the multiserver vacation/working vacation models is the conditional decomposition [52]. In this model, under the condition that all the servers are busy serving customers, the number of waiting customers is decomposed into the sum of two random variables. The first one is the number of waiting customers in the M/M/1 model with the same arrival rate and the service rate being the sum of those of all the servers. The second random variable depends on the vacations in a complex manner which has not a physical interpretation [52].

20.2.2   Models
with Workload /Queue-Length-Dependent
Service

Motivated by the balance of power saving and performance trade-off in data centers, models with queue length-dependent service rates are studied. Yajima and Phung-Duc [58, 60] study single server models with queue length-dependent service rates and setup time . In particular, when the server is in the active mode, the service rate of the server is the same as that of an infinity server system, i.e., the service rate is proportional to the number of customers in the system. Once the system becomes empty, the server is turned off and the first customer in the busy period activates the server and after the setup time the server becomes active again to serve waiting customers. In these models, customers arrive in batch and an interesting observation is that the stability condition is the finiteness of the expectation of the logarithm of the batch size. Furthermore, a special feature is that the sojourn time of a customer not only depends on the number of customers in the system upon arrival but also the customers who arrive later. In [58], the authors derive the LST (Laplace-Stieltjes transform) of the sojourn time distribution.

Sakuma et al. [49] study an M/G/1 vacation model in which the service rate of the server is a function of the workload in the system. Once the system becomes empty, the server takes a vacation and after the vacation the server becomes active if a threshold of positive workload is exceeded, otherwise the server takes another vacation. The distribution of the workload is obtained in this study in an integral form. In some special cases such as exponential service time distribution or linear service rate function, the distribution of the workload is obtained in a closed form. Sakuma et al. [50] further extend their study to the case that the service rate is a piece-wise constant function of the workload and the service time follows the phase-type distribution. They derive a matrix representation solution for the workload distribution. In this line, Yazici and Phung-Duc [61] study a related M/M/1 vacation model where the service rate is a piece-wise constant function of the workload. They obtain the workload distribution using the theory of fluid queues.

As a related model, we mention the one with cross selling [1] in which upon the completion of a service, the server will initiate a cross selling activity if the number of customers in the system is lower than a threshold. The service time of this model can be considered to be dependent on the number of customers in the system.

20.2.3 Models with Setup Time

Recently, motivated by applications in power-saving data centers, queues with setup time have been extensively studied. In single server queues with setup time, the server is immediately switched off once the system becomes idle. When the first customer of the busy period comes, the server needs some setup time to be active and serve customers [27]. In multiserver setting, the number of servers in setup depends on the number of customers in the system. Because of this property, the underlying Markov chain has an in-homogeneous structure which is a different point from models with vacations. Roughly speaking, models with setup time is different from that of the ones with vacations in the sense that in the former the servers are activated based on the number of jobs in the system while in the latter the servers return to the normal mode after their predetermined vacation period.

Because of the memory-less property of exponential distributions, an M/M/1 queue with exponential setup time is identical to that of the corresponding model with multiple vacations.

20.2.3.1 Multiserver Model with Setup Time

Multiserver queues with setup time are used as models for data centers where each server in a data center corresponds to a server in the queueing model. In the most basic model, a server is turned off if it completes a service and there is not a customer waiting job to process. When jobs arrive, off servers are turned on to process waiting jobs. For an easy explanation, we consider the simplest cases where we have c servers; the arrival process is Poisson process with rate λ; the service times of all servers follow the same exponential distribution with mean $1/\mu$ and the setup times follow the exponential distribution with mean $1/\alpha$. There are various setup policies but we consider two representative ones. Let $C(t)$ and $N(t)$ denote the number of active servers (serving a job) and the number of jobs in the system (including the ones in service), respectively. As usual, the quantity of interest is the joint stationary distribution $\pi_{i,j} = \mathrm{P}(C(t) = i, N(t) = j)$.

The first setup policy is the staggered setup policy in which only one server can be in the setup process at a time, i.e., the number of setup servers at time t is given by $\min(1, N(t) - C(t))$. The second policy is that the number of setup servers depends on the number of waiting jobs, i.e., the number of setup servers at time t is given by $\min(N(t) - C(t), c - C(t))$.

The staggered setup is first studied by Artalejo et al. [2] who derived the joint stationary distribution of $C(t)$ and $N(t)$. Later, Gandhi et al. [17]

derive a simpler solution for this model and proved that the waiting time of jobs in the staggered setup is decomposed into that of the model without setup time (M/M/c model) and the setup time . The same decomposition also holds for the number of waiting jobs. It is also turned out that $N(t) \overset{d}{=} N_0(t) + S(t)$, where $N(t)$ is the number of jobs in the corresponding M/M/c model without setup time and $S(t)$ is the number of jobs that arrive during the remaining setup time [41]. The feature that allows simple solution for the staggered policy is that as long as there are waiting jobs the number of setup servers $\min(1, N(t) - C(t)) = 1$ does not depend on the number of waiting jobs. As a result, the number of boundary states is only (i, i).

In the second case mentioned above (the number of setup servers is given by $\min(N(t) - C(t), c - C(t))$, the transition structure is more complicated. In particular, when the number of jobs in the system is smaller than the number of servers, the number of setup servers depends on the number of jobs in the system. The Quasi-Birth-and-Death (QBD) structure is only observed when the number of jobs in the systems is greater or equal to c. This QBD part has a special structure that the phase $C(t)$ has transition in only one direction ($C(t)$ only increases when $N(t) > c$). This allows us to obtain the explicit expression of the rate matrix. This property is also exploited in the recursive renewal reward approach [16]. However, the boundary parts (states that $N(t) \leq c$) has a more complex structure where $C(t)$ can both increase or decrease. Thus, the complexity of a naive algorithm is $O(c^6)$ for finding all the boundary probabilities. Phung-Duc [43] considers the same problem using the matrix analytic method and the generating function approach. Phung-Duc [43] derives a procedure to compute the joint stationary distribution (including the boundary part) with the complexity of only $O(c^2)$. In particular, explicit expressions are obtained for the partial generating function of homogeneous part $\Pi_i(z) = \sum_{j=c}^{\infty} \pi_{i,j} z^{j-c}$. The probabilities $\pi_{i,j}$ $(i = 0, 1, \ldots, c; i \leq j \leq c,)$ are calculated recursively in the following order.

$$
\begin{aligned}
\pi_{0,0} &\to \pi_{0,1} \to \cdots \to \pi_{0,c-1} \to \pi_{0,c} \\
&\to \pi_{1,1} \to \pi_{1,2} \to \cdots \to \pi_{1,c-1} \to \pi_{1,c} \\
&\qquad\qquad\qquad\qquad \vdots \qquad\quad \vdots \\
&\qquad\qquad\qquad \to \pi_{c-1,c-1} \to \pi_{c-1,c} \\
&\qquad\qquad\qquad \to \pi_{c,c}.
\end{aligned}
$$

.

It should be noted that the same decomposition property as in [17] does not hold for the model with multiple setup servers. However, if we restrict on the number of waiting jobs when all the servers are busy, a conditional stationary decomposition property holds. In particular, we are interested in the following distribution $\mathrm{P}(Q^{(c)} = j) = \mathrm{P}(N(t) = c+j | C(t) = c)$, where $Q^{(c)}$ represents the conditional number of waiting jobs when all the servers are active. Phung-Duc [43] shows that

$$Q^{(c)} \overset{d}{=} Q^{(c)}_{ON-IDLE} + Q_{Res}, \tag{20.1}$$

where $Q^{(c)}_{ON-IDLE}$ is the number of jobs in an M/M/1 queueing system with arrival rate λ and service rate $c\mu$ respectively. Furthermore, Q_{Res} represents the number of extra jobs incurred by the setup time and has a clear physical interpretation. In fact, it is shown in [43] that Q_{Res} represents the number of waiting jobs before an arbitrary customers in the setup model under the condition that $c - 1$ servers are active. It should be noted that Q_{Res} is expressed in terms of $\pi_{i,j}$. From this point of view, the conditional decomposition is not an explicit but an implicit one. The proof of (20.1) is simply obtained by showing that the generating function of the left hand is the same as that of the right hand side.

Phung-Duc [41] studies the staggered setup model with batch arrival, where only one server can be in setup mode at a time. The author derives recursive formulae for the partial generating functions $\Pi_i(z) = \sum_{j=i}^{\infty} \pi_{i,j} z^{j-i}$. Furthermore, the conditional decomposition property (20.1) is also established in which the $Q^{(c)}_{ON-IDLE}$ represents the number of jobs in an M^X/M/1 queue without setup time with the same arrival process and the service rate is given by $c\mu$. It should be noted that the same conditional decomposition is also established for the model with vacation [52].

In practice, data center traffic often has peak-on and peak-off nature meaning that the arrival of jobs to data centers is time-dependent. Taking this into account, a multiserver setup queue with nonstationary input and service capacity is studied in [39]. In [39], jobs arrive according to nonstationary Poisson process and the number of servers varies with time. The authors obtained the fluid limit of the model which can be used to obtain approximate results for the cases where the number of servers is large enough.

Models with block setup, i.e., a group of servers is turned on and off at a time are also studied [19, 31]. In Mitrani [31], setup time was not considered while in Hu and Phung-Duc [19] a block of servers is turned on at a time but each server has its own service time. These models can be analyzed using generating function or matrix analytic methods. Furthermore, setup models with finite buffer are also studied for which efficient numerical procedures are proposed [40, 42]

20.2.3.2   Retrial Model with Setup Time

Retrial queues are characterized by the feature that arriving customers who see all the servers being occupied join the orbit. Each blocked customer stays in the orbit for a random time before trying to occupy a free server again until he/she successfully occupies one. Retrial queues with always-on servers are extensively studied. When the servers are turned on and off, the possibility for customers to be blocked increases. The analysis of retrial models with vacation and/or setup is more challenging because we need to keep track of not only the number of active servers, the number of customers in the servers but also the number of customers in the orbit.

It is widely confirmed that the stability condition of a retrial queueing system (at least for the ones with classical retrial rate) is identical with that of the corresponding model with an infinite buffer [32]. Intuitively, when the number of jobs in the orbit tends to infinity, the time for a job in the orbit to find an idle server approaches to zero. Thus, there is no loss of capacity. In particular, the stability condition for an M/M/c/c retrial queue with arrival rate λ and service rate μ is given by $\lambda < c\mu$ and is independent of the retrial rate.

In the non-retrial models with vacation or setup, the stability condition is the same as that of the ones without vacation/setup. Intuitively, when there are infinite number of customers in the system, eventually all the servers will be active. Thus, the vacation/setup system behaves the same as conventional queue without these features.

From these observations, it is also expected that the retrial model with setup time also has the same stability condition with the corresponding one without retrials. Surprisingly, Phung-Duc and Kawanishi [47] find that the stability condition for the retrial model with setup time is more strict than the corresponding one without retrials for the case of more than one server. In particular, we consider an M/M/c/c retrial queue in which arriving customers are blocked and join the orbit if they see all the servers are either busy serving a customer or in setup process to serve a waiting customer. The arrival rate, the service rate and the setup rate are given by λ, μ and α, respectively. Each blocked customer stays in the orbit for an exponentially distributed time with mean $1/\sigma$. The stability condition is given as follows.

$$\frac{\lambda}{c\mu} < \frac{(c-1)\mu + \alpha}{c\mu + \alpha}. \tag{20.2}$$

It should be noted that in the case $c = 1$, this stability condition is the same as that of the corresponding model without setup time [44].

Nazarov et al. [33] study the asymptotic behavior of the number of jobs in the orbit for an M/M/c/c retrial queues with setup time. In particular, they consider the regime where the retrial rate is extremely small. In this regime, the number of jobs in the orbit $i(t)$ explodes. It is proved in [33] a fluid limit that $\sigma i(t) = \sigma i(\tau/\sigma)$ converges to a deterministic process $x(\tau)$ which is the solution of a differential equation of the following form.

$$x'(\tau) = a(x(\tau)),$$

where

$$a(x(\tau)) = \lambda E_1 R - x(\tau) E_2 R. \tag{20.3}$$

Here R is a matrix of $x(\tau)$ whose elements represent the stationary distribution of the finite Markov chain of the number of busy servers and that of setup servers for the dynamics of the corresponding M/M/c/c system with setup time with the arrival rate given by $\lambda + x(\tau)$ (See Figure 1 in [33]). The first term in the right hand side of (20.3) represents the arrival flow that is blocked and joins the orbit (E_1 is the operator that adds all the probabilities that an arrival is blocked, i.e., all c servers are either busy or in setup). The second term in the right hand side of (20.3) represents the repeated flow from the orbit that successfully enters the servers (E_2 is the operator that adds all the probabilities that at least one server is idle upon retrial) [33].

Furthermore, it is also proved in [33] a diffusion limit that $\sqrt{\sigma}(i(\tau/\sigma) - x(\tau)/\sigma)$ converges in distribution into a diffusion process, where the drift coefficient is given by $a(x(\tau))$ and the diffusion coefficient $b(x(\tau))$ is given in terms of $x(\tau)$ and other given parameters. The fluid limit and the diffusion limit can be interpreted as a functional law of large number and a functional central limit theorem for the number of jobs in the orbit, respectively.

As a related model, retrial queue with two-way communication is studied in [46], where after a service completion, the server is idle for a while before making an outgoing call. For this model, the stability condition is the same as that of the corresponding model without outgoing calls, i.e., $\lambda/c\mu < 1$.

Similarly, the fluid and diffusion limits when the retrial rate $\sigma \rightarrow 0$ are obtained in [34].

The authors in [33, 34] use the stationary distribution of the diffusion process to approximate the number of customers in the orbit. Simulations show that the approximation is accurate in a wide range of low retrial rate.

20.2.4 Open Problems

In all the models presented in this section, setup time or vacation time follows exponential distribution. Based on that these models are directly formulated using Markov chains where the matrix analytic method and/or the generating function method can be applied. When the vacation or setup time does not follow memory-less distributions further studies are expected.

In queues with workload-dependent service, the sojourn time distribution is challenging and thus needs further investigations.

In multiserver queues with setup time, while the queue length processes are well studied, little attention is devoted to the sojourn time distribution. For a finite buffer multiserver model with setup time, Phung-Duc and Kawanishi [45] obtain the waiting time distribution. However, for the infinite buffer version, the existence of closed-form solution for the waiting time distribution is still an open question. Furthermore, the case where the customers are strategic also calls for further investigation.

20.3 Infinite-Server Queues with Changeable Service

Infinite-server queues have infinitely many servers, and thus all arriving customers can receive service without waiting. Many researches have been devoted to infinite-server queues with constant parameters, because these models have applications in various areas such as road traffic systems, inventory systems and telecommunication systems. In recent years, infinite-server queues with variable service speeds have attracted much attention in addition to their special cases, i.e., models with constant parameters.

20.3.1 Stability Condition

Infinite-server queues have many applications in various areas, thus many researchers have studied stationary infinite-server queues (including both constant-speed models and variable-speed models). In this section, we review some studies on the stability condition of infinite-server queues. Note that the stability condition is the necessary and sufficient condition that there exists the unique limiting distribution of the queue length process.

In the case that customers arrive at the system one by one, stability conditions are often obtained in a relatively simple form. Kaplan [23] studies the stability for a GI/GI/∞ queue. He shows that a GI/GI/∞ queue is stable if and only if both inter-arrival times and service times have finite means. In addition, for some single-arrival infinite-server queues with changeable service, some researchers have studied the stability. O'cinneide and Purdue [35] study the stability of the M/M/∞ queue such that the service speed changes according to a background Markov chain. They show that the stability condition of this changeable-service queue is that at least one of the service rates is strictly positive. Keilson and Servi [26] extend the result of [35, Theorem 2.2] to the M/M/∞ queue such that the service speed changes at the moments that the background Markov chain changes, a customer arrives, or the service is completed. That is, they show the stability condition of such queues is that at least one of the service rates is strictly positive.

In the case that customers arrive in batches, infinite-server queues have more complex stability conditions than single-arrival models. For queueing models with constant service, Cong [8] establishes the stability condition of the multiclass $M^X/M/\infty$ queue. Note that the multiclass $M^X/M/\infty$ queue is the infinite-server queue such that customers arrive according to a multiclass batch Poisson process and service times are i.i.d. with a class-dependent exponential service time. The stability condition derived in [8] is that the first logarithmic moment of the batch-size distribution is finite. Pakes and Kaplan [36] show that a $GI^X/GI/\infty$ queue is stable if and only if the maximum service time of customers in a batch has finite mean, which is not explicitly presented. In [36], the stability condition for $GI^X/GI/\infty$ queue is obtained as a special case of the condition for the existence of a limiting distribution of the Bellman Harris process. Furthermore, Yajima and Masuyama [57] show the stability condition for the $GI^X/GI/\infty$ queue in a different way than [36]. In addition, they also show a tractable sufficient condition for the stability under a moderate condition on the tail of the service time distribution.

For batch-arrival infinite-server queues with changeable service, there are only a few previous studies which derived the stability condition. Yajima and Phung-Duc [59] study the stability for the $M^X/M/\infty$ queue such that the service speed changes according to a background Markov chain. Note that the $M^X/M/\infty$ queue (with constant service) is the infinite-server queue such that batches arrive according to a Poisson process, batch sizes are independent and identically distributed (i.i.d.) with a discrete distribution, and service times are i.i.d. with an exponential distribution. They show that the queueing model is stable if and only if the logarithmic moment of the batch-size distribution is finite.

20.3.2   Exact Analysis

In this section, we introduce some studies which explicitly analyze infinite-server queues with changeable service. Unfortunately, there are not many previous studies due to the complexity of models.

20.3.2.1   Two Types of Service Speeds

We now focus on some studies of changeable-service infinite-server queues such that service speeds are limited to two types. In such cases, relatively many studies exist.

Keilson and Servi [26] study M/M/∞ queues such that service speed changes in two types when a customer arrives, the service is completed, or the background Markov chain transitions. They derive the probability generating function (PGF) of the stationary queue length distribution. Baykal-Gursoy and Xiao [4] analyze M/M/∞ queues with two-type service speed such that the service speed switches to the other after independent exponential-distributed times. They show the stochastic decomposition of the stationary queue distribution; that is, the random variable of the stationary queue length can be expressed as the sum of two independent random variables. One of two random variables is identical to the stationary queue length of an ordinary M/M/∞ queue with higher service speed. The other is a randomized Poisson random variable whose parameter is explicitly derived in [4]. In addition, they obtain the mean and the variance of the stationary queue length by using the decomposition result. D'Auria [10] studies M/M/∞ queues whose service speed changes in two types according to the background semi-Markov process. Assuming that at least one of the two service time distributions is an exponential distribution, he derives explicitly factorial moments of the stationary queue length. Falin [13] considers M/M/∞ queues such that service speed changes in two types according to an alternating renewal process. He obtains the stationary mean queue length in the explicit form. Furthermore, assuming that one of the speeds is zero and that a period of strictly positive service speed is interrupted after an exponential-distributed time, he obtains the PGF of the stationary queue length.

If one of the two service speeds is zero, it is possible to represent a situation with server failures, service interruptions or service breakdown. Similar to [13], some researchers are interested in infinite-server queues with service interruptions (breakdowns). D'Auria [11] analyzes $M/M/\infty$ queues with interruptions such that up and down periods occur according to an alternating renewal process. He shows that the stationary queue length is stochastically decomposed into two independent terms. One of two terms is identical to the stationary queue length of an ordinary $M/M/\infty$ queue without interruptions. The other is a random variable whose distribution is determined by system parameters, which is explicitly shown in [11]. Jayawardene and Kella [21] study $M/G/\infty$ queues with interruptions such that up and down periods occur according to an alternative renewal process. Using a regenerative structure, they show the stochastic decomposition of the stationary queue length distribution. As similar to [11], one of the decomposed terms is identical to the stationary queue length in an ordinary $M/G/\infty$ queue without interruptions. However, for the other decomposed term, it is difficult to derive its distribution in an explicit form. Pang and Whitt [37] also present the stochastic decomposition for the stationary queue length distribution of $GI/M/\infty$ queue with service interruptions such that up and down periods occur according to an alternative renewal process.

20.3.2.2 More than Two Types of Service Speeds

Finally, we introduce some studies of changeable-service infinite-server queues such that the speed changes in more than two types. The explicit result can be obtained only when a model has a simple structure. O'cinneide and Purdue [35] analyze $M/M/\infty$ queues such that service speed changes according to the background Markov process. They obtain the stationary queue length distribution in a recursive form. In addition, they explicitly derive the factorial moments of the stationary queue length. D'Auria [9] extends the decomposition result of [4] to the $M/G/\infty$ queue whose service speed changes (into more than two types) according to the background semi-Markov process. However, the parameter of the randomized Poisson random variable is obtained only when some conditions are imposed, e.g., the case that there are two types of service speeds and the service time follows an exponential distribution. Falin [13] considers $M/M/\infty$ queues whose service speed changes according to the background semi-Markov process. He derives the mean queue length containing a solution of a set of linear equations.

Fralix and Adan [14] extend the stochastic decomposition result of [9] to allow the service speed to vary in more than two types. Blom et al. [5] study the M/G/∞ queue such that the service speed changes according to a background Markov chain. They derive the mean and variance of the queue length distribution in the explicit forms.

Even if the system of equations (e.g., for the queue length distribution) cannot be solved, they often help to capture the characteristic of the system. In limit analysis such as introduced in Section 20.3.3, researchers often start analysis from the system of equations. D'Auria [10] studies M/M/∞ queues such that service speed changes according to the background semi-Markov process. He represents this queueing model as a Poisson process on $\mathbb{R}^2$, and then computed the queue length by counting the number of points in this point process within a deterministic set (see e.g. [48]). By such a technique, he obtains the set of linear equations to compute row moments of the stationary queue length. Fralix and Adan [14] also analyze the same model as [10]. Assuming that service times follow an exponential distribution or hyperexponential distribution, they present the simultaneous integral equations for the PGF of the stationary queue length. Furthermore, in the case of hyperexponential services, they derive the simultaneous integral equations for the PGF of the stationary queue length.

20.3.3 Limit Analysis

Many researchers study limit analysis (e.g., large deviation theory, diffusion approximation, heavy traffic approximation) in order to capture characteristics of queueing models with changeable-service speed, because it is difficult to exactly analyze.

20.3.3.1 Limit analysis for a queue length distribution

The central limit theorem (CLT) describes the probability that a random variable slightly deviates from its mean. The CLT holds for the queue length of some infinite-server queues hold under a heavy traffic condition. For example, let us consider the M/M/∞ queue whose arrival rate is λ and service rate is μ. We denote $L^{(N)}$ as the stationary queue length of the scaled M/M/∞ queue such that the arrival rate is scaled by a factor N. Note that $L^{(N)}$ follows the Poisson distribution with mean $N\lambda/\mu$. By using the superposition theorem for Poisson point process and the classical CLT, it is obvious that the normalized queue length weakly converges to the normal distribution with mean 0 and variance $(\lambda/\mu)^2$ as $N \to \infty$; that is,

$$\sqrt{N}\left(\frac{L^{(N)}}{N} - \rho\right) \xrightarrow{d} \mathcal{N}\left(0, \frac{\lambda^2}{\mu^2}\right), \qquad N \to \infty,$$

where $\mathcal{N}(a, b)$ denotes a random variable following the normal distribution with mean a and variance b.

The CLT for some changeable-service infinite-server queues also holds as for the constant-service case. Blom et al. [5] study the M/G/∞ queue such that the service speed changes according to a background Markov chain. They consider the heavy traffic regime such that the arrival rate is scaled by N and the transition rate of the background Markov chain by N^{α} for $\alpha 1$; that is, the background Markov process speeds up faster than the arrival process. They show the CLT for the transient queue length in a finite dimensional setting; that is, at multiple points in time. Blom et al. [6] show the CLTs for the stationary and transient queue lengths of the Markov-modulated M/M/∞ queue. They consider a scaling scheme similar to [5], but they treat any positive α (i.e., all of $\alpha 1$, $\alpha = 1$ and $\alpha < 1$). They mention that the scaling regime is different based on the value of α: the rationale behind these different regimes lies in the fact that for $\alpha > 1$ the variances of the scaled queue length grow essentially linearly in N, while for $\alpha < 1$ they grow as $N^{2-\alpha}$. Yajima and Phung-Duc [59] show the CLT for the stationary queue length of the Markov-modulated M^X/M/∞ queue with binomial catastrophes via Lévy's continuity theorem. That is, they extend the study of [6] as customers arrive in a batch and catastrophes happen. Catastrophes represent the phenomenon in which jobs may leave without their service completions.

A diffusion approximation is a method in which a (continuous) diffusion process approximates a discrete stochastic process which is complicated and difficult to explicitly analyze. In order to investigate the detailed behavior of a queueing model which cannot be explained only by the average value, it is necessary to consider a model which incorporated the stochastic variation ignored in a fluid approximation.

Iglehart [20] shows that the functional central limit theorem (FCLT) holds for the M/M/∞ queue (with a constant-service speed); that is, the scaled queue length process converges to an Ornstein-Uhlenbeck (O-U) process. The O-U process is a diffusion process that models the velocity of particles undergoing Brownian motion. The O-U process $\{X(t)\}$ is a modification of the Wiener process such that

$$\mathrm{d}X(t) = -\theta X(t)\mathrm{d}t + \sigma \mathrm{d}W(t),$$

where $\{W(t)\}$ denotes the Wiener process and $\mu \in \mathbb{R}$ and $\theta, \sigma > 0$ are constant parameters [55].

The FCLT has been shown to hold in some changeable-service infinite-server queues as well as in the constant-service cases. Pang et al. [38] show the FCLT for the G/GI/∞ such that service interrupts and restarts according to an alternative renewal process under the assumption that a service time distribution has a finite positive support. They also show that the G/GI/∞ such that service interrupt and restart according to an alternative renewal process holds under the assumption of a weakly dependent service time.

20.3.3.2   Limit analysis for a queue length process

The CLT and FCLT show the probability concentrating on the average value. On the other hand, the large deviation principle (LDP) can handle the probability of an event far from the average value (including the probability of a rare event). The LDP describes the asymptotic behavior of a sequence of tails probability [54]. For some infinite-server queues, it has been shown that the LDP for the queue length distribution establishes. That is, there exists a lower semicontinuous function $I : [0, \infty) \mapsto [0, \infty)$ satisfying

$$\lim_{N \to \infty} \frac{1}{N} \log \mathsf{P}(M_N \geq x) = -I(x),$$

where M_N is the queue length of a scaled infinite-server queue whose arrival rate is sped up by N. The function $I(\cdot)$ is called the rate function, Cramér function, or entropy function.

Glynn [18] shows the LDP for the transition queue length of a GI/G/∞ (with constant service). For changeable-service case, Blom et al. [7] study the transient and stationary LDPs for the Markov-modulated M/M/∞ queue. For the stationary case, they explicitly derive the rate function. For the transient case, they show that the rate function jumps at most the number of background process states. Jansen et al. [22] show the LDP for the transient queue length of M/G/∞ queue in random environment. The service speed changes according to a stochastic process, but the service requirement distribution does not change regardless of the background state. They prove the LDP under various scale regimes. Lu et al. [30] study infinite-server queues such that batches of customers arrive according to a Markov additive process and service times follow a general distribution which is decided by the background Markov chain. They call the above queue the Markov-modulated

MMAP/G/∞ queue. They show the FCLT for the queue length process of the Markov-modulated MMAP/G/∞ queue.

References

1. Armony, M., Perel, E., Perel, N. and Yechiali, U. (2019). Exact analysis for multiserver queueing systems with cross selling. Annals of Operations Research, 274(1), 75–100.
2. Artalejo, J. R., Economou, A., and Lopez-Herrero, M. J. (2005). Analysis of a multiserver queue with setup times. Queueing Systems, 51(1–2), 53–76.
3. Baba, Y. (2005). Analysis of a GI/M/1 queue with multiple working vacations. Operations Research Letters, 33(2), 201–209.
4. Baykal-Gursoy, M. and Xiao, W. (2004). Stochastic decomposition in M/M/∞ queues with Markov modulated service rates. Queueing Systems, 48(1–2), 75–88.
5. Blom, J., De Turck, K., Kella, O. and Mandjes, M. (2014) Markov-modulated infinite-server queues with general service times. Queueing Systems, 78(4), 337–357.
6. Blom, J., De Turck, K. and Mandjes, M. (2015). Analysis of Markov-modulated infinite-server queues in the central-limit regime. Probability in the Engineering and Informational Sciences, 29(3), 433–459.
7. Blom, J., Kella, O., Mandjes, M. and Thorsdottir, H. (2014). Tail asymptotics of a Markov-modulated infinite-server queue. Queueing Systems, 76(4), 403–424.
8. Cong, T. D. (1994). On the M^X/G/∞ queue with heterogeneous customers in a batch. Journal of Applied Probability, 76(4), 403–424.
9. D'Auria, B. (2007). Stochastic decomposition of the M/G/∞ queue in a random environment. Operations Research Letters, 35(6), 805–812.
10. D'Auria, B. (2008). M/M/∞ queues in semi-Markovian random environment. Queueing Systems, 58(3), Article number 221.
11. D'Auria, Bernardo. M/M/∞ queue with on-off service speeds. *Journal of Mathematical Sciences*, 196(1): 37–42, 2014.
12. Doshi, B. T. (1986). Queueing systems with vacations-a survey. Queueing Systems, 1(1), 29–66.
13. Falin, Gennadi. (2008). The M/M/∞ queue in a random environment. Queueing Systems, 58(1), 65–76.
14. Fralix, B. H. and Adan, I. JBF. (2009) An infinite-server queue influenced by a semi-Markovian environment. Queueing Systems, 61(1), 65–84.
15. Fuhrmann, S. W. (1984). A note on the M/G/1 queue with server vacations. Operations Research, 32(6), 1368–1373.

16. Gandhi, A., Doroudi, S., Harchol-Balter, M., and Scheller-Wolf, A. (2014). Exact analysis of the M/M/k/setup class of Markov chains via recursive renewal reward. Queueing Systems, 77(2), 177–209.

17. Gandhi, A. Harchol-Balter, M. and Adan, I. (2010). Server farms with setup costs. Performance Evaluation, 67(11), 1123–1138.

18. Glynn, P. W. (1995). Large deviations for the infinite server queue in heavy traffic. Institute for Mathematics and its Applications, 71, 387–394.

19. Hu, J. and Phung-Duc, T. (2015). Power consumption analysis for data centers with independent setup times and threshold controls. In AIP Conference Proceedings, 1648, 170005.

20. Iglehart, D. L. (1965). Limiting diffusion approximations for the many server queue and the repairman problem. Journal of Applied Probability, 2(2), 429–441.

21. Jayawardene, A. K. and Kella, O. (1996). M/G/∞ with alternating renewal breakdowns. Queueing Systems, 22(1–2), 79–95.

22. Jansen, H. M., Mandjes, M. R. H., De Turck, K. and Wittevrongel, S. (2016). A large deviations principle for infinite-server queues in a random environment. Queueing Systems, 82(1–2), 199–235.

23. Kaplan, N. (1975). Limit theorems for a GI/G/∞ queue. The Annals of Probability, 22(1–2), 780–789.

24. Ke, J. C., Wu, C. H. and Zhang, Z. G. (2010). Recent developments in vacation queueing models: a short survey. International Journal of Operations Research, 7(4), 3–8.

25. Keilson, J. and Servi, L. D. (1990). The distributional form of Little's law and the Fuhrmann-Cooper decomposition. Operations Research Letters, 9(4), 239–247.

26. Keilson, J. and Servi, L.D. (1993). The matrix M/M/∞ system: retrial models and Markov modulated sources. Advances in Applied Probability, 25(2), 453–471.

27. Levy, H. Kleinrock, L. (1986). A queue with starter and a queue with vacations: delay analysis by decomposition. Operations Research, 34(3), 426–436.

28. Levy, Y. and Yechiali, U. (1976). An M/M/s queue with servers' vacations. INFOR: Information Systems and Operational Research, 14(2), 153–163.

29. Li, J. H., Tian, N. S., Zhang, Z. G. and Luh, H. P. (2009). Analysis of the M/G/1 queue with exponentially working vacations-a matrix analytic approach. Queueing Systems, 61(2-3), 139–166.

30. Lu, H., Pang, G. and Mandjes, M. (2016). A functional central limit theorem for Markov additive arrival processes and its applications to queueing systems. Queueing Systems, 84(3–4), 381–406.

31. Mitrani, I. (2013). Managing performance and power consumption in a server farm. Annals of Operations Research, 202(1), 121–134.

32. Morozov, E. and Phung-Duc, T. (2017). Stability analysis of a multiclass retrial system with classical retrial policy. Performance Evaluation, 112, 15–26.

33. Nazarov, A., Moiseev, A., Phung-Duc, T. and Paul, S. (2020). Diffusion Limit of Multi-Server Retrial Queue with Setup Time. Mathematics, 8(12), 2232.
34. Nazarov, A., Phung-Duc, T. and Izmailova, Y. (2021). Asymptotic-diffusion analysis of multiserver retrial queueing system with priority customers. To appear in Communications in Computer and Information Science, 2021.
35. O'cinneide, C. A. and Purdue, P. (1986). The $M/M/\infty$ queue in a random environment. Queueing Systems, 23(1), 175–184.
36. Pakes, A. G. and Kaplan, Norman. (1974). On the subcritical Bellman-Harris process with immigration. Journal of Applied Probability, 11(4), 652–668.
37. Pang, G. and Whitt, W. (1986). Heavy-traffic limits for many-server queues with service interruptions. Queueing Systems, 23(1), 167–202.
38. Pang, G. and Zhou, Y. (2016). $G/G/\infty$ queues with renewal alternating interruptions. Advances in Applied Probability, 48(3), 812–831.
39. Pender, J. and Phung-Duc, T. (2016). A law of large numbers for $M/M/c$/delayoff-setup queues with nonstationary arrivals. In International conference on analytical and stochastic modeling techniques and applications (pp. 253–268). Springer, Cham.
40. Phung-Duc, T. (2014). Impatient customers in power-saving data centers. In International conference on analytical and stochastic modeling techniques and applications (pp. 185–199). Springer, Cham.
41. Phung-Duc, T. (2014). Server farms with batch arrival and staggered setup. In Proceedings of the Fifth Symposium on Information and Communication Technology (pp. 240–247).
42. Phung-Duc, T. (2015). Multiserver queues with finite capacity and setup time. In International Conference on Analytical and Stochastic Modeling Techniques and Applications (pp. 173–187). Springer, Cham.
43. Phung-Duc, T. (2017). Exact solutions for $M/M/c$/setup queues. Telecommunication Systems, 64(2), 309–324.
44. Phung-Duc, T. (2017). Single server retrial queues with setup time. Journal of Industrial and Management Optimization, 13(3), 1329–1345.
45. Phung-Duc, T. and Kawanishi, K. (2019). Multiserver retrial queue with setup time and its application to data centers. Journal of Industrial and Management Optimization, 15(1), 15–35.
46. Phung-Duc, T. and Kawanishi, K (2014). An efficient method for performance analysis of blended call centers with redial. Asia-Pacific Journal of Operational Research, 31(02), 1440008.
47. Phung-Duc, T. and Kawanishi, K. (2019). Delay performance of data-center queue with setup policy and abandonment. Annals of Operations Research, 293, 1–25.
48. Resnick, S. I. (2013). Extreme values, regular variation and point processes. Springer.

49. Sakuma, Y., Boxma, O. and Phung-Duc, T. (2019). A single server queue with workload-dependent service speed and vacations. In International Conference on Queueing Theory and Network Applications (pp. 112–127). Springer, Cham.

50. Sakuma, Y., Boxma, O. and Phung-Duc, T. (2020). An M/PH/1 queue with workload-dependent processing speed and vacations. Submitted to Queueing Systems.

51. Servi , L. D. and Finn, S. G. (2002). M/M/1 queues with working vacations (m/m/1/wv). Performance Evaluation, 50(1), 41–52.

52. Tian, N., Li, Q. L. and Gao, J. (1999). Conditional stochastic decompositions in the M/M/c queue with server vacations. Stochastic Models, 15(2), 367–377.

53. Tian, N. and Zhang, Z. G. (2006). Vacation queueing models: theory and applications (Vol. 93). Springer Science & Business Media.

54. Touchette, H. (2009). The large deviation approach to statistical mechanics. Physics Reports, 478(1–3), 1–69.

55. Uhlenbeck, G. E. and Ornstein, L. S. (1930). On the theory of the Brownian motion. Physical review, 36(5), 823.

56. Wu, D. A. and Takagi, H. (2006). M/G/1 queue with multiple working vacations. Performance Evaluation, 63(7), 654–681.

57. Yajima, M. and Masuyama, H. (2019). Stability analysis of $GI^{X}X/GI/\infty$ queues. In Proceedings of the 14th International Conference on Queueing Theory and Network Applications (QTNA2019).

58. Yajima, M. and Phung-Duc, T. (2017). Batch arrival single-server queue with variable service speed and setup time. Queueing Systems, 86(3), 241–260.

59. Yajima, M. and Phung-Duc, T. (2019). A central limit theorem for a Markov-modulated infinite-server queue with batch Poisson arrivals and binomial catastrophes. Performance Evaluation, 129, 2–14.

60. Yajima, M. and Phung-Duc, T. (2020). Analysis of a variable service speed single server queue with batch arrivals and general setup time. Performance Evaluation, 138, 102082.

61. Yazici, M. A. and Phung-Duc, T. (2020). M/M/1 Vacation Queue with Multiple Thresholds: A Fluid Analysis. In International Conference on Quantitative Evaluation of Systems (pp. 148–152). Springer, Cham.

21

Forecasting and its Beneficiaries

Bahman Rostami-Tabar and John E. Boylan

21.1 Background

Forecasting informs critical decisions in public-, private- and third-sector organisations. Forecasts are used widely in such diverse areas as finance and economics, public policy, healthcare, transportation, supply chains and engineering. They can enable organisations to manage risk and deal with uncertainty.

A few examples illustrate the scope of forecasting. In public policy, forecasts can enhance the quality of decision-making by predicting changes in economic and social factors and their effects on the costs and benefits of policy options. Forecasting plays an important role in guiding government policy as well as business decisions regarding environmental challenges such as climate change, in situations ranging from CO_2 emissions to natural disasters and early warning systems [33]. Forecasting plays a crucial role in finance and economics, by anticipating how economies may evolve and informing

B. Rostami-Tabar
Cardiff Business School, Cardiff University, Cardiff CF10 3EU, UK
e-mail: rostami-tabarb@cardiff.ac.uk

J. E. Boylan (✉)
Department of Management Science, Lancaster University, Lancaster, England
e-mail: j.boylan@lancaster.ac.uk

© The Author(s), under exclusive license to Springer Nature Switzerland AG 2022
S. Salhi and J. Boylan (eds.), *The Palgrave Handbook of Operations Research*,
https://doi.org/10.1007/978-3-030-96935-6_21

the management of risk accordingly. In business and manufacturing, better forecasting can enable a more efficient supply chain and greater productivity. Forecasting is routinely used in the retail sector to ensure the availability of required items on the shelves.

In the forecasting literature, the main emphasis has been on the methods and techniques of forecasting. There is much less discussion on the questions of what purposes forecasts should serve and who should benefit from forecasting. If there is any discussion, the emphasis is on profit and other economic measures. Rostami-Tabar et al. [12] have challenged the notion that forecasting must necessarily serve economic or financial aims. They point to the potential of 'Forecasting for Social Good' (FSG) . They characterise FSG as forecasting that contributes towards strengthening social foundations and respecting the ecological ceiling. These social and ecological impacts can be assessed both locally and globally. Inspired by the FSG agenda, we ask who benefits from improved forecasting, and we discuss means by which more people can benefit.

Debate about the beneficiaries of modelling is not new. This issue was discussed in the Operational Research literature in a series of papers published in the 1970s and 1980s (e.g. [34–36]). Power was a common theme underpinning those papers. The authors noted that it tended to be more powerful organisations that benefit from OR, and OR projects had powerful people in these organisations as their clients.

If OR is mainly conducted on behalf of powerful people in powerful organisations, then it is natural that OR modelling will serve their interests. This is sometimes observed quite explicitly in a model with 'maximisation of profit' as its objective. Forecasting models, on the other hand, may appear to be more neutral. Surely, everyone would be supportive of 'minimising forecast error' (if appropriately measured) as an objective. This is to miss the fact that forecasting is generally part of a broader set of activities, whose objectives may not be shared so universally.

Many processes have indirect beneficiaries, and these beneficiaries may be internal or external to the organisation. Take an example of a forecasting system to predict the demand on an Accident and Emergency department of a hospital. The direct beneficiary of the system is the person (or people) with responsibility for using those forecasts to plan work rosters of doctors, nurses and allied health professionals. If this is well done, then the indirect beneficiaries are those health professionals for whom work is planned, and those patients for whom treatment is being planned. The importance of indirect beneficiaries such as these should be recognised when designing any forecasting process.

In this chapter, we examine the issue of forecasting beneficiaries from a number of perspectives. Firstly, we address the agenda of 'Forecasting for Social Good' and the different perspectives that may be called for. Then, we move on to the major barriers to spreading the benefits of better forecasting more widely. We review communication issues between stakeholders in forecasting. These issues are important in any setting, and must be addressed if real benefits are to be achieved and shared appropriately. We conclude by examining a recent initiative to improve forecasting capabilities in less well-developed economies. The initiative is called 'Democratising Forecasting' and it aims to extend the range of organisations and users who can benefit from developments in forecasting methods and software.

21.2 Forecasting for Social Good

What is the point of forecasting? If asked this question, most academics and practitioners would say 'to inform better decisions', or words to that effect. This immediately prompts two further questions: (i) what do we mean by better? and (ii) better for whom? Most of the organisations in which a more professional and analytical approach to forecasting is employed have economic and financial goals, such as minimising costs or maximising profits. Alternative goals may also be served by improved forecasting. Rostami-Tabar et al. [12] defined "Forecasting for Social Good' (FSG) as: "... *a forecasting process that aims to inform decisions that prioritise the thriving of humanity over the thriving of economies by enhancing the social foundation and ecological ceilings that impact the public as a whole on both global and local levels*". They remarked that FSG is inclusive and encompasses all organisations, irrespective of their industry or whether they are governmental, commercial or voluntary organisations. FSG can be considered as a self-contained area of inquiry that can lead to increased appreciation of forecasting as a worthwhile tool for a wide range of beneficiaries and their communities. The benefits should extend beyond the financial, although the forecasting process may also result in economic growth. It can still be considered as FSG if the main focus is to improve social and environmental conditions.

It is instructive to compare the concerns underpinning this definition of FSG with those of authors such as Bevan and Bryer, Dando and Bennett, and Rosenhead and Thunhurst, back in the 1970s and 1980s. Common to both is the disquiet that the less powerful members of society are not benefiting sufficiently from the rapid developments in modelling. The later work puts greater emphasis on global issues, although this had not been absent from earlier work, as summarised in the review of OR in developing countries by [37]. The later work also focuses more on environmental concerns, reflecting the growing awareness of ecological issues in recent years.

Traditionally, the success of forecasting has been assessed purely in terms of forecast accuracy. Boylan and Syntetos [38] argued that such accuracy measures should be complemented by accuracy-implication metrics. These measures assess the impact of forecast errors, for example on inventory costs and stock availability. Rostami-Tabar et al. [12] developed this idea further by prioritising social and environmental measures within the set of accuracy-implication metrics.

As well as considering an extended set of performance metrics, it may also be necessary to use more qualitative approaches to forecasting. Data in less well-resourced organisations may be patchy or non-existent. In such cases, quantitative forecasting methods are less helpful and processes relying on judgement will become more prominent. There is an interesting parallel, here, with the Community OR movement in the UK, which emphasised the use of softer OR methods in voluntary or community-based organisations. In situations like these, forecasting processes should be designed to be as transparent and interpretable as possible. This promotes trust in the modelling process, particularly if there is a wider group of beneficiaries than might normally be the case.

In summary, 'Forecasting for Social Good' may call for different perspectives on what constitutes success, and on the means of achieving success. Introducing these new perspectives in practice is not always straightforward. So, it may be fruitful to ask: what are the barriers to sharing the benefits of forecasting?

21.3   Barriers to Sharing the Benefits of Forecasting

In this section of the chapter, we review the barriers to 'Forecasting for Social Good', show how some are reducing in potency and point to ways of addressing the other barriers.

We suggest that there are three significant barriers to extending the benefits of forecasting: (i) lack of access to resources (e.g. software, people), (ii) lack of access to expertise and (iii) poor communication between the various stakeholders involved in forecasting (including the decision-makers). The first barrier has been particularly serious for resource-poor organisations but we shall argue that it is declining in significance. The second barrier is very important for poorer organisations and communities, and will be a major theme of this chapter. It actually affects richer organisations, too, who have the resources to invest in developing forecasting expertise, but fail to do so adequately. The final barrier is relevant to all organisations. It is sometimes under-emphasised in richer companies, to the detriment of their forecasting processes. It is understandable that concerns about resource issues may draw attention away from communication in poorer organisations, but to neglect this vital issue would be misguided.

21.3.1   Access to Resources

In the forecasting process, a number of resources—from skilled forecasters to specialist software—are required. Without them, forecasting model design and implementation become difficult [22]. To acquire these resources, funds are needed to purchase software, recruit appropriate staff and to educate stakeholders to increase awareness of the benefits of better forecasting. Unfortunately, the cost of the forecasting software, and of gaining modelling and statistical expertise can become very large [23].

The development of free open-source forecasting software over the past decade has been a breakthrough in making forecasting accessible to wider beneficiaries. This is because it can be installed and used at no cost to the user, while having huge support from the community of users, maintainers and developers. The most widely used open-source forecasting software is the forecast package for R [19], first released in 2006, and downloaded over 2 million times in 2019. Several other R packages for forecasting are listed on the CRAN Task View for Time Series [4]. Another high level programming language that has been used to create open-source forecasting software is Python. The Statsmodels library [5] in Python allows for statistical forecasting and the scikit-learn library [6] is used more for machine learning. The introduction of free open-source forecasting software has also led to the publication of free online educational resources (e.g. [1, 3]), which can also play a crucial role in learning about forecasting theory and practice.

Although the dissemination of open-source software has made sophisticated forecasting methods more accessible, there are other resourcing issues to be resolved. The most obvious is the cost of recruiting and retaining appropriate staff to work in a forecasting or planning capacity. Those who have power in organisations are in a position to make decisions relating to staffing levels and the deployment of staff. These decisions can have a significant impact on the success, or otherwise, of the implementation of new forecasting processes. Without the support of powerful people in an organisation and their commitment to making necessary resources available, the implementation of a forecasting process will fail and its potential benefit will be lost.

21.3.2   Access to Expertise

Although open-source developments are fundamental in making forecasting available to wider beneficiaries, they may also introduce some problems into practice. Anyone can easily find packages that let them produce forecasts with just a few lines of code. Many Machine Learning (ML) algorithms provide repositories of forecasting models, automate the hyperparameter tuning process and sometimes offer a way to put these models into production. The availability of such packages has led many people to think that the forecasting process can be fully automated, eliminating the need for forecasting expertise or interpretation. In fact, using forecasting models in practice requires various technical and non-technical skills that are lacking in many organisations. This becomes even more challenging in the public sector, third sector and almost any sector in resource-poor environments in low/middle income countries. These are communities that may have benefited less from forecasting, and they may end up making poor decisions if there is a lack of expertise in forecasting [25].

A rigorous forecasting process is not just about running code. The process includes discussing the context with stakeholders, understanding decision-making, identifying forecasting requirements, setting up the right evaluation metrics for the problem, including domain knowledge, forecast model testing, and gaining feedback from stakeholders, which all might be very specific to each forecasting problem [1]. Moreover, forecasts are not always produced using statistical or ML models relying on statistical software. In fact, in less developed countries (low/lower income) where the quality of the data may be an issue, relying on structured management judgement including the Delphi method, forecasting by analogy, surveys, scenario forecasting and other judgemental forecasting approaches can be more relevant [27].

Therefore, educating forecasters on the entire forecasting process so that they are able to understand what lies behind the forecasting models, the application of forecasting in various domains, and their implementation in practice, is imperative. This can help them to make better forecasts that are truly effective. Someone who just runs code might not be able to add value to real-world problems in organisations. We need to go beyond training and educate the potential users of forecasts on their impacts and how they can be used to inform decision-making process. Without such education, the benefits of forecasting cannot be assured.

21.3.3 Communication Issues

Even if finance is available to put software resources in place, and forecasters and planners have been recruited, this is still not a guarantee of success. It is also crucial that the right software is used, which is most appropriate to the needs of the organisation. Clear communication between software vendors and decision-makers, in both directions, is crucial here. Otherwise, and unless all needs are met by freeware, expensive mistakes can be made.

It is also very important that forecasts are being generated at the right frequency, over appropriate horizons, at the right level of aggregation (e.g. at product group or Stock Keeping Unit level) and are evaluated using appropriate criteria. Evaluations, of both forecasting accuracy and forecasting utility, need to be able to take into account the range of possible outcomes that may be expected. All of this requires effective communication channels between forecasters, planners and decision-makers.

In the sections that follow, we examine communication issues from different perspectives. The successful resolution of these issues is essential if knowledge and skills are to be developed and grown in organisations, thereby allowing them to benefit to the fullest extent from expertise in forecasting. It should be stated that effective communication channels are a necessary but not sufficient condition for success. Internal politics brings different kinds of instability within a forecasting process, especially where there are many human interventions. Each intervention becomes an opportunity to introduce bias and unnecessary inaccuracies [7]. Different stakeholders may have different political interests within the organisation that skew the forecasting process. Powerful people may seek confirmation from the forecasting outputs and if they do not get that confirmation, they tend to ignore it [21]. These issues are not unique to forecasting; they can affect other types of OR modelling too. Addressing these issues requires careful consideration of reward systems within an organisation and the promotion of a collaborative approach between different sectional interests.

21.4 More Effective Communications

It would be a mistake to think of organisations as homogeneous entities. There are often different people, with different roles, involved in forecasting, planning and decision-making activities. This is true not only in developed economies, but in developing ones as well.

Considered as a whole, a forecasting system can be viewed as a human activity system [2], embedded within a wider decision-making and monitoring system. In describing such a human activity system, three types of people are relevant: (i) actors—those that undertake the activity; (ii) customers—those for whom the activity is undertaken, and (iii) owners—those with the power to start or stop a system. The inclusion of the third, and most powerful, category of people recognises that human activity systems require decisions to be taken about investment in resources (e.g. hardware and software), processes to be followed (including data capture, reporting and monitoring) and deployment of staff (to specific forecasting and planning tasks). The responsibility for organising forecasting processes and tasks may be delegated by owners to less senior managers. Resource decisions, unless relatively trivial, are not usually delegated. For owners to take such decisions, they must have access to the necessary funds and to have some appreciation of the benefits that can accrue from better forecasting. Lack of funds or lack of this appreciation and understanding can inhibit progress in forecasting and planning.

Checkland [2] describes the second category of people as beneficiaries/victims, in a wry recognition that those who are said to benefit from a system may not do so in practice. The first category of people, the actors, play an essential role in the successful implementation of any forecasting system. The need to develop the knowledge and skills of these people has not always been fully recognised. It is certainly an issue in less developed economies, and this theme will be picked up in the next section of this chapter. It can be an issue in more advanced economies too. Forecasting education is often neglected in developed countries such as the United Kingdom. Our experience of running training courses in the UK is that demand planners can quickly absorb the principles of the methods they have been applying 'blind' and can use their forecasting systems much more effectively as a result.

For forecasting to be beneficial in organisations, effective communication between the 'actors', 'customers' and 'owners' is essential. However, the scope should be even wider. In this section, communications between three groups of 'forecast suppliers' and two groups of 'forecast recipients' will be considered. The forecast suppliers are defined broadly to embrace forecast producers, software developers and forecasting academics. (The term 'forecasting practitioners' is sometimes used to cover the first two categories). The forecast recipients include both the direct recipients (the 'customers') and indirect recipients (the 'owners').

21.4.1   Forecast Producers

It is important to recognise two important factors to increase acceptance and use of forecasting in practice: (i) how forecasts should be communicated with stakeholders and (ii) what should be communicated. Traditionally, forecasts are communicated as point forecasts (single numbers), which does not provide the information required for a decision-maker to manage risk. Communicating forecasts as forecast distributions will be more beneficial in that regard. Moreover, communicating not only the distributions of the forecast variable but also their impact on decisions is critical. Considering an Accident and Emergency department, providing the forecast distribution of the future patient admissions using a forecasting model is important. However, it is not something that a decision-maker can take action on. Complementing this information with the distributions of costs, number of staff required and waiting times resulting from the demand forecasts is more beneficial.

For communications to be effective, forecasters need to have a good awareness of how forecasts should be displayed visually. This is especially important when communicating forecast distributions, so that owners and customers (using Checkland's terminology) can appreciate the information that they are being given. Later, we shall discuss the development needs of forecast recipients. A little training should go a long way to improving communications of forecasts and plans.

21.4.2   Commercial Software Developers

Commercial software developers have a keen interest in communicating with system owners, as they have the power to commission and purchase a new forecasting system. This decision needs to take into account numerous factors, including interfaces with existing systems in general and Enterprise Resource Planning systems in particular.

Communication often focuses on factors other than forecasting accuracy because these issues will often be uppermost in the minds of the system owners. Moreover, given the lack of knowledge about forecasting, discussed previously, it is usually not possible to have an in-depth discussion on this matter.

When forecasting is discussed, system owners may be impressed by software developers' descriptions of the latest 'trendy' methods incorporated into their software, or by anecdotal evidence of forecasting accuracy improvements at other organisations. The problem is that there is hardly any objective evidence on the comparative accuracy of different forecasting software packages. Some information on a range of software packages is available in the biennial forecasting software review conducted on behalf of the Institute for Operations Research and Management Science (INFORMS) and published in *MSOR Today*. These surveys show comparisons of the features available in software packages but do not attempt to assess their forecasting performance.

After purchase, software developers often conduct training with forecasters and demand planners in the organisation. Boylan and Syntetos [28] have pointed out that there is great variation as to what may constitute training. If the training does not go beyond tuition in clicking the right buttons, then there will be little understanding of what to do when the forecasts decline in accuracy. There is also an important distinction between using a package to produce an operational forecast and using it as a 'what-if' scenario planner. To make the best use of these planners, users need to have an appreciation of the alternative methods available in their software and the parameters that control them.

21.4.3   Forecasting Academics

Although forecasting academics are usually at least two steps removed from forecasting clients, their contributions can be genuinely beneficial if harnessed appropriately. Their main impact, to date, has been in developed economies. In the next section, an initiative is described linking academics to less developed economies.

Singh [41] pointed to a widening gap between academic forecasting and business forecasting and, regrettably, his observation is still relevant five years later. There are three gaps that underpin the problem, namely the knowledge, research and implementation gaps [40].

The knowledge gap arises because of the lack of understanding of even basic forecasting theory by many practitioners, and the lack of appreciation, by many academics, of the practical settings in which forecasting is conducted. Filling these gaps is essential for meaningful communication to be established. Some progress has been made in this direction by the establishment of outlets such as *Foresight: the International Journal of Applied Forecasting*, which attracts pieces written in an accessible style by both practitioners and academics. Opportunities for face-to-face communications have been offered by the *Foresight Practitioner Conferences* and by events run by the *Institute of Business Forecasting and Planning*. Also, some universities offer training courses and events specifically targeted at practitioners. However, such publications and events attract the attention mainly of forecast producers and software developers, and often do not reach forecasting clients or system owners. Although these groups do not need a detailed appreciation of forecasting techniques, they do need to understand how to set realistic forecasting accuracy targets and to appreciate how the forecasts should inform their decision making. New communication channels are required to address this need.

The research gap arises from academics putting too much emphasis on solving stylised problems, which can be somewhat remote from real business situations. This can prompt doubts from practitioners about the relevance of academic research to their organisations. More researchers are now testing innovations on real-world data. Some researchers have gone further and evaluated the business implications of forecasting errors from different methods. For example, Wang and Petropoulos [39] examined the inventory implications of different forecasting approaches, including judgemental ones (often utilised in practice) on real business data. More research projects of this type are needed, together with good quality review articles and books, which synthesise the available empirical evidence.

The implementation gap refers to the delay between new methods being published and subsequently being adopted in software. It is here that software developers play a crucial role. When methods are adopted in commercial software, then their use follows soon after. Communication between academics and software developers has been enhanced in recent years by more researchers developing open-source software, in languages such as R and Python, to complement their academic papers. This is being picked up by some of the more adventurous developers, who are incorporating these new methods into their own commercial software offerings.

21.5 Democratising forecasting

While there are many initiatives such as Data Science for Social Good [8], Artificial Intelligence for Social Good [9], Pro Bono Operations Research [10], Statistics for Social Good [11] and Forecasting for Social Good [12] that investigate the potential benefits of using data, modelling and forecasting to tackle societal and environmental challenges, very few focus on educational issues. McClure [13] argued that the lack of educational processes for the potential beneficiaries of Operational Research (OR) and Management Science (MS) caused difficulties in securing benefits from OR/MS approaches in practice. In particular, the importance of education for the users of OR—those who do not necessarily develop models but use them in the decision-making process—was highlighted.

21.5.1 Data Science Initiatives

With the increase in data availability in the last decade and the interest in using the power of data, new data-driven areas such as Data Science (DS) have emerged [16]. Hill et al. [14] argued that it is important to make access to DS tools more widespread to ensure that end users benefit from them. To that end, they have designed a series of workshops and courses with the goal of giving users in online communities the ability to ask and answer their own questions and to build their skills to engage with other analysts and analyses. They also aim at reducing inequality by training under-represented groups in the field such as women, minorities, people with disabilities and veterans. Workshops are offered at times, and at a cost, that makes participation by diverse groups of people possible.

The National Institutes of Health (NIH) has launched the Big Data to Knowledge (BD2K) initiative to facilitate both in-person and online learning, and open up the concepts of Data Science to the widest possible audience in the biomedical sciences. BD2K has created the Educational Resource Discovery Index (ERuDIte), which identifies, collects, describes and organises online data science materials from various online sources to democratise novel insights and discoveries brought forth via large-scale data science training [15]. These initiatives cover a wide range of topics and may include forecasting but not necessarily so. There are some other initiatives that democratise access to Data Science such as R-Ladies [18]. The focus here is to make Data Science, using R programming, accessible to people of genders currently under-represented in the community worldwide. The organisation is articulated into 'chapters', groups hosting events in cities or remotely, the latter for the benefit of everyone, regardless of geographic location or personal circumstances. The focus of the group is to democratise programming skills in R via meetups (in-person and online), the abstract reviewers' network, the Slack channels and the mentorship programme. These initiatives are meeting with some success. Their main emphasis has been on broadening access within developed countries. Their principal focus has not been on developing countries.

21.5.2   Democratising Forecasting Initiative

Given the importance of educating stakeholders in order to increase the benefits of forecasting to wider communities, one of the co-authors of this book chapter launched the Democratising Forecasting (DF) initiative [17] in 2018, supported by the International Institute of Forecasters (IIF). The goal of this project is to provide forecasting education to individuals in developing countries around the world. This is born from a recognition of the benefits that forecasting knowledge can bring to advancing people's use of forecasting to inform decisions. However, it goes one step further by emphasising direct capacity building in deprived economies by educating future forecasters. This project aims to build skills, increase the systematic use of forecasting, and engage with stakeholders to make better decisions.

This work has involved designing a curriculum, and then running a series of workshops delivered to academics (students and lecturers) and practitioners in developing countries. The three-day training course concentrates on the foundations of forecasting, using R, for forecasters, analysts and modellers, focusing on the theoretical background of forecasting methods, their benefits and limitations and their implementations and use in R software [19]. The main emphasis of the workshops has been on educating learners about generating forecasts. Therefore, the primary audiences of the workshop have been academics and forecasters.

These workshops are used to explore the potential of, and challenges around, democratising forecasting. In designing and delivering the workshops, the intention is to broaden participation along several dimensions including geographical location, demographic characteristics and academic fields. Partners from academia, research institutes or industry are selected to coordinate and help organising the workshops. Partners are selected based on World Bank data from low, low-middle and middle income countries.

To make the workshops more widely accessible, the training comes at no cost for participants or the hosting organisation, thanks to sponsorship from the International Institute of Forecasters. This is important for participants from lower income countries, who might not be able to afford workshop fees. Beginners are targeted and, accordingly, participants are not assumed to have any prior forecasting knowledge or any programming experience in R. The training is designed around a project based on producing forecasts for hospital admissions, to inform decisions regarding resource allocation. Participants spend the majority of their time in the sessions identifying decisions that require forecasts, determining what to forecast and the associated data requirements, analysing data, writing code for producing forecasts and evaluating accuracy. In order to enrich the participants' learning experience, various guest speakers are invited from international organisations such as the National Health Service (NHS), the International Committee of the Red Cross (ICRC), the Australian Bureau of Agricultural and Resource Economics and Sciences and SAP to talk about specific forecasting topics. The topics range from retail forecasting to agricultural and food forecasting, forecasting for emergency services and forecasting for humanitarian operations. These talks provide a unique opportunity for learners in developing countries to engage with forecasters from prominent organisations around the world via an online platform. This creates a connection to the use of forecasting in the real world, as speakers share best practices on how forecasts are created and used and discuss challenges and practices that should be avoided.

21.5.3   Benefits and Impact of Democratising Forecasting

The aim of the Democratising Forecasting project is to reach wider communities with limited access to high-quality education, help participants to develop skills, increase awareness of the potential benefits of forecasting and empower participants to facilitate workshops in their country and create change.

The initial goal was to train 400 individuals, over 5 years in 20 countries. Nine workshops had been delivered in seven countries in Africa, the Middle East and South Asia by the end of 2019. Overall, 210 people have been trained, including undergraduate students, postgraduate students, academics and practitioners. An evaluation feedback survey has been sent to learners at the end of each workshop to assess whether the initiative has achieved its stated aims and had an impact so far. While it might not be easy to measure the success of the initiative using a post-workshop survey, we can provide some evidence from participants' feedback, which may serve as indications of the potential impact.

During the workshop, participants learn forecasting and R programming skills. They learn the theory and concepts of forecasting and how to implement methods in R. A participant explained how the workshop helped him to build skills in forecasting and R programming: "*The workshop helped me to manipulate and prepare data for forecasting and use R to generate forecast and evaluate its quality. I discovered how powerful R is for forecasting modeling*".

The workshop also emphasises the use of forecasting for planning and decision-making through various examples and guest speakers from different sectors. Although not relating directly to their own experience, this provides an opportunity for learners to think critically about the role of forecasting and its potential benefits for their organisations and wider society. A participant highlighted how the workshop increased her awareness about the potential use of forecasts:*"I couldn't have imagined a link between forecasting and social good utilities. You have shown that link and I thank you for that"*.

Democratising forecasting workshops are delivered in person. They are coordinated with institutions in developing countries, who host and organise the workshops. Tutors from the UK travel to the country and deliver the training. By doing so, the initiative achieves its aim of outreach to resource-poor countries where access to quality education might be an issue. Rostami-Tabar [25] discussed the knowledge and expertise gap in the area of forecasting in developing countries and emphasised that very little has been done over the past two decades to reduce this gap. A participant highlighted the importance of organising the forecasting workshop in her country:*"Not everyone in the world has the privilege or the chance to get a proper education and it is us, those who had this privilege, [who give] thanks for making the forecasting workshop accessible to us"*.

Ideally, the democratising forecasting initiative should empower participants and ultimately bring changes not only at the personal level but more widely in terms of enabling decisions to be more well informed. While it is difficult to measure the impact of the workshop on the latter, there are indications of the former from end-of-workshop feedback. A participant reported that the workshop had led to a significant change in her priorities for her professional life:

"Honestly, this workshop made me reset some of my priorities. In fact, I thought that I was determined and that I already chose the next steps in my career. Then, after this training, I found myself really interested in forecasting and especially forecasting for social good. So, I really welcome any opportunity to create the community that you talked about today and I would be honored to be part of it".

21.5.4 Challenges in Delivering Democratising Forecasting Workshops

Democratising Forecasting focuses on educating people about forecasting in developing countries and requires coordination with partners in those countries to make the workshops accessible to wider beneficiaries. Partners are responsible for in-country organisation. Tasks include advertising the workshop among potential participants, registration, communication and providing a venue.

While the idea of Democratising Forecasting is based on the distribution of forecasting knowledge, at no cost, in developing countries, it would be an oversimplification to assume that everyone is open to the idea. In fact, one of the most important challenges in the Democratising Forecasting workshops has been finding partners who are genuinely interested in knowledge distribution in this area and who are able and willing to coordinate effectively to meet the learning requirements of the workshop. The coordination with partners is needed prior to the workshop delivery to ensure that learning will take place, and requires having the right learners in the workshop with the right level of infrastructure and support. In the following, some challenges related to coordination and delivery are highlighted.

It had been agreed with partners that the workshop should be accessible to any learner at no cost. When delivering the workshops, it became evident that some institutions made it accessible only to their own students and staff. In one case, the hosting organisation was asking for money to organise the workshop, to provide a room and internet access. The amount they proposed was clearly aimed at making a profit from organising the event. Some partners brought in irrelevant people (e.g. secretaries) to show off the high number of attendees. These examples revealed, very clearly, that the concept of sharing knowledge and making it accessible to wider communities at no cost is not always understood or appreciated in some institutions.

Another challenge that was observed is related to the physical environment. Research highlights the importance of the physical environment on learning [26]. This was neglected by partners in some countries, especially in Africa. In one case, a workshop had to be delivered in a room without any windows or ventilation. Also, the layout of the room did not allow for any group discussion and it was difficult for the tutor to move around and help students who may have been having issues in using the software.

Overall, it is evident that the lack of dedicated partners who share the value of the Democratising Forecasting project can be an important barrier in achieving the project's aim.

21.5.5 Limitations of the Democratising Forecasting Initiative

One of the limitations of the Democratising Forecasting project has been the lack of assistance to learners after attending the workshop, to overcome the issues they face. This would include helping them at the transitional stage from the workshop to real-world settings or to become a trainer. This is highly desirable but additional financial and people resources would be required to support learners in this way.

The practical aspects of the workshop could be delivered based on problems/datasets that participants are familiar with. While this might be helpful for the learning process, it would require skilled mentors to help the instructor and such mentors have not been available.

So far, the Democratising Forecasting (DF) project has been mainly focusing on the theory of forecasting models and educating analysts to produce forecasts using R, rather than on the role of forecasts in the decision-making process. This limitation may not be restricted to the DF project and could be a more general tendency in designing forecasting education programmes, which may create issues in accepting forecasting as a useful tool. Similar issues have also been highlighted in the Management Science and Operations Research education literature [13, 30]. Also, the workshop content only covers forecasting using statistical methods, which assumes data availability. However, there are many situations where there is limited capacity to record data in developing countries, which means the data might not be available or the collected data might not be reliable. Including sessions on judgmental forecasting can enhance the curriculum in that regard.

In such programmes, there is often insufficient discussion on forecasting beneficiaries, the link between forecasting and decision making and how forecasts should be used. This raises the important question of whether learning theories about forecasting and applying models on datasets is enough to prepare learners for forecasting in practice. In the examples discussed in the DF training courses, there is usually no role for the user of forecasts to play. This may create an issue in using forecasts in practice, as learners may conclude that this is the end and generated forecasts are the solution to the problem. Putting more emphasis on the relationship between forecasts and decision-making in forecasting education programmes and educating the main beneficiaries of forecasting, such as managers and decision-makers, is fundamental in encouraging the systematic use of forecasting. It is intended that this aspect of Democratising Forecasting will become a focal point for future developments.

21.5.6   Future Agenda for Democratising Forecasting

Given the importance of judgemental forecasting in practice, especially in resource-poor environments where data is not available or is incomplete, and the fact that DF workshops have been covering only statistical methods, it is planned to introduce new sessions on judgemental forecasting in future workshops. The sessions will introduce different approaches in judgemental forecasting, and there will be a case study focusing on scenario forecasting, given its relevance in many situations for contingency planning.

To overcome the lack of support and communication with DF participants after workshops have finished, it is planned to create the Democratising Forecasting Slack channel and to invite attendees to join the channel. It will be used as a communication channel and, in particular, members can use it to post questions and/or answers. Previous attendees can also support new ones in their journey, help them to solve issues and create an online learning environment. The Slack platform has proved to be a very effective tool to assist learners, especially in data science-related programmes [31, 32]. It can be used as a single communication channel with attendees before, during and after attending a workshop. The aim is to use this channel to increase engagement, enhance the learning experience and assist learners during their transition stage, after attending the workshop.

Aligning with the principles of Forecasting for Social Good, the future agenda is to encourage workshop participants to put what they have learned into practice, and to empower them to create change by using forecasting to make better informed decisions and policies. To this end, the Forecasting for Social Good Research Grant has been introduced [29]. This grant will be awarded annually to researchers in developing countries as the project lead and its main objective is to improve the use of forecasting tools to inform decisions that prioritise the well-being of people and the planet.

Potential users of forecasts (e.g. managers, planners, decision makers) may not fully benefit from the current workshop, as it mainly focuses on forecasting methods and their implementation in R software. In recognition of this issue, it is planned to design and deliver a one-day workshop on forecasting for managers. The focus of this workshop will be on concepts and considerations about forecasting from the perspective of the consumers of forecasting, rather than the producers. The workshop will be aimed at increasing awareness of the potential benefits of forecasting for managers and decision-makers and encouraging the systematic use of forecasts. The workshop will be coordinated and hosted in developing countries by a leading international humanitarian organisation.

21.6   Conclusions

In many modern organisations, multiple decisions are made in the light of predictions generated by forecasting processes. A forecasting process should be perceived as successful if it enables better decisions to be made, bringing benefits to organisations and wider society. This requires a shift from the way forecasting success is assessed, which has been traditionally based on forecast accuracy alone. The potential benefits resulting from the use of forecasting should include not only economic outcomes but also social and environmental measures at both local and global levels. This would lead to an increased appreciation of forecasting as an activity with a much broader base of beneficiaries than has previously been contemplated.

Ensuring that forecasting benefits decision-making requires far more than developing the latest forecasting models, which has been the main emphasis in the academic forecasting literature. There are various factors that may act as barriers to realising the benefits that can arise from forecasting. We have discussed some of the principal reasons why benefits might not be shared, including lack of access to resources and expertise, and poor communication between the various stakeholders involved in the forecasting process. In addition to improving internal communications, it was argued that better communications are also needed with software developers and forecasting academics.

In recognition of the benefits that forecasting knowledge and skills can bring to organisations, and to overcome some of the barriers to realising these benefits, the Democratising Forecasting (DF) initiative has been established, to extend the range of users and organisations. This project builds capacity in developing countries by educating the potential beneficiaries of forecasting. Overall, the project has been a success so far. It has reached out to communities in lower/lower-middle/middle income countries, helping learners to develop forecasting and software skills, empowering them to create change and increasing awareness of the potential benefits of forecasting.

Reflecting on the experience of delivering workshops in the Democratising Forecasting project, we highlighted some issues and challenges that may have some broader relevance. It was concluded that perhaps the most important factor in making an international learning project a success is having a dedicated partner to coordinate and organise the workshop in the country. Without such a partner, all efforts to design a high-quality programme, and to make it more widely accessible, may prove fruitless.

In DF workshops, the main emphasis has been on statistical methods and software. However, there are many situations where data might not be available or incomplete, and this is where judgemental forecasting becomes essential. This will be included in future workshops and should, indeed, be a part of any business forecasting educational programme. We also recognise that it is critical to assist learners after attending a workshop in their transition to produce and use forecasts in the real world. To that end, a grant has been established, which helps participants to put in practice their learning in the forecasting for social good area.

Further reflection brought the realisation that the focus of the DF workshops has been mainly from the perspective of forecasters or forecasting modellers (i.e. on producing forecasts and using the software) rather than the perspective of the decision-makers. This omission is important, given their crucial role in adopting, gaining acceptance and sustaining new forecasting processes. New forms of engagement with these decision-makers are currently being planned. More generally, forecasting education should recognise the important role of decision-makers as the main beneficiaries and the relationship between forecasting and decision-making should be covered in any programme.

In similar initiatives such as Data Science for Social Good, there are indications of success such as peer review publications, number of organisations involved, number of projects completed and number of fellowships awarded. Democratising Forecasting has also been growing, in terms of outreach and number of participants benefiting from its workshops, since its launch in January 2018. However, a full set of measures has not yet been developed and so it is difficult to assess its impact objectively. Success might be best evaluated based on actions taken, and their effects, as a result of what was learned during the workshop and afterwards.

We believe that there is a broad demand for forecasting skills in communities that may have benefited less from forecasting, such as the public sector, third sector and almost any sector in resource-poor environments in low/middle income countries. We hope that we have provided a vision of what a democratised forecasting curriculum might look like. We believe that coupling Democratising Forecasting with Forecasting for Social Good creates opportunities for societal and environment benefits beyond what has been achieved so far.

References

1. Hyndman, R. & Athanasopoulos, G. Forecasting: principles and practice. (OTexts, 2021), http://OTexts.com/fpp3/
2. Checkland, P. Systems Thinking, Systems Practice. (Wiley, 1981)
3. Kuhn, M. & Silge, J. Tidy Modeling with R. (2021), https://www.tmwr.org/
4. Hyndman, R. Time Series CRAN Task View. (2020), https://cran.r-project.org/web/views/TimeSeries.html

5. Seabold, S. & Perktold, J. Econometric and statistical modeling with Python. *Proceedings Of The 9th Python In Science Conference.* **57** pp. 61 (2010)
6. Garreta, R. & Moncecchi, G. Learning scikit-learn: machine learning in Python. (Packt Publishing Ltd, 2013)
7. Makridakis, S., Bonnell, E., Clarke, S., Fildes, R., Gilliland, M., Hoover, J., Tashman, L. & Others The benefits of systematic forecasting for organizations: The UFO project. *Foresight: The International Journal Of Applied Forecasting.*, 45–56 (2020)
8. Ghani, R. Data science for social good and public policy: examples, opportunities, and challenges. *The 41st International ACM SIGIR Conference On Research & Development In Information Retrieval.* pp. 3–3 (2018)
9. Shi, Z., Wang, C. & Fang, F. Artificial intelligence for social good: A survey. *ArXiv Preprint* ArXiv:2001.01818. (2020)
10. Midgley, G., Johnson, M. & Chichirau, G. What is community Operational Research?. *European Journal Of Operational Research.* **268**, 771–783 (2018)
11. Hwang, J., Orenstein, P., Cohen, J., Pfeiffer, K. & Mackey, L. Improving subseasonal forecasting in the western US with machine learning. *Proceedings Of The 25th ACM SIGKDD International Conference On Knowledge Discovery & Data Mining.* pp. 2325–2335 (2019)
12. Rostami-Tabar, B., Ali, M., Hong, T., Hyndman, R., Porter, M. & Syntetos, A. Forecasting for social good. *International Journal Of Forecasting.* (2021), https://www.sciencedirect.com/science/article/pii/S0169207021000510
13. McClure, R. Educating the future users of OR. *Interfaces.* **11**, 108–112 (1981)
14. Hill, B., Dailey, D., Guy, R., Lewis, B., Matsuzaki, M. & Morgan, J. Democratizing data science: The community data science workshops and classes. *Big Data Factories.* pp. 115–135 (2017)
15. Van Horn, J., Fierro, L., Kamdar, J., Gordon, J., Stewart, C., Bhattrai, A., Abe, S., Lei, X., O'Driscoll, C., Sinha, A. & Others Democratizing data science through data science training. *Pacific Symposium On Biocomputing 2018: Proceedings Of The Pacific Symposium.* pp. 292–303 (2018)
16. Cuquet, M., Vega-Gorgojo, G., Lammerant, H., Finn, R. & Others Societal impacts of big data: challenges and opportunities in Europe. *ArXiv Preprint* ArXiv:1704.03361. (2017)
17. Rostami-Tabar, B. Democratising forecasting. (2020), https://forecasters.org/events/iif-workshops/, Sponsored by the International Institute of Forecasters
18. Bellini Saibene, Y., Vitolo, C., LeDell, E., Frick, H. & Acion, L. R-Ladies Global, a worldwide organisation to promote gender diversity in the R community.. *EGU General Assembly Conference Abstracts.* pp. 20530 (2020)
19. Hyndman, R., Athanasopoulos, G., Bergmeir, C., Caceres, G., Chhay, L., O'Hara-Wild, M., Petropoulos, F., Razbash, S., Wang, E. & Yasmeen, F. forecast: Forecasting functions for time series and linear models. (2020), https://pkg.robjhyndman.com/forecast/, R package version 8.12

20. Long, K., McDermott, F. & Meadows, G. Factors affecting the implementation of simulation modelling in healthcare: A longitudinal case study evaluation. *Journal Of The Operational Research Society*. **71**, 1927–1939 (2020)
21. Cipriano, M. & Gruca, T. The power of priors: How confirmation bias impacts market prices. *The Journal Of Prediction Markets*. **8**, 34–56 (2014)
22. LeVee, G. The key to understanding the forecasting process. *The Journal Of Business Forecasting*. **11**, 12 (1992)
23. Sanders, N. Forecasting: State-of-the-Art in Research and Practice. *The Routledge Companion To Production And Operations Management*. pp. 45–62 (2017)
24. KarpoviÄir A, R. & Others Learning skills for enhancing the use of Big Data. *World Journal On Educational Technology: Current Issues*. **12**, 23–36 (2020)
25. Rostami-Tabar, B. Business forecasting in developing countries. *Business Forecasting: The Emerging Role Of Artificial Intelligence And Machine Learning*. pp. 382 (2021)
26. Brooks, D. Space matters: The impact of formal learning environments on student learning. *British Journal Of Educational Technology*. **42**, 719–726 (2011)
27. Altay, N. & Narayanan, A. Forecasting in humanitarian operations: Literature review and research needs. *International Journal Of Forecasting*. (2020), https://www.sciencedirect.com/science/article/pii/S0169207020301151
28. Boylan, J. & Syntetos, A. Intermittent Demand Forecasting: Context, Methods and Applications. (John Wiley & Sons, 2021)
29. Rostami-Tabar Forecasting for Social Good Research Grant. (2021), https://forecasters.org/programs/research-awards/forecasting-for-social-good-research-grant/
30. Zahedi, F. MS/OR education: Meeting the new demands on MS education. *Interfaces*. **15**, 85–94 (1985)
31. Vela, K. Using Slack to communicate with medical students. *Journal Of The Medical Library Association: JMLA*. **106**, 504 (2018)
32. Perkel, J. How scientists use Slack. *Nature News*. **541**, 123 (2017)
33. Calder, M., Craig, C., Culley, D., Cani, R., Donnelly, C., Douglas, R., Edmonds, B., Gascoigne, J., Gilbert, N., Hargrove, C. & Others Computational modelling for decision-making: where, why, what, who and how. *Royal Society Open Science*. **5**, 172096 (2018)
34. Bevan, R. & Bryer, R. On measuring the contribution of OR. *Journal Of The Operational Research Society*. **29**, 409–418 (1978)
35. Dando, M. & Bennett, P. A Kuhnian crisis in Management Science?. *Journal Of The Operational Research Society*. **32**, 91–103 (1981)
36. Rosenhead, J. & Thunhurst, C. A materialist analysis of Operational Research. *Journal Of The Operational Research Society*. **33**, 111–122 (1982)
37. White, L., Smith, H. & Currie, C. OR in developing countries: A review. *European Journal Of Operational Research*. **208**, 1–11 (2011)
38. Boylan, J. & Syntetos, A. Accuracy and accuracy-implication metrics for intermittent demand. *Foresight: The International Journal Of Applied Forecasting*, 39–42 (2006)

39. Wang, X. & Petropoulos, F. To select or to combine? The inventory performance of model and expert forecasts. *International Journal Of Production Research*. **54**, 5271–5282 (2016)

40. Boylan, J. & Syntetos, A. Commentary: It takes two to tango. *Foresight: The International Journal Of Applied Forecasting*, 26–29 (2016)

41. Singh, S. Forecasting: Academia versus Business. *Foresight: The International Journal Of Applied Forecasting*, 46–47 (2016)

Part V

Problem Structuring and Behavioural OR

22

Behavioural OR: Recent developments and future perspectives

Martin Kunc and Konstantinos V. Katsikopoulos

22.1 Introduction

The study of the behavioural aspects of OR can be traced back to the 1960s and 1970s with authors such as Ackoff and Churchman, in the 1980s and 1990s within the field of systems thinking, and in the specialised domain of "soft" OR [5]). However, the need to merge behaviour and the practice of hard OR has been increasingly acknowledged due to the failures on implementing the results from models. A focus on human behaviour should help to develop models that capture behaviour realistically and focus the attention of scholars and decision makers on managing behavioural aspects of the system more realistically. This request is underpinned by experiments and theory in fields such as psychology, economics, and finance that are increasingly recognising aspects of individual behaviour such as decision-making heuristics and biases and adaptations, bounded rationality, and misperceptions of feedback affecting the results from quantitative models. Additionally, attributes of human behaviour both shape and are shaped by the physical

M. Kunc (✉) · K. V. Katsikopoulos
Southampton Business School, University of Southampton, Southampton, England
e-mail: M.H.Kunc@soton.ac.uk

K. V. Katsikopoulos
e-mail: K.Katsikopoulos@soton.ac.uk

© The Author(s), under exclusive license to Springer Nature Switzerland AG 2022

721

S. Salhi and J. Boylan (eds.), *The Palgrave Handbook of Operations Research*, https://doi.org/10.1007/978-3-030-96935-6_22

and institutional systems in which they are embedded [5]. Behavioural issues in decision-making are widely studied at the individual, group, and organisational levels by judgement and decision-making, cognitive psychology, organisation theory, game theory, and economics. Consequently, the rise of Behavioural OR (BOR) within OR/MS should not be surprising and it should naturally be part of any research on OR/MS modelling. The recent developments of BOR imply a focus on empirically examining what people actually do within a system or when engaged in OR-supported processes with the aim of identifying key behavioural dimensions that shape the conduct of OR in practice [5]. To summarise, scholars in BOR aim not only to describe but also to prescribe human behaviours in order to improve OR in practice. To summarise, among many definitions for BOR, we suggest "behavioural operational research (BOR) is defined as the study of behavioural aspects related to the use of operational research (OR) methods in modelling, problem solving and decision support" [10]". This chapter will cover recent developments in the field as well as future issues.

22.2 Recent Developments

This section divides recent developments into the conceptual frameworks defined by the BOR community and by a similar area of research in BOM. While they are not identical, BOR and BOM share some interesting aspects. The integration of their principles can provide a useful broader framework for considering behavioural aspects in the field of OR/MS.

22.2.1 Conceptual Framework of BOR

Franco and Hämäläinen [5] propose a framework for empirical studies in BOR. In their view, the behavioural aspects of OR practice depend on the type of OR actors, such as expert modellers, decision analysts, consultants, and users, the impact of OR methods (techniques/tools such as mathematical programming or simulation, and the routines for using those, such as building, communicating, and intervening, and OR praxis which reflects the behaviour of participants during the process of using OR methods. Finally, the context of the OR praxis, such that the type of the organisation or the level of decision-making defines the outcomes such as changes in cognition, attitudes, or interaction.

Relatedly, Kunc, Malpass, and White [22] suggested three areas of research related to BOR: behaviour in models, behaviour with models, and behaviour beyond models. The first area evaluates the representation of behaviour in OR/MS models where there can be different approaches such as modelling human behaviour as passive entities, which are predictable but unrealistic, to people with biases, sentiments, and traits, which are difficult to pin down, or to agents with capacities for adaptive and effective decision-making when the conditions are right. The representation of human behaviour depends on the assumptions of the modellers but the model can have very different results due to the impact of the behaviours on the dynamics of the system under study. The second area is related to the use of models by decision makers, for example, asking questions about what information is used and how it is processed.

Katsikopoulos [13] proposed psychological heuristics where decision-making is based on psychological capacities; decision makers do not necessarily use all available information and employ simple computations. The use of OR models can also impact dimensions such as affective or cognitive conflicts [11]. The final area of BOR research in this view is concerned with behaviour beyond the use of models. This area aims to understand the impact of models through the lens of the socially situated nature of OR practice [33]. Most models do not prescribe action because they are a guide to action and action is a collective activity aiming at system-level improvement. Therefore, behaviour beyond models intends to evaluate the externalisation of inclinations to act on and modifies the environment using models [33].

22.2.2   Comparison between BOR and BOM

Gino and Pisano [9] suggest that "behavioral operations is the study of attributes of human behaviour and cognition that impact the design, management, and improvement of operating systems, and the study of the interaction between such attributes and operating systems and processes". When comparing this with the BOR definition, it seems that the research focus in BOR is mainly related to behavioural facilitation for model building and communication of model results, whereas BOM seems to mostly focus directly on the impact of behavioural factors on solving problems within organisational contexts [20].

Ultimately, both BOR and BOM share the same goals: the design, management, and improvement of operating systems and processes assuming the impact of human behaviour [20]. However, BOM focuses on deviations from assuming that actors are motivated by self-interest expressed in monetary terms and the optimisation of a well-defined objective function. For example, activities like inventory management that can be explained

Table 22.1 Differences and similarities between BOM and BOR (adapted from [20])

Concept	BOM	BOR
Practice	Identify deviations from normative "rational" theories	Understanding behavioural aspects of the practice of OR
Scope	Activities in operations such as inventory, production, services, product development, supply chain management	The development and use of OR models in different organisational contexts and type of problems
Focus of attention	Operations	Models
Theories	Behavioural economics Organisational behaviour	Bounded rationality Group Dynamics
Research methods	Experiments Surveys Models Psychometric research	Action research Models Experiments Case studies
Target of research	Managers and workers	Consultants and analysts

with actors following "rational" theories in operations, are evaluated through experiments where participants do not follow such theories. Thus, BOM has focused on experimental research underpinned by, for example, behavioural-economics theories [20]. However, the most important aspect in BOM is the focus on the operational context such as the supply chain, service operations, forecasting, and so on, differently from BOR where the context is primarily the OR actor. Table 22.1 summarises the above comparison.

22.2.3   Empirical Basis of BOR

Of course, useful OR has always been taking into account the known evidence on human behaviour [5]. In 1940, Patrick Blackett's "circus" consisted of eleven members, three of which were physiologists [24]. In the wake of the second world war, behavioural sciences such as psychology and economics developed further rigorous methods of experimentation and data analysis, and are now able to provide an empirical basis for BOR. As with all science, some of the original findings has been called into question, but there have been systematic efforts of producing reliable findings and we can now be more confident about behavioural data [26].

Two areas of OR in which behavioural findings have played an important role in building and applying models are decision analysis and simulation [22]. In the case of BOM, behavioural game theory has provided modelling input to areas such as supply chain management [4]. A large chunk of the work on individual decision-making and strategic interaction can be found in the areas of judgement and decision-making, and behavioural economics. In recent years, some of such work is carried out within BOR itself [7, 12, 25, 27]. The literature on behavioural effects in simulation is partly found in human factors/engineering psychology, but it is now flourishing within BOR too [31, 3]. Because of the scientific need for experimental control, a big chunk of behavioural research can be criticised as taking place in the lab, which contradicts the need for rooting OR in practice, but there are also studies taking place in the field [6, 17].

The work referenced above provides behavioural evidence that interfaces more naturally with "hard" OR that employs formal models. Behavioural evidence that is better aligned with "soft" approaches is also available in both BOM and BOR [1, 34], but it is discussed in subsection 22.3.2. An interesting stream of this work gathers and reviews the evidence of behavioural interventions in the field [6].

The following section zooms into the input to OR from the areas of judgement and decision-making and behavioural economics, and abstracts some main themes, highlighting the spectrum of ideas present [14].

22.2.4   Behavioural Science and BOR

Herbert Simon was a serious polymath of the twentieth century, and contributed to both the human sciences, such as cognitive psychology and behavioural economics, as well as to what he called the "sciences of the artificial", such as the design of technical systems and AI. In 1958, in the pages of Operations Research, he engaged in a heated debate with Richard Bellman on how close were we to major advances in automating behaviours such as playing chess, proving theorems, and composing music. Simon thought that it was a matter of a decade but Bellman was dismissive (to put it politely). We shall discuss the connection between OR and AI that is emerging in recent years in the next section. Here, we consider how Simon's ideas on how people make decisions found their way into BOR.

Simon rejected the ideal of neoclassical economics that people make decisions "as-if" they optimise a utility function (an objective function in OR terminology). Rather, he posited, people use heuristics in order to satisfice [30]. This conception of heuristics resonates with how the concept features in OR: Optimisation is great when one can accomplish it, but in practice, who can? The data required might be of poor quality, the computational power needed might be unavailable, and so on. In both cases, heuristics, which are understood as formal entities, benefit decision makers by delivering feasible solutions. In fact, in the real world, these feasible solutions might well outper-form solutions that are optimal according to a model of the world, a point made repeatedly by the OR pioneers [19].

Simon's ideas on heuristic decision-making were mostly published in economics, psychology, or engineering, and seem to have had little immediate impact on OR. Eventually Simon did impact BOR, but this was through the work of two behavioural scientists that followed up on his ideas on heuris-tics, albeit in distinct ways. In their heuristics-and-biases program, Daniel Kahneman, together with his late colleague Amos Tversky, emphasised a conception of heuristics that "in general...are quite useful, but sometimes lead to severe and systematic errors" [32, p. 1124], and proposed verbal descriptions of heuristics. In the fast-and-frugal-heuristics program, Gerd Gigerenzer and his ABC research group developed and tested mathematical and computer models of heuristics that, they argued, "...when compared to standard benchmark strategies...can be faster, more frugal, and more accurate at the same time" [8, p. 22]. Both perspectives are represented in work on behavioural operations [16, 1, 22, 4], and researchers can choose an approach that fits their context [14].

22.3   Future Developments

In this section, we present three areas where research on BOR can see strong development. The first area is artificial intelligence (AI) where it can have profound impact on behaviour. The second area is the theories and method-ologies employed to do research in BOR since BOR is an inter-disciplinary field. Finally, teaching BOR is an untapped area with very few courses and no recognised book text.

22.3.1   BOR and AI

Simon might have been a little over-optimistic about the prospects of AI in the 1960s, but the new millennium could end up vindicating his vision. While some of us might remain un-impressed by AI-composed music, none should count on beating AI in games such as Go. Decision-making is now embedded in "technology-rich, data-driven" environments [2]. OR, and BOR, must interface well with AI; otherwise they might soon be seen as the mere precursors to an era of "analytics" or "big data".

Burger et al. [2] have pointed out that big data, by itself, does not guar-antee that OR/analytics methods and models will produce insights that are actionable by people. Drawing from areas such as sociology and philosophy of technology is key in figuring out how to do so well [34]. Such theoretical, methodological, as well as educational resources are provided in the next two sections. Here, we outline some model building and testing resources.

As any useful OR model, models induced by big data, should meet standards of performance and transparency. Transparency has entered, as it should, the public discourse, especially in sensitive domains such as health, wealth, and justice. There are many definitions of model transparency in AI. At a minimum, a model should be easily explainable to its users, especially not quantitatively sophisticated ones, and also easily usable by the users, again especially those who might lack some computer savviness [29, 15]. Candidate models should be compared with each other on these criteria, along with measures of performance such as predictive accuracy. Lazer et al. [23] have shown that this kind of crucial testing was missed in well-known applications such as nowcasting the incidence of influenza, and it is unfortunately not yet clear if such lessons have been heeded [18].

There might be multiple routes to building transparent models. An approach often taken in machine learning is to first build a model that is as accurate as possible without worrying about how complex this model is, and then trying to find a simpler model that is almost as accurate but much more explainable than the original model. Issue with this approach is that users are often confused by the mere existence of two models, their relationship, and their respective roles [28]. An alternative route is to attempt from the get-go to build models that are simultaneously simple, accurate, and transparent. While this might not always be straightforward, it has been accomplished in a range of applications, including peace-keeping operations and the monitoring of investment banks [17].

22.3.2 Theoretical and Methodological Resources for BOR

Kunc, Harper, and Katsikopoulos [21] presented three tables that summarise theoretical and methodological resources for the future developments of BOR, under the three main areas of behaviour in models (Table 22.2), behaviour with models (Table 22.3), and behaviour beyond the models (Table 22.4). The tables provide a useful summary for researchers and practitioners interested in applying behavioural sciences in OR. Table 22.2 has five columns. First column identifies the approach that has been taken by OR modellers to represent human behaviour. Second and third columns are a description of the way that human behaviour is considered. Fourth and fifth

Table 22.2 Behaviour in models: OR modelling and the representation of human behaviour (Adapted from Table 1, [21])

Approach taken to represent human behaviour	Description	Representation of human behaviour in the model	World view of the OR modeller	OR technique (example)
Simplify by not including any behaviour	Eliminate human behaviour by omission, aggregation and substitution	No representation or subsumed in one variable, e.g., a random one	Optimisation	Mathematical programming
Externalise from the model	Incorporate human behaviour outside the model by allowing decision makers to interact with the model	Since behaviour is too complex to codify, it is recorded from real decisions	Gaming, Naturalistic decision making	Management flight simulators, Experiments using models
Incorporate as a passive element	Model humans following similar rules without any difference	High-level variables representing average human behaviour	Continuous process over long term	Continuous simulation, System dynamics, Markov models
Incorporate as individual entities	Model humans as discrete entities such as machines	Discrete processes capture variables inside the model	Discrete elements controlled by rules	Discrete event simulation
Incorporate through activities	Model human performance in tasks	Output variables inside the model	Actions are response to pre-defined sequence of tasks	Discrete event simulation
Incorporate as free individuals	Model individual human behaviour with all its complexity	Micro-level variables inside the model represent states and process of change	Specific attributes of behaviour are presented individually and emergent from interactions with other humans	Agent-based simulation

columns show the type of OR method associated with each representation of human behaviour. As can be observed, there is a strong relationship between the type of models and how human behaviour is considered. Additionally, there is a suggestion of the use of multi-methodologies, e.g. experiments and OR models, to inform the models as a way of enhancing those models with more realistic behaviour.

Table 22.3 content is based on the field of psychology. The first column shows the type of behavioural change expected from using models, e.g. changes on the decision rules (heuristics), changes on the way of processing information (cognition), changes on the state of the mind when models are used (conflicts). This area implies the use of data collection methods that are related to soft OR methods, such as system dynamics models that consider mental models' complexity, and hard OR methods, such as decision analysis.

Finally, Table 22.4 is based on organisational behaviour literature. This is an area that has been particularly neglected in the OR field but it can very fruitful to indicate the impact of OR practice. For example, the implementation of a revenue management system can change the language used in the organisation and even the dialogue happening in the organisation while

Table 22.3 Behaviour with models: How OR models impact on decision makers' behaviour (Adapted from Table 2, [21])

Behavioural change in	Description	Representation of human behaviour	OR technique (examples)
Heuristics	Use of different heuristics under different interactions with the model	Elicitation of heuristics and their consequences	Decision analysis
Cognition	Change of mental models, Better understanding of complexity	Elements of mental models (variables, causal links)	System dynamics, Cognitive mapping
State of mind	Change in the state of mind is associated with two categories of conflict: functional task-related conflict (e.g. cognitive conflict) and dysfunctional emotion-related conflict (e.g. affective conflict)	Level of conflict	Problem-structuring methods

Table 22.4 Behaviour beyond models: The impact on organisational behaviour from the use of OR models (Adapted from Table 3, [21])

Organisational behaviour change expected	Description	Representation of collective behaviour
Interpreting / Integrating	Interpreting is a process of explaining an an insight or idea to others, Integrating is a process of developing shared understanding and taking coordinated action through mutual adjustment	Language Dialogue, Storytelling, Shared observations
Institutionalising	A process of routinisation where tasks and actions are specified together with organisational mechanisms to embed the learning	Systems, Procedures, Structures

the revenue management system also involves the implementation of new procedures and structures to embed in the organisation.

22.3.3   Education Resources for BOR

There exist two handbooks on behavioural OR [22, 34], and two handbooks on behavioural OM [1, 4], which cover the very wide spectrum of ideas, techniques, and applications in the two areas. A gap here is that there is currently no work that attempts to integrate the research performed in these two areas, by largely distinct communities. In the more specific area of building models of decision-making that are predictively accurate and at the same time transparent to first and end users, there is a "how-to" guide [17], which is accompanied by a freely available R package (ffcr) for statistically inducing and empirically testing such models.

22.4   Conclusions

The area of BOR is growing rapidly following the increasing attention to behaviour in multiple disciplines, such as economics, finance, operations, and marketing, and of course in the "sister" discipline of BOM. The growth of BOR is also sustained by excellent theoretical resources given the diversity of theories from, among others, disciplines such as psychology, economics, and sociology, which are supporting the analysis of human behaviour, and the lasting work of luminaries such as Herbert Simon. In terms of methodologies, there is a clear set of methods for supporting the collection of data describing human behaviour with many strengths, but also increasing levels of challenges. For example, an important development is the existence of more and more behavioural data coming from "big data" sources, and its automated processing via algorithms for predicting and influencing human behaviour. But it is unclear whether these algorithms always help build behavioural theory that is fit for practice. And, ethical implications have to be considered on the use of individual data. This is still an area where research is lagging and more transparency is needed.

References

1. Bendoly, E., van Wezel, W., and Bachrach, D. G. (Eds.) (2015). The Handbook of Behavioral Operations Management: Social and Psychological Dynamics in Production and Service Settings. Oxford University Press.
2. Burger, K., White, L., and Yearworth, M. (2019). Developing a smart operational research with hybrid practice theories. European Journal of Operational Research, 277(3), 1137–1150.
3. Currie, C. S., Fowler, J. W., Kotiadis, K., Monks, T., Onggo, B. S., Robertson, D. A., and Tako, A. A. (2020). How simulation modelling can help reduce the impact of COVID-19. Journal of Simulation, 14(2), 83–97.
4. Donohue, K., Katok, E., and Leider, S. (Eds.) (2018). The Handbook of Behavioral Operations. Wiley, New York.
5. Franco, L. A., and Hämäläinen, R. P. (2016). Engaging with behavioral operational research: On methods, actors and praxis. In M. Kunc, J. Malpass, and L. White (Eds.) Behavioral Operational Research (pp. 3–25). Palgrave Macmillan, London.
6. Franco, L. A., Hämäläinen, R. P., Rouwette, E. A., and Leppänen, I. (2020). Taking stock of Behavioural OR: A review of behavioural studies with an intervention focus. European Journal of Operational Research.
7. French, S., Maule, J., and Papamichail, N. (2009). Decision Behaviour, Analysis and Support. Cambridge University Press.
8. Gigerenzer, G., and Todd, P. M. (1999). Fast and frugal heuristics: The adaptive toolbox. In G. Gigerenzer, P. M. Todd, and the ABC research group, Simple Heuristics that Make us Smart (pp. 3–34). Oxford University Press.
9. Gino, F., and Pisano, G. (2008). Toward a theory of behavioral operations. Manufacturing & Service Operations Management, 10(4), 676–691.
10. Hämäläinen, R.P., Luoma, J. and Saarinen, E., (2013). On the importance of behavioral operational research: The case of understanding and communicating

about dynamic systems. European Journal of Operational Research, 228 (3), 623–634.

11. Huh, K. K., and Kunc, M. (2016). Supporting strategy: Behavioral influences on resource conceptualization processes In M. Kunc, J. Malpass, and L. White (Eds.) Behavioral Operational Research (pp. 337–356). Palgrave Macmillan, London.

12. Katsikopoulos, K. V. (2011). Psychological heuristics for making inferences: Definition, performance, and the emerging theory and practice. Decision Analysis, 8(1), 10–29.

13. Katsikopoulos, K. V. (2016). Behavior with models: The role of psychological heuristics. In M. Kunc, J. Malpass, and L. White (Eds.) Behavioral Operational Research (pp. 27–45). Palgrave Macmillan, London.

14. Katsikopoulos, K. V. (2022). Cognitive Operations: Modeling Psychological Processes and Predicting Decisions. Palgrave Macmillan, London.

15. Katsikopoulos, K. V., and Canellas, M. C. (in press). Decoding human behavior with big data? Critical, constructive input from the decision sciences. AI Magazine.

16. Katsikopoulos, K. V., and Gigerenzer, G. (2013). Behavioral operations management: A blind spot and a research program. Journal of Supply Chain Management, 49(1), 3–7.

17. Katsikopoulos, K. V., Şimşek, Ö., Buckmann, M., and Gigerenzer, G. (2020). Classification in the Wild: The Science and Art of Transparent Decision Making. MIT Press.

18. Katsikopoulos, K. V., Şimşek, Ö., Buckmann, M., and Gigerenzer, G. (2021). Transparent modeling of influenza incidence: Big data or a single data point from psychological theory? International Journal of Forecasting.

19. Kimball, G. E. (1958). A critique of operations research. Journal of the Washington Academy of Sciences, 48(2), 33–37.

20. Kunc, M. (2020). Behavioral Operations and Behavioral Operational Research: Similarities and Differences in Competences and Capabilities. In White, L, Kunc, M., Burger, K. and Malpass, J. (eds) Behavioral Operational Research A Capabilities Approach (pp. 3–22). Springer Nature, Germany.

21. Kunc, M., Harper, P., ans Katsikopoulos, K. (2020). A review of implementation of behavioural aspects in the application of OR in healthcare. Journal of the Operational Research Society, 71(7), 1055–1072.

22. Kunc, M., Malpass, J. and White, L. eds., (2016). Behavioral operational research: Theory, methodology and practice. Springer.

23. Lazer, D., Kennedy, R., King, G., and Vespignani, A. (2014). The parable of Google Flu: traps in big data analysis. Science, 343(6176), 1203–1205.

24. Mirowski, P. (1999). Cyborg agonistes: economics meets operations research in mid-century. Social Studies of Science, 29(5), 685–718.

25. Montibeller, G., and von Winterfeldt, D. (2015). Cognitive and motivational biases in decision and risk analysis. Risk Analysis, 35(7), 1230–1251.

26. Open Science Collaboration. (2012). An open, large-scale, collaborative effort to estimate the reproducibility of psychological science. Perspectives on Psychological Science, 7(6), 657–660.

27. Pande, S. M., Papamichail, K. N., and Kawalek, P. (2021). Compatibility effects in the prescriptive application of psychological heuristics: Inhibition, Integration and Selection. European Journal of Operational Research.

28. Passi, S., and Jackson, S. J. (2018). Trust in data science: Collaboration, translation, and accountability in corporate data science projects. Proceedings of the ACM on Human-Computer Interaction, 2(CSCW), 1–28.

29. Rudin, C., and Radin, J. (2019). Why are we using black box models in AI when we don't need to? A lesson from an explainable AI competition. Harvard Data Science Review, 1(2).

30. Simon, H. A. (1955). A behavioral model of rational choice. The Quarterly Journal of Economics, 69(1), 99–118.

31. Tako, A. A., Tsioptsias, N., and Robinson, S. (2020). Can we learn from simplified simulation models? An experimental study on user learning. Journal of Simulation, 14(2), 130-144.

32. Tversky, A., and Kahneman, D. (1974). Judgment under uncertainty: Heuristics and biases. science, 185(4157), 1124–1131.

33. White, L. (2016). Behavior beyond the model. In M. Kunc, J. Malpass, and L. White (Eds.) Behavioral Operational Research (pp. 65–84). Palgrave Macmillan, London.

34. White, L., Kunc, M., Burger, K., and Malpass, J. (Eds.). (2020). Behavioral Operational Research: A Capabilities Approach. Springer Nature, Germany.

23

Problem Structuring Methods: Taking Stock and Looking Ahead

L. Alberto Franco and Etiënne A. J. A. Rouwette

23.1 Introduction

On the morning of January 28, 1986, the space shuttle Challenger was launched from the Kennedy Space Center. The temperature that morning was around −5 °C, well below the previous low temperatures at which the shuttle engines had been tested before. Seventy-three seconds after launch, the Challenger exploded, killing all seven astronauts aboard, and becoming the worst disaster in space flight history. The catastrophe shocked the whole world, and for many Americans it was the most tragic event since the assassination of John F. Kennedy in 1963. The findings of the Presidential Commission on

L. A. Franco (✉)
Loughborough University, Loughborough, UK
e-mail: l.a.franco@lboro.ac.uk

L. A. Franco · E. A. J. A. Rouwette
Radboud University, Nijmegen, The Netherlands
e-mail: e.rouwette@ru.nl

L. A. Franco
Universidad del Pacifico, Lima, Peru

© The Author(s), under exclusive license to Springer Nature
Switzerland AG 2022
S. Salhi and J. Boylan (eds.), *The Palgrave Handbook of Operations Research*,
https://doi.org/10.1007/978-3-030-96935-6_23

the Space Shuttle Challenger Accident pointed to a flawed decision-making process as a primary contributory cause.[1]

Very few machines come near to the space shuttle in terms of its sheer complexity. Manufactured by Rockwell International and operated by NASA, the 250-ton machine operated at the very limit of human engineering. The launch of the Challenger was originally scheduled for January 22, 1986, but was postponed three times. The first two postponements occurred because the previous space mission was late, and the third postponement was based on an unacceptable weather forecast. Finally, a launch attempt on January 27 was cancelled because of high crosswinds and a balky bolt on a spaceship door. On the evening before the actual launch on January 28, NASA management and engineers met with the management and engineers of Morton Thiokol Inc, the contractors that produced the solid rocket boosters responsible for the shuttle's primary propulsion, to discuss the issue of launching the shuttle despite near freezing temperatures expected for the next morning. During that meeting, Morton Thiokol engineers expressed grave concerns about the effect of the low temperature on the functioning of the O-ring seal in the joint of the solid rocket booster. Roger Boisjoly was the key engineer expressing concerns. He believed that cold temperatures could lead to substantial O-ring erosion on the solid rocket boosters. And if the O-rings eroded substantially, the erosion could lead to a catastrophic accident during launch due to a leaking of hot gases.

Boisjoly found himself lacking sufficient data to prove his case. He had some data, but the evidence was inconclusive as the combination of O-ring erosion and low temperatures had been observed only in a very small number of previous shuttle launches. He also was relying on his intuition to come to the conclusion that cold temperatures were problematic. Without sufficient data, he could not persuade top managers. NASA and Morton Thiokol held very different interpretations about the decision that needed to be made about the launch. For Morton Thiokol management and engineers, the decision was about whether it was safe to launch the shuttle; for NASA management and engineers it was about whether the data suggested that the shuttle would fail. Clearly all parties in the meeting wanted to make the best possible decision, but the findings of the Presidential Commission indicate that NASA management tried to win the argument at all costs, presenting their views forcefully, suppressing dissenters, and seeing the other party as an opponent. They were not open to being influenced by arguments from the Morton Thiokol engineers. Had all the parties involved been willing and able

---

[1] Presidential Commission on the Space Shuttle Accident (1986) Report of the presidential commission on the space shuttle challenger accident. Washington, DC.

to understand whether there was a correlation between O-ring failure and temperature, they might have recognised that they had access to data that could have convinced everyone to delay the launch. Indeed, if data about previous flights that had not experienced O-ring erosion was added to the data that Boisjoly presented to NASA, it would have become apparent that O-ring erosion and temperature were indeed correlated, and that a launch delay was thus necessary.

Decision situations such as the one described above have received particular attention within the discipline of Operational Research (OR). Namely, complex situations that present high levels of uncertainty because full information or knowledge is not available, and that are subject to multiple contrasting interpretations and interests that can lead to high levels of conflict. This chapter will give an overview of a family of decision support approaches specifically developed to deal with complexity, uncertainty and conflict. Known as problem structuring methods (PSMs) [139, 140] and developed almost 50 years ago within OR, their general purpose is to assist a group of stakeholders in gaining a better understanding of a situation of concern through the provision of modelling and facilitation support [71], with a view to reaching consensus on problem structure, and usually, on initial stakeholder responses to the problem [140]. PSMs extended the scope of traditional OR decision support, which was already accessible to address problems with relatively low levels of uncertainty and conflict, and high levels of complexity, to problem situations with high levels of uncertainty and conflict. PSMs took from its OR origins the model-based approach and added facilitation processes [71] to enable groups of diverse composition to structure and thereby handle the problem situations they face more easily.

The use and study of PSMs have continued to grow over the years, although mainly confined to certain geographical areas [1, 78, 108, 124]. Advocates of PSMs maintain that the methods offer flexibility in their application and can be responsive to the dynamics of group work and/or the particularities of the problem situation at hand. In practice, this flexibility has allowed the possibility of their combined use, as well as their use in combination with non-OR and mainstream OR methods, in what has been termed 'multi-methodology' (or 'mixed-method') interventions [87, 107, 111, 116].

The original family of PSMs described in the widely referenced text by Rosenhead [139] and its revised version [140] was constrained to only five major methods.[2] However, increasing calls to extend the family of PSMs [16, 37, 79, 150, 162] has led some OR scholars to attempt redefining what a

[2] The original version contained six methods. In the revised version Metagame Analysis and Hypergame Analysis were fused into Drama Theory, resulting in five methods.

PSM is [153, 166]. A parallel development within PSM scholarship has been a gradual move from simply reporting case studies of PSM applications in various contexts, to rigorously testing or developing theories that explain how PSMs are used and their actual effects [63, 66, 141, 146, 172–174].

Against the above background, the aim of this chapter is to take stock of what we know about PSMs and highlight some areas of work that deserve critical attention for the continuing advance of PSM as a field of practice and research within OR. The chapter is structured as follows. First, we present the general nature of PSMs based on their shared characteristics regarding tools and process. Next, we review the use of PSMs in practice drawing from published surveys and academic reviews. This is followed by an examination of the evidence supporting or questioning the actual achievement of the products and impacts claimed by PSMs. Finally, we discuss what in our view are the most pressing issues confronting PSM practitioners and researchers, and offer some suggestions to address them.

23.2   The Characteristics of PSMs

What is a PSM? The PSM/non-PSM boundary has been somewhat arbitrary in the relevant literature, with key edited collections presenting different selections of methods [131, 137, 140]. Earlier attempts to characterise PSMs have mainly focused on their philosophical and sociological foundations, and on the type of problems for which they were specifically designed. That is, that PSMs operate within an interpretivist paradigm, and that they are suited to deal with 'messy' (i.e. ill-defined) problems [140]. These earlier characterisations position PSMs in sharp contrast to traditional OR methods based on a positivist paradigm, and focussed on 'tame' (i.e. well-defined) problems. The characterisation has remained the dominant portrayal of PSMs to the present time. The differences between traditional OR methods and PSMs are summarised in Table 23.1.

Although a useful starting point, portraying PSMs in this way is problematic. For example, whilst philosophical and sociological considerations are certainly important to raise awareness of the assumptions operational researchers are making about their interventions, knowing that we are interpretivists does not necessarily imply that the method we are using in a particular intervention can be considered a PSM. Indeed, it is possible to use many traditional OR methods such as decision analysis, system dynamics,

Table 23.1 Contrasting traditional OR methods and Problem Structuring Methods (based on Rosenhead [139])

Traditional OR methods	Problem Structuring Methods (PSMs)
Operate within a positivist paradigm, meaning that:	Operate within an interpretivist paradigm, meaning that:
• there is only one problem out there: objectives are set and the current situation can be known	• problems do not exist independently of human thought and are thus the constructs of people based on their worldviews
• the context of the problem is frozen: it does not change during analysis, current cause-effect relations carry on into the future	• people are considered active participants in the intervention deployed to tackle the problem
• the task of the operational researchers is to find the best way to get from the current to the desired situation	• operational researchers cannot act as objective outsiders
Suitable for well-defined (tame) problems, characterised by the existence of:	Suitable for ill-defined (messy) problem situations characterised by the existence of:
• passive stakeholders; unambiguous objectives and firm constraints; implementation is unproblematic due to a clear chain of command	• multiple stakeholders with potentially conflicting perspectives, values and interests regarding the problem; implementation cannot rely on authority or power
• certain or knowable relationships between causes and effects, based on an abundance of reliable and accessible data	• high levels of uncertainty regarding cause-and-effect relationships due to lack of reliable data, potential behaviours of others, or both

and mathematical modelling within an interpretivist paradigm.[3] That is, instead of assuming that the models produced by these methods are objective representations of a problem situation, the models are seen as representations of individuals' beliefs or views about that situation. And yet, even if these methods are used by adopting an interpretive stance, they would not be considered to be PSMs.

Similarly, the notion that PSMs are designed to tackle messy rather than tame problems is also problematic as a means of characterisation. Defining a problem as messy or tame always depends on who is doing the formulation. Indeed, seasoned OR practitioners and their clients would certainly be able to tame a messy problem (or formulate a tame problem as messy) to suit their particular methods, including PSMs. As Mingers and Rosenhead [112] aptly note: "the very construction of the situation as being a problem of a particular

---

[3] Mingers [108] makes a similar point.

type is a result of the process of problem structuring rather than being a given starting point" (p. 532).

There have been recent attempts to characterise PSMs in more practical ways. Yearworth and White [166] offer a set of nine testable propositions that can be applied to assess whether a given intervention can be considered to have used a PSM, even if the interventionists do not claim to have done so. An example of one of their testable propositions is 'the intervention uses systems ideas appropriate to the context and supported by systems modelling'. Although carefully crafted and grounded in literature, this framework allows for interventions that make use of 'hard' OR and systems methods in a 'soft' manner to be exemplars of PSM use, which in our view lessens the discriminatory power of the framework. Furthermore, whilst the language used in the propositions aligns well with systems-based PSMs, there are many PSMs that are not systems-based and thus the language of systems would be less appropriate to describe them. Similarly, Smith and Shaw [153] propose a set of 13 questions that can be used to determine if a given approach could be a PSM. This framework is also carefully formulated and supported by literature. However, several of the questions are related to the 'products' (see Sect. 23.4) claimed by PSMs (e.g. learning), which are aspects more related to PSM evaluation than actual characterisation.

Here, we provide a simpler (but hopefully useful) characterisation of PSMs based on their similarities in terms of available tools and the processes of applying them. We will leave the treatment of PSM products for a later discussion in the chapter. The characteristics listed in Table 23.2 are those which have been claimed for PSMs by OR scholars in relation to their use with stakeholder groups within and across organisations [53, 65, 140, 153].

Before we discuss PSM tools and processes in more depth, a short clarification of central terms may be helpful to the reader. First, the term 'problem structuring' will be used here to refer to any PSM-supported activity that adds clarity to the current situation, the desired situation, or actions to get from one to the other. This may, for instance, include activities for identifying different problem elements such as issues, uncertainties, stakeholders, and the relationships between these elements. As all PSMs are intended to facilitate agreements to act [52], a PSM-supported problem structuring activity will also include the identification of actions to tackle the problem of concern.[4] Second, and related to problem structuring, is the term 'frame',[5] which is

---

[4] Incidentally, many PSM pioneers reject the label 'PSMs' as it gives the (wrong) impression that the methods are only about structuring problems in a narrow sense [32, 53, 75].

[5] A related and frequently used concept is 'mental model'. In System Dynamics this term is typically used to refer to a person's understanding of a complex issue he or she is involved in. Doyle and

Table 23.2 PSM characteristics in terms of tools and process—based on Rosenhead and Mingers [140]

Tools	Process

• Model-based, where models are:
  – amenable to formal analysis of relationships
  – requisite
  – expressed in visual/diagrammatic form, and with reduced quantitative data requirements
  – transparent and accessible
• Open technology to support model building
	• Group-based
	• Participative
	• Facilitated
	• Iterative
	• Interactive
	• Phased
	• Non-Linear

widely used across various disciplines to refer to the sense-making devices that aid in organising and classifying our experiences of the world [20, 36, 60, 77, 101]. When we frame a problem situation of interest, we make use of our prior experience and knowledge to highlight one possible (but limited) view of that situation over other possible views. Our chosen frames will influence what we see or expect to see, and thus guide our responses to the problem situation. Consequently, when a stakeholder group engages in problem structuring , multiple problem frames will be exchanged and shared among those involved. Typically, the creation of an agreed problem frame will be needed to ensure stakeholder groups can make progress.

23.2.1 PSM Tools

The core tools available with PSMs are all model-based. According to Pidd [132], a model is "an external and explicit representation of part of reality as seen by the people who wish to use that model to understand, to change, to manage and to control that part of reality" (p. 12). This interpretation of part of reality includes cognitions, values, and expectations and may include elements of the present as well as the desired or ideal situation. As with the case of models developed with traditional OR methods, PSM models are amenable to formal analysis of relationships[6] of various types,

---

Ford [42] state that "A mental model of a dynamic system is a relatively enduring and accessible, but limited, internal conceptual representation of an external system (historical, existing or projected) whose structure is analogous to the perceived structure of that system" (p. 414).

[6] Some PSMs also offer explicit means of analysing uncertainties. In traditional OR models, the uncertainty about future values of a factor of interest is handled by deriving probability distributions across its possible values. By contrast, PSM models focus on the 'possibility' and implications of an uncertain event deemed to be important enough by the group to enter their deliberations [140].

namely, relationships between concepts, activities or stakeholders; relationships of similarity or influence; and relationships between options. Especially significant is the analysis of cause-and-effect relationships through which the different elements that make up the problem situation are identified. By enabling the analysis of relationships, PSM models and modelling are thought to help group members to 'look beneath the surface' by exchanging and sharing their individual problem frames. The use of models is thus the defining characteristic of these methods, which gives them their unambiguous OR identity [53, 66].[7]

The type of models built with PSMs are said to be requisite [127]. This means that they contain sufficient knowledge and information to help group members find a way forward. For instance, although considering the entire 'solution space' is in principle of interest as there is no single optimal solution to the problem at hand, the set of all possible solutions would be unmanageable large. Consequently, PSM models limit their scope at any time to a set of discrete 'solutions' or options for action selected using different screening procedures [76, 93]. By concentrating on a few significant discrete options (which may change during the analysis), PSM models seek to help stakeholder groups to handle the complexity of their problem situation.

PSM models are expressed in visual, diagrammatical form, and thus have reduced or no quantitative data requirements. Among the numerous examples of PSM models are: cognitive maps [26], soft systems models [33], decision graphs [76], causal loop diagrams [163], and means-ends objectives networks [93]. Furthermore, it has been claimed that diagrammatical methods are of particular value in representing complexity to lay audiences who might otherwise find traditional OR means of handling complexity opaque [52, 140]. In PSM models there is supposed to be nothing hidden, which makes them transparent (i.e. easy to understand) and accessible (i.e. simple to use).

Indeed, these attributes of transparency and accessibility have made it possible for some PSM scholars to promote PSMs as open technology

---

[7] It is worth noting that some prominent PSM scholars consider other cognate approaches as falling within the PSM family, though they do not use models and modelling in the sense described above [108]. However, whilst it is possible to support problem structuring without the type of models described here, we believe that the use of models amenable to formal analysis of relationships is a shared characteristic that locates all PSMs firmly and unequivocally within OR. PSMs are sometimes referred to as Soft OR approaches, a loosely defined term to indicate any use of OR that pays attention to the non-quantitative elements of a problem or uses traditional quantitative OR methods in a 'soft' way. Thus Soft OR would include, for example, approaches such as Interactive Planning [12] and Strategic Assumptions Surfacing and Testing [103], as well as particular forms of multimethodology [111] that combine hard and soft methods. In this chapter, however, we will stick to the term 'PSMs' as it is more sharply defined and firmly located within OR.

approaches [76]. This characteristic is aptly expressed in the settings and tools used for building PSM models: a room spacious enough for participants to move around freely and with movable chairs laid out in a horse-shoe fashion; large sheets of paper attached to the walls of the room; a simple, non-permanent means of sticking notes to these paper sheets; and a good supply of marker pens with contrasting colours are all that is usually needed for a PSM modelling session [45, 82, 88]. This suggests that PSM modelling is technically a relatively unsophisticated activity conducted in a workshop format.[8]

23.2.2 PSM Process

The aim of PSMs is to aid groups of stakeholders in coming to agreement on the nature of a problem situation they face so that progress can be made. This is because in a situation where there is a plurality of actors with different perspectives and interests, high levels of complexity , uncertainty, and conflict will be experienced by those involved and this needs to be managed. Consequently, unless the problem situation is resolved by an exercise of power, stakeholders will need to find an effective way to develop appropriate responses to the problem and commitment to the way forward [140].

When group members participate in a PSM process, they openly exchange their different frames about the problem situation that is being structured [62]. The PSM process is claimed to be participative in the sense that group members are able to jointly construct the problem situation, make sense of it, arrive at a shared problem definition, and develop a portfolio of options relevant to the problem so defined [140]. This participatory process is facilitated by external professionals [72, 122, 130, 148].

It has also been argued that the PSM process is interactive and phased [140]. Interactive because it requires interaction between the group and the model-supported analysis, and between the group members; this former interaction reshapes the analysis, and the analysis reshapes the group discussions. Phased in the sense that they are organised into stages or modes, which makes it possible for the users of the method to conclude without passing through all the stages that compose it, and still have a visible product which can be of use to them (more on the products of PSMs later). As Eden [44] argues, the characteristic 'phased-ness' of PSMs is a direct consequence of

---

[8] Some PSMs do, however, use software [4] and web technologies [167] to support their modelling processes.

acknowledging that participants in a stakeholder group will consider the prac-
ticality and political feasibility of possible actions [33, 51] at the same time
as the problem is formulated.[9] Finally, the process is claimed to be iterative,
because it is possible to cycle between the stages and thus the process can
be repeated until the problem situation is satisfactorily structured so that the
group feels sufficiently confident in making commitments to actions.

What have been described in the preceding sections are the typical shared
characteristics of the family of PSMs as a whole, though individual methods
may vary with respect to these in certain respects. Methods with these characteristics have been designed for one-off uses in particular problem situations.
And even those methods that have achieved a considerable weight of applications are commonly employed in creative variants that take account of local
circumstances. However, description and critique have naturally concentrated
on the more standard forms of the principal methods that arguably have trig-
gered the rise of PSMs as a recognised field of activity [3]. These methods
are: Strategic Options Development and Analysis [5, 56] and its development
Journey Making [6, 51], Soft Systems Methodology [30, 33], and Strategic
Choice Approach [76]. Following our preceding characterisation, and considering the number of published accounts of their use in practice (see next
section), we propose a slightly extended set of methods from that contained
in Rosenhead and Mingers [140] that can be considered PSMs.[10] These are
listed in Table 23.3.

23.3   The Use of PSMs in Practice

In this section we provide a short account of the practical application of PSMs
in two complementary ways. First, short descriptions of a small number of

---

[9] Built into some PSMs are features whose purpose is to enable participants to distance themselves
from previous bindings during the problem structuring process, effectively providing them with
a certain degree of ambiguity or 'equivocality' regarding their own positions [46]. This is often
facilitated by the possibility of group members entering their inputs to the model anonymously,
which can allow them to change their positions in response to what they have learned about the
problem without destroying the social order in the group [46]. Changing positions implies individuals
'changing their minds', i.e. changed beliefs, changed values, and changes in the salience of particular
issues or values [44]. The consequence of this adaptability is that it becomes easier for group members
to reconcile the position they eventually take both with principles and with past words and actions
during discussion.

[10] The list has similarities to the one proposed by Mingers [108], although we have not included
methods that do not build and use models (as defined here) in a facilitated mode. We also excluded
other facilitated modelling methods that would fit the characterisation presented here but which do
not have yet a substantive volume of applications published in the mainstream OR literature—see,
for example, Conklin's [35] Dialog Mapping and Ritchey's Morphological Analysis [138].

Table 23.3 Major PSMs—based on Mingers [108]

PSM	Starting point	Modelling	Developing a way forward	Key reference
Strategic Options Development and Analysis (SODA)-Journey Making (JM)/Causal Mapping (CM)	Elicitation of individuals' perceptions of the issues of concern in their own language	Psychological constructs and their interrelations captured through cognitive/causal mapping and analysed visually or with special purpose software	Identification and prioritisation of a portfolio of actions intended to resolve or alleviate issues while contributing to the achievement of goals	Eden and Ackermann [51]; Ackermann and Eden [5]
Soft Systems Methodology (SSM)	Elicitation of individuals' perceptions of the current problem situation in pictures	Models of 'ideal' human activity systems developed through the use of rich pictures, root definitions and systems models	Discussion of the differences between models of the ideal situation and the perceived current situation, leading to the identification of actions to improve the situation	Checkland and Scholes [33]
Group Model Building (GMB)	Elicitation of individuals' perceptions of the current problem situation in terms of variables and graphs of behaviour over time	Models that depict cause-effect relations between variables, which combine into feedback loops that are seen as the core structural drivers of problem behaviour	Identification of control variables (levers) that, via feedback loops, impact goal variables (performance indicators) in the right direction	Vennix [164]

(continued)

Table 23.3 (continued)

PSM	Starting point	Modelling	Developing a way forward	Key reference
Strategic Choice Approach (SCA)	Elicitation of individuals' perceptions of all the decisions concerning the current problem situation in graphs	Decision graphs and option graphs are used to develop a feasible set of interconnected options, which are then evaluated against a set of comparison areas which bring key uncertainties to the surface	Development of a commitment package comprising actions and explorations to be implemented now, as well as actions to be taken in the future	Friend and Hickling [76]
Value Focused Thinking (VFT)/ Decision Conferencing (DC)	Elicitation of individuals' values concerning the current decision of concern in the language of objectives	Means-ends objective networks are used to identify the set of fundamental objectives relevant to the decision problem being addressed, leading to the development of high-value options	Identification or development of measurements for achieving fundamental objectives, together with elicitation of preferences for different levels of achievement, and of value-trade-offs	Keeney [93, 94]; Phillips [128]; Phillips and Bana e Costa [129]
Viable System Model (VSM)[11]	Elicitation of individual's perceptions of how a relevant organisational system of interest functions in terms of its long-term sustainability	Characterisation of the situation of interest in terms of a viable system, comprising five systemic functions and two types of regulation	Identification of organisational changes to strengthen systemic functions and regulations	Beer [18]; Espejo and Reyes [58]; Espinosa and Walker [59]

[11] Although the VSM was originally developed with a prescriptive orientation (see, for example, Jackson [90]), an increasing body of published VSM applications show practitioners using the method in an interpretivist mode akin to PSM use, namely, they work with stakeholder groups to understand disfunctions in the system of interest, identify suitable responses to improve its effectiveness and viability, and help stakeholders in building a commitment to implementation (see Harwood [80]).

PSM	Starting point	Modelling	Developing a way forward	Key reference
Robustness Analysis	Identification of individual's commitments at present, in a situation of uncertainty, and comparing these to the future range of commitments with which they are compatible (number of options left open, flexibility)	Characterisation of relations between decision points and between decision points and end states, in combination with both system models of various kinds and cognate methods to identify alternative possible futures	Models are used to determine which possible system configurations perform acceptably in particular futures; atrices capture the relative accessibility of acceptable configurations from alternative initial decisions	Rosenhead and Mingers [140]; Wong [165]
Drama Theory	Representation of a conflictive situation involving different players and their interacting decisions	Characterisation of the main elements that determine interaction between participants (common reference scheme, positions and fallbacks, dilemmas) and its results (crisis, conflict, commitment, cooperation), option boards specifying each participant's position, fallback and default future	A set of players, their options and possible strategies are captured by developing a 'card table' and exploring the stability of solutions by analysing the different potential dilemmas faced by the players	Bennett and Huxham [19]; Bryant [24]; Howard [85, 86]

varied applications will be provided, in order to shed further light on what these methods can do in practice. Second, published survey evidence and academic reviews will be summarised, to capture actual use and the range and distribution of PSM applications.

23.3.1   Sample of PSM applications

In this section we sketch the process and products of three applications of PSMs. These applications are explicitly chosen to reflect the divergent contexts and ways in which the approaches are used. The examples cover systemic risk elicitation [10], public strategic planning [17], and child protection services [97].

The paper by Ackermann et al. [10] describes part of the Northern Isles New Energy Solutions (NINES) project. NINES aims to inform the design of a new power station for the Shetlands Islands, by assessing different energy generation portfolios and smart grid technologies in the light of current and future demand for electricity. This multi-million-pound project is extremely complex and involves a range of stakeholders. The role of Ackermann et al. was to identify, structure, quantify, and assess the implications of the risks involved in the options proposed. The understanding of risks here extends beyond standard technical and financial considerations, and also includes uncertainties arising from demands and actions of stakeholders. The research team designed and facilitated three workshops, each with different audiences: the NINES researchers and project managers, Shetland islanders, and technical staff of the electricity company. Participants were chosen in consultation with NINES project members and depending on availability on planned workshop days. The process followed in the workshops was supported by the use of Group Explorer,[12] a computer system that supports the implementation of the causal mapping technique (part of SODA), and enables the construction and utilisation of causal maps in a team environment. Each workshop followed roughly the same agenda: generation of risks (which were directly grouped into clusters by the facilitator), identification of relations between risks, and identification of priorities. Workshops had between eight and 16 participants, lasted four to five hours, and generated as much as 200 contributions each. The setup of the workshops included a computer console for each pair of participants, allowing them to contribute ideas, means-ends relations, and priorities in parallel, and see the results on a shared screen. A

---

[12] Group Explorer was originally developed by Colin Eden and Fran Ackermann at the University of Strathclyde.

round of interviews was held to gather additional input. As they were generated by different participant groups, the three resulting maps were analysed
separately and no attempt was made to integrate them. Across the maps,
clusters of highly interrelated risks were identified which pointed management to areas in which one risk could exacerbate another, and thus addressing
them in isolation would be less effective. On the basis of clusters and recurrent themes a prioritised agenda for risk management was provided to the
client organisation. Participants in particular valued the comprehensiveness
of the analysis, the consideration of relations between risks rather than seeing
them as independent, and the inclusion of different stakeholder groups in the
process.

Bana e Costa et al. [17] report on a project with the State Department
of Social Development and Human Rights (SESDH), part of the State of
Pernambuco in northeast Brazil. The aim was to develop a multi-annual
plan for the 2008–2011 period. Sessions were organised in the form of decision conferences and integrated various methods, in the main group causal
mapping (part of SODA) and multi-criteria decision analysis, supported by
value-focused thinking, analysis of interconnected decision areas (AIDA, part
of Strategic Choice Approach), strategic graphs and portfolio analysis. A total
of 30 participants took part in facilitated meetings, grouped into two separate work teams: a technical team bringing together representatives of the
SESDH's planning and budget units, and a decision-making team consisting
of secretaries, directors and superintendents of each administrative unit in
SESDH. After a first meeting attended by both teams, the technical team
continued into a three-day meeting aimed at structuring objectives, designing
actions and organising these into programmes, and identifying factual information on the contribution of programmes to objectives. The meeting of the
technical team started with listing ideas on Pernambuco's mission on post-it
notes. These were then clustered and by the end of the second day resulted
in a means-ends map in Decision Explorer.[13] The third day was spent on
clustering actions into intervention programmes. Following the principles
of AIDA, compatibilities and incompatibilities between actions were visualised. After coherent intervention programmes were formed, the technical
team organised factual information on the contribution of the programmes
to objectives. Both teams then met again, after which the decision-making
team took the lead in the next phase assisted by the technical team. Decision
makers in the next two days chose three fundamental objectives and validated

---

[13] Decision Explorer is a software tool to support the creation of causal maps. It is developed and
distributed by Banxia Software (www.banxia.com).

programmes. This laid the foundation for an evaluation of the contribution of programmes to objectives, weighing objectives, assessing doability of programmes and ultimately prioritisation of programmes. In formulating and weighing objectives, decision makers were supported by MACBETH.[14] Some participants scored programmes low on benefits because they were difficult to implement. This confusion of value and difficulty of implementation led to a separate analysis of benefit versus doability, leading to the conclusion that all programmes of high benefit were to be implemented regardless of their implementation difficulty. A sensitivity analysis was performed to test if a change in weights would alter the portfolio of chosen programmes. The conclusions were included in the multi-annual plan and implemented to various degrees.

Finally, Lane et al. [97] provide an in-depth review of the child protection services in England. The UK Department for Education (DfE) formed a reference group of individuals experienced in the sector: a judge, foster mother, paediatrician, two young people with experience of the child protection system, two academics, as well as representatives of children's services and a charity. An initial analysis of published research, expert interviews and additional qualitative and quantitative evidence indicated an addiction to compliance. The result was captured in a causal loop diagram, showing an emphasis on creating and strengthening procedures, generating a balancing loop aimed at error correction. This however limits the social worker's scope for using their professional judgement in working with children and families. In addition, learning by recognising and examining errors was replaced largely by avoiding the acknowledgement of errors and hiding behind procedures. The systems map was included in a first review report, which resonated widely within the sector. As a result, a series of facilitated meetings were held following a GMB format. Participants with a background in policy, practice, or academia were invited to participate and civil servants of the DfE gathered relevant qualitative and quantitative data on child protection services in England and other countries. An analysis of the diagram in terms of balancing and reinforcing loops allowed participants to see the ripple effects of compliance, as well as identifying why measures such as a Serious Case Review[15] do not result in allowing the system to improve its functioning again. Further discussions with the reference group and among the researchers involved led

---

[14] MACBETH is a software tool that supports the evaluation of options when multiple objectives need to be considered. It was originally developed by Carlos Bana e Costa at the University of Lisbon (m-macbeth.com).

[15] Serious Case Reviews (SCRs) were established in the UK under the 2004 Children Act to review cases where a child has died and abuse or neglect is known or suspected. SCRs could additionally be carried out where a child has not died, but has come to serious harm as a result of abuse or neglect.

to the formulation of 15 recommendations. These were directed at social workers, children's services, and other agencies involved in child protection and in the main aimed to create a child protection service that functions as a learning organisation, with a continued building of professional expertise and better ability to support safety and welfare of children. The Government's response was positive: 10 recommendations were accepted in full, five in principle and timescales for implementation were specified.

23.3.2 Evidence of Use and Applications

Published practical applications of PSMs have grown steadily over time, as evidenced in recent surveys of the field [1, 78, 136], although Mingers [108] notes that the bulk of applications is probably larger as most published accounts are written by OR scholars rather than practitioners. Below we start with a discussion of published surveys that cover the use of PSMs, before considering published academic reviews of their practical applications.

23.3.2.1 Surveys of PSM use in practice

Earlier published surveys into the use of PSMs focused on SSM. Mingers and Taylor [113] surveyed practitioners and academics in the UK with very high exposure to SSM, whereas Ledington and Donaldson [100] surveyed practitioners in Australia with lower levels of exposure to the method. Yet, both surveys report similar results, with the most common benefit attributed to the use of SSM being improved understanding and learning. In addition, the majority of respondents in both surveys evaluated their use of SSM as successful, although no objective criteria were provided for this evaluation. Another early survey evaluated PSM use indirectly by paying attention to the practice of multimethodology. Munro and Mingers [116] conducted a survey covering the combined use of PSMs, as well as their combination with other OR and non-OR methods. Like in the earlier surveys, practitioners reported their use of PSMs as successful albeit without an operational definition of success.

More recent surveys have examined the use of PSMs in specific areas. For example, O'Brien [117] surveyed OR practitioners in the UK to investigate the use of PSMs in strategic planning, which arguably is a natural domain of application given that strategic problems can be considered messy problems. The survey results indicate that whilst many traditional OR techniques are used to support the strategy process, PSMs are not regularly used despite practitioners being aware of these methods. A more positive picture is given by Ranyard et al. [136], who report the use of various OR techniques (including PSMs) in a survey commissioned by the International Federation of OR Societies (IFORS). Three methods, SODA, SSM, and Strategic Choice are reported as being used fairly regularly in the UK, but much less frequently in the rest of the world. The IFORS survey evidence confirms a gradual increase in the use of PSMs over time in the UK, though diffusion elsewhere remains low.

23.3.2.2   Academic Reviews of PSM Applications

A number of OR scholars have conducted literature reviews that focused on the application of particular PSMs. For example, Van der Water et al. [161] surveyed the published literature on SSM and found ecology and environment, and information and communication technology, as the main areas of application. Mingers and White [114] also surveyed SSM applications as part of their review of the use of systems-based approaches published in OR and non-OR journals from the mid-1990s to the late 2000s. They identified health, environment and agriculture, and supply chain, production, and project management as the main areas represented in SSM applications. Parnell et al. [123] surveyed VFT applications in selected OR journals from 1992 to 2010, and found that government and military were the most common problem domains of application. As part of an examination of the potential role of PSMs in the problem formulation stage of a simulation study, Powell and Mustafee [135] review published applications of SSM in healthcare. Of the 49 papers they selected to review, only eight papers reported an actual SSM application. Abuabara and Paucar-Caceres [1] surveyed published applications of SODA from 1989 to 2018 in OR and non-OR journals. They found a growing interest in SODA over the period of analysis, with applications reported in many sectors. Most areas where SODA had been used partially, fully or in combination with other methods included strategic management, sustainable development, information systems, and performance evaluation. Notably, only a very small proportion of the reported applications (less than ten per cent) involve facilitated model-supported workshops. Abuabara and Paucar-Caceres suggest the lack of facilitation skills as a barrier to deploy SODA in practice as originally intended.

Other OR scholars have undertaken broader reviews of PSMs applications. Mingers [107] surveyed reported PSMs applications published during the

1990s in reputable, peer-reviewed journals. The review covered applications of PSMs[16] used in isolation or in combination with other methods. The main areas of application were organisational design, planning, IS/IT, and health services. The partial or full use of SSM was quite common in these applications. Similarly, Marttunen et al. [102] surveyed the peer-reviewed literature covering the 2000–2015 period, reporting on the combined use of problem structuring approaches with multi-criteria decision analysis (MCDA) methods. Interestingly, the most popular combinations with MCDA methods did not include any of the PSMs listed in Table 23.3. The most recent review of PSMs at the time of writing was undertaken by Gomes Jr and Schramm [78], who surveyed an eclectic mix of journals covering articles published between 2010 and 2020. They found that PSMs were used to support the management of problems affecting businesses, society, healthcare services, and the environment. SSM was noted as the most frequently used PSM in these applications.

We conducted a cursory review of PSM applications published in the relevant OR literature during the 2010–2020 period. We used Web of Science (WOS) to search for applications published in the following mainstream OR journals: European Journal of the Operational Research, Journal of the Operational Research Society, and Omega. We did not survey US-based OR journals such as Management Science or Operations Research because they do not recognise Soft OR and PSMs as a legitimate part of OR [108] (but for a notable exception, see Dyson et al. [43]). We also surveyed two journals in which PSM scholars regularly publish their work: Group Decision and Negotiation, and Systems Research and Behavioral Science. Finally, we also included System Dynamics Review and Decision Analysis, because these journals are a natural home for PSMs such as GMB and VFT. We used various search terms including 'problem structuring methods', 'soft OR', and the names of each of the PSMs listed in Table 23.3. We need to emphasise that we did not intend to produce a comprehensive review of PSM applications as previous OR scholars have done (see above). We just wanted to give the reader a rough idea of the body of PSM applications published in selected journals over the last decade.

Our search criteria produced a total of 143 papers for initial analysis. After reading the abstracts we identified papers reporting PSM applications with actual stakeholder groups seeking assistance. If an abstract did not make this clear, we then read the whole paper to assess its suitability. We thus excluded papers reporting 'desktop' applications in which authors use PSMs to analyse

---

[16] The list of PSMs included in Mingers [107] also considered problem methods that do not use models as defined here.

a problem situation as outsiders, but without the involvement of an actual stakeholder group requesting support[17] [25, 95, 152]. Table 23.4 collates a corpus of 50 papers identified from our brief review of the selected literature. It shows the sector in which PSMs were used, the specific areas of application, split into several categories, the OR methods used, and the associated reference.

Several products have been claimed to be the result of the use of PSMs by stakeholder groups. The intended products of PSMs and the mechanisms claimed to facilitate their achievement, together with supporting evidence of their attainment after PSM use, are discussed in the following section.

23.4 PSM Products, Mechanisms, Supporting Evidence

23.4.1 Claimed Products and Facilitative Mechanisms

Table 23.5 displays those products that have been claimed for PSMs by numerous scholars in relation to their use with single and multi-organisational stakeholder groups [52, 63, 65, 112, 140, 163]. We use the term 'products' to refer to the visible and less visible outputs that result from using a PSM [76]. These products may be generated during or at the end of the PSM process, and their actual achievement is thought to be facilitated by specific mechanisms.

The most visible and common PSM product is obviously the final model built during the PSM process, which describes the agreed problem frame. The individual frames of stakeholder group members as well as the ensuing agreed problem frame are captured during the PSM modelling process, but each PSM model will represent problem frames in different ways. In SODA, for example, the problem frame represented by the model will contain a network of statements about issues, goals, and options. In VFT/DC, the final frame will contain a decision statement expressed in terms of the alternatives to choose to achieve the fundamental objectives concerning a given decision context. In GMB, the final frame will describe the structure underlying observed behaviour, with special emphasis on feedback loops, and so on.[18]

---

[17] Papers proposing new PSMs are mentioned in Sect. 23.5.

[18] In the case of VFT/DC and GMB, the problem frame represented in the model is often used to inform the development of a quantitative model.

Table 23.4 Sample of published papers reporting practical application of PSMs (2010–2020 period)

Sector Application	Area of application	OR method	Reference
Mining, agriculture, fishing Manufacturing, food production, construction, utilities, oil refining	Environmental management Energy Engineering Construction Family business Aircraft manufacturing Textile industry	SSM+Critical Systems Heuristics CM SSM+Technology Management VSM SSM SSM+SODA+VFT SSM+Quality Management+Linear Programming	Hart et al. (2014) Ackermann et al. (2014), Small et al. (2014), Espinosa et al. (2015), Paucar-Caceres et al. (2016), Abuabara et al. (2018), Castellini and Paucar-Caceres (2019)
Services (e.g. retail, transportation, banking, supermarkets, hospitality and leisure)	Banking Sports agency Regional transportation Social credit	CM+Multi-Criteria Decision Analysis SSM+Statistics+Geographical Information Systems SSM+Critical Systems Heuristics+Causal Loop Diagrams CM+Multiple Criteria Decision Analysis	Ferreira et al. (2011), Taylor et al. (2012), Setianto et al. (2014), and Ferreira et al. (2019)
Information and communication technologies, computing, education, consultancy, research and development	University ICT ICT University University Secondary school Peace program in schools ICT University and SME	CM+Large Group Intervention methods SSM+Balance Score Card+Strategy Maps SSM+Analytic Hierarchy Process SSM VSM+Utilisation-focused evaluation GMB SSM+Interactive Planning+Critical Systems Heuristics+Statistics+ conflict resolution methods SSM+VSM VSM	Bryant et al. (2011), Liu et al. (2012), Siriram and Rajenlall (2012), Wang et al. (2015), Hart et al. (2017), Kasman et al. (2017), Pinzon-Salcedo and Torres-Cuello (2018), Donaires and Martinelli (2019), and Preece and Shaw (2019)

(continued)

Table 23.4 (continued)

Sector Application	Area of application	OR method	Reference
Health	Hospital Primary care Health services Medical training Health Sugar consumption Health services Health policy	CM+Discrete Event Simulation GMB SSM+Process Modeling+Technology Management SSM + Linear Programming GMB GMB SSM+ethnography+Discrete Event Simulation DC+Delphi method	Pessoa et al. (2015), Ansah et al. (2018), Small and Wainwright (2018), Cardoso-Grilo et al. (2019), Hosseinichimeh et al. (2019), Urwannachotima et al. (2019), Lame et al. (2020), and Vieira et al. (2020)
Government	National government Government, criminal justice Public policy Public policy, control rooms Public policy Public policy Emergency relief Project management Urban planning Urban planning Urban planning Public policy	DC VSM VFT VSM CM+DC CM+Reciprocal Expectation Analysis VSM VSM+Hierarchical Process Modelling CM+Multi Criteria Decision Analysis SCA CM SSM+SCA+Situational Strategic Planning	Morton et al. (2011), Brocklesby (2012), Keeney (2012), Preece et al. (2015), Bana E Costa et al. (2014), Kato et al. (2014), Preece et al. (2015), Lowe et al. (2016), Ferreira et al. (2018), Todella et al. (2018), Pyrko et al. (2019), and Paucar-Caceres et al. (2020)

Sector Application	Area of application	OR method	Reference
Sustainability and community	Maritime sustainability Eco-community Food cooperative Indigenous community Indigenous community Local community Community organisations Access to healthy food Social capital Energy transition	GMB VSM VSM SSM VSM SSM VFT+ethnography SSM SSM VFT	Videira et al. (2012), Espinosa and Walker (2013), Tavella et al. (2017), Brocklesby et al. (2018), Espinosa and Duque (2018), Mirijamdotter et al. (2018), Mwiti and Goulding (2018), Wang et al. (2018), Weaver et al. (2018), and Hofer et al. (2020)

The full list of references listed in Table 23.4 is available from the authors upon request

Table 23.5 Products claimed for PSMs, with accompanying facilitative mechanisms—based on Rosenhead and Mingers [140], Vennix [163], and Franco [66]

Mechanisms	Claimed less visible products	Claimed visible products
• Taxonomy	• Improved communication	• Final model containing agreed problem frame
• Model as recording device	• Increased shared understanding	• Action plan to address the problem (typically in the form of 'partial commitments')
• Model as transitional object	• Accommodation of conflicting positions and interests	
• Model as boundary object	• New knowledge and cognitive change	
• Facilitated, participative modelling process	• Consensus on, and ownership of, final problem frame and action plan	
	• Commitment to support implementation of action plan	

Although it is possible to use PSMs only for structuring the problem, all PSMs are intended to facilitate agreements to act[19] [52, 53]. Consequently, a second visible product of a PSM intervention takes the form of an action plan or list of planned actions to tackle the problem. Actions plans are usually expressed as what Friend and Hickling call a 'commitment package' [76], which contains a mix of espoused or recommended decisions, policies, or research explorations, and which may or may not include supporting argumentation derived from the PSM model. Typically, action plans represent only partial commitments on the part of the stakeholder group because, it is argued, the only way to make progress in conditions of complexity, uncertainty, and conflict is by adopting an incremental approach and thus working on a less comprehensive solution [51, 74, 140].

The agreed problem frame and action plan are the consequence of achieving six less visible yet critical products during the PSM process: improved communication; increased shared understanding of the problem; accommodation of conflicting positions and interests; new knowledge and cognitive change; consensus on, and ownership of, the final problem frame and action plan; and, commitment to support implementation of the proposed action plan.

---

[19] See also, Footnote 4.

The achievement of these less visible products is thought to be facilitated by specific PSM mechanisms. First, the PSM model is built using a specific taxonomy (e.g. issues, goals, and actions in SODA; the CATWOE, RD, and 5Es mnemonics in SSM; decision, comparison and uncertainty areas in SCA; stock and flow variables in GMB). By using these taxonomies as a shared language to talk and think about the problem of concern, it is argued that communicative exchanges are more comprehensive and accurate because participants are able to better specify their different perspectives, dependencies, and knowledge about the problem [14, 62, 66], which results in an improved communication among those involved. Second, because PSM models can also act as recording devices that enable us to survey and trace content of group discussions 'on-the-hoof' [66], it is argued that PSM models can increase our ability to process and monitor large and complex information, which is another way to facilitate and improve communication within the stakeholder group.

Third, better specification of group members' views, dependencies, and knowledge is also thought to be facilitated by the PSM model acting as a transitional object [38, 52, 175] to experiment with problem structure. This means that through the analysis of relationships embedded in problem structure and the direct inputs of group members the model is constantly changing, which is thought to increase their shared understanding of the problem situation, of organisational processes and cultures, and of others' beliefs and values. Such increased understanding is also taken to be conducive to new knowledge and cognitive change (e.g. learning) [30, 31, 66, 76].

Fourth, increased shared understanding and learning can make particular perspectives, knowledge, and interests more salient and at stake, which generates conflict within the stakeholder group. If the conflict stays at the cognitive level, then it is claimed that the mutual exploration of problem structure as portrayed by the model as transitional object will further facilitate the creation of new knowledge, achieve cognitive change (i.e. people changing their minds), and develop consensus on, and ownership of, the final problem frame and the recommendations for action [46, 140].

However, group members' anticipations of the consequences, perceived or real, of their increased understanding and learning can sometimes escalate to a relational level [57], especially in situations characterised by complexity and uncertainty. Such conflict will commonly require group members to reach an accommodation regarding their positions and interests [30, 31], which is thought to be facilitated if the model, as a transitional object , also becomes a boundary object [21, 22, 28, 66] during group members' interactions. A model acts as a boundary object only if it is able to help group members defuse their entrenched positions and develop common interests. Achieving these accommodations[20] also facilitates new knowledge creation, cognitive change, consensus and ownership and, in addition, 'cognitive' and 'emotional' commitment [46, 140] to support the implementation of action plans.[21] Group members' active engagement in the PSM facilitated participative modelling process is also argued to produce strong ownership and commitment [71, 140].

23.4.2   Supporting Empirical Evidence

What has been described in the preceding section are the typical products and accompanying facilitative mechanisms claimed for PSMs as a whole, although individual PSMs may vary with respect to these in certain ways. What evidence is there, then, of the actual achievement of these products in the field? Looking at the number of PSM applications listed in Table 23.4 alone, it would be tempting to take it as a strong indication of supporting evidence. However, the justifications of the products claimed to have been achieved by using PSMs are often based on the personal reflections of those conducting the interventions. For example, in the case of GMB applications, Rouwette et al. [145] note that out of 107 applications, 88 gather evaluation data in the main through observation that informs personal reflection. And although we cannot disregard the reflections of highly experienced PSM scholars and practitioners, we should exercise caution: personal reflections alone are not reliable evidence of PSM impacts. In the few cases where questionnaires or interviews have been used to support the evaluation of PSM applications, very few or no details are given on the recruitment of the sample of respondents and interviewees, the impact of the sample on data collection, or the data analysis approach employed.[22] Similarly, previous surveys and academic reviews of PSMs (see Sect. 23.3.2) report high levels of satisfaction by users of PSMs, but no evidence is offered as to why users were satisfied. Overall, then, there is clearly a role for more formal, systematic evaluations of the actual achievement of claimed PSM products in the field [106, 146, 169].

However, systematic evaluations are rather scarce in the literature. For example, we searched for PSM evaluation studies in the same selected journals

---

[20] Accommodations between group members may also require coalition forming [44, 48, 54], which may produce a shift in power relations during the PSM process [46].

[21] In specific contexts, commitment to maintain the group membership has also been claimed [41].

[22] It is also worth noting that self-reports as a sole basis of evaluations are fraught with difficulties, as people struggle to distinguish between subjective and objective effects associated with PSM use [39, 142].

(see Section 23.3.2.2), but for the 20-year period between 2000 and 2020, and only found twelve studies that assessed whether the PSM products listed in Table 23.5 had been realised after PSM use. Notably, almost all studies evaluated GMB interventions. The remaining study evaluated DC interventions. Overall, evaluation studies of practical GMB interventions [142, 145, 149] provide some evidence for a positive impact on communication, cognitive change (learning), consensus, commitment and changes in behaviour, and implementation of results. Recent studies [39, 160] lend further support to an effect on consensus and alignment. However, it has proven difficult to reproduce these results in controlled environments [104]. For the case of DC interventions, Schilling et al. [147] use questionnaire data in six cases and found a positive effect on commitment and group alignment.

One of the earlier arguments against conducting systematic evaluations of PSM interventions was based on the notion that any approach to PSM evaluation must fit the complexity of the intervention because PSMs are complex technologies dealing with messy problems [47, 49, 50, 61]. This would render the use of an experimental approach to evaluation less appropriate. This does not mean that the need for PSM evaluation has dwindled within the PSM community. Indeed, now it is widely accepted that claims about the achievement of PSM products cannot only be based on self-reflective or impressionistic accounts of PSM intervention success [e.g. 154] or failure [e.g. 84], but also on empirically grounded evaluations [e.g. 64, 172].

Two approaches to non-experimental PSM evaluation have emerged in recent years. One approach is based on the development and use of an evaluation framework that relates the mechanisms of PSMs and their claimed products, and takes into account the context and purpose of the PSM intervention being evaluated. An example is the framework developed by Midgley and colleagues [106], which is based on the tradition of multi-method systemic intervention [91, 105, 110]. Another one is the meta-framework proposed by Donais et al. [40],[23] which draws from Chess' [34] environmental public participation framework. Whether these frameworks will be taken up by PSM scholars and practitioners is an open question, but the advantage of using an evaluation framework is clear for at least two reasons. First, an evaluation framework can inform the development of suitable questionnaires to elicit participants' views before and after the intervention [89], which can then be analysed to produce quantitative evidence of the achievement of PSM products from the perspective of those involved. Second,

---

[23] Although this meta-framework focuses on evaluating MCDA interventions, the framework could also be applied to evaluate PSM interventions.

repeated use of an evaluation framework can help build a corpus of accumulated evidence from different PSM evaluation studies, and subsequently inform the design of further evaluation studies that could add to the corpus of evidence.

The second approach is theory-based, and stems from the need to understand why the products claimed for PSMs were achieved (or not) in a particular application context. A theory-based approach could use an established theory in a 'top-down' fashion to analyse the data generated from the intervention to assess the actual achievement of PSM products. A good example is the study by Rouwette and colleagues [144], who use Ajzen's [13] Theory of Planned Behavior to evaluate seven GMB interventions. Overall, they found that GMB changed participants' attitudes, subjective norms, and intentions, each of which can be related to participants' problem frames, consensus, and commitment, respectively. Alternatively, a theory-based approach could analyse the data generated from the intervention to build a theory 'bottom-up'. Theories developed in this way can provide a locally meaningful evaluation based on how participants make sense of the intervention in which they are engaged [81]. Some PSM scholars argue that bottom-up explanations must also fit into the broader patterns of interactions within which the PSM intervention is embedded [172]. In this way, a 'mid-range' theory [125] can be built to explain why the PSM intervention products were realised (or not), and for whom. Such theory also recognises that using the same PSM intervention in one situation may work, but it may not work in another situation [66, 172].

It is our contention that the framework-based and theory-based approaches to PSM evaluation should be seen as being complementary rather than as competing or opposite. Combining the insights generated from the two approaches can provide a richer understanding of the actual achievement of PSM products than any one approach can provide by itself.

Finally, it is worth noting there is very little written about the impacts of PSMs beyond the intervention. For example, we know little about whether the use of PSMs can be linked to positive organisational change or performance. Indeed, the most cited textbook on PSMs [139] and its revised edition [140] steer away from claiming long-term PSM intervention impacts and, instead, focus mostly on PSM products within the intervention (see Table 23.5). This is not to say that PSMs cannot contribute to long-term impacts. Indeed, the high-profile cases by Ormerod at Sainsbury [118, 119] and by Eden and colleagues at Bombardier [8, 170] are a testimony that PSMs can indeed make a tangible and significant difference to organisations beyond the intervention. However, published accounts like these are rare in the literature. In a few cases, PSM scholars have gone back to stakeholder groups (or the organisations to which they belong) to identify any long-term effects following a PSM intervention [73, 81, 143]. Yet, again, these are the exception rather than the rule. Indeed, many published PSM applications do not report tangible results in terms of organisational change and improved performance. For example, the comprehensive review of SODA applications by Abuabara and Paucar-Caceres [1] indicated that SODA use has been mostly limited to achieving products within, rather than beyond, the interventions they surveyed. This should not come as a surprise: it would be very difficult to claim long-term impacts given the myriad of uncontrollable factors, both within and outside the stakeholder group using a PSM, that could affect the implementation and performance of PSM recommendations. Granted, it is plausible that for many interventions no action or change regarding the problem of concern is necessarily expected. But not being able to demonstrate the link between PSMs and long-term organisational impacts can make their dissemination and take up more difficult.

23.5 The Future of PSMs

The practical use of PSMs continues to represent an active field of activity judged by the increasing number of applications reported in the literature since PSMs were developed back in the 1970s, and the number of new methods introduced in the last decade as new PSMs [37, 79, 99, 150]. Furthermore, a wide variety of practical issues linked to PSM practice have already generated a significant amount of research since the start of the new century, from how to mix different PSMs with other methods [87, 110] to how to rigorously evaluate PSMs (see Sect. 23.4.2). However, there are still areas of work that remain critical to the future of PSMs as a field of practice and research within OR, and which deserve the continuing attention of PSM advocates. We discuss these areas in this final section, together with some suggestions for ways forward.

23.5.1 Becoming a Competent PSM Practitioner

What are the competences required to deploy PSMs in practice? In a review of the extant literature that examines PSM competences, Ormerod [120] identifies core competences under three broad headings: conducting analysis, designing and managing process, and appreciating context. Developing these competences is often best through apprenticeship, in which a novice has access to observing an expert in action, as well as applying the methods in practice. However, apprenticeship opportunities like this are not always available. Instead, university programmes that incorporate PSMs into the curriculum, as well as specialist PSM training courses offered by specialist providers, have traditionally addressed this gap. Here, there are two approaches to developing PSM competences. The first one aims to develop competences via small consulting projects with a real organisation, in which participants can have hands-on experience of using PSMs under the supervision of an academic with PSM expertise.[24] When conducting projects is a formal part of a university programme or training course, then this approach to develop PSM competences is the closest to the apprenticeship model. For example, in the European Master in System Dynamics program (www.europeansystemdynamics.eu), students take part in projects with client organisations as part of their studies.[25]

The second approach is to develop PSM competences in the classroom, but this is significantly more challenging for those teaching, and being taught, PSMs [2]. The size of the challenge will depend on the specific competences that are the target of development. For example, competence in conducting analysis requires mastery of qualitative modelling techniques, which can be developed via experiential learning [171], cases studies, and the understanding gained from textbook descriptions of various PSMs, such as those presented by Rosenhead and Mingers [140] or Reynolds and Holwell [137]. Although the use of experiential learning tasks, case studies, and textbooks cannot replicate the complex reality of PSM practice, this approach is nonetheless effective for helping novices develop a minimum level of desk-based analytic competence in PSMs. Similarly, the need to develop competences in appreciating the complexity of the context in which PSMs are deployed can somewhat be addressed by sharing the personal experiences of PSM teachers and trainers with students and trainees.[26] This could be complemented by bringing former clients into the classroom to talk about

---

[24] Ackermann [2] argues that an academic's PSM expertise can be real or vicarious. However, we would warn against the latter. Only academics with actual PSM expertise will be able to share their largely tacit, uncodified experience with their students, and in doing so help students appreciate the nuances and complexities of PSM practice, and know when and how to adapt a PSM intervention to fit the context in which it is deployed.

[25] A recent development is the OR apprenticeship approved in 2020 by the Institute for Apprenticeships and Technical Education in the UK (https://www.instituteforapprenticeships.org). The apprenticeship has not started at the time of writing. Notably, how to select and apply, a range of PSMs to understand complex problems is part of the knowledge, skills, and behaviours expected from the participants taking up the apprenticeship.

[26] Some PSMs also contain specific tools to gain an appreciation of context, for example, the use of rich pictures and analysis I, II, and III (cultural stream analysis) in SSM [31].

their experience of facing past problem situations, and discuss how useful they found PSMs in tackling those situations [2].

By contrast, developing competences in designing and managing process is significantly more challenging, particularly within the boundaries of a standard university programme or training course. This requires designing a learning environment that not only can bring the real world of PSM practice into the classroom, but also one that provides learning materials that capture the uncodified tacit knowledge of PSM experts, which is not revealed in textbooks [96]. To gain competence in designing and managing the process, the general approach seems to be engaging PSM novices in meaningful tasks in which they have a stake [2, 29], or tasks based on realistic consultancy projects [83]. Such tasks aim to provide opportunities for PSM novices to develop experience in performing tasks that are typical of PSM interventions such as, for example, preparing a proposal, interviewing, facilitating a group, presenting results, and recognising and justifying the added value brought by the use of PSMs. This is a useful approach to competence building, one that can help novices to move beyond just having desktop qualitative modelling skills and an appreciation of context.

It is worth noting that the learning tasks for competence building in the design and management of process are typically based on problems that do not exhibit the type of complexity, uncertainty, and conflict for which PSMs were developed. In addition, the scripts [9, 15] students are taught and instructed to follow to complete these tasks, are typically sanitised portrayals of real PSM practice, that is, they contain a clear and well-defined set of expected behaviours by PSM users. It is not so much that such scripts are divorced from real PSM practice. The main issue resides in their inability to capture the interactional and situated specifics of using PSMs in practice, which is an aspect certainly well known to PSM experts. In other words, scripts must be accomplished on the ground, and therefore cannot determine or prescribe what PSM users actually do in situ.

To the extent that the current approach to develop competences in designing and managing process, and its supporting learning materials, do not fully correspond to actual practice, PSM students and trainees are at a disadvantage. An approach to competence building based on real PSM practice will need to be informed by research that collects and analyses PSM practice as it is performed by experts on the ground [67, 72]. Analyses of multiple instances of recorded PSM practice can identify the actual organisation and trajectories of different PSM intervention tasks and activities, with a view to identify what works and what does not. With the knowledge accrued from these analyses it would be possible, for example, to develop facilitation role plays grounded in the actual, rather than simulated, activities of anonymised PSM facilitators. The structure of such role plays could be designed in a way that the trajectory of a given facilitated task would only be revealed after students and trainees do something at a particular point in time.[27]

23.5.2 Becoming a Competent PSM Researcher

Broadly speaking, OR practitioners conduct research in the sense of investigating a problem located within a system of interest, and using an analytic approach to solve that problem in order to improve the management of the system. This type of problem-solving research also enables OR academics to develop new methods or improve existing ones, and report these developments and their applications in peer-reviewed journals. PSM practitioners and academics are no exception to this type of research, although the use of problem and problem-solving is typically changed for problem situation and problem alleviation, respectively, to better reflect the context and purpose of PSMs. Methodology development and improvement is typically pursued via action research [55], and reporting applications of the use of PSMs in isolation or combinations with other methods is done through case studies [168].

The discussion in this section will focus on a different type of PSM research, namely, the empirical investigation of the practice of using PSMs as it happens on the ground [68]. This choice of research focus is deliberate. Research that is mostly aimed at creating or improving the methods or tools of PSMs, though important, tends to overlook the human, social and organisational challenges associated with their practical use. The latter aspects are well known to PSM practitioners, but their empirical interrogation is typically absent from published accounts of PSMs. This can only be done by examining what PSM practitioners and users actually do when they engage in a PSM intervention, which places the study of PSM practice within the domain of the behavioural and social sciences. A similar concern is shared by OR scholars working within the sub-discipline of Behavioural OR [23, 69, 70].[28] Treating PSM practice as a research problem demands specific competences that are distinct from those of mainstream PSM academics and practitioners. Here, the discussion will concentrate on what are more

---

[27] This approach to competence building has been pioneered in other professional fields such as mediation [155, 156] and education [92].

[28] It is worth clarifying that the concern of Behavioural OR scholars relates to OR practice in general, and not just PSM practice.

likely to be the main options regarding research methodology open to PSM researchers interested in studying practice, as well as the required competences for implementing these options.

First, PSM researchers can adopt the so-called variance approach [115, 134] to investigate PSM use. In general terms, variance research seeks explanations of change in terms of relationships among independent variables and dependent variables. Explanations take the form of causal statements captured in a theory-informed research model that incorporates these variables (e.g. A causes B, which causes C). The model is then tested with data generated by the PSM intervention, and the model findings are assessed in terms of their generality. The variance approach for investigating PSM use requires the implementation of quasi experimental or pre- and post-test research designs. This involves careful selection of independent variables, which might be either manipulated (e.g. method, computer support), or left untreated (e.g. experience, demographics). It also requires choosing and measuring dependent variables that act as surrogates of the products claimed for PSMs (e.g. learning, consensus). Measurements can be taken in absolute or relative terms, and can also include perceptions about intervention outcomes (e.g. commitment, confidence) and the intervention itself (e.g. satisfaction, usefulness), which can only be measured subjectively via self-reports. Variables that act as either covariates or moderators through which independent variables influence the dependent variables (e.g. conflict as moderating the relation between method and consensus) can also be included. Once information about all variables is collected, data is quantitatively analysed using a wide range of statistical techniques (e.g. analysis of variance, regression, structural equation modelling). Generally speaking, the competences that are required to conduct variance research align well with those used in typical OR investigations: review the literature and identify relevant theory, formulate hypotheses, test these empirically, and then develop a causal explanation that further specifies the theory. Indeed, the few systematic evaluation studies of PSM use discussed in the previous section adopt have adopted a variance approach. Thus competence building for undertaking variance-type research on the use of PSMs does not seem to be a critical issue.

Despite its obvious appeal to the mainstream PSM researcher, a variance approach will only produce explanations that contain a small number of variables, which will not always be applicable in cases where the overall intervention outcome is both complex and emergent. If the interest is on understanding how PSM users respond to events and circumstances within an intervention, and how their responses affect results, then PSM researchers can adopt what is known as the process approach [115, 134]. Generally speaking, process research seeks explanations of how a sequence of events leads to an outcome. Rather than using variables, a process approach considers an evolving actor (individual, group, organisation) to which events occur or who makes events happen as the unit of analysis. Process explanations provide thick narratives that account for how one event led to another, and that one to another, and so on to the final outcome [133]. Diverse and eclectic research designs are used to implement a process approach, and central to these designs is the task of identifying or reconstructing the intervention process through the analysis of activity and events taking place over time. Typically, process studies derive theory inductively from observation and ethnographic-type methods, which requires collecting and analysing large amounts of qualitative and quantitative data from which a process explanation is developed. It is also possible to test theory-informed models of the intervention process, or use theories to guide empirical observation in an abductive or retroductive mode [109], which then further specifies the theories [134]. It might be apparent that the demands placed on the PSM researcher wishing to implement a process approach are higher than if a variance approach is adopted. Specifically, becoming acquainted with theories from the social sciences, as well as gaining competence in social science research methodologies is not straightforward for the PSM researcher. Yet, the process approach has attracted growing attention of PSM scholars in recent years [7, 11, 27, 66, 67, 151, 157–159, 173, 174]. It is worth noting that not all process research presents the same challenges for those wishing to adopt it. As Brocklesby [23] notes, some types of process research represent a more feasible proposition for a wider population of PSM researchers [121]. For those interested in pursuing more complex types of process research, there are several heuristics and systems available in the non-OR literature that include both, qualitative [98, 126] and quantitative [134] process research.

23.6 Conclusion

The purpose of this chapter has been to take stock of what we know about PSMs. We noted that though the process of deploying PSMs is quite distinct from that used in mainstream OR, their model-based technology locates them firmly within the OR discipline. The chapter has documented the extent to which PSMs have been applied in practice, as well as the evidence regarding the products that are claimed to result from using PSMs. Whilst the range and variety of PSM applications is substantial, they remain limited in geographical coverage. Furthermore, evidence of PSM impacts remains patchy to date, with the notable exception of GMB evaluation studies. The chapter has also highlighted the development of PSM practice and research competences as critical to ensure the sustainability of PSMs within OR. We believe these are areas that might produce exciting further developments for the PSM field.

References

1. Abuabara, L., and Paucar-Caceres, A. 2021. Surveying applications of Strategic Options Development and Analysis (SODA) from 1989 to 2018. European Journal of Operational Research, 292(3): 1051–1065.
2. Ackermann, F. 2011. Getting messy with problems: The challenges of teaching soft OR. INFORMS Transactions on Education, 12(1): 55–64.
3. Ackermann, F. 2012. Problem structuring methods in the dock: Arguing the case for Soft OR. European Journal of Operational Research, 219(3): 652–658.
4. Ackermann, F., and Eden, C. 2001. Contrasting single user and networked group decision support systems for strategy making Group Decision and Negotiation, 10(1): 47–66.
5. Ackermann, F., and Eden, C. 2010. Strategic Options Development and Analysis. In M. Reynolds, and S. Holwell (Eds.), Systems Approaches to Managing Change: A Practical Guide: 135–190. London: Springer.
6. Ackermann, F., and Eden, C. 2011a. Making strategy: Mapping out strategic success (2nd ed.). London: Sage.
7. Ackermann, F., and Eden, C. 2011b. Negotiation in strategy making teams: Group support systems and the process of cognitive change. Group Decision and Negotiation, 20(3): 293–314.
8. Ackermann, F., Eden, C., and Williams, T. 1997. Modeling for litigation: Mixing qualitative and quantitative approaches. Interfaces, 27(2): 48–65.
9. Ackermann, F., Andersen, D. F., Eden, C., and Richardson, G. P. 2011. ScriptsMap: A tool for designing multi-method policy-making workshops. Omega, 39: 427–434.
10. Ackermann, F., Howick, S., Quigley, J., Walls, L. and Houghton, T., 2014. Systemic risk elicitation: Using causal maps to engage stakeholders and build a comprehensive view of risks. European Journal of Operational Research, 238(1): 290–299.
11. Ackermann, F., Yearworth, M., and White, L. 2018. Micro-processes in group decision and negotiation: Practices and routines for supporting decision making. Group Decision and Negotiation, 27(5): 709–713.
12. Ackoff, R. 1999. Re-Creating the Corporation: A design of organizations for the 21st century. New York: Oxford University Press.

13. Ajzen, I. 1991. The theory of planned behavior. Organizational Behavior and Human Decision Processes, 50(2): 179–211.
14. Akkermans, H. A., and Vennix, J. A. M. 1997. Client's opinions on group model building: An exploratory study. System Dynamics Review, 13(1): 3–31.
15. Andersen, D. F., and Richardson, G. 1997. Scripts for group model building. System Dynamics Review, 13(2): 107–129.
16. Andersen, D. F., Vennix, J. A. M., Richardson, G. P., and Rouwette, E. A. J. A. 2007. Group model building: problem structuring, policy simulation and decision support. Journal of the Operational Research Society, 58(5): 691–694.
17. Bana e Costa, C.A., Lourenço, J.C. Duarte, M. and Bana e Costa, J.C. 2014. A socio-technical approach for group decision support in public strategic planning: The Pernambuco PPA case. Group Decision and Negotiation, 23(1): 5–29.
18. Beer, S. 1985. Diagnosing the system for organizations: Wiley Chichester.
19. Bennett, P. G., and Huxham, C. 1982. Hypergames and what they do: a 'soft OR' approach. Journal of Operational Research Society, 33(1): 41–50.
20. Benford, R. D., and Snow, D. A. 2000. Framing processes and social movements: An overview and assessment. Annual Review of Sociology, 26(1): 611–639.
21. Black, L. J. 2013. When visuals are boundary objects in system dynamics work. System Dynamics Review, 29(2): 70–86.
22. Black, L. J., and Andersen, D. F. 2012. Using visual representations as boundary objects to resolve conflict in collaborative model-building approaches. Systems Research and Behavioral Science, 29(2): 194–208.
23. Brocklesby, J. 2016. The what, the why and the how of behavioural operational research: An invitation to potential sceptics. European Journal of Operational Research, 249(3): 796–805.
24. Bryant, J. W. 2003. The Six Dilemmas of Collaboration. Chichester: Wiley.
25. Bryant, J. 2014. Conflict Evolution: Tracking the Middle East Conflict with Drama Theory. Group Decision and Negotiation, 23(6): 1263–1279.
26. Bryson, J. M., Ackermann, F., Eden, C., and Finn, C. B. 2004. Visible Thinking: Unlocking causal mapping for practical business results. Chichester: Wiley.
27. Burger, K. 2020. Understanding participant engagement in problem structuring interventions with self-determination theory. Journal of the Operational Research Society.
28. Carlile, P. R. 2002. A pragmatic view of knowledge and boundaries: Boundary objects in new product development. Organization Science, 13: 442–455.
29. Carreras, A. L., and Kaur, P. 2011. Teaching Problem Structuring Methods: Improving understanding through meaningful learning. INFORMS Transactions on Education, 12(1): 20–30.
30. Checkland, P. 1981. Systems Thinking, Systems Practice. Chichester: Wiley.

31. Checkland, P. 2000. Soft Systems Methodology: A thirty year retrospective. Systems Research and Behavioral Science, 17: 11–58.
32. Checkland, P. 2006. Reply to Eden and Ackermann: Any future for problem structuring methods? Journal of the Operational Research Society, 57(7): 769–771.
33. Checkland, P., and Scholes, J. 1990. Soft Systems Methodology in action. Chichester: Wiley.
34. Chess, C. 2000. Evaluating environmental public participation: Methodological questions. Journal of Environmental Planning and Management, 43(6): 769–784.
35. Conklin, J. 2006. Dialog Mapping: Building shared understanding of wicked problems. Chichester: Wiley.
36. Creed, W. E. D., Langstraat, J. A., and Scully, M. A. 2002. A Picture of the Frame: Frame Analysis as Technique and as Politics. Organizational Research Methods, 5(1): 34–55.
37. Cronin, K., Midgley, G., and Jackson, L. 2014. Issues Mapping: A problem structuring method for addressing science and technology conflicts European Journal of Operational Research, 233(1): 145–158.
38. De Geus, A. 1988. Planning as Learning. Harvard Business Review, 66(2): 70–74.
39. De Gooyert, V., Rouwette, E., van Kranenburg, H., Freeman, E., and van Breen, H. 2021. Cognitive change and consensus forming in facilitated modelling: A comparison of experienced and observed outcomes. European Journal of Operational Research.
40. Donais, F. M., Abi-Zeid, I., Waygood, E. O. D., and Lavoie, R. 2021. A framework for post-project evaluation of multicriteria decision aiding processes from the stakeholders' perspective: Design and application. Group Decision and Negotiation, 30(5): 1161–1191.
41. Dooley, R., Fryxell, G., and Judge, W. 2000. Belaboring the not-so-obvious: consensus, commitment, and strategy implementation speed and success. Journal of Management, 26(6): 1237–1257
42. Doyle, J., and Ford, D. 1999. Mental models concepts revisited: Some clarifications and a reply to Lane. System Dynamics Review, 15(4): 411–415.
43. Dyson, R. G., O'Brien, F. A., and Shah, D. B. 2021. Soft OR and Practice: The Contribution of the Founders of Operations Research. Operations Research, 69(3): 727–738.
44. Eden, C. 1986. Problem Solving or Problem Finishing. In M. Jackson, and P. Keys (Eds.), New Directions in Management Science: 97–107. Aldershot: Gower.
45. Eden, C. 1990. Managing the Environment as a Means to Managing Complexity. In C. Eden, and J. Radford (Eds.), Tackling Strategic Problems: the role of group decision support: 154–161. London: Sage.
46. Eden, C. 1992. A framework for thinking about group decision support systems (GDSS). Group Decision and Negotiation, 1: 199–218.

47. Eden, C. 1995. On evaluating the performance of wide-band GDSS's. European Journal of Operational Research, 81: 302–311.

48. Eden, C. 1996. The Stakeholder/Collaborator Strategy Workshop. In C. Huxham (Ed.), Collaborative Advantage: 44–56. London: Sage.

49. Eden, C. 2000. On evaluating the performance of GSS: furthering the debate, by Paul Finlay (European Journal of Operational Research 107, pp 193-201) -a response by Colin Eden. European Journal of Operational Research, 81(120): 218–222.

50. Eden, C., and Ackermann, F. 1996. Horses for courses. A stakeholder approach to the evaluation of GDSSs. Group Decision and Negotiation, 5: 501–519.

51. Eden, C., and Ackermann, F. 1998. Making strategy: The journey of strategic management. London: Sage.

52. Eden, C., and Ackermann, F. 2004. Use of 'Soft OR' Models by Clients: What do they want from them? In M. Pidd (Ed.), Systems Modelling: theory and practice: 146–163. Chichester: Wiley.

53. Eden, C., and Ackermann, F. 2006. Where next for problem structuring methods. Journal of the Operational Research Society, 57(7): 766–768.

54. Eden, C., and Ackermann, F. 2010. Decision making in groups: Theory and practice. In P. C. Nutt, and D. C. Wilson (Eds.), Handbook of decision making: 231–272. Chichester, UK: Wiley-Blackwell.

55. Eden, C., and Ackermann, F. 2018. Theory into practice, practice to theory: Action research in method development. European Journal of Operational Research, 271(3): 1145–1155.

56. Eden, C., Jones, S., and Sims, D. 1983. Messing about in problems: An informal structured approach to their identification and management. Oxford: Pergamon.

57. Edmondson, A. C., and McLain Smith, D. 2006. Too hot to handle? How to manage relationship conflict. California Management Review, 49(1): 6–31.

58. Espejo, R., and Reyes, A. 2011. Organizational systems: Managing complexity with the viable system model: Springer Science & Business Media.

59. Espinosa, A., and Walker, J. 2017. Complexity approach to sustainability: Theory and application: World Scientific.

60. Fairhurst, G. T. 2010. The power of framing: Creating the language of leadership: Wiley.

61. Finlay, P. 1998. On evaluating the performance of GSS: Furthering the debate. European Journal of Operational Research, 107(1): 193–201.

62. Franco, L. A. 2006. Forms of conversation and problem structuring methods: a conceptual development Journal of the Operational Research Society, 57: 813–821.

63. Franco, L. A. 2007. Assessing the impact of problem structuring methods in multi-organisational settings: An empirical investigation. Journal of the Operational Research Society, 58(6): 760–768.

64. Franco, L. A. 2008. Facilitating collaboration with problem structuring methods: A case of an inter-organisational construction partnership. Group Decision and Negotiation, 17(4): 267–286.

65. Franco, L. A. 2009. Problem Structuring Methods as intervention tools: Reflections from their use with multi-organizational teams. OMEGA: The International Journal of Management Science, 37(1): 193–203.

66. Franco, L. A. 2013. Rethinking Soft OR interventions: Models as boundary objects. European Journal of Operational Research, 231(3): 720–733.

67. Franco, L. A., and Greiffenhagen, C. 2018. Making OR practice visible: Using ethnomethodology to analyse facilitated modelling workshops. European Journal of Operational Research, 265(2): 673–684.

68. Franco, L. A., and Greiffenhagen, C. 2021. Group decision support practice as it happens. In D. M. Kilgour, and C. Eden (Eds.), Handbook of Group Decision and Negotiation, 2nd ed., Vol. 2: 793–814. Cham: Springer International Publishing.

69. Franco, L. A., and Hämäläinen, R. P. 2016a. Behavioural operational research: Returning to the roots of the OR profession. European Journal of Operational Research, 249(3): 791–795.

70. Franco, L. A., and Hämäläinen, R. P. 2016b. Engaging with behavioural OR: On methods, actors, and praxis. In M. Kunc, J. Malpass, and L. White (Eds.), Behavioural operational research: Theory, methodology and practice: 3–26: Palgrave Macmillan.

71. Franco, L. A., and Montibeller, G. 2010. Facilitated modelling in operational research. European Journal of Operational Research, 205(3): 489–500.

72. Franco, L. A., and Nielsen, M. F. 2018. Examining group facilitation in situ: The use of formulations in facilitation practice. Group Decision and Negotiation, 27(5): 735–756.

73. Franco, L. A., Cushman, M., and Rosenhead, J. 2004. Project Review and Learning in the UK Construction Industry: Embedding a Problem Structuring Method within a partnership context. European Journal of Operational Research, 152(3): 586–601.

74. Friend, J. 2001. The Strategic Choice Approach. In J. Rosenhead, and J. Mingers (Eds.), Rational Analysis for a Problematic World Revisited: Problem structuring methods for complexity, uncertainty and conflict: 115–149. Chichester: Wiley.

75. Friend, J. 2006. Labels, methodologies and strategic decision making support. Journal of the Operational Research Society, 57(7): 772–775.

76. Friend, J., and Hickling, A. 2005. Planning Under Pressure: the Strategic Choice Approach (3rd ed.): Elsevier.

77. Goffman, E. 1974. Frame analysis: An essay on the organization of experience: Harvard University Press.

78. Gomes Jr, A. d. A., and Schramm, V. B. 2021. Problem Structuring Methods: A Review of Advances Over the Last Decade. Systemic Practice and Action Research: 1–34.

79. Gregory, A., Atkins, J., Burdon, D., and Elliott , M. 2012. A problem structuring method for ecosystem-based management: The DPSIR modelling process. European Journal of Operational Research, 227(3): 558–569.

80. Harwood, S. A. 2019. A question of interpretation: The viable system model (VSM). European Journal of Operational Research, 274(3): 1198–1201.

81. Henao, F., and Franco, L. A. 2016. Unpacking multimethodology: Impacts of a community development intervention. European Journal of Operational Research, 253(3): 681–696.

82. Hickling, A. 1990. 'Decision Spaces': A scenario about designing appropriate rooms for group decision management. In C. Eden, and J. Radford (Eds.), Tackling Strategic Problems: The role of group decision support: 169–177. London: Sage.

83. Hindle, G. A. 2011. Case Article-Teaching Soft Systems Methodology and a Blueprint for a Module. INFORMS Transactions on Education, 12(1): 31–40.

84. Houghton, L. 2013. Why can't we all just accommodate: A Soft Systems Methodology application on disagreeing stakeholders. Systems Research and Behavioral Science, 30(4): 430–443.

85. Howard, N. 1994a. Drama theory and its relation to game theory. Part 1: Dramatic resolution vs. Rational solution. Group Decision and Negotiation, 3(2): 187–206.

86. Howard, N. 1994b. Drama theory and its relation to game theory. Part 2: Formal model of the resolution process. Group Decision and Negotiation, 3(2): 207–235.

87. Howick, S., and Ackermann, F. 2011. Mixing OR methods in practice: Past, present and future directions. European Journal of Operational Research, 215(3): 503–511.

88. Huxham, C. 1990. On Trivialities in Process. In C. Eden, and J. Radford (Eds.), Tackling Strategic Problems: The role of group decision support: 162–168. London: Sage.

89. Huz, S., Andersen, D. F., Richardson, G. P., and Boothroyd, R. 1997. A framework for evaluating systems thinking interventions. An experimental approach to mental health system change. System Dynamics Review, 13(2): 149–169.

90. Jackson, M. C. 1993. The system of systems methodologies: A guide to researchers. Journal of the Operational Research Society, 44(2): 208–209.

91. Jackson, M. 2000. Systems approaches to management. New York: Kluwer.

92. Kane, T. J., and Staiger, D. O. 2012. Gathering feedback for teaching: Combining high-quality observations with student surveys and achievement gains (MET Project Research Paper). Seattle, WA: Bill & Melinda Gates Foundation.

93. Keeney, R. L. 1992. Value-Focused Thinking: A path to creative decision-making Cambridge, MA: Harvard University Press.

94. Keeney, R. L. 2012. Value-Focused Brainstorming. Decision Analysis, 9(4): 303–313.

95. Keeney, G. L., and Von Winterfeldt, D. 2010. Identifying and structuring the objectives of terrorists. Risk Analysis, 30(12): 1803–1816.

96. Keys, P. 2006. On becoming expert in the use of problem structuring methods. Journal of the Operational Research Society, 57: 822–829.

97. Lane, D.C., Munro, E. and Husemann, E., 2016. Blending systems thinking approaches for organisational analysis: Reviewing child protection in England. European Journal of Operational Research, 251(2): 613–623.

98. Langley, A. 1999. Strategies for theorising from process data. Academy of Management Review, 24(4): 691–710.

99. Laouris, Y., and Michaelides, M. 2018. Structured Democratic Dialogue: An application of a mathematical problem structuring method to facilitate reforms with local authorities in Cyprus. European Journal of Operational Research, 268(3): 918–931.

100. Ledington, P., and Donaldson, J. 1997. Soft OR and management practice: A study of the adoption and use of Soft Systems Methodology. Journal of Operational Research Society, 48(3): 229–240.

101. Levin, I. P., Schneider, S. L., and Gaeth, G. J. 1998. All frames are not created equal: A typology and critical analysis of framing effects. Organizational Behavior and Human Decision Processes, 76(2): 149–188.

102. Marttunen, M., Lienert, J., and Belton, V. (2017). Structuring problems for Multi-Criteria Decision Analysis in practice: A literature review of method combinations. European Journal of Operational Research, 263(1): 1–17.

103. Mason, O., and Mitroff, I. 1981. Challenging strategic planning assumptions: Theory, cases and techniques. New York: Wiley.

104. McCardle-Keurentjes, Marleen HF, Rouwette, E.A.J.A., Vennix, J.A.M, and Jacobs, E. (2018). Potential benefits of model use in group model building: Insights from an experimental investigation. System Dynamics Review, 34(1–2): 354–384.

105. Midgley, G. 2000. Systemic intervention: philosophy, methodology, and practice. New York: Kluwer Academic/ Plenum Publishers.

106. Midgley, G., Cavana, R., Brocklesby, J., Foote, J., Ahuriri-Drscoll, A., and Wood, D. 2013. Towards a new framework for evaluating systemic problem structuring methods. European Journal of Operational Research, 229(1): 143–154.

107. Mingers, J. 2000. Variety is the spice of life. Combining soft and hard OR/MS methods. International Transactions in Operational Research, 7: 673–691.

108. Mingers, J. 2011. Soft OR comes of age -But not everywhere! OMEGA: The International Journal of Management Science, 39(6): 729–741.

109. Mingers, J. 2012. Abduction: The missing link between deduction and induction. A comment on Ormerod's 'rational inference: deductive, inductive and probabilistic thinking'. Journal of the Operational Research Society, 63(6): 860–861.

110. Mingers, J., and Brocklesby, J. 1997. Multimethodology: Towards a framework for mixing methodologies. Omega, 25(5): 489–509.

111. Mingers, J., and Gill, A. (Eds.). 1997. Multimethodology: The theory and practice of combining Management Science methodologies. Chichester: Wiley.
112. Mingers, J. and Rosenhead, J. 2004. Problem structuring methods in action. European Journal of Operational Research, 152(3):530–554.
113. Mingers, J., and Taylor, S. 1992. The use of soft systems methodology in practice. Journal of Operational Research Society, 43(4): 321–332.
114. Mingers, J., and White, L. 2010. A review of the recent contribution of systems thinking to operational research and management science. European Journal of Operational Research, 207(3): 1147–1161.
115. Mohr, L. 1982. Explaining organizational behavior. San Francisco, CA: Jossey-Bass.
116. Munro, I., and Mingers, J. 2002. The use of multimethodology in practice: Results from a survey of practitioners. Journal of Operational Research Society, 53(4): 369–378.
117. O'Brien, F. A. 2011. Supporting the strategy process: A survey of UK OR/MS practitioners. Journal of the Operational Research Society, 62(5): 900–920.
118. Ormerod, R. J. 1995. Putting Soft OR methods to work: Information systems strategy development at Sainsbury's. Journal of Operational Research Society, 46(3): 277–293.
119. Ormerod, R. J. 1996. Information systems strategy development at Sainsbury's supermarkets using soft OR. Interfaces, 26(1): 102–130.
120. Ormerod, R. J. 2014a. OR competences: The demands of problem structuring methods. EURO Journal on Decision Processes, 2(3-4): 313–340.
121. Ormerod, R. J. 2014b. The mangle of OR practice: Towards more informative case studies of technical projects. Journal of the Operational Research Society, 65(8): 1245–1260.
122. Papamichail, K. N., Alves, G., French, S., Yang, J. B., and Snowdon, R. 2007. Facilitation practices in decision workshops. Journal of the Operational Research Society, 58(5): 614–632.
123. Parnell, G.S., Hughes, D.H.,Burk, R.C., Driscoll,P.J., Kucik, P.D., Morales, B.L. and Nunn, L.R. Invited review -Survey of value-focused thinking: Applications, research developments and areas for future research. Journal of Multi-Criteria Decision Analysis, 20(1-2): 49–60.
124. Paucar-Caceres, A. 2010. Mapping the changes in management science: A review of'soft' OR/MS articles published in Omega (1973-2008). OMEGA: The International Journal of Management Science, 38(1-2): 46–56.
125. Pawson, R. 2002. Evidence-based policy: The promise of realist synthesis. Evaluation, 8(3): 340–358.
126. Pentland, B. T. 1999. Building process theory with narrative: From description to explanation. Academy of Management Review, 24: 711–724.
127. Phillips, L. 1984. A Theory of Requisite Decision Models. Acta Psychologica, 56(1-3): 29–48.

128. Phillips, L. 2007. Decision Conferencing. In W. Edwards, R. Miles Jr, and D. von Winterfeldt (Eds.), Advances in Decision Analysis: from foundations to applications: 375–399. New York: Cambridge University Press.

129. Phillips, L. D. and Bana e Costa, C.A. 2007. Transparent prioritisation, budgeting and resource allocation with multi-criteria decision analysis and decision conferencing. Annals of Operations Research, 154(1): 51–68.

130. Phillips, L., and Phillips, M. 1993. Facilitated Work Groups: Theory and Practice. Journal of Operational Research Society, 44(6): 533–549.

131. Pidd, M. (Ed.). 2004. Systems Modelling: theory and practice. Chichester: Wiley.

132. Pidd, M. 2009. Tools for thinking. Modeling in management science (3rd ed.). Chichester: Wiley.

133. Poole, M. S. 2007. Generalization in process theories of communication. Communication Methods and Measures, 1(3): 181–190.

134. Poole, M. S., Van de Ven, A. H., Dooley, K., and Holmes, M. E. (Eds.). 2000. Organizational change and innovation processes: Theory and methods for research. New York: Oxford University Press.

135. Powell, J. H., and Mustafee, N. 2017. Widening requirements capture with soft methods: An investigation of hybrid M&S studies in health care. Journal of the Operational Research Society, 68(10): 1211–1222.

136. Ranyard, J. C., Fildes, R., and Hu, T.-I. 2015. Reassessing the scope of OR practice: The influences of Problem Structuring Methods and the Analytics movement. European Journal of Operational Research, 245(1): 1–13.

137. Reynolds, M., and Holwell, S. (Eds.). 2010. Systems approaches to managing change: A practical guide. London: Springer.

138. Ritchey, T. 2011. Wicked Problems-Social Messes: Decision support modelling with Morphological Analysis. Berlin Heidelberg: Springer-Verlag.

139. Rosenhead, J. 1989. Rational analysis for a problematic world: Problem structuring methods for complexity, uncertainty and conflict. Chichester: Wiley.

140. Rosenhead, J., and Mingers, J. (Eds.). 2001. Rational Analysis for a Problematic World Revisited: problem structuring methods for complexity, uncertainty and conflict. Chichester: Wiley.

141. Rouwette, E. A. J. A. 2011. Facilitated modelling in strategy development: Measuring the impact on communication, consensus and commitment. Journal of the Operational Research Society, 62: 879–887.

142. Rouwette, E. A. 2016. The impact of group model building on behavior, Behavioral operational research: 213–241: Springer.

143. Rouwette, E. A. J. A., and Smeets, S. 2016. Conflict, consensus and the management of a good debate: Exploring the deliberative assumptions of group facilitating techniques. In I. Bleijenbergh, H. Korzilius, and E. A. J. A. Rouwette (Eds.), Methods, Model Building and Management: A liber amicorum for Jac Vennix: 129–146. Nijmegen: Institute for Management Research.

144. Rouwette, E. A. J. A., Korzilius, H., Vennix, J. A. M., and Jacobs, E. 2011. Modeling as persuasion: The impact of group model building on attitudes and behavior. System Dynamics Review, 27(1): 1–21.

145. Rouwette, E. A. J. A., Vennix, J. A. M., and Van Mullekom, T. 2002. Group model building effectiveness. A review of assessment studies. System Dynamics Review, 18(1): 5–45.

146. Rouwette, E. A. J. A., Vennix, J. A. M., and Felling, A. J. A. 2009. On evaluating the performance of problem structuring methods: An attempt at formulating a conceptual model. Group Decision and Negotiation, 18(6): 567–587.

147. Schilling, M.S, Oeser, N., and Schaub, C. (2007). How effective are decision analyses? Assessing decision process and group alignment effects. Decision Analysis, 4(4): 227–242.

148. Schuman, S. P. (Ed.). 2005. The IAF Handbook of Group Facilitation: Best practices from the leading organization in facilitation. San Francisco, CA: Jossey-Bass.

149. Scott, R. J., Cavana, R. Y., and Cameron, D. 2016. Recent evidence on the effectiveness of group model building. European Journal of Operational Research, 249(3): 908–918.

150. Shaw, D., and Blundell, N. 2010. WASAN: The development of a facilitated methodology for structuring a waste minimisation problem. European Journal of Operational Research, 207(1): 350–362.

151. Shaw, D., Ackermann, F., and Eden, C. 2003. Approaches to sharing knowledge in group problem structuring. Journal of the Operational Research Society, 54(9): 936–948.

152. Shaw, D., Smith, C. M., and Scully, J. 2017. Why did Brexit happen? Using causal mapping to analyse secondary, longitudinal data. European Journal of Operational Research, 263(3): 1019–1032.

153. Smith, C. M., and Shaw, D. 2019. The characteristics of problem structuring methods: A literature review. European Journal of Operational Research, 274(2): 403–416.

154. Sorensen, L., Vidal, R., and Engstrom, E. 2004. Using soft OR in a small company: The case of Kirby. European Journal of Operational Research, 152(3): 555–570.

155. Stokoe, E. 2013. The (in)authenticity of simulated talk: Comparing role-played and actual conversation and the implications for communication training. Research on Language and Social Interaction, 46(2): 1–21.

156. Stokoe, E. 2014. The Conversation Analytic Role-play Method (CARM): A method for training communication skills as an alternative to simulated role-play. Research on Language and Social Interaction, 47(3): 255–265.

157. Tavella, E., and Franco, L. A. 2015. Dynamics of group knowledge production in facilitated modelling workshops: An exploratory study. Group Decision and Negotiation, 24(3): 451–475.

158. Tavella, E., Papadopoulos, T., and Paroutis, S. 2020. Artefact appropriation in facilitated modelling: An adaptive structuration theory approach. Journal of the Operational Research Society: 1–15.

159. Tully, P., White, L., and Yearworth, M. 2018. The value paradox of Problem Structuring Methods. Systems Research and Behavioral Science.

160. Valcourt, N., Walters, J., Javernick-Will, A., and Linden, K. 2020. Assessing the efficacy of group model building workshops in an applied setting through purposive text analysis. System Dynamics Review, 36(2): 135–157.

161. Van de Water, H., Schinkel, M., and Rozier, R. 2007. Fields of application of SSM: a categorization of publications. Journal of the Operational Research Society, 58(3): 271–287.

162. Veldhuis, G. A., van Scheepstal, P., Rouwette, E., and Logtens, T. 2015. Collaborative problem structuring using MARVEL. EURO Journal on Decision Processes, 3(3): 249–273.

163. Vennix, J. A. M. 1996. Group model building. Facilitating team learning using system dynamics. Chichester: Wiley.

164. Vennix, J. A. M. 1999. Group model-building: tackling messy problems. System Dynamics Review, 15(4): 379–401.

165. Wong, H. 2007. Using Robustness Analysis to structure online marketing and communication problems. Journal of the Operational Research Society, 58(5): 633–644.

166. Yearworth, M., and White, L. 2014. The non-codified use of problem structuring methods and the need for a generic constitutive definition. European Journal of Operational Research, 237(3): 932–945.

167. Yearworth, M., and White, L. 2021. Group support systems: Experiments with an online system and implications for same-time/different-places working. Handbook of Group Decision and Negotiation: 681–706.

168. Yin, R. K. 2018. Case study research and applications: Design and methods. (6th ed.). Los Angeles, CA: Sage.

169. Westcombe, M., Franco, L. A., and Shaw, D. 2006. Where next for PSMs— A grassroots revolution? Journal of the Operational Research Society, 57(7): 776–778.

170. Williams, T. M., Ackermann, F., and Eden, C. 2003. Structuring a delay and disruption claim: An application of cause-mapping and system dynamics. European Journal of Operational Research, 148(1): 192–204.

171. Williams, T., and Dickson, K. 2000. Teaching real-life OR to MSc students. Journal of the Operational Research Society, 51(12): 1440–1448.

172. White, L. 2006. Evaluating Problem Structuring Methods: Developing an approach to show the value and effectiveness of PSM interventions. Journal of the Operational Research Society, 57(7): 842–855.

173. White, L. 2009. Understanding Problem Structuring Methods Interventions. European Journal of Operational Research, 99(3): 823–833.

174. White, L., Burger, K., and Yearworth, M. 2016. Understanding behaviour in problem structuring methods interventions with activity theory. European Journal of Operational Research, 249(3): 983–1004.

175. Winnicott, D. W. 1953. Transitional objects and transitional phenomena: A study of the first not-me possession. International Journal of Psycho-analysis, 34(2): 89–97.

24

Are PSMs Relevant in a Digital Age? Towards an Ethical Dimension

Isabella M. Lami and Leroy White

24.1 Introduction

The aim of the paper is to explore the relevance of Problems Structuring Methods (PSMs) in the digital era. Today digital transformation , arising from the proliferation of digital technologies [71] is both affecting and altering organizations [82]. In tracing the progress of PSMs practice and theorizing, we argue that their place in this new world can hardly be denied, but there are some obvious consequences. In everyday organizational practices, it is questionable whether concerns for implementation, strategizing and planning, the sorts of issues PSMs were originally developed for, need PSMs. Even though these methods were developed with "wicked problems" in mind. Are the problems faced by stakeholders more amplified as a result of the digital transformation of organizational life? Does the promise of digital transformation bring an existential threat to PSMs? Primarily we ask: Is the concept of

I. M. Lami (✉)
Politecnico di Torino, Turin, Italy
e-mail: isabella.lami@polito.it

L. White
Management Department, University of Exeter, Exeter, UK
e-mail: L.White2@exeter.ac.uk

© The Author(s), under exclusive license to Springer Nature
Switzerland AG 2022
S. Salhi and J. Boylan (eds.), *The Palgrave Handbook of Operations Research*,
https://doi.org/10.1007/978-3-030-96935-6_24

PSM still relevant in a world accelerating with digital technology and innovation, where digital transformation is affecting and challenging organizational stakeholders?

This chapter takes a firm and justified position on their relevance: PSMs are still important but the challenging contextual conditions may have altered the way they are to be used and the purpose for which they are applied.

We make our case for the relevance of PSMs by first, arguing why the nature of the current organizational challenges still justifies the use of PSMs. Then, we examine further what is particularly special about PSM use, highlighting the need to shift from an emphasis on design to one on deliberation. Finally, we explore a new type of concern, an ethical one that heightens the relevance of PSMs We conclude with practical implications.

24.2   Where Are We Now?

PSMs were developed over 40 years ago, so the question of its relevance today appears legitimate. Defined as participative and interactive methods focused mainly on structuring the problems rather than directly solving them [67], they were developed to fill the gap that traditional Operational Research (OR) and decision analysis were not addressing satisfactorily, i.e., complex, ill-structured problems, also defined "wicked problems" [65], i.e., incomprehensible and resistant to solution [17], in a world of continuous change [11].

The assumption was that it is not always possible to find a single uncontested representation of the problem under consideration in real-world situations. PSMs were devoted to representing problems and observing their multiple perspectives [53]. Representation was necessary, using visually analytical models. In this perspective, the models are used to inform negotiations about the nature of the problem situation. In the process of representing the problem, stakeholders can understand and discuss the problem, engage with each other, and work towards identifying potential improvements. Thus, PSMs are often applied by groups of stakeholders in a workshop setting. Here, the stakeholders jointly develop suggestions on moving towards an agreement on the problem during interactive conversations [3]. Working on the models in the workshop is characterized by the way stakeholders can share and understand different perspectives, and the identification and agreement on possible solutions to alleviate the problems at hand and to act. Principally, the methods follow the notion expressed by Rorty ([66], p. 3), that the more accurately we represent the world, the better chances we have to improve our action in it (see White [85]).

24.2.1 What Is the Nature of the Problem Today?

In the early '70s PSMs were developed by academics and practitioners in response to practical commitments with real problems, involving complexity, uncertainty and conflict, recognizing that there are specific characteristics of problem situations that make the traditional mathematical modelling tools of OR ineffective. The 'unclear definition' of the problems, the presence of multiple interests and perspectives, many uncertainties and often a lack of reliable (or indeed any) data, highlighted how the process is primarily one of learning and negotiation rather than the technical solution of a problem [51]. These ill-structured problems, such as the planning problems, the environmental or social ones for instance, were defined by Rittel and Webber [65] "wicked problems", and later "messy problems" [7] or "social messes" [37]. Pioneers of PSMs developed methodologies to navigate many of these issues. Indeed, PSMs have been applied in many different fields (for a review of contributions, see Rosenhead [67], Mingers and Rosenhead [53], Mingers and White [54], Rosenhead [68].

However, we have recently witnessed quite dramatic events such the financial crash of 2010, COVID-19 and the ever-emergent climate crisis. These are characteristically complex and intractable [75]. Indeed, some say they are beset with wicked problems, contradictions, different world views, different mindset to name but a few. But are they different to problems OR has tackled in the past? These problems it seems are not only "wicked", but as some scholars recently suggest, they are "super wicked problem", because they have further exacerbated features [46, 49]. According to Lazarus (referring to climate change) are related to:

1. the quantitative and in somehow measurable aspects of the problem (the greenhouse gases, the stock/flow nature of physical and chemical processes underlying it with its enormous temporal dimension; the lack of homogeneity in the geographical distribution of the effects);
2. the limits of the human mind (human beings think mostly in physiological time; there is a human tendency to judge the likelihood of an occurrence based on the relative ability to imagine its happening and climate change is an unimaginable problem; the complexity of the causal chains of human actions makes their consequences seem very far from each other);

3. the absence of an adequate institutional framework able to "address a problem of climate change's tremendous spatial and temporal scope".

Drawing on climate change literature, it is possible to re-define several types of problems, in different realms, as super wicked problems, particularly the current disruptive events. Even before the pandemic of Covid 19 the scientific debate was discussing about climate change, infrastructural disruption, insecurity, pandemics, at local and global scales [91], to the point that this type of uncertainty has been proposed to be added in one of the most used PSMs, the Strategic Choice Approach [45]. These new issues, unpredictable, unknowable or unmanageable, which can vary from the health to the presence of transhumans in our society, pervade public and political debate about projections of uncertain futures.

In short, we still have wicked problems, even super wicked ones, but can we assert that the PSMs are still relevant?

24.2.2   PSMs Today

Over the years, the attention of researchers has been mainly devoted to the development of different PSMs [16, 26, 34]; their applications [2, 8, 19, 25, 30, 69, 86]; comparisons between different PSMs [36, 44, 76]. At the same time a literature developed on the theoretical and methodological position of PSMs [41, 50, 73, 81, 83].

There are several examples of the use of PSMs in the organizational field [1, 4, 5, 16, 30, 77]), in reshaping and restructuring the organization's structure and processes of government agencies, major corporations, communities and other bodies in general. They are also widely acknowledged in the health care and services sector [19, 27, 42, 47, 56, 87]), in cases of service provision, local care strategies, applying or developing simulation and systems modelling. Several applications to the information systems field have been published [15, 58–61, 90], developing IT strategies for different actors, such as supermarket chains, business organizations or even parliaments. Finally, PSMs have also often been used to develop planning strategies [8, 10, 18, 31–34, 78, 88], working at national and regional levels with local governments, transport systems, development planning, but also at urban and architecture scale, in urban renewal and reuse projects. These are among the main acknowledged uses in PSMs, nevertheless they have been used in other settings too—e.g., for strategic directions in the publishing industry [23], to support claims for damages [5], and more in general to support strategic decisions. Understanding the process of PSMs is also an ongoing research challenge [39, 40,

80]). More than a quarter of a century ago soft OR "pioneers" reported that interventions felt like a "playful toying with ideas" [22] and that they were "doing what feels good" [89] and yet it is unclear how these early soft OR insights can be used by today's OR practitioners. This is a pressing problem. The concern has led to recent attention to micro-process view of OR practice (e.g., Ackermann et al. [6]), which holds some potential for a more nuance understanding on the process of OR. This is a focus on research arising from the need to understand the interactional and collective behaviours that are difficult to predict based on knowledge of the constituent parts [62]. Hence, capturing the essence of "OR practice" requires further research [24].

24.2.3   So What's the Issue?

There is an exponential growth in the performance of available technologies and systems available to OR people. Approaches such as advanced algorithms and analytics are transforming the dynamics of work [43]. The so-called Moore's and Metcalf's laws are claimed to govern the broadening availability of digital technologies, in that computing hardware is becoming ever more powerful, cheaper, embedded and ubiquitous, while network effects yield increases in value by connecting individuals, organizations and objects [9]. Technologies typically associated with digital transformation are commonly abbreviated as SMAC: social, mobile, analytics and cloud [35]. Over the next decades, the adoption of analytics and artificial intelligence technologies will transform the workplace and organizations. These technologies are already bringing a profound change in the traditional way of organizing [20] and potentially could bring changes to OR practice [12, 55].

Digital transformation has completely changed context for OR compared to its origins. Therefore, it cannot but have consequences on the kind of contribution that PSMs can make. In order to reflect on this, we review the definition of PSM given by Rosenhead [67] (p. 117, bold is ours):

Problem structuring methods (PSMs) are a broad group of problem-handling approaches whose purpose is to **assist in structuring problems** rather than directly with solving them. They are **participative** and **interactive** in character and in principle offer operational research access to a range of **problem situations** for which more classical OR techniques have limited applicability.

In contrast to the above definition, fifteen years later, Mingers and Rosenhead [52] wrote that (p.1):

the question that PSMs aim to help with is: How can models based on the range of different perceptions and positions in a problematic situation help the participants in that situation to resolve what **actions they might agree to take**?

The emphasis is on the word *might*. There is a doubt. Does this last part imply that there is doubt about the efficacy of PSMs? Even after years of application the efficacy of PSMs is still in doubt? The phrase "actions they might agree to take" emphasizes the crisis at the heart of PSMs: do they allow action to be taken? Do they work?

This quote was 2011 and, as mentioned before, the world has dramatically changed due to the digital revolution. Who the clients are and what purpose the methods have has become vague or lost. Many clients are now online, virtual, clients are more experts, problems are more distributed with "tech savvy" professionals jumping in and out of the problem-solving space (see GitHub) and is much more about locality and globalization. The old way of thinking about hierarchy collaboration top-down/bottom-up public/private are all blurred in the digital world. Recently scholars are describing as new organizational forms such as Holacracy [72]. These are described as organizations with permeable, agile structures, that are agile, adaptable and without boundaries. These types of arrangements are made possible because data-driven processes enhanced through digital technologies [21]. In terms of actions and decision-making within these settings, before client characteristics and beliefs could be teased out by survey interviews or group work. Now organizations can scrape data from a variety of sources, apply analytics and learn all the characteristics of our colleagues and customers.

So Rosenhead & Mingers' doubt was right. But when they wrote this, we were in the middle of a far-reaching revolution that has now completely transformed how we work, live and relate. For example, who foresaw the collective events known as the Arab Spring where groups, communities and nations self-organized through their mobile phones and the social media apps? This has bearing with PSMs because decision-making was collective participation and problem structuring and self-organized at rapid speed with no impediment of time and space. Perhaps, the doubt in Rosenhead and Mingers definition was an unconscious realization that the world has changed and the PSMs relevance is in question.

In sum, given the dramatic changes in the environment for PSM practice, certain themes still make PSMs relevant. For instance, there are three words to observe in the original definition: (i) "structuring"; (ii) "participative and interacting"; (iii) problems situations.

Structuring. The challenges around the COVID-19 pandemic have spurred organizations into action by increasing their awareness of the need to accelerate digital transformation . Indeed, the pandemic emergency has forced us to move everything online. The consequence is that it has made any work much more designed. Perhaps problem structuring is a lesser need because there is currently a general tendency for any interaction to involve some online structuring [79], even if it is not explicitly aimed at solving a problem. This kind of reflection recalls the question that often appears in the debate on the topic, i.e., whether PSMs are more effective than self-structuring?

Participative and interactive. PSMs are still certainly participatory and interactive, but how this happens has changed. In most cases, participation takes place in a telematic forum where people interact simultaneously online; in more extreme cases, interaction takes place asynchronously. So, the interaction among the group has changed, but the role of the facilitator is also under question. This change, i.e., moving focus groups online, made necessary by Covid, but which will probably continue, at least in part, to be used even after the pandemic has ended, has required the introduction of new software developed specifically in the field of soft OR , or the use in this context of other software on the market.

Problem situations. Strategic problems continue to be of a nature that cannot be solved directly by mathematical models; indeed, in some ways, the level of complexity has increased further. In fact, the pandemic has highlighted the global scope of many decisions that until now we thought could only have local consequences.

In terms of the second definition, PSMs can be used as a basis for dealing with doubt through examining hunches, in that, as suggested by Weick [84] (p. 525) "plausibility is a substitute for validity". Therefore, "going with the flow" may be one way to deal with doubt. PSMs may also infer pragmatism [57] the notion of which is built on the early system philosophers who argued that pragmatic arises from people's need to solve problems quickly, using his limited understanding of the situation. A pragmatic perspective appears to have been predominantly applied to study the process of OR to inform a process view of PSMs [38]. In sum, the ideas present a very practical and applied philosophy that is orientated towards action, and it acknowledges that operational researchers' worldviews involve ethical and moral concerns. Finally, these ideas accord with the idea of abduction as Peirce [63], p. 216:

the only logical operation which introduces any new idea; for induction does nothing but determine a value, and deduction merely evolves the necessary consequences of a pure hypothesis.

24.3   The Ethical Boundary

This was certainly true in the "old world", where the PSM exercise was in a room, with a white board or a flip chart paper and a facilitator. But now, when the design phase is often supported by software, giving rise to a mediated form of problems structuring, helping people to self-facilitate and allowing distributed design and asynchronous design, we wonder if the contribution they can make today is more on **deliberation**. A first reflection connected to this is about the role of analytics in this realm. If we come back to the first ideals of PSMs: cognitive mapping, Strategic Choice Approach and SSM, they have at their core group work and facilitation. In the current world, we have technology. While software was available, the processes were more connected to the design and the *in-situ* issue of social interaction. Today, to bring PSMs to the actual world is perhaps to put digital first and see what characterize a decision currently. We can go to extremes and imagine a future where fully automated, decentered human facilitation algorithms that made recommendations.

The second reflection is about the nature of the decisions: decisions are not the responsibility of machines, but of human beings. According to the philosopher Maurizio Ferraris [28], for some decades now we have been witnessing a technological revolution, which is radical because it does not depend on people's beliefs, but on the tireless operation of machines. It is a revolution that can be defined as (p. VII):

> 'documedial' because it is based on the intersection between the growth of documentality, the production of documents as a constitutive element of social reality, and that of mediality, which in digital is no longer one-to-many but many-to-many.

The environment in which it is produced is the web, i.e., a potentially ubiquitous place, which easily explains the radicality of the transformations that have taken place. The importance and pervasiveness of today's technology, which has made this revolution possible, could generate the fear that the human is no longer needed in the face of the presence of the machine. Ferraris underlines the groundlessness of this fear (p. IX):

> artificial intelligence receives nourishment, meaning and purpose from the fact that there are human agents, mortal organisms that have an irreversible end, unlike machines, and are therefore able to prescribe an end to machines.

Taking these reflections back to the context of PSMs, it can be observed that machines and software can contribute to the structuring and representation of problems, but not to decision-making, which continues to remain in the purely human sphere. We come back to the initial discussion about the nature of the problem: in the fully automated process, wicked is ethical problem, which needs a human arbiter.

How do we take this forward? To reflect about the PSMs' contribution in a world accelerating with digital innovation, we started from the way scholars in PSMs categorize and define models as potential "boundary objects" [22, 29, 64, 74, 76, 86] and their performativity in facilitating or constraining group interactions. Boundary objects, indeed, can act by "transferring", to develop shared language between participants; by "translating", to develop shared meanings; moreover, by "transforming", with the aim to develop common interests among parties [29], based on Carlile [13, 14].

According to Franco [29] the models, as boundary objects, are (p. 731):

Focal points around which different knowledge, perspectives, dependencies and interests associated with the situation can be transferred, translated and transformed in interaction.

To this end, we can imagine adding a fourth type of boundary to Franco's [29] scheme, based on Carlile [13, 14]: the ethical boundary (Table 24.1).

Table 24.1 Modes, roles and effects at boundaries with the introduction of the ethical one (adapted from Franco [29])

Type of boundary faced	Model role	Model effects
Syntactic boundary	Transferring perspectives and Knowledge	Shared language
Semantic boundary	Translating perspective	Shared meanings
Pragmatic boundary	Transforming perspectives and Knowledge	Common interests
Ethical boundary	Deliberating	Ethical decision

This addition grounds a process in which to extend an understanding of the relevance of PSMs. This extension is also well-recognized in OR thinking (e.g., Le Menestrel and Van Wassenhove [48] and Mingers [51])

24.3.1   Case Vignette: Comparison of Two PSMs' Remote Applications

In this section, we use a synthetic illustration of the role of models as ethical boundary objects. We have selected a vignette related to two online applications of Strategic Choice Approach (in its classical version and in its combination with a multicriteria decision analysis) in a Master's degree course at the Politecnico di Torino for the development of transformation scenarios of a historical building. The students tackled the same decision-making problem with two different models, in both cases working virtually in groups and therefore only interacting remotely. In the first application, they were asked to apply the Strategic Choice Approach [34] with the support of the "Miro" software for the representations provided in the designing, shaping and comparing phases. In the second application, the same decision-making problem was tackled with a new software developed by the Politecnico di Torino, called Multi-Values Appraisal Methodology (MuVAM) (scientific referent is the first author of this chapter), where the first two SCA phases (Shaping Mode and Designing Mode) are combined with Analytic Hierarchy Process [70] for comparison and identification of the preferred option. During these two experiences, the students were asked to keep a "logbook", in order to develop some final comparative reflections on the two experiences. One of this logbook will be reappraised here in the light of the conceptualization of models as potential ethical boundary objects. It should be clear that the purpose of the empirical vignette is not to test this conceptualization but, rather, to illustrate its value in increasing the understanding of the new PSMs' contribution.

24.3.1.1   Analysis of the Case Vignette: Shaping

Decision Areas
The first phase of the Shaping is related to the identification of the decision areas. Using Politecnico's new software, MuVAM, each member of the group proposes decision areas, and the others react through written comments, leading to a vote that identifies which of these proposals will make up the model and which will be excluded. The reflections of the three group members were all in clear preference towards MuVAM over "classic SCA", precisely because of the interaction that took place through the written comments in the deliberation phase with respect to the selection of decision areas. Student 1 writes: "I found this first phase very quick and intuitive, personally more efficient than the 'traditional SCA' carried out manually, and

the key factor was the possibility of voting on the various Decision Areas without being overly influenced by my group colleagues". Student 2 points out that "it was essential to use the comments in the domains in which we disagreed, so as to try to find a solution or to try to convince classmates who had a different idea from mine". Student 3 writes: "The possibility of asking oneself questions independently and then being able to interact with group mates is a very good idea. Being able to put one's thoughts together and then compare them, through the software, by means of comments and actions finds its own logic in the identification of different problems".

Decision Graph and Problem Focus
In this phase the participants connect the various decision areas with decision links and the software determines which decision areas are "urgent", "important" and "secondary" based on the number of links (Fig. 24.1). The comments on this step are ambivalent: on the one hand all agree that the software considerably optimizes working time, on the other hand this reduction in time seems to be at the expense of understanding the graph. Student 3 emphasized that "in the manual SCA a clearer representation with Decision

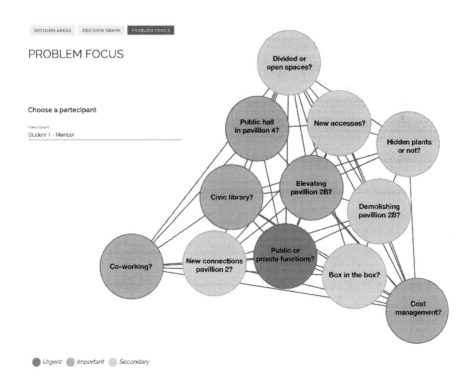

Fig. 24.1 Example of the problem focus (implemented with MuVAM)

Areas is possible with a process of identifying Important and Urgent areas leading to a much more informed focus".

24.3.1.2   Analysis of the Case Vignette: Design

Decision Options

In the first phase of the design the decision options are identified. A decision option is anyone of the mutually exclusive courses of action that can be considered within a decision area. With MuVAM, similar to the decision areas, each person can propose an option and the other participants can write comments or directly accept the proposed option. Here the speed of the deliberative process seems again to be perceived as a positive element of the method: "The simultaneity of the options that are sent is fundamental, as they all arrive very quickly, and this allows them to be read and approved without perhaps repeating them among the members of the group" (comment by student 1).

Incompatibility Grid

Once options have been identified, the question arises of what possibilities for choice are to be found, not merely within each decision area taken separately, but within linked pairs or sets of decision areas within the selected problem focus. It therefore becomes necessary to introduce assumptions about how far options from different decision areas can be combined. This phase is unanimously considered to be the one that has benefited most from the introduction of the software, not only in terms of its methods but also in terms of graphics (Fig. 24.2). The simultaneous filling in of identical boxes speeds up the work considerably, as do the graphics and ease of filling in. Student 3 writes: "This phase of the software is, in my opinion, of incredible value compared to the classic SCA carried out manually, it is much more efficient and faster. The graphic is well represented, clear and easy to handle, especially when dealing with a large number of Decision Options, I am really impressed".

Option Tree

The software processes all the data and produces the final option tree, reducing the work of the team to a minimum. The problem, however, is reading the tree in its entirety, especially when there are many options: in this case it is the technical limitation that does not allow a complete view of the route, reducing its effectiveness (Fig. 24.3). "If the software was excellent for the incompatibility phase, this is not the case for the Options Tree,

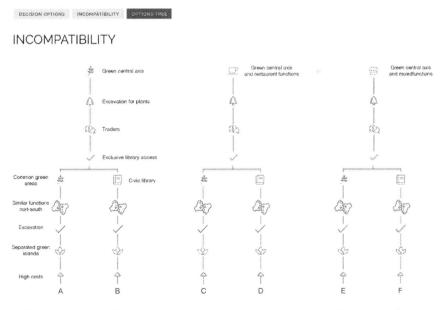

Fig. 24.2 Example of the incompatibility grid (implemented with MuVAM)

Fig. 24.3 Example of the option tree's section (implemented with MuVAM)

which completely loses its function of conveying clarity regarding the possible compatible solutions. On the web page it is practically impossible to see the whole graph, and the use of icons for each Decision Option is unclear, if they had been in text form it would have been better" (student 3). In this phase, where there is no need to decide but only to collect and represent information from the previous phase, the use of "classic SCA" is more effective and clearer, although it requires significantly more time and energy from the participants.

24.3.1.3   Analysis of the Case Vignette: Comparison

Solutions
At this stage of the methodology, the comparison is made through a multi-criteria analysis.

The first step concerns the decision whether to eliminate any of the solutions to the decision problem that emerged in the design, through a voting mechanism among the participants. This step was very much appreciated by the students, for two reasons: it was very quick and at the same time because "the option of being able to accept or exclude an option also makes one more reflect on the considerations of the other members of the group" (student 1).

Comparison Areas
Similarly, to the identification phase of decision areas in shaping, here also each member of the group proposes comparison areas, and the others react through written comments, leading to a vote that identifies which of these proposals will make up the model and which will be excluded. Again, participants said they preferred this approach to the less structured SCA. "My comments about this phase are limited to appreciating the clear and simple layout of voting in the various Comparison Areas, with the possibility of making a simple comment on the proposals of group colleagues, which again is a quicker approach than the communication problems with the traditional SCA" (Student 3).

Weighting and Comparison
In the weighting each criterion is assigned a degree of importance by each participant. This step is immediate thanks to the quality of the graphics.

In the comparison, each participant proceeds individually with the comparison of solution pairs. The evaluation phase represents one of the main innovations of MuVAM and takes place by placing the user in front of a graduated scale which allows him to define whether and to what extent a solution "A" is preferable to a solution "B", on a scale of 1 to 9 (Saaty), for each pair of opposing solutions. At the end of the evaluation phase, the software processes the data of each user: the individual analyses are then combined linearly to obtain a ranking of possible implementable solutions, ordered according to the combined score obtained by each solution. This ranking, accompanied by a set of additional information, is represented using schemes, graphs and tables that allow to analyse in depth the weight of each participant, of her/his choices and of the issues s/he brings in the whole decision-making process. This phase is much more structured than the comparison in the methodology defined by Friend and Hickling. According to the participants, "the traditional SCA is perhaps more elastic in both modification and representation, but this is at the expense of speed and efficiency, which make the software very good for managing multiple options" (student 2).

24.4 Conclusions

By reviewing the relevance of PSMs for a digital era, we have shown how the methods are still meaningful for organizational interventions as they embrace the complexities of digital transformation . Our chapter highlights the importance of deliberation aspect of PSMs in more detail, revealing the importance of embracing doubt via abduction. Specifically, via a case study we indicate a distinct emphasis on the ethical boundaries within problem situations. We thus propose future studies to focus on the ethical aspects of "wicked problems" to encourage more research into PSMs more generally.

References

1. Ackermann, F., & Eden E. (2011). Negotiation in strategy making teams: Group support systems and the process of cognitive change. Group Decision and Negotiation 20, 293–314.
2. Ackermann, F., & Eden, C. (2005). Using Causal Mapping with Group Support Systems to Elicit an Understanding of Failure in Complex Projects: Some Implications for Organizational Research. Group Decision and Negotiation, 14(5), 355–376.
3. Ackermann, F., & Eden, C. (1994). Issues in Computer and Non-computer Supported GDSSs. Decision Support Systems, 12(4,5), 381–390.
4. Ackermann, F., Eden, C., Pyrko, I. (2016). Accelerated multi-organization conflict resolution. Group Decision and Negotiation 25(5), 901–922.
5. Ackermann, F., Eden, C., Williams, T. (1997). Modeling for Litigation: Mixing Qualitative and Quantitative Approaches. Interfaces 27, 48–65.

6. Ackermann, F., Yearworth, M., White, L. (2018). Micro-processes in Group Decision and Negotiation: Practices and Routines for Supporting Decision Making. Group Decision and Negotiation 27(1), 709–713.

7. Ackoff, R.A. (1974). Redesigning the future: a systems approach to societal problems, New York - John Wiley & Sons.

8. Bana e Costa, C., Lourenço, J., Oliveira, M., Bana e Costa, J. (2013). A socio-technical approach for group decision support in public strategic planning: The Pernambuco PPA case. Group Decision and Negotiation 23, 1–25.

9. Bharadwaj, A., El Sawy, O., Pavlou P.A., Venkatraman, N. (2013). Digital Business Strategy: Toward A Next Generation Of Insights. MIS Quarterly 37(2), 471–482.

10. Bialecka-Colin E. (2007) Future with Uncertainties. Urban regeneration at Sodra Alvstranden, Goteborg, Archiprix Shanghai 2007.

11. Brown, S. L., & Eisenhardt, K. M. (1997). The Art of Continuous Change: Linking Complexity Theory and Time-Paced Evolution in Relentlessly Shifting Organizations. Administrative Science Quarterly, 42(1), 1–34.

12. Burger, K., White, L., Yearworth, M. (2018). Why so serious? Theorising playful model-driven group decision support with situated affectivity. Group Decision and Negotiation 27, 789–810.

13. Carlile, R.P. (2004). Transferring, translating, and transforming: an integrative framework for managing knowledge across boundaries. Organ Sci 15, 555–568.

14. Carlile, R.P. (2002). A pragmatic view of knowledge and boundaries: boundary objects in new product development. Organ Sci 13, 442–455.

15. Checkland, P., & Holwell S. (1998). Information, systems and information systems: making sense of the field. Chichester: John Wiley & Sons.

16. Checkland, P., & Scholes, J. (1990). Soft systems methodology in action. Chichester: Wiley.

17. Churchman, C. W. (1967). Guest Editorial: Wicked Problems. Management Science, 14(4), B141–B142.

18. Coelho, D., Antunes, C.H., Martins, A.G. (2010). Using SSM for structuring decision support in urban energy planning. Technological and Economic Development of Economy 16, 641–653.

19. Cushman, M., & Rosenhead, J. (2004). Planning in the face of politics: reshaping children's health services in Inner London. In M. Brandeau, F. Sainfort, W. Pierskalla (Eds.), International Series in Operations Research & Management Science. Operations research and health care: A handbook of methods and applications (pp. 555–592). Kluwer Academic: London.

20. Dehning, B., Stratopoulos, T. C. (2003). Determinants of a Sustainable Competitive Advantage Due to an IT-Enabled Strategy. The Journal of Strategic Information Systems, Vol. 12(1), 7–28.

21. Dutra, A., Tumasjan, A., Welpe, I.M. (2018). Blockchain is changing how media and entertainment companies compete. MIT Sloan Management Review, 39–45.

22. Eden, C. (1992). Strategy development as social process. Journal of Management Studies 29(6), 799–812.
23. Eden, C. (1985). Perish the Thought!. Journal of the Operational Research Society, 36(9), 809–819.
24. Eden, C., & Ackermann, F. (2018). Theory into practice, practice to theory: Action research in method development, European Journal of Operational Research 271(3), 1145–1155
25. Eden, C., & Ackermann, F. (2013). 'Joined-Up' Policy-Making: Group Decision and Negotiation Practice. Group Decision and Negotiation 23, 1–17.
26. Eden, C., & Ackermann, F. (2001). SODA: the principles. In J. Rosenhead, & J. Mingers (Eds.), Rational Analysis for a Problematic World Revisited: problem structuring methods for complexity, uncertainty and conflict: 21–41. Chichester: Wiley.
27. Fahey, D.K., Carson, E.R., Cramp, D.G., Gray, J.A.M. (2004). Applying systems modelling to public health. Systems Research and Behavioral Science 21(6), 635–649.
28. Ferraris, M. (2021). Documanità. Filosofia del mondo nuovo. Roma: Laterza.
29. Franco, L.A. (2013). Rethinking soft OR interventions: models as boundary objects. Eur J Oper Res 231(3), 720–733.
30. Franco, L.A. (2008). Facilitating collaboration with problem structuring methods: A case of an interorganisational construction partnership. Group Decision and Negotiation 17(4), 267–286.
31. Fregonese, E., Lami, I.M., Todella, E. (2020). Aesthetic Perspectives in Group Decision and Negotiation Practice. Group Decision and Negotiation 29, 993–1019.
32. Friend, J. K. (1993). Planning in the presence of uncertainty: Principles and practice. Journal of Infrastructure Planning and Management, 476, 1–9.
33. Friend, J. K., Hickling, A. (1987). Planning under pressure: The strategic choice approach. Pergamon (Urban and Regional Planning Series): Oxford.
34. Friend, J. K., Hickling, A. (2005). Planning under pressure: The strategic choice approach (3rd ed.). Routledge: London and New York.
35. Gimpel, H., Hosseini, S., Huber, R., Probst, L., Röglinger, M., Faisst, U. (2018). Structuring Digital Transformation: A Framework of Action Fields and its Application at ZEISS. Journal of Information Technology Theory and Application 19(1), 31–54.
36. Herrera, H. J., McCardle-Keurentjes, M. H. F., & Videira, N. (2016) Evaluating Facilitated Modelling Processes and Outcomes: An Experiment Comparing a Single and a Multimethod Approach in Group Model Building, Group Decision and Negotiation 25(6), 1277–1318.
37. Horn, R.E. (2001). Knowledge Mapping for Complex Social Messes, a presentation to the "Foundations in the Knowledge Economy" at the David and Lucile Packard Foundation, July 16.
38. Huxham, C. (2003). Theorizing collaboration practice. Public Management Review 5(3), 401–423.

39. Keys, P. (1997). Approaches to understanding the process of OR: Review, critique and extension. Omega 25(1), 1–13.
40. Keys, P. (1995). Reducing the process lacuna in operational research by taking a knowledge work perspective. Systems Research and Behavioral Science 24(3), 285–296.
41. Kotiadis, K., & Mingers, J. (2014). Combining problem structuring methods with simulation: The philosophical and practical challenges. In S. Brailsford, L. Churilov, & B. Dangerfild (Eds.), Discrete-event simulation and system dynamics for man- agement decision making (pp. 52–75). John Wiley & Sons Ltd: Chichester.
42. Kotiadis, K., & Mingers, J. (2006). Combining PSMs with Hard OR Methods: the Philosophical and Practical Challenges. J. Operational Research Society 57(7), 856–867.
43. Kreulich, K.; Dellmann, F.; Schutz, T.; Harth, T.; Zwingmann, K. (2016). Digitalisierung - Strategische Entwicklung einer kompetenzorientierten Lehre für die digitale Gesellschaft und Arbeitswelt. UAS7 e. V., Berlin.
44. Lami, I. M., & Tavella, E. (2019). On the usefulness of soft OR models in decision making: A comparison of Problem Structuring Methods supported and self-organized workshops. European Journal of Operational Research, 275, 1020–1036.
45. Lami I.M., & Todella E. (2019). Facing urban uncertainty with the strategic choiceapproach: the introduction of disruptive events. Rivista di Estetica 71, 222–240.
46. Lazarus, R.J. (2009). Super wicked problems and climate change: restraining the present to liberate the future. Cornell Law Rev. 94(5), 1153–1234.
47. Lehaney, B., & Paul, R.J. (1996). The use of soft systems methodology in the development of a simulation of outpatient services at Watford General Hospital. Journal of the Operational Research Society 47(7), 864–870.
48. Le Menestrel, M., Van Wassenhove, L.N. (2009). Ethics in Operations Research and Management Sciences: A never-ending effort to combine rigor and passion. Omega 37, 1039–1043.
49. Levin, K., Cashore, B., Bernstein, S., Auld, G. (2012). Overcoming the tragedy of super wicked problems: constraining our future selves to ameliorate global climate change. Policy Sci. 45, 123–152.
50. Midgley, G., Cavana, R. Y., Brocklesby, J., Foote, J. L., Wood, D. R.R., Ahuriri-Driscoll, A. (2013). Towards a new framework for evaluating systemic problem structuring methods, European Journal of Operational Research 229(1), 143–154.
51. Mingers, J. (2011). The Contribution of Systemic Thought to Critical Realism, Journal of Critical Realism, 10:3, 303–330.
52. Mingers, J., & Rosenhead, J. (2011). Introduction to the Special Issue: Teaching Soft O.R., Problem Structuring Methods, and Multimethodology. INFORMS Transactions on Education 12(1), 1–3.

53. Mingers, J., & Rosenhead, J. (2004). Problem structuring methods in action, European Journal of Operational Research 152, 530–554.
54. Mingers, J., & White, L. (2010). A review of the recent contribution of systems thinking to operational research and management science. European Journal of Operational Research, 207(3), 1147–1161.
55. Mortenson, M. J., Doherty, N. F., & Robinson, S. (2015). Operational research from Taylorism to Terabytes: A research agenda for the analytics age. European Journal of Operational Research, 241(3), 583–595.
56. Moulin, M. (1991). Getting planners to take notice. OR Insight 4(1), 25–29.
57. Ormerod, R. (2006). The history and ideas of pragmatism. Journal of the Operational Research Society, 57(8), 892–909.
58. Ormerod, R. (2005). Putting soft OR methods to work: the case of IS strategy development for the UK Parliament. Journal of the Operational Research Society 56(12), 1379–1398.
59. Ormerod, R. (1999). Putting soft OR methods to work: The case of the business improvement project at PowerGen. European Journal of Operational Research 118(1), 1–29.
60. Ormerod, R. (1996). Putting soft OR methods to work: information systems strategy development at Richards Bay. Journal of the Operational Research Society 47(9), 1083–1097.
61. Ormerod, R. (1995). Putting soft OR methods to work: information systems strategy development at Sainsbury's. Journal of the Operational Research Society 46(3), 277–293.
62. Paroutis, S., Franco, L.A., Papadopoulos, T. (2015). Visual Interactions with Strategy Tools: Producing Strategic Knowledge in Workshops. British Journal of Management 26(S1), S48–S66.
63. Peirce, C.S. (1958). 1931-1958. Collected Papers of Charles Sanders Peirce, vol. 1-8, eds. P. Weiss, C. Hartshorne, & A.W. Burks. Cambridge, MA: Harvard University Press.
64. Pidd, M. (2003). Tools for thinking: modelling in management science, 2nd ed. Wiley, Chichester.
65. Rittel, H. W. J., & Webber, M. M. (1973) Dilemmas in a General Theory of Planning. Policy Sciences, 4, 155–169.
66. Rorty, R. (1989). Contingency, Irony, and Solidarity. Cambridge: Cambridge University Press https://doi.org/10.1017/CBO9780511804397.
67. Rosenhead, J. (1996). What's the Problem? An Introduction to Problem Structuring Methods. Interfaces 26, 117–131.
68. Rosenhead, J. (2013). Problem structuring methods. In: S. Gass & F. Fu (Eds.), Encyclopedia of operations research and management science (pp. 1162–1172). New York: Springer.
69. Rouwette, E. A. J. A., Bastings, I., & Blokker, H. (2011). A comparison of Group Model Building and Strategic Options Development and Analysis. Group Decision and Negotiation, 20(6), 781–803.
70. Saaty, T. L. (1980) The Analytic Hierarchy Process. New York: McGraw-Hill.

71. Schallmo, D.R.A., Williams, C.A. (2018). History of Digital Transformation. In: Digital Transformation Now!. SpringerBriefs in Business (pp. 3–8). Springer, Cham.

72. Schwer, K., Hitz, K. (2018). Designing organizational structure in the age of digitization. Journal Of Eastern European And Central Asian Research 5(1), 1–11.

73. Smith, C. M., & Shaw, D. (2019). The characteristics of problem structuring methods: A literature review. European Journal of Operational Research, 274(2), 403–416.

74. Star, S.L., Griesemer, R.J. (1989). Institutional ecology, 'translations', and boundary objects: amateurs and professionals in Berkeley's museum of vertebrae zoology. Soc Stud Sci 19, 387–420.

75. Taleb, N.N. (2007). The Black Swan: The Impact of the Highly Improbable. Penguin Random House: New York.

76. Tavella E., & Lami, I.M. (2019). Negotiating perspectives and values through soft OR in the context of urban renewal. Journal of the Operational Research Society, 136–161.

77. Tavella, E., & Papadopoulos T. (2017). Applying OR to problem situations within community organisations: a case in a Danish non-profit, member-driven food cooperative. European Journal of Operational Research 258(2), 726–742.

78. Todella, E., Lami, I.M., Armando, A. (2018). Experimental Use of Strategic Choice Approach (SCA) by Individuals as an Architectural Design Tool. Group Decision and Negotiation 27(5), 811–826.

79. Yearworth, M., & White, L. (2021). A Problem Structuring Method implemented using a Group Support System. Paper presented at the 31st European Conference on Operational Research (EURO 2021), Athens, Greece.

80. Yearworth, M., & White, L. (2018). Spontaneous emergence of Community OR: self-initiating, self-organising problem structuring mediated by social media. European Journal of Operational Research, 268(3), 800–824.

81. Yearworth, M., & White, L. (2014). The non-codified use of problem structuring methods and the need for a generic constitutive definition. European Journal of Operational Research, 237(3), 932–945.

82. Weill, P., Woerner, S. (2018). Is Your Company Ready for a Digital Future? MIT Sloan Management Review; Cambridge 21–25.

83. Westcombe, M., Franco, L. A., & Shaw, D. (2006). Where Next for PSMs: A grassroots revolution? The Journal of the Operational Research Society, 57(7), 776–778.

84. Weick, K. E. (1989). Theory Construction as Disciplined Imagination. The Academy of Management Review 14(4), 516–531.

85. White, L. (2016). Behavioural operational research: Towards a framework for understanding behaviour in OR interventions. European Journal of Operational Research, 249(3), 827–841.

86. White, L. (2009). Understanding Problem Structuring Methods Interventions. European Journal of Operational Research, 99(3): 823–833.

87. White, L., 2003. The role of systems research and operational research in community involvement: A case study of a health action zone. Systems Research and Behavioral Science 20(2), 133–145.
88. White, L., & Lee, G.J. (2009). Operational research and sustainable development: Tackling the social dimension. European Journal of Operational Research 193(3), 683–692.
89. White, L., & Taket, A. R. (1993). Community OR-Doing what feels good. OR Insight 6(2), 20–23.
90. Wilson, J. M. (1998). Information systems provision: The contribution of soft systems methodology. Journal of the Operational Research Society 49(3), 296–297.
91. Zeiderman, A., Kaker, S., Silver, J., Wood, A., Ramakrishnan, K. (2017). Urban Uncertainty: Governing cities in turbulent times, London, LSE Cities.

Part VI

Recent OR Applications

25

Recent Advances in Big Data Analytics

Daoji Li, Yinfei Kong, Zemin Zheng, and Jianxin Pan

25.1 Introduction

With rapid development of information technologies, it is much easier and cheaper than before to collect data [22]. For example, satellites and surveillance cameras collect a large amount of image data with huge number of features; Walmart handles more than one million customer transactions

D. Li · Y. Kong (✉)
Department of Information Systems and Decision Sciences, California State University, Fullerton, CA, USA
e-mail: yikong@fullerton.edu

D. Li
e-mail: dali@fullerton.edu

Z. Zheng
International Institute of Finance, School of Management, University of Science and Technology of China, Hefei, China
e-mail: zhengzm@ustc.edu.cn

J. Pan
School of Mathematics, The University of Manchester, Manchester, UK
e-mail: Jianxin.Pan@manchester.ac.uk

© The Author(s), under exclusive license to Springer Nature
Switzerland AG 2022
S. Salhi and J. Boylan (eds.), *The Palgrave Handbook of Operations Research*,
https://doi.org/10.1007/978-3-030-96935-6_25

per hour; and Facebook generates billions of posts per week. Such examples also occur in agriculture, economics, finance, marketing, bioinformatics, medicine, biology, and social media studies.

Big Data cannot be processed or analyzed using traditional methods and tools. They are often accompanied by a large number of features and/or a large volume of observations. For example, in disease classification using microarray or proteomics data, tens of thousands of expressions of molecules or ions are potential predictors. When interactions are considered, the dimensionality is huge since the number of pairwise interactions increases quadratically with the number of features p and that of higher-order interactions grows even faster. Another example is the airline data set (http://stat-computing.org/dataexpo/2009/the-data.html), which includes more than one hundred million observations about flight arrival and departure information for all commercial flights within the USA, from October 1987 to April 2008. The number of covariates p is large in the first example while the number of observations n is huge in the second example. See Fan et al. [25] for more big data examples in different disciplines.

The availability of big data not only provides more information but also poses unprecedented challenges because traditional methods may fail in many big data applications. For example, the classical method of least squares for linear regression will fail for high-dimensional data because in this case the design matrix has more columns than rows, resulting in the Gram matrix is huge and singular. In addition, statistical inferences frequently involve numerical optimization. High-dimensional optimization is not only expensive in computation, but also slow in convergence [25]. It is well known that high dimensionality has a significant impact on computation, spurious correlation, noise accumulation, and theoretical studies [26]. For massive data, it is time-consuming to analyze the entire dataset. In some cases, the data is too large and beyond the capacity of standard machines and software tools for storage and analysis. Donoho [15] convincingly demonstrated the need to develop new statistical approaches and theories in high-dimensional data analysis. Fan and Li [24] provided a comprehensive overview of statistical challenges with high dimensionality in different problems. Fan et al. [22] presented various challenges in big data analysis.

To address the challenges in big data analytics, many new statistical methods have been developed in recent years. In this chapter, we will summarize some of these approaches to give a selective overview of the current state of the development. We will focus on two types of big data: ultrahigh-dimensional data and massive data, both of which are central to a spectrum of tasks of statistical learning and inference over the past two decades. Here, ultrahigh-dimensional data refers to the data in which the number of features may grow exponentially with the number of observations while massive data means that the number of observations is huge and much larger than the number of features.

The rest of the article is organized as follows. Section 25.2 presents recent advances in ultrahigh-dimensional data analysis with the focus on feature screening and interaction screening. Section 25.3 introduces divide-and-conquer methods and subsampling methods for massive data. We conclude the article with brief summary and discussions in Section 25.4.

25.2 Ultrahigh-Dimensional Data Analysis

As mentioned earlier, big data are typically characterized by high dimensionality and large sample size. In this section, we focus on ultrahigh-dimensional data in which the number of features p may grow exponentially with the number of observations n. In the past twenty-five years, variable selection and feature screening have been two central topics in ultrahigh-dimensional data analysis. Variable selection, also known as feature selection, aims at effectively identifying the subset of truly important features. It can increase the estimation accuracy and improve the model interpretability. Many variable selection methods have been proposed to select important covariates. Some examples include Lasso [78], SCAD [23], the Elastic Net [105], Adaptive Lasso [104], the Dantzig selector [7], SICA [61], and MCP [94]. See, for example [5, 27, 29], for overviews of recent developments in high-dimensional variable selection.

Scalability is a major challenge in high-dimensional variable selection. As pointed out in [26], when the dimension is extremely high, even though the aforementioned variable selection methods can be used to identify the important variables, the algorithms used for optimization can still be very expensive. To overcome such a challenge caused by ultrahigh dimensionality, one popular strategy is feature screening. The goal of feature screening is to reduce the dimensionality of the feature space from a very large scale to a moderate one in a computational fast way by discarding as many noise features as possible and meanwhile retaining all truly important features. In what follows, we will first briefly review feature screening methods and present some recent approaches for interaction screening.

25.2.1 Feature Screening

Suppose that we have n observations $(y_i, \mathbf{x}_i^T)$, which are independent and identically distributed copies of the pair $(y, \mathbf{x}^T)$, where $y \in \mathbb{R}$ is the response and $\mathbf{x} = (X_1, \cdots, X_p)^T$ is a p-dimensional covariate vector. Consider the linear regression model

$$y = \beta_1 X_1 + \cdots + \beta_p X_p + \varepsilon, \qquad (25.1)$$

where $\boldsymbol{\beta} = (\beta_1, \cdots, \beta_p)^T$ is a p-dimensional unknown regression coefficient vector, and ε is the random error with mean zero. We focus on the ultrahigh-dimensional setting in which $\log p = O(n^\alpha)$ for some $0 < \alpha < 1$. To ensure model identifiablilty, it is common to assume that the true regression coefficient vector $\boldsymbol{\beta}_0 = (\beta_{0,1}, \cdots, \beta_{0,p})^T$ is sparse, meaning that only a small number of covariates are truly associated with the response. Let $\mathcal{M}_* = \{1 \le j \le p : \beta_{0,j} \ne 0\}$ be the true sparse model with the size $s = |\mathcal{M}_*| = o(n)$. Then the set $\mathcal{M}_*$ contains all important variables.

The SIS method proposed in [26] is a two-scale learning approach in which large-scale feature screening is first applied to reduce the dimensionality from p to a moderate one d (say, below sample size n), and moderate-scale variable selection are then conducted on the much reduced feature space. In particular, the SIS method ranks the importance of all the p features $X_1, \cdots, X_p$ based on the marginal Pearson correlation between each covariate and the response, and estimate the set of $\mathcal{M}$ by

$$\widehat{\mathcal{M}} = \{1 \le j \le p : |\widehat{\mathrm{corr}}\,(X_j, Y)| \text{ is among the top } d \text{ largest ones}\}$$

where $\widehat{\mathrm{corr}}$ denotes the sample correlation. This is the feature screening step of SIS and reduces the ultrahigh dimensionality down to a relatively moderate scale d. Then the variable selection step of SIS using features in the estimated set $\widehat{\mathcal{M}}$ can be conducted with any existing variable selection method including Lasso [78], SCAD [23], the Elastic Net [105], Adaptive Lasso [104], the Dantzig selector [7], SICA [61], and MCP [94]. Under fairly general conditions, [26] proved that, with probability tending to one, all the important covariates are retained in the feature screening step of SIS, that is,

$$P(\mathcal{M}_* \subset \widehat{\mathcal{M}}) \to 1. \qquad (25.2)$$

This property in (25.2) was named as the sure screening property which is vital to the variable selection step of SIS.

Fan and Lv [26] suggested to take $d = \lfloor n / \log(n) \rfloor$ or $n - 1$ in practice, where $\lfloor a \rfloor$ is the smallest integer greater than a. It can also be tuned by some data-driven methods. For example [21, 96] proposed a simple permutation method that controls the false positive rate at a predetermined level.

Since the seminal work of Fan and Lv [26], the feature screening idea has been applied to many important problems including generalized linear model [31], classification [21], semi-parametric model [52, 102], nonparametric model [66], varying coefficient models [30, 57], generalized varying coefficient model [92], generalized varying coefficient mixed effect models [12], quantile regression [42, 65, 88], survival analysis [32, 36, 75, 97], compressed sensing [89], network autoregression model [44], and graphical models [20], among others. To avoid the issue of model misspecification, various model-free feature screening methods have been proposed [14, 54, 59, 67, 69, 71, 73, 77, 99–101]. See, for example [28, 58, 60] for overviews of feature screening procedures for ultrahigh-dimensional data.

25.2.2 Interaction Screening for Regression Models

Understanding how features interact with each other is fundamentally important in many scientific discoveries and contemporary applications, especially in areas such as medicine, genetics, and cancer studies [13, 68]. In practice, the models containing interaction effects are more flexible and powerful than main-effects-only models as they can improve both model interpretability and prediction accuracy. The following quadratic regression model

$$y = \alpha_0 + \sum_{j=1}^{p} \beta_j X_j + \sum_{k=1}^{p-1} \sum_{\ell=k+1}^{p} \gamma_{k\ell} X_k X_\ell + \varepsilon \tag{25.3}$$

is a natural extension of the linear model (25.1) by considering interaction effects between the covariates, where α_0 is the intercept, β_j's and $\gamma_{k\ell}$'s are regression coefficients for main effects and interactions, respectively. We assume that $E(X_j) = 0$ for each $j = 1, \ldots, p$. Otherwise, consider the interaction model (25.3) with each X_j replaced by $X_j - E(X_j)$.

Taking interactions into account in ultrahigh-dimensional data analysis poses great challenges in the computation for practical implementations and theory for analyzing the properties of the estimators. For example, the number of the possible pairwise interactions is $p(p-1)/2$, and p is typically growing at some exponential rate of the sample size n. For a dataset with n observations and p covariates, the augmented design matrix including all main effects and pairwise interaction terms is of size $n \times (p^2 + p + 2)/2$. When p is 10^5 or larger, it may not be possible to store the entire augmented design matrix for a desktop. In theory, interaction effects have heavier tails and more complex covariance structures than main effects in a random design, making theoretical analysis difficult, especially in ultrahigh-dimensional settings.

Similar to screening main effects, the goal of interaction screening is to screen out unimportant interaction terms in (25.3) while retaining important ones. A naive extension of the SIS idea for interaction screening would be to treat interactions as new features and screen them based on the marginal utility between each interaction and the response. It is easy to show this naive approach is inefficient and can result in undesirable results. See, for example [70] for a toy example.

To facilitate implementation, one commonly used strategy is to impose the heredity assumption. The strong heredity assumption requires that an interaction between two covariates be included in the model only if both main effects are important, while the weak one relaxes such as a constraint to the presence of at least one main effect being important. See, for example [4, 38–41, 53, 91] for the methods using this assumption.

However, the heredity assumptions can be violated or difficult to verify in real applications [13, 37]. To address this challenge [48] introduced a new screening approach, named the interaction pursuit with distance correlation (IPDC), in high-dimensional multi-response regression models, which exploits feature screening applied to transformed variables with distance correlation followed by feature selection. This approach is computationally efficient, and does not require the heredity assumptions. Here we only review the interaction screening step. To be more specific [48] consider the following high-dimensional multi-response interaction model

$$\mathbf{y} = \boldsymbol{\alpha} + \mathbf{B}_{\mathbf{x}}^T \mathbf{x} + \mathbf{B}_{\mathbf{z}}^T \mathbf{z} + \mathbf{w}, \qquad (25.4)$$

where $\mathbf{y} = (Y_1, \cdots, Y_q)^T$ is a q-dimensional vector of responses, $\mathbf{x} = (X_1, \cdots, X_p)^T$ is a p-dimensional vector of covariates, $\mathbf{z}$ is a $p(p-1)/2$-dimensional vector of all pairwise interactions between covariates X_j's, $\boldsymbol{\alpha} = (\alpha_1, \cdots, \alpha_q)^T$ is a q-dimensional vector of intercepts, $\mathbf{B}_{\mathbf{x}} \in \mathbb{R}^{p \times q}$ and $\mathbf{B}_{\mathbf{z}} \in \mathbb{R}^{p(p-1)/2 \times q}$ are regression coefficient matrices for the main effects and interactions, respectively, and $\mathbf{w} = (W_1, \cdots, W_q)^T$ is a q-dimensional vector of random errors with mean zero and being independent of $\mathbf{x}$. Each response in this model is allowed to have its own regression coefficients, and to simplify the presentation, the covariate vector $\mathbf{x}$ is assumed to be centered with mean zero. It is of practical importance to consider sparse models in which the rows of the coefficient matrices $\mathbf{B_z}$ and $\mathbf{B_z}$ are sparse with only a fraction of nonzeros. Obviously, the quadratic regression model in (25.3) is a special case of the interaction model (25.4) with $q = 1$.

To facilitate the presentation, we call $X_k X_\ell$ an important interaction if the corresponding row of $\mathbf{B_z}$ is nonzero, and X_k an active interaction variable if there exists some $1 \leq \ell \neq k \leq p$ such that $X_k X_\ell$ is an important interaction. Similarly, X_j is referred to as an important main effect if its associated row of $\mathbf{B_x}$ is nonzero. Define three sets

$$\mathcal{I} = \{(k, \ell) : 1 \leq k < \ell \leq p \text{ and } X_k X_\ell \text{ is an important interaction}\},$$
$$\mathcal{A} = \{1 \leq j \leq p : X_j \text{ is an active interaction variable}\},$$
$$\mathcal{M} = \{1 \leq j \leq p : X_j \text{ is an important main effect}\}.$$

Then $\mathcal{I}$, $\mathcal{A}$, and $\mathcal{M}$ the set of all important interactions, the set of all active interaction variables, and the set of all important main effects, respectively. Note that $\mathcal{I} \subset \{(k, l) : 1 \leq k < l \leq p \text{ and } k, l \in \mathcal{A}\}$. Thus, in order to identify the important interactions, it is sufficient to identify the set $\mathcal{A}$.

Kang et al. [48] proposed to construct the marginal utility function exploiting the distance correlation introduced in [74] and identified the set $\mathcal{A}$ by ranking the distance correlations between the squared covariates X_j^2 and the squared response vector $\mathbf{y} \circ \mathbf{y}$, where $\circ$ denotes the Hadamard (componentwise) product of two vectors. The distance correlation

$$\text{dcorr}(\mathbf{u}, \mathbf{v}) = \frac{\text{dcov}(\mathbf{u}, \mathbf{v})}{\sqrt{\text{dcov}(\mathbf{u}, \mathbf{u}) \text{ dcov}(\mathbf{v}, \mathbf{v})}}$$

is well defined for any two random vectors $\mathbf{u} \in \mathbb{R}^{d_u}$ and $\mathbf{v} \in \mathbb{R}^{d_v}$ of arbitrary mixed dimensions, where the distance covariance between $\mathbf{u}$ and $\mathbf{v}$ is given by

$$\text{dcov}^2(\mathbf{u}, \mathbf{v}) = \frac{1}{c_{d_u} c_{d_v}} \int_{\mathbb{R}^{d_u + d_v}} \frac{|\varphi_{\mathbf{u}, \mathbf{v}}(\mathbf{s}, \mathbf{t}) - \varphi_{\mathbf{u}}(\mathbf{s})\varphi_{\mathbf{v}}(\mathbf{t})|^2}{\|\mathbf{s}\|^{d_u + 1} \|\mathbf{t}\|^{d_v + 1}} d\mathbf{s} d\mathbf{t}.$$

Here $c_m = \pi^{(m+1)/2} / \Gamma\{(m + 1)/2\}$ is the half area of the unit sphere $S^m \subset \mathbb{R}^{m+1}$, $\varphi_{\mathbf{u}, \mathbf{v}}(\mathbf{s}, \mathbf{t})$, $\varphi_{\mathbf{u}}(\mathbf{s})$, and $\varphi_{\mathbf{v}}(\mathbf{t})$ are the characteristic functions of $(\mathbf{u}, \mathbf{v})$, $\mathbf{u}$, and $\mathbf{v}$, respectively, and $\| \cdot \|$ denotes the Euclidean norm. Compared to the Pearson correlation, it also has the advantage that the distance correlation of two random vectors is zero if and only if they are independent. See [74] for more properties of the distance correlation, and [45] for a fast algorithm for computing the distance correlation.

Suppose we have a sample $(\mathbf{y}_i, \mathbf{x}_i)_{i=1}^{n}$ of n independent and identically distributed (i.i.d.) observations from $(\mathbf{y}, \mathbf{x})$ in the multi-response interaction model (25.4). For each $1 \leq k \leq p$, denote by $\mathrm{dcorr}(X_k^2, \mathbf{y} \circ \mathbf{y})$ the distance correlation between the squared covariate X_k^2 and squared response vector $\mathbf{y} \circ \mathbf{y}$. For notational simplicity, we write $X_k^* = X_k^2$, $\tilde{\mathbf{y}} = \mathbf{y}/\sqrt{q}$, and $\mathbf{y}^* = \tilde{\mathbf{y}} \circ \tilde{\mathbf{y}} = \mathbf{y} \circ \mathbf{y}/q$. Define two population quantities

$$\omega_k^* = \frac{\mathrm{dcov}^2(X_k^*, \mathbf{y}^*)}{\sqrt{\mathrm{dcov}^2(X_k^*, X_k^*)}} \quad \text{and} \quad \omega_j = \frac{\mathrm{dcov}^2(X_j, \tilde{\mathbf{y}})}{\sqrt{\mathrm{dcov}^2(X_j, X_j)}} \quad (25.5)$$

with $1 \leq k, j \leq p$ for interaction variables and main effects, respectively. Denote by $\hat{\omega}_k^*$ and $\hat{\omega}_j$ the empirical versions of ω_k^* and ω_j, respectively, constructed by plugging in the corresponding sample distance covariances based on the sample $\{(\mathbf{y}_i, \mathbf{x}_i)\}_{i=1}^{n}$. According to [74], the sample distance covariance between any two random vectors $\mathbf{u}$ and $\mathbf{v}$ based on a sample $\{(\mathbf{u}_i, \mathbf{v}_i)\}_{i=1}^{n}$ is given by

$$\widehat{\mathrm{dcov}}^2(\mathbf{u}, \mathbf{v}) = \hat{S}_1 + \hat{S}_2 - 2\hat{S}_3,$$

where the three quantities are defined as $\hat{S}_1 = n^{-2} \sum_{i,j=1}^{n} \|\mathbf{u}_i - \mathbf{u}_j\| \|\mathbf{v}_i - \mathbf{v}_j\|$, $\hat{S}_2 = [n^{-2} \sum_{i,j=1}^{n} \|\mathbf{u}_i - \mathbf{u}_j\|][n^{-2} \sum_{i,j=1}^{n} \|\mathbf{v}_i - \mathbf{v}_j\|]$, and $\hat{S}_3 = n^{-3} \sum_{i,j,k=1}^{n} \|\mathbf{u}_i - \mathbf{u}_k\| \|\mathbf{v}_j - \mathbf{v}_k\|$. In view of $\mathrm{dcorr}^2(X_k^2, \mathbf{y} \circ \mathbf{y}) = \mathrm{dcorr}^2(X_k^*, \mathbf{y}^*) = \omega_k^*/\{\mathrm{dcov}^2(\mathbf{y}^*, \mathbf{y}^*)\}^{1/2}$ and $\mathrm{dcorr}^2(X_j, \mathbf{y}) = \mathrm{dcorr}^2(X_j, \tilde{\mathbf{y}}) = \omega_j/\{\mathrm{dcov}^2(\tilde{\mathbf{y}}, \tilde{\mathbf{y}})\}^{1/2}$, the procedure of screening the interaction variables and main effects via distance correlations $\mathrm{dcorr}(X_k^2, \mathbf{y} \circ \mathbf{y})$ and $\mathrm{dcorr}(X_j, \mathbf{y})$ suggested above is equivalent to that of thresholding the quantities ω_k^*'s and ω_j's, respectively.

Then one can estimate the sets of important main effects $\mathcal{M}$ and active interaction variables $\mathcal{A}$ as

$$\widehat{\mathcal{M}} = \{1 \leq j \leq p : \hat{\omega}_j \geq \tau_1\} \quad \text{and} \quad \widehat{\mathcal{A}} = \{1 \leq k \leq p : \hat{\omega}_k^* \geq \tau_2\}, \quad (25.6)$$

where τ_1 and τ_2 are some positive thresholds. With the set $\widehat{\mathcal{A}}$ of retained interaction variables, we construct a set of pairwise interactions

$$\widehat{\mathcal{I}} = \{(k, l) : 1 \leq k < l \leq p \text{ and } k, l \in \widehat{\mathcal{A}}\}. \quad (25.7)$$

This achieves the goal of interaction screening. Such a procedure is computationally efficient, generally applicable beyond the heredity assumption, and effective even when the number of responses diverges with the sample size. Under mild regularity conditions [48] showed that, the IPDC method enjoys the sure screening property that all important interactions and main effects can be retained in the reduced model with probability approaching to one even when the number of covariates p is growing at some exponential rate of the sample size n. In addition, for the special case of the interaction model (25.4) with $q = 1$ [51] further established the theoretical results of interaction selection on the oracle inequalities and false sign rate in ultrahighdimensional settings with random design. Moreover, the false sign rate can be asymptotically vanishing.

In practice, one may sort $\widehat{\omega}_k^*$ in descending order and keep the top d variables to estimate the set $\mathcal{A}$. One can also use the same idea to estimate the set $\mathcal{M}$. Similar to the SIS method in [26], one can take $d = \lfloor n/\log(n) \rfloor$ or choose d using some data-driven methods such as the permutation method in [21, 96]. It is worth mentioning that the screening procedure of IPDC replies only on the marginal statistics so that parallel computing can be further used to accelerate the computation for extremely large data sets.

25.2.3 Interaction Screening for Classification

Classification, aiming at identifying to which of a set of categories a new observation belongs, has been frequently encountered in various fields such as genomics, proteomics, face recognition, brain images, medicine, and machine learning. Unlike regression models, the values of the response variable in classification are discrete class labels, e.g., fraud vs. non-fraud.

For the ease of presentation, let us focus on binary classification problems in which observations are from two classes. Assume that the p-dimensional feature vector $\mathbf{x} = (X_1, \cdots, X_p)^T$ follows

$$\mathbf{x}|(Y = 1) \sim N(\boldsymbol{\mu}_1, \boldsymbol{\Sigma}_1) \quad \text{and} \quad \mathbf{x}|(Y = 2) \sim N(\boldsymbol{\mu}_2, \boldsymbol{\Sigma}_2),$$

where $Y \in \{1, 2\}$ is the class label, $\boldsymbol{\mu}_k \in \mathbb{R}^p$, $k = 1, 2$, are the mean vectors, and $\boldsymbol{\Sigma}_k \in \mathbb{R}^{p \times p}$, $k = 1, 2$, are the two covariance matrices. Bayes' rule classifies a new observation $\mathbf{x}$ to class 1 if and only if $\pi_1 f(\mathbf{x}|\boldsymbol{\mu}_1, \boldsymbol{\Sigma}_1) > \pi_2 f(\mathbf{x}|\boldsymbol{\mu}_2, \boldsymbol{\Sigma}_2)$, where $f(\mathbf{x}|\boldsymbol{\mu}, \boldsymbol{\Sigma})$ is the probability density function of a multivariate normal distribution $N(\boldsymbol{\mu}, \boldsymbol{\Sigma})$, and $\pi_k = P(Y = k)$, $k = 1, 2$, are the two prior probabilities. It is easy to show that the Bayes rule admits the following form

$$Q(\mathbf{x}) = 2^{-1}\mathbf{x}\boldsymbol{\Omega}\mathbf{x} + \boldsymbol{\delta}^T\mathbf{x} + \zeta, \qquad (25.8)$$

where $\boldsymbol{\Omega} = \boldsymbol{\Sigma}_2^{-1} - \boldsymbol{\Sigma}_1^{-1}$, $\boldsymbol{\delta} = \boldsymbol{\Sigma}_1^{-1}\boldsymbol{\mu}_1 - \boldsymbol{\Sigma}_2^{-1}\boldsymbol{\mu}_2$, and $\zeta = 2^{-1}\boldsymbol{\mu}_2^T\boldsymbol{\Sigma}_2^{-1}\boldsymbol{\mu}_2 - 2^{-1}\boldsymbol{\mu}_1^T\boldsymbol{\Sigma}_1^{-1}\boldsymbol{\mu}_1 + 2^{-1}\log(|\boldsymbol{\Sigma}_2|/|\boldsymbol{\Sigma}_1|) + \log(\pi_1/\pi_2)$. A new observation $\mathbf{x}$ is classified into class 1 if and only if $Q(\mathbf{x}) > 0$.

Throughout this subsection, we use the term "interaction" to refer to all second-order effects, including both two-way interactions $X_j X_\ell$ with $j \neq \ell$ and the quadratic terms X_j^2. So there are $p(p+1)/2$ possible interactions in total under our definition. We call $X_j X_\ell$, $1 \leq j, \ell \leq p$ an active interaction if its coefficient is nonzero in (25.8), and we call X_j an interaction variable if there exists some $\ell \in \{1, 2, \ldots, p\}$ such that $X_j X_\ell$ is an active interaction.

From (25.8), one can observe that an interaction term $X_j X_\ell$ is an active interaction if and only if $\boldsymbol{\Omega}_{j\ell} \neq 0$. Here we use $\mathbf{A}_{j\ell}$ to denote the (j, ℓ) element of any matrix $\mathbf{A}$. Motivated by this observation [33] proposed a new interaction screening approach, called the innovated interaction screening (IIS), by recovering the support of $\boldsymbol{\Omega}$. To be more specific, denote the index set of interaction variables by

$$\mathcal{A} = \{1 \leq j \leq p : X_j X_\ell \text{ is an active interaction for some } 1 \leq \ell \leq p\}. \qquad (25.9)$$

In light of (25.8), the above set can also be written as $\mathcal{A} = \{1 \leq j \leq p : \boldsymbol{\Omega}_{j\ell} \neq 0 \text{ for some } 1 \leq \ell \leq p\}$. If the index set $\mathcal{A}$ can be recovered, then all active interactions can be reconstructed by the set $\{(k, l) : 1 \leq j < l \leq p \text{ and } j, l \in \mathcal{A}\}$.

Identifying the index set $\mathcal{A}$ is challenging when p is large. Write $\boldsymbol{\Omega}_1 = \boldsymbol{\Sigma}_1^{-1}$ and $\boldsymbol{\Omega}_2 = \boldsymbol{\Sigma}_2^{-1}$. [33] proved that $\mathcal{A} = \mathcal{A}_1 \cup \mathcal{A}_2$ where

$$\mathcal{A}_1 = \{1 \leq j \leq p : (\widetilde{\boldsymbol{\Sigma}}_1)_{jj} \neq 0\} \text{ and } \mathcal{A}_2 = \{1 \leq j \leq p : (\widetilde{\boldsymbol{\Sigma}}_2)_{jj} \neq 0\} \qquad (25.10)$$

with $\widetilde{\boldsymbol{\Sigma}}_1 = \boldsymbol{\Omega}_1\boldsymbol{\Sigma}_2\boldsymbol{\Omega}_1 - \boldsymbol{\Omega}_1$ and $\widetilde{\boldsymbol{\Sigma}}_2 = \boldsymbol{\Omega}_2\boldsymbol{\Sigma}_1\boldsymbol{\Omega}_2 - \boldsymbol{\Omega}_2$. Observing that $(\widetilde{\boldsymbol{\Sigma}}_1)_{jj}$ is the difference of between-class variances of the jth component of the transformed variable vector $\boldsymbol{\Omega}_1\mathbf{x}$, the index set $\mathcal{A}_1$ can be obtained by examining which features have different variances across two classes after the transformation based on $\boldsymbol{\Omega}_1$. Similarly, the index set $\mathcal{A}_2$ can be obtained by examining which features have different variances across two classes after the transformation based on $\mathbf{\Omega}_2$.

Since IIS works with the transformed feature vectors $\tilde{\mathbf{x}} = \mathbf{\Omega}_1 \mathbf{x}$ and $\check{\mathbf{x}} = \mathbf{\Omega}_2 \mathbf{x}$ identically, for the ease of presentation, we only discuss in detail IIS based on the transformation $\tilde{\mathbf{x}} = (\widetilde{X}_1, \ldots, \widetilde{X}_p)^T = \mathbf{\Omega}_1 \mathbf{x}$. Suppose we observe n data points $\{(Y_i, \mathbf{z}_i^T)\}_{i=1}^n$, where $Y_i = 1$ or 2. Write $\widetilde{\mathbf{X}} = \mathbf{X}\mathbf{\Omega}_1$ as the transformed data matrix, where $\mathbf{X} = (\mathbf{x}_1, \ldots, \mathbf{x}_n)^T$ is the original data matrix. To test whether the jth transformed feature $\widetilde{X}_j$ has different variances across two classes [33] proposed to use the following test statistic

$$\widetilde{D}_j = \log \tilde{\sigma}_j^2 - \sum_{k=1}^{2}(n_k/n)\log\big[(\tilde{\sigma}_j^{(k)})^2\big], \qquad (25.11)$$

where $\tilde{\sigma}_j^2$ denotes the pooled sample variance estimate for $\widetilde{X}_j$, and $(\tilde{\sigma}_j^{(k)})^2$ is the within-class sample variance estimate for $\widetilde{X}_j$ in class k. As can be seen from (25.11), $\widetilde{D}_j$ is expected to be nonzero if variances of $\widetilde{X}_j$ are different across classes. This test statistic $\widetilde{D}_j$ was originally introduced in [46] in the sliced inverse index model setting for detecting important variables with pairwise or higher-order interactions among p predictors.

In most applications, the precision matrices $\mathbf{\Omega}_1$ and $\mathbf{\Omega}_2$ are unknown and need to be estimated. There is a large body of literature on estimating precision matrices. See, for example [3, 6, 34, 35, 84, 93], among others. For each $k = 1, 2$, given an estimator $\widehat{\mathbf{\Omega}}_k$ of $\mathbf{\Omega}_k$, the IIS approach transforms the data matrix as $\mathbf{X}\widehat{\mathbf{\Omega}}_k$. Consider the transformation $\mathbf{X}\widehat{\mathbf{\Omega}}_1$. Then the corresponding test statistic $\widehat{D}_j$ is

$$\widehat{D}_j = \log \hat{\sigma}_j^2 - \sum_{k=1}^{2}(n_k/n)\log\big[(\hat{\sigma}_j^{(k)})^2\big], \qquad (25.12)$$

where $\hat{\sigma}_j^2$ is the pooled sample variance estimate for the jth feature after the transformation $\mathbf{X}\widehat{\mathbf{\Omega}}_1$, and $(\hat{\sigma}_j^{(k)})^2$ is the class k sample variance estimate for the jth feature after the transformation for $k = 1, 2$.

Define $\widehat{\mathcal{A}}_1 = \{1 \leq j \leq p : \widehat{D}_j > \omega_n\}$ with $\omega_n > 0$ the threshold level depending only on n. Similarly, one can obtain $\widehat{\mathcal{A}}_2$, which is defined analogously to $\widehat{\mathcal{A}}_1$ using the test statistics calculated with data transformed by $\widehat{\mathbf{\Omega}}_2$. Then the set $\mathcal{A}$ can be estimated by $\widehat{\mathcal{A}} = \widehat{\mathcal{A}}_1 \cup \widehat{\mathcal{A}}_2$ and the set of all active interactions can be reconstructed by $\{(k, l) : 1 \leq j < l \leq p \text{ and } j, l \in \widehat{\mathcal{A}}\}$.

Fan et al. [33] showed that the IIS method enjoys sure screening property in interaction selection in the high-dimensional setting of p growing exponentially with the sample size. As we can see, the IIS method for classification share the same spirit as the IPDC approach for regression models in the sense that both use the marginal screening ideas on the transformed features and identify $O(p^2)$ important interactions by examining only p transformed features.

25.3   Massive Data Analysis

As we enter the era of big data, there has been an explosive growth of data size, not only in terms of the dimensionality but also sample size. In the previous section, we reviewed different methods for ultrahigh-dimensional data where $p >> n$. We now focus on massive data in which $n >> p$ and our goal is to analyze such a data with enormous size under limited computational resources. In the field of statistics, various techniques were developed to analyze massive datasets, such as divide-and-conquer methods [11, 56] and subsampling methods [17, 62, 63, 82, 83].

25.3.1   Divide-and-Conquer Methods

As discussed before, one major challenge in analyzing massive data sets is computational efficiency. When the data size n is too large to be analyzed entirely by one computer, or when datasets are already stored in distributed database systems, it is natural to consider a "divide-and-conquer" strategy for scalability. In such as strategy, one can split the entire dataset into K subsets of smaller sample sizes such that each smaller subset can be analyzed by one machine. Each subset is analyzed separately and K relevant subdata statistics are aggregated to obtain the final estimator.

To illustrate the idea of the "divide-and-conquer" strategy, let us consider the following linear regression model

$$y_i = \mathbf{x}_i^T \boldsymbol{\beta} + \varepsilon_i, \ \ i = 1, 2, \cdots, n, \tag{25.13}$$

where $y_i \in \mathbb{R}$ and $\mathbf{x}_i = (X_{i1}, \cdots, X_{ip})^T \in \mathbb{R}^p$ are the response variable and covariates vector for the ith observation, respectively, $\boldsymbol{\beta} = (\beta_1, \cdots, \beta_p)^T$ is a p-dimensional unknown regression coefficient vector, and ε_i is the random error for the ith observation. Here the sample size n is huge and $n >> p$. Denote by $\{(y_i, \mathbf{x}_i^T)\}_{i=1}^n$ the entire data. Let $\mathbf{X} = (\mathbf{x}_1, \cdots, \mathbf{x}_n)^T \in \mathbb{R}^{n \times p}$

and $\mathbf{y} = (y_1, \cdots, y_n)^T \in \mathbb{R}^n$ be the design matrix and the response vector for the entire data, respectively. Assume that p is finite and $\mathbf{X}^T\mathbf{X}$ is invertible, the ordinary least squares estimator using entire data all at once is

$$\widehat{\beta}^{(a)} = (\mathbf{X}^T\mathbf{X})^{-1}\mathbf{X}^T\mathbf{y}.$$

When one splits the entire dataset into K subsets such that each subset can be analyzed by one machine and assume $\mathbf{X}_k^T\mathbf{X}_k$ is invertible, the ordinary least squares estimator from the kth subset is $\widehat{\beta}^{(k)} = (\mathbf{X}_k^T\mathbf{X}_k)^{-1}\mathbf{X}_k^T\mathbf{y}_k$, where $\mathbf{X}_k \in \mathbb{R}^{n_k \times p}$ is the design matrix, $\mathbf{y}_k \in \mathbb{R}^{n_k}$ is the response vector for the data in the kth subset, and n_k is the number of observations in the kth subset. Write $S_k = (\mathbf{X}_k^T\mathbf{X}_k)^{-1}$ for $k = 1, \cdots, K$. Then one can combine these K least-square estimators to obtain a new estimator

$$\widehat{\beta}^{(c)} = \left(\sum_{k=1}^K S_k^{-1}\right)^{-1} \left(\sum_{k=1}^K S_k^{-1}\widehat{\beta}^{(k)}\right) = (\mathbf{X}^T\mathbf{X})^{-1}\mathbf{X}^T\mathbf{y} \qquad (25.14)$$

since $\mathbf{X}^T\mathbf{X} = \sum_{k=1}^K \mathbf{X}_k^T\mathbf{X}_k$ and $\mathbf{X}^T\mathbf{y} = \sum_{k=1}^K \mathbf{X}_k^T\mathbf{y}_k$. Compared with the traditional method, such a "divide-and-conquer" strategy utilizes the computing power of multiple machines. We illustrate this strategy in Fig. 25.1.

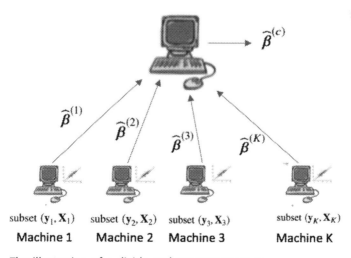

Fig. 25.1 The illustration of a divide-and-conquer strategy

It is interesting to see that the new estimator $\widehat{\boldsymbol{\beta}}^{(c)}$ is exactly same as $\widehat{\boldsymbol{\beta}}^{(a)}$ in this particular example. Note that obtaining $(\mathbf{X}_k^T \mathbf{X}_k, \widehat{\boldsymbol{\beta}}^{(k)})$ only needs to use the data in the kth subset and do not need to access the entire data. This means that using the divide-and-conquer approach, one can obtain the same estimator obtained from the entire data (assuming that there is a super-computer that could compute $\widehat{\boldsymbol{\beta}}^{(a)}$) when we pay a small price of requiring that the Gram matrix $\mathbf{X}_k^T \mathbf{X}_k$ from each subset is invertible. Of course, this assumption is slightly stronger than the original assumption on design matrix that $\mathbf{X}^T \mathbf{X}$ is invertible. Note that the size of $(\mathbf{X}_k^T \mathbf{X}_k, \widehat{\boldsymbol{\beta}}^{(k)})$ is $p^2 + p$, so we only need to save $K(p^2 + p)$ numbers, which significantly reduces commu-nication cost since both K and p are far less than n in practice for massive data.

Motivated by this interesting result, in the estimating equation framework [56] developed a computation and storage efficient algorithm for massive data using a similar "divide-and-conquer" strategy. To be more specific, suppose that the entire data are n independent observations $\{\mathbf{z}_i\}_{i=1}^n$ and $\boldsymbol{\beta} \in \mathbb{R}^p$ is the parameter of interest. Assume that the data model involving $\boldsymbol{\beta}$ is specified by

$$\mathbb{E}[g(\mathbf{z}_i, \boldsymbol{\beta}_0)] = 0, \tag{25.15}$$

where $g(\mathbf{z}, \boldsymbol{\beta}) = (g_1(\mathbf{z}, \boldsymbol{\beta}), \cdots, g_p(\mathbf{z}, \boldsymbol{\beta}))^T$ is a p-dimensional smooth esti-mating function, and $\boldsymbol{\beta}_0$ is the unknown true value of $\boldsymbol{\beta}$. In the above Gaussian linear regression example, we have $\mathbf{z}_i = (y_i, \mathbf{x}_i^T)$ with response variable y_i and predictors $\mathbf{x}_i$ and $g(\mathbf{z}_i, \boldsymbol{\beta}_0) = (y_i - \mathbf{x}_i^T \boldsymbol{\beta}_0)\mathbf{x}_i$. The esti-mating equation estimator $\widehat{\boldsymbol{\beta}}$ is defined as the solution to the equation $\sum_{i=1}^n g(\mathbf{z}_i, \boldsymbol{\beta}) = 0$.

Partition the entire data set $\{\mathbf{z}_i\}_{i=1}^n$ into K subsets and denote by $\{\mathbf{z}_{ik}\}_{i=1}^{n_k}$ the data in the kth subset. Let $\tilde{\boldsymbol{\beta}}^{(k)}$ be the solution to the estimating equation $\sum_{i=1}^{n_k} g(\mathbf{z}_{ik}, \boldsymbol{\beta}) = 0$ and write $D_k = -\sum_{i=1}^{n_k} \dot{g}(\mathbf{z}_{ik}, \tilde{\boldsymbol{\beta}}^{(k)})$ where $\dot{g} = \frac{\partial g}{\partial \boldsymbol{\beta}}$ is the gradient of g with respect to $\boldsymbol{\beta}$. Then the aggregated estimating equation estimator is defined as

$$\widehat{\boldsymbol{\beta}}^{\text{AEE}} = \left(\sum_{k=1}^K D_k \right)^{-1} \left(\sum_{k=1}^K D_k \tilde{\boldsymbol{\beta}}^{(k)} \right). \tag{25.16}$$

The divide-and-conquer method has an obvious benefit on computational efficiency because the entire data is processed subset by subset, and we only need to record $(D_k, \tilde{\boldsymbol{\beta}}^{(k)})$ for the kth subset. Under some regularity conditions [56] showed that $\widehat{\boldsymbol{\beta}}^{\text{AEE}}$ is consistent to the original full data estimation equation estimator $\widehat{\boldsymbol{\beta}}$ when p is finite.

The divide-and-conquer approach is also applied to the generalized linear model with high-dimensional data in [11] where the sample size n is exceedingly large and the covariate dimension p is not small but $n \gg p$. To be precise, let the penalized estimator using the entire data be

$$\widehat{\boldsymbol{\beta}}_{\text{PL}}^{(a)} = \underset{\boldsymbol{\beta}}{\operatorname{argmax}} \left\{ n^{-1} \sum_{i=1}^{n} \log f(y_i | \mathbf{x}_i, \boldsymbol{\beta}) - p(\boldsymbol{\beta}; \lambda) \right\}, \qquad (25.17)$$

where f is the density function, $p(\boldsymbol{\beta}; \lambda)$ is the penalty function with tuning parameter λ. Assume the entire dataset of size n is divided into K subsets and the kth subset has n_k observations. Let $\{(y_{ki}, \mathbf{x}_{ki}^T)\}_{i=1}^{n_k}$ be the data in the kth subset. Similar to (25.17), the penalized estimator for the kth subset is given by

$$\widehat{\boldsymbol{\beta}}_{\text{PL}}^{(k)} = \underset{\boldsymbol{\beta}}{\operatorname{argmax}} \left\{ n_k^{-1} \sum_{i=1}^{n_k} \log f(y_{ki} | \mathbf{x}_{ki}, \boldsymbol{\beta}) - p(\boldsymbol{\beta}; \lambda_k) \right\}, \qquad (25.18)$$

where λ_k is the tuning parameter for the kth subset. Since each $\widehat{\boldsymbol{\beta}}_{\text{PL}}^{(k)}$ is estimated from a different subset of data, the sparsity of $\widehat{\boldsymbol{\beta}}_{\text{PL}}^{(k)}$ can be different from one to another. In order to combine these K estimators $\widehat{\boldsymbol{\beta}}_{\text{PL}}^{(k)}$, $k = 1, \cdots, K$ [11] suggested a majority voting method to obtain the final estimator of $\boldsymbol{\beta}$, denoted as $\widehat{\boldsymbol{\beta}}^{\text{SC}} = (\widehat{\beta}_1^{\text{SC}}, \cdots, \widehat{\beta}_p^{\text{SC}})^T$. The proposed majority voting method in [11] sets

$$\widehat{\beta}_j^{\text{SC}} = 0 \ \text{ if } \ \sum_{k=1}^{K} I(\widehat{\beta}_{j,\text{PL}}^{(k)} \neq 0) \leq \omega \qquad (25.19)$$

for each $j = 1, \cdots, p$, where $\widehat{\beta}_{j,\text{PL}}^{(k)}$ is the jth component of $\widehat{\boldsymbol{\beta}}_{\text{PL}}^{(k)}$, $I(\cdot)$ is the indicator function, and $\omega \in [0, K)$ is another tuning parameter controlling the number of zeros in the final estimator. Obviously, if $\omega = 0$, then $\widehat{\beta}_j^{\text{SC}} = 0$ only if all $\widehat{\beta}_{j,\text{PL}}^{(k)}$ are zero. If $K - 1 \leq \omega < K$, then $\widehat{\beta}_j^{\text{SC}} = 0$ only if any

of $\widehat{\beta}_{j,\,\mathrm{PL}}^{(k)}$ is zero. [11] showed that under mild conditions the combined estimator $\widehat{\boldsymbol{\beta}}^{\mathrm{SC}}$ still retains desired properties of many commonly used penalized
estimators, such as the model selection consistency and asymptotic normality.
They also proved that $\widehat{\boldsymbol{\beta}}^{\mathrm{SC}}$ and the entire data estimator $\widehat{\boldsymbol{\beta}}_{\mathrm{PL}}^{(a)}$ are asymptotic
equivalent by showing that these two estimators have the same asymptotic
variances.

Some other related advances on the divide-and-conquer method include
[2, 47, 49, 76, 98, 103], among others. To be more specific [49] devised
a communication-efficient approach to distributed sparse regression in the
high-dimensional setting by averaging debiased lasso estimators. Zheng et al.
[98] suggested a new approach for statistical inference which divides the
entire sample set into subsamples for correcting the bias and constructs confidence intervals by aggregating the estimates based on subsamples. Battey et al.
[2] investigated hypothesis testing and parameter estimation in the context of
the divide-and-conquer algorithm for high-dimensional linear and generalized linear models. Jordan et al. [47] presented a communication-efficient
surrogate likelihood framework for solving distributed statistical inference
problems. The proposed framework can be used for low-dimensional estimation, high-dimensional regularized estimation, and Bayesian inference. Tang
et al. [76] proposed an alternative divide-and-conquer algorithm to fit generalized linear models with an extremely large sample size and a large p by
combining debiased LASSO estimates from each subset. By approximating
the local objective function using a local quadratic form and combining
estimator using a weighted average of local estimators [103] developed a
distributed least-square approximation method which can solve a large family
of regression problems (e.g., linear regression, logistic regression, and Cox's
model) on a distributed system. It has been proved that the resulting estimator is statistically as efficient as the global estimator using entire data.
The divide-and-conquer methods have also been used in different models
and settings; see, for example [95] for kernel ridge regression [10] and [8]
for quantile regression [86] for linear support vector machine [55] for feature
screening [87] for sparse cox models [9] for principal component analysis [85]
for multivariate survival analysis, and [43] for high-dimensional correlated
data analysis.

25.3.2 Subsampling Methods

Although divide-and-conquer methods can take advantage of distributed and
parallel computing facility, it may not reduce computing time if we only

have a single computer. Another simple and widely used method for massive data analysis with limited computing power is subsampling, which draws a small subsample from the entire dataset and estimates the parameters of interest using the chosen subsample only. To illustrate the idea of subsampling methods, let us revisit the linear regression model (25.13) in Section 25.3.1, that is,

$$y_i = \mathbf{x}_i^T \boldsymbol{\beta} + \varepsilon_i, \ i = 1, 2, \cdots, n,$$

where $y_i \in \mathbb{R}$ and $\mathbf{x}_i = (X_{i1}, \cdots, X_{ip})^T \in \mathbb{R}^p$ are the response variable and covariates vector for the ith observation, respectively, $\boldsymbol{\beta} = (\beta_1, \cdots, \beta_p)^T \in \mathbb{R}^p$ is an unknown regression coefficient vector, and $\{(y_i, \mathbf{x}_i^T)\}_{i=1}^n$ is the entire data. Algorithm 1 describes the general subsampling procedure for linear regression.

Algorithm 1: General subsampling procedure for linear regression

---

1 Draw a random subsample (with replacement) of size $r << n$ from the entire data $\{(y_i, \mathbf{x}_i^T)\}_{i=1}^n$ using the sampling distribution $\{\pi_i\}_{i=1}^n$ with $\pi_i \geq 0$ and $\sum_{i=1}^n \pi_i = 1$.
2 Denote by $\{(y_i^*, \mathbf{x}_i^{*T}, \pi_i^*)\}_{i=1}^r$ the selected subsample and the corresponding subsampling probabilities. Estimate $\boldsymbol{\beta}$ using the subsample $\{(y_i^*, \mathbf{x}_i^{*T})\}_{i=1}^r$.

The major challenge of the subsampling methods is how to select the subsample. This is equivalent to how to choose π_i. One might randomly sample a small number of observations using uniform subsampling in which $\pi_i = 1/n$, meaning that every observation is treated equally no matter how much information it carries. For many problems, it is easy to construct "worse-case" input for which uniform random sampling will perform very poorly [62]. Intuitively, one should choose a subsample with more informative observations. Motivated by this, there has been a great deal of work on subsampling in the existing literature; see, for example [17, 62, 63, 82, 83], among others. In what follows, we will concentrate on nonuniform subsampling via leveraging, optimal subsampling, and information-based optimal subdata selection.

25.3.2.1 Nonuniform Subsampling Via Leveraging

We start with nonuniform subsampling via leveraging, which was first developed in [17, 19] for linear regression problems. The main idea is to use the leverage scores to construct sampling probabilities $\{\pi_i\}_{i=1}^n$. Ma et al. [62] and Ma and Sun [63] further investigated the statistical properties of algorithmic leveraging for linear regression for massive data in terms of biases and variances of subsampling estimators.

To gain some insights for nonuniform subsampling via leveraging, consider the Gaussian linear regression model (25.13). Assume that p is fixed and $\mathbf{X}^T\mathbf{X}$ is invertible. Then the unknown regression coefficient $\boldsymbol{\beta}$ can be estimated via

$$\hat{\boldsymbol{\beta}}_{\text{OLS}} = \underset{\boldsymbol{\beta}}{\arg\min} \|\mathbf{y} - \mathbf{X}\boldsymbol{\beta}\|^2 = (\mathbf{X}^T\mathbf{X})^{-1}\mathbf{X}^T\mathbf{y}$$

and the predicted response vector is given by $\hat{\mathbf{y}} = (\hat{y}_1, \cdots, \hat{y}_n)^T = \mathbf{H}\mathbf{y}$ with $\mathbf{H} = \mathbf{X}(\mathbf{X}^T\mathbf{X})^{-1}\mathbf{X}^T$. Let $h_{ii} = \mathbf{x}_i^T(\mathbf{X}^T\mathbf{X})^{-1}\mathbf{x}_i$, which is the ith diagonal element of $\mathbf{H}$ and typically called the leverage score of ith observation in Statistics. It is easy to see that the predicted response of the ith observation $\hat{y}_i$ gets close to y_i as h_{ii} approaches to 1. Therefore, the leverage score h_{ii} measures how important the ith observation to the least squares estimator. Drineas et al. [17, 19] suggested to use normalized leverage scores

$$\pi_i = h_{ii} / \sum_{i=1}^n h_{ii}$$

to construct sampling probabilities in Algorithm 1. Then the resulting leveraging estimator of $\boldsymbol{\beta}$ can be written as

$$\hat{\boldsymbol{\beta}}_{\text{LEV}} = \left(\sum_{i=1}^r \frac{\mathbf{x}_i^* \mathbf{x}_i^{*T}}{\pi_i^*} \right)^{-1} \sum_{i=1}^r \frac{\mathbf{x}_i^* y_i^*}{\pi_i^*}. \tag{25.20}$$

[62, 63] investigated the statistical properties of the leveraging estimator and showed that $\hat{\boldsymbol{\beta}}_{\text{LEV}}$ is an approximately unbiased estimator of $\hat{\boldsymbol{\beta}}_{\text{OLS}}$. Ma et al. [64] established the asymptotic distribution of $\hat{\boldsymbol{\beta}}_{\text{LEV}}$. It can be seen from the definition of $\hat{\boldsymbol{\beta}}_{\text{LEV}}$ that the variance of $\hat{\boldsymbol{\beta}}_{\text{LEV}}$ may be inflated by the observations with small sampling probabilities. To address this issue [62] also proposed a shrinkage leveraging method which uses

$$\pi_i = \lambda \frac{h_{ii}}{\sum_{i=1}^n h_{ii}} + (1 - \lambda)\frac{1}{n}$$

with $\lambda \in (0, 1)$ and empirically showed that the resulting estimator has smaller mean squared error than $\hat{\boldsymbol{\beta}}_{\text{LEV}}$ when α is between 0.8 and 0.95.

Although the above leveraging method is simple and easy to implement, the computational cost can be expensive. The computing time of the leveraging method in [62, 63] comes from two sources: constructing the sampling probabilities π_{ii} and solving the least squares based on the subsample. The former needs $O(np^2)$ time for the exact computation of leverage scores h_{ii}, while the latter requires $O(rp^2)$ time to solve least squares based on subsample of size r [62]. Thus the total computing time for the leveraging method is dominated by $O(np^2)$, which can be large when n is huge or p is large. There are some existing approaches to reduce the computational burden of the leveraging method by fast approximation of leverage scores; see, for example [18].

25.3.2.2 Information-Based Optimal Subdata Selection

Wang et al. [82] showed that the asymptotic variance of the resulting estimator from the leveraging method discussed in Section 25.3.2.1 is typically at the order of the inverse of subsample size r, meaning that the subsample estimator is not consistent when r is fixed, regardless of how large the sample size of the entire data. Motivated by this observation [82] proposed a novel approach for the linear regression model, called information-based optimal subdata selection (IBOSS), to solve this issue. Consider the following linear regression model

$$y_i = \beta_0 + \beta_1 X_{i1} + \cdots + \beta_p X_{ip} + \varepsilon_i, \ i = 1, 2, \cdots, n,$$

where $y_i \in \mathbb{R}$ and $\mathbf{x}_i = (X_{i1}, \cdots, X_{ip})^T \in \mathbb{R}^p$ are the response variable and covariates vector for the ith observation, respectively, and ε_i is the random error for the ith observation. In this subsection, we slightly abuse the notation by writing $\mathbf{x}_i = (1, X_{i1}, \cdots, X_{ip})^T$ and $\boldsymbol{\beta} = (\beta_0, \beta_1, \cdots, \beta_p)^T$.

Unlike nonuniform subsampling via leveraging chooses data points randomly, the IBOSS method deterministically selects the most informative data points according to some optimality criterion so that subsample of a small size preserves most of the information contained in the entire data. Let $\mathcal{S} = \{(y_i^*, \mathbf{x}_i^{*T})\}_{i=1}^r$ is a deterministic subsample of size r from the entire data $\{(y_i, \mathbf{x}_i^T)\}_{i=1}^n$. Assume that the selection of $\mathcal{S}$ only depends on the design matrix $\mathbf{X} = (\mathbf{x}_1, \cdots, \mathbf{x}_n)^T$. Then the least-square estimator based on the subsample $\mathcal{S}$, given by

$$\tilde{\beta} = \left(\sum_{i=1}^{r} \mathbf{x}_i^* \mathbf{x}_i^{*T} \right)^{-1} \sum_{i=1}^{r} \mathbf{x}_i^* y_i^*. \tag{25.21}$$

is the best linear unbiased estimator of β. Denote by σ^2 the variance of the random error ε_i in the linear regression model (25.13). It is well known that the observed information matrix for β based on the subsample is

$$I(\mathcal{S}) = \left(\sum_{i=1}^{r} \mathbf{x}_i^* \mathbf{x}_i^{*T} \right) / \sigma^2,$$

which is the inverse of the covariance matrix of $\tilde{\beta}$. Intuitively, one should select a subsample that minimizes the covariance matrix of $\tilde{\beta}$, which is equivalent to maximize $I(\mathcal{S})$. The idea of the IBOSS method is to select a subsample that maximizes $I(\mathcal{S})$ under some optimality criterion. Wang et al. [82] showed that, under the D-optimality criterion, this can be cast as the following optimization problem

$$\underset{\delta}{\operatorname{argmin}} \left| \left(\sum_{i=1}^{n} \delta_i \mathbf{x}_i^* \mathbf{x}_i^{*T} \right) / \sigma^2 \right| \quad \text{subject to} \quad \sum_{i=1}^{n} \delta_i = r,$$

where $| \cdot |$ is the determinant of a matrix, $\delta = (\delta_1, \cdots, \delta_n)$, and $\delta_i \in \{0, 1\}$ indicates whether $(y_i, \mathbf{x}_i^T)$ is included in the subsample $\mathcal{S}$, i.e., $\delta_i = 1$ if $(y_i, \mathbf{x}_i^T) \in \mathcal{S}$ and $\delta_i = 0$ otherwise. Obtaining the exact solution to this optimization problem is computational infeasible because there are $\binom{n}{r}$ different possible choices for δ. To overcome this issue [82] established an upper bound of $\left| \sum_{i=1}^{n} \delta_i \mathbf{x}_i^* \mathbf{x}_i^{*T} \right|$ and showed that the resulting subsample is related to the extremes of the covariates. To be more precise, they suggested to select $k = \lceil \frac{r}{2p} \rceil$ observations with the smallest values and $k = \lceil \frac{r}{2p} \rceil$ observations with the largest values of each covariate. Here $\lceil a \rceil$ is the largest integer less than a. Algorithm 2 describes the IBOSS method for linear regression.

Algorithm 2: IBOSS

Input: The entire data $\{(y_i, \mathbf{x}_i^T)\}_{i=1}^n$, an integer $r << n$, and $k = \lceil \frac{r}{2p} \rceil$

Output: $\widehat{\beta}_{\text{IBOSS}}$

Initialization: $S \leftarrow \emptyset$ and $S^c \leftarrow \{(y_i, \mathbf{x}_i^T)\}_{i=1}^n$

for $j = 1, 2, \cdots, p$ **do**

> choose the observations in S^c with the k smallest values of X_{ij} and the k largest values of X_{ij}. Denote by S_j the set of these $2k$ observations. Update $S \leftarrow S \cup S_j$ and $S^c \leftarrow S^c \backslash S_j$.

end

Compute $\widehat{\beta}_{\text{IBOSS}}$ using the observations in S and the formula (25.21).

As we can see from Algorithm 2, the IBOSS method has the following appealing properties: (1) the computing time for the IBOSS method is in the order of np, which is significantly faster than the leveraging-based subsampling method in Section 25.3.2.1; (2) the IBOSS method selects informative data points by examining each covariate individually and thus can be implemented via distributed parallel computing; (3) as shown in [82], the variances of the slope parameter estimators converge to zero as the entire data size n increases even if the subsample size r is fixed. Here the slope parameters mean the parameters $\beta_1, \ldots, \beta_p$. In addition, when the entire data volume exceeds the capacity of available RAM of a single computer, one can first use the idea of divide-and-conquer approaches to split the entire data into K subsets of smaller sample sizes and then select data points from each partition using the IBOSS method [79].

25.3.2.3 Optimal Subsampling

We have reviewed two different subsampling methods, both of which do not use the information of the responses. Next, we will introduce optimal subsampling method in which the optimal subsampling probabilities depend on the responses and are obtained by minimizing the asymptotic mean square error of the subsampling estimator under certain optimality criterion. Wang et al. [83] first proposed an optimal subsampling method under the A-optimality criterion for logistic regression. To be more specific, consider the following logistic regression model

$$P(y_i = 1 | \mathbf{x}_i) = \frac{\exp(\mathbf{x}_i^T \boldsymbol{\beta})}{1 + \exp(\mathbf{x}_i^T \boldsymbol{\beta})} \quad i = 1, 2, \cdots, n,$$

where $y_i \in \{0, 1\}$ is the response variable for the ith observation, $\mathbf{x}_i = (X_{i1}, \cdots, X_{ip})^T \in \mathbb{R}^p$ is the associated covariates vector, and $\boldsymbol{\beta} \in \mathbb{R}^p$ is an unknown regression coefficient vector. Given the entire data $\{(y_i, \mathbf{x}_i^T)\}_{i=1}^n$, we can maximize the log-likelihood function to obtain the maximum likelihood estimator of $\boldsymbol{\beta}$, which is given by

$$\widehat{\boldsymbol{\beta}}_{\mathrm{MLE}} = \underset{\boldsymbol{\beta}}{\mathrm{argmax}} \sum_{i=1}^n \left\{ y_i \mathbf{x}_i^T \boldsymbol{\beta} - \log\left[1 + \exp(\mathbf{x}_i^T \boldsymbol{\beta})\right]\right\},$$

where $p_i(x_i; \boldsymbol{\beta}) = P(y_i = 1|\mathbf{x}_i)$. However, it is computationally difficult to obtain $\widehat{\boldsymbol{\beta}}_{\mathrm{MLE}}$ when the available computing resource cannot handle the entire data. Take a random subsample using sampling with replacement from the entire data according to the sampling probabilities $\{\pi_i\}_{i=1}^n$ such that $\pi_i \geq 0$ and $\sum_{i=1}^n \pi_i = 1$. Denote by $\{(y_i^*, \mathbf{x}_i^{*T})\}_{i=1}^r$ the resulting subsample, with associated subsampling probabilities $\{\pi_i^*\}_{i=1}^r$. Then the subsample estimator of $\boldsymbol{\beta}$ based on $\{(y_i^*, \mathbf{x}_i^{*T})\}_{i=1}^r$ is

$$\widehat{\boldsymbol{\beta}}_{\mathrm{sub}} = \underset{\boldsymbol{\beta}}{\mathrm{argmax}} \sum_{i=1}^r \frac{y_i^* \mathbf{x}_i^{*T} \boldsymbol{\beta} - \log\left[1 + \exp(\mathbf{x}_i^{*T} \boldsymbol{\beta})\right]}{\pi_i^*}. \tag{25.22}$$

Wang et al. [83] proved that $\widehat{\boldsymbol{\beta}}_{\mathrm{sub}}$ is consistent to $\widehat{\boldsymbol{\beta}}_{\mathrm{MLE}}$ and the approximation error $\widehat{\boldsymbol{\beta}}_{\mathrm{sub}} - \widehat{\boldsymbol{\beta}}_{\mathrm{MLE}}$ is asymptotically normal conditional on the entire data. By using the A-optimality criterion, which minimizes the trace of the asymptotic covariance matrix of $\widehat{\boldsymbol{\beta}}_{\mathrm{sub}} - \widehat{\boldsymbol{\beta}}_{\mathrm{MLE}}$ [83] obtained the following optimal subsampling probabilities

$$\pi_i^{\mathrm{opt}} = \frac{|y_i - p(\mathbf{x}_i; \widehat{\boldsymbol{\beta}}_{\mathrm{MLE}})|\|\mathbf{M}^{-1}\mathbf{x}_i\|}{\sum_{i=1}^n |y_i - p(\mathbf{x}_i; \widehat{\boldsymbol{\beta}}_{\mathrm{MLE}})|\|\mathbf{M}^{-1}\mathbf{x}_i\|},$$

where $\mathbf{M} = n^{-1} \sum_{i=1}^n p(\mathbf{x}_i; \widehat{\boldsymbol{\beta}}_{\mathrm{MLE}})[1 - p(\mathbf{x}_i; \widehat{\boldsymbol{\beta}}_{\mathrm{MLE}})]\mathbf{x}_i\mathbf{x}_i^T$ and $\|\cdot\|$ is the Euclidean norm. Since these optimal subsampling probabilities depend on $\widehat{\boldsymbol{\beta}}_{\mathrm{MLE}}$, which is not available, one has to approximate $\widehat{\boldsymbol{\beta}}_{\mathrm{MLE}}$ first. In addition, $\mathbf{M}$ can also be approximated by the pilot sample and pilot sample estimator to reduce the computational complexity. Wang et al. [83] proposed a two-step algorithm to approximate the optimal subsampling probabilities and obtain the resulting subsample estimator $\widehat{\boldsymbol{\beta}}_{\mathrm{sub}}$. In the first step, a pilot subsample of size r_0 is drawn to get a pilot estimate of $\widehat{\boldsymbol{\beta}}_{\mathrm{MLE}}$, which is then used to approximate the optimal subsampling probabilities for drawing another subsample of size r_1. The pilot sample can be drawn from the entire dataset by uniform subsampling with $\pi_i^0 = 1/n$ for each $i = 1, 2, \ldots, n$ or case control sampling with $\pi_i^0 = (2n_0)^{-1}$ if $y_i = 0$ and $\pi_i^0 = (2n_1)^{-1}$ if $y_i = 1$. For the latter, n_0 is the number of 0's in all y_i and n_1 is the number of 1's in all y_i. The details of the two-step algorithm are provided in Algorithm 3.

Algorithm 3: Two-step Optimal Subsamping for logistic regression

---

1 (Pilot sampling) Run Algorithm 1 with subsample size r_0 and subsampling probabilities $\{\pi_i^0\}_{i=1}^n$. Store the pilot subsmaple and the associated subsampling probabilities $\{(y_i^{*0}, \mathbf{x}_i^{*0^T}, \pi_i^{*0})\}_{i=1}^{r_0}$. Obtain the pilot subsample estimator $\tilde{\beta}_{\mathrm{sub},0}$ from (25.22) with $y_i^*, \mathbf{x}_i^{*T}, \pi_i^*$ replaced by $y_i^{*0}, \mathbf{x}_i^{*0^T}, \pi_i^{*0}$, respectively.

2 (Second step sampling) Compute the approximate optimal subsampling probabilities

$$\widetilde{\pi}_i^{\mathrm{opt}} = \frac{|y_i - p(\mathbf{x}_i; \tilde{\beta}_{\mathrm{sub},0})| \|\widehat{\mathbf{M}}^{-1} \mathbf{x}_i\|}{\sum_{i=1}^n |y_i - p(\mathbf{x}_i; \tilde{\beta}_{\mathrm{sub},0})| \|\widehat{\mathbf{M}}^{-1} \mathbf{x}_i\|}, \quad i = 1, 2, \cdots, n,$$

where $\widehat{\mathbf{M}} = (r_0 n)^{-1} \sum_{i=1}^r (\pi_i^{*0})^{-1} p(\mathbf{x}_i^{*0}; \tilde{\beta}_{\mathrm{sub}}) [1 - p(\mathbf{x}_i^{*0}; \tilde{\beta}_{\mathrm{sub}})] \mathbf{x}_i^{*0} \mathbf{x}_i^{*0^T}$. Run Algorithm 1 with subsample size r_1 and subsampling probabilities $\{\widetilde{\pi}_i^{\mathrm{opt}}\}_{i=1}^n$. Record the second step subsample and the associated subsampling probabilities $\{(y_i^*, \mathbf{x}_i^{*T}, \widehat{\pi}_i^{*,\mathrm{opt}})\}_{i=1}^{r_1}$.

3 (Final Estimation) Combine the samples from the two steps and obtain the final estimator $\widehat{\beta}_{\mathrm{OS}}$ by $\widehat{\beta}_{\mathrm{os}} = \mathrm{argmax}_\beta \ell_{\mathrm{OS}}(\beta)$ where

$$\ell_{\mathrm{OS}}(\beta) = \sum_{i=1}^{r_0} \frac{y_i^{*0} \mathbf{x}_i^{*0^T} \beta - \log\left[1 + \exp(\mathbf{x}_i^{*0^T} \beta)\right]}{\pi_i^{*0}}$$

$$+ \sum_{i=1}^{r_1} \frac{y_i^* \mathbf{x}_i^{*T} \beta - \log\left[1 + \exp(\mathbf{x}_i^{*T} \beta)\right]}{\widehat{\pi}_i^{*,\mathrm{opt}}}. \tag{25.23}$$

Wang et al. [83] showed that the final estimator $\widehat{\beta}_{\mathrm{OS}}$ from the above two-step algorithm is consistent and asymptotic normal distributed conditional on the entire data and pilot sample estimator. It is worth pointing out that Algorithm 3 is based on the assumption that the logistic regression model is correctly specified. Therefore, the model selection or the covariate transformation should be done before running this algorithm. In addition, the second step sample size r_1 should be always much larger than the pilot sample size r_0 when implementing Algorithm 3. This is a theoretical requirement to establish the asymptotic normality of the final estimator $\hat{\beta}_{OS}$.

Wang [80] proposed an improved estimation method for logistic regression based on the optimal subsampling method in [83]. They theoretically and empirically showed that the new estimator has a higher estimation efficiency. The optimal subsampling method in [83] has been extended to different model settings, including generalized linear models [1], multinomial logistic regression [90], additive hazards models [106], and quantile regression [81].

25.4 Summary and Discussion

In this chapter, we have provided a selective overview of big data analytics with the focus on two types of big data: ultrahigh-dimensional data and massive data. For the former, we briefly described the idea of feature screening and introduced the interaction screening procedures for regression models and classification problems. For the latter, we presented two popular strategies, divide-and-conquer approaches and subsampling methods.

However, the whole story of Big Data Analytics is far from complete. Except for high dimensionality and large sample size, other issues, including heterogeneity [72], measurement error [50], missing values [16], also arise frequently in Big data. More new innovative techniques are required to address these issues for big data analytics.

Acknowledgements We sincerely thank Professors Zvi Drezner and Saïd Salhi for their kind invitation to write this article.

References

1. Ai, M., Yu, J., Zhang, H., and Wang, H. (2021). Optimal subsampling algorithms for Big Data regressions. Stat. Sin. **31**, 749–772.
2. Battey, H., Fan, J., Liu, H., Lu, J., and Zhu, Z. (2018). Distributed testing and estimation under sparse high dimensional models. Ann. Stat. **46**, 1352–1382.
3. Bickel, P. J. and Levina, E. (2008). Regularized estimation of large covariance matrices. Ann. Stat. **36**, 199–227.
4. Bien, J., Taylor, J., and Tibshirani, R. (2013). A lasso for hierarchical interactions. Ann. Stat. **41**, 1111–1141.
5. Bühlmann, P. and Van De Geer, S. (2011). Statistics for high-dimensional data: methods, theory and applications, Springer Science & Business Media.

6. Cai, T., Liu, W., and Luo, X. (2011). A constrained ℓ_1 minimization approach to sparse precision matrix estimation. J. Amer. Statist. Assoc. **106**, 594–607.

7. Candés, E. and Tao, T. (2007). The Dantzig selector: Statistical estimation when p is much larger than n. Ann. Stat. **35**, 2313–2351.

8. Chen, L. and Zhou, Y. (2021). Quantile regression in big data: A divide and conquer based strategy. Comput. Statist. Data Anal. **144**, 106892.

9. Chen, X., Lee, J. D., Li, H., and Yang, Y. (2021). Distributed estimation for principal component analysis: an enlarged eigenspace analysis. J. Amer. Statist. Assoc., to appear.

10. Chen, X., Liu, W., and Zhang, Y. (2019). Quantile regression under memory constraint. Ann. Stat. **47**, 3244–3273.

11. Chen, X. and Xie, M. (2014). A split-and-conquer approach for analysis of extraordinarily large data. Stat. Sin. **24**, 1655–1684.

12. Chu, W., Li, R., Liu, J. and Reimherr, M. (2020). Feature screening for generalized varying coefficient mixed effect models with application to obesity GWAS. Ann. Appl. Stat. **14**, 276–298.

13. Cordell, H. J. (2009). Detecting gene-gene interactions that underlie human diseases. Nat. Rev. Genet. **10**, 392–404.

14. Cui, H., Li, R., and Zhong, W. (2015). Model-Free Feature Screening for Ultrahigh Dimensional Discriminant Analysis. J. Amer. Statist. Assoc. **110**, 630–641.

15. Donoho, D. L. (2000). High-dimensional data analysis: The curses and blessings of dimensionality; Aide-Memoire of a Lecture at AMS Conference on Math Challenges of the 21st Century.

16. Dong, R., Li, D., and Zheng, D. (2021). Parallel integrative learning for large-scale multi-response regression with incomplete outcomes. Comput. Statist. Data Anal. **160**, 107243.

17. Drineas, P., Mahoney, M. W., and Muthukrishnan, S. (2006). Sampling algorithms for ℓ_2 regression and applications. In Proceedings of the seventeenth annual ACM-SIAM symposium on discrete algorithm, 1127–1136.

18. Drineas, P., Magdon-Ismail, M., Mahoney, M. W., and Woodruff, D. P. (2012). Fast approximation of matrix coherence and statistical leverage. J. Mach. Learn. Res. **13**, 3475–3506.

19. Drineas, P., Mahoney M.W., Muthukrishnan S, and Sarlós, T. (2011). Faster least squares approximation. Numer. Math. **117**, 219–249.

20. Fan, J., Feng, Y., and Xia, L. (2020). A projection-based conditional dependence measure with applications to high-dimensional undirected graphical models. J. Econometrics **218**, 119–139.

21. Fan, J., Feng, Y., and Song, R. (2011). Nonparametric independence screening in sparse ultra-high dimensional additive models. J. Amer. Statist. Assoc. **106**, 544–557.

22. Fan, J., Han, F., and Liu, H. (2014). Challenges of big data analysis. Natl. Sci. Rev. **1**, 293-314.

23. Fan, J. and Li, R. (2001). Variable selection via nonconcave penalized likelihood and its oracle properties. J. Amer. Statist. Assoc. **96**, 1348–1360.
24. Fan, J. and Li, R. (2006). Statistical challenges with high dimensionality: Feature selection in knowledge discovery. In: Sanz-Sole M, Soria J, Varona JL, Verdera J, editors. Proceedings of the International Congress of Mathematicians, 595–622.
25. Fan, J., Li, R., Zhang, C.-H., and Zou, H. (2020). Statistical Foundations of Data Science. CRC Press.
26. Fan, J. and Lv, J. (2008). Sure independence screening for ultrahigh dimensional feature space (with discussion). J. R. Stat. Soc., Ser. B **70**, 849-911.
27. Fan, J. and Lv, J. (2010). A selective overview of variable selection in high dimensional feature space (invited review article). Stat. Sin. **20**, 101–148.
28. Fan, J. and Lv, J. (2018). Sure independence screening (invited review article). Wiley StatsRef: Statistics Reference Online.
29. Fan, J., Lv, J., and Qi, L. (2011). Sparse high dimensional models in economics (invited review article). Annu. Rev. Econ. **3**, 291–317.
30. Fan, J., Ma, Y., and Dai, W. (2014). Nonparametric independence screening in sparse ultra-high-dimensional varying coefficient models. J. Amer. Statist. Assoc. **109**, 1270–1284.
31. Fan, J. and Song, R. (2010). Sure independence screening in generalized linear models with NP-dimensionality. Ann. Stat. **38**, 3567–3604.
32. Fang, X. and Xu, J. Joint variable screening in accelerated failure time models. Stat. Sin. **30**, 467–485.
33. Fan, Y., Kong, Y., Li, D., and Zheng, Z. (2015). Innovated interaction screening for high-dimensional nonlinear classification. Ann. Stat. **43**, 1243–1272.
34. Fan, Y. and Lv, J. (2016). Innovated scalable efficient estimation in ultra-large Gaussian graphical models. Ann. Stat. **44**, 2098–2126.
35. Friedman, J., Hastie, T, and Tibshirani, R. (2008). Sparse inverse covariance estimation with the graphical lasso. Biostatistics **9**, 432–441.
36. Gorst-Rasmussen, A. and Scheike, T. (2013). Independent screening for single-index hazard rate models with ultrahigh dimensional features. J. R. Stat. Soc., Ser. B **75**, 217–245.
37. Gosik, K., Sun, L., Chinchilli, V. M., and Wu, R. (2018). An ultrahigh-dimensional mapping model of high-order epistatic networks for complex traits. Curr. Genomics **19**, 384–394.
38. Hall, P. and Xue, J.-H. (2014). On selecting interacting features from high-dimensional data. Comput. Stat. Data Anal. **71**, 694–708.
39. Hao, N., Feng, Y., and Zhang, H.H. (2018). Model selection for high dimensional quadratic regression via regularization. J. Amer. Statist. Assoc. **113**, 615–625.
40. Hao, N. and Zhang, H.H. (2014). Interaction screening for ultra-high dimensional data. J. Amer. Statist. Assoc. **109**, 1285–1301.

41. Haris, A., Witten, D., and Simon, N. (2016). Convex modeling of interactions with strong heredity. J. Comput. Graph. Stat. **25**, 981–1004.

42. He, X., Wang, L. and Hong, H. G. (2013). Quantile-adaptive model-free variable screening for high-dimensional heterogeneous data. Ann. Stat. **41**, 342–369.

43. Hector, E. and Song, P. (2021). A distributed and integrated method of moments for high-dimensional correlated data analysis. J. Amer. Statist. Assoc. **116**, 805–818.

44. Huang, D., Zhu, X., Li, R., and Wang, H. (2021). Feature screening for network autoregression model. Stat. Sin. **31**, 1–21.

45. Huo, X. and Székely, G. J. (2016). Fast Computing for Distance Covariance. Technometrics **58**, 435–447.

46. Jiang, B. and Liu, J. S. (2014). Variable selection for general index models via sliced inverse regression. Ann. Stat. **42**, 1751–1786.

47. Jordan, M. I., Lee, J. D., and Yang, Y. (2019). Communication-efficient distributed statistical learning. J. Amer. Statist. Assoc. **114**, 668–681.

48. Kong, Y., Li, D., Fan, Y., and Lv, J. (2017). Interaction pursuit in high-dimensional multi-response regression via distance correlation. Ann. Stat. **45**, 897–922.

49. Lee, J. D., Liu, Q., Sun, Y., and Taylor, J. E. (2017). Communication-efficient sparse regression. J. Mach. Learn. Res. **18**, 1–30.

50. Lee, J., Wang, H., and Schifano, E. (2020). Online updating method to correct for measurement error in big data streams. Comput. Statist. Data Anal. **149**, 106976

51. Li, D., Kong, Y., Fan, Y., and Lv, J. (2021). High-dimensional interaction detection with false sign rate control. J. Bus. Econom. Statist., in press.

52. Li, G., Peng, H., Zhang, J., and Zhu, L-X. (2012). Robust rank correlation based screening. Ann. Stat. **40**, 1846–1877.

53. Li, J., Zhong, W., Li, R. and Wu, R. (2014). A fast algorithm for detecting gene-gene interactions in genome-wide association studies. Ann. Appl. Stat. **8**, 2292–2318.

54. Li, R., Zhong, W., and Zhu, L.P. (2012). Feature screening via distance correlation Learning. J. Amer. Statist. Assoc. **107**, 1129–1139.

55. Li, X., Li, R., Xia, Z., and Xu, C. (2020). Distributed feature screening via componentwise debiasing. J. Mach. Learn. Res. **21**, 1–32.

56. Lin, N. and Xi, R. (2011). Aggregated estimating equation estimation. Stat. Interface **4**, 73–83.

57. Liu, J., Li, R., and Wu, R. (2014). Feature selection for varying coefficient models with ultrahigh-dimensional covariates. J. Amer. Statist. Assoc. **109**, 266–274.

58. Liu, J., Zhong, W., and Li, R. (2015). A selective overview of feature screening for ultrahigh-dimensional data. Sci. China Math. **58**, 1–22.

59. Liu, W., Ke, Y., Liu, J., and Li, R. (2020). Model-free feature screening and FDR control with Knockoff features. J. Amer. Statist. Assoc., in press.

60. Liu, W. and Li, R. (2020). Variable Selection and Feature Screening. Macroeconomic Forecasting in the Era of Big Data, 293–326.

61. Lv, J., and Fan, Y. (2009). A unified approach to model selection and sparse recovery using regularized least squares. Ann. Stat., **37**, 3498–3528.

62. Ma, P., Mahoney, M. W., and Yu, B. (2015). A statistical perspective on algorithmic leveraging. J. Mach. Learn. Res. **16**, 861–911.

63. Ma, P. and Sun, X. (2015). Leveraging for big data regression. Wiley Interdisciplinary Reviews: Computational Statistics **7**, 70–76.

64. Ma, P. , Zhang, X., Xing, X., Ma, J., and Mahoney, M. (2020). Asymptotic analysis of sampling estimators for randomized linear algebra algorithms, AISTATS, 1026–1035.

65. Ma, S., Li, R. and Tsai, C.L. (2017). Variable Screening via quantile partial correlation. J. Amer. Statist. Assoc. **112**, 650–663.

66. Mai, Q. and Zou, H. (2011). The Kolmogorov filter for variable screening in high-dimensional binary classification. Biometrika **100**, 229–234.

67. Mai, Q. and Zou, H. (2015). The fused Kolmogorov filter: A nonparametric model-free screening method. Ann. Stat. **43**, 1471–1497.

68. Musani, S. K., Shriner, D., Liu, N., Feng, R., Coffey, C. S., Yi, N., Tiwari, H. K., and Allison, D. B. (2007). Detection of gene×gene interactions in genome-wide association studies of human population data. Human Heredity **63**, 67–84.

69. Nandy, D., Chiaromonte, F., and Li, R. (2021). Covariate information number for feature screening in ultrahigh-dimensional supervised problems. J. Amer. Statist. Assoc., in press.

70. Niu, Y. S., Hao, N. and Zhang, H.H. (2018). Interaction screening by partial correlation. Stat. Interface **11**, 317–325.

71. Pan, W., Wang, X., Xiao, W., and Zhu, H. (2019). A generic sure independence screening procedure. J. Amer. Statist. Assoc. **114**, 928–937.

72. Ren, Z., Kang, Y., Fan, Y., and Lv, J. (2019). Tuning-free heterogeneous inference in massive networks. J. Amer. Statist. Assoc., **114**, 1908–1925.

73. Sheng, Y. and Wang, Q. (2020). Model-free feature screening for ultrahigh dimensional classification. J. Multivariate Anal. **178**, 104618.

74. Székely, G. J., Rizzo, M. L., and Bakirov, N. K. (2007). Measuring and testing dependence by correlation of distances.Ann. Stat. **35**, 2769-2794.

75. Song, R., Lu, W., Ma, S., and Jeng, J. (2014). Censored rank independence screening for high-dimensional survival data. Biometrika **101**, 799–814.

76. Tang, L., Zhou, L., and Song, P. (2020). Distributed simultaneous inference in generalized linear models via confidence distribution. J. Multivariate Anal. **176**, 104567.

77. Tian, Y. and Feng, Y. (2021). RaSE: A Variable Screening Framework via Random Subspace Ensembles. J. Amer. Statist. Assoc., in press.

78. Tibshirani, R. (1996). Regression shrinkage and selection via the Lasso. J. R. Stat. Soc., Ser. B **58**, 267–288.

79. Wang, H. (2019). Divide-and-conquer information-based optimal subdata selection algorithm. J. Stat. Theory Pract. **13**, 46.

80. Wang, H. (2019). More efficient estimation for logistic regression with optimal subsamples. J. Mach. Learn. Res. **20**, 1–59.

81. Wang, H. and Ma, Y. (2021). Optimal subsampling for quantile regression in big data, Biometrika, **108**, 99–112.

82. Wang, H., Yang, M., and Stufken, J. (2019). Information-based optimal subdata selection for big data linear regression. J. Amer. Statist. Assoc. **114**, 26393–405.

83. Wang, H., Zhu, R., and Ma, P. (2018). Optimal subsampling for large sample logistic regression. J. Amer. Statist. Assoc. **113**, 829-844.

84. Wang, L., Chen, Z., Wang, C.D., and Li, R. (2020). Ultrahigh dimensional precision matrix estimation via refitted cross validation. J. Econometrics **215**, 118–130.

85. Wang, W., Lu, S.-E., Cheng, J. Q., Xie, M., and Kostis, J. (2021). Multivariate survival analysis in big data: A divide-and-combine approach. Biometrics, to appear.

86. Wang, X., Yang, Z., Chen, X., and Liu, W. (2019). Distributed inference for linear support vector machine. J. Mach. Learn. Res. **20**, 1–41.

87. Wang, Y., Hong, C., Palmer, N., Di, Q., Schwartz, J., Ko-hane, I., and Cai, T. (2021). A fast divide-and-conquer sparse Cox regression. Biostatistics **22**, 381–401.

88. Wu, Y. and Yin, G. (2015). Conditional quantile screening in ultrahigh-dimensional heterogeneous data. Biometrika **102**, 65–76.

89. Xue, L. and Zou, H. (2011). Sure independence screening and compressed random sensing. Biometrika **98**, 371–380.

90. Yao, Y. and Wang, H. (2019). Optimal subsampling for softmax regression. Stat. Papers **60**, 235–249.

91. Yan, X. and Bien, J. (2017). Hierarchical sparse modeling: A choice of two group lasso formulations Stat. Sci. **32**, 531–560.

92. Yang, G., Yang, S. and Li, R. (2020). Feature screening in ultrahigh dimensional generalized varying-coefficient models. Stat. Sin., 30, 1049–1067.

93. Yuan, M. (2010). High dimensional inverse covariance matrix estimation via linear programming. J. Mach. Learn. Res. **11**, 2261–2286.

94. Zhang, C.-H. (2010). Nearly unbiased variable selection under minimax concave penalty. Ann. Stat. **38**, 894–942.

95. Zhang, Y., Duchi, J., and Wainwright, M. (2015). Divide and conquer kernel ridge regression: A distributed algorithm with minimax optimal rates. J. Mach. Learn. Res. **16**, 3299–3340.

96. Zhao, S.D. and Li, Y. (2012). Principled sure independence screening for Cox models with ultra-high-dimensional covariates. J. Multivariate Anal. **105**, 397–411.

97. Zhao, S. D. and Li, Y. (2014). Score test variable screening. Biometrics **70**, 862–871.

98. Zheng, Z., Zhang, J., Kong, Y., and Wu, Y. (2018). Scalable inference for massive data. Procedia Comput. Sci. **129**, 81–87.

99. Zhou, T., Zhu, L, Xu, C., and Li, R. (2020). Model-free forward screening via cumulative divergence. J. Amer. Statist. Assoc. **115**, 1393–1405.

100. Zhou, Y. and Zhu, L.P. (2018). Model-free feature screening for ultra-high dimensional data through a modified BLUM-KIEFER-ROSENBLATT correlation. Stat. Sin. **28**, 1351–1370.

101. Zhong, W. and Zhu, L. (2015). An iterative approach to distance correlation-based sure independence screening. J. Stat. Comput. Simul. **85**, 2331–2345.

102. Zhu, L.-P., Li, L., Li, R., and Zhu, L.-X. (2011). Model-free feature screening for ultrahigh-dimensional data. J. Amer. Statist. Assoc. **106**, 1464–1475.

103. Zhu, X., Li, F., and Wang, H. (2021). Least squares approximation for a distributed system. J. Comput. Graph. Statist., to appear.

104. Zou, H. (2006). The adaptive Lasso and its oracle properties. J. Amer. Statist. Assoc. **101**, 1418–1429.

105. Zou, H. and Hastie, T. (2005). Regularization and variable selection via the elastic net. J. R. Stat. Soc., Ser. B **67**, 301–320.

106. Zuo, L., Zhang, H., Wang, H., and Liu, L. (2021). Sampling-based estimation for massive survival data with additive hazards model. Stat. Med. **40**, 441–450.

26

OR/MS Models
for the Humanitarian-Business Partnership

Ali Ghavamifar and S. Ali Torabi

26.1 Introduction to Humanitarian Logistics

Unexpected events and natural disasters frequently give rise to enormous human and financial losses. In the recent decades, the severity of natural disasters has been increased considerably which highlights the significance of humanitarian relief operations [5], [46]. Humanitarian logistics is defined by [8] as a "special branch of logistics managing response supply chain of critical supplies and services with challenges such as demand surges, uncertain supplies, critical time windows and vast scope of its operations," whereas [45] refers to humanitarian logistics as "the process of planning, implementing and controlling the efficient, cost-effective flow and storage of goods and materials, as well as related information, from the point of origin to the point of consumption for the purpose of meeting the end beneficiaries' requirements."

In fact, humanitarian logistics relates to different operations for responding to a variety of catastrophes. The common aim of these operations is survival

A. Ghavamifar (✉) · S. A. Torabi (✉)
School of Industrial Engineering, College of Engineering, University of Tehran, Tehran, Iran
e-mail: Ali.ghavamifar@ut.ac.ir

S. A. Torabi
e-mail: satorabi@ut.ac.ir

© The Author(s), under exclusive license to Springer Nature Switzerland AG 2022
S. Salhi and J. Boylan (eds.), *The Palgrave Handbook of Operations Research*, https://doi.org/10.1007/978-3-030-96935-6_26

of affected people when a disaster occurs. It should be mentioned that the term "disaster" refers to unanticipated events with extreme suffering damage which might be either a natural disaster (such as earthquakes, hurricanes, flood, fires, etc.) or a man-made disaster (e.g. terrorist attacks, nuclear accidents, etc.) [25]. The pivotal goal of disaster relief operations might be the evacuation of injured individuals from affected areas in the shortest possible time as well as distribution of sufficient relief commodities for satisfying the initial needs of affected people at early post-disaster [12].

A humanitarian supply chain (HSC) is defined as the process of evacuating people from affected regions to safe places, planning for efficient and effective distribution of relief items, and collecting the related information from the supply point to the point of consumption in order to alleviate the suffering of affected people [13]. A conceptual framework of HSC is depicted in Fig. 26.1.

According to Fig. 26.1, the main goal of the HSC is to deliver the relief items to the affected regions from the supply points in a cost-effective way. Therefore, the prepositioned items from the HOs' warehouses or relief suppliers' warehouses are delivered to the affected regions through the central warehouses and regional relief distribution centers. It should be mentioned

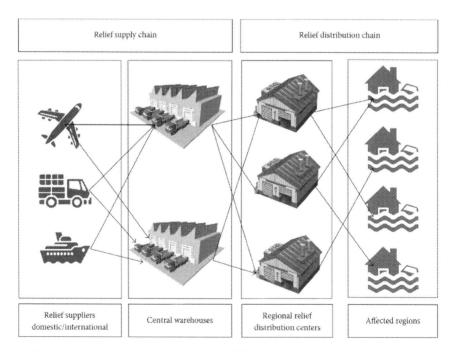

Fig. 26.1 A conceptual framework of HSC [23]

that this framework is applied in most of the research in the HSC context, however, other assumptions regarding the specific conditions of problems are considered. Due to the high uncertainty and unstable environment of disasters, HOs require specific strategies which provide them the opportunity to respond to risks and uncertainties in the demand and supply data of HSC in an efficient and effective manner. The main phases of the so-called disaster management include: mitigation, preparedness, response, and recovery phases, which are briefly illustrated in Fig. 26.2 [25]. Each phase needs distinct strategies with different challenges while facing a high level of uncertainty, which makes the planning of humanitarian relief chains very complicated. Examples of logistics operations in different phases include: strengthening the logistical infrastructure in the mitigation phase, prepositioning of relief items in diverse while safe locations in the preparedness phase, evacuation of affected people, and distributing the required relief items to affected areas in the response phase, and debris management in the recovery phase.

The main stakeholders of a relief supply chain include the affected people, governmental organizations, business sector and commercial institutions, non-governmental organizations (NGOs), military institutions, and donors.

Fig. 26.2 The main phases of disaster management [25]

The governmental organizations undertake making the strategic decisions in regard to, for example, establishing and strengthening of relief aid infrastructures, providing the relief prepositioning network, and determining the budget for the humanitarian operations. The NGOs may participate in each phase of disaster management according to their capabilities while they can be outside or inside of the country where the disasters occur. Donors provide in-kind donations including financial aids, relief items, and services which can be used in humanitarian operations. Military institutions are capable of giving some services at the onset of disasters like establishment of filed hospitals and shelters for affected people.

Similarly, the business sector and commercial institutions can play a pivotal role in the improvement of disaster relief operations as they possess considerable logistical knowledge, skill, expertise, and technology in managing their supply chains. For example, they utilize modern distribution centers, efficient transportation modes, and integrated decision support systems in their supply chains for informed decision-making, which can be leveraged by HSCs. Such a humanitarian-business partnership can enhance the effectiveness and efficiency of HSCs by sharing facilities (e.g. warehouses), relief items, knowledge, skill, and expertise of business sector in humanitarian operations. More precisely, either a supplier as a partner can share its products or services, or a logistics service provider (LSP) can help the HO by sharing its logistical capabilities at the pre- or post-disaster phase [18, 31]. In this study, we focus on the capabilities of business sector which can be employed in the humanitarian logistics. Firstly, we identify the challenges of humanitarian operations which HOs might face with and the main incentives of humanitarian-business partnership. Then, we review the recent OR/MS studies in the area of partnership between HOs and business sector based on the capabilities of business sector. According to the literature review, we perform a gap analysis in the context of humanitarian-business partnership. Then, a basic mathematical model is developed as a sample for quantitative modeling of decision problems related to such partnership whose results are described briefly. Finally, we propose some research avenues, which interested researchers can use in their future studies.

26.2   Humanitarian Supply Chains and Their Challenges

Humanitarian supply chains face unique challenges regarding the uncertainty in supply and demand sides, which may pose some challenges in the commodity flow of relief operations. Challenges of a HSC mainly relate to lack of sufficient and appropriate five entities, including commodities, transportation, facilities, personnel and staff, and coordination [34].

In the aftermath of a disaster, **relief commodities** are often supplied by HOs or donors. There is a high level of uncertainty in the in-kind donations due to the uncertainty in what will be received and the delivery time of these items. In addition, the delivered items could be perishable or unnecessary and unwanted which can clog up the material flow. The uncertain demand in the sudden-onset disasters make it too difficult to estimate the demand size precisely, while the needs of affected people can change dramatically on each day of post-disaster phase. Besides the high level of embedded uncertainty, the lack of relief commodities at the right time and the right place could be a huge challenge. The shortages of crucial items at the onset of a disaster could increase the mortality rate significantly, so lack of appropriate proactive plans to supply these crucial items could cause severe destructive damages [14].

Transportation has a significant role in the relief operations. The humanitarian sector often struggles with the lack of appropriate fleet for transportation of affected people, humanitarian staff, relief items (e.g. food and non-food items), and equipment for construction and other activities. Due to specific characteristics of developing countries (e.g. high population, dense urban districts, and in some cases being located in an earthquake-prone area), a natural disaster like an earthquake would result in a tragic mortality rate. Also, destruction of urban infrastructures will make the relief operations more difficult than it can be thought. Therefore, a mixed fleet of air and road transportation vehicles such as trucks and helicopters will be indispensable for evacuating the affected people and moving the relief items between different nodes in the network. However, the HOs' available fleets are not typically sufficient enough to be useful in a disastrous situation [33]. An important problem in the aftermath of disasters is the possibility of disruptions in the **facilities** like warehouses and distribution centers (DCs) as well as part of the road network. In some cases, it would be hard to find a place to store the relief items both in the pre- and post-disaster phases. In the pre-disaster, HOs may not afford to establish enough warehouses, especially for the prepositioning of relief items. In the same way, at the post-disaster it would be difficult to find some locations as a hub or DC to reconsolidate and distribute the delivered items (e.g. in-kind donations or relief aids supplied by HOs) from different regions to the affected areas [54].

Although the awareness and the experience of HSCs have been increased during the last decades, most of the **personnel** in charge of HOs and NGOs are not expert enough to immediately tackle the complex problems, mostly related to logistics and supply chain management issues. The low level of personnel's knowledge in some cases can cause delays in operations, waste of limited resources and thereby reducing the efficiency of relief operations [14].

Having an efficient and effective **coordination** between the HOs is often challenging. The problem becomes more complicated when cooperation with the business sector also should be taken into account. The challenges often ensue from lack of willingness to share information, different culture and mandates, technology barriers, lack of performance measurement, and undetermined outcomes and goals. Obviously, HOs are able to make their supply chain better by taking the advantages of the resources and expertise of the business sector. By engaging in a partnership, the HOs can achieve outcomes which are difficult to be reached individually [31].

According to the above issues, HSCs are dealing with different challenges whereas the business sector has many capabilities in solving these issues. It is expected that the potential contributions of the business sector to the humanitarian sector would be tangible but there is still lack of research on how this partnership should be formed, what contributions should be transferred, and how OR/MS models can contribute to the management of partnership between the humanitarian and business sectors. In the next section, we will review the recent studies in the literature of humanitarian logistics to find out how OR/MS models have been employed in humanitarian-business partnership as one of the main possibilities to improve the humanitarian operations and how the capabilities of business sector are employed to overcome the challenges that HOs are dealing with.

26.3   The Incentives of Partnership During the Disaster Phases

It can be indicated that the main reason for employing the business sector is their ability to provide HOs with the expertise that HOs do not have, or is not economical to have it themselves. The expertise, knowledge, and infrastructures are the most driving reasons forcing the HOs to collaborate with the business sector. This collaboration can reduce the capital investment of HOs in equipment, facilities, and man power and enables them to focus on their core competencies to scale up humanitarian response [37]. HOs' operations managers mostly prefer to shape relationship with the business sector in the pre-disaster phase to have more time for being ready to response. However, it needs a lot of efforts and resources. Firstly, establishing and maintaining a partnership needs financial supports, but most of HOs have faced with financial constraints and they are dependent on donations. Moreover, in the business sector, LSPs or other commercial companies participate in the humanitarian operations to generate profit, improve their social impacts, and increase their reputation and brand visibility. Collaboration with a HO can help the corporations to gain strategic customers. The private sectors can leverage their capabilities, network, facilities, and skills to help the relief partners in providing more effective preparedness plans [42].

The private companies also prefer to initiate the partnership during the pre-disaster phase. They are willing to have initial confrontation with HOs before their collaboration in the response phase because they feel more secure. The agreement can be made in the pre-disaster phase to clarify the domains and requirements of the partnership. In fact, the expectations of both sides will be clearer if the agreement is made in the pre-disaster phase. In the response phase, it seems the private sector has a tendency to attract a lot of attention from the media. The private sector often offers some free services in the early days after occurring a disaster and then they turn to normal contracts. Finally, business companies can take part in the recovery phase which seems to be a great opportunity for them to start their collaboration. Table 26.1 summarizes the dimensions of humanitarian-business partnership.

26.4   Literature Review

The business sector can collaborate with HOs in different kinds of logistics activities mainly including the procurement of relief items, warehousing, distribution, and transportation. Here, we are going to focus on the studies related to these logistical areas in which OR/MS tools have been used to model the humanitarian-business partnership. In other words, we limit our review to those studies using quantitative modeling techniques (especially optimization models) to analyze the humanitarian-business partnership schemes.

26.4.1   Relief Procurement

One of the main activities which the commercial sector can take part in humanitarian operations is the procurement of relief items. It should be mentioned that other relief operations like warehousing, distribution and transportation are directly affected by the procurement-related decisions [1]. Although some HOs prefer not to outsource the procurement due to having specific procurement procedures, collaboration with a supplier as a partner

Table 26.1 The dimensions of humanitarian-business partnership

Dimensions (Questions)	Answers
What kind of disasters the humanitarian-business partnership can be made for?	• Natural disasters • Man-made disasters
In which disaster phases can HOs and private sectors collaborate?	• Mitigation • Preparedness • Response • Recovery
What are the drivers of HOs to have partnership with the private sector?	• Capacity constraints • Lack of advanced IT Knowledge • Resource limitations • Financial constraints • Lack of expertise
What are the drivers of private sectors to have partnership with HOs?	• Corporate social responsibility (CSR) • Reputation • Motivation of employee • Profit • Branding • Entering to new markets • Networking
What are the main partnership risks for HOs?	• Financial risks • Price fluctuation • Lack of visibility of shipments • Single sourcing risks • Shortage of relief items • Dissatisfaction of the affected people • Uncertainties
What are the main partnership risks for private sectors?	• Financial risks • Unsuccessful collaboration with HOs • Loss of revenues • Loss of existing customers • Impact of disaster type on reputation risk

Dimensions (Questions)	Answers
What are the main barriers of humanitarian-business partnership?	• Conflicting goals and mandates • Lack of willingness to share information • Technology barriers • Structure conflict • Cultural conflict • Lack of performance metrics
What kind of commercial companies can participate in relief operations?	• Logistics service providers (LSPs) • Third party logistics (3PLs) • Fourth party logistics (4PLs) • Retailers • Wholesalers • Suppliers of relief items • Shipments companies
What are the main selection criteria of partners by HOs?	• Reliability • Responsiveness • Delivery quality • On-time delivery • Reputations • Logistical capabilities

(continued)

Table 26.1 (continued)

Dimensions (Questions)	Answers
What are the main logistical activities that HOs and private sectors can collaborate in?	• Transportation • Fleet management • Last mile transportation • Developing IT System • Procurement • Kitting service • Packaging • Labeling • Reverse logistics • Warehousing • Data analysis • Logistical trainings • Scheduling, routing and shipping of relief items distribution • Resource allocation • Material consolidation • Assessment of needs • Demand planning • Forecasting • Capacity building

and setting a procurement plan could facilitate the process and decrease the possibility of shortages at the sudden onset of disasters. In addition, the prepositioning of a huge amount of relief items by HOs could be ineffective, because the disasters are not frequent and it can lead to unutilized resources and waste of the limited budget. The procurement process could be different for different types of disasters (i.e. the sudden-onset and slow-onset disasters). In the slow-onset disasters, such as drought or famine, HOs have more time to find the appropriate suppliers for relief procurement and they can perform the supplier evaluation and selection process as it is employed in the business logistics [21]. Nevertheless, in the case of sudden-onset disasters, such as hurricane and earthquakes, HOs should decide to procure the relief items at pre- or post-disaster phase. When procuring the relief items in the post-disaster phase, HOs may face a variety of problems such as purchasing of low-quality and high-cost items, long lead times, and lack of items in the market [18]. However, pre-disaster relief procurement is very limited due to limited budget and lack of facilities for prepositioning of items.

Major of the studies in the literature have used contractual agreements to coordinate the supply of relief items. In the contractual agreements, HOs and suppliers commit to collaborate with each other at a specific price, delivery time, and payment term. Three major kinds of contracts which have been applied in the context of humanitarian procurement include the framework agreements, option contracts, and quantity flexible contracts. Balcik [10] developed a framework agreement using a mixed integer programming approach. In this agreement, the HO commits to purchase a minimum amount of items from the supplier during the agreement period while the supplier have to provide the items due to the agreement. Wang [50] proposed using the bonus contract into the framework agreement between governments and suppliers for relief procurement to increase the motivation of suppliers to enhance the quality of their services in the partnership. Falasca [21] developed a procurement plan by using a two-stage stochastic model for a HO. At the first stage, the demand of the items is unknown and in the second stage the demand and the available resources are realized.

Procurement auctions have been used by several HOs such as Federal Emergency Management Agency and Fritz institute [20]. For example, Ertem and Buyurgan [19] developed an auction process for procurement of relief items where they assumed the HO as the auctioneer and the suppliers as the sellers. Their study illustrates the impacts of auction strategies on the efficiency of relief procurement. Also, option contract is often used by signing a contract between HOs and suppliers. In this mode, HOs get into a contractual agreement in the preparedness phase to streamline the procurement process. These contracts provide more flexibility for HOs in the procurement process. Rabbani et al. [36] used the option contract mechanism for buying relief items from a supplier. They sought to determine the option and exercise price so as to motivate both parties to participate in the contract in which they can negotiate on the price obtained by a mathematical model. Hu et al. [24] introduced an option contract for relief supply chain management. They compared the buy-back, option, and wholesale price contracts in a collaboration between a supplier and public authorities and proved that the designed contract achieve win-win situation. Torabi et al. [41] proposed a specific option contract for vaccine supply through minimizing the procurement and social costs using an epidemic model, Stackelberg game model, and nonlinear programming approach. Wnag et al. [51] introduced a supply chain methodology in humanitarian operations management. They determined that the pre-purchasing from a supplier with an option contract is better than pre-purchasing with a buy-back contract and instant purchasing with a return policy. HOs mostly use a mixed procurement approach to both increase their efficiency and effectiveness. In this approach, HOs set a plan in which a percentage of relief commodities should be prepositioned at the pre-disaster phase and the supplier is committed to procure up to a specific amount. Akbarpour et al. [3] designed a pharmaceutical relief network under demand uncertainty using a framework agreement and option contract with the suppliers. Torabi et al. [48] offered a two-stage stochastic programming approach to determine prepositioning and procurement decisions. They developed a mixed integer programming model for relief procurement considering operational cost, inventory costs, purchasing price, and supply scarcity. Aghajani et al. [2] proposed a novel two-period option contract by using a two-stage stochastic programming approach. The decisions related to supplier selection and inventory prepositioning are determined in their model. In another study, Aghajani and Torabi [1] developed a mixed procurement/supply policy considering the possibility of spot market sourcing as well as using a multi-attribute and combinatorial reverse auction.

The explored literature validates that in the area of relief procurement, most of the studies have applied contractual agreement to coordinate suppliers and HOs in humanitarian operations. Here, we raise a question: Can the contractual agreement form a partnership? A partnership is "*an agreement between organizations, people, etc. to work together*" while a partnership agreement is "*a contract between two or more individuals who would like to manage and operate a business together in order to make a profit.*" Each partner shares a portion of the partnership's profits and losses and is personally liable for the debt and obligations of the partnership. In the vaccine of humanitarian relief procurement, partners are HOs and suppliers. The main motivation of supplier engagement in the partnership can be the profit expectation, but other reasons like supplier's social responsibility cannot be ignored as it has a great effect on the quality of partnership [43]. Additionally, HOs' engagement in the partnership is to ensure the supply of relief items required to meet the demands of each disaster. Since the aims of partnership here is different than what we have in commercial logistics, it would be difficult to make a partnership between the suppliers of relief items and HOs and it needs some incentives such as bonus, options and privilege. In the literature, most of the research only consider HO's preferences and ignore the supplier side's desires and limitations. In a few studies, like Liang et al. [28] and Nikkhoo et al. [30], the relief chains' goals are taken into account. Here, we reviewed the most recent while relevant studies in which the OR/MS tools have been used for the relief procurement. For more information, the interested readers can consult with [29].

26.5 Relief Warehousing, Transportation, and Distribution

In this type of partnership between HOs and business sector, consolidation can be utilized as the main approach to model the centralized coordination. The consolidation in humanitarian logistics is expected to be different than the one in the business sector. Consolidation often results in cost reduction and performance improvement while it needs planning and specific infrastructure. In the business sector, the decisions about demand planning, access to the resources are easily outsourced to third-party logistics companies while in the humanitarian logistics it is complicated to plan about demand and resource finding [4]. In addition, these issues could be doubled regarding the poor infrastructures in the public sector of developing countries, which makes the consolidation practices much harder in humanitarian logistics. Warehousing and transportation can be considered as the main activities of supply chains which can be consolidated. The consolidation of activities is done regarding the trade-offs between the overall goals of HO as well as controlling the costs in transportation and warehousing activities.

Transportation consolidation focuses on using the full capacity of transport modes. Therefore, in these problems, shipping policies are used to optimize the efficient use of vehicles. Interested readers can refer to [35], in which the innovative consolidation techniques for improved transportation efficiency is presented. Warehousing consolidation aims at managing the needs of clients and ensuring the availability of indispensable items in an appropriate time. If the consolidation is occurred in a large warehouse, it will allow pooling safety stocks and focusing on standard lead times while reducing holding costs. However, the rise in transportation costs is possibly due to increase in traveling distance [52]. In addition, decentralized warehouses allow the use of smaller warehouses closer to the main clients implying bigger safety costs, inventory costs, lower transportation costs, and less standardized lead times. An example of consolidation in the area of humanitarian logistics is what the United Nations Humanitarian Response Depot (UNHRD) do for storing, transporting, and procuring prepositioned goods across a worldwide network of warehouses. The cluster approach offered by the United Nations Office for the Coordination of Humanitarian Affairs to coordinate UN and non-UN agencies, additionally, managed the consolidation of items transportation between Santo-Domingo and Port-au-Prince during the 2010 Haiti earthquake.

In a review paper, Tomsini [47] reviewed the evolution of collaboration between public and private sectors for the period of 2000 to 2015 which is driven from analyzing the United Nation sets of policies related to the private sector engagement in humanitarian operations. We found that, there are limited studies in the area of humanitarian logistics which considered the partnership of public and private sectors in sharing transportation, warehouse, and distribution facilities while most of them have utilized the material consolidation. Schulz and Blecken [39] introduced the potential avenues for consolidation in sharing warehouse, transportation, and procurement through using horizontal cooperation. This study determines the partnership opportunities, while it mainly has focused on the coordination between HOs. However, other actors like private transportation companies and third-party logistics providers use consolidation to increase the productivity of their assets [27, 44]. Rodman [38] and Sebbah et al. [40] focused on using consolidation between HOs and military where warehousing and installation are shared in humanitarian operations. Cozzolino et al. [15] explained the contribution of LSPs to relief operations after investigating the difficulties of coordination. Dufour et al. [17] developed a mixed integer linear programming approach to analyze the potential costs of adding a DC to the network of United Nations Humanitarian Response Depot (UNHRD) which is an important LSP that manages a network of depots and provide multiple supply chain solutions to its partners of the humanitarian community.

Baharmand and Comes [9] investigated the role of LSPs in improving the efficiency and effectiveness of humanitarian assistance by proposing a block chain-based smart contract. Venkatesh et al. [49] proposed a multi-criteria decision-making model for partner selection in continuous-aid procurement. In another study, Kim et al. [26] developed a hybrid multi-criteria decision-making model for LSP selection in the pre-disaster phase. Balcik et al. [11] proposed a collaborative prepositioning strategy to strengthen the countries' regional response capacity against hurricane. They proposed a two-stage stochastic programming model to determine the locations and amounts of relief supplies to store, as well as the investment to be made by each country. Diehlmann et al. [16] contributed to the area of humanitarian logistics by evaluating the public–private partnership in emergency logistics using logistical and game-theory concepts. The incentives of private partner are modeled through developing game-theory models. In a recent study, Zhang et al. [53] developed a collaborative truck-and-drones system as an assessment tool for collecting the information from both nodes and links of a transportation network. The obtained information is then used by HOs in the routing problem at the post-disaster phase.

26.6 Gap Analysis of Extant Literature

Reviewing the literature validates that most of the studies have focused on the qualitative studies in the area of partnership between humanitarian and business sectors in the setting of disaster relief operations. Most of the studies highlight that humanitarian-business partnership enables HOs to provide a customized response, reduce waste, optimize resources, and reduce costs [49–32]. Although collaboration between HOs and private sector has been suggested by many scholars in the literature, a few studies have developed mathematical models to investigate the effects of such partnership. In addition, it can be found that HOs and private sector still have lots of partnership challenges which should be considered. It is hard to determine and measure whether the partners have met their partnership goals or not while there are not specific key performance indicators (KPIs) in the literature of humanitarian-business partnership for this assessment. In addition, it is highly needed to determine the affecting factors on this partnership.

As we mentioned before, partnership can take place in three main areas including procurement, warehousing, and transportation. Based upon the literature review, partnership in procurement is mostly modeled through designing supply contracts and framework agreements as well as supplier evaluation and selection. Partnership in warehousing and transportation activities is rarely modeled through quantitative approaches. By now, the researchers have mostly focused on the opportunities and barriers of the humanitarian-business partnership by doing qualitative studies. Our literature review shows a strong need for developing mathematical models for assessing humanitarian-business partnership, considering the opportunities and barriers identified in the literature. Considering the private sectors logistical capabilities in the relief operations along with the HOs capabilities through developing mathematical models enables the researchers and practitioners to accurately analyze the role and the responsibilities of each partner as well as their benefits. As a sample modeling, in the next section, we develop a simple mathematical model for a specific humanitarian-business partnership.

26.7   A Mathematical Model for Humanitarian-Business Partnership

Here, we model a specific partnership of humanitarian and business sectors through developing a sample mathematical model Ghavamifar and Torabi [22]. We assume that the partnership includes a HO, multiple suppliers, and multiple LSPs as the partners. The HO needs to collaborate with its partners for facilitating the procurement and storage of relief items. The suppliers are responsible for supplying the relief items and LSPs are responsible for providing warehousing space for storing the relief items. We assume that the HO outsources part of its need for relief items and storage capacity to its partner. The main assumptions made for the problem formulation include the following ones:

* Suppliers and LSPs have entered into the partnership to earn revenue.
* The HO has a limited budget.
* Suppliers have limited supply capacity.
* LSPs have limited warehouse capacity.
* All the procured relief items from the suppliers should be stored in LSPs' warehouses.
* At least one supplier and one LSP should be chosen.
* The HO can use more than one of the LSPs' warehouses.
* The HO should satisfy both the suppliers and LSPs' minimum expected income, otherwise, the partners would not participate in the partnership.

The HO wants to know which suppliers and LSPs should be selected for collaboration and how they can support the HO. We should mention that our model is proposed for the pre-disaster phase, when the HO plans to increase its capability against the possible upcoming disasters. Furthermore, the uncertainty in the parameters is not considered in our model as this is just a basic quantitative model for modeling the single-item humanitarian-business partnership aiming to show the problem setting of such partnerships in practice. We utilize the framework agreement approach, which has already been used by Wang et al. [50] and Balcik and Ak [10] in the context of humanitarian logistics. The following notations are used to formulate the partnership problem mathematically:

Set and indices:	
i	Set of suppliers
j	Set of LSPs
n	Set of warehouses
Parameters:	
fs_i	Fixed agreement cost with supplier i
fl_j	Fixed agreement cost with LSP j
D	Estimated demand for the relief item
sc_i	The supply capacity of supplier i
wc_j^n	The warehouse capacity of LSP j at the capacity level n
ms_i	The minimum acceptable income for supplier i
ml_j	The minimum acceptable income for LSP j
p_i	The procurement cost of relief item from supplier i
c_j^n	The warehouse sharing costs of LSP j with capacity level n
Decision variables:	
X_i	1, if the agreement with supplier i is executed; 0, otherwise.
Y_j	1, if the agreement with LSP j is executed; 0, otherwise.
Z_j^n	1, if the warehouse of LSP j at capacity level n is selected; 0, otherwise.
Q_i	The quantity of relief item procured from supplier i

Now, the developed mathematical model is presented as follows:

$$\min G = \sum_i fs_i X_i + \sum_j fs_j X_j + \sum_i p_i Q_i + \sum_j \sum_n c_j^n z_j^n \quad (26.1)$$

The objective function (26.1) minimizes the total costs of setting a framework agreement with suppliers and LSPs, the procurement costs, and the warehouse sharing costs.

$$\sum_i Q_i \geq D \, \forall i \in I \quad (26.2)$$

Constraint (26.2) implies that the demand of HO should be satisfied with the relief items delivered from the suppliers

$$Q_i \leq sc_i X_i \ \forall i \in I \tag{26.3}$$

Constraint (26.3) considers the supply capacity of each supplier.

$$Q_i \leq \sum_j \sum_n wc_j^n Z_j^n \ \forall i \in I \tag{26.4}$$

Constraint (26.4) takes into account the storage capacity of LSPs, where the relief items procured from the suppliers should be stored.

$$\sum_n Z_j^n \leq Y_j \ \forall j \in J \tag{26.5}$$

Constraint (26.5) indicates that a warehouse with specific capacity level can be shared if the agreement is set with the respective LSP. It also indicates that at most a specific capacity level can be chosen for each warehouse.

$$\sum_i X_i \geq 1 \tag{26.6}$$

$$\sum_j Y_j \geq 1 \tag{26.7}$$

Constraint (26.6) and (26.7) guarantee that at least one supplier and LSP are selected to collaborate with HO.

$$p_i Q_i \geq ms_i X_i \qquad \forall i \in I \tag{26.8}$$

$$\sum_n c_j^n Z_j^n \geq ml_j Y_j \qquad \forall j \in J \tag{26.9}$$

Constraint (26.8) and (26.9) consider the minimum acceptable income for the suppliers and LSPs in the partnership.

$$X_i, Y_j, Z_j^n \in \{0, 1\}, \ Q_i \geq 0 \forall i \in I, \forall j \in J, \forall n \in N \tag{26.10}$$

Finally, constraint (26.10) determines the domain of each variable.

The proposed model is a basic mathematical model which consider the potential capacity of the candidate suppliers and LSPs in procuring relief items and storing them. As we mentioned in the literature review, there is few studies focusing on mathematical modeling of humanitarian-business partnership. In this section, we have just proposed a basic model to give some clues about modeling of such partnerships while it can be extended in different ways. For example, the model can be extended by considering inherent uncertainties in the input data, incorporating other limitations of LSPs and suppliers in the partnership, and considering multiple HOs among other possibilities. The presented model has been solved for hypothetical data using CPLEX in GAMS whose numerical details can be found in Ghavam-ifar and Torabi[22]. Here, due to space limitation, we just explain the main managerial implications based on the numerical results:

1. Although we have not considered the possible disruption scenarios in our model, the HO would prefer to collaborate with more than one supplier and LSP due to capacity limitations.
2. Considering the minimum acceptable income for suppliers and LSPs forces the model to increase the items procuring from the suppliers, which may be not needed. Therefore, using the game-theory approach would be useful for modeling the problem.
3. The model selects the best set of candidate suppliers and LSPs for setting an agreement based upon the framework agreement costs, supply costs, and sharing costs. Considering other objective functions such as responsiveness measures (e.g. delivery time-related objective function) can be useful to achieve more informative results.
4. The warehouse capacities of chosen LSPs for storing the procured items, are not completely filled. So, by taking into account the location of suppliers and LSPs' warehouses, the results of our model can be improved. In addition, as mentioned in the literature review, considering the material consolidation between the suppliers and LSPs can reduce the total costs of partnership.
5. As the warehouse capacity of LSPs are not completely filled, the HO can use the additional capacity for storing the prepositioned items.
6. This model just considered the framework agreement concept for setting a partnership, while other contractual agreements such as quantity flexible and option contracts can be utilized in the modeling.

26.8 Conclusion and Suggestions

The aims of this research are to understand and explore how partnership with business sector can improve the humanitarian operations' performance. We have reviewed the literature to find out the opportunities of humanitarian-business partnership and the main challenges that HOs are dealing with and the barriers of the partnership between the partners. We observe that most of the studies have utilized qualitative methods in investigating the partnership of humanitarian and business sectors and have rarely applied quantitative modeling. Therefore, in this study, a basic mathematical model is developed by using the capability of some candidate suppliers and LSPs.

Our model is developed based upon the framework agreement concept while it can be extended by incorporating more real constraints into the model, which can be considered as avenues for the further research. As the main implication for practice, our study suggests the use of collaboration with the private sectors in the four disaster phases. With respect to the current state-of-the-art literature in humanitarian logistics context, there are various avenues for future research using OR/MS models. Among different possibilities, we can refer to:

1. addressing and prioritizing the various capabilities of business sector in the humanitarian operations using multi-attribute decision-making techniques,

2. utilizing other OR/MS tools for modeling of humanitarian-business partnership (e.g. game theory and dynamic programming),

3. using the capability of other partners like HOs, military, NGOs in the modeling to do material consolidation in the partnership,

4. developing heuristics, meta-heuristics, or exact solution algorithms to solve the developed mathematical models in the large-scale instances,

5. considering the possible disruptions in the modeling of humanitarian-business partnership, and

6. developing performance analysis models to measure and analysis of outcomes of humanitarian-business partnerships on the performance of humanitarian operations.

References

1. Aghajani, M. and S. A. Torabi (2019). "A mixed procurement model for humanitarian relief chains." Journal of Humanitarian Logistics and Supply Chain Management, Vol. 10, No. 1, pp. 45–74.

2. Aghajani, M., S. A. Torabi and J. Heydari (2020). "A novel option contract integrated with supplier selection and inventory prepositioning for humanitarian relief supply chains." Socio-Economic Planning Sciences 71: 100780.
3. Akbarpour, M., S. A. Torabi and A. Ghavamifar (2020). "Designing an integrated pharmaceutical relief chain network under demand uncertainty." Transportation Research Part E: Logistics and Transportation Review 136: 101867.
4. Akhtar, P., N. Marr and E. Garnevska (2012). "Coordination in humanitarian relief chains: chain coordinators." Journal of humanitarian logistics and supply chain management, Vol. 2 No. 1, pp. 85–103.
5. Ali, Ghavamifar Ahmad, Makui Ata Allah, Taleizadeh (2018). "Designing a resilient competitive supply chain network under disruption risks: A real-world application." Transportation Research Part E: Logistics and Transportation Review 115: 87–109. https://doi.org/10.1016/j.tre.2018.04.014
6. Aluisio, A. R., E. Zhu, G. Gil, T. Kenyon, V. Uzevski and A. C. Levine (2020). "Academic-humanitarian partnerships: leveraging strengths to combat COVID-19." Global Health Action 13(1): 1797296.
7. Andonova, L. B. and G. Carbonnier (2014). "Business-humanitarian partnerships: Processes of normative legitimation." Globalizations 11(3): 349–367.
8. Apte, A. (2010). Humanitarian logistics: A new field of research and action, Now Publishers Inc.
9. Baharmand, H. and T. Comes (2019). "Leveraging partnerships with logistics service providers in humanitarian supply chains by blockchain-based smart contracts." IFAC-PapersOnLine 52(13): 12–17.
10. Balcik, B. and D. Ak (2014). "Supplier selection for framework agreements in humanitarian relief." Production and Operations Management 23(6): 1028-1041.
11. Balcik, B., S. Silvestri, M. È. Rancourt and G. Laporte (2019). "Collaborative prepositioning network design for regional disaster response." Production and Operations Management 28(10): 2431–2455.
12. Bealt, J., J. C. Fernández Barrera and S. A. Mansouri (2016). "Collaborative relationships between logistics service providers and humanitarian organizations during disaster relief operations." Journal of Humanitarian Logistics and Supply Chain Management 6(2): 118–144.
13. Behl, A. and P. Dutta (2019). "Humanitarian supply chain management: a thematic literature review and future directions of research." Annals of Operations Research 283(1): 1001–1044.
14. Çelik, M., Ö. Ergun, B. Johnson, P. Keskinocak, Á. Lorca, P. Pekgün and J. Swann (2012). Humanitarian logistics. New directions in informatics, optimization, logistics, and production, INFORMS: 18–49.
15. Cozzolino, A., E. Wankowicz and E. Massaroni (2017). "Logistics service providers' engagement in disaster relief initiatives: an exploratory analysis." International Journal of Quality and Service Sciences, Vol. 9, No. 3/4, pp. 269–291.

16. Diehlmann, F., M. Lüttenberg, L. Verdonck, M. Wiens, A. Zienau and F. Schultmann (2021). "Public-private collaborations in emergency logistics: A framework based on logistical and game-theoretical concepts." Safety Science 141: 105301.

17. Dufour, É., G. Laporte, J. Paquette and M. È. Rancourt (2018). "Logistics service network design for humanitarian response in East Africa." Omega 74: 1–14.

18. Duran, S., Ö. Ergun, P. Keskinocak and J. L. Swann (2013). Humanitarian logistics: advanced purchasing and pre-positioning of relief items. Handbook of global logistics, Springer: 447–462.

19. Ertem, M. A. and N. Buyurgan (2013). A procurement auctions-based framework for coordinating platforms in humanitarian logistics. Humanitarian and relief logistics, Springer: 111–127.

20. Ertem, M. A., N. Buyurgan and M. D. Rossetti (2010). "Multiple-buyer procurement auctions framework for humanitarian supply chain management." International Journal of Physical Distribution & Logistics Management, Vol. 40, No. 3, pp. 202–227

21. Falasca, M. and C. W. Zobel (2011). "A two-stage procurement model for humanitarian relief supply chains." Journal of Humanitarian Logistics and Supply Chain Management, Vol. 1 No. 2, pp. 151–169.

22. Ghavamifar, Ali, S. A. Torabi (2021). "Collborative relief network design". Working paper.

23. Habib, Muhammad Salman, Young Hae Lee, and Muhammad Saad Memon. "Mathematical models in humanitarian supply chain management: A systematic literature review." Mathematical Problems in Engineering 2016 (2016).

24. Hu, Z., J. Tian and G. Feng (2019). "A relief supplies purchasing model based on a put option contract." Computers & Industrial Engineering 127: 253–262.

25. Jahre, M., G. Persson, G. Kovàcs and K. M. Spens (2007). "Humanitarian logistics in disaster relief operations." International journal of physical distribution & logistics management.

26. Kim, S., M. Ramkumar and N. Subramanian (2019). "Logistics service provider selection for disaster preparation: a socio-technical systems perspective." Annals of Operations Research 283(1): 1259–1282.

27. Knemeyer, A. M. and P. R. Murphy (2004). "Evaluating the performance of third-party logistics arrangements: a relationship marketing perspective." Journal of Supply chain management 40(4): 35–51.

28. Liang, L., X. Wang and J. Gao (2012). "An option contract pricing model of relief material supply chain." Omega 40(5): 594–600.

29. Moshtari, M., N. Altay, J. Heikkilä and P. Gonçalves (2021). "Procurement in humanitarian organizations: Body of knowledge and practitioner's challenges." International Journal of Production Economics: 108017.

30. Nikkhoo, F., A. Bozorgi-Amiri and J. Heydari (2018). "Coordination of relief items procurement in humanitarian logistic based on quantity flexibility contract." International Journal of Disaster Risk Reduction 31: 331–340.

31. Nurmala, N., S. de Leeuw and W. Dullaert (2017). "Humanitarian-business partnerships in managing humanitarian logistics." Supply Chain Management: An International Journal, Vol. 22 No. 1, pp. 82–94.

32. Pascucci, E. (2021). "More logistics, less aid: Humanitarian-business partnerships and sustainability in the refugee camp." World Development 142: 105424.

33. Pedraza-Martinez, A. J. and L. N. Van Wassenhove (2012). "Transportation and vehicle fleet management in humanitarian logistics: challenges for future research." EURO Journal on Transportation and Logistics 1(1-2): 185–196.

34. Petrudi, S. H. H., M. Tavana and M. Abdi (2020). "A comprehensive framework for analyzing challenges in humanitarian supply chain management: A case study of the Iranian Red Crescent Society." International Journal of Disaster Risk Reduction 42: 101340.

35. Piechnik, D. and O. Schaufenbuel (2021). "Innovative Consolidation Techniques for Improved Transportation Efficiency."

36. Rabbani, M., H. V. Arani and H. Rafiei (2015). "Option contract application in emergency supply chains." International Journal of Services and Operations Management 20(4): 385–397.

37. Razzaque, M. A. and C. C. Sheng (1998). "Outsourcing of logistics functions: a literature survey." International Journal of Physical Distribution & Logistics Management, Vol. 28 No. 2, pp. 89–107.

38. Rodman, W. K. (2004). "Supply chain management in humanitarian relief logistics."

39. Schulz, S. F. and A. Blecken (2010). "Horizontal cooperation in disaster relief logistics: benefits and impediments." International Journal of Physical Distribution & Logistics Management.

40. Sebbah, S., A. Boukhtouta, J. Berger and A. Ghanmi (2013). Military logistics planning in humanitarian relief operations. Humanitarian and Relief Logistics, Springer: 77–110.

41. Shamsi, G.N., S.A.Torabi and G.H.Shakouri (2018). "An option contract for vaccine procurement using the SIR epidemic model." European Journal of Operational Research 267(3): 1122–1140.

42. Sigala, I. F. and T. Wakolbinger (2019). "Outsourcing of humanitarian logistics to commercial logistics service providers: An empirical investigation." Journal of Humanitarian Logistics and Supply Chain Management, Vol. 9 No. 1, pp. 47–69.

43. da Silva Lamenza, A. A., T. C. Fontainha and A. Leiras (2019). "Purchasing strategies for relief items in humanitarian operations." Journal of Humanitarian Logistics and Supply Chain Management, Vol. 9, No. 2, pp. 151–171

44. Sohail, M., D. Maunder and S. Cavill (2006). "Effective regulation for sustainable public transport in developing countries." Transport policy 13(3): 177–190.

45. Thomas, A. and L. Fritz (2006). "Disaster relief, inc." Harvard business review 84(11): 114–122, 158.

46. Tofighi, S., S. A. Torabi and S. A. Mansouri (2016). "Humanitarian logistics network design under mixed uncertainty." European Journal of Operational Research 250(1): 239–250.
47. Tomasini, R. M. (2018). The Evolutions of Humanitarian-Private Partnerships: Collaborative Frameworks Under Review. The Palgrave Handbook of Humanitarian Logistics and Supply Chain Management, Springer: 627–635.
48. Torabi, S. A., I. Shokr, S. Tofighi and J. Heydari (2018). "Integrated relief pre-positioning and procurement planning in humanitarian supply chains." Transportation Research Part E: Logistics and Transportation Review 113: 123–146.
49. Venkatesh, V., A. Zhang, E. Deakins, S. Luthra and S. Mangla (2019). "A fuzzy AHP-TOPSIS approach to supply partner selection in continuous aid humanitarian supply chains." Annals of Operations Research 283(1): 1517–1550.
50. Wang, X., Y. Fan, L. Liang, H. De Vries and L. N. Van Wassenhove (2019). "Augmenting fixed framework agreements in humanitarian logistics with a bonus contract." Production and Operations Management 28(8): 1921–1938.
51. Wang, X., F. Li, L. Liang, Z. Huang and A. Ashley (2015). "Pre-purchasing with option contract and coordination in a relief supply chain." International Journal of Production Economics 167: 170–176.
52. Wanke, P. F. and E. Saliby (2009). "Consolidation effects: Whether and how inventories should be pooled." Transportation Research Part E: Logistics and Transportation Review 45(5): 678-692.
53. Zhang, Guowei, Ning Zhu, Shoufeng Ma, and Jun Xia. "Humanitarian relief network assessment using collaborative truck-and-drone system." Transportation Research Part E: Logistics and Transportation Review 152 (2021): 102417.
54. Zhao, M. and X. Liu (2018). "Development of decision support tool for optimizing urban emergency rescue facility locations to improve humanitarian logistics management." Safety science 102: 110–117.

27

Drones and Delivery Robots: Models and Applications to Last Mile Delivery

Cheng Chen and Emrah Demir

27.1 Introduction

In the last decade, the development of information technologies has shaped our lives and shopping habits greatly. One of the results of such development on economy is the huge volume of global parcel delivery activities in urban areas. From an environmental perspective, last mile logistics is the important part of a supply network and a significant source of negative externalities, such as congestion and emissions. Therefore, several last mile delivery services have emerged in recent years. For example, Sandra and Baptista [1] studied a case of incorporating electric cargo bikes into traditional van delivery system to improve traffic performance. In another application, to minimize traffic congestion and associated negative externalities in central London, Freight

C. Chen
School of Transportation and Civil Engineering, Fujian Agriculture and Forestry University, Fuzhou, China
e-mail: fjnlcc@fafu.edu.cn

E. Demir (✉)
PARC Institute of Manufacturing, Logistics and Inventory, Cardiff Business School, Cardiff University, Cardiff, Wales, UK
e-mail: demire@cardiff.ac.uk

© The Author(s), under exclusive license to Springer Nature Switzerland AG 2022
S. Salhi and J. Boylan (eds.), *The Palgrave Handbook of Operations Research*,
https://doi.org/10.1007/978-3-030-96935-6_27

Traffic Control 2050 [2] investigated the traditional portering system into the delivery operations.

Automation and robotic technologies have brought sustainable and efficient solutions in the context of last mile. For example, unmanned (autonomous) aerial vehicles (UAVs) are utilized by several logistics and online retailer companies, such as DHL international [3], United Parcel Service (UPS) [4], and Amazon [5]. Similarly, Starship Technologies has been trailing a delivery robot service (unmanned ground vehicle, UGVs) in London since March 2020.

The integration of small autonomous vehicles, like drones or delivery robots with delivery vans can offer greener solutions than using only diesel-fueled vehicles. Since they are powered by electricity, these new assistants do not produce CO_2e emissions, even though the generation of electricity may lead to emissions. In the study of Figliozzi [6], the authors showed that UAVs are more energy and emissions efficient per unit distance for low delivery density operations. Kirschstein [7] showed that the stationary drone delivery system can create an energy demand which is comparable to a standard delivery system with electric vehicles. Both these studies concluded that drones may lead to greener solutions. The autonomous delivery robot is another delivery service, which can cover limited areas under the surveillance of a driver. Chen et al. [8] presented three types of robots which are used in real-life traffic environments. These robots are also proved to be used as an efficient last mile delivery service in densely populated urban areas.

Since most drones are powered by batteries that last less than half an hour (on average), their loading capacities and flying ranges are limited. Puglia et al. [9] identified that the hybrid system where delivery vans are equipped with drones has the best tradeoffs between efficiency and environmental performance, i.e., CO_2e emissions and congestion. The authors compared three different transportation systems: delivering parcels without drone, deliveries performed solely by a fleet of drones, and the hybrid system. Jennings and Figliozzi [10] studied delivery time and number of customers served using delivery robots and a delivery van. Their results highlighted that delivery robots provide significant reduction in costs and operational times when compared with a standard parcel delivery system.

In the following sections, this chapter will investigate an innovative last mile service: van-assistant delivery system. Specifically designed delivery van loads assistants as well as goods for customer deliveries. While the van (driver) visits a customer, the assistants equipped in the vehicle can be dispatched to serve other nearby customers. When vans are used as the mothership and drones as assistants, the system turns to be a van-drone delivery system.

Similarly, when vans are used with delivery robots, the system turns to be a van-robot delivery system. The studied routing problem is known as a variant of the well-known Vehicle Routing Problem which aims to find a set of vehicle routes to serve a set of customers [11]. In this chapter, first, a brief discussion on the related studies and applications is presented. Then, a mixed-integer linear programming (MILP) formulation and a metaheuristics algorithm are introduced. Fourth, computational experiments and numerical results are presented. And finally, conclusion section is provided.

27.2 Literature Review

We now provide a brief literature review on drones and delivery robots that can be used collaboratively for the last mile delivery by retailers, logistics and transportation companies.

27.2.1 Drones: Last Mile Delivery Applications

Last mile logistics can be improved by considering new technological delivery resources, such as drones and delivery robots. In the study of Murray and Chu [12], who addressed a case where a single drone is operated in coordination with a delivery truck for serving a set of customers. The studied two types of vehicles may travel in tandem or independently and customers can be visited by either the driver or the drone. The drone is paired with a traditional delivery truck which departs from a depot with all customers' parcels being loaded. As the driver makes deliveries, the drone is launched from the truck. After its autonomous flight for the delivery, the drone rendezvouses with the vehicle at another customer's location in the same route. Then, the drone will be recharged (battery replaced) and reloaded for its next trip. The authors studied traveling salesman problem (TSP) that decides optimal customer assignments for a drone working with a delivery truck, named as flying sidekick traveling salesman problem (FSTSP). With an objective to minimize the total time to finish all deliveries, MILP formulations for the problem along with a heuristic algorithm are provided.

In another study, Agatz, Bouman, and Schmidt [13] analyzed a similar optimization problem, named as TSP with drone (TSP-D). The objective of the TSP-D is to minimize the costs of the tour. An integer programming (IP) formulations and several heuristics for the TSP-D are provided in the study. Carlsson and Song [14] determined the efficiency of a truck-drone coordinated system. A drone provides service to customers and can make a return trip to a truck. The truck is acting as a moving depot and the drone is dispatched and recovered at different locations. Based on continuous approximation techniques, it is shown that the improvement on route time is proportional to the square root of the ratio of the speeds of both truck and drone.

A case of multiple vehicles was studied by Wang et al. [15]. Trucks equipped with drones are employed to deliver packages to customers. The authors formulated a min-max problem to minimize the maximum duration of the routes and showed that the highest savings can be achieved using multiple UAVs. Schermer et al. [16] formulated the Vehicle Routing Problem with Drones (VRPD) as a MILP. Besides introducing several sets of valid inequalities to improve the performance of MILP solvers, they also proposed a matheuristic approach to effectively exploit the problem structure. Finally, based on extensive computational experiments, the potential of using drones as assistants in traditional van delivery system is shown. Chiang et al. [17] studied truck with drones for minimizing CO_2 emissions, compared to truck-only delivery system. A MILP model and a genetic algorithm are developed to solve the studied problem. The computational results highlight the benefits of using drones as assistants in last mile from cost saving and environmental friendliness perspectives.

Other types of delivery systems using the combination of traditional vehicles and drones are also investigated in the literature. Moshref-Javadi et al. [18] studied a delivery system with a single vehicle that stops at a customer site and launches self-driving drones to serve nearby customers. With an objective to minimize the total waiting times of all customers, the related routing problem is defined as multi-trip traveling repairman problem with drones (MTRPD). The problem is mathematically modeled as a MILP formulation and a hybrid algorithm with adaptive mechanism is developed to solve it. The authors studied real-life instances which show substantial reductions in customer waiting times. Kitjacharoenchai et al. [19] studied a case where a drone may visit several customers and the specific number of them is limited by its capacity and battery duration in a sortie. A mixed-integer programming is built and a large neighborhood search algorithm is developed. Sensitivity analyses have been conducted to show the improvement on the objective brought by allowing simultaneous services in a single dispatch.

In the literature, docking hubs or stations are also introduced into the delivery network. For example, Wang and Sheu [20] proposed a variant of classic capacitated VRP, where a drone may travel with a truck, take off from its stop and land at a docking hub to travel with another one. Also, backup drones at docking hubs are assumed. In Karak and Abdelghany [21], a hybrid vehicle-drone routing problem is investigated. It is assumed that there are several stations in the delivery network. Each station can be visited by the vehicle only once to drop off or collect drones. Vehicles are used to transport drones. A MILP is formulated to minimize the routing cost to serve all customers and three heuristic algorithms are developed to solve the studied problem.

In another study, Jeong et al. [22] extended the FSTSP to FSTSP with energy consumption and no-fly zone (FSTSP-ECNZ) by integrating payload-dependent energy consumption and restricted flight areas. A MILP formulation and an evolutionary-based heuristic algorithm are proposed. Li et al. [23] investigated the benefits of the vehicle-drone delivery system under traffic restrictions, i.e., vehicle-type restriction and half-side traffic. Based on a MILP formulation and a genetic algorithm, it is illustrated in the numerical experiments that both cost saving and CO_2 emissions reduction can be achieved by applying the vehicle-drone delivery system, especially when there is a vehicle-type restriction.

In a recent study, Ndiaye et al. [24] investigated the importance of the drones in the context of green technology for logistics, agriculture and healthcare. The authors have also presented a review of the recent applications of drone technology and discussed operational challenges. For more information on delivery systems using cooperated vehicle and drone(s), readers are referred to [25–27].

27.2.2   Delivery Robots: Last Mile Delivery Applications

Simoni et al. [28] investigated a van-robot delivery system. With a similar typology with truck-drone system, the authors modified the TSP-D to TSP with robot (TSP-R) by allowing the robot to visit multiple customers in a single trip. A MILP model and a heuristic algorithm are proposed to solve the studied problem. First, an initial truck-only route is created. Then, a dynamic programming is applied to obtain the corresponding optimal robot deployment. Last, the solution is improved using an adaptive perturbation. Numerical experiments in the study showed that robot delivery systems can be more effective if delivery robots are utilized in urban areas.

Chen et al. [8] studied an urban delivery problem using robots as assistants. In their proposed delivery system, the traditional delivery van serves customers and acts as a mothership for its robots at the same time. When the van is parked up safely, robots can be dispatched to their target customer(s) and return to the same place to rendezvous with the mothership van. However, not every customer can be served by a robot because of various factors, such as customers' preferences, geographical accessibility and regulations. Taking the total time duration of all routes as the objective, a MILP model and a two-stage matheuristic algorithm are developed. Although there are time windows constraints, this kind of delivery system benefits from the parallel delivery accomplished by delivery robots, especially when customers are clustered. In a related study, Chen et al. [29] proposed an adaptive large neighborhood search (ALNS) algorithm to solve the VRP with time windows and delivery robots. The authors provided insights and computational experiments on the use of delivery robots as an alternative last mile service.

In their study, Boysen et al. [30] considered trucks to transport autonomous robots. A single truck with shipments and several small autonomous robots travel from their starting point to their drop-off points. When the truck stopped at a point, robots with a single shipment loaded on each are launched to serve the customer before returning to a decentralized depot. At any depot, it is assumed that there are enough number of robots in the truck to replenish. With an objective to minimize the weighted number of late deliveries, this problem is named as the truck-based robot delivery scheduling problem (TBRD). A MILP formulation is provided for the TBRD and a multi-start local search procedure is proposed as a solution methodology. The results show that the decentralized depots increase the efficiency of delivery process. When there is no robot depot in the delivery network, trucks also need to recover all dispatched robots and take them back to the central depot.

In a recent study, Yu et al. [31] considered the routing of large vehicle-small autonomous robots delivery system as a two-stage routing problem. In the first stage, large vehicles carry robots and shipments for customers. Along its route, the large vehicle drops off and picks up robots at the rendezvous nodes. In the second stage, autonomous robots travel from drop-off nodes to serve several customers, then to the predetermined pick-up points to be recovered by large vehicles. Customers' time windows are also considered in the study. A construction heuristic for generating initial solutions and a multi-start hybrid metaheuristic approach with backtracking are developed. The sensitivity analysis reveals that the speed of robots has a very limited impact on the total transportation costs, including large vehicles and robots.

In this study, we specifically investigated the environmental benefits of a van-assistant delivery system where the assistant can be drone(s) or delivery robot(s). To achieve the purpose, we proposed: *i*) a so-called Green VRP with time windows and delivery assistants (GVRPTW-DA) and its mathematical model, *ii*) an enhanced Adaptive Large Neighborhood Search algorithm to solve the proposed routing problem. And finally, *iii*) several real-life instances are solved to investigate the environmental benefits of these new last mile delivery services.

27.3 Problem Description

The van-assistant delivery system (Fig. 27.1) studied here is a kind of mothership delivery system. Both the traditional diesel-powered vehicle and assistant(s) serve customers. The mothership van parks at a customer's parking place and releases assistants to make deliveries within a limited range. While the driver is serving the chosen customer, the assistants can also carry out deliveries in a certain proximity. After the completion of a single delivery, the drone/delivery robot comes back to the van and the delivery van is driven to next destination. With different parameter settings to capture assistants' characteristics, the van-assistant delivery system refers to van-drone or van-robot delivery system.

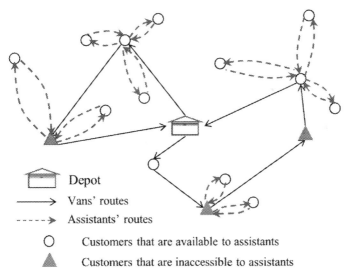

🏠 Depot

⟶ Vans' routes

----➤ Assistants' routes

○   Customers that are available to assistants

▲   Customers that are inaccessible to assistants

Fig. 27.1 A feasible solution with 2 vans and 3 assistants installed in diesel-powered delivery van to serve a set of 15 customers

27.3.1   The Estimation of Emissions

Emissions can be calculated based on payload and traveling distance. For assistants powered by electricity, like drones and robots, the energy consumption can be calculated using equation (27.1).

$$E_{ij}^a(w) = \varepsilon^e(\beta_0 + \beta_1 w)d_{ij}, \tag{27.1}$$

where $E_{ij}^a(w)$ is the amount of CO_2e emitted if a delivery assistant travels from node i to node j, d_{ij} is the corresponding distance (km), and w is the payload (kg). Moreover, ε^e is the amount of CO_2e generated from the power generation facilities per Wh, β_0 represents the required energy for the assistant and β_1 represents the required energy for the payload.

Because the forth-and-back route is assumed for assistants, the related emissions, $E_{i,j}^d(w)$, is calculated using equation (27.2), when customer j with a demand w is served by an assistant launched/dispatched at customer i.

$$E_{ij}^d(w) = \varepsilon^e(\beta_0 + \beta_1 w)d_{ij} + \varepsilon^e \beta_0 d_{ij} \tag{27.2}$$

$$= 2\varepsilon^e \beta_0 d_{ij} + \varepsilon^e \beta_1 w d_{ij} \tag{27.3}$$

$$= 2\varepsilon^e(\beta_0 + \beta_1 w/2)d_{ij} \tag{27.4}$$

$$= 2E_{ij}^d(w/2). \tag{27.5}$$

For the delivery van, a similar equation can be used. Equation (27.6) calculates the emissions of a delivery van traveling from a customer i to customer j with a payload w in it.

$$E_{ij}^v(w) = (\varepsilon_0^v + \varepsilon_1^v w)d_{ij} \tag{27.6}$$

where ε_0^v and ε_1^v are the amounts of CO_2e emitted from the delivery van and the unit mass of the delivery van per kilometer, respectively.

27.3.2   Mathematical Formulation

The GVRPTW-DA can be shown on a graph $G = (V, A)$, where $A = \{(i, j)i, j \in V, i \neq j\}$ is used to represent the set of arcs. $V = \{0\} \cup N$ denotes the set of nodes and includes a depot node and the customer set

$N = \{1, 2..., n\}$. Time interval $[l_i, u_i]$ is defined as the customer i's delivery slot (time window). The customer can only be served within its time window. The demand of customer i is denoted as q_i, which must be satisfied in one visit carried out by a van (driver) or an assistant (when possible).

Given that delivery robots and drones are emerging technologies, some customers may decline to be served by them. Also, customers may live at places where there are technical obstacles, or their demands may exceed the assistant's maximum payload capacity. Therefore, a binary parameter f_i^d is introduced to indicate situations mentioned above. If a customer i can be visited by the assistant, we set the value of f_i^d to be 1 and, 0 otherwise.

We consider a set of homogeneous diesel-powered vans $K = \{1, 2, ..., k\}$ and each van is installed with a set of delivery assistants $D = \{1, 2, ..., m\}$. Each van has a maximum capacity Q and each assistant has a limited radius r^d. Average speeds vel^v and vel^d are assumed for the delivery van and assistant, respectively. Accordingly, traveling times for each type of assistant on arc (i, j) are calculated as $t_{ij}^v = (d_{ij}/vel^v)\eta$ and $t_{ij}^d = (d_{ij}/vel^d)\eta$. Following de Freitas and Penna [32], a coefficient η is used to consider the time for acceleration, deceleration, traffic lights and road network.

Moreover, when drones are used as assistants, the time needed by a driver to prepare them for launch or to retrieve them is considered and defined by a parameter s^{LR}, and we have $t_{ij}^d = (d_{ij}/vel^d) + s^{LR}$. Furthermore, s_i^v and s_i^d represent service times of customer i for the delivery van and assistant, respectively. Finally, w^d is the weight of a single assistant. When a van is at parking place, it can launch/dispatch assistants to carry out nearby deliveries. For safety reasons, it is reasonable to assume that assistants must be recovered at the same place where they are launched or dispatched. Moreover, the assistant conducts only one delivery in each sortie to avoid longer waiting times. Furthermore, each assistant is launched/dispatched only once at a certain place. We now list all decision variables in Table 27.1.

The proposed GVRPTW-DA is formulated as a mixed-integer linear program as below.

$$\text{minimize} \quad \varepsilon_1^v p_{ij}^k d_{ij} + \left(\varepsilon_0^v + \varepsilon_1^v m w^d\right) d_{ij} \sum_{i \in V} \sum_{j \in V} \sum_{k \in K} x_{ij}^k$$

$$+ E_{ij}^d(q_j) \sum_{i \in N} \sum_{j \in N} \sum_{k \in K} \sum_{d \in D} y_{ij}^{kd} \qquad (27.7)$$

Table 27.1 A list of decision variables used in the model

Notation	Description
y_{ij}^{dk}	Binary variable; equals to 1 if an assistant (drone or delivery robot) d in delivery vehicle k is launched/dispatched at node i to serve node j, and 0 o/w.
x_{ij}^{k}	Binary variable; equals to 1 if a delivery vehicle k goes from node i to node j.
p_{ij}^{k}	Continuous variable; the payload on the delivery vehicle k between nodes i to j.
a_i	Continuous variable; the arrival time at node i, either a delivery vehicle or an assistant.
b_i	Continuous variable; the start time of service at node i.
w_i	Continuous variable; the waiting time at node i from the start time of service.

Subject to:

$$\sum_{i \in V} \sum_{k \in K} x_{ij}^{k} + \sum_{i \in N} \sum_{k \in K} \sum_{d \in D} y_{ij}^{kd} = 1 \qquad \forall j \in N \qquad (27.8)$$

$$\sum_{i \in N} \sum_{k \in K} \sum_{d \in D} y_{ij}^{kd} \leq f_j^d \qquad \forall j \in N \qquad (27.9)$$

$$\sum_{j \in N} \sum_{d \in D} y_{ij}^{kd} \leq m \sum_{j \in V} x_{ji}^{k} \qquad \forall i \in N, k \in K \qquad (27.10)$$

$$\sum_{j \in N} \sum_{d \in K} y_{ij}^{kd} \leq 1 \qquad \forall i \in N, d \in D \qquad (27.11)$$

$$\sum_{j \in N} x_{0j}^{k} \leq 1 \qquad \forall k \in K \qquad (27.12)$$

$$\sum_{i \in V} x_{ij}^{k} = \sum_{i \in V} x_{ji}^{k} \qquad \forall j \in V, k \in K \qquad (27.13)$$

$$\sum_{i \in V} \sum_{k \in K} p_{ij}^{k} - \sum_{i \in V} \sum_{k \in K} p_{ji}^{k} = q_j \sum_{i \in V} \sum_{k \in K} x_{ij}^{k} + \sum_{i \in N} \sum_{k \in K} \sum_{d \in D} q_i y_{ji}^{kd} \qquad \forall j \in V$$

$$(27.14)$$

$$p_{ij}^{k} \leq \left(Q - q_i - \sum_{l \in N} \sum_{d \in D} q_l y_{il}^{kd} \right) x_{ij}^{k} \qquad \forall i \in V, j \in N, k \in K$$

$$(27.15)$$

$$b_i - a_j + w_i + t_{ij}^{v} \leq M \left(1 - \sum_{k \in \mathcal{K}} x_{ij}^{k} \right) \qquad \forall i \in N, j \in N \qquad (27.16)$$

$$a_i - b_i - w_i - t_{ij}^v \leq M(1 - \sum_{k \in \mathcal{K}} x_{ij}^k) \qquad \forall i \in N, j \in N \quad (27.17)$$

$$a_j - a_j + t_{ij}^d \leq M(1 - \sum_{k \in \mathcal{K}} \sum_{d \in \mathcal{D}} y_{ij}^{kd}) \qquad \forall i \in N, j \in N \quad (27.18)$$

$$w_i \geq s_i^v \sum_{j \in \mathcal{V}} \sum_{k \in \mathcal{K}} x_{ji}^k \qquad \forall i \in N \quad (27.19)$$

$$b_j - b_i + s_j^d + t_{ij}^d - w_i \leq M(1 - \sum_{k \in \mathcal{K}} \sum_{d \in \mathcal{D}} y_{ij}^{kd}) \qquad \forall i \in N, j \in N$$

$$(27.20)$$

$$b_i \geq a_i \qquad \forall i \in N \quad (27.21)$$

$$u_i \leq b_i \leq l_i \qquad \forall i \in N \quad (27.22)$$

$$\sum_{i \in \mathcal{N}} \sum_{j \in \mathcal{N}} d_{ij} y_{ij}^{kd} \leq r^d \qquad \forall k \in K, d \in D \quad (27.23)$$

$$x_{ij}^k \in \{0, 1\} \qquad \forall i \in V, j \in V, k \in K \quad (27.24)$$

$$y_{ij}^{kd} \in \{0, 1\} \qquad \forall i \in N, j \in N, k \in K, d \in D \quad (27.25)$$

$$p_{ij}^k \geq 0 \qquad \forall i \in V, j \in V, k \in K \quad (27.26)$$

$$a_i \geq 0 \qquad \forall i \in N \quad (27.27)$$

$$b_i \geq 0 \qquad \forall i \in N \quad (27.28)$$

$$w_i \geq 0 \qquad \forall i \in N. \quad (27.29)$$

This mathematical formulation of the GVRPW-DA is developed by modifying the model of VRPTWDR presented by Chen et al. [29]. Objective (27.7) is considered to minimize the total amount of emissions for both vehicles and assistants. Constraints (27.8) ensure that each customer is served only once. Constraints (27.9) ensure that some customers cannot be served by assistants. Constraints (27.10) and (27.11) restrict that each assistant can be dispatched at most once at a certain place. Constraints (27.12) make sure that each van can be used no more than once. Constraints (27.13) balance the flow at each node. Constraints (27.14) and (27.15) guarantee the payload balance. Time windows are ensured by constraints (27.16)–(27.22), and they also eliminate the possibility of generating subtours together with the payload constraints. The maximum radius of each assistant is constrained by inequalities (27.23). Constraints (27.24–27.29) are used to define the binary and non-negativity constraints.

27.3.3   Solution Methodology

We now present an enhanced Adaptive Large Neighborhood Search (ALNS) algorithm proposed by Ropke and Pisinger [33] and Chen et al. [29]. Figure 27.2 illustrates the general framework of the ALNS algorithm. It uses different removal and insertion operators to achieve both diversification and intensification. For each current solution s, a removal operator and an insertion operator are chosen based on an adaptive mechanism. This leads to a neighborhood solution s'. The Simulated Annealing (SA) acceptance criterion is used to decide whether to update s with s': s' is accepted definitely

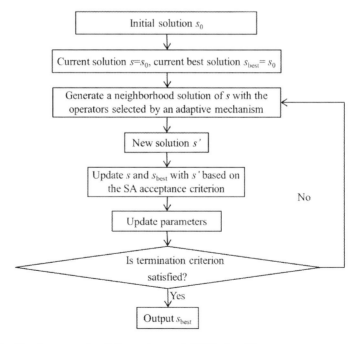

Fig. 27.2 The framework of the enhanced ALNS algorithm

when it has a lower objective value than s, otherwise it can be accepted with a probability calculated as the well-known formula $e - (f(s') - f(s))/T$. $f(s)$ is the objective value of solution s. T is a parameter representing the temperature. Let s_0 denote the initial solution. The value of T is originally set as $T_0 = \eta_1 f(s_0)$, where η_1 is a coefficient. The temperature T decreases as the iteration goes on and its value is revised at each iteration by multiplying a cooling rate c ($0 < c < 1$). The iteration lasts until the preset termination criteria is satisfied. All iterations are bundled into segments to facilitate the implementation of the adaptive mechanism for the selection of used operators.

27.3.4 Initial Solution Generation

We use a Greedy Insertion algorithm to generate an initial (feasible) solution. As assistants' routes are based on vans' routes, a customer who needs to be visited by a van is selected and a new van route is built (Step 1). Then, in Step 2, the insertion cost is calculated for each customer. The cost of insertion for a customer is the increase on the objective value after the customer is inserted. Taking the cost of building a new route, the lowest insertion cost is searched. During the search, every feasible position in route(s) is evaluated, including assistant only and van-assistant positions. Step 2 is repeated until there is no customer left out.

27.3.5 The Adaptive Mechanism for Deciding the Use of Operators

We use a score for each operator to record its performance in the past iterations, which is also used to calculate the probability to be selected in current iteration. With a same value as initial value, this score is updated at the end of every stage, using the following equation: $w_{mi} = w_{m,i-1}(1-r) + r\pi_{mi}/\theta_{mi}$, where w_{mi} is the score for operator m after segment i, $r \in [0, 1]$ acts as a factor, π_{mi} is the accumulated reward score of operator m in segment i, and θ_{mi} is the times that operator m is selected in segment i. The proposed scores (i.e., $\sigma_1, \sigma_2, \sigma_3$) are used to reward the pair of operators when the new solution obtained by them is accepted [33]. Specifically, the $\sigma_1, \sigma_2, \sigma_3$ are used when the new solution with an objective value that is lower than the best solution, the current solution or otherwise, respectively.

27.3.6 The Proposed Neighborhood Operators

The scheme of the ALNS algorithm is to destroy and reconstruct solutions for searching a new one. Hence, two types of operators are used: removal operators and insertion operators. At each iteration, two operators are selected. The removal operator destroys the current solution through removing some customers from its routes and the insertion operator reinserts them into existed routes or creates a new one. Seven removal and five insertion operators are proposed in this study, some of which are adapted by existing works [35–37].

27.3.6.1 Removal Operators

In the studied delivery system, as several assistants may be launched/dispatched at a certain customer's parking place, customers served by them need to be removed simultaneously when this specific customer is removed. In this regard, although the removal operator is intended to pick one customer, the total number of customers may exceed the predetermined removal number Γ.

Worst removal: It removes customer nodes which contribute the most to the objective value. The cost of customer i is defined as the decrease on the objective value if it is removed.

Worst assistant removal: This operator focuses on customers visited by assistants first. Then it turns to customers visited by vans when no customer visited by assistants is left but more customers need to be removed.

Route removal: This operator removes all the customers in the randomly selected route. It is useful for reducing the total number of routes (vans).

Shaw removal: This operator attempts to select customers that are related in a predefined way. At the beginning, a customer is selected randomly, and the related removal operation is applied. Then among customers in routes, the customer who is the most closely related to already removed customers is chosen and the removal operation is conducted. The process is repeated until sufficient number of customers are removed. Four factors are considered in the assessment of the relatedness in this study: geographical distance, time window, demand volume and route. Specifically, equation (27.30) is used to calculate the score.

$$RC(i, j) = \varphi_1 d_{ij} + \varphi_2(|l_i - l_j| + |u_i - u_j|) + \varphi_3|q_i - q_j| + \varphi_4 sr_{ij},$$
$$(27.30)$$

where $RC(i, j)$ represents the relatedness score between two customers i and j. $\theta_1, \theta_2, \theta_3$, and θ_4 are used to weight and harmonize the four aspects, and sr_{ij} is introduced to indicate whether customers i and j belong to the same route. If customers i and j are in the same route, we set sr_{ij} equal to -1, and 0 otherwise. Two customers with the lowest value of $RC(i, j)$ are with a highest relatedness.

Distance removal: With similar procedure to the Shaw removal, this operator tries to remove customers that are geographically related.

Time window removal: This operator is also similar to the Shaw removal operator. It focuses on the similarities among customers' time windows as the time window constraint plays an important role on the feasibility of a solution.

Random removal: It randomly selects a customer and conducts the corresponding removal operation. This process repeats until there are sufficient number of customers removed.

27.3.6.2 Insertion Operators

We define an insertion cost of a customer as the increase on the objective value after it is inserted. Fundamentally, a customer should be inserted into the position with the smallest insertion cost. However, for different configuration of current partial route, the best insertion position for a given customer varies. That is to say, the insertion sequence of customers influences final routes greatly. Therefore, we design a kind of best insertion operator based on several different insertion sequences. Then, the greedy scheme is applied to insert the customer with smallest insertion cost for current route configuration. We call this operator as a greedy insertion. Finally, minimum regret criterion is used, and the regret insertion is deduced. In addition, to diversify solutions for the myopic operators, a noise function is introduced, and other two corresponding operators are resulted. A brief explanation of each operator is provided below.

Best insertion: For each customer needs to be reinserted, this operator selects the position with the smallest insertion cost. Three ways to determine the insertion sequence are considered. The first one is to randomly select a customer at each time. The second one is related to the width of time window. Customers with smaller time window width have higher insertion priority. In the third one, customer who can only be served by a van has a higher priority.

Best insertion with a noise: This operator attaches a noise value $(d_{ist}\mu\varepsilon_1)$ to the insertion cost, where d_{ist} is the average van emissions value among all customers, μ is introduced here as a noise parameter, and $\varepsilon_1 \in [-1, 1]$ is a random number.

Greedy insertion: Based on the best insertion position of each customer, this operator inserts the customer with the smallest insertion cost at each iteration.

Greedy insertion with a noise: It is the variant of the greedy insertion with the same noise procedure described above.

Regret insertion: 2-regret operator is used in this research. The customer with the biggest difference between its first and second minimum costs is selected and inserted at each iteration.

27.4 Numerical Analyses

27.4.1 Instances and Parameters

27.4.1.1 Benchmark Instances

Chen et al. [29] created a library of real-life instances based on postcodes from Cardiff, United Kingdom. In these instances, customers' demand, time window and preference for assistants are randomly created. In this chapter, we choose the 100-node instances from this benchmark set to investigate the environmental benefits of the delivery system with autonomous delivery assistants.

27.4.1.2 Emissions-Related Parameters

According to Figliozzi [38], the summary of the characteristics of assistants is presented in Table 27.2. The emission parameters presented in this table are extracted from several publications in the literature. In addition, for safety consideration, the radius for both drone and robot is set to be 0.5 kilometers to facilitate a manual supervision for the deliveries.

The summary of the characteristics of the delivery van and the related emission parameters are presented in Table 27.3.

Furthermore, as drones need additional times for vertical takeoff and landing, one minute is assumed for takeoff and landing, respectively. Moreover, for vans and robots traveling on urban streets where traffic lights exist,

Table 27.2 Key parameters used for delivery assistants

Assistant	Speed (km/h)	Capacity (kg)	Radius (km)	ε_e (kg CO_2e/kWh)	β_0 (Wh/km)	β_1 (Wh/km/kg)
Drone	65	5	0.5	0.3773[a]	18.72[b]	10.94[b]
Robot	6.4	10	0.5	0.3773[a]	10.56[c]	0.58[c]

[a]Goodchild and Toy [39]
[b]Zhang et al. [40]
[c]Broderick et al. [41]

Table 27.3 Key parameters used for delivery van

Speed (km/h)	Capacity (kg)	ε_0^v (kg CO_2 e/km)	ε_1^v (kg CO_2 e/km/kg)
40	1,890	0.266	0.00041

10 percent additional time is included in their total traveling times. The tare weight of a single robot and a single drone is assumed to be 18 kg and 10 kg, respectively.

27.4.1.3 Parameters Used in the Algorithm

The ALNS is a parameter sensitive algorithm, and all parameters need to be prespecified. Preliminary experiments were conducted to decide the values of these parameters. We cannot claim that the values decided in our experiments is the best possible. However, we have decided parameters based on other well-performing ALNS applications found in the literature and our initial insights. We group all parameters used in our algorithm into three categories: SA framework parameters, adaptive mechanism parameters and operators' implementation parameters. We list parameters along with their values in Table 27.4.

27.4.2 Computational Results

In our experiments, we assumed three different delivery systems: van-only system ($m = 0$), using only drones as assistants and using only robots as assistants. Table 27.5 compares the total amount of emissions generated in each case. All values in Table 27.5 are the average values of 20 instances.

Generally, powered by electricity, both drones and robots contribute to emissions reduction. For the scenarios with assistants, the majority of carbon emissions come from delivery vans and the total amount of emissions from assistants just account for about 1% of that from delivery vans. When more

Table 27.4   Parameters used in the ALNS algorithm

Category	Definition	Value
SA framework parameters	Maximum iterations of non improvement	2,000
	Initial temperature parameter (η_1)	0.001
	Cooling rate (c)	0.99975
Adaptive mechanism parameters	Scores ($\sigma_1, \sigma_2, \sigma_3$)	(30, 10, 20)
	Reaction factor (r)	0.1
	Number of iterations in each segment (Max_{iter})	200
Parameters used in operators	Weights used in Shaw removal	(8, 2, 1, 1)
	Weights used in Best insertion	(0.5, 0.2, 0.2, 0.1)
	Randomization parameter	16
	Noise parameter	0.08

Table 27.5   The comparison of three scenarios

	Number of assistants installed on a van	Total emissions (kg CO_2e)	Emissions from vans (kg CO_2e)	Emissions from assistants (kg CO_2e)	Customers visited by assistants (%)	Reduction in total emissions
Van-only	–	16.75	–	–	–	–
With drone	1	15.18	15.03	0.15	20.5	9.37
	2	15.28	15.10	0.18	24.4	8.76
	3	15.39	15.21	0.18	25.0	8.08
With robot	1	14.71	14.61	0.09	35.0	12.17
	2	14.26	14.14	0.12	44.4	14.87
	4	14.04	13.90	0.14	50.4	16.18
	6	14.86	14.71	0.15	52.0	11.30

assistants are installed in a van, more customers can be allocated to be served by them. However, the total emissions may increase because of the increased payload resulting from more assistants installed in the van. As far as those instances used in this study, a single drone or four robots installed in each delivery van provided the best performance in terms of emissions reduction.

Compared to the number of customers served by drones, almost twice more customers are allocated to robots when the same number of assistants installed. That is because with a very limited capacity, the drone is restricted to a smaller set of customers. This is the main reason to explain the reduced environmental benefits of the van-drone delivery system than that of the van-robot delivery system in this study.

27.4.3 Sensitivity Analysis

27.4.3.1 Drone Capacity

The limited payload capacity is one of the main deficiencies that weaken the advantage of drone in delivery operations. In this regard, the influence of the drone capacity on total emissions is investigated in this study. We set different values for the drone capacity: 2.5 kg, 5 kg, 7.5 kg and 10 kg. Then, selected instances are solved under three scenarios with different number of drones installed in each van. The results are illustrated in Fig. 27.3.

When the drone has a larger capacity, more customers can be served by this service. As a result, lower total amount of emissions and more environmental benefits are achieved. Furthermore, when the drone has an ability to carry a weight up to 10 kg, installing more drones in each van becomes more beneficial. On the contrary, one drone is enough for each van to collaborate for the deliveries.

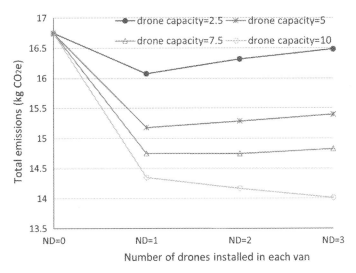

Fig. 27.3 Influence of the drone capacity (in kg) on total emissions

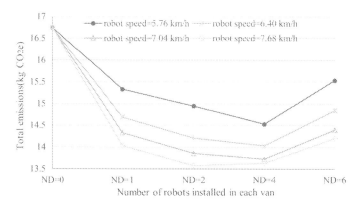

Fig. 27.4 Influence of the drone speed on total emissions

27.4.3.2 The Speed of Delivery Robot

Compared to the drone, delivery robots travel slowly. To this end, we look at the robot's speed on the environmental benefits. Based on primary speed setting, three additional scenarios with different changes on the robot speed are assumed: 10% decrease, 10% increase and 20% increase. Thus, besides the base speed (6.4 km/h), the deduced speeds are chosen accordingly: 5.76 km/h, 7.04 km/h and 7.68 km/h. Also, experiments are conducted with different number of robots installed in each van. Fig. 27.4 presents the results.

As expected, with higher speed of the robot, we obtained better solutions with lower total amount of emissions. It is noted that when the speed goes up by 20%, increasing the number of robots installed in each van from 4 to 6 leads to no improvement on total emissions. It is shown that installing more robots in a van compensates the disadvantage of robots to some extent.

27.5 Conclusions

In this chapter, drones and delivery robots are used in conjunction with a delivery van to serve customers. This could be a viable way to eliminate the negative externalities in last mile delivery as it can significantly reduce traveling distance of delivery vans.

Using drones and delivery robots as assistants in parcel delivery is a new service option, as seen in Amazon, UPS, Walmart, Alibaba, etc. With their joint work as assistants, the delivery services would be carried out more efficiently and environment friendly. When adequately number of assistants deployed, the cooperated delivery system would reduce the required energy consumption and the generated amount of CO_2e emissions. In addition, the improvements on the payload capacity of the drone or the speed of the robot would strengthen the benefits brought by those assistants and provide additional CO_2e reduction for last mile parcel delivery.

Studying optimization problems related to last mile logistics is essential for efficient and green parcel deliveries. It is important to explore different ways that efficiently cooperate multiple available resources including traditional vehicles and new autonomous vehicles under different circumstances. For example, a delivery fleet can consist of drones, robots and various types of vehicles (trucks or vans). Mathematical models should better reflect the characteristics of actual operations. First, characteristics of newly introduced delivery resources should be included into the modeling. Specifically, the assistant range constraints, such as the fundamental range limits (time and/or distance) should be based on realistic energy consumption functions. Second, actual application areas always result in different objectives and new constraints. Although minimizing total time duration or total cost are common practices in routing optimization problems, minimization of emissions, weighted number of late customer deliveries or the sum of customers' waiting times may also be investigated by decision-makers. Third, customers' acceptance of autonomous vehicles, technological accessibility to customers' location and other emergencies, like pandemic, would restrict delivery resources for those customers. Meanwhile, traffic legislation may influence the availability or the speed of delivery resources. Fourth, models and solution methods should be developed to handle stochastic factors of actual operations (e.g., travel times, delivery times, etc.). And finally, efficient metaheuristic algorithms are essential to solve routing problems rising in those cooperated delivery systems because exact algorithms may not work well for even medium-sized instances.

References

1. Melo, S. & Baptista, P. Evaluating the impacts of using cargo cycles on urban logistics: integrating traffic, environmental and operational boundaries. *European Transport Research Review.* **9**, 30 (2017)
2. Clarke, S., Cargo, G., Allen, J., Cherrett, T., McLeod, F. & Oakey, A. Report on the Portering Trial. (2018)
3. DHL: Logistic Trends Radar. Küchelhaus, Germany: DHL Customer Solution & Innovation (2016)
4. McFarland, Matt. In: UPS Broke in to Drone Deliveries Shuttling Medical Samples. CNN (2019)

5. Vincent, James, and Chaim Gartenberg: In: Here's Amazon's New Transforming Prime Air Delivery Drone. The Verge (2019)
6. Figliozzi, M. Lifecycle modeling and assessment of unmanned aerial vehicles (Drones) CO2e emissions. *Transportation Research Part D: Transport And Environment*. **57** pp. 251-261 (2017)
7. Kirschstein, T. Comparison of energy demands of drone-based and ground-based parcel delivery services. *Transportation Research Part D: Transport And Environment*. **78** pp. 102209 (2020)
8. Chen, C., Demir, E., Huang, Y. & Qiu, R. The adoption of self-driving delivery robots in last mile logistics. *Transportation Research Part E: Logistics And Transportation Review*. **146** pp. 102214 (2021a)
9. Pugliese, L., Guerriero, F. & Macrina, G. Using drones for parcels delivery process. *Procedia Manufacturing*. **42** pp. 488-497 (2020)
10. Jennings, D. & Figliozzi, M. Study of sidewalk autonomous delivery robots and their potential impacts on freight efficiency and travel. *Transportation Research Record*. **2673**, 317-326 (2019)
11. Demir, E., Huckle, K., Syntetos, A., Lahy, A. & Wilson, M. Vehicle routing problem: Past and future. *Contemporary Operations And Logistics*, pp. 97-117 (2019)
12. Murray, C. & Chu, A. The flying sidekick traveling salesman problem: Optimization of drone-assisted parcel delivery. *Transportation Research Part C: Emerging Technologies*. **54** pp. 86-109 (2015)
13. Agatz, N., Bouman, P. & Schmidt, M. Optimization approaches for the traveling salesman problem with drone. *Transportation Science*. **52**, 965-981 (2018)
14. Carlsson, J. & Song, S. Coordinated logistics with a truck and a drone. *Management Science*. **64**, 4052-4069 (2018)
15. Wang, X., Poikonen, S. & Golden, B. The vehicle routing problem with drones: several worst-case results. *Optimization Letters*. **11**, 679-697 (2017)
16. Schermer, D., Moeini, M. & Wendt, O. A matheuristic for the vehicle routing problem with drones and its variants. *Transportation Research Part C: Emerging Technologies*. **106** pp. 166-204 (2019)
17. Chiang, W., Li, Y., Shang, J. & Urban, T. Impact of drone delivery on sustainability and cost: Realizing the UAV potential through vehicle routing optimization. *Applied Energy*. **242** pp. 1164-1175 (2019)
18. Moshref-Javadi, M., Lee, S. & Winkenbach, M. Design and evaluation of a multi-trip delivery model with truck and drones. *Transportation Research Part E: Logistics And Transportation Review*. **136** pp. 101887 (2020)
19. Kitjacharoenchai, P., Min, B. & Lee, S. Two echelon vehicle routing problem with drones in last mile delivery. *International Journal Of Production Economics*. **225** pp. 107598 (2020)
20. Wang, Z. & Sheu, J. Vehicle routing problem with drones. *Transportation Research Part B: Methodological*. **122** pp. 350-364 (2019)

21. Karak, A. & Abdelghany, K. The hybrid vehicle-drone routing problem for pick-up and delivery services. *Transportation Research Part C: Emerging Technologies.* **102** pp. 427-449 (2019)

22. Jeong, H., Song, B. & Lee, S. Truck-drone hybrid delivery routing: Payload-energy dependency and No-Fly zones. *International Journal Of Production Economics.* **214** pp. 220-233 (2019)

23. Li, Y., Yang, W. & Huang, B. Impact of UAV delivery on sustainability and costs under traffic restrictions. *Mathematical Problems In Engineering.* **2020** (2020)

24. Ndiaye, M., Salhi, S. & Madani, B. When Green Technology Meets Optimization Modeling: The Case of Routing Drones in Logistics, Agriculture, and Healthcare. In Derbel H, Jarbaoui B and Siarry P (Eds), *Modeling And Optimization In Green Logistics.* pp. 127-145 (2020)

25. Chung, S.H., Sah, B. & Lee, J. Optimization for drone and drone-truck combined operations: A review of the state of the art and future directions. *Computers & Operations Research.* **123** pp. 105004 (2020)

26. Macrina, G., Pugliese, L., Guerriero, F. & Laporte, G. Drone-aided routing: A literature review. *Transportation Research Part C: Emerging Technologies.* **120** pp. 102762 (2020)

27. Otto, A., Agatz, N., Campbell, J., Golden, B. & Pesch, E. Optimization approaches for civil applications of unmanned aerial vehicles (UAVs) or aerial drones: A survey. *Networks.* **72**, 411-458 (2018)

28. Simoni, M., Kutanoglu, E. & Claudel, C. Optimization and analysis of a robot-assisted last mile delivery system. *Transportation Research Part E: Logistics And Transportation Review.* **142** pp. 102049 (2020)

29. Chen, C., Demir, E. & Huang, Y. An adaptive large neighborhood search heuristic for the vehicle routing problem with time windows and delivery robots. *European Journal Of Operational Research.* (2021b)

30. Boysen, N., Schwerdfeger, S. & Weidinger, F. Scheduling last-mile deliveries with truck-based autonomous robots. *European Journal Of Operational Research.* **271**, 1085-1099 (2018)

31. Yu, S., Puchinger, J. & Sun, S. Two-echelon urban deliveries using autonomous vehicles. *Transportation Research Part E: Logistics And Transportation Review.* **141** pp. 102018 (2020)

32. Freitas, J. & Penna, P. A variable neighborhood search for flying sidekick traveling salesman problem. *International Transactions In Operational Research.* **27**, 267-290 (2020)

33. Ropke, S. & Pisinger, D. An adaptive large neighborhood search heuristic for the pickup and delivery problem with time windows. *Transportation Science.* **40**, 455-472 (2006)

34. Shaw, P. Using constraint programming and local search methods to solve vehicle routing problems. *International Conference On Principles And Practice Of Constraint Programming.* pp. 417-431 (1998)

35. Pisinger, D. & Ropke, S. A general heuristic for vehicle routing problems. *Computers & Operations Research*. **34**, 2403-2435 (2007)

36. Demir, E., Bektaş, T. & Laporte, G. An adaptive large neighborhood search heuristic for the pollution-routing problem. *European Journal Of Operational Research*. **223**, 346-359 (2012)

37. Eshtehadi, R., Fathian, M. & Demir, E. Robust solutions to the pollution-routing problem with demand and travel time uncertainty. *Transportation Research Part D: Transport And Environment*. **51** pp. 351-363 (2017)

38. Figliozzi, M. Carbon emissions reductions in last mile and grocery deliveries utilizing air and ground autonomous vehicles. *Transportation Research Part D: Transport And Environment*. **85** pp. 102443 (2020)

39. Goodchild, A. & Toy, J. Delivery by drone: An evaluation of unmanned aerial vehicle technology in reducing CO2 emissions in the delivery service industry. *Transportation Research Part D: Transport And Environment*. **61** pp. 58-67 (2018)

40. Zhang, J., Campbell, J., Sweeney II, D. & Hupman, A. Energy consumption models for delivery drones: A comparison and assessment. *Transportation Research Part D: Transport And Environment*. **90** pp. 102668 (2021)

41. Broderick, J., Tilbury, D. & Atkins, E. Characterizing energy usage of a commercially available ground robot: Method and results. *Journal Of Field Robotics*. **31**, 441-454 (2014)

28

Evaluating the Quality of Radiation Therapy Treatment Plans Using Data Envelopment Analyis

Matthias Ehrgott, Andrea Raith, Glyn Shentall,
John Simpson, and Emma Stubington

28.1 Introduction

Apart from surgery and chemotherapy, the third main treatment modality for cancer is treatment with external high-energy ionising radiation. The radiation can alter the structure of cells, in particular their DNA. Externally generated radiation is beamed from outside the body through the skin to enter the body and interact with the cancer cells. Its goal is to damage the cancer cells and destroy them. Naturally, the radiation will have the same effect on healthy cells as well, i.e. healthy cells can be destroyed, too. However, healthy cells have a higher ability to recover from damage than cancer cells. Radiation therapy exploits this "therapeutic advantage" to destroy cancer cells while limiting damage to healthy cells.

M. Ehrgott (✉)
Department of Management Science, Lancaster University, Lancaster, UK
e-mail: m.ehrgott@lancaster.ac.uk

A. Raith
Department of Engineering Science, The University of Auckland, Auckland, New Zealand
e-mail: a.raith@auckland.ac.nz

G. Shentall
Rosemere Cancer Centre, Royal Preston Hospital, Preston, UK
e-mail: Glyn.Shentall@lthtr.nhs.uk

© The Author(s), under exclusive license to Springer Nature Switzerland AG 2022
S. Salhi and J. Boylan (eds.), *The Palgrave Handbook of Operations Research*,
https://doi.org/10.1007/978-3-030-96935-6_28

Before a patient undergoes a course of radiation therapy, the treatment has to be planned. This process starts with imaging the patient using CT and/or MRI scans. These images are used to build a 3D model of the patient's anatomy around the tumour site. Healthy tissues such as organs at risk (OAR), other normal tissue and cancer tissues are outlined in the images. A treatment planning software is then used to determine the angles and intensities of the radiation beams to be applied in the treatment. This planning problem can be considered as an optimisation problem (see [8, 18] for more information on the use of optimisation in radiation therapy treatment planning). The dilemma of trying to deliver a high dose to the tumour volume and at the same time a low dose of radiation to OARs and normal tissue puts this problem firmly into the field of multi-objective optimisation. Most treatment planning systems in fact optimise a parameterised model that is a single objective optimisation problem derived from the actual multi-objective optimisation problem of the treatment planning problem. Consequently, the treatment planning process often requires an iterative trial-and-error approach of computing a plan, evaluating the quality of this plan, identifying areas of improvement and modifying the parameters of the optimisation model to compute an improved plan of better quality.

In this process, the evaluation of the quality of the treatment plan in terms of the effect of the radiation dose delivered to the patient is essential and needs to be performed several times. This will be the focus of this chapter.

Treatment planning follows a clinical protocol, which prescribes a dose of radiation to the tumour, more precisely one or more planning target volumes (PTVs) outlined on the scans of the patient. For example, a typical prescription is to deliver a dose of $74\,Gy$ to the PTV of a prostate cancer case. The quality of a treatment plan is also described by indicators in the clinical protocol in terms of indicators D_x, the dose received by $x\%$ of the volume of a PTV, and V_x, the percentage of the volume of an OAR that receives a dose of $x\,Gy$. For prostate cancer, the clinical protocol may specify 20 such indicators. A plan that satisfies all of the indicators or criteria is considered

J. Simpson
Department of Radiation Oncology, Calvary Mater Newcastle, Waratah, NSW, Australia
e-mail: John.Simpson@calvarymater.org.au

E. Stubington
STOR-i, Lancaster University, Lancaster, UK
e-mail: e.stubington@lancaster.ac.uk

acceptable and would be signed off for treatment. However, this is unlikely to be possible.

In this chapter, we describe how the management science method of data envelopment analysis can be used to support the radiation therapy treatment planning process. In Sect. 28.2 we introduce the orientation and returns to scale of the DEA model used in this process. In Sect. 28.3 we consider the problem of feature selection, i.e. the selection of the inputs and outputs of the DEA model. Next, we address the inevitable issue of uncertainty in the values of the features and how uncertainty affects the results of the analysis (Sect. 28.4). Finally, we illustrate how the results of DEA can be used to provide guidance to treatment planners on how to improve treatment plans either in an offline manner or as an integral part of the planning process.

28.2 The DEA Model

There is not only a trade-off between achieving tumour control and OAR sparing, but even between different OAR criteria. Each of the goals of treatment could be achieved individually if the effect of the treatment on the other goals was ignored. Radiation therapy treatment planning is difficult because it is precisely this trade-off between the goals that has to be managed properly. It is very difficult to determine what the best choice of trade-off for an individual patient is [14]. This is one of the reasons why treatment planning is difficult. However, treatment centres do have a lot of experience with planning radiation therapy for cohorts of patients over time. Hence there is generally data about treatment plans, which have been delivered in the past. This makes it possible to compare a plan for a new patient to those of former patients with similar circumstances which have been considered "good".

This brings the problem of the evaluation of the quality of a treatment plan into the context of peer evaluation of a set of entities under a common set of criteria. This is the domain of data envelopment analysis (DEA). In an economic context, DEA aims at evaluating the performance of a set of "decision-making units" (DMUs) (such as hotels, bank branches etc.) in their ability to transform a set of inputs (e.g. number of employees, available capital) to a set of outputs (e.g. profit, customer satisfaction). A DMU is called efficient if there is no other DMU that achieves higher outputs with lower inputs, otherwise inefficient. DEA in its modern form goes back to [3] and a good introduction can be found in [5]. An important feature of DEA is that deciding whether a DMU i is efficient or not involves only the solution of a linear optimisation problem of the form (28.1) or (28.2). Let the number of DMUs be I, each DMU i having N inputs is summarised in the vector x^i and M outputs summarised in the vector y^i. The inputs of all DMUs are then collected in $N \times I$ matrix X, the outputs in $M \times I$ matrix Y.

$$\min\left\{\theta : -y^i + Y\lambda \geq 0; \theta x^i - X\lambda \geq 0; \lambda \in \Lambda\right\}, \tag{28.1}$$

$$\max\left\{\varphi : -\theta y^i + Y\lambda \geq 0; x^i - X\lambda \geq 0; \lambda \in \Lambda\right\}. \tag{28.2}$$

In (28.1) and (28.2), $\theta \in \mathbb{R}$, $\varphi \in \mathbb{R}$ and $\lambda \in \mathbb{R}^I$ are the decision variables. A DMU is considered efficient if the optimal value of either of these linear optimisation problems is 1. This implies it is impossible to proportionally decrease the inputs (28.1) or proportionally increase the outputs (28.2). An optimal value different from 1 indicates that this is possible, i.e. either inputs can be decreased or outputs increased without affecting outputs or inputs adversely. The set Λ determines the returns to scale of the DEA model, i.e. whether a proportional increase of inputs leads to a smaller, constant or larger proportional increase of outputs.

Thinking about radiation therapy, there is a clear similarity: If the radiation therapy plans are considered the DMUs, the goal is to determine whether a plan is efficient among a set of plans for the same cancer type treated at the same treatment centre using the same treatment protocol (to ensure comparability). Then the inputs are the doses delivered to OARs (and healthy tissue in general), reported by V_x indicators, and the outputs are the doses to the PTVs, reported by D_x indicators. Hence, if the optimal value of θ or φ of a treatment plan is 1, we conclude that there is no evidence in the data set that any plan in the data set is better. If it is different from one, the solution will identify a subset of plans (those plans j for which $\lambda_j \neq 0$ in an optimal solution to (28.1) or (28.2) that in combination have features that outperform the current plan, therefore providing guidance on how the current plan may be improved.

We now need to identify the type of DEA model that is appropriate for the radiation therapy treatment planning context. In Sect. 28.2.1 we identify the orientation and returns to scale for the DEA model. We then devote Section 28.3 to methods to determine the features, i.e. the inputs and outputs to be used as well as other factors that may be considered as influential for the quality of a plan, but that are not part of the treatment planning process.

28.2.1 Orientation and Returns to Scale

Working with clinical staff in the UK and New Zealand, we have learned that treatment planners are very good at using the treatment planning system to design plans that meet the primary prescriptions for a PTV (such as 74 Gy in a prostate cancer case). Hence planners focus on achieving tumour control. Since increasing dose to the tumour beyond the prescribed dose is not desirable they will in subsequent iterations of the planning process focus on reducing the dose to organs at risk to meet more criteria for V_x indicators. We have therefore used input-oriented model (28.1) in all work conducted on this topic, see [12, 16].

Because of the physics of radiation it is possible to obtain a constant increase of the dose to PTV for each unit change of dose to OARs by scaling the entire dose distribution we could assume constant returns to scale (CRS) in the DEA model. However, scaling the entire dose distribution may result in undesirable doses, such as hot spots in OARs or cold spots in a PTV. This implies that the CRS model might identify plans as efficient that are not clinically acceptable. Therefore, the assumption of variable returns to scale (VRS), in which linear combinations of DMUs that are most preferable for the corresponding input level, is more appropriate. Assuming that the DMUs with different input levels are all clinically acceptable plans, a VRS model offers a better approximation of what is clinically attainable for a given input level than a CRS model.

28.3 Feature Selection

In this section we describe the selection of features (inputs and outputs) considered in the DEA model. Recognising that we have already settled on an input-oriented model, we select inputs related to doses delivered to organs at risk and outputs related to doses delivered to PTVs.

28.3.1 Expert Opinions

In the first study [12] on this topic, we consulted clinicians on which indicators are most significant to determine the quality of a radiation therapy treatment plan for prostate cancer. The DEA model needs at least one input and one output. We decided to select D_{95}^{PTV}, i.e. the dose received by 95% of the PTV volume, as the single output. Clinicians consider the rectum as the OAR that most influences the ability to achieve the best dose to the PTV.

Hence the generalised equivalent uniform dose to the rectum was selected as the single input. Generalised equivalent uniform dose (gEUD [15]) is a theoretical dose value that if delivered uniformly would have the same effect as the actually delivered non-uniform dose distribution. Hence, the purpose of the DEA model is to compare plans in their efficiency to generate a dose distribution that matches the prescription dose in the PTV as closely as possible while maximising rectal sparing.

In [19] the study described in [12] has been extended to use different inputs and outputs and to gauge the technical requirements for using DEA for plan assessment.

Prostate cancer is of course the main type of cancer for males, so treatment centres usually have a lot of experience with planning radiation therapy for prostate cancer cases. The situation is very different for cancers in the head and neck area of a patient. Raith et al. [16] describe research that considers the DEA approach to plan evaluation for the more complex case of head and neck cancers.

In head and neck cancer cases often, two main PTV structures are defined: PTV70, which is treated with a prescription dose of 70 Gy and a larger volume denoted PTV54 with a prescription dose of 54 Gy. PTV70 is the target volume that contains the primary tumour and involved lymph nodes and therefore represents the primary treatment volume. Therefore, D_{98}^{PTV70} has been chosen as an output. Clinicians identified tumour volume, i.e. the volume of PTV70, as an important indicator of expected side effects and so it has been chosen as a second output. In an input-oriented DEA model, this means that any DMU (RT plan) is only compared to a benchmark plan with at least the same tumour volume, i.e. the volume of PTV70 acts as a non-discretionary environmental variable.

The inputs considered in this study are the average dose received by the oral cavity and the total swallowing volume. These values are adjusted statistically to model closeness of the OAR and PTV70. To include many other criteria relevant in quality assessment, two additional inputs are considered. These are aggregate scores for criterion attainment/violation modelled by empirical cumulative distribution functions. Further details on how these inputs and outputs are computed can be found in [16].

28.3.2   Principal Component Analysis

A drawback of relying on clinical expertise of physicians to define inputs and outputs is that the measures that are identified are not necessarily automatically computed for a plan once it has been created. On the other hand, indicators described in the clinical protocol will be computed and reported on for every plan. Therefore, selecting inputs and outputs from the indicators reported in the clinical protocol in an objective way makes this selection independent of the clinical expertise present at a particular treatment centre and enables comparisons to be made between treatment centres with similar clinical protocols. This also avoids additional effort to compute other measures not reported on by default.

Subington et al. [22] describe a procedure to use principal component analysis (PCA), see Joliffe [11] to select the inputs and outputs for the DEA model from a set of ten input and nine output indicators reported in the clinical protocol for a treatment centre in the UK. Let us first note that it is not possible to select all the criteria in the clinical protocol for the DEA model. This is because if the number of features $(M+N)$ is high in relation to the number of DMUs I, the DEA model loses its discrimination power and many DMUs will be classified as efficient because they perform particularly well for a single input or output. Dyson et al. [7] suggest that $I > 2 \times M \times N$ DMUs are required to achieve a reasonable level of discrimination and [4] suggest $I > \max\{M \times N, 3 \times (M + N)\}$.

In PCA, the variables in the data set (here the indicators reported due to the clinical protocol) are transformed into new variables called the principal components. These are directions in which the data are most dispersed. Subington et al. [22] describe an algorithm called AutoPCA that, for a cohort of radiation therapy treatment plans for prostate cancer from the treatment centre investigated selects one input variable each for the bladder and rectum as well as one output variable.

28.3.3 Environmental Factors

The quality of a radiation therapy treatment plan may be influenced by factors outside of the delivered radiation. These factors are called environmental variables or non-discretionary variables, to indicate that they are relevant for the performance of a plan but their values are outside the control of the DMU, i.e. they are not affected by the plan. For example, Lin et al. [12] consider the percentage volume of the rectum that overlaps the PTV as an environmental variable: The higher the overlap the more difficult it is to achieve good PTV coverage and low OAR dose simultaneously. In the input-oriented DEA model, an environmental variable is considered in the same way as an output:

$$-z^i + Z\lambda \geq 0. \tag{28.3}$$

In (28.3), like X and Y in (28.1) and (28.2), Z is an $L \times I$ matrix containing the data of all L environmental variables for all I DMUs, z^i is the ith column of Z and λ is a vector of decision variables. (28.3) guarantees that DMU i is only compared to DMUs $Z\lambda$ the value of which is at least as high as that of DMU i. In the same way, as PTV-rectum overlap in [12], the output tumour volume in [16] is essentially an environmental factor.

28.4 Dealing with Uncertainty

It is well known in radiation oncology that the doses delivered to structures are usually (slightly) different from those calculated during treatment planning. This uncertainty in predicting radiation dose delivered to PTVs and OARs has many sources. The first is the inherent uncertainty in the computational models for radiation dose. These are mathematical models of the physical interaction of radiation (photons, electrons) with biological tissue representing the deposition of dose in the body. This process accounts for some inaccuracy. Further factors are the physical design of the treatment machines delivering the radiation. Small amounts of radiation leakage cannot be prevented.

Apart from these mathematical and engineering factors, a compounding issue arises due to the delivery of the treatment over several fractions. Since patients return for treatment over a number of days, it is inevitable that the positioning of the relevant structures differs slightly from day to day. Roeske et al. [17] explore changes in size and location of the prostate, bladder, and rectum during a course of external beam radiation therapy. The authors conclude that the prostate volume can change by $\pm 10\%$ and the rectal and bladder volumes can change by up to $\pm 30\%$. Moiseenko et al. [13] report changes in bladder volume from $419 \ cm^3$ to $90 \ cm^3$ during the treatment and [2] investigate changes in prostate volume throughout treatment and find that averaged over all patients and not including setup errors, the mean displacements are slightly less than $0.5 cm$. However, for individuals the range of displacement is from $0.03 cm$ to more than $1.5 cm$. Das et al. [6] observe high variability among planners and institutions, reporting that the median dose to the tumour can vary by $\pm 10\%$ of the prescribed dose across 96% of the patient population.

The standard assumption is that uncertainty is proportional to the dose. The international commission on radiation units and measurements [1] conclude that the available evidence for certain types of tumour points to the need for accuracy $\pm 5\%$. Combining the standard uncertainty value for dose determination and the uncertainty associated with Pinnacle (a treat-ment planning system) for multileaf collimators [10] suggest an uncertainty of 3.6%

28.4.1 Simulation

One way of dealing with uncertain data is to run the DEA analysis several times with simulated data, fixing uncertainty sets, and randomly selecting values for X and Y from those uncertainty sets. This is the approach taken in [20]. The authors consider a data set of 51 radiation therapy treatment plans for prostate cancer. They replicate the DEA analysis for dose values $v \pm \varepsilon$ with $\varepsilon \leq u$ for the values of $u \in \{0.1, 0.5, 1, 1.8, 3.6, 5\}$ 1000 times for each value of u. They record the largest efficiency score for each u and observe that this increases as the value of u increases. The interpretation of the results allows differentiating between treatment plans that are inefficient assuming the data are exact, but become efficient with 5% uncertainty: These plans are probably good but have been classified as inefficient due to the uncertain data. In [20], 13 plans are efficient with an uncertainty level of u = 0.1%, 17 with u = 0.5%, 21 with u = 1%, and 23 with u = 1.8%. This increases to 37 when the uncertainty increases to 3.6% and 45 for u = 5%. Six treatment plans are still inefficient even with 5% uncertainty. Re-planning of those might in fact resolve structural problems with the original plans and improve them.

28.4.2 Uncertain DEA

A formal model of dealing with DEA in the presence of uncertain (input and output) data is developed in [9]. Following the principles of robust optimisa-tion, rather than assuming exact values for X and Y, input and output values are chosen from an uncertainty set. For given uncertainty sets, the robust efficiency score of DMU i is defined by changing the constraints in (28.1) to hold for all data in the uncertainty set. The authors show that as uncertainty increases (uncertainty sets get bigger in terms of set inclusion), the robust efficiency score increases, too. They introduce the notion of the amount of uncertainty and pose the uncertain DEA (uDEA) problem of determining the largest possible robust efficiency score and the minimal amount of uncer-tainty at which that can be obtained. If this value is 1, a DMU is termed capable, otherwise incapable. For the case of ellipsoidal uncertainty sets [9] propose a first-order algorithm to solve the uncertain DEA problem.

The model in [9] is rather general, even allowing relationships between the uncertainty sets for different inputs and outputs. Therefore [21] consider uncertain DEA for the case of box uncertainty, i.e. the uncertainty sets for each input and output are boxes. They demonstrate that without limit on the allowable amount of uncertainty all DMUs are capable in uncertain DEA with box uncertainty. Hence an interesting question in the application of DEA to radiation therapy treatment planning is to determine those plans that are capable under given upper bounds on the allowable amount of uncertainty in dose values reported in radiation therapy, e.g. those mentioned in Sect. 28.4. Because the robust DEA model of [9] reduces to a linear optimisation problem for fixed uncertainty sets, [21] propose an iterative linear optimisation procedure to solve the uncertain DEA problem for box uncertainty to some pre-specified accuracy.

28.5   Application in Practice

The ultimate goal of this research on evaluating the quality of radiation therapy treatment plans is to guide the treatment planning process to steer it towards a plan that is as good as possible for the individual patient. As indicated before, this involves identifying plans that are inefficient, respectively incapable and exploiting the information provided by the optimal solution of the (uncertain) DEA problem to provide the treatment planners with information that allows them to improve the plans.

28.5.1   Informing the Treatment Planning Process

The study of [12] works with a set of 37 plans for prostate cancer cases from a treatment centre in Auckland, New Zealand. Five inefficient plans were selected for re-optimisation. A planner was then instructed to further improve rectal sparing while maintaining overall clinical acceptance for the selected plans without access to the results of DEA. The efficiency scores of the selected plans were less than the original average efficiency score (0.985). The re-optimisation of plan 31 produced an additional efficient plan in the dataset. This plan extends the efficient frontier slightly and results in lower or equal efficiency scores of all other plans compared to those of the original dataset. The efficiency scores of the re-optimised plans were higher than those of the original plans, with an average improvement of 0.026. This improvement is quite substantial since the standard deviation of the efficiency scores was only 0.012. All of the re-optimised plans achieved an efficiency score higher than the re-optimised average efficiency score (0.98). A clinical peer review of the plans was performed by an independent radiation oncologist, who was not the clinician originally involved in the planning. In this review, clinical and DVH parameters not included in the DEA (i.e. bladder, femoral heads, dose maxima, hot spot percentage and site, etc.) were also taken into account. The review confirmed that three re-optimised plans were deemed superior when compared with the original plans. The other two were considered to be of similar quality than the original ones.

Figure 28.1 shows the DEA results with all plans plotted with their values of D_{95}^{PTV} against the values of $gEUD^{rectum}$. The environmental variable of PTV-rectum overlap is indicated by colour. Figure 28.2 shows the dose volume histograms (DVH) for one of the originally inefficient plans and its re-optimised version. A DVH plots the percentage volume of a structure of interest that receives at least a certain dose of radiation. The diagram shows that the PTV coverage of both plans is essentially the same. However, the curve for dose to the rectum of the re-optimised plan is below the curve for the original plan, illustrating the additional rectal sparing achieved.

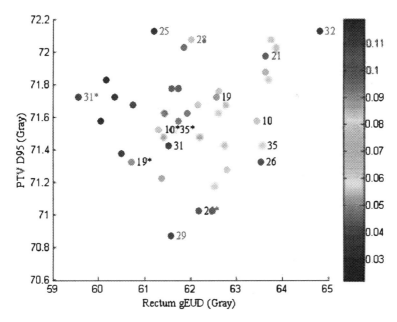

Fig. 28.1 (Figure 2(b) in [12]) Plot of the data points where colour represents PTV rectum overlap after re-optimisation of a subset of the plans. Red numbers indicate treatment plans considered efficient in the DEA analysis. Black numbers indicate treatment plans selected for re-optimisation

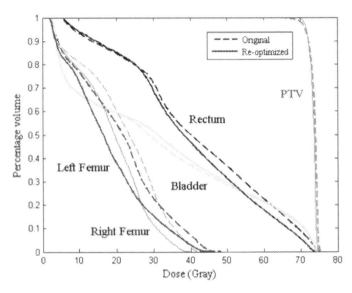

Fig. 28.2 (Figure 4(b) in [12]) Dose volume histogram for a radiation therapy treatment plan before and after re-optimisation following DEA

Considering uncertainty, in particular box uncertainty as described in [21] all of these 42 treatment plans (the 37 original ones plus five re-optimised ones) have been considered to determine what is the minimum amount of uncertainty required to deem each plan efficient. Figure 28.3 shows the nominal efficiency score (assuming D_{95}^{PTV} and $gEUD^{rectum}$ values are exact) on the horizontal axis versus this minimal amount of uncertainty on the vertical axis. These calculations have been performed with the iterative linear optimisation method using the method described in [21]. Note that plans that are efficient with the nominal data are all located at $(1, 0)$ in this diagram.

The software to extract the inputs and outputs for use in the DEA analysis has also been deployed at a treatment centre in the UK.

28.5.2   Integration in the Treatment Planning Process

Considering the use of DEA analysis as an integral part of the planning process that provides immediate feedback on the quality of a treatment plan to improve the next iteration, we refer to [16]. Similar to [12], five plans have been randomly selected for further improvement. The planner selected one of the final plans and aimed to improve plan quality as viewed holistically based

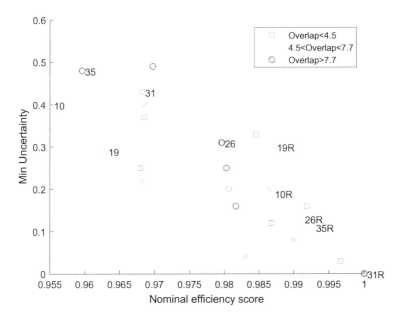

Fig. 28.3 (Figure 2(b) in [21]) Plot showing the minimal amount of uncertainty for which the 42 plans considered in [12] become capable

not only on the usual clinical criteria used for evaluation, but also the DEA-based feedback. The planner performed between two and four iterations and accepted the results for four out of the five plans, while the fifth was rejected due to remaining concerns regarding some OARs. This experiment demonstrates that the integration of the DEA tool in the planning process can lead to improved treatment plans without consuming additional time.

Acknowledgements The authors would like to acknowledge the contribution of other colleagues to prior research that has been published in references listed below. Thanks go to Fariza Fauzi, Kuan-Min Lin, Andrew Macann, Rachel Norris, Paul Rouse and Giuseppe Sasso. While the writing of this paper was not supported by any grant, the authors are grateful to EPSRC and Auckland Medical Foundation for their support in prior research.

References

1. Andreo, P., Cramb, J., Fraass, B., Ionescu-Farca, F., Izewska, J., Levin, V., Mijn-heer, B., Rosenwald, J., Scalliet, P., Shortt, K., *et al.* (2004). Commissioning and quality assurance of computerized planning systems for radiation treatment of cancer. *International Atomic Energy Agency Technical Report Series*, (430).

2. Antolak, J. A., Rosen, I. I., Childress, C. H., Zagars, G. K., and Pollack, A. (1998). Prostate target volume variations during a course of radiotherapy. *International Journal of Radiation Oncology Biology Physics*, **42**(3), 661–672.

3. Charnes, A., Cooper, W., and Rhodes, E. (1978). Measuring the efficiency of decision making units. *European Journal of Operational Research*, **2**(6), 429–444.

4. Cooper, W., Seiford, L. M., and Tone, K. (2006). *Introduction to data envelopment analysis and its uses: with DEA-solver software and references*. Springer Science & Business Media.

5. Cooper, W., Seiford, L., and Zhu, J. (2011). *Data Envelopment Analysis: History, Models and Interpretations. Handbook on Data Envelopment Analysis*. Springer Science and Business Media.

6. Das, I. J., Cheng, C.-W., Chopra, K. L., Mitra, R. K., Srivastava, S. P., and Glatstein, E. (2008). Intensity-modulated radiation therapy dose prescription, recording, and delivery: Patterns of variability among institutions and treatment planning systems. *Journal of the National Cancer Institute*, **100**(5), 300–307.

7. Dyson, R., Allen, A., Camanho, A., Podinovski, V., .Sarrico, C., and Shale, E. (2001). Pitfalls and protocols in DEA. *European Journal of Operational Research*, **132**(2), 245–259.

8. Ehrgott, M., Güler, c., Hamacher, H. W., and Shao, L. (2008). Mathematical optimization in intensity modulated radiation therapy. *4OR*, **6**(3), 199–262.

9. Ehrgott, M., Holder, A., and Nohadani, M. (2018). Uncertain data envelopment analysis. *European Journal of Operational Research*, **268**(1), 231–242.

10. Henríquez, F. and Castrillón, S. (2008). A novel method for the evaluation of uncertainty in dose-volume histogram computation. *International Journal of Radiation Oncology*Biology*Physics*, **70**(4), 1263 – 1271.

11. Joliffe, I. (2002). *Principal Component Analysis*. Springer Series in Statistics. Springer, second edition.

12. Lin, K.-M., Simpson, J., Sasso, G., Raith, A., and Ehrgott, M. (2013). Quality assessment for VMAT prostate radiotherapy planning based on data envelopment analysis. *Physics in Medicine & Biology*, **58**(16), 5753.

13. Moiseenko, V., Liu, M., Kristensen, S., Gelowitz, G., and Berthelet, E. (2007). Effect of bladder filling on doses to prostate and organs at risk: A treatment planning study. *Journal of Applied Clinical Medical Physics*, **6**(1), 55–68.

14. Moore, K. L., Brame, R. S., Low, D. A., and Mutic, S. (2011). Experience-based quality control of clinical intensity-modulated radiotherapy planning. *International Journal of Radiation Oncology* Biology* Physics*, **81**(2), 545–551.

15. Niemierko, A. . (1999). A generalized concept of equivalent uniform dose. *Medical Physics*, **26**, 1100.

16. Raith, A., Ehrgott, M., Fauzi, F., Lin, K.-M., Macann, A. amd Rouse, P., and Simpson, j. (2022). Integrating data envelopment analysis into radiotherapy treatment planning for head and neck cancer patients. *European Journal of Operational Research*, **296**(1), 289–303.

17. Roeske, J. C., Forman, J. D., Mesina, C., He, T., Pelizzari, C. A., and Fontenla, E. e. a. (1995). Evaluation of changes in the size and location of the prostate,

seminal vesicles, bladder, and rectum during a course of external beam radiation therapy. *International Journal of Radiation Oncology, Biology, Physics*, **33**(5), 1321–1329.

18. Shepard, D., Ferris, M., Olivera, G., and Mackie, T. (1999). Optimizing the delivery of radiation therapy to cancer patients. *SIAM Review*, **41**(4), 721–744.

19. Simpson, J., Raith, A., Rouse, P., and Ehrgott, M. (2017). Considerations for using data envelopment analysis for the assessment of radiotherapy treatment plan quality. *International Journal of Health Care Quality Assurance*, **30**(8), 703.

20. Stubington, E., Ehrgott, M., Shentall, G., and Nohadani, O. (2018). *Evaluating the Quality of Radiotherapy Treatment Plans for Prostate Cancer*, chapter 2, pages 41–65. Springer Science & Buisness Media.

21. Stubington, E., Ehrgott, M., and Nohadani, O. (2021a). Uncertain data envelopment analysis: Box uncertainty. Technical report, Lancaster University.

22. Stubington, E., Ehrgott, M., Shentall, G., and Norris, R. (2021b). Variable selection methods to evaluate the quality of radiotherapy treatment plans. Technical report, Lancaster University.

Index

© The Editor(s) (if applicable) and The Author(s), under exclusive
license to Springer Nature Switzerland AG 2022
S. Salhi and J. Boylan (eds.), *The Palgrave Handbook of Operations Research*,
https://doi.org/10.1007/978-3-030-96935-6

Printed in the United States
by Baker & Taylor Publisher Services